CORNERSTONE
BIBLICAL
COMMENTARY

CORNERSTONE BIBLICAL COMMENTARY

James, 1–2 Peter, Jude

Grant R. Osborne

Revelation

M. Robert Mulholland Jr.

GENERAL EDITOR

Philip W. Comfort

featuring the text of the

NEW LIVING TRANSLATION

TYNDALE HOUSE PUBLISHERS, INC. CAROL STREAM, ILLINOIS

Cornerstone Biblical Commentary, Volume 18

Visit Tyndale online at www.tyndale.com.

Designed by Luke Daab and Timothy R. Botts.

Library of Congress Cataloging-in-Publication Data

Cornerstone biblical commentary.
p. cm.
Includes bibliographical references and index.
ISBN 978-0-8423-8346-2 (hc : alk. paper)
1. Bible—Commentaries. I. Osborne, Grant R. II. Mulholland, M. Robert, Jr.
BS491.3.C67 2006
220.7′7—dc22 2005026928

Printed in the United States of America

17 16 15 14 13 12 11
7 6 5 4 3 2 1

CONTENTS

Contributors to Volume 18
vi

General Editor's Preface
vii

Abbreviations
ix

Transliteration and Numbering System
xiii

JAMES
1

1 PETER
129

2 PETER
273

JUDE
355

REVELATION
399

CONTRIBUTORS TO VOLUME 18

James, 1–2 Peter, Jude: Grant R. Osborne
BA, Fort Wayne Bible College;
MA, Trinity Evanglical Divinity School;
PhD, University of Aberdeen;
Professor of New Testament, Trinity Evangelical Divinity School.

Revelation: M. Robert Mulholland Jr.
BS, U.S. Naval Academy;
MDiv, Wesley Theological Seminary;
ThD, Harvard Divinity School;
Professor of New Testament, Asbury Theological Seminary.

GENERAL EDITOR'S PREFACE

The *Cornerstone Biblical Commentary* is based on the second edition of the New Living Translation (2007). Nearly 100 scholars from various church backgrounds and from several countries (United States, Canada, England, and Australia) participated in the creation of the NLT. Many of these same scholars are contributors to this commentary series. All the commentators, whether participants in the NLT or not, believe that the Bible is God's inspired word and have a desire to make God's word clear and accessible to his people.

This Bible commentary is the natural extension of our vision for the New Living Translation, which we believe is both exegetically accurate and idiomatically powerful. The NLT attempts to communicate God's inspired word in a lucid English translation of the original languages so that English readers can understand and appreciate the thought of the original writers. In the same way, the *Cornerstone Biblical Commentary* aims at helping teachers, pastors, students, and laypeople understand every thought contained in the Bible. As such, the commentary focuses first on the words of Scripture, then on the theological truths of Scripture—inasmuch as the words express the truths.

The commentary itself has been structured in such a way as to help readers get at the meaning of Scripture, passage by passage, through the entire Bible. Each Bible book is prefaced by a substantial book introduction that gives general historical background important for understanding. Then the reader is taken through the Bible text, passage by passage, starting with the New Living Translation text printed in full. This is followed by a section called "Notes," wherein the commentator helps the reader understand the Hebrew or Greek behind the English of the NLT, interacts with other scholars on important interpretive issues, and points the reader to significant textual and contextual matters. The "Notes" are followed by the "Commentary," wherein each scholar presents a lucid interpretation of the passage, giving special attention to context and major theological themes.

The commentators represent a wide spectrum of theological positions within the evangelical community. We believe this is good because it reflects the rich variety in Christ's church. All the commentators uphold the authority of God's word and believe it is essential to heed the old adage: "Wholly apply yourself to the Scriptures and apply them wholly to you." May this commentary help you know the truths of Scripture, and may this knowledge help you "grow in your knowledge of God and Jesus our Lord" (2 Pet 1:2, NLT).

PHILIP W. COMFORT
GENERAL EDITOR

ABBREVIATIONS

GENERAL ABBREVIATIONS

b.	Babylonian Gemara
bar.	baraita
c.	*circa,* around, approximately
cf.	*confer,* compare
ch, chs	chapter, chapters
contra	in contrast to
DSS	Dead Sea Scrolls
ed.	edition, editor
e.g.	*exempli gratia,* for example
et al.	*et alli,* and others
fem.	feminine
ff	following (verses, pages)
fl.	flourished
Gr.	Greek
Heb.	Hebrew
ibid.	*ibidem,* in the same place
i.e.	*id est,* the same
in loc.	*in loco,* in the place cited
lit.	literally
LXX	Septuagint
𝔐	Majority Text
m.	Mishnah
masc.	masculine
mg	margin
ms	manuscript
mss	manuscripts
MT	Masoretic Text
n.d.	no date
neut.	neuter
no.	number
NT	New Testament
OL	Old Latin
OS	Old Syriac
OT	Old Testament
p., pp.	page, pages
pl.	plural
Q	Quelle ("Sayings" as Gospel source)
rev.	revision
sg.	singular
t.	Tosefta
TR	Textus Receptus
v., vv.	verse, verses
vid.	*videtur,* it seems
viz.	*videlicet,* namely
vol.	volume
y.	Jerusalem Gemara

ABBREVIATIONS FOR BIBLE TRANSLATIONS

ASV	American Standard Version
CEV	Contemporary English Version
ESV	English Standard Version
GW	God's Word
HCSB	Holman Christian Standard Bible
JB	Jerusalem Bible
KJV	King James Version
NAB	New American Bible
NASB	New American Standard Bible
NCV	New Century Version
NEB	New English Bible
NET	The NET Bible
NIV	New International Version
NIrV	New International Reader's Version
NJB	New Jerusalem Bible
NJPS	The New Jewish Publication Society Translation (*Tanakh*)
NKJV	New King James Version
NRSV	New Revised Standard Version
NLT	New Living Translation
REB	Revised English Bible
RSV	Revised Standard Version
TEV	Today's English Version
TLB	The Living Bible

ABBREVIATIONS FOR DICTIONARIES, LEXICONS, COLLECTIONS OF TEXTS, ORIGINAL LANGUAGE EDITIONS

ABD *Anchor Bible Dictionary* (6 vols., Freedman) [1992]

ANEP *The Ancient Near East in Pictures* (Pritchard) [1965]

ANET *Ancient Near Eastern Texts Relating to the Old Testament* (Pritchard) [1969]

BAGD *Greek-English Lexicon of the New Testament and Other Early Christian Literature,* 2nd ed. (Bauer, Arndt, Gingrich, Danker) [1979]

BDAG *Greek-English Lexicon of the New Testament and Other Early Christian Literature,* 3rd ed. (Bauer, Danker, Arndt, Gingrich) [2000]

BDB *A Hebrew and English Lexicon of the Old Testament* (Brown, Driver, Briggs) [1907]

BDF *A Greek Grammar of the New Testament and Other Early Christian Literature* (Blass, Debrunner, Funk) [1961]

BHS *Biblia Hebraica Stuttgartensia* (Elliger and Rudolph) [1983]

CAD *Assyrian Dictionary of the Oriental Institute of the University of Chicago* [1956]

COS *The Context of Scripture* (3 vols., Hallo and Younger) [1997–2002]

DBI *Dictionary of Biblical Imagery* (Ryken, Wilhoit, Longman) [1998]

DBT *Dictionary of Biblical Theology* (2nd ed., Leon-Dufour) [1972]

DCH *Dictionary of Classical Hebrew* (7 vols., D. Clines) [2000]

DLNTD *Dictionary of the Later New Testament and Its Development* (R. Martin, P. Davids) [1997]

DJD *Discoveries in the Judean Desert* [1955–]

DJG *Dictionary of Jesus and the Gospels* (Green, McKnight, Marshall) [1992]

DOTP *Dictionary of the Old Testament: Pentateuch* (T. Alexander, D.W. Baker) [2003]

DPL *Dictionary of Paul and His Letters* (Hawthorne, Martin, Reid) [1993]

DTIB *Dictionary for Theological Interpretation of the Bible* (Vanhoozer) [2005]

EDNT *Exegetical Dictionary of the New Testament* (3 vols., H. Balz, G. Schneider. ET) [1990–1993]

GKC *Gesenius' Hebrew Grammar* (Gesenius, Kautzsch, trans. Cowley) [1910]

HALOT *The Hebrew and Aramaic Lexicon of the Old Testament* (L. Koehler, W. Baumgartner, J. Stamm; trans. M. Richardson) [1994–1999]

IBD *Illustrated Bible Dictionary* (3 vols., Douglas, Wiseman) [1980]

IDB *The Interpreter's Dictionary of the Bible* (4 vols., Buttrick) [1962]

ISBE *International Standard Bible Encyclopedia* (4 vols., Bromiley) [1979–1988]

KBL *Lexicon in Veteris Testamenti libros* (Koehler, Baumgartner) [1958]

LCL Loeb Classical Library

L&N *Greek-English Lexicon of the New Testament: Based on Semantic Domains* (Louw and Nida) [1989]

LSJ *A Greek-English Lexicon* (9th ed., Liddell, Scott, Jones) [1996]

MM *The Vocabulary of the Greek New Testament* (Moulton and Milligan) [1930; 1997]

NA^{26} *Novum Testamentum Graece* (26th ed., Nestle-Aland) [1979]

NA^{27} *Novum Testamentum Graece* (27th ed., Nestle-Aland) [1993]

NBD *New Bible Dictionary* (2nd ed., Douglas, Hillyer) [1982]

NIDB *New International Dictionary of the Bible* (Douglas, Tenney) [1987]

NIDBA *New International Dictionary of Biblical Archaeology* (Blaiklock and Harrison) [1983]

NIDNTT *New International Dictionary of New Testament Theology* (4 vols., C. Brown) [1975–1985]

NIDOTTE *New International Dictionary of Old Testament Theology and Exegesis* (5 vols., W. A. VanGemeren) [1997]

PG *Patrologia Graecae* (J. P. Migne) [1857–1886]

PGM *Papyri graecae magicae: Die griechischen Zauberpapyri.* (Preisendanz) [1928]

TBD *Tyndale Bible Dictionary* (Elwell, Comfort) [2001]

TDNT *Theological Dictionary of the New Testament* (10 vols., Kittel, Friedrich; trans. Bromiley) [1964–1976]

TDOT *Theological Dictionary of the Old Testament* (15 vols., Botterweck, Ringgren; trans. Willis, Bromiley, Green) [1974–]

TLNT *Theological Lexicon of the New Testament* (3 vols., C. Spicq) [1994]

TLOT *Theological Lexicon of the Old Testament* (3 vols., E. Jenni) [1997]

TWOT *Theological Wordbook of the Old Testament* (2 vols., Harris, Archer) [1980]

UBS^3 *United Bible Societies' Greek New Testament* (3rd ed., Metzger et al.) [1975]

UBS^4 *United Bible Societies' Greek New Testament* (4th corrected ed., Metzger et al.) [1993]

WH *The New Testament in the Original Greek* (Westcott and Hort) [1882]

ABBREVIATIONS FOR BOOKS OF THE BIBLE

Old Testament

Gen	Genesis	Deut	Deuteronomy	1 Sam	1 Samuel
Exod	Exodus	Josh	Joshua	2 Sam	2 Samuel
Lev	Leviticus	Judg	Judges	1 Kgs	1 Kings
Num	Numbers	Ruth	Ruth	2 Kgs	2 Kings

1 Chr	1 Chronicles	Song	Song of Songs	Obad	Obadiah
2 Chr	2 Chronicles	Isa	Isaiah	Jonah	Jonah
Ezra	Ezra	Jer	Jeremiah	Mic	Micah
Neh	Nehemiah	Lam	Lamentations	Nah	Nahum
Esth	Esther	Ezek	Ezekiel	Hab	Habakkuk
Job	Job	Dan	Daniel	Zeph	Zephaniah
Ps, Pss	Psalm, Psalms	Hos	Hosea	Hag	Haggai
Prov	Proverbs	Joel	Joel	Zech	Zechariah
Eccl	Ecclesiastes	Amos	Amos	Mal	Malachi

New Testament

Matt	Matthew	Eph	Ephesians	Heb	Hebrews
Mark	Mark	Phil	Philippians	Jas	James
Luke	Luke	Col	Colossians	1 Pet	1 Peter
John	John	1 Thess	1 Thessalonians	2 Pet	2 Peter
Acts	Acts	2 Thess	2 Thessalonians	1 John	1 John
Rom	Romans	1 Tim	1 Timothy	2 John	2 John
1 Cor	1 Corinthians	2 Tim	2 Timothy	3 John	3 John
2 Cor	2 Corinthians	Titus	Titus	Jude	Jude
Gal	Galatians	Phlm	Philemon	Rev	Revelation

Deuterocanonical

Bar	Baruch	1–2 Esdr	1–2 Esdras	Ps 151	Psalm 151
Add Dan	Additions to Daniel	Add Esth	Additions to Esther	Sir	Sirach
Pr Azar	Prayer of Azariah	Ep Jer	Epistle of Jeremiah	Tob	Tobit
Bel	Bel and the Dragon	Jdt	Judith	Wis	Wisdom of Solomon
Sg Three	Song of the Three Children	1–2 Macc	1–2 Maccabees		
		3–4 Macc	3–4 Maccabees		
Sus	Susanna	Pr Man	Prayer of Manasseh		

MANUSCRIPTS AND LITERATURE FROM QUMRAN

Initial numerals followed by "Q" indicate particular caves at Qumran. For example, the notation 4Q267 indicates text 267 from cave 4 at Qumran. Further, 1QS 4:9-10 indicates column 4, lines 9-10 of the *Rule of the Community*; and 4Q166 1 ii 2 indicates fragment 1, column ii, line 2 of text 166 from cave 4. More examples of common abbreviations are listed below.

CD	Cairo Geniza copy of the *Damascus Document*	1QIsa^{b}	Isaiah copy ^{b}	4QLam^{a}	Lamentations
		1QM	*War Scroll*	11QPs^{a}	Psalms
		1QpHab	*Pesher Habakkuk*	11QTemple^{a,b}	*Temple Scroll*
1QH	*Thanksgiving Hymns*	1QS	*Rule of the Community*	11QtgJob	*Targum of Job*
1QIsa^{a}	Isaiah copy ^{a}				

IMPORTANT NEW TESTAMENT MANUSCRIPTS

(all dates given are AD; ordinal numbers refer to centuries)

Significant Papyri (𝔓 = Papyrus)

𝔓1 Matt 1; early 3rd
𝔓4+𝔓64+𝔓67 Matt 3, 5, 26; Luke 1–6; late 2nd
𝔓5 John 1, 16, 20; early 3rd
𝔓13 Heb 2–5, 10–12; early 3rd
𝔓15+𝔓16 (probably part of same codex) 1 Cor 7–8, Phil 3–4; late 3rd
𝔓20 Jas 2–3; 3rd
𝔓22 John 15–16; mid 3rd
𝔓23 Jas 1; c. 200
𝔓27 Rom 8–9; 3rd
𝔓30 1 Thess 4–5; 2 Thess 1; early 3rd
𝔓32 Titus 1–2; late 2nd
𝔓37 Matt 26; late 3rd
𝔓39 John 8; first half of 3rd
𝔓40 Rom 1–4, 6, 9; 3rd

𝔓45 Gospels and Acts; early 3rd
𝔓46 Paul's Major Epistles (less Pastorals); late 2nd
𝔓47 Rev 9–17; 3rd
𝔓49+𝔓65 Eph 4–5; 1 Thess 1–2; 3rd
𝔓52 John 18; c. 125
𝔓53 Matt 26, Acts 9–10; middle 3rd
𝔓66 John; late 2nd
𝔓70 Matt 2–3, 11–12, 24; 3rd
𝔓72 1–2 Peter, Jude; c. 300
𝔓74 Acts, General Epistles; 7th
𝔓75 Luke and John; c. 200
𝔓77+𝔓103 (probably part of same codex) Matt 13–14, 23; late 2nd
𝔓87 Philemon; late 2nd
𝔓90 John 18–19; late 2nd
𝔓91 Acts 2–3; 3rd
𝔓92 Eph 1, 2 Thess 1; c. 300
𝔓98 Rev 1:13-20; late 2nd
𝔓100 Jas 3–5; c. 300
𝔓101 Matt 3–4; 3rd
𝔓104 Matt 21; 2nd
𝔓106 John 1; 3rd
𝔓115 Rev 2–3, 5–6, 8–15; 3rd

Significant Uncials

א (Sinaiticus) most of NT; 4th
A (Alexandrinus) most of NT; 5th
B (Vaticanus) most of NT; 4th
C (Ephraemi Rescriptus) most of NT with many lacunae; 5th
D (Bezae) Gospels, Acts; 5th
D (Claromontanus), Paul's Epistles; 6th (different MS than Bezae)
E (Laudianus 35) Acts; 6th
F (Augensis) Paul's Epistles; 9th
G (Boernerianus) Paul's Epistles; 9th
H (Coislinianus) Paul's Epistles; 6th
I (Freerianus or Washington) Paul's Epistles; 5th
L (Regius) Gospels; 8th
P (Porphyrianus) Acts—Revelation; 9th
Q (Guelferbytanus B) Luke, John; 5th
T (Borgianus) Luke, John; 5th
W (Washingtonianus or the Freer Gospels) Gospels; 5th
Z (Dublinensis) Matthew; 6th
037 (Δ; Sangallensis) Gospels; 9th
038 (Θ; Koridethi) Gospels; 9th
040 (Ξ; Zacynthius) Luke; 6th
043 (Φ; Beratinus) Matthew, Mark; 6th
044 (Ψ; Athous Laurae) Gospels, Acts, Paul's Epistles; 9th
048 Acts, Paul's Epistles, General Epistles; 5th
0171 Matt 10, Luke 22; c. 300
0189 Acts 5; c. 200

Significant Minuscules

1 Gospels, Acts, Paul's Epistles; 12th
33 All NT except Rev; 9th
81 Acts, Paul's Epistles, General Epistles; 1044
565 Gospels; 9th
700 Gospels; 11th
1424 (or Family 1424—a group of 29 manuscripts sharing nearly the same text) most of NT; 9th-10th
1739 Acts, Paul's Epistles; 10th
2053 Rev; 13th
2344 Rev; 11th
f^1 (a family of manuscripts including 1, 118, 131, 209) Gospels; 12th-14th
f^{13} (a family of manuscripts including 13, 69, 124, 174, 230, 346, 543, 788, 826, 828, 983, 1689, 1709—known as the Ferrar group) Gospels; 11th-15th

Significant Ancient Versions

SYRIAC (SYR)

syr^c (Syriac Curetonian) Gospels; 5th
syr^s (Syriac Sinaiticus) Gospels; 4th
syr^h (Syriac Harklensis) Entire NT; 616

OLD LATIN (IT)

it^a (Vercellenis) Gospels; 4th
it^b (Veronensis) Gospels; 5th
it^d (Cantabrigiensis—the Latin text of Bezae) Gospels, Acts, 3 John; 5th
it^e (Palantinus) Gospels; 5th
it^k (Bobiensis) Matthew, Mark; c. 400

COPTIC (COP)

cop^{bo} (Boharic—north Egypt)
cop^{fay} (Fayyumic—central Egypt)
cop^{sa} (Sahidic—southern Egypt)

OTHER VERSIONS

arm (Armenian)
eth (Ethiopic)
geo (Georgian)

TRANSLITERATION AND NUMBERING SYSTEM

Note: For words and roots from nonbiblical languages (e.g., Arabic, Ugaritic), only approximate transliterations are given.

HEBREW/ARAMAIC

Consonants

א	*aleph*	= *ʾ*	מ, ם	*mem*	= *m*
בּ, ב	*beth*	= *b*	נ, ן	*nun*	= *n*
גּ, ג	*gimel*	= *g*	ס	*samekh*	= *s*
דּ, ד	*daleth*	= *d*	ע	*ayin*	= *ʿ*
ה	*he*	= *h*	פּ, פ, ף	*pe*	= *p*
ו	*waw*	= *w*	צ, ץ	*tsadhe*	= *ts*
ז	*zayin*	= *z*	ק	*qoph*	= *q*
ח	*heth*	= *kh*	ר	*resh*	= *r*
ט	*teth*	= *t*	שׁ	*shin*	= *sh*
י	*yodh*	= *y*	שׂ	*sin*	= *s*
כּ, כ, ך	*kaph*	= *k*	תּ, ת	*taw*	= *t, th* (spirant)
ל	*lamedh*	= *l*			

Vowels

◌ַ	*patakh*	= *a*	◌ָ	*qamets khatuf*	= *o*
חַ	*furtive patakh*	= *a*	◌ֹ	*holem*	= *o*
◌ָ	*qamets*	= *a*	וֹ	*full holem*	= *o*
◌ָה	*final qamets he*	= *ah*	◌ֻ	*short qibbuts*	= *u*
◌ֶ	*segol*	= *e*	◌ֻ	*long qibbuts*	= *u*
◌ֵ	*tsere*	= *e*	וּ	*shureq*	= *u*
◌ֵי	*tsere yod*	= *e*	◌ֲ	*khatef patakh*	= *a*
◌ִ	*short hireq*	= *i*	◌ֳ	*khatef qamets*	= *o*
◌ִ	*long hireq*	= *i*	◌ְ	*vocalic shewa*	= *e*
◌ִי	*hireq yod*	= *i*	◌ַי	*patakh yodh*	= *a*

GREEK

α	*alpha*	= *a*	ι	*iota*	= *i*
β	*beta*	= *b*	κ	*kappa*	= *k*
γ	*gamma*	= *g, n (before* γ, κ, ξ, χ*)*	λ	*lamda*	= *l*
			μ	*mu*	= *m*
δ	*delta*	= *d*	ν	*nu*	= *n*
ε	*epsilon*	= *e*	ξ	*ksi*	= *x*
ζ	*zeta*	= *z*	ο	*omicron*	= *o*
η	*eta*	= *ē*	π	*pi*	= *p*
θ	*theta*	= *th*	ρ	*rho*	= *r* (ῥ = *rh)*

σ, ς	*sigma*	= *s*	ψ	*psi*	= *ps*
τ	*tau*	= *t*	ω	*omega*	= *ō*
υ	*upsilon*	= *u*	ʽ	*rough breathing mark*	= *h (with vowel or diphthong)*
φ	*phi*	= *ph*			
χ	*chi*	= *ch*			

THE TYNDALE-STRONG'S NUMBERING SYSTEM

The Cornerstone Biblical Commentary series uses a word-study numbering system to give both newer and more advanced Bible students alike quicker, more convenient access to helpful original-language tools (e.g., concordances, lexicons, and theological dictionaries). Those who are unfamiliar with the ancient Hebrew, Aramaic, and Greek alphabets can quickly find information on a given word by looking up the appropriate index number. Advanced students will find the system helpful because it allows them to quickly find the lexical form of obscure conjugations and inflections.

There are two main numbering systems used for biblical words today. The one familiar to most people is the Strong's numbering system (made popular by the *Strong's Exhaustive Concordance to the Bible*). Although the original Strong's system is still quite useful, the most up-to-date research has shed new light on the biblical languages and allows for more precision than is found in the original Strong's system. The Cornerstone Biblical Commentary series, therefore, features a newly revised version of the Strong's system, the Tyndale-Strong's numbering system. The Tyndale-Strong's system brings together the familiarity of the Strong's system and the best of modern scholarship. In most cases, the original Strong's numbers are preserved. In places where new research dictates, new or related numbers have been added.[1]

The second major numbering system today is the Goodrick-Kohlenberger system used in a number of study tools published by Zondervan. In order to give students broad access to a number of helpful tools, the Commentary provides index numbers for the Zondervan system as well.

The different index systems are designated as follows:

TG	Tyndale-Strong's Greek number	ZH	Zondervan Hebrew number
ZG	Zondervan Greek number	TA/ZA	Tyndale/Zondervan Aramaic number
TH	Tyndale-Strong's Hebrew number	S	Strong's Aramaic number

So in the example, "love" *agapē* [TG26, ZG27], the first number is the one to use with Greek tools keyed to the Tyndale-Strong's system, and the second applies to tools that use the Zondervan system.

The indexing of Aramaic terms differs slightly from that of Greek and Hebrew. Strong's original system mixed the Aramaic terms in with the Hebrew, but the Tyndale-Strong's system indexes Aramaic with a new set of numbers starting at 10,000. Since Tyndale's system for Aramaic diverges completely from original Strong's, the original Strong's number is listed separately so that those using tools keyed to Strong's can locate the information. This number is designated with an S, as in the example, "son" *bar* [TA/ZA10120, S1247].

1. Generally, one may simply use the original four-digit Strong's number to identify words in tools using Strong's system. If a Tyndale-Strong's number is followed by a capital letter (e.g., TG1692A), it generally indicates an added subdivision of meaning for the given term. Whenever a Tyndale-Strong's number has a number following a decimal point (e.g., TG2013.1), it reflects an instance where new research has yielded a separate, new classification of use for a biblical word. Forthcoming tools from Tyndale House Publishers will include these entries, which were not part of the original Strong's system.

James

GRANT R. OSBORNE

INTRODUCTION TO
James

The Epistle of James is dearly loved by many Christians. We know favorite statements like, "When troubles come your way, consider it an opportunity for great joy" (1:2); "Be quick to listen, slow to speak, and slow to get angry" (1:19); "Faith is dead without good works" (2:26); "If we could control our tongues, we would be perfect" (3:2); and "Resist the devil, and he will flee from you" (4:7). Moo (2000:1-2) provides three reasons why James is so popular: (1) It is incredibly practical, with each of its sections discussing issues that have relevance for our daily lives. There is a higher percentage of ethical commands in James than in any other New Testament book, and the stress is on living out the truth of the gospel. (2) His conciseness makes him easy to read and remember. Since there is little extensive development of ideas, readers can catch his points quite easily. (3) His colorful use of illustration and metaphor makes his points memorable. The divided mind, the unstable sea, the enticing trap, the shifting shadows, the look in the mirror, the roaring forest fire, the fancily dressed rich person, the untamable tongue, and the morning fog are all powerful word pictures that capture the imagination.

AUTHOR

The letter claims to be written by "James, a slave of God and of the Lord Jesus Christ." But who was this "James"? Calvin thought this was James the brother of John, one of the inner circle of the Twelve. But this James was executed by Herod Agrippa (Acts 12:2), and that event (which was around AD 44) seems a bit too early for this epistle (see discussion below under "Date"). Furthermore, there is no evidence in Acts that would fit James the son of Zebedee and brother of John as the author of this epistle.

The name James occurs two other times in lists of the Twelve: James the son of Alphaeus (Mark 3:18) and James the father of the other disciple named Judas (Luke 6:16). Neither has really been considered as the author because there is no evidence or knowledge of them other than their brief mention as being among Jesus' disciples. The most common critical view today is that this is a piece of pseudonymous literature, written by an unknown person or persons in the name of James the Lord's brother, perhaps as a response to Pauline ideas (Dibelius, Laws, Ropes).

There are several reasons why many scholars believe the epistle could not have been written by a Galilean who spent his adult life in Jerusalem. For one, the language is among the most literary in the New Testament, displaying many Hellenistic figures of speech (e.g., "course of life," 3:6; cf. NLT, "whole life") and lines of thought, as well as quotations drawn from the Septuagint rather than the Masoretic Text. But this argument is no longer persuasive. Hengel (1974), among others, has shown the widespread use of Greek in the Palestinian world of the first century. Especially in Galilee with its large Gentile population, Greek would have been spoken by Jesus' family from the start. It was the second language of the region, much like German, French, and English are spoken throughout Europe and not just in their respective countries. Moreover, if James was written to diasporate congregations, the Hellenistic style would be natural. It has also been shown that the Greek of James is not as sophisticated as some have thought. It would best be labeled "high Koine" in its style, and the language fits a highly literate Hellenistic Jewish work of its day. Martin (1988:lxx) says it follows "the literary conventions and idioms of hellenistic Judaism." The Greek of James, in other words, would not have the refined quality of the sophists (highly literate rhetoricians of the first century) or writers like Cicero, but it was still very good Greek.

Another reason James's authorship by a native Galilean has been challenged is the absence of references to Christ, which seems unusual in a letter written by the Lord's brother (only in 1:1; 2:1). For this reason, a few scholars like Spitta believe it to have been a Jewish writing "Christianized" with the additions of the two verses that reference Christ. While few have gone this far, the absence of references to Christ has led many away from apostolic authorship. Yet while explicit references are sparse, implicit material stemming from the Jesus Logia (Jesus' sayings) permeates James's epistle. Mayor (1913:lxxxv-lxxvii) notes 60 possible Synoptic references, and Davids (1982:47-48) notes 36 (with 9 more general allusions). It can fairly be said that James draws heavily from the thought-world of Jesus. Indeed, it is somewhat surprising that Christ is named so seldom, and the resurrection appearance to James (1 Cor 15:7) is not noted, but this is an ethical more than a purely theological work, and every sentence is Christian to the core.

In conclusion, the church has consistently held to authorship by James the Lord's brother for most of its history, and the evidence of the epistle itself supports that thesis. During Jesus' life, James was an unbeliever (John 7:5); he was converted via a resurrection appearance of Jesus (1 Cor 15:7). So he never actually knew Jesus on earth as a believer and disciple. However, he quickly became a major leader in the church. He is mentioned first in Acts 12:17, when Peter, just released from prison by the angel, asks the people at the house of prayer, "Tell James and the other brothers what happened." He already appears to be one of the primary leaders in Jerusalem. Then at the critical Jerusalem Council in Acts 15:13-21, it is his final speech that turns the tide and enables the church to accept that the Gentile mission is God's will. Then in the "Jerusalem decree" of Acts 15:22-29, James and the other leaders asked the Gentile converts to respect certain Jewish sensitivities. In both instances James was a central figure in the Jerusalem church, in a sense acting as its head elder. Bock (2007:502) says James represented "the Jewish Christian contingent in Jerusalem." Finally, in Acts 21:18-19 Paul meets with "James, and all the elders" (again presupposing his leadership among them) to report on the third missionary journey and to give them the collection taken for the poor.

Paul's further interaction with James appears in Galatians 1:19; 2:9, 12. The first verse recounts that Paul visited Peter and James (both called "apostles," meaning James was accepted alongside the Twelve as one of God's chosen leaders) on his first postconversion trip to Jerusalem. Longenecker (1990:39) calls him "the leading figure of that church," saying it resulted from "the need for someone to lead the growing number of scrupulously minded Christians in the Jerusalem church, and that his relationship to Jesus, his Davidic descent, and his personal qualities fitted him for the task." In Galatians 2:9, during Paul's second visit to Jerusalem (most likely the "famine visit" of Acts 11:27-30) Paul says he met with James, Peter, and John, "who were known as pillars of the church," probably meaning they had been chosen by the Christian community as the leaders of the church there and were modeled after the three patriarchs (Abraham, Isaac, and Jacob), who were considered the "pillars" of Israel (Longenecker 1990:57). The fact that James is named first shows his stature in the community.

Finally, the "friends of James" (lit., "certain men who came from James") in Galatians 2:12 could be the one sign of conflict between James and Paul. Some have thought they were the same Judaizers who went to the churches of Galatia and denounced Paul in Acts 15 and Galatians 1:7; 6:13. However, there is no evidence of that in Galatians 2:12, and they were probably representatives of the Jerusalem church sent by James to encourage the people to observe the requests of the Jerusalem letter of Acts 15:22-29. They were not opponents of Paul, but as Jewish Christian leaders their appearance led Peter to revert to his old scruples against table fellowship with Gentiles, so Paul had to chastise him as well as others who followed his example (Gal 2:13-16). It is wrong to surmise from this that James and Paul were opponents.

James was well-known in the early church for his Jewish piety and was called "James the Just" for his faithfulness to Torah (see Chilton and Evans 1999; Eusebius *Ecclesiastical History* 2.23.3-16). In early Christian sources like Hegesippus, Gospel of Hebrews, or the Pseudo-Clementine literature (see Johnson 2003:100-106; Martin 1988:xliii-lxi), James could seem as much Jewish as Christian. However, much of that is overstatement, and Johnson concludes (2003:106) that he "is never said to sponsor any kind of ritual observance, certainly not that of circumcision" and "is never identified as an active opponent of Paul or Paul's mission." Both James and Paul were thoroughly Jewish in their background and ideas, but the difference is that James always ministered in a Jewish setting while Paul became the apostle to the Gentiles.

DATE

Those who accept the problems regarding authorship enumerated above typically regard this epistle as pseudonymous and written at the end of the first century or beginning of the second (e.g., Dibelius, Laws, Ropes) and the Tübingen school placed it after AD 150. Yet as we have just stated, this is unnecessary, and pseudonymity was by no means as acceptable and commonplace as some have asserted (for a good discussion, see Moo 2000:337-350). For those who accept authorship by James the brother of the Lord, there are two possible dates, one towards the end of James's life around AD 62 (Eusebius *Ecclesiastical History* 2.23.3-16; Josephus

Antiquities 20.200-203 [20.9.1]) and the other earlier, before the Jerusalem council in the mid-40s AD. There are two reasons why some accept the later date around AD 60: (1) the church described here seems to have been settled and mature, with wealthy and knowledgeable members; (2) James in chapter 2 was addressing a perversion of Paul's teaching regarding justification by faith alone (Tasker 1956:31-32).

Yet neither of these reasons given for a late date is conclusive. The church addressed in James is not mature, as seen in the numerous ethical problems addressed in this book (Blomberg and Kamell 2008:30-31), and every aspect could fit the 40s as well as the 60s. Nor does the language of 2:14-26 demand awareness of Paul's teaching, for the issues of justification and Abraham and faith and works could easily precede Paul's writings. Moo (2000:26) believes that Paul's teaching in Tarsus from AD 36 (Acts 9:30) and in Antioch from AD 45 (Acts 11:25-26) could have led to misunderstandings of its implications, and James was trying to correct this "perverted Paulinism," writing a year or two later. This is certainly possible, but the language could also fit a general Jewish Christian setting, since the issues are Jewish in origin and not just Pauline. Either makes sense. However we see it, the date that has the strongest likelihood for the writing of James is the mid- to late 40s (so Adamson, Mayor, Moo, Stulac). If written after the Jew-Gentile controversy started and the council of Jerusalem had taken place, these would surely have been mentioned. Once the debates over Torah observance began (as seen in so many of Paul's epistles), a Jewish epistle could not have avoided the topic. So James was the first New Testament work to be written. Galatians was also early (AD 48–49), but it centers closely on issues arising from the Gentile mission (in particular, those of the first missionary journey) and so postdates James somewhat (for an excellent detailed recent discussion of these issues, see McCartney 2009:12-32).

OCCASION OF WRITING

As Jewish Christians living outside Jerusalem (1:1; see "Audience" below), the recipients of James's epistle faced oppression and anti-Christian sentiment. As a result, they were poverty-stricken, cheated by wealthy landowners (5:1-6), taken to court by their very persecutors (2:6), discriminated against even by fellow believers (2:1-6), and often lacking sufficient food or clothes (2:15-16). This difficult situation led to major dissension and backbiting in the church. With their difficulties they became "double minded," wavering between trust in God and dependence on their earthly situation (1:8; 4:8). They became self-centered and unwilling to add works to their faith in caring for others in the church (2:14-26). James wrote this epistle as an antidote to these problems.

AUDIENCE

James says he was writing "to the 'twelve tribes'—Jewish believers scattered abroad" (1:1). This fits the contents of the letter, with the use of "synagogue" in 2:2 (see NLT mg), the midrashic use of the Old Testament throughout, the Jewish Christian style of the argumentation, and the general tone of the epistle. If we take "diaspora" ("scattered") literally as a reference to the Jewish people living outside of Palestine (see commentary on 1:1), this would be a letter addressed to Jewish

Christian congregations in Syria and Asia Minor (e.g., "as far as Phoenicia, Cyprus, and Antioch of Syria" in Acts 11:19). As in Acts 8 and 11, this "scattering" could have been occasioned by persecution, but it should not be limited to Christian Jews who were "scattered" by the events of Acts 8:1-3, for it would also include Jewish residents in these lands converted by the Christian message.

This understanding of "diaspora," however, is uncertain. Davids (1982:30-34) places the epistle in the midst of the social upheaval in Palestine before the war of AD 66–70, with the wealthy landowners of Galilee and the materialism of the merchants. Martin (1988:lxii-lxix, lxxvii) finds two provenances: the first in Jerusalem in the early 60s addressing the situation of the Zealot uprising with its anger and violence; the second in Antioch of Syria, which accounts for the Pauline parallels and the Hellenistic flourishes. While Davids and Martin provide interesting possibilities, neither is particularly convincing; a more general situation better fits the tenor of the work as a whole, for there is no true evidence of the kind of social upheavals seen in Palestine in the 50s and 60s of the first century. Rather, the emphasis on rich and poor in James is more general, referring to social concern and proper treatment for those whom society has marginalized. So this was a pastoral letter to diasporate Jewish-Christian communities responding to ethical problems that had arisen in these congregations. James was writing as a Jewish Christian sage correcting matters in the Christian gatherings ("synagogues") outside Jerusalem.

CANONICITY AND TEXTUAL HISTORY

With respect to placement in the New Testament canon, there is no other epistle that has passed through the peaks and valleys that James has. An obviously Jewish epistle, it was rejected by Marcion and the Gnostics in the second century for its Jewish character. And it is missing in the Muratorian Canon (though the ending of this document is missing, and we cannot read too much into the absence of James). There are a few early allusions to James (e.g., *1 Clement*; *2 Clement* 6:3-4; *Shepherd of Hermas*; see Johnson 1995:71-79, 128), all late first- to early second-century writings, but there is no direct recognition of James until the third century, and Eusebius in the fourth century placed it among the "disputed books" (*Ecclesiastical History* 3.25.3). James found full acceptance in the Eastern church and was defended by Origen, Athanasius, and Cyril, among others. Yet it did not seem to be well-known in the Western church, though it was used frequently by Jerome and Augustine, guaranteeing James's popularity in the medieval church (see, e.g., the commentary on James by the Venerable Bede in the eighth century).

But things changed during the Reformation, when Martin Luther called James an "epistle of straw," due to its paucity of teaching about Christ, and made it of secondary importance compared with Paul and the Gospels. This view was not shared by all Reformers (Zwingli and Melanchthon used James extensively, and Calvin wrote a commentary on it), but Luther's position (and later German Lutheran scholarship) had enormous influence. In many circles James was neglected as a Jewish Christian (or even Jewish) epistle and relegated to the periphery of the early church. But that is not the case with the majority in the church today, who accept James's epistle and revere its teaching.

The epistle's seeming contradiction of Pauline thought has troubled many, like Luther. Since Paul demands faith alone and 2:14-26 centers on works, they are seen as antithetical. This commentary, however, will seek to show that this is wrong-headed: Paul speaks negatively of the idea that works result *in* faith (that is, faith coming from works), while James speaks positively of works that result *from* faith (that is, faith producing works). Putting them together, both Paul and James are saying that works cannot produce faith while faith must produce works (this is the teaching of Eph 2:8-10 as well as Jas 2:14-26). Johnson (2003:111) sums up the common misreading well: "These twelve verses (2:14-26) are measured against an (equally narrow and distorted) construal of Pauline theology. The fixation prevents the appreciation of each author in his own right and clouds the wide range of language and perception that they share beyond the narrow issue of faith and works."

James belongs at the head of the General Epistles, followed by 1 and 2 Peter, 1–3 John, and Jude. The text of James is attested to by many early manuscripts: 𝔓23 and 𝔓100 (third century), Codex Sinaiticus (fourth century), 𝔓54, A, and D (fifth century), and 𝔓74 (seventh century). Significant textual variants, of which there are few, are addressed throughout the commentary.

LITERARY STYLE AND STRUCTURE

James has one of the briefest epistolary introductions of any New Testament letter, with no greeting, thanksgiving, or opening prayer; it is also missing the conventional closing. It does contain the frequent use of "brothers and sisters" but shows little other signs of personal contact. It comes closer to a "treatise" rather than a personal letter like most of Paul's epistles. Though James was likely writing to people he had not met, the pastoral tone is obvious. Yet this is not a letter written to encourage beleaguered Christians but rather a pastoral challenge intended to exhort, indeed to admonish, believers who were not living out their faith. It has a higher percentage of imperatives than any other New Testament epistle, and the title of every single section of this work (see below) demonstrates this fact.

Several different suggestions have been made to define James's genre. Ropes (1916:10-16) calls it a "diatribe" similar to Romans. Popular in ancient debate, this genre used rhetorical questions, second-person address, and imaginary interlocutors (2:18-19) to draw the readers into the developing argument. While these elements are certainly present, few are willing to label the entire epistle a diatribe, because too many elements do not fit. A more general term like "paraenesis" (or "exhortation"; Dibelius 1975:5-6) fits better. Dibelius sees James as having general moral teachings without internal connections (to fit his view that James contains artificially and randomly connected isolated sayings). Johnson (1995:18-20) corrects this by showing that paraenetic material is a distinct form, containing traditional teaching that stresses memory of received truths, imitation of known models or paradigms of correct behavior, and maxims or brief instructions as to how to achieve that proper conduct. All this fits James very well. Still, this is not quite sufficient; James is better identified as a set of homilies utilizing wisdom material. In fact, both diatribe and paraenesis can be seen as aspects of Wisdom Literature. Davids (1982:23) describes the characteristics of a synagogue homily as containing "dialogue (including such features as rhetorical questions, questions and answers, and an imaginary opponent), the direct address of the auditor (e.g., 'my brothers'); variety in subject matter; and harsh speech." All three of the above (diatribe, paraenesis, wisdom) are found within the basic category of synagogue homily.

As to the literary structure of James, Dibelius (1975:2) set the tone for modern discussion when he said that "the entire document lacks continuity of thought . . . not only a lack of continuity of thought between individual sayings and other smaller units, but also between larger treatises." For Dibelius, James consists of a series of artificially strung-together minihomilies held together by hook-words but not by thematic development. However, not many have gone that far, and it is increasingly realized that James is a literary whole with a distinct structure. Blomberg and Kamell (2008:22) state that "James is comprised of a dozen or so passages of preachable length, with a few shorter introductory, transitional, and/or concluding sections." This could be understood to support Dibelius's contention, but I will be arguing that it is just the opposite—James comprises an artfully constructed series of ethical exhortations that fit together very well into a united discourse. The question is not whether there is a unified structure but how we delineate the organizing principles by which James developed that structure.

The best summary that I have seen regarding the various views on the overall structure of James is that of Blomberg and Kamell (2008:23-26). They point out four types of outlines that have been posited for the book. The first has already been noted: the view of Dibelius that James virtually has no outline but contains a mostly disconnected series of isolated challenges linked by catchwords. The second type proceeds via "a broad topical or thematic structure," in which James develops topic by topic, for example, Kistemaker's chapter-by-chapter movement (1986:21-22) from perseverance to faith to restraint to submission to patience; or Johnson's organization (1995:ix) around exhortation (1:1-27), the deeds of faith (2:1-26), the power and peril of speech (3:1-12), the call to conversion (3:13–4:10), examples of arrogance (4:11–5:6), patience in time of testing (5:7-11), and speech in the assembly of faith (5:12-20). Moo (2000:vi-vii) also has a seven-part outline: the opportunity afforded by trials (1:2-18), obedience to the word (1:19–2:26), pure speech and peace I (3:1–4:3), a summons to spiritual wholeness (4:4-10), pure speech and peace II (4:11-12), understanding time and eternity (4:13–5:11), and concluding exhortations (5:12-20).

The third type of outline sees key themes controlling the structure, with the author introducing the themes, then developing them in the middle section, and concluding them at the end. Davids (1982:25-28) finds three key themes—testing, wisdom, and poverty and wealth—introduced in two cycles in 1:2-11, 12-27, then developed in depth in reverse order (producing a chiasm) in 2:1-26 (poverty and wealth), 3:1–4:12 (speech and wisdom), and 4:13–5:6 (greed and testing), with a conclusion provided by 5:7-11. Blomberg and Kamell (2008:26-27) follow Davids closely, with the exception being that they take the expansion of the themes further (the third part is 4:13–5:18 rather than to 4:13–5:6). This approach has real promise, but the narrowing down of key themes to three may be overly simplistic. Neither 2:1-26 nor 4:13–5:6 can be narrowed down to poverty and wealth. The focus of

2:14-26 is living out one's faith, and the poverty aspect is only in the illustration of 2:15-16. The progression of thought seems more linear than this.

The fourth and final type of outline uses discourse analysis (on which see Osborne 2006:150-153) to organize James along the lines of Greco-Roman rhetorical patterns. Taylor and Guthrie (2006) find a twofold introduction (1:2-11, 12-27) and a closing (5:7-20) and then find a chiastic structure centering on the inclusion of 2:12-13; 4:11-12 (on proper speech and behavior), accompanied by a Hellenistic "body opening" in 2:1-11 and a "body closing" in 4:13–5:6. The central section is chiastic, with A = 2:12-26; B = 3:1-12; C = 3:13-18; B′ = 4:1-3; A′ = 4:4-10. This outline is both viable and illuminating. Yet while the third type of outline above is too simplistic, this is too complex. With two different sets of introductions as well a conclusion, and with the central part a chiasm, this becomes the polar opposite of Dibelius.

The second type of outline has always been the more popular approach (see McCartney 2009:62-67), and it accords well with the linear progression of James's epistle. The difficulty is with the short sections, which at first glance seem to be isolated sayings without connection to their context—1:9-11, 26-27; 2:12-13; 3:13-18; 4:4-10, 11-12; 5:7-11, 12, 19-20. Yet as the commentary will attempt to show, each does fit well into its context, and it is the task of a structural outline to demonstrate that literary connection.

In all my previous works (e.g., my recent work on the notes of the *ESV Study Bible*), I have taken James to be a series of exhortations centered one by one on the ethical problems of the Jewish church in James's day. I have since rethought that approach, and concluded that James organized his material into a series of triads like Matthew did (see Davies and Allison 1988:1.62-70). This is true at the macro level (each major section has three parts) and the micro level (e.g., the threefold structure of 1:2-11, 12-18, etc.). There is only one possible exception, 4:13–5:11, with two main sections, 4:13–5:6; 5:7-11; but there are in reality three sections there: 4:13-17; 5:1-6; 5:7-11 (many commentaries divide it this way). Thus, it seems those who think James is a disparate collection of isolated homilies have not adequately considered the literary cohesiveness of the book. James is in fact organized very tightly into a series of triads. (See "Outline" below for my detailed outline of the book.)

MAJOR THEMES

Luther and others have disparaged James because they believe he is weak theologically. When compared to Paul, he appears to have little Christology, a truncated soteriology, and not much on the Holy Spirit or the mission of the church. So Dibelius (1975:11) concludes that the letter of James has no theology and is simply an artificial collection of admonitions. However, this is one of the shorter epistles, and like the others, it is occasional, discussing the particular issues that were troubling James's congregations. As such, it does not provide a systematic presentation of dogma. Yet it is actually a very theological work, with several important themes that intersect the Christian life and beliefs. Moo correctly notes (2000:27), "So if by 'theology' one means a system of beliefs explicitly built on the person of Christ, then indeed the letter of James lacks a 'theology.' But such a definition of theology is much too narrow. If we expand the definition to include teaching grounded in an understanding of God and his purposes in the world, then James is thoroughly 'theological.'" Johnson adds (1995:85), "It is not far wrong to consider James one of the most 'theological' writings in the NT." If there is a single unifying theme (and such is widely denied), the best suggestion may come from Thielman (2005:500), who builds on the use of *dipsuchos* [TG1374/A, ZG1500] (unstable, double minded) in 1:8 and 4:8 to suggest that James is focused on "the undivided mind," that is, thoughts and actions that resonate against "friendship with the world" (4:4) and that follow God and his word.

God. The single most mentioned entity in James is "God." He is called *ho theos* [TG2316, ZG2536] (God) 16 times in the Greek (1:1, 5, 13 [twice], 20, 27; 2:5, 19, 23 [twice]; 3:9; 4:4 [twice], 6, 7, 8); "Father" three times (1:17, 27; 3:9); and "Lord" at least seven times (1:7; 3:9; 4:10, 15; 5:4, 10, 11, so Johnson 1995:85-86). Jesus is called "Lord" in 1:1; 2:1; 5:7, 8. The prayer "in the name of the Lord" in 5:14-15 could mean in the name of Jesus or God or both. Moo (2000:28-29) notes three characteristics of God emphasized in the epistle: First, God's oneness, which is hinted at in 1:5, where his "generous" giving also means he is "single-minded" in his giving. This is further emphasized in 1:17 with his "never-changing" character. The major place, however, is 2:19, where James challenges them, "You believe that there is one God. Good for you!" This refers to the Shema, the primary confession of Judaism, found in Deuteronomy 6:4, "The LORD is our God, the LORD alone." James's point is that the Shema is of little value unless it changes a person's perspective. "Even the demons believe this, and they tremble in terror." If God is truly one, then his people must live out that oneness in single-minded lives where their faith is expressed in works. Chester and Martin (1994:42) state, "God is portrayed as the *creator* (3.9; 1.17) and specifically as the Father of Lights, that is, as having supreme control over the universe. 1.17 shows in addition that he is seen as the *Father*, who is characterized by grace and giving freely. He is unchangeable, trustworthy and good. So also he is incorruptible, having nothing to do with evil; hence the importance of his role as eschatological judge and lawgiver."

The second characteristic Moo notes is God's jealousy, found in 4:5, "God longs jealously for the spirit he has caused to live in us" (my translation; see commentary on 4:5). When his people (= the bride of Yahweh) turn from him and become "friend[s] of the world" (4:4), God becomes a jealous husband (as in Exod 20:5; 34:14), and his divine wrath will fall on his straying wife. At the same time, he seeks repentance and reconciliation, whereby he "gives us even more grace" (4:6), so his people can overcome their sins, be forgiven, and return to their relationship with a loving God.

Third, the grace and mercy of God permeate his work. In 1:5 God is the "generous giver" who responds to our prayers; in 1:12 he gives "the crown of life" to his faithful people; and in 1:17 he gives every "good and perfect" gift to his people, especially the new birth (1:18). Then in 2:13 he shows "no mercy" to those who are not merciful to others, but at the same time his mercy is triumphant over his judgment, and that provides the model for us. The primary passage on the grace of

God is 4:6. When the pressure from our "evil desires" threatens to overwhelm us and make us "friend[s] of the world" (4:4), God "gives us even more grace" so that we can "come close" to him (4:8) and thereby "resist the devil" (4:7).

Trials and Temptation. This epistle begins with this theme, and it permeates virtually every section. Some issues that are trials, in fact, are discussed as separate aspects of James's theology, such as poverty or the effects of backbiting. In 1:2-3 he begins by noting that there are many kinds of trials and that their purpose is to test our faith, that is, to challenge our commitment to God and our separation from the world. The goal is to make believers "perfect and complete" (1:4; see "Wisdom and Practical Christianity" below) by teaching them endurance. In fact, "perseverance" is the title used by Thielman (2005:500-501) for this section, which he defines as remaining "firm in the faith" by lifting one's eyes to its good result before God and by single-mindedly committing oneself to "the wisdom from above" (3:17).

The primary trial James has in mind is persecution—the disapprobation faced by those who stand for Christ, the economic oppression of the Christian poor (5:1-6), and injustice in the courts (2:6-7). Davids (1982:343) sees three types of this persecution: disadvantages experienced as a result of living for Christ; opposition for spreading the Christian gospel; and the various kinds of suffering (emotional, economic, physical) inflicted by non-Christians. James's perspective is that God is the eschatological Judge who calls his followers to wait patiently for his final vindication (5:7-11). The believer is to return good for evil and maintain both their trust in God and their righteous conduct in the midst of evil.

With trials, however, also comes temptation (1:13-15). The same Greek word (*peirasmos* [TG3986, ZG4280]) means both "trial" (1:2, 12; NLT, "troubles" and "testing") and "temptation" (1:13-14). As we pass through these difficult tests, we are tempted to turn to self rather than God, resulting first in sin and then in spiritual death (1:15) if we give in. There are two sources of this temptation. First, there is what the Jewish people called the "evil *yetzer*" or impulse, the internal side. This tendency to self-centered living is also stressed in every section: in the "filth and evil" of 1:21, the favoritism of 2:1, the unconcern of 2:15-16, the fiery tongue of 3:6-10, the wars caused by "evil desires" in 4:1, and the apathy of 4:13. Second, there is the tempter, the devil (4:7), the external source, who brings jealousy and self-centered ways (3:15) that "set on fire" one's whole life (3:6).

Eschatology. James is not just a wisdom thinker calling for ethical accountability in a this-world environment; he is also an apocalyptic prophet who places it all in the context of final eschatology. This emphasis also flows throughout his epistle. The atmosphere behind 1:9-11, where the earthly perspectives of rich and poor (exaltation and humiliation) are reversed, is also found in 1:12, where the promised "crown of life" is said to await the faithful. Such will not happen with finality until the eschaton. The opposite to the "life" of 1:12 is found in 1:15, the eternal "death" that is the final stage of sin. Then in 2:5, the poor are described as those who "will inherit the Kingdom he promised." Next, the divine Judge of 2:12-13 and 4:12 points to the Last Judgment. The "greater condemnation" of 3:1 (see KJV), when teachers will be "judged more strictly," also refers to that final time when we will all give account to God (cf. Heb 13:17)—that is, we will answer to him for the quality of our ministries.

This stress culminates in the themes of chapter 5. The warning to the wealthy oppressors in 5:1-6 proceeds from this perspective of eternal judgment, as James says, "Weep and groan with anguish because of all the terrible troubles ahead" (5:1), and warns about "evidence against [them] on the day of judgment" (5:3) and about those who have "fattened [themselves] for the day of slaughter" (5:5). In contrast, the oppressed Christian poor are called to be "patient" for their vindication and "wait for the Lord's return" (5:7). Their courage is based on the imminent expectation that "the coming of the Lord is near" and "the Judge is standing at the door" (see commentary on 5:8-9). The ungodly face eternal punishment; the righteous will receive vindication and reward.

Of course, this does not mean that James is an apocalyptic work with an entirely future-oriented message. All of his ethical mandates are oriented to the present Christian life, and the promises of James begin in the present blessings poured out on those who have been given the new birth of 1:18, resulting in the fact that God's people even now are "his prized possession." There is an inaugurated eschatology in James, and as elsewhere in the New Testament, the saints are pictured as living in tension between the already and the not-yet, between the present possession of his rich blessings in the midst of this troubled world and the final realization of these promises in eternity. Chester and Martin (1994:20) conclude in this way: "The themes of judgment, testing, and threat are set over, and within, the work as a whole, but so also are those of hope for the messianic age and final reward, and the immediate, urgent implications of this for the way life should be lived in the present." In others words, the final eschatology and its realized implications function together in an inaugurated perspective.

Wealth and Poverty. Many have considered this the primary theme of James, but that is an overstatement. Still, it is one of the key issues. Moo (2000:35) provides background by noting three strands of the Old Testament/Jewish tradition: God's special concern as defender of the downtrodden (Deut 10:18; Ps 68:5); God's demands that his people show concern for the poor (Deut 10:19) and his condemnation when they do not (Amos 2:6-7); the association of the "poor" with the righteous (Pss 10; 37:8-17; 72:2, 4; Isa 29:19), as they throw themselves on the mercy of God and depend on him. Davids (1982:43) notes developments in the intertestamental period: The need to care for the poor became "a fundamental religious duty"; the wealthy more and more were seen as demonstrating a lack of piety; and "the poor" became a semitechnical name for pious groups who considered themselves to be oppressed.

In James, poverty and piety (i.e., dependence on God) are juxtaposed. When 1:2-8 (on trials and faithful prayer to God for wisdom) is followed by 1:9-11 (on the exaltation of the poor and the humility of the wealthy), the clear intention is to highlight poverty as a primary trial. As such, it must lead to endurance and to asking the generous God for wisdom to face the difficult trial. Also, the church must be involved in alleviating poverty; "pure and genuine religion" (i.e., if it is to be a truly biblical church) demands that God's people care for (i.e., help) the desperate "orphans and widows," the most destitute of the poor in the first century (1:27). In 2:3 the favoritism is for the rich against the poor, and in 2:15-16 the illustration of faith without works is a refusal to help a person without sufficient food or clothing. In 3:17 the "wisdom from above" is characterized by "mercy and good deeds." The issue of poverty is almost everywhere in James.

The theme comes to a head in 4:13–5:6. It is critical to realize that James never says that wealth is evil. In 1:10 the rich are told to glory in their humility in light of the brevity of life, and that is the point also in 4:13-17. The rich merchant Christians are admonished not because they are successful but because they have left God out of their plans and have a worldly (4:4) attitude toward their secular careers. Since life is fleeting, it must always be lived under God and his directions. The situation in 5:1-6 is different, but there too the wealth is evil not because it exists but because it is misused only to benefit the non-Christian landowners who were cheating their poor Christian workers out of the pay they deserved. Their sin was using all their wealth for luxurious living (5:2-3a), hoarding their treasures for themselves (5:3b), cheating their field workers (5:4), living only for pleasure (5:5b), and condemning innocent people to death by their actions (5:6). They would face judgment for their sins.

Wisdom and Practical Christianity. James is in a real sense Wisdom Literature, and biblical wisdom can be defined as "living life in God's world by God's rules," "a theological pattern of thinking that applies the wisdom of God to practical issues of life" (Osborne 2006:242-243). This fits James very well, for the demand is to use God's gift of wisdom to live rightly before him. In 1:4 the result of persevering in the midst of trials is to become "perfect and complete, needing nothing"; yet in 1:5 the one thing needed is "wisdom" to handle the many trials encountered. The solution is to "ask our generous God, and he will give it to you." In this context the "good and perfect" gift that "comes down to us from God our Father" (1:17) is precisely this wisdom. This is reiterated in 3:13, which calls for "doing good works with the humility that comes from wisdom." James 3:15,17 contrasts "jealousy and selfishness," which are "not God's kind of wisdom," with the "wisdom from above," which among other things is "full of mercy and good deeds." It is clear that for James, wisdom is tied to conduct, demanding a behavior that is in keeping with God's established way of life (see the excellent article by Johnson [2003]). Davids (1982:56-57) points to Luke 11:13, where God gives the Spirit to those who ask and says, "James has a wisdom pneumatology, for wisdom in James functions as the Spirit does in Paul," producing "the fruit of the Christian life."

This pattern of practical Christianity is found throughout the epistle. The key characteristic is what Thielman (2005:500) makes the central theme of James, the "undivided life," overcoming the danger of the "divided mind" (*dipsuchos* [TG1374/A, ZG1500]; 1:6-8; 4:8) by achieving the "perfect" or "complete" life in God (1:4, *teleios* [TG5046, ZG5455]; used also in 1:17, 25; 2:8, 22; 3:2). The theme begins in 1:22-25, where it commands that we be doers as well as hearers of the word; since the word is the "mirror" of our life, it must be lived out in "pure and genuine religion" (1:27) by caring for the marginalized in this world. This emphasis is continued in 2:8, challenging us to "obey the royal law" of love for our neighbor without favoritism (cf. Lev 19:18). The central passage on practical Christianity is, of course, 2:14-26, showing that faith is useless unless it is accompanied by good deeds. As will be said in the commentary, James is not contradicting Paul by developing a works-righteousness, but rather agreeing with Paul in Ephesians 2:10 by saying that real faith must always result in works. Our faith is meant to be lived out in our daily deeds.

In the section on speech and conflict (3:1–4:12), James challenges us to prove our wisdom and understanding by "living an honorable life, doing good works with the humility that comes from wisdom" (3:13). As was said above, wisdom is exceedingly practical and deals with the way we live—in this section meaning that we do not conduct ourselves out of jealousy and spite by speaking out against others (see "Speech, the Outward Sign of the Soul" below) but by gentle and merciful actions (3:17-18). There are two lifestyle choices: to live as a "friend of the world" (4:4) or to live in submission to God (4:7a, 8a). The unstable Christian is "divided between God and the world" (4:8b), and such a lifestyle will utterly fail.

The solution is a life of prayer, illustrated in three passages. First, in 1:5 the very wisdom we need to live rightly according to God can only come to us as a gift from above (1:17; 3:17) when we pray. We lack sufficient strength and understanding to do it on our own, but we have a generous God who gives us the wisdom to endure and overcome our difficulties (1:5). Second, we should place all our needs upon him. This is stated negatively in 4:2-3 ("You don't have what you want because you don't ask"), and it is in keeping with Matthew 6:11, "Give us today the food we need." The only way we can live a successful life is to relinquish control of our life to God (cf. also 4:13-16). Third, prayer for physical illness is highlighted in 5:13-18. The elders, who are likely the wise teachers of 3:1, 13, 17, seemingly have a special anointing and prayer power, yet at the same time all God's people are included, for "the earnest prayer of a righteous person has great power and produces wonderful results" (5:16), both in healing and in forgiveness of sins.

Speech, the Outward Sign of the Soul. The misuse of the tongue was a serious issue in James's churches. The topic is introduced in 1:19, which in one sense is the theme verse of the epistle: "Be quick to listen, slow to speak, and slow to get angry." All three of these uses of the tongue surface in 3:1–4:12, where envy and self-centered attitudes led many to backbiting and angry retorts rather than a wise use of the tongue. There is an A-B-A pattern in that central section, with 3:1-12 and 4:1-12 dealing with the misuse of the tongue to hurt others, and 3:13-18 stressing a wise use of the tongue to bring peace and "a harvest of righteousness" (3:18) to the community. For James, a person's speech habits reflect the true state of their relationship with God. Malicious speech can cause great damage (3:5b-8) and highlight hypocrisy (3:9-12). But lest all believers become afraid ever to speak, James also stresses the tongue's great power for good (3:3-5a). "If we listen to others carefully, think before we talk, and save our anger for rare occasions, in which it is truly justified (1:19), we will be wise indeed" (Blomberg and Kamell 2008:257).

Law and Grace. I have already spoken of the grace of God in James (under the section on "God" above), so here I am primarily tracing James's attitude to the law vis-à-vis Paul and the law-grace issue so often discussed today. The Torah is highlighted in three places—1:25 ("the perfect law that sets you free"); 2:8-12 ("the royal law as found in the Scriptures . . . you will be judged by the law that sets you free"); and 4:11-12 ("Your job is to obey the law. . . . God alone, who gave the law, is the Judge"). There are several things we must note: (1) James is completely positive about the law. (2) He always uses the law in terms of its ethical mandates, not its cultic requirements; he never demands adherence to the cultic rituals, but at the same time he never negates them either. (3) The law seems to be completely accepted by his churches; he uses it to support his arguments and needs no arguments for its validity. (4) James is Christian before he is Jewish; there is no atmosphere of what Sanders calls "covenantal nomism" (the belief in Judaism that they were right with God because they were the covenant people), no hint that salvation is in anything other than faith in Christ. (5) He is very Jewish regarding the law; it is the "perfect law" that liberates (1:25), the "royal law" and "the law that sets you free" (2:8, 12), and there is none of the negativism expressed in Paul, who says the law would "last only until the coming of the child who was promised" (Gal 3:19), that it was a "guardian until Christ came" (Gal 3:24), that a return to the law was a return to slavery (Gal 4:8-11), that we "no longer live under the requirements of the law" (Rom 6:14), and that we have "died to the power of the law" (Rom 7:4). So some scholars think that James is antithetical to Paul on the law, that Paul considers the law an enslaving force while James thinks it a liberating force. On the surface, that seems viable. But we have to remember that Paul held that attitude only regarding situations in which the law became a means of legalistic salvation. In Romans 7:12 Paul said, "The law itself is holy, and its commands are holy and right and good." Moreover, James is in agreement with Jesus in Matthew 5:18, "I tell you the truth . . . not even the smallest detail of God's law will disappear until its purpose is achieved." There is no contradiction; Paul stresses one aspect, James another aspect, of the place of the law in the age of Christ. Chester and Martin (1994:38) sum it up: "For James the law is specifically linked to the messianic kingdom and the new age. . . . Its requirements are summed up in Jewish tradition, are specific, concrete, and communal, as well as pointing to the nature of the messianic age." Davids (1982:51) adds, "James believes that through a gracious act of God one becomes a Christian. . . . This commitment ought to be expressed through appropriate moral action, the fruit of the renewed life. The authoritative guide to the character of this action is the law, particularly as interpreted by and in accordance with the sayings of Jesus."

OUTLINE

- I. Greeting (1:1)
- II. The Testing of Your Faith (1:2-18)
  - A. Trials and Testing (1:2-11)
    1. Joy in trials (1:2-4)
    2. Wisdom and faith in trials (1:5-8)
    3. A basis for trials—poverty and wealth (1:9-11)
  - B. Testing and Temptation in Relation to God (1:12-15)
  - C. God's Perfect Gift (1:16-18)

- III. Practical Christianity—Living Out the Word (1:19–2:26)
  - A. Hearing and Doing the Word (1:19-27)
    1. Hearers of the word (1:19-21)
    2. Doers of the word (1:22-25)
    3. Practical Christianity (1:26-27)
  - B. Preferring the Wealthy in the Assembly (2:1-13)
    1. The problem of prejudice (2:1-7)
    2. The royal law of love (2:8-11)
    3. Act in light of judgment (2:12-13)
  - C. Faith Must Be Accompanied by Works (2:14-26)
    1. Faith without works is dead (2:14-17)
    2. The response of a critic (2:18-20)
    3. The examples of Abraham and Rahab (2:21-26)
- IV. The Problem of the Tongue—The Sin of Dissension (3:1–4:12)
  - A. Taming the Tongue (3:1-12)
    1. Beware of becoming teachers (3:1-2a)
    2. Small things cause great results (3:2b-5a)
    3. The power of the tongue to destroy (3:5b-12)
  - B. The Solution—Wisdom from Above (3:13-18)
  - C. Warning against Worldliness (4:1-12)
    1. A friend of the world is an enemy of God (4:1-6)
    2. The solution—submit to God (4:7-10)
    3. Slander and judging (4:11-12)
- V. Admonitions to the Worldly and the Godly (4:13–5:11)
  - A. Warnings to the Worldly (4:13–5:6)
    1. The worldly Christian needs to trust in God (4:13-17)
    2. The worldly unbeliever will experience destruction (5:1-6)
  - B. Challenge to the Believers—Patience in Suffering (5:7-11)
- VI. Final Exhortations (5:12-20)
  - A. Avoidance of Oaths (5:12)
  - B. Promise to the Ill—Healing through Prayer (5:13-18)
  - C. Concluding Challenge—Restoring the Wanderer (5:19-20)

COMMENTARY ON
James

◆ I. Greeting (1:1)

This letter is from James, a slave of God and of the Lord Jesus Christ.

I am writing to the "twelve tribes"—Jewish believers scattered abroad.

Greetings!

NOTES

1:1 ***of God and of the Lord Jesus Christ.*** All the nouns in this series lack the article, and there is some discussion as to whether *theou* [TG2316, ZG2536] (of God) refers to God the Father or to the divine Christ. The latter would be translated "slave of Jesus Christ, who is God and Lord" (so Motyer). While this meaning is very possible, because the term "God" is utilized regarding the deity of Christ (e.g., John 1:1, 18; 20:28; Rom 9:5; Titus 2:13; Heb 1:8; 2 Pet 1:1), it is not likely here. In 2 Pet 1:1 (another place the title is used of Christ: "our God and Savior Jesus Christ"), Granville Sharp's rule (see Wallace 1996:270-290) makes it clear that the single article brings together "God" and "Savior" into a conceptual unity. That is not the case here; "God" must be seen here as the Father of Christ. Nevertheless, the two function together as the master of James, their slave; so the equality of God and Christ is implicit in this formula.

to the "twelve tribes"—Jewish believers scattered abroad. Lit., "to the twelve tribes of the Diaspora." This can be understood several ways: (1) it could be racial and geographical, referring to Jews and Jewish Christians living outside Palestine (Hort, Mayor); (2) it could more narrowly refer to those in Palestine but outside Jerusalem (Scaer); (3) it could be metaphorical, used as in 1 Pet 1:1 for the church as the new Israel "sojourning" in this world (Laws). The best understanding is most likely a combination of 1 and 3, that these were Jewish Christians living outside Israel, who considered themselves as the "scattered people of God."

COMMENTARY

The author of this epistle (as discussed in the Introduction) is neither James the brother of John and one of the inner circle of the apostles (martyred by Herod Agrippa I, Acts 12:2) nor James the son of Alphaeus (noted in Mark 3:18 as one of the Twelve, but hardly mentioned in the New Testament; some consider him to be Clopas, also known as James the younger, son of Mary in Mark 15:40, but that cannot be proven). The author of this epistle was likely James the brother of Jesus, an unbeliever during Jesus' life (John 7:5) and converted by the resurrected appearance of Jesus (1 Cor 15:7). He became chief elder of the church in Jerusalem and the leading figure in the Jerusalem council of Acts 15. According to Galatians

1:19, he was considered an "apostle," and in Galatians 2:9 he was labeled by Paul as one of the "pillars of the church" (with Peter and John). According to Galatians 2:11-14, a controversial episode took place in which some "friends of James" arrived and turned Peter against Paul on the issue of having table fellowship with uncircumcised Gentile followers. What cannot be known is the complicity of James in this incident, i.e., whether he sent them as emissaries or they simply used his name for their Judaistic demands. If he had sent them, it is clear that by the end of the Jerusalem council he had at least changed his mind on that issue. He was so pious as a Jewish Christian that the Jews labeled him "James the Just." The end for James came at the siege of Jerusalem when he was first denounced by the high priest Ananus and then thrown headlong down from a pillar atop the Temple (see Josephus *Antiquities* 20.200).

James does not call himself "the brother of our Lord," probably because his humility did not allow him to take advantage of that relationship. Besides, he was an unbeliever throughout his life (as a brother) until the resurrection appearance. Rather, he calls himself *doulos* [TG1401, ZG1528] ("slave"; see further on 1 Pet 2:16), a word often used at the beginning of New Testament letters (e.g., Rom 1:1; Phil 1:1; Titus 1:1; 2 Pet 1:1; Jude 1). This followed an Old Testament practice (e.g., Gen 32:10; Exod 14:31 [Moses]; Isa 41:8 [Israel]; 42:1; Jer 7:25 [the prophets]). The "slave of Yahweh" represented one who was a trusted official or envoy in the administration of the royal kingdom of Yahweh. It also speaks of absolute servanthood under the power of God. James's master here is God and Christ. There is no formula in the New Testament as full as this ("slave of God and of the Lord Jesus Christ"). James wanted the reader to understand fully that he served under the authority of his God and his Lord. They are fully sovereign, equally divine and master over James (see note on 1:1). We must note that while at the earthly level James was Jesus' brother, at the level of ultimate concern (and with James's whole being), he was Jesus' slave. While "Christ" here is without the article and thus part of his proper name ("Jesus Christ"), no Jew would have read this without thinking "Jesus the Messiah," and that is likely intended here. All of the first half of the verse is anarthrous (i.e., the definite article does not appear), emphasizing the theological aspects of Jesus' lordship and messianic office (cf. Acts 2:36, where Peter said in his Pentecost sermon, "God has made this Jesus, whom you crucified, to be both Lord and Messiah"). "Jesus is Lord" appears in several creedal passages (Rom 10:9-10; 1 Cor 8:6; 12:3; Phil 2:11; Col 2:6) and is part of his exaltation to the right hand of God (Rom 8:34; Col 3:1) and of his ultimate authority over God's kingdom.

The addressees are called "'the twelve tribes'—Jewish believers scattered abroad" (lit., "the twelve tribes of the Diaspora"). The twelve tribes were, of course, the descendants of the twelve patriarchs and were allotted territory in Israel after they conquered the Promised Land (Josh 13–21). However, in the Assyrian and Babylonian exiles, the tribes lost their place in the Holy Land and were "dispersed" throughout the nations (forming the Diaspora). The prophets frequently promised that God would regather his scattered people in exile and assemble the nation together once more (Isa 11:11-12; Jer 31:8-12; 50:19; Zech 10:8-12). It was commonly believed that the Exile would not be over until all the Jewish people had been returned to Zion, and that would only happen with the coming of the Messiah. Thus, the early church looked upon itself as the new Israel, Jew and Gentile alike, who were the regathered people of God. They were citizens of heaven and exiles living in a foreign land, alienated from and despised by the people of this world (see on 1 Pet 1:1, 17; 2:11). They were God's people of the last days. As Moo points out (2000:49-50), Jesus' choice of twelve disciples shows he was gathering together "eschatological Israel," depicted also in Revelation 7:5-8 by the 12,000 drawn from each of the twelve tribes, and in Revelation 21:12 by the twelve gates of the heavenly Jerusalem inscribed with "the names of the twelve tribes of Israel." So James was addressing a group of Jewish Christians who lived in pagan lands outside Palestine and considered themselves to be true Israel, living in exile far from their heavenly home.

◆ II. The Testing of Your Faith (1:2-18)
A. Trials and Testing (1:2-11)
1. Joy in trials (1:2-4)

2 Dear brothers and sisters,* when troubles come your way, consider it an opportunity for great joy. 3 For you know that when your faith is tested, your endurance has a chance to grow. 4 So let it grow, for when your endurance is fully developed, you will be perfect and complete, needing nothing.

1:2 Greek *brothers;* also in 1:16, 19.

NOTES

1:2 ***consider it an opportunity for great joy.*** The first two words in the sentence are *pasan charan* [TG3956/5479, ZG4246/5915] (all joy), emphasizing the proper response to trials. The verb ("consider") is an imperative and means that the mental decision to count all life's various difficulties to be completely joyous is not an option but a divine mandate.

1:3 ***For you know.*** This translates a causal participle, "knowing." This verb is often used in the NT (5:20; Rom 6:3, 6; 1 John 2:29) to bring to the reader's memory catechetical teaching they should be aware of. In a sense, this is like a teacher reminding students of something they already know.

COMMENTARY

The first section of James functions as an introduction to the contents of the entire letter. The basic themes—trials and tests (1:2-4, 12-15), the need for faith and wisdom (1:5-8), the social problem of poverty and wealth (1:9-11), and God's perfect gift of life (1:16-18)—are all introduced here. All four are intertwined: The basic trial is poverty, and the difficult situation of the majority of the readers calls for faith in God and his wisdom to overcome the temptations (1:13-15) produced by the trials. All four motifs will reverberate throughout the letter, once again showing the basic unity of James (against those who see it as a loose collection of homilies—see the Introduction). James begins with the problem of trials because all the other situations in the letter—prejudice, the need to put faith to work, the problem of the tongue, oppression by the wealthy, physical illness—are examples of the "various kinds of trials" (1:2, my translation) discussed here. Two other passages cover the same material as 1:2-4, namely, Romans 5:3-5 and 1 Peter 1:6-7. Romans 5:3-5 speaks of trials producing "endurance," which produces "strength of character," which produces "confident hope." In 1 Peter 1:6-7 we are told that we should "be truly glad" because trials test our faith like "fire tests and purifies gold." These three passages demonstrate a common thread of catechetical teaching in the early church.

James begins with "dear brothers and sisters," used often in this letter (2:1, 14; 3:1, 10; 4:11; 5:7, 9, 12, 19) to show that his admonitions stem from a heart of love and a family relationship with the readers. From this vantage point he delivers his impossible command: "Consider [your trials] an opportunity for great joy." "Consider" (*hēgēsasthe* [TG2233, ZG2451]) means to "think, regard, treat" something in a certain way; the idea is to make a mental switch so that a particular situation is "regarded" from a certain vantage point. Hebrews 12:11 states, "No discipline is enjoyable while it is happening—it's painful!" From the human perspective, discipline is painful. James takes the other perspective, from the viewpoint of eternity; he says it should be joyful. The first two words of the sentence (placed there for emphasis) are "great joy," with the word *pas* [TG3956, ZG4246] meaning "completely joyous" or "pure joy." This is only possible when we look at troubles from God's perspective. We must separate "joy" from happiness. We are happy when things go the way we want; joy can only occur when we see it God's way, when we surrender to his providential care. Then the afflictions become a source of "great joy."

This joy occurs as we encounter (lit., "fall into," often with a negative connotation of encountering thieves or difficult circumstances, see BDAG 804) *peirasmois . . . poikilois* [TG3986/4164, ZG4280/4476], which are "various kinds of troubles [trials]." James is here introducing all the myriad types of trouble that we pass through, especially the ones he will discuss throughout his letter. The word for "trial" here is used two different ways in this chapter: as a "test" that God allows in our lives (cf. 1 Pet 1:6; 4:12) and as a "temptation" in 1:13-15 (cf. 1 Cor 10:13; 1 Tim 6:9). God's purpose is to "test" the believers as he did Jesus, when the Spirit "led" or "drove" Jesus into the wilderness (Mark 1:12-13). Testing is common in Scripture: Abraham at the sacrifice of Isaac (Gen 22), Moses on the mountain for 40 days and nights (Exod 34:28), Israel in the wilderness for 40 years (Num 14:33-34), and Elijah in the wilderness on the way to Sinai for 40 days and nights (1 Kgs 19:8). So God uses the painful experience of trials to bring his people to joy in him. The way he does so is explored in the next two verses.

In 1:3 the meaning of trials is explained. He defines a trial as a situation "when your faith is tested" (lit., "the testing of your faith"). The Greek word for "testing" is *dokimion* [TG1383, ZG1510], which has two aspects, the process of testing or refining something, and the intended results of the test, the "approval" or "genuineness" of the thing. Most scholars agree that the stress here is on the means of testing, while in 1 Peter 1:7 (see commentary on that verse in this volume) it is on the results of the process. Putting the two together, God allows trials because they test one's faith with the refiner's fire, and in so doing strengthen one's faith so that it becomes "genuine" and "approved" by God. Like gold, one's faith must be placed in the crucible so that it can be purified; as the impurities are removed, it becomes acceptable to God as pure gold. This kind of purified faith is rewarded by "the crown of life" (see commentary on 1:12).

The process of proving one's faith leads to "endurance" (1:3), which as a result of the trial "has a chance to grow" (an agricultural metaphor showing what is "produced" by the growth process). The Greek term for "endurance" (*hupomonē* [TG5281, ZG5705]) literally means to "remain under" a weight, thus to "persevere" and remain "steadfast" under affliction. It became one of the primary characteristics of Christians in the first century due to the great amount of persecution they experienced. Jesus said that "everyone who endures to the end will be saved" (Matt 10:22; 24:13), and Paul said that as "true ministers" he and his associates "patiently endure troubles and hardships and calamities of every kind" (2 Cor 6:4). The book of Revelation makes perseverance a major theological emphasis, calling on believers to remain faithful and overcome temptation as well as opposition (Rev 1:9; 2:2, 3, 19; 3:10; 13:10; 14:12). As trials multiply in a believer's life, they progressively enable the person to place their trust entirely in God and rise above the difficulties to find that "joy" in the Lord mentioned in 1:2. Martin (1988:15-16) notes that Abraham was the primary model for this in Judaism, and that "endurance" also contains the ideas of "hope" and "expectancy" (1 Chr 29:15; Ps 71:5; Jer 14:8; 17:13).

James next (1:4) turns to the responsibility of the believers in the process. God sends the refining process; his people must put that to work in their lives. They are taught "endurance," but they must "let it grow" and "fully develop" in their lives. The literal wording is, "let endurance continue to have its perfect work," with the present tense "have" referring to a long period of time. There are two ideas here—the believer's responsibility to yield to God in the midst of the trials, and the effects of these difficulties that are at work in the Christian. The major desired effect is called *teleios* [TG5046, ZG5455], a term that can mean "perfect" but also connotes a "complete" or "mature" work. In this context it means to allow the process of learning perseverance come to "completion," to let it come to full fruition in one's life. Dibelius (1975:73-74) says this has an active rather than a passive force; the Christian must put the process to work with great effort, growing in character and dependence on God through difficulties.

There are three results for the believers, described by three different expressions in 1:4. The first is the same *teleios* used earlier in this verse. As Moo (2000:56) and Davids (1982:69) bring out, the Old Testament idea looks to Noah as the "complete" man (Gen 6:9; Sir 44:17; *Jubilees* 10:17). In the New Testament, there is little difference between "perfect" and "complete," since believers are to strive for the perfection of God (Matt 5:48, "Be perfect, even as your Father in heaven is perfect"). This does not mean that they attain perfection, but they strive for it at all times and become both "mature" and "complete" in him. James intends the full meaning of the term here. This is a major motif in James, occurring also in 1:17, 25; 3:2. Martin (1988:17) brings out three ideas in this: (1) It concerns one's character, not just one's actions or conduct; (2) it does not center just on "human endeavor" as in the Stoic model, but on the "divine pattern" at work in one's soul; and (3) it is eschatological, pointing ahead to the full maturity when God's plan has come to fulfillment.

The second result for believers is that they will be *holoklēroi* [TG3648, ZG3908], a medical metaphor that speaks of a "sound" or "whole" person. Louw and Nida (L&N 268) define its cognate as "a state of complete health or soundness in the whole body." And this refers to the moral and spiritual wholeness of the individual. Davids (1982:70) calls this "a fully rounded uprightness" and defines it as "not just a maturing of character, but a rounding out as more and more 'parts' of the righteous character are added (Ezek 15:5; Wisd 15:3)." This is at the core of James's message, and Moo considers it critical enough to entitle 1:2-18 "the pursuit of spiritual wholeness."

The third characteristic of the well-rounded Christian developed through life's trials is "needing [or lacking in] nothing." This restates the previous term ("complete, whole") and has a spiritual dimension (having no wants in Christ, who supplies all one's needs, Phil 4:19) and a moral dimension (blamelessness before God). The message of 1:2-4 is that the trials of life are allowed by God as a spiritual necessity that tests our Christian character and gives us an opportunity to strengthen our faith by learning steadfast endurance, thereby making us complete in Christ and whole (healthy) people of God.

◆ 2. Wisdom and faith in trials (1:5-8)

5 If you need wisdom, ask our generous God, and he will give it to you. He will not rebuke you for asking. 6 But when you ask him, be sure that your faith is in God alone. Do not waver, for a person with divided loyalty is as unsettled as a wave of the sea that is blown and tossed by the wind. 7 Such people should not expect to receive anything from the Lord. 8 Their loyalty is divided between God and the world, and they are unstable in everything they do.

NOTES

1:5-8 Dibelius (1975:77) sees only a "superficial" connection between 1:2-4 and 1:5-8, believing the latter a separate homily artificially attached to 1:2-4 by the catchword "lack" (1:4b, 5a). But Davids disagrees with Dibelius's conclusion that it is "futile" to find any "connection of thought" between the two paragraphs; Davids says that wisdom is the overarching theme uniting the two sets of ideas (1982:54). I agree with Davids but think that wisdom is not the dominant theme but part of the developing message. James 1:2-8 is similar to Phil 4:6-7 in that the solution to worry is deep-seated prayer and faith in God. Yet Dibelius is correct when he says that James adds a remarkable passage on the powerful reality of prayer and the kind of God who answers our prayers!

1:5 *ask our generous God.* The meaning of the adverb *haplōs* [TG574, ZG607] in this context is quite debated: It could be taken as (1) "generously, graciously, freely" (with regard to quantity) on the grounds that giving expresses such liberality of response (so Adamson, Johnson, Reicke, Ross); (2) "with singleness of heart, integrity" on the grounds that the emphasis is on God's undivided intent to meet our needs (Moo, Stulac); or (3) "without hesitation or reserve" on the grounds that it reflects the basic meaning of "sincerely" and pictures a God who responds immediately to the need (BDAG, Blomberg and Kamell, Davids, Dibelius, Martin, McCartney). All three are viable linguistically and can fit the context. Laws (1980:55) is probably correct in believing that James was conscious of these various meanings and may well have intended a richness of thought here, combining these meanings. There is a definite contrast with the double-minded person of 1:6—God is single-minded and gives without hesitation in his generosity.

1:7-8 There are two primary ways these two verses have been understood (see Laws, Moo): (1) as two separate statements about the doubter and the double-minded person, with the second expanding the meaning of the first (NLT, TNIV, NASB, ESV); (2) as a single statement for which the double-minded man is the one subject of 1:7-8, as in, "For that person [the doubter] must not suppose that a double-minded man . . . will receive anything from the Lord" (RSV). The latter is quite doubtful and was corrected in the NRSV to be like the majority understanding.

COMMENTARY

James uses a "chain-argument" utilizing catchwords ("need," 1:4b, 5a; "faith," 1:3, 6) to bring together the problem of trials and their solution (wisdom and prayer). When faith is tested by times of affliction and suffering, the Christian must turn to God in prayer and find the wisdom to turn the trial situation into a time of growing faith and ongoing endurance. As God's people realize that they lack wisdom to handle their trials, they must find that essential resource by turning to God and accepting that wisdom as a gift from him.

James begins by expressing the one need everyone has in difficult times: wisdom to endure trials. The word "if" (*ei* [TG1487, ZG1623]) in the phrase "If you need wisdom" is a first-class condition assuming the reality of the situation—virtually, "Since you need wisdom." In the Old Testament wisdom is an attribute of God (Dan 2:20-23) given to chosen leaders like Solomon (1 Kgs 10:23-24); it was also available to those who fear God (Prov 1:7; 9:10; 15:33). In the Wisdom Literature (Job, Proverbs, Ecclesiastes, Wisdom of Solomon, Sirach) wisdom means to live in God's world by his rules, with two foci, its practical orientation (embracing every area of life and conduct) and its dependence on God (reverence and submission to his dictates). Often wisdom was personified as a life-giving force in this world (see Osborne 2006:242-254; Patzia 2000:1200-1203). Jesus was a teacher of eschatological wisdom (Matt 11:2-19, 25-30; 23:34-39; et al.), and Paul speaks of "God's riches and wisdom and knowledge" (Rom 11:33), as well as "wisdom in its rich variety" (Eph 3:10).

James, building on the Jewish understanding of wisdom, saw it primarily as a gift from God (1:6-8) available only to those who ask him for it (1:5; see Gowan 1993, who points to 4 Maccabees as an example of this theme). In 3:13-18 it is called a "wisdom from above" that anchors the Christian virtues that control the tongue. Most recognize that in James wisdom functions in ways similar to the Holy Spirit. Yet at the same time the two "cannot be entirely equated, because believers could not lack the Holy Spirit," while they could lack wisdom (Blomberg and Kamell 2008:51). It is best to see the Spirit as mediating this gift from God.

Since the reality is that everyone lacks this wisdom, there is only one answer. One must turn to God and "ask" (a present imperative indicating ongoing prayer) for it. Then begins an incredible meditation on the kind of God we have—a God who responds to our prayers in love. The Greco-Romans had capricious gods who were disinterested in humanity's plight and whose involvement in people's lives often had to be bought (or bought off). The Old Testament paints quite a different picture; there we see a covenant God who loved his people and was constantly involved in their needs, who even in his judgment of their foolish wanderings from him acted redemptively to bring them back to himself. Here in James he is described as "the giving God" (*tou didontos* [TG1325, ZG1443] *theou*), with the present tense participle referring to a loving God "who never stops giving." In Matthew 7:7 Jesus says, "Keep on asking, and you will receive what you ask for." Both aspects of this challenge are found here as well. Our responsibility is to bring our needs to God, and his promise is that he will respond. This is as it says in 1 Peter 5:7, "Give all your worries and cares to God, for he cares about you."

God's free and continuous giving has two characteristics. First, it is "generous" (*haplōs* [TG574, ZG607]), a word that James uses dynamically (see note on 1:5) to connote not just the gracious extent of his liberality but also his single-minded focus and the unhesitating nature of his response to his children's needs. When we lack the basic wisdom to handle and overcome our trials, we can place ourselves in the hands of a Father whose constant vigilance over us and empowering presence in our lives mean we can find the strength and understanding to withstand all difficulties.

Second, God "will not rebuke you for asking," meaning that God does not give grudgingly or with a great deal of reproach for his children's inadequacies and lack of wisdom. There is no need to hesitate in prayer, as if one's finite, sinful condition will bring about only anger and recrimination from God. God does not belittle his people for their failures but forgives them when they come to him in repentance; he responds immediately to their prayers. James says simply that instead of mockery and condemnation, "he will give it to you" (this phrase occurs last in the sentence for emphasis). It is important to note what this doesn't say: It does not promise that believers can get anything they want from God. That will be addressed in 4:3; when we ask for "only what will give [us] pleasure," we will not get it. John 14:13 promises, "You can ask for anything in my name, and I will do it," but "in my name" means "in union with me and my purposes" (Osborne 2007:214). God will not give us what we want but rather what is best for us. Here the prayer is for wisdom, and that will always be given. Martin (1988:19) has a fine summary: "James has painted in some bold strokes the scope of such praying: It is universal (God gives to all who petition him), it is beneficent, it is without regard to merit, and it is a response with no equivocations."

The rest of this passage (1:6-8) centers on the importance of faith over doubting when coming to God in prayer. Petitions to God must be done "in faith," that is, with a total trust and dependence on God, taking him at his word. Many commentators (Adamson, Dibelius, Martin) see this as a complete confidence and certitude that God will answer. This is correct, but I also agree with those scholars (Blomberg and Kamell, Ropes) who say that the thrust is wider, referring to the basic reliance on God in every area of life, a God-centeredness that defines the Christian walk. Mainly, this confidence does not mean we are certain that we will receive whatever we ask for but rather that God will act in the way that is best in every situation. This does not teach a "name it and claim it" theology; such is utterly wrong because it teaches that we control God, while in reality only God is sovereign over every situation!

"Do not waver" is literally "not doubting" (*mēden diakrinomenos* [TG1252A, ZG1359]). The verb does not really mean to "doubt" that God is going to act but rather to have a divided mind that keeps one from trusting God in the first place. Moo (2000:60) says its basic meaning is "differentiate," often used in the sense of "create distinctions" (2:4), "judge" (1 Cor 14:29; NLT, "evaluate"), or "dispute" (Acts 11:2; NLT, "criticize"). In the middle voice, as here, this "doubt" means to "dispute with oneself." So the idea is that the person is internally divided, "wavering" between trusting God and trusting self. Nystrom (1997:61-62) notes that the duplicity or dishonest doubt James addresses here is different from honest doubt, which has "healthy and even helpful effects." Noting the honest emotions, even anger, of the psalmists directed at God (e.g., Pss 13:1; 39:1-3), he points out how "in the press of life, we, like the psalmist, often wonder where God is, whether he really cares, and why he waits." Such doubts force us to recall God's faithful character and all he has done. Moreover, God responds to such doubts and meets us in the midst of our human weakness.

In the next verses (1:6b-8) James describes those who "waver." Since they have a "divided loyalty" between God and this world, they are "as unsettled as a wave of the sea." The two participles, "blown and tossed," are virtual synonyms put together for poetic effect rather than to emphasize a violent force. Thus, they do not connote a typhoon or waves crashing on the shore, but rather the unsettled, ever-changing sea, driven by the wind. One moment such people are up (centered on God), the next moment they are down (centered on this world). You might call them spiritually "seasick"! The emphasis is on the instability of this kind of Christian life, which "oscillates between faith and skepticism, unwilling to trust in Christ once for all and to stay the course in allegiance to him" (Blomberg and Kamell 2008:53). The need is for perseverance in faith (1:3-4), a constancy of walk in which God and Christ are ever uppermost in facing the vicissitudes of life. We live in a fallen world, and in this world bad things happen to good people. Moreover, as Christians we must face the possibility of persecution, and this is a theme of James as well as of 1 Peter. There is only one way to handle such ups and downs in life, and that is by an unwavering trust in the providential care of God.

The people who waver "should not expect to receive anything from the Lord." "Expect" is *oiesthō* [TG3633, ZG3883] (think, suppose); the unstable person who depends as much on blind luck as they do on God should not really think God will reward their indecision by heeding their requests. God gives only "good and perfect" gifts (1:17), but he only gives when his people are centered on him and ask him (4:2). If you leave God out of your life for much of the time, you are on your own! Then 1:8 defines the doubter further as a person "divided between God and the world," literally "a double-minded person" (*dipsuchos* [TG1374A, ZG1500]; cf. discussion on 1:6). Porter (1990:469-498) states that this word appears here and in 4:8 for the first time in the Greek language and was therefore probably coined by James. In 4:8 the double-minded are linked with the "sinners" and need to purify themselves by getting right with God.

The idea of divided loyalty between God and the world has a lengthy background in Judeo-Christian ethics, as in the command to love God with a whole or undivided heart (Deut 6:5; 13:3; 18:13; 1 Sam 12:20). Laws (1980:58-59) links the Jewish idea of the two impulses (to do good and to do evil) with "the idea of doubleness as the essence of sin." Such duplicity is found in the Old Testament (e.g., Ps 12:2) and Jewish literature (*Testament of Asher* 1:3–6:2; *Testament of Benjamin* 6:5-7; 1QS 3:17-18; 4:23). We should also note Sirach 1:28, which says, "Do not disobey the fear of the Lord or approach him with a divided mind."

Another major New Testament passage on the teaching of undivided loyalty to God is Mark 12:29-30 (quoting Deut 6:5): "You must love the LORD your God with all your heart, all your soul, all your mind, and all your strength." The demand for undivided commitment to God is clear. Next, there is Matthew 6:24 (= Luke 16:13): "No one can serve two masters. For you will hate one and love the other; you will be devoted to one and despise the other. You cannot serve both God and money." The major area addressed in this saying and in the New Testament is poverty and wealth, an issue we will address in the next section. Paul calls greed "idolatry" in Ephesians 5:5 and Colossians 3:5; and 1 Timothy 6:10 states that "the love of money is the root of all kinds of evil." James was possibly anticipating this kind of divided mind in this verse (1:8).

People with divided loyalties are "unstable in everything they do" (1:8b). They vacillate, constantly switching allegiances from one thing to another. The actual word (*akatastatos* [TG182, ZG190]) is found in the Bible only in 1:8; 3:8, and Isaiah 54:11 (LXX). In the Isaiah passage it refers to a "storm-battered city," so this reiterates the wind-driven waves of 1:6b. "In everything they do" is literally, "in all his ways," a Jewish idiom (Ps 145:17; Prov 3:6; Jer 16:17) for the whole of life, one's conduct and regular activities. Such a person has no commitment and no stability. They are loyal to no one, and they constantly change, with no anchor except their ever-shifting concern for themselves.

◆ 3. A basis for trials—poverty and wealth (1:9-11)

9 Believers who are* poor have something
to boast about, for God has honored
them. 10 And those who are rich should
boast that God has humbled them. They
will fade away like a little flower in the
field. 11 The hot sun rises and the grass
withers; the little flower droops and falls,
and its beauty fades away. In the same
way, the rich will fade away with all of
their achievements.

1:9 Greek *The brother who is.*

NOTES

1:9-11 There are three possible interpretations of this section: (1) The poor believer is to glory in his status, for his position is actually "high" or elevated in Christ, while the rich believer should glory in his "humiliation," i.e., he is made lower in Christ. Both are equal before Christ; the rich are poor and the poor rich (so Adamson, Blomberg and Kamell, Mayor, Moo, Robertson, Ross, McCartney). (2) Christians should do their duty wherever God places them; some poor become wealthy, and some rich become poor. Whatever God's will is, glory in it. (3) The Christian poor are to regard themselves as fortunate (elevated) because they do not have a problem with Mammon, and the non-Christian rich should realize their problem with Mammon (which is causing their low status before

God). This accords with what Christ taught, "It is easier for a camel to go through the eye of a needle than for a rich person to enter the Kingdom of God" (Mark 10:25). Thus, many scholars (Davids, Dibelius, Laws, Martin, Maynard-Reid, Stulac) favor the last of these possibilities on the grounds that throughout the epistle the wealthy are viewed as being outside the congregation and as enemies of the faith. The interpretation hinges on the depiction of the wealthy here. They are not called "brothers," and there seems to be an emphasis on their downfall (with no hope for the future) as in 5:1-6. This favors the view that they are non-Christians. However, according to this third view the rich are sarcastically being told to "boast" in the fact that all that remains for them is condemnation and destruction (their "humiliation" when they will "fade away," 1:10) at the final judgment. While this could be the thrust, it does not make as much sense as the view that they are Christians who are being told not to take pride in their high earthly status but in their humble spiritual status in Christ, that is, their dependence on Christ and their equality with the poor before God.

COMMENTARY

This section introduces a type of trial that will become a primary emphasis in the book: experiencing poverty rather than wealth (2:2-4, 5-12, 15-16; 4:13-17; 5:1-6). Blomberg and Kamell (2008:54, from Martin 1988:24) make a valuable comment here that ties this passage into what comes before and after this section: "while riches often lead to temptations [1:13-15], poverty usually produces trials [1:2-4]." As stated in the previous verse, the poor are those who were undergoing serious trials and therefore must have faith in God (cf. the first beatitude in Luke 6:20, "God blesses you who are poor"), while the wealthy are the "double-minded" who too easily ignore their need for God. As stated in the note above (1:9-11), this does not mean they cannot be believers, only that their wealth too often draws them away from their commitment to God. Social stratification, even more deeply entrenched in the Roman world than in our day, is clearly the emphasis. People are not superior just because they have wealth. Before God, all are equal and must equally place their dependence on God rather than on their earthly resources.

James's point (1:9) is that the poor more easily depend on God and therefore can take joy in him. The expression "believers who are poor" is literally, "the humble brother"; it refers not to spiritual humility but the person of humble circumstances, of low status in the world due to poverty. In spite of their difficult situation, they "have something to boast about," since the necessity of their trusting in God in their circumstances means God is more central in their lives. Boasting is normally considered a sin (e.g., Rom 2:17, 23; 1 Cor 4:7; 2 Cor 5:12; Eph 2:9), but in Philippians 1:26 Paul speaks of taking "pride in Christ Jesus" and in Philippians 2:16 of being "proud" on the day of Christ that his ministry had not been for nothing (both verses use cognates of "boast"). Pride in self is a sin, but pride in what Christ is doing in one's life is a Christian privilege. They are told to boast "in their exaltation" (NLT, "for God has honored them"). The inaugurated thrust of this is apparent. They are now "honored" or "exalted" as citizens of heaven (Phil 3:20) and even inhabitants of heaven (Rev 12:12; 13:6), in spite of their alienation in an earthly, pagan society (1 Pet 1:1, 17; 2:11). This present glory will become absolute on the day when Christ returns, when death is defeated once for all (1 Cor 15:55), and the victory of God's people is made complete. This does not mean that poverty is a good thing to be commended; the Bible has more to say on alleviating the suffering of the poor (e.g., Acts 2:44-45; 4:32-34) than any other ethical topic. (Congregational care in every local church, including support for the poor, is a biblical mandate!) James's main point is that those experiencing poverty are honored by God.

In contrast, James addresses the rich (1:10; these are Christians, see note on 1:9-11), whose "boasting" is quite different. Instead of exaltation, these who have all the status and privileges in this life should take pride in their "humiliation." While this world has elevated them, God has brought them low. But what does this mean? Probably two things: (1) "Those who die with the most toys still die"—the wealthy too will die, and all their possessions will come to naught (Blomberg and Kamell, Martin). Possessions are empty in light of death, often emphasized in the Old Testament (Job 3:14-15; 15:29-30; Pss 49:16-20; 73:12, 18-20). (2) The rich should rejoice in the fact that they, like the poor, belong to Christ and depend on him alone, a reality that makes them despised in the eyes of the non-Christian world. The background for this is seen in Jeremiah 9:23-24: "Don't let the wise boast in their wisdom, or the powerful boast in their power, or the rich boast in their riches. But those who wish to boast should boast in this alone: that they truly know me and understand that I am the LORD who demonstrates unfailing love and who brings justice and righteousness to the earth." Since all, rich and poor, stand equal in the church before God, and since they are brothers and sisters belonging to the same family, the church today needs to join God in exalting the poor and humble and humbling the wealthy and proud (see 4:6; 1 Pet 5:5b).

James anchors his statements in 1:10b-11 by emphasizing the transitory nature of human life and thereby of all earthly wealth. In doing so, he uses a vegetation metaphor drawn from Isaiah 40:6-7 and Psalm 103:15-16. A "little flower in the field" or wildflower (Laws identifies them with poppies or anemones) lasts only a few days before dying. One moment the field is bursting with color and alive in its beauty, the next moment it is withered and gone. Such is life; as one who is now over retirement age, I can identify with this picture. To use a parallel metaphor, life is a flickering candle that brightens the world around it all too briefly, and then it is gone. Our task is to make certain the light of Christ shines through our flickering life while it can.

James 1:11 details the four destructive forces (using four gnomic aorists that describe these proverbial natural elements) that lead to the downfall of the beautiful flower. First, "the hot sun rises"; literally, "the sun rises with heat," possibly referring to the "scorching wind" (NASB) from the desert called the sirocco. It is said that when that wind hits, a flower can literally wilt in seconds. The last three verbs describe the result of the sun and wind: Green grass "withers," the little flower "droops and falls," and the beauty of both "fades away"—the entire process a graphic picture of what happens to all of us and our wealth (see Irwin 1991 on flowers as an ancient symbol for the brevity of life). James concludes that in the "same way" all the wealthy and "their achievements" will "fade away." While some take this as a message regarding final condemnation at the Last Judgment, it is more likely simply an image of death. In fact, this is a powerful metaphor for death, emphasizing the gradual process by which our biological life, as well as our financial accomplishments, pass away into nothingness. Moo (2000:69) sums the message up well: Rich and poor alike must "evaluate themselves by spiritual and not material standards." The poor, powerless in terms of money and status, rejoice because they are seated in the heavenlies with Christ (Eph 2:6-7). The rich, tempted to pride by their status, rejoice in their identity with the one "despised and rejected" (Isa 53:3) by the world.

◆ B. Testing and Temptation in Relation to God (1:12-15)

12God blesses those who patiently endure testing and temptation. Afterward they will receive the crown of life that God has promised to those who love him. 13And remember, when you are being tempted, do not say, "God is tempting me." God is never tempted to do wrong,* and he never tempts anyone else. 14Temptation comes from our own desires, which entice us and drag us away. 15These desires give birth to sinful actions. And when sin is allowed to grow, it gives birth to death.

1:13 Or *God should not be put to a test by evil people.*

NOTES

1:12 ***those who patiently endure testing and temptation. Afterward.*** Lit., "the person who endures trial/temptation, for having been tested." Does *peirasmos* [TG3986, ZG4280] mean "trial" (as in 1:2-4) or "temptation" (1:13-15)? If it is primarily part of what follows (as NLT, NRSV, KJV, NKJV, Martin, Ropes), it means the latter. If it mainly recapitulates 1:2-4 (as NASB, ESV, TNIV, HCSB, Blomberg and Kamell, Davids, Dibelius, Laws, Moo, Stulac), it means the former. As shown in the opening paragraph below, the whole of 1:12a points back to 1:2-4 and repeats the themes of that passage, so it is much more likely that the meaning here is the positive "trial" rather than the negative "temptation."

1:13 ***God is never tempted to do wrong.*** The genitive *kakōn* [TG2556B, ZG2805] (lit., "of wrong, of evil") can be taken three ways: (1) God cannot be tempted *by* evil, i.e., has no experience or contact with evil (Hort, Martin)—as Johnson says (1995:193), "God has nothing to do with evil"; (2) God cannot be tempted *to do* evil because he is "impervious" to it and not "susceptible" to it (Blomberg and Kamell, Dibelius, Laws, Moo, McCartney); (3) God "cannot be tempted by evil men," that is, the readers should quit doing so (Davids). The second is accepted by the majority and is still the best understanding (as in NLT), but the third may be somewhat in James's mind. The warning against "testing God" is biblical, as in Heb 3:1–4:13 and its midrashic exposition of Ps 95:7-11.

1:14 ***Temptation comes from our own desires.*** Behind James's discussion here is the Jewish doctrine of the two *yetzerim* [TH3336, ZH3671] or impulses: the *yetzer hattob* or tendency towards good, and the *yetzer hara'* (cf. Gen 6:5) or tendency toward evil (see Marcus 1982:606-621). Both were seen as part of human nature; the only debate was where the impulse to evil originated. In the *Apocalypse of Moses* 19:3 it is said that Satan put the poison of sin (or covetousness, the root of all sin) into the fruit of the tree, and the Jerusalem Targum on Genesis 3:6 says it was created by Adam. Only later, in the third century or so (*Bereshit Rabbah* 27; *b. Yoma* 69b, becoming the majority opinion in rabbinic circles), was it said that God created evil.

COMMENTARY

There is a certain cyclical relationship (or recapitulation) between 1:2-11 and 1:12-18. James returns in 1:12 to the issue of trials of the faith as developed in 1:2-4.

Almost every word in 1:12 recalls 1:2-4: "Blesses" reminds the reader of the "joy" of 1:2; "endure" repeats the term in 1:3-4; "testing" and "temptation" point back to 1:2-3. Then verse 12 expands the earlier scene (which centered on the realized eschatology of present reward) by pointing to final eschatology, the crown of life that will be given to God's people. For this reason some scholars (e.g., Johnson, Moo) place 1:12 with 1:1-11 and begin the new section with 1:13-15, but it is better to see 1:12 as summing up 1:2-4 in order to contrast with 1:13-15. The second part of this section (1:13-15) takes the word for "trial" (*peirasomos* [TG3986, ZG4280]) and develops the other side of the term, how the trial becomes "temptation" when Christians respond through self rather than through divinely given wisdom. The third part (1:16-18) expands on 1:13 by detailing what God *does* give: the perfect gift of new birth, the polar opposite of sin and temptation.

The only beatitude in James is in 1:12 (though 1:25 uses "bless" in a similar way). The word *makarios* [TG3107, ZG3421] is found throughout the Greek Old Testament (translating *'ashre* [TH843, ZH897], Pss 1:1; 34:8 [33:9]; 40:4 [39:5]; Prov 8:34; Isa 56:2, LXX), and in the New Testament (Matt 5:3-12; Rev 1:3; 14:13; 16:15). The Hebrew term and its Greek equivalent connote the ideas of "fortunate, happy," but the meaning goes far beyond that, especially since the persecution pictured in Matthew 5:10-11 and here can hardly be called "happy" circumstances. Rather, the term is eschatological, meaning "God blesses," with the final blessing taking place at the end of this world. The blessing falls on those who "patiently endure testing" (or, "trials"; see note on 1:12). Here is one major difference with 1:2-4: The earlier passage commands that we should endure trials and let the test produce endurance, while this verse looks back on those who have successfully done so and received God's reward for passing the test. The second part is grammatically a temporal aorist participle (lit., "after they have stood the test") building on 1:3. Both "trial" and "test" are collective singulars recapitulating the "various trials" of 1:2. In other words, the Christian is intended by God to pass through many kinds of trials that test their faith so that they can be "approved" by God. Then after they have victoriously endured those times of difficulty, allowing them to "fully develop" and produce their "perfect and complete" result (1:4), the mature believers will be "blessed" and rewarded by God.

In 1:2-4 James emphasized the present results, but here he turns to the final blessings to be "received" after Christ returns. The "crown of life" is not the ruler's crown (*diadēma* [TG1238, ZG1343]) but the victor's crown (*stephanos* [TG4735, ZG5109]), a laurel wreath awarded to those victorious on the athletic field or battlefield (1 Cor 9:25, cf. 1 Thess 2:19; 2 Tim 4:8; 1 Pet 5:4; Rev 2:10). This is "the crown" that means "life," i.e., the reward is eternal life. In ancient battles the victorious warriors were those who lived victoriously afterwards; so it is with us, but ours will be an eternal joy, not a temporary victory. Athletes shine for a moment and then are forgotten; after our race is won, we will share the joy with Jesus forever (Heb 12:1-3). Ours is a certain reward that "God has promised to those who love him," reminiscent of Romans 8:28, which says that "God causes everything to work together for the good of those who love God and are called according to his purpose." It is certainly true that we don't serve God for the reward but because we "love" him and want to do what is right. Still, throughout the New Testament the theme of rewards occurs frequently (e.g., in the Sermon on the Mount, at the end of every beatitude there is a reward for living out the ethical responsibility; see also Matt 6:4, 6, 18, 33; 7:7, 11). We don't do it for the rewards, but God wants us to know the rewards that await us.

In contrast to the "trial" as a positive "test" that brings reward, the same word (*peirasmos* [TG3986, ZG4280]) can also mean "temptation," the theme of 1:13-15. A "trial" is always accompanied by a "temptation." We might think of pilgrims on a quest suddenly encountering an obstacle. As they face the test, they have a choice to make: Turn to God for wisdom or turn to self and try to get around the obstruction on their own. One temptation of a trial is to blame God for our misfortunes. Illness tempts us to blame God for not healing; financial hardship tempts us to cheat and do anything to get more money; loneliness can lead to affairs; depression can lead to suicide. The first order of business when the temptation comes is to recognize the truth that "God is not tempting me." We can never blame God for our temptations. The last line of the Lord's Prayer (Matt 6:13) is best translated, "don't let us yield to temptation" rather than "lead us not into temptation" because God never tempts his people; he brings trials and tests but not temptation. In Jesus' confrontation in the desert (Matt 4:1-11) he was tested by God but tempted by Satan.

The reason (*gar* [TG1063, ZG1142], "for," omitted in NLT) we cannot blame God is stated two ways for emphasis: "God is never tempted to do wrong, and he never tempts anyone else." Sin and temptation are the absolute antithesis of a holy God, so he can neither be tempted by evil nor be tempted to do evil (see note on 1:13). The whole reason for the laws of clean/unclean and the sacrificial system was that sinful people dare not think they could walk into the home of a holy God and walk out alive. God must destroy all that has to do with evil. How could this kind of God ever be tempted? He cannot. At the same time, the God who cannot be tempted is not the kind of God who would tempt another. Temptation comes by Satan (4:7) or by self (1:14) but never by God. His entire work in redemption is to bring his people back from sin to himself. This is summed up perfectly in 1 Corinthians 10:13: "The temptations in your life are no different from what others experience. And God is faithful. He will not allow the temptation to be more than you can stand. When you are tempted, he will show you a way out so that you can endure." We have only ourselves to blame when we yield to temptation. This is developed in the next two verses.

Rather than being tempted by God, the true source is "our own desires" (the Greek emphasizes "each" and every one of us). A "desire" is a self-centered longing of what we ourselves want rather than a concern for what God wants for us. Calvin (1948:289) states, "As the inclination and excitement to sin are inward, in vain does the sinner seek an excuse from an external impulse. . . . It ensnares us by its allurements, and . . . it draws us away, each of which is sufficient to render us guilty." Temptation is described by James as a force that "entice[s] us and drag[s] us away;" both are hunting and fishing metaphors, used in fishing to describe the bait that lures the fish followed by the hook that drags it away to its destruction. In fishing it is an external force, but with sin it is an internal force; we destroy ourselves by producing the enticement and then willingly following it to our own defeat!

In 1:15 James changes his metaphors to describe "the havoc that *desire* can wreak in the spiritual life" (Moo 2000:75) and to "delineate the life cycle of sin" (Blomberg and Kamell 2008:72). Self-centered desires first "give birth to sinful actions"; the sin grows to maturity, and then bears its own child, "death." The conception-and-birth metaphor plays on the sexual connotation of *epithumia* [TG1939, ZG2123] ("desire"; see Johnson 1995:194). Temptation looks alluring and draws the person away from God into a cycle of lust and longing, and before long he or she capitulates. Then desire conceives and "gives birth" to "sinful actions." As those evil deeds take over the person's life, they "grow" in power and produce the child, spiritual "death."

The imagery in 1:15 stems from the wisdom theme of the seductress who leads God's people into spiritual adultery—in particular the immoral women of Proverbs 5–9 whose mouth seems "sweet as honey" (Prov 5:3) but is filled with poison and leads to death (Prov 5:4-5). The solution is to turn to wisdom (Prov 5:1; 7:4; 8:1, 11, 12; 9:1-6, 10-12) that will give you the understanding to be victorious. One path brings death; the other, life. Revelation 17 speaks likewise of the "great prostitute" who seduces the nations and leads them into the wrath of God (see Ortlund 2003 for this theme in Scripture). As Paul says in Romans 5:12, with sin, death entered the world and came upon every person. But we must separate temptation from sin in the sense that temptation does not have to result in sin. Temptation is not sin, and it becomes sin only when we yield to it. In 1 Corinthians 10:13 we are told once more that God always gives us a way out; whenever we center upon him and allow the Spirit to empower us, we will always defeat temptation and not fall into sin.

◆ C. God's Perfect Gift (1:16-18)

16So don't be misled, my dear brothers and sisters. 17Whatever is good and perfect comes down to us from God our Father, who created all the lights in the heavens.* He never changes or casts a shifting shadow.* 18He chose to give birth to us by giving us his true word. And we, out of all creation, became his prized possession.*

1:17a Greek *from above, from the Father of lights.* **1:17b** Some manuscripts read *He never changes, as a shifting shadow does.* **1:18** Greek *we became a kind of firstfruit of his creatures.*

NOTES

1:17 *Whatever is good and perfect.* Lit., "All good giving and every perfect gift"; this has a certain redundancy, and various explanations are given for the wording: (1) It could stress the abstract sense of a giving God as well as the concrete gifts he provides; (2) it may be a poetic device, as the Greek forms a rhythmical hexameter, a device often used in Greek poetic style (Moo); (3) it may be a traditional catechetical phrase borrowed by James (Davids, Dibelius, Ropes); (4) it could become a single sentence: "all giving is good, but every perfect gift stems from God" (Hort, Tasker). Probably the first two could be combined for the best interpretation (though it is likely also to be a traditional saying). The first (*dosis* [TG1394, ZG1521]) is the act of giving, and the second (*dōrēma* [TG1434, ZG1564]) is the gift given (Martin).

who created all the lights in the heavens. He never changes or casts a shifting shadow. Martin (1988:39) notes the two possible views on this: (1) God renders the astral forces powerless, thereby giving people the freedom to determine their destiny in trials (Davids, Dibelius, Ropes); (2) God is sovereign over the stars; while they constantly move, he never changes in himself or in the way he deals with people (Blomberg and Kamell, Martin, Reicke, McCartney). The difficulty of this metaphor led scribes to amend the text, with at least four different variations (see Comfort 2008:724-725 for a good discussion). ℵ* B read, "There is no variation which consists in the shifting of the shadow" (see NLT mg). 𝔓23 reads, "There is no variation or turning of the shadow." This image could possibly allude to the image of a sundial, which told time by the turning of the shadow. If so, James would be indicating that God is changeless and timeless (so Comfort 2008:724-725). The NLT text ("He never changes or casts a shifting shadow") is supported by ℵ[2] A C 1739 𝔐. Certainly "the lights" are the stars, understood here as reliable, constant guides in the heavens (used by voyagers for direction), and the emphasis is on the fact that God is the one who has created them. Thus, as the stars are an unchanging force in the heavens, the God who made them is an unchanging God.

1:18 ***He chose to give birth to us.*** There are two options for the birth image: (1) the gift of life, the "birth" referring to God's creating mankind in the first place (Elliott-Binns 1957, Hort, Laws, Spitta); (2) the gift of eternal life, stressing the new creation and God's redemptive work in giving people spiritual rebirth (Adamson, Blomberg and Kamell, Miller, Moo). The latter makes the best sense here, for while the meaning of redemption as regeneration is not emphasized in James like it is in 1 Peter, the context here is still centered on what God has done through Christ. As Moo (2000:80) brings out, the meaning would be creation if the Jewish and OT milieu was predominant here, but since James is a Christian document and reflects early Christian teaching (note "save your souls" in 1:21), then the redemptive regeneration thrust is likely.

COMMENTARY

From the human tendency to sin, James now turns to the divine side, God's desire to give only "good and perfect" gifts. God never tempts (1:13); rather, he always does what is best for his followers. The transition verse (1:16) is common in New Testament paraenesis (1 Cor 6:9; 15:33; Gal 6:7; 1 John 1:8), a warning against self-deception. The present-tense prohibition should be translated, "Do not at any time be misled." James calls them "dear" (lit., "beloved") brothers and sisters to emphasize that he says these things from feelings of loving concern. In one sense it points back to the section on the progression from temptation to sin and death; it warns that we dare not allow ourselves to be misled by rationalizing sin away. Mainly, however, it leads into the positive side: God's actual involvement in our lives. Martin (1988:37) calls it a "final call . . . of vigilance" that has "a serious situation in mind, akin to 5:19-20." To blame God and fail to realize our accountability to him can lead to disastrous consequences. We must live our lives in relationship to God and never give in to self-centered ways.

This is especially true when we realize the kind of God we serve (1:17). When we encounter trials of all stripes, we are faced with a choice by necessity. We can turn to self or we can turn to God. If we choose self, we begin the vicious cycle of the self giving in to temptation, followed by sin and then spiritual death. When we choose God, we yield to his providential care and realize the truth that he "causes *everything* to work together for the good." In the process we learn the truth that God gives only "good and perfect" gifts, proven especially in Luke 11:13, where God gives the greatest gift of all, the Holy Spirit, "to those who ask him." There is another connection with 1:2-5 here, as "perfect" looks back to "perfect and complete" in 1:4 and "gift" recalls the "giving God" of 1:5 (see commentary on 1:5). This does not mean that these are always pleasant gifts or bring happiness. No, they are often difficult to endure and bring great pain and hardship (Heb 12:11), but they are good because they are always best for us, and they are "perfect" in the sense that they lead us to spiritual wholeness in him (1:4). Thus, they result in a God-centered "great joy" (1:2). The wording here (the gifts, lit., "coming down from above") is unusual and probably reflects a traditional saying from the early church (so Davids, Dibelius, Mayor, Moo).

The Greek of 1:17 speaks of the gifts coming down "from above" (*anōthen* [TG509, ZG540]; cf. John 3:3, you must be "born again/from above"). In Jewish thinking, "from above" especially connotes divine origin; every truly good thing we have in life is actually not earthly but heavenly in origin. These gifts "come down" from God like the New Jerusalem, the eternal holy city, "coming down" out of heaven in Revelation 21:2 (cf. Gal 4:26).

God is here called "the Father of lights," translated well by the NLT as "from God our Father, who created all the lights in the heavens." Nowhere else in Scripture is God called "the Father of lights"; as Martin brings out (1988:38), this unites two Jewish ideas: God as the Lord of creation (Job 38:2-7) and as Father of the universe, whose sovereign power is especially "seen in his creation and control of the heavenly luminaries" (Ps 136:7; Jer 4:23).

This God who created the heavenly lights and so sustains his creation (and especially us) is immutable—"he never changes or casts a shifting shadow." There are two sides to this: God's nature and the goodness of his being never change; and nothing in this world can change him. Both "changes" and "shifting" are common terms in the ancient world for the movements of the heavenly bodies. James was building on that metaphor here. The sun, moon, and stars are in constant motion in the heavens, and they never seem to stop. Night turns into day, and day to night. The shadows cast by the heavenly bodies are always in motion. God is not like that; he is changeless and even timeless (see note on 1:17). His nature never changes, and his actions never waver. (There is a definite contrast between the immutable God and the unstable people with divided loyalty in 1:5-8.) We have a generous, giving God who is always at work for our good, and we must follow him and become like him.

The fact that God gives only the best gifts to his people is proven in the new birth of 1:18 (see note). The word for "chose" is not the one that speaks of God's election or predestining choice, but rather is *boulomai* [TG1014, ZG1089] (to will) and so speaks of "planning on a course of action," often after previous deliberation (BDAG 182). In other words, God deliberately willed or "chose" to "give birth to" a new people, the Christ-followers. This is the central part of the basic metanarrative of Scripture. God created mankind as an outlet for his love, but through Adam and then of our own free will (Rom 5:12), we chose sin against God. The rest of the biblical story is God's decision of his will to bring us back to him. The Old Testament story centers on God's choice of Israel, with everything pointing forward to the New Testament gift of Christ—his death as the atoning sacrifice for mankind and his resurrection as the means of God giving us new life. When we come to faith in Christ, that is the new birth described here, the greatest gift we will ever know.

The means "by" which (instrumental dative) we receive this gift is "his true word" (lit., "word of truth," using a descriptive genitive), elsewhere in the New Testament referring to the gospel (2 Cor 6:7; Eph 1:13; 2 Tim 2:15). James was thinking of the proclaimed gospel that confronts people with the truth and brings them to salvation. God spoke, and the first creation took place (Gen 1:3, 6, 9, 14, 20, 24), and now God has spoken again through "his true word" to produce the new creation. The Greek then adds the purpose of this new birth, that the believers become "a kind of firstfruit of his creatures" (NLT mg), with "kind of" reminding the reader that James was using this as an illustration. "Firstfruit" continues the creation motif; the word was used of the first gleanings of the harvest in the sacrificial system (Exod 23:16; Lev 23:10-11; Deut 14:23) and of Christ's resurrection in the New Testament (1 Cor 15:20, 23), as well as of the first converts in an area (Rom 16:5; 1 Cor 16:15). Here it likely refers to "believers as the eschatological creation of God" (Martin 1988:40), connoting "the first ripe fruit which promises the coming full harvest and as the special possession of God" (Davids 1982:90). The gracious and loving God is at work redemptively and regeneratively in bringing about his new creation. As a result, we have become God's "prized possession," a foretaste of God's plan to redeem not only his human creation but his whole creation (see Rom 8:18-22).

◆ III. Practical Christianity—Living Out the Word (1:19–2:26)
A. Hearing and Doing the Word (1:19-27)
1. Hearers of the word (1:19-21)

19 Understand this, my dear brothers and sisters: You must all be quick to listen, slow to speak, and slow to get angry. 20 Human anger* does not produce the righteousness* God desires. 21 So get rid of all the filth and evil in your lives, and humbly accept the word God has planted in your hearts, for it has the power to save your souls.

1:20a Greek *A man's anger.* **1:20b** Or *the justice.*

NOTES

1:19 ***Understand this.*** While the best manuscripts (𝔓74 ℵ A B C 1739) read *iste* (know, understand), an inferior reading is *hōste* [TG5620, ZG6063] (therefore): K P Ψ 𝔐.

1:20 ***the righteousness God desires.*** Lit., "the righteousness of God." James uses this phrase differently than Paul does in Rom 1:17; 3:22, where it means the righteousness that God imputes through the atoning sacrifice of Christ (i.e., justification). In James there is a parallel between the two genitives: anger of mankind and righteousness of God. Both are subjective genitives: the anger that people show versus the righteousness that God demands and his saving activity in the world. Martin (1988:47-48) notes three ways the phrase "righteousness of God" can be taken: (1) the righteousness God demands, that is, his standards required of us; (2) a "state of affairs" achieved by a righteous life; or (3) God's "saving deeds" bringing about salvation. Martin adds a fourth: James's opposition to a violent, Zealot-like attempt to produce God's "justice" or kingdom on earth (Martin's preference, as also Reicke). Yet a political interpretation seems very unlikely in this context, and a combination of the first two is more preferable.

1:21 ***get rid of all the filth.*** Scholars are divided as to whether this verse completes the first unit of this section (1:19-21; so Adamson, Blomberg and Kamell, Davids, Johnson,

Stulac, Tasker), on the grounds that it is addressing the sins of 1:19-20, or begins a new section (1:21-27; so Dibelius, Martin, Moo), on the grounds that a section on the "word" is introduced. The verse is probably transitional, both concluding the previous and beginning the new (so Laws). Nevertheless, the verse seems to be taking the twin problems of improper speech and anger as "filthy" sins that must be abandoned, so I have kept 1:21 with 1:19-20.

COMMENTARY

In this second major section of his epistle, James elaborates on the themes he introduced in 1:2-18, telling his readers that the wisdom to overcome involves practical obedience toward God's injunctions. The basic trial of poverty is found in all three sections (1:27; 2:2-3, 5-6, 15-16), and three temptations are used as examples (improper speech, 1:19-27; discrimination, 2:1-13; faith without deeds, 2:14-26). The section redefines wisdom as a dynamic process, a life-oriented attitude by which the Christian lives out God's admonitions in his word through works or deeds. The Christian life is not defined merely in the thought-life but also in the actions that result. This passage contains a serious warning against the type of halfhearted Christianity that listens to divine truth but is unwilling to do anything with it. As 1:27 states so clearly, "pure and genuine" Christianity is intensely practical and proves itself by turning internal understanding into external obedience.

The first third of this section (1:19-27) establishes the basic thesis, that the follower of Christ must not merely "listen" to God's truths but must "do" them. The three commands of 1:19 introduce the theme—our speech must proceed from careful listening and not from unreasoned, quick, and angry retorts. This leads into the first section, that anger and hasty speech must be jettisoned, along with all wicked behavior, and replaced with the life-giving word of God (1:19-21). This then leads into a section describing the difference between merely "hearing" God's truths without any effect on one's life and actually "doing" or "practicing" these in one's daily conduct (1:22-25). Finally, James defines true Christianity, first in terms of what it is not (untamed, deceptive speech, 1:26) and what it is (God-centered, people-helping behavior, 1:27).

The three injunctions of 1:19 stem from wisdom proverbs regarding anger and the misuse of the tongue. Dibelius (1975:109-110) finds parallels in Sirach 5:11 ("Be quick to hear and deliberate in answering"; cf. also Sir 6:33-35; 21:15), in Proverbs 29:20 (cf. Sir 4:29; *Pirqe Avot* 5:12), and in Proverbs 15:1 (cf. Eccl 7:9; Eph 4:26, 31; Col 3:8; Sir 1:22; *Pirqe Avot* 2:10) for the third part. Particularly apt is *Pirqe Avot* 5:12, "There are four types of disciples: swift to hear and swift to lose [i.e., forget]—his pain is cancelled by his loss; slow to hear and slow to lose—his loss is cancelled by his gain; swift to hear and slow to lose—this is a happy lot; slow to hear and swift to lose—this is an evil lot" (from Nystrom 1997:90). They are introduced by a traditional injunction to pay close attention ("Understand this," though NASB takes it as an indicative, "This you know"). This is similar to Jesus' expression, "Anyone with ears to hear should listen" (Matt 11:15; 13:9, 43; cf. Rev 2:7, et al.) and commands careful heeding of what follows. The wise are always searching for and heeding the truths of God.

The three admonitions themselves build a wordplay on "quick-slow," a rhetorical technique found often in Wisdom Literature. From the injunction to listen to God and his truths, the first command broadens that to a willingness to listen to others as well. The idea behind being "quick" or "swift" to listen means a constant readiness and openness to listen before speaking, first to God, and then to those around you. This is the heart of ministry, a love for others and a presence that tells them that you are there for them, that they can bare their souls and be accepted and aided in their needs. Kistemaker (1986:56-57) states, "Listening is the art of closing one's mouth and opening one's ears and heart. Listening is loving the neighbor as oneself; his concerns and problems are sufficiently important to be heard."

The flip side of this is "slow to speak," and the two are meant to be taken together. Many leaders are always willing to talk, often without any serious thought behind their perorations, but rarely willing to listen! It clearly means to give careful and serious forethought to what you say. Down through the centuries it has always been recognized how hasty words can ruin relationships, yet human nature continually forgets this incredibly important truth. Proverbs 10:19 says, "Too much talk leads to sin. Be sensible and keep your mouth shut," and Proverbs 13:3 states, "Those who control their tongue will have a long life; opening your mouth can ruin everything" (cf. also Prov 11:12-13; 17:28; 18:21; 21:23).

The third statement ("slow to get angry") introduces a slightly new topic. Speaking and anger are combined in Proverbs 17:27, "A truly wise person uses few words; a person with understanding is even-tempered." Moo (2000:82) states, "the quick tempered person, this proverb suggests, is the person who is likely to speak without careful consideration. Uncontrolled anger leads to uncontrolled speech." The problem of anger is frequently discussed in Wisdom Literature (Prov 15:1, 18; 22:24; 29:8, 11; Eccl 7:9; Sir 1:22; 27:30) and in the New Testament (Matt 5:22; Gal 5:20; Eph 4:26, 31; Col 3:8; 1 Tim 2:8). In a self-centered society like the one we live in today, rage is an ever-growing problem; the only answer is a self-effacing humility that leads people to quit thinking of themselves first and to place others ahead of their own interests (Phil 2:3-4). Even a casual reading of James makes us realize that his community was going through a time of conflict and dissension. Anger must be replaced by love and forgiveness if family or church is to survive!

The reason why we must control our frustrated rage, James says (1:20), is that "human anger does not produce the righteousness God desires." Human anger and God's righteousness are polar opposites; there is such a thing as "righteous indignation" (see Eph 4:26), but that is not the topic here. While this could be translated "Human anger does not produce justice," that is not the topic here either. The parallels are in 5:9 ("Don't grumble") and 3:9-10 ("Don't curse"). The emphasis is upon "of man" and "of God," and both are implied subjects here (see note on 1:20). The verb "produce" is literally "to work out" or "effect" something and refers to the product that results from work. So James is saying that acts of anger can never lead to the kind of righteous behavior that God demands. This is true at an individual level as well as a corporate one. James's community was endangered by dissension, and that could not be God's will or in keeping with God's standards. A bad temper is opposed to God's holiness and to his demands for a holy life. It is to be avoided.

The answer (*dio* [TG1352, ZG1475], "so," indicating an inference from the preceding) to the dilemma of human rage is both negative and positive (1:21). Negatively, you must "get rid of" the evil sins of hasty speech and anger. As in 1 Peter 2:1 (see commentary on that verse, also Rom 13:12; Eph 4:22, 25; Col 3:8; Heb 12:1), this verb was used in the early church as a renunciation formula in ethical exhortation. The image is of throwing away old, dirty, unwanted clothes. As several commentators note (Johnson, Martin, Nystrom, Reicke), the image of stripping off clothes in preparation for baptism provides an apt picture. Still, the image is not so much soiled garments that need to be cleaned but "filthy" (referring to moral filth) clothes too far gone to be salvaged. These are not sins to be endured and gradually eased out, but dangerous forces that must be entirely removed. The Greek is strong, literally, "get rid of all filth and abundance of evil," emphasizing how abominable the misuse of the tongue and anger are to God. The word "evil" in this context of rage might also refer to a malicious intent to hurt another person (Davids, Johnson).

The positive answer to the dilemma of human rage is the command to "humbly accept the word God has planted in your hearts." Humility or gentleness is the antithesis of anger and is the primary manner in which we are both to open ourselves to God and to relate to others. But for the Greeks, "meekness was weakness," since the Greco-Roman world stressed self-reliance and the ability to control others (essential in a patron-client society). Here "in humility" is placed between the two sections and may be a hinge idea referring to one's attitude "both while divesting oneself of sinfulness and while receiving our new selves from God" (Blomberg and Kamell 2008:87). To be in complete submission and reliance on God makes one ready to "receive" God's word. Note the movement from "taking off" sin and "receiving" (a type of "putting on") the word. God's truth is both the means whereby sin is defeated and the power that replaces sin in our lives.

James uses an agricultural metaphor to describe how God "plants" his word in the believer. There is some possibility that the term could have the Hellenistic sense of "inborn," that is, an innate ability to receive divine truth (so Hort, KJV's "engrafted"), but it is hard to see how this would enable one to "receive" God's teaching. More likely is the Jewish idea of something "implanted" by God (Davids, Dibelius, Martin). This is certainly the gospel that brings life (as in 1:18). It does not come from within but is that "perfect gift" that comes "from above" (see commentary on 1:17), planted by God and bearing fruit in a person's life. This is a message for Christians rather than non-Christians. The point is that God has planted the seed of his word in your heart (similar to the parable of the sower in Mark 4:1-20, which asks, "What kind of soil are you?"). You must place yourself under it, open yourself to it, listen carefully (cf. "quick to listen" in 1:19), and receive it into your life so it can revitalize and guide you. The reason you should do this is that "it has the power to save your souls [the whole person]." Here "save" does not so much point to the moment of regeneration as to the whole Christian life as the experience of "salvation," and especially to the believer's ultimate deliverance from sin and death at Christ's glorious return (see Rom 5:9-10; 13:11; Phil 2:12; 1 Thess 5:9; 1 Tim 4:16; 2 Tim 4:18; Heb 9:28; 1 Pet 1:5, 9; 2:2; 4:18). This is a major emphasis in James as well (1:12; 2:12-14; 3:1; 4:12; 5:5, 7, 15).

◆ 2. Doers of the word (1:22-25)

[22]But don't just listen to God's word. You must do what it says. Otherwise, you are only fooling yourselves. [23]For if you listen to the word and don't obey, it is like glancing at your face in a mirror. [24]You see yourself, walk away, and forget what you look like. [25]But if you look carefully into the perfect law that sets you free, and if you do what it says and don't forget what you heard, then God will bless you for doing it.

NOTES

1:23 ***glancing at your face.*** Lit., "observing the face of his origin" (*genesis* [TG1078, ZG1161]). Since the term *genesis* normally has the thrust of beginning or origins, some (Hort, Martin) see a reference to Gen 1:26-27 and the original "image of God," the ideal person that God intended. Others (Adamson, Laws) take it to be "the face they were born with," the persons they were created to be. However, the more general sense, "natural face" (NASB, ESV, Davids, Johnson, Moo), is best and means simply that they see "themselves" (NRSV) in the mirror.

1:25 ***the perfect law that sets you free.*** Lit., "the perfect law of liberty." This is the first use of "law" in James (found six times in 2:8-12 in the NLT). With his Jewish background, it could be that James had the Torah of Moses in mind, often described as "perfect" in Judaism (Ps 19:7) and as liberating the person (*m. Avot* 3:5; 6:2). In this context, however, "law" is closely linked with "the word" in 1:18, 21-23, so it must be understood as Jesus' gift of a "new law" (Matt 5:17-20), which is the new covenant written on the heart (Heb 8:7-13, quoting Jer 31:31-34). Jesus was the "end of the law" (Rom 10:4, NLT mg) who "has already accomplished the purpose for which the law was given" (Rom 10:4). As synonymous with the "word," the "law" refers to the gospel message, the truths of God, the canonical Scriptures.

COMMENTARY

These verses (1:22-25), which are the core of the second section, demand that true listening to the word of God must of necessity involve doing and obeying it. James was elaborating on 1:21, telling what it means to "accept the word God has planted." You have not "accepted" the word until you have lived it out in daily conduct. There is an A-B-A pattern in this paragraph, with the two admonitions to practice the word (1:22, 25) framing the illustration of looking in a mirror without doing anything about what one sees (1:23-24). The purpose of looking at God's truth is not just to become a focal point of study or a search for meaning. The purpose is for the whole person (the meaning of "souls" in 1:21) to be changed; every area of life must be affected.

The Greek text of 1:22 begins with a present-tense command (for ongoing action): "continue to be doers of the word." Johnson (1995:206) argues that the thrust of *ginesthe* [TG1096, ZG1181] should be "become" rather than "be," stressing the process of "turning profession into action." In 1:19 hearing was stressed, but now we see that by itself hearing is not enough. Listening must lead to practice. The reading of Torah was an essential part of synagogue life. "There were normally five readers on feast days, six on the Day of Atonement, and seven on the Sabbath (though in synagogues outside Palestine there tended to be more)" (Osborne 2002:57). We do not know the patterns in the early church, but we do know that the New Testament books were written to be read orally (see Col 4:16; 1 Tim 4:13; Rev 1:3).

After listening to the oral reading of Scripture, the hearers were to put into practice what they heard. For example, after Moses read the regulations in Exodus 24:3, the people responded, "We will do everything the LORD has commanded." Israel was often warned to follow all that was said (Deut 28:58; 29:29; Josh 1:8). In the justly famous meditation on God's word in Psalm 119, the poet promised repeatedly to "obey" God's decrees (e.g., Ps 119:8, 17, 34) and to "follow" them (Ps 119:1, 59, 67, 73, 173). Jesus said, "Anyone who hears my teaching and doesn't obey it is foolish" (in the parable of the wise and foolish builders, Matt 7:26; cf. Luke 11:28), and in Matthew 28:20 the great commission stresses teaching the nations "to obey all the commands I have given you." In John 14:15-24 Jesus emphasizes that loving him must always result in obedience. This emphasis continues in Paul, as in Romans 2:13, saying that it is not "merely listening" but "obeying the law that makes us right" with God; or in 1 Corinthians 9:21: "I do not ignore the law of God; I obey the law of Christ" (cf. Rom 16:26; 2 Cor 10:5-6; Gal 3:10; 2 Tim 3:15-16). James was following a rich precedent in his stress on being a "doer" as well as a hearer. Moo (2000:88-89) provides an important caveat that this does not obviate serious Bible study: "James would certainly endorse the need to pay careful attention to what the word says, studying it, meditating on it, and pondering its meaning and application. How else could one know what it commands us to do?"

When you merely hear and refuse to act on what you hear, James asserts, "You are only fooling yourselves." Rationalization and self-deception are virtually part of the DNA of sin. The verb (*paralogizomai* [TG3884, ZG4165]) for "fooling" (or, "deceiving") only occurs elsewhere in Colossians 2:4, where it describes false teachers "deceiving" the people "with well-crafted arguments" that are thinly disguised falsehoods. So this verb describes a person being untrue to himself or herself regarding eternally important truths. Such people may think they are in good standing with God, but they could not be more wrong. They can attend church regularly, even talk the talk, but those who do not walk the walk are in serious danger. The context is that of standing before God at the final judgment (see commentary on "save" in 1:21), so the danger is very serious indeed.

The argument then moves to a powerful short parable (1:23-24) regarding the kind of person who will listen or "look into" the word without doing anything about it. Apparently that is just what many of the readers have been doing, for James employs a condition of fact (*ei* [TG1487, ZG1623], "if") that assumes the reality of the hypothesis—they were "listening to the word" but not "obeying it," in contradistinction to the commands of 1:19, 22. James compares such people to those who look at themselves in a mirror, walk away, and immediately forget what they look like. Mirrors in the first century were made of polished copper or bronze (silver for the wealthy) and were fairly common in the average home (see Pilch 1998, who suggests this be translated "metal mirror"), so the illustration would have been widely understood by James's readers. To state the illustration another way, let's say you get out of bed in the morning, go to the bathroom, "see yourself" (the verb *katanoeō* [TG2657, ZG2917] has the sense of "look carefully" and "contemplate") in the mirror, checking your messy hair and blotchy complexion.

Who in their right mind would go to the trouble of looking in that mirror and then not only "walk away" without washing the face and straightening the hair but even "forget what you look like," going to school or work looking a mess? That would be ridiculous!

The contrast between 1:23 and 1:25, with the hearer "glancing" in the mirror and the doer "look[ing] carefully" into the "perfect law," is not between a hasty, careless glance and careful contemplation (as one could infer from the NLT), because, as just stated, the first verb (*katanoeō*) has the thrust of studied concentration and is virtually synonymous with "look carefully" (*parakuptō* [TG3879, ZG4160]) in 1:25. It is not a contrast but a continuation of the metaphor. The word is the mirror of the soul, and like looking in our bathroom mirror in the morning when we wake up, we must *do something* about what the word-mirror shows us about ourselves. It is absurd to see a dirty face or messy hair and ignore those blemishes, and it is equally ridiculous to see ourselves in the word and walk away ignoring our needs.

James applies this in 1:25. Like the person peering into a mirror, the doer looks carefully and contemplates the meaning and significance of the word, then acts on what they see. Blomberg and Kamell (2008:91) note that the verb connotes "to 'stoop down and look into closely,' much like the image of a child who bends over to get nearer to a bug they wish to examine." The idea would be study and meditation on the message of the text and its implications for daily life. God's word is described as "the perfect law that sets you free." This is equivalent to the "word" of 1:18, 21-23 and refers to the gospel truths they had been taught, that is, the new law or new covenant given by Christ (see note on 1:25) and proclaimed to them. As many have stated (Blomberg and Kamell, Davids, Moo, McCartney), this use of "law" must also include the fulfillment of the Old Testament Scriptures in Christ and the church he has established.

These truths are "perfect" because they perform a "perfect" or "complete" work in the believers, making them "perfect" or whole (1:4). Moreover, these principles have set them free (repeated in 2:12) by leading them to salvation in Christ. This new law brings us "freedom" from sin, both in terms of redemption (Christ providing the ransom payment with his blood that has purchased our freedom from sin) and of daily victory over sin. The latter is seen in the emphasis on "doing" and "remembering" the truths of God's word. The Greek says, "not a forgetful hearer but a doer of work" (an objective genitive meaning "who acts on it"), contrasting further the kind of Christian who does nothing with these truths as opposed to those who live them out in daily life.

The promise is that those who act on what they hear are "blessed" by God (cf. Luke 11:28; see 1:12 above). Literally, 1:25 says the doers of the word are "blessed in their doing." There are two directions one can take this. In terms of time, this could be present blessing—a life of meaning and fulfillment—or it could be future blessing, the final reward at the eschaton. In terms of the type of blessing, this could be upward, a blessing by God, or inward, a personal sense of satisfaction in doing what God wants. One cannot help but think all of these are part of the meaning.

◆ 3. Practical Christianity (1:26-27)

26 If you claim to be religious but don't
control your tongue, you are fooling your-
self, and your religion is worthless. 27 Pure
and genuine religion in the sight of God
the Father means caring for orphans and
widows in their distress and refusing to
let the world corrupt you.

NOTES

1:27 *Pure and genuine religion.* Dibelius (1975:121-122) and Davids (1982:102) see that this statement, as an admonition ("Have pure and genuine religion"), could pertain to three different things: (1) It is a Jewish or Jewish-Christian demand for proper legal observance of the laws of purity, perhaps in dealing with Gentile Christians; (2) it is a protest against Pharisaic ritualism that lacked spiritual genuineness; or (3) it denounces Christian Zealots who did not practice love. Yet in this context it must be more general; it probably addresses Christians among James's readers who practiced "faith without works" (see 2:14-26).

caring for orphans and widows in their distress and refusing to let the world corrupt you. Some scholars (Roberts 1972; Trudinger 2004) have opted for a different reading found in 𝔓74: "protecting" rather than "caring." They argue that James centers on the social concerns of this world. However, Johanson (1973) and Blomberg and Kamell (2008:95) show that "world" in James refers not only to social justice but also to the moral and spiritual sin of the world.

COMMENTARY

Continuing his practical emphasis on living out God's word, James now gives three examples that demonstrate what this might look like—controlling one's speech, caring for the oppressed, and refusing the corrupting influence of the world, all of which will become major emphases later in the letter. Note that he says, "If you claim [or seem] to be religious." This implies that the actual case is not so, but the hearers believe it to be so. They can fool others and obviously have fooled themselves (see commentary on "fooling yourselves" in 1:22), but they cannot fool God. The truth will emerge as to whether one is truly "religious" or not. "Religious" (*thrēskos* [TG2357, ZG2580]) was a general term used in both Jewish and Gentile circles for cultic worship in a temple or synagogue. As such, there is the idea of the practice of religion, not just of personal devotion. Certain people may have the basic elements of religion (church attendance, prayer, etc.), allowing them to "seem to be religious." They may claim to participate in the worship of God, but they show this to be false by the absence of genuine Christian living.

The first example James points to will be the theme in 3:1–4:10 and was already mentioned in 1:19—namely, controlling the tongue. The participle "controlling" (probably temporal) stems from the image of "bridling" a horse (see 3:3)—that is, placing a bit in its mouth to restrain and direct its movement. In both Jewish and Hellenistic circles, the wise person was expected to know when to be quiet and listen rather than to speak abruptly or harshly (as in 1:19). They would be expected to "rein in" the tongue. Misusing the tongue is a form of self-deception (see also 1:14, 16, 22). We can fool ourselves into thinking that we are strong leaders, but if we enjoy gossiping, our true religion (or lack thereof) will be exposed. Or, even worse, we might give way to slander (see ch 3). The point is that whenever our mouth gets away from us, it is leading us into sin. At the Last Judgment we will most likely discover that our mouths have been one of the primary sources of sin in our lives (as stated in 3:6).

When our tongues take over, James concludes that our religion is "worthless," a term (*mataios* [TG3152, ZG3469]) that BDAG (621) defines as "idle, empty, fruitless, useless, powerless, lacking truth" as well as "empty, futile, transitory, foolish." In the New Testament this concept is especially used of the "emptiness" or "foolishness" of idolatry (Acts 14:15; Rom 1:21-22; Eph 4:17) and the emptiness of life without God and hope (1 Cor 15:17; 1 Pet 1:18). James may well be saying that uncontrolled speech is a form of idolatry in the sense that it elevates self over God. It is devoid of any value and is empty, an arid wasteland.

In place of this false and empty form of religion, James encourages his readers to seek a "pure and genuine religion" (1:27). This becomes a swing verse in James's presentation. He has been moving more and more into the realm of ethical conduct in chapter 1; here he summarizes that developing theme and prepares the way for the ethical thrust of the rest of his book, especially in chapter 2. In contrast to the empty, meaningless "religion" of 1:26, he then defines true religion as being "pure and genuine." Both adjectives are used often in the Old Testament in a cultic sense, with "pure" defining purity laws, and "genuine" (or "undefiled") defining those who are ritually clean and fit to approach God. At the same time, both refer also to moral and ethical conduct, and here they are used in both senses to move from the ritual aspect of "religion" to the moral behavior demanded by God (2 Tim 2:22; Heb 7:26; 1 Pet 1:4, 22). The latter is emphasized by the fact that this conduct will be done "in the sight of God the Father," who judges without partiality (1 Pet 1:17). God sets the standards for true religion and judges whether our conduct is worthy.

James follows with the second and third examples of the conduct demanded by God for those who would claim to be truly religious. The verb "care for" often refers to God "visiting" people to bring them deliverance (Gen 50:24; Exod 3:16; Ruth 1:6); it came to be used for watchful care. Widows were in an especially distressful situation. In a patriarchal society, they were terribly vulnerable because they had no male protector. The inheritance went to the male children, and the wife was left only with her dowry and the protection of her parental family. Orphans were equally destitute because they no longer had a family to care for them. They were the two most impoverished groups in the ancient world (cf. 1 Kgs 17:8-24; 2 Kgs 4:1-7).

In the Old Testament, we see Yahweh as the protector of widows and orphans (Ps 68:5; Prov 15:25); Israel was commanded not to exploit them (Exod 22:22; Deut 10:18-19). The Israelites were to leave a part of the harvest in the field to take care of them (Deut 24:19-20), and every third year a special tithe from the crops was taken to provide for their needs (Deut 14:28-29). Ruth was the prototypical widow, and Boaz typified Israel in his care for her. The "sins . . . like scarlet" in Isaiah 1:18 refer to social sins: "Learn to do good. Seek justice. Help the oppressed. Defend the cause of orphans. Fight for the rights of widows" (Isa 1:17; cf. Isa 1:23; 10:2). Jeremiah 7:6 warns that God will only be merciful "if you stop exploiting foreigners, orphans, and widows" (cf. Mal 3:5). The concern of the early church for widows is seen in Acts 6:1-6 and 1 Timothy 5:3-16.

The third example is "refusing to let the world corrupt you." This is similar to Romans 12:2, which says, "Don't copy the behavior and customs of this world, but let God transform you into a new person by changing the way you think." Every culture has both positive and negative characteristics, and Paul commanded that the Christian respect and even cherish the positive cultural aspects of any society in which they found themselves (1 Cor 9:22, "I have become all things to all people," TNIV). Revelation 21:26 says that "all the nations will bring their glory and honor into the [heavenly] city." At the same time every culture partakes of human depravity and has its godless elements. These evil aspects are to be avoided at all cost, for they will "corrupt" or "defile" the believer. This admonition leads into the sections that follow—prejudice, unwillingness to help others, and an evil tongue—and James demands that we have nothing to do with such things, for they will corrupt us and the church.

◆ B. Preferring the Wealthy in the Assembly (2:1-13)

1. The problem of prejudice (2:1-7)

My dear brothers and sisters,* how can
you claim to have faith in our glorious
Lord Jesus Christ if you favor some people
over others?
2For example, suppose someone comes
into your meeting* dressed in fancy
clothes and expensive jewelry, and an-
other comes in who is poor and dressed in
dirty clothes. 3If you give special attention
and a good seat to the rich person, but
you say to the poor one, "You can stand
over there, or else sit on the floor"—well,
4doesn't this discrimination show that
your judgments are guided by evil mo-
tives?
5Listen to me, dear brothers and sisters.
Hasn't God chosen the poor in this world
to be rich in faith? Aren't they the ones
who will inherit the Kingdom he promised
to those who love him? 6But you dishonor
the poor! Isn't it the rich who oppress you
and drag you into court? 7Aren't they the
ones who slander Jesus Christ, whose
noble name* you bear?

2:1 Greek *brothers;* also in 2:5, 14. **2:2** Greek *your synagogue.* **2:7** Greek *slander the noble name.*

NOTES

2:1 ***faith in our glorious Lord Jesus Christ.*** "Glorious" is actually a genitive (*tēs doxēs* [TG1391, ZG1518], "of glory"). Martin (1988:60) notes four possible interpretations: (1) "faith in the glory of our Lord" (Zahn), thus his exaltation; (2) "faith in our Lord of glory, Jesus Christ" (Moo, KJV, RSV); (3) as a title, "faith in our Lord Jesus Christ, the Glory" (Blomberg and Kamell, Hort, Laws, Mayor), viewing Jesus as the shekinah or presence of divine glory; (4) as a descriptive genitive, "faith in our glorious Lord, Jesus Christ," looking at him as the exalted Lord (Davids, Johnson, Martin, Ropes, Stulac, McCartney, NASB, TNIV, NLT). It is difficult to choose between the last three. The expression "of glory" is placed last for emphasis, and there is definitely a sense that James is emphasizing Jesus as the exalted presence of God, the divine Majesty among us (see Rom 9:4; 1 Cor 2:8; Heb 1:3; 2 Pet 1:17), so a combination of the second and third options may be the best.

2:2 ***someone comes into your meeting.*** It is difficult to know whether this had actually occurred or was an illustration of the type of thing that could take place. In any event, there are two different understandings of the setting behind the episode described. Traditionally, this has been thought to be a church service, with "synagogue" (translated "meeting" in NLT) used either because these Jewish Christians were still attending the synagogues (Adamson) or with James using its more general meaning of a "meeting" place (Laws, Moo, McCartney, NLT). But another understanding has become increasingly popular, beginning with Ward's article (1969), picked up by a number of scholars (Blomberg and Kamell, Davids, Johnson, Martin), that this is not a worship service but a judicial courtroom sitting in assembly. They argue that the normal term for a worship service would be *ekklēsia* [TG1577, ZG1711] (church) and that the situation fits closely with Lev 19:15 ("Do not twist justice in legal matters by favoring the poor or being partial to the rich and powerful"), as reflected in rabbinic parallels like *Deuteronomy Rabbah* 5:6; *b. Shevu'ot* 31a; *t. Sanhedrin* 6:2. In 1 Cor 6:1-6 Paul urged the assembly of internal law courts to solve church problems; so it is argued that this is the situation described here. A legal setting is quite viable and appealing. However, the traditional understanding is slightly better because it is the more natural reading of the scenario ("your meeting" fits the worship setting better), as "synagogue" was used as late as the second century alongside the house church as a Christian place of worship. The issue of seating people could fit either hypothesis, and the wealthy person could be a visitor to a service or a participant in a dispute. In short, both suggestions are viable, but the worship setting is slightly better.

2:5 *the poor in this world.* There are several ways this expression (with the dative *tō kosmō* [TG2889, ZG3180]) can be read—as a possessive ("the world's poor"), as a locative dative ("the poor in the world"), or as a dative of reference ("the poor in the eyes of the world," called by Blomberg and Kamell 2008:112, "an ethical dative"). The third option is probably best. Johnson (1995:224) says, "it is not simply a question of fact but a matter of value, not only an issue of location, but of meaning. Those who are economically poor are thereby *regarded* 'by the world' as inferior to them." The people of the world judge worth by material gain and social status, so in the eyes of that false value system, the poor are degraded.

COMMENTARY

In 1:19-27 James introduced the key theme of his epistle, practical Christian living. Now he begins a series of three issues that build on that theme—favoritism (2:1-13), faith without works (2:14-26), and the misuse of the tongue (3:1–4:10). In all of these areas he asks that the reader allow the wisdom received from the implanted word to guide each one into living life God's way. This first section develops out of the implications of 1:9-11 and 1:27—namely, that God's people must elevate the poor and take care of them. When Christians discriminate against the poor (see also Rom 2:11; Eph 6:9; Col 3:25) and show favoritism toward the rich, they act against the "perfect law" that is supposed to liberate (1:25) rather than humiliate the needy. By the movement from 1:27 into 2:1-2, it is clear that prejudice against others is a major example of the world's "corrupting" influence. Stulac says, "impartiality is binding on us because of the same standard of justice that compels us to 'look after orphans and widows in their distress'" (1993:88). There are three parts to this section (2:1-7): the thesis (2:1), the example of favoritism shown in the worship service (2:2-4), and the incongruity of preferring their rich oppressors (2:6-7) over the very poor God has chosen to inherit his riches (2:5).

As in 1:2, 16, 19, James begins with "my dear brothers and sisters" to show he is challenging them because he loves them. He then states, "Do not hold faith with favoritism" (lit. translation), by which he means that prejudice is antithetical to faith. The present-tense prohibition could be translated as "Stop doing what you have been doing" but should probably be taken as a general prohibition, "Do not at any time show favoritism" (so Blomberg and Kamell, Johnson). The term itself (*prosōpolēmpsia* [TG4382, ZG4721]) combines two words, "face" and "receive," thus meaning in effect "to receive on the basis of looks." The denotative thrust is to accept a person on the basis of appearance or status in society, thereby discriminating against the poor.

"Faith in our glorious Lord Jesus Christ" begins with a genitive "faith of our Lord," which could be subjective (= "the faithfulness of our Lord") but here is much more likely to be objective ("faith in our Lord") and refer to the claim of faith that the people have as Christians (which will become a major issue in 2:14-26). James's question is, How can one claim faith in Jesus Christ and then obviate that claim with prejudice against the poor? Moreover, their claim is a belief "in our glorious Lord," which emphasizes the "glory" of Christ (see note on 2:1). If he is the presence of God among us, our "Lord," how can we deny that in the way we treat others? When we show favoritism, we are setting ourselves up in his place as judge (2:4, cf. Matt 7:2), but we will face his judgment (cf. 1 Pet 1:17).

James illustrates this principle with a hypothetical situation (suggested by the third-class condition *ean* [TG1437, ZG1569], "if") in 2:2-4. The picture is that of a worship service (see note on 2:2) with two different people, apparently visitors who need to be shown to a seat for the "meeting" (*sunagōgē* [TG4864, ZG5252], often used in the early church for Christian services). Adamson (1976:105) thinks this statement indicates an early date for the epistle because Jewish Christians still attended Jewish synagogue services in the early days of the church. That is plausible (in keeping with the use of the term in the Gospels and Acts) but not necessary, for James calls it "your meeting," probably indicating a Christian service. Moo (2000:102-103) says, "James's qualification of this synagogue as 'your synagogue' implies that Christians had control of the meetings," thus "a 'gathering' or 'assembly' . . . more likely the weekly meeting for worship and instruction."

One of the visitors to the meeting (this could be a woman; cf. 1 Tim 2:9; 1 Pet 3:3 for women dressing this way) is wealthy, with "fancy clothes" (the word means "bright, shining" and indicates resplendent dress) "and expensive jewelry" (lit., "gold-ringed," indicating fingers covered with rings). Gold jewelry signified both wealth and social status, so this was a prominent person in society. The other visitor is the polar opposite, extremely poor and wearing "dirty clothes," shabby and destitute.

The fact (2:3) that both the wealthy person and the poor person must be shown to a seat probably indicates that they are either visitors (Laws, Ropes, Tasker) or new converts (Martin, Moo). Either fits. The problem is that "you give special attention" (lit., "look upon with favor") to the wealthy person, showing favoritism. James likely wanted to draw our attention back to 1:19, "slow to speak," because he provided two examples of hasty, ill-considered speech here (Blomberg and Kamell 2008:108). First, the rich person is told, "You sit here well" (which probably means "sit in this special place"; or "give . . . a good seat to," as in NLT). This must refer to a seat of honor in the front of the sanctuary. In the ancient world (and often in our day as well), the seats closer to the front were reserved for important people (see Jesus' teaching in Luke 14:7-14 about taking seats at a banquet).

By contrast, the poor person is treated with contempt. The disdain is evident in the command: "You can stand over there, or else sit on the floor." The chairs are clearly reserved for people of status, and those of no consequence are allowed only to stand in the back or in a corner. If they sit, it is not in a seat but on the floor (lit., "under my footstool," a phrase used of defeated enemies in Ps 110:1; Acts 2:35; Heb 1:13; 10:13). This unfortunate person is being treated virtually as a slave, with no rights and no dignity whatsoever—the exact opposite of what James said in 1:9-11. The contrast is stark: The wealthy are shown great honor; the poor are shown only scorn and ridicule.

James draws two conclusions regarding such action (2:4), found in two questions that expect a "yes" response—the first of four consecutive verses (2:4-7) that utilize this. (The Greek construction is analogous to our use of tag questions in sentences such as "You are coming, aren't you?") First, "Doesn't this discrimination show that your judgments are guided by evil motives?" The Greek behind "discrimination" is *diekrithēte* [TG1252, ZG1359], used in 1:6 for those with "divided loyalty/minds." Here there may be a double meaning, defining the "discriminators" as those whose loyalty is mixed. Moo (2000:104) points out that this discrimination "in the community is another manifestation of a wavering, divided attitude toward God. The improper 'divisions' between rich and poor reflects the improper 'divisions' harbored in the minds of the believers." Hiebert (1979:138-139) discusses whether this refers to inner attitude or outward conduct, preferring the latter. It is better to say both are intended—the "double-minded" heart toward God (1:6-8) results in divisive conduct in the church. The NLT obscures the fact that such discrimination is being practiced "among yourselves" (Gr., *en heautois* [TG1722/1438, ZG1877/1571]), a phrase that shows that this is a corporate sin; the whole church is involved.

The second condemnation is that "your judgments are guided by evil motives." This is a powerful indictment and indicates that prejudice of any kind must always be identified as evil, not only racial and ethnic, but also economic prejudice. To consider any person superior on the basis of skin color, ethnic origin, gender, or economic status is to partake of the world's "evil" nature. Roman society was built on a client-patron system, and its laws favored the wealthy in every way (see Kloppenborg Verbin 1999). These Christians were secularists, letting culture rather than Christ determine their value system. But Christ has brought a new set of laws, and these principles centered on the equality of all people before God. The term behind "motives" is *dialogismōn* [TG1261, ZG1369], referring to thoughts and opinions as well as designs, thus building on the "double-minded" nature stressed in the first condemnation. It is sin that controls their minds, so their reasoning, as well as the resultant conduct, is faulty. In 4:12 (in a section on judging others) James states that "God alone, who gave the law, is the Judge. . . . So what right do you have to judge your neighbor?" That applies here as well. By discriminating against the poor, they have placed themselves in the role of judge and jury, arrogating authority that belongs only to God.

The last part of this section (2:5-7) centers on the incongruity of ignoring God's special election of the poor to favored status (2:5) and preferring the very rich, who have oppressed them and slandered the name of Jesus (2:6-7). For the fifth time

James addresses them as "brothers and sisters" (1:2, 16, 19; 2:1) to show the deep love and concern he had for them. Here he begins with the command to "listen to me." In 2:3 he built on 1:19, "slow to speak," and here he builds on the idea of "quick to listen." He was calling for alertness and spiritual vigilance in this area.

In 2:5 there are two questions expecting the "yes" response (cf. 2:4). First, James asks them to remember God's special election of the poor. The term "chosen" comes from *eklegomai* [TG1586, ZG1721], often used of predestination in the New Testament (Acts 13:17; 1 Cor 1:27-28; Eph 1:4); here it means God has a special place for the poor because he has elevated them to a whole new position of status in the community. The thrust is similar to 1:9, where James speaks of the special "honor" God has reserved for the downtrodden. The valuation of the world, here followed by the errant church members, is adamantly opposed by God.

This is similar to Paul's message to the biased Corinthians in 1 Corinthians 1:27-28, "God chose things the world considers foolish in order to shame those who think they are wise. And he chose things that are powerless . . . things despised by the world, things counted as nothing at all." In a startling reversal, the poor are called to be "wealthy," i.e., "rich in faith," meaning "in the sphere of faith." This is reminiscent of the first Matthean beatitude regarding "the poor in spirit," rightly translated by the NLT, "God blesses those who are poor and realize their need for him" (Matt 5:3). Without resources to overcome their oppressive situations, the poor must turn entirely to God and therefore find their wealth in trusting God. Luke 12:21 speaks of being, literally, "rich toward God" (cf. NLT, "have a rich relationship with God," which gets at the essence of the idea).

Second, they must realize that the poor more than the rich "will inherit the Kingdom he promised to those who love him." The theme of inheritance is central throughout Scripture (see Johnson 1995:225, as well as the discussion of 1 Pet 1:4 in this volume), beginning with the promise to Abraham and his descendants that they would inherit the Promised Land (Lev 20:24; Deut 1:8). Later, it came to be used of the kingdom blessings given by God to his people (Ps 16:5; Dan 12:13), and in Jesus' teaching it was used of the eschatological promise of a future inheritance of "the whole earth" (Matt 5:5) or the kingdom (Matt 25:34) or eternal life (Mark 10:17). Paul spoke of it often (Rom 8:17; Gal 5:21; Eph 1:14, 18), as did the author of Hebrews (Heb 1:2, 4, 14; 6:12, 17; 9:15; 11:7-8; 12:17). Once more, that first beatitude comes to the fore, "God blesses you who are poor, for the Kingdom of God is yours" (Luke 6:20). Adamson (1976:110) notes that this is the basic idea of the shekinah, the presence of God resting on his chosen people (= "the poor") who would in the kingdom become the rich (the Jewish doctrine of the reversal of roles).

The promise is that the poor will inherit "the Kingdom," which has both a present reality (God's kingdom already entered this world in Christ, Matt 12:28 = Luke 11:20) and future promise (the final coming of the kingdom at Christ's return). With the emphasis on the Parousia in 5:7-8, the latter may be uppermost in James's thinking. The "kingdom" as "God's reign" has already begun, yet it will not be finalized until the end. The basis of this is the "promises" of God, which are eternal and absolutely secure (see 1:4-5). The phrase "promised to those who love him" also appeared in 1:12 connected to the "crown of life," likely the primary "inheritance" intended here. The poor, who went through trials and temptations (1:9, 12), now receive a further trial when they are humiliated and rejected by their own church leaders. At the same time, they "love" God and Christ.

The honors heaped on the poor by God were enumerated in 2:5. But (in 2:6) the church members showed them only "dishonor" ("insult, shame, contempt"); they embraced the secular worldview by doing the polar opposite of what God does. In an honor-shame culture, this was one of the worst things they could have done to the already downtrodden poor members of their church.

For the third straight verse, James then utilizes a question that expects the answer "yes": "Isn't it the rich who oppress you?" The question is, "Why favor those who are using you?" Calvin (1948:303) says James's purpose was "to show that they were without reason or judgment who through ambition honored their executioners, and in the meantime injured their own friends." The Old Testament speaks often of the wealthy oppressing the poor (Isa 58:6; Ezek 18:12-13; Amos 4:1; Zech 7:10), and this has been commonplace as long as mankind has existed. The verb *katadunasteuousin* [TG2616, ZG2872] means also to "exploit" and may refer to the same situation as 5:1-6, with wealthy non-Christians cheating their field hands out of their proper pay so as to live in luxury.

A particular example of this economic exploitation is presented, as these wealthy oppressors "drag you into court," with a violent image behind "drag" that could be physical or legal (Johnson 1995:226). The "court" (more likely secular than a Christian tribunal) may refer to several legal means of cheating the poor, from collecting on debts (one of the major sources of slavery in the ancient world) to taking property for not paying mortgages to usury (high interest rates). Some think this refers to wealthy Jews who dragged Christians before synagogue tribunals (as Paul intended in Acts 9:1-2) and stole their property, but that cannot be proven. The misuse of law courts is frequently condemned by the prophets, as in Amos 5:7 ("You twist justice, making it a bitter pill for the oppressed"; cf. Amos 5:10-12) or Isaiah 10:2 ("They deprive the poor of justice and deny the rights of the needy"; cf. Isa 1:17; 29:21; 59:9, 11, 15).

These wealthy have not simply afflicted the poor; they have slandered the very name of Christ (2:7). The Greek term is *blasphēmeō* [TG987, ZG1059], which when used of people means "slander," but in its religious sense is "violation of the power and majesty of God" (TDNT 1.622). These people were mocking Christ in their opposition against his people, an action paralleled by the "beast" or Antichrist in Revelation 13:6. Moo (2000:109) says, "it can be extended to include any slander that involves God, even indirectly—such as criticism directed at Christian behavior by other believers (1 Cor 10:30; Rom 14:16) or abuse heaped on believers by unbelievers over differences in morality (1 Pet 4:4)." In this case, they were likely heaping abuse on believers as well as speaking against the God of the Christians.

Somewhat unusual is the added "whose noble name you bear" (lit., "that good name by which you were called"). The verb is a divine passive and means that God has given us his "good" (*kalos* [TG2570, ZG2819], "excellent, honorable") name. In the Old Testament and here it denotes ownership—that they are God's special possession (Num 6:27; 2 Chr 7:14; Isa 43:7; 63:19; Jer 14:9). Some think this stems from a baptismal context, as the name of the Lord is invoked over the initiate and in a sense placed upon the person (see Dibelius, Laws, Martin), but that is speculative.

The primary point is that they belong to God and are part of his family, bearing his name. When his followers are insulted, Christ is insulted with them. Therefore, when one shows favoritism, that person is preferring God's enemies over his own people.

◆ 2. The royal law of love (2:8-11)

8Yes indeed, it is good when you obey the royal law as found in the Scriptures: "Love your neighbor as yourself."* 9But if you favor some people over others, you are committing a sin. You are guilty of breaking the law.

10For the person who keeps all of the laws except one is as guilty as a person who has broken all of God's laws. 11For the same God who said, "You must not commit adultery," also said, "You must not murder."* So if you murder someone but do not commit adultery, you have still broken the law.

2:8 Lev 19:18. **2:11** Exod 20:13-14; Deut 5:17-18.

NOTES

2:8 ***Yes indeed.*** There are two ways to interpret *mentoi* [TG3305, ZG3530] here: (1) as a connective ("indeed," NLT; "really," TNIV, NRSV, Adamson, Hort, Johnson, Laws, Martin, Moo, McCartney), seeing it as affirming and continuing the argument; or (2) as an adversative "however" (NASB, REB, Blomberg and Kamell, Davids, Mayor), seeing it as in contrast to those who have blasphemed Christ. A close look at the connection shows this is not drawing a contrast with the wealthy unbelievers but is continuing the challenge to the believers. So the more positive sense as in the NLT is better.

the royal law. There are two issues here: (1) Does "law" refer to the Torah by itself, or does it include the "new law" brought by Christ? This is decided somewhat by our discussion of authorship; if James was writing as a believer (as argued throughout this commentary), the second is by far the better option. (2) Is the "royal law" the specific love command quoted from Lev 19:18 (Hort, Laws, Martin), or does it refer to the law as an entirety, including Jesus' teaching (Davids, Dibelius, Johnson, Moo, Ropes)? As Ropes (1916:198) says, the use of "law" here is broader and best describes "the law as a whole" rather than a single commandment. Still, Lev 19:18 is the apex of the ethical side of the law and sums up that aspect of the law as a whole.

2:11 ***if you murder someone.*** Some scholars have assumed James chose this with a particular scenario in mind. Martin (1988:70) thinks James in the 60s was mediating between the priests and the Zealots and thereby addressing a situation of escalating violence. Yet if that were the case, there would surely be more than this vague note. Moo (2000:115) discusses another possibility, that James was challenging the anger (connected to murder by Jesus in Matt 5:21-26) that may have led to the favoritism being shown here. Yet while Moo is drawn to this, he rightly recognizes its speculative nature. It can be no more than an interesting possibility, and the mention of adultery and murder is best seen simply as examples James was using.

COMMENTARY

The whole of 2:1-13 is on favoritism. The first section provides the "what"—that discrimination based on economic status is against God's regulations and endangers our faith. The next two sections (2:5-7 and 2:8-11) tell "why" it is wrong. First, 2:5 demonstrates that such prejudice is contrary to God's own special place for the poor; second, 2:6-7 asserts that it is completely illogical because the wealthy have shown themselves to be enemies of God and of his people. Now we are given a further pair of reasons why favoritism is a sin—it is against Scripture, and it breaks the royal law of love. There are two sections to this paragraph: (1) Two conditions of fact (*ei* [TG1487, ZG1623], "if") introduce a contrast in 2:8-9 between the right way to act toward others (2:8, love) and the wrong way (2:9, discrimination); and (2) two *gar* [TG1063, ZG1142] (for) clauses provide the basis in 2:10-11 for avoiding favoritism, namely, that it breaks God's law.

The condition of fact (*ei* [TG1487, ZG1623], "if") assumes the reality of the protasis, so the expression "if you fulfill" is rightly translated in the NLT, "it is good when you obey the royal law"— with "fulfill" meaning to "complete" the law by keeping or obeying it. "Royal" (*basilikon* [TG937, ZG997]) does not just mean it is the "supreme" law that takes precedence over all others (see Moo 2000:111); instead, it is closely connected to "kingdom" (*basileia* [TG932, ZG993]) in 2:5b, meaning it comes from the "king" and is "'kingly' in character or essence" (Johnson 1995:230). It is another way of saying "the perfect law that sets you free" in 1:25; the "laws" of God's word are kingly in essence and liberating in effect. Certainly both God's royal decrees in the Old Testament and Jesus' kingdom teaching in the New Testament are intended here. When James adds "as found in the Scriptures," he wanted to emphasize that he had biblical support for what he was saying. When these Christians show favoritism, they were not just doing what was morally wrong; they were breaking God's absolute laws as found in Scripture.

James's point is that the love command of Leviticus 19:18 belongs to the "royal laws" found in Scripture and sums up the ethical side of the law, as Jesus said in Mark 12:29-31, combining it with loving God and calling them "the most important commandment." (McKnight [2004] has validly labeled this part "the Jesus Creed" because it parallels the "Shema" in Deut 6:4-9 and sums up the ethical side of the Decalogue.) The command is simple yet profound: "Love your neighbor as yourself." In the Greek it is future, matching the Semitic original, often called a divine or eternal command: "Thou shalt (= 'you must') love." In Leviticus the "neighbor" is especially the fellow Israelite but includes foreigners in the land (Lev 19:33-34), as Jesus stressed in the parable of the Good Samaritan (Luke 10:30-37). So this commands love for Christians and non-Christians alike (cf. Gal 6:10, "do good to everyone—especially to those in the family of faith"), even love for enemies (Matt 5:43-47). Moreover, they must be loved "as yourself," meaning that you must have as deep and sacrificial a love for others as you have for yourself. However, this does not mean a "self-disregard" that involves denial of self, nor does "as yourself" reflect a narcissistic centering on self. Rather, it concerns a consideration and care for others as being part of yourself.

In direct contrast (*de* [TG1161, ZG1254], "but"; 2:9) to this law of love is the tendency to show prejudice. As 2:8 centers on Leviticus 19:18, 2:9 reflects Leviticus 19:15, "Do not twist justice in legal matters by favoring the poor or being partial to the rich and powerful. Always judge people fairly." Loving one's neighbor in Leviticus, as well as here, involves a refusal to show favoritism. In 2:9 James chose the verb form of the noun in 2:1 for "favoritism" (see discussion there), meaning to judge a person by outward appearance rather than inward reality. Two conclusions are drawn regarding acts of discrimination: First, "you are committing a sin." The verb *ergazesthe* [TG2038, ZG2237] means "working" and sets up a contrast with the "doer of works" (lit., in 1:25), who does good deeds as opposed to the evil deed of favoritism here. The term for sin is *hamartia* [TG266, ZG281], which means to "miss the mark," stressing the extent to which this breaks God's standard as stated in 2:8.

Second, James says it more directly: "You are guilty of breaking the law." The clause literally says "convicted by the law as lawbreakers." The verb "convicted" is the same one used of the Holy Spirit "convict[ing] the world of its sin" in John 16:8, meaning that the Spirit, as a prosecuting attorney, is proving the guilt of the world. That is the thrust here as well—those who show favoritism will be found guilty of breaking the law as stated in Leviticus 19:15, 18. The idea of "breaking [violating, transgressing] the law" connotes a deliberate act of disobedience, and there is no doubt regarding the guilt of such an act. The point is that any act of bias whatsoever—whether on the basis of race, gender, looks, social status, or economics—breaks the laws of God and is a sin. Before God all people stand equally as his creation. As Paul says, "You are all children of God through faith in Christ Jesus. . . . There is no longer Jew or Gentile, slave or free, male and female. For you are all one in Christ Jesus" (Gal 3:26-28).

The basis (*gar* [TG1063, ZG1142], "for") for James's argument is supplied in 2:10-11. Some among the readers may have thought discrimination a small sin that might escape the notice of God (many today have the same mistaken view). James wanted to disabuse them of such an error by stressing the equal status of all laws; the law is a united whole. So he provided a hypothetical situation of a person "who keeps [obeys] all of the laws except one" (in this case, Lev 19:15, against favoritism). Since the readers were Jewish Christians, James centered on the Torah. They might believe that since they assiduously followed all the Torah regulations except that one, they were all right. "Except one" could be literally translated, "but stumbles in one"—with the imagery of going astray and being lost (see BDAG 894). The point is that "failing" in one area is enough to lead a person away from God. Thus, such a one "is as guilty as a person who has broken all of God's laws." The courtroom metaphor continues, and the thrust is that God will judge them guilty. This does not mean that discrimination is the same as murder but rather that both are equally breaking God's law. Martin (1988:69) adds, "Though the Shema (Deut 6:4) is not explicitly mentioned here, there can be no doubt that for James love of one's neighbor goes hand in hand with love for God (see 2:14-26)."

Now we turn to an illustration (2:11) of James's point that to break one law is to break the whole law. He uses two examples taken from the second table of the Decalogue, the ethical side of the Ten Commandments. "God said" echoes the emphasis earlier on "the word" (1:18, 21, 22, 23), depicting God's speaking his true regulations for his people. "The individual commands are part and parcel of one indivisible whole, because they reflect the will of the one lawgiver" (Moo 2000:115). The two examples chosen are adultery and murder, the seventh and sixth commandments, respectively. Interestingly, these commandments are found in James's order in one major Septuagint document, Codex Vaticanus, and they may be found in this order in some Christian paraenetic traditions (see Luke 18:20, so Davids 1982:117).

These two were probably chosen because they reflect later emphases in this book (they were also used together by Jesus in Matt 5:21, 27; 19:18). In 4:4 James calls the weak Christians who lived for wealth and pleasure "adulterers," and in 4:2 murder is linked with the slander and fighting in the community (see also 5:6, where the rich have "killed" the innocent poor by withholding proper wages). Davids (1982:117) notes that "murder . . . is frequently associated with discrimination against the poor and failure to love the neighbor (Jer 7:6; 22:3; Sir 34:26; Test. Gad 4:6-7; 1 John 3:15; Amos 8:4)." So discrimination against the poor is a sin not unlike adultery and murder; all transgress the law of the one God, and all who commit any one of them stand guilty before the one God.

◆ 3. Act in light of judgment (2:12-13)

[12]So whatever you say or whatever you do, remember that you will be judged by the law that sets you free. [13]There will be no mercy for those who have not shown mercy to others. But if you have been merciful, God will be merciful when he judges you.

NOTES

2:13 *But if you have been merciful, God will be merciful when he judges you.* Lit., "Mercy triumphs over judgment." There is some question as to whether the "mercy" is God's or ours. If it is God's, it is saying that the mercy of God will predominate in the end and provide forgiveness for our shortcomings (Adamson, Hort, Martin). If it is human mercy, it means that by the grace of God people can overcome their prejudices and find mercy toward the less fortunate (Laws, Hiebert, Moo). Both aspects have their strengths, and both fit the context. Thus, it is best to see a "both-and" here. As McCartney (2009:150) states, this "specifically shows the relation between God's mercy in judgment toward people and the mercy of those people, who will be judged." "True believers (the ones showing mercy to others) will find God's mercy in Christ annuls the condemnation they otherwise would have received" (Blomberg and Kamell 2008:120). The NLT captures this well.

COMMENTARY

James has been arguing that those guilty of prejudice will be judged. Now he draws out the implications of this for the daily life of his readers, centering on the two ways discrimination was shown: by speech and by action. The present tense imperatives "say" and "do" here emphasize the ongoing necessity of watching their speech and action on a regular basis. The Greek has *houtōs* [TG3778, ZG4047] for both clauses: "Speak in this way" and "act in this way" on the basis of the realization that "you will be judged by the law that sets you free." In 2:10-11 James had centered on the Torah, but the "law that sets you free" returns to 1:25 and the new Torah of Jesus, the whole law of God. There is irony in noting that law that intends to liberate us from sin will also be our judge when we sin. The Greek reads "about to (*mellontes* [TG3195, ZG3516]) judge," stressing the imminence of the coming judgment. This is the holiness of God at work, with the two foci of his holiness being justice and love. His love frees us from sin and death to be his children and to enjoy his atoning forgiveness, but his justice demands that sin be condemned and eradicated.

We are saved by grace, but the Bible indicates that we will also be judged by works, a doctrine found often in the Old Testament (2 Chr 6:23; Ps 28:4; Prov 24:12;

Ezek 18:20), intertestamental literature (*1 Enoch* 41:1-2; *Psalms of Solomon* 2:16-17; 17:8 [10]; *4 Ezra* 7:35; *2 Baruch* 14:12), and the New Testament (Matt 16:27; Rom 14:12; 2 Cor 5:10; 2 Tim 4:14; 1 Pet 1:17; Rev 2:23; 22:12). The judgment will be for believers as well as unbelievers. While believers will be forgiven (e.g., for the sins of omission in 4:17), they will still "give account" to God and perhaps stand in shame (2 Tim 2:15; Heb 13:17) as they answer for sins like favoritism. In 1:19 James warned us to watch our speech, and in 1:22-25 he warned us to be careful that we do not just listen but "do" or "act" on what we see in the word. All this applies to the sin of showing bias toward others in 2:1-13. The law has told us to "love" others (2:8), and when we act on that, we will refuse to play favorites. If we give in to that temptation (1:13-15), we will face judgment "by the law." This does not mean the law will replace God on the throne of judgment but that it will provide the standard "by" which he judges us. The purpose of the new law in Christ is to free the poor and to alleviate their suffering, but if we disregard that law and discriminate against them, God by his law will become our judge.

James concludes this section (2:13) with a "'retribution' formula, in which people get, in effect, exactly what they have done to others" (Moo 2000:117). The statement was probably a "free-floating proverb" used by James to make his point (so Davids 1982:118, who notes Dibelius's error in seeing this as unconnected from its context). Behind this is the principle of justice that is also at the center of the book of Revelation, following the jurisprudential principle of Roman law, called *lex talionis*, "the law of retribution." It is also a good title for the law of God. His justice demands that people be "repaid" for exactly what they have done, whether good or bad (see the passages referenced in the previous paragraph). In fact, this provides a summary of New Testament ethics: What we do to others we do to God (for they are made in his image), and he will return those actions back upon our heads (again, whether good or bad). In the Lord's Prayer, the only element on which Jesus commented further was forgiveness (Matt 6:14-15); it is a perfect example of this point—if we forgive, we are forgiven; if we refuse to forgive, we will not be forgiven.

James used this principle here—"There will be no mercy for those who have not shown mercy to others." The Greek behind "show mercy" is *poiēsanti eleos* [TG1656, ZG1799], meaning "to do acts of mercy," and continues James's emphasis on "doing" (1:22, 23, 25; 2:8:12) rather than just listening and speaking. God is a God of mercy (Exod 34:6; Deut 4:31; 2 Sam 24:14; Neh 9:31; Ps 111:4) and demands that his people show mercy (Hos 6:6; Mic 6:8; Zech 7:9; Matt 18:33; 25:34-45). The statement here is the negative counterpart of Matthew 5:7, "God blesses those who are merciful, for they will be shown mercy." When we show favoritism against the poor, we are being merciless toward them, and we should expect "judgment" (*krisis* [TG2920, ZG3213]) from God, and that too will be "merciless." This could be saying that favoritism is an act of apostasy, and "those who discriminate against the poor are reckoned to be in danger of the same fate as the godless" (Martin 1988:72). This fits with the next section (faith without works is dead, 2:14-26) and with the serious warning at the end of James (5:19-20). Even though there is most likely a hyperbolic sense here, the warning of merciless judgment must be taken seriously.

James ends on a positive note, saying literally, "mercy triumphs over judgment," which should be read with a double meaning (see note on 2:13) that when our mercy towards others triumphs over our tendency to judge (see on 2:9), "God's attribute of mercy triumphs over the dictates of his justice" (Laws 1980:117), and we are forgiven and accepted by him. The verb for "triumphs" is *katakauchatai* [TG2620, ZG2878], which in some contexts means to "boast against, exult over" (Rom 11:18) but can also have the sense of "have triumph or victory over," and that is the meaning here. Our mercy must "conquer" our evil disposition toward prejudice. If we "have been merciful" to others, "God will be merciful when he judges" us (2:13).

◆ C. Faith Must Be Accompanied by Works (2:14-26)

1. Faith without works is dead (2:14-17)

14What good is it, dear brothers and sisters, if you say you have faith but don't show it by your actions? Can that kind of faith save anyone? 15Suppose you see a brother or sister who has no food or clothing, 16and you say, "Good-bye and have a good day; stay warm and eat well"—but then you don't give that person any food or clothing. What good does that do?

17So you see, faith by itself isn't enough. Unless it produces good deeds, it is dead and useless.

NOTES

2:14-26 Dibelius (1975:149) says, "A connection between this treatise and the preceding one cannot be established." Yet this is patently wrong, for both deal with practical issues (favoritism, adding works to our faith) that further develop the basic theme of 1:19-27, the need to work out one's Christian faith by doing or working at the ethical side of the Christian life. Martin (1988:78-79) finds several verbal connections between 2:1-13 and 2:14-26: my brothers/faith (2:1, 14); a poor person in shabby clothes (2:2, 15); faith seen in love/works (2:5, often in 2:14-26); "you do well" (2:8, 19); "called by a 'name'" (2:7, 23). Johnson (1995:246) sees similar rhetorical structures linking the two sections: a rhetorical question followed by a hypothetical case (2:1-3, 14-16); an argument showing the logical inconsistency of the actions (2:5-7, 18-19); a halachic argument for obeying the law of love paralleled by a haggadic argument from the examples of Abraham and Rahab (2:8-11, 20-25), a conclusion made by James utilizing *houtōs* [TG3778, ZG4047] (2:12, 26).

2:15 *brother or sister.* While earlier occurrences of the Greek term *adelphoi* [TG80, ZG81] have been translated "brothers and sisters" (2:1, 14; because the word refers to women as well as men), the specific term for "sister" (*adelphē* [TG79, ZG80]) is actually present in the text here. This is possibly due to the use of "widow" in 1:27 and emphasizes that true believers are mandated to "care for" needy people "in their distress."

2:16 *stay warm and eat well.* The verbs can be taken as middle or passive voice. The passive would seem to indicate something similar to a wish for God's blessing, "be warmed and filled." If the middle voice is understood, the hope is that the addressees may find these things.

2:17 *faith by itself isn't enough.* Since Martin Luther, scholars have differed on James's relationship to Paul. Ralph Martin (1988:82-84) gives four views: (1) They are irreconcilably opposed and demonstrate the diversity of perspectives in the early church (Bultmann 1955:2.163); (2) there is no conflict at all, since they respond to different problems (Ross 1954:53); (3) they can be reconciled by realizing that Paul starts with the commencement of the Christian life at regeneration while James begins later when one is professing faith (Snodgrass 1986); (4) Paul and James must be understood via differing historical contexts, as James was addressing a distortion of Paul's teaching of "saved by faith alone" (Goppelt 1982:2.200-211; Moo 2000:121). My preference is for the third view, primarily because James, writing in the 40s (see "Date of Writing" in the Introduction), would most likely not be facing such a mistaken form of Pauline teaching as the fourth view. The issue was alive in Jewish Christianity, and the terms were common (see also McCartney 2009:53-56). Both writers use the terms differently. Paul, when speaking of faith, means "saving faith," as the seeker opens to the Spirit's convicting presence; James means the faith of a professing Christian who claims already to know Christ. By works Paul means the "works of the law" that had salvific value for many Jews, while James means the good works that are exhibited in the Christian life. There is no true antithesis; Paul and James are not in conflict.

COMMENTARY

This is often called the central section of the book because this passage, calling for "a faith that works," focuses closely on the themes of rich and poor and of practical Christianity from chapter 1. As Davids (1982:119) puts it: "A faith which is purely doctrinal and does not result in pious action (i.e., charity) is a dead sham, totally useless for salvation. True faith reveals itself in pious deeds of love, as the examples of Abraham and Rahab show." So 2:14-26 could be called the fulcrum on which the whole epistle turns. The argument proceeds in three acts: (1) Two rhetorical questions on the saving efficacy of faith unaccompanied by works (2:14) are followed by a practical example involving refusal to care for the needs of the poor (2:15-16), then a statement of the central thesis—faith without works is dead (2:17). (2) A hypothetical interlocutor opposes the thesis (2:18a), and James responds (2:18b-19; see note on 2:18), concluding with a repetition of the basic thesis of 2:17 (2:20). (3) Two Old Testament examples—Abraham (2:21-24) and Rahab (2:25-26)—are given for those who combined faith and works.

James begins with another "dear brothers and sisters" (see on 2:1) followed by two rhetorical questions, this time expecting the answer "no." "What good is it" is a normal way to introduce a debate topic (cf. 1 Cor 15:32) and is meant to elicit the response, "There is no profit or value in this." The way the question is put is important. The person (*tis* [TG5100, ZG5516], "someone") "says" or "claims" to have faith; whether or not they truly believe in Christ is not answered. It is a claim or supposition. The problem is that this person does not "show" or demonstrate that claim by the "works" that accompany it. These are the two primary terms in this section. The Greek word for "faith" appears 11 times, and the Greek word for "actions/good deeds" appears 12 times in 2:14-26. Faith means a claim to believe in and follow Christ, and "actions/good deeds" are the deeds done in the name of Christ, acts of mercy meant to help others (1:25, lit., a "doer of works"). This is summed up in 3:13, where wisdom means "living an honorable life, doing good works." This emphasis on deeds required in the name of faith is found in the prophets (Isa 1:11, 17; Hos 6:6; Mic 6:8), in John the Baptist's preaching (Luke 3:7-14), in Jesus' teaching (Matt 7:15-21; John 15:5, 8, 16), and in Paul (Eph 2:10; cf. Rom 13:3; Gal 6:10; 1 Thess 5:15).

The second rhetorical question is, "Can that kind of faith save anyone?" (the expected answer: "No, it cannot"). From this it is clear that by "faith" James means "saving faith." As Blomberg and Kamell (2008:129) put it, "The verb 'save' (*sōsai* [TG4982, ZG5392]) in James refers to the entire process that begins with initial faith in

Christ and climaxes in heavenly glorification." So James is asking whether a faith that would fail to produce merciful deeds of kindness could ever be true or could ever be the kind of faith that would lead to eternal life. The merciless judgment of 2:13 could be in mind (Laws 1980:119, "it could not save him, presumably, from the judgment of vv. 12-13"). In other words, the "faith" claimed by the person in 2:14a was not actual faith at all, and the absence of accompanying works proves that the claim was false. James is neither denying the necessity of faith nor its reality. He is denying that true faith can exist without resulting in works. Paul says this in Ephesians 2:8-10: We are saved by grace not works (Eph 2:8-9), yet God has created us for good works (Eph 2:10).

Then James adds an example (2:15-16) of the kind of false "faith" named in 2:14. It is difficult to know how hypothetical the situation described here was (the use of *ean* [TG1437, ZG1569], "if," could point to a hypothetical example). As in 2:2-4, such things may well have occurred. Fellow Christians who are poverty-stricken come for help, literally, they are "naked and lacking in daily food." While "naked" does mean to have no clothes at all, in a context like this it refers to insufficient clothing as in 2:2. This also does not have to mean they are starving but are without enough food to meet their "daily" needs. Many bring out a possible link with the Lord's Prayer (Matt 6:11; Luke 11:3), "Give us each day the food we need." When people lack this basic need, God expects us to provide the necessary food and clothing.

The "faith" person responds (2:16) with a seemingly pious prayer that masks a cold heart. The statement "Go in peace" was the normal Jewish farewell (Judg 6:23; 1 Sam 1:17; 2 Kgs 5:19; Mark 5:34; Acts 16:36), translated well in NLT, "Good-bye and have a good day." The person is sending along best wishes for the journey. Also, "stay warm and eat well" (2:16) was a seemingly valid response to their need—may they find sufficient clothes and food to meet their needs. The prayer is that God would supply what they need; all well and good so far.

However, as Johnson (1995:239) says, "It is not the form of the statement that is reprehensible, but its functioning as a religious cover for the failure to act." The person is actually asking God to do what they are unwilling to do, and that is a false prayer. In effect, it says, "Go away. May God give you peace, clothes, and food, because I am not going to lift a finger to help you!" So James repeats what he began with in 2:14, "What good does that do?" Mere good wishes mean nothing without practical aid. Moreover, in the corporate Jewish Christian context, the whole church is indicted for allowing such things to occur in their midst, especially in light of the universal Jewish and Christian demand to care for the needy.

The conclusion is given in 2:17, and it restates 2:14—faith by itself is useless. As Ropes (1916:207) and Nystrom (1997:149) bring out, the contrast here is not between faith and works but between "dead, useless faith and living faith." To fail to care for the poor provides the death knell for any pretension of faith, for it is not faith and works but faith producing works that is demanded by God. Without good works, such faith is "by itself," which might mean that it stands alone, without merit, but it could also mean "in itself," meaning "by its inherent nature" (Hiebert, Ropes). Such a faith "is dead and useless"—with *nekros* [TG3498, ZG3738] meaning "lifeless, with no value whatsoever." Faith apart from works is no more faith than "a corpse without breath is a living person" (Adamson, Martin).

◆ 2. The response of a critic (2:18-20)

[18]Now someone may argue, "Some people have faith; others have good deeds." But I say, "How can you show me your faith if you don't have good deeds? I will show you my faith by my good deeds."

[19]You say you have faith, for you believe that there is one God.* Good for you! Even the demons believe this, and they tremble in terror. [20]How foolish! Can't you see that faith without good deeds is useless?

2:19 Some manuscripts read *that God is one;* see Deut 6:4.

NOTES

2:18 Dibelius (1975:154) says "the problematic v. 18" is "one of the most difficult New Testament passages in general." Everyone agrees that the verse introduces a hypothetical interlocutor, but there is wide disagreement as to how he functions in the argument and how to separate what he says from what James says. The major options are: (1) He is an ally of James, and his statement encompasses all of 2:18. He argues against the "faith" person that without works that person cannot prove there is any faith (NASB, Adamson, Mayor, Mussner). (2) He is an opponent or critic of James, and James responds to him in 2:18b (NLT, TNIV, ESV, Blomberg and Kamell, Davids, Dibelius, Johnson, Laws, Moo, Ropes, McCartney). See following notes.

Now someone may argue. In the ancient world this formula (lit., "But someone will say") always introduces an opponent to the thesis (see especially McKnight 1990). This supports the second view, that the interlocutor is a critic of James. Nearly all recent interpreters have been convinced by this evidence.

Some people have faith; others have good deeds. Lit., "You have faith; I have works." When translated literally, the interlocutor's statement supports James's position. Thus, the first view, that the interlocutor is an ally of James, makes better sense of the pronouns in this clause. The second view takes "you" (*su* [TG4771, ZG5148]) and "I" (*egō* [TG1473, ZG1609]) as rhetorical devices for "one" and "another" (hence NLT's "some . . . others").

But I say, "How can you show me your faith if you don't have good deeds? I will show you my faith by my good deeds." "But I say" is not present in the Greek; the NLT adds it in accordance with the second view, namely, that v. 18a is the opponent's critique of James, and 18b is James's response. Regarding the role of the interlocutor, I would like to suggest a third alternative that builds on the strength of both interpretations: (3) This is indeed an opponent, but one against the "faith" people rather than against James. To paraphrase, the verse would say, "But someone will argue against your position, 'You "faith" people can claim to have faith, but I have works.' You cannot prove that you have faith apart from good works, but I can show I have faith by the good works I do." When you translate the text literally ("You have faith, I have works"), it supports James's position, and this interpretation has the advantage of retaining that force.

2:19 ***there is one God.*** There are several different manuscript readings of this, but all agree that James is stating "God is one." The TR (followed by KJV) places "God" first for emphasis, but that is clearly a later development. The primary difference between the other two readings is whether "God" has the article (𝔓74 ℵ A, the most likely reading) or lacks it (B 614 630). Either way, James is saying that "there is one God."

COMMENTARY

To anchor his argument against the "faith" people, James introduces an interlocutor or critic of their position. The NLT follows the majority of recent interpreters in seeing this person as a critic of James, but I have argued for seeing him as a critic of the "faith" people in 2:14-17 (see notes on 2:18). "Now someone may argue" opposes their position and makes the issue starker. They claim to be people of faith in Jesus, but since there are no good deeds to prove their faith genuine, their claim is unsupportable. However, their opponent does not just *claim* to be a person of "works"; the works are visible for everyone to see. Thus, his challenge is completely valid, as "show" means to "make visible for all to see." Without visible deeds, the validity of their faith cannot be seen or known by others. Faith cannot be separated from works, for without the good deeds a true faith is impossible. The challenge is, "Where is the proof?"

In 2:19 James enters the argument again, adding a further perspective stemming from the Shema, which is central to Christian belief (Deut 6:4, "Listen, O Israel! The LORD is our God, the LORD alone"; cf. Mark 12:29). This is certainly a faith claim made by these people—"See, I can prove I have faith; I believe in the one God." James's response, "Good for you," is the same phrase used in 2:8: "It is good." While it may be "straightforward commendation" of basic understanding (Moo 2000:130), it goes no further than their Jewish background, and it is better to see this as "devastating irony" (Stulac 1993:113), even sarcasm. For Judaism, of course, this was a basic statement of faith, recited twice a day. But in this context, it was mere assent and did not go deep into the life of the person. Calvin (1948:313) speaks of "the common knowledge of God which can no more connect man with God than the sight of the sun carry him up to heaven."

This mental and verbal assent of creedal truth actually makes a person no better than the "demons" who "believe this" and "tremble in terror." In the sense of knowing who God really is, the fallen angels are more orthodox, more monotheistic, than we are! This is especially true in the Gospels, where the highest Christology comes out of the mouths of the unclean spirits. In Mark 1:24 a demon confesses, "I know who you are—the Holy One of God!" In Mark 3:11 they shriek, "You are the Son of God!" And in Mark 5:7 one screams, "Why are you interfering with me, Jesus, Son of the Most High God?" What is the result? They "tremble" or "shudder" (Hiebert 1979:168). The demons "tremble" (lit., "bristle") because they know the certainty of their judgment. Revelation 12:12 says it clearly, "But terror will come on the earth and the sea, for the devil has come down to you in great anger, knowing that he has little time." Satan and his minions are well aware of how it will all turn out. Their frustrated rage is caused by the certain knowledge of their final end. This is in contrast with the smug complacency of these "faith" people; the demons are the implacable enemy of God, but they tremble in the reality this produces. The "faith" people are also headed for judgment but unaware of their plight in their shallow confession of faith.

The rhetorical question in 2:20 restates 2:17; it is both a conclusion for 2:18-20 and a transition that introduces 2:21-26. It sums up what has come before and prepares for what is yet to be said on the issue. It begins with "How foolish!" This is part of the diatribe, the challenge made by debaters to turn the argument around. In the Greek text it is a bit more pointed: "Are you willing to know, *O foolish person*," stressing the fact that by an act of the will they did not want to "recognize" or "realize" the truth regarding their actual faith stance. In other words, they know the truth but refuse to face it. Therefore, they are "fools," defined by Blomberg and

Kamell (2008:136) as having "deficient understanding and moral error," with the moral sense predominant. They are more than empty-headed in this; they are guilty of serious moral sin!

What they refuse to see is the theme of 2:14-26 (cf. 2:14, 17, 26), "that faith without good deeds is useless." Note the buildup in the passages. In 2:14 faith apart from works has no "good" value or profit; in 2:17 it is "dead and useless"; now in 2:20 it is "unproductive." James uses a beautiful play on words for this. The Greek *argē* [TG692, ZG734] is *a* [TG01, ZG01] (the *a*-privative) + *ergon* [TG2041, ZG2240], meaning "without work" or "ineffective, useless" (cf. Matt 20:3, 6 of "idle workers"). One could say it is "worthless because it is work-less." So faith not accompanied by good deeds is unproductive and useless because by nature it fails to "work" at its faith.

3. The examples of Abraham and Rahab (2:21-26)

21 Don't you remember that our ancestor Abraham was shown to be right with God by his actions when he offered his son Isaac on the altar? 22 You see, his faith and his actions worked together. His actions made his faith complete. 23 And so it happened just as the Scriptures say: "Abraham believed God, and God counted him as righteous because of his faith."* He was even called the friend of God.* 24 So you see, we are shown to be right with God by what we do, not by faith alone.

25 Rahab the prostitute is another example. She was shown to be right with God by her actions when she hid those messengers and sent them safely away by a different road. 26 Just as the body is dead without breath,* so also faith is dead without good works.

2:23a Gen 15:6. **2:23b** See Isa 41:8. **2:26** Or *without spirit.*

NOTES

2:21 ***shown to be right with God by his actions.*** The Greek verb is *dikaioō* [TG1344, ZG1467], used for "being justified" by faith alone in Rom 3:24; 4:25; 8:30; 1 Cor 6:11; Gal 2:16-17; 3:6. Some have considered James to be in direct violation of the Pauline doctrine, since he seems to say "justified by works," while Paul says "not by works" in Eph 2:9 (cf. Rom 3:28; 4:2, 4-6). Yet this is not the case, for Paul and James use *dikaioō* in different ways (see Jenkins 2002; Laato 1997). Paul was emphasizing the forensic side of justification that takes place at conversion when, on the basis of Jesus' atoning sacrifice attributed to us, God "declares us to be right"; it is a forensic act of legal justification. There are two other ways this verb can be used, and James quite likely uses it in both ways. First, in an ethical sense it means "shown to be right" (NLT) or "vindicate," as in Matt 11:19, "Wisdom is shown to be right by its results" (Davids, Hort, Johnson, Moo). In this sense Abraham's act proved his ethical "rightness." Second, it can mean "vindicate in the judgment" (cf. 1 Kgs 8:31-32; Mic 6:11, LXX) and thus be used of "final, eschatological justification" (Blomberg and Kamell 2008:136). The binding of Isaac occurred in Gen 22, long after Abraham's faith had been "counted . . . as righteous" in Gen 15:6. So "James is asserting that Abraham was granted a positive verdict in the judgment of God on the basis of his pious acts" (Moo 2000:135).

2:25 ***Rahab the prostitute is another example.*** The question of the lie she told the king in Josh 2:4-5 is not mentioned here or in Heb 11:31. It is probably best to leave it there and not pursue the question too extensively, since it is speculative to guess what would have happened had she told the truth. Still, Blomberg and Kamell (2008:141) remark, "the example of Rahab may offer support for the hierarchical approach to ethics, in which at times a more fundamental moral principle must be kept even if it requires disobedience to a more subsidiary one. In this case, defending God's cause was a higher call than responding faithfully to an already doomed regime." This is worth pondering, but it may overstate the ethical implications of this incident.

COMMENTARY

James has made his argument for putting faith into practice logically and rhetorically; now he wants to anchor this point historically and scripturally by turning to two heroes of the faith, Abraham and Rahab. Abraham is the natural one to begin with as the "father" (NLT, "ancestor") of the nation. Abraham is literally called "father" in Isaiah 51:2 and Matthew 3:9; in Romans 4:1, 11-12, 17 he is called the father of "those who have faith." According to John 8:39, the Jewish people had found their self-identity in Abraham as their father—i.e., they were "the children of Abraham" and therefore a covenant people (cf. Luke 19:9; Acts 13:26). In Judaism Abraham became the paradigm of pious actions; so James had strong precedent for his use of Abraham here.

With another rhetorical question (this one expecting the answer "yes"; cf. 2:5, 6, 7, 14, 18, 20), James tries to rekindle their "memory" of how Abraham was proven to be right with God, namely, "by his actions" (on the conflict with Paul, see note on 2:21). Abraham's faith had already led him to be "counted . . . as righteous" in Genesis 15:6; then in Genesis 22 God tested his faith (a faith already present) in the incident of the "binding of Isaac" (called the *Akedah*), an episode often discussed in Jewish writings (1 Macc 2:52; cf. Sir 44:20; *Jubilees* 17:16-18; 18:12, 16) as evidence of Abraham's moral obedience and right standing with God. Laws (1980:134) says that "Abraham's faith was demonstrated in his trials, of which the requirement to sacrifice Isaac was the final and most crucial test." Davids (1982:128) adds: "This test of the reality of the faith forms the point at which God's verdict becomes clear, for while Abraham starts to offer Isaac, God ratifies the covenant by sparing the boy's life."

The point is that works are necessary to prove that one's faith is valid, and as Abraham showed, God was testing Abraham to show that his faith was real, and his final verdict will take one's "works" into account (see the note on 2:21 for this meaning as part of "shown to be right"). We are saved by grace through faith not works (cf. Eph 2:8-9), but works are the necessary result of a true faith and prove that the faith is real. Paul actually agrees with this in Ephesians 2:10, when he says those saved by faith were "created in Christ Jesus to do good works" (TNIV). Without works there is no evidence there was ever a faith to begin with, and that is the thrust in this section.

James explains his point about Abraham in 2:22, using the second-person singular "You see" to directly address the "faith" person from 2:14-16, clarifying that Abraham's "faith and his actions worked together." There is a play on words, "faith working with his works," to drive the point home that neither faith nor works can function properly apart from each other. The two are "coworkers" in the journey of the Christian life. Genesis 15:6 (faith and righteousness) had to be worked out in Genesis 22 (faith and works). Without the latter the former could not have been real; it would have been a claim that could not be verified.

Abraham's faith was "perfected" (Gr., *teleioō* [TG5048, ZG5457]) or "made complete" by his deeds. The verb recalls 1:4, where we are told to allow "endurance" to do its "perfect work" (NLT, "[be] fully developed"), so that we can become "perfect and complete." The term also means, "bring to maturity." Johnson (1995:243) says, "faith makes possible (co-works) the deeds, and the deeds bring faith to its mature expression." Blomberg and Kamell (2008:137) add, "Abraham's willingness to sacrifice his son not only showed his faith to be real, but also through his obedience his faith actually 'grew up.' Abraham's faith was not mature until he acted on it." Hebrews 2:10 says Christ was "perfected" (meaning his office was "completed" through suffering), and in 1 John 4:12, when we love one another God's love is "perfected" or "made complete" in us. In each of these and here, the idea is that one thing comes to full expression, to its God-intended goal, in another. Our faith can only attain fullness when we act on it, here via good deeds.

In 2:23 James uses a sister term (*plēroō* [TG4137, ZG4444], discussed side by side with *teleioō* [2:22] in L&N 658) in saying that Abraham's faithful act "fulfilled" (the basic term for fulfillment in the NT) or "brought to completion" what "the Scriptures" said in the faith statement of Genesis 15:6, "Abram believed the LORD, and the LORD counted him as righteous." Abraham's "action" at the binding of Isaac completed or "filled to the full" both his faith (2:22) and the basic faith statement about his relationship to God (2:23). James is not speaking of direct messianic fulfillment but to a "filling up" of meaning; at the binding of Isaac Abraham took the import of his "faith" to a new level. Of course, Genesis 15:6 reflects best the thrust of Romans 4:3 and Galatians 3:6, the forensic act by which God "credited" to Abraham's account a righteousness not naturally his own. Still, James's use of it fits as well, for in his righteous obedience in Genesis 22 Abraham proved or demonstrated the reality of God's declaration.

The result of Abraham's good deed and the faith it demonstrated is that Abraham "was even called the friend of God," perhaps a divine passive meaning, "God called him his friend," but at the least referring to how Abraham was known in Judaism. Yet there are several Old Testament passages that lead to this. In Genesis 18:17 (the passage where Abraham intercedes for Sodom), God says, "Should I hide my plan from Abraham?" indicating his intimate trust and acceptance. Philo (*Sobriety* 57) interpreted this as, "Shall I hide this from Abraham my friend?" Other sources in Judaism (*Jubilees* 19:9; *Testament of Abraham* 1:6; 2:3; *4 Ezra* 3:14) present Abraham as God's friend. In addition, several passages call Abraham "beloved of God" (2 Chr 20:7; Isa 41:8; cf. Isa 51:2, LXX; Dan 3:35, LXX), and there is a verbal connection between *philos* [TG5384A, ZG5813] (friend) in 2:23 and *phileō* [TG5368, ZG5797] (love). In John 15:15, Jesus said to his disciples, "Now you are my friends," and in John 20:17 he called them "my brothers." In addition, James is establishing a contrast between Abraham (and all who demonstrate their faith with works) and all those in 4:4 whose "friendship with the world" makes them an "enemy of God." Abraham's faith-exhibited-in-deeds gave him a deep, intimate relationship with God, while those who claim faith but deny it with their worthless worklessness are in reality friends with the world and thereby enemies of God.

In his concluding thought for the Abraham section (2:24), James switches to direct address and applies the point to his readers ("you see"), again restating his thesis (cf. 2:14, 17, 20) and adding the idea from 2:21-23 that this involved "justification" by God. So this becomes the heart of the whole section (2:14-26) and the core of James's theology, summing up the implications: "We are shown to be right with God by what we do, not by faith alone." Davids (1982:130) goes so far as to call this "a *crux interpretum*, not only for James, but for New Testament theology in general" because of its seeming conflict with Paul.

Nearly all commentators contrast 2:24 with Romans 3:28, where justification is said to be "through faith and not by obeying the law," while here it is "by what we do, not by faith alone." On the surface, there is an absolute contradiction between Paul and James at this point. This was discussed partly in the note on 2:21, but let us add a few thoughts here as well. Martin (1988:95) notes the differing situations addressed: "Whereas Paul's audience is in danger of relying on 'works' for salvation, James's readers are excusing themselves from good works, thereby showing only a faith that is dead." Let me note three areas where the two can be reconciled: (1) Paul is concerned with the issue of regeneration, James with the issue of sanctification; Paul with how a person is saved, James with how a person lives out their salvation. (2) For Paul justification refers to that moment when God declares a person right with him, while for James it refers to God vindicating a person's faith and showing it to be right with him, leading to the final vindication at the Last Judgment. (3) Paul fights against the "works of the law," i.e., following its stipulations as a means of being justified, while James fights for the good works that result from salvation. To put Paul and James together, works cannot bring about justification, but works must result from justification.

So James is arguing that God demands that the Christian life be demonstrated "by what we do," namely, by acts of mercy and caring. Interestingly, "by faith alone" is not a slogan found in Paul but only here in James. This means James acknowledges the importance of faith in the Christian life and is simply making the point that it does not function "alone." Unless faith produces works, it is "dead and useless" (2:17). Paul actually agrees with James on the place of good deeds in the Christian life (1 Cor 3:10-15; 2 Cor 9:8; Gal 6:4; Eph 2:10; Col 1:10; 1 Tim 2:10; 5:25; 6:18). As discussed in 2:12, the doctrine of "judged by works" occurs frequently in Scripture, and that fits well with the emphasis here, especially when we ascertain the eschatological understanding that James has of justification, that it refers to the final verdict of God when we give account to him of our lives.

The second example of faith producing works is found in Rahab (2:25), a very different model indeed, as she was the prostitute who in Joshua 2 saved the two spies in Jericho. She "hid those messengers" in her home and then "sent them safely away by a different road." Her house was part of the town wall. She lowered them with a rope, and they escaped (Josh 2:15). She was also one of the "heroes" of Jewish tradition, "celebrated as a proselyte and as a model of hospitality (see, e.g., *b. Megillah* 14b-15a; *Exodus Rabbah* 27:4; *Numbers Rabbah* 3:2; 8:9)" (Johnson 1995:245). She, like Abraham, was "shown to be right with God by her actions," and as a result she is in the messianic line of Jesus in Matthew 1:5. Though a pagan and citizen of Jericho, she confessed her faith in Joshua 2:11, saying "the LORD your

God is the supreme God of the heavens above and the earth below." Then she acted on that faith by hiding the messengers and saving them from the soldiers. As a result, she became a model of faith in Hebrews 11:31, and she along with Abraham are examples of faith in *1 Clement* 10-12. Now she is also a model of faith-based works and the right standing with God that results.

For the fifth and final time James states the thesis of this section (2:26; cf. 2:14, 17, 20, 24), "Faith is dead without good works." Davids (1982:134) calls this "dead orthodoxy" and says it "has absolutely no power to save and may in fact even hinder the person from coming to living faith, a faith enlivened by works of charity (i.e., acts of love and goodness)." James uses a strong analogy: "Just as the body is dead without breath (*pneuma* [TG4151, ZG4460], "spirit"), so also faith is dead without good works." A body is nothing but a corpse without a life-giving force to animate it. In Genesis 2:7 God "breathed the breath of life" into Adam so that he became a "living person." In this same way James is saying that good deeds "breathe life" into faith, and any faith that is not animated by works is no faith at all. "The principle is clear: a faith (body) that is not supported by works (spirit) is lifeless. As breath enables a body to live, likewise works produce a living faith" (Martin 1988:98).

◆ IV. The Problem of the Tongue—The Sin of Dissension (3:1–4:12)

A. Taming the Tongue (3:1–12)

1. Beware of becoming teachers (3:1-2a)

Dear brothers and sisters,* not many of you should become teachers in the church, for we who teach will be judged more strictly.
[2]Indeed, we all make many mistakes.

3:1 Greek *brothers;* also in 3:10.

NOTES

3:1 *not many of you should become teachers.* Martin (1988:104-106) argues that all of 3:1-12 is addressing teachers in the church who were misusing their speaking authority in the official meetings and worship in the church. He speaks of the misuse of "their tongues to the detriment of the community as evil report and rumor are spread to affect the entire range of their corporate life." Yet this narrows the force of the passage unnecessarily. There is no indication in 3:2-12 that the focus is just on leaders and on official worship settings. While certainly the "teachers" are a major focus, the material is addressed to all Christians.

COMMENTARY

At first glance, the section 3:1–4:12 (on the problem of the tongue) seems to have little relationship to the first two chapters and seems to be an artificially attached homily to the first part of the letter, supporting Dibelius's theory that a later editor has strung together independent units. But that is wrong, for chapter 3 is closely related to chapter 1 and actually is the third section (after 2:1-13; 2:14-26) of examples of practical ethical issues that have grown out of chapter 1. The two parts of chapter 2 developed the command to be doers as well as listeners (1:19, 22-25). This section develops the commands to avoid improper speech (1:19, 26). Several other parallels can be found (see Blomberg and Kamell 2008:147)—"judged" (3:1; 2:12-13); "perfect" (3:2; 1:4, 17, 25; 2:22); the bit in the horse's mouth (3:3; 1:26);

the ship in strong winds (3:4; 1:6); wickedness (3:6; 1:15); restless instability (3:8; 1:8); the curses/slander (3:9-10; 2:7). In short, this section is closely interwoven into the previous material in James and continues to develop ethical themes previously introduced.

There is an A-B-A structure in 3:1–4:12, with the problem of improper speech in 3:1-12 (taming the tongue) and 4:1-12 (the tongue causing conflict) framing the solution, which is wisdom-led speech (in 3:13-18). In 3:1-12 there are three sections: (1) Beware of becoming teachers (3:1-2a), since their greater responsibility will bring them stricter judgment; (2) small things like the tongue produce disproportionately great results (3:2b-5a); (3) the tongue has the power to destroy and cannot be tamed (3:5b-12), a power that is contrary to the way God intended.

James begins with the problem of leadership (3:1), warning his readers, "Not many of you should become teachers in the church." By repeating once again the intimate "brothers and sisters" (see 1:2, 16, 19; 2:1, 5, 14), he shows his concern for them. In the ancient world teachers had a great deal of status, whether the Hellenistic pedagogue or the Jewish rabbi. Jesus was called "rabbi" (Mark 9:5; John 1:38) or "teacher" (Matt 8:19; 12:38; Mark 5:35; 9:17, 38; Luke 7:40; 11:45; John 20:16), which showed the enormous respect the populace had for him. The scribes were the "teachers of religious law" (the way the term is translated in the NLT), and they and the Pharisees derived their status from the fact that they developed and disseminated the oral tradition in Judaism. In the early church teachers were the rabbis of the communities, and it was one of the highest offices (Acts 13:1; 1 Cor 12:28; Eph 4:11). The status and prestige this held meant that many people who were not gifted or called to that ministry would seek it anyway.

As leaders fought for power and prestige, bickering and dissension were the all-too-common result (1 Cor 10:10; Phil 2:3-4, 14; 1 Pet 3:9; Jude 16). Johnson (1995:263-264) says, "such a setting provides temptations to virtually every form of evil speech: arrogance and domination over students, anger and pettiness at contradiction or inattention; slander and meanness toward absent opponents; flattery of students for the sake of vainglory." One thinks of Diotrephes in 3 John 9-10, "who loves to be the leader" and made "evil accusations" against John.

The reason (causal participle "for you know") not to seek the teaching office is that "we who teach will be judged more strictly." Note that James included himself in this ("we") as a teacher; he wanted them to realize that he, too, understood the serious repercussions of his ministry. There are three levels to the meaning of divine "judgment" (*krima* [TG2917, ZG3210]) here (presented in logical order); while many scholars debate which of them is intended, I believe all three are part of James's thrust (so also Johnson): (1) They faced the danger of judgment as their continuous use of the tongue in the church exposed them to temptations to sin (Moo); (2) teachers are held to a higher standard since they have greater responsibility due to their office (Adamson, Laws); (3) since these teachers were misusing the tongue and damaging the church, they would face greater "condemnation" (KJV, Dibelius, Hiebert, Martin, Ropes).

Krima implies the "judgment" seat, the verdict by God at the Great Assize, but James was hardly saying he will face a negative verdict, nor that all the teachers in the church will do so. Rather, he means that each of those who choose to fulfill the teaching ministry will be held accountable for what they say, for the content of their teaching and the way they lead the church. Hebrews 13:17 says, "Obey your spiritual leaders" for "they are accountable to God." This means you can trust your leaders to do their best, for they realize they will answer to God for the quality of their leadership. In 2 Timothy 2:15 it says, "Work hard so you can present yourself to God" as "a good worker, one who does not need to be ashamed and who correctly explains the word of truth." This restates what James is saying here. A teacher who mishandles God's truth and "shoots off their mouth" in the wrong way will stand before God in shame at the final judgment. The quality of one's teaching and preaching matters a great deal to God, and too many preachers and teachers are guilty of shallowness and irrelevance.

The rest of this section will apply this principle to all Christians, and James begins this broader application in 3:2a, "Indeed, we all make many mistakes" (lit., "stumble in many ways"). The verb *ptaiō* [TG4417, ZG4760] means both to "make a mistake" (NLT) and to "fall into sin." (James will repeat this verb in 3:2b as he segues to the issue of the tongue.) The serious context of judgment means the latter is predominant, but both aspects are probably intended, namely, the misuse of the tongue accidentally (mistakes) and deliberately (sins). The use of "we all" shows that James continued to include himself and to universalize this to every Christian (not just all teachers). There is no one who has not fallen into improper speech. Yet "many" universalizes the sin of speech as part of "many kinds" of sins. Davids (1982:137) says *polla* [TG4183A, ZG4498] (many) "probably refers to all types of times as well as frequency" or variety of sins. The point is that we all make "mistakes" and commit sins; but that does not excuse us. We are still accountable to God for them, and that will be explored in the rest of this section.

◆ 2. Small things cause great results (3:2b–5a)

For if we could control our tongues, we would be perfect and could also control ourselves in every other way.

3We can make a large horse go wherever we want by means of a small bit in its mouth. 4And a small rudder makes a huge ship turn wherever the pilot chooses to go, even though the winds are strong. 5In the same way, the tongue is a small thing that makes grand speeches.

NOTES

3:4 ***a small rudder makes a huge ship turn wherever the pilot chooses to go.*** Baker (1995:125) sees three points in this analogy: Like the rudder, the tongue (1) does not contain power but channels power into directed action; (2) has an importance for the body "out of proportion to its relative size"; and (3) is controlled by the one directing it. This third point is seen in "wherever the pilot chooses to go," using the term *hormē* [TG3730, ZG3995], "impulse, inclination, desire" (BDAG 724), and the message is that in the final analysis we determine the course the tongue will take.

COMMENTARY

James now zeroes in on the issue of the tongue, segueing from the idea that we all make mistakes (of many kinds) to the mistakes we make with our words. No one can control their tongue perfectly, but that is the goal for which James wants us to strive. If we were to do so, we would be "perfect," i.e., a "complete" person who has arrived at full "maturity," for then we would "also control ourselves in every other way." Stulac (1993:123) says, "If you control what you say, you can control the rest of what you do." The desire is "to motivate us to diligence in speech because it is so influential over the rest of our lives." "Control" is the same verb as in 1:26 that uses the image of a horse's bridle that "reins in" the tongue (see 3:3) and therefore the rest of, literally, "the whole body," meaning every other area of one's life. The idea of keeping the tongue in check is found often in Proverbs (Prov 9:8-9; 10:8, 14, 19; 11:9; 12:18; 13:13; 15:1; 16:21; 17:7; 18:6-7; 21:23), so the control of the tongue as the key to the rest of one's being is a common emphasis in Wisdom Literature.

Some might doubt whether speech could make that great a difference, so in 3:3 James provides the first of four illustrations of small things controlling great things—a bit with a horse, a rudder on a ship, the tongue, and a spark with a forest fire (this last one is a negative image and begins the next section). These are all stock examples often used in the ancient world (see Dibelius 1975:186 for examples), and so the point would have been instantly recognized. The first, a small bit in a horse's mouth, would have been an apt illustration because of the general awe people had for the Roman cavalry and war horses, considered virtually invincible in battle. These powerful, large animals controlled the tide of a battle, yet the very small bit in the horse's mouth controlled its movement. Two further points are of interest. First, the mention of the "mouth" of the horse provides a strong connection with the tongue in the mouth of a person, so that the purpose of this section is enhanced. Second, the last clause in the Greek is "we guide their whole body" (NLT, "make a large horse go wherever we want") connecting this with the way the tongue controls "the whole body" or "self" in 3:2. The thrust is that the tongue, like a small bit in a horse's mouth, turns one's whole life around and directs the way it will go.

The second illustration is the small rudder on a large ship (3:4). The Romans built extremely large ships like the triremes with three banks of oars or the massive grain ships that brought tons of grain from Egypt to Rome. Paul was on one during his perilous trips in Acts 27:6-41. Barrett (1998:1145) notes one that measured 180 feet long, 45 feet wide, and 43.5 feet deep. While not overly large for our day, these were huge in the first century. The rudder, the smallest part of the ship, directed where the ship went, and that was true "even though the winds are strong." The emphasis on strong winds may go back to 1:6, where a Christian with "divided loyalty" is as unstable "as a wave of the sea that is blown and tossed by the wind." The point would be that if the tongue is under control, such winds can no longer toss the believer around. One is reminded of Ephesians 4:14, where Paul warned his readers to grow up spiritually lest they be "tossed and blown about by every wind of new teaching."

The question is, Will we control our tongue, or will we allow our tongue to control us? With "in the same way," James explains the illustrations explicitly. The tongue, the same as the bit or the rudder, is "a small thing," (lit., "a small member" of the body). It cannot even be seen when the mouth is closed, so this hints that the tongue seems to be (in terms of outward appearance) an "insignificant" part of the body. The last clause is somewhat surprising: literally, "it boasts great things." There is more than one level of meaning. The verb (*auchei* [TG849.1, ZG902]) is a *hapax legomenon* (i.e., it is used only here in the NT); it indicates pride in something that is expressed strongly. As such, it is a transition idea that is positive in the context of 3:3-5a (it has a lot to boast about because it can accomplish "great things") and negative as the introduction to 3:5b-8 (its boasting can cause great evil). Davids (1982:140) sums it up well: "The tongue is indeed powerful, but it is not always used for good" due to "the power of evil resident in the tongue." Thus, there is "a slow shift from the power of the tongue to the evil of the tongue to the need for proper control. It is not that the tongue steers the ship but that the proper helmsman is often not in control."

◆ 3. The power of the tongue to destroy (3:5b-12)

But a tiny spark can set a great forest on
fire. [6]And the tongue is a flame of fire. It
is a whole world of wickedness, corrupt-
ing your entire body. It can set your whole
life on fire, for it is set on fire by hell it-
self.*

[7]People can tame all kinds of animals,
birds, reptiles, and fish, [8]but no one can
tame the tongue. It is restless and evil,
full of deadly poison. [9]Sometimes it prais-
es our Lord and Father, and sometimes it
curses those who have been made in the
image of God. [10]And so blessing and curs-
ing come pouring out of the same mouth.
Surely, my brothers and sisters, this is not
right! [11]Does a spring of water bubble out
with both fresh water and bitter water?
[12]Does a fig tree produce olives, or a
grapevine produce figs? No, and you can't
draw fresh water from a salty spring.*

3:6 Or *for it will burn in hell* (Greek *Gehenna*). **3:12** Greek *from salt.*

NOTES

3:5 ***tiny spark . . . great forest.*** James used an interesting rhetorical play on words here, having the same term (*hēlikos* [TG2245, ZG2462]) for both "tiny" and "great." The word simply means "magnitude in either direction"; so it can refer to something very small or very large. This highlights the contrast between the very small spark and the very large fire. It does not matter whether a large forest is in view or brushwood and undergrowth in the woods (with Elliott-Binns 1955); the contrast is very much the same.

3:6 ***It is a whole world of wickedness.*** This is a very difficult verse to interpret, for it contains a series of nouns unconnected by verbs, and many scholars believe it so difficult that they must suggest emendations. Ropes (1916:233-234) says it cannot be understood in its present state, and Dibelius (1975:1194-1195) thinks it is the result of "textual corruption" (see also Adamson, Mayor). However, while difficult, it is not beyond understanding. But in order to get at the meaning we must ask several questions: What is the meaning of *kosmos* [TG2889, ZG3180] (world)? How does the genitive "of wickedness (or unrighteousness)" function? How do we interpret the Greek verb and predicate, lit., "it is appointed (or constituted) among its members"? *Kosmos* could be understood as "ornament" or "adorned" and mean it makes wickedness appealing (Chaine 1927:81), or it could mean "the sum total of wickedness" (the Latin Vulgate). While both are possible, neither is likely here, because everywhere the term is used in James (1:27; 2:5; 4:4) it refers to "the fallen, sinful world-system" (Moo 2000:157). The genitive is best seen as descriptive, "wicked world" (so Davids, Moo; cf. Luke 16:9, "unrighteous mammon"), though most translations, like the NLT, leave it as a genitive. The verb can mean "appoint" or "make/cause someone to be something" and could be in the middle voice ("makes itself to be") or passive voice ("is made to be"). The best here seems to be the middle voice (since there is no implied subject for a passive) with the latter meaning: "makes itself to be a wicked world."

3:8 ***deadly poison.*** Gr., *iou thanatēphorou* [TG2287, ZG2504], lit., "death-dealing poison." This would remind one of a poisonous snake, perhaps the serpent in Gen 3. See also Ps 58:4, which says, "They spit venom like deadly snakes; they are like cobras that refuse to listen," and Ps 140:3, which says, "Their tongues sting like a snake; the venom of a viper drips from their lips" (quoted in Rom 3:13).

3:9 ***praises our Lord and Father.*** While the best manuscripts (𝔓20 א A B C 1739) have "Lord," the TR (followed by KJV), supported by K L 𝔐, have "God and Father." Most likely later scribes used "God" to make it clear it was God rather than Christ who was intended here. As Comfort (2008:728-729) brings out, Jesus is called "Lord" in 1:1; 2:1; 5:7-8, 14-15, so the scribes wanted to avoid confusion.

COMMENTARY

This extended paragraph details the evil power of the tongue to act contrary to God's way with its terrible destructive power. There are three parts: (1) The tongue is like a small flame setting fire to a great area (3:5b-6); (2) the tongue cannot be tamed (3:7-8); (3) the tongue, which both blesses and curses, is antithetical to God's creation (3:9-11). The image of the small spark starting a great forest fire is in keeping with the other three small things making great results (3:3-5a). The three in verses 3-5a showed the positive effects the tongue can have, while the three in verses 5b-11 demonstrate the evil effects the tongue can have. The bit in the horse's mouth and the rudder on the ship were positive images having a good effect, but this is a negative image showing a destructive effect. James will now build on the image of fire from this analogy. We have all seen pictures on television of forest fires in the American West every summer and fall, and some of us have experienced them. They are horrific, and they all start by this same type of "tiny spark." That is the point here. The destructive power of small things like the tongue is immense.

What follows in 3:6 is a series of five further metaphors; it is a progressive series, building in intensity. In the first part of the verse what is implicit in 3:5b becomes explicit—"the tongue is a flame of fire." The *kai* [TG2532, ZG2779] (and) can be seen as emphatic ("also" or perhaps better, "indeed"). As in 3:5b, this fire of the tongue will destroy much around it. Dibelius (1975:192-193) points out that fire is a favorite metaphor in diatribe to represent the rule of the passions and desires in a person's life. Proverbs 16:27 and Sirach 28:21-23 show how the tongue, as an instrument of evil, expresses passion—"their words are a destructive blaze."

The second metaphor breaks the series because it appears as a sentence, though with "world" still in the nominative, functioning as if it were in apposition to "fire" (it also is first in its clause, thus immediately after "fire" in the sentence). As discussed in the note on 3:6, the idea is that the tongue, far from being a positive force in a person's life (and in the church), refashions ("makes") itself into "a whole world of wickedness" in our lives personally and in the church. (I believe the teaching encompasses both the personal and the corporate side here.) The emphasis clearly is on the power of sin to control the tongue whenever we do not maintain complete control of it. The tongue becomes in effect the "whole world" or focus of life. "Unrighteousness" or "wickedness" further defines the "world" as the system of evil in command of sinful humanity. The tongue "represents" or "constitutes" the power of unrighteous thinking and action that guides behavior all too often. James stresses the fact that it operates "among our members," referring to the parts of our body but also the church (Martin 1988:115). This is not exactly the Pauline metaphor of "body" (James was writing before Paul), but the meaning is very similar. His church was being torn apart by dissension, and he was addressing that problem in this section.

Next, the tongue is "corrupting your entire body," again meaning both the individual self ("body" referring to the whole self) and the church as a body. The verb *spiloō* means to "stain" or "blemish"; it has a religious force referring to that which defiles the body. The cognate is used in 1:27 in the expression "refusing to let the world corrupt you." Still more intensive is the fact that it can "set your whole life on fire"; the expression "whole life" is literally "the wheel of existence (or nature)." Some scholars (Adamson, Dibelius, Laws) see this as a semitechnical phrase from the Orphic mysteries referring to the circle of birth and existence. Most recent studies (Blomberg and Kamell, Martin, Moo) realize that the phrase had become a more popular idea by James's time, simply meaning the ups and downs of life. Since the tongue is at the center of our life, it sets in motion a conflagration that will destroy "the entire course of your life."

Finally, the tongue "is set on fire by hell itself." This is not "Hades" (the grave) but *gehenna* [TG1067, ZG1147], referring to the Valley of Hinnom outside the walls of Jerusalem, where there used to be child sacrifices to the god Molech (2 Kgs 23:10; Jer 32:35), and where in Jesus' day, the trash burned day and night. Jesus used this as a metaphor for eternal punishment (Matt 5:22, 29-30; 18:9). Blomberg and Kamell (2008:159, following Bauckham 1998:119-131) believe it is "punishment for wicked speech." This is an interesting possibility, but here it more likely functions like "death and [Hades]" in Revelation 6:8; 20:13-14, which uses it as a personification of demonic forces. This would mean the tongue becomes a tool of Satan to destroy the individual and the church. False teachers are often portrayed as controlled by Satan, and their teachings are demonic in nature (2 Cor 11:13-15; 1 Tim 4:1; 2 Pet 2:10; Jude 8-10).

James has been utilizing images of small things, in particular a fire, to teach the problem of the tongue. Then he switches the metaphor to God's animal creation. In 3:6 the fiery tongue could not be controlled; now the wild tongue cannot be tamed. The four categories of wild beasts are drawn from Genesis 1:26 (creation) and Genesis 9:2 (Noah's new world), especially the former where mankind is given dominion to "reign" over the animal world (cf. also Gen 2:19-20). "Animals," which included all four-legged creatures, together with the other three terms ("birds, reptiles, and fish") sums up all nonhuman animate creation. The point is that mankind's rule over the animal world has worked because all these "kinds of" (meaning every type or species of animal) creatures can be "tamed." Actually, the Greek has "is tamed" (gnomic present for the way it always is) and "has been tamed" (perfect tense for the constant state of affairs)—added for emphasis. Obviously this is hyperbole, for not every animal had been tamed; still, the ancient world took pride in mankind's ability to subdue the animal kingdom. Psalm 8:6-8 celebrates the dominion of mankind and "conveys the idea of humankind's superiority over animals both in terms of what is hunted and slain for food and what is domesticated for work and pleasure" (Martin 1988:116, from Adamson 1976:145). If this was the case in the first century, it is even truer now with whales and even sharks being trained to perform.

While lions and tigers, dolphins and whales have been tamed, the one "animal" that has never been "tamed" is the tongue (3:8). The expression "no one" is literally "no one among humanity"; it emphasizes the fact that it is not humanly possible to gain mastery over the tongue. This is an unusual emphasis. Augustine saw hope in this: "He does not say that no one can tame the tongue, but no one of men; so that when it is tamed we confess that this is brought about by the pity, the help, the grace of God" (*On Nature and Grace,* 15). This is doubted by Moo (2000:161) on the grounds that it would imply perfectionism, but I do not think that is Augustine's point. In the war against the tongue, there can be occasional victories, but only by the grace of God and the power of the Spirit. The tongue can be an implacable enemy, always tending to say the wrong thing. But with the help of God, it can be controlled.

Still, James's main point is the tongue's evil nature, as he goes on to say, "It is restless and evil, full of deadly poison." Used only here and in 1:8 in the New Testament, *akatastaton* [TG182, ZG190] denotes that which is "restless" and "unstable." It speaks of the nature of the double-minded person in 1:8, and this double nature is the theme of 3:9-10. The connotation is of something without a secure foundation; like an unstable building in the midst of an earthquake, the tongue can never be controlled. Here the basis for that disorderly conduct of the tongue is its "evil" nature. The wickedness described in 3:6 robs the tongue of any possibility of control, like an untamable predator. Martin (1988:117) states, "In the present context it forms the picture of a caged animal pacing back and forth and seeking an opportunity to escape." Due to this propensity to sin, it is a deadly force (see note on 3:8).

James then speaks of the inconsistent duplicity of the tongue (3:9-10). This is at the heart of the issue for James's churches in that it describes the spiritual problem behind their improper use of speech among themselves. At one level, their worship services were proceeding unabated, and at the other level, with the same mouths, they were bickering with each other and slandering each other. The message is, "This is not right!" The wickedness of the tongue is especially evident in this duplicitous conduct; God condemns this kind of hypocritical inconsistency. On the one hand, in their official worship they "bless" God. This is at the core of Jewish ideas of a proper relationship with God. From the time of the Old Testament even to today, whenever Jewish people name God, they often add, "Blessed be He!" (Pss 28:6; 31:21; 103:1-2; Rom 9:5; 2 Cor 1:3; 1 Pet 1:3; the ending of each of the Eighteen Benedictions; Tob 3:11; *1 Enoch* 77:2; 84:2; *m. Berakhot* 7:3). The double title "Lord and Father" appears only here in the Bible, but the two names occur in the same context several times (Isa 63:16; 64:8; Matt 11:25; 1 Cor 8:6). There is a strong liturgical background behind saying God's name in worship services.

At the same time and with the same mouths, as soon as the services were over, their hypocrisy continued unabated (James uses present tenses here) with their ongoing sniping at each other. The term for "curse" (*kataraomai* [TG2672, ZG2933]) often has a technical denotation; it indicated official curses placed on people in public forums ("to call down curses upon" someone). But it is doubtful that this is the case here. These curses were more like backbiting and bickering. Hiebert (1979:201) calls them "angry disputes and slanderous remarks in inner church party strife (cf. 4:1-2, 11-12) that resulted in the lack of self-control and elicited vicious invectives." God brought forth covenant blessings and curses on the people when they were faithful or unfaithful to his Torah stipulations, but God's people are not to curse others (Luke 6:28; Rom 12:14); in fact, the saints are supposed to return blessings when cursed (1 Pet 3:9). This does not mean that there will never be prophetic denouncement, as in the case of false teachers (2 Cor 11; Phil 3; 1 Tim 4; 2 Tim 3; 2 Pet 2; 1 John 4; Jude), but there is to be no slanderous invective uttered in anger.

People should not be cursed because they "have been made in the image of God." This stems from Genesis 1:26, where God said at creation, "Let us make human beings in our image, to be like us." With Genesis 1:27 alluded to in 3:9, there is a creation motif running through this section. To be created "in God's image" is to be in union with him. This is especially true because the people envisaged here were most likely other members of the church and therefore God's children, part of his family. To curse them is to curse God himself. Every parent feels that "what you do to my kid you do to me." So one moment they are praising God; the next they are in effect cursing God. This kind of hypocritical bifurcation cannot be tolerated. The duplicity of pretending you can do both must bring judgment.

In 3:10 James summarizes the issue—"so blessing and cursing come pouring out of the same mouth." The inconsistency of what we might label "bipolar mouth" is rather obvious. This is absolute proof of the "double-minded" person condemned in 1:6-8; the "double mouth" stems from the duplicitous mind. So it is condemned outright—"Surely . . . this is not right!" Davids (1982:146) calls this duplicity "moral and logical nonsense," and Stulac (1993:128) says it is "utterly unthinkable, abhorrent." Jesus deplored such behavior several times, and once again James seems to have drawn from the Jesus tradition. In Matthew 7:1-2 Jesus ordered, "Do not judge others," for "the standard you use in judging is the standard by which you will be judged." In Matthew 12:34-37 he says that evil speech comes from an evil heart, and "the words you say will either acquit you or condemn you." Finally, in Matthew 15:11, 18 Jesus says that evil words proceed from the heart and then come out of the mouth, defiling a person.

Finally, James concludes this section (3:11-12) with three illustrations from nature to depict how illogical and incompatible double-talk is in the divine order; all three are in the form of rhetorical questions that expect the answer "no" (2:14; cf. 2:4-5). They form almost a mini three-part message on the inconsistency of the tongue. He first deals with abnormality of the tongue producing both good and evil. The image of a spring was at the heart of Palestinian life; an area would be judged livable on the basis of its access to the "fresh" (*gluku* [TG1099A, ZG1184], lit., "sweet," where we get the English "glucose") water of a spring. Yet there were two dangers;

one would be an infusion of salt water from the Mediterranean or the Dead Sea, the other a combination of factors that could turn a spring brackish and foul (*pikros* [TG4089A, ZG4395] means "bitter" or "foul"). A comparison between the Jordan River and the Dead Sea would fit well; when fish from the Jordan hit the Dead Sea, they die instantly. James's image might also allude to the miracle at Marah during the Exodus, when the "bitter" (the meaning of "Marah") was turned sweet and drinkable (cf. Num 5:18). James's point is that a spring cannot "bubble out with both fresh water and bitter water." Springs could not "bubble" or gush forth (*bruei* [TG1032, ZG1108], "pour out") one kind on Monday and the other kind on Tuesday; they were not like modern faucets that could turn out hot or cold water with the turn of a spigot. They were either good or bad sources of water. When a spring had both fresh and salt water coming into it, it was unusable, for even a little salt (or foul) water turned the good water bad. The bottom line for this first point is that God did not make our tongue so that we would use it both to praise God and to abuse his people at the same time.

The second illustration (3:12a) looks at the problem from a slightly different perspective: The kind of person you are determines the type of things you will say. The illustrations about a fig tree producing olives and a grapevine producing figs (the two major fruits of Palestine) were stock examples with ancient writers. Jesus used it in Matthew 7:16 ("Can you pick grapes from thornbushes, or figs from thistles?"), in a section regarding false prophets. He says you can identify false teachers by their fruit; they will always act in kind. James's point is very similar. Plants will always bear fruit "of the same kind" (Gen 1:11-12). In the same way, a tongue that uses speech to hurt others by nature must act from an evil heart. A heart of goodness will never produce harmful, bitter speech.

The third and final illustration/point (3:12b) restates the previous. This time it is "a salty spring," one that drew its water from the Mediterranean. One could hardly expect such a spring to bubble up with sweet water. The type of speech you use is a barometer of the kind of person you are, and you will not control your tongue until you change your heart. An inconsistent tongue means an inconsistent Christian. God did not make you to use your divinely given gift of speech to tear others down.

◆ B. The Solution—Wisdom from Above (3:13-18)

13 If you are wise and understand God's ways, prove it by living an honorable life, doing good works with the humility that comes from wisdom. 14 But if you are bitterly jealous and there is selfish ambition in your heart, don't cover up the truth with boasting and lying. 15 For jealousy and selfishness are not God's kind of wisdom. Such things are earthly, unspiritual, and demonic. 16 For wherever there is jealousy and selfish ambition, there you will find disorder and evil of every kind.

17 But the wisdom from above is first of all pure. It is also peace loving, gentle at all times, and willing to yield to others. It is full of mercy and good deeds. It shows no favoritism and is always sincere. 18 And those who are peacemakers will plant seeds of peace and reap a harvest of righteousness.*

3:18 Or *of good things*, or *of justice*.

NOTES

3:13-18 This is a further section that Dibelius (1975:207-208) considers an isolated group of independent sayings added to the book by an unknown redactor. But Johnson (1995:268) finds "multiple links" between 3:1-12 and 3:13–4:10, e.g., *akatastasia* [TG181, ZG189] (disorder) in 3:8; 3:16; water and its fruit (i.e., the harvest produced by water, 3:11-12) = wisdom and its fruits (3:13-18); cursing (3:9) = wars (4:1); the teacher of 3:1 and the wise of 3:13. The whole section fits together in sermonic form as a challenge and indictment of those who conduct themselves in the church without regard to wisdom.

3:15 *unspiritual.* This term is sometimes translated "sensual" (KJV, NEB), but there is little sexual connotation here. It refers to the natural world, translated "natural" in the NASB and even "animal" in the JB. Yet the best translation is "unspiritual" as here (see commentary below).

3:17 *the wisdom from above.* Some scholars (Davids, Kirk, Martin, Windisch, McCartney) see "wisdom" in James as the equivalent to "the Spirit" in Paul's writings, since James does not refer to the Spirit and his work (with the possible exception of 4:5); the description of wisdom in James parallels in many ways the work of the Spirit in Paul's writings. Moreover, the two are often placed together in Jewish literature, where Wisdom is personified as the voice and presence of God. Still, it is best not to equate them but rather to note the similarities. Moo (2000:175) states, "The OT and Jewish writings provide a general profile of the godly person. James, following OT and Jewish precedents, attributes these qualities to the presence and power of wisdom; Paul, developing more fully the implications of new covenant fulfillment, attributes them to the Spirit."

3:18 Dibelius (1975:214) believes this to be an "isolated saying" added by an editor. But as before (see on 1:5-8; 2:13; 3:1ff), there is a close connection between this proverbial saying and its context. It plays a crucial role in the discussion of the "wisdom from above" in 3:13-18.

those who are peacemakers will plant seeds of peace. Lit., "[the fruit of righteousness] is sown in peace by (or for) those making peace." There is considerable discussion as to whether the dative participle *tois poiousin* is a dative of advantage ("for those making peace," stressing the peacemaker as the recipient, so NRSV, Dibelius, Laws, Martin, Mayor, McCartney) or a dative of agency ("by those making peace," stressing the peacemaker as producer of the harvest, so NASB, TNIV, NLT, Davids, Johnson, Moo, Ropes, Tasker). Since the emphasis throughout is on the contrast between the evil actions of the dissenters and the righteous actions of the godly, it is better to see this as agency, centering on the righteous conduct of those who exemplify godly wisdom. Another interesting possibility is provided by Hiebert (1979:213): "Perhaps James deliberately left the construction unlimited by a preposition in order to leave room for both meanings."

harvest of righteousness. The genitive "of righteousness" could be adjectival ("righteous fruit"), subjective ("the reward that righteousness brings," Ropes 1916:250), objective ("fruit producing righteousness"), source ("fruit produced from righteousness"); or epexegetical ("fruit that consists of righteousness," Adamson, Hort, Johnson, Martin, Moo). The last one makes the most sense in this context. The fruit of wisdom is the righteous behavior of the godly.

COMMENTARY

The solution to controlling the tongue is to live in wisdom. This returns somewhat to the qualifications of a teacher in 3:1 but adds the concept of wisdom from 1:5, 19-27 as the key characteristic of the good teacher. Some (e.g., Martin) believe that teachers have been the primary (almost the sole) focus of 3:1-12 leading into this section, but it is more likely that teachers and lay members have been the focus together, as the commentary above tries to demonstrate. The leaders may be the most guilty of misusing the tongue, but the whole church is guilty of dissension. Very few churches split due only to the leaders, and that is likely the case in the Jewish-Christian community of James, as well. At any rate, wisdom here is seen in the actions that flow out of it, and this proper conduct must replace jealousy and self-centeredness (3:14) with peace and mercy (3:17), resulting in righteousness (3:18). As such, this paragraph stands between the two sections on the bitter schisms that had resulted from the misuse of the tongue (3:1-12; 4:1-12), and it provides the answer for the malicious backbiting that brought war to the congregations. It concludes the earlier material, introduces the later, and acts as the antidote for both. Martin (1988:127-128) sees the negative setting as "congregational strife (as in a close-knit community . . .), leading to unruly behavior, disorderly worship, and a challenge to recognized authority, as at Corinth (1 Cor 14:33; 2 Cor 12:20; *1 Clement* 3:1-4; 14:1—texts that have several words or their equivalents in common with our passage—*zēlos* [TG2205, ZG2419], *eris* [TG2054, ZG2251], *akatastasia* [TG181, ZG189], *phronimos* [TG5429, ZG5861])."

In this section (3:13-18) there is an easily discernible three-part outline: (1) a thesis sentence calling for the kind of wisdom that shows itself in conduct (3:13), followed by (2) a vice list that is anchored in discord and self-centeredness (3:14-16), and then (3) a virtue list that is anchored in peace-seeking and selfless giving (3:17-18). Interestingly, in the latter two sections there is also a threefold contrast: (1) the origin—wisdom that is "not from above" (NLT, "not God's kind of wisdom") versus the "wisdom from above"; (2) the process—vices that center on strife versus virtues that center on peace; (3) the results—that which is "unspiritual, and demonic" versus that which "reap[s] a harvest of righteousness."

Once more James begins with a rhetorical question ("Who among you is . . . ?"; cf. 2:1, 14), equivalent to a conditional, "If you are" (as in the NLT). This challenges all the people (especially the leaders) to look seriously at their attitudes and actions, to see if they are "wise and understand God's ways." The point here is that knowledge is not enough; it must be coupled with wisdom. The term *epistēmōn* [TG1990, ZG2184] (understanding) speaks of a skilled person with technical knowledge, that is, with both theory and practice combined. "Wise" as in 1:5 connotes the proper use of knowledge for the higher goal (serving God), that is, the acquisition of insight into personal holiness and life (a basic term for Christian ethics). The two (wisdom and understanding) are found together in Deuteronomy 1:13, 15; 4:6 (cf. Isa 5:21), but are not combined in the New Testament apart from here. To be wise you have to know what is right and then do it. Hartin (1997) brings out the centrality of a God-given wisdom here ("the wisdom from above" in 3:17) and emphasizes the eschatological dimension of wisdom; the contrast is between a human-oriented "understanding" and a divinely illuminated "wisdom."

The emphasis in the second half of 3:13 is on the practical "proof" of God-given wisdom (*deiknumi* [TG1166, ZG1259], "demonstrate, show"; cf. 2:18) —"living an honorable life" and "doing good works with the humility that comes from wisdom."

The "honorable life" is "good conduct," with *kalos* [TG2570, ZG2819] connoting "a positive moral quality, with the implication of being favorably valued—'good, fine, praiseworthy'" (L&N 743). This parallels the emphasis in 1 Peter on living lives of goodness so as to disprove the slander of the non-Christians (1 Pet 2:12, 15, 19; 3:1-2, 10b-11, 16—see the commentary in this volume). It is in lives of moral excellence that the Christian's true worth is shown, and this is true in every practical ethical area of James—prejudice, faith that produces works, and the use of speech to build people up rather than tear them down.

The sphere within which this life of goodness is shown is the humility that comes from wisdom (NLT rightly sees the genitive "of wisdom" as one of source, "comes from wisdom"). The word for "humility" is *praütēs* [TG4240, ZG4559], which combines the idea of humility with that of a "meek, mild" temperament. The term was used in 1:21, where we were challenged to "humbly accept" the implanted word, an attitude that meekly accepts what God plants in the heart. Here the meekness is a gentle, open spirit toward others. To the Greco-Romans, this was one of the least desired qualities (see on 1:21; Laws 1980:160, says it was "linked with adjectives like ignoble, abject, servile, slavish, downcast, and low"), but Christ made a meek, humble attitude one of the most important Christian virtues. Jesus blessed the meek (Matt 5:5) and said, "I am humble and gentle at heart" (Matt 11:29). Johnson (1995:270) says this term "is not accidental; the entire passage takes up the contrast between the qualities of mildness associated with God's wisdom, and the harshness of a worldly wisdom based on envy."

The direct opposite (3:14) to a life of humble works is a "bitterly jealous" spirit (Hiebert, Ropes—"harsh zeal") and "selfish ambition." This begins with a condition of fact (*ei* [TG1487, ZG1623], "if") that assumes the reality of the problem; many leaders and their followers really were characterized by envy and an ambition that was splitting the church. In 3:14 the word for "jealousy" is *zēlos* [TG2205, ZG2419], which can be used positively for "zeal" or "eagerness" (e.g., for spiritual gifts, 1 Cor 12:31; for the law, Acts 21:20; or for God, Rom 10:2). As "jealousy" it can refer to God's jealousy (Exod 20:5, see below on 4:5) or negatively to people's envy and jealousy toward one another. When God is jealous, he is concerned for the holiness of his name, but when people are jealous they care only for what they desire from others. "Envy" is wanting what belongs to someone else without regard for their rights. James draws out the contentious side of this by adding *pikros* [TG4089, ZG4395] (bitter), a deep-seated anger when you don't get your way. Putting this together, it speaks of church dissension that is caused by leaders who care only for themselves and fight bitterly when they don't get their way. The contention that results is the poisonous tongue of 3:8, destroying the unity of the community.

In 3:14 another negative term (*eritheia* [TG2052, ZG2249], "selfish ambition") is joined with jealousy and refers to a party spirit (Aristotle uses it of politics in *Politics* 1303a14); selfish leaders so want to control the "party" or group that they are willing to split it into factions. The term is also used in 2 Corinthians 12:20 of the sins of the Corinthians; in Philippians 2:3 of those who caused dissension in Philippi; and in both Galatians 5:20 and Romans 2:8 of those who will face the fierce wrath of God. People who want power and authority gather those around them of like mind and sow discord in the fellowship of believers over their own self-centered ideas. They will face judgment from God. These sinful feelings take place "in your heart," with the plural "your" and singular "heart" likely referring to "a rotten core of key individuals in the church" (Blomberg and Kamell 2008:172) who have brought "bitter jealousy" and a contentious spirit into the church, resulting in factions or "parties." This has also led to the misuse of the tongue to go to war against rival factions (4:1-3) and destroy the cohesiveness of the church. The contrasts between 3:13 and 3:14 are many—humility versus envy, peace versus schism, and wisdom versus selfish ambition.

The basis of the envy and contention caused by these sinners in the church is the tendency to "boast" about themselves, so James commands that they stop such prideful misuses of the tongue (Gr., *mē katakauchasthe* [TG2620, ZG2878], present prohibition). The verb means to "exult against" or "boast at the expense of another" and thereby to "brag" about one's triumphs (cf. 2:13; BDAG 517), in this case their false claim to wisdom (3:13) and the jealousy that led to the discord sown by these pride-filled leaders. In Jeremiah 9:23-24 we are told, "Don't let the wise boast in their wisdom, or the powerful boast in their power. . . . But those who wish to boast should boast in this alone: that they truly know me and understand that I am the LORD."

For James this boasting constitutes "lying" and "cover[ing] up the truth" (lit., "lying against the truth"). These people stated that their claims stemmed from so-called wisdom and boasted that their teachings constituted God's truth, yet the arrogance and self-centered nature of everything they did proved it was all a lie. The actual truth was that there was no wisdom or God-given understanding behind anything they said, only ambition for power. This is a major problem in the church today, for the wealth and power of ministry have never been more easily attained for someone with charisma and a glib ability to communicate. The possibility of Christian leaders owning their own Lear jet and being worshiped by millions has never been so high, and this has led to an amazing number of charlatans who minister in the name of Christ but are actually controlled by "selfish ambition." There is no "truth," only a quest for prestige and glory.

James next (3:15) defines the true source of such attitudes and actions. Such is "not God's kind of wisdom" (lit., "not from above," meaning not a God-sent wisdom). In 1:17-18 God's "good and perfect" gifts come down to us, that is, from heaven, and here and in 3:17 the good gift of wisdom also is "from above." One of the greatest of these gifts is the kind of wisdom that allows us to endure trials and find spiritual wholeness (1:4-5). Such true wisdom centers on Christ, "the power of God and the wisdom of God" (1 Cor 1:24, 30), not on human eloquence or the half-baked ideas of this world.

This kind of false wisdom has nothing to do with God's truths. These people have a type of "wisdom," but it is like that of the Corinthians, who actually possessed a "wisdom of this world" (1 Cor 1:20) or a "human [or fleshly] wisdom" (1 Cor 1:22; 2 Cor 1:12) that God would prove to be "foolish" (1 Cor 1:20; 3:19) and would "destroy" (1 Cor 1:19). There are few words that have been so misused as "wisdom." Not all that purports to be wisdom is actually wise in any sense. Only that which stems from God and his revealed truth can ever truly be called "wisdom" and endure. Moo (2000:172) says well that "one can only speak of the self-oriented learning of these people who claim to be 'wise' as a phantom wisdom—a false representation of the real thing."

Instead, the so-called wisdom of these dissenters is "earthly, unspiritual, and demonic" (3:15b). The three adjectives form a descending spiral from bad to worse—"appertaining to the earth, not to the world above; to mere nature, not to the Spirit; and to the hostile spirits of evil, instead of to God" (Ropes 1916:248). The first (*epigeios* [TG1919, ZG2103]) can simply refer to something that belongs to this "earthly" sphere (1 Cor 15:40; Phil 2:10), but here it denotes that which is the antithesis of heaven or the realm of God, that which is opposed to the things of God. The second (*psuchikos* [TG5591, ZG6035]) is the opposite of "spiritual" (*pneumatikos* [TG4152, ZG4461]), "always denoting the life of the natural world and whatever belongs to it, in contrast to the supernatural world" (BDAG 1100; cf. 1 Cor 2:14; 15:44, 46; Jude 19), thus "unspiritual" (also NRSV, TNIV, TEV). In fact, the true origin of their wisdom lies in the satanic realm; it is "demonic" (*daimoniōdēs* [TG1141, ZG1229]) at the core. As in 3:6, it is "set on fire by hell itself." There is ample precedent for this, but elsewhere it describes false teachers. In 2 Corinthians 11:13-15 they, like Satan, "disguise themselves as servants of righteousness"; in 1 Timothy 4:1 they "follow deceptive spirits and teachings that come from demons"; in 2 Peter 2:10 and Jude 8 they even "scoff at supernatural beings." This is an extremely strong charge and shows that these arrogant, divisive people are playing a game that is incredibly dangerous; their counterfeit wisdom will bring God's wrath down upon them. As in 4:7 they must "resist the devil" and have nothing to do with his hellish ideas as exemplified in their unwise utterances.

James concludes the negative side (3:16) by repeating from 3:15 the spiritual problem these people have: They are controlled by "jealousy and selfish ambition." Their self-centered, power-hungry aspirations have made them envious of whatever others possess (especially power and authority) and brought backbiting and chaos to the church. All they have brought to God's people is "disorder," a term used in 1:8 (the "instability" of the double-minded person) and 3:8 (the tongue as "restless and evil"). The uncontrolled lust for power on the part of these self-appointed leaders/teachers has brought an anarchic instability, indeed "war" into the church (4:1; cf. Luke 21:9, where "wars and insurrections—same term as here: *akatastasia* [TG181, ZG189])—characterize the last days). This was as in the time of the judges, where everyone "did whatever seemed right in their own eyes" (Judg 17:6; 21:25; cf. Judg 18:1; 19:1), producing a tumultuous disorder that could not come from God (he is "not a God of disorder but of peace," 1 Cor 14:33).

The practices of these false leaders are then described as "evil of every kind" (lit., "every worthless deed"), referring to immoral actions that have taken place as light gave way to darkness. This is especially true of the sins of the tongue and the dissension this has wrought in the community of believers. The wording may reflect lawsuits, believers taking one another to court and shaming each other publicly (so Blomberg and Kamell, Johnson). In 2:6, the wealthy drag Christians into court (cf. 1 Cor 6:1-8 where Paul prohibits Christians from taking other believers to court).

While this may be part of the reference here, the "evil of every kind" is broader and refers to incendiary speech of every type that does irreparable harm to the community. Today, as well, a false wisdom on the part of church leaders allows them to rationalize their evil motives and thereby to practice all kinds of sin with impunity.

From what true wisdom is not (3:14-16), James turns to a discussion of what true wisdom "from above" actually is (3:17-18). Adamson (1976:154) calls 3:17 "this great Hymn of Wisdom," and all scholars recognize the literary artistry of this masterpiece, with the key designation of wisdom as "pure" followed by four adjectives beginning with *e* (the first three ending with an *ē*-sound) and then three beginning with *a* (the last two ending with *-kritos*). The text is also quite similar to Galatians 5:22-23 on the "fruit of the Spirit." James, like Paul, develops the attributes of the God-centered person. When divine wisdom controls the church and its members, these qualities demonstrate its presence and specify its results.

The preeminent ("first of all") characteristic is "pure," and the others develop aspects of it. The word (*hagnē* [TG53, ZG54]) refers to "innocence" but here especially "moral blamelessness," that which allows a person to be "unstained" and to have a "clear conscience." Such a person is "free of the moral and spiritual defects that are the marks of the double minded (1:7, 8; 4:8)" and that produce "the inevitable jealousy and strife that are characteristic of some in James's church" (Martin 1988:133-134; cf. 1:27; 4:8; 2 Cor 11:2; 1 Pet 3:2). This purity is the antithesis and the answer to the "disorder and evil" (3:16) of these self-centered, self-styled "wise" ones who are causing all the dissension.

The next three characteristics are introduced by *epeita* [TG1899, ZG2083] ("then"; NLT, "it is also") and define the "humility" or "meekness" commanded in 3:13 (Johnson 1995:274; Ropes 1916:250). The second term ("peace loving") is equally as important as purity, since it becomes the theme of 3:18. It is the exact opposite of the jealous, combative ambition that leads to the "quarrels and fights" of 4:1. Jesus said, "God blesses those who work for peace" (Matt 5:9), and the concept occurs frequently in Scripture (3:18; Ps 34:14; Isa 52:7; Rom 12:18; 14:19; Heb 12:14), connoting both peace with God and peace between people, with the latter flowing out of the former. "Gentle" is combined with a peaceful refusal to quarrel in 1 Timothy 3:3 and Titus 3:2; and in Philippians 4:5 it describes a "forbearing spirit" (Weymouth NT) that connotes an empathetic, considerate, gracious acceptance of others as they are. It involves a willingness to forgive and an attitude of magnanimity toward others.

Third, the pure heart is "willing to yield to others," in total contrast to the self-centered unwillingness to yield on the part of the ambitious leaders. Moo (2000:176) says this does not imply "a weak, credulous gullibility, but a willing deference to others when unalterable theological or moral principles are not involved." This was the command of Paul in Romans 14:1–15:13 regarding the dispute over eating Gentile foods. He told both sides to respect one another and defer to the religious sensitivities of each other. With Christians fighting over so many theological and practical issues, this should be the practice today. In the areas of both noncardinal doctrines (see Rom 14:3, 5, 9) and practical life issues (see Rom 14:13-14), "Christians must learn to accept each other and to forge a larger unity that recognizes and allows such differences" (Osborne 2004:385).

Next, the wisdom from above is "full of mercy and good deeds," the opposite of the "evil [practices] of every kind" resulting from the counterfeit wisdom. The use of "full of" provides a contrast with the description of the tongue as "full of deadly poison" in 3:8. "Mercy" is used in 2:13 to conclude the section on loving your neighbor without favoritism, stating, "There will be no mercy for those who have not shown mercy." So "mercy" refers to acts of love and compassion that reflect the mercy we have experienced from God. This in a sense refers to the gift of helps, the desire to show kindness concretely by aiding others. Mercy must be known by its "good fruits" (NLT, "good deeds"), looking forward to the "fruit of righteousness" that begins 3:18 (in the Greek) and to "the agricultural imagery of 5:17-18" (Johnson 1995:274). Merciful deeds are the natural "fruit" of a godly person.

The last two characteristics are that godly wisdom "shows no favoritism and is always sincere." *Adiakritos* [TG87, ZG88] is verbally related to "divided loyalty" and "discrimination" in 1:6 and 2:4. In 1:6 the emphasis is on a wavering mind divided between God and this world, and in 2:4 it is used with regard to discrimination against the poor. Both aspects are part of the meaning here. Instead of a "selfish ambition" that divides the church (3:14-16), true wisdom is characterized by a single-minded focus on accepting others without "favoritism." Then *anupokritos* [TG505, ZG537] means simply "without hypocrisy" (note that both terms begin with the *a*-privative that negates the quality—"without favoritism, without pretense"). There are two aspects of this term here: It connotes a person who is "genuine" or "trustworthy" and one who refuses to pretend to be something they are not. In Matthew 6:2, 5, 16 the "hypocrites" are those who give to the poor, pray, and fast just in order to be seen by others. They are pretending to be pious. In 1 Timothy 4:2 the false teachers are "hypocrites and liars," pretending to teach God's truths. So the "sincere" person refuses to "play act" and stands for what is right and true.

In the final part of this section, James turns from the description of godly wisdom to what it produces, describing the result of wisdom as "a harvest of righteousness" (first in the sentence for emphasis). Wisdom produces in its adherents a harvest of righteous behavior (as in 1:20, "righteousness" here refers to right conduct before God). The thrust of that behavior has already been defined in 3:17—"full of mercy and good deeds." The Sermon on the Mount especially develops this idea of "righteousness," beginning with Jesus' promise of divine blessings on those who "hunger and thirst for righteousness" (Matt 5:6, NLT mg; cf. Matt 5:10, 20; 6:1, 33). Clearly right conduct must be a defining characteristic of all those who wish to live godly lives.

In 3:18 the primary result of right behavior must be "plant[ing] seeds of peace" (the second quality of wisdom in 3:17) rather than discord in the community. Those who love God must be "peace loving" (3:17) and bring peace out of conflict. In the context of strife, conflict, and slander that governs 3:1–4:12, this provides "a suitable conclusion underlying the main point" (Davids 1982:155). The fact that it is found twice ("peacemakers will plant seeds of peace") shows how critical the point is, and the use of farming imagery (planting and harvest) makes it all the more emphatic. "*Peace* is the soil and *those who make peace* are the green-fingered gardeners" (Motyer 1985:138). The person who is controlled by divine wisdom will make sure that peace guides the community from start to finish. In the midst of the conflicts in the Roman church, Paul commanded, "make every effort to do what leads to peace" (Rom 14:19, TNIV), and Hebrews 12:14 says, "Work at living in peace with everyone." God has brought spiritual peace into our hearts through the atoning sacrifice of Jesus Christ, and we must in turn translate that into peace in the church and in our relationships with everyone around us.

◆ C. Warning against Worldliness (4:1-12)

1. A friend of the world is an enemy of God (4:1-6)

What is causing the quarrels and fights among you? Don't they come from the evil desires at war within you? [2]You want what you don't have, so you scheme and kill to get it. You are jealous of what others have, but you can't get it, so you fight and wage war to take it away from them. Yet you don't have what you want because you don't ask God for it. [3]And even when you ask, you don't get it because your motives are all wrong—you want only what will give you pleasure.

[4]You adulterers!* Don't you realize that friendship with the world makes you an enemy of God? I say it again: If you want to be a friend of the world, you make yourself an enemy of God. [5]What do you think the Scriptures mean when they say that the spirit God has placed within us is filled with envy?* [6]But he gives us even more grace to stand against such evil desires. As the Scriptures say,

"God opposes the proud
but favors the humble."*

4:4 Greek *You adulteresses!* 4:5 Or *that God longs jealously for the human spirit he has placed within us?* or *that the Holy Spirit, whom God has placed within us, opposes our envy?* 4:6 Prov 3:34 (Greek version).

NOTES

4:1 ***What is causing the quarrels and fights among you?*** Johnson (1995:276) argues that this strong language is neither literal nor metaphorical but simply part of a "Hellenistic topos on envy"; as such, he affirms that it is simply part of the rhetorical argument rather than based on any actual situation. Yet this language is very much in keeping with the situation described in 3:1-12, 14-16, that is, the atmosphere of conflict and infighting in the church. The language makes a great deal of sense as describing the serious discord in the community.

4:2 There is an exegetical problem regarding the punctuation of this verse, which affects the meaning. Some translators and commentators (KJV, NIV, Davids, Dibelius, Martin, McCartney) place stops after the negative clauses, arriving at a three-part structure:

> You want something but don't get it.
>
> You kill and covet, but you cannot have what you want.
>
> You quarrel and fight.

Others (NASB, NRSV, REB, TNIV, ESV, NLT, Blomberg and Kamell, Hort, Johnson, Kistemaker, Laws, Mayor, Moo, Ropes) see a two-part structure, with the evil desire highlighted and then the evil action that results:

> You want what you don't have, so you scheme and kill to get it.
>
> You are jealous of what others have, but you can't get it, so you fight and wage war to take it away from them.

The second reading makes a great deal more sense, for having "kill" before "covet" is difficult to comprehend, and the two-part structure has much better parallelism. The first reading centers on the ever-growing "violence as a way of securing religious freedom" (Martin 1988:146), which accords with Martin's view of Zealot influence behind the discord, but I find this scenario doubtful. Either way, the idea of an escalating conflict would be central in the first reading. The second reading fits better the selfish ambition and envy described in 3:14-16, which is said to be coming from their evil desires (4:1). They were willing to do anything to get what they didn't have.

kill. Some scholars (Adamson, from Erasmus; Dibelius; Mayor) think a textual error has occurred; they emend the text from *phoneuete* [TG5407, ZG5839] (to kill) to *phthoneite* [TG5354, ZG5783] (to envy), thereby connecting it even more closely to the envy and jealousy of 3:14-16. The problem with this emendation is that there is no textual evidence for it. Here a metaphorical sense for "kill" fits well with the same sense for "quarrels and fights" in 4:1.

4:4 ***You adulterers!*** Gr., *moichalides* [TG3428A, ZG3655] ("you adulteresses," so NLT mg); it is taken from the Old Testament portrait of unfaithful Israel as an adulterous wife (Ps 73:27, NKJV; Isa 50:1; Jer 13:27; Hos 9:1). This reading has good manuscript support (𝔓100 ℵ A B 33 1739). Some later manuscripts have "adulterers and adulteresses" (ℵ^c P Ψ 𝔐), undoubtedly due to discomfort with the simple feminine form (see Comfort 2008:729; Metzger 1994:682-683). For an article arguing for the longer reading, see Freedman (1999).

4:5 ***the spirit God has placed within us is filled with envy.*** This has rightly been called one of the most difficult exegetical passages in the New Testament. The problem is that the Greek can be translated three ways (all viable readings), and each gives a very different message:

1. The spirit God has caused to live in us is filled with envy (NIV, REB, NLT, Adamson, Johnson, Kistemaker, Laws, Motyer).
2. God longs jealously for the spirit he has caused to live in us (NRSV, TNIV, ESV, NLT mg, Blomberg and Kamell, Davids, Dibelius, Hort, Mayor, Moo, Ropes, McCartney).
3. The Spirit God has caused to live in us opposes our envy (NLT mg, Bauckham 2004, Martin).

Each can make sense, so we must look at the context in James to choose the best option. First, James elsewhere does not discuss the Holy Spirit, and so the third option is unlikely here. The context also does not hint at the Spirit being the subject of the action. Of the first two options, the first definitely fits the context well, and *phthonos* [TG5355, ZG5784] normally has a negative connotation for human envy or jealousy (Rom 1:29; Gal 5:21; Phil 1:15; 1 Tim 6:4; 1 Pet 2:1). However, as Moo (2000:189-190) points out, the word is used of the jealousy of the Olympian gods, and this fits the biblical emphasis on God's jealousy for his people. Moreover, the surrounding context (4:4, 6-8) centers on our relationship with God, so God is the most natural subject for the sentence. Therefore, with the grammar making the idea of divine jealousy over his people slightly better, it is best to take the second view as the more likely. It is interesting that the TNIV (followed by NIV 2011) switched to this view over the NIV 1984 reading (implying that the committee has changed its mind).

COMMENTARY

As stated at the beginning of chapter 3, there is an A-B-A pattern in 3:1–4:12, with the sins of the tongue (3:1-12; 4:1-12) framing the solution, which is the presence of divine wisdom in the church (3:13-18). Several scholars (Adamson, Hiebert, Laws, Martin) think chapter 4 begins a new, separate unit centered on the worldliness exhibited by these factious people and its solution in submission to God. However, the themes of 4:1-5 flow directly out of 3:13-18 and reflect the same problems addressed in 3:1-12, namely, conflict in the church as a result of the backbiting and slander of some members. In 4:1-12 there is another A-B-A three-part outline; it begins with the statement that the battles in the church are the result of "friendship with the world" (4:1-6) and then moves to the solution, namely, submission to God (4:7-10), and it concludes by returning to the theme of conflict, condemning the slander and atmosphere of judgmentalism in the church (4:11-12).

As in 2:1, 14, and 3:13, James begins with a rhetorical question regarding the causes behind the "quarrels and fights" in the community. This is the absolute antithesis to the peace-seeking spirit of the godly described in the previous two verses (3:17-18). The language combined with "kill" in 4:2 has led some to posit literal battles that led to murder. Martin (1988:144; cf. Reicke 1964:46; Townsend 1976) thinks the situation behind the letter is partly "a Zealot-infested society" (based on the view that the epistle reflects a situation in the 60s); he believes former Zealots in the church may have allowed the arguments to get out of hand, taking the lives of some opponents. However, the argumentative spirit and serious infighting described in 3:5b-12, 14-16 are naturally displayed in the hyperbolic language of 4:1-2, with the "war" and "killing" verbal rather than actual. Moo (2000:180) argues that *machai* [TG3163, ZG3480] (fights) in much of the Septuagint and always in the New Testament (2 Cor 7:5; 2 Tim 2:23; Titus 3:9) refers to verbal quarrels. The language then can refer to "verbal disputes as well as armed conflicts" and in this context is more likely metaphorical for the internal strife that was splitting the community.

Repeating the stress on their "selfish ambition" in 3:14, 16, James states that the true source for this contentious spirit is "the evil desires at war within you." The word for "desires" is *hēdonē* [TG2237, ZG2454], from which is derived "hedonism." The basic meaning of the term is "pleasure," but in a context like this it connotes a "desire for pleasure." Some see a sexual connotation, and that is indeed possible, but there is no hint of sexual perversion in the letter. It is likely a strong term for the sinful "desires" for dominance and power that led to the discord as well as for the "pleasures" that leaders enjoy. A parallel to this use is found in 4 Maccabees 1:25-26 (RSV): "in pleasure [*hēdonē*] there exists even a malevolent tendency, which is the most complex of all the emotions. In the soul it is boastfulness, covetousness, thirst for honor, rivalry, and malice." This passion for pleasure is "at war within you," literally, "among your members," which could refer to the individual (the members of your body) or the community (the members of the church). It is possible that both are intended. The military metaphors ("quarrels and fights," "at war") provide strong images of the seriousness of the conflict that threatened to destroy the cohesion and spiritual atmosphere of the churches.

In 4:2 the pattern taken by these "evil desires" is traced. In two consecutive sentences (see note on 4:2), the wicked path that their self-centered desires takes is traced, along with their frustrated coveting for what they cannot have. First, they "want what [they] don't have" (the very definition of envy), probably to be in control of the community among other things. "Want" translates another verb for "desire" (*epithumeite* [TG1937, ZG2121]), undoubtedly with the same meaning as in

4:1, "evil desires" to get what you want. The chosen path for achieving that desired object is to "scheme and kill," with "kill" used metaphorically to describe the character assassination they used to gain the upper hand. In Matthew 5:21-26 Jesus states that anger is murder in the mind, and that sense is likely behind this as well. These leaders have brought jealousy, anger, and backbiting into the church, and it is threatening to destroy the work of God among the members.

The second sentence restates the first and adds the idea of "envy" or "jealousy" (cf. 3:14, 16) to that of selfish desires in the first sentence. Also, it moves from "don't have" to "can't get it," adding the idea of frustrated envy. They are not getting what they selfishly desire, and in spite of their machinations they cannot achieve the object of their jealous envy (perhaps it is implied that God will not let them reach their goals). Though it is obscured somewhat in NLT, it is generally recognized (Blomberg and Kamell, Davids, Moo) that there is a chiasm in 4:1-2. A more literal rendering of these verses reveals the following structure: A (quarrels and fights), B (from evil desires), B′ (frustrated envy), A′ (fight and quarrel)—note the reversal of "quarrels and fights" in the second pair, adding to the inclusio. Their frustration makes them fight all the more. Instead of leading to repentance, it makes them even more jealous and contentious. This is a picture of the natural man—when they can't get what they want, they try to take it any way they can. The end justifies the means! Moo (2000:184) says these people want "the kind of wisdom that will enable them to gain recognition as leaders in the community. James has rebuked his leaders for wanting to become teachers (3:1) and for priding themselves on being 'wise and understanding.'" Their arrogant pride and their unwillingness to submit to God led to these problems.

These teachers clearly lacked the wisdom to achieve their desired goals, but unlike 1:5 ("If you need wisdom, ask our generous God"), their pride has made them unwilling to turn to God: "You don't have what you want because you don't ask God for it." Prayers without answers are the focus of 4:2b-3 in a kind of step parallelism—they rarely pray, and even when they do, their prayers are negated by evil desires. The first challenge (4:2b) centers on their self-sufficiency—they fail to go to God with their problems but instead rely on themselves. Jesus said clearly, "Keep on asking, and you will receive what you ask for" (Luke 11:9), but these people are too busy trying to achieve their desires in their own strength to realize their need to center on God. Baker and Carrier (1990:87) say, "The problem exposed here is a total collapse of healthy spiritual dependence on God. Some of us are so preoccupied with pleasures that we have forgotten about God." This is a problem we all have. As we get so busy with life, we more and more turn to ourselves and leave God out of these daily situations. Then when crises arrive, we waste so much time worrying about what we are going to do, and only much later, if at all, do we think of seeking God's wisdom and guidance!

Yet even on those rare times when the leaders do pray (4:3), their selfish desires for pleasure (4:1) dominate their requests. To their failure to pray, James then adds that they have sinful motives prompting their occasional prayers: Those motives "are all wrong—you want only what will give you pleasure." They are asking "wrongly" (*kakōs* [TG2560, ZG2809], "sinfully, with evil intentions") because their basic purpose is "pleasure" (*hēdonē* [TG2237, ZG2454], as in 4:1). The verb is *dapanaō* [TG1159, ZG1251], indicating their desire to freely spend the things that God gives on their own hedonistic desires, to "indulge" themselves in pleasure. Johnson (1995:278) says, "The gift-giving God is here manipulated as a kind of vending machine precisely for purposes of self-gratification (1:26, *apatōn kardian* [TG538/2588, ZG572/2840]). In this case, prayer is a form of idolatry and, as we shall see, expressive of 'friendship with the world.'" Blomberg and Kamell (2008:189) apply this well: "How dramatically this contrasts with the so-called 'health and wealth' gospel!" This "gospel of prosperity" is actually a "gospel of hedonism," as materialism is perversely made spiritual.

As a sort of conclusion (4:4), James castigates them, "You adulterers!" Actually, the Greek has "adulteresses," alluding to the Old Testament view of Israel as "the bride of Yahweh" (Isa 54:5-6; 61:10; 62:1-5; cf. the New Testament picture of the church as the bride of Christ, Eph 5:25-27; Rev 19:7-8; 21:2, 9). Thus, when the nation committed idolatry, it was committing adultery against Yahweh (Isa 57:3, 7-8; Jer 3:6, 20; Ezek 16:35-38). This is especially powerfully portrayed in Hosea, who was told by God to marry a prostitute; this was a symbol of Israel prostituting herself with other gods (see Ortlund 2003). Many of the readers were "adulteresses" because in their lust for pleasure and power, they made the world's standards their idol.

These arrogant pleasure-seekers courted "friendship with the world" (in contrast to Abraham, who was called "the friend of God" in 2:23), which constitutes spiritual adultery. Throughout James this worldly life is portrayed as prejudice for the wealthy against the poor (2:1-13), a refusal to help the needy and live out one's faith (2:14-26), a desire for the status of teachers (3:1), abuse of God's gift of speech to slander others (3:2-12), selfish ambition and envy (3:14, 16), introduction of conflict into the church for selfish reasons (4:1-2), a love for pleasure of all kinds (4:1, 3), backbiting (4:11-12), exclusion of God from business relationships (4:13-17), and pursuit of wealth (4:13; 5:1). In Hellenism the idea of "friend" meant a very serious relationship, connoting political and social allegiance, harmony of outlook ("to identify with its standards and priorities," Blomberg and Kamell 2008:190), and a "'sharing all things' in a unity both spiritual and physical" (Johnson 1995:279). The "world" is that entity and mind-set totally opposed to God and his moral requirements.

Thus, to be a "friend of the world" by its very nature means to be "an enemy of God." Note that James states this twice for emphasis (4:4; cf. 1 John 2:15). When we love the world, we commit spiritual adultery and become God's enemies, and his enemies are under his wrath and headed for divine judgment. In the Old Testament such enemies were subject to holy war. To turn to the world is to turn against God and to be subject to his covenant curses. Baker and Carrier (1990:88) apply this: "Perhaps some of us are in its clutches right now. . . . We have become contentious with people we used to consider friends. We have stopped praying except for things we want. Hear what James is saying! If this describes you, you are about to lose your closest friend."

God, as a husband, reacts jealously when his people, as his bride, live according to the world's standards. In the note on 4:5, I state why I prefer the NLT alternate reading, "God longs jealously for the human spirit he has placed within us." James supports this thrust by asking, "What do you think the Scriptures mean?" The problem is that there is no Scripture passage that matches any of the three options for the quote. So some say it means "scripture" with a small "s" or that the reference is back to 4:4 rather than to 4:5b. But the most natural sense is that the quote occurs in the second half of the verse, and that it is a sort of collage of passages on God being jealous for his people. Exodus 20:5 is part of the Ten Commandments and says, "You must not bow down to them or worship them [idols], for I, the LORD your God, am a jealous God." Several other passages also depict the jealous God yearning for his people (Exod 34:14; Deut 4:24; Josh 24:19-20; Nah 1:2; Zech 8:2). "The human spirit he has placed within us" refers to humanity created in the image of God and thus bearing the "spirit" or divinely given life force he has placed in us.

God and Christ love their people as a bride and therefore are "jealous" when they go astray after other gods or (here) after the world. This divine jealousy on the part of God, the metaphorical husband, connotes two things: First, when his bride strays after the world, it results in the anger expressed in 4:4, as divine wrath falls upon those who have become his "enemies." Second, God as a good husband seeks repentance from his people and wants to forgive them, so "he gives us even more grace" (4:6—Blomberg and Kamell 2008:192, following Carpenter 2001, takes 4:6a as part of the "Scripture" quote noted in 4:5a). If 4:5 centers on the human propensity toward envy, the "greater grace" would refer to God's gift of strength to overcome human envy (taking *de* [TG1161, ZG1254] as a full adversative, "but instead"). If, as I believe, it refers to God jealously watching over us, the "greater grace" would connote the good gifts of God (1:17) that enable us to live up to his requirements (mild adversative *de*, "but"). On the surface, 4:4 and 4:5 could bring despair, for the sins of God's people seem too much, and his wrath appears to be inevitable. But we can overcome sin, find forgiveness, and get right with God because his grace and mercy are "able, through his mighty power at work within us, to accomplish infinitely more than we might ask or think" (Eph 3:20). "God is tirelessly on our side. He never falters in respect of our needs; he always has more 'grace' at hand for us. He is never less than sufficient; he always has more and yet more to give" (Motyer 1985:150).

God gives us his grace overabundantly, but he also "demands response: the response of our humility" (Moo 2000:191). In making this point, James turns to Proverbs 3:34: "The LORD opposes the proud but favors the humble" (NLT mg; also quoted in 1 Pet 5:5). It is God's "grace" that ties 4:5b with 4:5a; the abundant "grace" of God is made available to the humble rather than to self-centered (3:14, 16), arrogant people. In this context, "humility" means a total dependence on God rather than on self or the world, seeking Christ rather than status or power or pleasure. This introduces the theme of 4:7-10, submitting to God and giving loyalty to him rather than to the world. The "proud" will find only "opposition" from God as he takes his stand against them. Johnson (1995:283) shows how frequently pride is connected to envy in Hellenistic writings; so James may well have been condemning further the misguided leaders of 3:5-12, 14-16; 4:1-3. The condemnation of the proud is also a frequent emphasis in the Old Testament (Pss 18:27; 34:18; Prov 6:17; 16:5, 18; Zeph 3:11-12).

◆ 2. The solution—submit to God (4:7-10)

**[7]So humble yourselves before God. Resist
the devil, and he will flee from you.
[8]Come close to God, and God will come
close to you. Wash your hands, you sin-
ners; purify your hearts, for your loyalty
is divided between God and the world.
[9]Let there be tears for what you have
done. Let there be sorrow and deep grief.
Let there be sadness instead of laughter,
and gloom instead of joy. [10]Humble your-
selves before the Lord, and he will lift
you up in honor.**

NOTES

4:7 *humble.* There is a wordplay between God "opposing" (*antitassomai* [TG498, ZG530], to "stand against") the proud (4:6) and the humble "submitting to" (*hupotassomai* [TG5293A, ZG5718], to "stand under") God (4:7). These are the two sides of our relationship to God. We either "stand under" his authority, or we will face God "standing against" us.

COMMENTARY

This section consists of a set of imperatives that expand the meaning of humility from 4:6, paralleled in large part by 1 Peter 5:5b-9 and possibly reflecting an early Christian catechetical tradition (cf. Davids, Dibelius, Moo). There are three parts: (1) The first (4:7-8a) has an A-B-A pattern, with A = 4:7a, 8a (submission to God) and B = 4:7b (resistance against the devil). The main thrust is that one can only find victory over Satan by relying entirely on God. (2) The second develops the meaning of repentance as the path that submission must follow (4:8b-9), a deep remorse and sorrow for sin. (3) The third (4:10) repeats the central point—submission to God is the only means by which a Christian can find exaltation.

This section provides the antidote for "friendship with the world" and the path by which one can be a "friend" rather than an "enemy of God" (4:4). Since (*oun* [TG3767, ZG4036], "therefore, so") God "favors the humble" (4:6), the only valid response is to "humble yourselves before God." Instead of the arrogance or pride that God resists, they should stand bowed before God in humility. Too many of James's readers aspired to be "teachers" or leaders (3:1); because of their "selfish ambition" (3:14, 16), they embroiled the church in their petty conflicts (4:1-2).

As Kistemaker (1986:139) puts it, submission "describes a voluntary act of placing yourself under the authority of someone else to show him respect and obedience." Two aspects of the Lord's Prayer apply (Matt 6:9-10)—"May your name be kept holy," an absolute concern that the sacredness of the name of God be magnified in our life; and "May your will be done," an acquiescence to God's will in everything we say and do. This becomes the basis of an entire set of hierarchical relationships at the heart of Christian ethics. Wives submit to their husbands "as to the Lord" (Eph 5:22), which does not mean "in the same way" they submit to God, but rather "as part of" their submission to God. To refuse to respect their husband's headship is to refuse to submit to God and his will. In the same way, children must submit to parents, slaves to their masters, and citizens to their government (Eph 5:21–6:9; Col 3:18-25; 1 Pet 2:13–3:7). However, this is not a one-way street. In the same way that God and Christ exercise their headship in love (sacrificial love in Eph 5:25-27, the model husbands must follow), so those who have leadership must at all times use it to build up those over whom God has placed them.

Two further actions define what it means to submit to God—"Resist the devil" and "Come close to God" (4:7b, 8a). If we belong to God, we will at all times place ourselves under and obey his stipulations. Also, if we belong to God, we are at the core of our being the absolute antithesis of everything that the "devil" (*diabolos* [TG1228, ZG1333], the Greek translation of the Hebrew *satan* [TH7854, ZH8477], meaning "adversary, enemy") stands for. We must oppose (*anthistēmi* [TG436, ZG468], "resist, stand in opposition against," BDAG 80) all that the devil stands for by standing against all his proud boasts and temptations. We cannot submit to God, on the one hand, and give in to Satan, on the other. The two are mutual opposites. Again, in the Lord's Prayer we ask, "Don't let us yield to temptation" (Matt 6:13), which means "Give us the strength to resist the temptations of the evil one." First Corinthians 10:13 states, "The temptations in your life are no different from what others experience. And God is faithful. He will not allow the temptation to be more than you can stand. When you are tempted, he will show you a way out so that you can endure." We can only resist the devil and defeat his temptations when we are completely dependent on God and find strength in him.

When we do rely upon God's Spirit to resist the devil, this evil power must "flee from" us! Satan is not an overpowering being who can gain control of us whenever he so wishes. All he can do as "the ancient serpent" is deceive us (Rev 12:9; 20:3). We are defeated only when we rely on ourselves and face temptation without the strength of Christ in us, not because Satan is irresistible. When we face him down through the Spirit in us, he will "flee" or run away as he did after the temptation in the wilderness when he "left [Jesus] until the next opportunity came" (Luke 4:13). That is an important point. The devil does not flee and stay away but has to leave in defeat "until the next opportunity." He will be back, so we must always be on our guard. Still, this is a very positive point—when we resist in the Spirit, he will have to go away!

Note that resistance to Satan is framed by submission to God in 4:7a, 8a; apart from God's strength we will succumb. "Come close" is *engizō* [TG1448, ZG1581], meaning "approach, draw near," used often for approaching God in worship, as at Sinai (Exod 19:21, LXX), the altar or sanctuary (Lev 21:21, 23; Num 8:19, LXX), or approaching the Lord himself (Ezek 40:46, LXX). In this context it undoubtedly prepares for 4:9, drawing near to God in repentance (see Hos 12:6; Heb 4:16; 7:19), especially for those who have been guilty of pride, backbiting, seeking pleasure, and bringing politics into the church (the sins enumerated in chs 3–4). Sorrow for sin is the first stage of submitting to God, and you cannot resist the devil until you have mourned for your moral and spiritual failures (as in the next verse). Moreover, when you do come close to God, you can be assured that he will "come close to you," reminiscent of 1 Peter 5:7, "Give all your worries and cares to God, for he cares about you." The gracious and forgiving God accepts our contrite spirit and in turn casts his loving presence upon us.

The mood of uncleanness and sorrow for sin is expanded in the Old Testament cultic (ritual) imagery of 4:8b-9. "Wash your hands" was used of priests purifying themselves in the laver; they must wash "or they will die" (Exod 30:19-21). God is a pure and holy God, and no sinful person can approach him and expect to live. Washing the hands was symbolic of their purification, and they were the means by which gifts were brought to God. "If, in the biblical idiom, the heart is the symbol of intention, then the hands are the symbol of action (Gen 3:22; 4:11; Exod 3:20; Deut 2:7; Ps 89:17)" (Johnson 1995:284). So this referred to a true repentance that involved actions as well as intentions. Intention or motive is seen in the next phrase, "purify your hearts," which states the same truth another way. The impurity of the readers means they should expect only judgment from God unless they repent and get right with him. Adamson (1976:174-175) says that these are "two aspects of one action" and "symbolize deeds and thoughts, respectively."

The readers are called two things here, "sinners" and "double-minded" (NLT, those whose "loyalty is divided between God and the world"). James earlier called them *adelphoi* [TG80, ZG81] (brothers and sisters), showing they were Christians (1:2, 16, 19; 2:1, 5). He will do so again (4:11; 5:7, 9, 10, 12), but now due to their intransigence and worldly attitudes he can only call them "sinners" and center on their need to repent, building on his derogatory address of them as "adulterers" in 4:4. Their basic problem (and his second negative address) is their "divided loyalty," a point already made in 1:8 (see the discussion there). They belonged partly to God and partly (for some of them, mostly) to the world. This divided mind is explored especially in 4:4, where they have sought "friendship with the world" more than they have tried to walk with God. Laws (1980:1184) states, "the *double-minded* are the archetypal *sinners*; for James doubleness is of the essence of human sin, seen in the divisive desires of the individual (4:1) and the 'adulterous' attempts to combine prayer to God and a quest for friendship of the world (4:3f)."

This sorrowful repentance is defined in 4:9. The NLT unpacks the terse opening that contains three commands, "Be miserable, mourn, and weep." The first ("tears for what you have done") refers to deep distress and misery induced by a terrible tragedy, here a tearful grief for the calamity of serious sin in your life. The second ("sorrow") is the period of public mourning for sin that reflects that tearful distress. The third ("deep grief") is the actual weeping caused by the mourning. All three are fairly synonymous and call for a serious sorrow for sin that is public, made known to all around. Moo (2000:195) alludes to the parallels in the prophets (Isa 15:2; Jer 4:13; Hos 10:5; Joel 1:9-10; 2:12; Mic 2:4) and concludes, "The biblical writers therefore suggest that all persons will inevitably 'mourn' for their spiritual state. They can wait to mourn until it is too late . . . [or] they can mourn now, turning sorrowfully from their sin so that they will have no occasion to mourn when the Lord returns."

In their worldly pursuit of pleasure (4:3) the readers have often participated in the false laughter and joy of secular society, for example, in the power and authority their boasting has won them in the church. But now they are warned that this false laughter must become sadness and their so-called joy must become gloom. They were guilty of serious sin but were treating it casually and even enjoying their sinful attitudes, finding joy in their power plays and worldly success. Jesus states this theme of reversal in his Sermon on the Plain in Luke 6:21, 25, "God blesses you who weep now, for in due time you will laugh. . . . What sorrow awaits you who laugh now, for your laughing will turn to mourning and sorrow" (cf. Prov 2:14; 10:23; 14:13; Lam 5:15; Amos 8:10).

True joy can only come after one has mourned for sin, and too much of modern preaching seems unaware of this fact. It seeks only to make people feel good about themselves, when in truth this is impossible until those very people have gotten right with God. Until then, all they can ever know is a counterfeit, secular "joy" that will turn to eternal sorrow! Sorrow for sin is necessary as the first step to feeling true joy, for such joy is only possible when we are "friends" with God.

James concludes this section and its list of imperatives by returning to the basic idea of 4:7: "Humble yourselves before the Lord" (4:10). The two choices were stated originally in 3:13-14: humility versus selfish ambition and pride. Exalt yourself or glorify God; you cannot do both (as with praising God while cursing others in 3:9-10). There will be no conflict and wars over power in the church when both sides are characterized by humility. But pride must become humility, and self-seeking must turn into obedience to God. Jesus often stated this truth—"Whoever wants to be first must take last place and be the servant of everyone else" (Mark 9:35; cf. Mark 10:43); "Those who exalt themselves will be humbled, and those who humble themselves will be exalted" (Matt 23:12; cf. Luke 14:11; 18:14). Thus, when you realize your desperate state and relinquish control entirely to God by obeying his will, he "will lift you up in honor" or "exalt you" both now and, more importantly, in eternity. Again there are two choices—self-glory, which will give temporary power but subsequent judgment, or self-humility, which leads to a servant heart and praise from God.

◆ 3. Slander and judging (4:11-12)

11 Don't speak evil against each other, dear brothers and sisters.* If you criticize and judge each other, then you are criticizing and judging God's law. But your job is to obey the law, not to judge whether it applies to you. 12 God alone, who gave the law, is the Judge. He alone has the power to save or to destroy. So what right do you have to judge your neighbor?

4:11 Greek *brothers.*

NOTES

4:11-12 *Don't speak evil.* There are some scholars who take 4:11-12 with what follows instead of what precedes. Moo (2000:197) notes Cargal (1993:170-171), who thinks the final section of the book is framed by the message that believers should not judge one another (4:11) but instead restore those who have gone astray from Christ. Laws (1980:186) considers it a separate, discrete section on passing judgment but connects it more with what follows. Martin (1988:160-161) considers it part of a section on arrogant speech (4:11-12, 13-17); and Johnson (1995:291-292) considers all of 4:11–5:6 as a rebuke against arrogance, slander (4:11-12), pretentious boasting (4:13-17), and luxurious living that condemns the poor (5:1-6). Most others consider it part of 4:1-12, and that fits the context best, as this recapitulates the sins of the tongue in 3:1-12. James does move to a different style of address, addressing *adelphoi* [TG80, ZG81] (brothers and sisters) rather than "adulterers" (4:4) or "sinners" (4:8), but the paraenetic style continues.

COMMENTARY

James now returns to the theme that has been central all along: the sins of speech in the community. In chapter 4, this has been explicit only in 4:1-3, but in reality everything in the chapter (friendship with the world, the problem of pride, the need for humility, and opposition against Satan) has related to the motif of the evils of the tongue. Moo (2000:197) notes the following connections with earlier material in the book: "speaking evil" as a manifestation of pride (4:6) as well as jealousy and selfishness (3:14, 16) and the law and judging (2:8-13). He concludes, "vv. 11-12 should be seen as a brief 'reprise' of the larger discussion of sins of speech that opened the section (3:1-12). We would then have an inclusion on speech that frames the section 3:1–4:12." So this section (4:11-12) concludes 3:1–4:12 by recapitulating the sins of the tongue—criticizing and judging others. As is often the case in James, there are three parts, beginning with (1) the condemnation of slander in the community (4:11a), proceeding to (2) the meaning of slander as setting yourself up as judge rather than follower of the law (4:11b), then concluding with (3) God as the only valid judge (4:12).

James returns to his familiar endearing address of them as "dear brothers and sisters," pleading with them as beloved family members in the church (departing from the addresses in 4:4, 8). Though they were seriously misguided and desperately in need of repentance and a changed lifestyle, they were fellow followers of Christ. The first prohibition (in the present tense, probably meaning "stop doing what you are doing") is "stop speaking against," referring probably not just to backbiting but to all "destructive verbal attacks," including slander, gossip, false accusations (Stulac 1990:152), harsh criticism, or condemnation in general (Laws 1980:186). When you engage in such vicious denunciation of others, "criticiz[ing] and judg[ing] each other," you commit the sin of Matthew 7:1-5, centering on the "speck" of sin in their eyes and ignoring the "log" in your own.

There is a massive difference between "judging" and "admonishing." When you judge, you are looking down on others and enjoying telling them how wrong they are; there is no love in the process. Tasker (1956:99) says, "Backbiting others is, in fact, a subtle form of self-exaltation" and quotes Calvin (1948:337), "Hypocrisy is always presumptuous, and we are by nature hypocrites, fondly exalting ourselves by calumniating others." When you admonish, you stand alongside them in love and try to restore them to the Lord (Gal 6:1) so they can defeat sin in their lives (Heb 3:13). It is the result of love, it is private rather than public, and there is no sense of superiority, no slander or gossip included. These people in the midst of their conflicts (4:1) were adding personal attacks to community debates. There was no love, only power politics. I remember a secretary once telling me about her boss, a major Christian leader: "You have to understand something; he never loses" (i.e., he had to get his way in every area of his ministry). That spoke volumes about the person. There was no search for truth, only victory, and the end justified the means.

Next, James expands his argument by stating that judging others is tantamount to criticizing and judging God's law. "The law" most likely refers to the Mosaic law, specifically the "royal law" (2:8) of Leviticus 19:18 to love one's neighbor. It also refers to Leviticus 19:16, where the royal law is negated by "slanderous gossip among your people" (Laws 1980:187, though see Hiebert 1979:242 for the possibility that the anarthrous "law" refers to "the law governing the Christian life"). James here refers to the Mosaic law from a new covenant perspective, as having been fulfilled in Christ's kingdom teaching (Blomberg and Kamell, Martin, Moo). The readers knew the biblical prohibition against such practices but deliberately ignored them. "To practice slander and judgment against a neighbor is, therefore, to assume not only an arrogant superiority toward an equal but also to assume an arrogant superiority to the law that forbids such behavior; one assumes the right to decide which laws apply and which ones don't" (Johnson 1995:293).

In light of this serious danger, James reminds them, "your job is to obey the law, not to judge whether it applies to you." This returns to 1:22-25 and its challenge to be not just listeners of the word but doers of it (*poiētēs logou* [TG4163/3056, ZG4475/3364], "doer of the word," found in 1:22, and *poiētēs nomou* [TG3551, ZG3795], "doer of the law" is in 4:11). In 2:8-11 they had been told to obey every precept of the law, not just those portions that are convenient, and in 2:12 they were warned that in everything they say and do, "you will be judged by the law that sets you free." By disregarding one portion of the law, they pretended that they could "judge" what portion was important and worth keeping, but in reality they would be judged by those parts they had broken. There is only one proper response to the divine regulations in God's law—practice and obey them.

In 4:12 a further implication is explored: When believers criticize and judge one another, they are not simply breaking God's law; they are usurping his rightful place as Judge. He alone "gave the law" (lit., "lawgiver") and is "the Judge." So these people were encroaching on territory reserved only for God. God is described as "lawgiver" often (e.g., Exod 24:12; 34:28; Pss 25:8, 12; 119:102, 104), and the thrust here is that all truth stems from him, and all his precepts must be obeyed (cf. Matt 28:20, "Teach these new disciples to obey all the commands I have given"). At the same time, God as Judge is found in virtually every book of the Bible (e.g., 5:9; Ps 94:2; 1 Cor 4:5; 2 Tim 4:8; Heb 12:23). To set yourself in his place as the one who decides what laws to follow and to critically "judge your neighbor" is to disobey Leviticus 19:18 and bring the wrath of God down upon your head.

The reminder that God "alone has the power to save or to destroy" is reminiscent of Matthew 10:28: "Don't be afraid of those who want to kill your body. . . . Fear only God, who can destroy both soul and body in hell." God alone is Savior (1 Sam 4:3; Pss 7:10; 18:2; Luke 19:10; Heb 7:25), and in the final analysis, he alone will destroy his enemies (Rev 11:18; cf. Pss 5:6; 17:14; Isa 11:14; Jer 25:9; 1 Cor 3:17). The message is clear: Those who repent and submit themselves to God will be "saved," while those who continue in their arrogant rebellion and bring backbiting and division into the church will be "destroyed" (contrast 1:21, "has the power to save your souls," with 5:20, "save that person from death").

◆ V. Admonitions to the Worldly and the Godly (4:13–5:11)

A. Warnings to the Worldly (4:13–5:6)

1. The worldly Christian needs to trust in God (4:13-17)

13 Look here, you who say, "Today or tomorrow we are going to a certain town and will stay there a year. We will do business there and make a profit." 14 How do you know what your life will be like tomorrow? Your life is like the morning fog—it's here a little while, then it's gone. 15 What you ought to say is, "If the Lord wants us to, we will live and do this or that." 16 Otherwise you are boasting about your own plans, and all such boasting is evil.

17 Remember, it is sin to know what you ought to do and then not do it.

NOTES

4:13 ***Look here, you who say.*** The delineation of the structural development of this section is difficult to ascertain. Some scholars (Johnson; Martin) see the shift occurring at 4:11, with slander being part of a section on arrogant, godless attitudes. However, 4:11-12 is too closely linked with the divisive spirit of the double-tongued in 3:1–4:10 to be a separate section; rather, it concludes that section. Dibelius (1975:230) goes too far in calling this "an independent section" with "no connection between the passage and the preceding list of imperatives," but he rightly sees a break in thought. The use of "look here" in 4:13 and 5:1 forms a prophetic address challenging and rebuking "the attitude of well-to-do people who arrogantly suppose that they can think and act without reference to God and to eternity. Arrogant selfishness is the problem in both paragraphs" (Moo 2000:200). For Moo this is "a clash of worldviews" between those who ignore God and those who center on God. James 4:13–5:6 describes those who seek wealth for its own sake and ignore God's guiding presence in their lives.

Today or tomorrow we are going to a certain town. There is some debate as to whether 4:13-17 is addressing merchants who are Christians or those (with 5:1-6) who are not believers. A few see these as wealthy unbelievers and make 4:13–5:6 a unit on the ungodly rich because of parallels like "look here" (4:13; 5:1) and the general tone of condemnation for the profit motive in both passages. However, the majority argue that the tone of 4:13-17 asks these merchants to consider God's will (4:15) and know what to do (4:17), things that would not be said to nonbelievers. So the better view is that they were indeed believers.

4:14 ***How do you know what your life will be like tomorrow?*** In the complicated Greek there might be one sentence, as in the NLT (following UBS^4; see also NASB, TEV, NJB), but there could also be two sentences: a statement followed by a question, as in the TNIV (also NRSV, ESV), "Why, you do not even know what will happen tomorrow. What is your life?" There are three separate issues: (1) the article before "tomorrow," which could read either "the things of tomorrow" or "about tomorrow" (the latter is more likely); (2) the insertion of *gar* [TG1063, ZG1142] (for) after the interrogative *poia* [TG4169, ZG4481] (what) in certain mss (𝔓74 𝔓100 ℵ^2 A P Ψ; for discussion, see Comfort 2008:731-732); and (3) the use of the future "it will be" or the present tense "you are" beginning the next clause (the present is more likely). While Moo (2000:203) argues for two sentences, it is better to go with Johnson (1995:296), who says "on the whole, however, it seems better to follow the text and punctuation of the 26th edition of Nestle-Aland . . . despite its awkwardness." UBS^4 agrees, and thus the single sentence (as in the NLT) is likely the better way to translate the statement.

4:16 ***you are boasting about your own plans.*** Blomberg and Kamell (2008:210) discuss the two ways to understand this (lit., "you are boasting in your pretensions"): (1) The preposition *en* [TG1722, ZG1877] (in) can be objective, saying that they are boasting "about" their "repeated acts of arrogance"; (2) it can be adverbial, telling how they are boasting, namely, "in a state of arrogance" or "proudly." Moo (2000:206-207) shows that in the New Testament the former is always the case, so the objective "about" (as in the NLT) is the best option.

4:17 ***Remember, it is sin.*** Dibelius (1975:235), as elsewhere, considers this to be "a thought unconnected with what precedes or follows" and thus a "general precept" artificially added to the paragraph. This time, however, he seems to have a point. It is a strange addition that appears to be a general principle simply building on the "evil" of 4:16. Yet while Dibelius is probably correct that this was a traditional saying, James connects it to 4:13-16 with *oun* [TG3767, ZG4036] (therefore), and it actually fits rather closely. These Christian merchants knew that they should include God in their plans but chose not to do so. That is a "sin of omission."

COMMENTARY

The final section of the epistle (4:13–5:18) sums up the arguments of the rest of the letter. One of the primary themes centers on wealth and poverty (see "Major Themes" in the Introduction), so the first part of this final unit, building on 1:9-11, addresses wealthy Christians (4:13-17) and non-Christians (5:1-6), warning them that God is the final judge (cf. 2:12-13; 4:11-12). The poor believers are then encouraged to be patient and stop grumbling; instead, they should wait for Christ's return when all will be made right (5:7-11). They, too, are warned of the coming judgment (5:9, 12). Finally, the Christ-followers are promised power in prayer to accomplish great things, even the healing of the sick (5:13-18). In this first section of 4:13-17 there are three parts: the false perspective for business plans (4:13), the true perspective centering on God's will (4:14-15), and a double conclusion regarding sin (4:16-17).

The opening words "look here" (*age nun* [TG33/3568, ZG72/3814], "come now") are found only here and 5:1 in the New Testament, but they were common in the Hellenistic world for demanding someone's full attention. It is similar to Jesus' "Anyone with ears to hear should listen and understand" (Matt 11:15; 13:9, 43). James is admonishing these people in a tone similar to that in 4:1-10, telling them they had better wake up and "look" at the reality of their situation. They have left God out of their future designs and will suffer the consequences. In James's mind such people are quasi-Christians. They are drawing their security from their wealth and are proving Jesus' saying, "It is easier for a camel to go through the eye of a needle than for a rich person to enter the Kingdom of God" (Matt 19:24). They don't feel the need for God in their daily lives; furthermore, they are committing idolatry by replacing God with their wealth, leading them to make their own plans without any dependence on God whatsoever.

Verse 13 does not replicate the actual words of any particular merchant; rather, James summarizes their attitude with a fictitious statement of a business trip "today or tomorrow" to "a certain town." The main thing is the clear confidence of their plans to "stay there a year" or so, conduct "business," and "make a profit." The future tenses demonstrate their absolute assurance that their infallible itineraries will work. On the surface, it sounds perfectly normal and fits virtually every merchant who has ever lived. This sentence could be taken from the *Wall Street Journal* and would certainly fit the Jewish merchant class from the first century who traveled throughout the Roman world and were famous for their ability to make money.

The problem, though, is not in their plans but in the independence of those intended projects from God; he is not a part of their business life, and his sovereign will is not considered at all. Motyer calls it "presumptuousness" and says it well (1985:160): "We speak to ourselves as if life were our right, as if our choice were the only deciding factor, as if we had in ourselves all that was needed to make a success of things, as if getting on, making money, doing well were life's sole objective." There is nothing wrong with a profit motive or a business goal when God is in charge. For business people today, the point is clear: God wants to be their "senior partner," to guide their portfolio and plans. A business career is as much a calling as being a pastor or a missionary. The goal must be to follow God's leading and glorify him in the business world, then use the profits not just to buy more and more "things" but more to enhance kingdom values in the church and among the downtrodden.

James begins 4:14 with *hoitines* [TG3748, ZG4015], a pronoun that means "people such as you" and so can be translated, "How can people like you know what tomorrow will bring?" You cannot determine the future, and if you leave God out of those designs, you are headed for disaster! There must be contingency in every plan, and the God of all contingencies must be at the center of all such planned itineraries. No one knows what will happen tomorrow, so the only possible reaction must be to allow God's providential care to be in charge of all decisions. Martin (1988:166) asks, "how does one approach life in the light of not knowing the outcome? The incorrect, that is, foolish, way is to assume that all will transpire as planned. The more sensible attitude—because it alone is safe—is to assume that whatever happens is always under the control of God."

James anchors this observation in the transitory nature of life: "Your life is like the morning fog—it's here a little while, then it's gone" (4:14b). The "fog" or "mist" was "a natural analogy for the ephemeral in the dry Palestinian climate, in which water droplets in the air formed from condensation near the sea but then quickly disappeared" (Blomberg and Kamell 2008:208). The brevity of life is emphasized often in the Old Testament (Job 7:7, 9; Pss 39:5-6; 103:15-16; Prov 27:1; Isa 40:6-7) and in the New Testament (1:10-11; Luke 12:16-20). Since we do not know whether we will live through the night, we must surrender control of the future to God. It is not wrong to make sound investments and prepare for the future; it is only wrong when we fail to depend on God in doing so.

In 4:13 James let us know what *not* to say regarding our future business plans, and now in 4:15 James tells us what we "ought to say" (an imperatival infinitive). Each time we think of future activities, we must always qualify it with "if (*ean* [TG1437, ZG1569], condition of possibility) the Lord wants us to"— with "Lord" referring to God but also including Jesus (so Martin). While the United States Constitution separates church and state, God refuses to do so. Every area of life has a spiritual dimension. "The will of God" infuses every single aspect of life and is emphasized in the Old Testament (Pss 40:8; 143:10; Isa 46:10; 53:10) and in the New Testament (Matt 6:10; Mark 3:35; Rom 12:2; 15:32; Heb 13:21; 1 Pet 3:17; 4:2). In every moment, every decision, we must seek God's will and the Spirit's guiding presence as we plan and implement our hopes and desires.

As any Christian knows, the very question as to whether we will be alive an hour from now is in the hands of God. I have a nephew who was in one of the buildings destroyed in the 9/11 disaster and ran out after the first plane struck, getting onto a ferry. He saw the second plane do a U-turn and fly over his ferry on its way to the second building. His wife worked on one of the top floors and would have been killed had she not been enrolling their child in nursery school that day. All her friends there perished. Our futures are in God's hands. Our actions ("do this or that") should be in his hands, as well. In all of our detailed planning (which is all well and good), we must always pray for God's guidance and will. The Gethsemane prayer is our guide (Mark 14:36), "Abba, Father . . . everything is possible for you. Please take this cup of suffering away from me. Yet I want your will to be done, not mine." Total surrender to God's providential will is the key to the successful Christian life. Motyer (1985:161) says that our walk with God can be lost if "we take the reins of life into our own hands, we forget our ignorance, frailty, and dependence and plan our day, our week and next year as if we were lords of earth and time, and there was no God in heaven."

In contrast to the proper attitude of 4:15, James in 4:16 returns to the presumptuous plans of 4:13, labeling it "boasting" (cf. "boasting and lying" in 3:14) about your own plans," with the term "plans" (*alazoneiais* [TG212, ZG224]) meaning "pretension, arrogance" (BDAG 40), thereby yielding the translation, "boasting about your pretentious plans." In itself "boasting" is not wrong, as in 1:9-10 where the poor "boast" in their exaltation and the rich "boast" in their humility. But these Jewish Christian merchants boasted to everyone about their "pretentious plans," that is, about all they were going to accomplish and how important they would become. In this they ignored God and became proud of all they planned to achieve; they were therefore pragmatic atheists who in effect did not believe God affected their secular lives.

The conclusion is obvious: "All such boasting is evil." Anyone who is proud of their achievements when those profitable actions are devoid of awareness and dependence upon God is guilty of "evil" actions (*ponēra* [TG4190, ZG4505]). Since James was addressing Christians this way, we must be aware of such tendencies in our own lives. Romans 12:2 warns, "Don't copy the behavior and customs of this world." I love the Phillips translation of this: "Don't let the world around you squeeze you into its own mould." A major way for a believer to fall into "friendship with the world" (4:4) is to allow its worldview to guide decision-making, to accept an autonomous, independent ownership over your life that leaves God out of the picture, then to brag about all you have accomplished. This is "evil" because it partakes entirely of the world's perspective and makes us an "enemy of God" (4:4). Stulac (1990:161) asserts, "It is a blasphemous denial of God's authority and grace to think that we instead of God control events." Kistemaker (1986:150) adds, "Paul is able to teach us that we can boast only in weakness; in this weakness the power of Christ becomes evident (2 Cor 11:30; 12:5, 9). A Christian, then, may boast of himself only in so far as his life is lived in dependence on God and in responsibility to him."

James concludes (*oun* [TG3767, ZG4036], "therefore"; NLT, "remember") this section with teaching about "the sin of omission." Virtually all commentators recognize this verse as a traditional saying or "maxim" (Johnson; Martin). James probably added it here as a conclusion not just to the paragraph of 4:13-16 but as a general conclusion that fits all the "sins" of chapters 1–4. Each of them (listening but not doing, discrimination and prejudice, failing to help the poor, conflict and backbiting in the church) are equally examples of Christians who know what God requires but fail to obey his precepts. Sins of "commission" would be sins we knowingly commit, while sins of "omission" are those sins in which we know better and yet fail ("omit") to make the correct decision. We likely sin more in the latter sense than in the former.

The sin of omission is explained well here. First, it involves "what you ought to do" (4:17)—literally, "the good/proper (*kalos* [TG2570A, ZG2819]) thing to do." To "know" or "understand" means you realize what God requires of you. The good or proper thing in this context is to depend on God and to yield to his will in our future planning. In the context of business and profit, it also means to use all our resources (especially financial) for the good of the kingdom. "Not do it" is present tense and means to never put your knowledge into practice. This repeats the sin of 1:19-27, to "hear the word" but refuse to be a "doer" of it. In this sense, the sin here also looks forward to the egregious misuse of wealth in 5:1-6.

Moo (2000:208) gives three examples of the sin of omission from Jesus' parables: the servant who fails to utilize the money entrusted to him (Luke 19:11-27); those who do not care for the unfortunate in society (Matt 25:31-46); and the servant who knows his master's will and refuses to do it (Luke 12:47). Tasker (1956:107) summarizes this well in his discussion of the parable of the rich man and Lazarus (Luke 16). The wealthy man was in torment "because he had yielded to the temptation, which especially besets the wealthy, to use his wealth to screen himself from any personal contact with those whom he had found uncongenial or who lived in circumstances more humble than his own. As a result, he failed to recognize and use opportunities of service which lay at his very doorstep."

So James's conclusion stands firm: "It is sin . . . not [to] do it." The "sin" (*hamartia*) in 4:17 is connected to the "evil" of 4:16. Presumptuous boasting regarding godless achievements is a grievous sin before God. The failure to use profits to benefit others and to enhance the work of the church is also sin. How often do we have choices to make regarding "practicing the presence" of Christ in our daily decisions? How often do we have discretionary funds that we can use for others or for God's work but instead use that money to purchase some trinket or toy for our own pleasure? We have much for which we must answer to God!

◆ 2. The worldly unbeliever will experience destruction (5:1-6)

Look here, you rich people: Weep and groan with anguish because of all the terrible troubles ahead of you. [2]Your wealth is rotting away, and your fine clothes are moth-eaten rags. [3]Your gold and silver have become worthless. The very wealth you were counting on will eat away your flesh like fire. This treasure you have accumulated will stand as evidence against you on the day of judgment. [4]For listen! Hear the cries of the field workers whom you have cheated of their pay. The wages you held back cry out against you. The cries of those who harvest your fields have reached the ears of the LORD of Heaven's Armies.

[5]You have spent your years on earth in luxury, satisfying your every desire. You have fattened yourselves for the day of slaughter. [6]You have condemned and killed innocent people,* who do not resist you.*

5:6a Or *killed the Righteous One.* 5:6b Or *Don't they resist you?* or *Doesn't God oppose you?* or *Aren't they now accusing you before God?*

NOTES

5:1-6 While some think the similarities between 4:13-17 and 5:1-6 (e.g., both begin with "Look here") mean that both groups must either be non-Christians or Christians, the differences are greater than the similarities. Stulac (1993:162-163) gives four reasons why these must be unbelievers and a different group than 4:13-17: (1) James refrains from using his frequent "brothers and sisters" but returns to it in 5:7, showing this is a different group;

(2) he calls them "you rich people" in 5:1, separating them from the others; (3) the entire paragraph centers on condemnation rather than exhortation; (4) the tone follows that of OT diatribes against rich oppressors, with all the affirmation going to the "needy, righteous victims."

5:1 ***Weep and groan with anguish.*** This translates the verbs *klaiō* [TG2799, ZG3081] and *ololuzō* [TG3649, ZG3909], both of which exemplify onomatopoeia, i.e., the words sound like wailing. The second verb also means "to howl." It describes "the sound a person utters when he suffers extraordinary pain or grief" (Kistemaker 1986:156). Such imagery is used often in prophetic writings to describe the laments of those condemned by God for their injustice and immoral lifestyles (Isa 10:30; 13:6; 14:31; 15:2-3; 16:7; 24:11; Ezek 21:12; Hos 7:14; Amos 5:16; 8:3; Zech 11:2-3). Many of these passages center on the Day of the Lord and include a call to repentance; that is likely the thrust here as well. Jesus warned that those who are "fat and prosperous" will face a time of "awful hunger" (Luke 6:25), and in Luke 23:28 Jesus calls upon Jerusalem to "weep for yourselves and for your children." In Rev 18:11, 15, 19, the kings, merchants, and shipping magnates who profited from the evil empire will "weep and mourn" for her absolute destruction.

5:2-3 ***is rotting away . . . are moth-eaten rags . . . have become worthless.*** The three verbs here are in the perfect tense, best seen as stative in this case (see Laws, Moo), describing a state of being that has already begun. However, Adamson (1976:185) calls this "prophetic anticipation," considering the future judgment to be so certain that it is described as having already taken place (so also Davids, Dibelius, Johnson, Martin, Mayor, McCartney). Others (Hiebert; Ropes) take these as equivalent to futures. While all three views are viable, the first fits the context better; Moo (2000:213) says, the tense "suggests that the material possessions of these rich people are already in the state of being 'rotted,' 'moth-eaten,' 'rusted.'"

5:3 ***This treasure you have accumulated will stand as evidence against you on the day of judgment.*** The image of evidence can be understood as positive ("testify to you," with *humin* [TG4771, ZG5148] an indirect object of the verbal idea in "testify"), thus calling them to repentance. But it is far more likely in light of the negative thrust of the context ("eat your flesh as fire") that it is negative: "testify against you" (with *humin* a dative of disadvantage). The rust first provides evidence at the final judgment and then actually becomes the sentence upon them, consuming them with fire.

Ropes (1916:287) argues that "like fire" is the object of "stored up treasure," and the Jerusalem Bible follows this reading: "It was a burning fire that you stored up as your treasure for the last days." Thus they are storing up punishment that will come at the Last Judgment (see Matt 19:21; Rom 2:5). While possible, this is unnecessary, and most commentators go with the traditional reading as the best way to understand the verse.

5:4 ***The wages you held back.*** There is wide disagreement whether the original should read *aphusterēmenos* [TG879.1, ZG935] ("withheld, held back," so ℵ B* with WH, NA[25], Comfort, Laws, Martin, NLT, NASB, TNIV) or *apesterēmenos* [TG650, ZG691] ("stolen, defrauded," in A B[2] Ψ 33 with NA[27], UBS[4], Blomberg and Kamell, Davids, Moo, McCartney, NRSV, ESV). It is a very difficult decision, but it may be best to opt for the more widely used verb, "defrauded," for it has wider manuscript support and is the kind of traditional language James would have utilized (though it could have been added as an assimilation to Mal 3:5). Metzger (1994:685) calls the first reading an "Alexandrian refinement" since both manuscripts (Sinaiticus [A] and Vaticanus [B]) normally agree and belong to the Alexandrian family of readings.

5:6 ***innocent people.*** Lit., "the righteous one." It has sometimes been said that this is Jesus, the quintessential "Righteous One" (cf. Johnson 1995:304, who notes Oecumenius, Bede,

Cassiodorus, and Feuillet as holding this), and others identify this with James the author of this epistle who was martyred (Mayor, with Dibelius, Martin holding it as possible [thus added by a later editor]). Neither is likely in this context of the poor being mistreated by wealthy landowners.

who do not resist you. The understood subject of this is "the righteous one." However, some make this a question, and there are two possibilities, either with "God" as the implied subject ("Does not God oppose you?" so Johnson) or with the innocent poor as the subject ("Should they not resist you [by calling on God for justice]?" so Davids, Ropes). "God" as the subject is not really viable, since he is not noted in the context. The resistance of the poor by calling on God for vindication and vengeance would fit in light of 5:4, but this is not as likely in this context. It is best to see here the nonresistance of the poor.

COMMENTARY

While 4:13-17 addresses worldly Christians, this one addresses non-Christians. The passage depicts prophetic doom in the same vein as Amos or Jeremiah (e.g., Jer 7:30–8:3; Amos 4:1-3; 6:1-7; 9:1-10), and the condemnation is far more harsh than in 4:13-17. The carnal Christians left God out of their plans in 4:13ff, but the nonbelievers here have gone an extra step, not only ignoring God but also cheating their poor workers in order to live even more luxuriously. This passage has a much more severe tone and judgment, as the sin is greater. There is no appeal to recognizing God, as in 4:15, for God is not in these wealthy pirates' lives. There is only the certitude of judgment, beginning with the disappearance of their wealth (5:3) and ending with their "slaughter" as fattened cattle ready to be sacrificed to God (5:5b).

This paragraph has four sections: (1) prophetic denunciation and a call to groan in light of the coming judgment (5:1); (2) the disappearance of the rich people's wealth, which will consume them like fire (5:2-3a); (3) their hoarded wealth and sins against the poor, which cry out to God (5:3b-4); and (4) the impending consequences of their sins, which have made them ripe for judgment (5:5-6). Another way one could look at this is to combine the third and fourth sections into one, with their sins first calling out to God (5:3b-4) and then getting them ready for the slaughter (5:5-6). Four specific sins are enumerated here: hoarding wealth (5:2-3), cheating field workers of their pay (5:4), living lives of self-centered luxury (5:5), and oppressing innocent people (5:6).

The paragraph begins (5:1) with the same denunciation formula as in 4:13, "Look here," meaning they have been blind to the reality of their situation before God and had better pay full attention. The hearers are called upon to "weep and groan with anguish," with the second verb also meaning to "howl." The language marks God's condemnation of injustice and immoral lifestyles (e.g., Isa 14:31; Ezek 21:12; Amos 5:16; see note on 5:1), and is often found together with a call to repentance; that is likely the thrust here, as well.

The corrupt who are condemned in 5:1-6 are wealthy landowners who, because of their avarice, essentially stole the property of the poor and then paid them virtually nothing to work the land. Martin (1988:174) notes four economic factors that "militated against the rural, independent farmer": (1) By controlling farming and commerce, the wealthy brought their produce to market more quickly and dominated the prices; (2) since the small farmers were poor, they could not keep their equipment and farms upgraded; (3) when famine or drought hit, the wealthy could maintain reserves, keep their produce stocks up, and give loans to the independent farmers that later could lead to foreclosure and seizing of the property by the large landowners; (4) the rural farmers would then become tenant farmers or even daily wage earners, toiling for the very wealthy who had taken their assets.

The "terrible troubles" (5:1) that will come upon these wealthy people refers primarily to the "wretchedness, distress, trouble, and misery" (BDAG 988) that they will suffer at the Last Judgment. "Ahead of you" (5:1) is literally "coming upon you," an eschatological phrase pointing to imminent judgment, which may include the idea of suffering in this life as well (so Martin 1988:176). Their luxurious living is about to end, and the polar opposite is awaiting them: intense suffering at the hands of the eternal Judge. Although unstated, the warning of terrible punishment to come may have a conditional element (as in the prophets, who often say God will relent if the people repent and change their ways).

It must be said that these wealthy people are not so judged merely because they are rich. Rather, it is because they were misusing their wealth for self-indulgent living rather than helping the poor. This is proven by the specific sins condemned in 5:2-5. Still, wealth is a major barrier to knowing God. Jesus says in Mark 10:23, "How hard it is for the rich to enter the Kingdom of God!" Far from riches being a sign of divine blessing (the Jewish belief), they make it nearly impossible to switch one's allegiance from the things of this world to God.

The actual state of the hoarded "wealth" is described in 5:2. These robbers of the poor may have kept the money for themselves and let it accumulate without helping any other person than themselves, but James lets them know that it is already "rotting away," using a perfect tense that means the riches are indeed in a state of decay even as James speaks. This is not just a future event; it has already begun. Then James gives two examples of wealth (clothes, gold and silver) in 5:2b-3, showing that every aspect of their riches is disappearing. "Rotting away" refers to the process of decay whereby food, clothes, or the human body in the grave last only a short time and then disappear forever. The transitoriness of life was emphasized in 4:14, and now the transitory nature of wealth is the focus. To place one's security and hope on that which is already "rotting away" is the height of folly.

Next, James says "your fine clothes are moth-eaten rags" (5:2b). Expensive garments have been a sign of great wealth down through history; in the first century, for instance, purple or scarlet clothes were worn only by the extremely wealthy (e.g., the "fancy clothes" of 2:2). It is amazing the lengths to which the rich then and now go to stand out from others. One young daughter of a billionaire never wears the same clothes twice and employs two buyers full-time just to help her select outfits, none of which cost less than a couple thousand dollars each! The idea of moth-eaten garments recalls Job 13:28, where Job complains he is wasting away "like a moth-eaten coat," or Matthew 6:19, where Jesus commands, "Don't store up treasures here on earth, where moths eat them and rust destroys them."

The primary example of wealth occurs in 5:3, where James says that "gold and silver" have "become worthless." The verb means to "become rusty, tarnished, corroded." The problem is that rust never affects gold. Some have thought that James was ignorant and did not realize this, but gold's resistance to rust was well-known among the ancients. Weiser (1999) believes it refers to counterfeit coins in which a copper piece is plated with gold or silver and passed off as a coin. Others have said impure gold mixed with other metals could tarnish, and while this is true, it is doubtful James was referring to this aspect. More likely, he intended it to be "jarring" and so used "the metaphorical meaning of becoming useless" (see Blomberg and Kamell 2008:221). The message is that what they trust the most (e.g., the "expensive jewelry" in 2:2) to ensure their future will pass away and return nothing for all their effort (see Matt 6:20). Not only is their gold "worthless"; it will also "eat away your flesh like fire." In the Greek it is corrosion itself that becomes the "flesh-eating fire," a powerful picture of rust eventually eating away metal. Blomberg and Kamell (2008:221) bring out that the term *ios* [TG2447, ZG2675] (corrosion) also means "poison" or "venom" in 3:8, and that this would also fit the idea of "flesh-eating fire" (creating the double meaning). Both aspects fit the picture of wealth as useless and destructive in the lives of those who have made it their idol. The image of fiery judgment is found also in Psalm 21:9 ("The LORD will consume them in his anger; fire will devour them") and Judith 16:17 ("The Lord Almighty will take vengeance on them in the day of judgment; he will send fire and worms into their flesh," NRSV). In 1 Peter 1:6-7 it is said that fire will "test" believers and prove them genuine; here, the fire will "consume" and destroy the unbeliever. In Jesus' teaching, this fiery judgment is Gehenna, the image of the trash dump in the Hinnom Valley outside the walls of Jerusalem, where the fires burned constantly (Matt 5:22, 29-30; 10:28). In Revelation 19:20; 20:14-15; 21:8 it is "the lake of fire," where the wicked will spend eternity in torment.

The analogy of rust/poison envisages a gradual destruction (both destroy over a period of time); it has already begun and will continue throughout eternity. Furthermore, this rust "will stand as evidence against you on the day of judgment." The picture is of a court of law, and the very corrosion of their wealth will provide incontrovertible evidence at God's Great White Throne Judgment (Rev 20:11-15) that they stand guilty before him. The metaphor is that the rust will be legal proof regarding the corruption of their wealth. In actuality, the order of the text is the opposite of the NLT, depicting the rust first as proving their guilt ("evidence") and then becoming the means of their execution ("consuming" them). Finally, they have "accumulated [stored or hoarded] this treasure in the last days" (the last of four clauses in this sentence). The preposition *en* ("in") must be taken seriously, for there is a kind of double meaning in the phrase: The wealthy are "hoarding" their riches for their retirement years ("last days"); but by keeping it for themselves rather than using it for God and others, they are actually storing up for themselves judgment that will come "on the last day." In the inaugurated eschatology of the New Testament (see also on 1:9), the tension between the "already" and the "not yet" means that the "last days" have already begun. Thus, their judgment has started (as in the perfect tenses used in 5:3; see note on 5:2-3) and is in process, preparing them for the final judgment before God. The wealthy believe they are storing up their riches for a comfortable retirement, but in actuality they are storing up divine wrath that will come on them at their eternal "retirement." Blomberg and Kamell (2008:222) say it well: "Where is our treasure? Are we laying it up on earth so that we might live in comfort, planning for a long life here (see cf. Luke 12:13-21), or do we focus more on amassing treasure in heaven with God, being merely grateful for the blessings he has given us here and now?" The sin is not being wealthy but using that wealth for selfish purposes. We are currently living "in the last days" and must always be vigilant, using all our resources to serve God rather than ourselves (see the three parables in Matt 24:42–25:30).

The second great sin of these wealthy landowners is presented in 5:4; namely, they cheated their field workers out of the pay they deserve. James is much more pointed in his accusation here. "Listen" (*idou* [TG2400, ZG2627], "behold, look"), he says, you must understand the gravity of your guilt before God. He states the charges against them two ways: First, the stolen wages cry out, and then the workers themselves cry out to God. The wealthy are seen as "defrauding" or "cheating" their workers of their pay. These were day laborers who were hired at harvest time to "mow" the wheat and other grains for the picking. Galilee and most agricultural provinces in the first century had for the most part been bought up by a small group of very wealthy landowners, and the small farmers had been forced off their land and made to hire themselves out to the very land barons who had displaced them.

The problem of withholding pay due to workers had been going on for centuries, and the poor had little redress, since the courts were controlled by the wealthy. Leviticus 19:11, 13 says, "Do not defraud or rob your neighbor"; Deuteronomy 24:14-15 states, "Never take advantage of poor and destitute laborers. . . . You must pay them their wages each day before sunset" (also Job 7:2; 31:38-40; Jer 22:13; Mal 3:5; Matt 20:1-16; Sir 7:20; Tob 4:14). The imagery of "crying out" from the place of wrong is strongly reminiscent of the blood of Abel crying out to God "from the ground" (Gen 4:10). Blomberg and Kamell (2008:223) think it should be "cry out from you" rather than "against you." The cries (as with Abel) emerge from the origin of the wrongdoing, that is, the pockets of the landowners where the stolen money was placed.

Second, the cries of the workers themselves "have reached the ears of the LORD of Heaven's Armies." These are cries for vengeance (Davids 1982:177 notes Gen 18:20; 19:13; Exod 2:23; 1 Sam 9:16; Pss 11:6; 12:5; Luke 18:7; Sir 21:5; 35:21), which the Lord always hears and offers a response. When God said, "I will take revenge; I will pay them back" (Deut 32:35; cf. Rom 12:19), he meant to leave the vengeance with him, and he would bring justice to the downtrodden. That is the significance of the cry of the martyrs in Revelation 6:10, "O Sovereign Lord, holy and true, how long before you judge the people who belong to this world and avenge our blood for what they have done to us?" God promised he would do so, and the rest of the book tells in part how God wrought vengeance on their behalf (see Osborne 2002:283-290). The emphasis here is that the one who hears and responds is "the LORD of Heaven's Armies," known in many versions as "the Lord of hosts" (Gr., *kurios sabaōth*—the last word being a transliteration of the Hebrew). The picture is that of God leading heaven's armies in defense and liberation of his people (cf. 1 Sam 17:45; 2 Sam 6:18; 7:27; Isa 1:24; 2:12; 6:3, 5; Jer 49:5, 7, 26;

Amos 3:13; 4:13; 5:14-16). He *will* answer the oppression of his people, and justice *will* be meted out, beginning in the present but especially at the eschaton. Those who defraud the poor will never get away with their evil deeds.

The third sin is derided in 5:5, namely, living a life of self-indulgent luxury. The two verbs, living "in luxury" and "satisfying your every desire," do not merely describe a wealthy lifestyle but rather a life of wanton indulgence and pleasure. The noun cognate of the first verb is found in Luke 7:25 ("people who . . . live in *luxury*") and 2 Peter 2:13 ("they love to indulge in evil *pleasures*"). The second verb is used in Ezekiel 16:49 (LXX; the sins of Sodom) and 1 Timothy 5:6 ("the widow who lives only for *pleasure*"). Such a person cares only for self and the satisfaction of every desire, like the one in the parable of the rich man and Lazarus in Luke 16:19-31. Similarly, the "great prostitute" of Revelation 17:4 symbolizes the economic exploitation of Rome, and for that luxuriant immorality she is destroyed (Rev 17:16-17). The lives of such people are entirely earth-centered, with no concern whatsoever for the future, heavenly realm.

Those who live for themselves on earth will find their path completely reversed in the afterlife. James used a powerful metaphor for this: "You have fattened yourselves for the day of slaughter," literally, "fattened your hearts," with *kardia* [TG2588, ZG2840] likely referring here to the stomach area and thus meaning "fattened your bellies" (Lerle 1985). Some interpret this as a further description of their profligate luxury, saying the poor are being "slaughtered" while the rich revel in style and grow fat (Dibelius 1975:239). But the context of eschatological reversal makes this quite unlikely. The "day of slaughter" is the final judgment day, and so the picture is of the hedonistic rich growing fat like animals made ready for the sacrifice. In Amos 4:1-2 (cf. NLT mg) the wealthy women who "oppress the poor and crush the needy" are called "cows of Bashan" (an area east of the Jordan known for its fat, well-fed cattle) and told that they will be taken into exile for their sins. In Jeremiah 12:3, the prophet asks for divine justice against his enemies, "Drag these people away like sheep to be butchered! Set them aside to be slaughtered." These wicked landowners are engaged in a feeding frenzy of grandiose consumption, and it "becomes, by implication, equivalent to 'stuffing' or force-feeding an animal to fatten it for the slaughter" (Johnson 1995:304). This day of reckoning has already begun, and these wealthy hedonists were foolishly making themselves ready for it. Martin (1988:180) states, "Though the event of catastrophic judgment is yet to begin, for this letter the death-knell of the rich has already sounded. The wealthy indulge themselves and ignore the poor as if the day of slaughter . . . were not only far away but did not exist at all!"

The fourth sin (5:6) of these wealthy landowners is their oppression of innocent righteous people. The expression "condemned and killed" at one level is hyperbolic language for the mistreatment of the poor as already seen in 5:2-5. At another level, it is forensic language for the misuse of the courts against the poor, who had no means of defending themselves in a system controlled by the powerful (Laws 1980:205 calls this "judicial murder"). Johnson (1995:304) notes how this "was recognized already in Torah under the rubric of 'perversion of justice' by moving landmarks (Deut 19:14; 27:17), by refusing to return what was taken in pledge from the poor (Exod 22:26; Deut 24:12-13), by the use of false weights and scales (Lev 19:35; Deut 25:13-16), or by the taking of bribes in making decisions (Exod 23:7-8; Lev 19:15; Deut 10:17-19; 16:18-20; 24:17; 27:19)."

The use of "kill" could refer to actual acts of violence (Martin 1988:181) but more likely is figurative—by withholding proper wages and legal rights, they condemn the poor to starvation (see Ps 10:8-9; Amos 2:6; Mic 2:6-9; 6:9-16; Sir 34:21-22; Wis 2:12-20; *1 Enoch* 95:7; 96:8). In 2:6-7, some of these were the very rich who had dragged these poor Christians into court and slandered the name of Christ. James used a strange term for those oppressed, *ton dikaion* [TG1342A, ZG1465], "the righteous/innocent one." Of the options (see note on 5:6) the most likely by far is that this is a generic singular for the "righteous, innocent" poor (seen in a collective sense as a whole group) who were being systematically beaten down by the oppressive policies of the rapacious rich. Moreover, these righteous poor "do not resist" (see note on 5:6) the selfish manipulation by their wealthy masters. This nonresistance is an implicit surrender of their lives to God, as well as a refusal to take the matter into their own hands and fight back. Like it is said of Jesus in 1 Peter 2:23, they do not "retaliate" or "threaten revenge" but instead leave their situation "in the hands of God, who always judges fairly."

◆ B. Challenge to the Believers—Patience in Suffering (5:7-11)

7 Dear brothers and sisters,* be patient as you wait for the Lord's return. Consider the farmers who patiently wait for the rains in the fall and in the spring. They eagerly look for the valuable harvest to ripen. 8 You, too, must be patient. Take courage, for the coming of the Lord is near.

9 Don't grumble about each other, brothers and sisters, or you will be judged. For look—the Judge is standing at the door!

10 For examples of patience in suffering, dear brothers and sisters, look at the prophets who spoke in the name of the Lord. 11 We give great honor to those who endure under suffering. For instance, you know about Job, a man of great endurance. You can see how the Lord was kind to him at the end, for the Lord is full of tenderness and mercy.

5:7 Greek *brothers;* also in 5:9, 10, 12, 19.

NOTES

5:9 *the Judge is standing at the door.* While it is common to think of the "Judge" of all as being God the Father (as in 4:12), the context of the Lord's return in 5:7-8 makes it best to think of Christ as the Judge here (so Johnson, Martin, and Moo; contra Laws and Ropes, who say God is the more prevalent figure as "judge" in the NT).

5:11 *those who endure.* The participle *hupomeinantas* [TG5278, ZG5702] (those who endure) is aorist, leading some scholars (Adamson, Martin) to restrict the blessing to the prophets in the past. However, this is not the sense of the aorist in this type of context. It is a culminative aorist and emphasizes not the past but the present endurance of the people of God, "those who (have) remained faithful to the end" (Blomberg and Kamell 2008:229).

the Lord was kind to him at the end. Lit., "you saw the *telos* [TG5056, ZG5465] of the Lord." This has been much discussed, and Moo (2000:229-230) summarizes the options well, since the term can mean "end" or "purpose." If it means "end," it can refer to the end of the

Lord's ministry or the end that the Lord "finally brought about" (TNIV) to Job's problems, i.e., restoring his fortune (as in NIV, REB, NLT). If "purpose," it refers to God's goal, the spiritual refining that the events produced in his life (as in NASB, NRSV, ESV). Moo opts for the meaning "end," which fits Job (Job 42:5-6), the NT as a whole (e.g., Matt 10:22; Mark 3:26; Rom 10:4; 1 Cor 1:8; Heb 3:14), and this passage. All of Job's suffering "ended" well, and God turned everything around.

COMMENTARY

The theme of this paragraph is the patience (used four times in 5:7-10) and endurance (twice in 5:11) of the believer in light of suffering and injustice. God's people are to follow the models of the farmer (5:7), the prophets (5:10), and Job (5:11), who exemplify patient waiting and trust in the Lord's promises. At one level this is intimately connected with 5:1-6, as the righteous refuse to retaliate (5:6b) but instead endure their exploitation by the rich with patience (so Laws, Blomberg and Kamell, who make 5:1-12 a single section). At another level this seems to introduce the concluding section of the letter, as James for the first time since 4:11 addresses them as "brothers and sisters" (see 5:7, 9, 10, 12, 19) and begins to encourage the readers in the final section of the letter (so Davids, Frankemölle, Martin, who consider 5:7-20 to be the conclusion of the epistle). Most likely, this provides a transition paragraph connecting what precedes to what follows (Johnson, Moo) and draws several motifs together. Johnson (1995:312) notes two themes: (1) 4:13–5:6 describes the negative side of the reversal asserted in 1:9-11, while 4:7-11 presents the positive side, the blessing on those who endure (cf. 1:12); (2) God's judgment, stated in 1:12; 2:12; 3:1; 4:12, comes to the fore "in terms of a vivid expectation of the *parousia* of the Lord" (Johnson 1995:312).

There is an A-B-A pattern in this paragraph: (A) a call for patient waiting in light of the Lord's return, following the example of the farmer (5:7-8); (B) an exhortation to avoid dissension in light of the coming of the Judge (5:9); and (A) a call for patient endurance in suffering, following the examples of the prophets and Job (5:10-11). Moo (2000:223) finds a close affinity between the themes here and Psalm 37, where the righteous "poor and the oppressed" (Ps 37:14) are encouraged in light of their persecution by the wicked (Ps 37:12-15, 32-33). Though tempted to be envious (5:1, 7), the believers are told to be patient (5:7) and refrain from anger (5:8), for the Lord would vindicate them.

The postpositive *oun* [TG3767, ZG4036] (therefore) of verse 7 links the command for patience with the denunciation of the wicked oppression of "innocent people" in 5:6. Since the believers know that God will justly vindicate them and condemn the landowners who have misused them, they can persevere in the midst of the current situation and wait for God to act. The verb itself (*makrothumeō* [TG3114, ZG3428]) occurs three times in 5:7-8 and once more in noun form in 5:10; it means both "patience" and "waiting." The primary nuance means to bear up under hard times and wait for God to act. There is a passive (waiting) and an active (trusting) sense, with the verb here emphasizing an active "forbearance" or bearing up under pressure. They should not take the law into their own hands and exact vengeance on the wealthy; instead, they should leave the "payback" with God, knowing that their future victory is certain. The latter is indicated in the added "wait for the Lord's return." The Greek term *parousia* [TG3952, ZG4242] was originally used for the "arrival" of a king or high official, but in the New Testament it became a technical word for the second "coming" or "arrival" of Christ, used this way in Matthew 24:3, 27, 37, 39; 1 Corinthians 15:23; 1 Thessalonians 2:19; 3:13; 4:15; 5:23; 2 Thessalonians 2:1; 2 Peter 1:16; 3:4, 12; 1 John 2:28. In this context "Lord" most likely refers to Christ, the one returning at the eschaton. Here it especially speaks of Jesus' "coming" as judge of the wicked (so Davids, Johnson, Laws) and vindicator of the righteous.

For an analogy of waiting, James turns to the farmer. "Consider" is *idou* [TG2400, ZG2627] ("behold, look," used this way in 3:4-5), calling for careful consideration. The "farmer" was one of the major occupations in Palestine. He is a perfect example here, because once he plants the seeds, virtually all the farmer can do is "wait" for nature to do its job (cf. 2 Tim 2:6). The harvest (*karpos* [TG2590, ZG2843]; "fruit") is "valuable" or "precious" (*timios* [TG5093, ZG5508]) especially to the farmer because it is his livelihood and it is a deciding factor in the ongoing life of his family. Johnson (1995:314) says this is "the only time in the biblical literature that something so lowly as produce is given a designation usually associated with jewels and crowns." James likely intended readers to see in it the "precious" nature of their future vindication and reward at the *parousia*.

The Palestinian farmer was especially dependent on "the rains in the fall and in the spring." These were the "early and late rains" mentioned several times in the Old Testament (Deut 11:14; Jer 5:24; Hos 6:3; Joel 2:23; Zech 10:1), those in October/November at the planting time and in March/April at the harvest time. Rain also fell in between, but these were the critical times. Throughout the Old Testament these rains are mentioned as affirming the faithfulness of Yahweh to his people (so Moo 2000:223), and that is the stress here as well. The point is critical: Like the farmer, we cannot control the movements of history; but we know that God does, and we can place our trust entirely in him. Baker and Carrier (1990:102-103) point out that "we live in a society that does not know very much about patience," one in which "we Americans expect quick service, and we do not like to wait. . . . But when we are put into situations where we have to wait . . . we can become easily distraught." That is true of us spiritually as well; when God does not answer our prayers immediately, we wonder if he has forgotten us. James reminds us that God's providential care comes in his time, not ours. He will vindicate us, but we must await his response and be patient for Christ to return.

In 5:8 James repeats his point for emphasis. As in the case of the farmer, God is calling us to patient waiting. But the point here is not passive but active. In this waiting there is no room for despair but rather for "courage," which translates the Greek verb *stērizō* [TG4741, ZG5114], meaning "stand firm" or "strengthen your hearts." The verb basically means to "establish" or "fix firmly in place" (e.g., an established city). So it speaks of a "strong" person in terms of one who is "resolute," set on a fixed path or firmly committed to a goal (BDAG 945). The "courage" or "strength of heart" stems from a life firmly committed to God and set on the path God has established. Waiting on the Lord in this sense becomes the natural thing to do. In Romans 1:11 Paul tells the Romans he wants to come and "bring you some spiritual gift" that will help them "grow strong" in the Lord, and in 1 Peter 5:10 Peter tells his readers that after they have "suffered a little while," God will "restore, support, and *strengthen*" them (my italics; see also Luke 22:32; Rom 16:25; 1 Thess 3:2; 2 Thess 2:17; 3:3). So here James asks believers to find an inner strength and take a firm stance for God in the midst of their difficulties. While the wealthy turn to their riches and hedonistic pleasures, believers will find the courage to turn to God and wait for him to act.

The other element that 5:8 adds to 5:7 is the reason (*hoti* [TG3754, ZG4022], "because") for the patience: the nearness of the Lord's return. This verb (*engizō* [TG1448, ZG1581]) was used in Jesus' summary of his kingdom proclamation in Mark 1:14-15, "The Kingdom of God is near," and the imminence of the *parousia* is mentioned often in the Gospels (Matt 3:2; 4:17; 10:7; 24:32-33; Luke 10:9, 11), Paul's writings (Rom 13:12; 1 Cor 16:22), Hebrews (Heb 10:25, 37), Peter (1 Pet 4:7), and Revelation (Rev 1:3; 3:11; 22:7, 12, 20). This has caused great controversy, for some critical scholars say Jesus and the New Testament writers expected the return in their lifetime and therefore were wrong. But this, while certainly a consideration, is not a necessary conclusion.

The answer normally given to this criticism comes from 2 Peter 3:8 (a thousand years is like a day) and 2 Peter 3:9 (God "does not want anyone to be destroyed, but wants everyone to repent"). Jesus did not truly believe he would return in a short time: His kingdom parables (e.g., Matt 24:36–25:30) looked to a lengthy period before his *parousia*, as did his great commissions (Matt 28:18-20; John 20:21-23; Acts 1:8). Moo (2000:234) puts it this way: "What is crucial is to understand this 'nearness' in the appropriate temporal framework: salvation-history. . . . This final age of salvation will find its climax in the return of Christ in glory. But—and this is the crucial point—the length of this age is unknown. Not even Jesus knew how long the 'last' days would last (cf. Mark 13:32)." The New Testament stresses imminence as the biblical demand to be ready at all times, to live our lives with the expectation of his soon return. There is also an inaugurated aspect, for the emphasis is that the process has begun. The result of Christ's first coming is that we are living in the last days, experiencing the tension between the "already" and the "not yet." Christ can return at any time, and when he does, we will be held accountable for how we have lived. This is the thrust of the New Testament.

Many have thought that 5:9 does not fit into this context, for it moves from the nearness of Christ's return to a prohibition against grumbling. Yet this is completely in keeping with the tenor of this epistle, with its continual concern for the practical issues involved and especially for the misuse of speech as condemned in 3:11–4:12. So James applies that problem to this situation, in which hard times and the pressure it produces lead to dissension. The stress of the work situation described in 5:1-6 and the inability of the Christians to greet it with patient endurance had led to the people venting their frustration by "grumbling" against each other. The verb *stenazō* [TG4727, ZG5100] basically means to "groan" and often is used of "complaining" or "expressing discontent" (BDAG 942), in this case Christians turning on one another. While groaning and moaning are an understandable response to painful experiences, the problem was that the believers were attacking each other (Davids 1982:184; note the preposition *kata* [TG2596, ZG2848], meaning "against"). "Perhaps they project their frustrations at the landlords on each other. Or perhaps they disagree on how they ought to deal with the oppression, and the different factions complain about each other in their anger. Maybe they are blaming one another for the problems they are facing as a congregation, or maybe they are accusing each other to avoid problems themselves" (Blomberg and Kamell 2008:228).

The warning "or you will be judged" shows that these complaints, as in 2:4 and 4:11-12, are a form of judging. Those doing so violate Matthew 7:1: "Do not judge others, and you will not be judged." As so often in James, the way we treat others is the way God will treat us (see on 2:13). If we set ourselves as judges of those around us and make bitter complaints against them, we must expect that we will face the same kind of judgment against ourselves, but this time from God. This danger becomes all the more intense with the added "the Judge is standing at the door." As in 5:2-3, *hestēken* [TG2476, ZG2705] is a stative perfect, emphasizing the continual nature of Jesus "standing" in readiness to judge (on Jesus as Judge, see note on 5:9). The image of Jesus "at the gate/door" continues the stress on imminence from 5:8 and is found also (so Johnson 1995:317) in Matthew 24:33 ("his return is very near, right at the door"). Those with critical spirits in the church will face a stern Judge, both now (in terms of divine displeasure) and at the final judgment. We must remember that God and Christ will not only judge the unsaved (5:3-5) but the saved as well (5:9). All will stand before God and give account for their lives (1 Cor 3:14-15; 2 Tim 2:15; Heb 13:17; 2 John 8; Rev 22:12; so also Davids, Moo).

The next two verses (5:10-11) return to the issue behind 5:7-8 and give two illustrations or models (the term means "pattern, model") of patient endurance from the Old Testament. This is a succinct parallel to the more extensive "roll call of heroes" in Hebrews 11, which presents a series of examples from the lives of Old Testament figures (as well as the martyrs of 2 Maccabees 6:28, 31) who exemplified endurance. The prophets as examples are especially emphasized in Hebrews 11:33-38:

> *They shut the mouths of lions, quenched the flames of fire. . . . Women received their loved ones back again from death. But others were tortured, refusing to turn from God in order to be set free. . . . Some were jeered at, and their backs were cut open with whips. Others were chained in prisons. Some died by stoning, some were sawed in half, and others were killed with the sword. Some went about wearing skins of sheep and goats, destitute and oppressed and mistreated. They were too good for this world, wandering over deserts and mountains, hiding in caves and holes in the ground.*

The key to their victorious lives was their "patience in suffering" (5:10)—using the noun form of the verb used three times in 5:7-8 for bearing up under pressure. When we read above what God's prophets went through, we realize how our own so-called suffering is slight indeed. An active trust in God and a radical surrender of every aspect of our lives, including our difficulties and hardships, are the only proper response to what Christ has done for us and in us.

Moreover, the prophets suffered especially because they "spoke in the name of the Lord." This is sometimes interpreted in terms of prophets who spoke out against injustice (for passages see note on 5:1, so Blomberg and Kamell 2008:229). While this would be included, it is not the main thrust here. They suffered in service to God, proclaiming the message he had given them. The message to James's readers is simple: No matter what the consequences, live for God and proclaim his word.

Often, the opposition will be severe (as in the list of Paul's experiences in 2 Cor 11:23-29). Often, in fact, the rejection will come from believers and not just unbelievers (again, with Paul's experience as the primary example; cf. 1 Cor 1–4; 2 Cor 11; Gal 3:1-6; Phil 1:15-17). God does not call us to a simple life of ease but to a good life of service. Kistemaker (1986:168) says, "Think of the persecution Elijah endured from King Ahab, the hardship Jeremiah suffered at the hands of the kings of Judah, and the perseverance Daniel displayed when he was put in the lion's den. . . . When they [James's readers] imitate the prophets, they will have to endure insult and persecution, and run the risk of losing their lives. Nevertheless, they ought to count themselves among those who are called blessed."

In the final verse of this section (5:11) James reflects the eighth beatitude, "God blesses those who are persecuted for doing right" (Matt 5:10). The NLT's rendering "we give great honor" is literally "we call blessed" (*makarizō* [TG3106, ZG3420]), meaning that we consider those who endure to be under the special blessing of God, not just that we bless them ourselves. Also, this does not mean that people who endure are "happy" or "fortunate" (see on 1:12); rather, they find "joy" (1:2) because God's blessing is upon them. This restates 1:12, "God blesses those who patiently endure testing and temptation. Afterward they will receive the crown of life that God has promised to those who love him." There the actual form that the eschatological blessing will take is stated directly: the crown of life. Here it is more general: all the blessings God will pour out on the faithful.

The second model for endurance in the midst of suffering—Job—makes sense on the surface, because Job is the paradigm of the suffering saint. But when considered more closely, Job does not seem to be an example of "patience," for he frequently, even bitterly, complained, asking God why these things had taken place (Job 7:11-21; 10:18-22; 13:20-27; 23:2-7; 30:20-23). Many think (Davids, Johnson, Martin, Moo) that James was either acquainted with the *Testament of Job* (that may have been written near the same time as James) or the tradition behind it, for that work also extols Job's patient endurance (Job 1:5; 25:4-5; 27:6-7; see Gray 2004, for the view that these are thematic parallels rather than literary dependence). This is a very real possibility, but we also must remember that in the canonical book of Job the hero never denounced either God or his faith but remained faithful to his hope. In Job 42:2, Job admits, "I know that you can do anything, and no one can stop you." Then in Job 42:7 God commends Job for "[speaking] accurately." Therefore, James could validly make the same conclusion as the author of the *Testament of Job*—that Job was a worthy example of endurance.

It is interesting that James mentions both hearing and seeing in reference to Job—"you heard" (NLT "know") of his patience, and "you saw" the results. He wanted the reader to take the example of Job seriously. In the second instance, James states, "You can see how the Lord was kind to him at the end." In the epilogue of Job (Job 42:7-17), Job received twice as much as he had before, and he learned the lesson to trust God through all his misfortune and difficulties (see note on 5:11). The lesson for us is the truth of Romans 8:26-28. When we face our trials, we don't know how we should pray (Rom 8:26a) and can only face the painful situation with patient endurance (5:7-8, 10-11). But we do know three things: The Spirit is groaning for us more deeply than we are (Rom 8:26b), he is interceding for us and knows the mind of God (Rom 8:27), and for that reason God will cause "everything to work together for [our] good" (Rom 8:28). What Job learned and what we learn from all the troubles of life is that "the Lord is full of tenderness and mercy." At the time this often does not seem to be so, for all trials "seem painful rather than pleasant" (Heb 12:11a, ESV) when they take place, but when their "end" or "goal" has been realized and the "peaceful harvest of right living" (Heb 12:11, NLT) has been attained, then we can understand the goodness of God in our lives, as we have become "perfect and complete, needing nothing" (1:4). Of course, this does not mean that God has granted our every request and given us the material prosperity or physical healing that we desire. Still, when God tells us to wait or says no to us, that is what is best for us and is part of God's "tenderness and mercy" to us. In the end we realize that in every way "God's will" is "good and pleasing and perfect" (Rom 12:2).

◆ VI. Final Exhortations (5:12-20)
A. Avoidance of Oaths (5:12)

12 But most of all, my brothers and sisters, never take an oath, by heaven or earth or anything else. Just say a simple yes or no, so that you will not sin and be condemned.

NOTES

5:12 Scholars are divided as to whether 5:12 goes with 5:7-11 (Adamson, Blomberg and Kamell, Hiebert, Reicke, Tasker), with 5:13-20 (as part of the closing exhortations, so Davids, Johnson, Laws, Martin, Moo), or simply by itself as an isolated saying (Dibelius, Mayor, McCartney). The second option is probably best. This prohibition of oath-taking continues the emphasis on misuse of speech in 3:1–4:12; 5:9, though at first glance it seems unrelated to its context. Johnson (1995:326) thinks it functions as a transition to the final section, arguing that 5:12-20 is "far from a disjointed series of exhortations. Rather, it is a unified discourse on the positive modes of speech in the community. The topic is speech: how can the tongue be used not for the destruction of humans, but for the building up of a community of solidarity?" As such, 5:12a is part of the series of negative commands (with 4:11; 5:9) on how the tongue should not be used in the community. At the same time, 5:12b is positive and begins the three positive exhortations of 5:12, 13-18, 19-20. As a transition, it is best to place it by itself as a section of the admonitions in 4:13–5:18 and as a beginning of the three-part concluding admonitions (5:12-20); it relates both to what precedes and to what follows.

COMMENTARY

The prohibition begins strangely with "but most of all." Does this mean that the avoidance of oaths is more important than the previous commands of the epistle or the specific admonition to patience in 5:7-11 (so Adamson, Reicke, Ropes)? Thus, some scholars (e.g., Davids, Martin) think it is a literary marker and functions like "finally" in Paul (2 Cor 13:11; Phil 4:8; 1 Thess 4:1) to introduce the conclusion of the letter. I agree with those scholars (Johnson, Moo) who see it functioning in both ways, highlighting the importance of integrity of speech and at the same time providing a transition to the community emphasis in the rest of the letter. The prohibition itself ("Never take an oath, by heaven or earth or anything else") echoes

Jesus' command in Matthew 5:33-37, where Jesus explicitly mentions oaths by heaven, by earth, by Jerusalem, and by one's head. This became the basis for similar prohibitions in the early church (2 Cor 1:17-18 and here; see Wenham 1986). There too the emphasis was on honesty and integrity of speech. The Old Testament has several passages on the taking of oaths (Exod 20:7; Lev 19:12; Num 30:2; Deut 23:21-23). The purpose of vows in the Old Testament was to anchor the truthfulness of a statement, and God in both testaments makes oaths to guarantee his future action (Num 14:23; Deut 1:34; Ps 95:11; Heb 3:11; 4:3; 6:13; 7:20-22, 28). The Old Testament did not prohibit oaths but rather demanded integrity in keeping those oaths. To break an oath was to profane the name of God (Lev 19:12), to "involve God in falsehood" (Baker and Carrier 1990:105). However, in Jesus' (and James's) time, oath-taking had become far too frequent and frivolous, and people often had little intention of fulfilling those promises.

In contrast with those who made lofty, insincere vows, Jesus (Matt 5:33-37) and James commanded that "a simple yes or no" was more than sufficient. Clearly the emphasis is on personal integrity and trustworthiness. God's people should stand by their word and not require an artificial oath to anchor the dependability of their promises. In this context, it is possible that James also has in mind the use of oaths by the poor to obtain credit or to settle debts (Baker and Carrier, Blomberg and Kamell). This would be a misuse of vows, especially when the person used them to replace money they did not have. The question is whether Jesus and James mean to prohibit vows of any kind (e.g., in a law court), as many Anabaptists interpret this. Paul did not think so, for he swears an oath on several occasions (Rom 1:9; 2 Cor 1:23; Gal 1:20; Phil 1:8). So these passages do not prohibit oaths of any kind, just the shallow use of them to ensure people's trust in the promises. Everything we say must have as its purpose the glory of God, and as before (2:12; 4:11-12; 5:9) false speech will cause us to "sin and be condemned." If we truly belong to God, we can stand on our own authority under him and do not need artificial vows to provide a veneer of trustworthiness. Stulac (1993:178) provides a good conclusion: "Do not try to impress each other or to manipulate God as if your works were what counted instead of God's grace. If you are trusting in God's grace, you have no need to impress God or people, and you can be at peace with saying honest words. Integrity should characterize Christians, and integrity will flow from wholehearted reliance on grace."

◆ B. Promise to the Ill—Healing through Prayer (5:13-18)

13Are any of you suffering hardships? You should pray. Are any of you happy? You should sing praises. 14Are any of you sick? You should call for the elders of the church to come and pray over you, anointing you with oil in the name of the Lord. 15Such a prayer offered in faith will heal the sick, and the Lord will make you well. And if you have committed any sins, you will be forgiven.

16Confess your sins to each other and pray for each other so that you may be healed. The earnest prayer of a righteous person has great power and produces wonderful results. 17Elijah was as human as we are, and yet when he prayed earnestly that no rain would fall, none fell for three and a half years! 18Then, when he prayed again, the sky sent down rain and the earth began to yield its crops.

NOTES

5:14 ***Are any of you sick?*** Moo (2000:236) notes several scholars (Armerding, Hayden, Pickar) who believe the "sick" here are spiritually rather than physically "weak." The elders then pray for the person so they can be "saved" or restored to the Lord, and the person is "healed" spiritually. While this is viable, it is not nearly as likely as physical illness, which fits the context much better. I will argue below that both aspects are in mind in the passage as a whole.

5:16 ***Confess your sins to each other.*** Motyer (1985:201-2) narrows this confession only to the one you have offended (cf. Matt 5:23-26) and states that it does not mean "affirm to each other that you are sinners." Yet this is neither likely nor necessary, since confession does mean a general affirmation of sinful actions, and the whole context is "to each other." The thrust is that we need to be involved in one another's spiritual lives, and that includes acknowledgment of sins.

has great power and produces wonderful results. Lit., "has great power, working," with *energoumenē* [TG1754, ZG1919] either temporal ("when it is at work," so Blomberg and Kamell, Hiebert, Ropes) or adjectival ("effective prayer," so Dibelius, Laws), and it can also be either passive ("made effective by God/the Spirit," so Davids, Mayor) or middle ("as it is at work," so Adamson, Martin, Moo; McCartney 2009:250, "is very powerful and effective"). The NLT catches it well, for the middle force still conveys God's power at work, as it may be best to see it as a circumstantial participle that becomes another main clause: "and produces wonderful results."

COMMENTARY

This paragraph exhibits features that often were found in the final sections of letters. Hellenistic letters frequently concluded with a wish for good health, and New Testament epistles often finished with an exhortation to prayer (Rom 15:30-32; Eph 6:18-20; Phil 4:6; Col 4:2-4; 1 Thess 5:17, 25; 2 Thess 3:1-2; Heb 13:18-19). These two elements are combined here (Moo 2000:34). In 5:12 the speech-problem is oath-taking; in 5:13 the speech-answer is praying. Prayer is the central theme of the passage. We rely on God rather than ourselves and surrender every situation (including ourselves) to him. The progression of the prayer is first hierarchical (centering on the leaders, 5:14), then corporate (5:14-15), then individual (5:16-18).

In this paragraph there are four points: (1) the general need for prayer and praise (5:13); (2) the response to illness with prayer and anointing with oil (5:14-15a); (3) the response to sin with confession (5:15b-16a); and (4) the power of righteous prayer to make a difference, using the model of Elijah (5:16b-18). James begins with a general introduction to the topic that centers on the two extreme situations in the church (note the central *en humin* [TG1722, ZG1877], "among you"; NLT, "of you"): suffering and happiness. These two function as a summary of the situation of the readers. Motyer (1985:187) summarizes the situation well:

> *Here, then, in two words are all life's experiences, and each of them in turn can so easily be the occasion of spiritual upset. Trouble can give rise to an attitude of surly rebellion against God and the abandonment of spiritual practices. Equally, times of ease and affluence beget complacency, laziness and the assumption that we are able of ourselves to cope with life, and God is forgotten. James is fully aware of this, for the persistence, throughout his letter, of the themes of trial, alongside warnings against allowing the heart to stray after riches, indicate his acquaintance with the full run of life, and his concern to armour us against its varied assaults.*

Some of the believers were going through various kinds of trials (1:2) and were "suffering." James used the verb *kakopatheō* [TG2553, ZG2802] (5:13), the verb cognate of the noun used for the "suffering" of the prophets in 5:10. In the passive sense it means "bearing misfortune" or "misery" and "in the active meaning . . . a *strenuous effort* that one makes, or *perseverance* that one practices" (BDAG 500). So this refers to both the experience of difficulties and the active endurance that results. In such occasions the proper response is to "pray" (*proseuchomai* [TG4336, ZG4667])—the basic term for prayer in the New Testament (used 85 times). This speaks of prayer in its broadest perspective, both leaving the situation in God's hands (petitionary prayer) and seeking the Lord in time of trouble (worshipful prayer). "Presumably, then, the prayer that he encourages here is for the spiritual strength to endure the trial with a godly spirit" (Moo 2000:235). Most likely the prayer here is corporate as well as individual (as indicated by "among you"; see Blomberg and Kamell 2008:242).

Other believers were doing very well and were "happy" (*euthumeō* [TG2114, ZG2313]), a verb that refers to a cheerfulness of heart, an inward joy that transcends circumstances; it is used in Acts 27:22, 25, 36 of "tak[ing] courage" during the storm that threatened to swamp the ship Paul was on. In chapter 5 it connotes a good situation, perhaps good health in light of 5:14 (Johnson 1995:329 translates it, "feeling good"). When things are going well, James commands, God's people should "sing praises"—with *psalletō* [TG5567, ZG6010] meaning literally "sing psalms." It was always used in the New Testament of singing praise to God (Rom 15:9; 1 Cor 14:15; Eph 5:19). In times of prosperity it is critical not to become complacent and self-centered like the church at Laodicea. In Revelation 3:17-18 they said, "I am rich. I have everything I want. I don't need a thing!" Christ retorted that in actuality they were "wretched and miserable and poor and blind and naked." It is easy for us to fall into the same trap in times of plenty, like the merchants of 4:13-16. We must continually (present-tense verbs) remind ourselves that everything good that is happening comes as a gift from God (1:17), and thus we will continue praising God for the good things he brings our way, trusting in him rather than ourselves for the future.

A third situation is enumerated in 5:14, forming an A-B-A pattern with the previous two: trial—doing well—trial. The first situation pertained to general "suffering," 5:14 with a specific type of suffering: sickness. The verb, *astheneō* [TG770, ZG820], and its cognates refer to "weakness" of many kinds—weak faith (Rom 4:19; 8:26), weak human nature (Rom 5:6; 6:19; 8:3), timidity (1 Cor 2:3), weak conscience (1 Cor 8:11-12), weak appearance (2 Cor 10:10). But it most frequently designates illness (Matt 8:17; 10:8; Mark 6:56; Luke 4:40; 5:15; 8:2; 10:9; 13:11-12; Gal 4:13; 1 Tim 5:23; 2 Tim 4:20), and that is most certainly the case here (see Davids 1982:192). The illness described seems fairly severe, for the person seems helpless and bedridden, being described in 5:15 as being "worn out" or "exhausted" (*kamnō* [TG2577, ZG2827]). Thus, the elders do all the praying "over" the sick person, having "faith" in his or her healing (Blomberg and Kamell 2008:242, from Mayor 1913:193-194). Thus, a small cold or flu does not need to be prayed for by the elders, just the more serious illnesses. In this section, a holistic understanding of illness in the community is expressed; it seems clear that the physical, the social (community), and the spiritual sides are integrated, with prayer the integrating power behind both aspects of healing (see Albl 2002).

The "elders" originally were heads of families and clans who led the people in their daily life (Exod 3:16, 18; 18:12; Num 11:16-17). In the Judaism of Jesus' day, a council of seven elders directed civic life, and the three "rulers" over the synagogues were usually chosen from among them, so they directed the civil and religious affairs of the community. They were also an important group in the Sanhedrin or ruling council in Jerusalem (Matt 16:21; 26:3, 57, 59). As the early church followed the synagogue style in worship, they also followed it in leadership, calling the heads of the house churches "elders." In Acts they led the church (Acts 11:30; 14:23; 15:2, 6; 16:4; 20:17; 21:18), and in Acts 20:17, 28 and in the Pastorals the three metaphors of elder, pastor, and overseer are one and the same office. So the "elders of the church" here refers to those with pastoral oversight in the congregations, present as the guardians of the flock. It is not that these elders had more prayer power than others, but rather that they had spiritual authority in the lives of the members of the flock and were known for their piety. It is natural to call upon the mature spiritual leaders in times of distress, and their intercession would constitute the "earnest prayer of a righteous person" in this situation (5:16). Note that the elders were praying "over" (*epi* [TG1909, ZG2093]) the person, the only place in the New Testament it is stated this way. This could hardly be a type of "exorcism" (so Dibelius 1975:252). Though the expression could be a type of a "gift of healing" (Moo 2000:237), that does not seem too likely here, for there are no real contextual hints in that direction. Perhaps it is best to see this simply as emphasizing the invocation of power "over" the situation "in the name of the Lord" (Johnson 1995:332), perhaps also indicating that the person was bedridden, so the elders stood "over" him or her.

As they prayed, they would also "anoint" the sick person "with oil in the name of the Lord" (5:14). The picture is that as they prayed, they were anointing the person (some mistake the use of the aorist participle as temporal, "after anointing," but it is circumstantial, thus simultaneous, see Ropes 1916:305). The only other place such a practice is mentioned is Mark 6:13 at the close of the mission of the Twelve (Mark 6:7-13), when they "healed many sick people, anointing them with olive oil." In the Old Testament oil was used medicinally (Isa 1:6; Jer 8:22; 51:8) and also to anoint kings and high priests (Exod 28:41; Lev 10:7; 1 Sam 16:13). It could also be used to refresh oneself (Eccl 9:8; Matt 6:17; Luke 7:46), perhaps looking to the anointing as a symbolic anticipation that God in his own time will indeed restore the person to health and well-being. In the Greco-Roman world, as well as in Judaism, it was used medicinally (*Testament of Solomon* 18:34; *2 Enoch* 22:8-9), and so it is often thought the disciples in Mark 6:13 were also using it as a healing balm. Jesus never used it so far as we know and mentioned it only with respect to his own anointing by the Spirit (Luke 4:18, from Isa 61:1) and in the parable of the Good Samaritan, where oil and wine were put on the wounds of the hurt man (Luke 10:34). In the New Testament anointing is mentioned with respect to the anointing of Jesus (Acts 4:27; 10:38; Heb 1:9) and of the believer (2 Cor 1:21). These symbolic anointings show God's special blessing, power, and status placed upon the person.

There are three main possibilities for the meaning of this anointing: (1) It might be *medicinal* (so Hayden, Mayor, Mitton, Robertson, Ross), for that is the primary way anointing with oil was used in Judaism, the Greco-Roman world, and even in the church. Thus, this would refer to the double duty of prayer mixed with medicine, and the elders functioned as both priest and doctor, working at the levels of cultic ritual and physical healing at the same time. However, the fact that only the elders were present and that they administered the oil "in the name of the Lord" argues against a medicinal understanding. This seems mainly spiritual in nature. (2) The *sacramental* interpretation arose in the early church in a practice called the *Euchelaion* (oil for prayer), and this led to the later priestly practice of extreme unction (originating in AD 852 and called "the anointing of the sick" from this James passage) to remove the presence of sin and prepare the dying person to meet God (see discussion in Moo 2000:239). Certainly, the anointing here does not have this much significance, but there could be sacramental effect in bringing the presence and power of God into the situation. (3) Most commentators today see this as a *symbolic* anointing with oil in which the sick person is consecrated and set apart to God (like priests and kings in the OT). In this way the anointing and prayer for God's presence are mediated or channeled to the ill person's life in a deeper way, and the compassionate, healing Father in all his *khesed* [TH2617, ZH2876] (loving-kindness) and *'emeth* [TH571, ZH622] (faithfulness) is seen at work at a deeper level.

This prayer and anointing are done by the elders "in the name of the Lord," meaning that God is behind the entire situation and guiding the process. The power of "the name" is especially emphasized in Acts 3–4, where Peter tells the crippled beggar, "In the name of Jesus Christ the Nazarene, get up and walk" (Acts 3:6) and then tells the crowd in the Temple, "Through faith in the name of Jesus, this man was healed" (Acts 3:16). Next he tells the Sanhedrin, "He was healed by the powerful name of Jesus Christ the Nazarene" (Acts 4:10). Clearly there is power in "the name," but this is not magic. The prayer and anointing bring the presence of "the name of God" into the situation of illness. The efficacy of this will be discussed in the next paragraph. The other question is how mandatory this practice should be. The fact that it is discussed only here in the Epistles must mean that it is not required. However, the fact that Jesus' disciples (Mark 6:13) as well as the church elders here did practice it on occasion means that it is a good thing to do. In terms of the details in 5:13-15, there is no indication it should be done in any and every situation of illness, such as the common cold or flu. But on serious occasions where the person is quite ill, it would be highly recommended. I would add fasting on the part of the elders as well. All three—prayer, fasting, anointing with oil—call the people of God into ever more serious reliance on God and his loving, healing presence in the person's life. All are valuable, even essential, tools of spiritual surrender of the community to the will of God.

Then James gives a startling promise (5:15): "Such a prayer offered in faith will heal the sick, and the Lord will make you well" (lit., "raise you up"). James used *sōzō* (save) here for "heal," a word often used in situations where the healed person was touched spiritually as well as physically (Matt 9:21-22; Mark 5:28, 34; 10:52). The major thrust here is physical healing, but still the presence of "in faith" as in Mark 10:52 brings in the spiritual side. When James adds that the sick person will be "raised up," he undoubtedly means to be "raised" from the sickbed (Davids 1982:194: "Standing up or rolling up one's bed was the natural consequence of healing"). This calls for a new boldness in prayer, an expectation that God's healing presence will be experienced in a new way. This was more natural in the first century, when people had a far greater awareness of the spiritual realm and the power of God at work in their lives. In our more materialistic age we must constantly challenge one another to greater faith and dependence on God. There should be a deeper level of anticipation of God at work in the midst of our prayers.

But does this expectation become a virtual demand, a certainty that God must and will heal due to the "prayer of faith," as many "prosperity" preachers say? We must answer with Paul in Romans 3:4, 6, 31; 6:2, 15: "Of course not!" or "God forbid!" Such a teaching is exceedingly dangerous, even heretical, for it means we control God. Here we are at the heart of the power of prayer to change things. Does prayer (and anointing with oil) make a difference? Is more of God's presence channeled into a situation through prayer (or fasting or anointing)? I believe the answer is yes, but there is mystery attached. Prayer does not guarantee that God will say yes, for he is sovereign over our lives; we are not sovereign over him! Martin (1988:208) says it best: "As we shall see, 5:15 shows that the uttering of a prayer for healing does not automatically ensure that the sick will recover. The reason why some people recover and others do not remains a mystery to faith, since the New Testament contains accounts of both recovery (in the Gospels and Acts) and non-recovery (1 Cor 11:30; 2 Cor 12:1-10; 2 Tim 4:20) and one illustration (Phil 2:25-30) of recovery without any procedure remotely resembling this Jacobean text."

Do prayer and anointing make a difference—do things happen that would not if God's people were not at prayer? I believe they do, but God is still sovereign and can say no if he so wills. That is where the mystery lies. Romans 8:26 admits, "We don't know what God wants us to pray for"—that is, what God's will is in a specific instance. But the Holy Spirit knows and intercedes for us with "groanings" deeper than ours. The Spirit's intercession guarantees that "everything" will "work together for the good" (8:28), but in each instance the best for us may lead God to say "wait" or even to say "no" to our request. Yet that "no" is a healing response on God's part, and we need the faith to accept that. God is responding and does bring his healing presence to bear on us as a result of the prayers of the faithful, and the result is always what is the very best for us.

The spiritual side of the equation is stated in the second half of 5:15: "If you have committed any sins, you will be forgiven." As before, this forgiveness is not automatic, but it does mean that God heals spiritually as well as physically (contra Moo 2000:242-246, who takes it only of physical healing). It is common to interpret this of instances where the illness is the result of past sin (as in Mark 2:11-12; 1 Cor 11:27-30; so Blomberg and Kamell, Hiebert, Johnson, Stulac). To be sure, this link is denied in John 9:1-3; 11:4; 2 Corinthians 12:8-10, but "if . . . any sins" leaves the possibility open in particular instances. Most likely James has both ideas in mind—those sins that led to the illness as God's judgment, as well as sin in the person's life in general. As in Jesus' healing miracles, God comes upon the person both physically and spiritually, and those healed will often get right with God and experience forgiveness of sin through the experience. "The statement is simple and straightforward: two promises, one for the body (the obvious, pressing need), the other for the soul. The person will be healed totally" (Davids 1982:195).

The corporate side continues in 5:16, where the churches that desire to experience God's healing presence must be communities that "confess your sins to each other." Once more, the question is whether this is entirely related to illness that is the result of sin in one's life. In light of the added, "and pray for each other so that you may be healed," that certainly is a major aspect of the verse. The verb for "heal" is *iaomai* [TG2390, ZG2615], a term that nearly always refers to physical healing (e.g., Matt 8:8; 15:28; Luke 6:18; John 4:47; 5:13; Acts 9:34; 10:38), so this implies that the spiritual state of the entire congregation is a factor in the healing presence of God. When there is serious sin in the life of the individual (5:15) or the congregation (5:16), the prayers are hindered (cf. 1 Pet 3:7b).

Two aspects of community spirituality are highlighted: confession of sins and prayer. "Confession" means to "accept, consent, or agree with" something and in a context like this means "to make an admission of wrong-doing" (BDAG 351). In Scripture confession is normally made to God (Matt 3:6; Acts 19:18; 1 John 1:9) but here it is made "to each other," connoting the mutual involvement of Christians in the spiritual growth of each other. This is the purpose of Galatians 6:1 (restore the sinner) and Hebrews 3:13 (admonish the sinner), in which the strong in the congregation strengthen the weak (Heb 12:12-13). None of us can defeat sin by ourselves; we need the help of each other to do so. When we are struggling with sin, we must "confess" it to others in the church and build on their strength in overcoming it. The same is the case with "pray for each other," meaning that mutual confession and prayer are essential to a congregation's spiritual health and that this has a bearing on the physical health of its members. Martin (1988:211) states that the text "widens" the perspective from the elders to all the members, so as "to make prayer and confession and so pastoral responsibility the 'privilege and responsibility' of all in the congregation." The purpose of the church is to establish a community and a family who will care and share in each other's lives and thereby ensure the spiritual health and power of all in the group. Such will make a difference in matters of healing.

James restates the true power of prayer in 5:16b: "The earnest prayer of a righteous person has great power and produces wonderful results." James uses three different words for prayer—*proseuchē* [TG4335, ZG4666] in 5:13-14, 17-18; *euchē* [TG2171, ZG2376] in 5:15; and *deēsis* [TG1162, ZG1255] in 5:16. These are fairly synonymous (the latter two emphasize the petition or intercession), so James was stressing the richness of the kind of prayer that places our needs in the hands of God. The "righteous person" is in one sense every believer (cf. the "righteous/innocent people" of 5:6), but in the context of 5:15-16 (and indeed all of James) it also emphasizes a person who has received forgiveness for sins (not just at conversion but on an ongoing basis) and is living "rightly" before God, that is, in light of the ethical imperatives of this epistle. All believers have the right and ability to pray, but those who are deeply committed to Christ will certainly pray more and be more dependent on him; thus, their prayers are even more effective. The power of prayer to accomplish great things is very evident here. There are two aspects of effective prayer uttered from a "right" relationship with God: (1) It "has great power," connoting the ability of prayer to accomplish much; and (2) it "produces wonderful results," stressing the "effective" results as prayer "goes to work" on behalf of others. As stated above, prayer changes things as it channels the healing presence of God into situations of illness and other difficulties.

As his model of a "righteous person" whose prayers had great effects, James holds out Elijah (5:17). First, we are told that Elijah "was as human as we are." He was the great miracle worker among the prophets, yet he had similar human failures to ours. He could feel all alone even though there were at least a hundred prophets around (1 Kgs 18:13, 22); after defeating and destroying the 450 prophets of Baal, he could fear for his life and flee from Jezebel's mere threat (1 Kgs 19:2); and he could yield to depression (1 Kgs 19:3-4, 9-10). God does not demand perfection on our part, only trust. When Elijah "prayed earnestly" (lit., "praying, he prayed"), he established a paradigm for the fervent prayers of any of the believers.

The incident James describes is the three-and-one-half-year drought that God sent upon Palestine and the surrounding lands in 1 Kings 18 because of Ahab and the apostasy of the nation. There are two questions: (1) First Kings 17:1 does not say that Elijah prayed for the drought but rather that he gave a prophecy from God. However, 1 Kings 18:42 does say that he prayed for it to end, and so his prayer was still central to the absence of rain. Jewish writers considered him to be a man of prayer (*4 Ezra* 7:108; *b. Sanhedrin* 113a; see other citations in Martin 1988:213). (2) First Kings 18:1 says the events took place three years later rather than three and a half, but that was the beginning of the Mount Carmel incident, and we do not know how much time there was between that and the rainstorm of 1 Kings 18:45. It may be that the number stems from Jewish tradition, where it symbolizes a period of judgment (Dan 7:25; Rev 11:11; 12:14; so Dibelius, Martin, Moo). Some also think that the ill person is symbolized in the rain-parched land, and the healing in the coming of the rain (Davids, Martin, Moo), but that may be too allegorical.

Elijah's prayer for rain brought immediate results, so that "the earth began to yield its crops" (5:18). "Crops" is *karpos* [TG2590, ZG2843], alluding back to 5:7, where the farmer waits for "the rains" that cause the "harvest to ripen." Both may look back to the good gifts of 1:17 and to "the seeds of peace" and "harvest of righteousness" (also *karpos*) in 3:18. The point is that prayer works. When God's people quit depending on themselves and turn to God, things happen. As stated above, this does not mean that God always gives us whatever we request, but it does mean that he always does what is best for us.

◆ C. Concluding Challenge—Restoring the Wanderer (5:19-20)

19 My dear brothers and sisters, if someone among you wanders away from the truth and is brought back, 20 you can be sure that whoever brings the sinner back will save that person from death and bring about the forgiveness of many sins.

NOTES

5:20 ***save that person from death.*** The manuscript evidence offers three possible readings: "save a soul from death" (K L Ψ, seen in KJV, NKJV); "save his soul from death" (ℵ A P 33, seen in NRSV, ESV, NASB, TNIV, NET); or "save a soul from death itself" (𝔓74 B 614, not found in the English versions). As Metzger (1994:686) explains, the best reading is likely "save his soul," and scribes changed it to avoid the ambiguity of "his soul" (i.e., the soul of the converter or of the converted).

bring about the forgiveness of many sins. Several commentators (Adamson, Dibelius, Laws, Ropes) think the first clause ("save a soul from death") refers to the sinner brought back, but the second clause ("the forgiveness of many sins") refers to the one bringing them back, on the grounds that one rescued from death does not need an added forgiveness of sins. But that is surely false logic—the forgiveness explains the rescue from death. They are not chronological but supplemental to one another. The grammar of the verse favors the two referring to the same person, the one saved from eternal death (so Davids, Johnson, Martin, Mayor, Moo, McCartney). Blomberg and Kamell (2008:249) think both are affected spiritually, but that seems to read more into the verse than is warranted; there is no indication that the act results in the forgiveness of sins for the restorer (see Hiebert 1979:311). Certainly the person who restores a failing fellow Christian is blessed by God, but that does not seem to be indicated in the text here.

COMMENTARY

The absence of any closing greetings, so common in Greco-Roman and New Testament epistles, shows the serious nature of James's concluding warning that spiritual vigilance is needed in the light of ethical and moral failure. The admonition here in one sense is part of the corporate command in 5:16 that the members of the church should confess their sins and pray for one another. This mutual involvement in one another's struggle with sin is a restoration process, and that is the issue here. In another sense this is the concluding thought of the epistle and "gives what must have been the author's purpose in publishing the epistle, i.e., turning or preserving people from error (cf. the similarity in 1 John 5:21)" (Davids 1982:198). "If someone among you wanders away from the truth" is a condition of possibility (*ean* [TG1437, ZG1569]) and notes a dangerous potential caused by the many ethical sins described in the letter. Anyone (*tis* [TG5100, ZG5516]) in the congregation could fall prey to this spiritual tragedy. One question is the meaning of *planēthē* [TG4105A, ZG4414] (NLT, "wanders [away from the truth]"; cf. BDAG 821-822). This verb can have either a passive thrust (led away by someone) or a middle force ("wander" of one's own accord). While either is possible, "wander" sums up the ethical sins of the epistle (failure to live out what one hears, prejudice, faith without works, misuse of the tongue, jealousy, dissension, misuse of wealth) and so emphasizes one's own conduct. "The truth" is the gospel, so the danger is falling away from the Christian faith.

While some have taken this straying from one's walk with Christ as tantamount to backsliding (Blomberg and Kamell, Hiebert, Tasker), it seems clear that with the idea of "sav[ing] that person from death" in 5:20, this is much more severe and refers to apostasy from the Christian faith (so Davids, Martin, Moo). In this sense it is similar to Hebrews 6:4-6; 10:26-27; 2 Peter 2:20-21; and 1 John 5:16-17. It is true that the language here is not as strong as in these other passages, and that has led many to conclude that "wandering" is not an image of apostasy. Yet it is better to think of two types of apostasy, one active (Heb 6; 1 John 5) and the other passive (James 5:19-20). Active apostasy occurs when one deliberately rejects Christ "with a high hand" or "brazenly," and there is no atonement for such an act; it constitutes an unpardonable sin (Heb 6:4-6; 1 John 5:16). Passive apostasy as here occurs when sin crowds Christ out of one's life, and that type is redeemable. Such a one can be brought back to Christ (as here).

In such cases it is essential that believers get involved and bring the fallen back to Christ. The task of the church is the restoration or reclamation of the straying sinner to Christ. Ethical sin is the basic thrust of this letter, and it is now seen as a very serious issue, for when it takes over the life of the erring follower, it can remove a person from the "truth," the Christian faith. Thus, the confession and prayer of 5:16 are here identified as potentially saving the person from spiritual death.

In light of this, James specifies (5:20) the significance for the vigilant fellow believers. "You can be sure" is literally "let them know," and it is a present-tense verb that means "at all times know/be sure." The results of the restoration (if successful) will always take place in this way. While the NLT has simply "brings the sinner back," the Greek adds "from the error of his way," stressing the Christian life as a pilgrimage or journey, with the sinner in this instance straying off God's path. One is reminded of Christ's parable about the wide and narrow gate, where Jesus says, "The highway to hell is broad, and its gate is wide for the many who choose that way" (Matt 7:13). Every believer has choices to make as to what "way" or path they will choose for their life. Those on the narrow way to salvation must watch out for each other to make sure none are straying from the "way of God" and joining the unsaved on the broad way to destruction.

The results of a person's turning back to God are that a soul is "save[d] . . . from death" and a sinner experiences "the forgiveness of many sins." Some have thought of "death" here as similar to 1 Corinthians 11:29-30, where those who had partaken of the Lord's Supper "in an unworthy manner" (NKJV) had actually "died" (lit., "fallen asleep"). The death here would then be physical death, and God would take the life of the person before they apostatized (Hiebert 1979:309, attributing this view to Harry Ironside and Lehman Strauss). But that makes little sense here; as Moo (2000:250) says, "'Death' here, as commonly in James and almost always in the NT where sin is the issue, is ultimately 'spiritual' death—the condemnation to eternal damnation that results from unforgiven sin (James uses the noun 'death' (*thanatos* [TG2288, ZG2505]) in this sense the one other time it occurs in his letter [1:15])." So the path they were walking leads to ultimate destruction, but they are rescued from the eternal wrath of God. As Romans 5:12 states, sin entered this world accompanied by death, and the final result of sin is an enslavement that ends finally in eternal separation from God.

The second result for the strayed sinner (see note on 5:20) is "forgiveness of many sins" (lit., "will cover a multitude of sins"). There are several Old Testament passages that James is echoing, including Psalm 32:1 ("Oh, what joy for those whose disobedience is forgiven, whose sin is put out of sight") or Proverbs 10:12 ("Hatred stirs up quarrels, but love makes up for all offenses"), echoed in 1 Peter 4:8 ("love covers a multitude of sins"). The idea of "covering sins" is behind the Old Testament idea of atonement, picturing God placing sins under the mercy seat so that they were "covered" by it (Lev 17:11). When a believer strays into such serious error as portrayed here and then is brought back to God by a faithful believer, the "many sins" committed during that period are "covered" or "forgiven" and the soul "saved." The restoration ministry of a truly biblical church is a wondrously effective part of the church's work and is desperately needed today. James's epistle is asking for a church that is intimately and lovingly involved with each other, encouraging and challenging one another in the Christian life and exercising vigilance to know when one of the flock is straying and in danger of falling into serious error and then into apostasy.

BIBLIOGRAPHY

Adamson, James B.

1976 *The Epistle of James.* New International Commentary on the New Testament. Grand Rapids: Eerdmans.

Albl, Martin C.

2002 "Are Any among You Sick?" The Health Care System in the Letter of James. *Journal of Biblical Literature* 121.1:123-143.

Armerding, Carl

1938 Is Any among You Afflicted: A Study of James 5:13-20. *Bibliotheca Sacra* 95:195-201.

Baker, William R.

1995 *Personal Speech-Ethics in the Epistle of James.* Tübingen: Mohr.

Baker, William R., and P. Carrier

1990 James. Pp. 9-112 in *James–Jude: Unlocking the Scripture for You.* Standard Bible Studies. Cincinnati: Standard.

Barrett, C. K.

1994, 1998 *The Acts of the Apostles.* 2 vols. International Critical Commentary. Edinburgh: T&T Clark.

Bauckham, Richard

1998 The Tongue Set on Fire by Hell Itself (James 3:6). Pp. 119-131 in *The Fate of the Dead: Studies in the Jewish and Christian Apocalypses.* Leiden: Brill.

1999 *James.* London: Routledge.

2004 The Spirit of God in Us Loathes Envy: James 4:5. Pp. 270-281 in *The Holy Spirit and Christian Origins.* Editors, G. N. Stanton, B. W. Longenecker, S. C. Barton. Grand Rapids: Eerdmans.

Blomberg, Craig L., and Mariam J. Kamell

2008 *James.* Zondervan Exegetical Commentary on the New Testament. Grand Rapids: Zondervan.

Bock, Darrell L.

2007 *Acts.* Baker Exegetical Commentary on the New Testament. Grand Rapids: Baker.

Brosend, William F., II

2004 *James and Jude.* New Cambridge Bible Commentary. Cambridge University Press.

Bultmann, Rudolf

1951, 1955 *The Theology of the New Testament.* 2 vols. New York: Scribners.

Calvin, John

1948 *Commentaries on the Catholic Epistles.* Grand Rapids: Eerdmans. (Orig. pub. 1551.)

Cargal, Timothy B.

1993 *Restoring the Diaspora: Discursive Structure and Purpose in the Epistle of James.* Atlanta: Scholars Press.

Carpenter, Craig B.

2001 James 4:5 Reconsidered. *New Testament Studies* 47:189-205.

Carson, D. A.

2007 James. Pp. 997-1013 in *Commentary on the New Testament Use of the Old Testament.* Editors, G. K. Beale and D. A. Carson. Grand Rapids: Baker.

Chaine, J.

1927 *L'épître de s. Jacques.* Etudes bibliques. Paris: Gabalda.

Chester, Andrew, and Ralph P. Martin

1994 *The Theology of the Letters of James, Peter, and Jude.* Cambridge: Cambridge University Press.

Chilton, Bruce, and Craig A. Evans

1999 *James the Just and Christian Origins.* Leiden: Brill.

Comfort, Philip

2008 *New Testament Text and Translation Commentary.* Carol Stream, IL: Tyndale House.

Davids, Peter H.
1982 *The Epistle of James.* New International Greek Testament Commentary. Grand Rapids: Eerdmans.

Davies, W., and D. Allison, Jr.
1988, 1991, 1997 *A Critical and Exegetical Commentary on the Gospel according to Saint Matthew.* 3 vols. International Critical Commentary. Edinburgh: T&T Clark.

Dibelius, Martin
1975 *James.* Hermeneia. Philadelphia: Fortress.

Doriani, Daniel M.
2007 *James.* Reformed Expository Commentary. Phillipsburgh, NJ: Presbyterian & Reformed.

Elliott-Binns, Leonard E.
1955 The Meaning of *hylē* in James 3:5. *New Testament Studies* 2:48-50.

1957 James i.18: Creation or Redemption? *New Testament Studies* 3:148-161.

Frankemölle, Hubert
1990 Das semantische Netz des Jakobusbriefes: Zur Einheit eines umstrittenen Briefes. *Biblische Zeitschrift* 34.2:161-197.

Freeborn, Jack
2000 Lord of Glory: A Study of James 2 and 1 Corinthians 2. *Expository Times* 111.6:185-189.

Freedman, D. N.
1999 Caution: Bible Critic at Work. *Bible Review* 15.1:42-43.

Goppelt, Leonhard
1981, 1982 *Theology of the New Testament.* 2 vols. Grand Rapids: Eerdmans.

Gowan, D. E.
1993 Wisdom and Endurance in James. *Horizons in Biblical Theology* 15.2:145-153.

Gray, Patrick
2004 Points and Lines: Thematic Parallelism in the Letter of James and the Testament of Job. *New Testament Studies* 50.3:406-424.

Guthrie, George H.
2006 James. Pp. 197-273 in *The Expositors Bible Commentary* 13. Rev. ed. Editors, Tremper Longman III, and David E. Garland. Grand Rapids: Zondervan.

Hartin, Patrick J.
1997 "Who Is Wise and Understanding among You" (Jas 3:13)? An Analysis of Wisdom, Eschatology and Apocalypticism in the Epistle of James. *Theological Studies* 53.4:969-999.

2003 *James.* Sacra Pagina. Collegeville, MN: Liturgical.

Hayden, Daniel R.
1981 Calling for the Elders to Pray. *Bibliotheca Sacra* 138:258-286.

Hengel, Martin
1974 *Judaism and Hellenism.* 2 vols. Philadelphia: Fortress.

Hiebert, D. Edmund
1979 *The Epistle of James: Tests of a Living Faith.* Chicago: Moody.

Hort, F. J. A.
1909 *The Epistle of St. James.* London: Macmillan.

Irwin, M. E.
1991 Considering the Lilies. *McMaster Journal of Theology* 2.2:20-28.

Jenkins, C. R.
2002 Faith and Works in Paul and James. *Bibliotheca Sacra* 159.633:62-78.

Johanson, Bruce C.
1973 The Definition of "Pure Religion" in James 1:27 Reconsidered. *Expository Times* 84:118-119.

Johnson, Luke T.
1995 *The Letter of James.* Anchor Bible 37A. New York: Doubleday.

2003 Reading Wisdom Wisely. *Louvain Studies* 28.2:99-112.

Keenan, John P.
2005 *The Wisdom of James.* Mahwah, NJ: Paulist.

Kirk, J. Andrew
1969–1970 The Meaning of Wisdom in James: Examination of a Hypothesis. *New Testament Studies* 16:24-38.

Kistemaker, Simon J.
1986 *Exposition of the Epistle of James and the Epistles of John.* Grand Rapids: Baker.

Kloppenborg Verbin, John S.
1999 Patronage Avoidance in James. *Theological Studies* 55.4:755-794.

Laato, Timo
1997 Justification according to James: A Comparison with Paul. *Trinity Journal* 18.1:43-84.

Laws, Sophie
1980 *A Commentary on the Epistle of James.* San Francisco: Harper & Row.

Lea, Thomas D.
1999 *Hebrews and James.* Holman New Testament Commentary. Nashville: Broadman & Holman.

Lerle, Ernst
1985 *Kardia* als Bezeichnung für den Mageneingang. *Zeitschrift für die Neutestamentliche Wissenschaft* 76.3-4:292-294.

Longenecker, Richard N.
1990 *Galatians.* Word Biblical Commentary 41. Dallas: Word.

Maier, Gerhard
2004 *Der Brief das Jacobus.* Wuppertal: Brockhaus.

Marcus, Joel
1982 The Evil Inclination in the Epistle of James. *Catholic Biblical Quarterly* 44:606-621.

Martin, Ralph P.
1988 *James.* Word Biblical Commentary 48. Waco: Word.

Maynard-Reid, Pedrito U.
1987 *Poverty and Wealth in James.* Maryknoll, NY: Orbis.

Mayor, Joseph B.
1913 *The Epistle of St. James.* London: Macmillan.

McCartney, Dan G.
2009 *James.* Baker Exegetical Commentary on the New Testament. Grand Rapids: Baker.

McKnight, Scot
1990 James 2:18a: The Unidentifiable Interlocutor. *Westminster Theological Journal* 52:355-364.

2004 *The Jesus Creed: Loving God, Loving Others.* Brewster, MA: Paraclete.

Metzger, Bruce M.
1994 *A Textual Commentary on the Greek New Testament.* 2nd ed. New York: United Bible Societies.

Miller, J. David
2005 Can the "Father of Lights" Give Birth? *Priscilla Papers* 19.1:5-7.

Mitton, C. L.
1966 *The Epistle of James.* Grand Rapids: Eerdmans.

Moo, Douglas J.
2000 *The Letter of James.* Pillar New Testament Commentary. Grand Rapids: Eerdmans.

Motyer, Alec
1985 *The Message of James: The Tests of Faith.* Bible Speaks Today. Leicester: Inter-Varsity.

Nystrom, David
1997 *James.* The NIV Application Commentary. Grand Rapids: Zondervan.

Ortlund, Raymond, Jr.
2003 *God's Unfaithful Wife: A Biblical Theology of Spiritual Adultery.* Downers Grove, IL: InterVarsity.

Osborne, Grant R.
2002 *Revelation.* Baker Exegetical Commentary. Grand Rapids: Baker.

2004 *Romans.* InterVarsity Press New Testament Commentary. Downers Grove, IL: InterVarsity.

2006 *The Hermeneutical Spiral: A Comprehensive Introduction to Biblical Interpretation.* 2nd ed. Downers Grove, IL: InterVarsity.

2007 John. Pp. 1-313 in *Cornerstone Biblical Commentary*, vol. 13. Carol Stream, IL: Tyndale House.

Patzia, Arthur G.
2000 Wisdom. Pp. 1200-1204 in *Dictionary of the Later New Testament and Its Developments*. Editors, R. P. Martin and P. H. Davids. Downers Grove, IL: InterVarsity.

Pickar, Charles
1945 Is Anyone Sick among You? *Catholic Biblical Quarterly* 7:165-174.

Pilch, J. J.
1998 Mirrors and Glass. *Bible Today* 36.6:382-386.

Porter, Stanley E.
1990 Is *dipsuchos* (James 1, 8; 4, 8) a "Christian" Word? *Biblica* 71:469-498.

Reicke, B.
1964 *The Epistles of James, Peter, and Jude*. New York: Doubleday.

Richardson, Kurt A.
1997 *James*. New American Commentary. Nashville: Broadman & Holman.

Roberts, David J.
1972 The Definition of "Pure Religion" in James 1:27. *Expository Times* 83:215-216.

Robertson, A. T.
1933 *Word Pictures in the New Testament*, vol. 6. Nashville: Broadman & Holman.

Ropes, James H.
1916 *A Critical and Exegetical Commentary on the Epistle of St. James*. International Critical Commentary. Edinburgh: T&T Clark.

Ross, Alexander
1954 *The Epistles of James and John*. New International Commentary on the New Testament. Grand Rapids: Eerdmans.

Sanders, E. P.
1977 *Paul and Palestinian Judaism: A Comparison of Patterns of Religion*. Philadelphia: Fortress.

Scaer, David P.
1993 *James: The Apostle of Faith*. St. Louis: Concordia.

Sleeper, C. Freeman
1998 *James*. Abingdon New Testament Commentary. Nashville: Abingdon.

Snodgrass, Klyne R.
1986 Justification by Grace—to the Doers: An Analysis of the Place of Romans 2 in the Theology of Paul. *New Testament Studies* 32:72-93.

Spitta, Friedrich
1896 *Der Brief des Jakobus untersucht*. Göttingen: Vandenhoeck & Ruprecht.

Stulac, George M.
1990 Who Are "the Rich" in James? *Presbyterion* 16.2:89-102.
1993 *James*. InterVarsity Press New Testament Commentary. Downers Grove, IL: InterVarsity.

Tasker, R. V. G.
1956 *The General Epistle of James*. Tyndale New Testament Commentaries. Downers Grove, IL: InterVarsity.

Taylor, Mark E., and George H. Guthrie
2006 The Structure of James. *Catholic Biblical Quarterly* 68:681-705.

Thielman, Frank
2005 *Theology of the New Testament: A Canonical and Synthetic Approach*. Grand Rapids: Zondervan.

Tidball, Derek
2003 *Wisdom from Heaven: The Message of the Letter of James for Today*. Fearn: Christian Focus.

Townsend, Michael J.
1976 James 4:1-4: A Warning against Zealotry? *Expository Times* 87:211-213.

Trudinger, Paul
2004 The Epistle of James: Down-to-Earth and Otherworldly? *Downside Review* 122.426:61-63.

Wall, Robert W.
1997 *Community of the Wise: The Letter of James*. New Testament in Context. Valley Forge: Trinity.

Wallace, Daniel B.
1996 *Greek Grammar Beyond the Basics: An Exegetical Syntax of the New Testament.* Grand Rapids: Zondervan.

Ward, Roy B.
1969 Partiality in the Assembly: James 2:2-4. *Harvard Theological Review* 62:87-97.

Webb, Robert L., and John S. Kloppenberg
2007 *Reading James with New Eyes: Methodological; Reassessment of the Letter of James.* London: T&T Clark.

Weiser, Wolfram
1999 Durch Grünspan verdorbenes Edelmetall? Zur Deutung des Wortes "IOS" im Brief des Jakobus. *Biblische Zeitschrift* 43.2:220-223.

Wenham, David
1986 2 Corinthians 1:17, 18: Echo of a Dominical Logion. *Novum Testamentum* 28.3:271-279.

Windisch, Hans
1951 *Die katholischen Briefe.* Tübingen: Mohr.

Zahn, Theodor
1909 *Introduction to the New Testament.* Translator, J. M. Trout. Edinburgh: T&T Clark.

1 Peter

GRANT R. OSBORNE

INTRODUCTION TO
1 Peter

I BEGAN TO APPRECIATE 1 Peter shortly after I arrived at Trinity Evangelical Divinity School in 1977 to begin teaching. We have always used this epistle as our example in the second course of Greek Exegesis, centering on how to preach through it. Teaching 1 Peter once a year for the next three decades led me to fall in love with the richness of its theological message and the practicality of its presentation of the Christian life. For many years I have longed for an opportunity to write a commentary on this incredible epistle, and it is with joy that I do so now.

AUTHOR

The text begins with the statement, "This letter is from Peter, an apostle of Jesus Christ"; furthermore, 2 Peter 3:1 refers to itself as "my second letter to you." First Peter is also alluded to often in Polycarp's epistle to the Philippians (*To the Philippians* 1:3; 2:1-2; 5:3; 7:2 et al.) and is generally accepted as Petrine by many ancient witnesses (Papias and Clement of Alexandria in Eusebius *Ecclesiastical History* 2.15.2; Irenaeus *Against Heresies* 4.9.2, 5.7.2; Tertullian *Scorpion's Sting* 12, among others).

Still, a large number of scholars (e.g., Achtemeier, Beare, Best, Elliott, Goppelt, Senior) believe it is pseudonymous, written by one of Peter's followers in his name somewhat late in the first century. Let us consider the five major reasons these scholars doubt that Peter was the author:

1-2. The Greek of 1 Peter is too good for a Galilean fisherman, and the author utilizes the Septuagint throughout. Elliott (2000:120) says, "The polished Attic style, classical vocabulary . . . and rhetorical quality of this Greek composition make it one of the more refined writings of the NT," concluding, "It is difficult to reconcile a composition of such quality with the Galilean fisherman Simon Peter whose mother tongue was Aramaic and who was described as 'unschooled' (Acts 4:13)." Achtemeier (1996:3-4) believes that the stylistic use of comparison, alliteration, synonyms, anaphora, antithetic and synthetic parallelism, rhythmic structure, and other literary devices meant the author had to have had at least a middle-level education in Hellenistic writing that would have included the study of classical authors like Homer.

A common solution to the problems posed by this incongruity is to suppose that Peter used an amanuensis to write his epistle—see 5:12, where Peter says he wrote the letter "with the help of" (lit., "through"; *dia* [TG1223, ZG1328]) Silvanus (another name for Silas). This verse, however, does not directly say that Silas penned the letter. Many argue that it actually means Silas was the carrier of the letter (so Achtemeier

1996:7-9; Jobes 2005:320). Nevertheless, there is no cogent reason to deny that Silas functioned in both capacities, taking Peter's content and fashioning it with better Greek (so Carson and Moo 2005:644-645) and then delivering the letter.

At the same time, there is nothing in the letter or its style that could not have been written by a former Galilean fisherman now become apostle and missionary. The Greek is very well done, but that is the case also for the very Jewish epistles of James and Hebrews. Jobes, in a careful excursus (2005:325-338), shows that the level of Greek spoken in Galilee is higher than was supposed, and the Septuagint was widely used in Palestine as well as in diaspora areas. Moreover, the statement that Peter was "uneducated" in Acts 4:13 was given from a Jewish standpoint and meant he had no formal rabbinic training. Finally, her syntactical study of 1 Peter shows it was written by someone for whom Greek was a second language.

Peter would have grown up with Greek as a second language in Galilee, and his years as a missionary leader in the Christian world would have given him a lot of experience with Gentiles. The old theory of the Tübingen school in the nineteenth century that Peter worked only with Jews has long been discounted. Moreover, the statement in Galatians 2:1-10 that Peter would center on the Jews was not meant to be a permanent situation, for Paul always evangelized Jews before Gentiles, and Peter had a following at the church in Corinth (1 Cor 1:12). In short, there is no reason in the Greek style of the book for denying Peter is the author, who had some help from Silas as an amanuensis.

3. The epistle is addressed to remote provinces in the north part of Asia Minor, and these were not likely reached until long after Peter had passed from the scene. It is true that neither Acts nor the Pauline epistles mention these northern provinces. But Paul in Romans 15:19 says he had ministered in every region "from Jerusalem all the way to Illyricum," a region on the Adriatic northeast of Italy. A land route from Jerusalem to there would include the northern regions of Asia Minor. In other words, we know too little about the evangelization of Cappadocia and Bithynia to assume Peter and Paul had no contact with people there. (On the objection that Peter ministered only to Jews, see the previous paragraph.) Moreover, we know that the church at Rome was founded by visiting business people rather than apostles, and these northern regions could easily have been reached the same way. Peter, like Paul in Romans, may have been writing to churches he had never visited.

4. The developed church situation in 1 Peter 5 and the level of the persecution described in the epistle fit the situation at the end of the century, not that of the 60s. Neither the church structure nor the persecution mentioned demands a late date. The view (called "early Catholicism") that dominated the 1960s and 1970s was that the presence of official offices like "elder" (5:1-4) developed late in the church (e.g., the AD 90s). This school of thought was influential for a while, but most scholars have strong doubts now as to the viability of this tenet (see especially in the Introduction to 2 Peter, page 277). The book of Acts tells us that there were elders very early in the life of the church (see, e.g., Acts 11:30; 14:23; 15:2, 4). Elders functioned both in Jewish and Hellenistic communities, and it makes sense that from the beginning (see Acts 11:30) such leaders were present in the church.

Similarly, some date 1 Peter during the time of Domitian (81–96) or Trajan

(98–117) due to the level of opposition and persecution it seems to portray. This, however, is problematic on two counts. First, there was no official persecution under Domitian, and no real empirewide conflagration even under Trajan. There is no situation in this letter that parallels that of Pliny's letters to Trajan, which tell of the arrest and torture of Christians (*Letters* 10.96-97). Second, the "fiery trials" of 4:12 do not in fact reflect an official empirewide persecution but rather the kind of serious opposition often experienced by Jews as well as Christians in the first century. The persecution mentioned in 5:9 was worldwide only in the sense that Christians everywhere were going through something similar, not in the sense that it was an official Roman persecution. In fact, this is true also for the book of Revelation; it, too, refers to a local yet severe persecution rather than a state-sponsored anti-Christian movement (see Osborne 2002:7-9).

5. The language of the epistle is too Pauline and shows too little cognizance of Jesus to have been written by Peter. Regarding the occurrences of Pauline language in this epistle, Jobes provides an excellent discussion (2005:11-13), noting that if there were such extensive Paulinisms, the epistle should be attributed to Paul, not Peter. The parallels, however, are better explained by a common early church tradition rather than a dependency on Paul. The closest affinity is with Romans, and that is easily explained by Peter's connection to Rome paralleling Paul's. Furthermore, in 5:1 the author calls himself "a witness to the sufferings of Christ" (likely reflecting Peter's presence at Jesus' trial), and in 2:23 he refers to Jesus' refusal to "retaliate" or "threaten revenge" at his trial (see Grudem 1988:20). In 3:18; 4:1-2, 13, he appeals to the model of Christ for Christian conduct. Moreover, there are few places in the epistle where it would have been natural to appeal to Christ's life (see 2 Pet 1:16-18, where Jesus' transfiguration is noted in a place where the argument called for it).

In sum, the arguments against Peter's authorship of 1 Peter are unconvincing. Marshall (1991:21) states the conclusion strongly: "if ever there was a weak case for pseudonymity, surely it is in respect to this letter."

DATE

Those who doubt Petrine authorship tend to date the epistle in the 80s or 90s since, as noted above, they think it reflects Pauline material and a late church organization, as well as an empirewide persecution. These arguments, however, are fairly weak and present an insufficient cause to reject Petrine authorship. Accepting Peter as author, the dating of the letter depends on one's view regarding his death. The commonly held view that Peter, as well as Paul, died around AD 65 during the Neronian persecution is based on Tacitus (*Annals* 15.44; cf. *1 Clement* 5–6), though Tacitus does not mention him by name. Peter's crucifixion upside down is portrayed in *Acts of Peter* 37–40, and is seen as prophesied in John 21:15-19. Yet this is challenged by Michaels (1988:vii-lxi), who says that John 21:19 ("to let him know by what kind of death he would glorify God") and 2 Peter 1:14 ("Christ has shown me that I must soon leave this earthly life") do not necessarily indicate martyrdom or death under Nero. He believes that Peter may have lived into the 80s, and firm conclusions about the date of this epistle cannot be tied to later reports of his early death.

Still, an earlier date remains more than reasonable since the general sense of widespread persecution fits closely the anti-Christian sentiment in the Roman Empire that made it possible for Nero to blame the burning of Rome on the Christians. While we cannot know for certain that Peter died under Nero, it makes good sense as a real possibility. Also, neither Peter in his writings nor Paul in his writings shows any overlapping of their ministries in Rome (where 1 Peter was penned; see 5:13), thus allowing for Peter's presence there in AD 62–64 (see Grudem 1988:36). In short, there can be no certainty, but there exists a valid possibility that Peter authored 1 Peter in 62–63 and 2 Peter in 63–64.

OCCASION OF WRITING

The Christians in Asia Minor were very distressed because of the hostility and persecution they were experiencing; as a result, they were deeply discouraged. Peter addressed their situation with great insight and in the process provided a well-thought-out theology of suffering. He wanted them to understand how special they were as God's chosen children, God's new temple, and the new Israel (1:3-13; 2:4-10). Recognizing their status in God's kingdom should help them put their marginalized position in this world into perspective. Though they were "temporary residents and foreigners" (1:1, 17; 2:11) in this world, they belonged to heaven and were God's own people; so they could "rejoice" in the midst of their trials (1:6, 8; 4:13-14). Their present circumstances were difficult, but their future was secure, which is a major focus of this epistle. In the future God would deliver them, ensure their victory, and both vindicate and reward them at the return of Christ (1:5, 7, 13; 4:13; 5:1, 10). In light of this special nature (namely, being strangers and aliens in this world) that they obtained from Christ, they must live as children of God and citizens of heaven, which demands a lifestyle of holiness. They were to respond to the abuse of their neighbors with good works and blessing (2:12; 3:9) and let their lives be a witness to the pagans who rejected them (3:15). Combining eschatology with ethics, Peter urged them to be Christ's witnesses to a hostile world.

AUDIENCE

Who were the recipients of this letter? Peter addresses the inhabitants of five Roman provinces in Asia Minor (modern-day Turkey)—Pontus, Galatia, Cappadocia, Asia, and Bithynia (1:1). These provinces of the Anatolian peninsula comprised all the area north and west of the Taurus Mountains. Cappadocia was in the eastern quadrant, Bithynia and Pontus in the north (considered one province by the Romans), Galatia in the center, and Asia to the west. Asia was a wealthy province, very pro-Roman, and inhabited by adherents of the imperial cult (the worship of the emperor as a god). It was the most urban of the five provinces, with a large number of wealthy cities due to the connections with Rome. Pontus and Bithynia had ports on the Black Sea and so were also moderately wealthy. Galatia and Cappadocia were generally rural and poor, with cities far apart. Apart from Asia, the peoples of these areas were very diverse, speaking several different languages; their populations included a large number of Jewish settlers (see Elliott 2000:84-90). This area eventually became central to the Christian movement, as Jobes (2005:22) points out:

> *And yet this untamed region became the cradle of Christianity. From Asia Minor emerged people whose names are immortalized in Christian history. From Pontus came Aquila, the Jewish tentmaker and husband of Priscilla (Acts 18:2), as well as Marcion. . . . From Hierapolis in Phrygia . . . came Epictetus, the famous Roman slave and Stoic philosopher . . . as well as Papias, bishop of Hierapolis. . . . In the fourth century came the Cappadocian fathers, such as Basil, bishop of Cappadocia's capital city, Caesarea, his brother Gregory of Nyssa, and Gregory of Nazianzus, bishop of Constantinople—all three defenders of the Nicene creed against the heresies of Arius.*

One debate is whether the recipients of the letter were mainly Jewish or Gentile. Most ancient interpreters (Origen, Eusebius, the Greek Fathers) tended to believe they were Jewish; modern interpreters think of them as predominantly Gentile. The use of the Old Testament, the allusion to the readers as "exiles of the Dispersion" (1:1, RSV), and the Jewish flavor of several passages could point to Jewish provenance, while the rhetorical traits would favor a Gentile origin. Yet the issue is wrongly put as an either-or. These provinces were primarily Gentile but with large numbers of Jews living in them. At Pentecost in Acts 2:9 there were pilgrims from "Cappadocia, Pontus, the province of Asia." Therefore, the churches in these regions were undoubtedly made up of Jews and Gentiles, and the epistle is addressed to both groups as forming one church.

CANONICITY AND TEXTUAL HISTORY

First Peter was among the earliest books to be accepted into the New Testament canon. It was generally accepted and quoted as Scripture by many ancient witnesses (Papias and Clement of Alexandria in Eusebius *Ecclesiastical History* 2.15.2; Irenaeus *Against Heresies* 4.9.2, 5.7.2; Tertullian *Scorpion's Sting* 12, among others). Michaels (1988:xxxiv) says that "aside from the four Gospels and the letters of Paul, the external attestation for 1 Peter is as strong or stronger than for any New Testament book."

The earliest manuscript containing 1 Peter is Papyrus Bodmer VII/VIII, known as 𝔓72 (dated to the late third century). The text of 𝔓72 is Alexandrian, closely related to the fourth-century Codex Vaticanus (B) and to Codex Alexandrinus (A, dated c. AD 400). These manuscripts present solid testimony to the original wording of 1 Peter. Other trustworthy manuscripts of 1 Peter are Codex Sinaiticus (א) of the fourth century, 𝔓81 of the fourth century, Codex Ephraemi Rescriptus (C) of the early fifth century, and 𝔓74 of the seventh century.

LITERARY STYLE

Most scholars today recognize 1 Peter as an apocalyptic epistle. It is not the type of apocalyptic work seen in Daniel, Zechariah, or Revelation (let alone *4 Ezra* or *2 Baruch*, two of the 25 or so Jewish apocalyptic works written between 200 BC and AD 100). First Peter is an "apocalyptic epistle" because of the centrality it places on the end of all things. First Peter is focused on eschatological salvation. Salvation is a present experience, but it progresses through life, and the end or goal of one's faith is the salvation of one's soul (1:9, NKJV)—an idea that agrees with 1:5, which says salvation is "ready to be revealed on the last day." Davids (1990:15-16) considers this the basic literary orientation of the book and discusses it in light of the two axes proposed by J. J. Collins in *Apocalyptic Imagination* (1992). The temporal axis concerns Peter's view of primordial events (e.g., 3:18-22) as paradigmatic of what the believers are going through. The current suffering is "an eschatological crisis" that prepares them for both final judgment and final salvation at the eschaton. The "spatial axis" concerns otherworldly regions like heaven (1:4, 12; 3:22) and hell (3:19) as well as otherworldly beings like angels (1:12), disobedient spirits (3:19), authorities and powers (3:22), and the devil (5:8-9). In terms of cosmic warfare, Peter clearly considered there to be demonic powers behind the persecutors (5:8-9); the Christians were embattled not merely by human opponents but by the devil who wanted to "devour" them. Christ had won the victory (3:19), proclaiming the defeat of these demonic forces after his resurrection. Believers participate in that victory by placing themselves under "the mighty power of God" (5:6) and by standing firm and strong in their faith (5:9).

The apocalyptic outlook begins with the primacy of Jesus' resurrection as the basis of our salvation (1:3; 3:21) and our hope (3:22). The moment after his resurrection (3:18), Christ proceeded through the heavens and proclaimed his victory to the cosmic forces that had sinned as recorded in Genesis 6 (3:19)—Christ had already won the battle against the evil forces and brought salvation to mankind (3:20-21). But the battle continues, and the dark forces had been at work using non-Christians to decimate the people of God (5:8-9). This is the eschatological trial that dominates this epistle. In the uncertainty of their crisis, God's people must center on Christ and look to the certainty of the future. The second major eschatological event is the second coming of Christ, called his "revelation" (1:7, 13; cf. 4:13). This is the eschatological center of the epistle and the basis of reflection for the afflicted saints, because it is at the Parousia that final victory will come.

MAJOR THEOLOGICAL THEMES

God. In 1 Peter, the name of God is found 39 times, more than any other term. As in all apocalyptic works (e.g., Revelation, *Similitudes of Enoch, 4 Ezra, Sibylline Oracles, Testaments of the Twelve Patriarchs*), the primary theme is God's absolute sovereignty and control over this world. The plan of God and his election of his people are made quite visible; this is an apocalyptic idea, linking the church with the righteous remnant in the Old Testament as those God will watch over and bring to victory for their suffering (Michaels 1988:7). The center of God's plan is his chosen, redeemed people (1:1-2; 2:4, 6, 9), called out of a suffering situation to find Christ and eternal life (1:4; 3:18), perform good deeds (1:15; 2:9, 21; 3:9), and be vindicated (5:10). In this he is the "God of all grace" (5:10, NIV), a primary theme of this epistle: He gives grace to his people (1:2), graciously gives life (3:7), and in him even suffering is "part of God's grace for you" (5:12). He will finalize his gracious love at Christ's return (1:10, 13). This gracious God always knows what is best and has his best always as part of his will for his downtrodden followers (see Howe 2000:432-438). Even hostility and suffering are part of this loving purpose, intended to produce glory for his own (see the heading "The End for the Believer—Hope and Glory," below). The will of God is mentioned five times (2:15; 3:17; 4:2, 19; 5:2 [*kata theon*;

see note on 5:2]), always bringing together the suffering of his people and his desire that they behave well in the midst of it.

His relationship to his people is highlighted at the very beginning, as he is called "God the Father [who] knew you and chose you long ago" (1:2), emphasizing his loving protection and care and his "foreknowledge" of his chosen ones even before creation. As the Father of Christ, he raised him from the dead (1:3) as the forerunner of all Christians, with the result that their "inheritance" and future are guaranteed (1:4-5). The other side of his fatherhood is that he is also the Judge of his children, one who "has no favorites," and "will . . . reward" them on the basis of their works (1:17). Still, they are a household or family under God's paternal care (2:5, NIV; 4:17). Even when he acts as Judge, it is an act of love. Upon the rebellious world, though, God's judgment centers on his justice on behalf of his people. Here Christ is the model: When he was insulted, he did not retaliate, but rather entrusted his situation to "God, who always judges fairly" (2:23). The believers, as well, can leave the vengeance with God who will bring justice (4:5), so that they are free to return "blessing" and good works when they are slandered (3:9; cf. 2:12).

Jesus Christ and Salvation. Christ is mentioned 22 times in the epistle. Michaels introduces this well (1988:lxviii), "If God is the Actor in the work of human salvation, Jesus Christ is the Agent, and therefore the one with whom the theology of 1 Peter is most directly concerned." At the beginning of the book where the emphasis is on the Trinitarian involvement with us (1:2, see "The Trinity and the Spirit," below), the believers are described as "cleansed by the blood of Jesus Christ," thus enacting the new covenant (built on Exod 24) and effecting salvation. As Peter enumerates the blessings of salvation (1:3-12), the core blessing is the "new birth" (1:3), the "faith" that enables us to ensure the future (1:7), and the final salvation that results (1:9). This core blessing is elaborated in five places: (1) Christ is the ransom or redemption payment as the perfect Lamb of God, whose sacrificial blood made salvation possible (1:18-20), becoming the basis for our trust in God (1:21). (2) He is the "living cornerstone" of God's final Temple, the church, on whom we as living stones are erected into God's new house (2:4-5). All this is realized because God raised Christ from the dead, thereby making hope and faith possible and ensuring our final salvation (1:3, 21). (3) In the strong catechetical section of 2:21-25, Jesus, the sinless person (2:22), "personally carried our sins in his body on the cross" so that we, the wandering sheep, can "be dead to sin" (2:24) and turn to our "Shepherd" (2:25). (4) In 3:18 Christ's death for our sins is mentioned twice, its purpose to bring us "safely home to God." Our response must be to "worship Christ as Lord" of our lives (3:15). Again, this is realized by Jesus' resurrection (3:18b). (5) In 5:10 Jesus is the means by which we "share in [God's] eternal glory"; he alone has made it possible. First Peter somewhat resembles Romans in its salvific thrust. There is a summary of the gospel and of the effects of Jesus Christ's sacrifice on our eternal salvation in each chapter! We no longer "see" Jesus, but because he brought salvation, we "love" him, "trust" him, and "rejoice" in the salvation that is our final destiny (1:8-9).

All of this was made possible when Jesus came to earth, and it will be consummated at the final "revelation" of Christ in glory (see below, "The Trinity and the Spirit"). In his first revelation he came not only as Savior but also as a "model" or pattern for us in suffering. Thus, in this book about endurance and faithfulness in the midst of hostility and suffering, Jesus Christ is also presented as the foundation and model for a beleaguered church. This begins in 1:10-12, which states that the prophets searched diligently to discover and experience the high point of their ministry, the coming of the Messiah—in particular, "Christ's suffering and his great glory afterward," which would become the guiding principle for the church to emulate. Later, Peter instructs the church to pattern itself after the incredible realization that Jesus is the elect and honored "living cornerstone" for God's house (2:4), and God's people follow that and become the "living stones" built upon Christ to become elect and honored (2:5, 9), as Jesus himself was (2:4), as both God's "house" (or temple) and as priests who offer "spiritual sacrifices" in that house (2:5).

The primary passage for *imitatio Christi* (or "imitation of Christ," so Michaels, who says [1988:lxx] it is "what distinguishes Peter from Paul") is 2:21-25, which occurs in the middle of the Household Codes of 2:13–3:7. This passage begins with the basic statement of this theme: "He is your example, and you must follow in his steps" (2:21), meaning that one should react to the various pressures and challenges of life as Jesus would. The meaning of discipleship in every area of life is "following" (the primary discipleship term in the Gospels) the way or pattern of Christ's life. He is especially our example in suffering. Fulfilling the image of the suffering servant depicted in Isaiah 53:7, he "did not open his mouth" in response to the slanders uttered against him (Matt 27:12-14; Luke 23:9)—that is Jesus' model for us as well (2:23a). On a parallel note, we are told not to trade insult for insult but instead to return a blessing (3:9). Like Jesus, the way to do that is to place our situation in "the hands of God, who always judges fairly" (2:23b). The next section using Jesus as a model is 4:1, saying we should "arm [our]selves with the same attitude he had," so that as a result of the suffering we can be "finished with sin"—that is, gain strength to defeat sin in our life and center on doing "the will of God" (4:2). Through Christ we will be blessed (3:9) as we become "partners with Christ in his suffering" (4:13) and experience the empowering presence of the Spirit of God. We are in process of "[sharing] in his eternal glory by means of Christ Jesus" (5:10), and we will be brought "safely home to God" (3:18).

The epistle as a whole centers on the future certainty of Christ's "revelation" at the Parousia and the glory that will bring (see below, "The End for the Believer—Hope and Glory"). The language is peculiar to Peter and centers on the worldwide implications of that coming. First, Christ was foreknown before creation, revealed to the prophets (1:10-12), and "revealed" (*phaneroō* [TG5319, ZG5746], 1:20; 5:4) to all at his first advent, inaugurating the "last days" (1:20) of human history. That was preparation for the final "revelation" (*apokaluptō* [TG601, ZG636], 1:5; 5:1) of Christ at his second coming, a manifestation of his glory that will "reveal" his salvation to all (1:5), provide final salvation (1:13), and give "praise and glory and honor" from God (1:7) to his followers. At that revelation the believers will rejoice to see and share in his eternal glory (4:13; 5:1, 10), receiving "a crown of never-ending glory and honor" (5:4). The resurrection and Parousia of Christ are the signature events that give the suffering saints a "great expectation" and a certainty that we have a sure inheritance waiting for us (1:3-4).

The Trinity and the Spirit. Peter includes a Trinitarian formula as he opens his epistle (1:2; cf. Rev 1:4b-5). The Father is the one who foreknows, the Spirit the one who sanctifies, and the Son the one who cleanses with his blood sacrifice. Davids (1990:23) states that "in his division of the functions of Father, Son, and Spirit he has laid part of the basis of what would develop into this (Trinitarian) concept. Furthermore, he shows how Christians of that day experienced God in their lives and what the relevance of this doctrine can be in a difficult situation." The place of the Father and Son in the book were discussed above; the Spirit plays a much less visible (but still important) role, being mentioned only six times. As noted, 1:2 speaks of the Spirit's sanctifying role in salvation. Since holiness is so important to 1 Peter (see below, "Responsibility—Lives of Holiness"), the Spirit in this sense is a critical figure in the book. The Spirit is also the one who inspires the prophets in predicting the suffering and glory of the Messiah (1:11); here he is "the Spirit of Christ," and his role was to make the coming presence of the Christ known to the prophets. Next, the "Holy Spirit sent from heaven" is the empowering presence behind the preaching of those who "announced" the gospel to the Christians (1:12). In this way, the Spirit is the divine representative sent from heaven to inspire both the ancient prophetic proclamation of Messiah and the gospel proclamation from the first century until now.

The Spirit's heavenly origin as part of the Trinity drives the people of God in past and present. In 3:18, Peter provides a creedal couplet, "died in the flesh/raised in the Spirit." There is double meaning behind *pneuma* [TG4151, ZG4460] (spirit) here; Jesus was raised into a new spiritual reality, and he was raised into the realm of the Holy Spirit. The Spirit as part of the Trinity raised Jesus from the dead and exalted him in heaven. All of these complex truths were in Peter's mind as he wrote. This new life that Christ enjoyed is given to the believer who will, like Christ, "live forever with God in the Spirit" (4:6). In other words, the believer will enter this new eternal heavenly reality that is only possible "in the Spirit." Finally, "the glorious Spirit of God rests upon" (4:14) the believers when they are persecuted, meaning that the Spirit becomes the shekinah glory resting on the suffering Christians (Isa 11:2) and making them a holy temple for God. (Shekinah [see Jastrow 2006:1573] is a Hebrew term designating God's glorious "indwelling" presence among his people, taken from the verb *shakan* [TH7931, ZH8905], "to dwell.")

The New Community—Aliens, Yet the Special People of God. There is no reason for Christians to be discouraged; they need to reflect on who they are and how they can live in that light. The first fact Peter gets across is that in this world believers are alienated foreigners who are marginalized and do not belong (1:1, 17; 2:11). As stated above, God "chose" and "called" them to be his special people; they have little in this world but await "a priceless inheritance" (1:4), a "crown of never-ending glory" (5:4). They have been rejected by the world, but they are protected by God's power (1:5) through all their suffering. They are the objects of the intense scrutiny and interest of both the prophets and the angels (1:10-12), meaning they are the fulfillment of the Old Testament hopes.

The Christians are also the community of the new covenant. Several images are found in 2:4-10. The church is constituted as the new Israel, joining believing Israel as the new people of God. Thielmann (2005:573-574) describes how the picture from Hosea 2:23 is applied in 1 Peter 2:10 and elsewhere in the epistle. "Not my people" (Hos 2:23; Israel's unfaithfulness) is transferred to the believers' time as pagans prior to conversion, when they were disobedient (2:8), lived in emptiness and ignorance (1:14, 18), led immoral lives (4:3), and were characterized by evil behavior (2:1, 12). Then God chose them to become "my people" (Hos 2:23), and they formed "a holy nation, God's very own possession" (2:9-10). Christ became the sacrifice (1:2, 18-20; 2:24) and the "living cornerstone" upon which they as "living stones" were erected to become both Temple and priesthood, offering "spiritual sacrifices" under the new covenant (2:4-5).

As a community, the church is also a "household" (4:17) or family (1:14, 17; 3:8; 4:9). They are "brothers and sisters" of one another (1:22; 2:17; 3:8; 5:9) and as such are duty-bound to care and share. Love must characterize the community, and it must be deep, energetic, and sincere (1:22). This communal relationship is explored in detail in 4:7-11. In light of the imminent return of Christ, the church must be a community of disciplined prayer and deep love expressed in both forgiveness and hospitality (4:8 restates 1:22). They must be a people using their spiritual gifts to strengthen and help each other. At the same time, they are a flock (5:2) under the Great Shepherd who guards their souls (2:25), but also one in need of shepherds; so the elders or pastors of the churches are told to "care for" and "watch over" their flocks with diligence and eagerness, leading their people by example (5:1-4). The whole church is called to humility before one another and especially under God's mighty hand, placing all their needs and worries under him (5:5-7). Davids (1990:18-19) calls this "communal holiness" and says it has two primary concerns: (1) "The sheer goodness of their life" is meant to improve their lot in the world and clarify the true basis of their suffering (i.e., highlight the world's injustice). (2) It strengthens the unity of the community and helps keep the faith of each individual intact.

Responsibility—Lives of Holiness. In light of their special place before God, Peter emphasizes that believers must live accordingly; their new status brings spiritual and ethical responsibility (1:13–2:3). Especially prominent is the call to a life of sanctification (1:2) or holiness (1:14-15). As "holy priests" (2:5) and a "holy nation" (2:9), they belong to God and not their former way of life (4:3). If the church is the people of God, she must resemble the God she follows, and his core characteristic is holiness (Lev 11:44-45; 19:2; quoted in 1:15). That means to be "holy in everything you do" (1:15). This is not an option, but a mandate, and God as Father will judge us on the basis of how we live (1:17; see commentary). Holiness means both to live apart from the world and to live for God, so the saints are to abstain from all the vices of their former way of life (1:14; 2:1, 11; 3:3, 11; 4:2-3, 15). Instead of living for pleasure, they are to live in hope (1:3, 13, 21; 3:5, 15) and place all their trust in God rather than the world (1:5, 7-9, 21; 2:6-7; 5:9).

This holiness becomes evident in the believer's ethics both in the decision to refrain from sin (1:14; 2:1, 11, 16, 24; 3:10-11; 4:2-3) and then in the active determination to "do good" (see next section). First Peter is similar to the other General Epistles and to the Pauline Epistles—the vertical aspect of the life of faith (new birth and salvation in Christ) must lead to the horizontal aspect (a life of holiness). When one is declared right with God (justification), the process begins by which the Spirit makes us right with God (sanctification), which results in our living right for God (holiness and ethics). Michaels (1988:lxxiv) comments, "faith validates itself in action to the extent that faith and action are indistinguishable. Salvation is gained by 'believing' (1:8, 21; 2:7), yet no less by 'growing' (2:2), 'coming' (2:4), or 'following' (2:21). . . . Because salvation is eschatological, 'hope,' no less than faith, is its watchword (1:3, 13, 21; 3:5, 15), and the doing of good (while there is still time) is its necessary expression."

Suffering and the Strategy for Victory over It. As we have already noted, the major situation addressed in this epistle is that of suffering. Whether Elliott (1981:xxxx) and Jobes (2005:32-41) are correct that the recipients of the letter were actual resident aliens, perhaps forcefully moved or even exiled to the provinces of Pontus, Galatia, Cappadocia, Asia, and Bithynia, is difficult to know for certain. I have my doubts (see note on 1:1). Nevertheless, these Christians felt like foreigners and exiles (1:1, 17; 2:11), so Peter encouraged them to not fall into despair. If they could realize with the old gospel lyric that "This world is not my home, I'm just a-passin' through," it would enable them to put their rejection by their neighbors in perspective. As new Israel, they could look upon their situation as a new diaspora, a scattering of the people of God into pagan lands, there to depend entirely upon God for their existence. "At the same time, they should not withdraw from their various societies but they should live under the scrutiny of unbelievers—and live in such a way that they both shame their accusers and lead them to conversion" (Thielmann 2005:576).

The primary form of persecution these people were experiencing was verbal abuse—they were accused as wrongdoers (2:12), insulted (3:9), spoken against (3:16), slandered (4:4), and mocked (4:14), but undoubtedly there was more. The abuse is referred to as "fiery trials" in 4:12, and these are the "many trials" of fire in 1:6-7. It is universally agreed by historians and commentators alike (see discussion in Osborne 2002:7-9) that there was no official Roman persecution at this time, but rather local opposition and slander by neighbors and former friends. They used to join these friends in wild living but no longer did so; therefore, they were mocked and slandered by them (4:3-4). In 5:9 we see that what they were going through is "the same kind of suffering" as experienced by "brothers and sisters all over the world." There is no mention of martyrs (cf. Acts 12:2; Rev 2:13) or Christians imprisoned (cf. Matt 25:36; Acts 16:23; 21:33; Col 4:18; Heb 13:3), although some physical persecution may be included among the "many [kinds of] trials" of 1:6.

Green (2007:192-197) explores the sociological and religious basis for this persecution. The Anatolian peninsula was an east-west thoroughfare that had become quite cosmopolitan with many ethnic groups that were intensely pro-Roman. So there was a lot of pressure to adapt to Roman mores and to show loyalty to Rome. As a trade route there was further pressure to be amenable to the many religious ideas circulating at that time. The area became more and more urban and wealthy, so demands for conformity to Roman cultural expectations increased exponentially. Old gods blended with the new, and the imperial cult (the worship of the emperors as gods) was also on the rise. Moreover, these diverse religious practices were more public than private, demanding participation by all. "Doing good" was defined as community benefaction—that is, doing one's duty to the state and city, rather than a moral or ethical practice of "good works." The honor and shame culture of the first-century Mediterranean world (encompassing Jews as well as Romans) was governed by public expectations, and verbal abuse was the heart of shame. Community and personal identity were aligned with making a valuable contribution to Roman life. With all this, it is no wonder that Christians stood out, were called "atheists" (refusing to recognize the Roman gods), and were seen as a menace to *Pax Romana*. Status was everything, and that meant assimilation into the cultural demands of the day. Christians refused to do that, considering themselves citizens of heaven rather than of Rome (as Peter argues), and so they were naturally marginalized and rejected.

Thielmann (2005:580-583) finds three elements in the eschatological perspective Peter develops for suffering. First, suffering is "a sign of faith's genuineness," in that faith, like gold, must be tested by trials to be purified (1:6-7). According to 4:1, the believers' willingness to be reviled and their Christlike attitude allow them to eschew sin in their lives. In 4:14, verbal abuse is described as a blessing because the Spirit of Christ empowers them to endure it, and they know that the glory of the final day has "broken into the present in their suffering." Second, the believers' faithfulness in suffering "leads to eschatological blessing" both as a promise of future glory and as a present evangelistic power in the gospel (as they experienced it, 4:6). Their suffering produces life in terms of present conversion and eternal glory. Third, God guarantees that the persecutors themselves will come to justice, as is clear in 4:5: "They will have to face God, who will judge everyone." In 2:23 we read that Jesus did not retaliate because he could place everything in the hands of God "who always judges fairly." The believers need not fear their persecutors; they will fear God (1:17; 2:17) and live for him (not vengeance), leaving the judgment up to him.

How were the followers of Christ to respond to this opposition and abuse? Peter is clear: They should respond through their goodness and good deeds. Though they could not "do good" in the Roman way, good deeds stand out in any society. There is a great deal of material about practicing good works in this epistle (2:12, 15, 19, 20, 21; 3:6, 13, 17; 4:11, 19). The core verse is 2:12, which says that Christians should, literally, "maintain goodness" at all times, so that when they are slandered, their enemies will observe that good conduct and be convicted (some even convinced) that they had told lies and even be converted. They also should respond with submission (2:13, 18; 3:1; 5:5), even to unbelievers (governing authorities, masters, husbands); Peter insists "that in these circumstances Christians show the effects of their obedience to the Lord by living according to the norms of ordered society" (Marshall 1991:656). They would thereby prove that belonging to Christ makes them better citizens, slaves, or wives. As in 2:12, believers are to use all these displays of public goodness and holiness as a witness to their neighbors (see O'Connor 1991:17-26); this is not a defensive strategy but an offensive one, motivated by a desire to see those around them converted. Their reaction of blessing rather than retaliation (3:9) will first convince their opponents they were wrong and then convict them of the superiority of Christ to their old pagan ways (3:16). So, the followers of Christ need to be "ready to explain" their "Christian hope" whenever they find opportunity (3:15). Michaels (1988:lxxiv) summarizes,

"To 'do good' is to do the will of God, especially in situations where one suffers for it (cf. 2:15; 3:17; 4:19), but even more specifically it is to fulfill the spirit (if not the letter) of Jesus' command to love one's enemies. . . . 1 Peter makes a serious attempt to do justice to the command . . . in its recurring emphasis on humility, gentleness, and non-retaliation as the response to those who slander and oppress the Christian community."

The End for the Believer—Hope and Glory. The Parousia of Christ is the basis of the believers' "great expectation" (1:3), which in this epistle means the central realization that God will vindicate them, and they will emerge with glory and honor in the end. In the midst of the difficult times they are experiencing, believers must set their hope on their final salvation when Christ returns (1:13). Their "faith and hope" are in the God who raised and exalted Jesus and who would do the same for them (1:21), and that hope will so stand out in a hopeless world that it will be noticed and people will ask about it (3:15).

Connected to hope is also the theology of "glory" in the book. In 1 Peter, this generally reflects the apocalyptic concept that the faithful will receive glory at the eschaton—the "end" (*eschatos* [TG2078, ZG2274]) of all things. The theme begins in 1:7, where a strong faith after fiery trials results in "praise and glory and honor" at Christ's return. The basic motif is established in 1:11, with Christ our model (see above on "Jesus Christ and Salvation")—suffering is the path to glory. The rest of the epistle will develop the implication of this for believers. The point is that God has called us to be faithful to him in this world, and with Jesus as our basic pattern, this means the world will turn against us. So suffering is the lot of Christians, yet that very suffering brings glory to God and will mean glory for them. When Christ suffered, "glory" or exaltation was the result, as is seen in 1:21 (God "raised Christ from the dead and gave him great glory"), in 2:4 (he was "chosen by God for great honor"), in 4:11 ("all glory and power [belong] to him forever and ever"), and in 4:13 (the believers should rejoice because they will see "his glory" when it is "revealed" at his coming).

Christ's glory was the end result of his faithfulness, and the same will be true of his followers who suffer for him, see that glory, and share in it (1:7; 2:7; 4:14; 5:1, 4, 6, 10). They will have glory after successfully enduring trials (1:7) and receive the honor given Christ the cornerstone (2:7; see note). When they endure verbal abuse, the result is that "the glorious Spirit of God rests upon [them]" (4:14), which means the shekinah presence of God dwells in them (see commentary at 4:14). The glory theme ends with a crescendo in chapter 5, with four occurrences: Peter testifies that he too will "share in [Christ's] glory" at his coming (5:1) and states that believers will receive "a crown of never-ending glory" at his appearing (5:4), that God will "lift [us] up in honor" at "the right time" (5:6), namely, at the end of all, and that "God called you to share in his eternal glory by means of Christ Jesus" (5:10). Yet this glory is not just a future reality we must wait for; it is inaugurated and has already begun. Jobes (2005:49) says, "Peter is not saying that Christians should complacently suffer through this life because the afterlife will be so much better. Peter's eschatology is not 'pie in the sky by and by.' Rather, it imparts an ethical quality of life *now* by setting present Christian experience within an eschatological perspective." In addition, this glory has begun in the lives of the saints. In 5:10 we currently "share" in Christ's glory, and that foretaste gives us strength to endure now in light of the time his glory will be consummated in us.

OUTLINE

- I. Salutation: A Trinitarian Message (1:1-2)
- II. The Blessings and Responsibilities of Salvation (1:3–2:10)
  - A. Doxology: The Blessings of Salvation (1:3-12)
    1. Primary blessing—regeneration (1:3-5)
    2. Two problems that threaten the blessing (1:6-9)
    3. Salvation fulfills the prophets and the angels (1:10-12)
  - B. The Ethical Responsibilities Resulting from Salvation (1:13–2:3)
    1. Preparation for holiness (1:13-16)
    2. The basis for our lifestyle—reverent fear (1:17-21)
    3. The heart of our lifestyle—love (1:22-25)
    4. The result of the blessings—craving God's food (2:1-3)
  - C. The Corporate Blessings of the Community of God (2:4-10)
    1. The core of the community—living stones on the living stone (2:4-5)
    2. Christ—honored cornerstone or stone of stumbling (2:6-8)
    3. The privileges of the community (2:9-10)
- III. The Relationships in the Community of God (2:11–3:12)
  - A. The Thesis—A Vital Witness (2:11-12)
  - B. Submission to Government (2:13-17)
  - C. Submission of Slaves to Their Masters (2:18-25)
    1. The extent of that submission (2:18-20)
    2. The model of Christ (2:21-25)
  - D. The Submission of Believing Wives to Pagan Husbands (3:1-6)
  - E. The Responsibility of the Husbands (3:7)
  - F. The Righteous Qualities Needed (3:8-12)
- IV. The Central Problem Developed—Persecution for the Sake of Christ (3:13–4:19)
  - A. Suffering for Righteousness' Sake (3:13-17)
  - B. The Model for Triumph over Suffering—Christ (3:18-22)
  - C. Right Response to Opposition (4:1-6)
  - D. Ethical Life in the Community (4:7-11)
  - E. A Christian Approach to Suffering (4:12-19)
- V. The Key to Community Life—Service (5:1-11)
  - A. A Challenge to the Leaders—Proper Leadership (5:1-5a)
  - B. A Challenge to the Community—Humility, Trust in God, Alertness 5:5b-11)
- VI. Final Greetings (5:12-14)

COMMENTARY ON
1 Peter

◆ I. Salutation: A Trinitarian Message (1:1-2)

This letter is from Peter, an apostle of Jesus Christ.

I am writing to God's chosen people who are living as foreigners in the provinces of Pontus, Galatia, Cappadocia, Asia, and Bithynia.* 2God the Father knew you and chose you long ago, and his Spirit has made you holy. As a result, you have obeyed him and have been cleansed by the blood of Jesus Christ.

May God give you more and more grace and peace.

1:1 *Pontus, Galatia, Cappadocia, Asia,* and *Bithynia* were Roman provinces in what is now Turkey.

NOTES

1:1 ***God's chosen people.*** It is debated whether "chosen" modifies "strangers" (so "elect exiles," ESV) or represents a separate idea ("chosen people who are living as foreigners," or "chosen to be foreigners," so NASB, NLT, TNIV). In the context, the latter is probably better. Peter is emphasizing Christians' special status as God's elect. The church is the new Israel, the people of God in continuity with Israel in the OT. Even though they are despised and oppressed in this evil world, they can know that they have been singled out by God as his chosen people.

living as foreigners. Most believe that this phrase (derived from *parepidēmos* [TG3927, ZG4215]) and the corresponding "foreigners in the land" (*paroikia* [TG3940, ZG4229], 1:17; both occur in 2:11) are metaphors that depict how Christians are to think of themselves in relationship to the world around them. The noun *parepidēmos* pictures a visitor who is in a location for only a short term. The noun *paroikia* (1:17) depicts the mode of life of a "resident alien" (or a sojourner) who is living in a foreign country for a time but does not "belong" there. They are "strangers" here and "exiled" from their true heavenly home. Both remind the followers of Christ that they do not truly belong in this world; they are citizens of heaven (Eph 2:19; Phil 3:20) and as such follow the ethical customs and standards of God's realm rather than those of this world. Achtemeier (1996:174-175; contra Elliott, below) says these two terms were not taken from their legal situation or their status in the Roman world but rather were based to some degree on the status of Israel, particularly Abraham, as he sojourned during his wanderings (cf. Gen 23:4; Ps 39:12). They relive the life of Israel and of the patriarchs as they "sojourn" in this world, never really belonging.

Elliott (1981:24-37; 2000:457-462; also McKnight 1996:48-50) believes that these are not metaphors but sociopolitical terms that describe a group of converts in Asia Minor that were marginalized because they belonged to the lower class. They thought their conversion would bring God's blessings and cause things to get better, but they discovered that they were now doubly oppressed because their neighbors turned against them when they became Christians. While an attractive theory, few have taken this route because there is insufficient evidence in 1 Peter for such a sociological approach. In similar fashion, Jobes (2005:28-40, 61) sees this as more than a metaphor; she believes it depicts Christians from Rome that were expelled and forced to recolonize in (or relocate to) Asia Minor, as with Priscilla and Aquila (Acts 18:2) in the expulsion under Claudius in AD 49. This "dispersion" led to discouragement, so Peter was addressing their plight. This suffers the same problem as Elliott's theory: There is not enough in the epistle to warrant so specific an identification.

in the provinces. Or, "dispersed (*diaspora* [TG1290, ZG1402]) among the provinces." In combination with the preceding "foreigners," Peter speaks of his readers literally as "aliens of the diaspora/dispersion." The Greek term *diaspora* had a particular Jewish usage, describing those who since the exile had been displaced and forced to live among the Gentiles in an "alien" environment (see Isa 49:6; Jer 15:7, LXX). Asia Minor, along with Babylon and Egypt, had the largest Jewish diaspora communities in the first century. So this is another term with a metaphorical sense describing Christians as the marginalized in society. There is also a possible thrust describing the Christian life as a journey of those "dispersed" in the world.

Pontus, Galatia, Cappadocia, Asia, and Bithynia. It is disputed whether Peter intended to depict the Roman provinces as official entities, for Pontus and Bithynia constituted a single Roman province. It is doubtful that he would be ignorant of this. Many think he was taking a geographical approach, describing the route a courier would take to deliver the letter—landing at the port of Sinope on the Black Sea at Pontus, then moving south to Cappadocia, west to Galatia and Asia, then north to Bithynia (see Achtemeier 1996:83-85; Hemer 1977–1978:239-243). The one difficulty is that this moves in the opposite direction (east to west) that one would expect of a letter coming from Rome. So it is possible that Peter was just naming them from memory without thinking of political changes, centering on regions rather than official provinces (so Green, Jobes).

1:2 *God the Father . . . his Spirit . . . Jesus Christ.* This verse is Trinitarian, expressing how each member of the triune Godhead relates to the scattered aliens and further describing the meaning of their election as the special people of God. Moreover, these are three prepositional phrases in the Greek that depict the parameters of God's choosing them: "according to" (*kata* [TG2596, ZG2848], the basis), "by" (*en* [TG1722, ZG1877], the means—though some prefer locative, "takes place in the sphere of"), and "for" (*eis* [TG1519, ZG1650], the purpose/result).

knew you . . . long ago. Lit., "according to the foreknowledge of God." This emphasizes that God, not Rome or any other human power, is in charge. It also parallels Rom 8:29; 11:2, where Paul talks of God knowing and choosing his people "in advance," "before he made the world" (Eph 1:4). (See 1:20 where Jesus was chosen "long before the world began.") God's foreordained purpose was that his people be separate and distinct from the people of this world. Marginalization is part of the plan of God!

COMMENTARY

With a three-part greeting consisting of the author, recipients, and salutation, this is a typical Christian letter exhibiting the regular epistolary conventions. However, it is written to the largest region of any epistle, with the provinces covering nearly 300,000 square miles (Achtemeier, Michaels). Simon, part of the inner circle (with James and John) of Jesus' apostolic band, was given the nickname Cephas (Aramaic) or Peter (Greek) by Jesus when they first met (John 1:42, reaffirmed at the Caesarea Philippi confession in Matt 16:18). This followed an Old Testament practice in which God would give certain people a special commission by renaming them, as with Abram/Abraham in Genesis 17:5 and with Jacob/Israel in Genesis 32:28. It was a virtual prophecy, for Peter never became "the rock" until after Pentecost; before then, he was shifting sand! We do not know whether or not Peter ministered in person in the parts of Asia Minor he mentions, but he twice calls the recipients "dear friends" (2:11; 4:12) and in 5:1 labels himself a "fellow elder" and "a witness." There is some familiarity between Peter and the addressees, but whether that means time spent together is difficult to ascertain. By calling himself "an apostle of Jesus Christ" (1:1), he makes this an authoritative letter (cf. the first verses of Romans, 1 and 2 Corinthians, Galatians, Ephesians, Colossians, 1 and 2 Timothy, and Titus) and tells the readers that he was led by Christ himself in writing this letter.

The three descriptions Peter uses here provide key themes for the book. First, they are the elect people of God (1:1). This term was used in the Greek translation of the Old Testament to express God's "choosing" a people from the nations to be his own (Deut 4:37; 1 Chr 16:13; Ps 105:6 [104:6, LXX]; Isa 45:4; 65:9). Michaels (1988:7) sees a background in Jewish apocalyptic as well, linking the believers with the righteous remnant in Israel who would be protected and vindicated by God for all that they suffer (see Wis 3:9; *1 Enoch* 1:1, 8; 39:6-7). This concept of being the "elect" was utilized by Jesus often to designate God's choice of the believers to be his own (Matt 22:14; Mark 13:20, 22, 27; John 13:18; 15:16, 19). Paul also frequently spoke of "the elect" (Rom 8:29-30; 9:6-26; Eph 1:4-5, 11; Col 3:12; 1 Thess 1:4; 2 Thess 2:13), as did Peter (1:1-2; 2:4, 6, 9—for discussion of this issue, see Osborne 2004:222-223, 280-281). The church is the new Israel, the "elect" people of God, including believing Jews and Gentiles. The church has not replaced Israel on the "olive tree" (Rom 11:17) but has joined Israel, and so there is direct continuity from the "elect" of the Old Testament to the "elect" of the New Testament. For us, this means that even when we are rejected by those around us, we can know that God has made us his special people (indeed, his children) chosen out of all of mankind to be his.

The NLT's "living as foreigners" is more literally, "foreigners of the diaspora" (see note on 1:1). "Foreigner" depicts the Christian as a temporary visitor or resident in a strange land—to quote one of the great spiritual hymns, "This world is not my home, I'm just a passin' through." It reminds us that when the world turns against us, we should not be surprised, because we do not belong anyway. We are strangers in it, and we belong to and live for God. *Diaspora* means that believers are reliving the experience of Israel after the exile; we are "dispersed" in strange places far from our true home, heaven. Since we are chosen by God and belong to him, we are alienated from those around us, seen as oddities, even dangerous oddities, by those who do not want God. We simply do not belong during this temporary sojourn, and problems arise when we try to belong to the world and be a part of it.

This designation of the believers is then followed by three prepositional phrases (1:2) that tell the basis, the sphere, and the purpose (see note on 1:2) of God choosing us to be strangers in this world. Theologically, this is the deepest greeting in the New Testament apart from Revelation 1:4-6 (another Trinitarian greeting). Peter wants us to know that the whole of the triune Godhead is involved in our God-ordained plight as the marginalized in society. First, we were known long before the events that happen to us. This salvific knowledge of us is held by our "Father" (1:2), a term stressing the intimate relationship we have with our sovereign Lord. Foreknowledge and election are closely connected, as Romans 8:29 demonstrates: "For God knew his people in advance, and he chose them." People may reject, oppose, and persecute us, but we must realize that God knew us and chose us long before they ever existed. Our lives, including our trials and hardships, are part of his plan, and as Job 42:2 says, "I know that you [God] can do anything, and no one can stop you."

Second, the means by which God chooses believers is the sanctifying work of the Spirit ("his Spirit has made you holy"). This refers to the process by which God sets us apart from the world and enables us to live by the power of the Spirit within. As Goppelt (1993:74) says, "Whoever is taken hold of by the Spirit is thus taken from the realm of the profane and placed into the sphere of the holy, i.e., of God. . . . This 'sanctification' corresponds in content to God's self-revelation expressed in corresponding human conduct." It includes the idea of the Spirit as the "seal" (Eph 1:13, 4:30), centering on our sanctified status before God and the idea of the Spirit's sanctifying activity in our lives, producing set-apart lives that please God.

Third, this chosenness and sanctification, the work of God and the Spirit, will result in the work of Christ in salvation, namely, in obedience and cleansing. There are two major questions: (1) Is "obedience" (1:2) the obedience of Jesus Christ to God's will (so Elliott, Green), our obeying the call of God in salvation (so Achtemeier, Best, Davids), or the obedience that follows salvation (so Grudem, Jobes, Marshall)? All three options can make sense, but the progression from foreknowledge to sanctification to obedience favors the third. This introduces the emphasis throughout the book on the good lives and conduct of the Christians (e.g., 1:14-15, 17; 2:5, 9, 12, 15, 19-20). (2) Why does "cleansing" (lit., "sprinkling") follow "obedience" in the text? This order follows the covenant passage of Exodus 24:1-8, in which the people pledge, "We will do everything the LORD has commanded. . . . We will obey" (Exod 24:3, 7), and then Moses sprinkles them with blood from the altar. Peter, then, reflects this order in his reference to the new covenant. The greeting follows Pauline precedent (some form of it is found in all his epistles), promising "grace" and "peace" to the readers, but only 1 Peter has "may God give you more and more" (possibly taken from the Old Greek version of Dan 4:37c), a Jewish type of prayer asking for bountiful blessings from God (as in many prayers for grace and deliverance, such as Pss 6; 17; 40). "Grace" (*charis* [TG5485, ZG5921], which "modifies and expands" the normal Greek greeting, *chairein* [TG5463A, ZG5897]; Jobes 2005:73), and "peace" (*eirēnē* [TG1515, ZG1645], representing *shalom* [TH7965, ZH8934], the normal Jewish greeting), are here combined. In the first century, these were for the most part dead metaphors, virtually equivalent to "hello." As early Christian greetings, though, the emphasis is on the eschatological fulfillment of these hopes. In effect, Peter says, "The blessings your greetings longed for have now become true in Christ, and God will increase them in your life as you turn and rely completely on him."

◆ II. The Blessings and Responsibilities of Salvation (1:3–2:10)
A. Doxology: The Blessings of Salvation (1:3-12)
1. Primary blessing—regeneration (1:3-5)

3All praise to God, the Father of our Lord
Jesus Christ. It is by his great mercy that
we have been born again, because God
raised Jesus Christ from the dead. Now we
live with great expectation, 4and we have
a priceless inheritance—an inheritance
that is kept in heaven for you, pure and
undefiled, beyond the reach of change
and decay. 5And through your faith, God
is protecting you by his power until you
receive this salvation, which is ready to be
revealed on the last day for all to see.

NOTES

1:3 *born again.* There has been a great deal of material written regarding the source and meaning of this concept. At the beginning of the twentieth century, it was seen as originating in the mystery religions, in particular, conversion as an initiation into a new life (against this, see Selwyn 1995:122-123, 305-310). More likely, its origin lies in Jewish thinking about proselytes entering a new life, possibly also in the Qumran sect's view that entering their community meant experiencing a new creation (Goppelt, Jobes). Most of all, it stems from Jesus' own teaching in John 3:3, 7 (Gundry 1967). Others believe this terminology refers mainly to baptism as a symbolic resurrection to new life (Elliott, Kelly, Selwyn), but it almost certainly is the language of conversion rather than baptism (Achtemeier, Michaels).

1:4 *inheritance.* Elliott (2000:335-336) brings out four ways the Christian concepts of inheritance and hope differ from their Israelite counterparts: (1) Christian inheritance does not center on reacquiring the land and finding "political autonomy" from its "colonial overlords"; (2) the hope is not linked with the land, for Christianity and its mission are worldwide in scope; (3) the holy community has replaced the idea of a holy land; its sense of identity stems from the binding force of being the reborn children of God; (4) the Christian inheritance, unlike that tied to the land, is permanent and will never perish. Marshall (1991:37-38) adds two further nuances: (1) it is not property received upon the death of our father but consists of that which is already ours while our father still lives; our name is already on the will, the gift is guaranteed; (2) it is a property that will come in the future, but God has already destined it for us; it has been prepared for our future property.

1:5 *through your faith . . . by his power.* The two prepositions ("through" and "by") are virtually synonymous, describing the means by which we are guarded. The power (*dunamis* [TG1411, ZG1539]) of God is the vertical instrument of our security, our faith in God the horizontal means of our security. In the Greek, the first and preeminent idea is God's power as the basis of protection; faith is our "passive" part in the process. This means that we rely entirely on the divine might exercised on our behalf, not on what we can do.

COMMENTARY

The focus now moves from the redemptive effects of the triune Godhead to the salvific parameters of our life in the new covenant reality. In the Greek text, 1:3-12 are a single sentence that describes the new hope and sure inheritance that flow out of our salvation (1:3-5), the joy that suffering brings as it anchors our faith and salvation (1:6-9), and the encouragement that comes when we realize we are living in the time of fulfillment, a time the prophets and even the angels longed to see (1:10-12).

It was common in the ancient world to begin a letter with a brief thanksgiving and prayer for the person being addressed. Paul usually followed this practice (e.g., 1 Cor 1:4-9). Peter used a variation on this, shifting the attention to God and beginning with a doxology celebrating the redemptive work by the Father, Spirit, and Son (expressed in 1:2), and then introducing the salvation that the divine work has produced. In light of what God has done, how can we not fall on our knees in grateful praise? The doxology was common in Jewish settings to show gratitude to God (cf. Gen 9:26; 14:20; Pss 28:6; 66:20; Dan 2:20; 3:28; as well as the Eighteen Benedictions that closed the synagogue service), and it became common Christian practice. The Christian form is seen here as praise to "the God and Father" (1:3, ESV) with a single Greek article bringing the two into a conceptual unity (in accordance with Sharp's rule—see Wallace 1996:270-290). In 1:2 God is our Father, and in 1:3 he is the Father "of our Lord Jesus Christ." There is emphasis on Jesus' lordship and especially on his unique sonship, as in John's "Son of God" language ("one and only Son," John 3:16; "the unique One," John 1:18). God is to be praised first for giving us his Son.

The next item for praise is God's "great mercy," which is further covenant language reflecting God as *rab-khesed* [TH7227/2617, ZH8041/2876] or "filled with unfailing love" (cf. Exod 34:6: "Yahweh! The LORD! The God of compassion and mercy! I am slow to anger and filled with unfailing love and faithfulness"). It is the God of the covenant who has given us his salvation and sent his Son to die in our stead. On the basis of his "great mercy," God has given us "new birth" (lit., "caused us to be born again"). This parallels Jesus' challenge to Nicodemus in John 3:7, "You must be born again [or 'born from above']" and has the same thrust, a God-given new creation in which the person enters a new reality as a child of God. As a result, believers are part of a new community and have become "foreigners" who do not belong to this world.

The result of this new birth (marked by the preposition *eis* [TG1519, ZG1650]) is that "we live with great expectation" (lit., "a living hope"), meaning a new assurance that the future is secured by God. The hope is "alive," a dynamic eschatological reality at work in the Christian that produces the "peace" of 1:2. As the first of three *eis* or purpose/result statements, it is intimately connected to the "inheritance" of 1:4 and the "salvation . . . ready to be revealed" of 1:5. All relate to the future vindication of God's children for all they have suffered. The world may have turned against them, but final victory is guaranteed. Those who live apart from God have no true hope, for all they can do is wait for seemingly random future events to take place. Only in God does hope have substance (see Heb 11:1). Hope is another major theme in 1 Peter (1:13, 21; 3:5, 15), an important truth needed for these beleaguered Christians. The means by which the new birth and the new hope are made possible is the Resurrection ("God raised Jesus Christ from the dead," 1:3; although the NLT has "because," the preposition *dia* [TG1223, ZG1328] denotes means rather than cause). While the Cross as an atoning sacrifice is the basis for regeneration, the Resurrection is the basis for eternal life.

The second result of this new birth is our "inheritance" (1:4). Eschatologically, this concept is related to God's future promises. In the Old Testament it was used of the Promised Land bequeathed to Israel as a gift from God (Lev 20:24; 25:23; Josh 22:19), as well as the allotments given to the tribes (Num 26:52-56; Josh 11:23). Next, it was used of the gifts given by God, the kingdom blessings (Ps 16:5; Dan 12:13). The emphasis was on the future possession of these blessings. This idea carried over into the New Testament in terms of Christ's followers inheriting "the whole earth" (Matt 5:5) or the kingdom (Matt 25:34; Gal 5:21) or eternal life (Mark 10:17). The emphasis is on the heavenly reward that those who live for Christ will inherit, as well as the eternal nature of that inheritance.

This is especially seen in the three terms that accompany it, a fine example of Hellenistic rhetoric with its alliteration (three alpha-privative negations—translated literally in English as "indestructible, undefilable, unfading"). Michaels (1988:21) says it well: "In general, *aphtharton* [TG862, ZG915] refers to freedom from death and decay, *amianton* [TG283, ZG299] to freedom from uncleanness or moral impurity, and *amaranton* [TG263, ZG278] to freedom from the natural ravages of time (as, e.g., in the fading of flowers, cf. 1:24)." God ensures the eternal validity of his inheritance for his followers.

After these three descriptors, the Greek text states that the inheritance is furthermore "kept in heaven for you" (1:4). This probably reflects Jesus' teachings, as in Matthew 6:19-20 ("Store your treasures in heaven, where moths and rust cannot destroy, and thieves do not break in and steal"; cf. Luke 12:33). God will preserve and protect all treasure deposited in heaven. The perfect tense ("kept"; 1:4) foregrounds this truth as being of major importance (see Porter 1994:23). While all earthly possessions are tenuous at best, with a complete lack of security (as evidenced by major firms in bankruptcy and massive worldwide drop in the stock market), God guarantees the continual and eternal growth of all deposits in heaven. The Jewish inheritance was lost first at the Exile and then to the Romans, who controlled the land for their own ends, but not so the future inheritance of Christ's followers! Moreover, it is reserved "for you." God is the acting subject in the transaction, and we are the recipients of his largesse.

Not only are our possessions and future reward guaranteed by God, but also we ourselves are protected "by his power" (1:5). The Greek verb *phroureō* [TG5432, ZG5864] (guarded, protected) is a military metaphor, speaking of a fortress with strong walls being guarded by a battalion of soldiers; it is used also in Philippians 4:7 (Philippi was a Roman garrison town) of God's peace standing guard over the "hearts and minds" of those who through prayer take their anxieties to God. In 1:5 it refers to the hosts of heaven, the "power of God," that stands against the vicissitudes of life. It is important to realize that this protection is entirely supplied by God, who exercises his might on our behalf. It is nothing we can do, as if we could control his power and so guard ourselves. We respond with "faith," that is, a total reliance on God who alone keeps us secure. This does not mean we are inactive, as if we sit back and wait for God to do everything for us. Rather, we actively seek God and both his might and wisdom as we work through our difficulties. The key is our utter dependence on him.

The third result or goal of our new birth (after "great expectation" and "inheritance") is "this salvation" (1:5), which in 1 Peter is the result of the "ransom" paid by Christ that saved us via his "precious blood" as the "sinless, spotless Lamb of God" (1:18-19), who also is yet to be "revealed," bringing our final "gracious salvation" (1:13). So salvation in this epistle is past, present, and especially future (emphasized here and in the rest of the book). The basic meaning of "ransom" is rescue or deliverance from danger, here from sin (1:18) and final judgment (1:17). The eschatological reality of our deliverance is demonstrated in what follows, "this salvation, which is ready to be revealed on the last day for all to see" (1:5). When Christ is revealed on the last day (1:13), our eternal salvation will also be made visible to all. The "last day" is the eschaton—the final events inaugurated by Jesus' return and final judgment (cf. Rev 19–20). The "great expectation" is faith in the certainty that our final "inheritance" and "salvation" are a secure promise awaiting us. At the present time we are "foreigners" (1:1, 17) living in alienation and rejection in a world that killed Christ and persecutes us. But we also live in the certain expectation of vindication and deliverance from this evil world. Jobes (2005:88) says it well: "The certainty of future salvation animates the hope in which Christians now live, making the eschatological future a present reality. This is a consolatory technique intended to relieve feelings of oppression by so closely interweaving the glories of the future with the present that the present is transformed in the thought-world of Peter's readers."

◆ 2. Two problems that threaten the blessing (1:6-9)

6 So be truly glad.* There is wonderful joy ahead, even though you have to endure many trials for a little while. 7 These trials will show that your faith is genuine. It is being tested as fire tests and purifies gold—though your faith is far more precious than mere gold. So when your faith remains strong through many trials, it will bring you much praise and glory and honor on the day when Jesus Christ is revealed to the whole world.

8 You love him even though you have never seen him. Though you do not see him now, you trust him; and you rejoice with a glorious, inexpressible joy. 9 The reward for trusting him will be the salvation of your souls.

1:6 Or *So you are truly glad.*

NOTES

1:6 *So be truly glad.* There are two issues here. First, "so" is lit., "in which" (*en hō*); there is a question whether the *hō* [TG3739, ZG4005] is masculine (thereby referring to "last time" and speaking of joy in light of our certain vindication) or neuter (referring to the whole of 1:3-5 and connoting joy in the reality of future salvation and the hope it brings in the midst of conflict). The latter, broader meaning fits the context better. The second question is whether the verb "be glad" is an imperative (commanding joy, so NLT) or indicative (expressing joy in the midst of conflict, so the NLT mg). While the imperative makes sense, most commentators (e.g., Achtemeier, Best, Michaels, Senior) note that exhortation begins in 1:13 rather than here, so the indicative is better in the context.

1:7 *show that your faith is genuine.* Lit., "the testing of your faith." The first term here is *dokimion* [TG1383, ZG1510], which means both a "test" and "genuine/true." Putting these together it means "proof of genuineness." The object of this is our "faith" (an objective genitive, "testing faith"), which God is testing to prove its validity. Several commentators (Achtemeier, Best, Elliott) rightly state that in this verse, *pistis* [TG4102, ZG4411] (faith) has more the connotation of "faithfulness" than of trust or belief in something. We can only know the reality of our faith when it is challenged and overcomes the obstacles by remaining faithful to God.

it will bring you. The Gr. *heurethē eis* [TG2147/1519, ZG2351/1650] lit. means "it may be found unto"; the verb is a divine passive with eschatological force. In other words, at the final judgment, God will look at our genuine faith and give us "praise and glory and honor."

1:8 ***You love him even though you have never seen him. Though you do not see him now, you trust him; and you rejoice.*** The grammar is the key to the verse. There is a problem, a solution, and a result. The *problem* is expressed in two concessive participles denoting the past ("though you have never seen him") and present ("though you do not see him now") situations. The *solution* is a circumstantial participle ("yet believing"). And with this ongoing faith, the *result* is that their love and joy are restored, as seen in the two main verbs, "you love" and "you rejoice" (same verb as in 1:6).

never seen him. The reading "seeing" (*idontes* [TG3708, ZG3972]) is found in the oldest and best witnesses, combining both Alexandrian and Western families of texts (𝔓72 ℵ B C 1739 Vulgate). A variant reading, "knowing" (*eidotes* [TG3708B, ZG3857]), is found in A K P Ψ 33 and some patristic writers, but it probably reflects a hearing error ("itacism": *ei* was pronounced like *i*). Moreover, "seen" makes much more sense in the context because believers are being addressed (cf. 2 Pet 1:2-3, 8).

glorious, inexpressible joy. Some have tried to make the "glory" and the "indescribable" joy a future thing only, which will occur at the final consummation (Goppelt, Michaels, Senior). But here and in 1:9, there is very much a present and ongoing aspect (Marshall, McKnight). Probably it is best to see here an inaugurated thrust (Best, Elliott), that is, we experience his glory now, but it will not be complete until he returns.

1:9 ***The reward for trusting him.*** In Greek this is another participle, telling us that a further result of "loving" and "rejoicing" (the two verbs in 1:8) is "receiving the goal of your faith" (1:9, NIV).

COMMENTARY

The central theme of the book, suffering and trials, is now introduced. This is what it means to be "foreigners" (1:1), to be disliked and mistreated. The purpose of 1:3-12 is to ask the readers to place their social marginalization in perspective. They don't belong to this world of affliction, but they do belong to the God of heaven. That is their true home, so as they suffer now, they can realize it is preparation for the future bliss. As they go through their myriad trials, they can "be truly glad" (lit., "in which you rejoice") in the reality of their eternal heritage. The word *agalliasthe* [TG21A, ZG22] (rejoice) frames this paragraph (1:6a, 8b) and provides a strong connotation of religious exultation. The word is used in Luke 1:44, 47 of the rejoicing of the unborn baby John in his mother's womb and of Mary at the coming birth of Jesus. In Acts 2:46 it refers to eucharistic joy, and in 1 Peter 4:13 and Jude 24 it is joy at the coming eschaton. So here in 1:6 and in 1:8 it is a future-oriented joy that Christ is in charge, and that God will turn all things into victory. But the verb itself is in the present tense, and while many believe it has strictly a future orientation, the stress is on the ongoing present. At all times the believers are to be filled with joy in their salvation, even when the world has turned against them.

God gives believers joy in the midst of "experiencing suffering" or "trials" (1:6).

This term (*peirasmos* [TG3986, ZG4280]) can mean several things—a test, a trial, a temptation. James 1:2 and this verse probably share a common early church tradition; both focus on various kinds of trials. This verse centers on the meanings "test" and "trial," as does James 1:2-4, 12. The adjective *poikilos* [TG4164, ZG4476] means "many kinds" or "various," as the believer undergoes a multitude of different types of difficulties. Mainly, the forms of abuse mentioned in the book are verbal—insult, mockery, slander (2:12; 3:9, 16; 4:4, 14)—but the expression "many kinds" could also suggest physical abuse.

There are two primary emphases here with respect to trials in the Christian life. First, they last "for a little while" (1:6, *oligon arti* [TG3641/737, ZG3900/785]; see also 5:10), stressing the temporary nature of our afflictions (contra Michaels 1988:28, who interprets this of the insignificant nature of trials in light of eternity). An exercise I often encourage people to do is to try to remember the trials they were going through a year ago; it is often difficult to reconstruct the vast majority of them, and in the future most won't remember the trials they are going through now any better. These earthly ordeals are part of the "first of the birth pains" (Matt 24:8) but are nothing more than present-time difficulties that will be overturned in Christ. Second, such ordeals are *ei deon* [TG1487/1163, ZG1623/1256] (1:6), translated here and in many versions as "have to," but there is a deeper meaning. I would translate this "as God deems them necessary," for *deon* is the neuter participle of *dei* (it is necessary), sometimes used of divine necessity in the New Testament (e.g., Luke 2:49, 4:43; John 3:7, 14; Acts 4:12; Heb 2:1, 11:6). God is in sovereign control of all trials and makes certain they "work together for the good" (Rom 8:28). Goppelt (1993:89-90) states, "If this 'must be' stands above all affliction that might be expected, then those who are called are no longer left to the caprice of fate or of humankind; then they are of themselves not to see martyrdom but only the path of obedience; then they are able to endure affliction as an expression of God's decision for salvation (2:20; 5:6)." This does not mean we are happy when such difficulties arise. As Hebrews 12:11 says, "No discipline is enjoyable . . . it's painful"; our joy comes from our trust in God's control over the situation and in both the salvation we now have through him and the final salvation that awaits us.

The purpose (1:7 is a *hina* [TG2443, ZG2671], or purpose, clause) of such trials is now expressed. As in 1:6, the idea is closely aligned with James 1:2-4, which defines a trial as "when your faith is tested." Faith is not a blind trust in God; it is always active, trusting God and remaining faithful to him in concrete circumstances. God allows such tests to force us not to trust ourselves or the world around us but to turn entirely to him in all situations. We must understand this carefully. James 1:13 says, "[God] never tempts," so this "test" is not a temptation. It can only become temptation when (as in Jas 1:13-15) we turn not to God but to ourselves and allow the test to arouse "our own desires, which entice us and drag us away" from God (Jas 1:14).

Peter uses a powerful metaphor to illustrate his point. The refining or smelting process by which gold was made pure in the ancient world was a frequent metaphor for the refining process of adversity (e.g., Ps 66:10; Jer 6:27; Zech 13:9; Wis 3:4-6; Sir 2:5; Seneca *On Providence* 5.10) and is very apropos here. Gold was placed in a crucible and brought to a boiling point. Since gold was the heaviest of metals, all the impure elements mixed in the ore were brought to the surface of the boiling metals and could be skimmed off by the goldsmith. This purifying process exactly depicts what the Christian goes through. The adversities we experience become the "crucible of life" that forces all our impure elements to the surface so that God can remove them and make us "genuine, pure gold" (a "24-karat" Christian!) that will never pass away. But Peter draws an important contrast: Gold, the most precious of metals, is still perishable. Peter may be thinking of what he will say in 2 Peter 3:10-11, that this natural world will be destroyed by fire at the eschaton to make way for the "new heaven and a new earth" (Rev 21:1). For all its value, the natural world will cease. Faith (as the genuine, proven character of the person) is of incredibly greater value because it is imperishable and will go into eternity.

The result of the refining is that "[your faith] will bring you much praise and glory and honor" (1:7). As our faith is tested by afflictions and persecution, we are proven genuine or valid. God rewards us in the present but especially in the future (emphasized here). In Revelation 5:12 (cf. Rev 4:11), the saints and angels are seen giving these rewards to God in worship; here God gives them to us. As we praise God, he blesses us (1:3-5; Eph 1:3). This is a catechetical triad of terms that describe the God-human relationship. Michaels (1988:31) defines this well: "If 'the God and Father of our Lord Jesus Christ' is a God of grace, then it is in giving that he receives. . . . In honoring he is honored, in glorifying he receives glory, and in praising he is praised." This is the heart of the concept of reward in the New Testament. What we do for God and for others is banked in heaven and returned to us "on the day when Jesus Christ is revealed" (1:7). Our proven character is given the honor it deserves. This is the message of Revelation: All human beings will receive from God exactly what they are worthy of getting (Rev 16:5-7). God is a just God and returns to us all the "glory" or judgment we have earned by the way we have lived.

In 1:8-9 Peter continues to describe the difficulties of his readers. In 1:6-7 he spoke of the horizontal problem of trials in their lives; here he addresses the vertical problem of the absence of Christ from them. The theme that links both together is faith, which gives them strength to endure trials and brings the presence of Christ into their lives. The readers, in the midst of their discouragement, wished Christ could be with them as he had been with Peter. But both in their past experience and at the time Peter wrote, Christ was not there; he is at the right hand of God (3:22; cf. Rom 8:34; Eph 1:20; Col 3:1—from Ps 110:1). There was only one way out of their dilemma—to trust completely in Christ and his presence with them. When that happens, their love wells up, and they feel a joy that is "glorious" and "inexpressible." We today can identify directly with this; we often feel as if we are on our own and Christ is nowhere to be found. In our hands-on, self-centered society, we too easily feel as if we have a hands-off God. Yet in our heart of hearts, we know that is not true. When we learn to live in an active, ongoing trust in Christ, we feel his presence and know that when we have said, "Whew, I lucked out on that," the truth is that God was providentially guiding our path!

This is also an eschatological promise; we know that we will see Christ at his second coming (1:4-5, 7b). Our joy is not in present circumstances but in future promises. In that sense, our joy is first "glorious" or "filled with glory." The glory of

Christ is in one sense ours now but will be ours in fullness only after his Parousia (see *parousia* [TG3952, ZG4242], "coming"). Yet this is the problem, called by Achtemeier (1996:102) "the discrepancy between their present experience of suffering and their anticipated future glory." Christ is not with them, and his promised return has still not occurred. The only reality they know is the present one of suffering. How to resolve this problem? By trust! Then unearthly joy is gained, a joy so deep it cannot be expressed in human words (the meaning of "inexpressible"). It is also so high that it reaches the mountaintop, where the glory of Christ becomes our "glory" (*doxa* [TG1391, ZG1518], 1:7; see also 2:7; 4:14; 5:1, 4, 6, 10).

A further result of the "love" and "joy" that this "faith" (1:5, 7, 8) has produced is our "reward" (1:9, *telos* [TG5056, ZG5465]; "end" or "goal"). As Michaels (1988:35) notes, obtaining the outcome/goal of faith "comes close to the idea of collecting a reward." Bringing 1:8-9 together, it says, "You love him and rejoice, with the result that you receive the reward of your faith, the salvation of your souls" (*psuchē* [TG5590, ZG6034], "soul," refers here to the whole person, not only the spiritual side). The participle "receiving" (1:9, unexpressed in NLT) is present tense, having an inaugurated thrust like those of 1:8 and referring to an ongoing act of "receiving"—namely, a salvation that begins now and culminates in eternity. With *telos*, there is also a distinct eschatological sense, so that "salvation" here agrees with 1:5, the "salvation, which is ready to be revealed on the last day." John states clearly that eternal life is a present possession (John 5:24; 11:25; 12:25), and Peter certainly agrees in his use of the present tenses in 1:8-9. But Peter's emphasis for these depressed people is on a future reward, an inheritance and a salvation that God is storing up for them and that will be their eternal vindication. This promise transcends present suffering with future hope, and it results in absolute joy.

◆ 3. Salvation fulfills the prophets and the angels (1:10-12)

[10]This salvation was something even the prophets wanted to know more about when they prophesied about this gracious salvation prepared for you. [11]They wondered what time or situation the Spirit of Christ within them was talking about when he told them in advance about Christ's suffering and his great glory afterward.

[12]They were told that their messages were not for themselves, but for you. And now this Good News has been announced to you by those who preached in the power of the Holy Spirit sent from heaven. It is all so wonderful that even the angels are eagerly watching these things happen.

NOTES

1:10 *the prophets.* There is some debate as to whether these are OT prophets (most interpreters) or NT prophets (Selwyn, Warden). The latter position argues that OT prophets did not search the Scripture, and that "the Spirit of Christ" is a NT phenomenon. Also, they understand "Christ's sufferings" in 1:11 as the persecution of God's people in the first century. However, the text does not say they searched the Scriptures but rather that they inquired after what the "Spirit" (who was active in the OT and not just the NT) had prophesied through them. Moreover, the verb in 1:11 says literally that the Spirit in them "testified beforehand," and that would be OT, not NT, prophets. Finally, "Christ's suffering" clearly denotes the messianic sufferings (the subject of 1:10-12a) and not those of his people (see especially Jobes 2005:99-100).

wanted to know more about. This actually combines two parallel verbs, "seek out" and "search out," both with a prefix called "perfective *ek*" [TG1537, ZG1666] intensifying the verbal idea. The best way to understand them is, "careful and diligent inquiry." The prophets searched intensely to find out the work the Messiah was to do.

1:11 ***what time or situation.*** There is considerable discussion on this phrase. Many translate it "what person or time" (NASB, ESV), which could fit the emphasis on the sufferings of Christ. However, the prophets were more interested in "when" than in "who," and Peter presupposes the identity of the Christ. So it is better to take the whole phrase as related to time, "what or what kind of time" (Michaels 1988:41; cf. Davids). Jobes (2005:102-103) states that *tina* ([TG5101, ZG5515], "what") is probably a pronoun and basically means "what circumstances," which supports renderings like those of NLT, TNIV.

Spirit of Christ. This Spirit of Christ is the same as the Holy Spirit who inspired first-century preaching (cf. Rom 8:9-11 where Paul uses "Spirit of Christ," "Spirit of God," and "the Spirit" interchangeably). Several commentators (Achtemeier, Best, Kelly) think this is Christ himself (as a preexistent spirit) speaking through the prophets (cf. John 12:41; Rom 1:4; 1 Cor 10:4; Heb 11:26).

1:12 ***the angels are eagerly watching.*** There are several theories regarding what this means: (1) Many in the past have surmised that the angels wish they could have participated in the results of salvation—but this makes no sense. Angels would hardly want to fall into sin so they could experience redemption. (2) More probable is the view that the angels were kept from knowing many of the mysteries of redemption (Mark 13:32; Rom 16:25; 1 Cor 2:8; Eph 3:10; *1 Enoch* 16:3; *2 Enoch* 24:3). This is the view of most (Best, Marshall, Michaels). (3) These might be fallen angels who "desire" (*epithumousin* [TG1937, ZG2121] in a hostile sense) to watch in order to oppose the work of God (Boring). (4) The angels are intimately involved and interested in the unfolding work of salvation and so are "watching" God's plan worked out in us (Davids, Grudem, Senior). The first and third do not fit the context of 1:3-12, and the best is a combination of the second and fourth; the angels knew God's Messiah would bring salvation to mankind (they revealed this through the prophets), but they did not know the details and so were eagerly and joyfully watching God's plan unfold.

COMMENTARY

Peter designed this section to climax his discussion to this point. In the three sections of 1:3-9 he has presented Christian blessings in terms of the new birth, the inheritance, and the certainty of final salvation. Then in relation to the current crisis he showed the viability of joy in time of suffering and finally love in this time of Jesus Christ's physical absence from earth. Now he concludes all these emphases by showing us the past as the recipient of prophetic and heavenly interest. Achtemeier catches the sense properly (1996:105): "If the first part had major emphasis on the future act of God's begetting believers anew (especially inheritance and salvation), and the second part put emphasis on the present results (suffering, love, and joy), this part lays emphasis on the past, in which the rudiments of this salvation were discerned, specifically through the intervention of the divine Spirit" (1:11-12). The purpose is to show the believers that in the midst of their suffering and discouragement, they live at the end of history and so are the focus of interest from the prophets who longed to see these events take place and be a part of the time of salvation fulfilled. These Christians are experiencing what those prophets longed to see. Salvation, present and future in 1:3-9, is now seen as fulfillment. This introduces the wide-ranging use of the Old Testament in 1 Peter. One way to summarize 1:10-12 is, the prophets were searching, the Spirit was predicting, and the angels were watching. This tells of the wonder of our salvation. We now live in the reality that the prophets in the past and the angels in the present long to see.

Salvation has been the key point thus far. Peter wanted his readers to place their trials and difficulties into perspective by meditating on the true meaning of their salvation (see 1:5, 9). When believers realize that they experience redemption now and await its finalization in eternity, present suffering is something they can endure. But Peter has more we need to understand on this. The completion of our salvation in the suffering Messiah was also the focus of the prophets, so the Old Testament prophets looked forward to our day as well. They ardently studied their prophecies to discover the meaning and method of the "salvation" that would come with the Messiah. Not only that, Peter wanted the believers to realize that the focus of the Old Testament prophets was "this gracious salvation prepared for you" (1:10). In other words, the prophets were intensely interested in seeing the fulfillment of their message, this new "grace" of God promised to his people through the coming of their Messiah. Peter was saying, "Think how special you are; you have experienced the fulfillment of that grace the prophets longed to see! They were part of the preparation for that day; you are living in that day."

In 1:11, Peter tells the subject of the prophets' search, namely, "what time or situation" the Spirit was "talking about" regarding the Messiah. The prophets were very interested in the "when" of the messianic age, as in Habakkuk 2:3 ("This vision is for a future time. . . . If it seems slow in coming, wait patiently, for it will surely take place"); Daniel 9 (the 70 weeks); Daniel 12:6 ("How long will it be?"; cf. *4 Ezra* 4:33, "How long when these things will happen?"). By pointing this fact out, Peter wanted his readers to direct their thoughts to the two-stage coming of the Messiah—in 1:3-9 the primary emphasis was on the second coming of the conquering Messiah, who will bring about the eschaton and eternal joy; here the thought turns to the first coming of the suffering Messiah, who brought redemption and present joy.

The prophecies about this were instituted by the direct inspiration of the Spirit of Christ who "was talking" (the imperfect tense emphasizing the ongoing work of the Spirit throughout the prophetic age) to and through the Old Testament prophets. The expression "Spirit of Christ" is found frequently in various forms in the New Testament: "Spirit of Christ" in Romans 8:9; "Spirit of Jesus" in Acts 16:7; "Spirit of Jesus Christ" in Philippians 1:19; "Spirit of his Son" in Galatians 4:6. The Spirit is the presence of God and Jesus Christ in this world; when "Spirit of God" is used the emphasis is on the presence of God, and when "Spirit of Christ" is used the emphasis is on the presence of Christ in this world. So this means that as the Old Testament prophets were writing their prophecies, the Holy Spirit made the presence of Jesus the Messiah real to them in that very process. The eternal Spirit of Christ (see Heb 9:14), freed from the constraints of time, was present "within [or 'among'] them" through the Spirit. Moreover, the Spirit "told them in advance" about the messianic coming and suffering as he prepared God's people for the arrival of Christ.

The last part of 1:11 introduces one of the primary themes of the book: "Christ's suffering and his great glory afterward." That suffering is the path to glory is a motif in the epistle and will later be applied to God's people. Jesus provides the primary model (see the Introduction, "Major Theological Themes: Jesus Christ and Salvation") for us to follow. Selwyn calls this "the sufferings of the Christward road" (1995:136). These are the sufferings of Christ—his rejection, passion, and crucifixion, as foretold in the prophets (especially Isa 52–53). An unusual phrase occurs in 1:11, literally, "the sufferings unto (*eis* [TG1519, ZG1650]) Christ." It is explained by a contrasting parallel in 1:10, "the grace that is unto (*eis* [TG1519, ZG1650]) us," and means "the sufferings that are Christ's." It may mean "the sufferings destined for Christ," referring to the divine necessity behind Jesus' suffering (Best 1979:81). The thrust of the "great glory afterward" sums up the resurrection, ascension, and exaltation that followed Jesus' death, as in Philippians 2:9 ("Therefore, God elevated him to the place of highest honor and gave him the name above all other names"). This glorious status also includes the salvation he procured for us, so that we share both his sufferings and his glory (emphasized throughout the epistle).

The point of 1:10-11 is summed up in 1:12 with its three parts: the message of the prophets, the "Good News" of present preachers, and the interested observation of the angels. The first two are closely connected. The message of the prophets was not for their own time; they proclaimed their messianic prophecies for the new covenant people of Peter's time (and of our time; cf. Rom 4:23-24; 15:4; 1 Cor 9:9-10; 10:11). This hardly means their prophetic activity was not meant for their own time; Peter was talking about their messianic prophecies. It is also critical to realize Peter was talking apocalyptically, seen in the verb "were told," which is literally "it was revealed" (*apokaluptō* [TG601, ZG636], which shares its stem with the English "apocalyptic"). Peter was speaking of all the future or "apocalyptic" truth he had presented in 1:3-9.

However, the major "revelation" (which began the last days) was the suffering and glory of the Messiah and the salvation purchased for us by Jesus' suffering. This same message is seen in the Christian "gospel" that has "now" (see also 2:10, 25; 3:21) been proclaimed by Christian prophets and teachers. Peter wanted to stress the continuity between old and new revelation from the Spirit. We know the contents of the Christian gospel from Romans 3:21-26; 1 Corinthians 15:3-5—the death of Christ on the cross as an atoning sacrifice for our sin, his resurrection, ascension, and exaltation in heaven, the salvation made available to us from the redemption procured for us by Jesus' death. Finally, the source for these revelations is identified as "the Holy Spirit sent from heaven" (1:12). This is similar to John's theme, where the Spirit joins Jesus as a "Sent One," built on the Jewish idea of the *shaliach* (cf. TDNT 1.414-420), a representative or ambassador sent from God to be his presence and spokesman in this world (Jesus—John 3:17; 5:24; 6:37-39 etc.; Holy Spirit—John 14:26; 15:26; 16:7-8). The divine origin of the Spirit as the revealing presence in the past and present is emphasized. This is a heavenly truth and so naturally involves the angels.

The final emphasis is the most mysterious. The idea of the angels "eagerly watching these things happen" has occasioned a great deal of speculation (see note on 1:12). The best understanding pictures the very angels who revealed the coming Messiah to the prophets but did not know exactly how God's plan would unfold, now with great interest and joy "glimpsing" or "peering down" from heaven (see Hort), "desiring" to watch God's plan work itself out on earth. Peter wanted his discouraged readers to realize just how interested heaven was in the redemptive events they were experiencing. Far from being a terrible time (due to their trials), it was the culmination of all of history!

◆ B. The Ethical Responsibilities Resulting from Salvation (1:13–2:3)

1. Preparation for holiness (1:13-16)

13 So think clearly and exercise self-control. Look forward to the gracious salvation that will come to you when Jesus Christ is revealed to the world. 14 So you must live as God's obedient children. Don't slip back into your old ways of living to satisfy your own desires. You didn't know any better then. 15 But now you must be holy in everything you do, just as God who chose you is holy. 16 For the Scriptures say, "You must be holy because I am holy."*

1:16 Lev 11:44-45; 19:2; 20:7.

NOTES

1:13 ***exercise self-control.*** There is a Greek term here (*teleiōs* [TG5049, ZG5458]; "fully, perfectly") that is not represented in the NLT. Also, there is some debate whether it modifies "self-control" (Beare, Marshall, McKnight, Michaels) or "look forward" (Achtemeier, Elliott, Jobes). It can fit either (the adverb comes between the two, and either order is viable), and it makes sense either way: "Exercise complete control" or "Set your hope completely." Yet, since the major verb is "look forward/set your hope," the latter option is slightly more probable.

1:15 ***just as God who chose you is holy.*** This could be either "just like the Holy One who called you" (with "holy" as a substantive) or "as the one who called you is holy" (with "holy" as an adjective). Several recent commentators prefer the substantive, or titular, use (Achtemeier, Elliott, Michaels), and the title is used often in the OT (Pss 71:22; 89:18; Isa 1:4; 12:6; 17:7; 41:20; 43:3). But it is used nowhere else in the NT as a title, and "the one who called you" is found often (5:10; Rom 9:12; Gal 1:6; 2 Pet 1:3), so the NLT reading is slightly more likely.

COMMENTARY

Here begins a series of imperatives and imperatival participles stating the new code of living (based on the Holiness Code of Lev 17–26). Several commentators (e.g., Elliott, Kelly) believe the ensuing paragraphs stem from a series of baptismal homilies strung together by the author. However, there is no evidence for such a haphazard collection and little evidence for the baptismal nature of the contents of 1:13–2:3. Rather, these verses provide ethical instruction, beginning here with the call to a life of holiness.

We may begin this section by asking: What are the implications of such a great salvation for life today? How then should we live in both the spiritual and secular realms? This is what Peter turns to in this section: the ethical ramifications of the present strength and future hope that Christ has provided for us. The ideas are presented in four paragraphs or principles, introduced by the first imperatives in 1 Peter (see note on 1:6). Each paragraph begins with an imperative introduced by a subordinate clause (1:13, 17, 22; 2:1-2) that defines the parameters of the ethical action: Hope in God and live a life of holiness, conduct your life in the fear of God, love one another deeply, long for God's milk. This section (1:13–2:3) translates the new birth and future promise that the believer has in Christ (1:3-12) into practical ethics, showing that redemption means a new way of living, both in society and in the church (see Botha 1988).

The first paragraph (1:13-16) repeats what has been said about hope and the inheritance waiting for us, then it calls for a life that models the holiness of God. It opens with a call for clear thinking and discipline. Literally it says, "gird up the loins of your mind" (1:13), picturing ancient men hiking up their lengthy outer tunic (reaching to their feet) and fastening it firmly in their belt as they prepared for work or swift action like running (see also Exod 12:11; Luke 12:35; Eph 6:14). In this case, believers were to ready their minds for the task of living for Christ, of enduring the vicissitudes of life in light of the promised prize. The mental framework for the Christian life is essential; McKnight (1996:99-100) applies this to planning for the future. What is the mind-set behind our decisions? Too often it is a preoccupation with temporary benefits or profit for ourselves rather than concern for service to God and others. For that, we also need "self-control," a disciplined mind that places its attention squarely on the goal.

The reason why the church is to focus its mind is our future hope (referencing the "great expectation" of 1:3). "Look forward" is literally "set your hope (completely) on" (see note on 1:13). We are to center absolutely not on our present circumstances but on our hope in the future inheritance (1:4) and glory (1:8) that is awaiting us. Peter describes this as "the gracious salvation that will come to you," alluding to both "praise and glory and honor" that will be given to the victorious faithful in 1:7 and "this gracious salvation prepared for you" in 1:10. God's gracious act at the eschaton (the last day) will vindicate and reward all the suffering and sacrifice of the saints. Peter's point is that it will all be worth it when "Christ is revealed to the world" (1:13) and our final victory is made eternal. Now we are characterized by hope, then we will be characterized by final joy. In this hope, however, there is a burgeoning joy, as our future is secure in Christ. In the present we gain control of our minds and, with discipline, consider this world temporary and live for the future. It is hope that enables us to do so.

The way we make this change in our ways of thinking is to determine to "live as God's obedient children" (1:14). Since we have been "born again" (1:3), we have a new Father (and address him as such, 1:17); so we are his children and are expected to be obedient. Moreover, the use of "child of" (it is a genitival phrase in the Greek) in the New Testament often refers to the basic characteristic of a person, so here it means that our lives are centered upon keeping his commandments. We no longer follow the world's ways but at all times seek to follow the path God has set out for us. We refuse to "slip back" into old ways of living (1:14), the lifestyle that characterized and controlled us before we were believers (4:3-4). Paul said this well in Romans 12:2: "Don't copy the behavior and customs of this world," or "Don't let the world around you squeeze you into its own mould" (J. B. Phillips's translation). This is the first step of a life of holiness, which means being set apart from the world (1:14) and then set apart for God (1:15-16). Until we have separated ourselves from "[our] own desires" (the basic pattern of a worldly life), as well as our conduct from the world's ways, we cannot belong to God and begin to be "holy." Self-centeredness is the core of sin and of the basic anti-God tendency of our age; in this life, we will always struggle between a life devoted to God and a life devoted to ourselves. Even though we lived this way in our pre-Christian "ignorance" (1:14; NLT, "You didn't know any better then"), there is now no excuse for falling back into the old patterns. When we know Christ, his love and sacrifice for us, and his mandate for a "born-again" lifestyle, there is simply no reason to fall back into "fleshly" pursuits.

The core of the first paragraph is 1:15-16. There is a chiastic pattern in the Greek order: God is the model for us in 1:15a and 16b, and we follow his pattern in 1:15b and 16a. We must gain control of our mind and focus our energy on rejecting the secular ways of our world and of our basic desires and instead (strong adversative *alla* [TG235, ZG247], "but rather") turn to holiness in every area of our life and conduct. Verse 15 emphasizes "in everything you do," meaning that every aspect of our conduct must reflect the holiness of God. Peter often addressees our "conduct" (1:17-18; 2:12; 3:1-2, 16) and stresses the fact that being a Christian is not just about believing or thinking but about doing. Until our behavior reflects God's own character, we are not fully Christian. The basis (*kata* [TG2596, ZG2848], "on the basis of") of our conduct is the holiness of God. At the same time Peter is saying that the result of our election or calling must also be the holiness of God. Holiness is "the quintessential nature of God" (DOTP 420) as seen in Leviticus 19:2, "I, the LORD your God, am holy." It is at "the center of God's being," seen in his covenant love, his majestic power, and his righteous character (DOTP 430).

The quote in 1:16 is found several places in Leviticus (Lev 11:44-45; 19:2; 20:7, 26) and is the heart of God's election of Israel to be his people. In the latter three passages, it is the heart of the Holiness Code (Lev 17–26). As Elliott (1966:361) says, "Here God's holiness and his mighty liberation of Israel are given as the motivating reasons for Israel's holy obedience to the covenant commands and its social and moral 'separateness' from the polluted ways of Israel's neighbors (Lev 18:1-5, 24; 20:23)." In the Torah this meant that Israel was to refuse to live by the standards of Egypt or Canaan and was to devote herself to imbibing the righteousness of God and living by his rules. As stated above, it is not just conduct that it is in view, but the character that leads to one's conduct. It is a demand to imitate God on the basis of his call; God's holiness becomes our holiness. This in a sense becomes Peter's prologue to his own "holiness code" (1:13–2:3). As Michaels (1988:60) says, this addresses Peter's readers "in distinctly priestly terms. . . . The priestly character of the church for Peter is simply an aspect of its identification with the Jewish people" as chosen and priestly in its holiness (2:9).

2. The basis for our lifestyle—reverent fear (1:17-21)

17And remember that the heavenly Father to whom you pray has no favorites. He will judge or reward you according to what you do. So you must live in reverent fear of him during your time as "foreigners in the land." 18For you know that God paid a ransom to save you from the empty life you inherited from your ancestors. And the ransom he paid was not mere gold or silver. 19It was the precious blood of Christ, the sinless, spotless Lamb of God. 20God chose him as your ransom long before the world began, but he has now revealed him to you in these last days.

21Through Christ you have come to trust in God. And you have placed your faith and hope in God because he raised Christ from the dead and gave him great glory.

NOTES

1:17 ***remember.*** In the Greek this is *ei* [TG1487, ZG1623], marking a "condition of fact" (meaning "if" but close to "since") and assuming the reality of the statement. "Remember" captures the idea well; Peter wanted them to center on what it means to be a child of God (1:14) and to be able to address him as a loving Father. They had been born into a new family with a new, loving father, but at the same time they have the responsibility to live by the rules of that new father.

has no favorites. Lit., "does not receive according to face," or "on the basis of their looks." God shows no partiality (unlike all too many people) and never prefers one over another on the basis of social status, external appearance, or natural abilities. As in Lev 19:15 and Ps 82:2, this looks at God as the judge of us all, but when he judges us, he never prefers anyone on the basis of looks or status in the community.

1:18 ***For you know.*** The causal participle *eidotes* [TG1492, ZG3857] tells the reason why they are responsible entirely to God and are "aliens" in this world. It often introduces a liturgical or catechetical formula (Rom 5:3; 1 Cor 15:58; 2 Cor 1:7), presenting material already known to the audience that anchors an author's point.

1:19 ***Christ.*** In the Greek, the possessive genitive "of Christ" is placed last for emphasis.

spotless Lamb of God. The reader is to think of OT lamb imagery first, with all its connection to the sacrificial system, Passover, and the suffering servant. Jesus the Messiah gave himself as the atoning sacrifice for us all.

1:20 ***chose.*** The Greek verb is a participle from *proginōskō* [TG4267, ZG4589] (foreknow), which includes the idea of God's omniscient awareness and his elective power. He "knew" long before creation what would happen when he created mankind and "chose" the only way that sin-laden mankind could be brought to him.

revealed. There is a double meaning in the verb "made manifest or visible" here: It refers both to the revelation of Christ and to his visible appearing. In the coming of God's Son into the world, God has made visible his plan for our salvation.

1:21 ***you have come to trust in God.*** Lit., "through him the believers in God" or "who through him are believers in God." There is a text-critical issue here as well: The majority of manuscripts (𝔓72 ℵ C P Ψ etc.) have "those who believe" rather than "the believers" (A B 398 Vulgate). "Those who believe" is the common way of expressing this and probably should be preferred (Metzger 1994:688). The emphasis is on the act of believing; they place their faith in God and only then join "the believers."

you have placed your faith and hope in God. Some scholars (Bultmann, Dalton, Elliott, Moffatt) believe that the lack of an article before "hope" in Greek makes it the predicate nominative, thus translated "so that your faith is also hope in God." While possible grammatically, it is better to see faith and hope as united (similar to Sharp's rule, in which the presence of the article before the first of two coordinated nouns brings them into conceptual unity), and to translate the phrase as in the NLT (Wallace 1996:270-290).

because he raised Christ. The Greek (and many versions) have a result clause here, "God has raised him . . . so that your faith and hope are in God." The NLT reverses the order of the clauses and uses a causal conjunction ("because") instead. Both mean the same thing, that our faith is based in God's act of raising Jesus from the dead.

COMMENTARY

The path to holiness is here seen as twofold—a special prayer relationship to our "Abba" or Father, and the reverential fear that results. This paragraph (1:17-21) is another single sentence in the Greek and could almost be called a midrash on the quotation from Leviticus (1:16; cf. Lev 11:44-45; 19:2; 20:7), exploring the meaning of the commandment, "Be holy because I am holy." Here we see the implications of a life of holiness, the responsibility that such a commitment invokes. At the outset, Peter asks us to realize what it means to know God as our father. There are few instances of Jewish prayers invoking God as "Abba" (for a good discussion see DJG 618-619), a term that connotes a child's intimate relationship with his or her father. With this term, Jesus gave Jewish prayer theology a particular richness (Matt 6:9; 11:25; Mark 14:36; Luke 11:2; 23:34; John 11:41; 12:27, 28; 17:1, 5, 11, 21, 24, 25—the only prayer of Jesus without "Father" is the cry of dereliction on the cross), stressing the new intimacy his followers have with God (and becoming a major confession in worship, Rom 8:15-17; Gal 4:6-7). When children cry out to their father, they know they will be heard and that he will respond. God has chosen us to be his children and given us a new birth, as well as new power in prayer.

Yet with privilege comes responsibility. As is the case with any good parent, God demands obedience (1:14) and therefore functions not just as loving parent but also as Judge. This is the Old Testament emphasis on God being holy, and thereby demanding that his people fulfill their covenant obligations, with the blessings and curses of the covenant as motivation. Moreover, as Judge, God "has no favorites"—that is, he treats every child as equal before him. The emphasis is on his absolute justice; every child is treated exactly as they deserve on the basis of what they have done. No one is ever shown favoritism because of their talents or wealth or community status. Instead, God always rewards us according to what we do. This is a biblical teaching called "judgment by works" that includes believers as well as nonbelievers and is quite frequent in the Old Testament (2 Chr 6:23; Job 34:11; Pss 28:4; 62:12; Prov 24:12; Jer 17:10; Ezek 18:20; Hos 12:2), in Jewish literature (*1 Enoch* 41:1-2; *Psalms of Solomon* 2:16; 17:8; *2 Esdras* [*4 Ezra*] 7:35; 8:33; *2 Baruch* 14:12), and in the New Testament (Matt 16:27; Rom 2:6; 14:12; 1 Cor 3:12-15; 2 Cor 5:10; 11:15; 2 Tim 4:14; Rev 2:23; 11:18; 14:13; 18:6; 20:12-13; 22:12). There is both promise (reward for obeying God) and warning (punishment for disobedience) connoted here. This is not "salvation by works," for our salvation comes only by the Cross. Rather, it deals with rewards: We take into heaven from our life only those things we have done for God and others. We know nothing in terms of whether this "reward" will proceed with us into heaven as memories (my preference) or some tangible form, but the New Testament often speaks of this (cf. Luke 12:47-48; Rom 14:12; 1 Cor 3:14-15; 2 Cor 5:10; 2 Tim 2:15; Rev 22:12). We are saved by grace (our salvation), and we will be judged by works (our accountability before God; Heb 13:17; Jas 3:1; 2 Tim 2:15).

As a result, the life of the holy person will be conducted "in fear." There has been a fad in the last several decades to avoid the concept of "fear" in the New Testament and to always translate *phobos* [TG5401, ZG5832] (fear) as "reverence." The NLT strikes a good balance here by translating "reverent fear" (1:17). The key is always to note the context and to recognize that in a worship context, the term means "reverence," and in a context of danger, means "fear" or "terror." Here it is responsibility towards God in light of the possibility of judgment; so it is closer to "fear." Still, since there is also the idea of prayer for strength in conducting our lives, "reverent fear" is viable. Beare (1961:74) says it well: "Our knowledge of Him as Father must not dispel our dread of Him as our Judge. It must not lead to presumption, but to humility; it must not induce moral laxity, as if by our new position we were exempted from rendering an account to Him." In short, the Christian life is one of privilege and responsibility. We are called, enabled, and protected; but we are also held responsible to live in accordance with our benefits, to walk in the life of holiness that a loving Father requires of his children. The present time is described as "your time as 'foreigners in the land'" (1:17). The last term (*paroikia* [TG3940, ZG4229]) is closely linked with "foreigners" in 1:1 (both terms occur in 2:11), reminding the readers that they are not a part of this world and should never expect to be accepted by the people of this world. The idea is that the believers are resident aliens; they are living here for a short time, but are citizens of another country—heaven (see notes on 1:1).

Why do they belong to heaven and not earth? It is because "God paid a ransom to save [lit., redeem]" them from a pagan, earthly way of life. "Redeem" is one of the basic terms for salvation in the New Testament (Mark 10:45; Rom 3:24; 1 Cor 1:30; Eph 1:7; Titus 2:14; Heb 9:15). It stems from the ancient practice of making payment to free a prisoner of war, purchase an animal, buy back land sold due to poverty, or free a slave. As pagans, Peter's readers were in bondage, enslaved to sin. To Gentile readers, the freedom from slavery was the most powerful image. A slave could deposit money in the pagan temple treasury in order to work toward his freedom. After a long period, when a certain amount was reached, the temple would keep a percentage as commission and purchase the slave from the owner (a "ransom" payment). The former slave would in a sense belong to the temple but in every other way be free (see Deissman 1927:318-328). The enslaving power is described here as "the empty life you inherited," speaking especially of the Gentile or pagan life. This lifestyle is futile and foolish; it is pointless and senseless because it has no lasting value and is completely devoid of hope. Since its origin was not in God but in their ancestors, it was entirely of this world and has no connection with eternity. Christ had purchased them and freed them from this futile way of life. Another way to phrase the question is whether one would be the slave of sin or the slave of Christ (see Rom 6); the latter way gives freedom in the life of the Spirit.

Christ's redemption payment is vastly superior to any other ransom, for Christ did not pay for us with "mere gold or silver," which Peter literally describes as "perishable" (1:18). Gold and silver, the most precious commodities today, are still of this world and will in the end be destroyed. In complete contrast is the eternal value of "the precious blood of Christ" (1:19), with the diametrical opposites of "perishable" versus "precious" commodities. Christ's payment is of inestimably greater value than mere earthly purchases, for he was the sinless, spotless Lamb of God. "Spotless" has a twofold meaning of "without blemish or defect," both terms describing a perfect lamb, fit to be offered in the sacrificial system (Exod 29:1; Lev 22:23). This description also fits the Passover lamb (Exod 12:5) and suffering servant (Isa 53:7) imagery. Since Isaiah 52:3 ("without money you will be redeemed," NIV) corresponds to "not mere gold or silver" in 1:18, the Isaianic Servant is certainly part of the imagery here. Christ as the perfect Lamb and suffering servant has purchased the believers with his blood, not with any temporal human payment.

Redemption is anchored in the distant past and the immediate present (1:20). Peter used the same term here as in 1:2, saying that God "foreknew" (NLT "chose," which catches part of the meaning) the necessity of Christ's ransom payment before "the world began." Before God ever created this world and mankind, he already knew the Fall would take place and that he would have to become incarnate and pay the price for our sin on our behalf. He not only foreknew his people (1:2), he also foreknew Christ's perfect sacrifice for us. The result of that divine knowledge and choice has now been "revealed" or "made visible" to us in Christ's sacrificial act. Two things have been revealed: his coming and the fact that in coming he has inaugurated "these last days" (lit., "the end of times"). Davids's comments on this are insightful:

> *That Christ was* revealed *implies that he pre-existed, as the hymn of 1 Tim 3:16 indicates (cf. Heb 9:26; 1 John 1:2; 3:5), just as he continues to exist before his final revelation at the close of time (Col 3:4; 1 Pet 5:4; 1 John 3:2). . . . Christians stand, as it were, on the brink: the last age of the world has already dawned and God's chosen ones expect . . . its close in the imminent future with the final manifestation of their King and Christ. (1990:74)*

The most amazing truth, though, is that all God's preparation and action were done not abstractly but emphatically—"for your sakes" (the "to you" of NLT is not quite specific enough). The incredible events foretold by prophets, watched by angels, and enacted by Christ took place for the eternal benefit of the people of God. Peter wanted his readers to realize that all the salvific work of God described in 1:3-21 was done for their sakes; thus, they can view their earthly hardships from the perspective of God's redemptive acts. They can persevere because they are the elect for whom Christ died, the focus of the ages and of the heavenly realm.

By becoming the atoning sacrifice for us, Christ made it possible for us to become "believers" (1:21; NLT, "you have come to trust"). He is the instrument through (*dia*

[TG1223, ZG1328]) whom we place our trust in God. Note that we don't just have faith in Christ but also in the God who sent him. This is salvific trust, placing our faith in Christ who died on the cross for our sins and in the God who gave him up for us so that we could have salvation. This is the kind of trust that makes the Christian life possible. Paul says it well in Romans 3:21–4:19. Romans 3:24-26 speaks of how Christ became the atoning sacrifice (propitiation) by paying the price for us on the cross (redemption) that brought about God's declaring us right with him (justification). We benefit from his work through faith, which is a response to God's working out his salvation in us. It is not active "works" (cf. Eph 2:8-9), but giving ourselves over to the Spirit, who changes our heart. It is an act of free will responding to the power of God in us. Of course, the relationship of human free will to God's sovereign regenerating grace is a mystery that has divided philosophers and theologians throughout the centuries. It is best simply to allow the antinomy to stand and not try to solve it (we never will until we get to heaven).

This God in whom we place our trust has done two things that provide a fulcrum for the faith of these discouraged Christians. First, he "raised Christ from the dead" (1:21), a major creedal emphasis in the New Testament tradition (Acts 2:24; Rom 4:24; 8:11; 10:9; 1 Cor 6:14; 2 Cor 4:14; Gal 1:1; Eph 1:20; 1 Thess 1:10). In his resurrection Jesus became a "firstfruits" of our future life (1 Cor 15:20), enabling us to rise above our earthly sorrows. For all we suffer in this life, we have the supreme promise that we will share in Jesus' resurrection and will be given by God a perfect, glorious "spiritual body" (1 Cor 15:44, 46) that will never fade away. Second, God "gave him great glory" (1:21), an emphasis found often in John (John 7:39; 12:23, 27-28; 17:1, 5, 22) and the rest of the New Testament (Phil 2:9-11; cf. 2 Cor 3:18; 4:4; 2 Thess 2:14). The exaltation of Christ is the theme behind 3:22 and its use of Psalm 110:1: "The LORD said to my Lord, 'Sit in the place of honor at my right hand'" (see also Eph 1:20; Col 3:1; Heb 1:3, 13; 8:1; 10:12; 12:2). This divine act of glorifying Christ involved his death, resurrection, ascension, and exaltation. As stated in the discussion of 1:11b, Jesus is the model for every Christian, proving that suffering is the path to glory. Implicit in what Peter is saying is that in the same way the readers share Jesus' suffering (4:13; Rom 8:17; 2 Cor 1:5; Phil 3:10; Col 1:24), they will also share his glory.

The intended result (*hōste* [TG5620, ZG6063]) or purpose of God's action becomes a kind of conclusion for the section. "Faith" (1:5, 7-9) and "hope" (1:3, 13) are major features of this section on the blessings of salvation and the responsibilities that ensue. Through faith our present salvation is experienced, and through hope our future salvation is realized. When faith is challenged by various afflictions (1:6-7), hope enables it to endure; it becomes "more precious" than any earthly reward only when it is centered in and results from the "precious" blood of the perfect Lamb, Jesus Christ. At the same time, our hope is grounded in our faith in the God who made hope possible by raising his Son as the guarantee of our future inheritance. This presentation prepares for the rest of 1 Peter, which emphasizes how this redemptive work, the basis of our faith and hope, is meant to be lived out in our lives; via redemption we are changed from the lifeless, empty world of our past (1:18; 4:4) and transformed into new life (see Kennard 1987).

◆ 3. The heart of our lifestyle—love (1:22-25)

22You were cleansed from your sins when you obeyed the truth, so now you must show sincere love to each other as brothers and sisters.* Love each other deeply with all your heart.*

23For you have been born again, but not to a life that will quickly end. Your new life will last forever because it comes from the eternal, living word of God. 24As the Scriptures say,

"People are like grass;
their beauty is like a flower in the field.
The grass withers and the flower fades.
25 But the word of the Lord remains forever."*

And that word is the Good News that was preached to you.

1:22a Greek *must have brotherly love.* **1:22b** Some manuscripts read *with a pure heart.* **1:24-25** Isa 40:6-8.

NOTES

1:22 ***You were cleansed . . . so now.*** The NLT has again (as in 1:21) reversed the clauses (for logical effect), making the subordinate clause of the Greek ("since you were cleansed") the main clause. Still, the meaning is the same; the cleansing becomes the basis for the communal love. There is debate on the participle *hēgnikotes* [TG48, ZG49] (having cleansed); it might be causal (Jobes), temporal (Achtemeier), or circumstantial (Elliott, Grudem), borrowing the imperatival force of "love." The first option is the best, making it the reason or basis of the command to love. Although it has been common to view this perfect-tense participle as having past force (Beare, Grudem, Michaels, Senior, Stibbs), it is better to see it as describing their current state of being (Achtemeier, Davids, Goppelt, Jobes), namely, that they live as cleansed and purified people. Also, the NLT has a passive participle ("you were cleansed") for the active participle in the Greek ("having purified your souls") to bring out the fact that God, not our own merit, is the basis of salvation.

obeyed the truth. Later witnesses (K P 049 056), followed by the Byzantine (and Textus Receptus, so KJV) tradition, add "with the Spirit," but that reading is not present in earlier manuscripts (𝔓72 א A B C Ψ). It was probably added by later scribes to emphasize the Spirit's work in salvation.

with all your heart. The majority of mss (𝔓72 א C P Ψ et al.) have "from a *pure* heart," but A B Vulgate and some Old Latin witnesses omit "pure." It is easy to see why a scribe would add "pure" here in light of the verb at the beginning of the verse ("you were cleansed/purified"). Though an accidental omission of "pure" is possible, it is slightly preferable to see the word as an expansion by later scribes.

1:23 ***you have been born again, but not to a life that will quickly end. . . . it comes from the . . . word.*** Lit., "you have been regenerated, not from perishable seed but from imperishable, through the word . . . of God." There is some question whether the regeneration is the work of the Holy Spirit, the God-generated new birth, or the word of God. Several (Achtemeier, Grudem, Marshall) prefer the latter, seeing the two prepositions *ek* [TG1537, ZG1666] ("of" the imperishable seed) and *dia* [TG1223, ZG1328] ("through" the word of God) as being virtually synonymous, bringing the "seed" and the "word" together as one entity. Yet it is better to see the seed as the origin of the new birth and the word as the instrument, so they are not the same thing. A combination of the first two options, the Holy Spirit producing the God-generated new birth, provides the best thrust.

the eternal, living word of God. This is lit., "the living and abiding word of God," but the unusual Greek word order also allows "the word of the living and enduring God" (Michaels). In fact, the word order could allow "through the living word and the abiding God." While the two are used to describe God in Dan 6:26 ("For he is the living God, and he will endure forever"), the context here does not fit that phrasing, for it is the "word of God" that is the focus both in the quote from Isa 40:6-8 in 1:24-25 ("the word of the Lord remains forever") and in 2:1-3 ("pure spiritual milk"). So the NLT's rendering is the better one (see Moffatt, Senior). Hort (1898:93) suggests that *logos* [TG3056, ZG3364] is not God's word but Jesus as the "Word" as in John 1:1-18; this on the grounds that he is "living" via his resurrection and "remaining" via his incarnation. While interesting, this does not fit the Isaiah quote, and indeed Jesus as "the Word" is not found anywhere but in John and Revelation.

1:24 *As the Scriptures say.* This verse begins with "because" (*dioti* [TG1360, ZG1484]), making the quote from Isa 40 the theological basis that grounds the emphasis on the transitory nature of life (1:4, 7, 18, 23) in contrast to the eternal life that awaits us (1:4, 5, 9, 13, 23). James 1:10-11 uses the same Isaiah passage to address the wealthy, but Peter uses it of all people.

1:25 *the word of the Lord . . . that word.* In 1:23 the "living word" is *logos* [TG3056, ZG3364], while 1:25 switches to the Greek word *rhēma* [TG4487, ZG4839]. Jobes (2005:133) states that the *logos* of 1:23 is the regenerating seed as opposed to the *rhēma* of 1:25 being the spoken "word," the gospel of the NT era. However, the two terms are synonymous in both LXX and NT and most likely refer together to both the spoken words of God and the written word of canonical revelation (so Davids). The use of *rhēma* in 1:25 is most probably due to its use in the LXX of Isa 40:6-8.

COMMENTARY

The ethics of 1 Peter are grounded in the reality of the conversion experience. The holiness of 1:13-16 is anchored in the God who made us his children, and the lives of reverent fear of 1:17-21 are based on the God who sent his Son as the sacrificial Lamb and then raised him from the dead for us. These two paragraphs (1:13-16; 1:17-21) describe the vertical aspect of our Christian life, namely, our relationship with God. This paragraph (1:22-25) turns to the horizontal side, our relationship with each other. Yet it too is framed by the reality of our salvation, that when we were born again (1:23a), we were cleansed from our sins (1:22a).

There may well be a double meaning in the cleansing of the believers (1:22; lit., "having purified your souls," with "soul" as the Hebrew concept of the whole person, thus "your lives, yourselves"). First, the idea of the believers purifying themselves can refer to the Old Testament ceremony (Exod 19:10; Num 8:21; Josh 3:5) that led to ritual purity. New Testament parallels point to moral purification (Acts 21:24, 26; Jas 4:8; 1 John 3:3), here referring to conversion as the grounds for love (Beare, Best, Michaels). Kelly and Elliott take the purification as baptismal conversion, but as in 1:3 (see note) and 1:13-16, this is highly unlikely since there is no reference to Christian baptism in the context. Second, the verb itself (*hagnizō* [TG48, ZG49], "make holy") refers to the process of sanctification, referring to the "setting apart" of themselves to God (Achtemeier, Grudem, Jobes). Conversion and sanctification are accomplished "in obedience to the truth," with "truth" an objective genitive ("obeying the truth") rather than a descriptive genitive ("true obedience"). Thus, "purifying yourselves" (cf. NLT, "You were cleansed"; see note on 1:22) refers both to obeying the gospel truth when coming to Christ and to the ongoing obedience to Christian truth that then characterizes the believer's life.

This obedience demands communal love. Jesus talked of love for enemies (Matt 5:43-47), and Paul talked of showing love to your persecutors (Rom 12:14, 17-21; Peter will do so in 2:12). But Peter here centers on that love expressed in the community of brothers and sisters. He certainly had the local church in mind, but it undoubtedly applies to relationships between all believers. Green (2007:51) speaks of the use of *philadelphia* [TG5360, ZG5789] (brotherly love) here: "A common image in early Christian discourse, familial love would have particular importance in the sort of world assumed by 1 Peter, in which a strong sense of 'family' identity would serve to counter the pervasive experience of 'strangerhood' (cf. 1:1, 17; 2:11)." The imagery conceives of the corporate church as a family. There are three stages a church should go through, from an "assembly" (the meaning of "church" or *ekklēsia* [TG1577, ZG1711]) to a "community" to a "family." Each step requires more commitment and love, more sharing and caring for one another. This has been a problem throughout church history, with unnecessary church schisms between the faithful (Paul discusses this in Rom 14:1–15:13).

This family love, which rises beyond personal conflicts in the church, goes against the ways of the world and takes enormous effort. This love must first be "sincere" (1:22; lit., "unhypocritical") or "genuine, authentic, without pretense." People must know it is authentic when they see it. Second, it must be done "deeply." Scholars are divided whether the emphasis of this word is on intensity or strength of effort (Davids, Grudem, Marshall) or on the constancy and endurance of their love (Achtemeier, Elliott, Michaels). Once again, I believe this is a both–and situation rather than an either–or one (so also McKnight). "Deeply" is a strong adverb emphasizing great effort and energy to accomplish something "intensely and heartily" as Mounce says (1982:22). But the term also connotes an ongoing energy that perseveres in working at loving relationships. I picture an Olympic runner with every muscle stretched out in an effort to cross the finish line. Third, such love must be done "with all your heart"; that is, it proceeds from the whole being. There is no middle ground; love must dominate church relationships.

The basis of this loving set of interrelationships, as in 1:22a, is the whole meaning of the Christian life, the "born-again" experience (1:23). This theme, of course, launched the body of the letter, when Peter praised God because "by his great mercy" he caused us to be "born again" (1:3). This link is strengthened by the connection to the "hope in God" of 1:21, for in 1:3 the first result of the new birth is "great expectation." The new birth, in which we become God's children and part of God's family, is characterized by hope because we are now aliens and strangers in this world (1:1, 17; 2:11) and citizens of heaven. We have a new present orientation and a new future hope. This new reality in God is further described as "not . . . a life that will quickly end. Your new life will last forever" (1:23; lit., "not from perishable seed but from imperishable"), a contrast already seen in 1:18 (see commentary on that text). The imagery of birth and seed stems from human procreation, but here the eternal seed from God and the new birth are in view. Our "seed" will "perish," while God's will live forever! There is also a strong contrast in 1 Peter between a life lived for the "perishable" things of this world with one centering on the "imperishable" things of the future inheritance (cf. 1:4). If that was true in the first century, how much more is it true of our current time?[1] Believers in each generation must quit centering on the "life that will quickly end" and start centering themselves and their decisions on the "new life" that "will last forever."

This new life is of inestimable value "because it comes from the eternal, living word of God" (1:23). The "imperishable seed" or God-produced regeneration of the first half of this verse is now seen as taking place "through" the "living word." The Greek sees "the word" as the instrument (*dia* [TG1223, ZG1328] with the genitive) more than the cause of our enduring life, but the meanings are fairly close to one another. The word of God here is probably both the gospel (the spoken word) and the Old Testament (the written word), as in the Isaiah quote in the next verse. In 2 Timothy 3:16 Scripture is "inspired by God" and "useful to teach us"; in Hebrews 4:12 it is "alive and powerful. . . . sharper than the sharpest two-edged sword"; in 2 Peter 1:20-21 the prophets "were moved by the Holy Spirit, and they spoke from God." Here the word is "living," or dynamic and powerful, in producing the regenerating power of God in the believer's life. It is also "eternal," or "enduring, remaining" at all times. As a living power, the word changes us, and as an enduring presence it gives us eternal life and enables us to persevere. Davids (1990:78) says this description has two effects: "(1) it helps the persecuted believers realize they have a firm foundation to build on, a better one than the corruptible world, and (2) it gives the inward action of God in conversion just as the phrase 'obedience to the truth' described the action of the Christian—both are kept in creative tension." I would add a third effect: The presence of the word of God provides the strength and spiritual grounding necessary to "love one another from the heart" (1:22, NASB).

Peter anchors his statement by quoting Isaiah 40:6-8 from the Septuagint (which lacks Isa 40:7b-8a MT). This is apropos as Isaiah sets the perishable (mortal mankind) in contrast to the immortal (the word of God). Isaiah 40 is the turning point from the first half of the work to the rest of the book. After the devastating prophecies of coming exile (Isa 39:5-7), God says, "Comfort, comfort my people" (Isa 40:1) and then promises to deliver them (Isa 40:1-11) through his power (Isa 40:12-26). The passage here is part of the prophetic message to be "shouted" to the people (Isa 40:6a), centering on the "voice shouting in the wilderness" to prepare the pathway (remove the obstacles) for the Lord, who will come in power to deliver his people (the return from exile). Mark 1:2-3 sees this role as fulfilled by John the Baptist as he prepared the way for Jesus' coming. The early church first called itself "the Way" (a title also used at Qumran, from Isa 40:3), believing they too were preparing the "highway to Zion" (Acts 9:2; 19:9, 23; 22:4; 24:14, 22; see Barrett 1994:448). Jobes (2005:126) links Isaiah's shouted message with the gospel proclaimed to Peter's readers, saying, "These promises were more than historical prophecies for the future of Israel; they were also, perhaps more importantly, eschatological revelations of God's final redemption of humankind." Peter intended his readers to see the whole context of Isaiah 40. Peter's readers were like Israel in Isaiah's day, discouraged and on the verge of catastrophe. So this quote is intended to be a word of "comfort" for them as well.

Peter's citation of Isaiah 40:6-8 in 1:24-25 begins with the temporary nature of all human life (applicable to the trials Peter's audience was encountering; see on 1:6

above). The first lines center on individual human frailty and the transitory nature of human society. "All flesh" (the literal words of 1:24) would communicate one's lifespan, and its "beauty" (lit., "its glory") would refer to how long a person (or a society) remains attractive or glorious. Peter had already spoken of the futility and emptiness of the pagan way of life (1:18), and this continues that thought. But just like a field of wildflowers, that outward beauty will be short-lived; it will "wither" and "fade," stressing the process by which all earthly beauty goes away. It flourishes for a while and then is gone. The image is that of the sirocco, the hot wind out of the desert in Palestine that can wilt a flower in seconds. All human "glory" pales into insignificance compared to the imperishable "glories" that await the people of God who will participate in the "glory" of Christ (1:7, 11, 21). All earthly glory will dissipate and disappear, but our glory in Christ is eternal. Thus, the people of God can endure their persecutors, whose lives and "glory" are ephemeral and will blow away like chaff in the wind, because believers have a certain hope in everlasting "praise and glory and honor" (1:7).

The reason for the confidence of the believers is that in total contrast to the human pronouncements of the Roman magistrates, "the word of the Lord remains forever" (1:25a, from Isa 40:8). This undergirds the statement of 1:23 about "the eternal, living word of God." In Isaiah, this centered especially on the prophecies and covenant promises God had made through Isaiah to a discouraged Israel. Here it refers to the covenant promises now made to a discouraged new Israel. The pronouncements and charges of the enemies of the church are short-lived, made by short-lived people in short-lived situations. What God says and what he does last forever, and they are delivered to a people who have eternal life. Roman proclamations and Roman building projects seemed long-lasting back then, as some do even today. For example, the arch of Titus on the *Via Sacra* still stands, with its depiction of the Roman army carrying off the treasures of the Temple in Jerusalem after they destroyed it in AD 70. But such monuments will last only as long as this world may last—and the majority of them far less time! This world will be destroyed (2 Pet 3:7, 10-13; Rev 21:1), and only the people of God will enter the new heaven and new earth (Rev 21:27–22:5). Those tempted to give up under the pressure of Rome and the people of Asia Minor should think twice and realize they were only choosing the transitory over the eternal. Likewise we, who are under far less pressure but tempted to surrender to the elusive power of affluence and materialistic success, should realize how temporary and senseless that success is when compared to the eternal glory we share with Christ.

Finally, Peter wants his readers to realize that the eternal word of God is identical with "the Good News that was preached to you" (1:25b). As stated above, there is the spoken word and the written word. Whenever the spoken message correctly exposits the gospel truth and the meaning of the biblical text, it is connected to the "eternal" truths of God. This is the purpose of hermeneutics today. The goal is to make certain that we in a sense follow the ancient rabbis and seek to give the *Bath qol*—the true "daughter of the voice" (see ISBE 1.438-439). Our exposition should faithfully follow the voice of God spoken in his written word. Whether in expository or topical messages, whether from the pulpit or in general biblical teaching inside or outside the church, we want to present what God has revealed in his word through our teaching and preaching. When we fail to exposit the meaning of the text, we are introducing dangerous elements, "perishable" speculations off the top of our heads, rather than the "imperishable" truths of the word of God (see the important warning in 2 Tim 2:15—my theme verse!). Peter wanted the Christians of Asia Minor to realize that even though they were beleaguered and beaten down in the Roman world, they had eternity on their side. When they heard the word of God and lived a life for God, they were the focus of all of prophesy and of the very angels in heaven. They had the eternal word on their side!

ENDNOTE

1. The pandemic of greedy speculation that has brought our world to its knees in the economic crisis of the past few years is described in an excellent critique entitled *Affluenza* (Hamilton and Denniss 2005).

◆ 4. The result of the blessings—craving God's food (2:1-3)

So get rid of all evil behavior. Be done with all deceit, hypocrisy, jealousy, and all unkind speech. [2]Like newborn babies, you must crave pure spiritual milk so that you will grow into a full experience of salvation. Cry out for this nourishment, [3]now that you have had a taste of the Lord's kindness.

NOTES

2:1 ***get rid of.*** The participle that begins this verse (*apothemenoi* [TG659, ZG700], "cast off, throw away") introduces a renunciation formula; it is a common term in ethical exhortation. It stems from an image of throwing away old, dirty, unwanted clothes. It is debated whether it is imperatival as in the NLT's rendering (cf. NRSV, NIV, ESV, Goppelt, Michaels)—the use of participles to give commands is common in 1 Peter—or circumstantial, providing an attendant circumstance to the main verb in 2:2 ("getting rid of . . . long for"; so NASB, Achtemeier, Davids). Since the second use would borrow the imperatival force of 2:2, it makes little difference. Once again, some (Elliott, Kelly) see in this a baptismal metaphor with the idea of removing clothes (encumbrances from the past) for baptism. But as in 1:3 and 1:13ff, this view has little to commend it. This verb is commonly used in vice lists (Rom 13:12-13; Eph 4:22, 25; Col 3:8; Heb 12:1; Jas 1:21) and has a broad paraenetic (exhortation) force rather than narrowly a baptismal one.

2:2 ***newborn babies.*** Once again, it is common for some to see here a baptismal image in which the converted emerge through baptism as "new" members of the church. This is possible, but as before there is little evidence to sustain this reading, for the metaphor centers on new babies rather than baptized believers (see Achtemeier).

pure spiritual milk. This can be understood in several ways, depending on how we understand "spiritual" (*logikon* [TG3050, ZG3358]) and how we see the referent to "milk." *Logikon* could be "reasonable" or "logical" (Jobes), "belonging to the word" (NASB, Achtemeier, Elliott, Kelly), "spiritual" (RSV, NLT, TNIV, ESV, Goppelt, Marshall), or even "figurative (not literal)" milk (Grudem, Michaels, Senior). If it is "reasonable," it would mean that the logical or appropriate choice for getting God's nourishment is this "milk"; this makes sense and is seen as the meaning by many in the only other place the word occurs in the NT, Rom 12:1. The second understanding, "belonging to the word," is accepted because of the relationship with *logos* [TG3056, ZG3364] (the word) in 1:23; yet, *logikon* is not a synonym for *logos*. The problem with "spiritual" is that when Peter speaks of "spiritual house" and "spiritual sacrifices" later, he uses *pneumatikos* [TG4152, ZG4461], the more natural word (2:5). It appears that Peter used the word *logikon* metaphorically to convey several meanings: First, it is "spiritual" because it deals with the Christian life that follows the regenerating work of the word in 1:23-25. Second, it is "reasonable" because this nourishment for continued growth is the next logical step in the Christian life. Third, it refers to the "word" (*logos* in 1:23) as the means by which the spiritual life grows into a life of obedience (1:14). In all this the "spiritual" nature of the milk/word is dominant, and the NLT translation fittingly connotes the idea.

into a full experience of salvation. This phrase (*eis sōtērian* [TG4991, ZG5401]) is omitted in the Textus Receptus (so KJV) and most of the later witnesses, probably due to a misunderstanding of its meaning as referring to a final eschatological reality. This reading, however, is found in all the earliest manuscripts and should be retained.

2:3 *had a taste of the Lord's kindness.* This phrase alludes to Ps 34:8. It is common to see here a special reference to the Eucharist (Ps 34 was used in early church eucharistic celebrations) and perhaps also baptism as times when the church has a special "taste" of the goodness of God (Beare, Davids, Kelly, Selwyn). However, most think it "may more immediately capture the joyous and life-giving experience of the Christians whose lives are rooted in Christ" (Senior 2003:49).

Some have queried whether "the Lord" in this verse refers to God or Christ. In one sense the title refers to both. The image with Ps 34:8 is certainly that of God the Father, whose kindness has been the subject of Peter thus far (the great mercy of 1:3, the powerful protection of 1:5, the salvation of our souls in 1:9, the word of God in 1:23-25). Yet Christ and the salvation he brought have been the subject of the last half of ch 1, and it is Christ as the "living stone" that will be at the forefront of 2:4-10. What settles the issue is that the one to whom "you are coming" at the start of 2:4 modifies "Lord" in 2:3 and identifies him as "the living stone," Christ. There may well be a double meaning here, but the lordship of Christ is clearly primary (cf. Goppelt, and Achtemeier, who notes a wordplay between *chrēstos* [TG5543, ZG5982], "kindness," and *Christos* [TG5547, ZG5986], "Christ").

COMMENTARY

The final ethical responsibility, in light of all God has done for us, is to "crave [God's] pure spiritual milk" (2:2). With the centrality of the emphasis on new birth (1:3, 23) and being part of the family of God (1:14, 17, 22), the idea of craving mother's milk is a beautiful metaphor (see below) for the Christian life. Moreover, the emphasis on the eternal word of God in 1:23-25 leads naturally to a command to crave that eternal truth. Since we are newborn babies in Christ, it is absolutely logical to want the milk of the word. Yet before we can do that, we must get rid of those forces that threaten our new existence in Christ. That is the topic of 2:1. "Get rid of" means to cast sins off like filthy old clothes; the sins make a person feel dirty just being near them. Behind this command is the holiness of God (1:15-16). Since God is the absolute antithesis of sin, those who become like him in his holiness must repudiate sin with all their strength. These sins are destructive to brotherly love; their renunciation is part of the social life entrusted to the believer.

The list of sins in 2:1 is made up of two singular nouns dealing with general attitudes (NLT, "evil behavior", better seen as an attitude of "malice" than as "behavior") and "deceit," each modified by *pas* ([TG3956, ZG4246] "every kind of"), and three plural nouns (often translated as singular) dealing with specific problems ("hypocrisy," "jealousy," "unkind speech"). The first general category is a heart of wickedness or malice—the desire to harm or act out of ill will against others. The second is "deceit"—the desire to take unfair advantage of others, to deal falsely and cheat people (the original idea is bait for fish). The first of the specific sins is "hypocrisy," a term found in negative form in 1:22 ("unhypocritical" or "sincere"). This term originated in Greek theater, picturing an actor placing a mask over his face to play another role. This is a specific form of "deceit." The other two specific sins are forms of malice: "Jealousies" or "envy" is to want something that belongs to another, to want to take for oneself what another deserves. "All unkind speech" refers to wanting to hurt another by speaking evil of them (in fact, this is the primary kind of persecution named in 1 Peter; cf. 2:12; 4:4). There are so many ways this is done—slander, disparagement, gossip, making fun of a person. All must be expunged from the Christian community if there is to be any love or fellowship possible. They must be removed at both the individual and corporate levels.

Normally, a catalogue of vices is contrasted to a list of virtues, but Peter did not do that. Rather, he tells how the community can come to the place of victory in their lives. He returns to the theme of 1:23-25, the triumphant role the eternal word of God must play in the lives of believers. As those reborn into a new family with a loving Father, the people of God must become "like newborn babies" (2:2). One major thing that characterizes all newborns is their "craving" (the term means to intensely desire, to demand; the NLT has a helpful metaphor for this—"cry out for this nourishment," 2:2) for mother's milk. Infants have a compelling need for milk; they manipulate everyone around them in order to get more of that nourishing food. Christians are to exemplify this in their intense yearning for the word of God (1:23-25; see note on 2:2). In this sense Peter is describing all Christians and not just spiritual infants or recent converts through this image; we all are to desire to be fed by the word. It is "pure" (*adolos* [TG97, ZG100]) because it enables believers to "get rid of" the vices noted in 2:1 (and other passages) and become free from "deceit" (*dolos* [TG1388, ZG1515]; 2:1) or "genuine" before God. It is "spiritual" in the sense that the word is the reasonable or logical way for Christians to become what God wishes them to be spiritually (see note on 2:2). It is "milk" in the sense that it is spiritual nourishment that allows believers to grow and prosper for God.

While the word of God is certainly a referent, Peter also intends that everything that helps the child of God grow and attain a life of holiness (1:15-16) be included in this "milk." This includes corporate fellowship, good Christian literature, general Christian teaching and dialogue, and so forth. Michaels (1988:88-89) says that while the proclamation of gospel truth is the medium, "the milk itself is more appropriately interpreted as the sustaining life of God given in his mercy to his children." Many do not believe the written word of God is the primary referent (e.g., Michaels and Jobes), and to an extent that is true. But it must be included as the means by which God's people are informed as to the conduct God requires.

The purpose of this nourishment from the word is for the believer to "grow into a full experience of salvation" (2:2). As milk enables children to grow up into adulthood, so God's spiritual food allows us to attain a mature life in Christ. The "pure spiritual milk" is the means by which (cf. Gr. *en* [TG1722, ZG1877]) this growth takes place. Every church must provide multiple opportunities for Christians to interact with and learn the deep truths of the faith. I believe there are two foci of a truly biblical church: the centrality of the word of God in both the preaching and teaching ministries, and the deep relationships that make the church a family. The goal (*eis* [TG1519, ZG1650]) of this growth is "salvation," which combines the ideas of spiritual salvation and deliverance (bringing vindication). In 1 Peter salvation is an eschatological concept referring to that deliverance "ready to be revealed on the last day," a salvation the prophets longed for (see 1:5, 9, 10). In 1 Peter there is an inaugurated aspect to it, that is, we experience the present salvation as a harbinger or proleptic anticipation of the final salvation we will receive when Christ returns (see notes on 2:2). This means that the whole of the Christian life, a process that continues until the Lord returns, is to be characterized by continual growth through the word of God and every kind of spiritual nourishment as we await our final salvation.

This truth is anchored further in 2:3 by an appeal to Psalm 34:8, "Taste and see that the LORD is good." "Now that you have [tasted]" (2:3) is an excellent translation of the condition of fact stated in the Greek (*ei* [TG1487, ZG1623]), which assumes the reality of the thing stated, here virtually synonymous with "Since you have tasted." The verb "taste" is a metaphor for one's experiences, here the experience of the Lord's goodness. Psalm 34 is a favorite of Peter's, quoted again in 3:10-12. The superscription of the psalm says David wrote it while fleeing from Saul, pretending to be insane in order to escape capture (cf. 1 Sam 21). It was a good psalm for Peter's discouraged readers because they, like David, were afflicted and rejected, and the second half of Psalm 34:8 says, "Oh, the joys of those who take refuge in him." The message is that believers, like David, know the goodness of God and have experienced his love and providential care for us. As a result, we need to take that past experience and apply it to our present afflictions, finding refuge in him and his word.

We crave God's milk because we have experienced how delicious, refreshing, and fulfilling it is. As we grow in him and realize his goodness, we naturally want more. "Kindness" in the NLT represents the adjective *chrēstos* [TG5543, ZG5982] (good, kind, gracious), which is a major descriptor of God, often similar to the Hebrew *khesed* [TH2617, ZH2876], the main term for God's "lovingkindness," his covenant love and mercy. This is his "goodness" at the highest level depicted by the metaphor of taste. It is amazing how often a person's favorite foods are those their mother made, and how frequently the marital complaint, "You don't cook like Mom," is heard. Home cooking becomes a criterion for good food. I tell my students they need to prepare gourmet meals from the word, so that the people in their churches will never again be satisfied with "fast food" Christianity, that is, with shallowness. There is so much depth in the word and in the great theological truths of the faith that no one should ever want to or have to be satisfied with half-baked teaching or books. There is also so much goodness in corporate fellowship, in the life of the church, that we all should gravitate to it again and again as we pass through the vicissitudes of life.

C. The Corporate Blessings of the Community of God (2:4-10)

1. The core of the community—living stones on the living stone (2:4-5)

4You are coming to Christ, who is the living cornerstone of God's temple. He was rejected by people, but he was chosen by God for great honor.

5And you are living stones that God is building into his spiritual temple. What's more, you are his holy priests.* Through the mediation of Jesus Christ, you offer spiritual sacrifices that please God.

2:5 Greek *holy priesthood.*

NOTES

2:4 *You are coming to Christ.* Lit., "to whom coming," and there is debate as to whether *proserchomenoi* [TG4334, ZG4665] is imperatival ("come to him," so NRSV, Goppelt, Moffatt, Senior), circumstantial and thereby borrowing from the indicative force of the main verb ("you are coming," NLT, Achtemeier, Beare, Grudem, Michaels), or temporal ("as you come," so TNIV, ESV, Grudem). The second is the most likely, since the participle here is connected to the main verb in 2:5.

2:5 *God is building.* Lit., "you are being built up." The verb can be seen as an imperative ("as for you, be built up," with a middle sense, "build yourselves up," so Bigg, Goppelt, Moffatt) but is most likely an indicative and a divine passive, thus "God is building you" (so Davids, Grudem, and Achtemeier, who notes that the passive of this verb is never an imperative in the LXX or NT). This construction metaphor pictures God building the church into a temple.

spiritual sacrifices. Some (e.g., Selwyn) see this pointing especially to the Eucharist as the Christian priest leads the community in offering a eucharistic sacrifice to Christ. However, the statement is certainly far more general, as there is no hint of sacramentalism in this context.

COMMENTARY

In this paragraph (2:4-10) there are two A-B-A patterns: A (Christ, 2:4), B (church, 2:5), A (Christ, 2:6a); and then A (believer, 2:6b-7a), B (unbeliever, 2:7b-8), A (believer, 2:9-10). The first pattern is comparative, with the church being built as a new temple of living stones upon the chief cornerstone, Christ. The second A-B-A pattern is contrastive, with believer and unbeliever in polar opposite positions. The purpose is to show the discouraged and suffering Christians how important they are, and to contrast their true status with those who are above them in this world but have no status with God.

Much discussion has arisen regarding the reason for the switch in imagery from infants feeding (2:2-3) to stones making up the construction of the temple (2:4-10). There are several possibilities (cf. Achtemeier, Hillyer, Jobes): (1) In the mystery religions, an initiate would drink ritual milk and then worship a stone idol; (2) it could be a contrast between the many-breasted Artemis (with her temple in Ephesus), who could not nourish her worshipers, and Jesus the living stone who could; (3) it might parallel a tradition in Qumran (1QH 9:28-32, 10:24) where it is said that God, the rock of strength, nourishes his people; (4) it could stem from Old Testament passages like Genesis 16:2; 30:3 (Sarah's and Rachel's desire for children combining ideas of family with building a house); Deuteronomy 32:18 (God the Rock who gives birth to his people); or Joel 3:18 (the hills will run with milk). The Genesis reference may be the best indication of the solution here, since it was common in Semitic thought to link building a house with having children (so Hillyer, Jobes).

The first major unit of Peter's letter (1:3–2:10) has moved from the blessings of salvation (1:3-12) to the responsibilities that those blessings entail (1:13–2:3). It now returns to the blessings of salvation, but shifts focus from the individual to the corporate body, from the hope and divine presence we each possess to the corporate identity we have as the people of God (2:4-10). These suffering Christians could be encouraged by realizing that the God who chose Jesus to be his cornerstone has chosen them to be the stones built upon that stone, which all would become the new temple of God.

Peter begins by centering on the moment of "coming" before Christ to serve him (see note on 2:4). The verb is used of worship in the Septuagint, often of a priest approaching God in the Temple. This same verb was used in Psalm 34:5a [33:6, LXX] ("Come to him and be made radiant with joy"). Psalm 34:5b ("their faces are never covered with shame") is quoted in part in 2:6 (the full quote comes from Isa 28:16, LXX, but the latter part of that quote ["will never be put to shame"] also connotes Ps 34:5b). This complex use of the Old Testament, with several passages brought together in one quote (called "intertextuality"), was common in the early church (e.g., in Hebrews and Revelation). As used here, the combination of Psalm 34 and Isaiah 28 in 2:4, 6 shows that we who are the despised in this world (whether in the times of the psalmist or Isaiah or Peter or today) are those honored by God and thus should be filled with joy.

The rest of 2:5-8 features stone imagery, taken from Psalm 118:22; Isaiah 8:14; 28:16 and used often in the New Testament as a symbol for Jesus Christ (Matt 21:42-44; Mark 12:10-11; Luke 20:17-18; Rom 9:32-33; Eph 2:20-22). The early church borrowed the "stone" passages from Jewish use (e.g., Isa 28:16 was taken messianically in Targum Jonathan)—and especially from Jesus' use of them in reference to himself. The "Lord" of 2:3 is identified in 2:4 literally as the "living stone," referring to the "cornerstone of God's temple" (2:4, NLT). In the Old Testament, God is called the "rock of salvation" (Deut 32:4, 15; Ps 62:2, 6), who had fathered Israel (Deut 32:18); the "Rock of Israel" (2 Sam 23:3); and Israel's "rock and redeemer" (Ps 19:14). The meaning is that God is the bulwark, the foundation for the nation.

Psalm 118:22 (alluded to in 2:4 and quoted in 2:7) tells us that "God has given prominence to his suffering servant like a 'capstone' . . . an important stone that held two rows of stones together in a corner ('cornerstone') or stabilized the stones at the foundation or elsewhere" (VanGemeren 2008:857). Both images, foundation and cornerstone, are applied to Christ as the rock on whom salvation is built and as the cornerstone (seen in the note on 2:6) that holds the people of God together. This stone is "living"; he is a dynamic, personal power—the "living God" in relation to his people. The description "living" especially points to Jesus as the "living One," raised from the dead, who can now give life to those who believe in him.

Psalm 118 is the last of the Hallel Psalms; it played an important role in the festivals and in synagogue worship. The contrast portrayed in Psalm 118:22 is the key to this section: "The stone that the builders rejected has now become the cornerstone" (the expression "chosen, honored" is taken by Peter from Isa 28:16). In Psalm 118 God's servant is said to be rejected by the "builders," which is apostate Israel (in Isa 8); here it alludes to the Jewish people in Jesus' time and the Greco-Roman world at the time of Peter's writing. The mission of the church is probably in view; Jesus is being rejected (2:4; the perfect participle "rejected" points to a current state) as his name is proclaimed all over the world. The primary emphasis, however, is on the fact that he at the same time is "chosen" or "elect" and "honored" or "precious." The whole of 2:4-10 is built on the fact that the church shares all of these with Jesus. Jesus was vindicated by God in the midst of his suffering and rejection, and as the people of God share his suffering (cf. Phil 3:10; Col 1:24), they will also share in his glory (see on 1:11). His "election" was described in 1:20 as occurring "long before the world began," and Christians are called a "chosen people" in 1:1. His "honor" stems from his ransom payment as the spotless Lamb (1:18-19) and is described as "glory" in 1:11, 21.

We share not only the rejection and honor of Jesus, the living stone; through him, we actually become "living stones" (2:5). He is the cornerstone or foundation of God's temple; the church becomes the building blocks erected upon him to become God's temple (an image also developed in Qumran; cf. 1QS 5:5-6, 8:4-6; 1QH[a] 14[6]:25-28; 4QFlor [4Q174] 1:1-7). When Peter wrote, the Temple had not yet been destroyed, so this statement that we are the "living stones" of the church, the new temple, is even more special. Peter was remembering the magnificent white marble, gold, and precious stones that went into that beautiful structure. So he was describing the beauty and splendor of the church as God's new "spiritual temple," meaning that the Holy Spirit has transformed it into God's "house." The Spirit dwells there, and as the Jerusalem Temple was viewed as God's literal home (Judg 18:31; Isa 56:7), so is the church now (see Acts 7:48; 17:24; 1 Cor 3:9, 16; 2 Cor 6:16; Eph 2:21-22; Heb 3:6). Moreover, we have the promise of eternity (the "great expectation") and know that we will be "living" just as Christ is in resurrection life (1:3b-4). Further, this implies the unity of the church, as Christians together make up this "temple" and are not meant to be disorganized or scattered piles but to be a corporate structure that works together. A major misunderstanding today is to apply rugged individualism to the concept of the church. The New Testament is united in demanding a corporate community "where the transformed lives of believers are offered as sacrifice to the glory of God" (Jobes 2005:149).

The extended metaphor developed here has one more step. Christians are living stones that make up God's temple, but they are also the priesthood that serves God in that temple. The word "priesthood" (2:5; NLT, "holy priests") is introduced by *eis* [TG1519, ZG1650], indicating that one goal or purpose of the building of the spiritual temple was for the work of this priesthood. So the metaphor shifts in a natural direction—the house describes the nature of the church, the priesthood the work or vocation of it. The church is a "holy" priesthood as it obeys the command of 1:15-16 to be like God, to be "holy in everything you do." The metaphor also pictures the church, like the priests of old, consecrating themselves to Yahweh, ministering to him in holy worship (cf. Exod 19; Lev 8). A spiritual house will naturally contain "holy priests" who are set apart from the world in service to God. In the same way that the church typologically fulfills the Jewish Temple, so the church typologically fulfills the Aaronic priesthood. Here we see Martin Luther's famous "priesthood of all believers." This image is true both individually (we are all "priests") and corporately (we form a "priesthood"). It is also ontological (we are his house) and functional (we are priests presenting sacrifices).

As priests we "offer spiritual sacrifices" (2:5). The background is obvious. The Aaronic priesthood offered five types of sacrifices—the burnt offering, the grain offering, the peace offering, the sin or purification offering, and the guilt offering (see Osborne 2006:193-198). Believers fulfill them all by first accepting the sacrificial offering of Christ and then presenting "spiritual sacrifices" to God, possibly meaning sacrifices guided by the Holy Spirit. This is to be acted out in every area of life—our daily activities belong to him. Moreover, this builds on the Old Testament emphasis on "sacrifices of the heart" being part of what God desires for proper worship (Pss 40:8; 50:7-15; 51:16-17; Hos 6:6; Mic 6:6-8), referring especially to nonmaterial sacrifices, such as good deeds and love, as worship celebrating Christ's atoning work via a new sacrificial lifestyle. It is only this Christ-centered lifestyle that will please God in the end. Another way to say this is to use the image of Old Testament sacrifice and say that such a life is "acceptable to God," a "pleasing aroma" to him (Exod 29:25, 41). Romans 12:1 is a close parallel, calling on believers to give their bodies as a sacrifice that God will find acceptable (cf. Phil 4:18, where a gift to Paul is called "a sweet-smelling sacrifice that is acceptable and pleasing to God"). Finally, all this is so only "through the mediation of Jesus Christ" (lit., "through Jesus Christ"). In 1:21 Christ was described as the instrument through which we could place our faith and hope in God. Now he is also described as the instrument through which we can live for God. Our faith in Christ makes it possible for us to become part of God's household; our life in Christ makes it possible to offer priestly sacrifices to God.

◆ 2. Christ—honored cornerstone or stone of stumbling (2:6-8)

6 As the Scriptures say,

"I am placing a cornerstone in
Jerusalem,*
chosen for great honor,
and anyone who trusts in him
will never be disgraced."*

7 Yes, you who trust him recognize the honor God has given him. But for those who reject him,

"The stone that the builders rejected
has now become the cornerstone."*

8 And,

"He is the stone that makes people
stumble,
the rock that makes them fall."*

They stumble because they do not obey God's word, and so they meet the fate that was planned for them.

2:6a Greek *in Zion.* **2:6b** Isa 28:16 (Greek version). **2:7** Ps 118:22. **2:8** Isa 8:14.

NOTES

2:6 ***cornerstone.*** Jeremias's argument (TDNT 1.791-793) that this refers to a keystone at the top of an arch rather than the foundation stone at the corner of a building (on the grounds that the term refers to a keystone in first-century texts) has had quite a bit of influence in the discussions about this verse. Yet the foundation stone at the corner of a building is the better understanding because in Isa 28:16 the picture is of God laying the foundation for his building, and in 2:8, this stone "makes people stumble," demanding that it be one on the ground. A third option, that it is a "capstone" or battlement placed at the top of the finished castle (Cahill 1999), is interesting but lacks final proof. As with the keystone Jeremias suggests, it would also be hard to "stumble" over a capstone.

2:7 *you who trust him recognize the honor God has given him.* There are two ways to understand this terse comment (lit., "to you who believe, honor"). Both center on "you who trust him," i.e., the believers. The question is how to translate *humin* [TG4771, ZG5148] . . . *hē timē* [TG5092, ZG5507], "to/for you (pl.) the honor." It can be either a dative of advantage: "there is honor *for you*" (NASB, ESV, Achtemeier, Goppelt, Marshall, Michaels, Selwyn), in which the Christians share in the honor of the cornerstone; or a dative of indirect object: "the honor (of Christ) is recognizable *to you*" (NLT, TNIV, NRSV, Best, Bigg, Davids, McKnight), in which the Christians give honor to the cornerstone. Either reading can fit the Greek, but because the theme in this section is that of the believers sharing in the election and honor of the cornerstone, it is better to take the first option as the more likely reading. This is especially so because the idea of "recognizable" is not in the Greek but has to be inferred from the context. In this light, the first option makes a lot more sense. As Davids (1990:104) says, *hē timē* is rightly seen as the subject of the sentence, "This honor belongs to you who believe."

2:8 *do not obey God's word.* There is some discussion on whether "the word" is the direct object of "stumble" ("stumble at the word") or "disobey" ("disobey the word"). Grammatically, it could be either. The primary thrust is the latter, but some (Hort, Michaels) see it intending both ("they stumble at the word because they disobey it").

COMMENTARY

Davids (1990:89) speaks of a chiastic structure in Peter's use of the stone passages in 2:4-5 and then 2:6-8:

- A. Psalm 118:22; rejection of the stone
  - B. Isaiah 28:16; God's election of the stone
    - C. Christians as "living stones"
  - B'. Isaiah 28 regarding the stone
- A'. Psalm 118 with Isaiah 8 on the rejection of the stone

This passage considers the effect that the honored cornerstone (2:6a) has on believers (2:6b-7a) and unbelievers (2:7b-8). First, the fact of the "living stones" built upon the "living stone" into a "spiritual house" is grounded (*dioti* [TG1360, ZG1484], "for") in Scripture (the anarthrous *graphē* [TG1124, ZG1210], probably pointing to the several texts quoted in ensuing verses). The quotation in 2:6 is taken from Isaiah 28:16, where Isaiah's themes of judgment and hope are applied to Jerusalem, whose foolish leaders had made a covenant with Egypt, a "bargain with death" (Isa 28:18a). Yet God had placed his "sure foundation" in Zion and would be faithful to his promises (Isa 28:16), even though the unfaithful nation would suffer "the terrible enemy" (Isa 28:18b; see Oswalt 1986:515-519). These two themes, hope and judgment, are applied by Peter in 2:6-8 to believers and unbelievers.

Jesus as the honored cornerstone was already spoken of in 2:4. God has established his "cornerstone," Jesus Christ, and the eternal salvation of all mankind depends on their response to him. The foundation stone (lit., "stone designed for the corner") was chosen for two reasons (Selwyn): It controlled the design of the edifice, and it was visible (the "foundation" often had a seal stating its owner and its purpose; cf. 2 Tim 2:19). Christ is both; indeed, he is the only basis for the salvation of every person (John 14:6; Acts 4:12). The stone cannot be ignored; everyone must encounter it and either share in its honor or stumble over it and fall. That is the message of 2:6-8.

The second half of Isaiah 28:16 turns to the righteous remnant of Israel who place their trust in Yahweh. In 2:6 it is the followers of Christ who, like him (2:4), were suffering the "disgrace" or "shame" of persecution. They needed to know that they would be vindicated. Their trials are temporary (1:6), and the believers' ultimate redemption is secure (1:5). As Elliott (2000:427) brings out, "Honor and shame were fundamental, central values of the cultural system of the ancient Mediterranean . . . and here it is God who is regarded as the ultimate conferrer or adjudicator of honor and shame." Thus, those who slander the Christian will receive ultimate shame (3:16) and those who experience earthly disgrace for being a Christian receive honor and give God glory (4:16). God will reverse all worldly standards when identifying recipients of honor and shame.

In a midrashic addition to Isaiah 28:16, Peter here (2:7a) shows that the believers share in the honor of the precious cornerstone. This is one of the themes of the book. As Jesus suffered and then received glory from God (1:10, 21b), so his followers will receive honor and glory from God for their suffering (1:7b, 9, 13b). They are "living stones" built upon their foundation stone into God's new temple; so they too will receive the honor of their cornerstone as part of that temple. They will "never be disgraced" but instead will receive final vindication, honor, and glory from God.

In contrast, "those who reject him" will find judgment. For these "unbelievers" (the literal term used), Psalm 118:22 (already used in 2:4) is quoted, followed by Isaiah 8:14 in 2:8a. In Psalm 118, the "builders" are the enemies of God's chosen cornerstone. This could possibly be the "nations" of Psalm 118:10-12 but is more likely Israel itself. As Marshall (1991:72) says, this is "a psalm about the king going to the temple to give his thanks to God for a military victory. It seems that even among his own people some rejected him and had doubts about his ability; now he has been vindicated by God, who caused his triumph." In Mark 12:10-11 Jesus uses this reference of the leaders of Israel in his day who had rejected him, the Davidic Messiah. Here it refers to the enemies of Christ in Peter's day, the persecutors of God's people (both the citizens and their leaders, so Achtemeier, Michaels; both Jew and Gentile, so Jobes). They wanted to build their lives and society apart from God and his Son, but in that endeavor they were destined to defeat. Their opposition is irrelevant because the sovereign God has made the rejected one into the "cornerstone" of his true edifice, his kingdom. The vindication of Christ as "head of the corner" includes his resurrection, ascension, and exaltation, as well as the universal mission of the church into all the world. In spite of the opposition of both Jews and Rome, the church is in the process of emerging triumphant (cf. the mustard seed parable of Mark 4:30-32). In 1 Peter, the final triumph of God's people at the second coming of Christ is especially intended; Christ and his people will have the final say.

The implications of the cornerstone for unbelievers is expressed in the quotation of Isaiah 8:14 in 2:8. In Isaiah 8 God gives the prophet the prophecy regarding the invasion of Assyria and the Exile. Isaiah was to name his son "Maher-shalal-hash-baz" (Isa 8:1), which means "swift to plunder and quick to carry away" to symbolize the coming devastation. In Isaiah 8:11-13 the southern kingdom of Judah is called to fear "the LORD of Heaven's Armies" rather than other nations. As for Israel and Judah, God will be the "stone that makes people stumble, the rock that makes them fall." For those who "wait for the LORD" and "put [their] hope in him" (Isa 8:17), "he will keep [them] safe" (Isa 8:14). This is the thrust of these "stone" passages: Jesus alone is the "rock of salvation," the "cornerstone" of the true building of God. It is only those who "believe" in him who have any future. Those who "reject" have only destruction in their future. Note the step parallelism in the two parts—they "stumble," then they "fall." The term for falling is *skandalon* [TG4625, ZG4998], a term used often in the Gospels for "falling away" into sin and rejection (Matt 13:41; 18:7; Mark 6:3; Luke 7:23) but here used for falling into destruction.

The reason for the judgment is "because they do not obey God's word," a reference back to the eternal word of God in 1:24-25. Here it is the spoken word, the gospel, rather than the written word. The unbelievers reject the cornerstone because of disobedience. They do not want to follow the dictates of God, especially the narrow path of Christ. This is why they stumble and fall; Peter makes it clear that it is not the power of sin that overwhelms them but the internal proclivity to sin. It is a deliberate act, and they stand guilty before God. More difficult is the last statement, "they meet the fate that was planned for them," literally, "unto which they also were destined." This has led to a great deal of discussion because on the surface it could imply double predestination—that is, God has chosen the sinner to go to eternal punishment as well as the Christian for salvation. The question is whether it modifies "stumble/fall" (the main verb—Beare, Best, Elliott, Marshall) or "disobey" (Achtemeier, Grudem, Kelly—a participle). Grammatically, it can modify either or both. If the former, God punishes those who choose to reject Christ; if the latter, God also chooses some for salvation and others for perdition, and everyone's choice is determined beforehand by God. Probably it is best to see it modifying the whole preceding statement of 2:8b, the disobedience as well as the stumbling. God has chosen to give two alternatives, to accept or reject his appointed cornerstone, and thus "has appointed two consequential outcomes with respect to acceptance or rejection of Christ" (Jobes 2005:155). God has sovereignly made our choices possible, and with that he has also determined the consequences. Here it means simply that he punishes those who reject Christ.

◆ 3. The privileges of the community (2:9-10)

9 But you are not like that, for you are a chosen people. You are royal priests,* a holy nation, God's very own possession. As a result, you can show others the goodness of God, for he called you out of the darkness into his wonderful light.

10 "Once you had no identity as
a people;
now you are God's people.
Once you received no mercy;
now you have received God's
mercy."*

2:9 Greek *a royal priesthood.* **2:10** Hos 1:6, 9; 2:23.

NOTES

2:9 *royal priests.* There is a major discussion as to whether this should be translated "royal priesthood" (so NLT mg, TNIV, NRSV, ESV, NASB, Davids, Grudem, Marshall, Michaels) or "a royal house, a priesthood" (so Best, Elliott). The question is whether *basileion* [TG934, ZG994] here is a noun ("royal palace, kingdom") or an adjective ("royal"); it can be either grammatically and morphologically. Exodus 19:6, LXX has exactly the same wording at this point and so has the same ambiguity as the present phrase. In favor of the adjectival understanding, it should be noted that the other three nouns in the list all have adjectives, and it makes more sense in the list of four to see this pattern of adjective/noun continuing. In favor of seeing it as a noun are the following points: Many ancient interpreters (2 Macc 2:17; Philo) have the two words as separate concepts; the MT has "kingdom" as the head noun in the construct; the other three terms have the adjectives following; and Rev 1:6; 5:10 have them as separate ideas. It is a difficult decision, but the evidence for keeping it a single phrase is stronger.

God's very own possession. Lit., "a people *eis* [TG1519, ZG1650] possession." Michaels (1988:109) sees an eschatological thrust in *eis* and translates "a people destined for vindication." He argues that "possession" here is synonymous with "for [*eis*] salvation" in 1:5; 2:2 and means final salvation. However, not many have followed this because the parallels are not so certain and the context here favors understanding this as a description of who the believers are now in contrast to pagan society, rather than who they will be at their vindication in glory. It may be possible to see a slight inaugurated sense (they are in process to their final goal of salvation), but even so, the emphasis remains on their present status.

show others. Lit., "proclaim the mighty acts" or "sound the praises." Michaels (1988:110) agrees with the theory that this is not preaching in mission but is praising in worship on the grounds that *exangellō* [TG1804, ZG1972] is used in the LXX for praising God in worship (Pss 9:14 [15]; 71:15 [70:15]; 73:28 [72:28], etc.). But as Achtemeier (1996:166) says, "the context of 1 Peter (e.g., 3:13-16) argues against restricting it here to the context of Christian worship." Most likely, it has connotations of both. Christians are to praise God for his salvific deeds and to proclaim it to the nations.

COMMENTARY

In contrast to the non-Christians (2:9), who are destined for shame and judgment due to unbelief, the Christians are destined to be God's special people. Peter gives four descriptions (see note on 2:9) of God's people, all drawn from Old Testament imagery of the people of God (primarily from Exod 19:6; Isa 43:20-21). These descriptions sum up the epistle thus far, reinforcing the believers' special status before God (the basic theme of 1:3-12) over against that of their persecutors. There is a kind of a chiasm in this list as well, as the two expressions from Isaiah 43 frame the two from Exodus 19:6.

First, the believers are called "a chosen people," referring to their election as the special people of God (see commentary on 1:2). This election is reflected in 1:1-2 with respect to the believer and in 2:4 and 2:6 (cf. 1:20) with respect to Christ, who is called the "cornerstone . . . chosen for great honor." The believers share in the honor of Christ (2:7a), and they share in his election as well. The idea of the Christians as a "race" (the meaning of *genos* [TG1085, ZG1169], "people") alongside Jews and Romans is connected to the idea of them being "citizens of heaven" (Phil 3:20; cf. Eph 2:19), as well as "heaven-dwellers" (Rev 12:12; 13:6). They are no longer citizens of this world, nor are they a "race" of people on the earth (this certainly challenges all forms of racial or ethnic prejudice). This designation became very popular in the second century and is important for our time as well. Since we are the elect, we form a new "people group," a new race.

Second, they are called "royal priests" (see note on 2:9), a phrase that comes from Exodus 19, which recounts the Hebrews' arrival at Mount Sinai and God's description to Moses of the purpose of the covenant that was about to be forged. He said, "If you will obey me and keep my covenant, you will be my own special treasure" (Exod 19:5) and will be "my kingdom of priests, my holy nation" (Exod 19:6). As a kingdom they would be his special nation in the world, and as priests they would mediate his reality to the world. This was a corporate reality, not individual. In Israel, one could be royalty or priesthood but not both. One of the reasons the Maccabean kings were rejected by the Hasidim in the second century BC was that under Simon they began to make themselves both kings and high priests. The pious Jews reacted strongly and refused to support them. Only the Messiah could assume both roles, and thus Jesus Messiah became both royalty and priest, fulfilling Exodus 19. In Hebrews 5:10; 7:1-25 this culminates in the claim that Jesus is "High Priest in the order of Melchizedek" in fulfillment of Psalm 110:4. The remarkable thing here is that his followers, again the new Israel, participate (as "heirs together" with Christ, see Rom 8:17) in this glorious role, as individuals and as a church. (On the priesthood of believers, see 2:5.)

Third, they are called "a holy nation." Holiness is a major theme of the letter (1:2, 15-16; 2:5; 3:5, 15). They are both a new race and a new nation, "set apart" from this world to be God's special people. Furthermore, as set apart for him, they are to live holy lives imitating the nature of God (2:15-16). All believers must live lives antithetical to sin, "[getting] rid of" all such behavior (2:1). As a new nation, they join Israel as God's holy people. (The "new Israel" concept is not a replacement theology, for the Jews are still God's people when they come to Christ.) In Exodus 19, holiness meant separating from the surrounding nations that had led Israel into idolatry at the golden calf incident. Here the conduct expected of believers by God is spelled out in 1:13–2:3 and 2:11–3:12: having nothing to do with the sinful practices of their neighbors (2:1, 11) and living lives of goodness in the midst of a pagan people who slandered them as evildoers (2:12). In every social relationship they must maintain their witness and holy conduct (2:13–3:7).

Fourth, through Christ they have become a people that are "God's very own possession," an expression taken from both Exodus 19:5 ("you will be my own special treasure" or "treasured possession") and Isaiah 43:21 ("I have made [this people] for myself"). Here, as in those Old Testament passages, God wants his righteous remnant to be aware of their special nature. They are a treasured, special people; they are his own. Christ has "paid a ransom" for them (1:18), and they are his. In Revelation, two images speak to this—when the saints are sealed (Rev 7:3-4), which pictures a religious tattoo, which in ancient society meant an individual belonged to their patron god (Jones 1987:144). The "seal" signifies that they are God's special possession. Then in Revelation 11:1-2, John (building on Ezek 40–42 concerning the man who measured the eschatological temple) measures the temple in heaven "and its worshipers." This is a symbolic picture (from surveying a property) of those who belong to God and are watched over by him. Being God's possession also means that Christians are "slaves of God" (2:16; Rom 6:18-22; 7:25; 1 Cor 7:22; Eph 6:6). This completely reverses an evil system. Believers belong to God and are objects of his love, care, and constant vigilance.

The intended purpose (*hopōs* [TG3704, ZG3968]) is that "you can show [lit., "proclaim to"] others the goodness of God." This is the mission of the church in the world. This reenacts Isaiah 43:21, where the people of Israel are to "honor me before the whole world." The term translated "goodness" (*tas aretas* [TG703, ZG746]) can mean "virtues" or "excellencies," but better for this context may well be "mighty deeds" or "saving acts" (so Achtemeier, Beare, Bigg, Elliott, Jobes, Michaels; Marshall—"praiseworthy deeds")—in light of the emphasis on God's salvation and its results in the immediate context and on the acts of Jesus' resurrection and his Parousia as guaranteeing the vindication of the saints (1:3, 5, 7, 11, 13, 21; 2:4-5). God has acted powerfully to call believers "out of the darkness into his wonderful light," an obvious reference to the act of salvation and our election (1:1, 2; 2:4, 6). The believer in 1 Peter is called to be holy (1:15), to suffer for doing good (2:21), to repay evil with blessing (3:9), and to receive eternal glory (5:10). Darkness and light symbolism is frequent in the Old Testament (Job 24:15-16; Ps 18:28; Prov 2:13; Isa 29:15), in Jesus' discourses in John (John 3:19-21; 5:35; 8:12; 9:5; 12:46), and in the early church (Acts 26:18; Eph 5:8; Col 1:13). The "darkness" here would be the believers' pagan past, a time of ignorance (1:14), futility (1:18), temporary things (1:18, 23), a wicked lifestyle (2:1; 4:3), and disobedience (2:8). But now they dwell in God's "wonderful light," possibly taken from Psalm 118:23 ("This is the LORD's doing, and it is wonderful to see"). Jesus is the divine "light" to bring God's salvation to the world and enable them to "see" it. Like a child standing before a 60-foot Christmas tree, the saints should be filled with "wonder" and delight when they contemplate the salvation God has given them.

This section closes (2:10) with two antitheses containing strong liturgical coloring from Hosea 1:6, 9 and 2:23. Hosea the prophet was told by God to marry the prostitute Gomer as a living symbol of God's relationship with the Jewish people, who had prostituted themselves with the gods of other nations. The two children who are born are a daughter named *Lo-rukhamah* [TH3808/7355, ZH4202/8163] ("Not loved," Hos 1:6) and a son named *Lo-ammi* [TH3808/5971A/2967.1, ZH4202/6639/3276] ("Not my people," Hos 1:9); these signify God's anger and rejection of Israel as his people. For Hosea this described the apostate nation of his day; for Peter this described the pagan past of his readers. However, God promises in Hosea 2:23 that this will all turn around for his righteous remnant: "At that time I will plant a crop of Israelites and raise them for myself. I will show love to those I called 'Not loved.' And to those I called 'Not my people,' I will say, 'Now you are my people.' And they will reply, 'You are our God!'" The names of the children will be reversed.

For Peter that day is the day of conversion. The two statements of 2:10 contrast "once" (*pote* [TG4218, ZG4537]) with "now" (*nun* [TG3568, ZG3814]), referring to their lives before and after they had found Christ. To be "not a people" does not mean they had no citizenship; many were Roman citizens, and all belonged to one or the other of the provinces mentioned in 1:1. Rather, it means they had no eternal home or nation; they did not belong to God's people. When God brought them to Christ, they suddenly became a true people with an eternal destiny. Also, they had never experienced the "mercy" of God. Hosea tells us that this truth cannot be restricted just to Gentiles. Those Jews who reject God's cornerstone will also have no mercy from God, but the repentant (as in Hosea) have forgiveness and mercy. The Christians may receive little mercy from the God-rejecting society, but that is merely temporary—now they have received mercy, and that will be eternal. Goppelt (1993:151) sums it up well: "While those living in the church's environment became a public entity or individuals through the Hellenistic-Roman imperial structure, Christians are called to be a new shared community, oriented toward the future; they are this because God out of his free mercy has bound them to himself and thereby to one another."

◆ III. The Relationships in the Community of God (2:11–3:12)
A. The Thesis—A Vital Witness (2:11-12)

[11] Dear friends, I warn you as "temporary residents and foreigners" to keep away from worldly desires that wage war against your very souls. [12] Be careful to live properly among your unbelieving neighbors. Then even if they accuse you of doing wrong, they will see your honorable behavior, and they will give honor to God when he judges the world.*

2:12 Or *on the day of visitation.*

NOTES

2:11 *worldly desires.* Some scholars (Marshall, Selwyn) see these as external pressures from the "unredeemed world" (Achtemeier) that lead the Christian into sinful conduct, while others (Davids, Grudem, Michaels) see them as internal forces leading the Christian to sin. There is little reason to separate these. The term *sarkikos* [TG4559, ZG4920] (fleshly, worldly) looks to the internal sins of the flesh, but the whole context is that of the non-Christian world pressuring the Christians to live like they did before. This is a case of both–and rather than either–or.

2:12 *Be careful.* The participle *echontes* [TG2192, ZG2400] here means to "maintain" or "keep" one's conduct exemplary. It could be imperatival (a command as in the NLT text, so Beare), circumstantial—modifying "keep away" in 2:11 (with imperatival force from that connection, so Michaels, Selwyn), or a participle of means (telling how to "keep away," so Achtemeier). All three are viable, but the second is probably best. There is a definite command aspect to the usage here.

even if. The Greek, *en hō* [TG1722/3739, ZG1877/4005], could be logical/sequential ("in the cases where, even if"), locatival ("in which"), causal ("because"), or temporal ("when"). The temporal understanding may be best (see Elliott, Michaels). This is describing concrete situations "when" people have denounced the Christians.

they will see your honorable behavior. The grammar is difficult here. The participle *epopteuontes* [TG2029, ZG2227] (seeing) modifies "glorify" in the next clause and could be either modal ("by observing," so Elliott, Michaels), causal ("because they observe," so Achtemeier, Jobes), or temporal ("when they observe," so BAGD). The stronger causal force seems closer to the context (see commentary), in which case the use of *ek* [TG1537, ZG1666] with the "good works" could have its basic sense of source ("observe [your conduct] *from* your good works") or be causal ("observe your goodness *because of* your good works"). The best is probably the former, more usual meaning. Thus the translation would be, "Because they observe [your life] from your good works, they will glorify."

give honor to God when he judges the world. Lit., "glorify God in the day of visitation." Many scholars (Achtemeier, Davids, Green, McKnight) think the "day of visitation" refers to the time of final judgment when the enemies of God and his people are forced to "give honor" to God by admitting that the saints were "good" after all. Others (Beare, Elliott, Kelly, Marshall, Selwyn, Senior) think it is a present time of testing, with implications for the conversion of the opponents because of the convicting presence of God in the good behavior of the slandered Christians. Michaels (1988:119-120) may be correct in seeing both aspects here. First, the "day of visitation" is most likely the final judgment, but that does not obviate the implicit thrust of conversion here. Second, he thinks Peter is developing a saying of Jesus found in Matt 5:16, where Jesus commands, "Let your good deeds shine out for all to see, so that everyone will praise your heavenly Father." A bold witness leads to conviction and conversion. Then at the final judgment God will be glorified as these former opponents praise his name.

COMMENTARY

Thus far Peter has spoken about who the Christians are in the world in light of what God has done for them (1:3-12; 2:4-10) and what their ethical and spiritual responsibilities are in light of these truths (1:13–2:3). But he has restricted himself to the inside perspective, the community and its relationship with God. It is almost as if the non-Christian world in 1:3–2:10 is a symbol, something to be discussed and endured but not to be confronted. The need for holiness (1:15-16) has led first to considering the community and now to considering the outside world. In the next two sections, Peter turns to the outsiders, the pagans and Jewish people who remain unbelievers, many of them enemies of the church. The first (2:11–3:12) speaks of the *Haustafeln* (German for "table manners" or "household code"), discussing the social implications of being a Christian in terms of their relational responsibilities to others (see also Eph 5:21–6:9; Col 3:18–4:1; Titus 2:1-10). The second (3:13–4:11) discusses the problem of persecution and how to live before God and alongside pagans when they are bringing you suffering.

This section begins with "Dear friends, I warn you . . . ," a normal way New Testament writers began a new section of an epistle (see Rom 12:1; 15:30; 1 Cor 1:10; 1 Thess 4:1; 5:14). It serves as an introductory statement for the section, establishing the basic theme: exhortation to lives characterized by godliness and goodness. It also summarizes the "holiness code" of 1:13–2:3. The question in this first section is, how does Christ require believers to conduct themselves as representatives of the new community of God? In the second section the question is, how should believers deal with the slander and persecution they experience? Marshall (1991:79) notes three interpretive problems here: (1) Since social relations today differ from ancient times, how do we formulate moral principles for such different times? (2) How do we apply teaching for situations that no longer exist (e.g., slave–master) and apply it today? (3) What do we understand about the spirit and power of Christian morality in the many modern areas where it is silent (e.g., liberation movements today or politics in differing systems)? We will try to answer these in the ensuing material.

Peter's first command (2:11) is for abstinence. As in 2:1, it is a prohibition centered on the private side, gaining control in the area of personal living. "Dear friends" (lit., "beloved") emphasizes that the believers are dearly loved by both God and the writer, and what is going to be said stems from that love. Peter then combines terms carried over from 1:1 and 1:17 (see further there), "temporary residents and foreigners," to remind them of their status in this world before they consider how they are to interact with the people in this world. They are temporary visitors, strangers and aliens in the land and so do not belong to this world. Michaels (1988:116) says Peter combines them here to add to the "notion of geographical displacement that of the lack of citizenship or legal rights." Achtemeier (1996:174) adds that as such they were "exiles from one's native land, [which] was one of the severest punishments that a city or state could impose." So Christians must live as if chosen by God to be foreigners in a strange land!

In 2:11 Peter uses a different but similar word to "get rid of" in 2:1; he tells them they must "keep away from" or "abstain from" (*apechesthai* [TG567, ZG600]) harmful things. The term comes from catechetical tradition (Acts 15:20, 29; 1 Thess 4:3; 5:22) taken from the Holiness Code (Lev 17–26), with the idea of separating one's self from the world. Especially, they must have nothing to do with "worldly desires," a phrase that looks to the selfish side of people, the appetites leading to indulgence. The outside world pressures Christians to conform to its way of conduct (Rom 12:2), and the internal "flesh" (*sarkikos* [TG4559, ZG4920]) tempts everyone to give in to their self-centered desires. Some have tried to see these as mostly sexual sins, but while these are certainly included, they are by no means exclusively intended here. Selfish desires are especially dangerous because they "wage war against your very souls," a strong military metaphor used often in the New Testament (Rom 7:23; 2 Cor 10:3; Jas 4:1). Selfishness has declared war against our whole being and wants to destroy us. The "soul" is emphasized often in 1 Peter (1:9, 22; 2:25; 3:20; 4:19) and refers to the whole self, not just the spiritual aspect. We (our souls) have been saved (1:9, 3:20) and cleansed (1:22); we are guarded by our Shepherd (2:25) and can trust our lives to our Creator, but we are also at war with our "worldly desires." Every part of one's life is involved—the physical and the spiritual, the internal and the external—when one gives in to sinful behavior. Satan is waging war against us, and sin is an invading army trying to enslave us (see Rom 6; Rev 12 for these images), yet we can emerge victorious (Rev 12:11). The key is to refuse to have anything to do with those desires that militate against our Christian lives.

As foreigners in an alien world, we must watch closely how the inhabitants of this world regard us, that is, "be careful to live properly among" them (2:12). This provides the positive counterpart to the negative "abstinence" of 2:11. The believer's everyday conduct (*anastrophē* [TG391, ZG419], denoting the "way of life") or pattern of living must at all times (present participle) manifest the "goodness" that is to typify the true follower. In 1:18 Christ's ransom payment freed them from an "empty life" so they could maintain holy conduct (1:15) in reverent fear (1:17). Their way of life is to be "good" (*kalos* [TG2570, ZG2819]; cf. NLT, "properly"), which as Best (1979:111) says, implies that their behavior should "not only be good but also seen to be good." Elliott (2000:466) adds that "it denotes conduct that is both morally just and aesthetically attractive, thus behavior that is in all senses worthy of honor." It connotes good deeds and ethical goodness in every area of life. The *ethnē* [TG1484, ZG1620] are not just the Gentiles (the way it is often used) but everyone among the "nations" who are not Christians, thus the "unbelieving neighbors" who watch and judge the believers.

The purpose (*hina* [TG2443, ZG2671]) of maintaining an impeccable lifestyle is the simple fact that these very neighbors often slandered the believers as "doing wrong," literally as "evildoers." This was a very difficult, but often occurring, situation (see 4:4, where the pagans are first "surprised," then react with "slander" when Christians refuse to follow them). The Christians could be completely innocent, yet destroyed by people who, without cause, accused them of doing wrong. This does not refer to legal indictments but to gossip and slander intended to harm one's reputation. It was this reputation of being "wrongdoers" that allowed Nero to make Christians the scapegoat for his burning of Rome. (It is possible that Peter was writing at the very time of this terrible event.) Peter's point is that the pagan neighbors who were slandering the saints were also watching them. So the people of God must make certain that what they see is the "honorable behavior," the good deeds and basic goodness, of the objects of their slander. The verb used here (*epopteuontes* [TG2029, ZG2227]) connotes studious observation. Elliott (2000:468) points out, "In a culture where such great weight is laid upon vision as the ultimate arbiter of truth, this stress upon the *visibility* of Christian behavior and its empirical apprehension makes eminent sense" (italics his).

Let us sum up the message. God's people must at all times make sure that their goodness of character and the good works that result are evident before unbelievers because they can expect to be falsely maligned by a society which rejects them and their message. At the same time, these very slanderers are observing them carefully. So when the pagans see only "honorable behavior" and the kind of good deeds noted in Romans 12:14-21, that will first prove their slander to be lies and then convict them regarding the truth of the Christian message. The result is described in Romans 12:20 (from Prov 25:21-22) as "burning coals of shame"—the convicting nature of impeccable lives on the believers' opponents. Many of these persecutors will thus eventually be converted and "give honor to God when he judges the world." Peter may be hinting at both aspects of the final judgment (see note on 2:12): The opponents will either find Christ and glorify God on judgment day in worship, or they will continue to reject him and "glorify God" via forced submission at the final judgment, admitting only then that the Christians were right all along.

Let us finish the discussion of this part of Peter's letter by quoting "An Anonymous Brief for Christianity Presented to Diognetus" from the second century AD (cited in Richardson 1953:213). It is powerful!

> *Christians are not different from the rest of men in nationality, speech, or customs; they do not live in states of their own, nor do they use a special language, nor adopt a peculiar way of life. Their teaching is not the kind of thing that could be discovered by the wisdom or reflection of mere active-minded men; indeed, they are not outstanding in human learning as others are. Whether fortune has given them a home in a Greek or foreign city, they follow local custom in the matter of dress, food, and way of*

life; yet the character of the culture they reveal is marvelous and, it must be admitted, unusual. They live, each in his native land but as though they were not really at home there. They share in all duties like citizens and suffer all hardships like strangers. Every foreign land is for them a fatherland and every fatherland a foreign land. They marry like the rest of men and beget children, but they do not abandon the babies that are born. They share a common board, but not a common bed. In the flesh as they are, they do not live according to the flesh. They dwell on earth, but they are citizens of heaven. They obey the laws that men make, but their lives are better than the laws. They love all men, but are persecuted by all. They are unknown, and yet they are condemned. They are put to death, yet are more alive than ever. They are paupers, but they make many rich. They lack all things, and yet in all things they abound. They are dishonored, yet glory in their dishonor. They are maligned, and yet are vindicated. They are reviled, and yet they bless. They suffer insult, yet they pay respect. They do good, yet are punished with the wicked. When they are punished, they rejoice, as though they were getting more of life. They are attacked by the Jews as Gentiles and are persecuted by the Greeks, yet those who hate them can give no reason for their hatred.

◆ B. Submission to Government (2:13-17)

13 For the Lord's sake, respect all human authority—whether the king as head of state, 14 or the officials he has appointed. For the king has sent them to punish those who do wrong and to honor those who do right.

15 It is God's will that your honorable lives should silence those ignorant people who make foolish accusations against you. 16 For you are free, yet you are God's slaves, so don't use your freedom as an excuse to do evil. 17 Respect everyone, and love your Christian brothers and sisters.* Fear God, and respect the king.

2:17 Greek *love the brotherhood.*

NOTES

2:15 *It is God's will that your honorable lives.* Lit., "because in this manner it is the will of God, that by doing good." There are some scholars (Hort, Michaels) who say this is a parenthesis that restates 2:11, with *houtōs* ([TG3779, ZG4048] "in this way") looking forward to "by doing good" and telling how the slander is to be silenced. However, others (Achtemeier, Beare, Goppelt, Selwyn) say it is indeed causal, telling the reason why the believer should "do good" among unbelievers ("in this way" looks back to 2:14). The latter view best fits the normal use of *hoti* [TG3754, ZG4022] (because) and *houtōs.*

silence. The verb *phimoō* [TG5392, ZG5821] can even mean to "muzzle"; one could call this a new way to "muzzle the ox"!

foolish. The term used here (*aphrōn* [TG878, ZG933]) is interesting because it is used in the LXX (Pss 14:1 [13:1]; 53:1 [52:2]; Prov 1:22) and the NT (1 Cor 15:36; 2 Cor 11:16; 12:6) of those who place themselves against God. This is certainly part of its use here (so Achtemeier, Kelly).

2:16 *For you are free.* Lit., "as free people"; the phrase stands without a main verb or a conjunction, such as "for." Thus, there is a question whether "as free people" modifies "respect/submit" of 2:13 (so Green, Hort, Marshall, McKnight, Selwyn, Senior), "your honorable lives" ("by doing good") of 2:15 (Beare, Elliott, Goppelt), or the four commands of 2:17 (Michaels). All are possible, but in this context it is best to see it as an extension of 2:15. The believers' good lives in the midst of the opposition of evil people are lived freely. Elliott 2000:496 says, "the point is that respect for order, doing what is right, and showing honor are voluntary actions of free persons (*eleutheroi* [TG1658A, ZG1801]) acting in accord with God's will."

2:17 ***Respect . . . love . . . Fear . . . respect.*** These are four consecutive imperatives; the first is an aorist, and the rest are present tenses. The question is why this organization, especially since 1 Peter normally uses aorists in commands. It is possible that the aorist is the general command, with the others specific examples ("everyone" then broken up into specifics), but it is difficult to conceive of "fear God" just being one of the group. Still, the aorist is the basic tense to use in commands, so the first is likely introductory, stressing the command structure of the whole—these are Christian obligations. Mainly this is a chiastic presentation (A-B-B-A) with A being the attitude toward those outside (everyone, the emperor) and B the attitude toward those inside (the brotherhood, God). The first pair is the people on the same level as the readers, the second pair those above the readers.

COMMENTARY

The thesis stated in 2:11-12, that the Christian living in this world has to realize his or her place as a stranger, highlights that we are not here to be loved or to discover pleasure; we are here to love God and give him pleasure. Yet that is because he chose us for pleasure; as we praise him, he blesses us (1:3). As Peter proceeds to discuss the government, this is all the more true. Rome was not a Christian-friendly empire, so these things were not said in happy times but in times of turmoil, rejection, and persecution.

The code of conduct Peter expounds in 2:13–3:7 is not quite a "household code" because it does not follow the expected order. Both of Paul's social codes (Eph 5:21–6:9; Col 3:18–4:1) are hierarchical, moving from the most to least influential members of the households, from parent to children to slaves (for a good introduction, see von Lips 1994). Peter's code addresses relationships of wife–husband, husband–wife, and slave–master (but not master–slave). Peter's list is controlled by a secular hierarchy in terms of worth to society: Governmental control is at the top of the societal order of importance and so is first. Slave–master is at the heart of commerce and business, so it must be second. The important thing in such societal orders is to maintain *dignitas* and smooth-running relationships. In all of these there are the same four themes: (1) The dominant theme is subordination, as the one placed under the other by God is to take the lower place of submission; the Christian's duty is inward loyalty and outward submission. (2) There is the divine sanction of civil power (ch 2 and Rom 13). (3) The Christian duty for God is twofold: Restrain evil and encourage good deeds. (4) The divine purpose is to make Christianity palatable to the pagan world so that the universal mission of the church can succeed.

Peter's first point is to "respect all human authority." It is possible that 2:13 introduces and applies to citizen, slave, and wife, because it literally is, "Submit to every created human being" (so Davids, Elliott, Marshall, Michaels). Although it could be rendered "every human institution/authority" and therefore specifically government (so NRSV, NEB, NLT, TNIV, Beare, Grudem, Hort, Jobes, Selwyn), the ones named are human beings, so the former is to be preferred. This first exhortation is primarily linked to humans who are in authority, and it provides a theme that will be found throughout, though it is not a general introduction in the same way 2:11-12 was. It is doubtful if many magistrates had become Christians; there is Sergius Paulus in Acts 13:12 in Cyprus, but there is no record of others in that part of the world. So Peter starts with an unfriendly element, but one that controlled their lives.

The word "submit" (*hupatassō* [TG5293A, ZG5718]) is the normal term for social exhortation in the New Testament (5:5; Rom 13:1; 1 Cor 14:34; 16:16; Eph 5:21; Col 3:18; Titus 2:5) and is used in all three here (2:13, 18; 3:1). It means to "place yourself under the authority of" or "subordinate yourself to" another, but it has no hint of inferiority attached to it. Michaels (1988:123-124) says, "The imperative *hupotagēte* implies that Peter regards the subjection of which he speaks as a matter of choice, not of nature or necessity. His readers are 'free' (*hōs eleutheroi* [TG5613/1658A, ZG6055/1801], v. 16) to cooperate or not cooperate with their fellow citizens and rulers, free to resist or comply with the demands of the civil authority." One does so "for the Lord's sake," meaning the primary subjugation is to the Lord, and all other acts of submission stem from that primary allegiance. There are three issues here: (1) Does "Lord" refer to God (Achtemeier, Elliott, Senior) or Christ (Davids, Green, Grudem, Selwyn)? Since "Lord" often designates Christ in 1 Peter (1:3; 2:3; 3:15) and is the subject of 2:4-10, the second option is quite viable. However, God is mentioned in 2:15-16 and is called "Lord" twice in the Septuagint passage quoted in 3:12. This issue comes to a stalemate. (2) Does this limit submission only to those areas that God or Christ would allow? Absolutely. As the apostles said in Acts 4:19 and 5:29, "We must obey God rather than any human authority." (3) If any person decides not to obey those placed over them (in a matter not addressed by issue 2 above), they are actually disobeying God. It is his will that we submit, and refusing to submit to any authority God has established (be it government, master, or husband) constitutes rebellion against God (see further below on 3:1).

Peter mentions two government officials as examples. First is the emperor (2:13b), "the king as head of state." As God is sovereign over all, he had established the emperor as "sovereign" over the empire the Christians inhabited at that time. Peter didn't say, like Paul in Romans 13:1, that "all authority comes from God," but that seems implicit in what he says here. We must remember Peter wrote this in the time of Nero, one of the worst emperors Rome produced. Yet the first part of the verse clearly defines him as a "created being." In the empire he may have had absolute authority, but he was a finite being who must answer to God for his actions. Still, as "head of state," he was to be obeyed in all areas that did not conflict with God's laws. Paul instructs believers to pray for rulers (1 Tim 2:1-2) and to obey them (Titus 3:1-2). It is clear that the early church, even as it was persecuted by them, continued to respect and defer to them as instituted by God.

Peter's second example is the "officials" or "governors" (2:14a) that the emperor had placed over regions of the Roman Empire. They might be legates over imperial provinces (where there was a military presence, such as Syria) or proconsuls over senatorial provinces (like Sergius Paulus in Cyprus in Acts 13). Herod the Great was king of a whole region (a client king of the emperor) and would have come under this as well. Pontius Pilate was a "prefect," in charge of a small province (Judea) and commanding auxiliary troops under the Syrian legate. All of these were to receive respect from Christians.

All of these imperial leaders were charged with two things (2:14b)—"to punish those who do wrong and to honor those who do right." The emphasis is on actions more than attitudes. It is what people do more than how they think. The idea of praise, as well as punishment, was more important in the ancient system than it is today. Public benefaction was expected as a sign of civic duty, and one's status in society was defined by it, as the governing powers would bestow "statues, inscriptions, crowns, or grants of money or special privilege to those who had in one way or another benefited the community" (Achtemeier 1996:184). Certainly this was not Peter's primary thrust, for such would be restricted to the wealthy and powerful, yet this overall perspective was part of it. Peter's point is that "doing good" (see also 2:15, 20; 3:6, 17) is a critical part of Christian behavior and should be evident both to neighbors and to authorities. While Christians could be prosecuted by the state, they were to make sure that if it happened, it was due to slanderous lies and not to wrong they had done. Their lives of goodness should prove their detractors wrong, as will be seen in the next verse.

Peter explains his point with further detail in 2:15. This tells the reason why Christians should be known among their neighbors as those who lead "honorable lives." It applies 2:12 (that the good lives of the believers show that the slander they are enduring is wrong) to the relationship of Christians to government. Doing "God's will" or "what is right" is a key component of any ethical mandate (2:20; 3:5, 17; 4:2, 19; 5:2). The way we live is of great interest to God, and he is strongly concerned that we maintain an impeccable lifestyle in the eyes of the surrounding world. It is part of our walk with him and part of our witness to a watching world. The purpose of our lives of goodness ("by doing good" is a modal participle telling how to thwart the slander) is to "silence those ignorant people" regarding their "foolish accusations" (the slander of 2:12).

The ignorance of the Romans about the Jewish people and the Christians was legion. They could not understand anyone who was not like them, nor did they try to do so. Pilate was continually getting into trouble, as when he brought the Roman standards into Jerusalem (they were idolatrous to the Jews) and was then surprised when they caused a riot. Christians were called everything at the time. They were accused of cannibalism because of the Eucharist (eating the flesh and drinking the blood of the Lord), murder (being "living sacrifices"), lies, treason (they wouldn't take part in idolatrous community feasts), and atheism (they wouldn't worship the Roman gods). Eventually, persistence in Christian faith itself was a capital offence. But by the time of Constantine (around 250 years later), this admonition worked and the "honorable behavior" Peter exhorts won the Romans over.

The qualification of 2:16 is interesting. The believers are to be subject to Rome and respect the secular authorities placed over them; they are to live lives of moral uprightness even as they are maligned by their neighbors. Yet they are to do so as a "free" people rather than under coercion. This could mean spiritual freedom provided by Christ (Michaels, freedom in Christ from the "ignorance" of the pagans) or civic freedom as Roman citizens (Elliott). Understanding a combination of the two may be best, though freedom in the Spirit is primary. In Matthew 17:24-27, Jesus said the "citizens" of God's kingdom are "free" but should pay taxes so as not to "offend" the people around them. Often in the New Testament, God's people are described as "free" (Luke 4:18-21; John 8:32; Rom 6:18, 22; 1 Cor 7:22; 9:19; 2 Cor 3:17; Gal 5:1), and the emphasis is freedom from sin and a freedom to follow Christ out of love. Here it means freedom to do what is right. But with it comes a danger; this freedom can actually become "an excuse to do evil" (2:16). The term *epikalumma* [TG1942, ZG2127] means a "cover" or "veil" used to hide something; in this case, the new freedom in Christ turned into a pretext for performing the evil deed that the person wants to do. The way to avoid doing this is to recognize that our liberation from the enslaving power of sin allows us to become "God's slaves" (cf. especially Rom 6:15-23, where "slaves to God" means "slaves to righteous living"). This is a difficult image today, and it was as difficult then (over half the population was or had been slaves). The major point is that Christ has paid the price and purchased (ransomed) us from sin so that we now belong to God and are his. Slavery has become freedom! That great paradox is the core of the joyful Christian gospel. We live in the secular world and both submit to its powers and accept its rejection as a free act, since we truly belong to God, not this world.

Peter now sums up this section with four commands. He begins with the general, "Respect [lit., 'give honor to'] everyone." Since the second command mentions fellow Christians, it is likely that "everyone" applies mainly to unbelievers. Then the contrast would be, give honor to all the unsaved but give love to the Christian community (as in John 13:34-35; 15:12, 17; Rom 12:9; Eph 1:15; Phil 2:2). This is similar to the command in Galatians 6:10, "do good to everyone—especially to those in the family of faith." It hardly means we do not love non-Christians but rather says that we have a special (family) relationship with those in the "brotherhood." We are bonded together in love. The third and fourth commands form a pair, emphasizing that we have no fear for the emperor, only for God. This fear is not just "reverence" as most commentaries translate it (though it may include both, see on 1:17). As Jesus says in Matthew 10:28, "Don't be afraid of those who want to kill your body. . . . Fear only God, who can destroy both soul and body in hell." "Fear" here has definite connotations of terror. Peter is probably deliberately building on Proverbs 24:21, "Fear the LORD and the king," altering it to stress his point. Jesus further says in Matthew 22:21, "Give to Caesar what belongs to Caesar, and give to God what belongs to God." Caesar deserves our honor and respect, but only God deserves our fear. Caesar can kill us or throw us in prison, but he is only human, deserving the same "honor" we give all people.

This is an important passage for all Christians. It is easy to apply in a democracy where there is a certain equality between everyone. It is difficult to apply in totalitarian and unjust societies—and there are many in this world. This is a hard passage, often ignored by liberation theology. What does it mean to respect and submit in a culture that is avowedly anti-Christian or a under a government that is evil? It must be admitted that Christians in the first century faced both and still practiced submission. Yet, as McKnight (1996:155) says, this submission "can now be understood to include obedience, protest, and at times even civil disobedience." Let us consider how both Israel and the early church understood this. The prophets often engaged in what we would call civil disobedience when it saw evil amongst its leaders, and the apostles refused to obey commands that did not allow them to evangelize in the Temple. Protest like that of Gandhi or Martin Luther King Jr. is justified, as is refusal to obey commands that go against God's deeper regulations (Acts 4:19; 5:29). In short, then, we are not to take up arms to destroy an evil government (we trust God to remove them), but protest against evil practices is part of love for government; it constitutes warning of judgment to come.

◆ C. Submission of Slaves to Their Masters (2:18-25)
1. The extent of that submission (2:18-20)

18You who are slaves must accept the authority of your masters with all respect.* Do what they tell you—not only if they are kind and reasonable, but even if they are cruel. 19For God is pleased with you when you do what you know is right and patiently endure unfair treatment. 20Of course, you get no credit for being patient if you are beaten for doing wrong. But if you suffer for doing good and endure it patiently, God is pleased with you.

2:18 Or *because you fear God.*

NOTES

2:18 *accept the authority.* The use of the participle *hupotassomenoi* ([TG5293A, ZG5718], "submit"), modifying the four commands of 2:17, could be understood as imperatival (Elliott, Kelly, Selwyn), circumstantial, or as denoting means. In the last case, it would tell how slaves continue the actions of the believers in 2:17. This latter is interesting but unlikely in the paraenetic context of these codes. The participle here is a separate command.

2:19-20 There is chiasm in the way these two verses are arranged, with an A (God is pleased), B (suffering unfairly), C (no credit when suffering justly), B′ (suffering unfairly), A′ (God is pleased).

God is pleased. Lit., "This is grace if," but the term *charis* [TG5485, ZG5921] can refer not only to the grace and mercy of God in salvation but as here to something that is pleasing and receives "credit" or praise from God (so Bigg, Elliott, Kelly, Marshall, Michaels, Selwyn, contra Goppelt).

what you know is right. Lit., "on account of conscience toward God" (an objective genitive). The difficulty is whether this phrase speaks of a God-given "conscience" in terms of a mental judgment and moral discernment regarding right or wrong actions (so Beare, Davids, Marshall, Selwyn) or whether it refers more generally to a consciousness or awareness of God's will (so Best, Green, Grudem, Michaels). The latter is probably to be preferred here. Ancient copyists also wrestled with the meaning of "conscience toward God," changing the text to read "a *good* conscience" (C 94 206) or "a *good* conscience toward God" (𝔓72 A* 33 81), but the reading as here is too strongly attested (א A^2 B K vg). As Elliott (2000:519) says, "conscience toward God" "implies not merely knowledge of God but also sensitivity of the divine will concerning conduct or 'compliance with God's will,'" thus the translation, "mindful of God's will."

2:20 *you get no credit.* This sentence is cast with strong rhetorical symmetry: Each clause has a condition of fact followed by two temporal participles that modify the main verb "endure." Put together, this produces a very balanced statement, lit., "What kind of credit is it, when doing wrong and being punished by beating, you patiently endure? But if when doing good and suffering you patiently endure, this is grace with God."

COMMENTARY

Slavery in the Greco-Roman world was the backbone of the economic system. The ancient world could not have existed the way it did without slave labor. It has been estimated that one-quarter to one-third of the population were slaves. But the differences with slavery in the Americas are immense: Racial factors played no role; education was greatly encouraged (some slaves were better educated than their owners) and enhanced a slave's value; many slaves carried out highly responsible social functions; slaves could own property (including other slaves!); their religious and cultural traditions were generally the same as those of the freeborn; no laws prohibited public assembly of slaves; and (perhaps above all) the majority of urban and domestic slaves could legitimately anticipate being emancipated by the age of 30 (ABD 6.66).

Another important point is that a slave was considered part of the family of the owner, and that is why master–slave relations are part of the "Household Codes" in the New Testament. This did not mean the slave was an equal; they were considered vastly inferior and could be mistreated or beaten with impunity at the whim of their master.

The Greeks, Jews, and Romans of Greco-Roman times had widely different attitudes about slaves. Greeks considered slaves as inferior chattel and fortunate to be owned by a Greek. Jews, with numerous exceptions (many were slaves by debt), did not really think it right to enslave another Jew since all had been liberated from Egyptian bondage and become "slaves of God." Romans were the most liberal, treating slaves generally on par with free people and regularly granting Rome citizenship when they were set free (ABD 6.66). What is surprising is the variety of services they rendered—teachers, accountants, business people, ship captains, merchants—many occupations considered today to be white-collar. Moreover, slaves were a sign of status—the more a person had, the more highly they were regarded. Wealthy women would have slaves just for their hair or for their clothes.

Peter did not use *douloi* [TG1401, ZG1528], the normal term for "slaves" (used in Eph 6:5; Col 3:22), but *oiketai* [TG3610, ZG3860], "household slaves," who were usually used for domestic work. This stresses the household emphasis throughout; it also distinguishes the term *douloi* for Christians as "God's slaves" (2:16). Nonetheless, *oiketai* was used for all sorts of slaves; Peter certainly did not want to exclude field or urban slaves. Like citizens and wives in this section, they are to "accept the authority of your masters," literally, "continue to submit" (with a present-tense imperatival participle), again meaning to "place themselves under" that master's authority. "Master" (*despotais* [TG1203, ZG1305]) sometimes fits the transliteration "despots"—it can have "the implication of absolute, and in some instances, arbitrary jurisdiction" (L&N 559). This may have been used here rather than the more normal *kurios* [TG2962, ZG3261] (Eph 6:5; Col 3:22) to prepare for the emphasis on their possible "cruelty." A major (and somewhat surprising) emphasis is *en panti phobō*, translated here "with all respect" but probably better "with all reverence" or "fear." As discussed on 1:17, *phobos* [TG5401, ZG5832] in certain contexts can mean "reverence" (it has been at least a 50-year fad to use "reverence" in English translations) or "fear/terror." Here in the context of responsibility for one's actions it is the latter, but it is not fear of the master, no matter how cruel (2:18) he might be. It is fear of God and answering to him for how you live your life that is the stress throughout 1 Peter. So "with a deep fear of God" (see NLT mg) is better than either "all respect" or "deep reverence."

Moreover, slaves are to submit to their masters "not only if they are kind and reasonable, but even if they are cruel" (2:18). Most likely, the majority of the owners fit the first category and treated their slaves fairly; again, the fact that most slaves eventually received their freedom attests to this. They were "good" to their slaves and "fair-minded" in the way they treated them. There is no indication whether or not any of the owners were Christians, and it does not really matter because Peter does not address owners here (unlike Eph 6:9; Col 4:1), possibly because "the situation of Christian slaves of unchristian masters here addressed was symbolic of the situation of the church as a whole, which was marginalized and vulnerable" (Boring 1999:117). The word for "cruel" (*skolios* [TG4646, ZG5021]) means "unjust, harsh, unscrupulous," the opposite of the two words for the good owners. The Christian slave was obeying God, not just the master, whether that person was wonderful or perverse. There are two reasons why this had to be so: (1) the way Christians related to others was a major part of their witness in the community and a major element of their relationship with God; and (2) "any attempt to carry out a social revolution in terms of eliminating the practice of slavery would have had terrible consequences, resulting in the slaves' crucifixion and the extermination of the Christian community" (Achtemeier 1996:195). God would eliminate that terrible institution in his own time.

In the rest of this section Peter centers on Christian slaves who suffer unjustly (2:19-20). The reason why (*gar* [TG1063, ZG1142], "for") they should be willing to submit, even if their masters are not kind, is that "God is pleased" with those who endure such harsh treatment. There are two aspects meant here: (1) God is pleased with their righteous conduct, and (2) he reacts with favor toward the person (see note on 2:19-20). The "if" (*ei*) is a condition of fact and assumes that the "unfair treatment" is happening to many (NLT, "when"). This assumes that many Christian slaves will suffer unfairly because they are Christians. To do "what you know is right" means they are aware or conscious of what God would have them do and can act on the basis of their knowledge of God's will in that instance (see note on 2:19-20). This assumes that the master has demanded something that goes against Christian scruples or practices (though it can include simple acts of cruelty). The Christian slave deserves to be commended for the action but instead receives "unfair treatment" (2:19). Because the Christian slave knows that God will right the wrong, they can endure the *lupas* [TG3077, ZG3383]—not only the "pain" or "affliction" but the "grief" and "sorrow" that result. Endurance or perseverance (synonymous with the verb in 2:20) is the primary Christian reaction to trials (1:6-7; cf. especially Rom 5:3-5; Jas 1:2-4) and the means to bear the troubles with a complete trust in the God who vindicates and rewards his people. His providential care never ceases. Therefore, God's people are long-suffering and patient in all difficulties. It also means that the Christian slave continues to submit and refuses to rebel (though see the discussion at the end of the comments on 2:17).

In 2:20 Peter clarifies what he has been saying in 2:19, stating the point both ways. First, there is no "credit" (*kleos* [TG2811, ZG3094], "praise, renown, fame"), no "glory," if a person deserves the ill treatment they get. The language used here is well chosen—they are guilty of "doing wrong" (*hamartanontes* [TG264, ZG279], "sinning"), with the word possibly chosen to assert that it is a wrong done in the eyes of God as well as the civil authorities—note the contrast with Christ in 2:22! The punishment mentioned in 2:20 is beating—denoted with the same verb used of Jesus in Mark 14:65. Here it probably refers to the frequent punishment meted out to slaves (see Exod 21:20, 26-27 regarding excesses in this area). However, there is credit for people who suffer for performing good deeds. As in 2:3 and 2:19, *ei* [TG1487, ZG1623] is a condition of fact that assumes such unfair treatment was occurring. (All 12 conditionals in 1 Peter are conditions of fact—he deals in reality!) Note that they again were "doing good" and suffering unjustly because of it. As Michaels (1988:142) says, it is unlikely these are the public benefactions that would benefit the state and the owner. No master would be stupid enough to beat a slave for benefiting him or her. Most likely, as we stated above, these were deeds that pleased God and were done according to his will but against the master's wishes. This again is a situation like 2:12, when a Christian is slandered (or beaten) for their faith, or 2:19, when the Christian slave is mindful of God's will and punished for acting accordingly. The verse ends with an inclusion (framing 2:19-20), as "God is pleased" (2:19a) and credits the suffering Christian for the decisions they made.

What is the relevance of this material? At one level, it forces us to think about the institution itself and remember the evils of slavery in the New World. At another level, it may be applied to employer–employee relations. But is that valid? McKnight (1996:172-173) greatly helps us, saying this is "reasonable and consistent with Petrine teaching in light of the broad kinds of activities that slaves performed in the ancient world (teaching, selling, farming etc.) and those same employment-type of activities that are done today. . . . Slaves were in some kind of employment relationship with their masters. This was how they 'made a living.'" In this case, the principles are as difficult today (think of union–management relations!) as they were in the first century. Respect the management team, submit to the foreman, be willing to be misused. The material here and in Ephesians-Colossians calls for mutual respect, working together, and seeking the common good. Mainly, it talks of the Christian witness among unbelieving colleagues in the workplace. One's secular career is actually a God-given ministry to which each person is called by God, and that call is every bit as important as the missionary or the pastor. Our secular life is part of our walk with God.

◆ 2. The model of Christ (2:21-25)

21 For God called you to do good, even if it means suffering, just as Christ suffered* for you. He is your example, and you must follow in his steps.

22 He never sinned,
nor ever deceived anyone.*
23 He did not retaliate when he was insulted,
nor threaten revenge when he suffered.
He left his case in the hands of God,
who always judges fairly.
24 He personally carried our sins
in his body on the cross
so that we can be dead to sin
and live for what is right.
By his wounds
you are healed.
25 Once you were like sheep
who wandered away.
But now you have turned to your Shepherd,
the Guardian of your souls.

2:21 Some manuscripts read *died.* **2:22** Isa 53:9.

NOTES

2:21 *Christ suffered.* This reading is supported by 𝔓72 A B 381 vg ; other mss (𝔓81 ℵ Ψ 209* arm) read "Christ died." The manuscript evidence is evenly balanced, as is the fact that scribes could have changed "died" to "suffered" to suit the immediate context or "suffered" to "died" because that is the common NT phrase (see Comfort 2008b:742). All things considered, "suffered" is the preferred reading. However, a number of scholars (Achtemeier, Elliott, Grudem, Michaels) believe this is not speaking of vicarious suffering in a redemptive sense but that "for you" should be understood in the sense of an "example" in accord with the emphasis later in the verse. Another option (Beare, Goppelt, Marshall) is to see this as anticipating 2:22-25 (which includes quotation of Isa 53) in a redemptive sense, producing a chiasm: A (vicarious suffering, 2:21a), B (Christ's example, 2:21b), B′ (teaching on the example, 2:22-23), A′ (teaching on the vicarious suffering, 2:24-25). This latter makes a great deal of sense and to me is the better path here. In reality, this is another both–and situation: Christ's suffering is an example, but its vicarious nature is also about to be highlighted.

2:22-25 This is presented in the NLT as a hymn, and several scholars have called it such (Bultmann, Goppelt, Martin). The arguments in behalf of this classification are (1) the introductory *hoti* [TG3754, ZG4022] (2:21) and use of the personal pronoun *hos* [TG3739, ZG4005] in 2:22, 23, 24, often a sign of a hymn (cf. Phil 2:6; 1 Tim 3:16); (2) the shift of pronouns from second person (2:21) to first (2:24a-b) back to second (2:24c-25); (3) the fact of contextual dislocation, that is, the teaching goes beyond the needs in the slave–master discussion; (4) the movement from addressing slaves in 2:21-23 to addressing the whole church in 2:24-25. This view was widely held from the 1930s through the 1970s, but in the 1980s the tide shifted, for the arguments came to have less weight. The particles *hoti* and *hos* are quite common to Peter, and the pronoun shifts are better seen as due to the use of Isa 53 in the text. The broader appeal to the wider community is also common to 1 Peter. The contextual dislocation can be seen as Petrine strategy, since there is so much emphasis on Jesus' passion and its salvific effects in this epistle (see Achtemeier, Elliott, Jobes, Michaels, T. P. Osborne). It is best to see this as Peter's contribution, not a borrowed Christian hymn; it is high prose that deserves to be set in poetic form.

2:23 *left his case in the hands of God.* In the Greek this is simply, "entrusted to the one who judges justly." There is no object to the verb, so it has been questioned what Jesus actually entrusted to God, whether his person (Beare, Best, Selwyn, Senior), his case or cause (Achtemeier, Kelly, Marshall, McKnight), or the judgment of his enemies (Goppelt, Michaels). As Grudem and Davids note, all may well be involved. Peter left the object unexpressed to stress all he has been describing in this section, so all three are probably intended. Still, with the addition of *krinonti* [TG2919, ZG3212] (who judges), there is special emphasis on the vindication of Jesus and the judgment of his enemies.

2:24 *we can be dead . . . and live.* While *apoginomai* [TG581, ZG614] is translated "die" in BAGD and accepted as such in most translations and commentaries, it can also have the meaning "have no part in" or "depart from," and this latter is seen as a likely translation by Achtemeier, Jobes, Michaels, T. P. Osborne (1983:400). It would thereby fit 2:1, 11 and provide the thrust "depart from sin and you will live." Still, the death/life antithesis is too strong, and "die" is a viable meaning of the verb. So of the two, this is the better reading. Also, "dying" is a participle here. If it is circumstantial, the translation, "die . . . and live," is correct. If it is a modal participle, it would be, "by dying to sin, you should live." While this also makes sense, the death/life theme implies that the two ideas are parallel, as in the NLT.

2:25 *wandered . . . turned.* Some (Beare, Elliott, Selwyn) see the language of straying and turning as a reference to the sacrament of baptism. However, there is no real evidence for this, and it is conversion from the pagan past that is in mind.

COMMENTARY

As elsewhere in the epistle (1:18-20, 23; 3:8-12; 4:7-11), a theological interlude places a challenge faced by believers in salvific perspective. Why should slaves be willing to suffer harsh treatment? They do so because it is their calling, and because Christ has already provided the model for such an approach to the Christian life. So Peter begins with the "purpose" (*eis touto* [TG1519/3778, ZG1650/4047]) for which they were "called," which is one of the primary themes of the epistle (1:15; 2:9; 3:9; 5:10). The believers were chosen and brought to salvation by God. In 1:15 they are "called" to holiness, in 2:9 to "his wonderful light," in 5:10 to "his eternal glory," and here and in 3:9 to nonretaliation when mistreated. God "calls" us first to his salvation and then to live out that salvation by exhibiting good, godly lives in a non-Christian world opposed to us. The reason we do so is because (*hoti* [TG3754, ZG4022]) Christ set us an example when he "suffered for" (*epathen huper* [TG3958/5228, ZG4248/5642]) us. These slaves as Christians are called to seek Christ in all things, and that would especially include his suffering, as Paul reflected so well, saying he considered his own troubles a fellowship in Christ's suffering (Phil 3:10) and sought to "fill up . . . what is still lacking in regard to Christ's afflictions" (Col 1:24, NIV). In this way the unjust suffering of the slaves was a participation in Christ's sufferings. The emphasis on Jesus suffering "for you" (2:21) has connotations of his vicarious death and prepares for the Isaiah 53 quotation that follows. As Marshall (1991:92-93) says, "The verb throbs like a repeated refrain throughout the letter from 2:19 onwards . . . and colors everything that is said. The same verb is used in the Gospels to refer to the dying of Jesus and all the associated suffering." He points out that this verb for "suffering" is found in 2:19, 20, 21, 23; 3:14, 17, 18; 4:1 [twice], 15, 19; 5:10 (12 of the 42 NT occurrences) and dominates the rest of the letter.

Moreover, Jesus' suffering is something he has "left behind" (*hupolimpanō* [TG5277, ZG5701]) as a legacy and an "example" (2:21; *hupogrammos* [TG5261, ZG5681]), a rare term used in ancient times for an outline of the letters of the alphabet that schoolchildren could copy or trace when learning to write, thus a "copy" or "paradigm" that people can follow. Peter calls Jesus' suffering an exact model "so that" (*hina* [TG2443, ZG2671]) the believer can "follow in his steps." This defines discipleship as *imitatio Christi*, an "imitation of Christ." Christ has established the pattern of suffering for God, and it is our privilege to walk where he walked and how he walked (this will be the theme of ch 4). "Following" is the primary New Testament term for discipleship, and that includes every area of life, including trials and suffering. Charles Sheldon's *In His Steps* has become a famous best seller and shows the meaning of Christ as our "model," a pattern to direct or guide every moment of our walk through life. According to the well-known adage of recent years, we ask, "What would Jesus do?" meaning we want always to act as he would act and seek to please God in our every action.

Jesus' model or pattern is spelled out in detail in the high prose (or possibly, poetry) of 2:22-25. The slaves were told to make certain they were innocent, that is, were punished wrongly and did not deserve the treatment they received. So the first thing said about Jesus is that "he never sinned nor ever deceived anyone" (2:22). The sinlessness of Jesus is stated in 2 Corinthians 5:21; Hebrews 4:15; 7:26; and

1 John 3:5. The statement here is a virtual quote of Isaiah 53:9 (except for "sin" in place of "wrong," possibly to prepare for "sins" in 2:24) and prepares for the further use of Isaiah 53 in 2:24. The suffering servant was a major title and theme Jesus used of himself; it was meditated on in the early church. In Isaiah 52:13–53:12 (the fourth of the Servant of Yahweh passages in Isa 42–54), the emphasis is upon the Servant's suffering as vicarious atonement to reconcile God with his people. In Isaiah 53:9 the stress is upon his innocence, that he had done nothing worthy of rejection. As the model to be copied, Jesus committed no sin whatsoever; Christian slaves (and all of us) must also renounce wrongdoing. The idea of the absence of deceit is taken from the Isaiah text but also repeats 2:1, "get rid of . . . all deceit," further defined there as "hypocrisy." In 2:11, this becomes "keep away from worldly desires." Holiness, the goal of discipleship, means to set yourself apart from sin, as well as set yourself apart for God. This determination alone will make certain that when you are mistreated, it is false rather than deserved.

The theme of Jesus as our example or paradigm for suffering continues in 2:23, which serves as "commentary on the last clause of 2:22" (Michaels 1988:145). The internal aspect (no sin) is provided in 2:22; the external aspect (no retaliation) of Jesus as paradigm for the persecuted is in 2:23. There is no direct quoting of Isaiah 53 in this verse, although the first part may well be built upon Isaiah 53:7, "He was oppressed and treated harshly, yet he never said a word. He was led like a lamb to the slaughter. And as a sheep is silent before the shearers, he did not open his mouth." There might also be a reflection here of Jesus' refusal to speak at his trial (Mark 14:61; 15:5), which alludes to Isaiah 53:7. Peter's wording is, "He did not retaliate when he was insulted, nor threaten revenge when he suffered." With the word "insult," the emphasis is upon verbal abuse and retaliation in kind, likely building on the last part of 2:22, "nor ever deceived anyone" (lit., "nor was deceit found in his mouth"; cf. also 3:9).

First Peter 2:23 points to Jesus' passion in three ways: (1) "insult" = verbal abuse by the Sanhedrin (Mark 14:65), the guards (Mark 15:16-20), and the thief (Mark 15:29-32); (2) "did not retaliate" = Jesus' silence in Mark 14:61; 15:5; and (3) "left his case" with God = Jesus' reply to the high priest in Mark 14:62. Peter often speaks of such verbal insults (2:15; 3:9, 16; 4:14) and says specifically not to return insult for insult (3:9). Furthermore, 2:23 represents the story of Jesus' life. In the Sermon on the Mount, he demanded that his followers refuse to seek revenge (Matt 5:38-42) and love their enemies (Matt 5:43-48). In Luke's version of the Sermon (Luke 6:28), Jesus says, "Bless those who curse you. Pray for those who hurt you." Jesus never retaliated against his enemies, instead walking through their midst or hiding when they tried to arrest him (Luke 4:29-30; John 7:30, 44; 8:20, 59). The use of imperfect tenses for "retaliate" and "threaten revenge" pictures the rejection he experienced his whole career, not only at the Passion (so Achtemeier).

Instead of getting even, Jesus "left his case in the hands of God, who always judges fairly" (2:23; cf. 4:19, "trust your lives to the God who created you"). This is an obvious paradigm for the readers in the midst of persecution. Many of them would be hauled before courts in fulfillment of Matthew 10:17-20; there Jesus said not to worry what to say because the Spirit would speak through them. Still, like

Jesus and Paul, many would unjustly suffer imprisonment or death. The picture of Jesus' "entrusting" (the verb meaning to "deliver, hand over, entrust, commit") is in the imperfect tense, and the participle "judging" is in the present tense, so it depicts Jesus' (and our) continuous trust in God through all circumstances.

The final section (2:24-25) in this segment returns to 2:21a and the theme of Jesus' vicarious suffering. With the expression "he personally carried our sins," Peter turned to Isaiah 53:4 ("It was our weaknesses he carried"), Isaiah 53:11 ("He will bear all their sins"), and Isaiah 53:12 ("He bore the sins of many"). Behind this is the nature of the Servant of Yahweh's suffering. As Oswalt (1988:386) states on Isaiah 53:4, "The language of carrying and bearing sets the stage for the substitutionary understanding of the Servant's suffering" that stems from the sacrificial system (Lev 10:17; 16:22), where the "animal carries (*nasa'* [TH5375, ZH5951]) the sins of the offerers away." On Isaiah 53:12 Oswalt (1988:405) adds, "Somehow this Servant has actually suffered the condemnation of all the sins ever committed, and by virtue of that fact, he is able to declare all those who will accept his offering as righteous, delivered, before God." This servant, Jesus Christ, has fulfilled the suffering servant's vicarious sacrifice with two results—salvation for all mankind was procured, and a pattern was set for all believers to follow in their own suffering. Two further points are added. First, this was done "in his body" (2:24), continuing the emphasis in the Old Testament as well as the New Testament on bodily sacrifice (Rom 7:4; Col 1:22), as seen in the words of institution in Luke 22:19, "This is my body, which is given for you." Second, he made this sacrifice "on the cross" (2:24), literally, "on the tree." The term (*xulon* [TG3586, ZG3833]) is used often for the cross (Acts 5:30; 10:39), and in Galatians 3:13 alludes to Deuteronomy 21:23, which says hanging "on a tree" is a curse, meaning that death on the cross cut Jesus off from the covenant. The amazing truth is that in offering himself on the cross, Jesus fulfilled the role of the high priest (see Heb 7) and that of the atoning sacrifice offered by the high priest. Here the emphasis is on his sacrifice for "our sins." Atonement has been made, and our sins forgiven.

There is an A-B-A pattern in 2:24, with the two mentions of vicarious healing surrounding the middle portion on its purpose and intended results for us. The movement reflects Jesus' death and resurrection as the basis for our own spiritual reliving of it, as through Christ we become "dead to sin" and "live for what is right" (see also Rom 6:2-4, 11, 13, 18). Again, there is a twofold thrust—a theological statement on the meaning of Christ's death for believers, and a model whereby slaves (and all of us) die to earthly ways and live for what is right. This is a major part of the gospel reality: Christ died on the cross for our salvation, and he was raised from the dead as our firstfruits (1 Cor 15:20, 23). When a person is converted, they die with Christ to the sin that enslaved them and then begin to live in Christ for the rest of their lives. When they physically die, they will experience resurrection from the dead and live eternally. The term *dikaiosunē* [TG1343, ZG1466] means "righteousness, justice, living rightly before God." Certainly the third idea is primary here, centering on a life lived well in terms of ethical goodness and good works (2:12, 15, 20). Yet the first idea may be included as well. It is the righteousness that we inherit from Christ that makes it possible to live rightly. So often these terms have double meaning in the New Testament (e.g., "hunger and thirst for righteousness" in Matt 5:6, NIV, is probably the second and third of the meanings).

The final pair of lines ("by his wounds you are healed") stems from Isaiah 53:5, changing Isaiah's first-person plural "we could be healed" to second-person plural "you are healed." This is Petrine style. Jobes (2005:198) tells us that the first person plural is only found in three places in 1 Peter (1:3; 2:24a; 4:17), while the second person plural is found 83 times. Some believe this is to make the Gentile readers feel they are a part of the church (Jobes, Michaels), but more likely it is general, wanting all the readers to think carefully about what Christ did for them and its implications for their own way of living. The "wounds," of course, refer to all the degradations of the Passion, the beatings and the taunting, as well as the crucifixion itself. There is great stress on "you are healed," with healing a metaphor for salvation (Ps 103:3; Mark 2:17; Luke 4:23). As Marshall (1991:95) asserts, "The readers are people who were suffering from illness but are now restored to health. Illness signifies weakness and inability to resist temptation. The person who is healed is not only delivered from illness—and possibly death—but has the strength to overcome temptation and to do good."

From Isaiah 53:5 Peter turned his attention to Isaiah 53:6, "All of us, like sheep, have strayed away. We have left God's paths to follow our own." Peter changed this into an image of the Shepherd saving the straying sheep. The idea of sheep straying was used often of Israel turning away from God because its "shepherds" had failed (Num 27:17; 1 Kgs 22:17; Isa 13:14; Jer 50:6; Ezek 34:1-10; Zech 10:2), so that God alone could return them as their Shepherd (Gen 48:15; 2 Sam 5:2; Isa 40:11; Ezek 34:11-16; Zech 11:4-17). In the New Testament Jesus is depicted as the Shepherd of God's people (5:4; John 10:1-18; Rev 7:17) who seeks lost sheep (Matt 10:6; 15:24; 18:10-14) and cares for his people (Heb 13:20).

Peter was speaking of the pagan past of his readers (lit., "were straying," a periphrastic imperfect emphasizing the ongoing nature of their pre-Christian past; cf. 1:18; 2:1) when, like wandering sheep, they were in danger of imminent destruction. Sheep are distracted by every little thing and in their aimlessness they easily fall into ditches or off cliffs. The picture is similar to the parable of the wide gate and the broad highway that leads to destruction (Matt 7:13-14). But our Shepherd has provided rescue. "Turned to" (*epestraphēte . . . epi* [TG1994/1909, ZG2188/2093]) continues the imagery with the straying, endangered sheep "turning back" to their shepherd. It is language of conversion (used in Acts 14:15; 15:19; 26:20), and the "now" (*nun* [TG3568, ZG3814]) stresses the difference from their past when they were "dying" and the present when they "live" in Christ (2:24b, cf. 2:10). Not only is Jesus "Shepherd," but he is also "the Guardian of your souls." "Guardian" (*episkopos* [TG1985, ZG2176], "overseer, superintendent, bishop") speaks of one who supervises by watching over and caring for the group. Here it further defines Jesus as the Shepherd who watches over and "guards" his flock. The people of God, including Christian slaves, can consider themselves secure in Christ, who both shepherds and watches over them in the insecure, non-Christian world in which they find themselves. They may be persecuted and rejected in the world, but both God and Christ have made each one their own.

◆ D. The Submission of Believing Wives to Pagan Husbands (3:1-6)

In the same way, you wives must accept the authority of your husbands. Then, even if some refuse to obey the Good News, your godly lives will speak to them without any words. They will be won over [2]by observing your pure and reverent lives.

[3]Don't be concerned about the outward beauty of fancy hairstyles, expensive jewelry, or beautiful clothes. [4]You should clothe yourselves instead with the beauty that comes from within, the unfading beauty of a gentle and quiet spirit, which is so precious to God. [5]This is how the holy women of old made themselves beautiful. They trusted God and accepted the authority of their husbands. [6]For instance, Sarah obeyed her husband, Abraham, and called him her master. You are her daughters when you do what is right without fear of what your husbands might do.

NOTES

3:1 ***must accept the authority.*** As in 2:18, *hupotassomenai* [TG5293A, ZG5718] is an imperatival participle, somewhat rare in the NT but common in the exhortation (paraenesis) of 1 Peter. In the present tense it is intended as an ongoing command, "you must at all times submit." This issue is very debated today, whether a wife should "submit" as her proper role in complementing her husband (the complementarian view) or whether husband and wife are equal and submit to each other as equals (the egalitarian view). This is too big an issue to cover thoroughly here, but a couple of things may be said. First, Gal 3:28 says that as a result of the Cross there is "no longer . . . male and female," meaning there is a new level of equality. Second, Eph 5:22-24 (written about 12 years [AD 61] after Galatians [AD 49]) still says that wives should "submit to your husbands" as "the head of his wife." While headship could mean source, in this context it has to connote a degree of authority. To me this means that while the husband is head of the home, both husband and wife look upon each other as equals, and that as an equal the wife voluntarily submits to her husband, while he uses his authority not for his own needs but only to enhance his wife (the sacrificial love of Eph 5:25). Thus, both come under the "mutual submission" of Eph 5:21.

refuse to obey the Good News. In the Greek this is "disbelieve/disobey the word," with "the word" the same as in 1:24-25 ("that word is the Good News"). "The word," or Scripture, demands that people adhere and obey, so when these husbands react against their wives they are actually denying the gospel. Grudem (1988:137) argues that "even if" implies that this is "an unexpected or uncommon occurrence" and that Peter assumed most Christian wives were married to Christian husbands. Actually, Peter makes no hint either way (so most commentators) and simply addressed the situation (most likely fairly common) of mixed marriages in the first-century church.

your godly lives. Lit., "through the conduct of the wives." Due to its place in the Greek (in between the clauses), there is some disagreement as to whether it modifies "refuse to obey" (the husbands rejected Christianity "through their wives' conduct") or "won" (that conduct leads to their conversion). The latter (as in the NLT) is certainly best for three reasons: (1) One would expect the coordination "because" rather than "through" if her conduct was the reason for his rejection; (2) the presence of "without a word" is linked with "through her conduct" and favors it being the basis of his conversion rather than of his rejection; (3) the context of 3:1-2 favors the emphasis upon the man's conversion rather than his rejection.

3:5 The grammar of this verse (especially its verbs) needs to be unpacked. First, a present participle (*elpizousai* [TG1679, ZG1827]) modifies "holy women," emphasizing their ongoing hope in God. The main verb is "adorned," an imperfect verb (*ekosmoun* [TG2885, ZG3175]) "designating habitual or customary action in the past" (Achtemeier 1996:215). Finally, this main verb is modified by a present-tense instrumental participle (*hupotassomenai* [TG5293A, ZG5718]), again with durative force ("by continually submitting"), telling how they adorned themselves. Putting all this together, Peter emphasizes that the OT holy women provided a model for Christian women by adorning themselves not with outward looks but first with an ongoing hope in God (the vertical or God-centered aspect) and then with a continual submission to their husbands (the horizontal or this-life aspect).

3:6 ***Sarah.*** There are some commentators (Elliott, Green, Kelly, Moffatt) who think Sarah and Abraham were chosen as the quintessential "aliens and strangers" (1:1, 17; 2:11; cf. Gen 23:4) and as such are intended to encourage the marginalized readers of 1 Peter, not just wives but the whole community. This is possible, but there is no indication in the text as such. Sarah is presented as the model of a godly wife, but Abraham is not presented as a model here.

You are her daughters. The verb for "are" is *egenēthēte* [TG1096, ZG1181], which can mean "you have become" as well as "you are." It is common to see this as an allusion to their conversion or baptism (Elliott, Goppelt, Michaels) or even to infer that they were Gentiles who through conversion had "become" Sarah's daughters (Kelly). But this reads too much into the term, for it is as common as *eimi* [TG1510, ZG1639] for the verb "to be," and here the best translation is the simple "you are." As Achtemeier (1996:216) says, "What is at issue is not when, or how, the women addressed became Christian; the point is how Christian wives are to act within the potentially hostile situation of marriage to nonbelieving husbands."

COMMENTARY

This is the third and final section of the "Household Code" (2:13–3:7), after citizens submitting to government and slaves submitting to owners. The basic message (built on 2:11-12) has special relevance because here a specific kind of marriage is addressed—Christian wives with pagan husbands. In this instance, there is a particular need: the conversion of the non-Christian husbands. Therefore, the need to avoid wrongdoing (2:11) and make sure your good Christian conduct is a testimony drawing unsaved people to God (2:12) is especially poignant. Submission is emphasized, framing the address to the wives (3:1, 5). There are three sections here: (1) the core—witness by your submission (3:1-2); (2) the proper adornment—not external looks but internal gentleness (3:3-4); and (3) the biblical example of submission—Sarah (3:5-6). The likely reason for addressing the wives in so much more detail than the husbands (Eph 5 is exactly the opposite) is because Peter was concerned with Christians in a non-Christian world, and there were probably few instances of Christian husbands with non-Christian wives (women tended to follow their husbands in religious matters) but many Christian wives with non-Christian husbands. The situation dictated the strategy, and Peter was addressing certain members of the Christian community—Christian wives.

It is critical to understand the place of women in the first century, the background for this section. For the first readers, this was primarily the Greco-Roman world (see Kroeger 2000). Earlier in the pagan world, women were considered to be decidedly inferior. They were secluded, and their living quarters tended to be small and dark. Men were rational; women were thought irrational and controlled by their emotions. They were thought to have worse morals than men and less thinking capacity, so in many homes women were not trusted in public or in conversations with men who were not their husbands (as often, some thinkers disputed this low view, but it was the norm). Women were not allowed to vote or hold office, and they did not write treatises or teach. They could not make legal decisions and were under the control of their father, husband, or a guardian/tutor. Things changed somewhat for the better under Caesar Augustus, so that a woman could inherit property and work in business (if she had three or more children). Still, the husband was dominant and had full power in marriage and family. The practice of exposure (placing an unwanted baby out in the natural elements to die) was common, and it was usually girls who were "disposed of" in this way. Some were rescued and made slaves. Women were thought good for three things—courtesans (some became quite wealthy as a result), companions (singers, dancers, some who would converse with men at banquets), or wives who would raise the children (especially sons). With this type of seclusion, wealthy women had to resort to games, gossip, and their external looks. Hordes of slaves looked after their adornment. They also became very involved in the Greco-Roman cults, always looking for the newest innovating movement. It is in this atmosphere that Peter addresses Christian wives about their God-given responsibilities.

Peter begins with "in the same way" (3:1), meaning that he was continuing the theme of submission. This does not mean that wives are "likewise" to be slaves to their husbands! Rather, they are to continually (present tense) place themselves under the authority of their husbands. The idea of the inferiority of women to men is absent in the New Testament. The presence of "your" (*idiois* [TG2398, ZG2625]; "your own") shows that it is not men and women in general that are in mind, but specifically husband–wife relationships. This expectation of submission to authority was to be expected in the ancient world, both Greco-Roman and Jewish, but we need to understand it also in light of Ephesians 5. There women are told to be submissive "in everything" (Eph 5:24), but this command is surrounded by two further factors. First, in Ephesians 5:21 the marital relationship is introduced by the fifth and final participle defining what it means to be "filled with the Holy Spirit" (Eph 5:18), that Spirit-filled Christians will "submit to one another." The submission of the wife is a major example of how all Christians must relate to one another. Second, the husband's sacrificial love for his wife is part of this mutual submission. As head of the house he will submit his desires and needs to making all decisions for the good of his wife, not for himself.

The motivation for submission is presented next. Peter was addressing Christian wives married to non-Christians ("even if some" in 3:1 indicating that not all fit this category), men who had refused "to obey the Good News," rejecting their wife's religion. In the first-century culture, wives were expected to follow their husband's religious choices, so for a wife to go against her husband and accept Christ was scandalous. Perhaps many husbands were among those slandering the church in 2:12, and the picture here is of intense opposition from husbands. Jobes (2005:203) states that a wife converting to Christianity would violate the expectation of an orderly home, and it would be seen as a danger to society as well as the home, since the gods would be displeased. Also, her worship of Christ would be perceived as rebellion, causing embarrassment to her husband and hurting his status in the community: He could be disqualified from offices, and she would have friends in her church (e.g., lower-class people) that would demean him in the eyes of others.

Note that the primary purpose was not to alleviate these social pressures but to convert the husband, in effect removing the tension points. The exhortation was evangelistic rather than social at heart. The Christian wife will react to these dangers by refusing to nag or browbeat her husband into the kingdom ("without any words") and instead to win him over to Christ by her "godly" life (3:1). The emphasis is on her "conduct" (the same word as in 1:15, 18). This continues the influence of 2:12, where the good "conduct" of the believer (here the wife) disproves the slander and then both convicts and converts ("won over" here means to "change the other's point of view," thus to convert) the former adversary (here the husband). Note the wordplay on *logos* [TG3056, ZG3364]. The husbands who had rejected "the word" could now be won without "a word" by the woman's conduct. The point is that Christ has made her into a better, more loving, and submissive wife than she ever was before, and that wins her husband over. This is called "lifestyle evangelism" today.

This conduct is clarified further in 3:2, beginning with another reminiscence from 2:12. The entire time her husband is rejecting and opposing her, he is also "observing" (from 2:12) her conduct. There are two aspects of this godly conduct stressed: First, it is "pure," which could refer particularly to sexual chastity, faithfulness to their husbands in marriage (Grudem, Marshall, Michaels), but probably is meant in a broader sense, Christian purity in general, akin to the holiness of 1:15-16 (Achtemeier, Best, Senior). These wives must evidence in their daily conduct a pure Christian, holy character. Davids (1990:116) calls this "Christian virtue," replacing the Old Testament emphasis on "cultic purity." The basis of this pure conduct is "reverence" for God (not "fear" of the husband). As stated above (1:17; 2:18) *phobos* [TG5401, ZG5832] can be "fear" or "reverence" depending on the context, and in this it is "reverence" (i.e., showing her godly character). In every aspect of her family life the love of Christ and the grace of God must be visible. As her husband watches this transformation, his coldness toward her will melt and opposition disappear. This will lead to his conversion.

The next section centers on "outward beauty" (3:3-4), with the key word being *kosmos* [TG2889, ZG3180], the term for "world" or "adornment." Peter was not using this term as a wordplay on "worldly," but that is a good image for today. This, of course, refers to a preoccupation with appearance, a problem that is as ancient as it is modern. Paul makes similar comments in 1 Timothy 2:9-10, and they could reflect Christian paraenetic tradition. Both use the foibles and egos of wealthy women to make an example about the desire for ostentation in general. As stated above, wealthy women would have slaves just to take care of their hair or their wardrobe. Before an important banquet, slaves would spend all day on hair, makeup, and the like. Many people today are no less ostentatious. Think of *haute couture*, the practice of making custom-fitted, hand-sewn, exclusive dresses that often cost hundreds of thousands of dollars. Many people's wardrobes could take care of an entire village in many parts of the world. However, note that the point here is not that it is a sin to wear makeup or dress well or have your hair cut and colored. The point is that we are not to center on the externals but on the internals. To me the best adage is to "try to look your best for Christ"—what will glorify him? We should not seek to draw attention to ourselves but to Christ. So I want to look my best in such a way that God will be pleased. That means to avoid extravagance but to seek moderate attractiveness.

Peter used three examples to demonstrate his point: fancy hairstyles, expensive jewelry, and beautiful clothes. Davids (1990:117-118) says this means there must have been wealthy women in the church, for only they could afford these three things (the poor and slaves usually had but one dress to their name). The list of ostentatious living is much the same as the similar passage in 1 Timothy 2:9-10 ("draw attention to themselves by the way they fix their hair or by wearing gold or pearls or expensive clothes"). This seems to be a traditional list of examples. The first area mentioned is "fancy hairstyles" (often worn at waist length). Fashions then had women wearing all kinds of nonsense in their hair—gold, jewelry, even in one recorded instance a birdcage! The second is "expensive jewelry," and not much need be said about that. This has throughout history separated the haves from the have-nots. As then, people today seek to have their bodies also covered by gold or jewels. Million-dollar items are fairly common among the superrich. "Beautiful clothes" does not mean a person cannot dress attractively; we should not go out of our way to be unattractive. This refers to the type of *haute couture* noted above, extravagant or sexually provocative clothing meant to bring out the wrong reactions.

In essence, Peter was exhorting these Christian women to live at the highest level of pagan morality, for many of the intelligentsia in Judaism and the Greco-Roman world also castigated women for placing external looks over internal character (e.g., Isa 3:18-24; *Testament of Reuben* 5:3-5; for examples from Philo, Aristotle, Seneca, Dio Chrysostom, Plutarch, Juvenal, Pliny, and Tacitus, see Achtemeier, Jobes, Michaels). Peter was not forbidding all hairstyles, makeup, jewelry, or nice clothes. He was denouncing a misuse of these things where the external appearance has absolute priority, where external looks are used to attract people in all the wrong ways. It is balance that is called for here.

There are several contrasts between 3:3 and 3:4—external versus internal, the visible versus the hidden, expensive jewelry and clothes versus the heart, adornment that seeks attention versus a gentle and quiet spirit, and temporary beauty versus lasting beauty. Peter declared what is truly attractive about a woman (again in agreement with other Jewish and Gentile writings); he advised Christian wives to put on the clothing that gives them "the beauty that comes from within." Expressions about this inner person of the heart are found often in the Old Testament (1 Sam 16:7; Ps 139:23), as well as the teaching of Jesus (Matt 6:3-4, 6, 18) and Paul (Rom 7:22; 2 Cor 4:16; Eph 3:16), centering upon a person's inner character rather than outward appearance. This realization is of utmost importance in our culture in which thin, busty movie stars are the standards of beauty, and plain but truly beautiful women are going unnoticed. This is the reason, too, why so many marriages are falling apart; the standards of beauty are horribly skewed in our day.

This inner garment that makes a wife especially radiant is identified as "the unfading beauty of a gentle and quiet spirit." This is definitely the human spirit rather than the Holy Spirit, the true definition of who we really are. "Unfading" means "imperishable" and is common in 1 Peter, corresponding with such expressions as "inheritance . . . beyond the reach of change and decay" (1:4), a ransom that was "not with perishable things" (1:18, NIV), and being born again "not of perishable seed, but of imperishable" (1:23, NIV). Our character is eternal; our looks are exceedingly temporary. Who we are inside, in our minds and hearts, is so much more important than how we look outside, yet we spend all our time and money on that external aspect that will disappear by the time we are even somewhat old. Meanwhile, that to which we give no importance will last for eternity. The "gentle" or "humble, meek" disposition refers to "an amiable friendliness" and defines "a person who does not attack back, for he or she waits on God to judge in the end; knowing God is just, the person can suffer evil without bitterness and vengeance (Num 12:2; Matt 5:5; 11:29)" (Davids 1990:119). The "quiet" person is "peaceful" rather than volatile, and this "denotes a state of inner peacefulness and calm, quite serenity, and tranquility, unruffled by the vicissitudes and disturbances of the daily round" (Elliott 2000:566). These characteristics will identify Christ in her and provide a powerful testimony of her inner goodness (2:12) to "win" her husband to Christ (3:1). Moreover, this will be "precious to God," with "precious" referring to "lavish, expensive" goods that are "of great worth." Note the distinct contrast between the "lavish" ("expensive," 3:3) jewelry and clothes, which are worthless to God, and the qualities of the inner person, which are truly "precious" to God (for a similar contrast, see the letter to Laodicea, especially Rev 3:18). Why spend our money and energy on that which is inconsequential to God, when we can cultivate what truly pleases our spouses and God?

The final section of this paragraph (3:5-6) provides an Old Testament illustration of the proper kind of wife Peter extols, general in 3:5, specific in 3:6. "This is how" presents a model or example of the beauty exemplified by "the holy women of old." They were "holy" both because they fulfilled Israel's "holy" calling and destiny (Peter may have in mind especially the four "matriarchs" of Israel—Sarah, Rebecca, Rachel, and Leah—the wives of the patriarchs) and because they were called and filled with the Holy Spirit. This is built, as in 2:4-10, on the church as the heir of Old Testament revelation, joining Israel as the people of God. These women were holy because instead of focusing on social standing or looks, they "trusted God" or "continuously set their hope in God" (see note on 3:5). "Hope" is future-oriented and God-directed, an important concept in 1 Peter (1:3, 13, 21; 3:15), and so these were special models of the godly wife. It was this hope that enabled them to truly "[make] themselves beautiful" (Gr., *kosmeō* [TG2885, ZG3175]; "adorn") in the eyes of God and their husbands by "submitting" or "[accepting] the authority of their husbands." Here we have a further contrast: adorning with expensive clothes or with submission. There is an *inclusio* as the passage is framed with the command to accept the husband's authority (3:1, 5). Once more, it is important to state that this does not negate the wearing of jewelry or nice clothes at all (as some have taken it); it negates making these things central and ignoring the more important thing, the kind of person we are.

Peter now moves from the general model to a specific example (*hōs* [TG5613, ZG6055]; "as"), Sarah (3:6), who "gave birth to [the] nation" (Isa 51:2). The Old Testament allusion is to Genesis 18:12, the scene where Abraham is told of the coming birth of Isaac, and Sarah, overhearing, laughs and says to herself, "How could a worn-out woman like me enjoy such pleasure, especially when my master . . . is also so old?" Peter draws upon her use of *kurios* [TG2962, ZG3261] ("master, lord," in LXX and here) and adds "obeyed her husband," thus making Sarah the model of the submissive wife. The problem is that in Genesis it is almost the other way around. In

Genesis 18:12, Sarah was more skeptical than submissive, and in other places Abraham obeyed Sarah (Gen 16:2, 6; 21:9-12). But Peter's midrashic exegesis centers on Sarah's use of the word "lord" (or "master") rather than on the whole context and connects it to the issue of submission. The rabbis used Sarah as a model, and the term "obey" is most likely chosen from the standpoint of "master" here rather than as an intensification of "submit" (see Balch 1981:104-105).

These wives then become "her daughters," a common analogy that indicates not actual offspring but rather those embodying her characteristics, which here is submission to husbands. Two aspects of this are highlighted by accompanying temporal present participles, stressing their ongoing conduct: First, they follow Sarah's example "when [they] do what is right." This continues the emphasis on embodying "good" in this section (2:12, 15, 20; 3:2, 10-12, 17; 4:17)—as a witness to the unbelievers. Second, they have no "fear of what [their] husbands might do" (lit., "not fearing any terror"). This alludes to Proverbs 3:25, "You need not be afraid of sudden disaster," meaning anything people can do to you. This entails a refusal to allow the pagan husbands to intimidate them in general, perhaps in trying to coerce them into disobeying God and into returning to their husband's religion (see 3:1). Once again, they are to be submissive but never when it means disobeying God; that is their higher allegiance (cf. Acts 4:19; 5:29).

◆ E. The Responsibility of the Husbands (3:7)

7 In the same way, you husbands must give honor to your wives. Treat your wife with understanding as you live together. She may be weaker than you are, but she is your equal partner in God's gift of new life. Treat her as you should so your prayers will not be hindered.

NOTES

3:7 ***you husbands must give honor to your wives.*** The strong consensus is that with this verse the focus changes to Christian husbands with believing wives. This has been challenged by Jobes (2005:207-209), who believes it is the obverse of 3:1-6, Christian husbands with nonbelieving wives. She argues that the language, asking the husband to honor her femininity and to treat her as if she were a coheir better fits a husband trying to convert a pagan wife. This is possible but is not the more likely hypothesis. Peter stated the issue of one unbelieving spouse directly in 3:1-2, but there is no evidence that this is the case in this verse. It is more likely that the convention in the Greco-Roman world that wives and children followed the husband's religious choice would apply in this case. The likelihood is that few wives refused to follow the "conversion" of a husband, while if the wife was converted first (3:1-6), many husbands would refuse to follow her choice.

She may be weaker than you are. Lit., "as a weaker vessel." Several views have predominated on this difficult statement. The idea of "weaker vessel" could be: (1) She was merely a sexual object in many Greek circles, with "vessel" referring to her as a sexual receptacle; but that can hardly fit in either OT or NT contexts. (2) She is weaker morally and intellectually; certainly this was a prevalent Greco-Roman opinion, but again there is nothing in this context or in the NT to suggest such a thing. Those who take "the woman was deceived" in 1 Tim 2:14 (cf. 2 Cor 11:3) this way misinterpret Paul there; Paul centers on Eve's sin but does not say she had a higher proclivity to sin. (3) It could refer to her lesser social status, the poor value women were given in the first-century world. This may be part of the picture, but the next is most likely the major thrust. (4) Virtually all commentators take this to mean physical frailty; the wife generally has less strength ("vessel" often means the physical body) than her husband and needs his help. Many now see these last two as the best understanding, seeing the wife as "weaker" and "more vulnerable" (Achtemeier, Davids, Elliott, Green).

she is your equal partner. There are two readings for the "equal partner" (lit., "coheirs"). Both use the same term, but one uses the nominative case, thus emphasizing the husband as coheir with the wife (A C P Ψ 81 Byz), while the other is dative, emphasizing the wife as coheir with the husband (𝔓72 𝔓81 ℵ[c] B 33). Due to better manuscript support and a better fit with the context, the dative is preferable.

your prayers will not be hindered. There is some question whether these are the prayers of both husband and wife (Beare, Craddock, Elliott, Marshall, McKnight, Michaels, Moffatt; Boring sees them as belonging to the community as a whole) or just the prayers of the husband (Bigg, Davids, Green, Grudem, Senior). While the plural "your" may include both, the whole statement is addressed to the husbands, and that is more likely here. As Achtemeier (1996:218) says, "there is nothing in the context to lead one to assume the pronoun refers to anyone but the men addressed in this verse" (*hoi andres* [TG435, ZG467]).

COMMENTARY

The key to understanding Peter's message here is to determine the grammatical relationships at work in the sentence. There are two participles and two *hōs* ([TG5613, ZG6055] "as") phrases; how they relate to each other determines the meaning. Let me lay out the Greek order with a literal translation: "You husbands likewise, live with (her) with understanding—as a weaker vessel—with her as a woman—showing her honor as also joint-heirs of the grace of life—so that your prayers be not hindered." The first present participle (*sunoikountes* [TG4924, ZG5324]) is definitely imperatival ("live with your wives," contra Achtemeier who sees it as instrumental and all the participles of 3:1-6 as modifying 3:17, producing a needlessly complex sentence). The second participial phrase, *aponemontes timēn* [TG632/5092, ZG671/5507] (showing honor) could also be imperatival (as NLT) or circumstantial, telling how to live with her—the latter is my preference. The next question is whether we take "as a weaker vessel" and "with her as a woman" with "live with" (her as a woman who is a weaker vessel—Elliott, Jobes, Marshall, McKnight, Selwyn) or "show honor" (to her as a woman who is a weaker vessel—Best, Davids, Michaels, Senior). On the basis of word order and context, it is best to follow the order of the text and see each *hōs* clause modifying a separate verb, thus: (1) live with her with understanding as a woman as a weaker vessel; (2) show her honor as a joint heir of the grace of life; (3) so that your prayers will not be hindered.

In Ephesians 5:22-33 the husband gets the greater attention; in 3:1-7 it is the wife, because Peter was addressing mixed marriages with non-Christian husbands. Still, it is clear that Peter, like Paul, did not believe that all the deference belonged with the wife. Paul speaks of mutual submission within headship (Eph 5:21 with Eph 5:22-33); Peter speaks of honor and deference to one's wife, commanding husbands to "give honor to [their] wives." "Honor" has appeared often in 1 Peter, both in terms of the honor and glory that is ours now and at the eschaton (1:7; 2:7), and the honor we give unbelievers and rulers (2:17). In one sense it means to "show respect" to wives, and while this is viable, it is a little weak. More likely, it is meant in the sense of 1:7 and 2:7—husbands must give them the honor and glory they deserve, and help them to realize how special they are.

Showing the wives honor means at one level that you "treat your wife with understanding as you live together" (lit., "live with them according to knowledge"). Obviously, this means that husbands should always seek to understand their wives' perspectives on things, their needs and desires, and at all times try to meet those needs. The phrase also connotes "with consideration" and is connected with "honor" in terms of husbands considering their wives greater than themselves and seeking to benefit their wives' interests rather than their own (the definition of humility in Phil 2:3b-4). There is a certain sexual orientation to the language (Michaels, on the basis of "live with"), but it cannot be restricted to this, for the context is that of life in the household. So this means in every area of marriage the husband must look out for his wife's point of view and her needs. In addition, the "knowledge" also refers to the husband's realization of God's will in regards to his duty vis-à-vis his wife. As Goppelt (1993:226-227) says, it is "the sensitive understanding that develops in love for God and one's fellow human beings when one knows oneself to be loved by God. For this reason it expresses itself especially in consideration for others." There is a twofold basis of this necessary understanding and consideration the wife deserves. First, she is "a woman," with the Greek using *gunaikeios* [TG1134, ZG1221] (rather than the normal *gunē* [TG1135, ZG1222]), a rare term meaning "feminine, female," perhaps to refer to all the women of the household (Jobes) but better to refer to her femininity as an object of consideration and honor. There may be a reference to creation as well (Gen 1:27, "male and female he created them") as an introduction to all that follows—giving honor and "joint-heirs"—as how precious all women are to God and to men. Second, the basis of such consideration is that she is "weaker than you are," literally, "a weaker vessel," with "vessel" meaning the physical body. This likely has a double connotation—"more vulnerable" in a society that denigrates women, and "weaker" physically (the major thrust). Husbands must give their wives the understanding and considerate help they need.

Two final considerations close out Peter's short homily on the husband's responsibility to his wife. First, he must realize his wife is his "equal partner in God's gift of new life" (lit., "joint-heir of the grace of life"). There is also a twofold message here: (1) He must treat his wife as an equal. This parallels Galatians 3:28, "no longer . . . male and female" and emphasizes the equality of all men and women before God. (2) "Gift" (lit., "grace") is an objective genitive (both "inherit God's grace"), and "life" is an epexegetical genitive (grace, which is life); putting these together, "both inherit that grace, which is life." In 1 Peter "grace" is both the basis of our present salvation (1:2, 10; 4:10) and our future hope (1:13; 5:10). "Life" also is present and future (1:3; 2:5, 24; 3:7, 10; 4:6). Both at heart are eschatological, "God's [gracious] gift of new life." Husbands are reminded that they are reflecting this "gift of life" in their relationship with their spouse. Their marriage is a gift of God's grace and a part of their walk with God.

The second consideration is a warning. If husbands fail to give their spouses the honor and consideration they are due, their "prayers will . . . be hindered." The New Testament principle is that our relationships with others are part of our relationship with God. Therefore, what we do to others we are doing to God, and that act will return upon our heads. It will be rewarded when we perform good deeds; it will bring judgment when we commit harm. This principle is found in Matthew 6:14-15 (God forgives when we forgive and does not forgive us when we refuse to forgive) and James 2:13 ("There will be no mercy for those who have not shown mercy to others"). When husbands do not show love, honor, and thoughtfulness to their wives, they are sinning against God, and thus their prayer life is negatively affected.

◆ F. The Righteous Qualities Needed (3:8-12)

8 Finally, all of you should be of one mind. Sympathize with each other. Love each other as brothers and sisters.* Be tender-hearted, and keep a humble attitude. 9 Don't repay evil for evil. Don't retaliate with insults when people insult you. Instead, pay them back with a blessing. That is what God has called you to do, and he will bless you for it. 10 For the Scriptures say,

"If you want to enjoy life
and see many happy days,
keep your tongue from speaking evil
and your lips from telling lies.
11 Turn away from evil and do good.
Search for peace, and work to maintain it.
12 The eyes of the Lord watch over those who do right,
and his ears are open to their prayers.
But the Lord turns his face
against those who do evil."*

3:8 Greek *Show brotherly love.* **3:10-12** Ps 34:12-16.

NOTES

3:8-9 There are a number of parallels with Rom 12:9-18, and many think there is a direct connection, implying that Peter had access to a copy of Romans (Michaels 1988:174-175). Goppelt (1993:224; cf. Gundry 1967; Piper 1981) believes that both go back to the Jesus tradition (cf. Matt 5:5-6, 44; Luke 6:27-28) and stem from a common source. However, the different vocabulary and organization make dependence unlikely (so Achtemeier 1996:221), so it is more likely that Paul and Peter were following early Christian paraenetic tradition rather than the Jesus logia (see Achtemeier; Best 1970; Goppelt; Michaels). In a final sense, however, it is impossible to adjudicate adequately. The stages are quite evident: Jesus' teaching -> Jesus logia in the Gospels -> catechetical tradition -> Peter and Paul. The exact relationships cannot be known for certain. Jobes (2005:217) concludes that at the least "this passage eloquently demonstrates that the two (Jesus' teaching and early tradition) cannot be separated."

pay them back with a blessing. While most scholars see the "blessing" as salvation, a few (Grudem, McKnight) believe the blessings relate to joy, peace, and longer life on this earth. This is possible but seems less likely than the conversion of the lost soul; see note on 2:12 regarding "give honor to God when he judges the world."

That is what God has called you to do. There is some question whether God's call here looks back to returning blessing for insult (Achtemeier, Best, Clowney, Grudem, Jobes, Marshall, Michaels, Piper) or forward to inheriting a blessing (Davids, Elliott, Goppelt, Kelly, Selwyn). Both make good sense grammatically, but with the strong emphasis in this section on maintaining a life of good works in the midst of such opposition, the former is the more likely. God has called us to bless our persecutors, and this will result in our receiving a blessing from him.

3:10 *If you want to enjoy life and see many happy days.* There is division between those who see this as present life (Bigg, Grudem, McKnight) and those who interpret it as future life with God (Beare, Best, Davids, Kelly, Michaels, Selwyn). It is best on the whole to take these as a "both-and" rather than an "either-or" (as Achtemeier, Goppelt, Jobes). Both in the immediate context (3:11-12) and in the following section (3:13-17) the emphasis is on the present life, while in 3:7 ("equal partner in God's gift of new life") and 3:9 ("he will bless you for it") there is strong emphasis on eternal life with God.

COMMENTARY

The "Household Code" (2:13–3:7) is framed by two passages that commend lives of goodness both in and outside the community (2:11-12; 3:8-12). This paragraph provides a conclusion for the Household Code that is based on community relationships rather than standing as the introduction to the next section (Best, Elliott, Marshall, Michaels, McKnight, contra Achtemeier—3:8–4:11, Davids—3:8-22). "Finally, all of you" (3:8) begins the concluding thoughts of the section and refers to every Christian (every person in the community) addressed in 2:13–3:7. This makes it evident that every section has principles for all the members of the church. The themes of goodness, respect, love, thoughtfulness, submission, and responsibility to God are characteristics to be exemplified by every believer, not just those addressed in the preceding sections. The thesis is stated in 3:8 (internal) and 3:9 (external), with the quote from Psalm 34:12-16 (in 3:10-12) providing a proper conclusion.

Davids (1990:124) and Elliott (2000:603) see chiasm in the five characteristics (given in Hellenistic style with rarely used terms) of a Christian community in 3:8: how one thinks (like-minded, humble), how one feels (sympathetic, tender-hearted), and the central concept being brotherly love. This makes a lot of sense. Achtemeier (1996:223) adds that all these are part of an attitude of general subordination of Christians to one another. This parallels Ephesians 5:21, "Submit to one another." Exhortation to unity of mind is found often in the New Testament (John 17:21-23; Acts 2:46; 4:32; Rom 15:5; 1 Cor 1:10; 2 Cor 13:11; Gal 5:13; Phil 2:2; 4:10) and does not mean that everyone will agree on everything (e.g., a system of doctrine imposed on all). Rather, it connotes a common goal or focus based on serving the same Lord (Davids, Goppelt) and means they share the same gospel and same purpose, serving God and Christ. Sympathy (3:8; *sumpathēs* [TG4835, ZG5218], "sharing feeling with") for the others in the community (cf. Heb 4:15 of Christ for us, Heb 10:34 of us with the imprisoned) means a loving understanding of another's situation (e.g., Rom 12:15 ["Be happy with those who are happy, and weep with those who weep"] or Heb 13:3 ["Remember those in prison, as if you were there yourself"]). Christians must share and care for one another deeply (as in 1:22), involving feeling the joys and hurts of others and then acting on that empathetic concern.

The central command is for brotherly love (3:8; *philadelphoi* [TG5361, ZG5790]), a major theme in the New Testament (1:22; John 13:34; 15:12; Rom 12:10; 1 Cor 13; 1 Thess 4:9; Heb 13:1; 2 Pet 1:7; 1 John 2:7-11; 3:11). There is no basis for any Christian living without community (see Heb 10:24-25). It is not "it's you and me, God" but "it's you and *we*, God." As Paul says in 1 Corinthians 13:13,

"Three things will last forever—faith, hope, and love—and the greatest of these is love." Parallel to "sympathetic" is "tenderhearted" (*eusplanchnos* [TG2155, ZG2359]), a term that can be translated also "compassionate, generous, or merciful," referring to a deep-seated concern for others. Finally, Peter speaks of "a humble attitude" (*tapeinophrones* [TG5012.1, ZG5426]), a mind that is consumed by humility. Best calls humility "a new quality of life which was introduced by Christianity into the Hellenistic world" (1979:130). The Greeks considered meekness to be weakness and disparaged humility in favor of strength of personality. It was Christ who made servanthood the chief virtue and who introduced a new concept: living for others, rather than yourself, in a spirit of humility (5:5; Matt 11:29; 18:4; 1 Cor 10:24; Gal 5:26; Phil 2:3-4, 7, 20; Col 3:12; Titus 3:2).

In 3:9 the emphasis changes from the internal church community to the external, depicting the Christian in a non-Christian society. The members of God's community (3:8) will gather strength from one another to respond properly to the slanderous attacks and persecution mentioned in 2:12. There the readers were told to respond to derision with goodness. Here Peter draws from the Jesus tradition to say, "Don't repay evil for evil." This is Jesus' teaching in the Sermon on the Mount on nonretaliation and love for enemies. In Matthew 5:44 Jesus says, "Love your enemies! Pray for those who persecute you!" Paul takes this theme and says never to repay evil for evil (Rom 12:17; cf. 1 Thess 5:15), but to leave the revenge with God (Rom 12:19, utilizing Deut 32:35), and instead give your enemies food and drink (Rom 12:20, building on Prov 25:21-22). In 1 Corinthians 4:12 we see parallels to the "bless those who curse" teaching. The flip side is said in Proverbs 17:13, "If you repay good with evil, evil will never leave your house." In 1 Peter evil must be gotten rid of (2:1) and avoided at all costs (2:11). Now it is to be endured without retaliation by trusting the Judge who does right (following Jesus' example, 2:23). We might call this "the Christian ethic of enemy-love," which "entails opting out of concerns for preserving one's own status and reputation in society and refusing to participate in the give-and-take of challenge-riposte that helped to define conventional social relations" (Green 2007:105).

"Insults" (3:9) were heaped upon Christ (2:23) and are another form of the slander mentioned in 2:12. Elliott (2000:607) states that this indicates "the kind of hostility that the author considers the believers to be experiencing: insult, defamation of character, and verbal abuse. These are the weapons typically employed in an agonistic honor-and-shame society for challenging the honor of others and publicly shaming and discrediting those who are different or regarded as one's competition." This differs little from the type of abuse heaped on people today, from cruel children in school to coworkers at the factory or office. Peter's point is that Christians should not retaliate in kind. Instead, when reviled they should "pay them back with a blessing." This is more than just saying nice things about them. There is a supremely spiritual, even an eschatological, element in the idea of calling down God's blessing on a person—namely, invoking his gracious presence in their lives. The "blessing" undoubtedly includes hope for their salvation as in 2:12, that they might "give honor to God when he judges the world." Some commentators (Best, Michaels) believe it possible that this is seen as part of the priestly function of the church in 2:5, 9 (in the OT, blessing was a priestly activity, Num 6:22-26; Deut

21:5). This shows a certain development from Romans 12:20b. There the acts of kindness pour "burning coals" on the heads of the opponents, meaning conviction of their deeds. In 2:12, good actions prove to them that their slanders were lies, and here in 3:9 this response includes a "blessing" that draws them to Christ. The result will be their conversion to Christ.

There are two reasons for doing this. First, "That is what God has called you to do," meaning God's will is that we pray for our persecutors (one meaning of "bless them") and offer them God's salvation in response to their verbal insults (see note on 3:9). The result of this is that God "will bless you for it," literally, "you will inherit a blessing." In 1:4-5 our "inheritance" is eternal life, "salvation, which is ready to be revealed on the last day," and in 3:7 husband and wife are equal partners "in God's gift of new life." Thus, the blessing referred to in 3:9 is a final blessing that will be received when Christ returns. Here it likely adds the idea of reward for returning blessing for insult (Best, Marshall). The idea of reward is found often in Jesus' teaching (Matt 5:12, 46; 6:1, 2, 5; 10:41-42) and elsewhere in the New Testament (1 Cor 3:8, 14; 2 John 8; Rev 11:18; 22:12). The basic thrust is that what we have done for others and for Christ will precede us into heaven and become our reward (cf. Luke 16:1-13; Rom 14:12; 1 Cor 3:12-15; 2 Cor 5:10; Heb 13:17).

Peter now grounds this in proof from Scripture (3:10-12), citing a slightly altered form of the Septuagint's rendering of Psalm 34:12-16 (see Jobes 2005:220 for explanation), a psalm already used in 2:3. This is a "psalm of deliverance" that is "quite congenial to 1 Peter's exile motif" (Jobes 2005:220, 221-223), because the difficulties David discussed in the psalm parallel those of the readers, and the ethics described there provide an important foundation for Peter's discussion here. In Psalm 34:12, God's people are asked whether they want to "live a life that is long and prosperous" in terms of this present life; in 3:10 the expression "enjoy life and see many happy days" most likely refers to both one's present existence and the eschatological future (see note on 3:10). Obeying God and living his way are the only path for living well now and enjoying the future "blessings" he will give us (3:9).

The lifestyle demanded begins with the verbal side (the movement from tongue to lips is poetic imagery). Those who want to enjoy life now and in eternity must make certain they do not "speak evil" or "tell lies" (3:10; cf. 2:1, 22), that is, use their mouth to hurt others. The misuse of the tongue is frequently addressed in both the Old Testament (Pss 12:2-4; 34:13; 39:1; Prov 18:6-8) and the New (Matt 12:36; Eph 4:29; 5:4; Col 3:8; Jas 1:26; 3:5-12; 4:1-10). God demands that we use our gift of speech to uphold people, not to deceive them and do them harm (as in the slander of 2:12). We do not return "evil for evil" or "insult for insult" (3:9a) but instead use our lips to utter a "blessing" over our enemies (3:9b).

Then the psalm turns from our speech to our actions (3:11 = Ps 34:14), beginning with "Turn away from evil and do good." This is the second time *kakos* [TG2556B, ZG2805] (evil, harm) has appeared (with 3:10b), and it is obviously emphasized. All five times it is found in 1 Peter occur in 3:9-12, and cognates appear in 2:1, 12, 14, 15, 16; 3:13, 17; 4:15, all with the idea of evil intentions (malice) or actions (evildoers). It is clear that evil thoughts embodied in evil speech lead to evil acts. The term emphasizes the central danger of wrongdoing in the social sphere, both within the community and in contacts with unbelievers. The antithesis is obviously to "do good," the primary positive duty of the Christian in 1 Peter (2:12, 14-15, 20; 3:6, 17; 4:19). These ideas of avoiding evil and doing good may be one major element that led Peter to this psalm. Another has to be the command to "search for peace, and work to maintain it" (3:11). Peacemakers were highly prized people in the early church. Commended everywhere from Jesus' beatitude (Matt 5:9) to Paul's teaching (Rom 12:18; 14:19; 1 Cor 7:15; 2 Cor 13:11; 2 Tim 2:22) to Hebrews (Heb 12:14) and James (Jas 3:18), those who would seek to bring peace both with outsiders and insiders were desperately needed in a world of conflict. The verbs "search" and "work to maintain" speak to the conscious effort needed by Christians to make "peace" an ongoing reality behind all relationships.

The motivation for such righteous conduct is found in 3:12 (Ps 34:15-16). Note the anthropomorphic language; the text moves from the Lord's eyes to his ears to his face, showing the total involvement of God among his people. Elliott (2000:615) says, "The face is the part of the anatomy through which one's attitudes are most clearly expressed. Eyes, like ears, were regarded as the organs of perception and 'emotion-fused thought,' as part of the traditional three-zone concept of human (and divine) personality." The "righteous" or "those who do right" are those believers who live rightly before God, who eschew evil talk and deeds and seek both goodness and peace in their time on earth. When it says "the eyes of the LORD watch over" them, it means that God sees their good deeds and blesses them; he cares for them, protects them, and guides their steps. When God's "eyes" are mentioned in the Old Testament, it can be with righteous anger in judgment (the "eyes like flames of fire" of Dan 10:6; cf. Rev 1:14; 19:12), in knowledge and awareness (Exod 3:16; Ps 66:7), or in understanding and watching over his people (2 Kgs 19:16; 2 Chr 6:20; Ps 33:18). Here it is his awareness and care that are in view. The psalm adds, "his ears are open to their prayers" (cf. 4:7), which adds God's hearing to his sight. Jesus promised a new depth of prayer power in his Farewell Discourse (John 13:31–17:26, cf. John 14:13-14; 15:7, 16; 16:23-24, 26) and in John 16:23 said, "At that time you won't need to ask me for anything. I tell you the truth, you will ask the Father directly, and he will grant your request because you use my name." Still, as in 3:7, righteous living is a necessary prerequisite for effective prayer (cf. Jas 5:16b).

The element of warning now centers on the "face" of God; Moses could not look on the face of God and live (Exod 33:20; cf. John 1:18) because the face exhibited the true being of an individual. So when God turns his face "against those who do evil" (and here these would be God's people), it means he moves against them in judgment. The same ideas are found in Psalm 102:1-2, "LORD, hear my prayer! Listen to my plea! Don't turn [your face] away from me in my time of distress." Hearing prayer and turning his face away are antitheses in God's dealings with his people. The antithesis is very powerful, both in right versus wrong and in divine blessing versus the divine curse (see DOTP 83-87). Those whose actions are "evil" can expect nothing but anger and judgment from God. The message of the psalm quotation as a whole is powerful. Both in the internal life of the church and in external dealings with non-Christians, the believers must make certain they exemplify uplifting speech and good deeds rather than evil speech or actions. That will determine whether they receive God's present and final blessings or God's anger and judgment.

◆ IV. The Central Problem Developed—Persecution for the Sake of Christ (3:13–4:19)

A. Suffering for Righteousness' Sake (3:13-17)

13 Now, who will want to harm you if you
are eager to do good? 14 But even if you
suffer for doing what is right, God will
reward you for it. So don't worry or be
afraid of their threats. 15 Instead, you must
worship Christ as Lord of your life. And if
someone asks about your Christian hope,
always be ready to explain it. 16 But do this
in a gentle and respectful way.* Keep your
conscience clear. Then if people speak
against you, they will be ashamed when
they see what a good life you live because
you belong to Christ. 17 Remember, it is
better to suffer for doing good, if that is
what God wants, than to suffer for doing
wrong!

3:16 Some English translations put this sentence in verse 15.

NOTES

3:13 ***want to harm you.*** Achtemeier (1996:229) thinks the verb here (*kakoō* [TG2559, ZG2808], "harm, do evil") is too strong for "social rejection or even persecution" and therefore it refers to the type of harm "that can separate them from . . . God," causing God to turn against them and withdraw his divine favor. Yet there is no real evidence for such an interpretation. The term is used most often in Acts for persecution (Acts 7:6, 19; 12:1; 14:2; 18:10), and this passage, too, refers to mistreatment at the hands of unbelievers.

3:14 ***you suffer.*** This verb (*paschoite* [TG3958, ZG4248], also in 3:17) is in the optative mood, which leads some to call the persecution a remote or "rare contingency" (Marshall) and "unlikely" (Grudem) rather than viewing it as something that was currently taking place (since the optative mood centers on contingency, see Porter 1994:59-60). Yet at the same time Peter has indicated that "some of his readers have in fact been the targets of accusations (1 Pet 2:12), ignorant talk (2:15), evil and insult (3:9; 4:14), threats (3:14), and malicious talk (3:16)" (Jobes 2005:227). Thus Achtemeier labels it a "sporadic reality" that is not regular but can erupt at any time, and Davids calls it "a possible situation." Yet again the entire epistle reflects the discouragement that these Christians were experiencing and the reality of the hostility they were enduring. It is probably best to state that the optatives here and in 3:17 (with Elliott 2000:622) "point less to what is possible than to what is desirable, namely, upright behavior even if it leads to suffering." This is in keeping with the optative, which is often used for formal prayers and requests (e.g., 1:2).

3:15 ***Christ as Lord.*** Gr., *kurion ton Christon* [TG5547, ZG5986]. The relationship between the two nouns can be understood as apposition ("the Lord, namely, Christ" or "Christ the Lord"—so Bigg, Elliott, Jobes, Kelly) or as predicate ("Christ as Lord"—so Achtemeier, Best, Michaels, Selwyn). Either is possible, but the use of the article and the context of the statement make the predictive use better. The lordship of Christ is central, and probably *ton Christon* is not meant as a title ("the Messiah") but is the direct object referring to Jesus, "set apart Christ as Lord." Later mss (K L P, most minuscules, Textus Receptus) have the reading "God as Lord," but the earlier and better mss (𝔓72 ℵ A B C Ψ 33) have "Christ as Lord."

Christian hope. Lit., "the hope that is in you." There is a question whether this means "in you" (i.e., in every individual's heart—so Goppelt, Kelly) or "among you" (i.e., referring to the community of faith that unites the church—so Achtemeier, Best, Michaels, Selwyn). So often the distinction between the individual and the corporate is overdone. In the NT most defenses are performed by individuals, but the "hope" is at the same time a community concept. I doubt Peter would make the distinction.

3:17 ***if that is what God wants.*** This brings up one of the difficult theological questions in Scripture. Does God determine when we suffer? Jobes (2005:232-233) likes Elliott's answer (2000:635), "The qualification, *if this should be God's will,* refers to suffering *for doing what is right* and not simply suffering per se. The point is not that God wills suffering but that God *wills doing what is right* . . . even if and when this results in suffering" (emphasis original). While this could fit the passage here, it does not fit 1:6, and it is likely this verse has the same meaning as 1:6. God does not tempt us (Jas 1:13), but he does test us. He is lovingly sovereign, and believers should look upon the difficult side of their providential care as an opportunity to depend more closely on him. The NT principle is that every trial is a chance to allow the Spirit to work.

COMMENTARY

The first section of 1 Peter centered on our true status as the community of God both individually (1:3-12) and corporately (2:4-10), emphasizing the ethical responsibility we have as God's people in between (1:13–2:3). The second major section zeroed in on our relationships, primarily with outsiders (2:11–3:6) but also within the community (3:7-8). Implicit in all this has been the fact of opposition, hostility, and persecution suffered by Christians at the hands of unbelievers (see 1:6-7; 2:19). Peter now addresses this issue directly in the third section of the epistle (3:13–4:19). Many today feel disconnected from the thoughts of this section because most are suffering little persecution in their lives. Yet let us consider three perspectives: (1) While we are not being persecuted now, this could come soon. A great deal of anti-Christian opposition, fueled by political correctness, is looming on the horizon, and the church is already being attacked on several fronts (e.g., postmodern pluralism, the gay rights movement). (2) While we are not being persecuted, more people every day are losing their jobs, their homes, their very lives, for Christ (e.g., Sudan, the Middle East, India, China); we are to "weep with those who weep" (Rom 12:15; Heb 13:3). (3) Many of us are not being persecuted because we are compromising ourselves on various issues so as not to stand out or invite hostility.

Verses 13-17 form an introduction to the section and in a sense are almost a midrash on 2:12, developing the idea of suffering for doing what is right and reacting with such a "good life" that people are "ashamed" for slandering you (3:16). As elsewhere (1:18-20; 2:4, 21-25), Christ is presented as the theological foundation and model for suffering (3:18-22)—with the implications of following Christ's model presented in 4:1-6, the ethical ramifications (like 1:13–2:3) in 4:7-11, and finally a conclusion summing up the Christian approach to suffering in 4:12-19. In 4:13-17 we can divide the structure into three parts: the problem of unjust suffering (4:13-14a), a series of admonitions regarding how to handle such difficult experiences (4:14b-16), and a concluding challenge that such may be God's will, so make certain it comes from doing good (4:17-19).

This present section (3:13-17) begins with a logical premise: Why would anyone hurt us for doing good (3:13)? This could be a rhetorical question, though it may better be called a "general expectation" (Jobes 2005:227) or perhaps a "general rule" with 3:14 an "exception" (Marshall 1991:114). Many of those addressed would have answered, "Do you want names? How many should I list?" This may have been written during the persecution in Rome under Nero, and Christians everywhere were afraid. So this is a good way to begin the topic of the next five sections. The phrase for the one who will "harm" or hurt" us is *ho kakōsōn* [TG2559, ZG2808], tying this with 3:8-12, where the cognate *kakos* [TG2556, ZG2805] appeared five times. Since God is watching over us and hearing our prayers, whatever people do to us will not "hurt" us in the long run. This may reflect Isaiah 50:8-9, "He who gives me justice is near. Who will dare to bring charges against me now? . . . See, the Sovereign LORD is on my side! Who will declare me guilty?" In "eager to do good," Peter uses a strong word for "eager," *zēlōtēs* [TG2207, ZG2421], referring to someone who arduously pursues a goal. It became the title for the political "Zealots" of AD 50–70, the group whose anti-Roman zeal led to the destruction of the nation and the Temple by the Romans (Jobes, Michaels—it is doubtful whether there is an intended contrast here). The point is that God's people should "eagerly" seek to do good (see on 3:11) with all their energy.

The reality of suffering is described in 3:14, beginning with "but even if," a reality that fit the experience of all too many of the readers to whom this epistle was written. When a believer suffers, it should be the result of "doing what is right" rather than a result of committing wrong acts (2:16, 19-20, 21; 3:11; 4:14-16). When that is the case, "God will reward you" (3:14; lit., "you are blessed"), a promise that likely goes back to the beatitude of Matthew 5:10, "God blesses those who are persecuted for doing right." As in 3:9b and 4:14, the blessing is both present and future. God honors such a believer in the present, and there will be eternal reward. In Acts 5:41, the apostles, after being beaten by the Sanhedrin, rejoiced "that God had counted them worthy to suffer disgrace for the name of Jesus." Oh, that such a realization regarding hostility could predominate in our current church.

The proper reactions to suffering are found in the admonitions of 3:14b-16. First, Peter begins with what not to do in reacting to hostility. He utilizes a quote (actually in the first two admonitions, 3:14b and 15a) from the Septuagint of Isaiah 8:12b-13. In the Septuagint, the object of fear is singular (*autou* [TG846, ZG899]) because it was fear of the Assyrian king (though it could also mean the fear held by the "people" who spoke of conspiracy); Peter changed it to plural (*autōn*) because here it is fear of all the persecutors (see Moyise 2005). The literal translation would be "Now don't be afraid with fear of them nor be troubled." The use of these two verbs from Isaiah 8:12 (LXX) in 3:14 ("worry or be afraid") stems from the believers' deep distress and further proves the persecution was very real (see note on 3:14). Jesus said, "Don't be afraid of those who want to kill your body" (Matt 10:28a) and "Don't let your hearts be troubled" (John 14:1, 27). Paul added, "Don't worry about anything" (Phil 4:6a). When a Christian knows the sovereign God and trusts in his providential care, the troubles of this world, though still very real and painful (Heb 12:11), recede in importance.

The second admonition (3:15) provides the positive side (what to do when encountering opposition): "worship Christ as Lord of your life." The idea is very similar to the opening request of the Lord's Prayer, "May your name be kept holy" (Matt 6:9) and stems from Isaiah 8:13 ("Make the LORD of Heaven's Armies holy in your life"). Peter's admonition is literally to "make Christ holy in your hearts as

Lord." The heart refers to the mind as the core of one's feelings, thoughts, and volition; it is the basic self. So Jesus must be sovereign Lord at the core of one's self. The verb (*hagiazō* [TG37, ZG39]) combines reverence and the act of the will; to "make Christ holy" is to recognize and reverence his holiness in every area of your life. Worship is the best antidote to worry and depression. At the same time, as in the Lord's Prayer, worship means living a life of holiness before him (as in 1:15-16) and making his holiness known to the very persecutors who are harassing you (as in 3:15b).

Third, the believer must "be ready to explain" the Christian faith and lifestyle to non-Christians. Often this will be in response to slander or disparaging the believers (as in 2:12, 15; 3:12, 14, 16; 4:14), but also many will honestly ask "about your Christian hope." Note the progression thus far: Don't be afraid of rejection; instead, set apart Christ as Lord over the situation, and be ready for an aggressive defense of Christianity. In that sense this teaching is the harbinger of "apologetics," which means to "defend" the truth behind an idea. In fact, the NLT's "to explain" represents the Greek *pros apologian* [TG4314/627, ZG4639/665]. "Apology" or "defense" is legal terminology, and so this might reflect actual trial situations (Acts 25:16; 26:1-2—so Beare), but that is not the primary thrust. Believers must "always be ready" to answer "anyone," including those involved in legal trials and personal challenges, but the situation behind the book is verbal abuse (2:12; 3:9, 16) rather than imprisonment. The questions will center on "your Christian hope," meaning their basic Christian belief in the "hope" of Christ (1:3). Jobes asks the key question, "How many Christians today could make an articulate statement of the reasons for their faith in Christ in terms that would be understood by modern society?" (2005:230).

Jesus promised that in any of these circumstances "the Holy Spirit will teach you at that time what needs to be said" (Luke 12:12; cf. Matt 10:20; Mark 13:11; Acts 4:8). The point is that there is no need for fear (3:14b) but rather need for a reverential dependence on Christ (3:15a) and the Spirit, whether responding to either interrogation or to simple questions. Yet these apologetic defenses must at all times be done "in a gentle and respectful way" (3:16a). The difficult question is whether these refer to meekness and reverence toward God (Michaels) or gentle and respectful answers to the pagans (Grudem, Jobes). In 1 Peter "gentleness" is usually related to people (3:4) and "reverence/fear" often to God (1:17; 2:17; 3:2); thus, many take the first in relation to people and the second in relation to God (Achtemeier, Beare, Davids, Goppelt, Marshall). Perhaps it is best to slightly modify this: The "gentleness" is to those probing your allegiance to Christ; treat them well and with kindness, as Paul says in 2 Timothy 2:24-25, "Be kind to everyone, . . . be patient with difficult people. Gently instruct those who oppose the truth." The "fear" is first of all a reverence toward God and then the respectful approach to everyone.

Fourth, Peter reminded believers, "Keep your conscience clear" (3:16). In the Greek this is a participial phrase, "maintaining a good conscience," utilized circumstantially to identify a third desired quality when defending the faith: gentleness, reverence (3:16a), and a good conscience (3:16b). At the same time, it partakes of the imperatival force of 3:15 and so can be seen as a further admonition (as in the NLT). The conscience (as in 2:19; 3:21) is the spiritual ability or awareness that allows one to make moral choices between good and evil, both in terms of the earthly situation and the God who judges. A "good" or "clear" or "clean" conscience is noted also in Acts 23:1; 1 Timothy 1:5, 19; 3:9; 2 Timothy 1:3; Hebrews 13:18 and refers to a personal realization that one is just and fair before God and people. Paul exemplified this in his defenses before Festus in Acts 25:8, and before Festus and Agrippa in Acts 25:24–26:31.

The purpose stated in 3:16 returns to the message of 2:12, that a life of goodness will show slander to be a lie and make opponents ashamed at what they had spread about Christians. The introductions for the two central sections of the book (2:11-12 introducing 2:13–3:12 and 3:13-17 introducing 3:18–4:19) end with this same message. Yet there is one difference; in 2:12 the goodness leads to people's conversion, while here it leads to their shame. This is the step discussed in 2:12 (see comments there) that convicts the people regarding their need for salvation, but the emphasis stands differently in this verse. The source of abusive speech is further defined here as "those who abuse, disparage, malign" (*hoi epēreazontes* [TG1908, ZG2092]), which also connotes contempt in the speakers. They are mocking and mistreating the believers, and as Elliott (2000:631) notes, this does not speak of official or legal governmental action but of the informal reproach heaped on them by neighbors and associates. Still, as in 2:12, they are obviously watching, and the "good life" (lit., "good conduct") they observe (as noted in 1:15; 2:12; 3:1-2) will "put" them "to shame," which in the New Testament means a lot more than being embarrassed. It is a divine passive (God is the one who will "shame" them), and again there is an inaugurated thrust: In the present time he will use the exemplary conduct of the Christians to prove how wrong their opponents' lies are; but more importantly, the persecutors will be put to eternal shame at the Last Judgment (cf. 2:6; Mark 8:38; Rom 9:33; 10:11; Phil 1:20; 1 John 2:28). Shame means not just embarrassment but certain judgment. Finally, this good conduct must be done "in Christ," a phrase normally found as a technical idea in Paul (connoting both union with Christ and membership in his body) but found in 3:16; 5:10, 14 in 1 Peter in the sense of the centrality of Christ in everything the believer thinks and does. Their "goodness" is not done or defined in the eyes of society but refers to what is "good" before God and Christ, with the Spirit prompting them.

A second theme that binds the two sections of 2:11–3:12 and 3:13–4:19 is provided in 3:17—make certain when suffering that the cause is your good deeds rather than your bad behavior (see also 2:19-21a; 3:6, 9, 11, 13-14a; 4:14-16, 19). This is spoken to slaves in 2:19—why should there be any credit or reward if you suffer because you did something wrong? But if you suffer unjustly because you lived rightly before God and others, that deserves vindication and honor. The point is that God is in absolute control. When Peter says "if that is what God wants" (or, "if God so wills") he is restating 1:6 ("you have to endure," literally, "if God thinks it necessary to endure"). The verb (*theloi* [TG2309, ZG2527]) is in the optative mood (see note on 3:14), which at times can connote contingency and at other times a desire for something. There is probably more of an atmosphere of contingency than in 3:14; God may or may not will suffering to occur, but he is in complete charge. Peter's point is to make every opportunity to suffer count. God is behind the situation and will take it and use it for your glory as well as your opponents' shame (3:16b) and possible conversion (2:12b). Your responsibility is to be sure you respond by living rightly.

When you experience hostility and are abused for your faith, it is the better path; in this world there is injustice, and the preference is to suffer it for Christ. The use of "it is better" terminology stems from both Hellenistic and Jewish precedent, and there are two aspects here (Marshall 1991:117): It is "better to suffer persecution than to be punished for breaking the law"; and "to suffer persecution from men for doing good is better than to incur God's judgment for doing wrong." Suffering for being a believer is special in the New Testament. The apostles rejoiced that they were "counted . . . worthy" to suffer (Acts 5:41), and Paul considered himself to be experiencing the messianic woes (Col 1:24; see on 4:13, 16) and "the fellowship of [Christ's] sufferings" (Phil 3:10, NIV). Peter later says "these trials make you partners with Christ in his suffering" and as a result "you will have the wonderful joy of seeing his glory" (4:13). We should "praise God for the privilege" (4:16b).

◆ B. The Model for Triumph over Suffering—Christ (3:18-22)

18 Christ suffered* for our sins once for all time. He never sinned, but he died for sinners to bring you safely home to God. He suffered physical death, but he was raised to life in the Spirit.*

19 So he went and preached to the spirits in prison—20 those who disobeyed God long ago when God waited patiently while Noah was building his boat. Only eight people were saved from drowning in that terrible flood.* 21 And that water is a picture of baptism, which now saves you, not by removing dirt from your body, but as a response to God from* a clean conscience. It is effective because of the resurrection of Jesus Christ.

22 Now Christ has gone to heaven. He is seated in the place of honor next to God, and all the angels and authorities and powers accept his authority.

3:18a Some manuscripts read *died.* **3:18b** Or *in spirit.* **3:20** Greek *saved through water.* **3:21** Or *as an appeal to God for.*

NOTES

3:18 *suffered for our sins.* The ancient manuscripts present a bewildering array of different readings for this phrase. The major options are "suffered for our sins" (B K P, many later minuscules) or "died for our sins" (𝔓72 ℵ A C Ψ). "Suffered" would be Petrine style (used 11 times) and "died" more Pauline style. While "died" has stronger manuscript evidence (see Comfort 2008b:746-747), it is more likely that later scribes would have employed Paul's preferred wording, and "died" is rare in the General Epistles (nowhere in 1 Peter). Overall, the reading adopted here is more natural and in keeping with Petrine style.

once for all time. Beare (1961:142) understands *hapax* [TG530, ZG562] (once) as the "final and sufficient" nature of Christ's death, so that death has no more power over Christ, emphasizing the eternal triumph of Christ over death. Better, however, is the view that sees this as once for all, "so that no other sacrifices for sin are ever again necessary" (Best 1979:138).

physical . . . in the Spirit. The Greek has two parallel prepositional phrases, "in the flesh" and "in the spirit." The meaning of this is difficult. It is possible to separate them and have Christ dying "*in* the flesh" while being raised "*by* the Spirit" (so NIV 1984). But nearly everyone agrees that the two datives should be understood the same (so TNIV, followed by NIV 2011, rendering it "in the Spirit"). It is also generally agreed that these are not the two aspects of Jesus' human nature (his material body and his immaterial soul) or of his being (his human nature and his divine nature). The two datives are most likely locative (perhaps datives of reference, so Davids, Michaels), referring to the two spheres or modes of his existence, his physical existence on earth, and his new life in spirit in heaven following his resurrection. First Corinthians 15:45 actually provides an explanation: Christ became life-giving spirit in resurrection. Still, as Michaels (1988:204-205) says, "he was raised from the dead, not as a spirit, but bodily (as resurrection always is in the NT), and in a sphere in which the Spirit and power of God are displayed without hindrance or human limitation (cf. 1:21)," thus the capitalized "Spirit" found in the NLT.

3:19 ***he went and preached to the spirits in prison.*** This extremely difficult assertion has innumerable difficulties: Who are "the spirits" and what is the "prison"? Is the "went" a descent into Hades? Is the "preaching" an offer of salvation to departed spirits or a proclamation of the victory to other "spirits"? When did this occur—in the time of Noah, after Christ's death, or after his resurrection? There are three major interpretations:

(1) It was a "descent into Hades," so Irenaeus, Clement of Alexandria, Origen, Beare, Goppelt. Between his death and resurrection, Jesus descended into the realm of death (prison = Hades) and proclaimed salvation to either those who had died in the Flood (Beare, Goppelt) or to the OT saints (who lived before Christ), thereafter taking those saints from the compartment of the dead (Luke 16:22) to heaven (so Calvin). The problems with this view are many: (a) this would involve a second chance for salvation, but Scripture is clear that no such chance after death is possible (Heb 9:27); (b) there is no other passage that refers to a descent into Hades (Eph 4:9-10 refers to Jesus' ascension and incarnation; Rom 10:7 is not Jesus descending but is rhetorical about us going down to the grave to find Christ); (c) the parable of the rich man and Lazarus (Luke 16:19-31) is not a statement on the state of the dead but a story form, and "Abraham's bosom" most likely "represents the patriarch's reception of the faithful into heaven" (Bock 1996:1368).

(2) It refers to Christ in his preincarnate state preaching repentance through Noah to his contemporaries (the "spirits") while they were alive and imprisoned in sin (so Augustine, Bigg, Erickson, Feinberg, Grudem, Skilton). Although Grudem and Feinberg have certainly shown the viability of this, there are several reasons for rejecting this in the final analysis: (a) It is simply too allegorical, as there is no biblical evidence for a Christophany in the form of Noah (Jesus entering Noah and speaking through him); 2 Pet 2:5 speaks of Noah preaching, but not of Christ speaking through him. (b) Although the "Spirit" inspiring the prophets in 1:11 could refer to the preincarnate Christ preaching through Noah, it is something of a stretch. It is more likely the Holy Spirit inspiring the OT prophets (could they include Noah?). (c) The term "spirits" by itself is hardly ever used in the Bible for departed human "spirits." (The one exception is Heb 12:23.) (d) The phrase "raised to life in the Spirit" in 3:18 does not fit a time in the days of Noah. How could he be "raised to life" by speaking through Noah?

(3) The consensus view today and the one that best fits the contextual and historical data is that Jesus after his death and resurrection made proclamation to the demonic forces (the "unclean spirits" of the Gospels) of his victory and their defeat. This journey of Jesus ("went") was at his ascension (cf. 3:22) through the heavens, and the "prison" for the evil spirits was this earthly sphere (perhaps the upper heavens of it, perhaps the abyss of Rev 9:1-2; 11:7; cf. Jude 6) to which Satan and the fallen angels were "thrown down" (Rev 12:7-9)—mainly a symbol of the confinement of the fallen angels to this world. The proclamation told the evil spirits that their power had been broken. Dalton and France have done an especially fine job showing the likelihood of this view (see also Achtemeier, Davids, Elliott, Jobes, Kelly, Marshall, McKnight, Michaels, Selwyn, Stibbs).

The connection with the Flood is seen in the intertestamental connection between the fall of the angels just prior to the days of Noah in Gen 6:1-4 (the "sons of God" [fallen angels] cohabiting with women and producing giants) and the Flood in Gen 6:9–8:22, events also connected in 2 Pet 2:4-5 (cf. Jude 6-7). In Jewish literature, the connection of Gen 6:1-4 with the Flood is found in *1 Enoch* 6:1–7:6; 9:8–10:16; 12:1-4; 15:4-12; 21:1-10; *2 Enoch* 18:2-9; *2 Baruch* 56:7-16; *Jubilees* 5:1-11, 10:1-13; *Testament of Naphtali* 3:1-5. Michaels and Jobes think it is primarily *1 Enoch* behind 3:19-20. So Peter here (and in 2 Pet 2) built on the Jewish tradition of the evil union between the fallen angels and certain women who lived in the generation before the Flood and the Flood itself. He connected this with the triumphal proclamation of Christ at his ascension to produce this passage. One final note: Many scholars (Achtemeier, Jobes, Marshall, Michaels) emphasize Enoch because they see *1 Enoch* as central, and thus Enoch becomes the Christ-figure in the Jewish story. Some have even seen the name "Enoch" in the Greek *en hō kai* (in which also) that begins the verse, but that is farfetched and has no manuscript evidence whatsoever. On this, Marshall (1991:129) says, "Peter appears to have expressed the significance of Jesus' death and resurrection by using imagery and language from the Enoch story to depict dramatically Christ's victory over all the powers of evil." However, I do not see Enoch being so central, for I think Peter drew on the whole Jewish tradition in developing this little side story here. His emphasis is on what the glorified Jesus did (not on the tradition) and its significance for the readers' encouragement by realizing they share not just in Jesus' suffering but in his glory as well. This was not nearly so complex to them as it is for us, for they knew the stories and did not have to work through the options like we do.

3:21 ***And that water is a picture of baptism, which now saves you.*** Lit., "which also baptism, an antitype, now saves you." The first question is whether the *hō* [TG3739, ZG4005] (which) has as its antecedent "water" or the whole of 3:20b. The former is the more likely and is accepted by most modern translations and commentaries. Second, how do the three ("which," "baptism," "antitype") relate to each other and to the expression "saves you"? Again, most agree they are appositional to each other—"which baptism as an antitype now saves you." The NLT is a good rendering of the resultant meaning.

a response to God from a clean conscience. There are two issues here: First, what is the "response to God" (*eperōtēma,* [TG1906, ZG2090], lit., "pledge")? It means an "answer, demand, enquiry" and was used in the formal question and consultation sealed into a legal contract. The question is whether the forensic aspect is intended or a more general "response/answer" is the force. If the latter, is it a "response" to God or a "request" for a good conscience? That leads to the second issue: Is "good conscience" an objective genitive (a request "for" a good conscience—NRSV, NASB, ESV, Achtemeier, Best, Elliott, Kelly, Senior) or a subjective genitive (a response "by" a good conscience—NLT, TNIV, Davids, Grudem, Marshall, Michaels, Selwyn)? The commentary will argue that baptism here is seen as a formal "pledge" made before God "by" a good conscience.

COMMENTARY

As in 1:18-21 and 2:21-25, Peter turns to Christ to provide a pattern or model to be followed when suffering persecution. In 3:13-17 the section on persecution was introduced, centering on the issue of unjust suffering, even when the believer is doing right in the presence of God and man. This section tells us the reason (*hoti* [TG3754, ZG4022]; "because," 3:18; not translated in NLT) why it is better to suffer this way (3:17)—namely, because this is what Christ himself experienced. According to the previous sections, Christ had purchased the believers with his blood as the perfect lamb (1:18-21) and refused to retaliate for those insults when he healed his followers with his wounds (2:21-25). Now his death produces victory on our behalf. He has defeated the cosmic powers of evil and brought salvation to his people. His physical death was overturned in resurrection and ascension, and his followers will share in that salvation, vindication, and victory. Yes, there is a great deal of rejection and hardship ahead for them, but the greater reality is that, like Jesus, suffering is the path to glory (a theme begun in 1:11).

This passage has often been called one of the most difficult to understand in the New Testament. Martin Luther himself stated, "This is a strange text and certainly a more obscure passage than any other passage in the New Testament. I still do not know for sure what the apostle meant" (cited in Jobes 2005:236). Every scholar wrestles with its difficult syntax and meaning. Yet it is not an impossible passage, nor was it a later interpolation into 1 Peter as some have tried to say. It is intimately connected to its context and provides a vital component to the message of the whole, as we will see. The key is understanding its Jewish background, and I will attempt to provide that for the reader. The passage is framed with creedal material on the death, resurrection, and ascension into glory in 3:18, 22 (cf. 1 Tim 3:16). Furthermore, many have considered it a hymn (see the discussion in Goppelt 1993:247-250), but it is more likely a compilation of traditional material in a high prose form (i.e., creedal themes in a poetic format). The other two passages from tradition (1:18-21, 2:21-25) centered on Jesus' death, while this moves on to his exaltation. So Christ becomes a model of the suffering that ends in glory. The middle portions center on the victory he won over the cosmic powers (3:19-20a) and the salvation that was produced and in which we have participated (3:20b-21).

We begin with Christ as victor (3:18), who provides the basis for victory in suffering. God's people who suffer unjustly need to look to Jesus, who provided the model for suffering (3:17). He "suffered for our sins once for all time," obviously here referring to the cross. The expression *peri hamartiōn* [TG4012/266, ZG4309/281] (for sins) is used in the Septuagint for the sin offering (Lev 5:6-7; 6:24-25; Ezek 43:21), as well as in the New Testament (Rom 8:3; 1 Thess 5:10; Heb 5:3; 10:26; 1 John 2:2; 4:10). Christ became the sacrifice for sins, but the difference is that his sacrifice is *hapax* [TG530, ZG562] ("once for all time," never needing to be repeated like OT sacrifices), especially prominent in Hebrews (Heb 7:27; 9:12, 26, 28; 10:10). While there is not here the emphasis as in Hebrews on the inadequacy of the Jewish sacrificial system, the stress is still on the complete adequacy and completeness of our salvation as a result of Christ's sacrifice. Our suffering can bring glory to God and lead to our own vindication and glory, but Christ's has produced eternal salvation. Ours is a sacrifice, Christ's *the* sacrifice.

Moreover, "he never sinned, but he died for sinners" (lit., "the just for the unjust"). We who are suffering are the beneficiaries of his suffering; we are the "unjust" for whom the one "just" man (1:19; 2:22-23) died. Jesus did not die for us because we deserved it. Romans 5:8 says it best: "God showed his great love for us by sending Christ to die for us while we were still sinners." The purpose was "to bring you safely home to God" (3:18). This is not the Greek idea for bringing priests or initiates to a deity (see Selwyn) but a reference first to conversion and then also to the whole progression of the Christian life to the final "bringing home" at Christ's return (as the NLT recognizes by adding "safely"). The picture is the death of Christ as bringing about our redemption (1:18) from sin to God. As Michaels (1988:203) puts it, "If the immediate benefit of Christ's sacrificial death is religious conversion, its ultimate benefit is eschatological salvation."

The last half of 3:18 provides a creedal couplet that sums up the meaning of Christ's suffering and glory: "He suffered physical death, but he was raised to life in the Spirit." The meaning of the verbs is certain—Jesus' death and his resurrection. The second verb is "made alive," unusual for Jesus' resurrection, used only here (Davids, Michaels) but normally used of others' resurrection (John 5:21; Rom 4:17; 8:11; 1 Cor 15:22, 36; Eph 2:5). The modifiers, literally "in the flesh" and "in the spirit" (see note on 3:18), refer to Jesus' two modes of existence: He died physically as the incarnate God-man on earth but was raised to a new mode, the spiritual new life in heaven. It is important that we do not separate this into anthropological spheres of life (e.g., body and soul), or see this as Jesus' earthly nature versus his divine nature. Jesus died as a whole person, as the God-man, and his resurrection was physical as well as spiritual. Therefore, "in the Spirit" means not that the Spirit was the means of his resurrection but that he was raised into the realm of the Spirit. There is double meaning behind *pneuma* [TG4151, ZG4460] here; Jesus was raised into a new spiritual reality, and he was raised into the kingdom of the Spirit. Peter's point is that Jesus died as our "firstfruits" (1 Cor 15:20, 23); that is, in Christ we too will experience physical death and resurrection to life. This is explained further by 1 Corinthians 15:45, which says "the last Adam—that is, Christ—is a life-giving Spirit," meaning that Christ as resurrected "Spirit" has brought resurrection "life" to all believers.

One would expect the text to move directly to 3:22 concerning the ascension of Christ. Instead, 3:19-21 contains two illustrations of the victory wrought by Christ in his death and resurrection. He begins by establishing a connection between Jesus' death and resurrection in 3:18 by opening 3:19 with *en hō*, which in 2:12 and 3:16 means "when" but here (as in 1:6) means "in which"—namely, in the "spirit"-form of Jesus after his resurrection. As raised "in the Spirit" he "went and preached to the spirits in prison." The basic thrust of this is that Jesus after his death and at his resurrection "went" (the same word is used for "gone to heaven" in 3:22) and "proclaimed" (= "preached"; the verb refers to an announcement made by a herald to a people) his victory over the demonic spirits (see note on 3:19). So after he was "made alive" following his death on the cross, Jesus during his ascension to his Father disarmed the spirits, then led them in a Roman-type triumph across the heavens (Col 2:15). At that time he "proclaimed" and then demonstrated his absolute triumph over them; the two passages (3:19 and Col 2:15) describe the same event in different ways, as both proclamation and event. Achtemeier (1996:260-261) points out that Jesus had already defeated and in a sense imprisoned the cosmic powers by exorcism, that is, "the binding" of Satan and his forces (Mark 3:27); he then confirmed their final defeat on his way to the right hand of power. This victory was won on behalf of his followers, who share in his triumph and can take heart in the midst of their own suffering.

Peter in 3:20 turns to the Noah's Flood story, pointing out that the fallen spirits Jesus triumphed over were the same ones "who disobeyed God long ago when God waited patiently while Noah was building his boat." There was frequent comment in Jewish literature on the evil spirits of Genesis 6:1-4 as the basis for the Flood (see passages in note on 3:20), and Noah was often seen as the representative righteous man (e.g., Ezek 14:14, 20), so that the twin themes of judgment (the Flood) and mercy (the preservation of Noah's family through the Flood) stood out. As stated in the note on 3:20, this connection stems from the Genesis 6 story regarding the "sons of God" (best seen as evil spirits on the basis of Job 1:6; Ps 29:1; 2 Pet 2:4—see Michaels 1988:207) who cohabited with human women and produced a race of "giants," thereby causing God to reject corrupt humanity (Gen 6:11-13) and send the Flood (Gen 7). These cosmic beings are described as "disobeying God," a term used in 1 Peter (2:8; 3:1; 4:17) for those who reject the gospel and turn against God. The readers would see the connection between these evil spirits and their own persecutors. As Michaels (1988:211) says, "the 'disobedient spirits' of long ago still exist, and it is not unlikely that Peter saw their influence behind the ridicule and slander of pagans actively opposed to the Christian movement in his day (cf. Eph 2:2, where 'the ruler of the power of the air' is further identified as 'the spirit now at work among the children of disobedience.')"

There is particular emphasis on how "God waited patiently" (*makrothumia* [TG3115, ZG3429], "longsuffering") during the days of Noah, which was a time of disobedience. The period is specified here as "while Noah was building his boat" (3:20). The patience of God stems from Genesis 6:3 ("Then the LORD said, 'My Spirit will not put up with humans for such a long time. . . . Their normal lifespan will be no more than 120 years'"), which Jewish writers took as referring to God's mercy in giving people a period to repent (*1 Enoch* 66; cf. 2 Pet 3:5-9). The exact period is never specified, though some Jewish writers took it to be the 120-year lifespan of Genesis 6:3 (*Mishnah Avot* 5:2—10 generations). Genesis 7:6 says Noah was 600 years old when the Flood came, so the period from the sons of God to the Flood was considerable, however long it was. Whatever the exact period, this "longsuffering" delayed but did not preclude judgment, so in that sense there is also in the metaphor of the Flood a warning that God's patience will not wait forever. Peter and his readers would likely see in this a parallel with the interval between their present suffering and the final judgment, an idea Peter explores also in 2 Peter 3:5-9. This is the time of mercy and patience when God allows their enemies a chance for repentance. Their task is to bear the hostility of sinners with the same patience and longsuffering that God did and to offer their enemies a chance to repent (2:12; 3:1-2, 9, 15; 4:6).

At this stage, Peter turns from judgment to mercy. The imagery of water provides the transition, now the source of salvation (3:20b-21) rather than of judgment (3:19-20a). Building on the traditions about the Flood, he reports, "Only eight people were saved"—Noah, his wife, his three sons, and their wives. The emphasis is on the God of salvation who can judge the nations and yet rescue his people both from earthly danger and from the cosmic powers, bringing them physical deliverance and spiritual salvation—both are implied here. It is difficult to decide whether "eight" has symbolic significance; is there an "eighth day" theme centering on the day (Sunday the "eighth day," the day of a new creation) Christ was raised from the dead? While possible, that particular symbolism developed a little later, and here the emphasis is on the fact that only a few were saved, paralleling the situation in Peter's day when only a "few" were faithful to Christ and would be saved. It reminded the readers that though they were a small minority, they would certainly be saved from judgment. The eight "people" are referred to as *psuchai* [TG5590, ZG6034] ("souls"; cf. 1:9, 22; 2:25; 4:19) but reference is to their physical lives, not spiritual "souls." The emphasis is on "saved from drowning" (lit., "saved through water"); the verb is a divine passive, "God saved them"; the preposition *dia* [TG1223, ZG1328] has instrumental force, "by means of" water. This leads into the main point in 3:21, that "water" was the means of salvation for the "few" who were redeemed from the Flood: Not the ark but water was the means of rescue.

The "water" through which the "few" were saved is a "picture" (lit., "an antitype") of "baptism" (3:21). The background is Jewish typology, referring to a technique of interpretation in which the Old Testament event (type) is relived or reenacted by a contemporary fulfillment (antitype). It is a correspondence in history as the Old Testament event foreshadows the New Testament reality, and so there is a continuity of divine action as God reworks current history along the lines of the past event (e.g., Heb 7 on Melchizedek/Christ; 1 Cor 10 on manna/Lord's Supper—see Osborne 2006:328-329). In this way, the saving of the "few" souls through the water is reenacted by God in the salvation of "few" in Peter's day. The primary thrust (and greatest difficulty) is the statement, "baptism, which now saves you." At first glance, this means that the deliverance of Noah's family "through water" prefigured salvation through Christian water baptism. It is clear that Peter was not interested in the rite of baptism, that is, in its methods and means, but rather in the effect of baptism, what it produces. In the immediate context the thrust is first, that we are saved from death (like Noah) and, second, that salvation is a participation in Christ's resurrection and victory over the evil powers.

Peter qualifies this basic statement in terms of the effects of baptism in two directions. First, he tells us what it does not mean: It does not constitute "removing dirt from your body." He may have meant the simple fact that it is not just the physical act of taking a dip in the river to clean yourself. But that seems too obvious. Why would he need to say that? Some interpret Peter to be saying that baptism is not merely an outward religious ritual of washing that becomes almost magic (Beare, Boring, Davids, Elliott, France, Marshall). That is viable and probably part of the thrust, but could there be more to it? Several (Achtemeier, Best, Dalton, Kelly, Selwyn) believe it is a reference to circumcision, the cutting off of the unclean foreskin ("the flesh"; cf. Lev 19:23, NLT mg). This might fit Colossians 2:11, where Paul says baptism is "not by a physical procedure" like circumcision, but Colossians compares circumcision with baptism, while 1 Peter does not. Here baptism as an inward act would be contrasted to the external act of circumcision. However, the language here would be very obscure for circumcision, and it simply does not fit very well.

The best view is to see a moral aspect—Peter was saying that baptism does not produce the removal of moral defilement from the "flesh." Michaels (1988:214) says that this would fit Josephus's description of John the Baptist, who told Jews to lead righteous and just lives as "a necessary preliminary if baptism was to be acceptable to God. They must not employ it to gain pardon for whatever sins they committed, but as a consecration of the body implying that the soul was already cleansed by right behavior" (*Antiquities* 18.117). Peter's point would then be that baptism does provide "inward moral cleansing" (Michaels 1988:216). Baptism is a Godward act and proceeds from an inward act that has already taken place. There is no automatic cleansing from all sin that takes place in baptism. As the next statement here says, that inward act must already have taken place.

Peter next tells us what baptism *does* mean: It is "a response to God from a clean conscience" (on this term see 2:19; 3:16). The "response" (*eperōtēma* [TG1906, ZG2090]) can be either a general "request" (even a "prayer"—so Beare, Grudem, Michaels) or a technical term for a "pledge" made in a legal contract. This fits well here (baptism is not seen in the NT as a prayer, and it is hard to see it "appealing" to God), for it looks at baptism in a sense as a seal of the salvation contract, involving the "response" or assent to the spiritual and ethical stipulations made by God to his followers. This makes a great deal of sense given the high ethical content of 1 Peter (so Achtemeier, Dalton, Davids, Elliott, France, Goppelt, Jobes, Kelly, Selwyn). As said above (see note on 3:21), it is best to see this as a pledge to God made "by/from a good conscience." Baptism in this sense is not baptismal regeneration, but it is part of the salvation experience in the sense that the contract has been made at conversion, after which one has a "clean conscience" toward God. The baptism event then seals that contract and pledges to live by God's standards, namely, the stipulations of the salvation contract (what Jobes [2005:256] rightly calls "the moral imperative").

The final comment is especially important: "It is effective because of the resurrection of Jesus Christ" (3:21). This recalls the early Christian connection between the resurrection and baptism; the baptism command came in the great commission of Matthew 28:19, so it was instituted as a sacrament during the 40 days of Jesus' resurrection appearances. As Michaels (1988:217) points out, "through the resurrection" (the literal Greek rendering) actually modifies "baptism, which now saves you" in 3:21a. Thus, in effect it makes the resurrection the basis for salvation, as also seen in the sermons of Acts (Acts 2:32-41; 3:15-19; 4:10-12; 10:39-43; 13:28-39). This clause further answers the question regarding baptismal regeneration; the Resurrection is the instrument or power of regeneration (as the effective vindication of Christ's sacrificial death, cf. 3:18—see Best, Michaels, Reicke). The Cross is the theological basis, the Resurrection the apologetic basis of our salvation (the two are together in Rom 4:25; 6:1-4). It is not baptism that saves us, but the death and resurrection of Christ as a single salvific moment in history. We experience justification at the moment of faith decision, when our "rightness with God" is declared and our conscience made right with him. In baptism, that clear conscience makes a "pledge" to live rightly before God, and baptism is the sacrament that seals our faith decision when our "conscience" is made "clean" and finalizes its salvific experience in that baptismal event.

Peter frames this victory and salvation remembrance of 3:19-21 with his creedal material on the death, resurrection, and ascension of Christ in 3:18, 22. The wording of the two verses is very similar to 1 Timothy 3:16, showing their creedal origins (most believe Peter put these verses together from catechetical content that he inherited—see Goppelt). So Christology provides the heart of the matter, and Christ's exaltation is the foundation for the vindication and glory of the believer. In our trials and troubles, we must center on the glory of the Christ who ascended to heaven and is seated with power above all the cosmic powers, including those threatening us. There are three parts to this incredible statement, and we must consider each in turn. Their importance is shown in that the first two are found in the Apostles' Creed.

The fact of Christ having "gone to heaven" (the Ascension) is the natural denouement to the Resurrection that concludes 3:18 and 3:21 on the theme of the exalted, glorified Christ. The effects of baptism come to us "because of the resurrection" (3:21c), and that leads naturally to the exaltation and glory of Christ in 3:22. At the Ascension Jesus passed through the heavens, and at this time he "went and preached" his victory to the cosmic powers, telling them their power had been stripped (also Col 2:15). Yet the Ascension was probably not a single event, for his ascension began at the moment of his death and was concluded at the end of his resurrection appearances 40 days later (see Osborne 2007:288-289 on John 20:17). Most likely 3:19 refers to the beginning of the process, this verse to the end of that process.

After Jesus ascended, he was "seated in the place of honor next to God," literally, "at the right hand of God," an allusion to Psalm 110:1, the most frequently quoted Old Testament passage in the New Testament (cf. Mark 12:36; 14:62; Acts 2:33-35; 5:31; 7:55-56; Rom 8:34; Eph 1:20; Col 3:1; Heb 1:3; 8:1; 10:12; 12:2). The right hand was the place of honor and power where the king's primary advisor or military general sat. The second half of Psalm 110:1 says, "until I humble your enemies, making them a footstool under your feet," and that is seen in the subjugation of the angels and authorities in the third clause of this verse. This also reflects Psalm 8:6, "You gave them charge of everything you made, putting all things under their authority," referring to the dominion of mankind over God's created order (cf. Ps 8:5). In John 1:1-2, 14; 1 Corinthians 15:25-27; Ephesians 1:22; Colossians 1:16, this psalm passage is used to anchor Christ's authority over all of creation that God has made subject to him (in Heb 2:6-8 Christ returns dominion to mankind).

At the same time, in Jewish writings there is a tradition that evil powers have certain authority over human affairs (*1 Enoch* 61:10-11; 99:7; *2 Enoch* 20:1; *Jubilees* 1:11; 22:17; *Ascension of Isaiah* 1:3; 2:1-4; *Testament of Levi* 3:8—see Best 1979:142-143), and this fits the titles for Satan as "ruler of this world" (John 12:31; 14:30; 16:11) and "god of this world" (2 Cor 4:4), as well as Pauline material on demonic involvement in this world (Rom 8:38; 1 Cor 10:20-21; 15:24; Eph 1:21; 2:2; 3:10; 6:12; Col 1:16). This subjugation is definitely connected to 3:19, where Christ told these evil beings that their power had been broken and their defeat was certain. Of course, Satan was bound (Mark 3:27) during Jesus' ministry, and he had already been cast out of heaven (Luke 10:18; Rev 12:7-9), but after the Resurrection and Ascension, this defeat took on a new intensity. Of course, in the expression "all the angels and authorities and powers," good angels as well as fallen angels are seen as subject to Christ, but the emphasis is on the evil powers in this context. Good angels are by nature and intent willingly under Jesus' authority; but in this context of conflict with the pagan and cosmic authorities, the stress is on the negative side. In the context of all of 1 Peter, the hostility of nonbelievers is seen as due partly to the influence of "rulers of this world," and the truth is that all of these will answer to Christ, who has already won the victory and has absolute power over them. That victory has not yet been finalized, but it is in process; and the Christians can be encouraged and rest assured that this triumph is absolutely certain and that they will share in it.

◆ C. Right Response to Opposition (4:1-6)

**So then, since Christ suffered physical
pain, you must arm yourselves with the
same attitude he had, and be ready to
suffer, too. For if you have suffered
physically for Christ, you have finished
with sin.* [2]You won't spend the rest of
your lives chasing your own desires, but
you will be anxious to do the will of
God. [3]You have had enough in the past
of the evil things that godless people
enjoy—their immorality and lust, their
feasting and drunkenness and wild
parties, and their terrible worship of
idols.**

**[4]Of course, your former friends are
surprised when you no longer plunge into
the flood of wild and destructive things they
do. So they slander you. [5]But remember that
they will have to face God, who will judge
everyone, both the living and the dead.
[6]That is why the Good News was preached
to those who are now dead*—so although
they were destined to die like all people,*
they now live forever with God in the Spirit.***

4:1 Or *For the one* [or *One*] *who has suffered physically has finished with sin.* **4:6a** Greek *preached even to the dead.* **4:6b** Or *so although people had judged them worthy of death.* **4:6c** Or *in spirit.*

NOTES

4:1 ***since Christ suffered physical pain.*** The verse opens with a phrase in the genitive absolute with causal force ("because, since"). "Suffered physical pain" is lit., "suffered in the flesh" and as such takes the reader back to 3:18 and Jesus' bodily suffering (especially his death) that makes him the perfect paradigm for us. Some mss (א A K P 33 Byz) and the KJV have added "for us" to clarify the suffering of Christ, but good mss of both the Alexandrian and Western families (𝔓72 B C Ψ 330) do not have the added material. The reading that best explains the others is the one followed by the NLT.

For if you have suffered physically for Christ. Lit., "because the one having suffered in flesh." There are two related issues here. The Greek conjunction *hoti* [TG3754, ZG4022] could be causal ("for, because"—so Beare, Clowney, Elliott, Goppelt, Michaels) or epexegetical/explanatory ("namely"), leading to a translation like "arm yourselves with the mind of Christ, namely, the one having suffered in the flesh" (so Achtemeier, Davids, Jobes). The related issue is whether "the one who suffered" is the believer (Achtemeier, Best, Elliott, Jobes, Marshall, Senior) or Christ (Davids, Michaels). It would seem that those who take *hoti* as a causal would see "the one who suffered" applying to Christians, while those who take *hoti* as explanatory would see the phrase applying to Christ, but scholars have fallen on both sides on this. The arguments for the phrase referring to Christ are: (1) the "mind of Christ" has to do with his own suffering rather than ours; (2) the one who "suffers physically" in the context is Christ, not the believer (3:18; 4:1a); (3) this could mean that Christ, as a result of his death, has conquered and is free from the power of sin; (4) Peter often emphasizes Christ's sinlessness and power over sin (1:19; 2:22). The arguments on behalf of the phrase referring to Christians are: (1) the context centers on exhorting the believers, and this would seem to be part of that thrust; (2) the thought parallels Rom 6:6, which says the old self was "crucified with Christ so that sin might lose its power in our lives"; (3) it might be proverbial in saying that suffering will give us strength so that we can defeat sin; (4) for Christ to have "finished with sin," there seems implied that Christ has at one time sinned, which 2:22 would deny. While there is a good chance that in one sense both are involved, since Christ is the paradigm for the suffering person defeating sin, Peter's point most likely concerns the Christian, for the context of 4:1-6 concerns the Christian defeating sin. Also, *hoti* is better seen as causal than as explanatory, since 4:1b provides the reason for being ready to suffer.

One other option under the "Christian" understanding must be discussed: the view that the text refers to baptism. Since Rom 6:7 is connected to the baptismal passage in Rom 6:2-3 (baptism is joining "[Christ] in his death" and so in it "we have died to sin"), some see this as a reference to baptism (Cranfield, Dalton, Kelly). Goppelt (1993:281) provides two answers: "But in 1 Peter suffering unto death is never purely spiritual, but is always bodily suffering. And ceasing from sin is never simply freedom from sin but is always also desisting from offences, as in v. 2a, according to which one should live no longer 'for human lusts.'" Therefore, the baptism interpretation is not very likely.

4:4 *they slander you.* The Greek verb is *blasphēmeō* [TG987, ZG1059], and it likely has double meaning here. The surface thrust, of course, is the slander of Christians by their former comrades in profligate living who now mock and denounce them. There is also another aspect (perhaps the primary one) in which the pagans are at the same time "blaspheming" God. This principle is found throughout the NT—what is done to God's people is done to God, and the perpetrators will be judged accordingly (cf. Matt 10:40-42; 25:31-46).

4:5 *will judge.* Lit., "being ready to judge." It is also possible to take this in an inaugurated sense that God is "prepared to judge" the unsaved now, and this process will continue until the eschaton. But the phrase "the living and the dead" makes this view virtually impossible, since the dead are awaiting judgment rather than being judged now. At the final judgment "the sea gave up its dead, and death and the grave gave up their dead. And all were judged according to their deeds" (Rev 20:13).

4:6 *the Good News was preached to those who are now dead.* This is the only passage in the NT that hints of Christ proclaiming the gospel to the dead, so like 3:19 this is a famous *crux interpretum* and has generated a great deal of literature. Many commentators (e.g., Beare, Best, Goppelt, Green) tie it together with 3:19 and believe that this details Christ preaching to the "spirits in prison" in 3:19 and giving them a second chance for salvation. But this makes little sense in the context and in fact has been disproven in 3:19. In the NT, choices to accept or reject Christ are made in this life, not after a person has died (cf. Heb 9:27). Another view is that this refers to the spiritually dead who receive the gospel, but the problem is 4:5, which refers to the literal dead, and that must be the sense here as well ("the dead" in 4:6 must be the same as "the dead" in 4:5). The best view (see Achtemeier, Dalton, Elliott, Grudem, Jobes, Marshall, Selwyn, Senior) is that the dead here are NT believers who had passed away (cf. 1 Thess 4:13). Peter obviously wanted to clarify the judgment of "the living and the dead" by encouraging the Christians that judgment will be experienced by all, but that Christians can be assured that death, for them, does not obviate their standing before God.

destined to die like all people. Lit., "judged according to men in the flesh." There is a question as to whether this refers to the inevitable nature of death (NRSV, NLT, ESV, Beare, Best, Dalton) or the fact that the world of mankind is going to continue judging God's people (so NLT mg, TNIV, Jobes, Marshall, Michaels, Selwyn, Senior). In the first case, Christians do receive God's "judgment" in the sense that they die; in the second, the judgment is something that Christians receive by human hands (in 4:3-4). Both views make sense in

4:6. The first fits the context of 4:1-6, but the second fits the use of "judge" as divine judgment in 4:5 and is more in keeping with the whole message of 3:13–4:19. The pagans have heaped human judgment on God's people, but they will face God's judgment (4:5).

COMMENTARY

Peter now returns to the theme begun in 3:18 (4:1 and 4:6 both deliberately recall 3:18), the example of Christ's suffering and the encouragement that it gives believers to suffer patiently, depending on God. There are two points in this paragraph—seek the mind of Christ because that will give you strength over sin, and make a decisive break with the mind-set of your pagan past, realizing that those who torment you will answer to God. The basic point is the choice Christians have between living by the will of God (4:2) or by the dictates and pressure from their pagan friends (4:3-4). What is at stake is the judgment of God (4:5). This further points out that the pressure does not come from official governmental requirements but from their neighbors who expect them to conform with their immoral lifestyle. When Christians do not, the surprise turns to anger and slander (4:4). There are three parts to this paragraph (so Jobes): the mind-set that leads to victory over sin (4:1-2), their relationship to past and present sin (4:3-4), and the accountability of all to God's judgment (4:5-6). An alternative way to look at this (Michaels) is to see 4:1-3 on the behavior of Christians (subject is "you"), and 4:4-6 on the pagan response (subject is "they").

On the basis of the exaltation and victory of Christ in 3:18-22 ("So then" moves into a conclusion from that paragraph), 4:1 returns to the model of Christ in his suffering. In 3:18 we are told how Christ "suffered" and "died" on our behalf, and 4:1 resumes that emphasis and once more makes this the archetypal example for all Christian reaction to antagonism. The admonition to "arm yourselves" (*hoplizomai* [TG3695, ZG3959]) draws on the powerful military metaphor of the Roman hoplite infantryman, the core of Roman battlefield success. The related noun is often used of equipment for spiritual warfare as in Romans 13:12 ("put on the shining *armor* of right living"), 2 Corinthians 6:7 ("the *weapons* of righteousness") and 2 Corinthians 10:4 ("We use God's mighty *weapons*, not worldly *weapons*, to knock down the strongholds of human reasoning"). The picture is quite similar to Ephesians 6:10-17 in which the believers put on "all of God's armor" and wage war against the principalities and powers. Here the major weapon that will bring us victory is the "attitude" or "mind" of Christ that will enable us to "be ready to suffer, too." The reference to Christ's mind-set reminds us of Gethsemane, where Christ asked the Father to be released from his destiny, yet said, "I want your will to be done, not mine" (Mark 14:36). Peter was not saying that we should seek suffering (like some monks in the Middle Ages) but rather that if and when it comes, we should be "ready."

Peter now adds the reason for taking "the mind of Christ" in readiness for the possibility of hostility: "If you have suffered physically for Christ, you have finished with sin." In the note on 4:1, it is argued that Peter is speaking of the Christian rather than of Christ here. "Physically" is *sarki* [TG4561, ZG4922] (in flesh), and this term, as Jobes (2005:264-265) argues, is defined in 4:2 by "living out the rest of your time in the flesh" and so means "the time of earthly life before death," rather than the Pauline use of the term for the fallen human nature. So when one experiences "the fellowship of sharing in his sufferings" (Phil 3:10, NIV), a spiritual strength is imparted as the believer gains "the mind of Christ." With the decision to follow Christ to the extent of actual bodily suffering, a spiritual power (Phil 3:10, "the mighty power that raised him from the dead") infuses followers so that they begin to live a life obedient to "the will of God" (4:2) and to "keep away from worldly desires" (2:11) in their daily conduct. They desist from ("cease, are finished with") sin. "Have finished" is perfect tense (*pepautai* [TG3973A, ZG4264]), which refers to a state of being; they will from that point be in a state of obedience to God and "cease" to allow sin to have control. The mind of Christ honed in suffering provides armor and weapons by which believers can defeat sin in their lives. Yet this hardly means believers will live sinless lives from that time on. As Grudem (1988:167) says, this means "a clear break with sin." The believer is strengthened spiritually and morally to triumph over the desire to live for self, but this does not ensure a life of sinless perfection.

Peter details in 4:2 the purpose for and implications of the state of being "finished with sin" (4:1). For "the rest of [their] lives" (4:2; a virtual definition of that state), believers will refuse to chase their "own desires" and instead "be anxious to do the will of God." This is certainly not an automatic state; it is clear that all depends on how believers conduct their lives. "Spend the rest of your lives" is literally "live (*biōsai* [TG980, ZG1051], your "biological" existence) the remaining time in the flesh" and means that so long as they live on earth, believers continue to walk with God and have the same attitude as Christ. The negative command is to forego "your own desires" (lit., "human lusts/passions"), denoting not just sexual lusts but all the self-centered impulses that tend to control "human" (cf. 2:4, 15; 4:6) desires (see the discussion and lists in 1:14; 2:1, 11; 3:9; especially 4:3). "The use of 'desire' for this generalized 'I want' within ('If it feels good, do it') has already been noted . . . earlier in 1 Peter (1:14; 2:11)" (Davids 1990:150). The positive counterpart that should control Christians' lives is "the will of God." In a very real sense "God's will" sums up the spiritual and ethical content of the letter. It "connotes the direction and guidance for life that must come from God. It is a moral and ethical concept that defines proper Christian thoughts and conduct before God" (Osborne 2004:322). It basically means to know God's dictates and to obey them in every area of life. According to Matthew 7:21, only those who do God's will enter the kingdom; and according to Matthew 12:50, Jesus' true family are those who do "the will of [his] Father in heaven." In John 7:17 the choice to do God's will is necessary to understand Jesus' teaching. In Hebrews 13:21, doing God's will and pleasing him are virtually synonymous (cf. Rom 12:2, his will is "good and pleasing and perfect").

From the discussion of the mind of Christ that makes it possible to obey God's will and defeat sin, Peter turns to the issue of his readers' past and present relationship to these very sins (4:3-4); one's lifetime is divided into two eras—before and after conversion. In terms of the temptation to indulge in these self-centered desires, the readers are told they have had more than enough time for these destructive urges. The hook word, left untranslated in the NLT, is *chronos* [TG5550, ZG5989], "chronological" time. In 4:2 the "remaining time" of life on earth is mentioned; in 4:3, it is "sufficient time" in the past. This naturally speaks of the time before conversion, when the believers were pagans. Their life in sin was more than long enough for them to discover the true reality behind a life of sin. "The evil things that godless people enjoy" (4:3) is literally "the will of the Gentiles" (referring to all the unsaved, not just the Gentiles), and stands in contrast to "the will of God" (4:2). The term for the Gentiles' will is *boulēma* [TG1013, ZG1088], which adds to the *thelēma* [TG2307, ZG2525] (will) of God in 4:2 the idea of a plan to achieve the goal (see L&N 289). The contrast is that God "desires" to have us live for him, but the pagans have a plan to fulfill their own "desires" that are counter to God's. Every Christian feels pressure from two directions—live out God's will in daily life or allow the desired goals of the unbelievers around us to control our decisions.

To demonstrate what those pagan desires were that controlled their lives before conversion, Peter lists six items, a vice catalogue similar to those in 2:1; Romans 13:13; 1 Corinthians 5:10-11; 6:9-10; Galatians 5:19-21; Colossians 3:5; and in other writings in the Jewish and Greco-Roman worlds. The first five vices are acts of debauchery and were not only acceptable but expected in Roman society; these are uniformly condemned in Scripture. All are plurals to emphasize specific acts and not just attitudes, and the language is that the Christians were tempted to "go along" (*peporeumenous* [TG4198, ZG4513]) with the godless in these practices.

"Immorality" (4:3) refers to sensual acts and is highlighted in 2 Peter 2:2, 7, 18 as characteristic of false teachers. "Lust" (same term as "desire" in 4:2) refers specifically to sexual lust; parallel actions today would be viewing pornography, going to adult stores, etc. Michaels (1988:231) provides a good comparison with 2 Peter here: "It is obviously no accident that 1 Peter sounds most like 2 Peter when it denounces the same kinds of behavior 2 Peter denounces. The difference is that 1 Peter is directing its scorn against the world outside the Christian community, while 2 Peter is combating the intrusion of that world into the church itself." "Drunkenness" is perhaps even greater a problem today than in Peter's day; it is a worldwide disgrace, and the number of deaths attributed to excess or binge drinking is catastrophic. "Feasting" and "wild parties" are similar terms and combine the ideas of both excess wine and sexual immorality. In the Roman world this was especially well-known at the feasts of Bacchus and Saturnalia, but today such parties are celebrated every weekend! Jobes sums them up: "All five terms refer to practices that have in common a lack of self-control, a character flaw leading to behaviors that are a self-destructive violation of God's standards and are harmful to others" (2005:267). The sixth and final item, "terrible worship of idols" (lit., "lawless idolatry"), stands by itself and looks at idolatry from a Christian perspective. This is not just temple worship but idolatrous banquets (1 Cor 10:20-22)—indeed, the worship of anything that replaces God (for us today, for instance, our bank accounts!).

In 4:4 Peter segues from the past to the present pressure on believers to conform to "the desires" of the surrounding culture. There is a presupposition here that these people who are surprised are "former friends," meaning that the Christians are no longer moving in the same circles as those with whom they used to carouse. This is what Paul meant when he challenged the believers not to "team up with those who are unbelievers" (2 Cor 6:14); it does not mean to have no friends among non-Christians but rather not to run in their circles. Our closest friends and advisers are to be in the church. So Peter means that these people with whom the Christians used to attend "wild parties" are shocked when they no longer do so. The wording here is terrific—"plunge into the flood of wild and destructive things they do" (4:4).

There is a development from 4:3 in that they are pressured to "go along" and then "plunge" into sin. The picture is so apt! The unbelievers are like lemmings following each other as they plunge to their deaths over a cliff into a wild flood. The sins of 4:3 become a "flood of debauchery/dissipation." The idea of "wild and destructive" behavior is behind the term and sums up this self-indulgent lifestyle that exists only for pleasure. When they realize the Christians are not going to cave into the pressure, they "slander" (or denounce), revile, and heap abuse on the believers (discussed in 2:12; 3:16). History tells us how the Christians were labeled traitors, murderers, atheists, enemies of all the Romans held dear. Today the idea of separating from one's old friends and influences has become a major part of all recovery programs (whether alcohol, drugs, or sexual addictions); one of the first things that must be done is to remove the person from that circle of so-called "friends" who keep leading them down that destructive path. These two verses (4:3-4) are more true today than ever!

The third and final section of this is 4:5-6 on the accountability of all before God, first the enemies of God's people and then both "the living and the dead." Those who defame the children of God may have the upper hand in the present, but they will literally "give account" (*apodidōmi* [TG591, ZG625]) to God. This is legal language for answering to charges in a court of law (see Matt 12:36; Luke 16:2; Acts 19:40; Heb 13:17). Beare (1961:155) contrasts it with the Christian being hauled before the authorities in 3:15 and says, "The Christian may be called to account before an earthly tribunal; his enemies will be called to account before the tribunal of heaven." The judge could be Christ (Acts 10:42; Rom 14:9; 2 Tim 4:1—so Beare, Best, Selwyn—Goppelt points out that the Apostles' Creed takes it this way), but in the context the judge is most likely God (cf. 1:17; 2:23). In the long run, of course, the triune Godhead will be the eschatological judge. He will judge "the living and the dead" (4:5), meaning every human being who has ever lived, in the past as well as the present. Some have thought of "the dead" as the spiritually dead, but here it is simply an expression for every person, whether alive or dead (as clarified in 4:6).

Verse 6 is almost an appendix explaining the significance of God judging "the living and the dead" in 4:5. Because final judgment is coming, the "Good News" was "preached" to those believers now dead (see note on 4:6). The first clause contains a passive verb ("was preached") and no subject, so some (Achtemeier) believe Christ was preached, but as in 3:19, it is the gospel (which would certainly include Christ!) that has been preached. The passive refers to all first-century teachers and preachers who had "proclaimed" the gospel to the unsaved, with the Christians accepting the message, leaving behind their worldly pursuits and friends (4:2b-3) and coming to Christ before they died. Peter's point is that everyone, living and dead, will give account to God, but believers, even though they die, are safe in the Spirit. So there is both warning for the unbeliever as well as comfort for the believer; there is a judgment after death, and both are affected. The gospel is not being proclaimed to people who have died (see note on 4:6), and this verse is not connected to 3:19. There is no second chance for salvation, in keeping with the rest of the New Testament. Nor in this verse is the Good News preached to the spiritually dead (true as this may be); rather, it centers on a different issue, discussing believers who have died and their relation to the final judgment described in 4:5. Jobes (2005:271) provides Calvin's (1963:302) excellent quote here: "We see . . . that death does not hinder Christ from being always our defender. It is a remarkable consolation to the godly that death itself brings no loss to their salvation. Even if Christ does not appear as Deliverer in this life, yet His redemption is not void, or without effect, for His power extends even to the dead."

Death is an inescapable fact, but the text concerns the judgment that follows. Every human being will "give account" to God at the final assize, and that will determine whether they face judgment or reward, entrance into heaven (4:6) or eternal punishment (4:5). It is more likely that "destined to die" refers to the judgment that the pagans have heaped on them ("although people had judged them worthy of death"; 4:6, NLT mg). Therefore, the contrast in the two clauses, "like all people" (*kata anthrōpous* [TG2596/444, ZG2848/476]; judged "by human standards") and "with God" (*kata theon* [TG2596/2316, ZG2848/2536]; live "on the basis of God's standard"), refers to temporary human hostility set over against God's eternal blessing. The believers who accepted the "preaching" of the gospel also experienced opposition and persecution before they died, but that is completely countered by the promise that they will "live forever with God in the Spirit" (like Christ in 2:4). As Christ was "raised to life in the Spirit" in 3:18, so Christians will "live . . . in the Spirit" forever. As Elliott (2000:738-739) says, this is not life in the Holy Spirit but, as in 3:18, life in the new sphere of existence, a spiritual life "animated by the life-giving Spirit of God (see Ezek 37:14; Rom 8:10; 1 Cor 5:5; 15:42-46)." The Spirit is behind this new dimension, but it is linked to the "spiritual body" of 1 Corinthians 15:44, a new spiritual reality.

◆ D. Ethical Life in the Community (4:7-11)

7The end of the world is coming soon. Therefore, be earnest and disciplined in your prayers. 8Most important of all, continue to show deep love for each other, for love covers a multitude of sins. 9Cheerfully share your home with those who need a meal or a place to stay.

10God has given each of you a gift from his great variety of spiritual gifts. Use them well to serve one another. 11Do you have the gift of speaking? Then speak as though God himself were speaking through you. Do you have the gift of helping others? Do it with all the strength and energy that God supplies. Then everything you do will bring glory to God through Jesus Christ. All glory and power to him forever and ever! Amen.

NOTES

4:8 ***love covers a multitude of sins.*** This is an enigmatic saying and can have several possible meanings: (1) God's love has "covered" our sins, so we can as a result "cover" other people's sins (cf. Matt 6:14-15; Mark 11:25; so Goppelt, Selwyn). (2) When we truly love another, we will forgive (cover) people's offenses (sins against us, so Achtemeier, Beare, Jobes, Michaels, Reicke). (3) When we exercise love, God will forgive our sins (Luke 7:47; so Kelly, Kline). All are attractive and viable. However, the context of 1 Peter in terms of community forbearance and unity makes the second (our forbearance and forgiveness of others) the best option.

4:11 ***All glory and power to him.*** Lit., "to whom be glory and power." The question is whether "to whom" refers to God (the center of the context, so Achtemeier, Best, Goppelt, Kelly) or Jesus Christ (the immediately preceding name in the verse, so Bigg, Davids, Michaels, Selwyn). As Jobes states, Peter does not seem to be troubled by the ambiguity, and it may well be that Peter intended this to apply to "God through Christ." Still, God is the primary focus, as seen in the parallel 5:10-11, where the praise is ascribed to God, again in a context where our calling is "by means of Christ Jesus."

COMMENTARY

Due to the brevity and terseness of this section, it is common to think of it as a concluding paragraph, either to the book (Beare) or to the section (Achtemeier, Jobes, Michaels). But paraenetic (exhortation) sections often come in the middle of a discourse (Rom 13:11-14; Phil 4:4-8; Heb 10:19-25), and this section is closely connected to both the preceding and following material on the issue of suffering. Thus, it belongs in 3:13–4:19, detailing how the church should conduct itself internally in light of the external hostility. As we will see, most of the issues addressed parallel material elsewhere in the epistle (e.g., 1:22; 2:2-3, 5, 17; 3:8; 5:1-11), and so this section acts as a focal point of admonition regarding relationships and ministry in the church. The church needs togetherness in light of the current crisis, so the paragraph centers on "each other" (4:8), "one another" (4:9, NIV), and "each of you" (4:10) as defining the unity and mutual love that should typify the church. There are four parts of this paragraph: the basis—the imminent eschaton (4:7a); the vertical dimension—disciplined prayer (4:7b); the horizontal dimension A—love and hospitality (4:8-9); the horizontal dimension B—spiritual gifts and ministry (4:10-11).

As a summary of the central theme in the epistle concerning the eschatological end of the age, Peter begins 4:7 with "the end of the world is coming soon." The Greek has "the end of all things is at hand" with "all things" in the emphatic position at the start of the sentence. God's entire creation has been tainted with sin and is longing for its release (Rom 8:18-22), and the whole of the created order must be destroyed (2 Pet 3:7, 10) for the new order to be released. The theme of the eschatological end is stressed in "great expectation" (1:3), the "inheritance" (1:4), the "salvation, which is ready to be revealed" (1:5), "the day when Jesus Christ is revealed" (1:7, 13; 4:13), the "reward for trusting him" (1:9), God as final judge (1:17; 2:12; 4:5, 17-19), Christ as judge (2:8), and "eternal glory" (5:10). The statement in 4:7 draws together all those images and stresses the "soon" arrival of that day. The intensive perfect "is coming soon" (*ēngiken* [TG1448, ZG1581], "draws near, is at hand") strongly stresses the imminence of the event. This is the exact same verb form as in Mark 1:15, Jesus' proclamation that "the Kingdom of God is near."

There is a constant emphasis on imminence in the New Testament. John the Baptist (Matt 3:2) and Jesus (Matt 10:7; Mark 1:15) both said "the Kingdom of God is near," and Jesus added he would come like "a thief" (Matt 24:43-44; cf. 1 Thess 5:2; 2 Pet 3:10; Rev 3:3; 16:15). In Romans 13:12, Paul says, "The night is almost gone" and in Philippians 4:5 he states that "the Lord is coming soon" (cf. 1 Cor 16:22; Heb 10:37). In Hebrews 10:25 we are told that "the day of his return is drawing near" (cf. Jas 5:8; Rev 1:3). The purpose established by Jesus and continued through the rest of the New Testament is clear—since the Lord is returning soon, the believers must be ready at all times, for when he arrives they will be held accountable for the way they are living—whether for God or for themselves. This is the theme in 1 Peter, as well. Yet at the same time the imminent expectation constitutes both a living hope and a huge problem, for after nearly 2,000 years, the Lord has still not returned. If anyone had told Peter or Paul that, they might have labeled him a heretic! The classical answer is still true—God's timetable is not ours (2 Pet 3:8), and God patiently waits for more people to repent (2 Pet 3:9). Moreover, in the kingdom parables of Jesus (e.g., Matt 24:36–25:30) and in the commissions to mission (e.g., Matt 28:18-20; Acts 1:8), it is clear Jesus expected a lengthy time before he returned. The purpose of imminence is to stress the biblical demand to be ready at all times, and there is an inaugurated thrust as well, accentuating the beginning of the process. The result of this inaugurated series is that we are living in the last days, in tension between the already and the not yet. God's final intervention is on the way, and we must be ready for it at every moment.

In the rest of the paragraph, the implications of Christ's soon return are explored. At the outset, the vertical dimension is the necessity of disciplined, earnest prayer. Jesus established prayer as the great power of the new age of the Spirit, both in his model prayer (Matt 6:9-13) and in his personal prayers (e.g., Gethsemane, Mark 14:38) and teaching (e.g., Luke 11:1-13; in the Farewell Discourse—John 14:12-14; 15:7, 16; 16:23-24, 26). This new power is based on a new direct relationship with the Father and on the resurrection power given by Jesus and the Spirit (Eph 1:19-23), resulting in the new efficacy of prayer (Luke 18:1; Rom 1:10; 12:12; Eph 6:18; Col 4:2; 1 Thess 5:17). Prayer does change things. Here it must be noted that Peter has corporate prayer in mind, the church on its knees together, but this teaching does not exclude the individual prayer life. The two aorist imperatives (looking at prayer as a complete whole in our lives) are similar in meaning and center on the need of discipline in general, particularly in the prayer life. It is likely that they actually set the tone for the whole section, and the need for clear disciplined action permeates all of 4:7-11. The first imperative (*sōphronēsate* [TG4993, ZG5404]) stresses a clearheaded sensibility that allows a person to appraise a situation and act appropriately. The second (*nēpsate* [TG3525, ZG3768]) is the opposite of drunkenness (their old way of life in 4:3) and emphasizes self-control and clarity of thought (see also 1:13; 5:8). What this says is that the believer's mind must be clear of all encumbrances, focused, under the control of the Spirit in every area of life, and especially *eis proseuchas* [TG1519/4335, ZG1650/4666], "directed to prayer." A realistic, sober assessment of the world and our true situation in it will drive us to our knees (see Green 2007:142-143). The church moves forward on its knees, and this calls for alert, disciplined prayer at all times. Believers must assess their situation, clearly be aware of all their circumstances, and in light of the imminent end of all things, give everything over to the Lord, asking for the wisdom to react as God would have them react and asking for the empowering presence of the Spirit.

The rest of the paragraph will present the horizontal dimension, life in the church. In 4:8-9 relationships are addressed with respect to love and hospitality. Lack of love (anger, bitterness, refusal to forgive, even indifference) in the church or individual destroys the prayer life. So Peter returns to the exhortation of 1:22,

"Love each other deeply with all your heart." The church (meaning "assembly") must become a community and then a family. The basis for this divine mandate is caring and sharing among the brothers and sisters in the "household of God" (4:17; 1 Tim 3:15). It must be a "deep love," which, as in 1:22, means both intense and enduring love; it never quits and demands great effort. Marshall (1991:143) calls it love "at full stretch . . . because this love will be stretched to the limit by the demands made on it." Peter then parallels the literal phrase "directed to prayer" in 4:7 with "directed to each other" in 4:8, emphasizing the congregational side of believers' lives. Believers must love the world as God and Christ did (John 3:16; Rom 5:8; 1 John 4:9-10), but there is a special love within the community (John 13:34-35; 15:12, 17; Gal 6:10; 1 John 2:7-11; 3:11).

One reason that love is so critical in the church is that it "covers a multitude of sins," which is a loose paraphrase of Proverbs 10:12 (it follows neither the Hebrew nor the LXX) and is also found in James 5:20 (also *1 Clement* 49:5; *2 Clement* 16:4), and is thus a traditional saying. Proverbs 10:12 also states the converse, "Hatred stirs up quarrels, but love makes up for all offenses." Love and forgiveness are intertwined. Two of the sins in 2:1 are connected to retaliation for being wronged—jealousy and unkind speech—and 3:8 tells the accompanying attitudes that make such forgiveness possible—kindness, sympathy, compassion, and humility. In time of crisis, stress and worry produce irritability and frayed tempers. Small slights are expanded into major offenses, and it is easy for relationships to fall apart. These Christians were threatened from without by the slander and persecution of the church's enemies, and they were threatened from within by dissension and bitterness. The remedy was a deep-seated, energetic love that would fulfill 1 Corinthians 13:5, keeping "no record of being wronged"—wrongs including not only acts committed against us but also anything in others that irks us, like character flaws.

Love must be expressed in hospitality, as 4:9 tells us. Christians were on the move in the mobile Roman world, and both merchants and church emissaries, as well as missionaries, were frequently visiting other congregations. The inns in those days were black holes, and people could disappear in them. In one Greek play the characters judged the value of inns by cockroaches—all had them, but the one with the fewest was judged best. Therefore, Christians were expected to open their homes to visitors, not just due to the bad state of lodgings but even more on account of the love they felt for other brothers and sisters in the faith. Here in 1 Peter the emphasis is on the local church members cheerfully sharing their homes with one another. There were no church structures in the first three centuries of the church; rather, they met in the larger homes of the members of the church. Therefore, many believers were not only allowing their homes to be used as meeting space, they were also treating out-of-town visitors as houseguests. This does not just mean a willingness to use their home as a house church for worship but also to use it to welcome the other believers outside the service in love and fellowship, as the NLT says, "with those who need a meal or a place to stay" (4:9).

Hospitality was critical in the ancient world as a sign of friendship and even for social status (e.g., the powerful were expected to have lavish parties). There was even a tradition of the gods visiting people in disguise to check their character (similar to "entertained angels without realizing it," Heb 13:2). The friendliness of the host and the responses of the guests created a bond that was important to the patron-client culture of the Roman world, often with a gift given by the visitor that would cement the friendship established. Nations even had officials called *proxenoi* whose major function was to show hospitality and promote goodwill toward their government (see Fitzgerald 2000).

There is much on this issue in the New Testament. In a section on communal love, Romans 12:13 says, "Be eager to practice hospitality," and in 1 Timothy 3:2 and Titus 1:8 hospitality is one of the criteria for leadership. In several other places, hospitality is implicitly expected (Matt 10:11-14; 25:35, 38, 43-44; Acts 16:15; Rom 16:5, 23; 1 Tim 5:10; Jas 2:15-16, 25; 2 John 10; 3 John 5—so Davids). Finally, this is to be done "cheerfully" (4:9; lit., "without grumbling"). Both the negative and positive sides are intended; it is a type of litotes, in which the negative statement (no grumbling) intends to express the positive side (Achtemeier). There was a certain obligation to open your home in a society like the first-century world, especially with the church so small and marginalized. In this situation, it would be easy to feel put upon and used. All hospitality situations too frequently lead to complaining about the food and service on the one side or about the selfishness or bad manners (e.g., dress, eating habits) on the other side. Christian love demands cheerfulness above all. I remember a friend who wrote a pamphlet about the Christian family and said that not only are their homes their castles, but they have built moats around them and keep the drawbridge forever raised! All too many families do not want their "castle" invaded. Yet there may be no area more needed in our age of lonely people!

The other aspect of the horizontal dimension is that of spiritual gifts and ministry (4:10-11). The theology of spiritual gifts described in 1 Corinthians 12:12-26 and Romans 12:3-8 lies behind Peter's short summary here and is critical to understanding it. God has made many spiritual gifts available to his people; the gifts are controlled by the Spirit, and he distributes them as he wills (1 Cor 12:11), *not* as we want. We should be thrilled with what God gives us and use our gifts with joy rather than complaining that we want a different spiritual gift or demanding more of whatever gift he has given us (e.g., to be smarter or a better speaker or an even better musician). Talents become spiritual gifts when dedicated to and used for God and his church. The purpose of gifts is never to exalt the person but rather to serve the community. So every Christian (there are no Christians without a gift from God, though many neither realize it nor use it) is given exactly the gifts God wants, and each is meant to use them for the benefit of the church and the glory of God. This leads to the interdependence of all the believers. We need each other, to be the dispensers and also the recipients of the gifts God has given to the church through his people. The church is a family with each member supporting the others by using their gifts—not for status but for the enrichment of the others. Gifts do not confer status; they confer responsibility. Just as it says in James 3:1, many should not "become teachers in the church, for we who teach will be judged more strictly." The teaching office is very important to God; so it has more responsibility and will be judged more strictly. Such gifts contain both privilege and responsibility.

With this in mind, Peter centers on two ideas discussed in the preceding paragraph: Each person's ministry (in the broad sense) in church is "a gift from [the] great variety of spiritual gifts," and the purpose or goal of each is "to serve one another." At times "gift" (*charisma* [TG5486, ZG5922]) refers specifically to the more supernatural gifts such as tongues, interpretation, healing, and knowledge, but here it has the more general sense of all God's gracious gifts available to the church (e.g., carpentry, music, children's ministry). Here the great "variety" or diversity is stressed; there are more than enough for everyone—literally, the gifts stem from "the varied grace of God." The gifts are ours only because of the "grace" (*charis* [TG5485, ZG5921]) of God; they are "grace-gifts." And it is the incredible depth and variation of divine grace that provides for the multiform needs of the church. As each of us receive these loving gifts and have the privilege and joy of using them in the church to enhance each other's lives and to glorify God, we must utilize them consciously "to serve" (lit., "as good stewards of the varied grace of God"). The combination of "minister" (*diakonountes* [TG1247, ZG1354]) and "steward" (*oikonomos* [TG3623, ZG3874]) indicates that the ministry of the church is more in view than our daily lives in this service, but the theme encompasses both. A steward was the manager of a household (*oikos* [TG3614, ZG3864], "house"; *nomos* [TG3551, ZG3795], "law") or business and oversaw its affairs. Slaves often filled this position. This was a common metaphor (Luke 16:1-8; 1 Cor 4:1-2; 9:17; Eph 3:2, 9; Col 1:25; Titus 1:7) for one who serves the church and is responsible to God accordingly.

When Peter moves into specific gifts (4:11), he does not mention several types of gifts the way Paul does (nine in 1 Cor 12:7-10; seven in Rom 12:6-8). At the same time he is not just using two general kinds of gifts among others (Davids, Senior) but wants to enumerate the two basic types of gifts, namely, gifts of speech and of action (Achtemeier, Jobes). In 4:11, there is an "if . . . then" format (*ei* [TG1487, ZG1623], a condition of fact that assumes many have these gifts), best translated "whoever has." The gift of speaking is not general conversation but corporate teaching and preaching to the congregation. Of course, this should not be restricted to that only, for it can include more charismatic gifts like prophecy, wisdom, and tongues. The main thing is that in any of these gifts of speech, we must exercise them under the empowering presence of God. If God grants us this gift, we must "speak as though God himself were speaking" through us (4:11; lit., "as oracles of God"). This is the language of prophecy, dealing with revelation from God (cf. Num 24:4, 16; Ps 107:11; Acts 7:38; Rom 3:2; Heb 5:12), and here it means that God is behind what is taught, with the Spirit guiding and using everything said (Achtemeier, Beare, Michaels). We do not speak, as it were, off the top of our heads but center on God's word and are led by his Spirit. The gift of "service" or "ministering" (NLT, "helping others") refers to all that Christians do to help or serve each other, such as benevolence, caring for others, or fixing things in a house. We are to do this not on our own but "with all the strength and energy that God supplies" (4:11). In 1 Peter, terms for "strength" are normally used for the strength of God (1:5; 5:11), and so this may well mean that God gives his own strength to us when we serve his people in the church (so Michaels). As Paul says in Philippians 4:13, "I can do everything through Christ, who gives me strength." The supply of his Spirit and his strength are the keys to success in anything we do, especially in our service to the saints.

The purpose of all spiritual gifts is that "everything you do will bring glory to God through Jesus Christ" (4:11). The Westminster Confession says that mankind was created "to glorify God and enjoy him forever." Life is a two-way street: The more we glorify God on the one side, the more joy we get out of life on the other side. As we exercise our gifts, our service to others in the community is also bringing glory to God, for what we do for his children we do for him. Our ministry to each other is also an act of worship (the Greek word for worship, *latreuō* [TG3000, ZG3302], also means "to serve"). The glory of God in all its fullness as shared with his suffering people is the goal of the letter as a whole. In 1:7 the goal of trials is stated as bringing believers "praise and glory and honor" at the Parousia, and in 1:11, 21, the sufferings of Christ are said to result in glory. In 4:13-14, Peter reminds believers that they experience Christ's glory (which they will one day see) through the Spirit even now. Finally, in 5:1, 4, 10 there is the promise that believers will share his glory. This glory comes "through Jesus Christ" (cf. 1:3, 21; 2:5; 3:21), the means by which we accomplish anything worthwhile. He is the instrument through which we glorify God. His death gives us salvation, his resurrection the power to live for God, and his presence through the Spirit gives us the enabling presence of God by which everything is made possible.

Peter has been reflecting on God and Christ as the source of all we do, so at the end of 4:11 he naturally ends the section with praise. The doxology centers on the glory due to God through Christ (see note on 4:11). God is to be ascribed not only glory but also power, a recognition of the omnipotence and sovereign control over our world that he has exerted on our behalf. His glory and his power are eternal and form the basis of our present victory over evil and our guaranteed eternal future. Thus, when Peter ends with the characteristic "Amen" (cf. Rom 11:36; 16:27; Gal 1:5; Eph 3:21; Phil 4:20; Rev 7:12), its basic meaning of "so be it" or "may this come to pass" is absolutely true.

◆ E. A Christian Approach to Suffering (4:12-19)

**12 Dear friends, don't be surprised at the
fiery trials you are going through, as if
something strange were happening to
you. 13 Instead, be very glad—for these tri-
als make you partners with Christ in his
suffering, so that you will have the won-
derful joy of seeing his glory when it is
revealed to all the world.**

**14 So be happy when you are insulted for
being a Christian,* for then the glorious
Spirit of God* rests upon you.* 15 If you
suffer, however, it must not be for murder,
stealing, making trouble, or prying into
other people's affairs. 16 But it is no shame
to suffer for being a Christian. Praise God
for the privilege of being called by his
name! 17 For the time has come for judg-
ment, and it must begin with God's
household. And if judgment begins with
us, what terrible fate awaits those who
have never obeyed God's Good News?
18 And also,**

**"If the righteous are barely saved,
what will happen to godless
sinners?"***

**19 So if you are suffering in a manner that
pleases God, keep on doing what is right,
and trust your lives to the God who cre-
ated you, for he will never fail you.**

4:14a Greek *for the name of Christ.* **4:14b** Or *for the glory of God, which is his Spirit.* **4:14c** Some manuscripts add *On their part he is blasphemed, but on your part he is glorified.* **4:18** Prov 11:31 (Greek version).

NOTES

4:12 *Dear friends.* It is common to see the presence of this endearment as proof Peter begins a new section (as in 2:11, so Achtemeier, Goppelt, Michaels). This makes sense, but the content of 4:12-19 fits 3:13–4:11 so well (suffering for Christ) that it is better to take this as the conclusion of the previous section rather than the start of a new section, with 5:1-11 the final segment of the epistle addressing the elders and young men (5:1-5), then the community as a whole (5:6-9).

4:13 *partners with Christ in his suffering.* Marshall (1991:151) notes four options for understanding this: (1) Christian suffering as imitating the sufferings of Christ (cf. 2:20-21); (2) sharing mystically in his sufferings through baptism (as becoming part of his body); (3) becoming partners through "the fellowship of sharing in his sufferings" (Phil 3:10, NIV), i.e., the "messianic woes"; and (4) all Christians share in the suffering that leads to righteousness (Marshall's view). In the commentary below, the third and fourth views will be combined.

4:14 Several later mss (K L P and many minuscules) as well as the Textus Receptus and KJV add "On their part he is blasphemed, but on your part he is glorified." However, the older witnesses (𝔓72 א A B) do not have it, and it was almost certainly added later. For an argument that the reading should be retained, see Michaels (1988:265), who believes it fits Petrine style and should be included. For an argument for the shorter text, see Comfort (2008b:750).

4:15 *prying into other people's affairs.* This is based on a single Greek word, *allotriepiskopos* [TG244, ZG258], a difficult term that appears nowhere else in the NT, LXX, or Greek writings before the fourth century. A great deal has been written about the word, mostly in terms of its makeup, as it combines *allotrios* [TG245, ZG259] (belonging to another) and *episkopos* [TG1985, ZG2176] (overseer, manager, bishop). Achtemeier (1996:311-313) and Elliott (2000:785-788) provide excellent surveys of suggested meanings: (1) political ("revolutionary"— Beare, Moffatt) or economic gain ("embezzler"—Achtemeier) at the expense of others; (2) one who oversees the church poorly (Sander); (3) a person who is a "meddler" or "busybody" in the affairs of others (Davids, Elliott, Jobes, McKnight). The first type is argued on the basis that the other three are criminal activities (murderer, thief, evildoer), but the third is general, and this could be as well. The second view is not likely in this context (why would a sinful bishop be persecuted for it by outsiders?) and has not received very wide acceptance. The third is the most likely, and there is evidence that those who meddled in other people's lives were condemned in the Roman world, as well as in the church.

4:18 *barely saved.* The term *molis* [TG3433, ZG3660] here does not mean "barely" (so NLT) or "scarcely" (so ESV) as if the righteous are barely going to make it. Rather, the idea is that the believers undergo great difficulty (e.g., persecution) in being saved (cf. NASB).

4:19 *So.* Lit., "therefore, so then" (*hōste kai* [TG5620/2532, ZG6063/2779]). This phrase marks the verse as a conclusion; it closes 3:13–4:19.

COMMENTARY

We arrive at the conclusion for the central section on suffering (3:13–4:19). There is an A-B-A-B-A pattern, with the first, third, and fifth paragraphs (3:13-17; 4:1-6, 12-19) discussing the problem of the hostility the readers were experiencing, and the intervening B-sections noting the model for suffering (3:18-22) and the ethical needs when suffering (4:7-11). So here we turn back to the issue of the proper approach to suffering. As such, this sums up much of the epistle thus far, since the themes reach back into the first two chapters as well. Suffering for Christ is considered to be a fiery trial (4:12; cf. 1:6-7), a new partnership with Christ that brings joy (4:13a, 14a; cf. 1:6), a source of final glory (4:13b; cf. 1:7; 4:11), experiencing the Spirit of God (4:14b; cf. 1:2, 11; 3:18), a privilege (4:16b), the beginning of judgment (4:17; cf. 2:8; 3:12b; 4:5), and a reason to entrust yourself to God (4:19; cf. 2:23b). The paragraph (4:12-19) is organized into four parts: the personal responses to suffering (4:12-13), the proper reason for suffering (4:14-16), suffering as an aspect of divine judgment (4:17-18), and the response to God when suffering (4:19). Note that the passage is framed by the proper responses to suffering (4:12-13, 19).

Peter begins by addressing them as "beloved" friends (*agapētoi* [TG27, ZG28], see 2:11), which is meant to show that the admonitions to follow flow from a heart of love, as often occurs in hortatory contexts (Rom 12:19; 1 Cor 4:14; 10:14; Eph 5:1; Phil 2:12). In this challenge, he again uses *xenizontai* [TG3579A, ZG3826] as in 4:4 (there, former pagan friends were "surprised" by the Christians' new behavior), this time cautioning Christians against being "surprised" at their "fiery trials" (4:12). This image stems from the Old Testament account of the fiery destruction of Sodom (Gen 19:28), and especially from the use of the "testing by fire" image in Psalm 66:10; Proverbs 17:3; 27:21; Jeremiah 9:7; Amos 4:11; Zechariah 13:9; Matthew 3:10-12; 1 Corinthians 3:13; and Revelation 3:18. God does not tempt (Jas 1:13), but he does test, and the "testing" of Christians is similar to the testing of God's own Son in the wilderness (Matt 4:1-11); its purpose is to drive believers to God and to greater dependence on him (see Jas 1:2-4).

Here Peter is moving back to the issues at the beginning of the epistle: The Christians were marginalized as "foreigners" (1:1, one meaning of *xenos* [TG3581, ZG3828] here) and thereby passed through such "fiery trials" (1:6-7) that they were in shock "as if something strange [*xenos*] were happening" (4:12). Peter was consoling them that they should not be so bewildered by this turn of events (for background see Holloway 2002). The church had always been under one cloud or another. Jesus was rejected at every turn. The apostles had two trials before the Sanhedrin at the start of their ministry (Acts 4, 5). Paul, in almost every city he visited on his three missionary journeys (Acts 13–14, 16–18), was first rejected by the Jews, then by the Gentiles, and then left under duress. To understand all that Paul went through in terms of opposition and hostility, read 2 Corinthians 11:22-33. Then ask yourself, "Am I better than Paul? Should my life have constant ease and worldly success unlike his?"

We in the "first-world" church today expect an untroubled life and are surprised, depressed, and often embittered toward God when things fail to go the way we expect (and demand). As Jobes (2005:286) says, "The idea that normal life should always be harmonious and free from suffering, despite universal suffering and death, remains a lingering echo of life in Eden as God created it before the fall." But we are living after the Fall, so dislike and persecution (as well as general trials!) should never be "foreign" or unexpected. As in John 3:19-20, the people of darkness must always hate the light, because God's light in us proves they are of the darkness. So they reject and fight that light in us. In the first century (sadly, more than in our day with the church growing increasingly secular), the Christian life contrasted sharply with the pagan way of life. One of the reasons there is not a great deal of persecution in the West today is that too many Christians resemble the world more than Christ. One poll several years ago said that evangelicalism has never been more popular and yet has never had less effect on society. The reason, that poll concluded, was that the church in America has become more and more secular, resembling the world around it (see Gallup and Lindsay [1999:45], who say "Spirituality in America may be three thousand miles wide, but it remains only three inches deep"). When we truly live the "set apart" life of holiness in a New Testament sense, we should expect that trouble will occur (see John 15:18–16:4; 17:14; 1 Thess 3:3; 2 Tim 3:12; 1 John 3:13).

Instead of being shocked, Christians should "be very glad," full of joy, when they encounter the hard times (4:13). This joy does not mean happiness; we are happy when things are going the way we want, but all trials are painful while they are happening (Heb 12:11). Joy, however, is centered on God, who is in control and will work all things for good (Rom 8:28). We never enjoy our afflictions, but we rejoice because God is in charge and because we know what the future holds. Peter details the present and future ramifications of suffering. In the present, the reason (*katho* [TG2526, ZG2771]; "in so far as, inasmuch as") for joy is that in suffering those who belong to God become "partners with Christ in his suffering" (4:13). This is a reference to what is called the "messianic woes," that is, the suffering of God's people as participation in the suffering of the Messiah. Paul spoke of the fellowship of Christ's suffering in Philippians 3:10 (cf. Rom 8:17; 2 Cor 4:10-12), and in Colossians 1:24 of filling up "what is lacking in the sufferings of Christ" (NET). This does not mean Jesus failed to suffer enough and needed Paul's suffering; rather, it refers to the suffering of God's people that would accompany the Messiah's suffering before the final consummation (cf. Rev 6:9-11; see Davids 2008:262-263). In our troubles in life we share in Christ's suffering. In this sense there is also a deeper experience and a deeper spiritual awareness of Christ and the Spirit in our lives. There is so much truth in the adage, "The blood of the martyrs is the seed of the church," as shown in China and Africa in our generation. With suffering comes a new depth of spiritual power.

Suffering for Christ eventually brings joy: "You will have the wonderful joy of seeing his glory when it is revealed to all the world" (4:13). There is movement from gladness (*chairete* [TG5463, ZG5897]) in the first clause to joy (*charēte agalliōmenoi* [TG5463/21A, ZG5897/22]) here. Michaels (1988:262) thinks that the first clause looks at present joy in Christ, while the second (cf. 1:6, 8) is future joy in an "ascending parallelism from present 'gladness' in the experience of suffering for Christ to eschatological joy or jubilation on the day 'when his glory is revealed.'" The emphasis on the day when Christ is "revealed" is found often in 1 Peter (1:5, 7, 13; 5:1), and the final eschaton permeates the whole epistle. Here it is the final "glory" that is the emphasis, viewed through the lens of the theme set in 1:11, "suffering is the path to glory," for Christ (1:11, 21; 2:4; 4:11) and for his people who suffer with him (1:7; 2:7, 9; 5:1, 4, 6, 10). The revelation of Christ's glory will involve our own glory as "together with Christ we are heirs of God's glory" (Rom 8:17; cf. Heb 10:35-39; 11:26, 39-40; 13:13-14; Rev 22:12, 14).

Now the discussion moves from the proper response to the proper reasons for suffering (4:14-16). The situation is one of verbal abuse (see 2:12, 23; 3:9), with the combination of *ei* [TG1487, ZG1623] (if) in 4:14 with the present tense "are insulted" (or, "are reproached, reviled") meaning virtually "when" rather than "if" (so NLT, see Achtemeier, Elliott, Michaels, Selwyn). "Be happy" is better rendered "count yourself blessed"; *makarios* [TG3107, ZG3421] will often produce "happiness," but it connotes far more, because it is the very blessing of God that is experienced. This restates the "be very glad" of 4:13 but uses the language of 3:9 ("he will bless you for it"). So this is another beatitude resembling Matthew 5:11, "God blesses you when people mock you," and Luke 6:22, "What blessings await you when people . . . mock you and curse you as evil because you follow the Son of Man." As is the case in Matthew and Luke, the blessing here is inaugurated eschatology, with the divine blessing beginning now and growing until the eschaton. In a shame culture, this type of public humiliation was particularly grievous (Ps 69; Rom 15:3; Heb 13:13), yet in biblical terms such verbal abuse is not shame but blessing because it is "for the name of Christ" (4:14, NLT mg), meaning we are suffering it in the sphere of who Christ is.

The blessing itself is spelled out, and the reason for it (marked by *hoti* [TG3754, ZG4022]) is provided—"the glorious Spirit of God rests upon you." The Greek says "the Spirit of glory and of God," reflecting Isaiah 11:2 ("The Spirit of the LORD will rest on him"), which describes the Branch of David. *Tēs doxēs* [TG1391, ZG1518] could be a descriptive genitive, "glorious Spirit" (NLT), but it is most likely epexegetical, "the Spirit of glory." This is a reference to the shekinah glory (i.e., the glory of God "dwelling" among his people, especially connected to his presence in the Most Holy Place), given to Christ by the Spirit (see, e.g., John 1:14) and now shared with us (so NASB, TNIV, ESV, NRSV). This is more in keeping with the "glory" theme in 1 Peter (see on 4:11). The point is that the glory that rested alone in God, that shekinah presence dwelling among his people, was first given to his Messiah in Isaiah 11:2 and now rests upon them in further fulfillment of the spread of God's glory to the church through suffering (see 4:13). The movement from Father to Son to Spirit (a Trinitarian thrust reminiscent of 1:2) to believer is momentous, and it is all due to our participation in Christ via a faith decision and then via suffering. As the shekinah rested on the Tabernacle and upon the Most Holy Place in the Temple, so the Spirit as the shekinah rests on the church and its priestly people as the new temple of God (cf. 2:5). In one sense this builds on Matthew 10:19-20, as the Spirit in trial situations tells the Christian what to say; but this goes beyond that to the presence of the Spirit "resting" on the believer in every area of life.

As in 2:12, 20, and 3:17, Peter reiterates in 4:15-16 an important theme—suffering will come again and again (note the present tense in 4:15), but the Christian should make certain it is undeserved. He uses four examples of wrong reasons to suffer, in a descending order of severity. "Murder" is addressed in the sixth commandment (Exod 20:13; Deut 5:17), and "stealing" is addressed in the eighth (Exod 20:15; Deut 5:19), covering a whole series of crimes in the Old Testament. "Making trouble" is "wrongdoing" (Selwyn's "magician, sorcerer" is based on second-century evidence and does not fit), a general term for anyone who commits "evil" acts (cf. similar terms in 2:12, 14). The last category, "prying into other people's affairs," is set off from the others by *hos* [TG5613, ZG6055] (as), possibly because it is not a criminal activity but rather something that "can bring reproach on Christians as a group" (Michaels 1988:268). Christians who are known as "busybodies" (that would include gossips) would be looked down upon by everyone, pagans as well as Christians. All four are examples of activity that might result in deserved suffering that cannot be considered suffering for Christ. However, there is no "shame" (unlike the sins of 4:15) when one is called "to suffer for being a Christian" (4:16). The use of "Christian" for Christ-followers was not chosen by the early church (they called themselves "the Way," Acts 9:2; 19:9, 23; 22:4; 24:14, 22) but was first used in Antioch by outsiders (Acts 11:26), possibly to distinguish them from Jews. The term is used one other time, in Acts 26:28, when Agrippa says to Paul, "Do you think you can persuade me to become a Christian so quickly?" So the term was widely used to identify the movement. By the time of Peter, Christians seem to be using it of themselves, and they were definitely using it in the second century. There was great public shame in such suffering, although at this time it was not official persecution but sporadic and personal opposition; the only two official Roman persecutions in the first 100 years of the church were under Nero and Trajan, but neither was extensive (movies like *The Robe* and *Ben-Hur* overstate the actual situation). Under Domitian there was also significant persecution (the theme of the book of Revelation), but it, too, was local rather than official (see Osborne 2002:10-11).

Peter wanted them to realize there is no shame before God; in fact, their suffering was an occasion to "praise God for the privilege" (4:16; lit., "glorify God"). In Acts 5:41, after the apostles had been beaten for preaching in the Temple, we are told that they rejoiced "that God had counted them worthy to suffer disgrace for the name of Jesus." What seems disgraceful or shameful to the world is a cause for joy for Christians. There may be another nuance as well: To "glorify God" means to bring glory to God by responding to hostility with witness (3:15) "in the name of" Christ (Achtemeier, Michaels). The reason is that suffering for being a "Christian" is actually suffering for "being called by his name" (4:16). That is a great "privilege," especially since it is part of the "messianic woes" (see on 4:13), namely, participating in Christ's suffering as part of God's plan and bearing the "name" of Christ even when it means terrible affliction and rejection. Note the antithesis between "shame" (the world's perspective) and "glory" (God's perspective). In his shame-honor culture, Peter was reversing the categories. Honor and glory belong to the Christ-follower, especially when sharing the "shame" of Christ!

Suffering is not shame, but it is an aspect of divine judgment (4:17-18). Peter is commenting further on the "fiery trials" of 4:12, telling us now that these are also the fires of divine judgment, and that the "time" (*kairos* [TG2540, ZG2789], the "propitious" or "critical" moment), for the eschatological judgment of humanity has arrived and "must begin with God's household" (4:17). Since believers are the children of God, they are part of his "household" (1 Tim 3:15). It is natural for a father to begin with his own house. Still, it is difficult for us to understand how the word "judgment" applies to us in light of Paul's words in Romans 8:1, "So now there is no condemnation for those who belong to Christ Jesus." However, judgment is broader than the condemnation Paul speaks of. As Grudem (1988:181) says, this "can refer to a judgment which results in good and bad evaluations, a judgment which may issue in approval or discipline as well as condemnation. . . . The refining fire of judgment is leaving no one untouched, but Christians are being purified and strengthened by it."

Peter was drawing on Old Testament background for his statement about judgment beginning with God's household (*oikos* [TG3624, ZG3875]), and at the same time returning to the picture of the church as the house or temple of God in 2:5. The Old Testament contains quite a few passages on God's judgment starting with his people, indeed with his Temple (Isa 10:11-12; Jer 7:8-15; 25:29; Amos 3:2; Zech 13:7-9). Especially important are Ezekiel 9:6-7 and Malachi 3:1-2. Ezekiel 9 tells how God sent his executioners to slaughter the idolaters in Jerusalem, and Ezekiel 9:6 says, "Begin right here at the Temple." They begin with the 70 elders there. Malachi 3 speaks of the coming day of judgment and says, "Then the Lord you are seeking will suddenly come to his Temple . . . like a blazing fire that refines metal" (Mal 3:1-2). The picture stemming from these passages helps us to understand Peter's point. The last days have begun, and the judgment God is sending to earth has been inaugurated. The persecution that has come upon Peter's readers is part of that "refining fire," and God is using it to purge his people. All trials (1:6-7; Heb 12:1-11; Jas 1:2-4) have as their purpose drawing God's people to break their ties to this life and to center on God. The refining fire forces believers to learn how to endure and put their whole trust in God. Marshall adds another nuance: "The period of time has begun in which God is judging the world: he is 'weeding out' those who are opposed to him and those whose faith in him is hypocritical (which is not the same thing as a weak but genuine faith)" (1991:156). Such trials separate the true from the quasi-Christians.

Returning to his point regarding divine judgment on the ungodly in 4:5, Peter adds that if the suffering of God's people is just the beginning, "what terrible fate awaits those who have never obeyed God's Good News?" (4:17). As Hebrews 10:31 states, "It is a terrible thing to fall into the hands of the living God." Eternal judgment, called the "second death" in Revelation 20:6, 14, is depicted graphically in Revelation 14:10-11—"tormented with fire and burning sulfur" with "the smoke of their torment" rising "forever and ever" and "no relief day or night." Those who face this terrible fate are the disobedient, a title that highlights not mere failure to obey God's standards but rejection, rebellion, and studied refusal to heed "God's Good News," and opposition to both Christ and his followers. The "Good News" refers not only to the call to repentance and belief in Christ and his atoning sacrifice for salvation but also to God's ethical requirements for living in right relationship with him. Those who are consigned to his wrath have rejected all of that.

To anchor his point, Peter in 4:18 quotes Proverbs 11:31 (LXX). The "righteous" are obviously those who are committed to Christ and to following his precepts. They were experiencing hostility and persecution and so were "barely saved," meaning they were saved "with difficulty"—namely, the difficulty of all the suffering they were going through that was refining and strengthening them. One dangerous myth perpetuated by some overzealous and shallow evangelists is that when people come to Christ, their lives get easier and better. Joy and peace increase exponentially, but the new believer's ease does not. Walking with Christ takes dedication, discipline, and great effort, as even a casual reading of the New Testament will demonstrate. But the main point of the quote is the second half, reinforcing 4:17b, that the "godless sinners" who oppose God and his people will have it much worse. The Christians in Asia Minor were called to realize that the "difficulties" they faced would be worth it in the future. Achtemeier (1996:317) says it well: "Thus the contrast between the (evil) present with its suffering and the (better) future with its salvation sets the parameter of these verses, as the contrast between the (more evil) past, with its unacceptable behavior, and the (better) present, with its acceptable behavior, set the parameter in the earlier discussion" of 4:3-4.

Verse 19 provides a conclusion, not just to the paragraph of 4:12-19, but to the whole unit on suffering in 3:13–4:19. It addresses those who are "suffering in a manner that pleases God," literally, "suffering according to God's will," which could have several thrusts: (1) The messianic woes (see 4:13, 16 and notes) are pictured as part of God's plan (Best, Green). (2) Those who live according to God's will are going to suffer unjust persecution and thereby glorify God (Achtemeier, Davids, Elliott, Jobes, Senior). (3) When suffering comes, it is God's will so that you can place your trust entirely in him, the faithful Creator, and know the suffering will produce good (Grudem, McKnight). (4) Undeserved suffering is part of the beginning of God's judgment on the world (4:17), so the Christian can endure it because they know its certain end (Boring, Michaels, Selwyn). (5) The persecutors only have power because God allows it, so God's people can put their trust in him (Beare). There is some truth in all of these, but those especially close to Peter's intention here are the first four. Putting them together, God is sovereign over this world and in these last days has begun his judgment with the church, his temple. So when believers inevitably suffer hostility, God is there in these messianic woes and is moving history to its inexorable consummation, and the believers can know their final victory is certain.

Christ's followers are told to do two things. First, with 1:15; 2:12, 15, 19-21; 3:2, 9, 11, 13-14, 16-17; 4:2, 11, they must continually "do right"—living a life of goodness and good works according to God's will. The ongoing emphasis in this whole unit is on making certain that we suffer for doing right as a Christian and not because we have broken laws and done evil. Senior (2003:133) says this "is emphatic and gives the final punch to the author's exhortation. 'Doing good' is not an additional bit of advice, but expresses what 'entrusting one's life to God' means. . . . Trust in God and an active commitment to doing good constitutes the stance the Christian must take as the day of judgment approaches." Second, Christ's followers are to trust their lives to God their creator, who will never fail them (4:19). Christ likewise did this when he "left his case" to the God "who always judges fairly" (2:23). "Trust" (4:19; *paratithemai* [TG3908A, ZG4192]) is a strong term meaning to give one's possessions into the safekeeping of a friend who then has a sacred duty to watch over them (Elliott, Grudem). The reason we can trust God to be vigilant over us in our time of suffering is that he is our "creator" who will "never fail" (lit., "faithful"). Creation theology is at the heart of all of Scripture. When Israel was in despair thinking God had forgotten about them, they were told, "The LORD is the everlasting God, the Creator of all the earth" (Isa 40:28). This means God has both the power and the compassion (he cares about his creation) to care for and protect his people. The very power that created the universe is at work on behalf of God's people, and so they can trust God to guarantee their futures. God is not only omnipotent and compassionate, but also trustworthy and faithful, so naturally we can trust our present and our future to him. (On God's faithfulness, see also Rom 3:3; 1 Cor 1:9; 10:13; 2 Cor 1:18; 1 Thess 5:24; 2 Tim 2:13; Heb 10:23.)

◆ V. The Key to Community Life—Service (5:1-11)
A. A Challenge to the Leaders—Proper Leadership (5:1-5a)

**And now, a word to you who are elders in
the churches. I, too, am an elder and a wit-
ness to the sufferings of Christ. And I, too,
will share in his glory when he is revealed
to the whole world. As a fellow elder, I ap-
peal to you: [2]Care for the flock that God
has entrusted to you. Watch over it will-
ingly, not grudgingly—not for what you
will get out of it, but because you are eager
to serve God. [3]Don't lord it over the people
assigned to your care, but lead them by
your own good example. [4]And when the
Great Shepherd appears, you will receive a
crown of never-ending glory and honor.**

**[5]In the same way, you younger men
must accept the authority of the elders.**

NOTES

5:1 ***And now.*** Many find *oun* [TG3767, ZG4036] (now, therefore) enigmatic and wonder what connection it makes between 4:12-19 and 5:1-5. Elliott (2000:811) says it is "not immediately clear." Some think this verse becomes an example of the good deeds in 4:19 (Beare, Elliott), some that it points to the "leaders" in Ezek 9:6 (behind 4:17, so Grudem, Michaels), some that the leaders in particular would face the brunt of the opposition (Davids), some that it is merely a transitional particle ("now," Goppelt), and some that the pressure on the church led to addressing the need for good leadership (Achtemeier, Senior). The strongest connection is provided by the last view: "given the crisis the community faces—with the need for discipline and fortitude in dealing with a hostile environment and the responsibility to maintain mutual love within the community—it is crucial that it have the support of authentic and understanding leaders" (Senior 2003:137). So the particle means Peter is now turning to the leadership as a solution to the crisis (as Heb 13:7, 17).

5:2-3 The main clause in these verses is at the beginning, consisting of an aorist imperative ("care for/shepherd") followed by an adverbial participle that qualifies the shepherding image (see next note) with "managing" the church well. The verbal idea is qualified further in a series of three antitheses or disjunctions, introduced by two adverbs and then a participle. The organization, then, can be described as stating the proper work (the command and first participle) and then the proper method (the three antitheses that modify the command and participle).

5:2 ***Watch over it.*** This represents a participle that is missing in ℵ B 33, but it is present in the majority of mss, including 𝔓72, A, P, Ψ, Old Latin. While it could have been added on the basis of 2:25, it is more likely that it was original and omitted because it seemed redundant after the shepherd image. Besides, Codex Vaticanus (B), usually trustworthy, omits several other words in this section. Overall, most scholars consider the participle original here. (For further arguments on retaining the participle, see Comfort 2008b:751-752.)

to serve God. Gr., *kata theon* [TG2596/2316, ZG2848/2536], "in accord with God." This phrase (which is lacking in the Textus Receptus; cf. KJV, NKJV) follows the word translated "willingly" in this verse in the NLT, and is usually taken as modifying it. Though generally understood in this verse as a reference to God's will (ASV, ESV, NIV, NASB, HCSB), its force can be understood variously as in the NLT or the NET, which renders "under God's direction."

5:3 ***the people assigned to your care.*** Because *klēros* [TG2819, ZG3102] (lot, portion) was later used for "ecclesiastical office," some have said it is warning leaders not to be high-handed when they allocate assignments in the church (Kelly), or to be dictatorial over the clergy under them. But since the parallel statement in 5:2 speaks of the "flock," this is almost certainly the elder's house-church congregation that is in view (so Achtemeier).

5:4 ***a crown of never-ending glory and honor.*** There has long been a debate over the doctrine of rewards. Blomberg (1992) says there are not degrees of reward but only one reward for all, the crown of life (1 Cor 9:25; 2 Tim 4:8; Jas 1:12), and that Matt 20:1-16 shows there are no degrees of reward in heaven. However, this does not quite fit all the data. The idea of being "judged by works" occurs at least 24 times in Scripture (see passages on 1:17) and points to degrees of reward—we will take into eternity what we have done for the Lord and for others. The equality here does not mean we all receive only the same reward (the crown of glory) but rather that we will all equally stand before the Lord without any disadvantage and be rewarded for what we have done (see also Matt 5:3-12; 6:1, 4, 6, 18; 7:11; 10:41-42; 13:12, 43; 19:28-29; 25:20-21, 23, 34). God will be gracious to every one of us.

5:5 ***younger men.*** Several explanations for the contrast between "elder" and "younger" have been offered: (1) Peter turns to the age distinction of "older people" and "younger people" (Kelly); (2) these are a subordinate, lesser group of officials like deacons (Moffatt); (3) it could be new believers, perhaps newly baptized (Elliott); (4) this could be a specific group of youth in the church (Spicq). None of these quite work, for there is too little evidence that *neōteroi* [TG3501B, ZG3742] was ever used in these ways. The elders were normally older and more mature in the faith, so it fits for Peter to use "younger" to refer to those less mature spiritually. So it is best to read this, with most commentators, as a convenient reference for the rest of the congregation.

COMMENTARY

The letter now turns to the subject that dominated 2:4-10; 3:9; and 4:7-11, namely, relationships within the church (5:1-11). It moves from the elders (5:1-4) to the younger men (5:5a) to the corporate body (5:5b-9) and then concluding with a doxology (5:10-11). Green (2007:162-163) shows that the whole passage combines a discussion of "honor/glory" with one of "mutuality/humility," stating that the church as a united whole must not adopt the elitist strategies of the world, but the leaders need to conduct themselves with humility in the service of the church. The church as a community must live together in mutual harmony (note parallels with Paul's farewell to the Ephesian elders in Acts 20:18-35). This is the first time in Peter that the leaders of the church are addressed (5:1-5a). The elders were the key to the reaction of the church in difficult times, for they set the tone and became examples for the believers in reacting to the adverse circumstances (Heb 13:7). The church was to follow their guidance during such times (Heb 13:17a). Moreover, they were accountable to God for their leadership (Heb 13:17b). As "shepherds" they were the "pastors" (see 5:2, 4) and were responsible to care for and watch over the flock. The paragraph consists of the address, centering on what Peter shares with the elders (5:1); the proper method and means for conducting their ministry (5:2-3); the reward for faithful service (5:4); and a charge to the youth to respect the elders' authority (5:5a).

Peter addresses the "elders" of the church first (5:1). These are not "elderly people," as some have thought, but leaders in the church; still, most of them were older than the average church member or at least more senior in the faith (see note on 5:5). The centrality of elders in the early church appears often (Acts 11:30; 14:23; 15:2, 4, 6; 16:4; 20:17; 1 Tim 5:1, 17; Titus 1:5; Jas 5:14; 3 John 1), and the office was one and the same with "pastor" and "overseer" (Marshall 1999:170-182). This is evident here, as they are called "elders" in 5:1 and then charged to "do the work of a pastor" (the main verb in 5:1). The office itself seems to have grown out of the place of "elders" as Jewish community leaders (e.g., Exod 24:9-10; Josh 24:1; Judg 11:5-6; Acts 4:5; 6:12). In both Jewish and Greco-Roman backgrounds, the office developed as the leaders of households became community heads (Campbell). Elders would pastor individual house churches and gather together perhaps in a church council over the city churches.

Peter notes three parallels between himself and these leaders: (1) He placed himself among them not as having a privileged status but as a "fellow elder" (5:1, "I, too, am an elder"; cf. 2 John 1; 3 John 1) who stood beside the others. In so doing he was a model of humble leadership (remember that he was the first leader or the first "rock"—Matt 16:18—of the church), refusing to place himself above others. At the same time, he elevated their position and importance in the church to his level (Marshall). (2) He was also a "witness to the sufferings of Christ," which does not mean that he was present at the Crucifixion (the Gospels are clear that only John saw Christ on the cross, although Peter was present at the trial), but either that he bore apostolic "witness" to the Passion and meaning of the Cross (Best, Senior) or that he participated in Jesus' suffering, the messianic woes (see on 4:13) via his own suffering (Davids, Marshall, Michaels). Likely both are intended (Achtemeier). (3) Peter "will share in his glory when he is revealed." Some (Selwyn) see this as a reference to the Transfiguration, as in 2 Peter 1:16-18, but that is unlikely because the context is future glory, not past glory, and the language here is too obscure for such a reference. It is better to see this as the messianic woes (see commentary on 4:13); Peter and his readers, including the elders he addresses, experience a foretaste of future glory in their present suffering.

In 5:2-3 a positive exhortation to the elders to "care for the flock" and "watch over" it is followed by a series of antitheses on how they should conduct their responsibilities. The word behind "care for" is *poimainō* [TG4165, ZG4477], meaning "shepherd, tend," and is the major image behind the work of "pastoring" in the New Testament. Every aspect of the shepherd is intended here (Selwyn), and this parallels the reinstatement of Peter (John 21:15-17), with Jesus' threefold conclusion, "Feed my lambs. . . . Take care of my sheep. . . . Feed my sheep." So this is a broad concept—feed, tend, protect, guide, care for. Behind this is the Old Testament image of God as the shepherd of Israel (Pss 23:1-4; 74:1; 78:52; 100:3; Isa 40:11; Jer 23:1-4). Ezekiel 34 is especially relevant, as it speaks of the false shepherds, the leaders (Ezek 34:1-10), from whom God will rescue his people; God, the true shepherd, will then tend and feed them (Ezek 34:11-24). Jesus then became the "good shepherd" (John 10:11-18; Heb 13:20), who rescued the wandering flock (Matt 9:36; 10:6; 18:12-14; Mark 6:34). The idea of Christian leaders as "shepherd/pastor" grew out of John 21:15-17 (cf. Acts 20:28; Eph 4:11). But there is also, in 5:2, an emphasis on the fact that the community is "the flock *of God*," not the shepherd's. The leaders are responsible to watch *God's* flock and are watching over it, not controlling it. The charge to "watch over it" (see note on 5:2) refers to both oversight and vigilance. In both Greek and Jewish contexts, the idea was to "manage" the flock well, to be its guardian (see 2:25) and protect it. This defines the administrative side of church work, as well as pastoral care. The shepherds are also overseers.

Then three contrasting pairs further clarify how the pastoral responsibility is to be conducted. The first is "willingly, not grudgingly." The latter is *anankastōs* [TG317, ZG339], and occurs only here in the New Testament. It indicates some form of coercion or compulsion, as in the cognate words of 2 Corinthians 9:7 ("don't give . . . in response to pressure") and Philemon 1:14 (asking Philemon to "help because you were willing, not because you were forced"). Some might be forced into leadership due to pressure from the church or parents or an overdeveloped sense of duty in light of the crisis. But Peter calls for service done freely or voluntarily, using a term that can refer to the cheerful cooperation of "a person who placed himself at God's disposal, either in terms of military service (Judg. 5:2, 9; 1 Macc. 2:42) or of sacrifice (Ps. 54:6)" (Davids 1990:179). Implicit in the NLT and explicit in the Greek, this willing service is to be done "according to God," that is, due to the realization that God has called them to his work. God is in control, and the leaders are responding to God. This includes the idea of devotion to God (Best, Kelly) but is even more the joyful response to his call.

The second contrast is "not for what you will get out of it, but because you are eager to serve God." The term *aischrokerdōs* [TG147, ZG154] combines two words, "shameful, dishonest" and "gain"; in this case both are part of the meaning, seeking gain through sordid means, or simply being "greedy." Paul called greed "idolatry" in Ephesians 5:5 and Colossians 3:5 because the person's god became the accumulation of wealth. Jesus said that those who work deserve to be taken care of (Matt 10:10), and Paul agreed (1 Cor 9:4, 7; Gal 6:6; 1 Tim 5:18). There is Jewish background for this potential for greedy service, since "elders" controlled community finances as well as relief funds for the poor. This structure was echoed in the church (Acts 6:1-4; 11:30; 2 Cor 8:20). With this came the temptation to use part of that money for themselves, much like Judas, who had charge of the purse of the apostolic band and often stole from it (John 12:6). Paul frequently castigated leaders for using their ministry as a money-making device (1 Tim 3:3, 8; 6:9-10; Titus 1:7, 11; cf. Heb 13:5; 2 Pet 2:3, 14; Jude 11). If this was true in Paul's day when the church was a relatively small movement, how much more does this fit our time when Christian leaders can become millionaires! Too many ministers change churches not because God is calling them but because the salary and benefits are calling them. At the same time, this cannot be restricted to monetary gain; it encompasses all forms of gain, for status or benefits or any type of ministering in order to get ahead. Instead, the leaders must serve "eagerly," a term that refers to the enthusiasm, zeal, and energetic spirit that should characterize serving the Lord.

The third contrast (5:3) is a refusal to "lord it over" God's people and a determination to "lead" by their "good example." This speaks against leaders abusing their authority by dominating others and imposing their will. This is reminiscent of Mark 10:40-45, where Jesus warned James and John that their desire to sit in the seats of power in the kingdom made them like Gentile rulers who "lord it over" their charges and "flaunt their authority" (unlike himself, who gave his life as a "ransom"; cf. 1:18). "The people assigned to [the elders'] care" (5:3) are literally "your lot, portion." The word is similar to "inheritance" and is used of a person chosen by lot (Acts 1:23-26; cf. Acts 1:17), allocations of land assigned by lot, or a portion of funds set aside for a community. So here it refers to the "portion" of the congregation God has assigned the leader. They belong to God, and the leaders are accountable to God for the quality of their care (Heb 13:17; Jas 3:1). They are to conduct their ministry by setting their "own good example" (*tupos* [TG5179, ZG5596], "model," like an architectural blueprint)—that is, using their lives humbly as models for people to follow, much like Christ did (2:21-25; 4:1, 19). Jesus often made himself a pattern to follow (Matt 10:24-25; Mark 10:44-45; John 13:16), and Paul centered his idea of discipleship on the theme of "imitating a model" both in terms of himself ("Imitate me, just as I imitate Christ," 1 Cor 11:1; cf. 1 Cor 4:16; Phil 3:17; 2 Thess 3:9) and telling others to become examples (1 Tim 4:12; Titus 2:7; cf. 1 Thess 1:6-7). As the leaders show servanthood, the others in their churches will learn by following their lead.

For those who conduct their ministries well and become sterling examples for the flock, there is a promise of final reward (5:4). The "crown of never-ending glory" utilizes a strong image, for *amarantinon* [TG262, ZG277] (unfading) refers to the amaranth flower, "a red blossom whose color was unfading" (Jobes 2005:306). The *stephanos* [TG4735, ZG5109] (crown) was a well-known wreath given to those who won athletic or military victories (Caesar Augustus received a "grass crown"; cf. Pliny *Natural History* 22.4-6), with a gold wreath given to citizens who significantly benefited their city. In both cases, the idea was reward for significant good deeds. Here it is a crown of "glory" or honor. The emphasis here is on servanthood. Final glory has been a major theme throughout this epistle (see on 4:13), and it is promised to all believers, not just to elders. While earlier the theme was "suffering is the path to glory" (1:11), now it is "faithful service is the path to glory" (5:3-4). Every person, including Christians, will be "judged by works" (for the many passages, see commentary on 1:17-21), and for believers it will include reward on the basis of faithful works. The leaders will receive this crown from "the Great Shepherd," a fact that reminds them that they are under-shepherds (5:2) serving their Lord. Peter's own charge came from Christ in John 21:15-17. It is God's flock, not theirs (5:3). The leaders will receive their reward not in the present but on the day when Christ "appears" or is "revealed" (cf. 1:5, 7, 13; 4:13; 5:1). The choice they face is whether to seek honor and reward (often monetary) in this life, or serve the Lord and wait for his certain reward at the eschaton. The present gain is only temporary, but the final reward is never-ending.

Peter turns to the "youth" next (5:5a), a reference to those younger in the faith, meaning the congregation as a whole (see note on 5:5). God has sent the elders as leaders (cf. Eph 4:11-12) to this group. This approach of addressing age groups is found elsewhere (1 Tim 5:1-2; Titus 2:2-8; 1 John 2:12-14), and Peter has already addressed various groups in the Household Code section of 2:13–3:8. The problem of youth rebelling against older authority (whether parents or bosses or pastors) is universal. It is difficult to know why Peter felt he must exhort the youth to "accept the authority" of the elders. Jobes believes it may connote that this was a young church; Davids sees them as junior leaders in training who are impatient with their elders. It seems better simply to take this along the lines of 1 Corinthians 16:15-16;

1 Thessalonians 5:12-14; Hebrews 13:17 as well as the social codes of 1 Peter as a general call for respect and submission to authority. There is no specific problem behind this exhortation, just a gentle reminder regarding the authority God has given to his chosen leaders. The verb for "accept authority" is *hupotassomai* [TG5293A, ZG5718], the same verb used of citizens, slaves, and wives in 2:13, 18; 3:1; so in a sense Peter was continuing the principle of the Household Code and saying submission to authority should characterize the church as a whole. The elders serve the congregation humbly, and the people defer to and respect their authority.

◆ B. A Challenge to the Community—Humility, Trust in God, Alertness (5:5b-11)

And all of you, serve each other in humility, for

> **"God opposes the proud**
> **but favors the humble."***

6So humble yourselves under the mighty power of God, and at the right time he will lift you up in honor. 7Give all your worries and cares to God, for he cares about you.

8Stay alert! Watch out for your great enemy, the devil. He prowls around like a roaring lion, looking for someone to devour. 9Stand firm against him, and be strong in your faith. Remember that your Christian brothers and sisters* all over the world are going through the same kind of suffering you are.

10In his kindness God called you to share in his eternal glory by means of Christ Jesus. So after you have suffered a little while, he will restore, support, and strengthen you, and he will place you on a firm foundation. 11All power to him forever! Amen.

5:5 Prov 3:34 (Greek version). 5:9 Greek *your brothers.*

NOTES

5:6 ***at the right time.*** Some mss (A P 33) read "at the time of visitation," but most older mss (𝔓72 ℵ B) support the NLT text. The change was made by way of assimilation to 2:12 and possibly to Jer 6:15 (LXX).

5:9 ***Stand firm against him.*** Several commentators (Elliott, Kelly, Selwyn contra Goppelt) see this as stemming from baptismal rituals that had as part of their liturgy a renunciation of the devil. However, there is little evidence for such a ritual this early.

Remember that. The connection of this participle with the preceding clause is difficult to determine. It might be imperatival (as in NLT, Michaels) or perhaps instrumental, telling how to resist ("by remembering . . ." so Achtemeier). Probably it is best is to take it as a simple circumstantial, "as you remember that." Throughout the NT (and ancient Greek), such a construction was used to remind the readers of something they knew and should be remembering.

going through the same kind of suffering. Beare (1961:180) and Best (1979:175) take the verb *epiteleisthai* [TG2005, ZG2200] as a middle rather than a passive, and translate it "fulfill the obligation (to God) of suffering" (Beare) or in a legal sense "knowing that the same tax of suffering will be paid by your brotherhood" (Best). But there is no hint of a religious duty (or paying a tax) in this context, and it is better to translate the verb in the passive: "is being carried out" or "accomplished" (Davids, Elliott). Senior (2003:148) recognizes both intentionality and purpose (by God—a divine passive) and translates that the suffering "is placed upon" the believers for redemptive purposes. This captures the idea well.

COMMENTARY

Building on the submission of the congregation in 5:5a, Peter turns to the humility that should characterize every member (elder and others), in a sense equivalent to the mutual submission of Ephesians 5:21. This humility is horizontal in 5:5b (to each other) and vertical in 5:6 (to God). As Michaels (1988:293) aptly puts it, the whole paragraph is "most appropriately understood as Peter's exposition of the text of Prov 3:34, LXX, quoted in v. 5b." It also functions as a conclusion to the letter, describing the relationships of Christians to God, the devil, and outsiders. What is interesting is how similar this section is to James 4:6-10. Both contain the Proverbs quote as well as the commands to humble yourself before God and to stand firm against the devil. It is likely that both build on a common catechetical tradition (Achtemeier, Goppelt, Kelly). The text then turns to the issue of suffering (seen as a tool of Satan) and encourages the beleaguered believers to allow God to deliver them so that they are victorious (5:9c-10), closing with a brief doxology (5:11). The basic message of this section is that behind the pagans who are marginalizing and berating the believers are the cosmic powers, and a war is taking place. The only solution is for God's people to place themselves entirely under God's powerful hand. As in the Old Testament, God fights the battles for his people and brings them the victory. When they humble themselves, their present situation will likely continue to be one of suffering (the battle rages on), but their future exaltation will be guaranteed.

The opening command to "serve each other in humility" (5:5) is literally "clothe yourself (*enkomboomai* [TG1463, ZG1599]) with humility," a vivid image. In some contexts, it depicts a slave tying an apron around his garments to keep them from getting dirty as he goes about his menial tasks (Davids, Selwyn). Some connect this with Jesus' act of servanthood, tying the apron around himself as he washed the disciples' feet (John 13:4). There is no evidence Peter was thinking of this event, but Marshall (1991:165) rightly says, "Whether a conscious allusion is present or not, the story in John undoubtedly provides forceful backing for the teaching here." Humility is the garment, a virtue emphasized already in 3:8 and a primary ethical emphasis of Jesus (Matt 11:29; 18:4; Luke 14:11; 18:14) and Paul (Eph 4:2; Phil 2:3; Col 3:12). Elliott (2000:847) points out that this attitude is the polar opposite of the Gentile world, for whom "humility was typical of slaves and an unworthy, servile attitude for those who were free," while in Christianity it was "renunciation of ambition and domination over others, submission to God's will, and trust in God's generous favor and support, all of which contribute to the social harmony and cohesion of the community." The meaning here is to clothe ourselves with humility as we serve each other.

Peter then anchors this in Scripture by quoting Proverbs 3:34, where God reverses the worldly approach by opposing the proud on the one hand and favoring the humble on the other. One could think in light of 5:3, 5a that the "proud" are arrogant pastors and the "humble" are faithful parishioners, but in the larger context of 1 Peter, the proud are likely the pagan persecutors (the Hebrew of Prov 3:34 calls them "scornful mockers") and the humble the persecuted faithful. The general sense of the proverb applies even to situations where persecution isn't a major factor—all the proud will face God's opposition, and anyone who is humble will feel his gracious favor. The exhortation of Paul in Philippians 2:3-4 is entirely apt:

"Don't be selfish; don't try to impress others. Be humble, thinking of others as better than yourselves. Don't look out only for your own interests, but take an interest in others, too."

The focus now shifts (5:6) to the vertical side of humility, our relationship with God. Humility before people means to take the lower position, to care more for them than for ourselves. Humility before God adds the aspect of total surrender and complete dependence. What both have in common is the idea of service. We submit to "the mighty power of God" (lit., "the mighty hand"), a metaphor for God's disciplining his people (Job 30:21; cf. 4:12-13, 17) and also for his sovereign intervention on behalf of his people, especially connected to his delivering them from bondage in Egypt at the Exodus (Exod 3:19; 6:1; 13:3; Deut 3:24; 4:34; 5:15; 7:8). This becomes the model for the promise of future help (Isa 25:9-10; 26:11; Jer 6:12; 15:6; see TDNT 9.427). God's "hand," symbolizing divine help in time of need, is also a New Testament image (Luke 1:66; Acts 4:28, 30; 11:21; even in Jesus' death, Acts 4:28). As Davids surmises, "Thus they are to see God at work behind their suffering and submit, allowing themselves to be brought low, for his purpose is that 'he may exalt you in due time'" (1990:186).

Only when we turn ourselves over completely to God will we be lifted "up in honor" (5:6), a phrase referring to the exaltation and glory that will be ours at the final judgment (see on 4:13-14; 5:1, 4). In fact, this exaltation is the purpose and goal of the "mighty power of God" (5:6). All through this epistle, the theme is that suffering leads to glory (see on 1:11; 4:19), and glory will come "at the right time" (5:6), referring to the revelation of Christ (1:5, 7, 13; 4:13) at the last time (1:5, 20; 4:7; cf. 2 Pet 3:3). The struggling Christians must submit to their suffering as the hand of God in their lives now, triumphing over it via their goodness (2:12a) and good works (2:12b, 15, 19; 3:11, 13, 17; 4:7-11), so that they may triumph over it finally at the Parousia, when their enemies will receive their just due (1 Thess 5:1-11; 2 Thess 1:7-10). Following the pattern of Jesus, portrayed in the Philippians hymn as a paradigm for Christians, God's people must seek humility (Phil 2:6-8) and leave the exaltation up to God—he will give the glory (Phil 2:9-11).

In light of this complete submission to God, Christians must not try to solve their problems by themselves but give all their worries and cares to God (5:7). This provides a practical example of what humility means, taking all of the sources of your anxiety and giving them over to God. The word for "give" is *epiripsantes* [TG1977, ZG2166], a circumstantial participle that modifies "humble" and may share its imperative force but could also be instrumental, telling how to humble oneself (so Achtemeier). It is an action verb for "throwing" or "casting," which pictures the follower throwing every single anxiety on God's shoulders one at a time. The "worries and cares" (*merimnan* [TG3308, ZG3533], a collective singular) are life's problems that cause us to worry. Background for this can be found in Psalm 55:22, possibly the source of this reflection ("Give your burdens to the LORD, and he will take care of you"). Other verses with a similar theme are 4:19 ("Trust your lives to the God who created you"); Matthew 6:25 ("I tell you not to worry about everyday life"; cf. Luke 12:11, 22); and Philippians 4:6-7 ("Don't worry about anything").

The reason for this absolute submission and trust is that "he cares about you." We do not need to fret overmuch about our difficulties, for God is more concerned about our needs than we are, and he knows far better what we need. As Paul said in Romans 8:26, "We don't know what God wants us to pray for," (i.e., we don't know God's will when we pray), but we do know that the Spirit intercedes for us, and he prays "with groanings" that are deeper than ours! Moreover, he prays "in harmony with God's own will" (Rom 8:27), and that is why everything works together for good (Rom 8:28). This concern over life's difficulties is found in many passages (Deut 31:6, 8; Josh 1:5; 1 Kgs 8:57; Matt 6:26-30; Luke 12:24-28; Rom 8:31, 39; Heb 13:5). There is no need for anxiety, for God cares about us more than we care about ourselves. Beare (1961:178) makes an excellent comment: "The conception of God as concerned with the afflictions of man is the peculiar treasure of Judaic and Christian faith; Greek philosophy at its highest could formulate a doctrine of His perfect goodness, but could not even imagine in Him an active concern for mankind."

Following this, Peter says, "Stay alert" (5:8). "Divine protection does not eliminate the need for constant vigilance" (Elliott 2000:853). This is not a new section (contra Grudem), for the connections are too close. In light of God's overwhelming concern for us (5:7), we must place ourselves entirely under his care (5:6a) in these last days (5:6b) and be vigilant (5:8). Since the time of God's final intervention has begun, and in light of the evil times the readers were living within, it was time to get serious. *Nēpsate* [TG3525, ZG3768] (stay alert) has been used twice earlier, in 1:13 ("exercise self-control") and 4:7 ("be . . . disciplined"), and refers to a state of alertness and disciplined readiness for action. *Grēgorēsate* [TG1127, ZG1213] (watch out) means to be "vigilant, watchful," and both verbs have the idea of "staying awake" (these are aorist imperatives and may have ingressive force—"begin" right now). The same two verbs appear together in 1 Thessalonians 5:6 with respect to the coming Day of the Lord. One or the other appears often in passages pertaining to the end of time (1 Thess 5:8; 2 Tim 4:5—alert; Matt 24:42, 43; 1 Cor 16:13; Col 4:2; Rev 16:15—watchful). Since the Lord is returning and this day is the time of trial and testing, God's people must stay alert in prayer (cf. 4:7 [alert prayer] and Mark 14:37 [being watchful to pray]).

The primary reason for alert vigilance is the presence of the "great enemy, the devil" (5:8). The "great enemy" (*antidikos* [TG476, ZG508]) designates an opponent or adversary (often in a court of law), and is a virtual synonym for "devil" (*diabolos* [TG1228A, ZG1333], "slanderer") and for "Satan" (*satanas* [TG4567, ZG4928], "accuser, adversary"), a word borrowed from Hebrew and Aramaic (*satan* [TH7854, ZH8477]). He is called "the ruler of this world" (John 12:31; 14:30), "the god of this world" (2 Cor 4:4), "the evil one" (Matt 5:37; 13:19), and "the dragon—that old serpent" (Rev 12:3, 9; 20:2). He is the leader of the demonic realm and the one who strategizes and oversees the war against God and the attacks on human beings. His appearance here is as the force behind the persecution. The special need for vigilance is because this enemy "prowls around like a roaring lion, looking for someone to devour" (5:8). Found only here in Scripture, this image is quite apt, as Satan is pictured as the greatest of the predatory animals (Prov 30:30), naturally connected with destruction and death, as in the lion's den of Daniel 6:14-24 or sheep rescued "from a lion's mouth" (Amos 3:12). Those who threaten the people of God are often compared to lions (Pss 7:2; 10:9; 17:12; Lam 3:10-11), and the "roar" symbolizes the fright of the destructive force (the devil and the persecutors). Especially relevant is

Psalm 22:13, where David's enemies are "like lions [who] open their jaws against me, roaring and tearing into their prey." As this psalm was used often in the Passion narratives (Matt 27:35, 39, 43, 46; Luke 23:34; John 19:28; 20:25), the image would be particularly apt for the messianic woes (see commentary on 4:13, 16). "Devour" (*katapiein* [TG2667, ZG2927]) means to "drink down" or "swallow" a person, thus, to utterly destroy them. It was common to see cosmic powers behind the enemies of the church, both false teachers (1 Tim 4:1; 2 Tim 3:8, 13; 2 Pet 2:19; Jude 10; Rev 2:14) and persecutors (5:8-9; Rev 12–13), and such are called the "many . . . antichrists" in 1 John 2:18.

In light of the devil's prowling, the Christians are commanded in 5:9 to "stand firm against him" (with emphatic force—"do it now"). Easier said than done! Nonetheless, God's people are called to this; the resistance is only possible with the "power" (5:6; lit., "mighty hand") of God behind it. This does not mean physical or revolutionary resistance but a determination to remain faithful to God in spite of the suffering. Matthew 5:39 in fact says, "Do not resist an evil person." Combining this command with that in 5:9 results in an approach that resists the evil in the opposers (the work of the devil through them) but does not physically fight back against them. This is also seen in Ephesians 6:12, where our fight is not "against flesh-and-blood enemies, but against evil rulers and authorities of the unseen world." The way to withstand the cosmic powers is to remain "strong in your faith" (5:9; lit., "firm in the faith," with faith being the sphere within which we resist). The adjective "strong" (*stereos* [TG4731, ZG5104]) means "firm, hard, solid, steadfast" and may borrow from the "living stone" image of 2:4-5 to mean "rock-like" in strength and firmness (Michaels, Selwyn). The sphere within which we are victorious is the Christian faith ("the faith"; cf. Eph 4:13), grasping tightly and totally committed to the truths of the faith.

Peter then reminds them that they are not alone in what they are going through. They "know" and should "remember" that they have "brothers and sisters all over the world" who are enduring "the same kind of suffering" (5:9). The idea of the "brotherhood" was already seen in 2:17, NLT mg, "love the brotherhood." This continues the family atmosphere of 1 Peter. With God our Father, we all belong to one family, the church, and thus all over the world (the Roman Empire at this stage), the Christians of Asia Minor had family members who were also suffering. This does not mean Christianity had been outlawed or that there was an official worldwide persecution, only that similar suffering was being experienced in many other places (so Marshall). It is probably correct to see here a further reflection of the messianic woes (see commentary on 4:13, 16). As Marshall (1991:171) says, "Perhaps he is saying that there is a fixed amount of suffering appointed for God's people and that it is rapidly exhausted by this worldwide persecution, in which case it cannot last forever" (cf. Rev 6:11, "And they were told to rest a little longer until the full number of their brothers and sisters . . . had joined them [lit., 'the full number to be killed was complete']").

Continuing the theme of suffering from 5:9c, 5:10-11 becomes a "body closing" for the book (Achtemeier, Goppelt, McKnight). In this closing, we are told of God's grace. The expression "in his kindness God" (5:10) is literally "the God of all grace." It sums up all the divine grace acts of the epistle: God gives "more and more grace and peace" (1:2); the prophets spoke of "this gracious salvation prepared for you" with Christ (1:10); we are to hope fully on "the gracious salvation that will come" at the Parousia (1:13); it is "God's gift of new life" (3:7); when we use our spiritual gifts we are "stewards of the varied grace of God" (4:10, NET); "God gives grace to/favors the humble" (5:5); and finally, Peter assures the suffering believers that this is "truly part of God's grace for you" (5:12). What these expressions all have in common is the assurance that all of life and its experiences, even the negative ones, are the result of God's gracious providence at work, and the final proof of that grace will come when Christ returns and the believers' vindication is finalized. Especially providential is that Christians have been "called . . . to share in his eternal glory by means of Christ Jesus" (5:10). This "calling" or election is another major theme in 1 Peter (1:15; 2:9, 21; 3:9). As has been seen so often, the "eternal glory" that will result from this call to suffering is one of the primary themes of the book (1:7, 11, 21; 4:11, 13-14; 5:1, 4, 10). For Christ and then for us in the messianic woes, suffering is the path to glory, a glory that will become eternal at the revelation of Christ. Christ is both the sphere and the instrument (double meaning of *en* [TG1722, ZG1877], 5:10) of this calling and glory. He has brought redemption and hope (1:3-4, 18-20; 2:21, 24-25) and will inaugurate eternity at his coming (1:7, 13; 4:13; 5:1).

Echoing a point made in 1:6, suffering is said to be temporary, in complete contrast to the "eternal glory" that will come (5:10). In 2 Corinthians 4:17 Paul says "our present troubles are small and won't last very long," stressing both the insignificance and the brevity of trials, especially compared with "a glory that vastly outweighs them and will last forever." In the letter to Smyrna in Revelation 2:10, the Christians in Smyrna are told they "will suffer for ten days," most likely a Semitic idiom for a small, limited period (Gen 24:55; Num 11:19; Dan 1:12); the result is that Christ "will give [them] the crown of life." The theme of short trials resulting in eternal glory is a firm doctrine in Scripture.

The four verbs in the second half of 5:10 (restore, support, strengthen, place) are future indicatives (preceded by the emphatic *autos* [TG846, ZG899], "he himself") and have the force of a benediction, as in Romans 16:20; 2 Corinthians 13:11; and Philippians 4:9 (so Michaels). They tell how the grace of God (5:5, 10) will "lift you up" (5:6) and enable you to "stand firm" (5:9). Each builds on the other to describe how the "mighty power of God" (5:6) will give you the strength to stand against Satan (5:8b-9a) and achieve the final victory of "glory" (5:10). "Restore" means that God will supply what is needed to complete you or "make you whole." In a persecution context, the idea is that God will repair what has been damaged by the ordeal; he will give you what you lack so that his victory will be finalized in you and for you. The other three verbs are almost synonyms. "Support" means to "establish, confirm, reinforce," allowing someone or something to "be strong" (it is a cognate of the term in 5:9) in the midst of adversity. "Strengthen" means virtually the same as the preceding, making someone strong enough to win the victory. Finally, "place you on a firm foundation" means to "establish" or "anchor" and pictures God supplying a firm foundation for his house (see Matt 7:25; Eph 3:17; Col 1:23; Heb 1:10). It is likely that these future tense verbs present inaugurated eschatology—that is, the strength that is available now begins a process that will continue until consummation at the return of Christ.

This section closes with a short doxology, "All power to him forever! Amen" (5:11). In 4:11, a similar doxology was presented to both God and Christ, adding "glory" to "power." This one is addressed to "the God of all grace" (5:10, NIV), who has promised to uphold and strengthen his people. "Power" (*kratos* [TG2904, ZG3197]) describes "God's inexhaustible power to create and rule" (Michaels 1988:254), and it sums up the major apocalyptic theme in 1 Peter regarding God's sovereign control over this world, including over those who are persecuting the Christians. In every chapter, God, not Rome, is portrayed as the true ruler of this world, and only those who come to Christ and align themselves with his Father can be victorious in the end. So this is a fitting end to the message of the book. Only God and Christ are worthy of worship (see "worthy" in Rev 4:11; 5:9, 12-13), and all who submit themselves to his "mighty power" (5:6) will enter his "eternal glory" (5:4, 10).

◆ VI. Final Greetings (5:12-14)

12 I have written and sent this short letter to you with the help of Silas,* whom I commend to you as a faithful brother. My purpose in writing is to encourage you and assure you that what you are experiencing is truly part of God's grace for you. Stand firm in this grace.

13 Your sister church here in Babylon* sends you greetings, and so does my son Mark. 14 Greet each other with Christian love.*

Peace be with all of you who are in Christ.

5:12 Greek *Silvanus.* **5:13** Greek *The elect one in Babylon.* Babylon was probably symbolic for Rome. **5:14** Greek *with a kiss of love.*

NOTES

5:12 ***I have written and sent.*** Peter does not close with a Hellenistic form but with an early Christian form like Paul's closings to his letters. Normally, a Greek letter closed with "be strong" (cf. Acts 15:29, "Farewell") or "prosper" followed by the date the letter was written. Paul and Peter closed with: (1) a commendation of the one who helped write or delivered the letter (5:12, cf. Rom 16:1; Eph 6:21; Col 4:7, 9); (2) a summary of the basic message of the epistle (5:12b); (3) greetings (as in 5:13) and for Paul a benediction in his own hand (1 Cor 16:21; Gal 6:11; Col 4:18); (4) the liturgical kiss (5:14; cf. Rom 16:16; 1 Cor 16:20; 2 Cor 13:12; 1 Thess 5:26); and (5) a wish for "grace" (e.g., Paul in 2 Thess 3:18) or "peace" (5:14b).

with the help of Silas. Lit., "through (*dia* [TG1223, ZG1328]) Silvanus." The meaning of this expression is much debated. Does it designate the amanuensis or secretary who wrote the letter (cf. Rom 16:22, so Beare, Davids, Goppelt, Kelly, Moffatt) either in part or in whole, or could it designate the one who delivered the letter to the churches (cf. Acts 15:23, so Achtemeier, Elliott, Grudem, Jobes, McKnight, Michaels, Senior)? In the Introduction, I argued that Silvanus did help Peter draft the letter; the ideas are Peter's and the language Silvanus's (as also in 1 Thess 1:1 and 2 Thess 1:1). At the same time, the expression "through Silvanus" is also language that fits a courier delivering a letter. Therefore, it is likely that both are correct (with Best, Bigg, Selwyn); as the NLT puts it, this epistle was "written and sent . . . with the help of Silas."

I commend. Lit., "in my opinion/estimate, as I consider" (*hōs logizomai* [TG3049A, ZG3357]), meaning this was Peter's apostolic testimony.

what you are experiencing is truly part of God's grace for you. Lit., "that *this* is the true grace of God." There is a question concerning the reference of "this" (see Davids 1990:200). It may be (1) the previous mentions of "grace" (1:13; 5:5, 10) with the emphasis on both God's present relationship with the believers and their future reward (so Elliott, Goppelt, Kelly); (2) the suffering itself, the very thing they consider evil, is actually part of God's gracious plan (5:10, so Senior); or (3) the letter as a whole, so that the teaching content is a grace-gift in itself (so Achtemeier, Bigg, Davids, Michaels). These three options are not really disjunctive (either–or), and it is likely that each contains part of the meaning here. Peter was stating that the content of this letter is meant to address the Christians about the true grace of God at work in their lives, to help them understand that in suffering they were experiencing God's grace in a new way.

5:13 *Your sister church.* Lit., "the elect one" (feminine gender). Nearly all agree that while "the elect one" could be Peter's wife (according to 1 Cor 9:5, he often brought her on his travels) or a coworker like Priscilla (Rom 16:3), Euodia, or Syntyche (Phil 4:2-3; Applegate 1992), it most likely refers to the church in Rome. Such a reference to a person would be far too subtle here (he would certainly have named her), and the churches in 2 John 1, 13 are called "chosen lady" and "your sister, chosen by God." Further, the *sun*-compound (*suneklektē* [TG4899A, ZG5293]) in 1 Peter normally reflects interrelationships in the church, what they experience "together" (see 1:4; 3:7, 9; 5:1).

here in Babylon. There are three options for its meaning: (1) It could refer to that once-great city in Mesopotamia that had ruled the world centuries before the days of the apostles. But that city was in great decline in the first century, and Josephus (*Antiquities* 18.371-379) said that under Claudius (AD 41–54) most Jews there moved to Seleucia. When Trajan visited (AD 113) it was virtually deserted. Moreover, there is no record of Peter ever being there. (2) There was a military garrison housing a Roman legion called "Babylon" in Egypt near Memphis, and Eusebius (*Ecclesiastical History* 2.16.1) links Mark with the founding of the Egyptian church, but again there is no record of Peter being there. (3) The most likely interpretation is that Babylon was a euphemism for Rome because it had opposed God's people, destroyed Jerusalem, and lived in luxury. Rome was called Babylon in Jewish (*2 Baruch, 4 Ezra, Sibylline Oracles*) as well as Christian circles, and "Babylon the Great" in Rev 14:8; 16:19; 17:5; 18:2, 10 is most likely Rome. There is firm early tradition that Peter ministered in Rome and was martyred there (e.g., Eusebius *Ecclesiastical History* 3.1).

5:14 *who are in Christ.* Several mss (א K P 1739) along with the Textus Receptus have "Jesus Christ," but other mss (A B Ψ 33) have just "Christ." There was a tendency among later scribes to expand the sacred names, so the shorter form is to be preferred.

COMMENTARY

There are two parts to the closing of this letter, first a commendation of "Silvanus" (the NLT uses the shortened form of this name, "Silas"), and second the greetings and blessing from Peter and his congregation in Rome ("Babylon"). The Greek begins 5:12 with "Through Silvanus to you," indicating the bearer and the recipients of the epistle for emphasis. Silvanus/Silas is first mentioned as one of the two prophets who accompanied Paul and Barnabas when they brought the Jerusalem decree to the Gentile believers (Acts 15:22-23, 32), and then he joined Paul as a coworker (and possible apostle, 1 Thess 2:7) for the second missionary journey (Acts 15:40). He was jailed with Paul in Philippi (Acts 16:19, 25) and, with Timothy, gathered information about Thessalonica, reporting back to Paul in Corinth (Acts 18:5). Silvanus was also Paul's cowriter for the letters of 1 Thessalonians and 2 Thessalonians (see Comfort 2008a:315-318). As such, he helped two well-known apostles with writing letters, first Paul (in the Thessalonian letters) and then Peter (in 1 Peter). Peter calls him his "faithful brother," commending him as the letter-bearer to any who did not know him (common in epistles, as in Rom 16:1; Eph 6:21; Col 4:7). "Faithful" means both that he lived what he believed ("faithful" to God) and that he was a reliable coworker and friend of Peter's who could be trusted by these churches.

"Encourage" (5:12, *parakalōn* [TG3870, ZG4151]; "exhort") and "assure" (5:12, *epimarturōn* [TG1957, ZG2148]; "bear witness to, declare") are present-tense participles of purpose detailing the ongoing intent of Peter in "writing" the epistle. Achtemeier (1996:352) states well the thrust when he comments that these "provide an admirable summary of the entire letter which has consisted of alternating blocks of witnessing to the content of the faith (1:3-12, 18-21, 23-25; 2:6-10, 21-25; 3:10-12, 18-22; 4:4-6, 17-18; 5:10-12) and exhorting to appropriate response (1:13-17, 22; 2:1-5, 11-20; 3:1-9, 13-17; 4:1-3, 7-16, 19; 5:1-9)." While one could quibble with his breakdown, his basic point is sound. Peter does move back and forth from paraenesis (exhortation) to gospel tradition (catechetical) material throughout. He hoped to attest for them the truths of the faith they must know and to exhort them to the proper response: right Christian living. The content of this encouraging witness is that all they have gone through is "truly part of God's grace" (5:12) or literally, "the true grace of God." They have suffered and been marginalized and alienated from their neighbors, but in the process, they have experienced the varied grace of God in brand-new ways and now look to the future and God's active participation in that future in a final display of his power to deliver.

The final phrase of 5:12, *eis hēn stēte* [TG2476, ZG2705], "in which, stand!" (with *eis* [TG1519, ZG1650] having the force of *en* [TG1722, ZG1877]—fairly common in Koine Greek; cf. 3:20 and Moule 1959:67-71), is adequately translated in the NLT, "Stand firm in this grace." The imperatival aspect tells the Christians to govern their lives by a firm grip on God's grace at work in every area. In the pagan way of life described in 4:2-4, there is neither truth nor grace, and they would miss any redemptive quality in it. So by an act of the will believers must keep a firm hold on experiencing God's grace in these difficult areas of their lives. This is the message of the epistle. Again, grace in 1 Peter is more than that divine mercy that brings salvation and deliverance from sin; it is that compassionate mercy, that divine will, that empowering presence that makes it possible to live a life pleasing to God. It is in this precious reality that we must take our stand.

The final greetings typical of biblical epistles are next (cf. Rom 16:3-15; 1 Cor 16:19-20; Phil 4:21-22; Col 4:7-15; Heb 13:24). The first greeting comes from "your sister church here in Babylon" (5:13), literally, "your fellow-elect one in Babylon" (see note on 5:13). The emphasis on "elect" brings back that major theme in 1:1; 2:4, 6, 9, with Christ the elect stone and the believers "called" (1:15; 2:9, 21; 3:9; 5:10) to belong to God in Christ. In 1 Peter "elect" is a term for those God has saved and brought to himself, thus the Christians. The "elect" in their sister church send them greetings from "Babylon," undoubtedly a reference to Rome as the persecutor of the church in the same way that Babylon was in the Old Testament (see note on 5:13). The sobriquet "Babylon" was used not because Peter was afraid to name "Rome," but as a symbol of exile (Babylon took Israel into exile; 2 Kgs 24–25). It forms a kind of literary inclusion by connecting with the themes of exile and sojourning from 1:1, 17 and 2:11, reminding the readers that the true home they long to see is heaven, where they will be vindicated and rewarded with eternal glory.

"Mark," like Silas, cannot be identified with absolute certainty, but is most likely the John Mark whose mother had one of the early house churches (Acts 12:12-17) and who went with Paul on the first missionary journey (Acts 12:12; 13:5). Paul and Mark were estranged when Mark failed and returned home (Acts 13:13), and Paul and Barnabas split up over the issue of allowing Mark to join the second missionary journey (Acts 15:36-39). It likely took Mark years to overcome his failures, but he later became a trusted associate of Paul (Col 4:10; 2 Tim 4:11; Phlm 1:24) and of Peter as well, whom he certainly knew from his mother's house church in Jerusalem. Probably sometime earlier than this letter, he wrote the first Gospel, likely with help from Peter (Papias and others in the early church believed the contents of Mark came mainly from Peter). Peter calls him "my son," which may well mean Peter was instrumental in converting John Mark, as "son" was often used of a convert or spiritual "son" (1 Cor 4:15, 17; Gal 4:19; 1 Tim 1:2; Phlm 1:10, so Achtemeier, Marshall), although it may simply be the kind of older–younger language used in 5:1, 5, with Peter using it either to note Mark as a younger colleague (Davids, Elliott) or to continue his emphasis on the church as family (so Michaels). The first option may be slightly better, for Peter and Mark must have had a relationship from the earliest days of the church.

The request to "greet each other with Christian love" (5:14) is literally "with a kiss of love"; it was urged by Paul also at the close of several letters (Rom 16:16; 1 Cor 16:20; 2 Cor 13:12; 1 Thess 5:26). Paul called it a "holy kiss," which some take to mean it was a liturgical or "sacred," even eucharistic, rite (see TDNT 9.138-141). So far as we know, it became part of liturgy about the time of Justin Martyr (*Apology* 1.65) when it was labeled "the kiss of peace" in the second century. This may have been part of the meaning, but it is not the whole. It was "holy" because it was exchanged by church members in the name of Christlike love. The kiss was common in Judaism as a sign of love and affection, as well as respect and even of reconciliation, and it was adopted by Christians for the same reasons. Peter calls it "the kiss of love" to highlight two of his emphases, the church as a family (1:14, 17, 22; 2:17; 3:8; 4:9; 5:9), and the centrality of brotherly love in the church (1:22; 4:8). The kiss was especially connected to the family in the ancient world, and so this was meant as further proof of the church community as a loving family.

Peter concludes his letter and his final greeting by pronouncing a blessing upon the congregation (5:14): "Peace be with all of you who are in Christ" (cf. Rom 15:33; 2 Cor 13:11; Gal 6:16; Eph 6:23). His epistle is framed by the promise of "peace" (with 1:2; its only other occurrence is in the quotation of Ps 34 in 3:11). This third use combines the first two, with "peace" meaning both that peace with God and tranquility of soul that comes from being "born again" (1:2, 4) and that corporate peace and reconciliation that is the hallmark of Christian community (both within and outside the church, 3:11). The phrase "all of you who are in Christ" (5:14) is meant to extend this peace to all who belong to the churches. In a world of chaos and difficulty, a world that has turned against God's people, Peter sums up his message with the promise of peace "in Christ." Everything in this epistle points to this: When we are "in Christ," that is, united with him and part of his body, we truly have "God's peace, which exceeds anything we can understand" (Phil 4:7).

BIBLIOGRAPHY

Achtemeier, Paul J.

1996 *1 Peter: A Commentary.* Hermeneia. Minneapolis: Fortress.

Applegate, Judith K.

1992 The Co-Elect Woman of 1 Peter. *New Testament Studies* 38.4:587-604.

Balch, David L.

1981 *Let Wives Be Submissive: The Domestic Code in 1 Peter.* Society of Biblical Literature Monograph Series 26. Chico, CA: Scholars Press.

Barclay, William

1976 *The Letters of James and Peter.* Minneapolis: Westminster.

Barrett, C. K.

1994 *A Critical and Exegetical Commentary on the Acts of the Apostles.* 2 vols. Edinburgh: T&T Clark.

Beare, Francis W.

1961 *The First Epistle of Peter.* 2nd ed. Oxford: Blackwell.

Best, Ernest

1970 1 Peter and the Gospel Tradition. *New Testament Studies* 16.2:95-113.

1979 *1 Peter.* New Century Bible. Greenwood, SC: Attic.

Bigg, Charles

1956 *A Critical and Exegetical Commentary on the Epistles of St. Peter and St. Jude.* International Critical Commentary. Edinburgh: T&T Clark.

Blomberg, Craig L.

1992 Degrees of Reward in the Kingdom of Heaven. *Journal of the Evangelical Theological Society* 35:159-172.

Bock, Darrell L.

1996 *Luke 9:51–24:53.* Baker Exegetical Commentary. Grand Rapids: Baker.

Boring, M. Eugene

1999 *1 Peter.* Abingdon New Testament Commentary. Nashville: Abingdon.

Botha, J.

1988 Christian and Society in 1 Peter: Critical Solidarity. *Scriptura* 24:27-37.

Bultmann, Rudolf

1947 Bekenntnis- und Liedfragmente im ersten Petrusbrief. Pp. 1-14 in *Coniectanea Neotestamentica in Honorem Antonii Fridrichsen.* Lund: C.W.K. Gleerup.

Cahill, Michael

1999 Not a Cornerstone! Translating Ps 118,22 in the Jewish and Christian Scriptures. *Revue Biblique* 106.3:345-357.

Calvin, John

1963 *The Epistle of Paul the Apostle to the Hebrews and the First and Second Epistles of St. Peter.* Translator, W. B. Johnson. Grand Rapids: Eerdmans.

Campbell, R. Alistair

1994 *The Elders: Seniority within Earliest Christianity.* Edinburgh: T&T Clark.

Carson, D. A., and Douglas J. Moo

2005 *An Introduction to the New Testament.* 2nd ed. Grand Rapids: Zondervan.

Clowney, Edmund

1988 *The Message of 1 Peter: The Way of the Cross.* Downers Grove, IL: InterVarsity.

Collins, John J.

1992 *The Apocalyptic Imagination: An Introduction to the Jewish Matrix of Christianity.* 2nd ed. New York: Crossroad.

Comfort, Philip
2008a 1 & 2 Thessalonians. Pp. 313-414 in *Cornerstone Biblical Commentary*, vol 16. Carol Stream, IL: Tyndale House.
2008b *New Testament Text and Translation Commentary*. Carol Stream, IL: Tyndale House.

Craddock, Fred B.
1995 *First and Second Peter and Jude*. Westminster Bible Companion. Louisville: Westminster John Knox.

Cranfield, C. E. B.
1958 *The First Epistle of Peter*. London: SCM.

Dalton, William J.
1965 *Christ's Proclamation to the Spirits*. Rome: Pontifical Biblical Institute.
1974 So That Your Faith May Also Be Your Hope in God. Pp. 262-274 in *Reconciliation and Hope: New Testament Essays on Atonement and Eschatology Presented to L. L. Morris on His 60th Birthday*. Editor, R. Banks. Grand Rapids: Eerdmans.

Davids, Peter H.
1990 *The First Epistle of Peter*. New International Commentary. Grand Rapids: Eerdmans.
2008 *Colossians*. Cornerstone Biblical Commentary. Carol Stream, IL: Tyndale House.

Deissman, G. A.
1927 *Light from the Ancient East*. New York: Doran.

Elliott, John H.
1966 *The Elect and the Holy*. Leiden: Brill.
1981 *A Home for the Homeless: A Sociological Exegesis of 1 Peter, Its Situation and Strategy*. Philadelphia: Fortress.
2000 *1 Peter*. Anchor Bible 37B. New York: Doubleday.

Erickson, Millard J.
1995 Is There Opportunity for Salvation after Death? *Bibliotheca Sacra* 152:131-144.

Feinberg, John S.
1986 I Peter 3:18-20, Ancient Mythology, and the Intermediate State. *Westminster Theological Journal* 48:303-336.

Feldmeier, Reinhard
2008 *The First Letter of Peter: A Commentary on the Greek Text*. Translator, P. Davids. Waco: Baylor University Press.

Fitzgerald, John T.
2000 Hospitality. Pp. 522-525 in *Dictionary of New Testament Background*. Editors, C. A. Evans and S. E. Porter. Downers Grove, IL: InterVarsity.

France, Richard T.
1977 Exegesis in Practice: Two Samples. Pp. 252-281 in *New Testament Interpretation: Essays on Principles and Methods*. Editor, I. H. Marshall. Grand Rapids: Eerdmans.

Gallup, George, Jr., and D. Michael Lindsay
1999 *Surveying the Religious Landscape: Trends in U.S. Beliefs*. Harrisburg, PA: Morehouse.

Goppelt, Leonard
1993 *A Commentary on 1 Peter*. Translator, J. E. Alsup. Grand Rapids: Eerdmans.

Green, Joel B.
2007 *1 Peter*. Two Horizons New Testament Commentary. Grand Rapids: Eerdmans.

Grudem, Wayne
1988 *1 Peter*. Tyndale New Testament Commentaries. Grand Rapids: Eerdmans.

Gundry, Robert H.
1967 "Verba Christi" in 1 Peter: Their Implications concerning the Authorship of 1 Peter and the Authenticity of the Gospel Tradition. *New Testament Studies* 13:336-350.
1974 Further "Verba" on "Verba Christi" in First Peter. *Biblica* 55:211-232.

Hamilton, Clive, and Richard Denniss
2005 *Affluenza: When Too Much Is Never Enough*. Sydney: Allen & Unwin.

Hemer, Colin J.
1977–1978 The Address of 1 Peter. *Expository Times* 89:239-243.

Hillyer, Norman

1970 Rock-Stone Imagery in 1 Peter. *Tyndale Bulletin* 21:39-70.

Holloway, Paul A.

2002 Nihil inopinati accidisse—"Nothing unexpected has happened": A Cyrenaic Consolatory Topos in 1 Pet 4.12ff. *New Testament Studies* 48.3:433-448.

Hort, F. J. A.

1898 *The First Epistle of St. Peter I.1-II.17: The Greek Text with Introductory Lecture, Commentary, and Additional Notes*. London: Macmillan.

Howe, Frederic R.

2000 God's Grace in Peter's Theology. *Bibliotheca Sacra* 157:432-438.

Jastrow, Marcus

2006 *Dictionary of the Targumim, the Talmud Babli and Yerushalmi, and the Midrashic Literature*. Peabody, MA: Hendrickson.

Jobes, Karen H.

2005 *1 Peter*. Baker Exegetical Commentary. Grand Rapids: Baker.

Jones, C. P.

1987 Stigma: Tattooing and Branding in Graeco-Roman Antiquity. *The Journal of Roman Studies* 77:139-155.

Kelly, J. N. D.

1969 *A Commentary on the Epistles of Peter and Jude*. New York: Harper & Row.

Kennard, Douglas W.

1987 Petrine Redemption: Its Meaning and Extent. *Journal of the Evangelical Theological Society* 30.4:399-405.

Kline, Leslie

1963 Ethics for the End Time: An Exegesis of 1 Peter 4:7-11. *Restoration Quarterly* 7:113-123.

Kroeger, Catherine C.

2000 Women in Greco-Roman World and Judaism. Pp. 1276-1280 in *Dictionary of New Testament Backgrounds*. Editors, C. A. Evans and S. E. Porter. Downers Grove, IL: InterVarsity.

LaVerdiere, Eugene A.

1974 A Grammatical Ambiguity in 1 Peter 1:23. *Catholic Biblical Quarterly* 36:89-94.

Lips, Hermann von

1994 Die Haustafel als "Topos" im Rahmen der urchristlichen Paränese: Beobachtungen anhand des 1. Petrusbriefes und des Titusbriefes. *New Testament Studies* 40.2:261-280.

Marshall, I. Howard.

1991 *1 Peter*. Downers Grove, IL: InterVarsity.

1999 *The Pastoral Epistles*. International Critical Commentary. Edinburgh: T&T Clark.

Martin, Ralph P.

1962 The Composition of 1 Peter in Recent Study. *Vox Evangelica* 1:29-42.

McKnight, Scot

1996 *1 Peter*. NIV Application Commentary. Grand Rapids: Zondervan.

2004 Aliens and Exiles: Social Location and Christian Vocation. *Word & World* 24.4:378-386.

Metzger, Bruce M.

1994 *A Textual Commentary on the Greek New Testament*. 2nd ed. New York: United Bible Societies.

Michaels, J. Ramsey

1988 *1 Peter*. Word Biblical Commentary 49. Waco: Word.

Moffatt, James

1928 *The General Epistles: James, Peter, and Judas*. Moffatt New Testament Commentaries. Garden City, NY: Doubleday.

Moule, C. F. D.

1959 *An Idiom Book of New Testament Greek*. Cambridge: Cambridge University Press.

Mounce, Robert H.

1982 *A Living Hope: A Commentary on 1 and 2 Peter*. Grand Rapids: Eerdmans.

Moyise, Steve

2005 Intertextuality and Historical Approaches to the Use of Scripture in the New Testament. *Verbum et Ecclesia* 26.2:447-458.

O'Connor, Daniel

1991 Holiness of Life as a Way of Christian Witness. *International Review of Mission* 80:17-26.

Osborne, Grant R.

2002 *Revelation.* Baker Exegetical Commentary. Grand Rapids: Baker.

2004 *Romans.* The InterVarsity Press New Testament Commentary. Downers Grove, IL: InterVarsity.

2006 *The Hermeneutical Spiral: A Comprehensive Introduction to Biblical Interpretation.* 2nd ed. Downers Grove, IL: InterVarsity.

2007 John. Pp. 1-314 in *Cornerstone Biblical Commentary,* vol. 13. Carol Stream, IL: Tyndale House.

Osborne, Thomas P.

1983 Guide Lines for Christian Suffering: A Source-Critical and Theological Study of 1 Peter 2,21-25. *Biblica* 64:381-408.

Oswalt, John

1986 *The Book of Isaiah: Chapters 1–39.* New International Commentary on the Old Testament. Grand Rapids: Eerdmans.

1988 *The Book of Isaiah: Chapters 40–66.* New International Commentary on the Old Testament. Grand Rapids: Eerdmans.

Piper, John

1981 Hope as the Motivation of Love: 1 Peter 3:9-12. *New Testament Studies* 26:212-231.

Porter, Stanley E.

1994 *Idioms of the Greek New Testament.* 2nd ed. Sheffield: Academic.

Reicke, Bo

1964 *The Epistles of James, Peter, and Jude.* Anchor Bible 37. Garden City, NY: Doubleday.

Richardson, Cyril C.

1953 *Early Christian Fathers.* Philadelphia: Westminster.

Sander, Emilie T.

1967 *PYRŌSIS* and the First Epistle of Peter. Diss., Harvard.

Selwyn, Edward G.

1995 *The First Epistle of St. Peter.* New York: St. Martin's.

Senior, Donald P.

2003 *1 Peter.* Sacra Pagina. Collegeville, MN: Liturgical.

Skilton, John H.

1996 A Glance at Some Old Problems in First Peter. *Westminster Theological Journal* 58.1:1-9.

Spicq, Ceslas

1966 *Les Épîtres de saint Pierre.* Paris: Gabalda.

Stibbs, Alan M.

1979 *The First Epistle General of Peter.* Tyndale New Testament Commentaries. Grand Rapids: Eerdmans.

Thielmann, Frank

2005 *Theology of the New Testament: A Canonical and Synthetic Approach.* Grand Rapids: Zondervan.

VanGemeren, Willem A.

2008 Psalms. Pp. 1-880 in *The Expositor's Bible Commentary,* vol. 5. Grand Rapids: Zondervan.

Wallace, Daniel B.

1996 *Greek Grammar Beyond the Basics: An Exegetical Syntax of the New Testament.* Grand Rapids: Zondervan.

Warden, Duane

1989 The Prophets of 1 Peter 1:10-12. *Restoration Quarterly* 31:1-12.

Winter, Bruce W.

1988 The Public Honouring of Christian Benefactors: Romans 13.3-4 and 1 Peter 2.14-15. *Journal for the Study of the New Testament* 34:87-103.

2 Peter

GRANT R. OSBORNE

INTRODUCTION TO
2 Peter

THERE IS probably no other New Testament epistle so universally contested as 2 Peter. Many scholars consider it a pseudonymous work written at the end of the first century or beginning of the second. Many Christians tend to ignore it due to the fact that it fights heresy throughout, which is not appealing to many today. It does not feature the centrality of the gospel and salvation as is found in Romans or the ethical cast found in James or 1 Peter. And the centrality of apocalyptic issues has led many to conclude that its message is inferior to that of the other New Testament books. Yet there is a clear emphasis in 2 Peter on the grace of God and on the implications of that grace for the believer's ethical responsibilities. All the New Testament epistles are occasional letters addressing the problems encountered in individual church settings, and 2 Peter is no exception. The apocalyptic perspective of the book pulsates with a Jewish mind-set, and what it says is in complete agreement with Jesus and Paul (as Peter claims in 3:15-16). Furthermore, the number of cults and false teachers in our day indicates that we need to consider the teachings of this epistle more seriously.

AUTHOR

The author claims to be the apostle Peter (1:1), who was present at the transfiguration of Jesus (1:17-18). Only three apostles were present at Jesus' transfiguration: Peter, James, and John. He also says that this was the second letter he had written to them (3:1), the first being the epistle known as 1 Peter. Further, the author believes he is soon to die as indeed Jesus revealed to him, an incident we identify with John 21:18-23, where Jesus spoke of Peter's demise. Finally, he speaks of "our beloved brother Paul" (3:15), placing himself on a par with that apostle (see G. Green 2008:139). Who could fit all this except Simon Peter, one of the 12 apostles? While it is possible that a pseudonymous author was using all this information to appear apostolic, it is not very likely. Yet the vast majority of critical scholars, and indeed several in the early centuries of the church age (see Eusebius *History* 3.3.4; 6.25.8), have great doubts that Simon Peter was the author of this epistle. They believe the aspects just discussed were written by a later author (possibly a member of a Petrine circle) in the name of Peter, making it a pseudonymous (meaning "false name") work. Let us consider the reasons for doubting its authenticity.

Probably the single greatest factor against the authenticity of the authorship of 2 Peter is the Hellenistic language and style of the epistle. Bauckham (1983:135-136) concludes that the author was well read and rhetorically gifted, seeking literary effect, and was at times even grandiose in style. He bases this conclusion on the high incidence of 57 hapax legomena (words occurring only once in the NT), 32 of which are not found in the Septuagint either. Of these 32 words, 15 can be found in other Hellenistic Jewish writers; 17 of 2 Peter's 57 hapax legomena are found in the apostolic fathers. Critics wonder how a mere Galilean fisherman could produce such style. Yet it must be reckoned that people from Galilee tended to be familiar with the Greek language because of the large number of Greek speakers in that part of Palestine (see Introduction to 1 Peter, "Author"). Moreover, just as Paul's language was affected strongly by the groups he was addressing (e.g., in the Colossians hymn [Col 1:15-20] or the Pastorals, which have similar problems), so Peter could easily have adapted his style to the people and opponents of Asia Minor (so Watson 1988:144-146, Carson and Moo 2005:661, who speak of the "Asiatic" style adopted here). It must also be noted that as Peter used one amanuensis (Silvanus, see 1 Pet 5:12) for his first epistle, he could have used a different one for 2 Peter. This would account for the difference in style between 1 Peter and 2 Peter.

But there are other reasons that explain why the style and themes are different in the two letters. The general perspective of each epistle shows that quite diverse issues are being discussed, and even the apocalyptic emphases are fairly distinct, with 1 Peter more interested in the believer sharing in Jesus' resurrection and 2 Peter in the Second Coming and final judgment (1 Peter centers on the Christians and 2 Peter on the condemned false teachers). Yet emphases are occasioned by audience, and while it is certainly true that the situation behind the two epistles is very different, that is also the case behind the epistles of Paul. The problems addressed in all epistles are controlled by the audiences themselves, but that never demands separate authors. Every one of us writes very different letters to various friends depending on the circumstances being addressed, and that no doubt is also the case between 1 Peter and 2 Peter (see M. Green 1987:20-21).

The use of Jude in 2 Peter 2 has led many to place 2 Peter late (after the death of Peter), largely because of a predisposition to accept Jude also as postapostolic. However, this is circular reasoning, and if we can support the apostolic authorship of Jude (see the Introduction to that book), then there again is little reason to doubt the authorship of 2 Peter. Michael Green (1987:144) discusses the implications of a person in the ancient world copying another (which often denoted the inferior status of the copier) and notes that as the brother of Jesus, Jude would have a place and status alongside of Peter. Yet at the same time, such distinctions were not followed by Christ's followers, as seen in Matthew using Mark's Gospel when writing his own. Jesus stressed the equality of status on the part of all believers, and that was followed throughout the New Testament. There is no problem with Peter using Jude.

Another argument posed by critics is that the opponents in 2 Peter should be identified as second-century Gnostic teachers, on the basis of their claim to *gnōsis* [TG1108, ZG1194] and their superiority to the angels. However, there is no evidence for a developed Gnosticism in 2 Peter (see further below, "Occasion of Writing"), and everything said about the false teachers in 2 Peter can fit into a situation in Asia Minor in the 60s of the first century (e.g., their libertine antinomianism, their "knowledge," their hedonism). Further, some of Paul's references to "knowledge" in 1 Corinthians (cf. 1 Cor 8:1, 11; 13:2, 8) suggest that the concept was an issue in the church even early on. Again, there is no basis for doubt on this score.

The centrality of "tradition" in 2 Peter (3:2, 16) is also seen as evidence of a late date. It is common (so Schreiner 2003:253-254; Bauckham 1983:51) to note Ernst Käsemann in this respect: He believed that tradition and the church as an institution in 2 Peter had replaced the Spirit, and both Christology and justification by faith had been watered down and sublimated to anthropology (i.e., individual piety), with faith becoming "mere assent to the dogmas of orthodoxy" (1964:195). When viewed from the perspective of a close reading of 2 Peter, this is a gross misrepresentation of the contents of the epistle. The so-called institutionalization (called "early Catholicism" by Käsemann and others) is based on the mistaken assumption that the early church was charismatic in the beginning and only became institutional late in the apostolic period. There is no evidence for that (see Marshall 1974). The charismatic and institutional aspects developed side by side from the beginning. The emphasis on right teaching and creedal truth is found in Romans and Corinthians, as well as in the Pastorals and 2 Peter.

It is also common today to identify 2 Peter as a fictive "farewell testament," a viewpoint especially developed by Bauckham (1983:58-62), who states it was written by a member of the "Petrine circle" after Peter's death as a testament to his apostolic message for the postapostolic period. The genre known as "farewell testament" was quite common in Second Temple Jewish literature (as in *Testament of the Twelve Patriarchs*, the *Testament of Moses*) and is summarized well by Moo (1996:64): The speaker knows he is soon to die, gathers around an audience, emphasizes the need to remember what he is about to say, predicts the future, and stresses moral exhortation." All of these are paralleled in 2 Peter, but there are some significant differences. The farewell testaments are pseudohistorical in form and written centuries after the Old Testament hero died. There are usually apocalyptic revelations attached, and the death of the speaker is often noted. It is better to see that Peter himself uses some aspects of the testamentary form in 2 Peter than that it is a later pseudonymous work (so M. Green, Moo, G. Green). Also, in an extensive excursus on pseudonymity, Carson and Moo (2005:337-350) show that such falsely ascribed works in the ancient world inevitably involve an attempt to deceive and were not ultimately received well by ancient readers.

In conclusion, there are many reasons to accept Peter's authorship of 2 Peter, and too few reasons to reject it. While not mentioned often in the time of the apostolic fathers (see discussion under "Canonicity and Textual History"), it is noted often enough to justify the traditional ascription of this epistle as 2 Peter.

DATE

The date one assigns to the epistle is affected by one's decision regarding authorship. In 1:14 the author says, "Our Lord Jesus Christ has shown me that I must soon leave this earthly life," most likely referring to Peter's death during the Neronian persecution, a terrible time that probably also took the life of Paul. So if we accept Peter as the author, then the letter was written somewhere around AD 64–65 (the fire in Rome took place in AD 64; Nero committed suicide in AD 68). If we do not accept Peter as the author, the date could be 80–90 (when the delay of the Parousia would have been regarded as an acute problem, so Bauckham 1983:158-159), late in the first century (Harrington 2003:237), or perhaps 110 or later (Kelly 1969:237; Mayor 1907:138). Most likely Peter was in Rome at this time, prior to his martyrdom (1 Peter was also written from Rome—see commentary on 1 Pet 5:13 in this volume).

OCCASION OF WRITING

One of the primary differences between 1 Peter and 2 Peter is that the first epistle centers on persecution from outside the church, while the second epistle addresses schism from inside the church caused by false teachers. We know little about these heretics apart from the twofold nature of their teaching: (1) Morally, they were propagating a licentious lifestyle, centering mainly on "shameful immorality" but also on "greed" (2:2-3). Their "twisted sexual desire" (2:10, 18) made them little more than "unthinking animals" (2:12). They "love[d] to indulge in evil pleasures" (2:13) and "commit adultery" (2:14), so much so that they had become "slaves of sin and corruption" (2:19). (2) Theologically, they were justifying that lifestyle by stating there would be no return of Christ in judgment. They taught "destructive heresies" that denied the Lord (2:1), "slandered" the truth (2:2), and "scoff[ed] at supernatural beings" (2:10). Mainly, they claimed that "everything has remained the same since the world was first created" (3:4), concluding that there will be no second coming of Christ (on the grounds of the delay of the Parousia) and no final judgment (1:16; 3:3-10). They denied that any prophetic texts predicted the Parousia (1:20-21), and so for them the sins of the body remained within their body; God would never call them to account for their earthly sins.

In response Peter labels their views "evil teaching" (2:2) employing "clever lies" (2:3) intended to deceive the "ignorant and unstable" (2:14; 3:16). They are apostates (2:20-22) who have "wandered" from the faith (2:15); they "promise freedom" (their liberty was actually a libertinism) but have themselves been enslaved by sin (2:19). This is one difference with Jude: In Jude the heretics come from outside the church; in 2 Peter they stem from within the church. Thus, there will not only be a final judgment (2:4-9; 3:4-10), but it will especially result in the "destruction" of the heretics and their followers (2:1, 3, 12-13, 17; 3:16).

Throughout much of the twentieth century it was common to identify these false teachers with second-century Gnostics due to the emphasis on *gnōsis* [TG1108, ZG1194] in the epistle, the place of "myths" in 1:16 ("clever stories," NLT), and the denial of the Parousia, perhaps involving rejection of a physical resurrection and thereby of the material realm. However, in recent years there has been a growing reluctance to embrace this view, because there is no evidence in the letter of either a rejection of resurrection or of the material world, and the hedonism described in this epistle existed throughout the pagan world and is not endemic to Gnosticism. Nor is there any kind of dualistic separation between the material and spiritual realms as later became true of Gnosticism. The idea of the unchanging nature of the world (3:4) was stated in many segments of Hellenism, not just in Gnosticism. So there has now been a reappraisal of the evidence.

More promising is the connection with Epicurean philosophy, especially as developed by Neyrey (1980:407-431; 1993:122-128). The Epicureans rejected any idea of the providential intervention of the gods and believed the world was ruled by chance. This would parallel 3:4 (the unchangeable nature of creation) and 1:19-21 (the rejection of prophecy). There would be no future judgment or just end to this world, and human beings are free to pursue their own desires. There are very real parallels in 2 Peter, but I must agree with Schreiner (2003:279-280) and G. Green (2008:155-157) that the false teachers were not full-fledged Epicureans but rather were influenced by Epicurean thought, adding it to their basic theism and generally Christian worldview. They were "seed-pickers" of the kind noted in Acts 17:18 ("babbler," NLT), pulling together various aspects of pagan and Christian realms into a new syncretistic kind of religion.

AUDIENCE

If this letter was written by Simon Peter (as we have argued above), several factors guide us in determining the audience. First, in 3:1, Peter calls this "my second letter to you," meaning it was sent to the same group addressed in 1 Peter (see the commentary on 3:1), namely, a group of churches in northern Asia Minor (modern-day Turkey), the provinces of Pontus, Galatia, Cappadocia, Asia, and Bithynia. The salutation of 1:1 did not designate the recipients, identifying them only as "you who share the same precious faith we have." Yet this cannot be a catholic or general epistle, for Peter in this letter centers on a very specific group of false teachers. So a specific Asia Minor setting with a strong Gentile presence (befitting the language and style of the epistle) is the best solution.

CANONICITY AND TEXTUAL HISTORY

The external witnesses to 2 Peter's canonicity are admittedly not as strong as most other epistles. It is not mentioned in the Muratorian Canon, but then neither is 1 Peter, and the list seems to break off in the middle of the General Epistles. There seem to be some allusions in works like the Epistles of Clement, Barnabas, Hippolytus, or the *Shepherd of Hermas*, but 2 Peter is nowhere named in them. Origen and Eusebius both recognize the doubt regarding its authenticity, but Irenaeus uses it, and Clement of Alexandria may even have written a commentary on 2 Peter. It was accepted in the canon of Laodicea and by the councils of Hippo and Carthage in the second century (see Schreiner 2003:260-264). In short, the evidence is somewhat sparse but still significant, and there was some recognition of the book from the start.

The earliest manuscript to include 2 Peter is Papyrus Bodmer VII-VIII (𝔓72), dated about AD 300. The epistle is also found in Codex Vaticanus (c. 325), Codex Sinaiticus (c. 350), Codex Alexandrinus (c. 400), and Codex Ephraemi Rescriptus (c. 400). These and other manuscripts provide good evidence to the text of 2 Peter. While there are some textual differences between the manuscripts, they are no more numerous than in any other epistle and do not obviate our claim that 2 Peter has good textual evidence behind it.

LITERARY STYLE

The idea that 2 Peter is a "farewell testament" has already been discussed. We must address here the additional literary issue of the great number of parallels between 2 Peter 2 and Jude: (1) secret teaching denying Jesus (2:1 = Jude 4); (2) false teachers condemned long ago (2:3 = Jude 4); (3) fallen angels put in dark dungeons (2:4 = Jude 6); (4) destruction of Sodom and Gomorrah (2:6 = Jude 7); (5) slander of celestial beings, which not even angels do (2:10-11 = Jude 8-9); (6) lack of understanding like unthinking animals (2:12 = Jude 10); (7) wandering off into Balaam's error (2:15 = Jude 11); (8) teachers being like waterless springs, doomed to blackest darkness (2:17 = Jude 12-13); (9) teachers filled with boasting (2:18 = Jude 16); (10) scoffers in the last days who follow their own desires (3:3 = Jude 18).

This extensive list of parallels demands some type of literary relationship between 2 Peter and Jude (much like the synoptic Gospels). Three have been suggested: (1) Jude used 2 Peter. When Jude 17 says, "Remember what the apostles . . . said," it may refer to 2 Peter (Bigg 1901:216-224). (2) Peter may have been using Jude, a view held by the majority of scholars (Kelly 1969:226-227; Bauckham 1983:141-142; Davids 2006:136-143; Callan 2004; G. Green 2008:159-162). (3) Both 2 Peter and Jude could have used a common source (M. Green 1987:58-64). The third, while possible, is the more complex, and there is no evidence for any such document. The other two are almost equally viable, and I would echo Moo's statement (1996:21), "My own conclusion is that none of the usual theories has enough positive evidence in its favor to accept as a working hypothesis." Still, when we seek the more viable of the two, it is more likely that Peter used Jude. If Jude were using 2 Peter, one would think he would use more material from chapters 1 and 3, and not restrict his borrowing just to 2:1–3:3. Moreover, as Bauckham (1983:142) says, Jude seems more carefully arranged, so it seems more likely that Peter rearranged and added material to Jude's text than that Jude removed material from Peter's text.

MAJOR THEMES

Jesus as Lord and Savior. "Lord" occurs eight times describing Jesus Christ (1:2, 8, 11, 14, 16; 2:20; 3:2, 18), and "Savior" occurs five times (1:1, 11; 2:20; 3:2, 18—only Titus has more [six]). The two occur together four times and form a key emphasis in the book. First, Jesus is cosmic "Lord" or ruler over God's creation, especially emphasized in 2:1, where Peter asserts that the heretics are denying the "Master" (Gr., *despotēs* [TG1203, ZG1305]), a strong term for the ruler of a household or kingdom. As Davids (2006:152) says, "Jesus has taken over the functions of Caesar (and any client king) for these people. . . . There is one sovereign Lord, namely, Jesus." The false teachers said God no longer intervenes in this world, and in 3:4-10 Peter gives three proofs that God has and will intervene in world history—Creation, the Flood, and the end of this world. In Jesus there is a fourth intervention—God has sent his Son, the divine ruler over this world. By emphasizing the Transfiguration in 1:16-18 Peter centers on the majesty and glory of Christ, showing that the glorious Lord revealed on the mountain is the same Lord who will return again.

The second emphasis is that this ruler is also the Savior, who has brought salvation to this world. In the Old Testament it is God who saves or delivers his people.

Jesus Christ is "God and Savior" (1:1b), the one and only God (see the commentary) who delivers people via the "faith . . . given to you" (1:1a). All things necessary for salvation come as gifts from God—faith (1:1), election (1:10), and "everything we need for living a godly life" (1:3). "Faith" is the primary virtue in the golden chain of 1:5-7; it is faith in his blood (Callan 2001) that enables us to "escape from the wickedness of the world" (2:20) so that we can "grow in the grace and knowledge" (3:18) and enter his "eternal Kingdom" (1:11). Again there is an implied contrast with Caesar, seen as the one who brought deliverance and prosperity to the world. Davids (2006:153) brings out the similarity to Paul, who also used the title "Savior" to designate the cosmic victory to be attained at the Second Coming (Phil 3:20; 2 Tim 1:10; Titus 2:13). The false teachers denied his cosmic eschatological role. Moreover, they failed to realize that his lordship meant he would reign over them as eschatological Judge.

God. God the Father is not as central to 2 Peter as he was in 1 Peter. Still, he is Creator of the heavens and the earth (3:5), the Lord over time (3:8-9); it is he who will destroy the cosmos with fire (3:7a, 10-12) as well as the ungodly (2:9b; 3:7b) and create a "new heavens and new earth" for his people (3:13). He rules over the angelic realm (2:4), has heaped "honor and glory" on Christ at the Transfiguration (1:16-18), and "rescue[s] godly people from their trials" (2:9). The "day of the Lord" (3:10; "day of God" in 3:12) is the penultimate event in this epistle, when the wicked will be destroyed and the righteous will inherit the new eternal realm God will create for them.

Eschatology. The false teachers had a realized eschatology that said God had turned this world over to his creation, was no longer involved in the affairs of this world, and would never intervene in judgment against his creation. In response, Peter emphasizes an apocalyptic eschatology that centered on God's sovereign control over his creation and especially the final judgment by which he would end this present evil world. There are two interdependent aspects—the certainty of both the return of Christ and final judgment. The opponents called these "clever stories" (or "myths") and stated that the apostles and the prophets created imaginary tales in their stories about the Parousia and the judgment of the world. Peter responds that his own experience of the reality of the Transfiguration should give us "even greater confidence" in the reality of the future visions of the prophets and apostles (1:19).

Davids (2006:350) notes six parts to the eschatological presentation: (1) Jesus' return is prefigured in the Transfiguration and confirmed by prophetic pronouncements (1:16-21). (2) The final fiery judgment is anticipated in the judgment by water in Noah's day (3:5-7). (3) The Parousia has been delayed due to God's patience in seeking redemption for all (3:8-10, 15). (4) God's people understand the transitory nature of life and live in the light of the new world promised in Isaiah 65:17-25 (3:13). (5) That day will come like "a thief" (3:10), so God's people must live in light of its coming. (6) Christians not only await the coming of the Parousia but can hasten it (3:12) by living faithful lives in the midst of suffering.

The point of 2 Peter is that this world will end, and this close of human history will come unexpectedly. The loving nature of God has led to his "patience," desiring time for more and more people to repent (3:8-9), but when that cataclysm arrives, it will be final. Then will come the final "destruction," but those who have opposed God's purposes and perverted God's truths are headed for it already (2:1, 13; 3:16). There are three aspects of this final destruction: It will destroy the enemies of God and his people; it will renew God's creation and restore it to its pristine purity; and it will mean reward and an eternity in peace and joy for his people.

Ethics. Throughout the New Testament, eschatology always moves to ethics, for the promised Parousia means not only reward but responsibility for the believer. We will all be "accountable to God" (Heb 13:17; cf. 2 Tim 2:15; Jas 3:1). Christians are called to live their lives in light of the imminent end. Thielman (2005:527) calls this "the way of truth and righteousness" in the sense that Peter views the Christian life as a "road" or "path" in statements like "the way of truth" (2:2), the "right road" (2:15), and "the way to righteousness" (2:21). When God's people have finished walking that path, God will give them "a grand entrance into the eternal Kingdom" (1:11). The false teachers corrupted this road with their licentious behavior, and so they are headed for final destruction.

God demands a life of piety and virtuous practices on the part of those who walk on what Jesus calls the "narrow" and "difficult" road (Matt 7:14) to life everlasting. If God's people are to "share his divine nature" (1:4, see the commentary there), they must live lives characterized by faith leading to moral excellence, then to knowledge, self-control, patient endurance, godliness, brotherly affection, and love (1:5-7). To ensure their "grand entrance" into God's kingdom, believers must "work hard" to "prove" they are the "called and chosen" by the way they live (1:10-11). They must live lives opposite of the false teachers, whose pride, mockery of the things of God, and immorality are bringing the wrath of God down on them. They must "escape the world's corruption" (1:4).

In light of the certainty of the return of Christ and final judgment, Christians are called to live in constant readiness for that event. In light of the certain destruction of "everything around us," Peter says, "what holy and godly lives you should live" (3:11). By our righteous conduct we should make every effort to hurry along the day (3:12), meaning that God takes into account the lives of his people in terms of their suffering (the messianic woes) and godly living in determining the eschaton (see further on 3:12). Part of this is God's demand that his followers live "peaceful lives" that are "pure and blameless" in light of that coming end-time event (3:14). He wants his people to exercise spiritual vigilance in watching out for one another, lest any fall away and be lost (3:17). In this sense 2 Peter parallels Hebrews in warning against apostasy (1:10; 2:20-22; 3:17).

Scripture. One of the two best-known passages on the inspiration of Scripture (with 2 Tim 3:16-17) occurs in 1:20-21. The reason Peter emphasizes this is because the false teachers have denigrated the worth of biblical prophecy in foretelling the second coming of Christ and the last judgment. So Peter claims that no single true prophecy ever emerged from the mind of the prophet (contra the "clever stories" charge of the heretics, 1:16), but rather all stem from the Holy Spirit, indeed the very voice of God (1:21). They are Spirit-inspired truths and binding for that reason.

One important contribution of 2 Peter is his witness to the growing canonical status of Paul's epistles in the apostolic age. In 3:15-16 he shows that Paul's writings agree with his own teaching in the letter, and as part of this emphasis he relates how the "ignorant and unstable" (the false teachers and their followers) have distorted the meaning of Paul's comments "just as they do with other parts of Scripture," implying that Paul's writings are equivalent to Holy Scripture. There are three stages of inspired writings in 2 Peter—the prophets (1:20-21), the apostolic witness (3:2), and Paul's writings in particular (3:16). Certainly Peter is not describing a final collection of the Pauline writings. "All of his letters" in 3:16 refers to those written to the churches Peter was addressing. Still, this demonstrates a step in the canonical consciousness of the early church that later led to the collection and recognition of the New Testament.

OUTLINE

It is always difficult to determine a book's exact structure, and in fact for every book of the Bible there are nearly as many different outlines as there are commentaries. The problem is that we are forcing Western-style outlines on Near Eastern works, and they did not think the way we do. There are always several different possible ways to structure a book, and transition passages can belong to what comes before or what comes after. Watson (1988:141-142, followed by Davids 2006:144-145) sees 2 Peter as Greek rhetoric and so sees the flow as: *prescript* (1:1-2), *exordium* (prologue, 1:3-15), *probatio* (proof of the argument, 1:16–3:13), and *peroratio* (conclusion, 3:14-18). Bauckham (1983:134-135) thinks it a testamentary form and sees 1:3-11 as Peter's basic message, with a reply to four objections (1:16-19, 20-21; 2:3-10; 3:5-10) as the core of his epistle. Differences in outlines often occur at two places: Do we place 1:12-15 (the testament of Peter) with 1:1-11 or 1:16-21? And do we place 3:11-13 with 3:1-10 or with 3:14-18? These are transitional in nature and can fit either way. My own outline is as follows and will be explained in the ensuing commentary:

- I. Salutation (1:1-2)
- II. The Opening: A Life Worth Living (1:3-15)
    - A. Proving the Reality of the Promises (1:3-11)
        - 1. The gift of God's promises for living (1:3-4)
        - 2. The divine virtues that typify the godly life (1:5-9)
        - 3. The need to confirm your calling with godly living (1:10-11)
    - B. Peter's Testament: A Call to Remember (1:12-15)
- III. The Body of the Letter: Response to the False Teachers (1:16–3:10)
    - A. Supernatural Intervention and the Return of Christ (1:16-21)
        - 1. Proof of supernatural intervention: the Transfiguration (1:16-18)
        - 2. Proof of supernatural revelation: the place of prophecy (1:19-21)
    - B. Condemnation of the False Teachers (2:1-22)
        - 1. The rise and coming judgment of the false teachers (2:1-3)
        - 2. The condemnation of the ungodly and the rescue of the righteous (2:4-10a)
        - 3. The arrogance and evil deeds of the false teachers (2:10b-16)
        - 4. Seduction and apostasy—the effects of the false teachers (2:17-22)

- C. Scoffers and the Day of the Lord (3:1-10)
  1. Answers for those who deny the return of the Lord (3:1-7)
  2. Reasons for the delay (3:8-10)

IV. The Challenge of the Letter: Living in Light of the Day of the Lord (3:11-18a)

- A. Encouragement to Godly Living (3:11-13)
- B. Call to Lives of Purity (3:14-16)
- C. Call to Be Vigilant (3:17-18a)

V. Closing Praise (3:18b)

COMMENTARY ON

2 Peter

◆ I. Salutation (1:1-2)

This letter is from Simon* Peter, a slave and apostle of Jesus Christ.

I am writing to you who share the same precious faith we have. This faith was given to you because of the justice and fairness* of Jesus Christ, our God and Savior.

2 May God give you more and more grace and peace as you grow in your knowledge of God and Jesus our Lord.

1:1a Greek *Symeon.* 1:1b Or *to you in the righteousness.*

NOTES

1:1 ***from Simon Peter.*** The text does not have the normal *Simōn* [TG4613, ZG4981] but *Sumeōn,* a transliteration of the Aramaic, used elsewhere of Peter only in Acts 15:14, where James utters it in a Palestinian setting (for the text-critical authenticity of "Simeon" over "Simon," see Comfort 2008:757-758). The use of it here stresses the Palestinian origins of the author, but scholars are divided as to whether it favors the authenticity of this letter from Simon Peter (Bigg, Mayor, G. Green), demonstrates the attempt by a pseudepigrapher to look more authentic (Kelly), or was the name used for Simon in the Petrine circle that penned the letter (Bauckham). I would agree with Schreiner (2003:284) who says, "The terms 'Peter' and 'apostle' in this verse show that the letter claims to be from Peter himself. I conclude that the Semitic *Simeōn* [TG4826, ZG5208] comes from Peter himself, and further it represents an authentic touch from the apostle Peter."

the same precious faith we have. There are three options for this comparison: (1) They, the Gentile community, have the same faith as the Jewish Christians (Mayor, Plumptre, Moo), but there is no Jewish-Gentile tension in this epistle. (2) These Christians have the same faith as the apostles (perhaps on the basis of 1:16-18, so Calvin, Reicke, Kelly, Bauckham), and this is possible but probably too narrow. (3) The best solution is to see this as general—the readers share the same faith with all other believers and churches around the world (Hillyer, Schreiner, G. Green).

because of the justice and fairness. Gr., *en dikaiosunē* [TG1343, ZG1466], meaning "in righteousness" (so NLT mg); in Rom 1:17; 3:21 "the righteousness of God" refers to justification, the forensic act whereby God declares us to be right with him because Christ bore our sins on the cross. So scholars are divided as to whether we translate this "justice" (NLT; Mayor, Kelly, Bauckham, G. Green) on the basis of the ethical and moral use of this term in 2:5, 21; 3:13 (*dikaios* [TG1342, ZG1465] in 1:13; 2:7-8); or "righteousness" (NASB, TNIV, ESV; Moo, Schreiner) on the basis of God's grace and the gift of faith in this section. It is a difficult decision, but the idea of "justice and fairness" fits well on the basis of the free gift and equal honor accorded the readers by God.

COMMENTARY

This letter begins in the normal Greco-Roman style, moving from the author to the recipients to the greeting itself. The author combines his familial name, "Simeon" (see note on 1:1) with the nickname "Peter," given him by Jesus when they first met (John 1:42, reaffirmed at the Caesarea Philippi confession in Matt 16:18). This was a prophecy of the rocklike strength Simon would demonstrate as the first leader of the church after Pentecost. "This would set the stage for his appeals to them to be stable in their faith (1:10-12; 2:14; 3:16-17)" (Harvey and Towner 2009:25).

Peter called himself "a slave and apostle." New Testament writers often labeled themselves as "slaves" of God and of Christ (Rom 1:1; Gal 1:10; Phil 1:1; Titus 1:1; Jas 1:1; Jude 1), a term denoting not only servitude but the privilege of being "God's very own possession" (1 Pet 2:9). In the Old Testament the great leaders were known as "slaves of God": Abraham, Isaac, and Jacob (Exod 32:13; Deut 9:27); Moses (Num 12:7; Deut 34:5), Samuel (1 Sam 3:9-10), David (2 Sam 7:8), and Daniel (Dan 6:20). First Corinthians 7:23 says that Christ purchased our freedom from slavery to sin so that we could become his slaves (cf. Rom 6:15-23). The Old Testament heroes and New Testament apostles belonged to God; in that role they acted on his behalf as official envoys of the one who sent them. Both ideas—ownership and authority—are intended here. The latter is highlighted with the added "apostle" (*apostolos* [TG652, ZG693]) indicating one "sent" (*apostellō* [TG649, ZG690]) as God's envoy to speak for him. Peter was commissioned by Christ to proclaim his kingdom truths with authority (Mark 3:14-15) and to counter the false teachers plaguing his readers.

The audience is not identified by location (the usual form in Paul's letters and 1 Peter); however, 3:1 tells us they were the same group as in 1 Peter (see commentary on 3:1). Peter called them those "who share the same precious faith we have." "You who share" translates the Greek participle *lachousin* [TG2975, ZG3275], meaning to "receive a portion," sometimes by drawing lots (cf. John 19:24); here it means that their faith is a gift from God, a divine blessing they have received. The gift is "the same precious faith we have," with "faith" perhaps being subjective for that personal belief in God and Christ (so M. Green, Bauckham, Moo, Schreiner) but more likely referring to the gospel or "body of faith" they all share (Kelly, Davids, G. Green), for it is the gospel that binds all Christians together. This faith contains equal "honor" or "precious" content. The term (*isotimon* [TG2472, ZG2700]) combines two words, equal (*isos* [TG2470, ZG2698]) and honor (*timē* [TG5092, ZG5507]) and conveys both value ("precious") and status ("honor") here. These believers had honor and privilege as the children of God.

The basis of this faith and the new status of the Christians is the "justice and fairness" (see note on 1:1) of Christ. He has justly made all believers to stand before God in equal honor, and he has refused to show partiality toward any group or individual. All are the recipients of his gracious love. Moreover, this just acceptance of us has been extended not only by God the Father but by "Jesus Christ, our God and Savior." This is one of the New Testament passages that affirms the deity of Christ (see also John 1:1, 18; 20:28; Rom 9:5; 2 Thess 1:2; Titus 2:13; Heb 1:8; 1 John 5:20, on which see Harris 1992), as seen in the single article (*tou* [TG3588, ZG3836] *theou hēmōn kai sōtēros* [TG2316/4990, ZG2536/5400], very lit., "the God of us and

Savior") that binds together "God and Savior" as a single idea modifying Christ (called Sharp's rule; see Wallace 1996:270-290). While some believe the rule is not at work here and so separate God and Jesus in the phrase (Mayor, Plumptre), this is highly unlikely, and the majority agree that Jesus is seen here as the divine Savior.

In 2 Peter, Jesus is called "Savior" 5 times (1:1, 11; 2:20; 3:2, 18) of the 16 in the New Testament, more often than anywhere else in the New Testament. Usually combined with "Lord" in 2 Peter, "Savior" was a divine title in Judaism and the Roman world (often used of the emperor); it refers to that "deliverance" from sin and the realm of darkness that Christ achieved on the cross. Jesus is God incarnate, who assumed human flesh, gave himself as the atoning sacrifice and died as the substitute for our sins, and brought about our salvation and deliverance so that we could be the people of God.

The salutation in 1:2 begins with the traditional New Testament combination of the Greek *charis* [TG5485, ZG5921] (grace) and Jewish *eirēnē* [TG1515, ZG1645] (cf. Heb., *shalom* [TH7965, ZH8934], "peace"). In the epistles this is an eschatological promise meaning, "The grace and peace you implicitly have longed for is now offered you in Christ." As in 1 Peter 1:2, the wish here is that God would "multiply" this or "give you more and more of it" (possibly an allusion to Dan 4:37c in the Old Greek version). God's "grace" or "unmerited favor" (Acts 15:40; 2 Cor 8:1; Gal 2:9) and God's "peace" (Rom 5:1) sum up the offer of salvation in its fullness to the readers.

This salvation comes "in your knowledge of God and Jesus our Lord." While some think that the term "knowledge" (*epignōsis* [TG1922, ZG2106]) appears here because of the false teachers and stresses Christian knowledge rather than false knowledge (so Kelly, M. Green), it is better to see this as referring to conversion (Bigg, Bauckham, Schreiner, G. Green) and to the process by which we get to "know" (1:3, 8; 2:20, where the term is equal to the use of *gnōsis* in 1:5-6; 3:18) God and Christ personally. The emphasis is upon coming to know Jesus as "Lord," used throughout the Greco-Roman world as well as Judaism for deity.

◆ II. The Opening: A Life Worth Living (1:3-15)
A. Proving the Reality of the Promises (1:3-11)
1. The gift of God's promises for living (1:3-4)

3By his divine power, God has given us everything we need for living a godly life. We have received all of this by coming to know him, the one who called us to himself by means of his marvelous glory and excellence. 4And because of his glory and excellence, he has given us great and precious promises. These are the promises that enable you to share his divine nature and escape the world's corruption caused by human desires.

NOTES

1:3 *living a godly life.* Scholars are divided as to whether the Gr. *zōēn kai eusebeian* [TG2222/2150, ZG2437/2354] is a hendiadys ("godly life," so NLT, TNIV, Reicke, Davids, Bauckham, Harvey and Towner) or whether the two should remain separate ideas, e.g., "life and godliness" (NASB, NRSV, ESV), "eternal life and godliness" (Schreiner), or "life and duty" (G. Green). Since 2 Peter tends to use pairs of words with related meanings, this is likely a hendiadys.

by means of his marvelous glory and excellence. There are two possibilities in the manuscripts, which either have *dia* [TG1223, ZG1328] (𝔓72 B 0209 𝔐) or *idia* [TG2398, ZG2625] (א A C P 33). The first is understood as "*by means of* his glory and excellence," connoting the glorious excellence of the Godhead as the means or instrument of our calling. The second reading means "*to* his own glory and excellence," meaning that we would grow spiritually to share in these attributes. Both are viable and would make good sense here, but the first is likely the best reading because God is seen as our benefactor/giver, who through his own glorious excellence pours out his promises on us (1:4).

COMMENTARY

Some scholars (see G. Green 2008:179-180) have argued that this section (1:3-11) follows a "decretal form," a Hellenistic style of writing used often in imperial and civic contexts in which the honorable and generous deeds of a benefactor are extolled. While Green especially does a fine job of showing the viability of this parallel, I must agree with Bauckham (1983:174), who says, "The most that might be said is that the highly rhetorical style of 1:3-11 echoes some of the kind of language used in official decrees." Still, there is definitely an air of the more general patron-client relationship that characterized the Greco-Roman world. We will see that often in the verses that follow.

It was normal in letters of the first century to begin with a thanksgiving and prayer for the recipients (Rom 1:8-15; Phil 1:3-11; Col 1:3-14) or a blessing (Eph 1:3-6; 1 Pet 1:3-5). When such is missing, it indicates a serious situation that needs to be addressed. Gene Green (2008:170) shows how the author here prefaces his primary themes: "He introduces God's engagement with the readers in salvation (1:3-4) and underscores the necessity of moral growth (1:5-9) in anticipation of entrance into God's eternal kingdom (1:10-11)," all "in juxtaposition to the immoral bent of the heretics who assailed the church as they denied the providential care of God as well as the final judgment." These are the three divisions of this first section: the wondrous promises of God that enable us to find spiritual victory (1:3-4), the divine virtues that define the contours of that spiritual growth (1:5-9), and the necessity of confirming our calling in light of God's promised eternal kingdom (1:10-11).

In Greek, 1:1-4 is a single sentence, with 1:3 introduced by *hōs* [TG5613, ZG6055] (seeing that), which shows that the "grace and peace" provided by God (1:2) is anchored in his power for living (1:3). The central term in 1:3-4 (the main verb in both verses) is *dōreomai* [TG1433, ZG1563] (to bestow, grant, present a gift) and means that all the benefits of the kingdom are given to God's people as a free gift by his grace. The source of these gifts is "his divine power." The Greek word behind "divine" appears elsewhere in the New Testament only in 1:4 and Acts 17:29, but is frequently used in the Hellenistic world and is probably used here from the standpoint of Peter's readers (see Davids, Bauckham, G. Green). The phrase is equivalent to "the power of God" or "the power of Christ" elsewhere (Matt 10:28; Luke 4:14; 5:17; Rom 1:16, 20; 1 Cor 5:4; Heb 1:3; 1 Pet 1:5) and means that the power of almighty God is at work on our behalf. There is some debate whether this refers to God (Kelly, Davids, on the basis of its usual meaning) or Christ (Bigg, Bauckham, Moo, since Jesus in 1:2 is the nearest antecedent of "his"), but in this context it is best to see it referring to both God and Christ (with Schreiner 2003:291). The power of the Godhead is the source of strength for "living a godly life."

In Greek, the phrase "everything we need" (lit., "everything necessary for") is first in the sentence for emphasis. Paul says the same in Philippians 4:19, "And this same God who takes care of me will supply all your needs from his glorious riches, which have been given to us in Christ Jesus." There is no need—material, social, spiritual—that God cannot supply. The goal of this is that we live "a godly life" (lit., "for life and godliness"). Here the two terms are meant to be drawn together (see note on 1:3), with "life" intended ethically for the Christian life and "godliness" referring to a life lived by God's principles and will.

The means by which (*dia* [TG1223, ZG1328], "by, through") we receive this power for living godly lives is "coming to know" him, based on the same word (*epignōsis* [TG1922, ZG2106], "knowledge") as in 1:2. This refers to the process initiated at conversion by which we grow in our knowledge of God and of Christ. It is God who is sovereign over salvation, not us, for it is he who has "called us to himself," an emphasis stressed often in 1 Peter (1 Pet 1:15; 2:9, 21; 3:9; 5:10) and 2 Peter (1:3, 10). We do not come to know him by our own power, for salvation is a divine action, and a faith decision takes place due to the convicting presence of the Spirit, not by a human choice of the will (on this issue see Osborne 2003:280-281). We do "choose" Christ, but that choice is made possible only by the Spirit. Therefore, it is not a "work" (Eph 2:9-10) but a gift from God.

All of this is available only "by means of his marvelous glory and excellence," a further combination of terms in Hellenistic style. His "glory" (*doxa* [TG1391, ZG1518]) would be either his "honor" or praiseworthy status (Davids 2006:170) or his "splendor, majesty" (Schreiner 2003:293). Most likely, both aspects are present. As Bauckham (1983:179) states, this is related to the "divine power" in the beginning of the verse that bestowed on us everything necessary for our Christian life. His "excellence" (*aretē* [TG703, ZG746]) refers to his perfect moral virtue. We share his "glory" (2 Cor 4:17; 2 Thess 2:14; 1 Pet 5:10), and we seek to exemplify his moral "excellence" (1:5; Phil 4:8). Both in our calling to salvation and in the godly life that follows, the "glory and excellence" of our God and Christ are evident and provide the spiritual and moral paradigm for living the Christian life.

In the next verse (1:4) Peter recognizes that the "glory and excellence" of God and Christ are the instrument or basis (lit., "through which") of our receiving his promises. As God's people feel the presence of Christ's goodness, this becomes the means by which they experience and receive his promises. As G. Green (2008:184) points out, God appears as the benefactor who pours out his benefits or promises upon a grateful people. The promises are "great" because they demonstrate the power of God, and they are "precious" because they affect the believer so completely.

But what promises are they? We could go through the New Testament and catalogue the various promises—Christ (Acts 13:23), the Spirit (Acts 1:4; 2:39; Gal 3:14; Eph 1:13), salvation (Acts 26:6; 2 Cor 6:18–7:1; Eph 3:6), the covenant promises (Gal 3:16-18; 4:23, 28; Eph 2:12; Heb 8:6), inheritance (Rom 4:13-16; Gal 3:29; Heb 6:12), eternal life (2 Tim 1:1; Heb 4:1; 9:15; 11:33, 39; 1 John 2:25), and the Parousia (3:4; Heb 10:36-37). The "promises" here could be the past promises made and given by God, perhaps Christian conversion and baptism, the contents of the gospel (Reicke). But in 2 Peter, with the heretics denying the reality of God's future eschatological promises, these certainly pertain primarily to the promises of the Parousia of Christ (3:4, "What happened to the promise that Jesus is coming again?") and of the believer's inheritance of those promises (see 1:11, 14, 19; 3:9, 11, 13). This unbelievably valuable and powerful promise is nothing less than our share in the "new heavens and new earth." We have been "promised a world filled with God's righteousness" (3:13).

Yet these promises also have present ramifications. Throughout the New Testament, beginning with the Olivet discourse (Matt 24:36–25:30), the future eschatological promises regarding the Parousia have always produced present warning, that on that day of glory every believer will also give account of his or her life and be held responsible for the ethical responsibility to live rightly before God (Rom 13:11-14; 1 Cor 15:58; 2 Cor 5:9-10; Phil 4:5-6; 1 Thess 5:6, 8, 10-11; 2 Thess 2:13-15; Heb 10:35-39; Jas 5:7; 1 Pet 4:7). The point is that Christ will come back like a thief (3:10; Matt 24:43-44; cf. 1 Thess 5:2; Rev 3:3; 16:15), and when he returns he will hold his servants accountable for the quality of their Christian walk.

The present aspects or purposes of these future promises are twofold here. First, they "enable you to share his divine nature"—with "sharing" being *koinōnoi* [TG2844, ZG3128], "partners" who participate in God's nature. To partake of the "divine nature" (*theias . . . phuseōs* [TG2304/5449, ZG2521/5882]) speaks of *theiosis* or "deification," a major theological emphasis in Orthodox circles. For the Greeks it was that internal spark of the divine defined as immortality and the ability to reason. The soul could live above the material world and contemplate divine realities. Within Hellenistic Judaism (e.g., Philo, Josephus, Wisdom of Solomon) the individual was "divinized" via the physical resurrection, when the person shares the divine immortality and incorruptibility (see Bauckham 1983:180). There is debate whether Peter here is speaking entirely of this future "sharing" at Christ's return (Bauckham 1983:181-182) or whether it also includes the ethical life of the believer in the present as becoming more like God (so Davids, Schreiner, G. Green). In this context the present moral character of the individual is almost certainly the primary thought, especially in light of the second half of the admonition (see below). Thus, it refers to Christlikeness as in Ephesians 4:13, "measuring up to the full and complete standard of Christ" or in Romans 8:29, "chose them to become like his Son." Christians are "partakers of the divine nature" (1:4, NASB) when they are holy as God is holy (Lev 11:44; 1 Pet 1:16) or are perfect (i.e., mature, whole) as he is perfect (Matt 5:48). This takes place to the extent they are "filled with the Holy Spirit" (Eph 5:18), which O'Brien (1999:392) says pictures the Spirit "mediating the fullness of God and Christ to believers," so that they are "transformed by the Spirit into the likeness of God and Christ."

The second purpose of God's promises is that his people "escape the world's corruption caused by human desires." The Greeks believed that this "corruption" (*phthora* [TG5356, ZG5785], "dissolution, that headed for destruction," see BDAG 1055) is that which is in process of perishing; hence, it was entirely confined to the material world. But Peter, following Jewish belief, relates it to internal sin or self-centeredness. The "desire" here is the *yetzer hara'* or "impulse (tendency) to evil" (cf. Gen 6:5; 4Q417 Frg. 1 ii:12; *Mishnah Berakhot* 9:5) that was always present in a human being. In 2:20 (speaking of the false teachers) Peter speaks of people who "escape from the wickedness of the world by knowing our Lord and Savior Jesus Christ." In Christ the strength comes to defeat these tendencies within. The "escape" takes place step-by-step as we become more like Christ and progress in "the upward calling of God in Christ Jesus" (Phil 3:14, my translation), completed only when we have died and gone to be with the Lord.

2. The divine virtues that typify the godly life (1:5-9)

5 In view of all this, make every effort to respond to God's promises. Supplement your faith with a generous provision of moral excellence, and moral excellence with knowledge, 6 and knowledge with self-control, and self-control with patient endurance, and patient endurance with godliness, 7 and godliness with brotherly affection, and brotherly affection with love for everyone.

8 The more you grow like this, the more productive and useful you will be in your knowledge of our Lord Jesus Christ. 9 But those who fail to develop in this way are shortsighted or blind, forgetting that they have been cleansed from their old sins.

NOTES

1:8 *in your knowledge.* Gr., *eis tēn . . . epignōsin* [TG1922, ZG2106]. There are two possible interpretations of this: to see *eis* [TG1519, ZG1650] as reference or respect ("with respect to" or "in the knowledge," so Bigg, Kelly, Bauckham, Davids) or to see *eis* as denoting result ("resulting in" or "leading to the knowledge," so Mayor, Reicke, M. Green). The use of "knowledge" thus far in this section (1:2-3) for personal knowledge of Christ makes the former more likely. Knowing Christ is the basis and sphere within which Christian growth will occur.

1:9 *shortsighted or blind.* Some scholars (Kelly, M. Green) see "blind" as deliberately closing the eyes, thus willful blindness. Shortsighted people squint in order to see better (Mayor, Bauckham), so the two words are used as near synonyms. The idea is that these people see only what is in front of them and thus are blind to true reality; theirs is a "refusal to see the truth," with spiritual and moral blindness resulting.

COMMENTARY

The subject or active agent in 1:3-4 is God/Christ, and the active agent of 1:5-7 is the believer. Therefore, the basis or foundation for the "godly life" is the salvation effected by God (1:3-4), but that salvation must be put into practice by the "godly living" of the Christian (1:5-7). This is not "righteousness by works," but it does agree with James 2:14-26 that true faith must lead to works if it is real. In 1:5-7 Peter presents a "virtue list," of which there are many examples in the New Testament (2 Cor 6:6-8; Gal 5:22-23; Phil 4:8-9; Col 3:12-14; 1 Tim 3:2-7; 6:11; Titus 3:1-3; Jas 3:13, 17-18; 1 Pet 3:8-9). But the verses in 2 Peter 1 portray a very particular kind of virtue list called *sorites*, a chain list that proceeds step-by-step to a climax, with each one mentioned twice. The closest parallel is the "golden chain" of Romans 8:29-30; Davids (2006:177) also finds similar progressions in Romans 5:3-5; Galatians 5:22-23; and James 1:3-4 (for Jewish parallels see Bauckham 1983:185-189; Davids

2006:178). What nearly all agree on is that the order is rhetorical. There is no distinct logical order or progression in which each virtue leads into the next; they are not to be worked on one at a time in the order presented but are all to be developed together (see especially Schreiner 2003:297-298). The list is comprised of two sections: the virtues themselves (1:5-7) and the importance of possessing and growing in them (1:8-9).

"In view of all this" (1:5) means that the salvific gifts of God (1:3-4) provide the true basis for the Christian life. We could not begin to work upon these divine virtues without the empowering presence of Christ and the Spirit within. With these gifts, however, comes strenuous activity on our part as we "make every effort" to grow in them. We do not grow in Christ by sitting back and waiting for God to do it for us; he demands an intense work ethic, where we put every ounce of energy we possess into our Christian walk. Most of us today work very hard at our secular jobs, sacrificing greatly to be successful. Does God deserve any less?

The main verb in this section is difficult to translate. The normal translation "add to" does not fit the term used, *epichorēgeō* [TG2023, ZG2220], which means to "provide at one's own expense, supply, furnish" that which is needed for the well-being of another (BDAG 387). In the Roman world it would reflect a patron or benefactor supplying the needs of a client. The word itself depicts a wealthy person (a *chorēgos*) who financed the training and equipping of the chorus for a dramatic festival. Each virtue supplies the means of the next, but the rhetorical effect of the whole is that all work together to provide for the needs of the believer. Thus, the NLT's rendering "supplement . . . with a generous provision of" captures the intent well; each virtue supplements the others.

The first and foundational virtue is "faith" (*pistis* [TG4102, ZG4411]), already noted as "the same precious faith we have" in 1:1. There we concluded that the term was most likely referring to "the faith," the body of doctrine that the church has inherited from Christ and the apostles and that guides its belief. Yet this is probably not the case here, for this is an ethical list of virtues to be lived out as constituting the "godly life" of 1:3. "Faith" often occurs in ethical lists (1 Cor 13:13; 2 Cor 8:7; Gal 5:22; 1 Tim 4:12; 6:11; 2 Tim 3:10); here it likely refers both to that trust in God that allows us to accept and obey all that he says (so Moo, Lucas and Green, Bauckham, Schreiner, Harvey and Towner), as well as that life of "faithfulness" to him and to others that results (so Davids, G. Green). In patron-client relationships, faithfulness was a requirement.

"Moral excellence" is the same *aretē* [TG703, ZG746] (excellence) that described God and Christ in 1:3. In light of the demand to be like God and Christ ("share his divine nature") in 1:4, this makes a great deal of sense. In New Testament virtue lists it appears elsewhere only in Philippians 4:8, but it is quite common in Hellenistic lists as the basic term for "virtue" or "honorable" behavior. Gene Green (2008:192) points out that this not only connotes moral character but emphasizes the "social context" in which this is seen. "The person of 'virtue' demonstrates excellence of character, shown in generosity toward others, surpassing what normal constraints of duty demand," with emphasis on "the acts that demonstrate the character" and that are "worthy of praise."

This leads to "knowledge"—here *gnōsis* [TG1108, ZG1194] but synonymous with *epignōsis* [TG1922, ZG2106] in 1:2-3 above (see there, contra Bauckham 1983:186, who understands the term in 1:3 as conversion and the one here as wisdom or discernment for Christian living). This is not philosophical or intellectual knowledge of facts but a combination of personal "knowledge" of Christ gained at conversion with "knowing" God and his will in daily life. Thus, the emphasis is not on content (knowing about truth or God) but on practical Christian living. Knowing Christ and God's will enables us to live for him. The two terms in 1:3, 5 are not different, for "wisdom and discernment come from knowing God/Christ and adopting his character" (Davids 2006:180).

Knowledge then produces "self-control" (*enkrateia* [TG1466, ZG1602], 1:6), connoting the discipline and mastery over our impulses and desires that enable us to harness our passions and live the life God requires. This is one of the fruits of the Spirit (Gal 5:23) and is critical for spiritual growth. In every area of life we must learn to control ourselves and let Christ reign rather than our own self-centered desires. Peter may have had in mind the false teachers, whom he will describe as shamefully immoral (2:2, 18), greedy (2:3, 14), like animals (2:12), indulging in evil pleasures (2:13), and enslaved to lust and sin (2:14, 19). We are called to a life of self-restraint, living for God and serving others rather than our own selves.

Discipline produces "endurance" as it reacts to the difficulties of life. This virtue was prized in athletic contests (marathon races) and in war (marching over difficult terrain, fighting for hours on end), and both of these areas are metaphors for the Christian life. The term (*hupomonē* [TG5281, ZG5705]) means not only bearing up in the midst of hardship but also remaining resolute or steadfast in life in general. "Peter does not have in mind, however, endurance in the midst of persecution . . . but rather moral endurance amid the pressures of temptation (cf. 4 Macc 7:9; 17:12; Rom 2:7). In light of the tactics of the heretics to draw the church into their error and immorality, the importance of this virtue is evident (cf. 2:1-3, 18-19)" (G. Green 2008:194).

Next comes "godliness" or "piety" (*eusebeia* [TG2150, ZG2354]), also found in 1:3 (and 3:11) with "life" (translated "living a godly life"). God has given us all we need to live lives of godliness (1:3), but now we have to put that in practice in our daily conduct (1:6). The term denotes a life of piety and reverence for God and for the way of life he has regulated. Several scholars (e.g., Davids, Harvey and Towner) have noted that this works two ways: respect or piety toward God along with a corresponding respect and consideration toward all who are related to him, namely, our fellow human beings. As G. Green (2008:194) says, "In the ancient world this virtue was understood as the demonstration of due reverence and loyalty to the gods, parents, relatives . . . and fellow citizens," so for Peter "the virtue points up the necessity of loyalty to God and to the community in which the readers are embedded."

Therefore, a life of godliness must lead to "brotherly affection" (*philadelphia* [TG5360, ZG5789], 1:7). It is very appropriate that the final two of the eight virtues center on community love, since this is the core of community life in the church. The term expresses the early Christian view that the church is a family, and the members are brothers and sisters. This is at the heart of the Christian life; as 1 Peter 1:22 puts it, "you have purified your souls for (the purpose of) brotherly love" (my translation). As such, Christians are to "love each other with genuine affection" (Rom 12:10), as "God himself has taught you" (1 Thess 4:9). Love and hospitality are to be the hallmarks of Christian relationships (Heb 13:1-2). Since the early Christians looked upon themselves as family, they "felt that what they owned was not their own" and so "shared everything they had" (Acts 2:44; 4:32). The result was that "there were no needy people among them" (Acts 4:34). In other words, they gave concrete expression to their "brotherly love."

Finally, *agapē* [TG26, ZG27] (love) must characterize God's people. According to 1 Corinthians 13:13 the highest virtue of them all is "love," and in Colossians 3:14 love is named as the virtue "which binds us all together in perfect harmony." Love crowns the other virtues because along with holiness it best exemplifies the presence of God in the individual. As Harvey and Towner (2009:46) put it, "We are being recreated in the image of the One who loved us with this exact kind of love, and we therefore must give as we have received from him." The three chief virtues (faith, hope, love) often appear together in the New Testament writings (Rom 5:1-5; 1 Cor 13:13; Gal 5:5-6; Col 1:4-5; 1 Thess 1:3; Heb 10:22-24), and in each passage the other two find themselves completed in love. It is fitting that of these chief virtues faith and love frame the list here in 1:5-7. Knowledge without love is nothing (1 Cor 8:1-3), and miracles without love are irrelevant (1 Cor 13:1-2). The Father's love is reciprocated by the Son, and the Son's love for us is reciprocated by our love for him. These two levels of love must produce a deep love that characterizes God's new community and becomes the basis of our mission to the world (John 15:9-17; cf. the "new commandment" of John 13:34-35).

The effective benefits produced by the virtues are explained in 1:8-9. Note that the emphasis is on progressive personal growth ("the more you grow," lit., "These things [the virtues in 1:5-7] are present and are increasing"). God does not magically infuse them in us through the Spirit. We are expected to work very hard at putting them to practice in our daily lives. There is a conditional nature to the participles ("if they are present and increasing"), not questioning their presence but rather challenging us as to whether they are at work in us. This is how to live "a godly life" (1:3), by allowing these godly characteristics to be exemplified "more and more" in our thoughts and actions.

When this takes place, we will become "productive and useful" both to God and to those around us. These are presented negatively in the Greek and produce another near hendiadys (see note on 1:3), with *argous* [TG692, ZG734] (idle, lazy, unproductive, useless) and *akarpous* [TG175, ZG182] (unfruitful, useless, unproductive) meaning in effect "keep you from being lazy and worthless" or "unproductive and useless." There seems to be a progression in both words from idleness to an absence of productivity to complete uselessness. Peter was picturing a person who could be working but preferred to sit idly in the marketplace doing nothing, of no use to anyone. Fruitfulness in the Christian life is a primary demand. With the Spirit comes the "fruit" of Christian virtues (Gal 5:22-23), but those "in the vine" must bear fruit or grow in this area, lest they be removed from the vine, gathered in bundles, and cast into fiery judgment (John 15:1-6). Spiritual fruit was a goal of Paul's ministry (Rom 1:13), and the result of this fruitfulness is to be righteousness (Phil 1:11), holiness (Rom 6:22), and goodness (Eph 5:9). To produce this fruit takes hard work (2 Tim 2:6), and the result will be a "harvest of right living" (Heb 12:11; Jas 3:18). Peter's point is that we must work with all our energy to produce these virtues under the empowering presence of the Spirit, and we must yield to the Spirit so that they progressively grow and produce a harvest of right living.

The basis for this growth in the fruit or virtues of the Spirit is "in your knowledge of our Lord Jesus Christ." This refers to personally knowing Christ (see also on 1:2-3, 5) as "Lord" (see on 1:2) of our lives. Knowing Christ both in conversion and in the life of sanctification results in the basis for spiritual growth (see note on 1:8). As we come to know him and surrender to him as Lord of our lives, we will become more and more fruitful as the divine virtues abound in us. But we dare not be idle, that is, refuse to work at our Christian walk, for then we will become useless to God and to all around us.

This danger of spiritual idleness becomes especially evident in 1:9, which addresses those Christians who "fail to develop in this way," meaning they allow these fruits of the Spirit to lie fallow in them. Such people are "shortsighted or blind." The Greek has "blind, being nearsighted" (the latter word occurs only here in the NT), or "so shortsighted that they cannot see" (TEV in Davids 2006:186). I happen to be nearsighted and have worn glasses since I was in high school. My vision became so bad a few years ago that I had to have cataract surgery, and everything I looked at was incredibly blurry. To read I had to have books really close to my ultrathick glasses. That is the problem with those in the church who focus only on themselves and their own desires (as in 1:4b). They cannot see anyone but themselves and fail to focus on God or others in their lives. They should "know Christ," but they have failed to see beyond themselves, and so the light of Christ has been shut out in their lives.

A major aspect of this blindness is the fact that they have also been deliberately "forgetting that they have been cleansed from their old sins." As G. Green (2008:198) points out, this is not a mere memory lapse but "a willful act of ignoring something." These people have returned to their former way of life and are acting as if their sins had never been forgiven. It is common to think that this "cleansing" or "purification" from sins is a reference to baptism (Acts 22:16; 1 Cor 6:11; Eph 5:26; Titus 3:5; so Mayor, Bauckham, Davids). Yet while baptism is certainly part of the image as symbolizing cleansing from previous sins (1 Pet 3:21; so Schreiner 2003:303), it is best to see here primarily the Old Testament and early Christian metaphor of washing or cleansing from sin (Lev 16:19; Ps 51:2; Ezek 36:33; Titus 2:14; Heb 9:14; 1 Pet 1:22; 1 John 1:7; so Moo 1996:48). Peter undoubtedly had in mind the immoral behavior of the false teachers and their followers. They were living like pagans and were ignoring, even pragmatically denying by their behavior, that their sins had been cleansed by the blood of Christ. One's actions matter; once you have been cleansed from sin, you must refuse to commit that sin. There is room here, too, for the sense in which "cleansed" might refer to the sense of release from sin's power over us and its destructive effect on us.

◆ 3. The need to confirm your calling with godly living (1:10-11)

[10]So, dear brothers and sisters,* work hard to prove that you really are among those God has called and chosen. Do these things, and you will never fall away. [11]Then God will give you a grand entrance into the eternal Kingdom of our Lord and Savior Jesus Christ.

1:10 Greek *brothers.*

NOTES

1:10 *Do these things.* The participle *poiountes* [TG4160, ZG4472] can be conditional ("if you do these things," TNIV), imperatival ("Do these things," NLT), or modal ("by doing these things," G. Green 2008:201). A combination of the first two seems best, for Peter was challenging his readers, especially those following the false teachers, regarding their obedience to God.

COMMENTARY

The Christian life is hard work. We have not read our Bible very well if we think that when we become the "King's kids," life will become easy, and we can bask in the privileges and sumptuous life God will bring our way. God is not a "sugar daddy" who simply lavishes the good life on his followers. He demands we "work hard" (1:5, "make every effort") and sacrifice much to follow him. The verb *spoudazō* [TG4704, ZG5079] connotes the ideas of zeal, priority decisions, and energetic effort (see Eph 4:3; Heb 4:11), but Peter adds that we need even "more" (*mallon* [TG3123, ZG3437]) strenuous effort in the Christian life. This great energy is to be exerted in order "to prove that you really are" among the chosen. This phrase is *bebaian* [TG949, ZG1010] . . . *poieisthai* [TG4160, ZG4472], to "confirm" or "make sure" that something is correct. It is a legal concept referring to ratifying or guaranteeing a contract. In other words, by living by or exercising the Christian virtues of 1:5-7 (and working hard at them), the believer "ratifies" their calling from God.

What is proven or confirmed is that "God has called and chosen" us—literally, our "calling and election." Here we have another word pair that forms a hendiadys (see on 1:3, 8, 9) and might be translated "elective calling" or perhaps "chosen election." It is interesting that Peter has brought together in one sentence the two sides of our salvation that have been the subject of such vociferous debate, God's sovereign choice of us to be his people and our own decision to put that to work in our lives. A similar balance is found in Philippians 2:12-13, with our side being "Work hard to show the results of your salvation, obeying God with deep reverence and fear," and God's side being "For God is working in you, giving you the desire and the power to do what pleases him." In both these places, there is balance between God's sovereign choice and our serious responsibility. Here Peter is saying that we must prove by our lives that God has indeed chosen us and given us life. There has been some debate as to whether this "proof" is to ourselves (assurance of salvation) or to others (evangelism and apologetics). Most likely, both are intended (see Schreiner 2003:305).

It requires strenuous effort (1:10a) to put the virtues (1:5-7) into practice in our lives. Note that throughout 2 Peter it is not enough simply to have the Christian virtues; they must be lived out or "done/practiced" in our daily conduct. When this occurs, Peter promises that "you will never fall away," using the term *ptaiō* [TG4417, ZG4760], which means to "stumble, fall into sin." This could mean simple backsliding, but it is generally agreed that it is used as in Jude 24 (God is "able to keep you from falling") of apostasy or falling into eternal ruin (Bigg, Kelly, Bauckham, Davids, Moo). This danger is very real in 2 Peter, as exemplified in the heretics (2:1, 20).

The antithesis of eternal punishment is the promise of eternal glory in 1:11. The reason for faithfully pursuing the godly life and placing their trust completely in Christ rather than in the false promises of the heretics is that thereby they will have a "grand entrance into the eternal Kingdom of our Lord and Savior Jesus Christ." The idea of "entering the Kingdom" is quite frequent in Jesus' teaching (Matt 18:3; 19:23; Mark 10:23-24; Luke 18:24-25; John 3:5) as is also the danger of failing to enter it (Matt 5:20; 7:21; Luke 18:17). The picture of God "giving" entrance is *plousiōs epichorēgēthēsetai* [TG4146/2023, ZG4455/2220] in Greek, meaning that he "will richly provide" (the future tense refers to entrance into heaven rather than present promises), and it pictures a wealthy patron lavishing his gifts on the fortunate client. The incredible grace of God means that he will sumptuously provide for his followers who turn to Christ in faith and live according to his regulations. The contrast between verses 10 and 11 is quite stark—committing apostasy and finding eternal ruin versus living a godly life and finding eternal joy.

This is the "eternal Kingdom," where the emphasis is on the eternal nature of our future reward in contrast to the temporary pleasures of a worldly existence (like that of the false teachers). The background for this is found in Daniel 7:27 ("His kingdom will last forever") and is echoed in Luke 1:33 ("His Kingdom will never end"), Revelation 11:15 ("He will reign forever and ever"), and Revelation 22:5 ("They [the victorious saints] will reign forever and ever"). Moreover, the emphasis here (as throughout ch 1) is on Christ. Peter speaks of Christ's kingdom, whereas the rest of the New Testament usually speaks of the Kingdom of God. It is Christ (and belief in him) that will provide entrance into eternal life. Jesus Christ is "Lord and Savior"; the emphasis is on Christ as cosmic Lord (eight times in 2 Peter) and the "Savior" (see 1:1, 11; 2:20; 3:2, 18) who has brought salvation to humanity—the two appear together also in 2:20; 3:2, 18. As in 1:1, Jesus is seen as the divine Lord who makes entrance into the eternal kingdom possible.

◆ B. Peter's Testament: A Call to Remember (1:12-15)

[12]Therefore, I will always remind you about these things—even though you already know them and are standing firm in the truth you have been taught. [13]And it is only right that I should keep on reminding you as long as I live.* [14]For our Lord Jesus Christ has shown me that I must soon leave this earthly life,* [15]so I will work hard to make sure you always remember these things after I am gone.

1:13 Greek *as long as I am in this tent* [or *tabernacle*]. 1:14 Greek *I must soon put off my tent* [or *tabernacle*].

NOTES

1:12 *I will always remind you.* This future tense, *mellēsō aei humas hupomimnēskein* [TG5279, ZG5703] (lit., "I will always be ready to remind you"), could be taken as delineating Peter's intention to keep on writing them in the future (thus not a reference to this present letter), but that does not fit the context, which must refer to this letter. So most likely it is a periphrastic construction for the future tense, as the NLT properly translates, "I will always remind you." Peter undoubtedly refers to the letter as a whole and is saying, "Throughout this letter (= 'always') it is my intention to remind you of these things."

1:15 ***I will work hard to make sure you always remember.*** The future tense (as in 1:12) here has led to many different interpretations of the meaning of Peter's promise here. Many see this as an intention to write other works after 2 Peter (the issue also in 1:12 above), perhaps the Gospel of Mark (on the basis of Papias's statement that Mark was Peter's Gospel, so Mayor, Bigg, M. Green). This is unlikely, for it is too enigmatic a statement to refer to the second Gospel, which after all was written by Mark, not Peter. Once more the best option by far is to take this as referring to 2 Peter as a whole (Kelly, Davids, Moo), perhaps centering on the letter's future ministry among them after his death (Bauckham 1983:201).

COMMENTARY

Many scholars place this section with what follows (Schreiner, G. Green), but it is better to see it as a transition from the basic statement of Peter's positive message (1:1-11) to his responses to his opponents (1:16–3:10). Virtually everyone recognizes it as a final "testament" on the part of Peter, stating his purpose for writing. It has most of the characteristics of the "testament" form (Bauckham, Neyrey, Davids): The author is aware of his impending death and wants his message to be remembered afterward; he is aware of a crisis and wishes to avert that crisis and leave his legacy. There are many such testamentary or farewell speeches in Scripture (Moses in Deut 33; Joshua in Josh 24; Jesus in John 13:34–17:26) and Jewish literature (*Testament of the Twelve Patriarchs; 2 Baruch* 78–87; *Testament of Moses*).

Peter began (1:12) by stating the reason for writing his thesis statement of verses 3-11: "I will always remind you about these things." As in 1:10, "these things" refers to the basic message of 1:3-11, the need to work hard at living a godly life in light of all that God and Christ have done for us. Peter wanted them to know that throughout this letter (see note on 1:12) he would be bringing to their remembrance these deep truths about the Christian life, as he countered the false teachers. Peter's intention to remind them of the truths they need to keep uppermost in their minds will guide them through this letter (1:13, 15; 3:1-2).

In fact, Peter writes about this even though there are two reasons why he does not really need to do so. First, they already "know" all this. He was aware that they had been believers for some time and that they had been taught the same truths he had just reiterated in verses 3-11. Still, "knowing" something and putting that into practice in one's life are two different things. Most sermons are composed of material that people have heard before, but it is packaged in such a way that the message both reminds and stimulates the listeners to deepen their walk in these areas. Still, Peter added that they not only "know" this but are now "standing firm in the truth" (lit., "established in the truth present with you"). The verb (*stērizō* [TG4741, ZG5114]), in its base meaning, means to "support" and connotes the idea of "fixing something so that it stands upright and immovable" (TDNT 7.653) and thus to be "stable, grounded, strengthened." Peter was saying that the truths of his letter were firmly fixed in their lives. They have not only known it but were well grounded in this material, and in light of it the false teachers should not be able to make much headway into their community. So Peter was reminding them of spiritual realities that have a firm foundation in their community, and this very stability should protect them against the heresies Peter will be discussing shortly.

So Peter repeats his intention (1:13), saying it is "only right" (*dikaios* [TG1342, ZG1465], the "right" or "just" thing to do as God leads him) for him to "keep on reminding" them of these things as long as he was still alive, which apparently would not be very much longer (1:14). It is one thing to know something and even to be grounded in it, yet quite another to continue abiding in it. So constant prompting is essential, especially in a situation in which false teachers were opposing these very truths. "Keep on reminding" contains a strong idea here, as Peter says the reminder is supposed to "wake up, arouse, stir up" (BDAG 243) the readers. They were not asleep or in lethargy (1:12), but their passions still needed strong stimulation so they would join Peter in further developing the Christian virtues of verses 5-7 and in opposing the heretics.

"As long as I live" is an interesting choice of words, for Peter literally says, "so long as I inhabit this earthly tent" (*skēnōma* [TG4638, ZG5013]), a metaphor for the human body "as a temporary dwelling-place for the soul, folded up and abandoned when the soul leaves it at death" (Bauckham 1983:198). Paul used this metaphor in 2 Corinthians 5:1, where he discusses the time when "this earthly tent (*skēnos* [TG4636, ZG5011]) we live in is taken down." This idea is also found in John 1:14, where at his incarnation, Jesus "made his home" (lit., "pitched his tent") among us. This language is quite appropriate since Peter was contemplating his imminent death (1:14). So for the rest of his time on earth, he wanted to anchor these truths in their minds by bringing them to their remembrance and arousing them to even greater effort in light of the danger posed to their community by the heretics.

In 1:14 Peter explains why (causal participle, "Because I know") he spoke of prompting their memories "as long as I live." He knew he did not have a long time left in his mortal body. The adverb *tachinē* [TG5031, ZG5442] (soon) can imply a "sudden" or violent death (so Plumptre, M. Green) but more likely here means "soon" in terms of an imminent death (the more common thrust, so Bauckham, Schreiner, G. Green). Peter was not aware of his soon demise only because Christ revealed it to him; the Greek says, "knowing this . . . as also" the Lord "showed me." In other words, Christ's revelation confirmed what he already knew.

But what was this revelation? A vision or oral prophesy recently given to Peter? While this is possible, it is more likely that Peter was referring to Jesus' own prophecy regarding his martyrdom in John 21:18-19, "'I tell you the truth, when you were young, you were able to do as you liked; you dressed yourself and went wherever you wanted to go. But when you are old, you will stretch out your hands, and others will dress you and take you where you don't want to go.' Jesus said this to let him know by what kind of death he would glorify God." Probably Jesus adapted a parable on the infirmities of old age to prophesy Peter's later death by crucifixion—"stretch out your hands" is a metaphor for one's hands "stretched out on the crossbeam at crucifixion" (see Osborne 2007:301-302). This follows another prophecy of Peter's martyrdom at Jesus' farewell discourse in John 13:36, "You can't go with me now, but you will follow me later."

Peter's death by crucifixion under Nero was later reported in *Acts of Peter* 35–39; Eusebius *History* 3.1; *Epistle of Clement to James* 1–2. The first is the famous "Quo Vadis" story where Peter, trying to escape the persecution in Rome, meets Jesus, who says he is going to Rome to be crucified again. Peter then turns around and returns to Rome to die (for all of this, see Bauckham 1983:200-201). This *Acts of Peter* story is later mythology, and Peter most likely had in mind the John 21 incident. He was writing as the Neronian persecution was in full swing, and he had come to believe that soon Christ's prophecy would come to pass, and he would soon "lay aside" (the Greek word here) his mortal body.

So in 1:15 Peter repeats his injunction of 1:12, thereby framing the paragraph with his intention to "make sure you always remember these things after I am gone." In 1:10 Peter challenged the readers to "work hard" to prove that God's calling was effective in their lives; now he promises to "work hard" himself to make certain they remembered these truths. It is Peter's purpose that God would use this epistle to strengthen their resolve and give them the material by which they can overcome the false teachers and continue to grow in Christ long after Peter's death. "After I am gone" is literally, "after my departure," and this is not a reference to the discussion of Jesus' coming "departure" (or "exodus") at the Transfiguration in Luke 9:31 (as some have said) but a euphemism for Peter's own death, likely with a wordplay between the "entrance" (*eisodos* [TG1529, ZG1658]) into the "eternal Kingdom" in 1:11 and the "departure" (*exodus* [TG1841, ZG2016]) from this world (see Harvey and Towner 2009:59).

◆ III. The Body of the Letter: Response to the False Teachers (1:16–3:10)

A. Supernatural Intervention and the Return of Christ (1:16–21)

1. Proof of supernatural intervention: the Transfiguration (1:16–18)

16 For we were not making up clever stories when we told you about the powerful coming of our Lord Jesus Christ. We saw his majestic splendor with our own eyes 17 when he received honor and glory from God the Father. The voice from the majestic glory of God said to him, "This is my dearly loved Son, who brings me great joy."* 18 We ourselves heard that voice from heaven when we were with him on the holy mountain.

1:17 Matt 17:5; Mark 9:7; Luke 9:35.

NOTES

1:16 ***We saw . . . with our own eyes.*** This term (*epoptai* [TG2030, ZG2228]) was also used of initiating followers into the Eleusinian mysteries (and in other mystery religions), and so some scholars (M. Green, Neyrey) see this as language used by the false teachers. However, the word was a common one for observers of an event, and the emphasis here is on the public nature of the apostolic witness, not the secret nature of mystery rites. The emphasis in the NLT translation is best.

1:17 ***when he received honor and glory.*** Why did Peter choose the Transfiguration rather than Jesus' resurrection as proof of the veracity of the belief in the later return of Christ? Moo (1996:74-75) provides four reasons for this "intimate relationship to the parousia": (1) Jesus' promise that some would not die before they saw the kingdom arrive in power

(Mark 9:1) pointed to a salvation-historical link between the Transfiguration, Resurrection, and Parousia. (2) The term "glory" here is normally used in the Synoptics in connection with Christ's return, thus forging a link between the Transfiguration and Parousia as similar events. (3) Later church tradition also linked the two events apologetically. (4) The transformation of Jesus' appearance in the Transfiguration revealed his true nature, and the final revelation of this "honor and glory" will not take place until the Parousia.

COMMENTARY

Peter's account of the Transfiguration here is closest to Matthew's narrative (e.g., only 1:17 and Matt 17:5 have "who brings me great joy"), but there are significant differences, and both Bauckham (1983:210) and Davids (2006:199) believe the wording here reflects independent tradition. It is most likely that Peter is drawing on his own memories rather than the synoptic accounts.

There is wide disagreement regarding the place of 1:16-21 in the structure of the letter. Since 1:16-18 (the Transfiguration) and 1:19-21 (the prophets) are events from the past, it is possible to place them with 1:12-15 as "a call to remember" (Schreiner 2003:311; G. Green 2008:217). However, it is clear that Peter's response to the heretics, who deny the supernatural intervention of God in the world and especially the Parousia, begins here. Thus, it is best to make the first section of that response to be 1:16-18, and to see this central section as continuing through 3:10. In 3:4 these "scoffers" say, "What happened to the promise that Jesus is coming again?" and use this as the linchpin for their claim that "everything has remained the same since the world was first created." They called the doctrine of Christ's future return little more than a "clever story" (1:16). Peter will respond to this in eight successive arguments—1:16-18, 19-21; 2:1-3, 4-10a, 10b-16, 17-22; 3:1-7, 8-10.

We do not know what the heretics said about other doctrines like Christology or soteriology, for Peter's response centers on their eschatology. Most likely these other issues were affected as well, but the primary teaching was their denial that God intervenes in this world, leading to a corresponding denial of Christ's second coming and of a final judgment. So this is Peter's opening salvo against their false doctrine. The topic of the Lord's return has already been broached in 1:11, which spoke of our "grand entrance into the eternal Kingdom of our Lord and Savior Jesus Christ." There the purpose was providing a reason for living a virtuous Christian life (eternal destruction versus eternal glory). Here the purpose is responding to the denial of the Parousia by the false teachers. Peter saw his experience of God's intervention into history via the Transfiguration as positive proof that there is a sovereign God who acts supernaturally. The future return of Christ is simply the second installment of Christ's transfiguration, which prefigures or proleptically anticipates the Parousia. There are three parts to this section: (1) the denial that this Parousia teaching was merely "clever stories" (1:16a); (2) the eyewitness testimony to the reality of the Transfiguration as a glorious appearance of the Christ (1:16b-17a); and (3) the witness of the divine voice affirming the sonship of Christ (1:17b-18).

At the start (1:16), Peter states, "We [all the apostles, not just Peter] were not making up clever stories." The term *muthos* [TG3454, ZG3680] refers to a "fable, invented story or myth," used often in the ancient world for fictional stories about the gods that centered on moral lessons rather than factual events. Moreover, he says these were not *sesophismenois* [TG4679, ZG5054], "craftily concocted" or even "deceitfully crafted." Some scholars (Neyrey, Bauckham) point out that the Epicureans despised "myths" as unedifying, and Philo denied that the biblical narratives were "myths." Put together, Peter was denying the false teachers' claims that the return of Christ was a fictional creation of the church, and he did so by relating the true story about a parallel event, the Transfiguration. Neither story could be labeled "clever fiction," for both were based on the testimony of eyewitnesses, one of whom was Peter himself. This is important for the historicity of the Gospels as well, for it is a third eyewitness claim alongside Luke 1:1-4 (a "careful account" based on "eyewitness reports") and John 19:35; 21:24 ("an eyewitness giving an accurate account").

Those like Bultmann and the Jesus Seminar who deny the historical trustworthiness of the Gospel accounts must reckon with these three claims. We are at the heart of what it means to be a Christian here. In our age where there are so many atheists denying any reality behind our belief in God, it is critical to realize that the Transfiguration and the Resurrection were actual events that hold up to historical scrutiny (see Blomberg, as well as Bock and Webb, on the historicity of the Gospels); furthermore, they provide evidence that there will be another powerful intervention of God yet to come—the Second Coming.

The apostolic witness was "about the powerful coming of our Lord Jesus Christ." In the Greek this is "power and coming," another hendiadys (a word pair that becomes a single idea; see note on 1:3) deliberately worded to remind the readers of the Second Coming, the main issue with the false teachers. The term *parousia* [TG3952, ZG4242] means "arrival" or "presence" and was often used of the "coming" of an emperor or a god. While some think this refers to the incarnation and ministry of Christ (Calvin), this became a technical term for the glorious return of Christ in the New Testament (Matt 24:27, 37, 39; 1 Cor 15:23; 1 Thess 3:13; 4:15; 2 Thess 2:1, 8; Jas 5:7-8; 1 John 2:28) and elsewhere in this epistle (3:4, 12). This event will be an act of "power" akin to God's raising Jesus from the dead (the "mighty power that raised Christ from the dead," Eph 1:19-20) and will involve the raising of the saints (1 Cor 15:51-53; 1 Thess 4:15-17), the destruction of God's enemies (1 Thess 5:1-3; Rev 19:11-21), and the final judgment (Rev 20:11-15).

Proof of the reality of the supernatural events linked with the Parousia is the apostolic witness: "We saw his majestic splendor with our own eyes." They (Peter, James, and John, the inner circle among the disciples) were "eyewitnesses" or "careful observers" (*epoptai* [TG2030, ZG2228]) who were actually there. Something physically "seen" cannot be a myth! The New Testament is absolutely clear on this topic. In Jesus the transcendent God became immanently involved in human history, and the supernatural entered the natural world. The disciples watched as Jesus stilled nature, healed the sick, cast out demons, and raised the dead. They were present when God revealed his majesty at the Transfiguration. They "were watching" as he "was taken up into a cloud" at his Ascension and were told by angels that "he will return from heaven in the same way you saw him go" (Acts 1:9-11). Jesus experienced a physical resurrection and a physical ascension, and he will return in glory physically.

"Majestic" is *megaleiotēs* [TG3168, ZG3484] in Greek; it has "divine overtones as it refers to God's grandeur and majesty" (G. Green 2008:221). At the Transfiguration,

Jesus' true nature as the one and only God shone through his incarnate flesh. Jesus was declared deity in 1:1, and now Peter describes seeing that divine splendor with their own eyes.

The emphasis on the Transfiguration as majesty and glory continues in 1:17, which speaks of this as the time "when he received honor and glory from God the Father," a scene called Jesus' "investiture" by Neyrey (1993:172) and Davids (2006:203-204). The two words may form a further hendiadys (as in 1:3, 8, 9, 10, 16), translated "glorious honor," but it may be best to keep them separate since the pair had attained a near-creedal status (Rom 2:7, 10; 1 Tim 1:17; Heb 2:7, 9; 1 Pet 1:7; Rev 4:9, 11; 5:12, 13; 7:12; 21:26). There is some discussion whether they emphasize the visible glory of the transfigured face and clothes or the implicit honor given by God's own message (see Bauckham 1983:217, who favors the former), but one wonders why we have to choose between the two. The entire scene centers on the glory of Christ. It could be that "honor" stresses his exaltation by God and "glory" his glorious appearance (so Mayor, M. Green, Kelly, Moo, Schreiner).

In the Gospels' presentation of the scene, the glory of Christ frames the story. At the outset, it is seen in his face, which "shone like the sun" (Matt 17:2), and then in his clothes that became "dazzling white" (Mark 9:3; Luke 9:29), as white as "light" (Matt 17:2). At the end of the story his glory is manifest in the shekinah cloud that envelopes them and the voice of God that comes from the cloud. (Shekinah is a Hebrew term designating God's glorious presence dwelling among his people; see Jastrow 2006:1573.) Both aspects recall the scene with Moses at Sinai, but in Moses's case he reflected the glory of God, while Christ radiated the divine glory from within, "the glory that was intrinsic to him as both Messiah and God" (Moo 1996:73).

The fatherhood of God is probably being stressed because he calls Jesus "my dearly loved Son." The divine message is introduced in a somber tone, literally, "when such a voice solemnly conveyed [lit., 'was brought'] to him"; this is language of divine revelation. The emphasis is on the solemn declaration of the transcendent, sovereign God. God is then called "the majestic glory," a title found only here in the New Testament but echoing Psalm 145:5, 12 [144:5, 12, LXX]: "your majestic, glorious splendor . . . the majesty and glory of your reign." While Bauckham (1983:218) is correct that there is little Moses typology in 1:16-18, this language is connected to the shekinah glory of God in the cloud scene of Mark 9:7, and Mark 9:7 alludes to Exodus 24:16, which says, "The glory of the LORD settled down on Mount Sinai, and the cloud covered it for six days." The glorious, majestic God was announcing the "glory and honor" that belongs to Jesus, thereby announcing that the shekinah glory belongs to him as well.

The message of the divine voice is closest to Matthew's rendition but is most likely Peter's own reminiscence: "This is my dearly loved Son, who brings me great joy." Mark 1:11 and Luke 3:22 read, "You are my dearly loved Son," while 1:17 and Matthew 17:5 read, "This is my dearly loved Son." So for Peter and Matthew the message is intended for the disciples (and the readers), being in effect an annunciation formula and an investiture of Jesus. The formula echoes Psalm 2:7 ("You are my son"), a coronation psalm for the Davidic king/Messiah, thereby showing that Jesus is King of kings (Rev 19:16). Psalm 2 was recognized as messianic in Jesus' day (4Q Flor 1:118–2:1; *Psalms of Solomon* 17:23-24), and in it the Messiah is declared the "Son of God" and anointed as king to subdue the nations who have rebelled against God. This psalm is often used in Revelation in terms of the Parousia and the judgment of the nations (Rev 2:28-29; 11:15-18; 12:5; 19:15), thereby "presenting Jesus as eschatological divine viceregent" and "eschatological judge" (Bauckham 1983:219). This fits well with Peter's purpose to prove the future reality of Jesus' coming by pointing to the past reality of his Transfiguration. The fact that Jesus is "the dearly loved" Son brings added emphasis to the "Son of God" language here, which throughout the New Testament portrays Jesus in terms of his unique sonship and relationship to the Father.

The second part of the divine announcement is "who brings me great joy" (lit., "in whom I am well pleased"), an allusion to Isaiah 42:1, "Look at my servant, whom I strengthen. He is my chosen one, who pleases me." This was the first of the Servant songs (Isa 42–54), and probably Jesus' elect status (implicit) as well as God's "great joy" in him (explicit) are both connoted here in 2 Peter. So Jesus is both messianic king and suffering servant, and as such he will be judge of all, conquering the antagonistic nations as well as the false teachers who have joined the nations as God's enemies.

Two aspects of the Transfiguration are highlighted in 1:18: the source of the divine investiture ("from heaven") and the place where the Transfiguration took place ("the holy mountain"). In 1:16, Peter and the apostles were observers of the Transfiguration, and now they are referred to as hearers as well (Moo 1996:73 speaks of "eyewitness" and "ear-witness"), reinforcing the emphasis on official witness to the Transfiguration and to the truthfulness of the Second Coming. The heavenly source of the voice is slightly different than the synoptic accounts where the voice comes from the cloud (Mark 9:7), but "from heaven" often speaks of divine origin, and that is implicit in the Gospel accounts as well. Since Jesus would return "from heaven" (1 Thess 4:16; Rev 19:11), this also is part of the connection between the Transfiguration and the Parousia. The stress on the "holy [sacred] mountain" would naturally recall for the reader the connection between Mount Sinai and the "high mountain" (Matt 17:1) where the Transfiguration took place, especially in Matthew, where mountains are emphasized as the place of divine revelation (cf. Matt 4:8; 5:1; 8:1; 14:23; 15:29; 28:16).

◆ 2. Proof of supernatural revelation: the place of prophecy (1:19-21)

19 Because of that experience, we have even greater confidence in the message proclaimed by the prophets. You must pay close attention to what they wrote, for their words are like a lamp shining in a dark place—until the Day dawns, and Christ the Morning Star shines* in your hearts. 20 Above all, you must realize that no prophecy in Scripture ever came from the prophet's own understanding,* 21 or from human initiative. No, those prophets were moved by the Holy Spirit, and they spoke from God.

1:19 Or *rises.* **1:20** Or *is a matter of one's own interpretation.*

NOTES

1:19 ***even greater confidence.*** Behind this is the comparative adjective *bebaioteron* [TG949, ZG1010], and scholars have interpreted it several ways: (1) as a comparative, saying that prophecy is a "more certain" argument for the Parousia than is the Transfiguration, since the latter was personal experience rather than divine revelation (Bigg, M. Green); (2) as an elative, that the apostles have a "very firm hold" on the truth (Bauckham 1983:223); (3) not really comparing anything, but simply a statement that the apostles are "ever more certain" about the truth value of prophecy (Davids, Schreiner). The best is a combination of the second and the third, as developed below. There is no real possibility that Peter would be saying the Transfiguration is less reliable than prophecy; both together prove the truth about the coming return of Christ.

message proclaimed by the prophets. Lit., "the prophetic word." There are many suggested meanings of this. Bauckham (1983:224) lists six: (1) OT messianic prophecy (Bigg, Mayor, Moffatt, Davids, Moo, Schreiner, Harvey and Towner); (2) the entire OT seen as messianic prophecy (Kelly, Bauckham, G. Green); (3) one particular messianic prophecy; (4) OT and NT prophecies; (5) 1:20–2:19; (6) the Transfiguration as prophecy (Neyrey). The likely thrust is one of the first two, more likely the first, for it is referring to the OT prophecies of the Day of the Lord and the end of this evil world.

shines in your hearts. This has been interpreted several ways since it seems strange in the context of the "rising" of the Morning Star: (1) Some scholars (Plumptre, Mayor) say it refers to present enlightenment of the "heart," perhaps modifying "realize/know" in 1:20 (so Callan 2006; against which see Porter and Pitts 2008), but the apocalyptic context makes this unlikely. (2) Others (e.g., Kelly) refer this to an inner "spiritualizing" or present spiritual experience of the apocalyptic hope of Christ's return. Yet the context is entirely apocalyptic, and this most likely refers to the Parousia itself. At that time, our partial knowledge of these final events of history that we have attained from prophecy will become complete, and we will know everything "in our hearts."

1:20 ***the prophet's own understanding.*** There are several different interpretations of this, as the grammar is ambiguous, reading, "No prophecy of Scripture comes from *one's own* interpretation." The ambiguous "one's own" could refer to the prophets in the past (so M. Green, Bauckham, Davids, Moo, G. Green, NLT, NIV, NET) or to understandings in the present (Kelly, Neyrey, Schreiner, NRSV, NKJV, REB, ESV). The latter would be a special denunciation of the false teachers who were using the prophecies to their own ends rather than properly allowing them to speak, especially on the Day of the Lord and the Parousia. This second possibility is attractive, but Bauckham (1983:229-230) shows that *idios* (one's own) in such Greek passages is almost always used of the "origin" of prophecies rather than of current interpretations, and so the first possibility (as in the NLT) is the more likely. In another sense both are still applicable, for Peter was contrasting the prophet's faithful understanding with the false teachers' false use of the prophecies.

1:21 ***they spoke from God.*** Some mss read "holy men spoke from God" (א A Ψ 33 Byz, followed by KJV, NKJV), but that is more likely added by later scribes as a further description of the "holy" prophets. The NLT reading follows 𝔓72 B P 1739, as do NRSV, NASB, NIV, TNIV, NET, ESV.

COMMENTARY

The first argument against the false teachers and their denial of the second coming of Christ is the reality of the Transfiguration (not a "clever story"), an event that Peter and the other apostles (Peter along with James and John, the inner circle

Christ had taken with him up the mount) had seen as eyewitnesses (1:16-18). If the transcendent God had intervened in human history by glorifying Christ in that way, of course he could glorify Christ at the end of history with his coming in final victory and judgment. The second argument is presented in 1:19-21. The message of 1:16-18 is that God does enter supernaturally into history; now Peter needs to argue that the prophecies of the Parousia are also correct. He does that by supporting the truth of divine prophecy.

Divine revelation has already been noted twice—in 1:14 Peter told of the revelation given to him (recounted in John 21:18-19) of his early demise, and in 1:16 he spoke of the revelation/prophecy that the apostolic teaching had made known to the readers about the return of Christ. It is this latter revelation that is the subject here. Peter supports the veracity of this by speaking of the divine origin of Old Testament prophecies and the implication of this for New Testament prophecies regarding the Second Coming. This is the second New Testament statement on the inspiration of Scripture, along with 2 Timothy 3:16-17. There are two parts to this short paragraph: (1) the need to "pay close attention" to the prophetic message, since it alone illumines this dark world (1:19); and (2) the assertion that the prophetic message did not come from the prophet himself but from God through the Holy Spirit (1:20-21).

Due to Peter's "experience" of witnessing Christ's transfiguration, he tells his readers that he and the other apostolic eyewitnesses have "even greater confidence" in God's revelation. "Confidence" (*bebaios* [TG949, ZG1010]) means to be "certain" that it is completely "reliable" or "trustworthy"; it has elative force here; Peter was saying in effect that he was "very sure" that God's revelation is "absolutely reliable." The "message proclaimed by the prophets" refers to Old Testament prophecies regarding the end of the age (see note on 1:19), and Peter was telling his readers that he was absolutely certain that these prophecies can be trusted, for they have come from God. The prophecy of Joel 2:28-32 ("I will pour out my Spirit upon all people"), used by Peter at Pentecost in Acts 2:17-21 (also Acts 3:21), is one case in point (see also Isa 2:2; Hos 3:5; Joel 1:15; 2:1; Amos 5:18; Mic 4:1; Zech 14:1).

Since the truth of Christ's return is proven to be completely reliable by both the Transfiguration and Old Testament prophecy, we all must pay extremely "close attention" to what is being said. The literal command is "Do well to pay heed" and is a mild injunction encouraging them to center on the prophetic teaching. The idea of "heeding" or "paying attention" is true here at the macro level (following all of Scripture) and the micro level (spiritual vigilance due to the soon return of Christ). The latter is a special emphasis of the Olivet discourse in Matthew (the parables of the faithful servant, the 10 bridesmaids, and the talents all teach constant readiness in light of the master's unexpected return), and much of the rest of the New Testament demands a deeper spiritual walk in light of the Parousia (e.g., Rom 13:12; 1 Cor 15:58; 2 Cor 5:10; Phil 4:5; 1 Thess 5:2; Heb 10:37; Jas 5:8; 1 Pet 4:7; Rev 16:15). To "heed" something means both to understand its meaning and to follow its mandates. For us it means both deep Bible study and obedience.

The reason for heeding Scripture is that it is "like a lamp shining in a dark place." Psalm 119:105 says, "Your word is a lamp to guide my feet and a light for my path," and Proverbs 20:27 states, "The LORD's light penetrates the human spirit, exposing every hidden motive" (see also Wis 18:4; *4 Ezra* 12:42; Davids 2006:208). In first-century homes an oil lamp was the only light people had, and they counted on it to stave off the darkness and to guide their way through the dark paths. The "dark" or "gloomy place" is often the netherworld, but here it refers to the darkness of the human mind under sin. Travelers cannot make their way in the darkness until a light is there to guide them over the rough terrain. For us, only the word of God can do that, and it is sad that so few Christians study the word deeply. It is like having a powerful flashlight and failing to use it when the lights go out.

Peter then describes the prophetic "words" as lasting "until the Day dawns, and Christ the Morning Star shines in your hearts." This may allude to Numbers 24:17, "A star will rise from Jacob; a scepter will emerge from Israel," Balaam's prophecy of a future ruler who would defeat Israel's enemies. This passage was understood messianically by many Jews (*Testament of Levi* 18:3; *Testament of Judah* 24:1; 1QM 11:6-7; cf. Bauckham 1983:226). A similar messianic image is found in Malachi 4:2, "The Sun of Righteousness will rise with healing in his wings" and destroy the wicked. The dawning of "the Day" could refer to the Day of the Lord, but it may be referring more broadly of the coming eschatological age as a whole, since this context centers on the positive image of the coming of the light more than the negative image of destruction (Bauckham 1983:225). Of course, the Day of the Lord is still present (implicit in the imagery from Numbers and Malachi), and the idea of judgment will be central in 2:4, 9b-10; 3:7, 11-12.

The rising of the Morning Star clearly refers to the Parousia of Christ. Revelation also presents the idea of the glory of Christ coming to conquer all and establish righteousness on the earth. Revelation 2:28 and 22:16 use the imagery of the "bright morning star" (i.e., Venus), a symbol of sovereignty found on Roman shields and used by many emperors. The interesting point in 2 Peter is that the star "shines [lit., "rises" as in Num 24:17] in your hearts." As stated in the note on 1:19, this means that our "hearts" (or minds, since the "heart" in Scripture often connotes the mind) at the Parousia will finally know "the whole truth and nothing but the truth." Prophecy has given us part of the picture, but there is much we will not understand until Christ returns. This is implicit in 1 Corinthians 13:9, 12, which says, "Even the gift of prophecy reveals only part of the whole picture! . . . Now we see things imperfectly, . . . but then we will see everything with perfect clarity. All that I know now is partial and incomplete, but then I will know everything completely."

The next two verses (1:20-21) provide the second comprehensive statement in the New Testament on biblical inspiration, along with 2 Timothy 3:16-17. "You must realize" translates an imperatival participle: "Know this." It does not mean Peter was giving them new information they did not previously possess, because the Spirit's inspiring the prophets is clearly stated in 1 Peter 1:10-12 and was widely understood among early Christians. Rather, Peter wanted them to realize it anew in light of the claims of the false teachers. These heretics gave their own "understandings" without recourse to the inspired statements of Scripture; but the prophets, Peter says clearly, refused to give their "own understanding" but relied on God entirely to provide the meaning of his revelations to them.

The Greek word for "understanding" (*epilusis* [TG1955, ZG2146]) refers to the "explanation" or "interpretation" of ecstatic revelations like dreams, riddles, or prophecy. Harvey and Towner (2009:71) show that this charge of personal interpretation was made about false prophets in the Old Testament, who spoke the "foolishness made up in their own lying hearts" (Jer 14:14) and who "do not speak for the LORD" (Jer 23:16), and so, in effect, have "seen nothing" (Ezek 13:3). So the emphasis is on the divine origin of the prophecies and of their understanding by the prophets themselves, in contradistinction to the false teachers of Peter's day. Peter was saying that their creative rereading of the Old Testament was a denial of divine inspiration. This is significant for us today. We are required by God to interpret his word as accurately as we can (2 Tim 2:15, "correctly explains the word of truth"), and shallow sermons are in themselves also a denial of inspiration, for those who preach them in effect are saying that they don't care what God meant to say in his word!

In 1:21, Peter contrasts "human initiative" (lit., "human will") with divine inspiration from the Spirit. The human will is antithetical to divine truth, as exemplified in the flesh/Spirit conflict of Romans 8:1-13. Prophets were supposed to focus on the mind of God and speak only the message of God. Interestingly, Peter has the same verb (*pherō* [TG5342, ZG5770]) in both 1:21 and 1:17, the "voice conveyed [or "carried"] to him," which I called (see the commentary there) "language of divine revelation." To bring the meaning of that word in 1:17 to 1:21, Peter was saying, "No prophecy was carried out by the human will, but human beings were carried along by the Holy Spirit" (so Davids 2006:213). Prophets refused to fall back on their own "initiative" or understanding, but at all times they made certain that what they said came directly from God.

Most likely the false teachers of Peter's day, like the later Ebionites, a group of Jewish Christians of the second century, rejected the prophets of the Old Testament as speaking for themselves rather than God (Methodius of Olympus *Symposium on Virginity* 8.10; Epiphanius *Panarion* 30.18.5). So Peter responded by asserting that the prophets "were moved by the Holy Spirit" and so "spoke from God." The present participle *pheromenoi* [TG5342, ZG5770] is durative, stressing that the Spirit "continually moved" or "carried them along" as he inspired their prophetic ministry. Michael Green (1987:91) sees a sailing metaphor here, picturing the prophets "raising their sails," which are then "filled" and "carried along" by the Spirit. For those with a Gentile background, the idea would be similar to being possessed by the gods; for Jewish Christians, it would be being "filled with the Holy Spirit" (Eph 5:18), but in a special way connected to divine inspiration for the writers of canonical Scripture. The Old Testament often speaks of the Spirit's place in prophetic inspiration (Num 11:25; 1 Sam 10:5-6; 18:10; 19:20-24; Neh 9:30; Isa 61:1; Joel 2:28-32), as does the New Testament (Luke 1:41, 67; Acts 1:16; 19:6; 28:25; Eph 3:5; Heb 3; 10:15; 1 Pet 1:11). Thus, the prophets spoke not for themselves but "from God," as their prophecies entirely bore witness to the divine agency speaking through them. This is not the dictation view of inspiration, however. The Spirit guided their hand, yet the words reflected their personality, background, and way of speaking. Moo (1996:85-86) speaks of the doctrine of "concurrence," as the writers "genuinely spoke their own words" and at the same time employed "just those words that God wanted them to use." There is both a divine and a human element in Scripture.

B. Condemnation of the False Teachers (2:1-22)

1. The rise and coming judgment of the false teachers (2:1-3)

But there were also false prophets in Israel, just as there will be false teachers among you. They will cleverly teach destructive heresies and even deny the Master who bought them. In this way, they will bring sudden destruction on themselves. [2]Many will follow their evil teaching and shameful immorality. And because of these teachers, the way of truth will be slandered. [3]In their greed they will make up clever lies to get hold of your money. But God condemned them long ago, and their destruction will not be delayed.

NOTES

2:1b-3 ***will be . . . will cleverly teach . . . will bring . . . will follow . . . will be slandered . . . will make up.*** These future tenses occur in a context where the false teachers seem to be present in the church, as can be seen in the present tenses in 2:12-13 ("[They] are like unthinking animals. . . . They do not understand. . . . They love to indulge. . . . They are a disgrace . . . even as they eat with you"). Four options for interpreting the future tenses have arisen: (1) 2 Peter is a pseudonymous work, and a later author is quoting the predictions of Peter and other apostles, which are now coming to fruition after Peter's death (Bauckham 1983:239; Harrington 2003:261); but this is not likely a pseudonymous work (see Introduction, "Author"). (2) The false teachers have not yet come, but they have infested other churches and may arrive soon (Bigg 1901:231), yet the present tenses and tenor of the chapter favor their presence now. (3) Peter was alluding to earlier Christian prophecies about the coming of false teachers in the last days (Mark 13:22), so he wanted his readers to know that the arrival of heretics should not be thought unexpected (Moo, Schreiner). However, there are no formal hints that these were earlier prophecies. (4) Present and future can be intertwined, with differences used for purely rhetorical purposes in strong eschatological or exhortatory contexts, and this likely is one of those times (G. Green 2008:238-239; Davids 2006:218). A combination of the third and fourth is probably best. Peter was saying that the future arrival of false prophets/teachers is now here, and the people of God must be ready for them. Harvey and Towner (2009:76) explain, "Moving effectively between tenses, Peter warns us of just such an unpleasant reality, a threat to the purity of the church that had occurred before and will occur again."

COMMENTARY

All of chapter 1 prepared for Peter's primary purpose of exposing and condemning the group of false teachers who had so corrupted the churches to which he was writing. In 1:3-11 he challenged the readers to live godly lives, contrary to the immorality and evil lifestyles promulgated and demonstrated in the heretics. In 1:12-15 Peter asked them to remember these truths and obey them, important reminders in light of the false ethics taught by these evil people. In 1:16-21 Peter introduced one of the chief heresies—their rejection of God's intervention in this world, specifically their denial of a future Parousia (which will be combated further in ch 3). Davids (2006:217) sees a chiastic pattern in 1:16–2:3 that emphasizes the contrasting link with the past:

A. New Testament prophets (1:16-18)
    B. Old Testament prophets (1:19-21)
    B′. Old Testament false prophets (2:1a)
A′. New Testament false prophets (2:1b-3)

So here in chapter 2, Peter warns his readers that these pernicious people were replicating the false prophets that plagued Israel in the past (2:1-3), bringing the same judgment upon themselves as was heaped upon the fallen angels and the people of Noah's day (2:4-6, in contrast to the salvation experienced by the godly, 2:7-10a). Their certain judgment was caused by their arrogance and immoral lifestyles (2:10b-16), and in their folly they seduced many in the church and led them into their own apostate state (2:17-22).

This chapter begins with "But . . . also," linking 2:1-3 closely with 1:19-21, where Peter argued for the validity of divine revelation on the basis of God speaking through the Old Testament prophets and the implications of that for New Testament prophecy. His point was that the prophetic message of old came directly from God through the Holy Spirit, who inspired the prophets; thus, those revealed truths must be accepted as completely reliable and true. Now the attention shifts to the false prophets in Peter's churches. While we should "pay close attention" to the inspired prophets and their message, we must at the same time realize that false prophets usually exist side by side with true prophets. Peter was making the point that this was exactly the case in ancient Israel. Bauckham (1983:238) provides a threefold description of their activity: (1) There was no divine authority behind their messages; (2) they pretended their proclamation was "good news" because they altered the prophetic warnings of judgment to a false promise of peace and security; (3) they were condemned by God for their lies.

False prophets appeared often in Old Testament times. The Torah warned of prophets who would utilize signs and wonders to seduce the people to worship other gods (Deut 13:1-5), and 1 Kings 22:5-28 tells of a group of 400 prophets who encouraged the king to go to war but were accused by the true prophet Micaiah of speaking with a "lying spirit." Isaiah (Isa 9:15; 28:7-13; 29:10-12; 44:20) and especially Jeremiah (Jer 2:8, 26-28; 4:9; 5:31; 6:13; 11:21; 14:13-16; 18:18-23; 23:9-40; 27:9-18; 28:1–29:32) and Ezekiel (Ezek 13:9; 22:28) frequently encountered false prophets. There was a huge problem with lying prophets in the past, and it had raised its ugly head again in Peter's day. We might note seven characteristics of false prophets in the Old Testament (Osborne 1991:210-211): (1) divination, forbidden in Deuteronomy 18:9-14 (cf. Jer 14:14; Mic 3:7); (2) their unfulfilled prophecies (cf. 1 Kgs 22:28; Isa 30:8; Jer 28:9); (3) desire to please the rulers and the people rather than speak for God (Jer 8:11; Mic 3:5, 11); (4) lack of call from God, thus drawing the people away from God (Deut 13:1-3; Jer 28:15; cf. Amos 7:14-15); (5) failure to uphold the Torah and remain faithful to its regulations (Jer 6:10-15; 8:9-10); (6) lack of authentication by a miracle (1 Kgs 18); (7) immoral character that invalidated the message—seen in lies (Jer 8:11), drunkenness (Isa 28:7), and immorality (Jer 23:14). These are the types of things Peter wanted his churches to see in the false teachers and false prophets among them.

It is possible that these heretics did not claim prophetic authority (so Bauckham, Moo), for Peter calls them "false teachers" (*pseudodidaskaloi* [TG5572, ZG6015]), a term that appears only here in the New Testament. But there are semantic equivalents elsewhere: "false brother" (2 Cor 11:26, NLT mg; Gal 2:4, NLT mg), "deceitful workers" (2 Cor 11:13), "false witness" (cf. "lie/lying," NLT; Matt 15:19; 26:59; 1 Cor

15:15), "false messiah" (Matt 24:24; Mark 13:22). The problem of false teachers comes up frequently in the New Testament (e.g., Paul's prophecy to the Ephesian elders in Acts 20:29-31, which came to pass later and is referred to in the letter to the Colossians and in the Pastoral Epistles).

Peter tells us seven things about these false teachers. First, they "cleverly teach destructive heresies" (2:1). The verb *pareisagō* [TG3919, ZG4206] means to "bring in" or "introduce," but in a negative context like this can connote "secret" or "clever" infiltration of false ideas into a group (like the Judaizers in Gal 2:4). In a similar vein the noun *hairesis* [TG139, ZG146] refers to the distinctive views of a particular group like the Sadducees or Pharisees (Acts 5:17; 15:5). So its basic meaning is sectarian beliefs in general, but again in a context like this it connotes dangerous or false tenets, "heresies." This must be defined carefully. A "heresy" is not just any doctrine that is disputed between Christian groups. Believers can debate issues like the timing of the return of Christ, the charismatic gifts, or predestination without using this terminology. "Heresy" concerns the cardinal doctrines of the faith, the essential truths, issues like the Trinity, the deity of Christ, the substitutionary atonement of Christ, the resurrection of Christ, and the return of Christ. On other issues we can agree to disagree, but on the essentials the very reality of the Christian faith is at stake. To teach contrary to these truths is to promote "destructive heresies"—with "destruction" (*apōleia* [TG684, ZG724]) appearing three times in 2:1b-3 for emphasis. To deny or change these cardinal beliefs will bring God's "destruction" down upon one's head. To embrace such false teachings is to commit apostasy (see on 2:20-21 below, where this issue will be discussed) and face what Hebrews 10:27 calls "the terrible expectation of God's judgment and the raging fire that will consume his enemies."

Second, these heretics have denied "the Master," meaning that their false doctrine constitutes a denial of the God of the Bible. One question to ask of the cult movements of our day is whether their "god" is the same as the God of the Bible. In 2:1 he is called *despotēs* [TG1203, ZG1305] (master, slaveowner), meaning "Master, Sovereign Lord" when used of God (Luke 2:29; Acts 4:24; Rev 6:10) or Christ (Jude 4) and denoting their absolute authority and power over creation. Here, the "Master" is probably Christ, who "bought" or "purchased" us with his blood (1 Cor 6:20; Rev 1:5; 5:9; 14:3-4). This is redemption language, referring to the payment of Christ's blood to "purchase" us for God and free us from the bondage of sin. There are two levels on which the "denial" has taken place, first in terms of adherence to the false teaching, and second by their profligate and decadent behavior, the "shameful immorality" of 2:2. This latter will be emphasized in the rest of the chapter.

Third, they "bring sudden destruction" down on their heads (2:1). The idea of "sudden" or "swift" (*tachinēn* [TG5031, ZG5442]) action stresses the imminence of judgment that is coming soon, as well as the certainty of that judgment (Moo 1996:93). These evil leaders were convinced that God no longer intervened in this world (see on 1:16-21) and that there would be neither a second coming of Christ nor a final judgment. Their arrogance was foolhardy and completely wrong. Their destruction was nigh. In this letter Peter tries to maintain a critical balance between imminence (2:1) and a delayed or distant event (3:8-9). Their judgment was already beginning but will fully come at God's ordained time. It is sure, and it will be final.

Fourth, they will seduce "many" who will "follow their evil teaching and shameful immorality" (2:2). The verb (*exakoloutheō* [TG1811, ZG1979]) literally means to "follow out," with the idea that they have moved "outside" the church to pursue these false ideas and conduct. Their behavior is described as *aselgeia* [TG766, ZG816], "licentious, lewd conduct," stressing sexual profligacy devoid of moral constraint (cf. Rom 13:13; 2 Cor 12:21; Gal 5:19; Eph 4:19). This type of libertine or indecent action was even recognized in the pagan world as wrong. It is clear that sexual sin is a major hallmark of this heretical movement (2:7, 10, 12-14; 3:3), and undoubtedly part of its appeal came from the extent to which it condoned, indeed encouraged, immoral activity.

Fifth, "the way of truth will be slandered" (lit., "blasphemed") or "reviled, defamed" (2:2). Non-Christians were looking for reasons to denounce believers, and these heretics were giving them the ammunition they wanted. Constant lies were being spread about Christianity in the early centuries, such as cannibalism (from the Eucharist) and hatred of others (due to intolerance for Greco-Roman temple practices). These people were making this easy by bringing shame to the cause of Christ. When Christ's name is slandered, it should be in spite of Christian conduct, not because of their sinful behavior (Rom 2:24; 1 Tim 5:14; 6:1; Titus 2:5, 8), and the good deeds of the saints should prove these lies to be wrong (1 Pet 2:12; 4:3-4). The "way (*hodos* [TG3598, ZG3847]) of truth" refers not just to right beliefs but to right behavior or "way" of life. As in 2:1, Peter blends together correct doctrine (truth) with correct conduct (way). As James 1:22 says, God's people must be both listeners and doers.

Sixth, "in their greed they will make up clever lies" (2:3), a common characteristic of all cult leaders. They're in it for the money! It is a get-rich-quick scam, and it usually works (see 2:14, "They are well trained in greed"). Paul emphasizes this about the false teachers in Asia Minor (1 Tim 6:5, 9-10). Greed (*pleonexia* [TG4124, ZG4432]) has from time immemorial been a major factor in the development of new religions or philosophies (for Hellenistic comments regarding the desire for gain among sophists and others, see G. Green 2008:244-245). Paul calls greed idolatry in Ephesians 5:5 and Colossians 3:5 because in reality the accumulation of wealth becomes one's god. In this sense these heretics were apostates to avarice as well as to sensuality and false doctrines. As a result, they "make up clever lies to get hold of your money." The verb *emporeuomai* [TG1710, ZG1864] means "to engage in a business transaction" and in a negative context like this can connote the "misrepresentation of merchandise" (BAGD 324). Louw and Nida (L&N 759) call this "exploiting by deception" and translate "to take advantage of someone by implying that what is offered is more valuable than it is." In other words, this was a monetary swindle, and the merchandise they were foisting on an unsuspecting public was "clever lies" (*plastois logois* [TG4112, ZG4422]) or teaching that is "made up, fabricated, filled with pretentious ideas." In other words, they knew they were lying and did so deliberately to get rich.

Seventh, their end is certain: "God condemned them long ago, and their destruction will not be delayed" (2:3). This point was already made in 2:1 ("sudden destruction"), but here it is developed further. This is courtroom language, with judgment pronounced from the very throne of God. We are not told when exactly this "long ago" was, whether it refers to the Old Testament condemnation of false prophets or perhaps to the omniscience of God, who knew about them and condemned them from the very beginning of creation. The emphasis is the certainty of coming judgment. The heretics in 3:4 claim that God's intervention has never been experienced and is never coming, so they feel secure in their pretensions. Peter says that this is preposterous, for there will be no "delay" when God acts. Literally, the second clause is, "their destruction is not slumbering." The picture is that of God becoming drowsy and falling asleep on his throne, failing to act. Such a view is insanity! Their condemnation will lead to their destruction, and the sentence has already been pronounced, soon to come to effect.

◆ 2. The condemnation of the ungodly and the rescue of the righteous (2:4-10a)

**[4]For God did not spare even the angels
who sinned. He threw them into hell,* in
gloomy pits of darkness,* where they are
being held until the day of judgment.
[5]And God did not spare the ancient
world—except for Noah and the seven
others in his family. Noah warned the
world of God's righteous judgment. So
God protected Noah when he destroyed
the world of ungodly people with a vast
flood. [6]Later, God condemned the cities of
Sodom and Gomorrah and turned them
into heaps of ashes. He made them an
example of what will happen to ungodly
people. [7]But God also rescued Lot out of
Sodom because he was a righteous man
who was sick of the shameful immorality
of the wicked people around him. [8]Yes,
Lot was a righteous man who was tormented
in his soul by the wickedness he
saw and heard day after day. [9]So you see,
the Lord knows how to rescue godly
people from their trials, even while keeping
the wicked under punishment until
the day of final judgment. [10]He is especially
hard on those who follow their own
twisted sexual desire, and who despise
authority.**

2:4a Greek *Tartarus.* **2:4b** Some manuscripts read *in chains of gloom.*

NOTES

2:4-10a This is all one single conditional sentence, from "For [if] God" in 2:4 through "[then] the Lord knows" in 2:9 (and on to the end of 2:10a). No English translation can keep this lengthy sentence and still be comprehensible. All break this into separate sentences. There have been two ways to represent the conditional nature of the sentence. Many translations (NASB, NRSV, NIV, TNIV, ESV) repeat the "if" clause before each of the examples (2:4, 5, 6, 7) and place "then" or "and if so" at the beginning of 2:9. Others (NLT, JB, NEB) omit the "if" and begin 2:9 with "so you see" or "thus." Both ways emphasize the fact that 2:9-10a form a conclusion from the examples in 2:4-8.

2:4 *gloomy pits of darkness.* There is a text-critical problem as to whether Peter wrote *sirois* [TG4617.1, ZG4938], meaning "caves" or "pits" (א A B C, so NASB, NIV, NLT, Moo, Davids) or *seirais* [TG4577, ZG4937], meaning "chains" (𝔓72 K P Ψ, so KJV, NRSV, TEV, TNIV, NET, ESV, Comfort, Bauckham, G. Green, Harvey and Towner). The manuscript evidence is fairly balanced, but it is slightly more likely that later scribes introduced the term from Jude 6 ("chained") while Peter used the term found in the Book of the Watchers in *1 Enoch* 10:4, 12; 18:11, etc., where they were consigned to "dungeons." Therefore, "pits" is to be preferred here.

2:6 ***an example of what will happen to ungodly people.*** There are two possible text-critical readings for this: "people who live in an ungodly way" (a verb, *asebein* [TG764, ZG814], "to act ungodly"; so ℵ A C K); or "ungodly people" (a noun, *asebesin* [TG765A, ZG815]; so 𝔓72 B P). In a difficult decision (the manuscript evidence again is fairly even), the noun makes more intrinsic sense in this context (so Mayor, Kelly, Bauckham).

2:9 ***keeping the wicked under punishment.*** The difficulty is the present-tense participle *kolazomenous* [TG2849, ZG3134], "keeping under punishment" or as in the NIV, "while continuing their punishment." Does this connote a present state of punishment or a future (final) judgment? Some (Bigg, Kelly, Moo) believe this is present judgment along the lines of Rom 1:18-32; God is allowing the terrible results of human depravity to be experienced by sinners. Others (M. Green, Bauckham, Davids, Schreiner, G. Green) see the present participle used rhetorically to emphasize the certainty of final judgment. It may well be best to take a middle position—present sufferings are a harbinger of the final torment awaiting those who turn against God.

COMMENTARY

This paragraph builds on 2:3 (the claim by the heretics that God has not acted in the past) and consists of a single lengthy conditional sentence, beginning with "For [if] God" in verse 4 (see note) and continuing with "[then] the Lord" in 2:9, ending with 2:10a. The basic message, then, is that since God did not fail to judge sinners in the past (2:4-5a, 6—fallen angels, the world of Noah's day, Sodom and Gomorrah) and to rescue the godly (2:5b, 7-8—Noah, Lot), then of course God will rescue the godly today and judge the wicked (2:9-10a). Note the chiasm: A. past judgment, B. past rescue, B'. present rescue, A'. present and future judgment. The first paragraph (2:1-3) says that the judgment of the false teachers is certain because of their wicked lives and their evil lies. This paragraph (2:4-10a) stresses the certainty further by showing that God's condemnation of the wicked and rescue of the godly definitely took place in the past and so is guaranteed now and in the future. Peter is building on Jude 5-7 here (see the Introduction, "Author"). Jude stresses God's judgment on the Egyptians, the fallen angels, and Sodom and Gomorrah. Peter replaces Egypt with Noah and places them in chronological order, adding the preservation of the godly to Jude's coverage. The purpose is to emphasize both aspects of God's judicial activity and to stress the choice his readers must make: Follow the heretics to destruction or turn to God for salvation.

The first of the examples of God's past condemnation (2:4) centers on "the angels who sinned." Some suggest this alludes to Isaiah 14:12-14 or Ezekiel 28:1-19, but these passages are not really about Satan but about the kings of Babylon and Tyre, respectively (see Moo 1996:101, 111-112; Jones 2006). It is much more likely that this is the same event discussed in the comments on 1 Peter 3:19 and Jude 6, namely, Genesis 6:1-4, in which the "sons of God" came to earth, cohabited with women, and produced children who became "the heroes and famous warriors of ancient times" (Gen 6:4). Fallen angels as "sons of God" fits the use of this phrase for celestial beings in Job 1:6; 2:1; 38:7; Psalms 29:1; 89:6. Moreover, Jewish tradition frequently discussed the sin of the angels who had sexual intercourse with human women (*1 Enoch* 6:1–7:6; 9:8–10:16; 12:1-4; 15:4-12; 21:1-10; *2 Enoch* 18:2-9; *2 Baruch* 56:7-16; *Jubilees* 5:1-11; 10:1-13; *Testament of Naphtali* 3:1-5). Second Temple Jewish writings said that this was the basis of human wickedness (especially in the *1 Enoch* passages) and led directly to the Flood. The defeat of Satan and his angels and their expulsion from heaven is narrated in Revelation 12:7-9, though I think that occurred before Genesis 6 in the primordial past, before the serpent entered the garden (see Osborne 2002:468-469).

Because of their evil God refused to "spare" them, that is, did not show them any mercy whatsoever. Instead, he cast them into "hell, in gloomy pits of darkness, where they are being held until the day of judgment." "Hell" does not represent Greek *gehenna* [TG1067, ZG1147] or *hadēs* [TG86, ZG87], the usual terms, but *tartaroō* [TG5020, ZG5434], "thrown into Tartarus," the place in Greek mythology that was the lowest dungeon of the underworld, to which rebellious gods and evil mortals were consigned. Peter's use of this fits the Hellenistic cast of his epistle but also stems from the use of this term in the Septuagint at Job 40:20; 41:24; Proverbs 30:16; and in Jewish writings (*1 Enoch* 20:2; *Sibylline Oracles* 2:303). This term also fits the added "gloomy pits of darkness," similar to the "bottomless pit" of Revelation 9:1-2; 11:7; 17:8, the home of the demons, viewed in Jewish tradition as a "prison" where demons are chained (*1 Enoch* 10:4-6; 18:9-16; *Jubilees* 5:3-11; cf. Luke 8:31). The "day of judgment" is the final judgment, the "great white throne" of Revelation 20:11-15, when the demons and all who oppose God are thrown into the lake of fire. That day is a certain event. (See Charles 2005 for the use of these fallen angels to warn the readers of God's incontrovertible judgment for such wickedness.)

How do we reconcile this picture of fallen angels imprisoned in dark dungeons with the picture in the Gospels and Epistles of demons free to roam the world, possess people, and do all kinds of mischief against God and his people? Are there two kinds of demons, lucky ones who are free and unlucky ones who are in prison? That is unlikely. Probably the best way to understand this is to see in 2:4 and Jude 6 a metaphor for a deeper reality. When Satan and his followers were cast out of heaven, this world became their prison. When Satan is called "the god of this world" (2 Cor 4:4), we need to understand that he is only the "god" of his prison block. In Luke 8:31 when the demons ask Christ not to cast them into the abyss, it refers to the place of final judgment. This twofold thrust fits Peter's statement here, for they are currently in the abyss (this world as their prison) awaiting the final abyss (eternal punishment).

The second example of divine judgment (2:5) is the people of Noah's time, the generation of the Flood (Gen 6:5–7:24). This was the quintessential judgment scene of the Old Testament, and Peter will use it again in 3:5-7 to show the error of the heretics that taught that God has never intervened sovereignly in this world. As with the fallen angels, God "did not spare the ancient world" when it fell into serious sin after the fallen angels had introduced wickedness in a new way (Gen 6:1-4). That harbinger of final judgment was proof positive that divine judgment was a reality, and therefore the coming condemnation and destruction of the heretics and their followers was also a guaranteed event (2:1b, 1d, 3b). God has already poured out his judgment in ancient times and surely will do so again. The Flood depicted not just judgment on heavenly beings (2:4) but now a judgment that encompassed the whole world, the world of humanity, not just the earth itself, though both are intended (so Bauckham 1983:250). This coming judgment will be universal, and none will escape who have turned against God.

First Peter 3:19-20 also connects the Flood with the fall of the angels, and it stresses the "patience of God" that allows any human being to be saved. Here Peter reflects that tradition by relating how God "protected Noah" and brought him and his family through that ordeal. The message here in 2 Peter 2 is clear—choose whether to follow the heretics (and suffer a similar destruction like the Flood) or turn to and follow Christ (and be saved). God "protected" ("kept, preserved, guarded") Noah from harm "when he destroyed the world of ungodly people with a vast flood" (2:5). The Bible is uniform in the belief that the Flood destroyed all humanity, a picture of the fact that no "ungodly" person will escape. Interestingly, Peter emphasizes that seven other family members were saved with Noah (his wife, three sons, and their wives; cf. 1 Pet 3:20, "Eight people were saved"). Many have seen numerical symbolism in both passages, with "eight" the "eighth" day or resurrection (deliverance and new creation) theme. That is an interesting possibility, but in neither epistle is there much evidence for such a motif. Most likely the emphasis here is similar to 1 Peter, that "few" were saved, and even though Christians are a real minority in this world, their final deliverance and victory are assured. God's people should never be discouraged because they are outnumbered.

Noah is depicted as "a preacher of righteousness" (NLT, "warned the world of God's righteous judgment," 2:5), with "righteousness" likely having a double meaning as "righteous judgment" (NLT) but also repentance so as to attain a state of being right with God (so also Schreiner 2003:339). The Old Testament does not depict Noah as preaching to his contemporaries, but he undoubtedly did so, and Jewish tradition (*Sibylline Oracles* 1:128-198; *Jubilees* 7:20-29; Josephus *Antiquities* 1.74) relates Noah's attempts to warn the people and turn them to God. This is a similar theme as in the book of Revelation, where the beleaguered saints respond to severe persecution not by fighting back (Rev 13:9-10) but by bold witness (Rev 11:3-7), as indeed the persecuted church has done in China and Africa today.

The third example of sudden judgment—Sodom and Gomorrah (2:6; Gen 19:23-29)—proceeds naturally from the others. In keeping with his later argument in 3:6-10, Peter moves from water to fire. After the Flood, God promised never again to destroy the world by water, giving the rainbow as a covenant sign and promise (Gen 9:11-17). The next judgment will be a judgment of fire (3:7, 10), necessary to purge this world of sin forever, and so Sodom and Gomorrah are the perfect examples. Jude 5-7 has a different order and slightly different emphasis than Peter here. Jude moves from Egypt to the fallen angels to Sodom and Gomorrah (omitting Noah) with the emphasis entirely on divine judgment for wicked conduct. The sexual nature of Sodom's sin fits the licentious conduct of the false teachers and so is a perfect example here. Peter here stresses the two sides—judgment of the ungodly versus deliverance for the righteous. He wanted his readers to understand at the deepest level that they must not join false teachers in their folly, for judgment will definitely come upon those who do so.

Genesis 19 explicitly says that destruction fell upon Sodom and Gomorrah because of their terribly wicked actions. Peter here presupposes this and centers upon the cities' judgment, relating how God "turned them into heaps of ashes." Genesis 19:24, 28 states that "the LORD rained down fire and burning sulfur" resulting in "smoke [rising] from the cities like smoke from a furnace." Peter paraphrases this by saying all that remained were "heaps of ashes" (thought to be still evident in the Dead Sea area in the first century; cf. Wis 10:7; Josephus *War* 4.483-485). Total destruction of the people and the buildings in fiery judgment was an apt metaphor for the coming fiery judgment that the heretics were denying, but which they were doomed to experience themselves. So Peter adds that this was intended as an "example of what will happen to ungodly people" (2:6). This is borne out by the frequent references to the destruction of Sodom and Gomorrah in the Old Testament (Deut 29:23; Isa 1:8-10; 13:19; Jer 23:14; 49:18; 50:39-40; Ezek 16:46-58; Amos 4:11; Zeph 2:9), in Jewish writings (3 Macc 2:4-5; Wis 10:7; *Jubilees* 20:5), and in the New Testament (Matt 10:15; 11:23-24; Rom 9:29).

As with Noah in 2:5, Peter stresses the positive rescue of "Lot . . . a righteous man" (2:7) to counterbalance the judgment of the "ungodly"; Noah and Lot are "rescued" or "delivered, saved" while their contemporaries are annihilated. Some have noted the difficulty with the reference to Lot's "righteous" character here, because in the Genesis account (Gen 19:1-38) Lot does not appear very righteous. When the men of Sodom wanted to sodomize the two angels, Lot was ready to hand his two daughters over to them in order to placate those evil men (Gen 19:8). When the angels told Lot to take his family and flee the coming conflagration, Lot "hesitated" (Gen 19:16), vacillating over the decision. The angels had to force him to take his family and flee. Still, Lot never turned against God, he did try to protect the angels and give them hospitality, and he did grow "sick of the shameful immorality," begging the townspeople not to do "such a wicked thing" (Gen 19:7). The Greek has Lot "distressed by the shameful conduct of the lawless people," stressing their libertine rejection of God's laws. So in a broad sense he trusted God and could be called "righteous" in spite of his many weaknesses. Jewish and Christian writings assigned him a place among the righteous (Wis 10:6; 19:17 also speak of God "rescuing a righteous man" in apparent reference to Lot; see also *1 Clement* 11:1), and Peter was likely following this tradition.

Peter's emphasis on Lot's righteous character is continued in 2:8, telling us that Lot was "tormented in his soul by the wickedness." This repeats the last part of 2:7, that Lot was "sick of" the "shameful immorality," referring to the incident with the two angels. His distress in the story was with the homosexual congress the evil townspeople wanted to take with his guests, and he tried to dissuade them of their evil intentions. Here Peter emphasizes the undoubtedly true fact that for the entire time Lot lived there he "saw and heard" the evil hearts and deeds of the townspeople and was "tormented" or "deeply distressed" by it. "Wickedness" is literally "lawless deeds" (*anomos* [TG459, ZG491]), the polar opposite of *dikaios* [TG1342, ZG1465] (righteous) actions. This is intended in its most general sense, connoting not only God's laws but also all human moral standards. Such behavior is evil in any society. This is a point for the reader. When we see this kind of evil occurring around us, we should never let ourselves become used to such rampant immorality; we should be distressed like Lot was. Lot saw this taking place on a daily basis; so do we, through magazines, TV, Internet porn, and such. We dare never become inured to it.

In 2:9 we finally arrive at the apodosis (then-clause) of the very long protasis (if-clause) in 2:4-8—"for [if] God" (2:4-8) . . . "[then] the Lord" (2:9-10a). It provides the lesson to be learned: If God delivered Noah and Lot while destroying their evil contemporaries, he will do the same for us in our day. The introductory "So you see" makes clear that Peter was drawing a conclusion to what he had been saying in the paragraph so far. If throughout the Old Testament God was saving the righteous and condemning the wicked, then of course he will continue to do so in our day as well.

The first conclusion is, "The Lord knows how to rescue godly people from their trials." The "godly" (*eusebēs* [TG2152, ZG2356]) are the antithesis of the "ungodly" in 2:5-6, namely, those who "show uncommon reverence or respect" for God (BAGD 413), in their daily conduct as well as in worship settings. Peter promises that the God who rescued Noah and Lot can also do so for all his people in "their trials"; *peirasmos* [TG3986, ZG4280] can mean either "trial" or "temptation," and James brings out both in his epistle. The difficulties and afflictions of life are "trials" intended to drive us to depend on God according to James 1:2-4, but at the same time they become "temptations" when we are "enticed" by our own "selfish desires" in the midst of them (Jas 1:13-15).

If Peter's meaning was that the Lord can "rescue from temptation," this would restate the Lord's Prayer (Matt 6:13; so Bigg 1901:227; Kelly 1969:335). But in this context (Noah and Lot are not so much tempted as rescued from their trials) the thrust is clearly on the side of the trials of life (cf. 1 Pet 1:6; 4:12; though see Hiebert 1989:106; Schreiner 2003:343, who see it as both the external trial and the internal temptations that result). Others believe that in this context of the Lord's return and final judgment, this refers to that "test" or "trial" when the Lord returns to "test the quality of every Christian's service" (M. Green 1987:113). While the eschatological trial is certainly present here, it is unlikely that this is the entire thrust. It is best to see this in an inaugurated sense as all the trials of living that Christians experience in a non-Christian world, as these current tests lead up to the final trial at the eschaton (so Bauckham, Harrington, Moo, G. Green, Harvey and Towner). The point is not that God will keep us from going through the difficulties of life but that God will bring us through them successfully.

The second conclusion is that the Lord also keeps "the wicked under punishment until the day of final judgment." This sums up the judgments on the fallen angels (2:4), the contemporaries of Noah (2:5b), the people of Sodom and Gomorrah (2:6), and the false teachers. The wicked or "unrighteous" of every age, including our own, live in a state of "punishment," of God's displeasure, awaiting their certain condemnation and punishment at the eschaton. The old adage, "Be sure your sins will find you out," is absolutely true. The current sufferings of sinners in this sin-sick world are a proleptic anticipation of "the day of final judgment," when those opposed to God will be cast into the lake of fire (Rev 20:11-15). Peter's point here is that God has sovereign power over the final harvest, when God's angels will "throw" those who do evil "into the fiery furnace," while "the righteous will shine like the sun in their Father's Kingdom" (Matt 13:42-43).

Two aspects of the sins of the false teachers are singled out in 2:10a. First, they "follow their own twisted sexual desire." This is a particularly strong charge, literally, "They continually go after the flesh in their shameful (defiling) desires" (probably an objective genitive, "lust for defilement"). These licentious heretics don't simply fall into acts of depravity; they actively pursue such (as also in Jude 7). Primarily, this refers to sexual sin, probably including the homosexuality connected to Sodom (so M. Green, Moo, Schreiner). Second, they "despise authority," similar to Jude 8, "defy authority." At first glance, one would think this meant the leaders in the church, but the word for authority here is *kuriotēs* [TG2963, ZG3262], "lordship," so most interpreters take it to mean they flaunted the authority of God and Christ (so Bigg, Kelly, Neyrey, Bauckham, Davids). An interesting (and quite possible) variation is that of Moo (1996:108), who considers it "a general charge to the effect that the false teachers are self-willed and rebellious," opposed to the very "principle of authority." This is directed to God and leaders of the church and will be exemplified in the last half of this verse (2:10b) in the contempt they show the "supernatural beings" (angels).

◆ 3. The arrogance and evil deeds of the false teachers (2:10b-16)

These people are proud and arrogant, daring even to scoff at supernatural beings* without so much as trembling.
11But the angels, who are far greater in power and strength, do not dare to bring from the Lord* a charge of blasphemy against those supernatural beings.

12 These false teachers are like unthinking animals, creatures of instinct, born to be caught and destroyed. They scoff at things they do not understand, and like animals, they will be destroyed.
13Their destruction is their reward for the harm they have done. They love to indulge in evil pleasures in broad daylight. They are a disgrace and a stain among you. They delight in deception* even as they eat with you in your fellowship meals.
14They commit adultery with their eyes, and their desire for sin is never satisfied. They lure unstable people into sin, and they are well trained in greed. They live under God's curse.
15They have wandered off the right road and followed the footsteps of Balaam son of Beor,* who loved to earn money by doing wrong.
16But Balaam was stopped from his mad course when his donkey rebuked him with a human voice.

2:10 Greek *at glorious ones*, which are probably evil angels. **2:11** Other manuscripts read *to the Lord;* still others do not include this phrase at all. **2:13** Some manuscripts read *in fellowship meals.* **2:15** Some manuscripts read *Bosor.*

NOTES

2:10b-11 ***scoff at supernatural beings . . . do not dare to bring from the Lord a charge of blasphemy against those supernatural beings.*** There is considerable debate as to which group Peter has in mind in these two verses. The word for these "beings" is *doxas* [TG1391, ZG1518], meaning "glories" or "glorious ones." While the term could refer to church officials (so Bigg 1901:279-280; M. Green 1987:116-117) or civic leaders as those "glorified" in the church or community, in this context it almost certainly refers to celestial beings or angels. The traditional view has been that these are fallen angels on the grounds that these are central in 2:4-5 and seen in contrast with good angels in the next verse (2:11), thus connoting evil angels (so Kelly, Bauckham, Moo, Schreiner, Harvey and Towner). But a view that is gaining prominence is that these are good angels on the grounds that these are more likely the angels that have participated in the final judgment (rejected by the false teachers). In this sense, the contrast in 2:11 states that the good angels will not, in turn, slander the false teachers (so Davids, Neyrey, G. Green). Both views are viable—in the first, the false teachers revile the demonic powers, but even God's angels refuse to do so; in the second, the heretics mock God's angels, but these glorious celestial beings refuse to revile the heretics in turn. Of the two, I slightly favor the first due to my view of the parallel in Jude 8-10 (see the commentary there), and that in this context the "glorious ones" in 2:10b (NLT mg) should be distinguished from the "angels" in 2:11a.

2:11 ***bring from the Lord.*** This reading, found in 𝔓72 056 0142, is generally preferred as the more difficult reading over "to the Lord," which has stronger manuscript evidence (א B C P 𝔐). Later scribes would have changed it because it has the slanderous charge coming from God, while "to the Lord" follows courtroom imagery and is easier theologically (so Comfort 2008:763; Metzger 1994:633).

2:12 ***like animals, they will be destroyed.*** Lit., "in their destruction they will be destroyed." Davids (2006:237) notes three possible interpretations of this: (1) "They will be destroyed in their own destruction" (cf. Exod 18:18; Isa 24:3; Mic 2:10); (2) "They will be destroyed in the same destruction with them" (the swiftness of the final judgment or that it will destroy both animals and the teachers); (3) "They will be destroyed in the same destruction" (with the very evil angels they slander). The key is the pronoun *autōn* [TG846, ZG899] (their). Is the "their" the fallen angels (Bauckham 1983:263-264) or the animals (most other scholars)? The nearest antecedent is the animals, and that is more likely. But does it mean "perish with them" (NASB, NRSV, ESV) or "perish like they do" (REB, NIV, NLT). The former does not make a lot of sense here, and the idea of being hunted down and perishing like wild animals fits the context well and so is to be preferred.

2:13 ***destruction is their reward for the harm they have done.*** There is difficult wording here, reading lit., "suffering harm as the reward of harm." Some later scribes smooth this out by changing it to "receiving harm as the reward" (א A C K 𝔐), but this is more likely a change for theological reasons. Some also translate the text, "defrauded of the profits of their evil actions" (so M. Green, Reicke, G. Green), but while greed for monetary gain is stressed in 2:3, 14, it is not stressed in the immediate context of this paragraph. The more likely meaning is found in the NLT.

They delight in deception. This is found in the majority of manuscripts (*apatais* [TG539, ZG573] in 𝔓72 א A* C K P), while a few have "delight in their love feasts" (*agapais* [TG26, ZG27] in A B Ψ), undoubtedly in assimilation to Jude 12.

2:15 ***Balaam son of Beor.*** It is interesting that many versions (NASB, NIV, ESV, NKJV, NLT) have "son of Beor" (from Num 22:5; 24:3), found in some manuscripts (B 453), while most manuscripts (𝔓72 א A C K P Ψ 048 33) have the reading "Bosor." It is more likely that later scribes would have replaced "Bosor" with the Old Testament "Beor." The reason for "Bosor" is probably a play on words with the Heb. *basar* [TH1320, ZH1414] (flesh), thus saying that Balaam is "a son of the flesh," thereby primarily a fleshly, sinful person (Comfort 2008:764-765).

COMMENTARY

This third paragraph in this central section returns to the issue of the "false prophets" (2:1-3). In the previous section Peter centered upon their coming judgment as a reenactment of the Old Testament judgments upon the fallen angels, the people of Noah's day, and the wicked in Sodom and Gomorrah (2:4-9). The conclusion of that section (and a transition to this section, 2:10a) told why these heretics were condemned—sexual sin and defiance against divine authority. Peter now expands upon that and provides a lengthy description of these evil interlopers into the church. This material is built upon Jude 8-12, centering on Balaam (Jude 11) while omitting the story of Michael and Satan (Jude 9). Reversing the order of 2:10a, there are two sections in this paragraph: sins of arrogance and their reward (2:10-13a), and sins of a sexual nature (2:13b-16).

Anyone who would blithely spurn the authority of God would, of course, have no respect for people either (2:10b). These false teachers are "proud and arrogant" individuals, boldly demanding an obeisance they neither deserve nor are entitled to receive. As Bauckham (1983:261) says regarding the parallel in Jude 9, "Where the archangel Michael feared to tread, these fools rush in" in their "presumptuousness, arrogance, and obstinacy." The proof of their self-willed audacity is the fact that they dare to "scoff at supernatural beings" (*doxas* [TG1391, ZG1518], "glorious ones") "without so much as trembling." These beings are most likely the fallen angels discussed in 2:4-5 (see note on 2:10b-11); they had become evil powers but are still celestial beings created by God, still "glorious." These people were "fearless" in their stupidity! The term for "scoff" is *blasphēmeō* [TG987, ZG1059], to "slander, blaspheme." Most likely, this does not refer merely to the fact that they denied the existence of such beings; rather, they mocked and denigrated not only teaching about such, but the beings themselves. As Harvey and Towner (2009:90) say, these heretics "may even have mocked the power of demons and challenged them to interfere with their enjoyment of their free indulgence of sensuality."

In contrast to these foolish false teachers, Peter turns to the good angels (2:11). God's holy angels are "greater in power and strength" than the fallen angels (see Rev 12:7-9), yet they refuse "to bring from the Lord a charge of blasphemy against those supernatural beings." The verb "blaspheme" is used in both 2:10b and 2:11. Note the irony. The false teachers in their foolish arrogance slander fallen angels, and yet God's angels, so much more powerful, refuse to slander the very cosmic powers over which they have power (cf. Jude 8-9, "Even Michael . . . did not dare accuse the devil of blasphemy"). The angels show the demons the respect that is their due, even if they are supremely evil. The first (the heretics) have no right to do so; the second (the angels) have every right, but do not do so. The heretics showed no respect whatsoever for "the god of this world" (2 Cor 4:4), while the angels did. Most likely Peter means that the angels left the judicial charge of blasphemy up to God. On the other hand, the false teachers, who deny the supernatural realm and God's intervention into this world, not only deny but "are mocking the possibility that their sins might put them at the mercy of such evil spiritual beings" (Moo 1996:123). It is a spiritual principle that sin by its nature is both a giving in to self and a surrender to the false deceptions of Satan. So when we surrender to sin, we place ourselves at the mercy and control of evil spiritual beings.

In 2:12, Peter turns to the reasons for the certain destruction of the false teachers. As elsewhere, he has adapted Jude, "Like unthinking animals, they do whatever their instincts tell them, and so they bring about their own destruction" (Jude 10). Peter further describes these "unthinking [unreasoning] animals" as "creatures of instinct, born to be caught and destroyed." These foolhardy people have denied God's presence in this world, flouted his moral laws, and scoffed at the celestial beings God created. So what could cause them to teach and behave so absurdly in their hubris? The best analogy is to liken them to "irrational beasts," going purely on their "instinct," which here probably is linked both to their licentious behavior and to their ignorant claims as nothing but pure animal instinct. These people have allowed their basic carnal instincts to control them, so of course they are liable for judgment. The statement that they are "born to be caught and destroyed" is based on a common ancient belief that certain animals were placed on earth ("born to be") in order to be killed and eaten (for passages see G. Green 2008:275). By their blatant dismissal of God's standards regarding truth and morality, these people had become animals good for nothing but to be captured and slaughtered. For an interesting comparison of the fallen angels, false teachers, and the animals they have become, see Billings (2008) and Callan (2009). Both scholars note the use of this motif among ancient writers and show how Peter used it in similar ways.

In the last half of 2:12, Peter restates why they are under such an indictment; they "scoff at things they do not understand" (cf. Jude 10). As "unthinking animals" (2:12a) they live only on instinct and have no concept of right and wrong. As Paul says in 1 Timothy 4:2, their "consciences are dead." The scoffing is *blasphēmeō* [TG987, ZG1059], the same verb used in "the way of truth [being] slandered" in 2:2 and "daring even to scoff at supernatural beings" in 2:10. As brute animals snort at and charge anyone without discrimination, so these brute teachers scoff at beings and things no thinking person would dare to mock. "These people speak great, bombastic nonsense (2:18), but in the end they are no more well informed than the beasts and are proper objects of retribution" (G. Green 2008:277).

Sadly, this description fits not just cult leaders in our day but far too many Christian leaders and churches. The popular church has too often developed a philosophy devoid of theology and the deep things of the word, and this has led to a worldliness typified in many churches. As Moo (1996:138) states, "Too many of our churches are devoting too much energy to the periphery of Christian ministry and too little to its heart. For at the heart of Christian ministry must always be the molding of people into the image of Christ, and the full and faithful teaching of God's truth is the means the Spirit uses to accomplish the goal."

Therefore, "like animals, they will be destroyed." The heretics are like animals in their carnal appetites and in the unreasoning nature of their foolish teaching, so it is absolutely just that they be hunted down and destroyed (imagery of the final harvest/hunt). Jesus in the parable of the fishing net states that they "threw the bad [fish] away," likening this to final judgment when "the angels will come and separate the wicked people from the righteous, throwing the wicked into the fiery furnace" (Matt 13:48-50). That is the point here: These false teachers are like the bad fish in Jesus' parable, destined to be hunted at the final "harvest," caught, and destroyed like the wild animals that they are.

The first part of 2:13 continues the thought of their certain judgment—"Their destruction is their reward for the harm they have done." There is a strong use of cognates for emphasis: "God will see to it that they suffer harm for all the harm they have caused." As we have seen, final judgment is the major emphasis of chapters 2–3. These foolish and ignorant leaders were denying the central fact of the Bible—God's continuing involvement and intervention in this world. They were destroying the faith of countless people, and so it is true justice that they experience the destruction they had wrought—as Revelation 11:18 says, God will "destroy all who have caused destruction on the earth." This is indeed the "reward" they have earned, and God will see to it that they receive the proper recompense for their work.

The next section (2:13b-16) centers again on their immorality, their "love" for indulging "in evil pleasures in broad daylight." Their evil proclivities for licentious behavior (the Greek term is "hedonistic" pleasures) were so ingrained that they broke conventions by reveling in them throughout the day. They were shameless and didn't even have the decency to wait until it was dark! In Jude 12 their sin is gluttony (NIV, "blemishes at your love feasts, eating with you without the slightest qualm—shepherds who feed only themselves"), and this is likely part of Peter's condemnation as well. But the ancient world believed these orgies of food and sex were to be done at night (Eccl 10:16; Isa 5:11; Rom 13:12-13; 1 Thess 5:7). So these people were even more of "a disgrace and a stain" on the church. They are the kind of "spots and blemishes" that make an animal unworthy to be sacrificed to God. They again are pictured as unclean animals. In 3:14 Peter tells the Christians to be "pure and blameless in his sight," the polar opposite of the terms here (2:13—*spiloi, mōmoi* [TG4696/3470, ZG5070/3700]; 3:14—*aspiloi, amōmētoi* [TG784/298, ZG834/318]; Moo 1996:125). These evil people are the exact antithesis of what a true follower of Christ should be.

This denunciation of their wicked orgies continues, as "they delight in deception even as they eat with you in your fellowship meals." The word is "reveling" or "carousing" as they "indulge" in their "delights." The word *apatē* [TG539, ZG573] refers to "deceitful pleasure," enticing people to indulge themselves in what was obviously wrong. What made this all the more crass and wicked was the fact that they were doing so at the primary Christian festival, what Jude 12 calls the "love feasts" (NIV), the fellowship meal early Christians shared when they celebrated the Eucharist (reenacting the Last Supper). This was also the scene of the sins of the Corinthians; see 1 Corinthians 11:17-34, where Paul condemns the wealthy for refusing to share with the poor in the feast. So these people were desecrating the love feast in a similar way, by turning this sacred meal into a gluttonous, perhaps even a profligate, event. Likely they treated it like any other Hellenistic feast. Gene Green (2008:280) explains the two parts of Greek dinners, the time of eating and the time of drinking, with the latter moving inexorably toward drunkenness and revelry.

In 2:14 their evil lusts continue; the image Peter uses is of their eyes being "filled with adulteresses" as they "never stop sinning." This means that at all times they sin by looking at every woman with sexual intent. Their lust never ceases, and they undress every woman they see with their eyes. This accords with Jesus' statement about lust (Matt 5:28) and John's statement about "the lust of the eyes" (1 John 2:16, NASB). Moreover, their constant sin is a communicable disease, as they "lure unstable people into sin." In Revelation 17:5 the prostitute is entitled the "Mother of All Prostitutes" because she does not just prostitute herself but seduces the nations (her children) into committing prostitution with her. That is the case here as well. These licentious people did not just practice a dissolute lifestyle, they also enticed others to do the same. They were not just teachers of falsehood, they had become trainers of evil. This is a fishing metaphor, "to lure by the use of bait" (BAGD 217), picturing the sexual temptations by which these people snare the "unstable" or weak (connoting those with no foundation who are easily moved), who are not firmly anchored in their faith (the opposite of those in 1:12 who are "standing firm in the truth"). Such people are easily moved with the "high-sounding nonsense" (Col 2:8) that spouts from these heretics. Like a house built on the sand (Matt 7:26-27), such people are easily swept away. This is an apt description of the American way of life; at no time since the Roman Empire has sexual perversion been so readily accessible or so widely accepted. The warning here must be heeded by all of us!

From sexual sin Peter then turns to the "greed" for money and possessions he previously noted in 2:3. Peter says they are "well trained in greed," using *gegumnasmenēn* [TG1128, ZG1214], from which "gymnasium" is derived. Like a well-honed athlete, these have become "experts" in greed, with great discipline becoming all-pro profiteers who exploit the gullible in order to become rich. Summing up the consequences of the three areas of wickedness—false teaching, sexual sin, and greed—Peter states they "live under God's curse," literally, "children of a curse." "Child of" was a Semitic idiom for a person's primary characteristic, as in "children of the light" (1 Thess 5:5) or "children of obedience" (1 Pet 1:14, literal translation). Similar to this is "children of wrath" (Eph 2:3, literal translation), meaning that their destiny is to face God's wrath. Here their major characteristic is that they are under God's curse. They promised their followers the blessing of God, but in reality all they can deliver is God's condemnation.

In the final section of this paragraph (2:15-16), Peter notes the analogy of Balaam. Jude 11 calls the false movement "Balaam's error" (NIV, ESV), since they like Balaam "deceive people for money" (NLT). Here Peter begins, "They have wandered off the right road," literally, "wandering from the straight way." The Greek term *hodos* [TG3598, ZG3847] (cf. 2:2, "way of truth"; 2:21, "way to righteousness") was often a semitechnical term for a philosophical or religious "way," and the early church called itself not "Christians" (see Acts 11:26) but "the Way" (Acts 9:2; 19:9; 22:4; 24:14) on the basis of Isaiah 40:3 ("Clear the way through the wilderness for the LORD! Make a straight highway through the wasteland"; cf. 1QS 8:13-14; Osborne 2010:111). They viewed themselves as the messianic people preparing the way for Christ. Unfortunately, the people in 2:15 had "wandered off" God's highway and left the "right road" of the Messiah into apostasy and heresy. The straight path "comprises both doctrinal and moral matters" (Harrington 2003:273) and is often used for those who have walked through life faithful to God (e.g., Isa 35:8; Hos 14:9 [10, MT]; Acts 13:10). The idea of "wandering" from that path (*eplanēthēsan* [TG4105, ZG4414]) can speak of an inadvertent "going astray" due to spiritual weakness (Jas 5:19-20), but here it seems stronger, depicting a deliberate "leaving" of the faith to follow after false teachings (cf. Deut 11:28; Prov 2:13). As G. Green (2008:284) says, "The heretics' wandering is not due to disorientation or 'getting lost' but is rather willful apostasy from God (Deut 4:19; 13:1-18; 30:17; Wis 12:24). Living in obedience to God constitutes walking in that way; departing from it is the core of apostasy and rebellion against him."

The "road" to which Peter likens their wandering is that of "Balaam son of Beor" (see note on 2:15). Balaam entered the story of the conquest of Canaan at Numbers 22–24. Israel was encamped on the plains of Moab and about to enter the Promised Land. Balak, the Moabite king, was alarmed by Israelite successes, and so he hired Balaam, a prophet, seer, and diviner from Pethor near the Euphrates, to come and place a curse on Israel. At first, Balaam refused to go because God had forbidden him, but Balak promised a lot more money, and God relented, allowing him to go. Probably because of Balaam's pecuniary interests, God changed his mind and sent an angel to stop Balaam. Balaam did not see any angel, but his donkey did, so she refused to go forward. Balaam beat the donkey, which was then given a voice by God and rebuked her master (2:16). The key is that the donkey could see, but Balaam was blind to God's angel and had wrong motives. Still, Balaam refused to curse Israel and blessed them four times. Peter called this Balaam's "mad course" or "madness" because his love for money led him to contemplate the foolish, irrational act of trying to curse God's people, Israel. The false teachers were far more "mad" because they were slandering God himself! They were "unthinking animals" (2:12), and it was an unthinking animal, a donkey, who corrected Balaam. Even the donkey could reason better than the false teachers (see Bauckham 1983:269).

Later texts expand on this and tell of Balaam "who loved to earn money by doing wrong" (2:15). In Numbers 31:15-16 it was Balaam's advice that led the Moabite women to seduce the Israelite men and lead them into apostasy (see also Num 25:1-3). Several other Old Testament passages retell the story of Balak wanting a curse and Balaam's recital of blessing (Josh 24:9-10; Neh 13:1-2; Mic 6:5). Davids (2006:253-256) provides an interesting study of Balaam in rabbinic literature, which says he was a sorcerer who had sexual relations with a cow (a play on words on "Beor") or his donkey (*b. Sanhedrin* 105-106). In *Sifre Numbers* 157 on Numbers 31:8 the rabbis commented on his "wages." The Israelites paid him his full salary and did not deprive him because he had come to give them (the Moabites) counsel" (Davids 2006:242). In Jude 11 and here, the emphasis is upon Balaam's greed as a picture of the false teachers who were also seeking "money by doing wrong" (i.e., the wages of sin).

◆ 4. Seduction and apostasy—the effects of the false teachers (2:17-22)

17 These people are as useless as dried-up springs or as mist blown away by the wind. They are doomed to blackest darkness. 18 They brag about themselves with empty, foolish boasting. With an appeal to twisted sexual desires, they lure back into sin those who have barely escaped from a lifestyle of deception. 19 They promise freedom, but they themselves are slaves of sin and corruption. For you are a slave to whatever controls you. 20 And when people escape from the wickedness of the world by knowing our Lord and Savior Jesus Christ and then get tangled up and enslaved by sin again, they are worse off than before. 21 It would be better if they had never known the way to righteousness than to know it and then reject the command they were given to live a holy life. 22 They prove the truth of this proverb: "A dog returns to its vomit."* And another says, "A washed pig returns to the mud."

2:22 Prov 26:11.

NOTES

2:18 *They brag about themselves with empty, foolish boasting.* In the NLT (and NIV), this is a main clause. In the Greek it is a participle, probably modal, and tells how the heretics entice people "by bragging about themselves." This is followed by a prepositional phrase (instrumental *en* [TG1722, ZG1877]) that tells a second way Christians are lured away from Christ. Putting this together, Peter is saying, "By their empty boasting, they seduce people away from Christ by appealing to their sensual desires."

those who have barely escaped. There are two possible readings. Some manuscripts (א* C P 1739 𝔐) have *ontōs* [TG3689, ZG3953] (really, actually, fully), while slightly superior readings (𝔓72 א2 A B Ψ 33) have *oligōs* [TG3641F, ZG3903] (scarcely, barely). If the former, these are established believers who are mature in the faith; if the latter, these are recent believers who are weak in the faith. The latter is preferred by a strong majority of versions and commentaries.

2:19 *They promise freedom.* Bauckham (1983:275-276) notes five options for the kind of freedom they promised: (1) liberty from moral law or moral constraints (Bigg, Kelly, Hiebert, M. Green); (2) a Gnostic freedom from the "archons" or demiurge (inferior powers who created this world); (3) freedom from "perishability" or moral corruption; (4) political freedom (Reicke); (5) freedom from final judgment at the Parousia. The second to the fourth options do not have much evidence from 2 Peter in their favor, leaving the first and fifth as the primary options. Some prefer the first (Moo, G. Green, Harrington); some the last (Bauckham). I agree with those who say that both are likely intended here (Davids, Schreiner, Harvey and Towner).

you are a slave to whatever controls you. A few commentators (Kelly 1969:347; Bauckham 1983:277) believe it should be "the slave of someone who masters him." However, maxims build on metaphors, and the context of 2:19 makes it clear that the false teachers were enslaved by their sensual appetites, not by some military or enslaving person.

2:20 *when people escape from the wickedness of the world.* There is some debate as to the identity of the "people" here. Kelly (1969:347-348) thinks they are the young converts who were seduced by the heresy on the grounds that "escape" here refers back to those who "barely escaped" in 2:18. Thus the *gar* [TG1063, ZG1142] ("for"; NLT, "and") refers back to 2:18 rather than 2:19. The majority of scholars (Mayor, Reicke, Bauckham, Harrington, Davids, Moo, G. Green) argue that 2:20 refers back to the false teachers themselves from 2:19, the more natural referent and the primary subject of 2:20. If one is to be the subject, the false teachers are the more natural referent. However, I agree with Schreiner (2003:360) that there is no reason to separate the two. Verses 20-22 refer to all who are part of the cult, teachers and adherents alike.

2:21 *It would be better . . . than to.* Several scholars (Snyder 1977; Davids 2006:250; G. Green 2008:303) note that this kind of "better . . . than" construction fits a proverbial form called *Tobspruch* (meaning "better-speech") found quite often in biblical literature (Ps 37:16; Prov 3:14; 8:11, 19; 15:16-17; 16:19, 32; Eccl 7:1-5; Mark 9:42-43; Rom 14:21; 1 Cor 7:9; 1 Pet 3:17).

COMMENTARY

In the central section (2:10b-16) Peter centered on the actions (sexual sins and greed) of the heretics. Now he returns to their false teaching and its effects (in 2:17-19) and to the judgment on them for their apostasy (2:20-22). The first part is built loosely upon Jude 12-13, 16, which describes the wicked teachers as "dangerous reefs" and "shameless shepherds" who are like "clouds blowing over the land without giving any rain" and like "wandering stars, doomed forever to blackest darkness" because they "brag loudly about themselves" and "flatter others." The effect is a denunciation of the lies by which they have seduced the weak Christians into embracing their false ideas, and it is a frightening description of the effects those falsehoods will have on these foolish followers.

The first picture (2:17) centers upon how "useless" and frustrating their teaching was. The imagery builds on the parched, barren lands of the Judean wilderness.

The tired, thirst-driven travelers seeing "springs" in the distance would have been intensely disappointed to discover they were "dried up," with no water to refresh them. All promise but no deliverance; this characterizes the false teachers as well. The same can be said of "mist blown away by the wind." Early morning fog or mists seem on the surface to hold promise of future rain, but all too often it is followed by the heat of the sun and withered land. "Wind" was often a picture of the "hot air" of false teachers, as in Ephesians 4:14, "tossed and blown about by every wind of new teaching . . . people [who] trick us with lies so clever they sound like the truth." Kelly (1969:345) calls it a "bitter symbol of disillusionment" that derives from "the insubstantiality and flimsiness of the teaching." M. Green (1987:126) adds, "Heterodoxy is all very novel in the classroom; it is extremely unsatisfactory in the parish."

Because of the worthless, dangerous nature of these people, "they are doomed to blackest darkness" (lit., "gloom of darkness"), taken from Jude 13. The same language ("gloomy pits of darkness") was used in 2:4 to describe the prison house where the fallen angels are kept awaiting their doom. "Gloom" describes the frightening, dark places of the underworld in Jewish and Hellenistic imagery. Jesus used two different metaphors for eternal punishment: "Gehenna" or fiery judgment, and "outer darkness, where there will be weeping and gnashing of teeth" (Matt 8:12; 22:13; 25:30). "Doomed" is *tetērētai* [TG5083, ZG5498] ("kept, reserved," a perfect tense indicating their "state of being") and means that eternal torment is their destiny for twisting God's truths.

Following Jude 16, Peter returns to the matter of their arrogance (see 2:10b) in 2:18, stating that "they brag about themselves with empty, foolish boasting." They are devoid of value (2:17a) and destined for judgment (2:17b) because of their braggadocio and utter lack of humility. The verb is *phthengomai* (to utter, to proclaim) and was interestingly used also in 2:16 of the donkey speaking "with a human voice" to Balaam. Moo (1996:142) speaks of the irony involved: "Even a donkey 'mouthed' better doctrine than these false teachers do!" The term for their "foolish boasting" is *huperonka* [TG5246, ZG5665], meaning it was "haughty, pompous, bombastic" (BAGD 1034). Their high-sounding musings sound magnificent, and people are quite impressed. But in reality they are "empty" or devoid of any worth whatsoever. To listen to it is to walk away "empty" of any value at all. The only thing they are pushing is themselves, and such bragging should never be countenanced. This happens all too often today; some television preachers even have their wives telling everyone how wonderful they are. Teachers should always be judged by the truth content behind what they say, not by their claims for themselves.

Worst of all, the content of their teaching appeals only to the "twisted sexual desires" of their audience. As Bigg (1901:284) says appropriately, "Grandiose sophistry is the hook, filthy lust is the bait." They enticed their listeners with the oldest appeal there is: the sensual desires of the flesh. Like the heretics of 1 John 1:8, 10, they claimed that their followers could do anything they wished and yet have no sin. There would be no final judgment, and Jesus would not come again to hold them to account (3:4). Therefore, they were free to do whatever felt good at the moment; there are no constraints (note how similar this attitude is to that of our own time). The word used here is *aselgeia* [TG766, ZG816], used above of the "shameful immorality" of the false teachers (2:2) and of Sodom and Gomorrah (2:7). It speaks of the licentious conduct of those who have no moral compass and live only for their pleasures.

With their foolish boasting and their twisted appeals, these heretics "lure" weak Christians "back into sin." The use of *oligōs* [TG3641F, ZG3903] here can refer to degree (they have "barely" or "scarcely" escaped) or time (they have "recently, newly, just" escaped). The latter makes best sense (they are recent converts), but probably both ideas are present. As new believers, they are just beginning to grow. Moreover, the expression "have barely escaped" renders a present-tense participle (lit., "are just in the process of escaping") and so are at the beginning stages. It is clear that the target of the false teachers was not pagans who already lived that wicked lifestyle but recent converts who had only recently left that world behind. They had the same strategy as all predators: Look for the weak and defenseless, lure them into the open, and then pounce on them. These recent converts were just beginning to escape "a lifestyle of deception" or "error" (*planē* [TG4106, ZG4415])—that is, the way of life from their pagan past. It was a brilliant strategy, to lure those who have interest but little knowledge, and apparently it was working, as it so often does today with slick pseudoteachers seen so frequently on television and in megachurches.

In 2:19 Peter turns to the means by which these heretics lure the unwary into their trap: They "promise freedom," freedom both from moral restraints (there may have been some antinomian influence against any constraining laws) and from any final judgment arising from their libertine lifestyle (see note on 2:19). But these promises were pretentious and false; their "freedom" was actually enslavement, because the very people who promised such "freedom" were themselves "slaves of sin and corruption." Slaves cannot promise others freedom, especially when their own claim to be "free" is only a lie. The NLT ("slaves of sin and corruption") combines the NIV ("slaves of depravity") with the more common "slaves of corruption" (NASB, NRSV, ESV). The term is *phthora* [TG5356, ZG5785], which means "corruption," but can speak of the moral corruption of sin or refer to human mortality and "perishability." The word is used in two earlier verses in 2 Peter. In 1:4 it tells how God's promises have allowed his people to "escape the world's corruption caused by human desires," where it meant "headed for destruction" due to sin. Then in 2:12 the term is used twice, both times of the certain "destruction" awaiting the false teachers who were "unthinking animals." So it combines the thoughts of moral corruption with its necessary corollary, ultimate destruction.

This verse ends with what is most likely a common proverb or maxim: "For you are a slave to whatever controls you." This proverb draws its image from a tragic fact of life in the ancient world—a major source of slaves was military conquest (the second major source being debt). For instance, G. Green (2008:299-300) points out that thousands of Jews captured in the AD 66–70 revolt were enslaved and forced to construct a canal across the isthmus at Corinth. Paul uses this image of slavery by conquest in Romans 6–7, where he depicts sin as an invading army that uses the law to establish a bridgehead in "enemy" territory (our lives, Rom 7:8, 11) and then proceeds to conquer us and become our "master" (Rom 6:14), so that we become its slaves (Rom 6:15-20). Peter's point is exactly the same—these false leaders promised freedom but were themselves slaves to the licentious living with which they were enthralled (the perfect tenses of the verbs mean they remain in the state of slavery). Davids (2006:247-248) challenges the church today to "look at its own situation, asking which powers have mastered the church in general and many of its members in particular. . . . Often the church is so busy pointing the finger at obvious corruption outside her walls that she does not see rampant enslavement within them."

From the effects of the false teaching in 2:17-19, Peter moves to the judgment that is guaranteed to "people" (see note on 2:20) who embrace the heresy and the wanton life it produces (2:20-22). The introductory "And when" in the Greek is *ei gar* (for if), a condition of fact describing a real situation or event that has actually occurred. Thus, the NLT "when" is appropriate. At the outset, two things tell us that these were formerly Christians. First, they have escaped "from the wickedness of the world," language reminiscent of escaping the world's corruption in 1:4 and escaping from "a lifestyle of deception" in 2:18. In the former passage Peter described God's promises given to believers, and in the latter passage he described the state of recent converts. Both point to Peter's statement here that these were once members of the church and true believers. "Wickedness" is *miasmata* [TG3393, ZG3621], connoting "defilement connected with a crime" and meaning "shameful deed, misdeed, crime" (BDAG 650). The point is that they had escaped the moral defilement of the world, the very thing that characterized the movement.

Second, the means by which they have escaped is "by knowing our Lord and Savior Jesus Christ," repeating the title for Christ in 1:11 (to be used again in 3:2, 18). The message is that Christ is sovereign "Lord" over all and at the same time the "Savior" who makes it possible for people to enter God's kingdom. Davids (2006:190) says, "The one who provides a triumphal welcome is the one we have served as Lord and are experiencing as Savior as he delivers us from the powers of this world." This is the one we have come to "know" (*epignōsis* [TG1922, ZG2106]; cf. 1:2, 3, 8; 2:20, 21). The reality of salvation is seen in its effect, "knowing" Christ and God. Thus, in the first part of this verse Peter is describing those who have experienced Christ as Savior and come to know him as Lord.

The tragedy is that some who have known Christ (the members of this cult) would "get tangled up and enslaved by sin again." The picture behind getting "entangled" could be a similar fishing metaphor as that in 2:14, 18 (with the false teachers getting caught in the very nets they had set to "lure" the unsuspecting, so M. Green 1987:129; Moo 1996:146), or perhaps the idea of an animal caught in thorns and thistles (G. Green 2008:302). Either way, this depicts people moving back into the world and becoming "enslaved" or "overcome," developing the image from 2:19 of a person conquered and then enslaved by an invading army. These people have been invaded, conquered, and made slaves by the very profligate lifestyle and pernicious teaching that promised "freedom" (2:19a)!

All of 2:20 thus far is an "if" clause; we now come to the "then" clause. "If" (since) they had experienced the things of Christ and yet fell away into terrible sin, then "they are worse off than before" (lit., "The last state is worse than the first"). This reflects the dominical saying at the end of Jesus' parable regarding the demon returning with seven more to the empty house/person in Matthew 12:43-45 (Luke 11:24-26), with the result being that "that person is worse off than before." From this there may be a hint of demonic presence with the false teachers (see 2:4, 10b-11), and so the "worse off" has two dimensions—they are even deeper into sin and false ideas than before, and their ultimate judgment will be worse. There may indeed be an atmosphere here similar to Hebrews 6:4-6 ("It is impossible to bring back to repentance"), Hebrews 10:26-31 ("only the terrible expectation of God's judgment"), and 1 John 5:16 ("a sin that leads to death"). If this is correct (and it is likely), then the current state as well as the eternal state is far worse.

This is developed further in 2:21-22. As in 2:15, Peter sees the Christian life as a "way" or path to be walked carefully. The Christian walk is the "way [of] righteousness," an ethical phrase that means "the way of righteous living" here, a "right way" characterized by Christ (1:1), proclaimed by Noah (2:5), exemplified by Lot (2:7-8), and which would become the protocol for the new heavens and new earth (3:13). These people had embarked on the path established by God and had begun to conduct their lives the "right way" as required by God. Moreover, as discussed in the last verse, they had "known" or realized the "way" God had established for them to live. Peter expresses this with a perfect infinitive ("to have known"), stressing the existing state resulting from previous action. They had experienced conversion and so knew how they were to live their lives. Yet they had forsaken what they knew to be the God-ordained path.

So Peter is saying it would be better "if they had never known" that way "than to know it and then reject the command" of God. The infinitive is *hupostrepsai* [TG5290, ZG5715], to "reverse, turn back" from something. They were headed the right direction but made a U-turn on God's highway and rejected the directions they had been given so that they could "live a holy life." These holy commands had been "given" or "passed on" to them (*paradidōmi* [TG3860, ZG4140], used of the "passing on" of tradition in 1 Cor 11:2, 23; 15:3; Jude 3), and they were sacred truths. Not only to ignore but to consciously reject these eternal realities is the height of depravity and demands divine judgment. These people repudiated the transcendent God and his revelation, so it would have been better never to have known these truths than to have turned their back on God and his sacred commands.

In 2:22, Peter gives two proverbial examples to demonstrate the horror of this rejection. Actually, both together are presented as a single "proverb," because they contain the same message. Also, it is critical to realize that both dogs (Exod 22:31; Lev 11:27) and pigs (Lev 11:7) were considered to be unclean animals, and Jesus used them both in Matthew 7:6 (NLT mg), "Don't give the sacred to dogs. Don't throw your pearls to pigs." Throughout Mark (e.g., Mark 1:23, 26; 3:11, NLT mg) demons are called "unclean spirits" to show they were despised by God. These demonically controlled teachers and their followers were unclean animals (cf. 2:12, "unthinking animals"). The saying that the dog "returns to its vomit" stems from Proverbs 26:11, where it describes a fool repeating his foolhardy behavior. Dogs were never pets in Old Testament times; they were looked upon with disgust and roamed in packs like wolves today. These heretics spewed out their filth and then returned to their disgusting practices.

Peter's pig saying must have come from a Gentile context, because Jews allowed no pigs in their territory. Nevertheless, pig farms surrounded Palestine (Mark 5:1-20), so it was probably widely known even there. There are two ways of understanding this proverb. It could be saying, "Pigs delight to wallow in the mud," thereby emphasizing the immoral lifestyle of the false teachers. But the parallelism with the first saying makes it more likely we should read, "A washed pig returns to the mud," thus making the point that these people were once followers of Christ but then returned to the corrupt practices of the world.

Schreiner (2003:363-365; see also Moo 1996:151-155) questions whether a true believer can commit this kind of apostasy, concluding that the "conversion" language is phenomenological, i.e., these people *appeared* to be believers but could not have been since true Christians cannot lose their salvation. We are at the heart of the dilemma: In the Bible there are passages that teach the security of the believer (e.g., John 6:35-40, 44-45; 10:27-30; Acts 13:48; Rom 8:28-39; Eph 1:13-14; 4:30; 1 Pet 1:5) and others that warn about the possibility of losing one's salvation (e.g., 2:20-22; John 15:1-6; Rom 11:19-21; Heb 6:4-6; 10:26-31; Jas 5:19-20; 1 John 5:16; Rev 2:5; 21:8). This is an age-old debate that will only be solved when we get to heaven. I believe that the most natural reading favors the latter, that these were genuine believers who lost their salvation. Moo (1996:155) believes these could not have been "truly regenerate believers" but admits, "I am not finally satisfied with this conclusion," adding, "I am in process on this issue, still convinced that eternal security is a biblical doctrine, but less convinced of it than I used to be." This is one of the more difficult issues in Scripture, since there are so many seemingly convincing passages on both sides. Yet both cannot be correct. The issue calls for more humility than we all too often see! It is likely that God did not intend to give us the final answer but wanted us to live within the tension of our security and of our responsibility. Still, the issue demands preliminary resolution, and I believe the stronger biblical view holds to the possibility of Christians losing their salvation (on this issue, see further Bateman 2007).

◆ C. Scoffers and the Day of the Lord (3:1-10)

1. Answers for those who deny the return of the Lord (3:1-7)

This is my second letter to you, dear friends, and in both of them I have tried to stimulate your wholesome thinking and refresh your memory. [2]I want you to remember what the holy prophets said long ago and what our Lord and Savior commanded through your apostles.

[3]Most importantly, I want to remind you that in the last days scoffers will come, mocking the truth and following their own desires. [4]They will say, "What happened to the promise that Jesus is coming again? From before the times of our ancestors, everything has remained the same since the world was first created."

[5]They deliberately forget that God made the heavens by the word of his command, and he brought the earth out from the water and surrounded it with water. [6]Then he used the water to destroy the ancient world with a mighty flood. [7]And by the same word, the present heavens and earth have been stored up for fire. They are being kept for the day of judgment, when ungodly people will be destroyed.

NOTES

3:1 *This is my second letter to you.* The question is whether the first letter is 1 Peter, Jude (due to the parallels with ch 2), or a lost letter (since there are not many parallels in subject matter with 1 Peter). Jude is extremely unlikely because it is clear Peter could not have written it. Many scholars (M. Green, Moo, Davids) think it refers to a lost letter, just as there are several lost letters attributed to Paul (1 Cor 5:9; 2 Cor 7:8; Col 4:16), but that is difficult to prove. The best option is that it is indeed 1 Peter (so Bigg, Kelly, Neyrey, Bauckham, Schreiner, G. Green). Peter's point is not that the letters covered the same material but that in both there is an appeal to the eschatological hope and to clear thinking on the part of the readers.

3:4 *From before the times of our ancestors.* The term for "ancestors" is *pateres* [TG3962, ZG4252] (fathers), and several scholars (Kelly, Reicke, Bauckham, Vögtle, Harrington) think this refers to the first generation of believers, who died without seeing the promise fulfilled. (They use this as one argument that the author of 2 Peter was not the apostle Peter, since he belonged to that first generation.) However, in Jewish literature and in the NT (e.g., John 7:22; Rom 9:5; 11:28; 1 Cor 10:1; Heb 1:1) this term referred to the Jewish ancestors (often the patriarchs), and that is certainly the thrust here (see M. Green, Moo, Davids, Schreiner). If the scoffers were referring only to the original generation of the church, they would not have added "since the world was first created." Every generation from Adam to the present (thus "our ancestors") is intended.

3:5 *They deliberately forget.* There are two different ways to translate these opening words. The NLT rendering is also found in NRSV, TEV, NIV (see Bigg, Mayor, Harrington, G. Green), but depending on how we translate the two verbs, it could also be, "When maintaining this, it escapes their notice that" (NASB, REB; see Kelly, Bauckham, Moo, Davids, Schreiner). The main verb *lanthanō* [TG2990, ZG3291] can mean "fail to notice" or "forget," but the key is whether *touto* [TG3778, ZG4047] (this) is the object of this main verb or the participle (*thelontas* [TG2309, ZG2527]), which can mean either "willingly, deliberately" or "resolve, maintain," depending on which translation choice one makes. The order of words better fits the second choice ("maintaining this"), but the whole tenor of this epistle favors the view that these teachers are deliberately ignoring the truth rather than inadvertently neglecting it. So while one cannot be certain, the NLT reading seems more likely.

he brought the earth out. This verb (*sunestōsa* [TG4921, ZG5319]) can be translated either "bring into existence, establish" or "sustain, cause to cohere." Therefore, there is disagreement as to whether it refers to the creation of the earth (Schreiner 2003:376) or to the sustaining of creation (G. Green 2008:319). On the basis of the parallel in Col 1:17 and the movement of ideas between the two clauses, probably the verb is intended to connote both ideas. The earth was both "formed" and "sustained" by God's command.

COMMENTARY

Of the three sections at the center of this epistle, the first (1:16-21) presents proof for the reality of the second coming of Christ, dealing with eschatological realities that have been denied by the false teachers. The second section (2:1-22) deals with the heretics themselves, condemning them for their blasphemous teaching and for their profligate lifestyle. This section (3:1-10) draws the two together and goes further into both the teaching of the "scoffers" and their claims that God will not intervene and that there will be no Second Coming or final judgment. Peter addresses the Christians directly, calling them "dear friends" (lit., "beloved," 3:1) and challenging them to act on the information in these three sections by living lives morally pleasing to God and by "remembering" (3:1-2, 5 recalling 1:20) and "knowing" or "understanding" God's truths (3:3, 17 recalling 1:20; 2:20-21, see Moo 1996:160-161). Peter especially returns to their refusal to accept Scripture's teaching about the Parousia and final judgment. There are three sections here: (1) 3:1-2, reminding his readers to remember the prophecies of the prophets and of Christ himself on these matters; (2) 3:3-4, calling on them to realize that the coming of the "scoffers" was prophesied, so their denials that God has acted in the past are to be expected; and (3) 3:5-7, containing the evidence that disproves the erroneous claims of the false teachers, since Creation, the Flood, and the coming fiery destruction of this present world are all proof of God's sovereign intervention into this world.

The term "beloved," which dominates this section (3:1, 8, 14, 17), shows Peter's close relationship with these believers and brings out the three levels of Christian reality: the incredible love of God for us, leading him to send his Son to die on the cross; the love that characterizes Christian interrelationships as a family (including Peter's love for them); and God's love for the lost, which is the heart of Christian mission (including their mission to the cult of the false teachers). Those who have experienced this love will not give in to their false teaching or the immoral way of life it engenders. Peter then reminds his readers that this is the "second letter" he has written, wanting his readers to remember the themes in 1 Peter dealing with the promises of the prophets (1 Pet 1:10; cf. 2:16; 3:2) and the return of Christ (1 Pet 1:5, 7, 13; 4:13; 5:1, 4, 10), including the blessed hope that arises from that doctrine.

This section expands on 1 Peter in these areas in order "to stimulate your wholesome thinking and refresh your memory." Peter had earlier talked about "clear thinking" (*dianoia* [TG1271, ZG1379] as here, indicating "correct or pure understanding"—so Bauckham, Hiebert, Neyrey—that entails "the ability to discern spiritual truth and apply it"—so Moo 1996:162]) in terms of the "gracious salvation that will come to you when Jesus Christ is revealed" (1 Pet 1:13). Peter wants to "remind" or recall to their memory these precious truths and then use them to counter the horrific lies the heretics were spreading. Davids (2006:259) recalls two purposes of "reminder" language from 1:12-15: (1) It assumes the readers have already been instructed on the issue and so "ascribes a more honorable status" to those people; (2) it was a critical element in an oral culture for teaching through repetition, here of the Lord's return and future judgment, thereby protecting the readers from the errors of the false teachers.

The specific points Peter wanted them to remember and understand are made clear in 3:2. The first thing he wanted them to recollect was "what the holy prophets said long ago." The false teachers made light of past revelation and sought to convince their adherents that their new revelation had eclipsed and replaced all past teaching. In 1:19-21 he had told them to "pay close attention" to the prophets because they were "moved by the Holy Spirit" and "spoke from God." Peter does not specify at this time what part of the message of the Old Testament prophets (certainly a better option than NT prophets, which do not fit this context) he has in mind, but the content of 1:16-21 and 3:2-10 makes it clear that he was speaking specifically about the prophecies of the end times, specifically of the second coming of the Messiah, the end of the world, and the final judgment.

Second, Peter wants to remind them about "what our Lord and Savior commanded through your apostles" (3:2). This refers to the apostolic preaching and teaching as actually originating in "our Lord and Savior," the favored title in 2 Peter, found also in 1:11; 2:20; 3:18 (1:1, "God and Savior," see on these passages). With the idea of "passing on" tradition seen in 1:4, 21, the emphasis here is on the faithful transmission of the sacred truths from God through Jesus to the apostles, who "passed them on" to the Christians. These traditional truths consisted of moral "commands" (the primary thrust of "command"—to counter the immorality of these people) and doctrinal teaching (an implicit secondary thrust—to counter the dogmatic falsehood of these false teachers). Yet whom does "your apostles" denote? It is unlikely that it includes Peter himself as one of "your apostles," for there is implicitly an emphasis on the particular group who brought the gospel to these people. It is also difficult to think just of the Twelve here and best to see "apostles" in the sense of the church representatives and missionaries who took the Good News to them, possibly including Paul and Barnabas (3:15; Acts 14:14). So Peter asks his readers to "remember" one more thing—those God-sent "apostolic" missionaries who had brought them the gospel truths back when their church was established. He wanted them to realize how different their message was from the lies of the false teachers.

In the second half of this section (3:3-4), Peter moves from the past reception of God's moral and doctrinal truths (through the prophets and apostles sent from Christ) to the "scoffing" heretics themselves. He shows that their arrival at this time is hardly unexpected, for their coming was predicted long ago. "Most importantly" means that for them this is the most critical aspect of the prophecies they should remember. "I want to remind you" is literally "know" (an imperatival participle), and the phrase was used earlier in 1:20, where it introduced the statement that prophecies came not from the prophets themselves but from the Holy Spirit. This is similar, as Peter asks them to realize anew that these Spirit-inspired prophecies must be heeded. Especially critical was their need to remember the prophetic background behind the emergence "in the last days" of these "scoffers." From 3:2 the reference would be to both Old Testament and New Testament prophecies. From the Old Testament there is Ezekiel 38:16 (the rising of Gog "in the distant future"), Hosea 3:5 (the return of Israel "in the last days"), Micah 4:1 (the mountain of the Lord's Temple established "in the last days"), and also denunciations of false prophets (Jer 6:13-14; 8:10-11; 23:10-22; Lam 2:14; 4:13; Ezek 13:1-23; Mic 3:5-12). In the New Testament Jesus warned of false messiahs (Mark 13:5-6, 21-23), Paul spoke of the rising of false teachers "in the last times" (1 Tim 4:1; 2 Tim 3:1; cf. Acts 20:29-30), and John says that the appearance of "many . . . antichrists" is proof that "the last hour has come" (1 John 2:18). Especially relevant is the parallel in Jude 18: "In the last times there would be scoffers whose purpose in life is to satisfy their ungodly desires." The "last days" began with the coming of Jesus and would be consummated in his Parousia, one of the major things these heretics denied. Peter's point was that the believers should not be shocked at such heretics; they are to be expected in these times.

A "scoffer" is a person who has scorn or contempt for God and so ridicules or mocks him and his people. Such people, filled with derision for the things of God, are found frequently in the Old Testament (Pss 1:1; 35:15; Prov 1:22; 9:7-8; 13:1; 14:6). In an honor-shame culture, such attempts to bring dishonor to the name of

God are all the more blasphemous. Worse, these people claimed to do so in the name of God. Peter's point is that they were really "following their own desires." Peter uses this term (*epithumia* [TG1939, ZG2123]) often (1:4; 2:10, 18) to describe the immoral sexual desires and "ungodly" impulses (cf. Jude 18) of this movement.

In 2 Peter it is clear that the false doctrine arose from licentious living. As G. Green (2008:316) says, "The doctrinal denial warrants their behavior, but their character and praxis give rise to their skepticism. Heteropraxis begets heterodoxy." In order to justify and explain away their behavior, these false teachers mocked the return of Christ and a future judgment. (Adams [2005] thinks the emphasis here is more on the end of the world than on the Parousia.) They wanted to feel safe from the universal biblical condemnation of their profligate ways. So they scoffed (3:4), "What happened to the promise that Jesus is coming again?" This type of skeptical rhetorical query is found several times in the Old Testament, such as Psalm 42:3, 10 ("Where is this God of yours?"), Psalm 79:10 ("Where is their God?"), Jeremiah 17:15 ("What is this 'message from the LORD' you talk about? Why don't your predictions come true?"), or Micah 7:10 ("So where is the LORD—that God of yours?"). Notice the derision in their use of "promise" (on which see also 1:4). They were deriding the whole idea of promise and fulfillment, which are at the heart of Christian belief in the second coming of Christ and final judgment. Obviously, the delay of the Parousia was being used by these people to make fun of the belief in an imminent return (cf. Matt 10:23; Mark 9:1; 13:30; Rom 13:11; Heb 10:25; Jas 5:9; 1 Pet 4:7; Rev 1:3). Since that "promise" has still not come to fruition, these teachers were ridiculing any such belief. The Epicureans in the first century denied that the gods were involved at all in human affairs. They lived apart from humanity and had little to do with the things of this world. These heretics applied this same idea to the God of Christianity.

The reason for such derisive skepticism is that "from before the times of our ancestors, everything has remained the same." This refers to the Old Testament times, and it is echoed in Peter's response that both Creation and the Flood demonstrate God's sovereign intervention in the world he made. The mocking heretics had a worldview that had no place in it for salvation history, that is, God's supernatural hand in control of history. "Since the world was first created," they argued, "nothing has changed, and our world just keeps rolling on with no sign of such cataclysmic events." It is doubtful that they denied the very presence of God (there is no evidence of that here, and they did claim to be Christians); they probably taught that God allowed history to develop on its own and did not intervene. Their reasoning was that since the world continues unchanged, there is no room for an idea of a Parousia or final judgment, and one need not fear any divine condemnation for immoral behavior.

The final section of this paragraph (3:5-7) contains Peter's response to this false doctrine, whereby he argues that God has intervened supernaturally in this world on several occasions: (1) He created the earth and the heavens not only by water but also by his word (3:5); (2) he destroyed that earth by water in the Flood (3:6); and (3) he will destroy it again by fire on "the day of judgment" (3:7). Peter argued that the false teachers knew these truths but "deliberately [willingly] forget" it in order to support their heinous views. "Their ignorance is not merely an unfortunate circumstance. They are marked as those who have willfully passed over the fundamental truths from Scripture that Peter now elaborates. Faced with these facts, they have turned their backs" (G. Green 2008:319).

In his first point regarding the Creation, Peter remarks that long ago God "made the heavens" (not only the sky but the entire universe, including possibly "the unseen spiritual realm," so Moo 1996:169) and the earth. The phrase "by the word of his command" modifies both clauses and emphasizes the creative power of God's commands. These intentionally ignorant people have ignored the fact that divine intervention in the cosmos was most evident in the ancient and cataclysmic act of Creation. The potency and wonder of that event will be repeated only when God creates "a new heaven and a new earth" (Rev 21:1). The language is taken from the Genesis account. Creation is referred to by the copulative verb *ēsan* [TG1510, ZG1639], which here means "came into being." We are told further that these acts of creation were brought about "by the word of his command," which occurs last in the sentence and modifies both parts (both the heavens and the earth). Creation via God's command is found often in Scripture (Gen 1:3-30; Pss 33:6; 148:5; John 1:3; Heb 11:3) and Second Temple literature (Wis 9:1; Sir 48:3; *4 Ezra* 6:38; *Sibylline Oracles* 3:30). The whole of creation is the result not of unseen forces continually at work in a stable world but of a God who acts powerfully to create a world *ex nihilo* with his very command.

In addition, God at Creation "brought the earth out from the water and surrounded it with water." "Brought out" is the perfect participle *sunestōsa* [TG4921, ZG5319], which stresses the state of the earth resulting from creation and means the earth is "sustained" or "held together" by God. This is also seen in Colossians 1:17, where the same verb is used (NLT, "he holds all creation together"), which O'Brien interprets as, "He is the sustainer of the universe and the unifying principle of its life" (1982:47). There is the creative power of God that forms the world, and there is his sustaining presence through which our creation coheres or is preserved.

Finally, the earth was formed *ex hudatos kai di hudatos* [TG5204, ZG5623] (lit., "out of water and through water"). This phrase has occasioned a great deal of discussion because it is so mysterious. Bigg (1901:293) argues that it teaches the Greek notion that water is the basic element out of which this world was made. That is unlikely, however, and it is much better to see here the language of creation from Genesis 1. At Creation (Gen 1:2) the Spirit hovered "over the surface of the waters," and God separated the waters of the earth and the sky in making the heavens (Gen 1:6-8). What are we to make of the phrase "through water"? Some (M. Green 1987:141) think the second ("through water") refers to rain as the substance by which God sustains the world. But it is better to take the two uses of "water" as referring to the same thing. Therefore, this means water was both the source ("out of") and the instrument ("through") of creation. Peter's point is quite simple—God intervened directly in this world first by creating it from water, with water emphasized here in order to prepare for the Flood in the next verse. Water was used to make this world on the one hand, and to destroy wicked humanity on the other hand. "In this way Peter points out that the history of the world has been and can be sovereignly altered, for it is still governed by God, who is both Creator and Judge" (Harvey and Towner 2009:117).

Most important for these false teachers is the idea of judgment (3:6), for that is what they were denying. So Peter uses the same image ("water") to show that the very same God who has the power to create and sovereignly controls this world is the God who can destroy it. The NLT begins with "then he used the water," but the verse in Greek begins with "through these things" (*dia hōn* [TG3739, ZG4005]), with the plural most likely referring both to "water" and "the word" (the nearer antecedent). So we would translate, "Then through his word he used the water." God's command set in motion both Creation and the Flood. The "word of God" dominates the entire section—his command brought about Creation (3:5), it destroyed antediluvian mankind with the Flood (3:6), and it has reserved the evil humanity of the present day for a final judgment (3:7). It is the divine word, not the words of the heretics, that contains ultimate truth, and it *does* intervene decisively and cataclysmically in our world.

That which was destroyed was "the ancient world" (see also 2:5 for a reference to "the ancient world" as the people of Noah's day); Peter believed it was the whole world, not a portion of it, as is often stated on scientific grounds. Also, the world itself was not annihilated; rather, the wicked people of Noah's day were killed in the Flood. In a very real sense it was returning God's created earth back to the chaos of the waters at Creation, and Noah and the seven others (cf. 1 Pet 3:20) became the new Adam and Eve, the only righteous souls on God's new inhabited earth. So while there is a continuity of life and history taking place at the present time, as the false teachers were saying, that was not fully accurate, for this is the second age of mankind, and the first was destroyed in the divine Deluge of Genesis 6. So the world has not continued as it was or "remained the same since the world was first created." God divided the waters twice, at Creation and at the Flood, and both constituted a discontinuity in this world, divine interventions that interrupted the smooth operation of this world.

For the third time, God will speak via "the same word" (3:7), and this will be the second judgment command, leading to destruction. The "same word" that sustained this world after Creation and after the Flood is once more sustaining it in the present time (G. Green 2008:322). But sin has once more become the dominant force in our world, so as a result "the present heavens and earth have been stored up for fire." Water was the agent of God for Creation and the Flood, but now fire will be the divine medium of judgment and will introduce the third and final age of humanity. An unusual word is used for "stored up" (*thēsaurizō*), which normally speaks of the "treasures" stored up or saved for the future, but it was also used for reward and punishment awaiting individuals (Matt 6:19-21; Rom 2:5; 1 Cor 16:2; 2 Cor 12:14; *Psalms of Solomon* 9:5; *4 Ezra* 7:77-84). Synonymous with "stored up" is "kept (*tēreō* [TG5083, ZG5498]) for judgment." God is reserving our world and its inhabitants for the purifying (i.e., destroying evil) fire of judgment. God's "treasure" for his people will be the destruction of the present evil world and also of the evil people (including the heretics) in this world.

God has used fire before to purge evil and destroy a place of wickedness, as at Sodom and Gomorrah in Genesis 19, which in 2:6 above (cf. Jude 7) was seen as a harbinger of final judgment. The concept of a fiery judgment reserved for this world is frequent in the Old Testament (Deut 32:22; Ps 97:3; Isa 29:6; 33:11-14; 66:15-16; Ezek 38:22; Joel 2:30; Nah 1:6; Zeph 1:18; Zech 12:6; Mal 4:1) and Second

Temple literature (*1 Enoch* 1:6-7; 52:6; 1QH 3:29-36; *Sibylline Oracles* 2:196-213; 4:173-182), as well as in the New Testament (3:7, 10; Matt 5:22, 29-30; 10:28; 18:9; Acts 2:19-20; 2 Thess 1:8; Rev 9:17-18; 16:8; 20:11-15). For the most part, however, it is the people of the world rather than the physical world itself that are the subject of this judgment, and this and 3:10 are the only unequivocal statements regarding the fiery destruction of this world. But for Peter judgment was universal. Paul in Romans 8:18-22 states that all of creation groans, waiting for its release, and Revelation 20:11 and 21:1 speak of earth and heaven fleeing from God's presence and disappearing, so these are commensurate with what Peter says here. As Schreiner (2003:378) says, "The future destruction of the world was inseparable, in Peter's mind, from judgment. . . . It will also involve the day of destruction for the ungodly." Here we find the answer for the false teachers, the "ungodly people" Peter was addressing. Unless they repented and changed both their views and their ways, this destruction of evil would involve them as well.

◆ 2. Reasons for the delay (3:8-10)

8But you must not forget this one thing, dear friends: A day is like a thousand years to the Lord, and a thousand years is like a day. 9The Lord isn't really being slow about his promise, as some people think. No, he is being patient for your sake. He does not want anyone to be destroyed, but wants everyone to repent. 10But the day of the Lord will come as unexpectedly as a thief. Then the heavens will pass away with a terrible noise, and the very elements themselves will disappear in fire, and the earth and everything on it will be found to deserve judgment.*

3:10 Other manuscripts read *will be burned up;* still others read *will be found destroyed.*

NOTES

3:8 ***A day is like a thousand years.*** Some have used this text to establish a timeline, as if all of human history will last six "days" (as in Gen 1) or 6,000 years, with the eschaton then lasting a "day" (= 1,000 years). As interesting as this is, it fails to interpret this text, for here a "day" is *like* a thousand years, rather than constituting a millennium of years (see the extensive discussion in Bauckham 1983:306-310; Davids 2006:275-277). Peter, like Jewish writers before him (Sir 18:9-11; *Pirqe Rabbi Eliezer* 28; *Apocalypse of Abraham* 28-30; *2 Baruch* 48:12-13), was establishing "the contrast between the brevity of human life and God's eternity" to show "that although this period may seem long by human reckoning, in God's eternal perspective it is short" (Bauckham 1983:309).

3:10 ***will be found.*** There is a great deal of variety in the manuscripts on this point. One variant reading is "burned up," found in A and numerous manuscripts, as well as in KJV, NKJV, RSV, but that is most likely a scribal emendation to conform a difficult reading with a verb that fits the rest of the verse. The more difficult and also better supported reading (with א B P and followed by NRSV, NIV, REB, ESV, NET) is the one here.

COMMENTARY

The "scoffers" (false teachers) rejected the biblical teaching about the Second Coming and final judgment in order to justify their immoral lifestyle. In 3:1-7 Peter has proven both that their denials of God's sovereign intervention are fatally flawed and that the believers should heed the prophecies regarding God's future intentions. "How foolish to think that God cannot judge and even destroy the world (3:7), when he himself has created it (3:5) and 'destroyed' it once already (3:6)!" (Moo 1996:185). But there is one question that this has raised for all Christians, namely, why so much time has passed without God fulfilling his promises. If this was a problem in the first century, it is a much greater difficulty today, almost two millennia later. So Peter now addresses this and answers it two ways: first, the completely different reckoning of time from God's perspective (3:8), and second, God's salvific desire regarding all humanity that leads him to delay the final judgment (3:9).

The first part of Peter's response to the delay of the Parousia centers on the "what" of the waiting period. In 3:1-2 Peter said he wanted to "refresh your memory" regarding the prophecies made by the Old Testament prophets and the New Testament apostles, undoubtedly about the coming judgment. Then in 3:3 he reminded the readers that the presence of "scoffers" in the church was one of those prophetic predictions. Finally, in 3:5 he stated that those very scoffers knew but "deliberately forget" the Old Testament teaching regarding Creation, the Flood, and the coming destruction of the world. Now for the fourth time he challenges these "dear friends" (see on 3:1) that they "must not forget" two further truths. We today must be careful not to allow the false ideas of the world around us to muddy the waters of divine truth; we must not forget critical teachings we have inherited from the word and our church traditions as shaped by the history of Christian dogma.

These critics had been arguing that so much time has passed that people should discount the teaching about Christ's soon return. Peter responded: "A day is like a thousand years to the Lord, and a thousand years is like a day." This alludes to Psalm 90:4, labeled "a prayer of Moses"; it centers on the destruction (Ps 90:3, 5, 9, 11) that awaits those who give themselves over to sin (Ps 90:7-8) and includes a prayer for God to "come back to us" (Ps 90:13). Undoubtedly, Peter wanted them to reflect on the whole psalm as part of his message. God's calendar is nothing like ours—what we consider an inordinate amount of time is but a passing instant to God. This statement has even more meaning for us than for Peter, because it is saying that the last 2,000 years of time since Christ's promise to return are merely a couple of days to God! Peter was not saying that the Second Coming is no longer imminent (e.g., 3:11-13 seems to imply living godly lives in light of a soon return). What he was saying is that God is in control, and he decides the timing of the eschaton. Our part is to wait patiently for his chosen time.

The second part of the argument (3:9) centers on the "why" of the delay. The "promises" of God are the polar opposite of the false teachers. They "promise[d] freedom" but brought only bondage (2:19), while God's promise to bring back his Son is guaranteed to come to pass, as is his promise of a "new heavens and new earth" in 3:13 (cf. the "great and precious promises" of 1:4). But the issue is its delay, so Peter states unequivocally, "The Lord isn't really being slow about his promise, as some people think." The key term is *bradunō* [TG1019, ZG1094] and its noun cognate, meaning "slow, hesitant, delayed." The idea of delay was a frequent subject in the Old Testament, as shown in Exodus 34:6 or Numbers 14:18, saying God is "slow to anger" (cf. Neh 9:17; Pss 86:15; 145:8; Joel 2:13; Jonah 4:2). Yet also, Deuteronomy 7:10 says he "does not hesitate" to judge, and Habakkuk 2:3 says the judgment of the Babylonians "will surely take place. It will not be delayed" (also Isa 13:22; 46:13; 51:14). Still, the passage of years made even the Christians of the first century question the holdup of the final events of history. G. Green (2008:327) shows parallels with the Epicurean rejection of the idea of divine providence; perhaps influenced by them, the false teachers believed that God's seeming reluctance to end this world is proof that he is not involved in human affairs.

Peter does not deny the fact of the delay of the Parousia (from a human perspective); he simply explains the reason for it. Far from being uninvolved, God is deeply involved in the salvation of men and women and so holds back the forces of destruction. The basis is the divine "patience" (*makrothumia* [TG3115, ZG3429], "longsuffering, forbearance") at work in this world: "He does not want anyone to be destroyed, but wants everyone to repent." The basic thrust is quite evident: God is interested in the salvation of everyone, so he holds back his anger in order that people can repent. This is called the doctrine of God's "universal salvific will" and is also reflected in John 1:4 ("brought light to everyone"), John 1:7 ("so that everyone might believe"), and John 1:9 ("gives light to everyone"). In Romans 2:4 we are told God's "kindness" is meant for repentance (cf. Rom 11:32, "so he could have mercy on everyone"), and in 1 Timothy 2:4 we see how God "wants everyone to be saved." In Revelation 7:1 the winds of destruction are held back so the saints could be sealed, and even the judgments had as their purpose the repentance of the nations (Rev 14:6-7; cf. Rev 9:20; 16:9, 11).

Yet here too is a problem: If an omnipotent, loving God wants every person to be saved, how is it that so few are? Some respond that there are two wills of God, one reflecting his compassionate desire for all, and the other his "decretive" will for the elect. This fits the view that his grace is sufficient for all but efficient only for those he has predestined for salvation (the Calvinist approach, see Schreiner 2003:381-382). One such view sees "anyone/everyone" here in light of "patient for *your* sake" (italics added) earlier in the verse, so that God's desire is not for the false teachers or sinners in general but only for the believers who are in process of turning to God (Bauckham 1983:312; Moo 1996:188). Yet that does not really fit the language of 3:9, nor its equivalent in 1 Timothy 2:4. An alternative approach understands God's universal will making it possible for all to repent, with the convicting presence of the Spirit encountering each person and making faith decisions possible, resulting in some converting and others rejecting (the Arminian position). This seems better here, for the emphasis in 2 Peter is on the wrong choices of the false teachers and their followers. God (and Peter) wants them to repent, and surely that is a possibility (though on the unpardonable sin see Heb 6:4-6; 10:26-31; 1 John 5:16). Either way, however, there is no universalism here, for while God desires all to come to him, a significant portion of the world refuses to do so, mandating the final judgment that is the point of the next verse.

Those who are following the falsehood that "the day of the Lord" (3:10) will never come are now warned of their folly. It will arrive "as unexpectedly as a thief," alluding to the teaching of Jesus (Matt 24:43; Luke 12:39), Paul (1 Thess 5:2) and John (Rev 3:3; 16:15) on this issue. A robber cases a home to make certain that when he comes the people are unaware and unprepared. Christ had several parables to that effect. The idea of servants awaiting the return of their master who arrives unexpectedly is seen positively in terms of reward in Luke 12:35-40 (Matt 24:45-47) and negatively in terms of judgment in Matthew 24:48-51. Throughout the New Testament the thrust is the need for spiritual vigilance lest any of us be found unprepared when he comes.

In 3:7 Peter spoke of the fiery destruction reserved for the evil world. Now Peter adds further detail about "the day of the Lord," which is stressed repeatedly in the Old Testament (e.g., Isa 13:6-10; Ezek 30:3; Joel 1:15; 2:1, 11; 3:14; Zech 14:1) and the New Testament (Acts 2:20; 1 Cor 5:5; 2 Thess 2:2) and refers to divine judgment on the wicked. The shaking of the heavens and the cataclysm in which this world will end is found in Isaiah 34:4, as reflected in Revelation 6:14 ("The heavens above will melt away and disappear like a rolled-up scroll. The stars will fall from the sky"). (Similar imagery is found in Isa 13:10, 13; Ezek 32:7-8; Joel 3:15-16; Amos 1:2; *1 Enoch* 91:16; *Sibylline Oracles* 3:82; 1QH 3:32-36; *4 Ezra* 13:4.)

Here three aspects characterize this fiery destruction: First, "the heavens will pass away with a terrible noise," referring to the destruction of this world as Jesus taught (Matt 24:35; Luke 16:17). God the divine warrior will lead his celestial army against the world of evil, and it will end in a "roar," perhaps the roar of the flames at the conflagration (so Bauckham 1983:315). In Revelation 20:11 and 21:1 this destruction of the present world is necessary before the "new heavens and new earth" can appear.

Second, "the very elements themselves will disappear in fire," repeating the fiery end prophesied in 3:7. These "elements" (*stoicheia* [TG4747, ZG5122]) could be what the Greeks called the four elements that make up the universe (air, earth, water, fire), or the "elementary spirits" (spiritual powers) as in Colossians 2:8, 20, or the sun, moon, and stars themselves. Probably best is a combination of the first and third, that is, the total elements that make up the universe (Harrington 2003:284—"cosmic conflagration"). This verse speaks of the heavens and the earth, and 3:12 of the heavens and the elements, so "elements" should be linked with the physical makeup of this world. As Davids (2006:284) notes, "We are talking about a total dissolution of the earth as we know it," but we must understand it is the earth and the heavenly bodies that are destroyed by fire to make way for the "new heavens and new earth" that will be our eternal home. What isn't completely clarified is whether or not the galaxies (still expanding and millions of light-years in actual size) are included in this destructive force. Is it our solar system or our entire intergalactic universe that will be destroyed? This is not entirely clear (though see below on 3:11a).

Third, "the earth and everything on it will be found to deserve judgment." The passive "will be found" has occasioned much comment, even a comment that it seems "devoid of meaning" (Metzger 1994:636), but it is best to realize that this verb "suggests a judicial inquiry through which God will discover the deeds of humanity and will execute his judgment on the basis of what he finds" (G. Green 2008:330). The idea is that the evil of this world order will be "made manifest" (Bauckham 1983:319; Neyrey 1993:243) or "laid bare" (NIV) and the justice of God in his judgment will be evident to all. In Romans 8:18-22 Paul states that all of creation groans in frustration at the bondage to "death and decay" that our sin has thrust upon it. It longs for the "freedom" and deliverance that the eschaton will bring. The evil that controls this world order must be destroyed so that newness and life can replace the death that now dominates.

◆ IV. The Challenge of the Letter: Living in Light of the Day of the Lord (3:11-18a)

A. Encouragement to Godly Living (3:11-13)

[11]Since everything around us is going to be destroyed like this, what holy and godly lives you should live, [12]looking forward to the day of God and hurrying it along. On that day, he will set the heavens on fire, and the elements will melt away in the flames. [13]But we are looking forward to the new heavens and new earth he has promised, a world filled with God's righteousness.

NOTES

3:11 ***everything around us is going to be destroyed.*** The causal participle *luomenōn* [TG3089, ZG3395] is present tense, so some scholars (Mayor, Kelly, Moo, Harver and Towner) think that the process of dissolution has already begun. But as the NLT correctly surmises, it has a futuristic force and is best translated "is going to be destroyed," emphasizing the certainty of the event (see Bigg, Bauckham, Schreiner, G. Green).

COMMENTARY

Nearly all commentators place 3:11-13 with 3:1-10 and consider 3:14-18 to be the closing of the letter. Yet at the same time the three sections (3:11-13, 14-16, 17-18a) move from condemnation of the false teachers and prediction of final judgment to a challenge of the Christians in the churches to remain true to Christ and to live out their Christian commitment. The first section centers on godly living (3:11-13), the second on blameless conduct (3:14-16), and the third on vigilance in the church (3:17-18a). To be sure, there is still censure (3:16b, 17b) and promise of judgment (3:11a, 12, 16c), but these are all parts of Peter's challenge to the readers to live differently in light of these truths. Therefore, I have concluded that 3:11-18a is the third section of the epistle, wherein we see that, contra the cult movement fostered by the heretics, the true followers of Christ will live lives worthy of Christ and his second coming. They are to place their trust in the rewards God has promised and live according to his will as a result. There are three sections in 3:11-13, with (1) the command to live a godly life (3:11b) grounded in (2) the coming destruction of the present world and its evil (3:11a-12), then in (3) the promise of the new righteous world we will inherit in eternity (3:13).

Verse 11a draws a conclusion from the teaching of 3:7, 10, asking the reader to understand the implication, "since everything around us is going to be destroyed like this." It provides a distinctive summary of the event, as well as a reason and basis for the godly living called for in 3:11b. There will be a completely transformed and pristine "new heaven and new earth" (see Rev 21:1) with the old destroyed by fire. In 3:7, 10 we are told "the present heavens and earth" will pass away; the question is whether the term "heavens" refers only to the sky of this world or to the entire universe, including the stars. Peter's use of "everything" makes it likely that for him the whole universe is intended. This entire cosmos—earth, sky, sun, moon, stars—will be engulfed in flames and remade anew in the new eternal order God is preparing for his people (see Davids 2006:287-288). As it says in 3:10, "the very elements themselves" will disappear, and God's people are called to be ready at all times for that certain cataclysm.

The challenge that ensues is natural in light of this: "What holy and godly lives you should live!" The Greek says, literally, "What sort of people must you be in holy conduct and godliness?" Every passage on the return of Christ affirms that eschatology must lead to ethics. Let us begin with the Olivet discourse, especially Matthew 24–25. The parables that follow Jesus' teaching on the destruction of Jerusalem and his future return all center on the responsibility to be ready for his sudden and unexpected return, and all have catastrophic ends for those not living right. And every Parousia passage stresses lifestyle issues—1 Corinthians 15 ends with "Be strong and immovable" (1 Cor 15:58); 2 Corinthians 5:10 has "We must all stand before Christ to be judged. We will each receive whatever we deserve"; 1 Thessalonians 4–5 closes with "Encourage each other and build each other up" (1 Thess 5:11); 2 Thessalonians 2 has "Stand firm and keep a strong grip" (2 Thess 2:15); James 5:8 has "Be patient. Take courage"; 1 Peter 4:7 says, "Be earnest and disciplined in your prayers." The whole book of Revelation contains passages that call for faithful, persevering lives (Rev 2:2-3, 10, 19; 3:8; 7:14; 12:11; 13:9-10; 14:12; 16:15; 17:14; 21:7; 22:10, 12, 14). Throughout the New Testament, the return of Christ has promise but also responsibility. His followers must, at all times, be ready and will be held accountable for their lives.

The message in 3:11 is on our "conduct" (*anastrophē* [TG391, ZG419]) or the way we manage our lives. The stress is on daily decisions regarding our lifestyle and actions. God gives directions as to what sort of people we must strive to be, to live our lives on the basis of "holiness" and "godliness" (both nouns are plurals, indicating "holy and godly actions"; see note on 3:11). This was discussed in 1 Peter 1:15-16, where the teaching centers on imitating God's character in our character and conduct, in our attitudes as well as in our actions. We are called to be "set apart" from the world and live for God at all times. The call to "godly conduct" reiterates 1:3, 7, where we noted that the concept concerns a life of both reverence and piety toward God and respect toward our fellow human beings. We live a forward-looking life centered on the hope of vindication at Christ's return, but we also live a present-centered existence focused on our responsibility to walk with God and live as he would have us: "Be holy because I am holy" (1 Pet 1:16, from Lev 11:44).

Peter then adds (3:12) another aspect of Parousia-living, "looking forward to the day of God and hurrying it along." The return of Christ for the believer (rather than for the cult followers, who were denying it, and for whom it would bring destruction) is the basis of great anticipation, as seen in the Lord's Prayer, "May your Kingdom come." For us it connotes vindication and reward, the absolutely certain fulfillment of all our hopes and the beginning of an eternity without sin and suffering in the very presence of God (cf. Rev 21:1-6). The idea of "looking forward" or "greatly anticipating" has the idea of "eager expectation" and is found three times in 3:12-14, reflecting the desire for "the *parousia* of the day of God" (connected to "day of the Lord" in 3:10 and to "that great judgment day of God the Almighty" in Rev 16:14).

More unusual is Peter's further statement that we are to hurry the Parousia along, which comes from the Greek *speudō* [TG4692, ZG5067], meaning to "hasten" or "speed" the occurrence of an event. The verb also connotes the idea of "striving" or exercising "great effort" to make something happen, perhaps even "eagerly waiting" for it to take place (as in NIV mg). Here, however, the emphasis is certainly on working hard to hasten Christ's return, as in several Jewish and Christian texts (see Bauckham 1983:325). Isaiah 60:22 says of the time of future glory, "At the right time, I . . . will make it happen," and several intertestamental texts interpreted this as God's hastening the time of the end (Sir 36:8; *2 Baruch* 20:1-2; 54:1; *4 Ezra* 4:26). Some rabbinic texts believed that the repentance of God's people would bring the end sooner (*b. Sanhedrin* 97b-98a; *b. Yoma* 86b); and Acts 3:19-20 says, "Repent of your sins and turn to God. . . . Then times of refreshment will come from the presence of the Lord, and he will again send you Jesus, your appointed Messiah." There is also the Jewish doctrine of the "messianic woes" reflected in several New Testament passages (Rom 8:17; 2 Cor 4:10-12; Phil 3:10; Col 1:24; Rev 6:9-11; see discussion at 1 Pet 4:13 in this volume). This states that God has established a certain amount of suffering that the messianic community would have to endure before he would intervene and bring about the Day of the Lord. In this sense, the faithful suffering of the saints would hasten the day. Here Peter adds that living godly lives will also hurry it along. As Bauckham (1983:325) asserts, "This does not detract from God's sovereignty in determining the time of the End . . . but only means that his sovereign determination graciously takes human affairs into account."

As was already made clear in 3:7 (earth and heavens "kept for the day of judgment") and 3:10 ("disappear in fire"), this day "will set the heavens on fire, and the elements will melt away in the flames." As in 3:10 the very elements of this world (air, earth, water, fire) are going to disappear in a fiery conflagration, utilizing the powerful idea of "melting," as in Isaiah 34:4 ("The heavens above will melt away"), Isaiah 64:1-2 ("The mountains would quake in your presence! As fire causes wood to burn"), and Micah 1:4 ("The mountains melt beneath his feet"). The false teachers could not be more wrong about the reality of the future eschaton. This world, tainted by sin and death, has been "found to deserve judgment" and therefore must cease to exist in order to make way for the promised new world and the eternal delights that await the faithful. Those (like the cult condemned in this book) who ignore the God-ordained destiny of this evil world will be part of that "judgment."

God's promises (3:13) are not just concerned with the future destruction of the present world; the promises pertain to the "new heavens and new earth" that will follow that cataclysm. This has already been introduced in the discussion of 3:11a above—this world must disappear (Rev 20:11; 21:1) to make way for a brand-new world. Sinners will be judged and their world destroyed, but that is preliminary to the true purpose of the Second Coming, to vindicate and reward the righteous for all they have suffered and for their godly living on earth. Thus, the Christ-followers "are looking forward to" (same verb as in 3:12) God's "promised" reality stated in Isaiah 65:17 ("Look! I am creating new heavens and a new earth"; cf. Isa 66:22), which is often reflected upon in Jewish literature (*1 Enoch* 45:4-5; 72:1; *Jubilees* 1:29; *Sibylline Oracles* 5:211-213; *2 Baruch* 32:6; *4 Ezra* 7:75). This is also seen in the New Testament teaching about the new creation that will liberate the old creation (Rom 8:18-22), provide a "world [that] is made new" (Matt 19:28), and bring about eternal life for God's people.

Further, this will be "a world filled with God's righteousness," (lit., "in which righteousness dwells"). There are several levels to the meaning of *dikaiosunē* [TG1343, ZG1466] (without the definite article the qualitative or theological thrust is stressed):

(1) Primarily (as in the NLT translation), it refers to God's righteousness. Presently, evil makes its home in this world; in the final reality God and his righteousness will inhabit the new world, as stated in Revelation 21:3, "God's home is now among his people! He will live with them, and they will be his people." (2) It also refers to God's justice, which will prevail, and the injustice that dominates now will be no more (cf. Isa 9:7; 11:4; 16:5; 42:1; Jer 23:5). Both these are combined in Isaiah 32:16, "Justice will rule in the wilderness and righteousness in the fertile field." (3) It also refers to a world where God's "righteous people" will dwell. Peter has often spoken of the standard of righteousness expected (2:5, 7-8, 21), and only those who live as God's righteous people will inherit and inhabit this final Promised Land.

◆ B. Call to Lives of Purity (3:14-16)

14And so, dear friends, while you are waiting for these things to happen, make every effort to be found living peaceful lives that are pure and blameless in his sight.

15And remember, our Lord's patience gives people time to be saved. This is what our beloved brother Paul also wrote to you with the wisdom God gave him—16speaking of these things in all of his letters. Some of his comments are hard to understand, and those who are ignorant and unstable have twisted his letters to mean something quite different, just as they do with other parts of Scripture. And this will result in their destruction.

NOTES

3:14 ***peaceful lives.*** The last two words of this sentence are *en eirēnē* [TG1515, ZG1645], lit., "in peace." The question is whether "peace" here refers to inner tranquility, peaceful relations with those around us, or peace with God. Since the whole context centers on our walk with God, the third is taken by nearly all commentators.

3:15 ***our beloved brother Paul.*** Some scholars (e.g., Kelly 1969:370) think this could not have been written by Peter due to the fact that he was apostle to the Jews and Paul the apostle to the Gentiles (assuming there was competition between them, based on Gal 2:11-13). However, in Acts 15, Peter (Acts 15:6-11) and Paul (Acts 15:12) clearly agreed regarding the inclusion of the Gentiles in the church. The so-called war between Peter and Paul over the law and the Gentile mission was engineered by F. C. Baur (the Tübingen school of "tendency criticism" from 1830 onward) and accepted by many critical scholars, but it is not solidly based on NT evidence. Peter was not opposed to the Pauline mission, and the conflict in Gal 2 was a single instance, the type that we all experience with friends and colleagues from time to time. Silvanus (also called "Silas") was an associate of both Paul (Acts 15:40; 1 Thess 1:1) and Peter (1 Pet 5:12). The two were not at odds with one another.

3:16 ***all of his letters.*** This does not mean the Pauline corpus had been collected by this time; rather, it likely refers to "all" the letters Peter and the churches knew about. Still, we know that Paul's epistles already circulated somewhat by this time (Col 4:16). Thus, some preliminary form of a Pauline corpus was likely in existence, as was stated later in Clement's writings (*1 Clement* 47:1). Still, this does not demand a late date of this epistle as a pseudonymous work (cf. Mayor 1907:165; Kelly 1969:370-371); all it means is that Paul's epistles had begun to be collected and that several were known to Peter and his readers. As Bauckham (1983:331) says, "Small local collections probably preceded the formation of the corpus of ten letters."

COMMENTARY

The final section of Peter's epistle (3:11-18a) centers on the conduct of believers in light of the warnings regarding Christ's return and the judgment that will ensue. Throughout the New Testament, passages on the Second Coming conclude with paraenesis (i.e., exhortation; see above on 3:11) that challenges believers to live at all times in light of the fact that at the Parousia we will all have to give account to God. The first part of this section (3:11-13) charges Christians to live in a godly manner. This section (3:14-16) challenges them to blameless conduct in light of the salvation God has provided (3:14-15a) and then uses Paul to confirm the correctness of this teaching (3:15b-16a). The section concludes with a further warning for the false teachers (3:16b).

Peter begins with *dio* [TG1352, ZG1475] (and so), drawing an inference from the promises and warnings of 3:11-13. He adds his typical "dear friends" (*agapētoi* [TG27A, ZG28]), used earlier in 3:1, 8 to emphasize his loving relationship with these churches), leading into the exhortation. As in 3:12-13 he points out the fact that they are "waiting for" (connoting eager anticipation) the final events of human history to "happen." This includes the promise of a new world and the warning of judgment that will take place then. These are the two prominent themes of this letter (Christ's return and final judgment) because these were the two areas denied by the false teachers in order to justify their immoral lifestyles. The present evil world (and its people) is doomed and must be destroyed to make way for the eternal realm of goodness and light reserved for God's people. A holy God must destroy evil (note that OT and NT theologies are in complete agreement on this point). This "Day of the Lord" will take place at God's final intervention into world history, which will end that sinful realm and make it possible for goodness and joy to reign forever. Believers and unbelievers alike will be "judged by their works" and receive either the reward or judgment that is their due (Rom 14:12; 1 Cor 3:12-15; 2 Cor 5:10; 2 Tim 4:14; 1 Pet 1:17; Rev 20:13; 22:12).

In 3:11 Peter exhorted them to holy and godly living; here in 3:14 he adds to that the command to be "pure and blameless." They must "make every effort," a term used also in 1:10, 15 to emphasize energetic, diligent effort to accomplish a goal. God's people should work very hard at conforming to his standards of conduct. The Christian life was never meant to be easy; it demands incredible effort to live in ways contrary to the world around us. As Moo (1996:207) says, "'To be found' has judicial overtones. It conjures up the scene of the court of law, where the judge 'finds' the defendants guilty or innocent." Thus, the wording does not mean that believers are simply to appear "pure and blameless" to others, but that we will all answer to God for the "spotless" character of our lives. These two words ("pure and blameless") appear together often (cf. Eph 1:4; 5:27; Col 1:22; 1 Tim 6:14; 1 Pet 1:19) and are virtual synonyms with sacrificial overtones of the spotless lamb sacrificed before God. These became metaphors for moral purity, meaning that as the Old Testament follower gave the best of the flock to God, believers are to give God only the best of their lives, namely, blameless behavior. As Jesus was "the sinless, spotless Lamb of God" (1 Pet 1:19; cf. Heb 9:14), so his followers must lead "pure" lives (Jas 1:27). In Jude 24 God is celebrated as the one who is "able to keep you from falling" and bring you "into his glorious presence without a single fault" (the same Greek word as "blameless" in 3:14). So the saints are responsible here to "make every effort" to live the "faultless" life God has made possible. These are the two sides of the Christian life—God's part (we are protected "by his power," 1 Pet 1:5) and our part ("Work hard to show the results of your salvation," Phil 2:12). This moral purity will be lived out "in peace" (NLT, "peaceful lives"), referring not to tranquility of spirit or peaceful relations with those around us but peace with God. As G. Green (2008:337) states, this is "the objective condition of being reconciled with God (Rom 5:1) and being found acceptable before him (1 Pet 1:2; 5:14; 2 Pet 1:2)." When we are in right relationship with God, centered on the hope we have in him, it is possible to find the spiritual strength in his Spirit to live pure lives.

Peter told them three times in 3:12-14 to "look forward" to the end, but they saw just one delay after another. The false teachers used this to claim that the delay of the Parousia meant that God had become "slow" in terms of his "promise" (3:9), interpreting this to signify that he would never intervene in human affairs. They believed that God would never call them to account for their immoral practices. So now in the first part of 3:15, Peter returns to that issue and calls the readers (as in 3:8-9) to "remember" ("consider," "be cognizant of the fact") that the delay reflects "our Lord's patience" that "gives people time to be saved." In 3:9 he had said that the Lord's patience was due to the fact that he "wants everyone to repent." The actual wording here in 3:15 is, "Regard our Lord's patience to be salvation." The heretics considered their "evil pleasures" (2:13) to be evidence that their salvation was certain no matter how they acted, but Peter wanted the believers to have a different mind-set centered on the gracious mercy of God rather than on hedonistic practices. There is probably a twofold meaning in "salvation." First, God wants as many as possible "to be saved" or find salvation; second, he wants Christians to have the time to "show the results of [their] salvation" (as in Phil 2:12-13), that is, to make certain they were walking worthily before the Lord. "Consider the Lord's patience, that is, his delay in coming, as an opportunity to repent and be saved" (Schreiner 2003:294) and a chance for Christians to change their patterns and live rightly before God.

Peter then turned to Paul (3:15b) to confirm what he had been saying in 3:14-15a, calling Paul in affectionate terms "our beloved brother," with "our brother" most likely referring to Paul as a fellow apostle, a companion in the work of the gospel (though Mayor [1907:164] takes it generally of all Christians, and Davids [2006:300] of Paul and his coworkers). It seems clear that Paul and Peter had become good friends (see the note on 3:15) and felt a kinship as colleagues in the service of Christ. We know of three instances of contact between the two. According to Galatians 1:18, on his postconversion visit to Jerusalem, Paul spent 15 days with Peter, and it is likely that they became friends. Then, according to Galatians 2:11-13, they came into conflict when Peter surrendered to pressure from Jewish Christians and stopped eating with Gentiles, and Paul had to rebuke him for his error. However, that was short-lived, for Peter joined Paul at the Jerusalem council in witnessing on behalf of the inclusion of Gentiles into the church (Acts 15:6-12). It is probable that they remained friends after that, as seen in the expression "our beloved brother."

Paul undoubtedly was the founder of many of the churches Peter was addressing in this letter, and among the churches in Asia Minor, Paul had written the Galatians, Ephesians, Colossians, and Laodiceans (Col 4:16). But the heretics had twisted Paul's writings to support their own heinous teachings. So Peter wanted his readers to know that Paul supported what he had just said about the necessity of purity of conduct and about the Lord's patience in 3:14-15a. These were the two major issues in the false teaching (immorality versus purity and the Second Coming), so Peter stressed that Paul, using "the wisdom God gave him," agreed entirely with Peter. This means that Peter recognized that Paul's writings were inspired by God. Peter was placing Paul's letters in a category similar to that of the writings of the inspired prophets in 1:20-21. This is further supported by Peter's added comment "just as they do with *other* parts of Scripture" (italics added). This implicitly seems to say Peter is placing Paul's writings within the category of Scripture (so Bauckham 1983:333; G. Green 2008:340). Here we have an important step toward the development of a canon consciousness at a very early date. Mainly Peter wanted his readers to realize that not only Paul but the God who inspired Paul was confirming Peter's teaching over against that of the false teachers.

With divinely sent wisdom, then, Paul wrote of "these things" (3:16), namely, the need to center on purity in conduct and on the Lord's "patience" in delaying the Parousia (3:14-15a), in "all of his letters." Peter was anchoring his teaching in Paul, the other apostolic authority his readers followed, and he wanted everyone to know that Paul was entirely on his side. Still, he must admit that many teachings in Paul's works "are hard to understand," connoting the idea "difficult to interpret" (Bauckham 1983:331). No one who has ever studied Paul's epistles carefully would fail to agree with this observation. Peter, however, was speaking of the fact that such difficult passages are capable of being understood in more than one way; he was not saying that they can mean many different things. This makes it easy for "ignorant and unstable" people (the false teachers) to twist the meaning of passages. The "ignorant" are the "unlearned" and "uninstructed," rather than those unable to learn, and the "unstable" (as in 2:14) are the "weak" people with no firm anchor in truth who are easily moved into false understandings. As such, this could apply to the followers of the false teachers (as in 2:14). But the attention here is on the false teachers themselves, and Peter most likely combined both the heretics and their duped adherents as "ignorant and unstable." These people deliberately "twist" the true teachings of Scripture to suit their nefarious purposes. Truth is not an interest of theirs; supporting their lifestyle is all that matters.

It is difficult to know specifically what aspect of Paul's teaching the false teachers were distorting. However, 3:14-15a combined with the basic aspects Peter emphasizes throughout his epistle suggest several points. First, there are false eschatological views regarding the return of Christ and final judgment, both of which were denied by the false teachers. It may be that these heretics took Paul's teaching about the Resurrection and emphasized the idea of a "spiritual" resurrection (Rom 6:4-5; 1 Cor 15:44; Eph 1:3; 2:5-7; Col 2:12). Second, there is Paul's teaching about the grace of God and freedom in Christ (Rom 6:18, 22; Gal 5:1, 5, 13). They may have distorted this and said that the believers are "free" from the effects of sin and therefore can live however they please (cf. 1 John 1:8, 10). Yet Paul was not the only part of the canonical Scriptures twisted by these dangerous leaders; the other Scriptures, probably the Old Testament, were also distorted in service to these heretical ideas.

Peter then returned to an earlier theme and stated that the result of this will be "their [certain] destruction." This shows the serious nature of their error. This is not a failure to interpret a portion of Scripture accurately or a mistaken view of a doctrine. They distorted cardinal doctrines and developed a type of "Christianity" directly opposed to God and to true religion. It will have eternal consequences. In 2:1 these were called "destructive heresies" because they in effect "[denied] the Master who bought them" (with his blood). In 2:3 God's condemnation of them for their heresy was so severe that their destruction "will not be delayed," meaning it is absolutely certain; their judgment had already been pronounced on them. Then in 3:7 Peter says that all "ungodly people" will be "destroyed" at the final judgment when the present creation itself will disappear in fire. As it states in Hebrews, "It is a terrible thing to fall into the hands of the living God" (Heb 10:31), for "our God is a devouring fire" (Heb 12:29).

◆ C. Call to Be Vigilant (3:17-18a)

17 I am warning you ahead of time, dear friends. Be on guard so that you will not be carried away by the errors of these wicked people and lose your own secure footing.

18 Rather, you must grow in the grace and knowledge of our Lord and Savior Jesus Christ.

NOTES

3:17 ***warning you ahead of time.*** Lit., "knowing beforehand." Bauckham (1983:337) speaks for those who hold to the pseudonymity of 2 Peter when he maintains that "knew this beforehand" (see below) refers to a deliberate "fiction" on the part of the unknown later author who refers to a prophecy of Peter before his death. But as Moo (1996:213) points out, the seriousness of this warning goes far beyond the words of Peter himself to "what the holy prophets said long ago and what our Lord and Savior commanded through your apostles" (3:2). There is no reason whatsoever to take this as a "fictional" creation of a later author.

COMMENTARY

At the close of his letter Peter gives a final charge to his readers (seen in the emphatic "you" that begins this verse), warning them not to fall into the clutches of the false teachers. This charge acts as a summary of the basic exhortation of the epistle as a whole. The expression "ahead of time" renders a causal participle, "since you knew this before," referring to their knowledge of eschatological and ethical truths from the previous apostolic teaching they had heard (e.g., through Paul), as well as what they had read earlier in this epistle (so Moo 1996:213; Schreiner 2003:399-400). The readers should recognize the serious deviation from truth on the part of the heretics; they should rely on their knowledge of true doctrine through previous teaching they had learned.

"Be on guard" (*phulassō* [TG5442, ZG5875]) is present tense, meaning "at all times be vigilant." The verb pictures a watchful prison guard (the semantic domain) and speaks of constant vigilance. If the community did not maintain its alert vigil, the danger was that some may "be carried away by the errors of these wicked people." The verb speaks of "causing someone along with others to go astray in belief" (BDAG 965) and depicts the false teachers morally kidnapping their followers by means of their deliberate lies. The term for "error" is *planē* [TG4106, ZG4415], emphasizing the "deceit" by which the heretics manipulated the thinking of their adherents. It can also mean "wandering" and should probably be seen both in a passive sense (their "wandering" from the truth) and in an active sense (causing others to "wander" from the faith, see Bauckham 1983:82, 337). The term is used for the "error" of Balaam in 2:15 and Jude 11. These heretics were "wicked" or "lawless," linking them with the people of Sodom in 2:7, who also rejected God's moral laws. The danger is that many of Peter's readers were being influenced by their perverse teachings and might be "carried away" into their destructive practices.

If this were to occur, these believers would "lose [their] own secure footing" in Christ. There is a difference between the "unstable" in the community (2:14; 3:16) who are easily led astray and the "firm" or secure Christians who are anchored in their faith. But this does not mean there was no danger for the latter, for the warning here is "losing" or "falling from" (the literal meaning) their place in Christ. Peter stresses here the necessity of the "secure" maintaining constant vigilance over each other. The term for "secure footing" is *stērigmos* [TG4740, ZG5113], referring to a "fixed, secure, or safe" position. The verb form of this is found in 1:12, speaking of believers who are "standing firm" or well-grounded in God's truths. The idea of "losing" or "falling away from" their secure place in Christ's community is language of apostasy, similar to the drifting away of Hebrews 2:1 or the falling away of Hebrews 4:11; 6:4-6. This is a theme in 2 Peter, seen in the "never fall away" of 1:10 and the "enslaved by sin" and "reject the command" of 2:20-21. The obvious question is whether this can happen to a true believer, and that was discussed in 2:20-22; 2 Peter (like Hebrews or 1 John 5) teaches that Christians who fail to "stand firm" (1:12; 3:17) in Christ are in danger of losing their salvation. The answer is continual vigilance, as is stated in Hebrews 3:13, "You must warn each other every day, while it is still 'today,' so that none of you will be deceived by sin and hardened against God."

The first antidote for apostasy is vigilance (3:17); the second (3:18) is spiritual growth, again a present-tense command, meaning "keep on working at your growth." The two spheres in which they are to grow are "grace and knowledge." "Grace" would refer to the blessings of salvation and their experience of God's mercies in their life. "Knowledge" is strongly stressed in 2 Peter (1:2-3, 5-6, 8, 20; 2:20-21; 3:3, with the two terms, *gnōsis* [TG1108, ZG1194] and *epignōsis* [TG1922, ZG2106] being synonyms in 2 Peter) due to the false teaching. But in this case it is primarily experiential knowledge—knowing God and Christ. "Of our Lord and Savior Jesus Christ" (a frequent title; see 1:1, 11; 2:20; 3:2) could modify just "knowledge" (so Moo 1996:214; Schreiner 2003:401), but "grace and knowledge" are linked by a single preposition, so it is slightly better to see that the phrase modifies both. With "grace" it is a subjective genitive ("the grace shown by Jesus Christ") and with "knowledge" it is an objective genitive ("knowing Christ Jesus"), though both could be subjective ("the grace and knowledge Jesus gives," so Davids 2006:316-317).

Either would fit, though I prefer the former. As Bauckham (1983:338) states, "knowing Christ" means "that deepening experience of Christ and understanding of the truth of Christ which should continue to increase until the Parousia brings a full revelation of him (cf. 1 Cor 13:8-9, 12)." The main thing is that ongoing spiritual growth in our relationship to Christ is a prerequisite, lest the slide downward into spiritual ruin start to take place.

◆ V. Closing Praise (3:18b)

All glory to him, both now and forever!
Amen.

NOTES

3:18 ***Amen.*** While the closing "Amen" [TG281, ZG297] is present in the majority of manuscripts (e.g., 𝔓72 א A C P Ψ), it is missing in a few (B 1739 1881). Since NT doxologies regularly conclude with "amen," it is more likely that later scribes added it rather than removed it. Therefore, it is better to see "amen" as a later scribal insertion (so Comfort 2008:769; Metzger 1994:637-638; Bauckham 1983:336).

COMMENTARY

Most epistles end with a closing wish or prayer, "May the grace of our Lord be with you" (most of Paul's letters). A few have a doxology, but most of those are addressed to God (Rom 16:27; Phil 4:20; 1 Pet 5:11; Jude 25). Doxologies to Christ only occur in 2 Timothy 4:18; Hebrews 13:21; here; and Revelation 1:5-6 (obviously not a letter closing). This doxology to Christ is very natural given the high Christology of 2 Peter, which begins by calling Christ "our God and Savior" (1:1). The answer to the false teachers is the centrality of Christ as God and as Savior, so "glory" belongs to him and him alone. In 1:3 Christ's "glory" is the means by which believers receive the divine promises, and 1:17 celebrates the "honor and glory" Christ received on the Mount of Transfiguration. The heretics had dishonored Christ, and Peter wanted to restore that honor by proclaiming at the end that "glory" belongs to him and him alone.

This glory belongs first to him "now," referring to present worship and praise. Jesus as part of the triune Godhead deserves a central place in the church's liturgy and hymnody as well as in the personal adoration of every believer. Yet that worship is not only for the present time but is to be eternal in duration. Most doxologies have "forever and ever," but Peter here has, literally, "into the day of eternity." It might be best to translate this "both now and from the day that inaugurates eternity," a reference to the Parousia of Christ (= "the Day of the Lord," the core of the issue in this epistle), which itself is the eschaton and means the onset of the eternal reign of God. The false teachers denied that there will be a return of Christ, and Peter ends his epistle by saying that there will not only be a return but that that return will inaugurate eternity. "The 'day' that Peter and his readers anticipate will signal the destruction of the present order (3:10, 12) and will also inaugurate a new era that will last throughout eternity (1:19; 3:13)" (G. Green 2008:344).

BIBLIOGRAPHY

Adams, E.

2005 Where Is the Promise of His Coming: The Complaint of the Scoffers in 2 Peter 3.4. *New Testament Studies* 51:106-122.

Barclay, William

1976 *The Letters of James and Peter.* Philadelphia: Westminster.

Bateman, Herbert W., IV, editor

2007 *Four Views on the Warning Passages in Hebrews.* Grand Rapids: Kregel.

Bauckham, Richard J.

1983 *Jude, 2 Peter.* Word Biblical Commentary 50. Waco: Word.

1988 James, 1 and 2 Peter, Jude. Pp. 303-317 in *It Is Written: Scripture Citing Scripture; Essays in Honour of Barnabas Lindars.* Editors, D. A. Carson and H. G. M. Williamson. Cambridge: Cambridge University Press.

Bigg, Charles

1901 *A Critical and Exegetical Commentary on the Epistles of St. Peter and St. Jude.* International Critical Commentary. Edinburgh: T&T Clark.

Billings, Bradly S.

2008 The Angels Who Sinned . . . He Cast into Tartarus (2 Peter 2:4): Its Ancient Meaning and Present Relevance. *Expository Times* 119 11:532-537.

Blomberg, Craig L.

2007 *The Historical Reliability of the Gospels.* 2nd ed. Downers Grove, IL: InterVarsity.

Bock, Darrel, and Robert Webb

2010 *Key Events in the Life of the Historical Jesus: A Collaborative Exploration of Context and Coherence.* Grand Rapids: Eerdmans.

Bray, Gerald, editor

2000 *Ancient Christian Commentary on Scripture: James, 1–2 Peter, 1–3 John, Jude.* Downers Grove, IL: InterVarsity.

Callan, T.

2001 The Soteriology of the Second Letter of Peter. *Biblica* 82:549-559.

2004 Use of the Letter of Jude by the Second Letter of Peter. *Biblica* 85:42-64.

2006 A Note on 2 Peter 1:19-20. *Journal of Biblical Literature* 125:143-150.

2009 Comparison of Humans to Animals in 2 Peter 2,10b-22. *Biblica* 90/1:110-113.

Calvin, John

1979 *Commentaries on the Catholic Epistles.* Translator, J. Owen. Grand Rapids: Baker.

Carson, D. A., and Douglas J. Moo

2005 *An Introduction to the New Testament.* 2nd ed. Grand Rapids: Zondervan.

Charles, J. D.

2005 The Angels under Reserve in 2 Peter and Jude. *Bulletin for Biblical Research* 15:39-48.

Chester, Andrew, and Ralph P. Martin, editors

1994 *The Theology of the Letters of James, Peter, and Jude.* Cambridge: Cambridge University Press.

Comfort, Philip W.

2008 *New Testament Text and Translation Commentary.* Carol Stream, IL: Tyndale House.

Cranfield, C. E. B.

1960 *1 and 2 Peter and Jude: Introduction and Commentary.* London: SCM.

Davids, Peter H.

2000 2 Peter. Pp. 350-351 in *New Dictionary of Biblical Theology.* Editor, T. D. Alexander. Downers Grove, IL: InterVarsity.

2006 *The Letters of 2 Peter and Jude.* Pillar New Testament Commentary. Grand Rapids: Eerdmans.

Green, Gene L.
2008 *2 Peter and Jude*. Baker Exegetical Commentary on the New Testament. Grand Rapids: Baker.

Green, Michael
1987 *The Second Epistle General of Peter and the General Epistle of Jude*. Tyndale New Testament Commentaries. Grand Rapids: Eerdmans.

Harrington, Daniel J.
2003 *Jude and 2 Peter*. Sacra Pagina. Collegeville, MN: Liturgical Press.

Harris, Murray J.
1992 *Jesus as God:* Theos *as a Christological Term in the New Testament*. Grand Rapids: Baker.

Harvey, Robert, and Philip H. Towner
2009 *2 Peter & Jude*. InterVarsity Press New Testament Commentaries. Downers Grove, IL: InterVarsity.

Hiebert, D. Edmond
1989 *Second Peter and Jude: An Expositional Commentary*. Greenville, SC: Unusual Publications.

Hillyer, Norman
1992 *1 and 2 Peter, Jude*. New International Biblical Commentary. Peabody, MA: Hendrickson.

Jastrow, Marcus
2006 *Dictionary of the Targumim, the Talmud Babli and Yerushalmi, and the Midrashic Literature*. Peabody, MA: Hendrickson.

Jones, D. W.
2006 The Apostate Angels of 2 Pet. 2:4 and Jude 6. *Faith and Mission* 23:19-30.

Käsemann, Ernst
1964 An Apologia for Primitive Christian Eschatology. Pp. 169-195 in *Essays on New Testament Themes*. Philadelphia: Fortress.

Kelly, J. N. D.
1969 *A Commentary on the Epistles of Peter and Jude*. Black's New Testament Commentary. London: Black.

Kistemaker, Simon J.
1987 *Exposition of the Epistles of Peter and of the Epistle of Jude*. Grand Rapids: Baker.

Kraftchick, S. J.
2002 *Jude, 2 Peter*. Abingdon New Testament Commentary. Nashville: Abingdon.

Lloyd-Jones, D. M.
1983 *Expository Sermons on 2 Peter*. London: Banner of Truth.

Lucas, Dick, and Christopher Green
1995 *The Message of 2 Peter and Jude*. The Bible Speaks Today. Downers Grove, IL: InterVarsity.

Marshall, I. Howard
1974 Early Catholicism in the New Testament. Pp. 217-231 in *New Dimensions in New Testament Study*. Editors, R. N. Longenecker and M. C. Tenney. Grand Rapids: Zondervan.

Mayor, Joseph B.
1907 *The Epistle of St. Jude and the Second Epistle of St. Peter: Greek Text with Introduction, Notes and Comments*. New York: Macmillan.

Metzger, Bruce M.
1994 *A Textual Commentary on the Greek New Testament*. New York: United Bible Societies.

Miller, T. A.
2000 Dogs, Adulterers, and the Way of Balaam: The Forms and Socio-Rhetorical Function of the Polemical Rhetoric in 2 Peter (Parts I & II). *Irish Biblical Studies* 22:123-144, 182-191.

Moffat, James
1928 *The General Epistles: James, Peter and Judas*. Moffatt New Testament Commentaries. Garden City, NY: Doubleday.

Moo, Douglas J.
1996 *2 Peter and Jude*. NIV Application Commentary. Grand Rapids: Zondervan.

Mounce, Robert H.
1982 *A Living Hope: A Commentary of 1 and 2 Peter*. Grand Rapids: Eerdmans.

Neyrey, Jerome H.
1980 The Form and Background of the Polemic in 2 Peter. *Journal of Biblical Literature* 99:407-431.

1993 *2 Peter, Jude: A New Translation with Introduction and Commentary*. Anchor Bible 37C. New York: Doubleday.

O'Brien, Peter

1982 *Colossians, Philemon.* Word Biblical Commentary 44. Waco: Word.

1999 *The Letter to the Ephesians.* Pillar New Testament Commentaries. Grand Rapids: Eerdmans.

Osborne, Grant R.

1991 *The Hermeneutical Spiral: A Comprehensive Introduction to Biblical Interpretation.* Downers Grove, IL: InterVarsity.

2002 *Revelation.* Baker Exegetical Commentary on the New Testament. Grand Rapids: Baker.

2003 *Romans.* InterVarsity New Testament Commentaries. Downers Grove, IL: InterVarsity.

2007 John. Pp. 1-314 in *Cornerstone Biblical Commentary*, vol. 13. Carol Stream, IL: Tyndale House.

2010 *Matthew.* Zondervan Exegetical Commentary on the New Testament. Editor, C. E. Arnold. Grand Rapids: Zondervan.

Plumptre, E. H.

1879 *The General Epistles of St. Peter and St. Jude: with Notes and Introduction.* Cambridge: Cambridge University Press.

Porter, Stanley E., and A. W. Pitts

2008 τοῦτο πρῶτον γινώσκοντες ὅτι in 2 Peter 1:20 and Hellenistic Epistolary Convention. *Journal of Biblical Literature* 127:165-171.

Reese, Ruth Ann

2007 *2 Peter and Jude.* Two Horizons New Testament Commentary. Grand Rapids: Eerdmans.

Reicke, Bo

1964 *The Epistles of James, Peter, and Jude.* Garden City, NY: Doubleday.

Richard, E.

2000 *Reading 1 Peter, Jude and 2 Peter: A Literary and Theological Commentary.* Macon, GA: Smyth & Helwys.

Schreiner, Thomas R.

2003 *1, 2 Peter, Jude.* New American Commentary. Nashville: Broadman & Holman.

Senior, Donald

2005 The Petrine Letters and the Petrine Ministry. *Bible Today* 43:233-237.

Snyder, G. F.

1977 The *Tobspruch* in the New Testament. *New Testament Studies* 23:117-120.

Thielman, Frank

2005 *Theology of the New Testament.* Grand Rapids: Zondervan.

Vögtle, A.

1994 *Der Judasbrief; Der 2. Petrusbrief.* Evangelisch-katholischer Kommentar zum Neuen Testament. Düsseldorf: Neukirchen.

Wallace, Daniel B.

1996 *Greek Grammar Beyond the Basics: An Exegetical Syntax of the New Testament.* Grand Rapids: Zondervan.

Watson, Duane F.

1988 *Invention, Arrangement, and Style: Rhetorical Criticism of Jude and 2 Peter.* Atlanta: Scholars Press.

Jude

GRANT R. OSBORNE

INTRODUCTION TO

Jude

JUDE IS certainly not one of the more recognized New Testament books. It is rarely made the subject of sermon series or Bible studies, rarely studied in survey courses of seminaries or Christian colleges, probably because, along with 2 Peter, it has a basically negative cast (opposing a false movement in the church) and has a highly apocalyptic orientation. People just do not warm up to works that center on final judgment and going to battle against false teachers. In our postmodern world with its emphasis on radical pluralism and tolerance and its soft approach to theological issues, Jude's harsh demand for truth and condemnation of those who reject that truth strikes a difficult chord. Then there is the book's use of apocryphal and pseudepigraphical works like *The Testament of Moses* and *1 Enoch*. Nevertheless, Jude is indeed worthy of study as a first-century work placed in the Canon by God's providence. Jude has an important message for the church both in terms of the importance of maintaining a purity of doctrine and of building up the church so that it recognizes truth (as well as error) when it hears it.

AUTHOR

The author identifies himself as "Jude" and probably added "brother of James" (v. 1) because Jude was such a common name in the first century. This personal name was always used of a Jewish male and could be rendered by a plethora of equivalents—Judas, Judah, Jude, and, in geographic use, Judea. The "James" named here is certainly the brother of Jesus. It could not refer to James the brother of John, because that James had been martyred earlier (Acts 12), and Judas (son of James), one of the Twelve (Luke 6:16; Acts 1:13) was not a brother of that (otherwise unknown) James, ruling him out as a candidate here as well. Judas Barsabbas, noted in Acts 15:22, 27, 32, does not fit well either, for there is little likelihood of any such connection with James. The "James" named here was clearly a well-known figure in the early church, and by far the best candidate is the James who was the brother of Jesus (Mark 6:3; John 7:5; Gal 1:19) and a prominent elder in Jerusalem (Acts 15:13-21; 21:18; "a pillar of the church" in Gal 2:9). Jude probably mentioned James to anchor his authority for writing this letter (see commentary). But why didn't Jude mention he was a brother of Jesus himself? Probably because he had already called himself "a slave of Jesus Christ" and wanted to center on his spiritual relationship to Jesus rather than on his earthly connection to him (so Clement of Alexandria *Comments on the Epistle of Jude* 1-4).

We do not know much about Jude or his life. In the two lists of Jesus' family (Matt 13:55; Mark 6:3) "Judas" is listed as last and third (respectively) among the four brothers of Jesus (with James, Joseph, and Simon), with his "sisters" interspersed among them. So Jude could have been four or more siblings removed from Jesus, and Davids (2006:11) estimates he "could have been younger than twenty when Jesus died." Furthermore, Jude and his brothers were unbelievers during Jesus' life (John 7:5; cf. Mark 3:21), and like James he may have been converted via a resurrection appearance (1 Cor 15:7). Acts 1:14 tells us that Mary "and the brothers of Jesus" were part of the 120 gathered together in the upper room between Jesus' ascension and Pentecost, so they were all believers by then. First Corinthians 9:5 tells us that Jesus' brothers engaged in the same type of pioneer missionary work as Paul, and that likely included Jude. On the basis of this epistle, Jude had become a major leader in the church, for there is a distinct tone of authority in this letter. According to Eusebius (*History* 3.19-20), his family continued to serve the Lord, for his grandsons were arrested and forced to appear before Domitian to answer for their loyalty to Rome.

In modern times, Jude's authorship has been doubted because the quality of its Greek (cf. Kelly, Vögtle) is seen as too good for a Galilean Jew, but many have noted the Greek-speaking ability of residents in Galilee (with its high percentage of Gentiles). While there are some who assert that only the upper-class elite in Galilee spoke Greek well, G. Green (2008:7-8) rightly notes that Jude's itinerant ministry in Gentile areas would not be possible unless he knew Greek fairly well. Moreover, if Jude ministered regularly in the Greek-speaking world, he would have learned to speak and write Greek with facility (so Bauckham 1983:15).

Some scholars think Jude to be pseudonymous because they understand verse 17 as referring to the apostolic age as past. But Jude was not saying the apostles wrote in the distant past. If Jude was written in the 60s, the prophecies of Jesus and Paul would clearly fit the apostolic witness alluded to. Another reason some regard Jude as pseudonymous lies in the assumption, as in the case of 2 Peter (see the Introduction to that book), that the heretics addressed in this work were a type of Gnostic thinkers who arose much later than the middle of the first century. However, there is no evidence for this (see below regarding the heresy itself), and the heretics Jude describes would easily fit the 60s. Overall, it is best to see this epistle as written by Jude, the brother of Jesus and James.

DATE

If Jude was the author (as I have argued), then the date of writing must be somewhere between AD 50 and 95. On the basis of the expression "the faith that God has entrusted . . . to his holy people" in verse 3, many think Jude was writing at a time after Christian doctrines had been codified; they argue that this is an example of "early Catholicism," marking Jude as a late epistle (see the discussion under "Author" in the Introduction to 2 Peter). However, this line of reasoning is completely unnecessary; in the commentary I point out that Jude refers to the gospel truths transmitted to the church, something that happened in the 50s (as in 1 Cor 11:2, 16; 15:1, 3; 2 Thess 2:15; 3:6), as well as the 90s.

More significant than the dating of Jude is the literary relationship between 2 Peter and Jude. If Jude used 2 Peter, then any date would be possible for Jude after the mid-60s. But if Peter used Jude (as I argue in the Introduction to 2 Peter), then there is a *terminus ad quem* for Jude, since Peter died during the Neronian persecution in the mid-60s. On that basis I would date Jude in the late 50s or early 60s.

OCCASION OF WRITING

There is a certain connection between the false teachers mentioned in Jude and those opposed in 2 Peter, for Peter used much of Jude in his epistle. Jude originally had intended to write about their common salvation (v. 3a) but was forced to change the focus of his letter when he heard that dangerous teachers had "wormed their way" into the good graces of these churches (vv. 3b-4). So Jude called the faithful to battle, to "defend the faith" (v. 3b) against these people. It is very difficult to describe the movement itself, for Jude simply highlighted certain aspects he wished to stress, but he expected his readers to be aware of the whole. All we get are the snippets Jude has decided to point out as examples of the heinous nature of their doctrine and practices. There is no attempt to summarize what they stood for, and so all we can do is determine generalities about their teaching.

Still, it is not as though we have nothing to say. Davids (2006:20) lists the following characteristics:

1. impiety ("ungodly," vv. 4, 15, 18)
2. arrogance, claiming a false authority ("denied . . . Jesus," v. 4; "claim authority," v. 8; "brag loudly about themselves," v. 16) and even "scoff at supernatural beings" (v. 8)
3. immorality ("grace allows us to live immoral lives," v. 4; "live immoral lives," v. 8; "ungodly desires," vv. 16, 18; "follow their natural instincts," v. 19)
4. greed ("deceive people for money," v. 11; "care only for themselves," v. 12; "flatter others to get what they want," v. 16)
5. rebellion ("defy authority," v. 8; "scoff at supernatural beings," v. 8, and at "things they do not understand," v. 10; likened to Korah's rebellion, v. 11)
6. divisiveness ("grumblers and complainers," v. 16; "insults . . . spoken against him," v. 15; "creating divisions among you," v. 19)

While the emphasis is upon the actions of the false teachers, both doctrine and praxis are involved, although we know more about the latter. The very first thing mentioned is "the faith" (v. 3), which means the set of beliefs. The only direct reference to doctrine in the epistle occurs in 1:4, clearly presenting the false teachers as arguing that "God's marvelous grace" freed Christians from all law and allowed them to practice a libertine (and immoral) lifestyle (v. 4). From this and the practices Peter mentions, most conclude that some form of antinomianism (lit., "against law") characterized the movement, in this case a view that their heightened spirituality freed them from any ethical or moral restraints. Verse 4 also implies that these were interlopers who had infiltrated the church from outside ("wormed their way into," v. 4), unlike the false teachers in 2 Peter, who developed from within the church.

It is very difficult to align these false teachers with any particular movement of the first century. They were not Gnostics, for there is no evidence of secret teaching or initiations, no view of God creating the aeons, no dualism between the natural and spiritual realms. Still, there were some connections with the later Carpocratians who flourished in Alexandria early in the second century. While there are some similarities, there are also some significant differences. The Carpocratians were separatists and practiced the "agape meal" by themselves and never pretended to be part of "apostolic tradition" (vv. 4, 12). If there is any commonality, it is general, and at best this could be an early form of the later movement (see G. Green 2008:24-25). We should probably recognize we will never know for certain how the false teachers addressed in Jude exactly fit into the movements of the first and second century. We dare not leave out the Jewish elements in the apocalyptic heritage of the group, and we should also see some connection between the heresies of Jude and 2 Peter (see the Introduction to 2 Peter). This was likely a syncretistic movement combining Jewish and Gentile notions into a quasi-Christian cult.

AUDIENCE

Jude does not contain any opening designation of addressees or any salutations at the end, so we cannot know for certain where it was sent. There are two somewhat conflicting pieces of evidence as to the makeup of the recipients of the epistle. On the basis of the use of Jewish apocalyptic literature (*1 Enoch, Testament of Moses*), the audience seems to be Jewish. Yet at the same time, the licentious behavior would point more to Gentiles. Many think the Jewish aspects predominate and see a Palestinian provenance (Kelly, Bauckham, Schreiner), but the fact of the excellent Greek, as well as the problem of severe immorality, has many favoring a Gentile destination. Syria is often mentioned (Bigg, M. Green), but the problem here is that Syria was the last region to accept Jude as a canonical work. Others prefer Egypt, in particular Alexandria (Neyrey, Gunther), because the letter was well received and widely known there (as in Clement of Alexandria's commentary).

Overall, my preference is for a more Gentile provenance, for the reasons above and also because the desecration of the Lord's Supper (v. 12) is similar to the situation in 1 Corinthians 11, also a Gentile setting. I argued that 2 Peter was written to Asia Minor, and Jude was used in 2 Peter 2, indicating a possible connection between the audiences. The primary difference is that Jude does not refer to the issues of the Lord's return and the denial of final judgment, both central to 2 Peter (on this issue see the Introduction to 2 Peter). However, the general situation is similar. I do not believe we can go any further and specify exactly where Jude's churches were located. It is best to see a general Gentile setting, possibly with a few Jewish Christian house churches, as in Rome. Bauckham (1983:16) likewise speaks of "a Jewish-Christian community in a Gentile setting."

CANONICITY AND TEXTUAL HISTORY

While the Western church generally accepted the epistle, some parts of the Eastern church did not (it was omitted in the Peshitta). Some doubted it because of its quote from *1 Enoch*. However, it was accepted in the Muratorian Canon, and Clement of Alexandria even wrote a commentary on it (see the helpful discussion in G. Green 2008:5-6). Jude was included among the 27 books of the New Testament listed by Athanasius of Alexandria in his *Festal Letter* for Easter in 367. It was also included in the list of canonical Scriptures by the Council of Carthage in 397.

The text of Jude is best attested to by the fourth-century manuscripts Codex Vaticanus and Codex Sinaiticus, as well as by the third-century Bodmer Papyrus VII/VIII (𝔓72), which preserves the entire epistle. Another third-century papyrus, 𝔓78, preserves a small portion of Jude (vv. 4-5, 7-8). Differences in texts will be discussed throughout the course of the commentary.

LITERARY STYLE

As discussed above, Jude is both a Hellenistic and a Jewish epistle. It contains excellent Greek, both in grammar and in vocabulary. It is carefully organized in terms of rhetorical skill (see Charles 1991). Jude likes triads, or sets of three, seen in several places (vv. 1-2, 8, 12-13, 15, 19, 22-23). At the same time, there is also clearly Jewish argumentation and use of Old Testament and Second Temple Jewish literature. Jude also employed the "story" form to embed narratives into his rhetorical strategy (see Webb 2008). The two different approaches (Jewish and Hellenistic) are seen in the structure worked out by various scholars. Bauckham (1983:4-6) believes the argumentation is midrashic, centering on a series of Jewish "texts" (vv. 5-7, 11, 14-15, 17-18) and employing a pesher type of exegesis centering on "this people" or "these people" and eschatological prophecies applied to the current situation. His outline is:

- 1-2 Address
- 3-4 Occasion and theme
- 5-19 Background of the appeal: a midrash on the prophecies of doom of the ungodly
  - 5-9 Three Old Testament types plus interpretation
  - 10-13 Three more Old Testament types
  - 14-16 Prophecy of Enoch plus interpretation
  - 17-19 Prophecy of the apostles plus interpretation
- 20-23 The appeal
- 24-25 Closing doxology

Many others see a more Hellenistic structure, exemplified by Watson (1988:77-78), who sees an organization that follows Greek rhetoric:

- 1-2 *Prescript*
- 3 *Exordium*, stating the purpose
- 4 *Narratio*, stating common assumptions
- 5-16 *Probatio*, presenting the arguments of the epistle
  - 5-10 First proof
  - 11-13 Second proof
  - 14-16 Third proof
- 17-23 *Peroratio*, providing the closing exhortation
- 24-25 Doxology

It is clear that Jude had both Jewish background and some Hellenistic level of education, for his epistle shows awareness of both approaches. Likely his readers had both as well.

MAJOR THEMES

Although Jude is obviously one of the shorter epistles in the New Testament, it contains a rich theological perspective. Harvey and Towner (2009:149-150) see a Trinitarian aspect, especially in verses 20-21, "Pray in the power of the Holy Spirit . . . await the mercy of our Lord Jesus Christ . . . keep yourselves safe in God's love." As they say, "What is evident from a statement like this is the understanding of the significant presence and role of each divine person in the life of the community." The Spirit is the least mentioned, found only in verse 19 (the heretics do not have the Spirit) and verse 20 (the believers have the Spirit and pray in the Spirit). While the false teachers may claim to have God's revelation behind their tenets, Jude makes it clear that the presence of the Spirit makes the difference, and thus the truly faithful, not the cult leaders, are the ones inspired by God.

God is more central than the Spirit. The love of God opens the epistle (v. 1) and God as "Savior" closes the epistle (v. 25). God is our Father (v. 1), his "grace" defines salvation in contrast to the perversion of it by the false teachers (v. 4), and his love preserves us (v. 21). As Savior he not only "keeps" us now but will "bring" us into his "presence"; thus, he is deserving of our praise and glory (vv. 24-25).

As one would expect, it is Christ who permeates Jude's epistle. In the opening salutation, Jude presents himself as the "slave of Jesus Christ" (v. 1), indicating that Jesus was his "Master and Lord," the very thing the false teachers denied (v. 4). Jesus is at all times sovereign and cosmic Lord, standing alongside God in his dominion over all creation. True theology must begin by acknowledging Jesus' lordship. In fact, Jude describes the return of Christ in verses 14-15 via a quote from *1 Enoch* 1:9 about God's coming in judgment, transforming Enoch's vision of theophany into a promise regarding the Parousia: "The Lord is coming." As Lord, Jesus will be eschatological judge and will destroy the heretics for their blasphemy and immorality. The epistle is framed by Jesus' power to safeguard the faithful—God's preservation of his people will be conducted in "Jesus Christ" (v. 1), and that protection and presentation at the eschaton will occur "through Jesus Christ our Lord" (v. 25). In fact, Jude presents Jesus as the one who "rescued the nation of Israel from Egypt" (v. 5, see note and commentary on this), a precursor of Jesus delivering his people now. Finally, it is "the mercy of our Lord Jesus Christ" (v. 21) that will "bring you eternal life." Throughout Jude the work of God (preserving, coming, judging, bringing eternal life) is conducted by Christ.

Sin and salvation are another primary theme in Jude. Davids (2006:31) points out that two primary problems are stressed in Jude: the rejection of the sovereignty of God and Christ (v. 4) and the "giving in to desire" (vv. 4, 16, 19)—not only sexual perversion but also greed and slander. Such sins "contaminate" or "pollute" the lives of those who commit them (v. 23c). The result of the depravity of their actions will be their "condemnation" (vv. 4, 6, 15) and certain "destruction" (vv. 5, 10-11, 23). Yet God through Christ has shown mercy (vv. 2, 21-23) by providing salvation and allowing his people to rescue such from the "flames of judgment" (v. 23). Salvation means to embrace the faith entrusted once for all time (v. 3) and the "marvelous grace" of God (v. 4), to dwell in the power of the Holy Spirit (v. 20), and to center on the security to be found only in Christ (vv. 1c, 21, 24).

Finally, Jude demonstrates the same kind of final eschatology found in 2 Peter. Two aspects are emphasized. First, the final judgment is stressed throughout: The fallen angels are imprisoned, "waiting for the great day of judgment" (v. 6), and Sodom and Gomorrah were "destroyed by fire" to "serve as a warning of the eternal fire of God's judgment" (v. 7). The final destruction of the false teachers in verses 10-11, 13 is the antitype of these judgments, and when the adherents are rescued, they are "snatch[ed] . . . from the flames of judgment" (v. 23). Second, this judgment will take place in accordance with the second coming of the Lord with his holy angels (vv. 14-15). At that return, which is awaited by the saints, God's "mercy" will bring "eternal life" (v. 21) and bring the faithful "into his glorious presence" (v. 24).

OUTLINE

A structural outline needs to find a balance between Bauckham's and Watson's approaches (see "Literary Style" above). While recognizing the difficulties of any attempt, I suggest the following outline:

- I. Salutation (vv. 1-2)
- II. Purpose and Theme (vv. 3-4)
- III. Condemnation of the False Teachers (vv. 5-16)
  - A. Biblical Examples of Their Condemnation (vv. 5-10)
    - 1. Three examples presented (vv. 5-7)
    - 2. Application to the false teachers (vv. 8-10)
  - B. Further Biblical Examples of Their Depravity (vv. 11-13)
  - C. An Illustration from Enoch's Prophecy (vv. 14-16)
- IV. Closing Appeal to the Genuine Believers (vv. 17-23)
  - A. Call to Remember Apostolic Prophecy (vv. 17-19)
  - B. Exhortation to Remain Faithful (vv. 20-23)
- V. Concluding Doxology (vv. 24-25)

COMMENTARY ON

Jude

◆ I. Salutation (vv. 1-2)

This letter is from Jude, a slave of Jesus Christ and a brother of James.

I am writing to all who have been called by God the Father, who loves you and keeps you safe in the care of Jesus Christ.*

[2]May God give you more and more mercy, peace, and love.

1 Or *keeps you for Jesus Christ.*

NOTES

1 ***called by God the Father, who loves you and keeps you.*** In the NLT "God" modifies the verb "called" and itself is the subject of the verbs "loves" and "keeps." But in the Greek the two latter verbs are connected grammatically with "the called," and "God" better modifies "loves," producing better balance in the two phrases modifying "the called." Therefore, a better translation of this is, "to those who have been called, who are loved by God the Father and kept for Christ Jesus."

loves. The KJV and NKJV read "sanctified," following another textual tradition (K P 048 056 𝔐), but the best and oldest manuscripts (𝔓72 א A B Ψ) contain the reading followed here.

COMMENTARY

Ancient letters began with the sender, the recipients, and a greeting. Most also contained a thanksgiving and prayer, as in Paul's epistles, and when the latter two are missing (as in Galatians or the Pastorals), it usually indicates that the occasion for writing was serious enough that it demanded the author get right to the point. That is the case with Jude (and with 2 Peter). The problem with the false teachers was so severe that Jude had to move right into the issues.

The author identifies himself as "Jude" (*Ioudas* [TG2455, ZG2683]), a very common name in Jewish circles, as shown by the fact that two of the twelve disciples were named "Judas/Jude." In the Introduction I concluded that the likely identification of the sender is Jude, the brother of Jesus (Mark 6:3) and of James. It is important to realize that Jude did not identify himself as Jesus' brother but rather as his "slave" (*doulos* [TG1401, ZG1528]). The latter was, for Jude, the more significant. Jesus may have been Jude's earthly brother, but he was more importantly Jude's cosmic Lord and Master (v. 4). It was Jude's privilege to give his life in service to his Lord.

At the same time "slave" (often translated "servant") was a title of honor, with the great leaders of Israel called "slave/servant of God": Abraham, Isaac, and Jacob (Exod 32:13; Deut 9:27); Moses (Num 12:7; Deut 34:5); Samuel (1 Sam 3:9-10); David (2 Sam 7:5, 8, 19); and Daniel (Dan 6:20). The writers of the New Testament epistles commonly labeled themselves and others "slaves of Christ" (Rom 1:1; Gal 1:10; Phil 1:1; Col 4:12; Titus 1:1; Jas 1:1; 2 Pet 1:1). As a title of distinction it meant they were part of God's royal family and official envoys of the King of kings. As G. Green (2008:45) says, "The higher the social status of the master, the more weighty the power of the managerial slave. Since Jude is the slave-agent of Jesus Christ . . . we should understand his self-designation as a claim to authority, divine commission, and perhaps even inspiration."

At the same time Jude identified himself as James's brother. This was undoubtedly James the brother of Jesus (Mark 6:3) and elder/leader of the Jerusalem church (Acts 12:17; 15:13-21; 21:18; Gal 2:9, 12). Neither of them were believers during Jesus' life (John 7:5), and Jude, like James (1 Cor 15:7), probably came to faith during the resurrection appearances. Other than that, we know almost nothing about the life and ministry of Jude. While some take this as evidence of pseudonymity (Kelly 1969:242), it most likely meant the opposite. Jude, possibly not well known to his readers, demonstrates his authority by showing his blood relationship to one of the "pillars" of the church (Gal 2:9; so Neyrey, Schreiner).

We do not know who the recipients of this letter were, for like 2 Peter, Jude identified the readers not by location but by spiritual description. They are the ones "who have been called by God the Father." As stated in the note on verse 1, it is better to see this simply addressed to "the called." As Davids (2006:36) notes, this title is found 10 times in the New Testament, especially in Romans (Rom 1:1, 6-7; 8:28) and 1 Corinthians (1 Cor 1:1-2, 24). The major thrust seems to be that believers are "called" as the "holy people" of God (Rom 1:7; 8:28; 1 Cor 1:2), the children of destiny who are the special people of God. The concept builds on the Old Testament imagery of Israel as the "elect people of God" (especially in the Servant Songs of Isa 42:6; 45:3-4; 49:1; 51:2; 54:6). It is somewhat common to read a theology of *ordo salutis* into this phrase (e.g., Schreiner, Moo) and to see the call as bringing the elect into the kingdom, with the result that they are irresistibly drawn to God by his powerful "love" and then "kept" secure in his grace. While this is an aspect of Romans 8:28, I doubt that this is intended in all cases, especially in introductory sections like those of Jude, Romans, and 1 Corinthians. The emphasis is likely on the church as the new Israel, the community of God. The initiative is God's (who "calls" in Rom 9:11; 1 Thess 2:12; 1 Pet 1:15; 2 Pet 1:3), and those who respond become his people, called to be faithful (Rev 17:14).

Two participles further clarify this idea of "being called." Both are in the perfect tense, emphasizing the ongoing state of love and protection involved in being "the called." First, they are "loved by God the Father" (v. 1). The actual preposition is *en* [TG1722, ZG1877], which could have a local force ("in God," NRSV, NASB, REB, ESV) or an instrumental force ("by God," NIV, NLT). If local, God becomes the sphere within which we experience love, and the love could be love in the church (a horizontal thrust) or divine love (a vertical thrust). While possible, it may be better and clearer to see this as agency, where God is the source of the love (so Kelly, M. Green, Moo, Schreiner).

The Old Testament often centers on God's love as the basis of Israel's election (Deut 4:37; Ps 78:68; Isa 41:8-9; 44:2; Jer 31:3; Hos 11:1). The new Israel, the church, reexperiences the calling and the love of God. God brings us to himself and calls us to be his own on the basis of his absolute love, and everything we are and have is the result of that unfathomable love. The emphasis on a "Father's love" here leads into the rest of the letter, for the readers are called "dear friends" (literally, "beloved") in verses 3, 17, 20, stressing the way a father would address his child as "my beloved" and "the familial bond that exists between members of the Christian community" (G. Green 2008:52) as a result of their sharing God's love.

Second, the idea of being called is modified by "[kept] safe in the care of Jesus Christ." The verb signifies that the believer is "kept safe" or "secure," with an eschatological force connoting that we are preserved in our present salvation for our future salvation (cf. John 17:11; 1 Thess 5:23; 1 Pet 1:4-5; Rev 3:20). Here there are three options for translating the dative case that is applied to "Jesus Christ": kept "by" (thus parallel to the preposition *en*, "by," so Bigg, Kelly, M. Green, Schreiner); kept "for" (indicating Jesus' return as the goal, NRSV, TNIV, NJB, ESV, Bauckham, Moo, Davids, Harrington, G. Green), or kept "in" (Jesus as the sphere within which we are protected, KJV, NKJV, NLT). Interestingly, few scholars present the third as an option, but it makes a great deal of sense and actually encapsulates the other two. All the security of the believer takes place "in Christ." He is the sphere, the means, and the goal of our spiritual safety because we remain "in Christ."

The greeting itself (v. 2) is somewhat unique with its threefold emphasis (with "mercy, peace, and love" paralleling the threefold "called, loved, kept" in v. 1). Paul and Peter normally have "grace and peace," and in three epistles "mercy" is added (1 Tim 1:2; 2 Tim 1:2; 2 John 3). Only here does "love" replace "grace." "Mercy and peace" was used as a Jewish greeting (e.g., *2 Baruch* 78:2-3, which later mentions "love": "Mercy and peace be with you. I remember, my brothers, the love of him who created me, who loved us from the beginning"). God's "mercy" (*eleos* [TG1656, ZG1799]) harks back to the Hebrew term for his "lovingkindness" (*khesed* [TH2617, ZH2876]), a major covenant concept that centers on the "steadfast love" through which God has chosen his chosen people. In the New Testament, it centers on the grace shown through Jesus Christ.

"Peace" (*eirēnē* [TG1515, ZG1645]) harks back to the Hebrew *shalom* [TH7965, ZH8934]—that tranquility, wholeness, and well-being of soul that results from experiencing the mercy of God. "Love" is added to emphasize further the divine love already noted in verse 1. These three terms introduce major themes throughout the book, with "mercy" in verses 2, 21-22 and "love" in verses 1-2, 12, 21. "Peace" is found only here, but in a sense the whole book concerns finding God's peace in the midst of the volume of lies propounded by the heretics. Jude asked that God grant his readers "more and more" (lit., "May [they] be multiplied")—namely, that they experience increasing spiritual blessings as they progress in their Christian walk.

◆ II. Purpose and Theme (vv. 3-4)

3Dear friends, I had been eagerly planning to write to you about the salvation we all share. But now I find that I must write about something else, urging you to defend the faith that God has entrusted once for all time to his holy people. 4I say this because some ungodly people have wormed their way into your churches, saying that God's marvelous grace allows us to live immoral lives. The condemnation of such people was recorded long ago, for they have denied our only Master and Lord, Jesus Christ.

NOTES

3 ***I had been eagerly planning to write.*** There are various ways to understand this clause. One is to see it as temporal ("while eagerly preparing to write," NRSV, NKJV, NASB, Reicke, Davids), which indicates Jude had intended this letter all along, namely, to write both about their salvation and about the false teachers. Another option is to take it as concessive ("although I was very eager to write," NIV, NLT, ESV, Kelly, Bauckham, Schreiner), which would mean that Jude had originally intended to write them a general letter but changed his plans when he received word about the false teachers. This second option fits the context best, for a change of tone seems indicated in the rest of the verse.

the salvation we all share. Most commentators and translators (including NLT) interpret this as "our common salvation," but G. Green (2008:53-54) opts for "common security" on the grounds that *sōtēria* [TG4991, ZG5401] can also mean "bodily health, well-being," or "safety" depending on context. While this could refer to the "salvation" or "deliverance" God has achieved on behalf of his people, Green thinks that in the context of Jude the idea of the "security" or "safety" of the people of God from their common enemy, the heretics, was paramount. This would be viable if the clause was referring to the contents of this letter. But since this refers to a letter that Jude had been intending to write but then had to jettison, "common salvation" is the better alternative.

4 ***recorded long ago.*** There are four options for what Jude means here: (1) If Jude was using 2 Peter, it could be a reference to 2 Peter (so Bigg 1901:326) since *palai* [TG3819, ZG4093] can mean "a short time ago" as well as in the distant past. But it is more likely that 2 Peter used Jude (see the Introductions to both epistles in this work). (2) It could refer to the "heavenly books" kept by God, which record each person's destiny (as in *2 Baruch* 24:1; *1 Enoch* 89:61-71; 98:7; so Clement of Alexandria; Kelly 1969:250). However, Jude does not demonstrate this kind of predestinarian thought. (3) It might refer to early Christian prophecies as in Acts 20:29-30; 1 Tim 4:1-3; 2 Tim 3:1-13; 2 Pet 2:1 (so Zahn 1909:249-252). While possible, this is not as strong a view as the following one. (4) Jude here refers to OT prophets, particularly those alluded to in vv. 5-8, 11, and probably including the Jewish writers noted in vv. 9, 14-16. The fourth interpretation is favored by most scholars.

our only Master and Lord, Jesus Christ. Some scholars (e.g., M. Green 1987:175; Kelly 1969:252) think that *despotēs* [TG1203, ZG1305] (master, sovereign lord) refers to God, since elsewhere it usually is a title for God (Luke 2:29; Acts 4:24; Rev 6:10). In this case it would read, "They deny our only Master, as well as the Lord Jesus Christ." However, one article governs both terms, and so this parallels 2 Pet 2:1, which is likely also an allusion to Christ.

COMMENTARY

In first-century letters people would either open with a brief thanksgiving and prayer, or if it was a serious issue, proceed to state the occasion of the letter and give a précis of what the message would be. Jude does the latter in verses 3-4. Bauckham

(1983:28) tells us that Jude uses the form of a petition, "urging" or "appealing" (*parakalein* [TG3870, ZG4151]) to them in an intensely personal way and stating first the purpose or theme of the book (defending the faith, v. 3) and then the reason or occasion (ungodly and immoral false teachers, v. 4). Jude was calling for the faithful to go to war against these outsiders and to fight for the true Christian faith.

He begins by addressing his recipients as "dear friends" (*agapētoi* [TG27A, ZG28]), literally, "beloved," drawing the conclusion from his stress on "God's love" in verses 1-2 (see note on v. 1 on the connection) and highlighting the results: They are those "loved by God." The term appears often in 2 Peter 1:17; 3:1, 8, 14-15, 17, and we will see it again in Jude 17, 20. He then moved into the purpose and occasion and discussed his previous plans, beginning with the letter he had originally intended to write. In fact, he had been very "eager" (lit., "making every effort" or "with great diligence") to write these churches about "the salvation we all share," that is, their common life in Christ and the blessings that salvation had brought into their lives (perhaps including the eschatological salvation awaiting them at the Parousia, so Bauckham 1983:31). One can picture him sitting down to write when he received the bad news.

Having received the bad news, he found himself under "constraint" or "compulsion" (*anangkē* [TG318, ZG340]) to write a very different letter. His new purpose was to "urge" or "exhort" (this is a paraenetic letter challenging them to a God-given duty) the readers to "defend [contend for] the faith"—with *epagōnizomai* [TG1864, ZG2043] an athletic or military metaphor for strenuous effort made to win the contest (1 Cor 9:25; Heb 12:1). Jude was calling not for a mere defense but for an energetic struggle to defeat the false teachers; this was offense more than defense. Moreover, this was not just a negative fight to defeat the heretics but rather included a positive effort to build up and safeguard the saints (vv. 20-21), as well as to rescue those endangered by the false teaching (v. 23).

The object of this intense effort is "the faith that God has entrusted once for all time to his holy people." "The faith" (articular *tē . . . pistei* [TG4102, ZG4411]) does not refer to subjective trust in God but to the full content of Christian truth and teaching (Rom 10:8; Gal 1:23; Eph 4:13), tantamount to the gospel (so Neyrey, Schreiner, Harvey and Towner). "Entrusted" literally is "handed down, passed on" and speaks of traditional truths passed from one generation to the next (1 Cor 11:2; Col 2:8; 2 Thess 2:15; 3:6; cf. 2 Tim 2:2), in this case, from God to the apostles to the church. The stress on these doctrines being transmitted "once for all" underscores the eternal nature of God's truth and contrasts it with the novel, false teachings of these heretics.

An important caveat is provided by Harvey and Towner (2009:179), stating that "this in no way suggests that the early Christians had completely plumbed the depths of the gospel's meaning or practical implications for life. In each generation the churches are charged with the responsibility to make sense of the story of redemption and the Christ event at its center." This includes the need for commentaries like this one and other works that help us to understand the ancient message of Scripture. Yet all our writing, teaching, and preaching must explicate and make more understandable the "once for all faith" given its final form in Scripture. All teaching today must be held up to the light of God's word to determine its truth value.

The actual situation that called for Jude to change the content of his letter is spelled out in verse 4. He learned that "some ungodly people have wormed their way into your churches." This is different from 2 Peter, where the false teachers arose from within. Here they are outsiders who have snuck into the churches. "Wormed their way" is literally "secretly slipped in among you" or "infiltrated" (Bauckham 1983:35). These were probably itinerant prophets or so-called Christian teachers similar to the wandering philosophers who went town to town in the first century. They undoubtedly had presented themselves (possibly with false credentials) and pretended to be pious teachers who could take these believers to a new level spiritually. They were wolves in sheep's clothing (Matt 7:15), "vicious wolves [who would] come in among" the church (Acts 20:29).

Let us note what Jude has to say about them. First, they are "ungodly people," a key term in Jude (vv. 4, 15, 18) that refers to those "godless" who have no place for God in their lives and are headed for eternal destruction (cf. Rom 1:18; 1 Tim 1:9; 2 Tim 2:16; 1 Pet 4:18; 2 Pet 2:5-6; 3:7). As Bauckham (1983:38) brings out, their "irreverent attitude to God is manifested in unrighteous conduct." They were not just "ungodly" in holding beliefs that are counter to God's truths; they were guilty of ungodly conduct and lived their lives apart from the Lord of all.

Second, they taught "that God's marvelous grace allows us to live immoral lives," literally, they "alter [or pervert] the grace of our God into immorality." The Greek verb (*metatithēmi* [TG3346, ZG3572]) means to "change" or "exchange" and in a context like this speaks of a blasphemous "perversion" of divine grace. The "grace of God" is that divine favor and love that provided redemption for mankind on the basis of Christ's atoning sacrifice. What should have been liberation from sin had been exchanged in their hands for a libertinism that allowed them to freely pursue sin. Like the false teachers described in 2 Peter, these people said that when God through his grace removed sin, he did so absolutely; so whatever we do is no longer sin, and there will never be any judgment on our activities. "Immorality" (*aselgeia* [TG766, ZG816], "ungodly actions") was used in both Jewish and Hellenistic contexts for sins of the flesh, referring to indulgence and debauchery of any kind but most often sexual perversions.

Third, Jude notes "the condemnation of such people was recorded long ago," meaning that Old Testament prophecy centuries previous (see note on v. 4) had predicted these false teachers' sin and the judgment they would face. This is not a kind of double predestination, meaning that "long ago" from eternity past God had determined their condemnation, for Jude says it was "recorded" or "written down" rather than "decided" or "preordained." What was predetermined was the punishment for all who would choose to prophesy or teach falsehood in the name of God. The condemnation of false prophets was a constant emphasis in the prophetic books of the Old Testament (e.g., Jer 6:13-14; 8:10-11; Ezek 13:1-23), and these false teachers were seen in direct line with them.

Fourth, "they have denied our only Master and Lord, Jesus Christ." Since "Master" or "Sovereign" is used elsewhere primarily of God, Jesus' divinity is again being emphasized (as in 2 Pet 1:1; 2:1; so Bauckham, Schreiner). In what way were they "denying" the sovereignty and lordship of Christ? Most likely this combines both doctrinal (rejection of Jesus' authority over them and possibly "his nature and status," Moo 1996:231) and practical denials, as their ungodly, immoral behavior denied everything Jesus demanded of his followers. If Jesus is truly our "Master and Lord," we cannot indulge in any behavior he rejects. He has absolute authority, but these false teachers were serving other masters (note the stress on *only* Master) and so were denying his lordship over their lives.

◆ III. Condemnation of the False Teachers (vv. 5-16)

A. Biblical Examples of Their Condemnation (vv. 5-10)

1. Three examples presented (vv. 5-7)

5So I want to remind you, though you already know these things, that Jesus* first rescued the nation of Israel from Egypt, but later he destroyed those who did not remain faithful. 6And I remind you of the angels who did not stay within the limits of authority God gave them but left the place where they belonged. God has kept them securely chained in prisons of darkness, waiting for the great day of judgment. 7And don't forget Sodom and Gomorrah and their neighboring towns, which were filled with immorality and every kind of sexual perversion. Those cities were destroyed by fire and serve as a warning of the eternal fire of God's judgment.

5 As in the best manuscripts; various other manuscripts read *[the] Lord*, or *God*, or *Christ;* one reads *God Christ*.

NOTES

5 *that Jesus first rescued.* There are two text-critical issues here. First, does *hapax* [TG530, ZG562] ("once," "already"; NLT, "first") belong after "Lord/Jesus" (א Ψ C* etc., so NRSV, REB, TNIV, NLT) or should it be placed after "knowing all these things" (𝔓72 A B L 049 et al., so Metzger, Bauckham, Schreiner)? Most likely it was originally connected with "knowing" and was moved to conform with the next clause that says God "later [lit., 'a second time'] destroyed those who did not remain faithful." Second, should we read "Lord" (א Ψ C* 630, so NASB, NRSV, NIV, TNIV) or "Jesus" (A B 33 81, so NLT, NET, ESV) or "God" (C^2; cf. NLT mg) or "God Christ" (𝔓72c; cf. NLT mg) here? It is slightly more likely to place "Jesus" in the text because it is the better attested reading and because later scribes changed it to fit better with the Exodus event described (i.e., reading "Jesus" at the Exodus seemed strange; see Metzger 1994:726; Comfort 2008:802-803; Bartholomä 2008).

COMMENTARY

There is typological interpretation taking place in this section, with three "types" of the heretical infiltrators presented in verses 5-7 and the "antitype" or application of them explained in verses 8-10 (with three examples of their sin—Jude likes triads). The three types presented center on the theme of the ungodly and their doom. These examples are the unfaithful in Israel at the Exodus (v. 5), the fallen angels (v. 6), and Sodom and Gomorrah (v. 7). All three are seen in their disobedience and in the judgment they received. This is paralleled in 2 Peter 2:4-6, where the triad is the angels who sinned, the world of Noah's day, and Sodom and Gomorrah. The theme in 2 Peter and Jude is the same: sin followed by judgment. Moo (1996:243) says, "by following the order he does, Jude achieves a crescendo in punishment—from physical death (v. 5) to binding in darkness (v. 6) to the 'punishment of eternal fire (v. 7).'"

Verses 5-10 introduce Jude's central section regarding God's condemnation of evil. They are followed in verses 11-13 with three more types (Cain, Balaam, Korah) applied to the false teachers (vv. 12-13), then by Enoch's prophecy of divine judgment (vv. 14-15) also applied to these doomed interlopers (v. 16). In all three sections (vv. 5-10, 11-13, 14-16) the typological examples from the prophetic past (v. 4, "The condemnation of such people was recorded long ago") lead into a description of these false teachers and the reasons why God's judgment is going to fall on them.

Jude begins with what is called a "disclosure formula" (cf., e.g., Rom 1:13; 1 Cor 11:3; Col 2:1), leading into an important truth that the author wanted to bring up (Bauckham 1983:44). So Jude begins, "I want to remind you," thereby introducing the theme of remembering, which is important to 2 Peter as well (2 Pet 1:12-13, 15; 3:1-2). Such remembering normally has as its object the deep traditional truths of the Christian faith (v. 3); here, these will prove the serious error behind the ideas of the infiltrators. As in 2 Peter "remember" means not only to bring something to mind but to act on it as well—to allow it to change both thinking and actions. This could refer back to what Jude said in verses 3-4 about defending the faith (thus reminding them of gospel truths). Yet more likely it refers to what he discusses in the rest of the letter, truths tied to their knowledge of the Old Testament and Jewish material he was going to utilize.

First, Jude reminds them of the Exodus, when Israel was "rescued" (Gr., *sōzō* [TG4982, ZG5392]) from Egypt. If "Jesus" rather than "Lord" is the correct reading here (see note on v. 5), then Jude linked Jesus with God in Old Testament events. There is ample precedent for this. Paul called Christ the "spiritual rock" who accompanied Israel in the wilderness, and Jesus is frequently identified with Yahweh (cf. John 12:41; Rev 1:12-16). There is nothing strange in Jude connecting Christ with the judgments of verses 5-7. The emphasis is upon Israel experiencing divine "deliverance" at the Exodus (Exod 6–14) and then being "unfaithful" in the wilderness. In the plagues God had shown that the Egyptian gods were not divine but were mere forces of nature under his control. He proved his sovereignty to both the Egyptians and the Israelites. Then he delivered them from the Egyptian chariots at the Red Sea and took his people to Mount Sinai, where he gave them the law.

But in the wilderness the people of Israel failed to put their trust in Yahweh. In the golden calf incident (Exod 32), in the constant murmuring and rebellion in the wilderness (Num 14), and in the worship of Baal at Peor (Num 25), Israel angered God, and only Joshua and Caleb (the faithful witnesses) were allowed to enter the Promised Land (see also 1 Cor 10:8-10). God "destroyed" that generation in the wilderness. After committing immorality with Moabite women (Num 25:1-9), 24,000 of the Israelite men were killed. The deaths of the rest of the people are recorded in Numbers 26:64-65, which says "not one of them survived" apart from Caleb and Joshua. The reason for this judgment, according to Psalms 95:7-11; 106:25; Hebrews 3:19; 4:6, 11, was disbelief and hardness of heart toward God. Jude was warning his readers that if they fell into the same kind of sin (with the false teachers) the same judgment would fall upon them.

The second example (v. 6) stems from Genesis 6:1-4 and the story of the "sons of God" (a description of fallen angels in Job 1:6; 2:2; 38:7; Pss 29:1; 89:6) who cohabited with women and produced the Nephilim or "giants," namely, "the heroes and famous warriors of ancient times" (Gen 6:4). Jude followed the common Jewish interpretation of that day (e.g., *1 Enoch* 6–19, 86–88; *Jubilees* 4:15, 22; 5:1-11; *2 Baruch* 56:10-16) regarding the "watchers" or fallen angels who rebelled against God and were punished. In 2 Peter 2:4 they are called simply "the angels who sinned," but Jude describes them with two parallel clauses. First, they "did not stay within the limits of authority God gave them"—their *archēn* [TG746, ZG794] or "domain," "sphere of authority." That God-given domain was heaven, and they as angels were to be servants of God and messengers to humanity. Second, Jude says they rebelled and "left the place where they belonged." In Jewish tradition this is what occurred in Genesis 6:1-4.

The result was judgment, and "God has kept them securely chained in prisons of darkness, waiting for the great day of judgment" (v. 6). The text literally speaks of "eternal chains," building on the binding of the watchers in *1 Enoch* 14:5; 56:1-4; 88:1. "Eternal" means that their defeat is final, as in the everlasting binding and imprisonment of Azazel in *1 Enoch* 10:4-6 (Bauckham 1983:52-53). The "darkness" was used by Jesus as a description of eternal punishment in Matthew 8:12; 22:13 ("darkness, where there will be weeping and gnashing of teeth"). Yet in Jude the everlasting darkness emphasizes the fallen angels' present state, not their final state, for they are awaiting "the great day of judgment," a phrase that builds on the "Day of the Lord" in the Old Testament (Joel 1:15; 2:11; Zeph 1:7, 14; Mal 4:5).

In the New Testament this phrase refers especially to the final judgment (Rev 20:11-15) and the casting of the demonic forces into the eternal lake of fire (Rev 19:20; 20:10, 14), which in Matthew 25:41 is described as "the eternal fire prepared for the devil and his demons." Satan and his demonic hordes are already in a state of defeat, bound by Christ (Mark 3:27), imprisoned in this world (Satan is only "the god of *this* world," 2 Cor 4:4, italics added), and knowing that their time is short (Rev 12:12). They do have some authority in this world, primarily with their followers, and they tempt and test believers, trying to "devour" or defeat them (1 Pet 5:8). But God's people have already been given authority over them (Mark 3:15; 6:7) and strength over their temptations (Matt 6:13; 1 Cor 10:13), so believers can only be defeated by giving in to the satanic deceptions.

The third example (v. 7) or "type" of the false teachers is Sodom and Gomorrah (cf. 2 Pet 2:6; also Isa 13:19; Jer 49:18; Amos 4:11; Matt 10:15; Luke 17:29; Rev 11:8) and the neighboring towns (Admah, Zeboiim, Zoar; Gen 19:22; Deut 29:23). The three angels visiting Abraham had planned judgment against these cities because of the "outcry . . . their sin is so flagrant" (Gen 18:20), but Abraham had interceded and saved the city. Then two angels visited Lot in Sodom, warned Lot and his family to flee, and then destroyed the area. Jude describes the people as "filled with immorality and every kind of sexual perversion," with the immorality referring to their homosexuality and the "perversion" possibly to their desire to have sex with angels (so Kelly, Bauckham, Davids). Moo (1996:242) says that this association between the sin of the angels (v. 6) and the men of Sodom (v. 7) "would make a neat transition here. As angels are condemned for sex with humans, so the people of Sodom are condemned for seeking to have sex with angels." The emphasis here on their sexual perversions provided an apt warning for the readers of this epistle, for sins of immorality were evidently a major part of the false religion spawned by the heretics Jude was combating. This false, new religion (Jude emphasizes that it is not part of the Christian religion) tried to bring together Christian ideas with a pagan lifestyle, but it failed.

Sodom and Gomorrah were destroyed by "fire and burning sulfur" (Gen 19:24-25). As such, they provide another "warning of the eternal fire of God's judgment." As stated in 2 Peter 2:7, there was still evidence of this judgment in Jude's day. The message on the danger of eternal punishment in the lake of fire is incredibly plentiful in the New Testament. The fact of eternal fiery punishment is quite prevalent in the New Testament (Matt 5:22, 29-30; 10:28; 18:9; 23:15, 33; Mark 9:43, 48), especially in the Apocalypse (Rev 14:9-11; 19:3; 20:12-15). While the idea of God condemning sinners to eternal torment is offensive to many today, we must be cognizant that this is partly because we do not understand how God detests sin. The laws of clean and unclean and the sacrificial system developed because people did not see how they could approach God and come back alive. God must punish sin. He is not just a loving God, he is a *holy* God. His holiness is expressed in his love and his justice; these are interchangeable aspects of his being.

◆ 2. Application to the false teachers (vv. 8-10)

8 In the same way, these people—who claim authority from their dreams—live immoral lives, defy authority, and scoff at supernatural beings.* 9 But even Michael, one of the mightiest of the angels,* did not dare accuse the devil of blasphemy, but simply said, "The Lord rebuke you!" (This took place when Michael was arguing with the devil about Moses' body.) 10 But these people scoff at things they do not understand. Like unthinking animals, they do whatever their instincts tell them, and so they bring about their own destruction.

8 Greek *at glorious ones*, which are probably evil angels. 9 Greek *Michael, the archangel.*

NOTES

8 ***scoff at supernatural beings.*** Lit., "They blaspheme glories." There are several possibilities for understanding this (see Bauckham 1983:57-58), depending on how we understand these celestial beings. If they are good angels (on the grounds that "glories" would not be used of evil powers), this could mean: (1) Jude's anti-Gnostic polemic against the false teachers on the basis of their disparaging the angels for their role in creating the world. This is unlikely, given that Gnosticism was a second-century movement. (2) On the basis of their visions, the false teachers believed they had entered the heavenly realm and were superior to the angels (1 Cor 6:3, "judge angels," so Harrington 2003:207). The problem with this is that visions normally accompanied the elevation of angels rather than the reverse. (3) They criticized the angels as mediators and guardians of the law (Acts 7:38; Gal 3:19-20; Heb 2:2), since they rejected all authority over their practices (i.e., they were antinomians, so Bauckham 1983:58; Harvey and Towner 2009:198). (4) They rejected the place of the angels in the final judgment, since the heretics denied any divine judgment on their actions (Neyrey 1993:66). (5) They dishonored the angels in general by their teaching and actions rather than with specific statements (Davids 2006:58-59). Either of these latter two are possible if these are good angels. If they are evil angels, which is likely in view of v. 9, then (6) they were mocking the power of demons, claiming that they had no authority or power to affect or hurt them in any way (so Moo 1996:245-246; Schreiner 2003:458).

9 ***Michael, one of the mightiest of the angels.*** We do not truly know the source of this story. It is not found in the OT, and while Clement of Alexandria believed it came from *The Assumption of Moses* (*Fragments on the Epistles of Jude*), the story cannot be found there. Bauckham (1983:67-76) argues it is found in the lost ending of *The Testament of Moses*, a piece that many believe is the same work, but Bauckham argues is separate. Jude was not accepting this work as canonical but was only using this story from Jewish tradition to make his point. He was not so much quoting a book as telling a story. As Moo (1996:246) says, we cannot even know for sure whether Jude thought the story ever "really happened," though the implicit sense is that Jude believed it was a true story.

COMMENTARY

After showing three examples of sin and punishment from God, Jude showed how each was fulfilled in the pretenders who had "wormed their way" into the believers' midst (v. 3-4). While the divine judgment was stressed in the biblical types of verses 5-7, Jude centered on the sinful actions of the false teachers and left the judgment implicit, stressing that the sins of the past were being repeated in the sins of the present. Continuing his preference for triads, three sins are presented in verse 8 that parallel the sins of verses 5-7 (note how v. 8 begins with "In the same way").

They are "dreamers," correctly interpreted in the NLT as "claim[ing] authority from their dreams." This does not mean they "dreamed big dreams" or spent their time dreaming up new ideas. Rather, they apparently justified their aberrant behavior by claiming their dreams were apocalyptic visions (the same word is used in Acts 2:17 from Joel 2:28 [3:1, LXX], "Your old men will dream dreams"), thereby anchoring their deceptive teachings by calling them revelations from God. These were apparently erotic dreams, for they led this cult to "live immoral lives" (lit., "defile the flesh"), paralleling those of the people of Sodom in verse 7. Their licentious behavior was defended by turning their erotic fantasies and dreams into visionary directions from God. This led them to commit all the sins of Sodom (probably including homosexuality, which was popular in the Hellenistic world), pretending they were following God's leading.

They were defying authority (v. 8), which could be defined as a rejection of human authority. If so, it was perhaps governmental but more likely the authority of church leaders who told them they were wrong. But the word here is not the normal word for "authority" but rather *kuriotēs* [TG2963, ZG3262], "lordship," and most likely refers to the authority of both God and of Christ (better than some who argue that one or the other is intended). According to Jesus' teaching and the word of God, immoral activity is sin. By explaining away their licentious behavior, the false teachers had rejected the lordship of God and Christ.

Finally, they were "scoff[ing] at supernatural beings," literally, "slandering (*blasphēmeō* [TG987, ZG1059]) the glorious ones" (see also vv. 10, 18; 2 Pet 2:2, 10-12). The "glories" were celestial beings or angels, called "glorious ones" on occasion (*2 Enoch* 22:7; *Ascension of Isaiah* 9:32; 1QH 10:8) because they dwell in heaven and serve the glorious God. Jude does not tell us exactly how they "blasphemed" these beings. Still, we can surmise a likely understanding (see note on v. 8). I think these are probably evil angels (on the basis of v. 9; Peter follows this in 2 Pet 2:10-11). The difficulty is why Jude would call fallen angels "glorious ones," but they were still celestial beings and cosmic powers, so the title is apt. The heretics were probably making fun of the fallen angels as powerless to act against them or to influence their behavior (since they taught that God had inspired their immorality through visions). Their twisted views left no place for the reality of sin or of judgment in their lives.

In contrast to the foolish bravado of the false teachers in dishonoring the evil powers, Jude rehearsed the encounter Michael had with Satan (v. 9). This is a difficult verse, because the story does not appear in the Old Testament. The closest parallel is Zechariah 3:1-2 in which an "angel of the LORD" "rebukes" Satan when the latter tried to bring accusations against Joshua the high priest. The death and burial of Moses are recounted in Deuteronomy 34:1-12, in which Moses goes up Mount Nebo in Moab, is shown the Promised Land by God, then dies and is buried there. The story behind Jude's statements (apparently from *The Testament of Moses;* see note on v. 9) is summed up by Davids (2006:60):

> *After the death of Moses Michael came to bury his body. The devil (Samma'el, one of a variety of Jewish names for the devil) came and argued that the body should be given to him, for Moses had been a murderer (i.e., he had murdered the Egyptian, Exod 2:12-14) and thus did not deserve an honorable burial. When Michael appealed to the judgment of God with "The Lord rebuke you!" the devil withdrew, knowing that God would decide in Moses' honor and against his slander.*

Michael is mentioned three times in the Old Testament (Dan 10:13, 21; 12:1) as a "chief prince" and protector of Israel, and he is mentioned in Revelation 12:7 as the leader of heaven's army that casts Satan and his followers out of heaven. In Jude he is an "archangel" (NLT, "one of the mightiest of the angels"), one of four (*1 Enoch* 40:1-4) or seven (*1 Enoch* 20:1-7) chief angels that seem to preside over the heavenly council and are often called "the angels of the Presence." In Jewish literature, Michael seems to be the leader of this group. His presence here in a dispute over Moses's body makes sense in light of the fact that he is the guardian over Israel (Dan 12:1). The language is that of a legal dispute, with the devil trying to prove Moses guilty and therefore unworthy of an honorable burial so that Satan could claim the body (so Bauckham, Davids, Schreiner).

Michael's response showed the kind of proper respect for the cosmic powers that the false teachers did not. He "did not dare [or presume to] accuse the devil of blasphemy" (v. 9), contra the false presumptions of superiority shown by the heretics. As G. Green (2008:83) explains, the language here also refers to legal charges, so it "is not that Michael did not dare to bring a 'slanderous accusation' (NIV) but that he did not bring the verdict or the judgment itself." The false teachers had made the slanderous remarks; Michael accepted his proper place and refused to become judge in the matter. He left that to God and simply pronounced, "The Lord rebuke you," the very thing said by the angel of the Lord in Zechariah 3:2. According to Zechariah 3, Satan had brought accusations to discredit Joshua the high priest; but God responded with forgiveness, the very response God made to Moses. This is the point of the story. Michael left the judgment up to God; it was the divine rebuke, not Michael's, that mattered. The sin was the presumption of Satan and the false teachers to take God's authority upon themselves. Only God can forgive, and only God can pronounce judgment.

After the counterexample of verse 9, Jude returns in verse 10 to the subject of verse 8, the fact that the heretics take it upon themselves to "scoff" (again, *blasphēmeō* [TG987, ZG1059]) at the evil angels, one of the many things, Jude says, that "they do not understand" (v. 10). These interlopers pretended to have wisdom and disseminate truth, while in reality they, like Satan, understood little and disseminated slanderous lies. Rather than being wise teachers, they were "unthinking animals," which (as in 2 Pet 2:12) emphasizes especially their sexual appetites. They claimed understanding but actually were "unthinking" and controlled by their animal "instincts." "Thus these teachers, who probably claimed a higher spirituality, a higher knowledge, actually are ignorant of the true spiritual world; all that they really know about is their instinctual desires, probably referring to their sexual desires" (Davids 2006:63). They had no spiritual or moral control; they had become soulless beings, pure animals, driven by their base desires.

The result is that like animals "they bring about their own destruction" (v. 10). This is not physical death (of an animal) but the eternal destruction of the enemies of God. It is possible (with G. Green 2008:85-86) to take this of their moral "corruption," in keeping with the use of this verb (*phtheirō* [TG5351, ZG5780]) elsewhere in the New Testament (1 Cor 15:33; 2 Cor 7:2; Eph 4:22; Rev 19:2) and with the emphasis on animal corruption in the verse. However, in the parallel 2 Peter 2:12 it means destruction, and that is a major emphasis in Jude (vv. 5, 10-11) and 2 Peter (2 Pet 2:1, 3, 12; 3:6-7, 10-12, 16). The theme is that of condemnation and judgment, and that makes the best sense here. These false teachers, like unthinking animals, were headed for destruction, and their own moral degeneracy was determining their final destiny.

◆ B. Further Biblical Examples of Their Depravity (vv. 11-13)

11What sorrow awaits them! For they follow in the footsteps of Cain, who killed his brother. Like Balaam, they deceive people for money. And like Korah, they perish in their rebellion.

12When these people eat with you in your fellowship meals commemorating the Lord's love, they are like dangerous reefs that can shipwreck you.* They are like shameless shepherds who care only for themselves. They are like clouds blowing over the land without giving any rain. They are like trees in autumn that are doubly dead, for they bear no fruit and have been pulled up by the roots.
13They are like wild waves of the sea, churning up the foam of their shameful deeds. They are like wandering stars, doomed forever to blackest darkness.

12 Or *they are contaminants among you;* or *they are stains.*

NOTES

12 *dangerous reefs.* The NRSV and NIV have "blemishes" ("stains") while the NLT, NJB, and ESV have "dangerous reefs." The parallel in 2 Pet 2:13 uses *spilos* [TG4696, ZG5070], meaning "stain," "blots," or "blemishes," but the term here is the similarly spelled *spilas* [TG4694, ZG5069], which has the idea of a "hidden reef" or "rocky hazard hidden by waves" (BDAG 938; cf. Josephus *War* 3.420), and this is the better meaning here (so also Mayor, Kelly, Moo, Schreiner). Davids (2006:69) thinks there may be a wordplay with *spilos* here, stressing also that these people are also "a danger to the purity of the community," and that is indeed possible.

shameless shepherds. There is some question as to whether *aphobōs* [TG870, ZG925] (which is placed between the two clauses) goes with "eat" ("eat in your fellowship meals *without fear*," so NIV, ESV, Bauckham 1983:85; Schreiner 2003:465) or with "shepherds" ("like *shameless* shepherds," so NLT, Kelly 1969:271; Davids 2006:70). In terms of word order, either is possible. Overall, it is probably slightly better to take it with "eat," meaning they "share in your feasts fearlessly."

trees in autumn . . . bear no fruit. There have been two interpretations of this. One (Biggs, Kelly) takes this as late autumn after the harvest season, so the image is of dead trees that bear no fruit. The other (Bauckham, Davids, Harvey and Towner) see this as autumn at the end of harvest season when there should be fruit but isn't. Both are viable, but the second is more in keeping with the first image of clouds without rain, an image of unfulfilled expectations.

COMMENTARY

These three verses follow the organization of verses 5-10, beginning with a triad of biblical examples (v. 11) and then applying it to the heretics (vv. 12-13). The difference from the presentation of examples in verses 5-7 is their brevity here and their literary form, for these are "woe oracles" that begin with the pronouncement of judgment (*ouai* [TG3759, ZG4026], "woe" or "what terrors await")—a specific type of judgment prophecy centering upon the imminent sorrow and doom that will fall upon resolute sinners (cf. Isa 5:8-24; Amos 5:18-20; Mic 2:1-4). The evil teachers Jude warns against are likened to specific false teachers and archetypal sinners in the Old Testament. The three examples in verses 5-7 were groups that brought judgment on themselves, the three in verse 11 are individuals who committed great sins and led Israel astray. This is further typology, in which the heretics are seen as fulfilling the terrible example of these notorious sinners.

First, they walk "in the footsteps of Cain" (v. 11). Cain is used as the archetype of hatred in 1 John 3:12, and at first glance one might think verse 11 refers to "the sin of Cain" and that the false teachers were being accused of murder. But that is not the case when we see how Cain was reflected in Second Temple Jewish literature (see Bauckham 1983:79-80; G. Green 2008:79-80). Cain's first "sin" was in his self-centeredness, anger, and jealousy when God accepted Abel's sacrifice of a lamb rather than Cain's crop sacrifice (Gen 4:3-7). Jewish writers considered him the prototype of luxury, greed, and violence (Josephus *Antiquities* 1:52-66), who taught others to experience lust and thievery (Philo *The Posterity and Exile of Cain* 38-39). According to the Jerusalem Targum at Genesis 4:8 (an Aramaic paraphrase of the OT used in synagogues), Cain taught that there was no future judgment. In other words, Cain was a viable type of those who taught falsehood and practiced sin in Jude's day.

Second, they are like Balaam (also in 2 Pet 2:15-16), the false prophet who "deceive[d] people for money" (v. 11). The Greek says they have "dedicated themselves" to Balaam's error for profit, with the verb meaning "to be consumed with, give oneself totally in commitment to" (BDAG 312). The picture is that of total immersion into a movement. Balaam was a prophet from Pethor hired by Balak, king of Moab, to curse the people of Israel. At first he refused, but Balak offered more money (see the more detailed story in the commentary on 2 Pet 2:15-16). When his efforts to curse Israel failed, he advised (Num 31:15-16) the Midianites to use their women to entice the Israelites into sin and apostasy (cf. Num 25:1-3).

Later Jewish writers emphasized his greed and guilt in the apostasy of Israel that led to the deaths of 24,000 in Numbers 25 (see the Targum on Numbers 22; Philo *Moses* 1:266-268; Josephus *Antiquities* 4.126-140 [4.6.6-9]). Jude's point is that the heretics were consumed with the same greed and immorality that characterized the Balaam story. The emphasis here is on their desire for "profit" (a frequent emphasis in the NT; cf. 1 Thess 2:5; 1 Tim 6:5, 10; Titus 1:11; 2 Pet 2:3, 14), and like so many cults today, their movement was little more than a "get rich quick" scheme.

Third, they were like Korah and "perish in their rebellion" (v. 11). In Numbers 16, we read that Korah led 250 leaders in rebellion against Moses, trying to usurp his leadership and the Levitical authority of Aaron. God quashed the rebellion by having the earth open up and swallow all 250 rebels. These false teachers were also "rebelling" and "disputing" the authority of God and of his apostolic leaders (also the point above on vv. 8-9). They would share the fate of Korah, who was "destroyed" or "perished," as already stressed in verse 10. As Davids (2006:68) brings out, the shared fate is why the example of Korah is placed last (chronologically, he would be second): "Cain was exiled and Balaam died in the context of a battle, but Korah's fate was public and dramatic. He went down into the ground, and so these teachers will go down, for Jude is implying that they will end up in hell."

From past examples of the sin and fate that await the false teachers and their followers, Jude turns to their present effect on the community (v. 12). As in verse 8, Jude was applying these examples to the current situation. The first point of application Jude chose was participation in "fellowship meals commemorating the Lord's love" (v. 12). This is a lengthy but fine translation of *tais agapais* [TG26, ZG27], "love feasts," a term found only in Jude for early Christian eucharistic practice in which the celebration of the Eucharist was combined with a re-creation of the Passover meal/Last Supper that was characterized by "love" in the community. Davids (2006:68-69) thinks this combined celebration was practiced throughout the time of the early church until at least AD 250. A very important aspect of both Jewish and Greco-Roman life was "table fellowship," and shared meals cemented community life and achieved love and unity.

The problem was that the false teachers were participating in these love feasts and using them as a forum to draw adherents into their movement. Since this sacred meal (celebrated every "Lord's Day"—Acts 20:7; Rev 1:10) centered on the "love" relation between members of the community, it was a brilliant ploy on the part of the heretics (remember that they were outsiders, v. 4) to insert themselves into those celebrations and thus to become known as insiders who could also be loved and trusted. So Jude warned the true believers about them, calling them "dangerous reefs that can shipwreck you" (see note on v. 11). The stress is that these dangerous people were like hidden rocks waiting to tear the bottom out of the church. Moreover, they were doing so "without fear" (see note on v. 12, "shameless shepherds") most likely meaning "without fear of God's judgment," but possibly including "without fear of opposition" from within the community. There is a sense of irreverence here, perhaps like the Corinthians of 1 Corinthians 11:17-34 who treated the sacred meal as just another gluttonous feast.

Moreover, they are "shepherds who care only for themselves" (lit., "shepherding themselves"). By their very nature, shepherds give of themselves in order to take care of their sheep. These people didn't care about the flock but were entirely self-centered. God was the "shepherd of Israel" (Gen 48:15; 49:24; 2 Sam 5:2; Pss 23:1; 80:1; Isa 40:11), and the early leaders of the church were "pastor/shepherds" (Acts 20:28; Eph 4:11; 1 Pet 5:2-3). These interlopers, however, were like the "false shepherds of Israel" who fed only themselves (Ezek 34:2), failed to take care of the weak (Ezek 34:4a), never searched for those who had "wandered away" (Ezek 34:4b; in fact, they caused them to "wander" off!), leading the flock to become "sheep . . . without a shepherd" (Ezek 34:5). They lived in comfort and debauchery without any concern whatsoever for their followers.

Jude closed this section (vv. 12b-13) with four further metaphors, all derived from the natural realm, perhaps reflecting "the order of the universe in terms of the heavens, the earth, and the waters" (Schreiner 2003:466). First, the false teachers are "like clouds blowing over the land without giving any rain" (v. 12). In the Mediterranean (even more so in dry Palestine), rain was essential for crops and therefore for life. The picture here is derived from Proverbs 25:14, "A person who promises a gift but doesn't give it is like clouds and wind that bring no rain." One would see the clouds driven in from the sea with the promise of moisture, only to be sadly disappointed. Similarly, these false teachers gave the hope of life from their teaching but failed to deliver anything but empty promises.

Second, they are compared to "trees in autumn that are doubly dead" (v. 12). As G. Green (2008:96) says, this is harvest time in the Julian calendar (August 11 to November 10) when the hope of fruit (particularly olives and figs, and also pomegranates) is at its highest. Yet the trees are found fruitless. Like the first image of clouds without rain, there is all the hope of fruit but a complete failure to deliver on that promise. But here Jude adds a further image, that of judgment. These trees (metaphorically, the false teachers) are "doubly dead," since they have been "pulled up by the roots." Some (Bauckham, Moo) see this as an apocalyptic image referring to the false teachers experiencing the "second death" (Rev 20:6, 14; 21:8). But with the image of trees, it is probably better to see this as part of the imagery, that these trees are dead first by the fact that they have stopped bearing fruit and by virtue of being torn out at the roots (Mayor, Davids, Schreiner). The false teachers fit this very well. They were dead in their own fruitlessness and then doubly dead in the judgment they faced from God. Two sayings of Christ are apropos here: first, the good and bad trees in Matthew 7:16-20, in which false prophets are known by their bad fruit, with the result that they are "chopped down and thrown into the fire" (Matt 7:19); second, John 15:1-8 speaks of the branch that stops bearing fruit being "thrown away" and then "gathered into a pile to be burned" (John 15:6). In both, the judgment of the fruitless tree is emphasized.

Third, the heretics are also "like wild waves of the sea, churning up the foam of their shameful deeds" (v. 13). This metaphor is taken from Isaiah 57:20: "Those who still reject me are like the restless sea, which is never still but continually churns up mud and dirt." This is part of a section (Isa 56–59) calling on God's people to put their trust in him (Isa 57:13), but they are not doing so, so God must act (Oswalt 1998:485). The truth is that there is "no peace" for the wicked (Isa 57:19, 21), but it is their own fault, for they are restless and do not choose to allow God's peace to enter their lives. Jude was saying that this was the case with the false teachers as well, who produced "wild waves" and were closed to God. In Isaiah the storm-tossed sea casts up "mud and dirt," the detritus of wasted lives. Here it is more serious, for they are "churning up the foam of their shameful deeds" (lit., "abominations"), probably referring to both their teaching and their actions. They shamed themselves (in an honor/shame society as in the first century, this was especially serious) before God and brought his wrath down upon them and their followers.

Fourth, they are "like wandering stars," which builds on ancient astrological beliefs that the planets and stars move according to set patterns set by the gods and represent the divine forces that regulate life. When the planets (probably more in view than stars, but including shooting stars and meteors) became restless and "wandered" (note the connection to the "restless sea" above), it was cause for great consternation. Also, as shown in *1 Enoch* 82 (e.g., Uriel in *1 Enoch* 82:7-8 who has "the power in the heaven both day and night" to establish "the orders of the stars"), the ancient Jews believed that the angels regulated the movements of the planets. When the planets wandered from their proper place, it was believed that this was due to disobedient angels, and falling stars were fallen angels being cast out of heaven. In *1 Enoch* 18:13-15; 21:1-10 the "watchers" (see commentary on v. 6) are depicted as seven stars or "burning mountains" that are cast by the archangels from heaven into their prison house. So here Jude likens the false teachers with the fallen angels whose final condemnation is certain. Also, "wandering" is *planētēs*, related to a term meaning to "lead astray, deceive" that is frequently used of false teachers in the New Testament (Matt 24:11, 24; Eph 4:14; 1 Tim 4:1; 2 Tim 3:13; 1 John 4:6; Rev 13:14). The false teachers had been deceived and in turn are leading others astray.

This terrible judgment concludes the section. Jude adds that they are "doomed forever to blackest darkness" (v. 13 = 2 Pet 2:17). He used a perfect tense (lit., "has been reserved"), which indicates an eternal state that has already been prepared for them. According to 2 Peter 2:4, the fallen angels were thrown into "gloomy pits of darkness" until the Day of Judgment, but here the image of "darkness" is not a temporary but an eternal place of punishment. Jesus spoke often of eternal punishment not just as Gehenna, a place of fire, but as a place of "darkness, where there will be weeping and gnashing of teeth" (Matt 8:12; 13:42, 50; 22:13; 24:51; 25:30; Luke 13:28; cf. also Tob 14:10; *1 Enoch* 17:5-6; *Psalms of Solomon* 14:9). The fire of Gehenna emphasizes punishment, and darkness the absolute separation from God. The point is that the heretics will join the cosmic powers in the place of eternal punishment far from God.

◆ C. An Illustration from Enoch's Prophecy (vv. 14-16)

[14]Enoch, who lived in the seventh generation after Adam, prophesied about these people. He said, "Listen! The Lord is coming with countless thousands of his holy ones [15]to execute judgment on the people of the world. He will convict every person of all the ungodly things they have done and for all the insults that ungodly sinners have spoken against him."*

[16]These people are grumblers and complainers, living only to satisfy their desires. They brag loudly about themselves, and they flatter others to get what they want.

14-15 The quotation comes from intertestamental literature: Enoch 1:9.

NOTES

16 *grumblers and complainers.* The first word (*gongustai* [TG1113, ZG1199]) is onomatopoeia, as the very sound of the word reminds one of the low murmur of angry speech. The second term (*mempsimoiroi* [TG3202, ZG3523]) pictures people who are discontented and "complaining about one's lot" in life (BDAG 629).

COMMENTARY

Jude has employed several Old Testament examples to illustrate the wickedness and apostasy of the false teachers (vv. 5-7, 9, 11), and now he adds a further prophetic example to provide an authoritative denunciation of their actions and teaching. His point is that these godless people were part of an ongoing chain of battle with evil that the prophets spoke of long ago and that is under the control of God. But here he chooses a text that is not from the Old Testament but from *1 Enoch*. Moreover, he attributes the prophecy directly to "Enoch, who lived in the seventh generation after Adam" (v. 14), whose story is told in Genesis 5:18-24. Yet there is nothing in Genesis about any prophecy from this Enoch, and *1 Enoch* is a composite work written for the most part in the second century BC. What Jude records here was taken from *1 Enoch* 1:9 (probably from the Aramaic version, see Davids 2006:77-78), which says, "Behold, he will arrive with ten million of the holy ones in order to execute judgment upon all. He will destroy the wicked ones and consume all flesh on account of everything that they have done, that which the sinners and the wicked ones committed against him."

There are three ways to understand the implications of this quote for the issue of canonicity, and all three are represented by the church fathers (see Moo 1996:272): (1) Since Jude quoted *1 Enoch*, it must be an inspired work (Clement of Alexandria *Extracts from the Prophets* 3; Tertullian *Idolatry* 15:6); (2) since Jude quotes a noncanonical work, Jude also must be noncanonical (Jerome *De viris illustribus* 4); (3) Jude thought this particular prophecy was inspired but not the whole of *1 Enoch* (Augustine *City of God* 15.23). The first is unlikely because all the evidence we have shows that *1 Enoch* was never considered an inspired canonical work in Judaism or in first-century Christianity. The Old Testament canon was closed for the most part by the first century, and only a few books (e.g., Esther, Song of Songs, Ezekiel) were questioned. For instance, at Qumran *1 Enoch* was appreciated but not regarded as canonical. The second option is unnecessary and unlikely, for Jude is certainly a canonical work (see the Introduction). The third is by far the best option. Note that Jude carefully does not say that *1 Enoch* is "Scripture" but rather that this one particular quote is "prophecy." Moreover, Jude was not saying that Enoch actually gave the prophecy but rather that the prophecy found in *1 Enoch* was true and from God (Schreiner 2003:469). In other words, *1 Enoch* did give a "prophecy," but just this one time; the whole work was not canonical prophecy.

When Jude said Enoch was the seventh generation from Adam, he was reflecting the order from Genesis 5:1-18—Adam, Seth, Enosh, Kenan, Mahalalel, Jared, Enoch. Since the same thing is stated in *1 Enoch* 60:8; 93:3, he might have been simply citing the traditional title for the book rather than saying Enoch had actually uttered the prophecy. Since it was widely known that *1 Enoch* was a pseudepigraphical work, it is unlikely that Jude was saying here that it was the product of the historical Enoch. Rather, he established a further contrast, namely, one between the godly Enoch, so pious that he did not die but was translated into heaven by God (Gen 5:23-24) and the ungodly false teachers who were "doubly dead" (v. 12).

The prophecy itself is very apt, centering (as does the rest of Jude) on two facts: the wickedness of the false teachers and the divine judgment awaiting them. The primary difference is that Jude specifies that "the Lord is coming," referring to the Parousia of Christ as the arrival of the eschaton and final judgment. Gene Green (2008:105) states, "Jude has taken a text that speaks of a divine theophany and has transformed it into a passage that refers to the advent of Christ." In a Jewish context "the Lord" would be God, and his "coming" the arrival of the kingdom accompanied by the destruction of Israel's enemies. The statement that he is coming with "countless thousands of his holy ones" stems from Deuteronomy 33:2, which says, "The LORD came from Mount Sinai" with "myriads of holy ones" (NLT mg). In the Deuteronomy text these could be the people of God, but in both *1 Enoch* 1:9 and Jewish tradition they were seen as angels. Angels are called "holy ones" often (e.g., Ps 89:5, 7, NIV), and Zechariah 14:5 says, "Then the LORD my God will come, and all his holy ones with him." Throughout the New Testament, the return of Christ is accompanied by angels (Matt 16:27; 24:30-31; 25:31; Mark 8:38; Luke 9:26; 2 Thess 1:7), and they are involved in the harvest of both the saints and the sinners.

The purpose of Christ's coming (v. 15) is "to execute judgment on the people of the world," referring to the condemnation of all the unbelievers. This is the judgment of the wicked at Christ's return, in keeping with New Testament texts like 1 Thessalonians 5:1-3; 2 Thessalonians 2:1-12; Revelation 19:11-21. The emphasis here is that no one will escape, for it literally says, "judgment on all and the conviction of every person." The word for "convict" (*elenxai* [TG1651, ZG1794]) is a legal term also used in John 16:8 of the Holy Spirit who "will convict [prove the guilt] the world of its sin, and of God's righteousness, and of the coming judgment." In the book of Revelation, judgment is depicted as later, after the final battle and the millennial reign of Christ (Rev 20:11-15), but in both cases it is part of the Day of the Lord, the eschaton or end of all things (see Schnabel 2011). The theme of the inevitable and final judgment for the ungodly is a major emphasis in 2 Peter (2 Pet 2:1, 3-6, 9, 12-13, 17; 3:7, 10-12, 16) and Jude (vv. 4-7, 10-11, 13, 15, 23).

The nature of the heretics as "ungodly" (an idea introduced in v. 4; see commentary there) is another primary theme. Reference to it is made three times in verse 15, literally, "convict the ungodly people of all the ungodly deeds that they have godlessly committed." Their practices have priority over their teaching here, for it is their godless action that is highlighted. Their irreverent attitude towards God and all supernatural forces (vv. 8-10) led them to godless living, to "violate the norms of a proper or professed relation to deity" (BDAG 141). The false teachers were impious and cared little for God's ways, and so they developed patterns of action that flouted God's rules of conduct and showed irreverence toward his will. In both Jewish and Greco-Roman worlds this was a serious breach of socially acceptable behavior, for proper reverence for God and lives that exhibited piety were expected of upstanding citizens.

The final part of the quote deals with sins of speech, as Jude moves from deeds to words. These heretics were also being condemned "for all the insults that ungodly sinners have spoken against" God (v. 15). This is not found in *1 Enoch* 1:9 but may come from other phrases in *1 Enoch* like "spoken slanderously grave and harsh words" (*1 Enoch* 5:4), or "speak with their mouth unbecoming words against the Lord and utter hard words concerning his glory" (*1 Enoch* 27:2), or "you utter bold and hard words against his righteousness" (*1 Enoch* 101:3). Jude most likely added this in order to segue into the sins of speech in verse 16. The dangerous teaching and words of these people are discussed in verses 4, 8, 10, hinted at in verses 12-13, and summed up in verses 16, 19. By their terrible actions and harsh words they were turning many away from God.

Jude applies all this directly to the heretics by making three indictments against them in verse 16. First, these false teachers were like the rebellious Israelites in the wilderness. The theme of the rebellion and God's judgment upon it is also utilized in verse 5 ("He destroyed those who did not remain faithful") and verse 11 ("Like Korah, they perish in their rebellion"). Here the emphasis is on the sins of speech from verse 15b, for Jude begins by decrying the fact that they were "grumblers and complainers." In the Exodus the Israelites complained about the way God was taking care of them (Exod 16:7-12; Num 14:2-3, 27-29) and showed a distinct lack of faith (Num 14:11). It is difficult to ascertain just what the false teachers were complaining about. They may have been upset with the moral restrictions placed upon them by God and the church (Bauckham 1983:98), and wanted to be free to act as they wished (Moo 1996:270). This is shown in the added comment that they were "living only to satisfy their desires," meaning that their grievance was fueled entirely by their lascivious appetites.

Second, not only were they murmuring protests against God and the church, they were bragging "loudly about themselves," returning to the charge of their arrogance in verse 8. Such proud boasting is absolutely opposite the "humility that comes from wisdom" (Jas 3:13) that should characterize Christian speech. This haughty language is also decried in Daniel 7:8 ("a mouth that was boasting arrogantly"), *1 Enoch* 5:4 ("proud and hard words"), and *Testament of Moses* 7:9 ("their mouths will speak enormous things"), so this was a common emphasis in Jewish thought. Arrogant claims have always been a problem and continue to be so, especially proud speech about God and one's knowledge of his ways.

Third, the text says that "they flatter others to get what they want" (v. 16). Since the false teachers had no truth to offer, the best way to gain adherents was to cajole them with false praise. The Greek phrase means to "show partiality or favoritism" to a person, thus to "flatter" a person, in this case "for the sake of gain"—first monetary advantage and then simply to gain influence over another. The greed of these people was already noted in verse 11. Gene Green (2008:110) notes that this "implies that these people were *not* people of extremely modest means. The flatterer's goal is consumption, and such a person uses others while pretending to be their friend." Harvey and Towner (2009:218) speak of "the ingratiating bias of the false teachers toward those with influence in the community," resulting in their "teaching (instead of what God's word demanded) what certain people wished to hear." This tendency of false teachers is called teaching for "itching ears" in 2 Timothy 4:3. Truth all too often dies on the altar of gaining influence.

◆ IV. Closing Appeal to the Genuine Believers (vv. 17-23)
A. Call to Remember Apostolic Prophecy (vv. 17-19)

17 But you, my dear friends, must remember what the apostles of our Lord Jesus Christ said. 18 They told you that in the last times there would be scoffers whose purpose in life is to satisfy their ungodly desires. 19 These people are the ones who are creating divisions among you. They follow their natural instincts because they do not have God's Spirit in them.

NOTES

19 ***creating divisions.*** The word for "divisions" or "conflict" is *apodiorizontes* [TG592, ZG626], a hapax legomena in the NT that normally means "draw a boundary through" and was used in the Hellenistic world for classifying animals or other things. Therefore, some have said the movement was "making distinctions" between people in the congregation, classifying people in Gnostic fashion as "worldly" (*psuchikoi* [TG5591, ZG6035]) or as "spiritual" (*pneumatokoi* [TG4152, ZG4461]) (Mayor, Kelly, M. Green). While this certainly fits some of the language that follows, the meaning of "separating, dividing" and thus bringing "divisions" and "conflict" is closer to what was happening (so Bigg, Reicke, Bauckham, Moo, Schreiner). These divisions are behind the challenge in vv. 22-23, as Jude asks the faithful to "rescue" those caught in the trap of the heresy.

COMMENTARY

In the middle section (vv. 5-16), Jude spent his time warning his readers about the false teachers. Now he turns and tells them how they are to act on this information. Some scholars take this with the preceding, since it does continue the denunciation, but he begins with "beloved" and addresses the faithful directly ("you"), asking them to "remember" the truths handed down to them by the apostles. Jude was doing much more than just denouncing the false teachers; he was also trying to build up the genuine believers in their faith and give them spiritual strength to both grow in the Lord and to overcome the heretical teachers. The negative vituperation in verses 5-16 is framed by positive reassurance in verses 3-4 and 17-23. As in verse 3, Jude first establishes his relationship with them by calling them "beloved" or "dear friends," reminding them again of the love from God and within the church that binds them as a community into a family. The interlopers are always spoken of in this epistle in the third person, stressing that they were not part of the community. The believers here as in verse 3 are always addressed in the second person ("you") as treasured friends/members of the community. As Moo (1996:280) brings out, in this closing section (vv. 17-23), Jude was challenging believers to do three things: (1) remember apostolic predictions (vv. 17-19) about these false teachers so they could realize God knew about them all along and was still in control; (2) build each other up spiritually (vv. 20-21) so the heretics could not deceive them; and (3) rescue those who had given in to these deceptions and show mercy to others (vv. 22-23).

This passage (vv. 17-19) begins much the same as verse 5, where the community is asked to remember past prophecies about the enemies of God and the church. In verse 5 as well as in 2 Peter (2 Pet 1:12-13, 15; 3:1-2) "remembering" is a critical action with regard to the interlopers; it connotes not just bringing facts to mind but allowing those truths to change both thinking and actions. Verse 5 referred to Old Testament types that were fulfilled in the false teachers. Here it is apostolic prophecies about the "scoffers" (see vv. 8, 10 on the "scoffers") who have now come. These prophecies about false teachers to come were delivered first by Jesus (Matt 24:4-5, 11, 23-24), then by Paul at Miletus (Acts 20:29-31) and in his epistles (2 Thess 2:3-12; 1 Tim 4:1-5; 2 Tim 3:1-5), and later by John (1 John 4:1-3, most likely postdating Jude; cf. also 2 Pet 3:3, though it builds on Jude). The point here is that the prophecies were already coming to pass. The prophets are the apostles "of our Lord Jesus Christ," emphasizing that he is cosmic Lord and sovereign over both creation and history. Here Christ is clearly the true source of these prophetic truths and will bring to pass his judgment against these enemies of God.

The false teachers are "scoffers" or "mockers" (v. 18; *empaiktai* [TG1703, ZG1851]) who laugh and make fun of divine realities (similar to those who "slander" or "blaspheme" the heavenly truths in vv. 8, 10; 2 Pet 2:2, 10-12). These are people who despise the things of God and disparage theological and moral demands (see Pss 1:1; 35:16; Prov 9:7-8; 14:6) and are paralleled by the authorities who taunted Jesus on the cross (Mark 15:29-32). Second Peter differs with Jude in the sense that there the heretics are especially centered on denying the Parousia and the Last Judgment, while in Jude their "scoffing" is broader, centering on the authority of God and Christ in general. In their hubris they dishonor God (G. Green 2008:115-116). The "last times" refers not only to the events at the end of history but to the entire period between Christ's advents. With the Incarnation, God's Kingdom arrived (Mark 1:14-15; Luke 11:20), and so the "last days" were inaugurated. We are living in these final times before the end (the doctrine is called "inaugurated eschatology"). During these days there will be many false teachers twisting and distorting the teachings of the word of God, drawing many in the community away from Christ.

These false teachers are people "whose purpose in life is to satisfy their ungodly desires" (v. 18). Their "ungodly" nature is stressed in verses 15-16. They were irreverent in word and deed, and the term "desires" (*epithumias* [TG1939, ZG2123]) here especially centers on their immoral sexual desires. In their demand for lascivious living, they derisively mocked the standards of God and made fun of the church's moral teaching. We all have the same choice—to satisfy God or satisfy ourselves. We must decide between going the way of the world or following the way of God. Clearly these people made the wrong choice, and they would suffer as a result of that choice for eternity.

The church was fractured (v. 19), filled with "divisions" and discord because of these people. The false teachers, by participating in normal Christian gatherings like the love feast (v. 12), were polarizing influences, as they spent a great deal of their time trying to talk the members of the community into joining their faction. They were similar to but much worse than the Christian pneumatists at Corinth (1 Cor 12–14) who considered themselves superior to the other believers and tried to brainwash the faithful over to their side.

These false teachers are said to "follow their natural instincts because they do not have God's Spirit in them" (v. 19). It is they who are the *psuchikoi* [TG5591, ZG6035] (worldly, natural) and have no "spiritual" (*pneumatikoi* [TG4152, ZG4461]) presence within them (see note on v. 19). They were "natural," purely of this world, and had no instincts that could make them in any sense part of the spiritual realm. Their entire value system, their morals and their ethics, was wholly worldly and had nothing of the Spirit in it. In 1 Corinthians 3:1 Paul speaks of the spiritual (*pneumatikoi*) and the carnal (*sarkinoi* [TG4560, ZG4921]), and in 1 Corinthians 2:14-15 he contrasts the *psuchikoi* and the *pneumatokoi* from the standpoint of the natural and spiritual mind, saying the natural person cannot understand the things of the Spirit. So these leaders were completely devoid of anything pertaining to the Spirit, a very frightening thing to contemplate. We today must also make certain that those we listen to (e.g., television preachers and so-called Christian talk shows) are of the Spirit and not of the natural mind. There is an incredible amount of very bad theology out there, and the frightening thing is that many Christians care little if anything about theological truth. They are prime fodder for these charlatans.

◆ B. Exhortation to Remain Faithful (vv. 20-23)

[20]But you, dear friends, must build each other up in your most holy faith, pray in the power of the Holy Spirit,* [21]and await the mercy of our Lord Jesus Christ, who will bring you eternal life. In this way, you will keep yourselves safe in God's love.

[22]And you must show mercy to* those whose faith is wavering. [23]Rescue others by snatching them from the flames of judgment. Show mercy to still others,* but do so with great caution, hating the sins that contaminate their lives.*

20 Greek *pray in the Holy Spirit.* 22 Some manuscripts read *must reprove.* 22-23a Some manuscripts have only two categories of people: (1) those whose faith is wavering and therefore need to be snatched from the flames of judgment, and (2) those who need to be shown mercy. 23b Greek *with fear, hating even the clothing stained by the flesh.*

NOTES

20 *pray in the power of the Holy Spirit.* It is often believed (so M. Green, Bauckham, Davids, Harvey and Towner; see Dunn 1975:239-240) that prayer "in the Spirit" here refers to *glossolalia,* a charismatic prayer in tongues, on the basis of 1 Cor 14:15-16, where Paul seems to contrast prayer "in the Spirit" with prayer "in words I understand." While this may be included (as one type of prayer), there is no evidence in the context that this is primary in Jude's thinking. Rather, it is a more general reference to the Spirit as the sphere within which prayer is to occur (see commentary).

22-23 This is one of the most complex and difficult text-critical passages in the NT, as there are at least six different readings of these verses. In brief, some manuscripts divide the text into two clauses, others into three. The two-clause approach is supported by B C* 𝔐 and is followed by KJV, NKJV, NEB as well as several scholars (Bigg, Kelly, Bauckham, Neyrey, Davids, G. Green). The KJV reads, "And of some have compassion, making a difference: And others save with fear, pulling *them* out of the fire." The three-clause approach is supported by א A and is followed by NRSV, NASB, NIV, REB, NJB, NET, ESV, and NLT, as well as several other scholars (Metzger, Comfort, M. Green, Vögtle, Osburn [who changed his mind from an earlier article], Kubo, Moo, Schreiner) and reads similar to the NLT text above. It is impossible to decide with certainty, but overall the three-clause option fits with Jude's predilection for triads and best accounts for the other version. So I tentatively side with the version represented in the NLT.

whose faith is wavering. There are three possible understandings for the meaning of the verb *diakrinomenous* [TG1252A, ZG1359] here: (1) As in NIV, NLT, and ESV, it might mean "doubt" or "waver" as often in the NT (Matt 21:21; Mark 11:23; Acts 10:20; Rom 4:20; 14:23; Jas 1:6), referring to those who had been influenced by the false teachers and were "doubting" what they had been taught (so Kelly, Moo, Schreiner, Ross, Harvey and Towner). (2) It might mean "those under judgment" and refer to followers of the heretics who had been excommunicated (so Birdsall 1963). (3) It can have the same meaning as it does in v. 9, "dispute," and refer to the adherents of the false teachers who rejected the discipline Jude and others were trying to impose and who therefore remained in conflict with the church (so Bauckham, Spitaler). The second is the least likely, for it is not a regular meaning of the term. The other two are both viable, but in the movement between the three levels of vv. 22-23, "waver" fits better.

COMMENTARY

Verses 20-23 are the second half of the address directed to the faithful in the church and consist of an ethical exhortation addressing their spiritual needs directly. Every challenge is directed to their situation, telling them how to respond to the heresy and remain firm under the pressure. In verse 3 Jude directed them to "defend the faith," and in verses 5-16 and then 17-19 they were to defend it by taking action against the false teachers and exposing their heresy. Now he tells them to defend the faith by strengthening their own faith and keeping the church "safe in God's love" (v. 21). Bauckham (1983:4) calls this the true epicenter of the letter, asserting that the argument of verses 5-19 becomes "necessary background" to the appeal here, which is "the climax of the letter to which all the rest leads up." There are two parts to this section, beginning with the command to develop their own faith (vv. 20-21) and then the command to rescue as many of those who had strayed after the false teachers as they could (vv. 22-23).

As in verse 17, Jude opens verse 20 with "But you, dear friends," addressing the believers directly as "beloved" friends in the church and separating them from the false teachers and those of their cult. The Spirit was not absent in them as he was in the heretics, but they dare not remain spiritually idle. To try to be neutral in the Christian faith is to begin the downward spiral to spiritual defeat. They are therefore enjoined to do four things.

First, they "must build each other up in [their] most holy faith" (v. 20). The verb is a construction metaphor that pictures the erection of a foundation and a structure upon it (cf. Rom 15:20; 1 Cor 8:1; 14:3-5; 2 Cor 10:8; Eph 2:21). Most agree that the image here is of the community becoming an "eschatological temple" (Bauckham 1983:112), as in 1 Peter 2:4-6 where the members are "living stones" built on the "living cornerstone" (Jesus) to become both the "spiritual temple" and the priesthood that offers sacrifices in it (see also 1 Cor 3:9-15; 2 Cor 6:16; Eph 2:19-22). But the primary stress is upon the responsibility of the church to maintain corporate vigilance and fellowship, to continue to grow as God's house.

The foundation or sphere within which this growth takes place is the "most holy faith" (v. 20), namely, the Christian system of belief. It is "most holy" because it centers on the sacred truths revealed by God to his people, and it is "your faith" because it belongs to the church in contrast to the false teachers. This is one of the most emphatic statements in Scripture on the true significance of right Christian theology. Our sacred deposit is not just important; it is sacred ("holy") truth, and it is "exceedingly great" in importance, "incredibly holy" in significance. Those traditions in our time that denigrate theology and play lightly with the critical nature of truth (in our postmodern age) are playing with fire. There is nothing more critical than God's revealed truth.

Second, the believers must "pray in the power of the Holy Spirit" (v. 20). There are two triads in verses 20-21, namely, faith, hope (in "await the mercy"), and love, which sum up the core experiences of what it means to be a Christian (so Bauckham, Moo, Harvey and Towner). Furthermore, there is a Trinitarian aspect, as the text moves from the Spirit to Jesus to God. For the believers, the Spirit draws them up to God. Here it is prayer that centers on the presence of the Spirit. This is in keeping with passages throughout the New Testament in which Christian activity is to be done "in the Spirit," including prophesying (Mark 12:36), going from place to place (Acts 19:21), speaking (1 Cor 12:3), and expressing joy (Rom 14:17). It can all be summed up in "be filled with the Holy Spirit" (Eph 5:18). In Romans 8:26-27 our own inadequate human prayers are effective because behind our prayers is the intercessory prayer of the Spirit. This is why "all things work together for good" (Rom 8:28, NKJV). Davids (2006:95) says this "refers to prayer *controlled* or *guided* by the Spirit" as "the Spirit inspires true prayer." The faithful live for God, and their lives are centered on Spirit-enhanced prayer; by contrast, the worldly members of the cult lived for pleasure, and their lives were centered on self and the desires of the flesh.

Third, they should "await the mercy of our Lord Jesus Christ" (v. 21), undoubtedly referring to the merciful rewards awaiting believers when Christ returns, in contrast to the judgment awaiting the sinners (vv. 4-5, 7, 10-11, 13, 15). The idea of "waiting" for the final kingdom often has the nuance of confident expectation, as with Simeon and Anna waiting for the Christ (Luke 2:25, 38), the eschatological image of servants "waiting" for their master to return (Luke 12:36), and Paul's image of the believers, who "wait for the blessed hope" (Titus 2:13, NIV). "Mercy" coincides with the Old Testament concept of God's lovingkindness and grace, which in the New Testament is extended also to the mercy of Christ (included in many epistolary salutations, see commentary on v. 2; cf. Matt 5:7; Rom 9:23; 2 Tim 1:18; Jas 2:13). This mercy will be shown to the righteous, while the sinners will face judgment, for they lived only for present appeasement of the baser appetites, but the person of faith has the joy of looking forward to a future victory.

At the final harvest, the wheat will be separated from the weeds (Matt 13:24-30, 36-43) and the good fish from the bad (Matt 13:47-51), with the result that the "righteous" will "shine like the sun in their Father's Kingdom" (Matt 13:43). In the "waiting" there is both anxiety and hope, and the believer finds the balance between them via prayer. Trust in God becomes "the substance of things hoped for" (Heb 11:1, KJV). Moreover, the one we await is "the Lord Jesus Christ" (see vv. 4, 17) who is cosmic Lord over all and who "will bring . . . eternal life" (v. 21) for the faithful. In John's Gospel eternal life is a present possession (see John 3:15-16; 5:24; 6:40, 47), but Jude emphasizes another aspect, that the believer receives eternal life at the Second Coming (also Matt 19:29; Rom 2:7; Titus 3:7). Both, of course, are true. The primary point is the vastly different futures that await the wicked and the saints.

Fourth, they are commanded to, literally, "keep yourselves (*tēreō* [TG5083, ZG5498]) in God's love" (cf. NLT, "In this way, you will keep yourselves safe in God's love"). This is the fifth time the verb *tēreō* appears in Jude: In verse 1 God "keeps you safe"; in verse 6 the angels did not "stay" (lit., "keep themselves") within their God-given limits, so God "kept" them chained up; and in verse 13 the "blackest darkness" is reserved (kept) for the false teachers. Here in verse 21 the verb is used positively as in verse 1—there God "keeps" us in Christ; here we "keep ourselves" in God.

In these verses we have the two sides of the security of the believer: God keeps us safe, and at the same time we keep ourselves safe in him, as in Philippians 2:12 ("Work hard to show the results of your salvation") and Philippians 2:13 ("For God is working in you"). "Keeping" ourselves in God means obedience to his will; it is by "keeping" his commands that we remain in him. In John 15:9-10 "remain in my love" is defined as "obey my commandments." Moreover, this is not just an individual act of each believer; the plurals make this a corporate act of the whole church in its spiritual vigilance. We are to maintain watch over one another to maintain our security in God. The book of Hebrews speaks of two antidotes for apostasy: the vertical faith and hope in God (Heb 3:14; 4:3; 10:22-23; 12:1-3; 13:21) and the horizontal involvement of every member of the church in each other's walk with God (Heb 3:13; 10:24-25; 12:12-13; 13:17). Jude emphasizes that "God's love" is the central factor in our security. It is the love of God that brought Christ to the cross and made salvation possible. It is God's love that keeps us secure in Christ.

In the first half of this section (vv. 21-22a) the trajectory has been internal, as God's people worked at their faith walk and built up the body of Christ. In verses 22b-23 the trajectory is external, as the believers reach out to those sucked into the heretical movement and try to "rescue" them from the flames. As Moo (1996:286) says, "With their own spiritual condition secure, they can now reach out to others whose position is not so certain." Jude addresses three levels of people who have been influenced by the false teachers. First are those who have been led to doubt the truth (the term means "dispute" in v. 9 but "doubt" here; see note), and Jude commands the saints here to "show mercy to those whose faith is wavering." The saints have experienced mercy from God and Christ (vv. 2, 21), and now they must show the same grace to those who have fallen under the influence of the heretics.

These people had not yet deserted their faith and joined the false movement, and Jude wanted to make certain the believers did not overreact and reject or dispel these people from the church. In 2 Timothy 2:24-26 Paul instructed Timothy and the other leaders to "be kind to everyone . . . gently instruct those who oppose the truth" so that they can "come to their senses and escape from the devil's trap." The goal was to help these people realize the lies they were being told and return to Christ; in other words, Jude wanted a redemptive rather than a punitive response. This is an apologetic as well as redemptive move, helping these people realize the error and fully embrace the truth, and bringing them back fully into the "most holy faith" (v. 20).

The second group (v. 23) consisted of those who had moved further to the other side and joined the heretics, for they must be "rescued" (*sōzō* [TG4982, ZG5392]) and snatched "from the flames of judgment [lit., 'the fire']." This has to be a reference to the theme of final judgment that has dominated this epistle. The emphasis on "fire" refers to eternal torment in the "lake of fire" (Rev 19:20; 20:10, 14-15), pictured as fiery judgment (1 Cor 3:13-15; Heb 10:27; Jas 3:6; 5:3; 2 Pet 3:7), and called "Gehenna" by Jesus (Matt 5:22, 29-30; 10:28; 18:9; 23:15; Mark 9:47-48). Gehenna referred to the constantly burning trash dump in the Kidron Valley on the south side of Jerusalem, picturing the fiery judgment awaiting the wicked. Those in this second group had joined the false teachers' movement and were in danger of this fiery judgment. Yet there was still hope, as James 5:19-20 states, "If someone among you wanders away from the truth and is brought back, you can be sure that whoever brings the sinner back will save that person from death and bring about the forgiveness of many sins." Jude was asking for that very kind of rescue operation in this instance. They were on the brink of divine judgment, and Jude asked the faithful to "snatch" them from the burning embers.

Behind this is undoubtedly Zechariah 3:1-4 (see also Amos 4:11), already alluded to in verse 9. In Zechariah 3:1-4, the Lord rebukes Satan for bringing accusations against Joshua the high priest and describes Joshua as "like a burning stick that has been snatched from the fire," referring both to the exiles who were snatched away from near destruction in Babylon and to Joshua's own experience of forgiveness from God. Both aspects are intended here as well, as these people, brought back to the Lord, would have their sins forgiven and would be plucked away from fiery judgment (as indicated in Jas 5:20). There needs to be more of this activity in our own day, rescuing people who are being sucked into the false movements of our time.

The third group refers to those who have fully joined the heresy, including the false teachers themselves. The reason for this interpretation is the command here to approach them "with fear, hating even the clothing stained by the flesh" (NLT mg). The idea of their very clothing "stained by the flesh" speaks of the members of the cult who were engaging in the corrupt sins described earlier in the epistle. The very clothing they wore when participating in such evil acts became contaminated by their fleshly corruption. This is a further reference back to Joshua in Zechariah 3:3-4, where it says his "clothing was filthy as he stood there before the angel," signifying the sin and guilt of the nation. But the angel commanded that Joshua remove his filthy clothes, saying, "See, I have taken away your sins, and now I am giving you these fine new clothes." The message was one of forgiveness.

Jude told the believers to "show mercy" to this third group, combining prayer for their conversion and evangelistic opportunities to bring them to Christ and his forgiveness. There is no hint that they had committed the "sin that leads to death" of 1 John 5:16-17 (cf. Heb 6:4-6; 10:26-31), so there was still hope for their future salvation. Yet that mercy must be accompanied "with great caution" (lit., "fear")—in this case, not fear of God (so Kelly 1969:289; Bauckham 1983:116) but fear of being contaminated by the sin "stain" of the false movement. In every effort of reclamation there is danger of being drawn into the flames yourself. Their very clothes (the Greek word indicates the tunic or inner garment closest to their "flesh") were "stained" (v. 23, NLT mg), and the word here may refer to human excrement (see Harvey and Towner 2009:230). The picture is that of underclothes fouled by human filth, so polluted they can never again be worn.

The corruption of the world brings great temptation to bear on the people trying to bring the false teachers back. The faithful are drawn to the very sins of the flesh they should hate. So great caution is called for, a caution caused by the fear that the rescuers might fall into the very pit from which they are trying to save the endangered. As Galatians 6:1 says, when restoring a sinner, "Be careful not to fall into the same temptation yourself." The question we should each ask ourselves is, "How much do I hate these sins, and how much am I drawn to them." When the appeal outweighs the dislike, we are in deep trouble! We must love the sinner yet hate the sin.

◆ V. Concluding Doxology (vv. 24-25)

24Now all glory to God, who is able to keep you from falling away and will bring you with great joy into his glorious presence without a single fault. 25All glory to him who alone is God, our Savior through Jesus Christ our Lord. All glory, majesty, power, and authority are his before all time, and in the present, and beyond all time! Amen.

NOTES

25 *who alone is God.* Those who grew up with the KJV (and NKJV) expect to read "To the only wise God," but that reading is attested only in P 𝔐 and is missing in the oldest manuscripts (𝔓72 ℵ A B C). It was most likely added by influence from the doxology in Rom 16:27 (as was a similar text in 1 Tim 1:17, so Comfort 2008:807). So the reading as in NLT is correct.

through Jesus Christ our Lord. There is debate as to whether this modifies what precedes (as in the NLT, so M. Green) or with what follows ("all glory, majesty, power, and authority are his *through Jesus Christ our Lord*"; so NIV, Mayor, Bigg, Kelly, Davids, G. Green). If a choice has to be made, the evidence from the other NT doxologies favors the latter, that glory and majesty belong to God "through Jesus Christ" (Rom 16:27; 2 Cor 1:20; Col 3:17; 1 Pet 4:11). Yet I agree with Bauckham (1983:123-124) that this does not have to be an either-or decision: "The phrase may be deliberately ambiguous, combining the two thoughts" (in the Greek the phrase "through Jesus Christ" comes right between the two parts, indicating it may be meant to modify both and provide a transition from the one to the other). The NRSV, NASB, and ESV catch this well with their punctuation, following the order of the Greek: "To the only God our Savior, through Jesus Christ our Lord, be glory, majesty, dominion, and authority" (NASB).

COMMENTARY

Instead of the normal closing of a letter with greetings, wishes, and so on, Jude concludes with a doxology that has become one of the most beloved in the Bible, used to close countless services in various churches. It also sums up the positive part of the message of this epistle, namely, that God has the power to preserve his people from dangerous teachers and enable them to both "defend the faith" (v. 3) and bring back the fallen (vv. 22-23). Doxologies are often used at the close of major sections in New Testament epistles (Rom 11:36; Gal 1:5; Eph 3:20-21; 1 Tim 1:17; 6:16) and sometimes at the close of letters (either just before the greetings—Phil 4:20; 2 Tim 4:18; Heb 13:21; 1 Pet 5:10-11—or as the conclusion itself—Rom

16:25-27; 2 Pet 3:18; cf. *1 Clement* 65:2). Doxologies normally are composed of four parts—attribution to God or Christ, lengthy word of praise, a desire for the glory to last forever, and the "amen" close. All are found here. There are four parts of the ascription of glory to God, the first pair telling what God has the power to do for his people, the second pair describing the glory that belongs to God and Christ alone.

First, God "is able to keep you from falling away," emphasizing that God has the strength ("able to" = "has the power to") to keep his people secure ("protecting you by his power," 1 Pet 1:5). The idea of God "keeping" in Jude is used positively of keeping Christians "safe" in verses 1, 21 and negatively of reserving the wicked for judgment (vv. 6, 13). Here the term is *phulassō* [TG5442, ZG5875], normally used of imprisoning criminals but also used positively of God "guarding" or "protecting" his people, as here (John 17:11-12; 2 Thess 3:3; 2 Tim 1:12; 2 Pet 2:5; cf. Phil 4:7; Rev 3:10). God is at work and watching over his people, keeping them safe from dangers like the false teachers.

What God protects the believers from is "stumbling" or "falling away," with athletic imagery of stumbling in a race and falling down, as in the "weak knees" of Hebrews 12:12-13; the danger is growing weak in the race of life and falling into the ditch. In James 2:10 and 3:2 the idea is losing "control" and falling into sin, but Romans 11:11 is closer to this context (Paul asks, "Did [the Jews] stumble and fall beyond recovery?"). In 2 Peter 1:10, Peter demands that the righteous work hard to prove that they are "called and chosen" so that they "will never fall away." The idea is that of apostasy; what Jude is saying is that God works to preserve his people from the blandishments of the false teachers and therefore from apostasy and the final judgment (cf. Rom 8:31-39).

Second, God "will bring you with great joy into his glorious presence without a single fault" (v. 24). Grammatically, this is a second infinitive telling what God has the power to accomplish: "to him who is able to keep . . . and to bring you." The idea of God bringing us without fault into his presence is frequent in the New Testament (1 Cor 1:8; Eph 5:27; Col 1:22; 1 Thess 3:13). The idea is an image of a pure sacrifice "presented" to God, so the Christian is seen presented as a living sacrifice (Rom 12:1). The idea of the "faultless" sacrifice, of course, can be true only when the blood of Christ has atoned for sins, but Revelation 14:4-5 speaks of believers keeping "themselves as pure as virgins" so that they are "without blame," and Revelation 7:14 speaks of the victorious saints having "washed their robes in the blood of the Lamb and made them white." Both are part of the metaphor here—the blood of Christ and the moral purity of the Christian life as agents that keep the believer safe in Christ.

The false teachers have been warned throughout that they will suffer eternal damnation at the final judgment (vv. 10, 13, 15, 23; cf. vv. 5-7), but the faithful are promised that their eternal future is "great joy" in God's "glorious presence." There are two stages by which the righteous enter God's presence, first at death (2 Cor 5:8—"away from these earthly bodies . . . at home with the Lord"; cf. Phil 1:22-23), known to us as the intermediate state, and at the Parousia (1 Cor 1:8; Eph 5:27; Col 1:22; 1 Thess 3:13). Revelation 21:3-4 describes this latter moment when "God's home is now among his people! He will live with them, and they will be his people." At that time the final covenant will be established, and the believers will spend eternity experiencing the living presence and glory of God. "Glory" and "joy" throughout the New Testament are associated with the present and future experiences of the faithful. Bauckham (1983:123) speaks of this "eschatological joy" pictured here as "a cultic festival" in which rejoicing is an essential element (cf. Isa 12:6; 25:9; 1 Pet 4:13; Rev 19:7; *4 Ezra* 7:98; *1 Enoch* 5:9; 103:4).

Third, this God who exercises his power to bring us to himself is now described (v. 25) as "him who alone is God, our Savior through Jesus Christ our Lord." Monotheism is the distinctive feature of the Judeo-Christian heritage, and the emphasis on God as the "one and only God" is frequent in the Old Testament (the Shema [cf. Deut 6:4-9]; 2 Kgs 19:15; Neh 9:6; Pss 83:18; 89:6; Isa 37:16), Second Temple Jewish writings (2 Macc 1:24-25; 7:37; *Odes of Solomon* 7:45) and the New Testament (John 5:44; 17:3; Rom 3:30; 1 Tim 2:5; Rev 15:4), especially in doxologies (Rom 16:27; 1 Tim 1:17; 6:15-16). When Jesus was included in doxologies and designated "one and only God" (the meaning of *monogenēs* [TG3439, ZG3666] in John 1:14, 18; 3:16, 18), we have what Hurtado (1999:101-102) calls "a binitarian form of monotheism," where the worship of Jesus does not violate the worship of "the one true God." Here the emphasis is on God the Father, yet Harvey and Towner (2009:236) rightly note the comparison of this with verse 4: "There is in the sharing of epithets and attributes a noticeable inclination of an elevated Christology, a coalescing of the Godhead into what would later be described in more Trinitarian terms." It is unlikely that the false teachers were teaching a form of polytheism, for there is no evidence of this in either Jude or 2 Peter, so the emphasis in the doxology is probably purely for the sake of worship. This is a liturgical section celebrating the wonder of worshiping God.

In 2 Peter, the emphasis is on Christ as "Savior" (2 Pet 1:1, 11; 2:20; 3:2, 18), but here God is described as "Savior" or "Deliverer." This is a central confession in the Old Testament (Deut 32:15; Pss 24:5; 27:9; 65:5; 79:9) as well as in intertestamental literature (Sir 51:1; *Psalms of Solomon* 3:6; 17:3; *Odes of Solomon* 2:15) and the New Testament (Luke 1:47; 1 Tim 1:1; 2:3; 4:10; Titus 1:3; 2:10; 3:4). There is a slight hint that God would "deliver" the saints from the deadly teaching of the heretics, but the main purpose here is to place a capstone on the positive emphasis in the epistle that the righteous have been delivered from their sins and given salvation by the grace and mercy of God (vv. 1-3, 20-21). Still, this deliverance (and glory) has come "through Jesus Christ our Lord." Our salvation was accomplished by God, who sent his Son to the cross as the atoning sacrifice for us, so that we could be delivered from sin.

Fourth, the formal ascription of praise is given: "All glory, majesty, power, and authority are his before all time, and in the present, and beyond all time" (v. 25). Most New Testament doxologies have one or two elements, usually "to him be the glory" (the exceptions being 1 Tim 6:16—honor and power; and 1 Pet 5:11—power). The best parallel to Jude can be found in the praise song of Revelation 5:13, also having four elements (praise, honor, glory, and power). That is also a climactic doxology, for it is the fifth worship hymn to God and the Lamb in Revelation and highlights the oneness motif there—that is, the unity of God and the Lamb as one being. The doxology here closes Jude's epistle on the note of the worthiness of God to be worshiped.

Each of the four attributes that Jude mentions provides an important glimpse into the wondrous God we worship and into the reasons for rejecting the false God of the heretics. "Glory" (*doxa* [TG1391, ZG1518]) is the primary biblical term for the recognition of God's transcendent worth. Its basic thrust is "repute, honor" seen in a public affirmation. "It denotes 'divine and heavenly radiance,' the 'loftiness and majesty' of God, and even the 'being of God' and His world" (TDNT 2.237). All three of the other terms flow out of the sense of God's "glory." "Majesty" (*megalōsunē* [TG3172, ZG3488]) refers to "his state of greatness, preeminence" and, like "glory," can be used as a periphrasis for the name of God (Heb 1:3; BDAG 123). As it "shares semantic space with 'glory' . . . this doubling contributes to the impression of God's overwhelming grandeur" and "frame the whole moral argument of the epistle. To dishonor such a one would be unconscionable" (G. Green 2008:136).

The first two attributes center on God's exquisite honor, and the next two center on his sovereign control over his creation. "Power" or "might" (*kratos* [TG2904, ZG3197]) is used frequently in doxologies (1 Tim 6:16; 1 Pet 4:11; 5:11; Rev 1:6; 5:13) to extol God for exercising his strength on behalf of his people (Eph 1:19; cf. 1 Pet 1:5) and making it available to his people (Eph 6:10; Col 1:11). The "power" of God created this world, sustains it, and will bring it to an end at the time of his choosing. God's people place their trust entirely in his "mighty" hand of justice to end this world and destroy evil, thereby vindicating the believers for all they have sacrificed and suffered. This will all take place on the basis of his "authority" (*exousia* [TG1849, ZG2026]), a word that in many contexts means "power." God's "power" is exercised on the basis of his "authority" over his creation. He is Lord and ruler over his domain and will work out his "authoritative will" at the eschaton (Luke 12:5; Acts 1:7). Justice and power are in control of this world, and all Christians must live life God's way and seek only his truths.

Jude has the lengthiest temporal reference of any New Testament doxology, emphasizing God's timeless control of the past ("before all time"), present ("in the present," simply *nun* [TG3568, ZG3814], "now"), and future ("beyond all time," lit., "for all eternity"). This is similar to the teaching of two titles of God in Revelation: "the one who is, who always was, and who is still to come" (Rev 1:4, 8; 4:8; 11:17; 16:5) and the "Alpha and Omega" (Rev 1:8, 17; 21:6; 22:13), meaning that God as sovereign majesty is "Lord over history." He was in control before history began, will be in control throughout history, and will remain in control when history is over and eternity begins. Moreover, it is only those who follow him who will share and "reign with him" (Rev 20:4; 22:5). The doxology ends with the "Amen" that normally ends doxologies and prayers (e.g., Deut 27:15-16; Matt 6:13 [NLT mg]; Rom 16:27; 1 Pet 4:11; Rev 1:6; 19:4; 22:20, 21 [NLT mg]). "Amen" is a Hebrew prayer affirmation, meaning "so be it" or "may it come to pass" but also carrying with it "the commitment of the writer and readers to the truth found in the worshipful utterance" (Osborne 2002:68). To all of this we can only lift our faces to heaven and shout with Jude, "Amen!"

BIBLIOGRAPHY

Bartholomä, P. F.
2008 Did Jesus Save the People out of Egypt? A Re-examination of a Textual Problem in Jude 5. *Novum Testamentum* 50:143-158.

Bauckham, Richard J.
1983 *Jude, 2 Peter.* Word Biblical Commentary. Waco: Word.
1988 James, 1 and 2 Peter, Jude. Pp. 303-317 in *It Is Written: Scripture Citing Scripture; Essays in Honour of Barnabas Lindars.* Editors, D. A. Carson and H. G. M. Williamson. Cambridge: Cambridge University Press.

Bigg, Charles
1901 *A Critical and Exegetical Commentary on the Epistles of St. Peter and St. Jude.* International Critical Commentary. Edinburgh: T&T Clark.

Birdsall, J. N.
1963 The Text of Jude in 𝔓72. *Journal of Theological Studies* 14:394-399.

Bray, Gerald, editor
2000 *Ancient Christian Commentary on Scripture: James, 1–2 Peter, 1–3 John, Jude.* Downers Grove, IL: InterVarsity.

Callan, T.
2004 Use of the Letter of Jude by the Second Letter of Peter. *Biblica* 85:42-64.

Charles, J. Daryl
1991 Literary Artifice in the Epistle of Jude. *Zeitschrift für die neutestamentliche Wissenschaft* 82:106-124.
2005 The Angels under Reserve in 2 Peter and Jude. *Bulletin for Biblical Research* 15:39-48.

Charlesworth, James H.
1983 *The Old Testament Pseudepigrapha.* 2 vols. Garden City, NY: Doubleday.

Chatelion Counet, P.
2006 Pseudepigraphy and the Petrine School: Spirit and Tradition in 1 and 2 Peter and Jude. *Theological Studies* 62:403-424.

Chester, Andrew, and Ralph P. Martin, editors
1994 *The Theology of the Letters of James, Peter, and Jude.* Cambridge: Cambridge University Press.

Comfort, Philip W.
2008 *New Testament Text and Translation Commentary.* Carol Stream, IL: Tyndale House.

Craddock, F. B.
1995 *The Message of Second Peter and Jude.* Leicester: Inter-Varsity.

Davids, Peter H.
2006 *The Letters of 2 Peter and Jude.* Pillar New Testament Commentary. Grand Rapids: Eerdmans.

Dunn, James D. G.
1975 *Jesus and the Spirit.* London: SCM.

Elliott, John H.
1982 *I and II Peter/Jude.* Augsburg Commentary on the New Testament. Minneapolis: Augsburg.

Green, Gene L.
2008 *2 Peter and Jude.* Baker Exegetical Commentary on the New Testament. Grand Rapids: Baker.

Green, Michael
1987 *The Second Epistle General of Peter and the General Epistle of Jude.* Tyndale New Testament Commentaries. Grand Rapids: Eerdmans.

Gunther, John J.
1984 The Alexandrian Epistle of Jude. *New Testament Studies* 30:549-562.

Harrington, Daniel J.
2003 *Jude and 2 Peter.* Sacra Pagina. Collegeville, MN: Liturgical Press.

Harvey, Robert, and Philip H. Towner
2009 *2 Peter & Jude*. InterVarsity Press New Testament Commentaries. Downers Grove, IL: InterVarsity.

Hiebert, D. Edmond
1989 *Second Peter and Jude: An Expositional Commentary*. Greenville, SC: Unusual Publications.

Hillyer, Norman
1992 *1 and 2 Peter, Jude*. New International Biblical Commentary. Peabody, MA: Hendrickson.

Hurtado, Larry W.
1999 *At the Origins of Christian Worship: The Context and Character of Earliest Christian Devotion*. Grand Rapids: Eerdmans.

Jones, D. W.
2006 The Apostate Angels of 2 Pet. 2:4 and Jude 6. *Faith and Mission* 23:19-30.

Kelly, J. N. D.
1969 *A Commentary on the Epistles of Peter and Jude*. Black's New Testament Commentary. London: Black.

Kubo, Sakae
1981 Jude 22-23: Two Division Form or Three? Pp. 239-253 in *New Testament Textual Criticism: Its Significance for Exegesis: Essays in Honour of Bruce M. Metzger*. Editors, E. J. Epp and G. D. Fee. Oxford: Clarendon.

Leaney, A. R. C.
1967 *The Letters of Peter and Jude*. Cambridge: Cambridge University Press.

Lucas, Dick, and Christopher Green
1995 *The Message of 2 Peter and Jude*. The Bible Speaks Today. Downers Grove, IL: InterVarsity.

Mayor, Joseph B.
1907 *The Epistle of St. Jude and the Second Epistle of St. Peter: Greek Text with Introduction, Notes and Comments*. New York: Macmillan.

Metzger, Bruce M.
1994 *A Textual Commentary on the Greek New Testament*. New York: United Bible Societies.

Moo, Douglas J.
1996 *2 Peter and Jude*. NIV Application Commentary. Grand Rapids: Zondervan.

Neyrey, Jerome H.
1993 *2 Peter, Jude: A New Translation with Introduction and Commentary*. Anchor Bible 37C. New York: Doubleday.

Osborne, Grant
2002 *Revelation*. Baker Exegetical Commentary on the New Testament. Grand Rapids: Baker.

Osburn, Carroll D.
1992 Discourse Analysis and Jewish Apocalyptic in the Epistle of Jude. Pp. 287-319 in *Linguistics and New Testament Interpretation: Essays on Discourse Analysis*. Editor, D. A. Black and K. Barnwell. Nashville: Broadman.

Oswalt, John N.
1998 *The Book of Isaiah, Chapters 40-66*. The New International Commentary on the Old Testament. Grand Rapids: Eerdmans.

Reese, Ruth Ann
2007 *2 Peter and Jude*. Two Horizons New Testament Commentary. Grand Rapids: Eerdmans.

Reicke, Bo
1964 *The Epistles of James, Peter, and Jude*. Garden City, NY: Doubleday.

Ross, J. M.
1989 Church Discipline in Jude 22-23. *Expository Times* 100:297-298.

Schnabel, Eckhard J.
2011 *40 Questions about the End Times*. Grand Rapids: Kregel.

Schreiner, Thomas R.
2003 *1, 2 Peter, Jude*. New American Commentary. Nashville: Broadman & Holman.

Spitaler, P.
2006 Doubt or Dispute (Jude 9 and 22-23): Rereading a Special New Testament Meaning through the Lens of Internal Evidence. *Biblica* 87:201-222.

Vögtle, A.
1994 *Der Judasbrief; Der 2. Petrusbrief.* Evangelisch-katholischer Kommentar zum Neuen Testament. Düsseldorf: Neukirchen.

Watson, Duane F.
1988 *Invention, Arrangement, and Style: Rhetorical Criticism of Jude and 2 Peter.* Atlanta: Scholars Press.

Webb, Robert L.
2008 The Use of "Story" in the Letter of Jude: Rhetorical Strategies of Jude's Narrative Episodes. *Journal for the Study of the New Testament* 31:83-117.

Zahn, Theodor
1909 *Introduction to the New Testament.* Edinburgh: T&T Clark.

Revelation

M. ROBERT MULHOLLAND JR.

INTRODUCTION TO *Revelation*

THE FACT that there have been so many interpretations of Revelation from every conceivable perspective is a daunting reality for anyone bold or foolish enough to consider yet another contribution. One wonders whether there is any possible way to get a handle on what has already been done so as to avoid reinventing the hermeneutical wheel, and whether there can be anything new to add. It is possible to divide most interpretations of Revelation into two very broad, general groups. One group works from the presumption that the author was simply reporting a visionary experience more or less exactly as it was experienced. The other group works from the presumption that the author was simply employing the literary genre of apocalyptic to convey a message to an intended audience. There is great diversity both within each group and among those who attempt to work within both groups as to the "meaning" of Revelation. In many cases, "meaning" becomes dependent upon the presumption one brings to the text.

If genre (apocalyptic) is the starting point, there is a strong tendency to presume that there was no visionary experience, and John is simply utilizing the apocalyptic genre to promulgate his own particular agenda. Those who see Revelation as belonging to this literary genre bring to the text a preunderstanding of that genre that is often imposed upon the book as its meaning. If form (vision) is the starting point, there is a tendency to ignore the role of apocalyptic in Jewish literature and to bring to the text a preunderstanding of visionary experiences in general and the author's vision in particular, which is often overlaid upon the material as its meaning.

It may be that one aspect of narrative criticism can provide us an alternative starting point that will shed light upon Revelation rather than fuel the heat that exists in much of its interpretation. One of the essential aspects of narrative criticism is the understanding that a literary work operates within a narrative world. This world consists of the perceptual framework(s), value system(s), and behavior pattern(s) within which and/or against which a writer frames his or her work. A narrative world can utilize a variety of genres to convey the writer's purpose, and contains whatever entities are needed for the writer to present his or her purpose. The narrative world of a literary work may be that of the writer (real or putative), or it may be the narrative world of the reader (intended or imagined). Careful reading of a text can help tease out the narrative worlds within which it operates. (For more on narrative criticism, see Powell 1990.) The narrative world operates at a deeper level than form (report of a vision) or genre (apocalyptic), and thus can help us move beyond the impasse that often results from starting with form or genre as the key to interpretation, recognizing the place of each, for John utilizes the apocalyptic genre as the vehicle for conveying a visionary experience.

JOHN'S NARRATIVE WORLD: THE JEWISH STORY

When we approach Revelation to uncover its narrative world, John, the author, gives us some wonderful assistance. He provides us three introductions to his visionary experience: an apocalyptic introduction (1:1-3), an epistolary introduction (1:4-8), and a personal introduction (1:9). Since these introductions are distinct from the "vision" itself, they can be mined for evidences of John's narrative world without getting into the strange world of the vision itself.

The first clue John gives us to his narrative world is the "title" of his work: "A revelation from Jesus Christ" (1:1). "Christ" is the Greek for the Jewish term "Messiah." This suggests that John's narrative world is at least cognizant of the Jewish expectations of his time—a group of ideas and themes that I sometimes refer to in the commentary as the Jewish story. The essence of these expectations is epitomized in the disciples' question to the risen Jesus: "Lord, has the time come for you to free Israel and restore our kingdom?" (Acts 1:6). The Jews were eagerly awaiting God's intervention to free them from Rome's domination and restore their kingdom—that is, to make them an independent nation on their Promised Land, free to be God's covenant people without interference, and perhaps even to make them rulers of the world with the Gentiles as their subjects. Some Jews, such as the Zealots and Sicarii, actively sought (often by violent means) to force this issue with Rome.

These expectations were variously framed by several common understandings. First, Israel was still in exile, clearly manifested in the facts that their Promised Land was under Gentile control (cf. Jer 30:3), they lacked a Davidic king (cf. Jer 33:7, 15, 17), and God's presence had not returned to the Temple (cf. Isa 52:8; Ezek 43:1-7; Mal 3:1). Second, the reason for continued exile was sin; before God would restore the kingdom, the covenant community had to be cleansed of sin (cf. Jer 31:34; Ezek 36:25; Zech 13:1; 2 Macc 7:32). Third, diverse messianic expectations orbited around the hope for the restoration of the kingdom. A sense of this informs John 1:20-21, where John the Baptist tells the authorities he is not the Messiah (most likely the Davidic Messiah, the primary expectation [cf. 1 Kgs 8:25; Zech 12:8-10; 13:1]), nor Elijah, the forerunner to the Messiah (Mal 4:5), nor the prophet Moses promised (Deut 18:15-18). Some expectations looked also for the priestly Messiah of the order of Melchizedek (Ps 110:4), a concept seen in the book of Hebrews. Fourth, the restoration would fulfill the prophetic promises and consummate the old covenant (cf. Matt 5:17, esp. with the use of "fulfill" in Matt 1:22; 2:15; 8:17; 12:17; 13:35; 21:4). Fifth, when God restored the kingdom, the righteous dead, especially those martyred for their faithfulness, would be resurrected (Isa 26:19; Ezek 37; Dan 12:2; Luke 14:14; John 11:24; 2 Macc 7:9, 14, 23, 29). While there were many variations on these themes within first-century Judaism (including some, like the Sadducees, who rejected most of these ideas), this sketches the key points of Jewish expectations.

The apocalyptic introduction (1:1-8) provides us a wealth of information about John's narrative world. It is the narrative world laced with Jewish expectations for the Messiah and their promised kingdom; it is a story in which the creator/covenant God is involved with his covenant people in the midst of history to fulfill his purposes. Within this macro-story, John indicates that his narrative world is a version in which Jesus is the Messiah whom the Jews had been expecting.

John's second introduction (1:4-8) helps us to flesh out more of the details of the particular form of the Jewish expectations that shaped his narrative world. These are found primarily in John's descriptions of the Messiah (1:5-7) as follows:

1. Jesus the Messiah is the faithful martyr (1:5a). Especially in intertestamental Judaism, the image of the faithful martyr (or witness) was widespread.[1] Those who suffered death at the hands of the enemies of God's faithful people hastened the day when God would avenge them and restore the kingdom to Israel. In the Jewish story of John's narrative world, Jesus the Messiah also joins the ranks of these faithful martyrs.

2. Jesus is the firstborn from the dead (1:5b). In the intertestamental period, many Jews believed that when God restored the kingdom to Israel, those who had been faithful in their obedience to the covenant, especially the martyrs, would be raised to life in the restored kingdom. The theme seems to have originated in Daniel 12:2, which says, "Many of those whose bodies lie dead and buried will rise up, some to everlasting life." This is set in a context of deliverance out of great anguish (Dan 12:1).[2] There are textual echoes to Zechariah throughout Revelation's introduction, and here Zechariah 14:5 comes to mind. In that vision of the restoration of Israel, all the "holy ones" are to come with God, an early allusion to the resurrection of the pious to enjoy the restored kingdom. But rather than the resurrection just being a future hope, John implies that the resurrection of the righteous has already begun with Jesus as the first of the group. This also implies that the restoration of the kingdom has also begun.

3. The Messiah is the ruler of the kings of the world (1:5c). One of the crucial aspects of the expectation of the restoration of the kingdom to Israel was that God would become the king of the whole world and that the Gentile nations would become subservient to God and the restored Israel. The text echoes Zechariah 14:9: "And the LORD will be king over all the earth. On that day there will be one LORD—his name alone will be worshiped" (cf. Pss 10:16; 29:10; 47:2, 7-8; 93:1; 96:10; Isa 33:22; Jer 10:7, 10; Ezek 20:33; Zeph 3:15; Zech 9:9-10). John here confirms what was implicit above—that the restoration has come and Jesus the Messiah is God's regent over the kingdom.

4. Jesus' martyrdom had cleansed Israel from its sin (1:5d), a necessary step before the kingdom could be restored to Israel.[3] John's fourth description of Jesus the Messiah (lit., "he has freed us from sins through his blood," 1:5d) gives a radical subversion of the Jewish expectations. He claims that the martyrdom of the Messiah resulted in the release of Israel from her sin. The textual echoes of Zechariah 13:1 are unavoidable: "On that day a fountain will be opened for the dynasty of David and for the people of Jerusalem, a fountain to cleanse them from all their sins and impurity," especially when it appears in a context where the house of David and people of Jerusalem will mourn for the one *whom* they have pierced (Zech 12:10).

5. Jesus the Messiah has established the kingdom and made its members priests (1:6). The textual echoes from Exodus are unmistakable here. God's purpose for the consummation of the original Exodus was to make Israel a kingdom of priests (Exod 19:6). The consummation of the exile Israel was in at John's time would be God's restoration of the kingdom to Israel and the fulfillment of God's original purposes for his people. Through Jesus, the martyred Messiah, God has restored the kingdom to Israel and formed them as the kingdom of priests originally planned. There is, again, a textual echo from Zechariah here. The last aspect of Zechariah's vision is that the entire kingdom will be as holy as the Temple (Zech 14:20), at least implying that the people are priests. This "restoration," however, was not the geopolitical restoration of Israel to the Promised Land, though that was a primary aspect of Jewish expectation. It was the restoration of "Israel" as a new entity, a new covenant community of God's people that included not only Jews but also Gentiles (cf. 7:1-8 for the Jews, and 7:9-10 for the Gentiles).

6. Jesus the Messiah will come with the clouds (1:7). This reference to Daniel 7:13 shows that John's narrative world not only has a past and present, it also has a future. Wright (1992:291-297) has convincingly argued for an understanding of the "son of man" figure in Daniel as a representation of Israel vindicated after its affliction at the hands of the Gentiles (the beasts of Dan 7:3-12; cf. Dan 7:17-18). Here again, however, John appears to subvert the normal Jewish expectations. Jesus is placed in the role of the vindicated Israel. John linked this image to his earlier image of Jesus as the faithful martyr through the textual echoes of Zechariah 12:10: "They will look on me whom they have pierced and mourn for him as for an only son. They will grieve bitterly for him as for a firstborn son who has died." Here John introduces another variation from Jewish expectations. While Jesus has already restored the kingdom to Israel, there will also be a future consummation.

The epistolary introduction, therefore, provides specificity and clarity regarding John's narrative world: It is still the world of Jewish messianic expectations, but now changed in several ways. Jesus is a faithful martyr who has been raised from the dead, signaling the restoration of the kingdom to Israel. Through his martyrdom, Jesus has freed Israel from her sins and made her a kingdom of priests in fulfillment of God's original purposes for her. But the ultimate consummation of the kingdom is yet to come.

Finally, John told his readers that he was a coparticipant with them in tribulation, the kingdom, and patient endurance (1:9). This indicates that John's intended readers were participants with him in his narrative world. Together they were already coparticipants in the restored kingdom. But they were also coparticipants in persecution, which calls for patient endurance. This provides another new twist on broader Jewish expectations for the kingdom, which held the view that faithful Jews who endured persecution at the hands of their enemies would ultimately be vindicated and participate in the restored kingdom. Here, however, the faithful already participate in the restored kingdom, yet they still must endure persecution, apparently until the kingdom is consummated at some point in the future.

Let's summarize the information that John's introductions provide us with regarding the narrative world within which he is writing. We see that John's narrative world is the world of Jewish expectations of the first century. But it is a highly subverted form of these expectations. Jesus is the Messiah whose martyrdom has cleansed Israel from her sins and whose rising from the dead inaugurated the restored kingdom of priests over which he rules. This restored kingdom, however, while a present reality for the faithful, is not yet consummated. For anyone whose worldview was shaped by these Jewish expectations, the narrative world implicit in John's introductions would certainly entice them to read on and find out what it was all about. From this starting point, we can see that although John uses the apocalyptic genre to communicate the essence of his visionary experience, the narrative world he creates in his introduction subverts the typical expectations for the genre of apocalyptic by its affirmation that in the Messiah Jesus the future restoration has already begun.

AUTHOR

On first blush, there is no problem with the authorship of Revelation because the author identifies himself as "John" (1:1, 4, 9; 22:8). The issue is which John. The Christian writers of the first couple of centuries all attest to John the apostle, the author of the Gospel of John and letters of 1–3 John, as the author of Revelation. One of those writers, Irenaeus, was a disciple of Polycarp, who, Irenaeus reports, was a disciple of John the apostle. Irenaeus attributed Revelation to "John, the Lord's disciple" (*Against Heresies* 4.20.11). In addition, Justin Martyr wrote of "John, one of the apostles of Christ, who prophesied by a revelation that was made to him" (*Dialogue with Trypho* 81). These second-century church fathers are joined by the third-century writers Tertullian (*Against Marcion* 3.24) and Hippolytus (*On the Antichrist* 36) in affirming the apostle John as the author of Revelation.

As early as the third century, however, questions about John's authorship were raised on the basis of the linguistic differences between Revelation and the Gospel and letters of John. The Greek of Revelation, like the Greek of John's Gospel, is fairly simple. In Revelation, however, there are numerous grammatical anomalies that do not appear in the Gospel. At most points these anomalies can be linked to aspects of the author's visionary experience. That is, the author was wrestling with some aspect of the vision that did not communicate well in the normal, grammatical use of Greek. Therefore, the author "bent" the language in an attempt to convey as much of the reality of the vision as possible (see the note on 1:4 regarding John's misuse of grammar to emphasize a crucial aspect of the vision as an example of this phenomenon). On this basis, there is no reason not to side with the early Christian writers and accept John the apostle as the author.

In addition, there are a number of images and features in Revelation that find their parallel primarily, and often only, in the Gospel of John in the New Testament: (1) reference to Jesus as the "Lamb" (5:6, and 27 other uses; cf. John 1:29, 36); (2) the image of Jesus as the "door" (4:1—see note in commentary; cf. John 10:7); (3) Jesus as the Word (19:13; cf. John 1:1, 14); (4) the cross as the judgment of Satan (11:4-18; 19:11–20:3—see notes in commentary; cf. John 12:31-32; 16:11);

(5) Jesus as "light" (21:23; cf. John 1:4, 9; 3:19; 8:12; 9:5; 12:35-36, 46); (6) Jesus' preexistence (13:8, NLT mg; cf. John 8:58; 17:5, 24; Col 1:17); (7) the "I am" statements (*egō eimi* [TG1473/1510, ZG1609/1639]), which appear most often in John and Revelation (1:8, 17; 2:23; 21:6; 22:13, 16; cf. more than 20 uses as self-identification in John's Gospel).

DATE AND OCCASION OF WRITING

There are two primary choices for the date of Revelation. One is the mid-90s of the first century AD. The other is the mid- to late 60s. Scholars have been divided on this almost from the beginning of Christian history. Early church writers provide support for both dates (and a number of others), and modern scholars have joined them in their diversity. In the nineteenth century the predominant dating of Revelation was in the 60s. In the twentieth century it has been the 90s—although, in the last generation of scholars, many have been returning to the 60s for the date of Revelation.

There are several evidences from within Revelation that may support a date in the 60s: (1) John's vision of the division of "the Great City" (Rome) into three parts (16:19) could allude to the civil war that broke out among three factions following the suicide of Nero in AD 68. (2) John's description of the seven heads of the beast as seven kings, five of whom have fallen (17:9-10), also suggests a date in the 60s since the first emperor of Rome was Augustus (31 BC–AD 14), followed by Tiberius (14–37), Gaius (37–41), Claudius (41–54), and Nero (54–67). (3) A subtle pointer to the 60s might be the boast of the church in Laodicea, "I am rich. I have everything I want. I don't need a thing!" (3:17). In the early 60s Laodicea was destroyed by an earthquake. The inhabitants refused Nero's offer of financial assistance and rebuilt themselves to greater magnificence than before. While these pointers to the 60s are by no means proof positive for that dating of Revelation, there are no pointers as suggestive as these that point to the 90s. On this basis it is probably judicious to cautiously suggest a date in the late 60s.

The occasion of the writing of Revelation was a vision John received while in exile on the island of Patmos in the Aegean (cf. Caird 1966:22, who cites Tertullian *Prescription against Heretics* 36). In his vision of Jesus, John was instructed to "write in a book everything you see, and send it to the seven churches in the cities of Ephesus, Smyrna, Pergamum, Thyatira, Sardis, Philadelphia, and Laodicea" (1:11). The situation that seemed to engender the concern for these churches was that they were under pressure, if not attack, from the world in which they lived. Some of them were holding fast to the faith (Smyrna and Philadelphia), some of them had almost made shipwreck of their faith (Sardis and Laodicea), and some of them were waffling between faithfulness and apostasy (Ephesus, Pergamum, Thyatira). The vision was given to John so that he might convey to these churches a loud and clear call to faithfulness as citizens of God's New Jerusalem in the midst of their fallen Babylon world.

AUDIENCE

The primary implied audience of Revelation, as we have just seen, was the seven historical churches of the Roman provinces of Asia Minor in the first century. These churches were located on Roman routes that would enable a person carrying Revelation to begin at Ephesus, proceed to the other six churches in the order in which the cities are listed, and return to Ephesus without retracing any steps.

Since seven is one of the major recurring images in John's vision, both explicitly and implicitly,[4] and the number seven is the symbol for completeness, wholeness, and fullness, it is also possible that Revelation was written for the entire church, of which the seven churches in Asia Minor are paradigms. This would not only make the wider church of John's day part of the audience, but would also extend the audience throughout Christian history.

A primary issue for understanding John's vision is the ethnic composition of the seven churches. Were these churches predominately Gentile, Jewish, or mixed? If mixed, what percentage of the community might have been Gentile or Jewish? To answer this question we must quickly trace the history of Jewish presence in the Roman provinces of the Anatolian peninsula (modern-day Turkey), and, especially, the Roman province of Asia where the seven churches were located.

It is possible that some Jews who were scattered by the Assyrian conquest of Israel in 722 BC and the Babylonian conquest of Judah in 587 BC may have settled in this area and formed Jewish communities. The first documented presence of Jews in this area, however, is from Aristotle who, in 348–345 BC, encountered an educated Jew in the province of Asia.[5] More reliable, though not uncontested, evidence comes from the reign of Antiochus III (d. 187 BC). Josephus preserves a letter from Antiochus according to which 2,000 Jewish families were transferred from the region of Babylon to the central Anatolian area (Lydia and Phrygia) to provide a garrison of mercenaries to protect Seleucid interests (*Antiquities* 12.148-153).[6] These families were the beginning of the Jewish dispersion throughout Asia Minor. Both documentary and archaeological evidence indicates that this group became the nucleus for the spread of Jewish communities throughout the Anatolian peninsula.[7] The presence of Jews in Ephesus, Sardis, Pergamum, Thyatira, Philadelphia, and Laodicea is attested, with evidence of a heavy Jewish presence in Ephesus.

Both Josephus and Philo, first-century Jewish writers, tend to focus in various ways upon the Anatolian peninsula when making reference to diaspora Judaism in the first century. This suggests a major presence of Jews in this area. Both writers also testify to numerous legal actions between Jewish communities and Roman officials, indicating that Jewish communities were large enough to be a matter of interest or concern to the ruling powers.

In this light, it is interesting to note that Paul's first missionary journey was primarily to Jews. Acts 13:5-6 seems to indicate that Jewish synagogues were the sole focus of the mission to Cyprus, and the extension of this mission into Galatia (Acts 13:14–14:23) was, as noted above, into an area with strong Jewish populations. An inferential, yet telling event is found early in Paul's second missionary journey through Galatia. After the Jerusalem council (Acts 15), where it was determined that Gentiles did not need to be circumcised to become believers, Paul circumcised Timothy (Acts 16:3) "in deference to the Jews of the area." It appears that Paul's focus was primarily upon the Jews. As he moved from Galatia, Luke tells us that Paul first wanted to go into Asia and then to Bithynia (Acts 16:6-7), both areas with attested populations of Jews. Other than approximately two years spent in Greece (Philippi, Thessalonica, Berea, Athens, Corinth), the rest of the 12 to 15 years involved in Paul's three missionary journeys were spent in the Anatolian peninsula. It is not unlikely that this was because of the heavy Jewish population of this region.

Other evidence for the Jewish presence in the region comes from the record of the Temple tax that diaspora Judaism sent to the Temple in Jerusalem. In 88 BC, Mithridates seized a large amount of money at Cos; the Temple tax from Asian Jews was included.[8] Thirty years later, in his defense of Flaccus, Cicero noted that Flaccus, while proconsul of Asia, had confiscated the Jewish Temple tax from the province of Asia.[9] (Cicero was his defense attorney in his trial before the Roman Senate in Rome.) The amount confiscated must have been large, indicating a strong Jewish population in precisely the area of the seven churches to whom John's vision was addressed. Also during the trial of Flaccus, Cicero noted the presence of Jewish communities and their importance and leverage, not only in Rome, but also in the Diaspora. Since Flaccus was being tried for seizing the funds of the Jews of Asia, they must have constituted a significant presence in that area.

Further evidence of the significant presence of the Jews appears during the military mobilization that took place in Asia in 49 BC. The Roman consul, L. Lentulus Crus, issued an edict exempting Jews who were Roman citizens from military service. This edict was endorsed by C. Fannius, the propraetor of Asia, and subsequently applied to all Jews in Asia by P. Cornelius Dolabella, the Caesarian governor of Syria, who had seized Asia.[10] Such official action would not have been necessary for an insignificant minority. Augustus, sometime after his accession, reenacted the Lex Julia banning the *collegia* (voluntary associations).[11] In the Lex Julia (c. 48 BC), Julius Caesar disbanded all the *collegia* except those of ancient foundation. It appears that the Jews and their synagogues were specifically exempted from this ban. They were allowed to assemble for worship and common meals, to observe their Sabbath, to live by their ancestral customs, to observe their festivals, to hold funds, to build synagogues, and to have their communal properties safeguarded. This was the formative universal legislation that gave the Jews a legal standing in the Roman Empire. We know that this status continued because during Augustus's reign (c. AD 2–3), there was a decree to Asia that confirmed the Jews' rights as under Caesar.[12] Again, the Jews must have had a significant presence in the province to have warranted the attentions of the emperor.

Finally, sometime during the first decade of the second century, Ignatius, the bishop of Syrian Antioch, was taken in captivity through the Anatolian peninsula to Rome for execution. He wrote letters to a number of churches in the area addressed in Revelation (including Ephesus, Magnesia, Tralles, Philadelphia, and Smyrna). Particularly in his letters to the Philadelphians and Magnesians, he presents strong diatribes against Judaism and Judaizers. Given the seriousness of this problem in the first decade of the second century in the very area of the seven churches of Revelation, especially in one of those churches (Philadelphia—where the Jews are specifically mentioned), it would be reasonable to assume that former Jews comprised a considerable proportion of the membership of the Christian communities—particularly at the earlier date of John's vision (whether 60s or 90s, it still predates Ignatius). Also, Ignatius's understanding of Christianity as the true fulfillment of the prophetic promise of Judaism works thoroughly from within a Jewish frame of reference, even though (as in John's vision) that Jewish frame of reference is fulfilled in Christ.

Since, however, we are undoubtedly dealing with an indeterminate proportion of Gentile Christians in the seven churches addressed by John, it seems probable that Gentile believers would have been socialized into the Jewish frames of reference of the early church. Believers, whether Jewish or Gentile, were assimilated into a community that understood itself to be the "true" Israel for whom Jesus was the promised Messiah and in whom God was in the process of restoring the kingdom (cf. Rom 9–11, especially 11:8, 16-18; Gal 3–4; and Eph 2:11-22, which imply the nurturing of Gentiles into the redeemed Israel). Such a perspective would have been primary in the catechesis of new believers.

All this points to the high probability that even if the composition of the seven churches of Revelation were predominately Gentile, these Gentiles would have been nurtured by a community whose core had been Jews, Jewish proselytes, and Gentile God-fearers, whose former Jewish frame of reference and later reframed Jewish perspective would have provided a matrix of understanding within which they could explain to Gentile believers the imagery of the vision.

CANONICITY AND TEXTUAL HISTORY

There have always been concerns within the Christian movement as to the authority and canonicity of the book of Revelation. The origin of these concerns appears to have been a reaction to Montanus who, in the second century, led a heretical, charismatic movement that relied heavily upon Revelation for its authority. As a result of the usurpation of Revelation by the Montanists, the "orthodox" church tended to shy away from the writing. While this was especially the case in the eastern Mediterranean where Montanism had its strength, there were also concerns about Revelation voiced by Christian leaders in the West. This may, in part, have been due to the strongly Jewish nature of John's imagery, which would have been somewhat incomprehensible to the later Gentile church of the West. Even after the final establishment of the New Testament canon in the fourth century in the East by the Festal Letter of Bishop Athanasius of Alexandria (AD 367), and in the West by the councils of Hippo (393) and Carthage (397), there have continued to be questions raised as to its inclusion. Even today, for various reasons, there are many Christians for whom the New Testament ends, for all practical purposes, with the letter of Jude. It is hoped that this commentary will, among other things, help people realize that Revelation is as authoritative an expression of the essence of the Christian faith and life as any New Testament writing and that it shares with them the same understanding of Christian faith and life.

The textual history of Revelation has been largely independent of the rest of the New Testament, probably in large part due to the early rejection of the book in the Eastern church, where the earliest manuscript tradition arose. Having said this, however, one of the strongest manuscripts of Revelation is Codex Alexandrinus (A), which seems to have originated with the Egyptian church. While this manuscript is quite poor in the Gospels, in Acts it is comparable to Codex Sinaiticus (א), one of the best manuscripts. In Revelation, Codex Alexandrinus even exceeds Sinaiticus in reliability, although in the earlier part of Revelation it is not as reliable as in the later chapters. Codex Alexandrinus is usually supported in its readings in Revelation by another important early manuscript, Codex Ephraemi Rescriptus (C), which is usually somewhat inferior in other parts of the New Testament but one of the strongest textual witnesses in Revelation. The recently published papyrus, P^{115} (dated third century), generally accords with codices Alexandrinus (A) and Ephraemi Rescriptus (C). The second-best group of witnesses to the text of Revelation consists of the papyrus $\mathfrak{P}^{47}$ (a third-century manuscript and the earliest textual witness to 9:10–17:2) and Codex Sinaiticus (Comfort 2005:77-80).

While each variant reading must be considered on its own merits, when Alexandrinus (A), Ephraemi Rescriptus (C), and $\mathfrak{P}^{115}$ agree, their witness is usually superior to $\mathfrak{P}^{47}$ and Sinaiticus. The grammatical anomalies of the text, often caused by John's "bending" of grammar in the attempt to convey the reality of the vision, have spawned a host of textual variants that attempt to correct grammatical errors and infelicities.

LITERARY STYLE

The primary literary form of Revelation is that of an apocalypse. The noun "apocalypse" is derived from the Greek verb *apokaluptō* [TG601, ZG636], which means to reveal or disclose. John titled his work "An apocalypse of Jesus the Messiah" (1:1). Apocalyptic literature, generally, recounts an experience the writer allegedly had with a heavenly being or in the heavenly realm. The question is: Was John's visionary experience real or did he simply use the apocalyptic literary form to convey a message? As a way of answering this question, we need to consider the nature of visionary experience.

Throughout Christian history there have been men and women who have experienced genuine visionary experiences. The apostle Paul is the earliest Christian to attest to such experiences (2 Cor 12:2-4), and he is followed by a long train of women and men such as Julian of Norwich, Hildegard of Bingen, Teresa of Avila, and St. John of the Cross, just to name a few. When we study these persons' reports of their experiences, three things stand out. First, the vision comes unexpectedly and without any "manipulation" on the part of the visionary. It is an experience "graced" to them by God. Paul, for example, described it as being "caught up" (2 Cor 12:2). In the same manner, John's vision came totally unexpectedly (1:10). Second, the experience transports them into an altered state of consciousness. The "normal" sphere of consciousness is transcended, and the visionary moves into a supranormal sphere of consciousness. Again, Paul described this as "the third heaven" and "paradise" (2 Cor 12:2, 4), and as a situation where he didn't know whether he was in the body or not (2 Cor 12:2-3). John, apparently, was taken up into heaven (4:1-2) and transported in the Spirit (17:3; 21:10). Third, the visionary has great difficulty in trying to convey his or her experience to those who are living within the "normal" sphere of consciousness. Paul, once again, reported that he "heard things so astounding that they cannot be expressed in words" (2 Cor 12:4).

Even after 20 years of reflection upon her visionary experience, Julian of Norwich bemoaned the fact that she could not fully convey the profound reality of what she experienced.[13]

How, then, can the visionary convey something of the reality of their experience to others? John did it by using the pool of images that comprised the lingua franca of Jewish apocalyptic literature. That is, rather than attempting to use the ineffable images of his vision, John chose other, more familiar images to convey his experience to his readers. As strange and outlandish as the images and symbols of Revelation are to us, these were images and symbols that were known to John and his readers. Think, for example, how strange and ludicrous our American political cartoons of donkeys and elephants (Democrats and Republicans) must appear to those whose culture lacks any such imagery. John's symbols and images are drawn largely from the Jewish scriptures and intertestamental literature that informed the Jewish story within which he and his readers found their identity. But even a common pool of images is not adequate to convey the profound reality that John experiences. He repeatedly indicates this inadequacy by using the Greek terms translated by "like" or "as." For instance, he hears "a loud voice *like* a trumpet blast" (1:10). Jesus' eyes "were *like* flames of fire," and "his feet were *like* polished bronze refined in a furnace" (1:14-15, my italics). More than 80 times in his writing, John used these terms to indicate that the image he was using didn't fully convey the reality he experienced. This is a sign of a genuine visionary experience.

John also modulated his imagery as another signal that the images were inadequate. As we have just seen, Jesus' voice was "a loud voice like a trumpet blast" (1:10). In 1:15, however, Jesus' voice "thundered like mighty ocean waves." Which is it? It is both, and more. Neither image can encompass John's experience of Jesus' voice. The presence of such modulations of imagery is another pointer to the presence of a genuine visionary experience.

It would seem likely, therefore, that John had a visionary experience. In order to convey something of the reality of that experience to his audience, he utilized a pool of images he held in common with his readers. But repeatedly he told them that the images only partially conveyed the reality of his experience. The most ready-made literary form for this type of communication is apocalyptic.

Apocalyptic, while a literary form, was even more a means to bring the multitextured and polyvalent imagery of the Jewish tradition into the service of alternative experiences and perceptions of God's actions in the history of the Jewish people. This prompted Wright to write: "The different layers of meaning in vision-literature of this type thus demand to be heard in their full polyphony, not flattened out into a single level of meaning" (1992:282). The thrust of such writing is to enter fully into the perceptual world of the audience, employ all the nuanced and multidimensional imagery, symbols, and stories of their perceptual world, but use them in a radical restructuring of their perceptual world. Wright again frames it well: "Apocalyptic . . . is at least in part to be understood as the literature of subversion, of the cryptic undermining of a dominant and powerful worldview, and the encouraging and supporting of a revolutionary one" (1996:179). It is this aspect we have already seen in our preliminary look at John's introductions. That a discredited and crucified Galilean peasant is the Messiah through whom God has consummated the covenant and fulfilled the promises to restore the kingdom to Israel was subversive beyond belief to the perceptual world of a first-century Jew.

Thomas Merton wrote something that is relevant at this point:

> *Words lose their capacity to convey the reality of holiness in proportion as men focus on the symbol rather than on what it symbolizes. The sense of the sacred, of the "numinous" without which there can hardly be any real or living religion, depends entirely on our ability to transcend our own human signs, to penetrate them and pass beyond their manifest intelligibility into the darkness of mystery, to grasp the reality they can suggest but never fully contain.* (1961:87)

What John was seeking to do in the presentation of his vision was to utilize the Jewish pool of images to convey a "reality they can suggest but never fully contain." If we allow ourselves to become fixated on the symbols, rather than on what they represent, we will miss the mystery of John's vision.

At a secondary level, Revelation also has the form of an epistle, at least in its introduction (1:4-8). The epistolary introduction was utilized by John since the vision was to be conveyed to the seven churches, but few other epistolary elements are employed thereafter. The closing of Revelation is certainly epistolary in its benediction, but it lacks the usual greetings from others, future plans of the writer, etc., as one sees in other epistles (cf. Rom 16; 1 Cor 16:5-24; Eph 6:21-24; Col 4:7-18; Heb 13:22-25; 1 Pet 5:12-14).

MAJOR THEMES

There are at least three major themes in John's vision. First, John tells us that his vision is "a revelation from Jesus Christ" (1:1). This is the title of the writing. This is also the primary theme of the vision. This is not a vision of "end times" (see notes on 1:1). It is not a vision of the "rapture." It is a vision of Jesus the Messiah. John is seeing the profound depths of what God has done, is doing, and will ultimately consummate in and through Jesus.

Second, a closely related theme is the role of the cross in what God has done and will accomplish. John sees ever deeper levels of the meaning of the cross. Through the cross, God's people have been cleansed of their sin and have been made a kingdom of priests (1:5-6). Through the cross, the profound depths of God's purposes have been revealed (5:5).[14] Through the cross, Gentiles have been brought into God's kingdom of priests (5:9). Through the cross, the old covenant has been fulfilled (11:4-12). Through the cross, the depths of God's very being has been manifest (12:1-6). John saw that the cross even goes back "before the world was made" (13:8, NLT mg). Through the cross, God overcomes the forces of rebellion (19:11–20:3). In a very real sense, John's vision is a revelation of the meaning of the cross of Jesus the Messiah.

Third, two interrelated themes emerge from the action of God through the Messiah: New Jerusalem and fallen Babylon. New Jerusalem is John's image for the realm of God's people, a synonym for God's kingdom of priests. New Jerusalem is a realm in which human beings find cleansing from sin, liberation from destructive bondages, healing of woundedness, wholeness for their brokenness, and transformation from death to life. The citizens of New Jerusalem are those who have God's name on their forehead (7:3; 14:1; 22:4), who have "the word of God and the testimony of Jesus" (1:2, 9; 3:8; 6:9; 12:17; 14:12; 20:4), and who worship God and the Lamb (7:9-10). The citizens of the New Jerusalem, however, experience tribulation at the hands of fallen Babylon in whose midst they dwell (1:9; 2:9; 7:14). Fallen Babylon is John's image for the realm of rebellion against God. Fallen Babylon is a realm that is inherently destructive of human wholeness. Its citizens are described as "the people who belong to this world" (6:10; 8:13; 11:10; 13:8-14) and those of "every tribe and language and people and nation" (5:9; 7:9; 10:11; 11:9; 13:7; 14:6; 17:15). They worship the beast and its image and have the number of its name upon their foreheads (13:4, 12; 14:9, 11; 16:2; 19:20).

These two realms, like Jesus' parable of the wheat and the weeds (Matt 13:24-30), coexist in the context of human history. In a very real sense, John's vision is a clarion call to the followers of Jesus to live their lives as faithful citizens of New Jerusalem in the midst of their fallen Babylon world.

THEOLOGICAL CONCERNS

John's vision, while thoroughly consonant with the theological perspectives of the rest of the New Testament, is not primarily a theological treatise. The basic thrust of the vision is not orthodoxy but orthopraxy. The vision reveals what it means to live as a faithful member of God's realm in the midst of a world in rebellion against God. It is not so much a matter of holding right beliefs as manifesting the fruits of faithful discipleship. This is seen in the repeated attention given to "works" or "deeds" (9:20; 14:13; 16:11; 18:6; 19:8; 20:12; 22:11-12; see the note on "works" at 2:23), as well as the repeated litany to the churches: "I know all the things you do" (2:2, 19; 3:1, 15). Perhaps this is summarized best in John's description of the garments of the bride of the Lamb as "the good deeds of God's holy people" (19:8).

A companion piece to works is worship, also a matter of praxis, not doctrine. John's vision is filled with the acts of worship of the faithful, together with their hymns and ascriptions of praise to God and the Lamb. This may be summarized best by John's vision of the actions of the 24 elders who represent the faithful priests of God's kingdom of priests. (There were 24 orders of priests in Judaism in the first century; Luke 1:5; cf. 1 Chr 24:7-18.) Since the vision repeatedly identifies God's faithful people as priests (1:6; 5:10; 20:6), the elders represent the people of God's new covenant. Rather than focusing on right theology about God, they model right relationship with God by bowing (acknowledging God to be God), worshiping (letting God be God in their lives on his own terms), and casting their crowns before the throne (yielding control of their lives to God).

This is not to say that there is no theology in John's vision. It is just that it is more subtle, more submerged, more nuanced. There is a very strong emphasis upon the unity of the Trinity. In an unusual formulation, John places the Holy Spirit between God and Jesus (1:4-5), as if to emphasize that the Holy Spirit is not a "second-class" member of the Godhead. He does this again by linking the Holy Spirit closely to God (4:5) and the Lamb (5:6).

There is also a strong emphasis upon God's sovereignty in John's vision. This is especially seen in God's relationship to the rebellious realm. God is always pictured as sovereign over fallen Babylon, the beast and false prophet, Satan, and the whole realm of evil. There is no metaphysical dualism here such as is found in the Gnostic heresies of the second century. Satan and his realm are never an equal and opposite power over against God. Neither is there any dualism between the created order and the heavenly realm in John's vision. God is not only the Creator (ch 4), but creation is so closely bound to God as to be almost inseparable, yet without any hint of pantheism, as can be seen in creation's worship and praise of God (4:6-8).

Undoubtedly, the greatest theological issue in John's vision is the subversion of the Jewish narrative world discussed at the beginning of this introduction. Jesus is the Messiah through whose death God has consummated the old covenant, restored the kingdom, and included Gentiles in the new people of God. But this consummation of the old covenant is an incomplete one that does not overcome the enemies of God's people. God's people find themselves continuing through history in the midst of a world still deeply stained by the rebellion, awaiting the final consummation of the victory God achieved in the cross of Jesus. If anything, John's vision is a *theologia crucis*—a theology of the cross. As we have noted above, the vision plumbs the depths of the cross, carrying its reality back to the very heart of God's being before the foundation of the world.

OUTLINE

Outlining Revelation is difficult because there are so many overlapping themes, subthemes, harmonics, and echoes, that trying to reduce the "symphony" of Revelation to an outline is somewhat akin to taking a picture of a juggler. While the snapshot may provide an accurate portrayal of the juggler at the moment it was taken, it cannot capture the reality of juggling. A video or movie could better capture this, but unfortunately, there are no literary equivalents to videos or movies that enable us to capture the full dimensions of John's vision. The best we can do is to chop up the multifaceted interconnectedness of the text into a sequence of units wherein each provides one picture of the juggler but not the reality of juggling. Before doing that, however, it might help to have a "picture" of the vision that enables us to see the whole in a more interconnected structure than the outline.

A wide-sweeping outline would be as follows:

I. Introduction (1:1-9)
II. Earthly vision (1:10-20)
III. Seven churches; Heavenly vision; Seven seals (2:1–3:22; 4:1–5:14; 6:1–8:5)
IV. Seven trumpets; Heavenly vision; Seven bowls (8:6–11:18; 11:19–15:4; 15:5–16:21)
V. Harlot vision; Heavenly vision; Bride vision (17:1–19:10; 19:11–21:8; 21:9–22:9)
VI. Conclusion (22:10-21)

It can be seen here that the four groups of seven in the vision (points III and IV) and the vision of the harlot and bride (point V) pair themselves around a core containing a heavenly vision introduced by the earthly vision of Jesus to John. One of the interesting features here is that each of the heavenly visions begins with something "open." In 4:1, John sees "a door standing open in heaven." In 11:19, John sees "in heaven, the Temple of God was opened." In 19:11, John sees "heaven opened." This suggests that the "revelation from Jesus Christ" (1:1), which begins with John's vision of Jesus on Patmos (1:10-20), moves to progressively deeper or greater portrayals of what God has done, is doing, and will do in Jesus (door open in heaven; Temple in heaven open; all of heaven open). On each side of this "core" of heavenly visions are the groups of seven and the vision of the harlot and bride, all of which relate in various ways to the realities of human life and history. Although the passages are not broken down for comment according to the preceding outline, the overall structure it represents, along with features such as the core visions, will be a point of reference in the commentary. (See also the diagram in the commentary on 4:1-11.)

The following outline, which breaks the facets of this unified whole into smaller pieces, is the one that this commentary follows:

- I. Introduction (1:1-9)
  - A. Introduction to the Vision (1:1-8)
  - B. Personal Introduction (1:9)
- II. Earthly Vision of the Son of Man (1:10-20)
- III. The State of Affairs (2:1–8:5)
  - A. The Seven Churches (2:1–3:22)
    1. Ephesus (2:1-7)
    2. Smyrna (2:8-11)
    3. Pergamum (2:12-17)
    4. Thyatira (2:18-29)
    5. Sardis (3:1-6)
    6. Philadelphia (3:7-13)
    7. Laodicea (3:14-22)
  - B. God and the Lamb (4:1–5:14)
    1. God the Creator (4:1-11)
    2. The redeemer Lamb (5:1-14)
  - C. The Seven Seals (6:1–8:5)
    1. The four horsemen (6:1-8)
    2. Saints and sinners (6:9-17)
    3. Interlude: The composition of New Jerusalem (7:1-17)
    4. The power of prayer (8:1-5)
- IV. The Problem and Its Solution (8:6–16:21)
  - A. The Seven Trumpets (8:6–11:18)
    1. Flawed creation (8:6-12)
    2. Fatally flawed creatures (8:13–9:21)
    3. Interlude: God's radical solution (10:1–11:14)
    4. The song of victory (11:15-18)

- B. What's Really Going On (11:19–15:4)
  1. The real roots of the cross (11:19–12:6)
  2. The mother of all wars (12:7-17)
  3. The nature of fallen Babylon (12:18–13:18)
  4. The nature of New Jerusalem (14:1-5)
  5. Opportunity and outcome (14:6-13)
  6. Harvest (14:14–15:4)
- C. The Seven Bowls (15:5–16:21)
  1. Judgment on the citizens of fallen Babylon (15:5–16:9)
  2. The results of the refusal of redemption (16:10-21)

V. The Consequences (17:1–22:9)
- A. Babylon's Present Fallenness and Future Demise (17:1–19:10)
  1. Babylon's fragile facade (17:1-18)
  2. Doom and gloom (18:1-24)
  3. Praises for victory (19:1-10)
- B. The Lamb's Present and Future Victory (19:11–21:8)
  1. The Lamb's victory (19:11-21)
  2. The firstfruits of victory (20:1-10)
  3. The final fruits of victory (20:11–21:8)
- C. New Jerusalem's Present Hope and Future Glory (21:9–22:9)
  1. The nature of New Jerusalem (21:9-21)
  2. The people of New Jerusalem (21:22–22:9)

VI. Conclusion (22:10-21)

ENDNOTES

1. Second Maccabees 7 documents well the ideal of the faithful martyrs. This chapter is later picked up by the writer of 4 Maccabees and expanded in a more Hellenistic mode, downplaying the idea of resurrection, but retaining the efficacy of faithful martyrdom. Josephus also attests to the theme in *War* (3.374), where the faithful martyrs have a special place in heaven from which they will return to enjoy the restored kingdom. Wright summarizes it well: "We are here in touch with a tradition that was reasonably widespread and well known in the period of the second Temple. According to this tradition, the suffering and perhaps the death of certain Jews could function within YHWH's plan to redeem his people from pagan oppression: to win for them, in other words, rescue from wrath, forgiveness of sins, and covenant renewal" (1996:583).
2. Josephus articulates the theme in the first century: "Each individual is firmly persuaded that to those who observe the laws and, if they must needs die for them, willingly meet death, God has granted a renewed existence and in the revolution of the ages the gift of a better life" (*Against Apion* 2.218).
3. Wright said, "Throughout both major and minor prophets there runs the twin theme: Israel's exile is the result of her own sin, idolatry and apostasy, and the problem will be solved by YHWH's dealing with the sin and thus restoring his people to their inheritance" (1992:273).
4. The explicit uses of seven are the seven churches, the seven seals, the seven trumpets, the seven bowls, as well as the seven spirits of God (1:4), seven lampstands (1:12), and seven stars (1:16). The implicit use consists of the seven blessings (1:3; 14:13; 16:15; 19:9; 20:6; 22:7, 14).

5. Aristotle's encounter is reported by his pupil Clearchus in his work, *On Sleep*. This is preserved by Josephus in *Against Apion* 1.176-182. Tcherikover, however, rightly notes that this is no proof of Jewish communities at this time; further, he questions the historical reliability of the account (1961:287).
6. Tcherikover (1961:287) upholds the historical reliability of this account, but others have questioned it.
7. See Tcherikover 1961:288-289, and, especially, Schürer 1986:3.17-33.
8. Josephus *Antiquities* 14.112-113 (quoting Strabo).
9. Cicero *Pro Flacco* 28 (66-69).
10. Josephus *Antiquities* 14.223-240.
11. Suetonius *Augustus* 32.1.
12. Philo *Embassy to Gaius* 156-159; Josephus *Antiquities* 16.160-166.
13. Some examples from Julian of Norwich illustrate this: "And about the spiritual vision, I have told a part, but can never tell it in full" (1978:322); "Christ's clothing . . . is so marvelous that I cannot describe it" (1978:278); "the number of the words surpasses my intelligence and my understanding and all my powers, for they were the most exalted, . . . for in them is comprehended I cannot tell what; but the joy which I saw when they were revealed surpasses all that the heart can think or the soul may desire. And therefore these words are not explained here" (1978:223-224); "I saw that all that I can say is inadequate, for it cannot be described" (1978:209); "but I may not and cannot show the spiritual vision as plainly and fully as I should wish" (1978:192).
14. The Greek of the passage indicates that the "conquering" is the same as the opening of the scroll in God's right hand. The larger context of John's vision indicates that the "conquering" of the Lamb happened at the cross (cf. commentary on 6:2; also on 1:18; 2:7; 5:5).

COMMENTARY ON

Revelation

◆ I. Introduction (1:1-9)

A. Introduction to the Vision (1:1-8)

This is a revelation from* Jesus Christ,
which God gave him to show his servants
the events that must soon* take place. He
sent an angel to present this revelation to
his servant John, [2]who faithfully reported
everything he saw. This is his report of the
word of God and the testimony of Jesus
Christ.
[3]God blesses the one who reads the
words of this prophecy to the church, and
he blesses all who listen to its message
and obey what it says, for the time is near.
[4]This letter is from John to the seven
churches in the province of Asia.*
Grace and peace to you from the one
who is, who always was, and who is still to
come; from the sevenfold Spirit* before
his throne; [5]and from Jesus Christ. He is
the faithful witness to these things, the
first to rise from the dead, and the ruler
of all the kings of the world.
All glory to him who loves us and has
freed us from our sins by shedding his
blood for us. [6]He has made us a Kingdom
of priests for God his Father. All glory and
power to him forever and ever! Amen.

[7]Look! He comes with the clouds
of heaven.
And everyone will see him—
even those who pierced him.
And all the nations of the world
will mourn for him.
Yes! Amen!

[8]"I am the Alpha and the Omega—the
beginning and the end,"* says the Lord God.
"I am the one who is, who always was, and
who is still to come—the Almighty One."

1:1a Or *of.* 1:1b Or *suddenly,* or *quickly.* 1:4a *Asia* was a Roman province in what is now western Turkey. 1:4b Greek *the seven spirits.* 1:8 Greek *I am the Alpha and the Omega,* referring to the first and last letters of the Greek alphabet.

NOTES

1:1 *a revelation from.* The NLT translation "from," while legitimate from a syntactical perspective, limits the understanding of the phrase to appear as though Jesus gives a revelation to John when, as the rest of the vision discloses, the vision is also a revelation of (about) Jesus, i.e., what God has done, is doing, and will do in and through Jesus. The Greek genitive case has within its range of uses two basic ones, the subjective genitive (Jesus himself as the revelation) and the objective genitive (the revelation as an object that Jesus possesses [and passes on]). Since this is a revelation "which God gave him," it would seem that either the subjective or possessive genitive could be operative here. In typical Jewish fashion, John most likely plays upon both dimensions—i.e., the revelation that Jesus "possesses" is the very nature of his being and is the image of God that Jesus then reveals to John.

Jesus Christ. The Greek term translated "Christ" (*christos* [TG5547, ZG5986]) means "Messiah" (*mashiakh* [TH4899, ZH5431]; cf. *messias* [TG3323, ZG3549]) in the Jewish context (see Introduction). John seems to be operating within the narrative world of the Jewish story with its various messianic expectations of there being one person, anointed by God, who would advance or fulfill God's purposes.

which God gave him. The revelation is not only an object that Jesus then passes on; it is Jesus himself as the manifestation of God's purposes.

his servants. The Jewish people are frequently described as God's servants in the OT (Lev 25:42, 55; Deut 32:36; Ezra 5:11; Neh 1:6, 10; Ps 34:22; Isa 54:17). While believers in the NT are also called God's "servants," there was no NT book through which John could contextualize this phrase for his readers, since the NT books were not likely widely known at this time period and the NT doesn't fully use the phrase in the same way as the OT.

the events that must soon take place. This would be better translated, "the things necessary to be in God's timing."

an angel. This angel is probably Jesus (see 1:13). Several of the other angels in the book may also be Jesus (7:2; 10:1; 18:1, 21; 20:1).[1] Beale (1999:183) comments: "This scheme of communication probably explains why in some sayings later in the book it is difficult to discern whether the speaker is God, Christ, or an angel, since the message actually derives from all three (note likewise that in the OT, the angel of the Lord and God himself are sometimes indistinguishable [e.g., Gen. 18:1-33; 22:12-18; Judg. 6:11-18; 13:1-24])."

1:2 ***the word of God and the testimony of Jesus Christ.*** Elsewhere in his vision, John describes the faithful followers of Jesus as those who have the testimony of Jesus (12:11, 17; 19:10). This is a designator for the citizens of God's new order. John later identifies this new order as God's kingdom (1:6) and as the New Jerusalem (3:12; 21:2).

1:3 ***God blesses the one who reads the words of this prophecy to the church.*** In the early church, one person read the Scriptures to the congregation. He was the lector, here referred to lit., as "the messenger of the church" (see note on 2:1).

1:4 ***This letter is from John.*** After the apocalyptic introduction (1:1-3), the author introduces himself as "John" in a typical Hellenistic letter introduction.[2] The typical Hellenistic letter introduction began with the identification of the writer, then indicated the recipient(s), and concluded with an expression of blessing or goodwill.

the seven churches. In the pool of images John employs, the number seven is a symbol for totality, completeness (Rengstorf 1964). Since there were, in the Roman province of Asia, more than the seven churches, it seems likely that the seven churches represent the entire church throughout the province, if not the Roman world.

from the one who is, who always was, and who is still to come. The Greek preposition *apo* [TG575, ZG608] takes the genitive case when used in a sentence like this one, but John uses the nominative case here. It is a glaring grammatical error that calls attention to itself. While there are numerous attempts to resolve the anomaly (cf. Beale 1999:188-189; Caird 1966:16; Mounce 1977:68), none take into account the repetition of the phrase in both correct (1:8; 4:8) and incorrect (1:4) grammatical forms. In 11:17 and 16:5, however, it is only "who is and who always was." This suggests a crucial shift at 11:17. It is there (11:3-13), as we shall see, that John sees the old covenant consummated in the cross of Jesus. Prior to that event, God always was, is, and was still to come in the promised Messiah who would consummate the covenant and fulfill the promise to restore the kingdom to Israel. The strange grammar John used in 1:4 functions to indicate to the hearers that they should pay attention to this phrase throughout the message.

sevenfold Spirit. This expression represents, through the image of "seven," the fullness of the Spirit of God. In Isa 11:2, LXX, seven attributes of the Spirit are given.

before his throne. In this book, there are a number of things before God's throne: seven torches of fire (representing the fullness of the Spirit of God; 4:5); the sea like glass, which represents the rebellious order (see the discussion of the image of the sea at 4:6), the great numberless multitude of the redeemed (7:9, 15); the golden altar of incense (8:3; 9:13); and the dead of the rebellious order (20:12).

1:5 *ruler of all the kings of the world.* In one version of the Jewish expectation of the restoration, the "rulers of the world" would be overthrown, and Israel's king would rule over all.[3]

has freed us from our sins. This statement touches upon another aspect of the expectation of the restoration. Before God could restore Israel, she would have to be cleansed from her sins.[4] Some mss (P 046 𝔐[K]) read *lousanti* [TG3068, ZG3374] (having washed) instead of *lusanti* [TG3089, ZG3395] (having freed), found in superior mss (𝔓[18] *a* A C). "Washed" appears to be scribal assimilation to 7:14 where the redeemed are those who have "washed their robes in the blood of the Lamb."

1:6 *All glory and power to him forever and ever!* This is an exclamation of God's absolute sovereignty.

glory. This word (*doxa* [TG1391, ZG1518]) denotes the very essence of God's nature, which endures forever. The term *doxa* signified those aspects of a person or thing that identify their nature. This can be seen in a Pauline parallelism: "We all, beholding the glory of the Lord, are being changed into his likeness" (author's translation of 2 Cor 3:18). The "glory" is the "likeness."

1:7 *Look! He comes with the clouds.* This is an expectation that was given by Jesus (Matt 24:30; 26:64; and parallels), was an early expectation of the church (Acts 1:9-11), and was affirmed by Paul (1 Thess 4:17). The image originated in the OT with Isa 19:1 and Dan 7:13. John saw this in his vision in 14:14-16.

everyone will see him—even those who pierced him. And all the nations of the world will mourn for him. This is a variation on Zech 12:10 where, in the context of the restoration of the kingdom to Israel, all the tribes of Judah will mourn when they look on him whom they have pierced.

1:8 *Alpha and the Omega.* God is the origin (*alpha* [TG1A, ZG270]—the first letter of the Greek alphabet) and consummation (*ōmega* [TG5598, ZG6042]—the last letter of the Greek alphabet) of all things (cf. Isa 44:6). Jesus applies this title to himself in 22:13, one of several instances where Jesus is described or portrayed in a position previously reserved for God alone.

who is, who always was, and who is still to come. See note on 1:4.

the Almighty One. This is a title of God used seven times in the vision (1:8; 4:8; 11:17; 15:3; 16:7; 19:6; 21:22—the only other NT use is in 2 Cor 6:18). In light of what John will see as the seemingly invincible power of fallen Babylon, this title sets the proper perspective from the beginning.

COMMENTARY

The book begins with the words, "This is a revelation from Jesus Christ." God gave Jesus an apocalyptic unveiling, which Jesus then passed on to John through an angel. The revelation came from Jesus and in many ways is a revelation about Jesus himself. As the revelation is unfolded in the coming chapters, the readers will see more and more of Jesus himself, his actions, and his words (see note on 1:1).

The opening verse says that this revelation pertains to "events that must soon take place." No matter how John's readers would have read this, nearly 2,000 years of Christian history reveal that "soon" must be understood in other than purely temporal terms. Behind the word "soon" is the unusual Greek phrase *en tachei* [TG1722/5034, ZG1877/5443]. The root of *tachei* is *tach*, meaning "to set in order." Thus, the phrase could be translated, "the things that must come to be in their proper order." Revelation 1:3 says, "the time is near." Again, nearly 2,000 years of Christian history give us perspective on this. The Greek term here *kairos* [TG2540, ZG2789] indicates a special or significant time, as opposed to *chronos* [TG5550, ZG5989], which is simply the passage of minutes, hours, days, etc. John may be reflecting the same perspective as Jesus' message: "The *kairos* has come at last! . . . The Kingdom of God is near" (Mark 1:15).

John received the revelation and "reported everything he saw." This means that the book is a record of his visionary experience (see Introduction). John then tells us that he testified to "the word of God and the testimony of Jesus Christ" (1:2). To do so meant that he had his inner being fully aligned with God's purposes and that he had a radical commitment to serve Jesus Christ. To have the witness of Jesus[5] is to live like Jesus in the world, so profoundly abandoned to God that we may become, like Jesus, faithful martyrs who manifest God's victory through suffering (see note on 1:9).

In 1:3, John proclaims that God "blesses all who listen to [the vision's] message and obey what it says." The content of the vision is not merely to be known; it is to be lived and obeyed. In the Jewish tradition, there is an inescapable link between hearing and obeying. There is no such thing as "hearing" without obeying. If hearing does not lead to obedience, there has been no hearing. The link between hearing and obeying is exemplified in Isaiah 42:20 (where God's wayward people have ears but do not hear), Isaiah 48:8 (where rebels from birth are characterized as having ears that have never been opened), Isaiah 50:5 (where God's faithful servant is the one who has listened and not rebelled or turned away), and Jeremiah 5:21 (where God's rebellious people are described as having ears but not hearing). In every instance obedience or rebellion is linked to hearing. Thus, the blessing is for those who listen—that is, who obey. This is the first of seven blessings in the book (see 14:13; 16:15; 19:9; 20:6; 22:7, 14 for the other six).

John then provides an introduction containing blessings from the triune God: "the one who is, who always was, and who is still to come" (the Father), "the sevenfold Spirit," and "Jesus Christ" (1:4-5). In 4:5 the image of the sevenfold Spirit before the throne of God is repeated, and in 5:6 the Lamb has the sevenfold Spirit sent out into all the earth. In 22:1, the river of the water of life, another image for the Spirit, flows from the throne of God and the Lamb.

John then describes Jesus as "the faithful witness" (1:5). This is the first designation of Jesus the Messiah as the "martyr" (*martus* [TG3144, ZG3459]); it provides a significant focus in a vision where martyrdom at the hands of fallen Babylon is always possible (2:13; 6:9; 12:11; 13:7; 17:6; 18:24; 20:4). For John's Jewish-Christian audience, faithful martyrs were those who, by their death for the faith, advanced the restoration of the kingdom and the fulfillment of God's promises to his people.[6] As a companion piece to "martyr," John says that Jesus was "the first to rise from the dead." Jewish expectations were that when God restored the kingdom to Israel and fulfilled his promises to his people, the righteous dead would be raised to life and participate in the restored kingdom.[7] John was indicating that in Jesus the restoration had begun.

Following this, John offers praise to Jesus Christ for freeing his people from their sins and making them a "Kingdom of priests" (1:6). The image of the redeemed ones being a kingdom of priests is found throughout the vision. It is specific in 5:10 and 20:6 and inferred in the linen garments of 19:8, 14 (linen was the material for the garments of the priests; see Lev 6:10), together with the mention of the redeemed as "firstfruits" in 14:4 (see NLT mg). The Levitical priesthood was the surrogate for the firstborn of Israel; thus, they were the "firstfruits" offered to God (see Exod 13:2; 22:29; Num 3:12). They are also pictured as serving God day and night in the Temple (7:15).

For John's Jewish-Christian audience, well-acquainted with the Jewish expectations of the restoration of the kingdom, the epistolary introduction is a profoundly radical statement. John indicates that in Jesus the Messiah God has fulfilled his promise to his people through the prophets to restore the kingdom to Israel. The focal element is that the death of the Messiah has cleansed Israel from her sin and made her God's kingdom and priests in fulfillment of the purpose of the covenant (Exod 19:6). The authentication of this reality is the resurrection of Jesus, the faithful martyr—this is the unmistakable sign that the restoration has begun. As we shall see, God's restoration of the kingdom extends far beyond Israel's limitation of it to Jews only. Gentiles have also been incorporated into God's kingdom as priests (see notes on 5:9-10; 7:9; 14:1-5).

The full implications of John's apocalyptic introduction cannot be fully grasped until the larger reality of his vision begins to become clear (see the Introduction for a brief overview). For his audience, however, both Jewish Christians and Gentiles instructed in the Jewish-Christian tradition, John indicates that Jesus is the Messiah in whom God has revealed the fulfillment of his purposes for his chosen people. John also indicates that God's fulfillment, begun in Jesus, is continuing to be played out according to God's purposes. Those who participate fully in what God is doing ("listen . . . and obey," 1:3) will experience the blessings of being God's people in his fulfilled purposes.

For us today, the apocalyptic introduction is almost incomprehensible outside of the full sweep of John's vision. The larger vision reveals that God fulfilled the purposes he set forth in his covenant to Abraham (Gen 12:2-3). There God promised that all the nations of the earth would be blessed through Abraham's descendants. We will see that the people of God are those redeemed from every tribe, nation, language, and people (5:9; 7:9).

God has also fulfilled the purposes he set forth in his covenant with Moses—that his people would be a kingdom of priests (Exod 19:6). This expectation was quite alive in the intertestamental period, as evidenced in the second-century BC book *Jubilees*, which says that God's people "should become a kingdom and priests and a holy nation" (*Jubilees* 16:18). This is the previously unfulfilled purpose of the old covenant, which is now fulfilled in what God did in the Messiah. The kingdom is also the fulfillment of God's promise to restore the kingdom to Israel. This is a "preview" of what John will see in chapter 11, where the old covenant is consummated in the death, resurrection, and ascension of the Messiah. We will shortly see that in his death and resurrection, the Messiah has made us a kingdom of priests (1:6). And Gentiles have also been brought into God's covenant people and been made a kingdom of priests (see 1 Pet 2:9-10). As believers, we are called to live lives in the world as members of God's kingdom and as priests of God in such radical obedience to God that we may become witnesses of Jesus.

To live as members of God's kingdom is to incarnate the values, perspectives, and relationships of God's kingdom in our daily living. To be priests of God is to be agents of God's redeeming, healing, liberating, and transforming grace to a broken and hurting world. When we hear this call through John's vision and live it out obediently in our lives, we experience God's blessing of wholeness. We are also called to live as faithful citizens of God's new kingdom, looking expectantly for its ultimate consummation in the return of Jesus, which John first notes in 1:7.

The final consummation of God's purposes will be completed in the second coming of Jesus. John's Jewish-Christian audience, as well as the Gentile believers, would be puzzled at this two-stage presentation of what they had conceived of as one event. Up to 1:7 everything has pointed to the fact that in Jesus the Messiah God has restored the kingdom to Israel and fulfilled his promises to his people. When that was done, there would be nothing more for God to do. John suggests that while God had indeed fulfilled his promise of restoration and made them a kingdom of priests, there was yet a further consummation to come. In a very real sense, John's vision reveals God's unexpected way of fulfilling the promises and the ongoing reality of life "between" God's victory and its final consummation.

John concludes his epistolary introduction by citing Isaiah 44:6, "I am the First and the Last," which is found in a section of Isaiah that tells of the restoration of the kingdom (Isa 44:1-5) after the desolation of exile (Isa 43:28). John nuances this citation by repeating the affirmation with which he began his introduction, "who is, who always was, and who is still to come" (1:4). Thus John frames his radical affirmation that in Jesus God has restored the kingdom as a priestly kingdom of believers in the context of Jewish expectations.

ENDNOTES

1. In 7:2, the angel comes literally "from the rising of the sun," a messianic image and a "harbinger of grace," as Beale has noted (1999:408). This angel has the "seal of the living God," reminiscent of the role of the Holy Spirit elsewhere in the NT (2 Cor 1:22; Eph 1:13; 4:30; cf. Beale 1999:415). In John's Gospel the gift of the Holy Spirit is the consequence of Jesus' glorification (John 7:39; 16:7). Thus, there is at least the possibility that John understood this angel to be Jesus. In 10:1-3, the angel has numerous likenesses to Jesus: He is wrapped in a cloud (cf. 1:7), has a face like the sun (cf. 1:16), legs like pillars of fire (cf. 1:15), a great voice (cf. 1:10), and a voice like a lion roaring

(cf. 5:5). As Beale notes, the angel in 10:1-3 "is either the divine Christ himself or the divine angel of Yahweh" (1999:522-523). In 18:1, the angel has brightness as does Jesus in 1:14-16, and "great authority" would certainly apply to Jesus. With respect to the angel in 18:1, Beale states, "That the angel is Christ is confirmed by the fact that every ascription of 'glory' to a heavenly figure in the Apocalypse refers to either God or Christ" (1999:892). In 20:1, the angel has the key to the bottomless pit (cf. 1:18) and the power and authority to bind Satan (cf. John 12:31), which are attributes most suitable to Jesus. Beale notes that "'the key of the abyss' is probably the same as 'the key of death and of Hades,' which Christ holds in ch. 1" (1999:984).

2. While the nature of Revelation differs from the Gospel and letters of John, the content and perspective seem to be those of the writer of the Gospel and three epistles. See "Author" in the Introduction. These connections will be noted throughout the commentary.
3. One antecedent appears in Ezek 20:33ff and in Ps 47. See Josephus *Antiquities* 18.23, which says that one sect of the Jews believed they should have no king but God. In *Psalms of Solomon* 17:21-32, it is said that God will raise up for the Jews a king, the son of David, who would drive the Gentiles out of Jerusalem and gather a righteous people whose king would be the Messiah.
4. The linking of cleansing of sin with restoration appears in Isa 40:1-2; Ezek 36:24-28. In 4 Maccabees the martyrdom of the faithful is portrayed as purification for the sins of the whole people (4 Macc 6:27-29).
5. "Witness" is a better translation of *marturia* [TG3141, ZG3456] than is "testimony." Testimony suggests a verbal affirmation, while witness implies a quality of life. It is the latter that is focal in John's vision.
6. According to 2 Macc 7, seven brothers and their mother suffered for the sins of the Jewish people (2 Macc 7:18, 32, 38), which would hasten the day when God acts against their enemies (2 Macc 7:17, 19, 31, 34-36) and restores them to life (2 Macc 7:9, 14, 23, 29). Clearly, here, martyrdom is linked to faithfulness to God, suffering for the sins of the people, hastening the restoration of the kingdom, and resurrection in the restored kingdom. The witnesses to the restoration being an "eternal kingdom" are manifold in the OT: Ps 145:13; Isa 25:6-9 ("He will swallow up death forever!" Isa 25:8); 35:10; 45:17 ("eternal salvation"); 60:15, 19-21; Ezek 37:22-28; Dan 7:14, 18, 27; 12:2 (the resurrection is to "everlasting life"). The perception is carried forward in the intertestamental period: *1 Enoch* 58:1-3; *Testament of Reuben* 6:12.
7. 1QpHab (Pesher Habakkuk) 8:1-3 applies Hab 2:4 to "all in Judah who carry out the Torah. On account of their labor (faithfully living by Torah) and their faith in the one who expounded the Torah correctly (the Teacher of Righteousness), God will deliver them from the house of judgment (i.e., they will participate in the restored Kingdom)." Josephus reports how the two famous and revered scribes, Judas and Matthias, urged their youthful adherents to tear down the eagle Herod had placed over the Temple gate with the assurance that even if they were killed for their action, it was noble to die for the Torah and their souls would be deathless and attain eternal felicity (*War* 1.649-650), i.e., they would live in the restored kingdom forever. The idea of resurrection to life in the restored kingdom continued in Judaism as evidenced in the Mishnah: "All Israelites have a share in the world to come. . . . And these are they that have no share in the world to come: he that says that there is no resurrection of the dead" (*m. Sanhedrin* 10:1). *Second Baruch* 30:1-2 says that when the Messiah comes, "all who have fallen asleep in hope of Him shall rise again."

◆ B. Personal Introduction (1:9)

9 I, John, am your brother and your partner in suffering and in God's Kingdom and in the patient endurance to which Jesus calls us. I was exiled to the island of Patmos for preaching the word of God and for my testimony about Jesus.

NOTES

1:9 ***I, John.*** The writer of this apocalypse identifies himself as John, whom I understand to be the apostle John, author of the fourth Gospel and three epistles (see "Author" in Introduction).

your brother and your partner in suffering. This is the first of five uses of "suffering" (often translated "tribulation"—see NASB, ESV) by John. Four of these (1:9; 2:9, 10; 7:14) describe what faithful followers of the Lamb experience at the hands of fallen Babylon. The fifth is what the apostates of "Jezebel" will experience if they don't repent (2:22). Obviously, "tribulation" is not some future event for John and his readers. It was and has been a present reality of faithful Christian discipleship. Experiencing suffering is a corollary of following Jesus, the faithful martyr (1:5).

in God's Kingdom. When Christians live as faithful followers of the Lamb in a fallen Babylon world, they experience tribulation at the hands of that world.

patient endurance. The vision calls the faithful to, or commends them for, patient endurance seven times (1:9; 2:2, 3, 19; 3:10; 13:10; 14:12). Here, at the beginning of his vision, John sets the theme of endurance in the context of tribulation coming upon the citizens of God's kingdom.

I was exiled to the island of Patmos. John's faithfulness to Jesus had resulted in his banishment to Patmos. The historian Pliny tells us that Patmos was a place of banishment in this period (*Natural History* 4.12.23).

for preaching the word of God and for my testimony about Jesus. See note on 1:2.

COMMENTARY

John understood himself and his readers to be participants in God's kingdom. This confirms all that John had said up to this point with regard to the restoration of the kingdom. This kingdom, however, is not a place of peace and prosperity. Participation in the kingdom brings tribulation and therefore requires patient endurance. This certainly did not fit the expectations of those in his audience who were Jewish Christians. They foresaw the future kingdom as a place of peace and plenty (Isa 11:6-8; 60:5-7, 18; 61:6). John made it unmistakably clear that God's restoration of the kingdom (which is his fulfillment of the covenant) did not follow the lines of these expectations.

John sets for us, with his personal introduction, the context of our life as Christians. We are now members of God's kingdom, his priestly people. But we live in a world whose destructive and dehumanizing values, perspectives, relationships, and actions are part of what John saw as the fallen Babylon, a realm in rebellion against God. When we, as citizens of God's kingdom (later to be seen as "the New Jerusalem"), live our lives by the values and perspectives of that kingdom, we become an uncomfortable presence in the midst of fallen Babylon. In the words of the Thessalonian Jews' charge against Paul, we become those who "have turned the world upside down" (Acts 17:6, RSV). When we do, those whose power, prestige, and possessions depend upon the values and perspectives of the fallen Babylon will not tolerate the witness of the New Jerusalem. Faithful citizens of the New Jerusalem will soon experience "tribulation" at the hands of those in the fallen Babylon—that is, they will experience ridicule, character assassination, marginalization, ostracization, even persecution, imprisonment, torture, and death. When these things come, God's faithful people are called to patient endurance.

For John's original audience, as for us, the question is "why?" If God has restored the kingdom, fulfilled the promises, and consummated the old covenant in the Messiah, Jesus, then why are God's faithful people still experiencing tribulation? This is the question that is answered by John's tremendous vision.

◆ II. Earthly Vision of the Son of Man (1:10-20)

10 It was the Lord's Day, and I was worshiping in the Spirit.* Suddenly, I heard behind me a loud voice like a trumpet blast. 11 It said, "Write in a book* everything you see, and send it to the seven churches in the cities of Ephesus, Smyrna, Pergamum, Thyatira, Sardis, Philadelphia, and Laodicea."

12 When I turned to see who was speaking to me, I saw seven gold lampstands. 13 And standing in the middle of the lampstands was someone like the Son of Man.* He was wearing a long robe with a gold sash across his chest. 14 His head and his hair were white like wool, as white as snow. And his eyes were like flames of fire. 15 His feet were like polished bronze refined in a furnace, and his voice thundered like mighty ocean waves. 16 He held seven stars in his right hand, and a sharp two-edged sword came from his mouth. And his face was like the sun in all its brilliance.

17 When I saw him, I fell at his feet as if I were dead. But he laid his right hand on me and said, "Don't be afraid! I am the First and the Last. 18 I am the living one. I died, but look—I am alive forever and ever! And I hold the keys of death and the grave.*

19 "Write down what you have seen—both the things that are now happening and the things that will happen.* 20 This is the meaning of the mystery of the seven stars you saw in my right hand and the seven gold lampstands: The seven stars are the angels* of the seven churches, and the seven lampstands are the seven churches.

1:10 Or *in spirit.* 1:11 Or *on a scroll.* 1:13 Or *like a son of man.* See Dan 7:13. "Son of Man" is a title Jesus used for himself. 1:18 Greek *and Hades.* 1:19 Or *what you have seen and what they mean—the things that have already begun to happen.* 1:20 Or *the messengers.*

NOTES

1:10 *It was the Lord's Day.* The "Lord's Day" was Sunday, in contrast to the Jewish Sabbath on Saturday. It was the day Christians celebrated the Resurrection (the sign of the restoration of the kingdom), and joined together in the kingdom banquet (the Eucharist). The Gospels stress the fact that Jesus rose on the first day of the week (i.e., Sunday—Matt 28:1; Mark 16:2; Luke 24:1; John 20:1, 19). Acts 20:7 notes that on the first day of the week the Christian community met to break bread. The *Didache* (14:1) uses the same term (*kuriakē* [TG2960, ZG3258]) as John, noting that it is the day the Christian community met to celebrate the Eucharist.

1:11 *everything you see.* The expression in Greek is singular (*ho blepeis* [TG3739/991, ZG4005/1063] = "that which you see"). In 1:19 it becomes plural (Gr., *ha eides* [TG3739/3708B,

ZG4005/1625], "the things which you see") and is further defined as "the things that are now happening" and "the things that will happen" (see note on 1:19). The vision now provides a new perspective on the restoration of the kingdom. It is already a present reality ("the things that are now happening") but also has a future component ("the things that will happen").

1:13 ***in the middle . . . the Son of Man.*** John saw Jesus in the middle of the lampstands. He is the one in whose presence the lampstands, symbolizing the churches, stand. Just as the sevenfold lampstand in the Temple is in the presence of the Lord, so the church lives in the presence of Jesus.

He was wearing a long robe with a gold sash across his chest. This depicts Jesus as a priest (cf. Exod 28–29). The term John uses for "robe" (*podērēs* [TG4158, ZG4468]) is used in the LXX almost exclusively for the garment of the high priest (Exod 25:7; 28:4, 31; 29:5; 35:9; Zech 3:4; the exception being Ezekiel's strange "man dressed in linen"—Ezek 9:2-3, 11). The same term is used in Sirach 45:8 to describe Aaron's robe. The term for "sash" (*zōnē* [TG2223, ZG2438]), while used more generically in the LXX for belts of various sorts, is also used to describe the sash of the high priests (Exod 28:4, 39-40; 29:9; 39:29 [36:36, LXX]; Lev 8:7, 13; 16:4). Since John has just described believers as "priests" (1:6), a description of Jesus as High Priest follows logically. John also draws strongly upon Daniel's vision of one "like a son of man" to describe his vision of Jesus (cf. Dan 7:9, 13; 10:5-6, 9-10). Since Daniel's "son of man" receives "authority, honor, and sovereignty over all the nations of the world, so that people of every race and nation and language would obey him" (Dan 7:14), it seems John is amplifying Jesus' position as "the ruler of all the kings of the world" (1:5).

1:14 ***His head and his hair were white like wool, as white as snow.*** In Dan 7:9, the vision depicts God (the Ancient One) with "his clothing . . . white as snow, his hair like purest wool." John may be mixing images to denote that Jesus and God are two manifestations of the same reality. Later, John sees that the throne is the throne of both God and the Lamb (3:21; 7:17; 22:1, 3; and by inference in 7:9-10 and 12:5; and by deduction 5:13 and 6:16).

his eyes were like flames of fire. This image is consistent with Dan 10:6, and is repeated in Rev 2:18 and 19:12. Daniel's vision is of a person dressed in linen with a sash of gold around his waist, who subsequently tells Daniel of God's future restoration of Israel after a long period of subjugation by foreign powers (Dan 10:1–12:1). Since, as noted, John presents Jesus as the one through whom God has restored the kingdom, the use of Daniel's imagery is most suitable.

1:15 ***feet were like polished bronze refined in a furnace.*** This accords with the image in Dan 10:6, although for Daniel it was the legs (cf. ESV).

his voice thundered like mighty ocean waves. In Ezek 43:2 the coming of the glory of God is like "the roar of rushing waters" rather than "mighty ocean waves," but this is the only OT use of a similar image. The vision is somewhat similar to Daniel's image of "his voice roared like a vast multitude of people" (Dan 10:6). John uses the image again in 14:2 and 19:6, but there it stands in reference to the redeemed and the host of heaven.

1:16 ***seven stars.*** John is told in 1:20 that the seven stars are the angels of the seven churches (cf. note on 2:1 for the meaning of the angels of the churches).

right hand. This is John's first use of the image of a right hand; it appears again in 1:17, 20; 2:1; 5:1, 7; 10:5; 13:16. In the OT, the right hand denotes the action or the fulfillment of the purpose of the person whose hand it is (Exod 15:6, 12; Judg 5:26; Job 40:14; Pss 16:8, 11; 20:6; 60:5; 77:10; 118:15-16; 138:7; Isa 45:1). The same use is found in the NT (Matt 5:30; Acts 3:7)—note especially the image of Jesus at the right hand of God (Matt 26:64; Acts 2:33; 5:31; 7:55-56; Rom 8:34; Eph 1:20; Col 3:1; Heb 1:13) as an indication that Jesus is the action of God in the world, the fulfillment of God's purpose.

sharp two-edged sword. This image for the word of God seems to appear first in Heb 4:12, although Paul speaks of the word of God as the sword of the Spirit (Eph 6:17), an image that originates with the servant of God in Isa 49:2: "He made my words of judgment as sharp as a sword." Isaiah then identifies the servant as Israel: "You are my servant, Israel" (Isa 49:3). The vision is doing the same thing with Isaiah's image as with Daniel's (see note on 1:14): Jesus is the one in whom Israel has been embodied and through whom God's purposes for Israel have been fulfilled (cf. Wright 1996:538-539 for Jesus as the representative of Israel).

his face was like the sun in all its brilliance. This image is a variation of Daniel's vision of the one whose face was like lightning (Dan 10:6).

1:17 ***I fell at his feet as if I were dead.*** John, like Daniel (Dan 10:8-9), was overcome by the vision and fell at his feet as if dead.

1:18 ***grave.*** The NLT consistently translates *hadēs* [TG86, ZG87] as "grave" (1:18; 6:8; 20:13-14). Although this communicates to modern audiences, readers need to know that Hades represents a realm of being "dead." The Hebrew concept of *sheol* [TH7585, ZH8619] (= *hadēs* in the LXX) is a realm in which all are at least separated from God (Ps 6:5), if not outright alienated from God (Num 16:30; Job 24:19; Ps 9:17). While Hades can be a synonym for "dead" (2 Macc 6:23; Sir 17:27; Wis 16:13), it is also the place of sinners (Sir 21:10; *Sibylline Oracles* 5:178), the realm of false gods (*Sibylline Oracles* 1:22), and the place of the dragon (cf. Rev 12:3) who devours the wicked (*3 Baruch* 4:4-6; 5:3).

1:19 ***things that will happen.*** Lit., "things that will happen after this" or, possibly, "things that will happen along with this." John never used the preposition *sun* [TG4862, ZG5250] (with) in Revelation. Its presence in the Gospel, however, indicates his familiarity with it. In classical Greek prose, *sun* was largely replaced by *meta* [TG3326, ZG3552] (Smyth 1920:§1696), which has a base meaning of "accompaniment." According to Smyth, the original meaning of *meta* was "amid," or "among" (1920:§1691), and its use with the accusative (as here) can indicate "into the midst of" (1920:§1691.3). *Meta* is usually the prose preposition for *sun* (1920:§1691.4). I suggest that John, for some unknown reason, was using the prose convention rather than employing *sun*, although it must be admitted that this is the classical prose convention rather than a Hellenistic one. As I note at 4:1; 7:9; 15:5; and 19:1, *meta tauta* [TG3326/3778A, ZG3552/4047] stands between two integral units: At 4:1 it links what follows back to the vision of Jesus in 1:10ff, and the connection is reinforced by the reference to the "loud voice like a trumpet" and being "in the Spirit" (1:10). Thus, the two trajectories that flow from the vision of Jesus, namely the letters to the seven churches and the material of 4:1–22:21, are connected by *meta tauta*, which, it would seem, connects the first trajectory "with" the second rather than "after" it. At 7:9 *meta tauta* connects the Jewish (7:1-8) and Gentile (7:9-10) components of the redeemed so that "along with" the expected Jewish population of New Jerusalem, John sees the unexpected (at least in the Jewish mind) and innumerable multitude of Gentiles. At 15:5, the bridge verse between 11:19–15:4 and the Bowls of Wrath (see note on 11:19 for the chiastic structure of 11:19–15:5), it seems that *meta tauta* serves to join the introduction of the angels who have the plagues (15:1) "with" their action (15:6ff). Finally, at 19:1, *meta tauta* seems to join the ultimate demise of fallen Babylon (18:21-24) "with" the praise of the heavenly host at this demise (19:1ff). These rather clear uses of *meta tauta* to join two segments of the vision suggests that perhaps some of the other uses of *meta tauta* follow this convention.

1:20 ***The seven stars are the angels of the seven churches.*** This is the first explanation John receives in the vision. Jesus holds the "angels" of the churches. (See note on 2:1 for who these "angels" are.)

COMMENTARY

In the beginning of this section, John indicates two contexts for his life simultaneously: "I was exiled to the island of Patmos" (1:9) and "I was worshiping in the Spirit" (1:10). The Greek has "I was in (*egenomēn en* [TG1096/1722, ZG1181/1877]) the island called Patmos. . . . I was in (*egenomēn en*) the Spirit." John positioned himself in two different but contiguous locations; at one and the same time he was both on Patmos and in the Spirit.

John's faithfulness to Jesus had resulted in his banishment to Patmos (see Pliny *Natural History* 4.12.23). While on Patmos, John tells us, "I was . . . in the Spirit." This is John's first of four attestations of being "in the Spirit" (see 1:10; 4:2; 17:3; 21:10). While it might refer to the condition in which he experienced his vision, it must be remembered that while "in the Spirit," Christians made decisions (Acts 13:2-4; 19:21), lived the Christian life (Rom 8:9, 13-14; Gal 5:16, 25), spoke to God (1 Cor 14:2), prayed (1 Cor 14:15; Eph 6:17-18), sang (1 Cor 14:15), and worshiped (Phil 3:3). The phrase reflects a consciousness of living in vital relationship with God.

While in the Spirit, John heard a voice. God's address came to John from a direction opposite to his orientation ("I heard *behind* me a loud voice," 1:10; my italics). Often we presume that God will come to us and enter into our situations in ways that are compatible with our status quo. However, God usually doesn't come to us in the way we have oriented ourselves for God's coming. God's presence is often a disorienting presence (cf. Mulholland 1998:25-31 for a development of this reality in the book of Acts.) It requires that we relinquish the comfortable orientations of our life in order to enter into experience with God. To enter into transforming experience with God we may have to make a 180-degree restructuring of our life.

The voice John heard sounded like a trumpet blast, whereas in 1:15 Jesus' voice is "like mighty ocean waves." This is the first instance where John used images to attempt to convey to his readers something of the profound reality he experienced. Such an experience cannot be fully contained within human images. The primary reference for a trumpet blast was Israel's experience of God at Sinai in the establishment of the covenant (Exod 19:13, 16, 19; 20:18). The trumpet blast was also characteristic of the Day of Atonement (Lev 25:9), where Israel was brought once again into perfect covenant relationship with God. The trumpet blast also preceded important announcements (1 Sam 13:3; 2 Sam 20:1; 1 Kgs 1:34; 2 Kgs 9:13; Isa 18:3), and it would also herald the restoration of the kingdom to Israel (Isa 27:13; Zech 9:14). The image, therefore, would have evoked multiple resonances for those who knew the Old Testament Scriptures.

The voice told John to write down what he saw and to send it to "seven churches" (1:11). The seven churches probably represent the entire church (see note on 1:4 and the discussion introducing 2:1). Beale (1999:204) said, "the number 'seven' refers to the church universal in both a geographical and temporal sense. . . . Therefore, what we find in the letters is potentially relevant for the church of every time and place." The particular churches mentioned could be visited in a circuit without backtracking. Ephesus would be the first encountered by someone coming from Patmos, and if one took the Roman road to the north, Smyrna would be next and so on. From Laodicea the Roman road to the west would bring one back to Ephesus.

These seven churches were represented by "seven gold lampstands" (1:12). Exodus 25:37 and Zechariah 4:2 speak of a single lampstand with seven lamps that the priests were to keep burning before the Lord perpetually. The image is a priestly one, consistent with John's description of his audience as "priests" (1:6). In 1:20, John is told that the seven gold lampstands are the seven churches. The image is rounded out at the end of the vision: In 21:23, John sees that there is no sun or moon in the New Jerusalem because "the glory of God illuminates the city [lit., "is its light"], and the Lamb is its light [lit., "its lamp is the Lamb"]." This defines the image of the church being the lampstand! The church is to lift up Christ, the lamp, who bears the light of God to the world.

Then John saw Jesus as the Son of Man (1:13-14). The images John uses to describe Jesus are largely parallel to Daniel 7:9-13 and 10:5-9. The Son of Man figure originates in Daniel 7:13, a passage that has resonance with what John has already written in his introduction. Daniel 10:5-9 says, "I . . . saw a man dressed in linen clothing, with a belt of pure gold around his waist. . . . His face flashed like lightning [cf. 1:16], and his eyes flamed like torches [cf. 1:14]. His . . . feet shone like polished bronze [cf. 1:15], and his voice roared like a vast multitude of people [cf. 1:15]." Daniel's response, like John's (1:17) was to fall at the feet of this person (Dan 10:9). This reaction is a common one for people who have overpowering experiences of God (see Gen 17:3; Lev 9:24; Num 16:22; 20:6; Josh 5:14; Judg 13:20; Ezek 1:28; 3:23; 43:3; 44:4; Dan 8:17-18; 10:9; Acts 9:4). Also common to visionary experiences is that the person who has been seen in the vision comforts the person who has seen the overwhelming vision (Ezek 2:1-2; Dan 8:18; 10:10).

Jesus comforted John and then said, "I am the First and the Last." This is a variation on the title "the Alpha and the Omega" in 1:8. Jesus brings them both together in 22:13, clearly indicating his inseparable identity with God, who is identified by the same phrase at Isaiah 44:6. In the Isaiah passage, God is more particularly identified as Israel's king and redeemer. John has already depicted Jesus as "ruler of all the kings of the world" (1:5), and stated that he had made his people a kingdom (1:6), intimating that through his death and resurrection Jesus has restored the kingdom to Israel.

Jesus also said, "I am the living one" (1:18a). This may indicate that Jesus is not simply the start and finish (First and Last), but also the living presence that fills the space between. "The living one" is also used as a designation for God in 2 Esdras 2:14 and thereby provides another possible link between Jesus and God.

Jesus then told John, "I died, but look—I am alive forever and ever! And I hold the keys of death and the grave" (1:18b). This is one of the primary themes of the vision: Jesus died (via crucifixion), is alive forever and ever (via resurrection), and now has the keys of Death and Hades, which means he has conquered the entire realm of rebellion. As we move into the vision, we will see deeper and deeper dimensions of the cross, but always it is the mode by which God has overcome the power of evil. For example, in chapter 5, the cross is the means by which God has redeemed humanity; in chapter 11, the consummation of the old covenant; in chapter 12, a revelation of the deep nature of God; and in chapter 19, God's victory over the realm of evil.

For John's audience, born into or nurtured with certain Jewish messianic expectations, the vision of Jesus would have been extremely jarring to their perceptions and expectations. They would have had to undergo major changes in orientation. In his introductions John has implied that Jesus is the Messiah whose death inaugurated the restoration of the kingdom, the fulfillment of the promises given through the prophets and the consummation of the covenant with Israel. Now John clearly indicates that this Jesus is, in some way, equal to the very God. We should not be surprised at John's imaging of Jesus as God, for it is in John's Gospel that Jesus says, "The Father and I are one" (John 10:30) and that his opponents accuse him of making himself equal with God (John 5:18).

John also saw that the exalted Messiah was present in the midst of the church. There is no problem, in the modulation of visionary images, with Jesus being the lamp that the lampstands hold and, at the same time, the one in whose presence they exist. We tend to make two mistakes with respect to Jesus. On one hand, we make Jesus so transcendent that there is no realization of his living presence in the midst of the church. On the other hand, we often reduce Jesus to a "pal" who accompanies us through life primarily to ensure that things go our way. John saw Jesus as the awesome presence of God in the midst of the churches. As we will see next, this awesome presence did comfort the faithful churches but also confronted those who were falling short of being faithful priests in God's kingdom.

◆ III. The State of Affairs (2:1–8:5)

A. The Seven Churches (2:1–3:22)

1. Ephesus (2:1-7)

"Write this letter to the angel* of the church in Ephesus. This is the message from the one who holds the seven stars in his right hand, the one who walks among the seven gold lampstands:

2"I know all the things you do. I have seen your hard work and your patient endurance. I know you don't tolerate evil people. You have examined the claims of those who say they are apostles but are not. You have discovered they are liars. 3You have patiently suffered for me without quitting.

4"But I have this complaint against you. You don't love me or each other as you did at first!* 5Look how far you have fallen! Turn back to me and do the works you did at first. If you don't repent, I will come and remove your lampstand from its place among the churches. 6But this is in your favor: You hate the evil deeds of the Nicolaitans, just as I do.

7"Anyone with ears to hear must listen to the Spirit and understand what he is saying to the churches. To everyone who is victorious I will give fruit from the tree of life in the paradise of God.

2:1 Or *the messenger;* also in 2:8, 12, 18. 2:4 Greek *You have lost your first love.*

NOTES

2:1 ***the angel of the church.*** The word for "angel" is *angelos* [TG32, ZG34]; it means "messenger." I think it has been incorrectly translated "angel" here and in many other translations. Jesus was addressing not a supernatural being, but that person in each community who represented the community before God; he was speaking to a human messenger. This has to be understood within the structure of synagogue worship out of which the early church emerged. In the synagogue, different roles were assigned to different members of the community for varying periods of time (Safrai 1976:915; Schürer 1979:2.433-439). One of those roles was to lead the congregation in prayer and to represent the community before God. This person was known as "the messenger of the congregation," the *"shaliakh tsibbur"* (cf. *m. Berakhot* 5:5; Jastrow 2006:1274, 1583).

the one who holds the seven stars in his right hand. In several of the letters (to Ephesus, Smyrna, Pergamum, Thyatira, and Sardis), Jesus identifies himself by one of the attributes of the vision in ch 1. Here, Jesus reminds the Ephesians that he is "the one who holds the seven stars." Since the seven stars represent the messengers of the seven churches (1:20), the messenger who represents the Ephesian church before God was held in Jesus' right hand. Since the right hand represents the action of fulfillment of the purpose of the person (see note on 1:16), the messenger of each church now becomes the agent of Jesus' action in the midst of the church—an agent of commendation, correction, or confrontation.

the one who walks among the seven gold lampstands. This means that he is intimately present with the church, and the church exists in his presence.

2:2 ***I know.*** Jesus knows each church, its situation, and its condition in relationship to its particular situation.

2:3 ***You have patiently suffered.*** Jesus repeats his affirmation of the Ephesians' "patient endurance," mentioned in 2:2. That phrase and "patiently suffered" both reflect the term *hupomonē* [TG5281, ZG5705] (endurance).

2:4 ***You don't love me or each other as you did at first!*** Lit., "your first love you have abandoned" (see NLT mg)—not giving any indication as to the nature of that love. The NLT has added "me" and "each other" as objects of the verb "love," but this misses the force of the grammatical structure and the idea of the noun "love" (*agapē* [TG26, ZG27]), which connotes a radically others-referenced structure or mode of being.

2:5 ***remove your lampstand.*** Jesus' call to turn back contains a most serious threat. To have their lampstand removed would mean the Ephesians would cease to be a church. It is as strong an image as Jesus' later threat to spit the Laodicean church out of his mouth (3:16).

2:6 ***the Nicolaitans.*** They are an unknown group, the object of much scholarly speculation. (For an overview of some of the speculation, see Buchanan 1993:87-88; Caird 1966:31.) In the letter to Pergamum (2:12-17) we discover that this group was involved in some way in fellowship meals of pagan deities and thus committing spiritual fornication. Given the orthodoxy of the Ephesian church, it is no wonder they hated this group and its activities.

2:7 ***Anyone with ears to hear.*** This statement appears in each letter, as well as later in the vision (13:9). In the Jewish context, "to hear" is a synonym for "to obey" (see note on 1:3).

understand what he is saying to the churches. The fact that all the churches are to listen to what is being said to each church highlights the probability that the seven churches represent the totality of the Christian community in the world.

everyone who is victorious. In each letter, there is an exhortation for the believers to be conquerors. "Conquering," in the vision, is an expression for victorious discipleship in the face of the temptation to succumb to fallen Babylon (see 2:11, 17, 26; 3:5, 12, 21; 12:11; 15:2; 21:7). John used the present tense here and in all other places except 12:11, thereby indicating that conquering is the ongoing expression of faithful discipleship. "Conquering" is the consequence of obeying what the Spirit is saying to the churches.

COMMENTARY

How are we to understand the identity of the seven churches? The primary understanding, of course, must be the seven historical churches in the Roman province of Asia Minor in John's day. Their historical grounding in the culture of their Roman cities is basic for our understanding of the messages they received from Jesus. At another level, however, each letter to an individual church is to be heard by all the churches (2:7, 11, 17, 29; 3:6, 13, 22). In some sense, therefore, the letters are to all the churches. But there were other churches in Asia Minor in John's day. Are they excluded? Is there no word here for them, or for the churches throughout the Roman world? Since all churches in John's day would face the same pressures and temptations as the seven addressed, it is reasonable to presume the vision was for them as well.

But was the vision only for the churches in the first century? Does not the church in every age face from its culture similar pressures to assimilate the world's values, perspectives, and lifestyles? At its broadest level, John's vision speaks to the church throughout the ages (Beale 1999:204; Mounce 1977:84).

Some have understood the seven churches as representing seven ages of church history. But there is nothing integral to the text to support this, and nothing in the first 2,000 years of church history suggests this. The seven churches are ordered in an interesting pattern of "perfect" churches, "problem" churches, and "perverse" churches:

Ephesus: Problem
Smyrna: Perfect
Pergamum: Problem
Thyatira: Perfect, Problem, and Perverse
Sardis: Perverse
Philadelphia: Perfect
Laodicea: Perverse

The middle church of the seven, Thyatira, embodies all three conditions. Only by highly contrived constructs of history can this be made to be an outline of church history.

Now let's turn our attention to the church at Ephesus. Some historical background information is helpful in understanding this letter to the Ephesians. Ephesus was one of the leading cities of the Roman Empire. With a population from 250,000 to 500,000, it ranked in size and importance with Alexandria in Egypt and Antioch in Syria. Only Rome itself was greater. Ephesus was the major seaport of the Roman province of Asia, located on the western end of the overland trade routes to China and India. From ancient times Ephesus had been the center for the worship of a mother goddess who came to be associated with Artemis by the Greeks and Diana by the Romans. Her temple, one of the seven wonders of the ancient world, was the goal of religious pilgrims from across the empire. Due to its importance, the political, economic, and cultural presence of Rome was strongly manifest in Ephesus. One evidence of this is the colossal statue of Domitian (emperor from AD 81–96) that has been found in Ephesus. The church in Ephesus was immersed in the fullness of the values, perspectives, and life of the Roman world.

In such a context, the Ephesian church was characterized by hard work, patient endurance, and not tolerating evil people. John had already established a context for understanding "patient endurance" (1:9). It is the hard work of resisting the pressures of the world to conform to its values, perspectives, and lifestyles. The Ephesian church was working hard to maintain its holiness as people of God's New Jerusalem in the midst of a fallen Babylon world. But Jesus told them they had abandoned the love they had at first (2:4).

We see in Acts 19:1–20:1 that the church in Ephesus was so alive in Christ, so profoundly in love with Jesus, that it was making a powerful impact upon the world around it. All the residents of the province of Asia heard the gospel (Acts 19:10), the name of Jesus was extolled (Acts 19:17), and a burning of magic books revealed a radical paradigm shift in the lives of believers in the midst of the culture of Ephesus (Acts 19:19).[1] In addition, the economy of the city was affected so much that the metalsmiths stirred up the entire citizenship body to hold an unscheduled meeting (Acts 19:23-41). Obviously, the church in Ephesus was impacting its world with the gospel.

But then the church seemed to have fallen back into the defensive posture of orthodoxy rather than continue the offensive of evangelism. This may have been due to the pressures that the society of Ephesus was putting upon the church, thus the double reference to endurance (2:2-3). The church maintained their allegiance to Jesus and had not become tired of being faithful citizens of New Jerusalem. They were not, however, reaching out to their world with the liberating, healing, cleansing, transforming reality of God's grace in Jesus. While they were profoundly orthodox, they were no longer evangelistic. Jesus praised their orthodoxy, but indicated that their evangelistic failure had them on the verge of ceasing to be a community of God's people (their lampstand was about to be removed).

If I am correct in my analysis of the problem in Ephesus, then we see that orthodoxy and evangelism are the inseparable foci of a healthy church. Both must be kept in dynamic balance. Evangelism without orthodoxy becomes a tolerant pluralism and results in a community formed around diffuse human values and criteria. Orthodoxy without evangelism becomes a cold, harsh legalism and results in a community formed around debilitating "do's and don'ts." Sound orthodoxy and fervent evangelism result in a community of faith whose growing wholeness of life is a powerful witness of the cleansing, healing, liberating life in Christ to a soiled, wounded, and imprisoned world.

In the end, Jesus promised the conquerors in Ephesus (i.e., those who obeyed Jesus' charge for them to turn around and regain their first love) that they would eat of the tree of life (2:7). Each promise to the seven churches is related in some way to the New Jerusalem; here, the promise pertains to partaking of the tree of life (see 22:2). The tree of life appears first in the Garden of Eden (Gen 2:9) and was lost to humanity due to the fall (Gen 3:24). Jews expected that the tree of life would be restored to the righteous in the consummation of God's purposes.[2] The image appears again in 22:2, as the source of nurture for the citizens of the New Jerusalem and as the means of healing for the nations.

ENDNOTES

1. The Roman culture was shaped predominately by the worldview of Stoic philosophy. Stoicism was a very deterministic philosophy. A person's life was under the control of spiritual powers and forces of the cosmos, what Paul often describes as "the spiritual powers of this world" (Col 2:20) and "evil rulers and authorities of the unseen world, . . . mighty powers in this dark world, . . . evil spirits in the heavenly places" (Eph 6:12). Magic was the antidote to such a rigid determinism. If you knew the right spells, the right power terms, the right potions, you could release yourself and others from these powers. Thus, to burn one's magic books was an action that evinced a radical change in one's worldview.
2. *First Enoch* 25:4-5 says: "And as for this fragrant tree no mortal is permitted to touch it until the great judgment, when he [God] shall take vengeance on all and bring everything to its consummation for ever. It shall then be given to the righteous and holy. Its fruit shall be for food to the elect; it shall be transplanted to the holy place, to the temple of the Lord, the Eternal King." Note the parallels to John's vision: The fruit is for food for the righteous, it grows in "the holy place . . . the temple," which in John's vision is the New Jerusalem itself (21:22).

◆ 2. Smyrna (2:8-11)

8"Write this letter to the angel of the church in Smyrna. This is the message from the one who is the First and the Last, who was dead but is now alive:

9"I know about your suffering and your poverty—but you are rich! I know the blasphemy of those opposing you. They say they are Jews, but they are not, because their synagogue belongs to Satan. 10Don't be afraid of what you are about to suffer. The devil will throw some of you into prison to test you. You will suffer for ten days. But if you remain faithful even when facing death, I will give you the crown of life.

11"Anyone with ears to hear must listen to the Spirit and understand what he is saying to the churches. Whoever is victorious will not be harmed by the second death.

NOTES

2:8 ***angel.*** Better translated as "messenger" (see note on 2:1).

2:9 ***I know about your suffering and your poverty.*** It appears that the consequence of the Smyrnans' faithfulness was suffering (lit., "tribulation," see note on 1:9), presumably material poverty, although they were spiritually rich.

They say they are Jews. The reference to Jews reflects a situation also seen in Paul's ministry. Paul went first to the Jews (Acts 13:5, 14; 14:1; 16:13; 17:1, 10, 17; 18:4, 19; 19:8). When they rejected him and the gospel, he went to the Gentiles (Acts 13:45-48; 18:6; 19:9).

2:10 ***prison.*** In the Roman system of justice, prison was a place where persons were held until their case was adjudicated. During this time they would be tested (i.e., tortured; cf. Acts 22:24) on the premise that if enough pain was inflicted, the truth would come out.

ten days. Like seven, the number ten is another image for completeness, fullness, totality. The Torah was built around ten commandments; it took ten men to form a legitimate community for worship; ten righteous people would have spared Sodom (Gen 18:32); the Tabernacle had ten curtains enclosing it (Exod 26:1). Here it may mean that the tribulation will run its full course.

remain faithful even when facing death. Part of the full course of tribulation might lead to death, either through the "testing" or as the outcome of the case. Here Jesus' identification of himself as the one "who was dead but is now alive" (2:8) becomes crucial when he calls them to be faithful even when facing death.

crown of life. The outcome of such death will be a consummated life: "the crown of life." (For this image, see 2 Tim 4:8; Jas 1:12; 1 Pet 5:4; all of which refer to the outcome of faithfulness.)

2:11 *Whoever is victorious will not be harmed by the second death.* Being victorious for the church in Smyrna might well mean physical death. The promise for those who remain faithful citizens of the New Jerusalem in the face of fallen Babylon's most intense pressure is that they are assured that the second death will not touch them (see 20:14). The imagery suggests that the "first death" is physical death. The "second death" is the spiritual death of those whose name is not in the Lamb's book of life (20:12, 15).

COMMENTARY

Smyrna, modern Izmir, was founded in the second millennium BC. About 600 BC, however, Smyrna was destroyed by the Lydians and remained "dead" for about three centuries. It became "alive" again in 290 BC, when refounded by Lysimachus. Smyrna, together with Ephesus and Pergamum, was one of the leading cities in the Roman province of Asia. It was about 35 miles north of Ephesus, and boasted a deep harbor and well-protected gulf that enabled it to vie with Ephesus as a major center of the shipping trade. Smyrna had been loyal to Rome since Rome's conquest of Asia Minor from 200 to 190 BC. In the first century, Smyrna was the center of the imperial cult in the province. Its close allegiance with Rome meant that Smyrna was a city in which the values, perspectives, and culture of Rome predominated. John's vision makes it clear that faithfulness may result in suffering at the hands of the fallen Babylon world, specifically those Jews in what is called the synagogue of Satan (2:9).

Various Jews, concerned that the Roman authorities would view Paul's evangelization of the Gentiles as Jewish proselytization (a situation that had caused the Jews serious problems in the past), allied themselves with the local authorities against the Christians (Acts 13:7-8, 50; 14:5, 19; 17:5, 14; 18:12; 19:33).[1] In the perspective of John's vision, Rome is the incarnation of fallen Babylon (see notes on 13:18; 16:19; 17:4-5, 9-11), Satan's dominion. Thus, when the Jews joined themselves with the Roman authorities against the Christians, they became a synagogue of Satan.

Smyrna was suffering persecution from these Jews joined to the Roman system. Jesus identified himself to this faithful church as the one "who was dead but is now alive," a fitting word to a city that had died and come to life again—but even more so to Christians facing the possibility of being faithful martyrs. How relevant this is for our time, when more Christians have been martyred in the twentieth century than the preceding nineteen centuries.[2] Christians will always be called to account for their faith and its genuine incarnation in their lives. The values and perspectives of God's kingdom are always a threat to the dehumanizing perspectives and destructive values of the fallen Babylon world.

Jesus' word to Smyrna is in sharp contrast to those who proclaim a gospel of prosperity. We will see a "prosperity" church shortly—namely, Laodicea. In Smyrna we see one of the faithful churches, a community of God's people living out their lives as disciples of the kingdom. The terms associated with this faithful church are not comfortable: suffering, poverty, being blasphemed by others, being afraid, prison, being put to the test, facing death. These are not terms or experiences that would induce people to sign on for the Christian pilgrimage. How often have we "domesticated" the gospel to make it palatable to those of our fallen Babylon world? Are we willing to be faithful citizens of God's New Jerusalem no matter what the cost?

ENDNOTE

1. The Jews had a very special privilege in the Roman world. They were a licit religion, meaning they were allowed to worship and to govern their community according to their own ancestral laws (Torah). Rome's toleration was limited, however. Whenever the Jews began to make inroads into the Roman culture through proselytizing activities, Rome stepped in and stopped it. About AD 19, the Jews were expelled from Rome due to proselytizing activities (Tacitus *Annals* 2.85.5; Suetonius *Tiberius* 36.1; Josephus *Antiquities* 18.65-84). In 41, Claudius recognized the Jewish rights in Egypt, but also warned them not to intrude themselves into the sociopolitical structure (Tcherikover and Fuks 1960). About 49, Claudius expelled the Jews from Rome (Acts 18:2; Suetonius *Claudius* 25.5). These actions would make the Jewish communities very sensitive to Roman perceptions of Christian proselytizing. Note also the charges against Paul and Silas in Philippi: "The whole city is in an uproar because of these Jews! . . . They are teaching customs that are illegal for us Romans to practice [i.e., proselytizing]" (Acts 16:20-21).
2. EWTN News, "A Century of Blood and Faith," May 10, 2000, http://www.santegidio.org/news/rassegna/00001/20000510_ewtnews_EN.htm.

◆ 3. Pergamum (2:12-17)

12"Write this letter to the angel of the church in Pergamum. This is the message from the one with the sharp two-edged sword:

13"I know that you live in the city where Satan has his throne, yet you have remained loyal to me. You refused to deny me even when Antipas, my faithful witness, was martyred among you there in Satan's city.

14"But I have a few complaints against you. You tolerate some among you whose teaching is like that of Balaam, who showed Balak how to trip up the people of Israel. He taught them to sin by eating food offered to idols and by committing sexual sin.
15In a similar way, you have some Nicolaitans among you who follow the same teaching.
16Repent of your sin, or I will come to you suddenly and fight against them with the sword of my mouth.

17"Anyone with ears to hear must listen to the Spirit and understand what he is saying to the churches. To everyone who is victorious I will give some of the manna that has been hidden away in heaven. And I will give to each one a white stone, and on the stone will be engraved a new name that no one understands except the one who receives it.

NOTES

2:12 ***angel.*** This is better rendered as "messenger" (see note on 2:1).

Pergamum. This magnificent city was the capital of the Roman province of Asia.

sharp two-edged sword. This calls to mind the Roman sword of the proconsul's judgment and, at the same time, the word of God by which all things are judged (see note on 1:16).

2:13 ***where Satan has his throne.*** This undoubtedly refers to the seat of the Roman proconsul, the governor of the Roman province of Asia. The presence of the power of Rome in this manner would have strengthened the perspectives and values of the Roman world and heightened the contrast between faithful citizens of God's kingdom and the Roman ethos.

you have remained loyal to me. Lit., "you are holding fast my name." Biblically, "name" relates to the nature of the one named. That is why, when persons have transforming encounters with God, their name is sometimes changed. For example, Abram became Abraham (Gen 17:1-5), and Jacob became Israel (Gen 32:24-28).

2:14 ***Balaam, who showed Balak how to trip up the people of Israel.*** There is nothing in the account of Balaam (Num 22–24) that implicates him in the apostasy of Israel in Moab. In Jewish traditions, however, Balaam is regularly characterized as evil (Buchanan 1993:96). The origin of the tradition may have been Moses (Num 31:16), subsequently reinforced by Josh 13:22, where it is said that Balaam was put to death by the Israelites for practicing divination. (See 2 Pet 2:15 for an example in Jewish Christian literature.) Immediately following the account of Balaam, however, is the account of Israel being led into apostasy by the Moabites (Num 25).

sexual sin. This is an unfortunate translation of the word *porneusai* [TG4203, ZG4519] (to fornicate). The OT often uses sexual terminology (adultery, fornication) to characterize apostasy and idolatry (see Jer 3:9; Ezek 23; Hosea). John's vision plays upon this image consistently. While there certainly were many instances of sacred prostitution in pagan temples, the issue was not "sexual sin." The issue was much deeper; it was spiritual adultery (see commentary).

2:15 ***Nicolaitans . . . follow the same teaching.*** Here we gain a little insight into the heresy of this group. Obviously, they were teaching that it was acceptable for Christians to participate in the worship of guild deities and to eat meat that had been sacrificed to those deities. (See Paul's discussions of this in 1 Cor 8:4-13; 10:14-21; and see commentary.)

2:16 ***the sword of my mouth.*** See discussion of this image in the note on 1:16 and commentary on 19:15, 21. The sword, which is the Lord's word, always cuts through all subterfuges and is the corrective for accommodation and heresy.

COMMENTARY

Pergamum was the capital of the Roman province of Asia, the seat of the proconsul, whose office possessed the *ius gladii* (the law of the sword) to dispense Roman justice. Pergamum's ties to Rome went back to 240 BC, when the Attalid kings allied themselves with Rome. In 133 BC Attalus III willed his kingdom to Rome upon his death. In 29 BC, the emperor Augustus allowed the city to build a temple to "the divine Augustus and the goddess Roma" (Tacitus *Annals* 4.37), the first city in the East to be given this privilege.

Pergamum was located about 55 miles northeast of Smyrna and about 10 miles inland from the Aegean. Its location did not allow it the mercantile significance of Ephesus or Smyrna, but its long history as the capital of the Pergamene kings together with its role as the Roman capital of the province made it one of the wealthier cities of the area. The Roman world was incarnate here, perhaps more than any of the other six cities.

Like the Ephesian church (2:1-7), the Pergamum church received praise from Jesus for aspects of its faithfulness (2:13). It even held fast in the face of a persecution in which one of its members was martyred. Like Ephesus, it seems to have been a faithful church, living as citizens of God's New Jerusalem in the midst of the pressures of their fallen Babylon world. The Christians of Pergamum had not only been resistant to denying their faith in Jesus as Messiah and Lord, they had been manifesting "the witness of Jesus" in their living (see note on 1:2). Their lives manifested a Christlike quality. This is emphasized in the martyrdom of Antipas, who had been put to death by forces associated with the Roman power structure (2:13).

But Pergamum, like Ephesus, had problems. Their problems differed from Ephesus, however. In Ephesus, the entire church seemed to be involved in its cold orthodoxy. In Pergamum there were two groups creating problems. One group was verging on apostasy with its advocacy of eating food offered to idols and spiritual fornication, participating in the worship of other gods. The rest, who appeared not to participate in this activity, were nonetheless tolerant of those who did.

The background for this is important for us to understand. Most trades in the Roman world formed guilds that served as the security network for their members. The guild ensured one's livelihood, provided support during illness, and even handled the affairs of burial for their dead. Each guild had a patron deity whose worship was an integral part of membership. To fail to participate in the worship and sacred meals of the deity would result in removal from the guild and loss of one's livelihood. An additional aspect of life in the Roman world was that meat markets, generally, were outlets of pagan temples. Meat left over from sacrifices to pagan deities was sold to the public. Apparently there were those in the church at Pergamum who were teaching that it was all right for Christians to participate in guild activities and to purchase meat from temple outlets (2:14). Such involvement in idolatry constituted spiritual fornication—the breaking of one's bond with God and joining oneself to another god.

In a culture like ours, where toleration has become the primary virtue, it is easy for the community of faith to "Christianize" tolerance and allow all sorts of destructive perspectives and behaviors into its fellowship. Since the surrounding culture cultivates and promotes toleration as the ultimate level of maturity and caring, who would want to be accused of being "intolerant?" This is even more the case when we consider that Ephesian-type churches tend to manifest a brand of intolerance that rightly brings the world's scorn and ridicule down upon them. If the Ephesian church represents the intolerance of cold orthodoxy, the Pergamum church represents the toleration of mild heterodoxy.

In the midst of the problems at Pergamum, Jesus gave a call for the believers to rise up and be "victorious" (2:17). The promise to those who become "victorious" relates directly to the situation of the church in Pergamum. In contrast to "food offered to idols," Jesus promised "the manna that has been hidden away" (there is no mention of "in heaven" in the Greek text of 2:17). This promise would resonate with John's audience, shaped by Jewish understanding. One of the Jewish expectations associated with the restoration of the kingdom was the full restoration of the Temple in Jerusalem. This meant the return of the manna that had been in the Ark of the Covenant in the Holy of Holies until Jeremiah took it out and hid it just before the destruction of the Temple by the Babylonians. (See Heb 9:4 for the tradition of manna in the Ark of the Covenant, 2 Macc 2:4-8 for Jeremiah hiding the sacred objects from the Temple [although the manna is not explicitly mentioned], and 2 *Baruch* 29:8 for the restoration of the manna in the consummation.) By promising this manna, Jesus was giving the church another intimation that the restoration of the kingdom had come.

Jesus also promised the victorious ones a "white stone" with "a new name" (2:17). This may refer to the ballot that was used by citizens of a Roman city to cast their votes during meetings. To have such a stone, one's name had to be on the citizenship rolls of the city. Jesus seems to be indicating that God's faithful people are citizens of God's kingdom. This would appear to be confirmed by the presence of the new name on the white stone. Since a person's "name" is representative of their nature (see note on 2:13), faithful believers have a new nature as citizens of God's New Jerusalem. Jesus' final remark that "no one understands" the new name "except the one who receives it," points to the experiential reality of citizenship in the New Jerusalem. Citizenship is not a legal formality conferred from without, but an existential reality of life in intimate union with Christ.

◆ 4. Thyatira (2:18-29)

18"Write this letter to the angel of the church in Thyatira. This is the message from the Son of God, whose eyes are like flames of fire, whose feet are like polished bronze:

19"I know all the things you do. I have seen your love, your faith, your service, and your patient endurance. And I can see your constant improvement in all these things.

20"But I have this complaint against you. You are permitting that woman—that Jezebel who calls herself a prophet—to lead my servants astray. She teaches them to commit sexual sin and to eat food offered to idols. 21I gave her time to repent, but she does not want to turn away from her immorality.

22"Therefore, I will throw her on a bed of suffering,* and those who commit adultery with her will suffer greatly unless they repent and turn away from her evil deeds. 23I will strike her children dead. Then all the churches will know that I am the one who searches out the thoughts and intentions of every person. And I will give to each of you whatever you deserve.

24"But I also have a message for the rest of you in Thyatira who have not followed this false teaching ('deeper truths,' as they call them—depths of Satan, actually). I will ask nothing more of you 25except that you hold tightly to what you have until I come. 26To all who are victorious, who obey me to the very end,

To them I will give authority over
all the nations.
27 They will rule the nations with an
iron rod
and smash them like clay pots.*

28They will have the same authority I received from my Father, and I will also give them the morning star!

29"Anyone with ears to hear must listen to the Spirit and understand what he is saying to the churches.

2:22 Greek *a bed*. **2:26-27** Ps 2:8-9 (Greek Version).

NOTES

2:18 ***angel.*** This is better rendered as "messenger" (see note on 2:1).

eyes are like flames of fire. Jesus is introduced to this church as "the one who searches out the thoughts and intentions of every person" (2:23). Jesus sees through the outer facade and discerns the inner perspectives and motivations of the heart (Heb 4:12-13).

feet are like polished bronze. This may relate to the promise to those who are victorious and thereby receive authority over all the nations (2:26). The image, from Dan 10:6, suggests the tremendous power and authority of God who tramples his enemies under his feet (1 Kgs 5:3; Pss 60:12; 68:30; 108:13; Isa 14:25). By relating Jesus to God through this imagery, his authority over the nations can be promised to the victorious. All the images of brightness would also contrast Jesus to Apollo, the sun god, whose temple was in Thyatira.

2:20 ***Jezebel.*** This woman clearly calls to mind the pagan queen of Israel who substituted the worship of Baal for the worship of Yahweh (1 Kgs 18–21; 2 Kgs 9). There would, undoubtedly, also be an allusion to the Sibyl, Sambathe, who was located in Thyatira. The situation seems even more serious than at Pergamum, although the basic issues are the same: eating food offered to idols and spiritual adultery (see note on 2:14). The added word, that she "lead[s] my servants astray," seems to indicate a more serious apostasy.

2:21 ***I gave her time to repent.*** This suggests that there have been warnings to this woman and her followers. Obviously, the warnings had gone unheeded.

2:22 ***I will throw her on a bed of suffering.*** Lit., "I am casting her into bed"—with no mention of suffering (so NLT mg). The "bed" may imply sickness, but not explicitly. The context strongly implies that "Jezebel" was going to experience the destructive consequences of her activities.

unless they repent. For her followers, however, there was still an option. They could repent of her works. Otherwise, they would experience great tribulation.

2:23 ***I will strike her children dead.*** Lit., "I will kill her children with death." At first glance this seems to be a redundancy, but John's vision, like Paul, uses "death" to speak of the spiritual condition of those in rebellion against God (see 20:5, where "the rest of the dead" are unredeemed humanity who have not "come back to life" with the redeemed [20:4]; cf. Eph 2:1-6). Jesus seems to be indicating that unless "Jezebel's" followers repent, they would return to the spiritual death from which they were redeemed. The same image appears again in the letter to Sardis (3:1-2), where most of the church is "dead."

I am the one who searches out the thoughts and intentions of every person. And I will give to each of you whatever you deserve. "Whatever you deserve" is lit., "according to your works." Though "works" play a significant role in John's vision (cf. 2:2, 5, 6, 19, 26; 3:1, 2, 8, 15; 14:13; 18:6; 20:12-13), Jesus made it clear here that works are not the sole criteria of faithfulness (cf. 20:12-14). Faithful works are the incarnation of a faithful heart and motives. This will come forcefully to mind in the next letter where the church at Sardis has a reputation for being alive—that is, it has works and yet is dead (3:1).

2:24-25 ***the rest of you in Thyatira who have not followed this false teaching.*** This indicates a third group, distinct from the followers of Jezebel and those who tolerated her presence in the church. Jesus had nothing to say against this group but urged them to "hold tightly to what you have."

depths of Satan. The meaning of this phrase is a puzzle. It may refer to Jezebel and her followers thinking that they were able to comprehend Satan's wiles and thus escape bondage to evil. Caird (1966:44) describes this option well: "One possibility is that the followers of Jezebel actually claimed, in so many words . . . believed that it was their Christian duty to participate as fully as possible in the pagan society around them, to identify themselves with the common life of their city. They recognized that pagan social life was an open field for the operations of Satan, and that those who entered it did so at their peril. They were confident that their baptism gave them supernatural protection from the onslaughts of Satan, so that they could touch pitch without being defiled and handle fire without being burnt."

COMMENTARY

Thyatira was located about 40 miles east of Pergamum in the fertile Lycus valley. It was founded by Seleucus I (301–280 BC), and came under Rome in 190 BC. Thyatira was known for its trade and industry. It was a transshipment point for trade between the Mediterranean and the East, and inscriptions reveal a large number of industries: bronze- and coppersmiths, tanners, leather workers, dyers, wool and linen workers, potters, and bakers. Lydia, a dealer in purple goods worn only by the elite, was from Thyatira (Acts 16:14). Along with the many deities associated with the industrial guilds, Apollo, the sun-god, was worshiped in Thyatira. The shrine of the sibyl Sambathe was also located here. (Sibyls were a class of prophetesses throughout the Roman world; they were sought out for their ability to foretell events and give sagacious advice to seekers.) While Thyatira was of minor political importance, the economic and religious arenas of the Roman culture were strong.

Among the seven letters to the seven churches in Revelation 2–3, Thyatira is the central church of the seven. As noted in the commentary on 2:1-7, the first three churches are in this pattern: problem church—perfect church—problem church. The last three are in this pattern: perverse church—perfect church—perverse church. Thyatira appears to combine all three types: perfect, problem, and perverse. Not only did Jesus praise them for their faithfulness, he also indicated that they evidenced "constant improvement in all these things" (2:19). Some among them, however, were perverse in that they followed the apostasy of "Jezebel." Jezebel and her followers were participating in the life of the fallen Babylon world around them, perhaps thinking it was possible to be citizens both of the New Jerusalem and fallen Babylon at the same time (see note on 2:24-25). These would return to spiritual deadness if they didn't repent (see notes on 2:22-23).

Another element in the church was problematic—there were those who simply tolerated Jezebel and her followers. These were the ones who, while they had "love . . . faith . . . service, and . . . patient endurance," were warned for this toleration of perversity. The more we understand what is represented in these churches, the more we see that John's vision speaks strongly to the church in every age. In many "mainline" denominations today there is a three-way division. On the one side are those who, at various levels and in diverse ways, seek to live lives of faithful Christian discipleship. These are often labeled "conservatives" or "fundamentalists" or "evangelicals." On the other side are those who, in equal diversity, adopt various apostate or heretical perspectives and behaviors. These are often labeled "liberals" or "radicals." In the middle are those who, for various reasons, ally themselves with neither side but "tolerate" the extremes of both sides for the sake of preserving the myth of structural or denominational "loyalty" or "unity." The Thyatiran church is alive and as sick as ever in our day.

Jesus makes a promise to those who rise above the sickness. These are the ones who keep Jesus' works until the end and those whose lives have the "testimony of Jesus" (see note on 1:2). The promise of giving them "authority over all the nations" would be clear to John's audience, which was steeped in Jewish messianic expectations. When God restored the kingdom to Israel, they would have this authority (Ps 149:5-9; Isa 49:23; 60:11; Dan 7:27). The image would also indicate a radical shift of understanding. John clearly indicated that God had restored the kingdom through the death and resurrection of Jesus (1:6; 5:10), yet the final consummation of this event, along with the rule of the new covenant community, is still in the future (see commentary on 1:7).

The promise in 2:26-27 is a paraphrase of Psalm 2:8-9, a messianic psalm that envisions the rule of God's Messiah over the nations. The image appears again in John's vision at 12:5 and 19:15. Here the action of the Messiah is now associated with God's people ("They will have the same authority I received from my Father," 2:28a). In this promise, Jesus says he will give them the "morning star" (2:28b). In 22:16, Jesus identifies himself as the bright morning star. This Messianic image has its source in Numbers 24:17, where Balaam prophesied, "A star will rise from Jacob." Jacob is closely associated with David in the Jewish tradition (see 2 Sam 23:1; Jer 33:26; Ezek 37:25; for a full discussion, see Beale 1999:268-269). John thus continues his portrayal of Jesus as the Davidic Messiah. In short, the image of the overcomers having Jesus as the "morning star" is a parallel to having "the same authority" Jesus received from God. Thus, Jesus seems to be indicating that he will give himself to those who are being victorious so that they would become the presence of Christ in their world.

◆ 5. Sardis (3:1-6)

"Write this letter to the angel* of the church in Sardis. This is the message from the one who has the sevenfold Spirit* of God and the seven stars:

"I know all the things you do, and that you have a reputation for being alive—but you are dead. 2Wake up! Strengthen what little remains, for even what is left is almost dead. I find that your actions do not meet the requirements of my God. 3Go back to what you heard and believed at first; hold to it firmly. Repent and turn to me again. If you don't wake up, I will come to you suddenly, as unexpected as a thief.

4"Yet there are some in the church in Sardis who have not soiled their clothes with evil. They will walk with me in white, for they are worthy. 5All who are victorious will be clothed in white. I will never erase their names from the Book of Life, but I will announce before my Father and his angels that they are mine.

6"Anyone with ears to hear must listen to the Spirit and understand what he is saying to the churches.

3:1a Or *the messenger;* also in 3:7, 14. 3:1b Greek *the seven spirits.*

NOTES

3:1 *angel.* This is better rendered as "messenger" (see note on 2:1).

the sevenfold Spirit of God. Lit., "the seven spirits of God." Since the same title appears in

1:4, together with Jesus and the Father, it is a title for the Holy Spirit of God—hence the translation "sevenfold Spirit."

the one who has . . . the seven stars. Jesus reminds the church in Sardis that their messenger, the one who represents them in his presence, is held in his hand.

you have a reputation for being alive—but you are dead. The same kind of reversal is seen again in the other "perverse" church, Laodicea (3:17), who think they are rich, prosperous, and need nothing, but whom Jesus describes as wretched, miserable, poor, blind, and naked.

3:2-3 ***Wake up!*** The Greek term here (*grēgoreo* [TG1127, ZG1213]), although it can be translated "wake up," essentially means "to be watchful," "to be on the alert," "to be alive" (BDAG 1689, §§1, 2, 3). There would have been a double meaning here, reminding the church in Sardis both of Sardis's past military defeats (see commentary) and the church's present condition of being "dead" (3:1).

Strengthen what little remains, for even what is left is almost dead. Jesus indicates that there is only a little life left in the church and even that is almost dead. If we take "death" as a spiritual condition (see note on 2:23), it appears that this church was on the verge of ceasing to be a community of faith.

your actions do not meet the requirements. Once again the issue is their "actions" (see note on 2:23). Their life does not manifest the "witness of Jesus" (see note on 1:2).

3:3 ***Go back to what you heard and believed at first.*** Jesus basically told this church that it needed to start from scratch. The Greek has "remember how you received and heard." That is, Jesus was calling them back to the experience of redemption, not an intellectual or propositional construct. The Greek then says, "keep" it; that is, "obey." Again the conjunction of hearing and obeying is highlighted (see note on 1:3). The church in Sardis needed to recover and live out the experience of its relationship with Jesus as Messiah and Lord.

I will come to you suddenly, as unexpected as a thief. The image of Jesus coming as a thief appears again in 16:15 (cf. Matt 24:43; Luke 12:39; 1 Thess 5:2-4; 2 Pet 3:10) and seems to militate against all attempts to compute the time of his return. This further substantiates Jesus' response to the disciples' inquiry as to the time of the end: "No one knows the day or hour when these things will happen, not even the angels in heaven or the Son himself. Only the Father knows" (Mark 13:32).

3:4 ***clothes.*** This is significant in John's vision. In the Roman world, persons were identified by their clothing. Only the emperor and the patrician class could wear togas with purple, the equestrian class could wear red, and so on. A person's clothing manifested to the world the nature of the person. John seems to play upon this feature of his world. A Christian's "garment" was the witness of their faithful discipleship.

some . . . have not soiled their clothes. Jesus described the faithful few in Sardis as those who had not soiled their clothes. The term appears again in 14:4, where the text says that the followers of the Lamb are those who have not "soiled" themselves with women (see note there). In the context of a church that seems to have almost completely returned to the spiritual death of the Roman world, the few faithful who have not "soiled their clothes" (like those undefiled "by women") are those who have not fallen back into the destructive and dehumanizing values, perspectives, and lifestyle of their surroundings. They had not adorned themselves with the clothing of the sinful world around them, nor entered into spiritual fornication with the prostitute, fallen Babylon, incarnate as the Roman culture around them.

COMMENTARY

Sardis was about 30 miles southeast of Thyatira. From the sixth century BC, it was the capital of the Lydian Empire and, under its last king, Croesus, was known for its tremendous wealth. It later fell under the control of the Pergamene kings and was also left to Rome in the will of Attalus III, in 133 BC.

Sardis was an interesting city. It was the site of a huge temple of Artemis (160 feet by 300 feet, with columns 58 feet high), who had been known as Cybele from Lydian times. Cybele was believed to have the power to bring the dead to life (cf. 3:1). It also possessed a seemingly impregnable acropolis that insured it against being taken by its foes. On two occasions, however, Sardis was captured because it failed to keep watch on a portion of its walls presumed to be unassailable (cf. 3:2). The first was by Cyrus in 549 BC, the second by Antiochus the Great in 218 BC (cf. Herodotus *Histories* 1.84). The besieging forces sent men up the steep cliffs at night to scale the wall at the vulnerable point and capture the city. When the people of Sardis arose in the morning, they were captives!

In the first part of the letter to Sardis, John broke with his normal pattern for the introductions to the letters. Up to this point, each letter began with attributes of Jesus taken from the vision in chapter 1. The image for Jesus having the sevenfold Spirit (3:1) doesn't emerge until 5:6, where the Lamb's seven eyes are "the sevenfold Spirit of God that is sent out into every part of the earth." It is interesting that the same thing happens in the letters to Philadelphia and Laodicea (3:7-13, 14-22). There, too, the attributes of Jesus come from the vision that follows rather than from the vision in chapter 1. It is almost as if the initial vision of Jesus wasn't enough for these churches. The two perverse churches needed to be confronted with the deeper realities of Jesus as revealed in the vision. Powerless Philadelphia needed the deeper assurance of God's victory through the "powerlessness" of the cross. It would seem that Jesus gave these messages to John in a manner that serves to transition between the introductory vision in chapter 1 and the succeeding vision in chapters 4–22. In the case of Sardis, Jesus is seen as the fullness of the presence of God in their midst (the one who has the sevenfold Spirit of God).

Once again, as with the previous churches, Jesus indicated his knowledge of the church. But this time there was no general praise for the church. Instead, there was condemnation for the church's condition. With the exception of a few faithful souls, the church at Sardis was in dire straits. They were so spiritually dead that they were on the verge of having their name erased from the Book of Life (3:5). Unlike the previous "problem" churches, repentance was not enough. They needed to return to the essentials of their experience of redemption, and once again begin to live out that reality in their life.

The crucial problem with the church in Sardis was that they had a reputation for being alive but were actually spiritually dead (3:1). Thus Jesus exhorts them to "come alive" (see note on 3:2). There are many such Sardis-type churches in the world today. They might be alive with "exciting" worship that appeals to the tastes of the culture but dead to the genuine awe and humility of true worship. They might be alive with "entertaining" programs for children, youth, and adults but dead to the transforming grace of God. They might be alive with "socially aware" attitudes and activities but dead to the liberating power of God. They might be "alive" with the world's perspectives, values, and behaviors but "dead" to those of the kingdom.

As with each of the seven churches in chapters 2–3, Jesus offered promises to those who would overcome the situation and be victorious conquerors over the insidious pressures of the fallen Babylon world, pressures that tempt Christians to live by its perspectives and values (see note on 2:7). The first promise is that the victorious ones "will be clothed in white" (3:5a). Later in the vision we see that the faithful have "washed their robes in the blood of the Lamb and made them white" (7:14). Since John already indicated that Jesus freed us from our sins by shedding his blood for us (1:5), the white garment here represents a life delivered from the power of sin.

The victorious ones are also promised that their names will never be erased from "the Book of Life" (3:5b). This book appears again and again in John's vision. It is identified as the Lamb's Book of Life (13:8). No citizen of fallen Babylon has their name in it (13:8; 17:8); only the citizens of the New Jerusalem are written in the book (21:27). The image is not peculiar to John or to the Bible. Paul used the same image (Phil 4:3). It seems to have its origin in Exodus where Moses said to God, "But now, if you will only forgive their sin—but if not, erase my name from the record you have written!" (Exod 32:32). To which God responded, "I will erase the name of everyone who has sinned against me" (Exod 32:33). The image continued to be used in the Jewish tradition (Pss 56:8; 69:28; 139:16; Dan 12:1; *1 Enoch* 47:3; *Jubilees* 30:20-22—here, especially, note the possibility of being removed from the book of the living), and is more fully developed in 20:12-15. All people are judged by whether or not their names are written in it (20:12, 15), and those not found there are spiritually dead (20:15).

The implication of Jesus telling the conquerors that they would not have their names erased from the Book of Life is that it is possible to have one's name erased from this book. In essence, Jesus was warning those in Sardis who had soiled their clothes and become "dead" (3:1) that their names would be erased from the Book of Life. This is John's way of describing those who are spiritually dead, as is clearly seen in 17:8 and 20:15.

The final promise to the conquerors is that Jesus would announce them before his Father and his angels (3:5). This reflects the imagery Jesus used in Matthew 10:32 and Luke 12:8, where the issue is acknowledging Jesus publicly. In the terms of John's vision, this is the same as having the testimony of Jesus (see note on 1:2). Those who do so are thereby acknowledged by Jesus before God.

◆ 6. Philadelphia (3:7-13)

7 "Write this letter to the angel of the church in Philadelphia.

This is the message from the one
who is holy and true,
the one who has the key of David.
What he opens, no one can close;
and what he closes, no one can
open:*

8 "I know all the things you do, and
I have opened a door for you that no
one can close. You have little strength,
yet you obeyed my word and did not
deny me. 9 Look, I will force those who
belong to Satan's synagogue—those
liars who say they are Jews but are
not—to come and bow down at your

feet. They will acknowledge that you are the ones I love.

[10]"Because you have obeyed my command to persevere, I will protect you from the great time of testing that will come upon the whole world to test those who belong to this world. [11]I am coming soon.* Hold on to what you have, so that no one will take away your crown. [12]All who are victorious will become pillars in the Temple of my God, and they will never have to leave it. And I will write on them the name of my God, and they will be citizens in the city of my God—the new Jerusalem that comes down from heaven from my God. And I will also write on them my new name.

[13]"Anyone with ears to hear must listen to the Spirit and understand what he is saying to the churches."

3:7 Isa 22:22. 3:11 Or *suddenly*, or *quickly*.

NOTES

3:7 ***angel.*** This is better rendered as "messenger" (see note on 2:1).

key of David. This phrase, when taken with "What he opens, no one can close; and what he closes, no one can open" refers to Isa 22:22. There God tells Shebna, the apostate "prime minister" (palace administrator) of the Davidic house, that he will be overthrown and the key of the house of David will be given to Eliakim son of Hilkiah. The image is one of the restoration of Israel in the face of its enemies within.

3:8 ***You have little strength.*** This may refer to its size, but most Christian communities in this time were quite small. It may refer to the influence of its members in the larger community since Christians were not drawn from the socially influential classes for the most part (cf. 1 Cor 1:26; for a fuller discussion see Beale 1999:285-286). The latter is more likely.

3:9 ***those who belong to Satan's synagogue.*** Lit., "synagogue of Satan," as in 2:9 (see note) with respect to the other "perfect" church, Smyrna.

3:10 ***persevere.*** Lit., "patient endurance" as in 1:9 (see note). This is another confirmation to the church that as members of the restored kingdom they would experience tribulation, which calls for patient endurance (1:9).

those who belong to this world. Lit., "those who dwell upon the earth." This phrase is introduced here and used throughout the vision to describe the citizens of fallen Babylon (6:10; 8:13; 11:10; 13:8, 12, 14; 14:6; 17:2, 8). In trying to describe his vision John drew the image from the pool of Jewish apocryphal literature, as evidenced in *1 Enoch* where the phrase is often used for those in rebellion against God (*1 Enoch* 54:9; 55:1; 60:5; 65:6, 12; 66:1; 67:8—although it is sometimes used positively as well). Thus, "earth," for John, is an image for the rebellious realm and is used as such at many points throughout the vision (3:10; 6:10, 15; 7:1-2; 8:5; 9:15, 18; 12:9, 12; 14:3, 18, 19; 16:1-2; 17:5; 18:3, 9, 11; 19:2, 19; 20:8). While the faithful citizens of God's kingdom experience tribulation at the hands of fallen Babylon, in the end the citizens of fallen Babylon will experience tribulation ("the great time of testing") at the consummation of God's kingdom.

3:11 ***I am coming soon.*** Jesus already told the church in Pergamum that he would come suddenly (2:16); the promise is reiterated in 22:7, 12, and 20 (where the NLT uses "soon," as here in 3:11). The Greek phrase is identical in all these places (*erchomai tachu* [TG2064/5035, ZG2262/5444]), and the translation should be consistent. As in 1:1, 2,000 years of Christian history provide us with a broader perspective on "soon." The Greek term for "soon" is part of the same family of terms as the phrase in 1:1. Although Christians should always live as though each moment was their last, and Jesus' return will be unexpected (3:3; 16:15), it seems likely Jesus was indicating that his return would be at the precise moment of God's purposes (see note on 1:1). An alternative understanding is to use "suddenly" (so NLT mg), as in 2:16, not indicating the time of his coming but the manner.

so that no one will take away your crown. In his letter to the other "perfect" church, Smyrna, Jesus promised them the "crown of life" (2:10), and in 4:4 and 10, the 24 elders who represent the kingdom of priests (see note on 4:4) have crowns.

3:12 *I will write on them the name of my God, and they will be citizens in the city of my God.* Biblically, "name" relates to the very nature or essence of that which is named. See note on 2:13 and commentary on 2:17.

the new Jerusalem that comes down from heaven. The grammar of the Greek indicates that it is continually coming. On the continuous nature of the New Jerusalem's coming, see the last paragraph of commentary on 20:11–21:8.

COMMENTARY

Philadelphia was located about 30 miles southeast of Sardis in an area known primarily for vineyards and, with the rest of the seven cities, earthquakes. Philadelphia had been devastated by an earthquake in AD 17. While the city was rebuilt, most people no longer lived in the city but in the outskirts to minimize the danger lest the city fall again.

Philadelphia was founded either by Eumenes II (197–159 BC) or Attalus II "Philadelphos" (159–138 BC). It, too, passed into Roman control through the will of Attalus III in 133 BC. As the center of a fertile vine-growing area, the worship of Dionysus, the god of wine, was one of the city's major religious expressions.

Jesus introduced himself to the church in Philadelphia as "the one who is holy and true" (3:7), a combination of terms used elsewhere in the vision only of God (6:10). The two terms separately are also used primarily for God in John's vision ("holy" in 4:8; 15:4; 16:5; "true" in 15:3; 16:7; 19:2, 9; 21:5; 22:6). To a church that certainly might have felt abandoned (see note on 3:8), this gave assurance that the one whom they followed was indeed God and that God's presence was with them. (As with the letter to Sardis, the attributes of Jesus are not drawn from John's vision of Jesus in ch 1.)

Jesus then told them that he had the key of David (3:7), which indicates that God had transferred the control of the house of David (Israel) to Jesus. He told them, "I have opened a door for you that no one can close" (3:8). From the content of the letter, this is the door into the New Jerusalem (3:12), the new people of God (3:9). In the later vision of the New Jerusalem, the gates are never shut (21:25), while outside is fallen Babylon (22:15). This reference might forge a link between the key of David here and the keys of Death and Hades in 1:18. Jesus' keys open the way out of the dehumanizing and destructive bondage of fallen Babylon and the way into the restored and transformed life of the New Jerusalem.

Even though the church had little strength, this church had been faithful. They had the word of God ("obeyed my word") and the testimony of Jesus ("did not deny me"), the chief characteristics of the faithful (see note on 1:2). Their "little strength" may refer to the church's relationship to the synagogue, which had a privileged status in the Roman system (see endnote on 2:8-11). In Philadelphia it seems that the synagogue was claiming its "privileged" role as God's covenant people ("who say they are Jews") and denying any participation in the covenant by the Jewish-Christians and, especially, the Gentiles in their number. Jesus said he would make them "come and bow down at your feet" (3:9). The image of the "false Jews" bowing at the feet of the Christians, especially the Gentile ones, is a radical reversal of Isaiah's imagery of the Gentiles bowing at the feet of Israel in the restored kingdom (Isa 45:14; 49:23; 60:14). Jesus' words of assurance, "you are the ones I love," affirmed for the church that they were, indeed, participants in God's restored kingdom, the true Israel, New Jerusalem.

Even though Jesus affirmed them, he also warned them not to lose their crown (3:11). Whatever the crown represents (authority, control, power), it is possible for persons to lose their crowns. This is a parallel image to having the lampstand removed (see note on 2:5), being "killed with death" (see note on 2:23), being erased from the Book of Life (see commentary on 3:5), and being vomited out of Jesus' mouth (see note on 3:16). All point to the fact that salvation (i.e., being a member of God's kingdom) does not guarantee eternal security but is a dynamic relationship with God that can be broken and lost.

Immediately following this warning, Jesus gives assurance of salvation to those "who are victorious" (3:12). It should be noted that in all of the letters, this phrase is in the present tense in Greek, denoting a continuing experience, not a one-time or final state. This, again, suggests that "salvation" is a relationship with God that must be continually lived out, developed, matured, and perfected by God's grace, not a static "possession" that needs no attention. The promise for the one who perseveres in "growing in every way more and more like Christ" (Eph 4:15) points to the ultimate goal of God's purposes for us.

What Jesus is saying is that those who persevere in faithful discipleship will be restored in the image of Christ who is the image of God (Col 1:15) and that this is also the very nature of the New Jerusalem citizens. This becomes manifest in 21:11 where John sees the New Jerusalem filled "with the glory of God"—or, more literally, "having the glory (*doxa* [TG1391, ZG1518]) of God." The Greek word translated "glory" relates to the nature of the one being described. The New Jerusalem, therefore, has the essence of God's nature.

Those who are continually conquering "will become pillars in the Temple of my God, and they will never have to leave it" (3:12). The image originates in the description of Solomon's Temple (1 Kgs 7:15-22), where two huge pillars were erected on each side of the entrance into the presence of God. There may be a dual play upon the image. Those conquering live their lives of faithful discipleship in the presence of God. At the same time they are, for those who come to faith as a result of their witness, the entry into the presence of God. These are awesome promises to a weak yet faithful church.

How often in history has the church been weak, powerless, marginalized, and under tribulation at the hands of its culture? One thinks of the church in Romania under Communist rule: hounded, persecuted, imprisoned, tortured, and martyred. Yet it was the church that triggered the movement that ultimately brought down the brutal, dictatorial regime in 1989. After the fall of the regime an announcement appeared on the bulletin board of the Hungarian Reformed Church in Timişoara, which had been at the center of the storm: "The Lamb Won!" This church knew what it was to be a Philadelphia-type church—true followers of the powerless Lamb that was slain (Colson and Vaughn 2003:246-252).

And how often has a faithful group of disciples had to withstand not only the pressures of the state, but also the power of a state church? One thinks of the Confessing Church in Nazi Germany during World War II. They, too, knew what it was like to be a Philadelphia-type church.

In the words of Kenneth Leech: "Following the leadership of Jesus, his Church needs to stand as a sign of contradiction and of conflict, affecting and, as it were, upsetting through the power of the Gospel, mankind's criteria of judgment, determining values, points of interest, lines of thought, sources of inspiration, and models of life which are in contrast with the Word of God and the plan of salvation" (1985:391).

Always, at some level of its life, the church lives against the grain of its culture. When it does so, it loses the power and prestige that comes with being a supporter of the status quo. There is a powerful temptation to "play the world's games," to let the world set the agenda, to operate by the world's rules so as to be an "influence for God" in the world. After all, if, individually or corporately, we give up our positions of influence, prestige, and power in the world, how can we advance the kingdom? But in a kingdom established by a crucified Messiah, life comes through death, victory through defeat, strength through weakness, and power through powerlessness. We need a lot more Philadelphia-type churches in the world today.

◆ 7. Laodicea (3:14-22)

14 "Write this letter to the angel of the church in Laodicea. This is the message from the one who is the Amen—the faithful and true witness, the beginning* of God's new creation:

15 "I know all the things you do, that
you are neither hot nor cold. I wish
that you were one or the other! 16 But
since you are like lukewarm water,
neither hot nor cold, I will spit you out
of my mouth! 17 You say, 'I am rich. I
have everything I want. I don't need a
thing!' And you don't realize that you
are wretched and miserable and poor
and blind and naked. 18 So I advise you
to buy gold from me—gold that has
been purified by fire. Then you will be
rich. Also buy white garments from
me so you will not be shamed by your
nakedness, and ointment for your eyes
so you will be able to see. 19 I correct
and discipline everyone I love. So be
diligent and turn from your
indifference.

20 "Look! I stand at the door and
knock. If you hear my voice and open
the door, I will come in, and we will
share a meal together as friends.
21 Those who are victorious will sit
with me on my throne, just as I was
victorious and sat with my Father on
his throne.

22 "Anyone with ears to hear must
listen to the Spirit and understand
what he is saying to the churches."

3:14 Or *the ruler,* or *the source.*

NOTES

3:14 *angel.* Better translated as "messenger" (see note on 2:1).

the Amen. This is the only place in Revelation where Jesus is called "the Amen." "Amen" (*amēn* [TG281, ZG297]) comes from Hebrew and means "truly," "so be it." The term almost always follows an assertion of some sort in Revelation (1:6-7; 5:14; 19:4; 22:20-21). In 7:12, however, it both precedes and follows the assertion so as to heighten and emphasize that, "Blessing and glory and wisdom and thanksgiving and honor and power and strength belong to our God forever and ever!" This may be our clue to John's use at 3:14. "The Amen" precedes the attributes of Jesus to emphasize them.

faithful and true witness. Lit., "faithful martyr and true." In 1:5, Jesus was introduced as the "faithful witness" (see commentary there), and in 19:11 he is described as "faithful" and "true." To one of the most unfaithful churches, with a totally false self-perception (3:17), Jesus' attributes are a confrontation.

the beginning of God's new creation. In 21:6, God is described as "the Alpha and the Omega—the Beginning and the End," and in 22:13, Jesus says, "I am the Alpha and the Omega . . . the Beginning and the End." In 3:14, Jesus is the beginning of God's new creation. Jesus clearly indicates to the Laodicean church that "business as usual" is not what Christian life is all about. It is a new creation whose beginning in Jesus forecloses the old manner of life.

3:15-16 *you are neither hot nor cold . . . you are like lukewarm water.* The lukewarm image would not have been lost on the Laodiceans. The city had no fresh water supply. Drinking water had to be carried from the springs or the river in the valley below. Utility water was piped to Laodicea from hot mineral springs about six miles away near Hierapolis. By the time it reached the city it was lukewarm and, because of its high mineral content, would cause a person to vomit if it were drunk (Beale 1999:303; Witherington 2003:107). Jesus used this language to tell the Laodicean church that it did not stand out against the culture in which it lived, for it was neither cold nor hot.

Probably too much has been made over Jesus' statement, "I wish you were cold or hot." Some have suggested that "hot" referred to the healing mineral waters of the hot springs near Hierapolis and "cold" to the refreshing waters of Colossae. (For a full discussion of this view, see Hemer 1986.) It seems best, however, to simply infer that Jesus was indicating they should be distinct from their culture.

I will spit you out of my mouth! This is better translated as "I am about to vomit you out." Laodicea's accommodation to its culture made Jesus sick. Again, we see the possibility of people falling away from the faith. This element has been present in each of the "problem" and "perverse" churches. Ephesus was on the verge of having their lampstand removed (2:5), Pergamum was about to experience Jesus' warring against them (2:16), Thyatira had those who were about to be "killed with death" (see note on 2:23), and Sardis was in danger of having their name erased from the Book of Life (3:5).

3:17 *rich . . . have everything . . . you are wretched and miserable.* It would be hard to imagine two more radically different evaluations of the same group. The Laodiceans perceived themselves as rich, having everything they wanted, and not needing a thing. *First Enoch* 97:8 contains a similar image: "Woe to you who acquire silver and gold in unrighteousness and say: 'We have become rich with riches and have possessions; and have acquired everything we have desired.'"

3:18 *I advise you to buy gold from me . . . white garments . . . and ointment.* That the Laodiceans had, indeed, adopted the values of their culture becomes manifest as Jesus played off their three claims to fame. Laodicea was an extremely wealthy city rich in gold, it was the center of a garment industry for luxurious black garments, and it was famous for its eye salve.

3:19 ***correct and discipline.*** Or, "reprove and nurture." The first word, *elenchō* [TG1651, ZG1794], means to rebuke, to reprove, to convict. It is a stronger term than the English "correct," especially since Jesus was dealing with a church with such profound problems. The second word, *paideuō* [TG3811, ZG4084], represents the entire process by which an infant was nurtured, guided, trained, educated, disciplined, and brought to mature adulthood as a productive member of the community. Jesus was sharply confronting the Laodiceans with their failures yet, at the same time, offering them remedies for restoration.

everyone I love. Jesus indicated that this was not a vindictive, punitive action, but that of love, desiring their perfect wholeness.

be diligent. Lit., "be zealous." The term *zēleue* [TG2206A, ZG2418] means "to burn with zeal."

turn from your indifference. Lit., "repent" (NLT adds "from your indifference" based on context). "Repent" is the same term found in the letters to Ephesus (2:5), Pergamum (2:16), Thyatira (2:21-22), and Sardis (3:3), most of which are translated "repent" by the NLT. One of the two occurrences in 2:5 is translated "repent," the other "turn back." Two of the three occurrences in 2:21-22 are translated "repent," and the third "turn back." This is not merely turning from indifference. It is a call to a radical restructuring of one's perspectives and values.

3:20 ***I stand at the door.*** Jesus' position at the door is an enduring stance. The perfect tense can indicate that Jesus took this stance at some previous point and continues to maintain it. Perhaps John, in good rhetorical fashion, is here introducing, very obliquely, the cruciform nature of God/the Lamb, which he sees as the very essence of their being (12:1-5; 13:8)—that is, Christ's stance at the door that shuts him out of a person's life is inherent in his very nature as the Lamb who was slain from the foundation of the world.

knock. If you. Lit., "I am knocking. If anyone." The verb is in the present tense in Greek, as are the terms for "reprove" and "nurture" (3:19). The individual believer rather than the church is indicated as the subject/object by the singular terms that follow in the verse, lit., "anyone," "come in to him," "eat with him," "and he with me." Jesus continually stands at the closed doors of our lives and knocks. This is, most likely, the loving knock of reproof, as well as the invitation to open to nurture.

share a meal. The term *deipnēsō* [TG1172, ZG1268], is found in the NT for the Eucharist (Luke 17:8; 22:20; 1 Cor 11:25). The noun form, *deipnon* [TG1173, ZG1270], while used of other gatherings (Matt 23:6; Mark 6:21; Luke 14:12ff; John 12:2) during the ministry of Jesus, after the Resurrection is used only for the Eucharist (1 Cor 11:20ff). The Gospel of John uses it in association with Jesus' last meal with his disciples (John 13:2, 4; 21:20). In 19:9 and 17, John again uses this term in what seems to be a non-Eucharistic setting. However, the "wedding feast of the Lamb" (19:9) could be understood as the ultimate consummation of all Eucharists. By contrast, "the great banquet God has prepared" (19:17) could be seen as the obverse of the Eucharist for fallen Babylon. This meal is the "sacrament" of his presence that liberates, cleanses, heals, and transforms. Eating with the Son of Man is also an image of the restoration of the kingdom (see *1 Enoch* 62:13-14).

3:21 ***Those who are victorious.*** Lit., "the one who is conquering." The conquering ones are those who will be fully transformed into the image of Christ, which was God's initial purpose in creation (Gen 1:26-27) and God's redemptive purpose in Christ.

sat with my Father on his throne. Throughout the vision Jesus, the Lamb, is pictured with God on the throne. The throne is the place of God. It is the principle locus of the presence of God and, consequently, God's status and nature (cf. 7:17; 22:1, 3 for explicit images, and 5:6, 8, 13; 6:16; 7:9-10; 21:22 for implicit images).

COMMENTARY

Laodicea was one of the wealthiest cities of the Roman province of Asia. It was a major banking center located on both east-west and north-south trade routes about 40 miles southeast of Philadelphia and 100 miles east of Ephesus (cf. Mounce 1977:123). Like Philadelphia, Sardis, and Pergamum, Laodicea passed into Roman control through the will of Attalus III, the last of the Pergamene kings. In AD 60, Laodicea was destroyed by a major earthquake. Although offered assistance by Nero, Laodicea was so wealthy it rebuilt itself to even greater splendor than before.

Laodicea was also famous for its medical school whose "Phrygian powder," when mixed with oil, made an eye salve that was very effective in treating an eye disease prevalent in the area. It was also known for its luxurious black wool garments, which only the wealthy could afford. These local factors play a significant role in what Jesus said to the church.

The two churches receiving the severest rebuke from Jesus were Sardis and Laodicea. Sardis had the reputation of being alive, and Laodicea thought they were rich, had prospered, and needed nothing. The Laodicean church had almost totally accommodated the perspectives and values of its culture. The norms of the culture had become the standards by which they evaluated themselves. They fit comfortably and smoothly into the ebb and flow of their world. They did not exhibit compassion for the marginalized, concern for institutionalized injustice, or zeal to be agents of God's transforming grace in their broken and hurting world. They were not "hot." Neither did they exhibit coolness toward the destructive and dehumanizing values of their fallen Babylon world. They were not "cold." Their tepid, banal "lukewarmness" was totally innocuous in the world of Laodicea, confirming for those outside the church that their perspectives and values were perfectly fine.

Jesus told such a church that true riches come only through "fire" (3:18). On the one hand, this is the fire of God's holiness that purges the soul of all impurities, refines habits, burnishes behaviors, purifies relationships, and enables Christians to be the presence of God's love, truth, and grace in the world. On the other hand, it is the "fire" of adversity and opposition that reveals the weakness of our reliance upon our own strength, that probes our dependence upon popularity, power, or possessions as the source of our identity and signs of our success, drives us into the heart of God, and leads us to entrust our entire being to him. The life that has been through these "fires," in total reliance upon God, becomes "rich" in the quality of its wholeness, the depths of its peace, the heights of its joy, and the fullness of its love for God and others. With Charles Wesley it sings, "Refining fire, go through my heart, illuminate my soul; scatter thy life through every part, and sanctify the whole" ("Jesus, Thine All Victorious Love").

In contrast to the luxurious black garments produced in Laodicea, Jesus counseled the church to buy from him white garments to cover the shame of their nakedness (3:18). Unless we are "clothed with Christ" we stand vulnerable and exposed to the powers of the world's values and perspectives. The "body" of our being becomes wounded by the manipulations of others. That "body," the structure of perceptions, values, and behaviors unique to each individual, becomes scarred by rejection, broken by abuses, crippled by destructive relationships, deformed by dehumanizing structures of life. But when we "put on" a white garment in a world clothed in black, we stand out. To put on the garment Jesus offers sets us apart from our world. Instead of participating in the wounding of others by our manipulations, we become the means of their healing. Instead of scarring others with our rejection of them, we become agents of God's love that receives them into God's loving embrace. Instead of breaking others by our abuse of them, we become those through whom God heals. Instead of crippling others by controlling relationships, we become those in whom the love of God calls them to wholeness. Instead of participating in dehumanizing economic, political, or social structures that marginalize and dehumanize others, we become those through whom God affirms the full humanity of others.

When salve or "ointment" (3:18) is applied to the eyes, the initial result is a blurring of vision, a clouding of one's perceptions and perspectives. When we allow God to begin to apply to our eyes the salve of a Christlike perspective, our normal perspectives get changed. We perhaps experience what I believe G. K. Chesterton described well. He said the first time he read the Sermon on the Mount (Matt 5–7) he thought it was all upside down, but on a more reflective reading he came to realize that it was the world that was "upside down." Christ calls us to a radical new way of seeing our world, ourselves, and others.

Where do these "purchases" of true riches, true garments, and healing salve take place? These transactions wait to take place at those points in our lives where we have shut Jesus out and imprisoned ourselves within our own poverty, woundedness, and blindness. Jesus constantly stands at those closed doors and, in profound and costly love, knocks with his nail-scarred hand. He knocks in reproof of those attitudes, those habits, those perspectives, and those values in our lives that shut him out and imprison us within. He knocks with the offer of nurture to wholeness at the closed door of our brokenness, the offer of healing at the closed door of our woundedness, the offer of cleansing at the closed door of our sin, the offer of liberation at the closed door of our destructive bondages, and the offer of resurrection at the closed door of our deadness.

Jesus continually knocks, but only we can open. Opening can be scary. This may be why Jesus says, "If you hear my voice . . . open the door." We may hear the call (knock) of love, but it is powerless unless we open to its invasion. To open to love is to jeopardize our entire status quo. It is much more comfortable to stay safe behind our closed doors. To open to love is to endanger the entire false self we have constructed out of the world's false values and perspectives. If we open, however, we experience the invasion of love. Christ comes in and nurtures us toward wholeness. He enters into the most intimate fellowship (eating) with us and we with him. This is the heart of the Eucharist: It is the sacramental presence of Christ who cleanses us, liberates us, heals us, and nurtures us to wholeness in his own image (see note on 3:20; cf. Rom 8:29; 1 Cor 15:49; 2 Cor 3:18; Col 3:10).

This is, indeed, good news for the multitude of Laodicean-type churches in the world today, many of which espouse a "prosperity gospel"—a message that they should be wealthy and healthy because they are God's children. What Jesus said to the Laodicean church should give pause to the proclaimers and adherents of the "prosperity gospel."

◆ B. God and the Lamb (4:1–5:14)
1. God the Creator (4:1-11)

Then as I looked, I saw a door standing
open in heaven, and the same voice I had
heard before spoke to me like a trumpet
blast. The voice said, "Come up here, and
I will show you what must happen after
this." [2]And instantly I was in the Spirit,*
and I saw a throne in heaven and some-
one sitting on it. [3]The one sitting on the
throne was as brilliant as gemstones—like
jasper and carnelian. And the glow of an
emerald circled his throne like a rainbow.
[4]Twenty-four thrones surrounded him,
and twenty-four elders sat on them. They
were all clothed in white and had gold
crowns on their heads. [5]From the throne
came flashes of lightning and the rumble
of thunder. And in front of the throne
were seven torches with burning flames.
This is the sevenfold Spirit* of God. [6]In
front of the throne was a shiny sea of
glass, sparkling like crystal.

In the center and around the throne
were four living beings, each covered with
eyes, front and back. [7]The first of these
living beings was like a lion; the second
was like an ox; the third had a human face;
and the fourth was like an eagle in flight.
[8]Each of these living beings had six wings,
and their wings were covered all over with
eyes, inside and out. Day after day and
night after night they keep on saying,

"Holy, holy, holy is the Lord God,
the Almighty—
the one who always was, who is,
and who is still to come."

[9]Whenever the living beings give glory
and honor and thanks to the one sitting
on the throne (the one who lives forever
and ever), [10]the twenty-four elders fall
down and worship the one sitting on the
throne (the one who lives forever and
ever). And they lay their crowns before
the throne and say,

[11] "You are worthy, O Lord our God,
to receive glory and honor and
power.
For you created all things,
and they exist because you created
what you pleased."

4:2 Or *in spirit.* 4:5 Greek *They are the seven spirits.*

NOTES

4:1 *Then as I looked.* Lit., "After these things I saw." The term "looked" or "saw" (*eidon* [TG3708B, ZG3972]) appears 43 times in the vision (chs 4–22). Only five of those usages follow the phrase "after these things" (*meta tauta* [TG3326/3778A, ZG3552/4047]; 4:1; 7:1, 9; 15:5; 18:1). The uses in 7:1 and 7:9 may inform our understanding of John's style. Verses 7:1 and 7:9 introduce two halves of the interlude between the sixth and seventh seals. Since the interlude is integral to the opening of the seals, it doesn't seem logical to use "after" to translate either of them. It would make sense to use "in the midst of" or "along with." That is, the interlude is an integral part of the seals, not something separate and distinct (see note on 1:19). It may well be that John is indicating in 4:1 that what he is now seeing is an integral part of what went before and not a separate or subsequent element. That is, John's visionary experience coincided with his writing of the letters to the churches—while writing, he saw an open door in heaven and heard the voice dictating the letters and inviting him to come up. We must not make the mistake of thinking that because John presents his vision in a structure and content his hearers will understand that this is how he experienced it. (Visionary experience is further discussed under "Literary Style" in the Introduction and at the notes on 4:2.) In 15:5, John expands on the open Temple in heaven from 11:19, both passages representing the "bridge" verses between the second heavenly vision (11:19–15:4) and the seven trumpets (8:6–11:18) and the seven bowls (15:5–16:21). Again, it would seem better in the structure of John's recounting of his vision to translate 15:5 as "in the midst of these things" or "along with these things," although "then" is certainly acceptable. Verse 18:1 also continues the flow and deepens the focus of the vision of the judgment of the harlot, fallen Babylon (17:1–19:10), and implies "in the midst of" or "along with." The other uses of the phrase translated "after these things" (1:19; 9:12; 20:3) all require the "after" because of the clearly temporal setting of the context.

I saw a door standing open in heaven. Each of the three pieces of the core of the heavenly vision begins with a statement of something being opened. Here it is merely a door in heaven, in 11:19 the whole Temple in heaven is open (repeated at the close of the unit in 15:5), and in 19:11 all of heaven is open.

the same voice I had heard before. See 1:10. The fact that Jesus invited John to enter the door ("Come up here"), suggests that Jesus is the open door into God's realm. The "door" may echo John's Gospel where Jesus is the "door" of the sheepfold (John 10:7, 9). Another textual echo might be John 14:6, where Jesus says, "No one can come to the Father except through me." Through the "door" of Jesus we see God. Thus, an essential part of the revelation of Jesus the Messiah is the revelation of God, God's purposes, and God's action.

I will show you what must happen. The Greek terms behind "show" and "what must happen" are repeated from 1:1 (see note), where the revelation of Jesus the Messiah is to show God's servants things that "must soon take place." (The same phrase is also found in 22:6.) John is returning to the core of the vision.

after this. In 1:19, John is told to write, lit., "the things that will happen after these things," while in 1:1 it is things that must happen "soon" (or "quickly" or "in proper order") that are to be shown. The Greek represented in 4:1 as "after this" is the same as that in 1:19. It would seem that John's use of "after these things" here and in 1:19 confirms the interpretation of "soon" at 1:1 (see note) as not indicative of a short time frame; rather, God is fulfilling his purposes according to his own plan (i.e., "in proper order").

4:2 ***instantly I was in the Spirit.*** This is John's only use of the word (*eutheōs* [TG2112, ZG2311]) in the vision. When coupled with "I was in the Spirit," it forces us back to the exact same phrase that begins John's visionary experience in 1:10 (see commentary). By this link and the mention of the voice he had heard before (4:1; cf. 1:10), John indicates that 1:10 and 4:1 are inseparably conjoined. Thus, I don't think we are being told of a new vision. Rather, I believe we are up against the reality of visionary experience.

A visionary experience is a unitive experience, similar to standing in the center of a cyclorama. One is immersed in an enveloping reality, often with sound and lights added to the visual representation. (The cyclorama at Gettysburg National Military Park, Gettysburg, PA, is a good example: You find yourself in the midst of the hottest part of the battle that is portrayed all around you on the walls; you hear the whine and buzz of bullets, the roar of cannon, and you see the flashes of light at their discharge; you hear the cries of the dying and wounded, the shouts of orders, etc.) But how would you describe the experience to someone who has never been there? You would have to break it into segments and describe each segment separately. I think this is what John was doing. The repetition of "I was in spirit" (*egenomēn en pneumati* [TG1096/1722/4151, ZG1181/1877/4460]) in 1:10 and 4:2 indicates that what follows 4:2 is another aspect of John's vision of Jesus in 1:10ff. John was simply shifting our focus to another facet of the cyclorama, not to a new vision. So the vision of Jesus carrying him into heaven is, at the same instant, what provided John the message of Jesus for the churches in 1:10–3:22.

I saw a throne in heaven and someone sitting on it. The throne is representative of God's sovereignty and rule. This is the image of God as the king who rules over the kingdom that has been created by the Messiah (1:5-6; 5:10). In a good study of the role of "throne" in the NT, Ekola (2001:362-363, 367-368) indicates that "the enthroned Christ sits where the King of Israel should be sitting, [thus] Old Testament passages and ideas were given a Christocentric rendering. Furthermore, Christ was revered as a divine being on the throne. . . . [Thus,] exaltation Christology reinterpreted the core of traditional Jewish theology, the basic idea of theocracy, i.e., meeting with God. In the New Testament theocracy became Christocracy."

4:3 ***jasper and carnelian.*** These were the last (jasper) and first (carnelian) jewels on the breastplate of the high priest (Exod 39:8-14). Thus, God is imaged in the role of High Priest, which is consistent with the following image of the 24 elders who, we will see, represent God's kingdom of priests (see note on 4:4). God is not only King, he is also High Priest over the priests (1:6; 5:10). For those in John's audience acquainted with the OT, this would indicate the fulfillment of God's purposes for the original covenant (Exod 19:6). The reversal of the order of the stones (from that in the OT) may hint at the idea that God's fulfillment has come in a manner radically different from what the Jews had expected. This may be reiterated in 21:19-20 where the foundations of the walls of New Jerusalem are pictured as the 12 stones on the breastplate, but with their order rearranged (see notes on 21:18-21).

the glow of an emerald circled his throne like a rainbow. Normally, this image would be expected to have its origins in the Noah story and represent God's mercy in the midst of judgment. But, as Beale (1999:321) notes, the image likely also represents God's glory, the manifestation of his nature, which the NLT has picked up well. The emerald nature of the rainbow gives the image still another nuance. Since John had already pointed his readers in the direction of the breastplate of the High Priest in his use of jasper and carnelian to describe God, it would be reasonable to assume that the use of emerald is to be understood in the same frame of reference. The emerald was the third stone in the breastplate (Exod 28:17; 39:10) and, in some numerations of the tribes of Israel, Judah is the third tribe (Num 1:7; 13:6; Deut 27:12). If the emerald is to be equated with Judah, the rainbow may represent the manifestation of God's glorious being in Christ—the Lamb (also the Lion of the tribe of Judah—5:5) that is with God on the throne (7:9, 17; 22:1; 22:3).

4:4 ***Twenty-four thrones surrounded him, and twenty-four elders sat on them.*** The number is significant in the OT with respect to the number of the divisions of the priesthood. There were 24 courses of priests whose role was to maintain the perpetual service and worship of God at the Temple in Jerusalem (1 Chr 24:1-19). The elders represent those whom the Messiah has made "priests" (1:6; 5:10). Just as the priests represented the entire Jewish community before God, the elders represent the priests of God created by the Messiah. Thus, the elders represent all believers.

The reason the elders are seated on thrones probably has its origin in Jesus' promise to the disciples that they would sit on thrones "judging" (i.e., "leading," as in the book of Judges) the 12 tribes of Israel (Matt 19:28; Luke 22:30). Perhaps more relevant to John's vision than the Gospel references is Paul's image in his statement that those who have been made alive together with Christ have been raised up with him and seated with him in the heavenly places (Eph 2:6).

They were all clothed in white. White garments are the garb of the redeemed, another implication that the elders represent the people of God (see note on 3:4). The image of white garments is also found in 3:4-5, 18; 6:11; 7:9, 14; 19:8, 14. The last reference to white garments in the vision (19:14) also introduces the fabric of the garment as linen. Those who follow the Word of God are clothed in "the finest of pure white linen." In 19:8, the bride of the Lamb (the church) "has been given the finest of pure white linen," which, John tells us, "represents the good deeds of God's holy people." The permission for the bride to wear the finest linen is somewhat unusual since linen was the cloth of kings (1 Chr 15:27) and priests (Exod 39:27-29). But the people of God are God's kingdom and priests!

gold crowns on their heads. We have already seen that the faithful citizens of New Jerusalem have crowns (3:11), indicating again that the elders represent God's people. Such imagery is not foreign to first-century Judaism. The book of 2 Esdras has the following account:

> I, Ezra, saw on Mount Zion a great multitude that I could not number, and they all were praising the Lord with songs. In their midst was a young man of great stature, taller than any of the others, and on the head of each of them he placed a crown, but he was more exalted than they. And I was held spellbound. Then I asked an angel, "Who are these, my lord?" He answered and said to me, "These are they who have put off mortal clothing and have put on the immortal, and have confessed the name of God. Now they are being crowned, and receive palms." Then I said to the angel, "Who is that young man who is placing crowns on them and putting palms in their hands?" He answered and said to me, "He is the Son of God, whom they confessed in the world" (2 Esdr 2:42-47, NRSV).

This imagery reinforces the idea that John's imagery indicates that the elders represent the priestly people of God's kingdom.

4:5 ***flashes of lightning and the rumble of thunder.*** Lit., "lightning, voices, and thunders." These are typical manifestations of God (Exod 19:16), which recur again throughout John's vision (8:5; 11:19; 16:18).

seven torches with burning flames. This is the sevenfold Spirit of God. This continues the priestly imagery because in the sanctuary of the Temple in Jerusalem was the lampstand with seven lamps (Exod 25:31) that stood before the Lord (Lev 24:4). The imagery is repeated in 1:4; 3:1; and 5:6, and represents the fullness of the Spirit of God.

4:6 ***a shiny sea of glass, sparkling like crystal.*** This demands attention because in the vision of the new creation, John explicitly says, "The sea was also gone" (21:1). It is also to be noted that the first of the core of heavenly visions (4:1–5:14) opens with the image of the sea (4:6) and the last of the core heavenly visions (19:11–21:8) closes with the image of the sea (21:1). Furthermore, in the second heavenly vision (11:19–15:4) the beast that exercises Satan's power comes from the sea (13:1) and, at the close of the vision, the redeemed (defined as "the people who had been victorious over the beast") are seen with the sea of glass beneath their feet (15:2). In both the Roman and Jewish pool of images, "sea" represented the abode of demonic and evil powers (Caird 1966:65ff; Beale 1999:327). It would seem that John used the image of the sea to represent the realm of evil from which the beast emerges (13:1), over which the saints are victorious (15:2—both introduced with the phrase "like a glass sea"), and which has no place in God's new creation (21:2). The image of such a sea before the throne is a powerful picture of the sovereignty of God over the realm of evil.

In the center and around the throne were four living beings. These living beings (*zōa* [TG2226, ZG2442]) seem to represent the created order, in particular the animate order of creation (Beale 1999:329). John seems to be indicating that creation is not something separate and independent from God—the four living beings are "in the center of the throne." Creation emerges out of the very presence of God and continues to be the place of God's abiding presence—the four living beings are "around the throne." There is no "spirit/matter" dualism in John's vision.

each covered with eyes. See note on 4:8.

4:7 ***lion . . . ox . . . human . . . eagle.*** This is a modulation of Ezekiel's vision of God where four living creatures have the same attributes but in a very different configuration (Ezek 1:4-18). See Beale (1999:329-332) for a full analysis of the options regarding the four living creatures. Beale's position, like mine, is that these creatures "represent the whole of animate life" (1999:332). Witherington concurs that they are "heavenly archetypes of the whole of the animate creation" (2003:118). Malina goes further in seeing them as symbolizing "the whole created cosmos" (1993:80). It may be enough to see them as archetypes of the created order, the heavenly reality of which the natural order is the Incarnation.

4:8 ***Each of these living beings had six wings.*** The image of six wings is taken from Isaiah's vision of God (Isa 6:2), but John doesn't describe their use, as Isaiah did, presuming his readers would understand the image.

covered all over with eyes. This concurs with Ezek 1:18. Neither there nor here is any explanation given. In Rev 5:6, however, the Lamb has seven eyes, which are identified as the sevenfold Spirit of God present in the world. Since John presents creation as so intimately associated with God, the fullness of eyes may represent a way of expressing the omnipresence of God in all creation.

Day after day and night after night. John emphasizes that creation never ceases to praise God. Like the seraphim of Isaiah (Isa 6:1-3), the four creatures praise God for his holiness using a triple repetition of the word "holy." The triple repetition emphasizes the absolute holiness of God, three being another image of totality in the Jewish pool of images.

the one who always was, who is, and who is still to come. This same expression is found in 1:4 (see note).

4:9-10 ***the twenty four elders fall down and worship.*** The elders are continually falling, worshiping, and casting their crowns. The Greek has the future tense here since it is describing what the elders will do "whenever" the four living beings praise God. Since the beings do this unceasingly, the elders will continually bow, worship, and cast their crowns.

4:11 ***they exist because you created what you pleased.*** Lit., "by your will they existed and were created." John indicated that creation existed in the heart of God ("they existed") before it was incarnate as creation ("and were created").

COMMENTARY

A major crux of interpretation arises at this point in Revelation. How does the section 4:1–22:21 relate to what has come before (1:1–3:22)? One school of interpretation holds that at 4:1, John begins to see what will take place in the last days, although there is much diversity among interpreters as to the details. This school most often interprets the seven churches as seven ages of church history (see commentary on 2:1), after which God will bring history to a close. If, however, we realize that the seven churches are representative of the entire church in every age of Christian history and that the "core" of heavenly vision is balanced by pairs of visionary elements that relate to human life in history, the distinction between 4:1–22:21 and the first three chapters can be viewed in an alternative way.

	Introduction (1:1-9)	
	Earthly Vision (1:10-20)	
Seven Churches (2:1–3:22)	Heavenly Vision (4:1–5:14)	Seven Seals (6:1–8:5)
Seven Trumpets (8:6–11:18)	Heavenly Vision (11:19–15:4)	Seven Bowls (15:5–16:21)
Harlot = Fallen Babylon (17:1–19:10)	Heavenly Vision (19:11–21:8)	Bride = New Jerusalem (21:9–22:9)
	Conclusion (22:10-21)	

The groups of seven (churches in 2:1–3:22; seals in 6:1–8:5; trumpets in 8:6–11:18; bowls in 15:5–16:21), together with the visions of the harlot (17:1–19:10) and bride (21:9–22:9), all reveal the past, present, and future realities of two realms of human existence—New Jerusalem and fallen Babylon. These two realms, like Jesus' parable of the wheat and the weeds (Matt 13:24-30), exist throughout history as mutually inimical—New Jerusalem experiencing tribulation at the hands of fallen Babylon, and fallen Babylon experiencing radical disruption at the presence of New Jerusalem in its midst. The "core" of heavenly vision (4:1–5:14; 11:19–15:4; 19:11–21:8) reveals the profound realities of what God has done, is doing, and will do in Jesus the Messiah, especially in the cross, and its effects on the two realms of human existence. This is previewed in John's introduction and inaugural vision of Jesus. Jesus is the ruler of the kings of the earth (1:5) who has the keys of Death and Hades (1:18)—images of radical disruption for fallen Babylon; and he has made his people a kingdom (1:6) and is present in their midst (1:12)—images of enduring permanence for New Jerusalem, even though its citizens experience tribulation at the hands of fallen Babylon (1:9).

With the interplay of earthly and heavenly in the rest of the vision, John's expression "instantly I was in the Spirit" may have been a signal to his audience that, having given them the "earthly" aspect of the vision (1:9–3:22), he was now giving them the "heavenly" aspect. In the earthly portion of his experience, John saw seven gold lampstands with the Son of Man standing in the midst (1:12-13). Along with this, in the heavenly portion, he saw "a throne in heaven and someone sitting on it" (4:2). Since the vision reveals that Jesus is the Lamb who shares the throne with God, it seems that John was here describing the heavenly side of the same reality of which he just described the earthly side in 1:9–3:22. I think chapters 1–3 and 4–5 are two aspects of a single reality that has both earthly (chs 1–3) and heavenly (chs 4–5) dimensions. In John's portrayal of the earthly dimension, Jesus is seen in the midst of the seven lampstands, later identified as the seven churches. In chapter 5, Jesus is closely linked to God and the throne (5:6, 13), and in the rest of the vision God and the Lamb are conjoined on the throne (3:21—which conjoins Jesus and the faithful believers with God on the throne, thus conjoining the earthly and heavenly aspects!—7:9-10, 17; 22:1, 3). Thus, John is introducing the heavenly dimension of the vision for which the earthly dimension was given in chapters 1–3. As John's original audience moved from Jesus' address to the churches (2:1–3:22) into the first heavenly vision (4:1–5:14), they would have begun to comprehend through 4:1–22:21 the larger reality within which their life in the world was set, and to see more fully what faithful discipleship entailed.

John's vision in chapter 4 includes several profound theological truths. First, God is absolutely sovereign over the realm of rebellion. The rebellious realm is not a realm equal and opposite to God's realm. John sees it imaged as the sea under God's feet (4:6). In the rest of the vision we will see, again and again, that God is in complete control over the realm of rebellion. Second, there is no spirit/matter dualism in John's vision. The created order is not seen as "evil" as opposed to the spiritual realm—a view of the world held by those with a dualistic philosophy (e.g., the nascent Gnostic movements of John's time). The creation is intimately and inseparably linked with God. Third, there is no pantheism in John's vision. Creation is not God, nor is God confined within creation. Creation emerges out of God and is subordinate to God as seen in the constant praise creation gives to God. Fourth, the vision reveals the place of humanity in God's creation. While humanity is part of the entire created order (one of the four creatures is human), humanity also sits on thrones with golden crowns (4:4). This may be the vision's way of indicating that humanity, while part of creation, is intended to be in the image and likeness of God.

In the action of the elders, John sees the essence of what our relationship with God is to be. John tells us that the elders are constantly falling before the throne, worshiping God, and casting their crowns before the throne (4:9-11). Yet, in 5:5, and again in 7:13, an elder is seen talking with John. This suggests that the action of the elders before the throne is the inner dynamic of their relationship with God, which prevails in the midst of all other activities. What is that inner dynamic?

First, the elders fall before the throne. This posture represents an acknowledgment of God as absolute deity. Second, they worship God. How is this different from acknowledging God to be God? It is one thing to acknowledge God to be God, quite something else to allow God to be God in your life. According to many polls, the great majority of people in America today acknowledge belief in God, but it certainly doesn't appear that anywhere near as many allow God to be God in their lives. Even the demons believe that God is God (Jas 2:19), and while they shudder, they certainly do not allow God to be God in their being, though presumably they could. Third, the elders continually cast their crowns before the throne. The crown represents authority, rule, control. Here we see the elders yielding the control of their lives to God. They are allowing God to be God in their life on God's terms, not theirs.

It is possible for us to acknowledge God to be God and to allow God to be God in our lives—but on our terms! We define God for ourselves in ways that allow us to cling to many attitudes, habits, and relationships that are precious to us but actually damaging. We set the boundaries with respect to what God can and cannot do in our life. We attempt to appease God or manipulate him for our own purposes. We want a God who will fit more or less comfortably into our agendas, not upset our status quo, not impact the structures of our relationships, not question our values, not turn our world upside down. This kind of relationship with God will never lead us out of our brokenness into the wholeness of being in God's image; it will never heal our woundedness and bring light to our darkness. Only the radical abandonment of ourselves to God—casting the crown—will lead us into such transformation.

The casting of the crown is a continual process, not a one-time act. God has created us to have the kind of relationship with him that if our "yes" of obedience is to have any meaning, we must be equally free to say "no." If we cannot say "no" to God, then we cease to be beings created with free will. The holy life is a life whose steady habit is saying "yes" to God—casting the crown—in each and every situation and relationship even though there is always the possibility to say "no" in that situation or relationship.

The action of the elders reveals to us the deep inner dynamics of God's priests, the members of his kingdom and citizens of the New Jerusalem. It is interesting that later in the vision John sees the deep inner dynamics of the citizens of fallen Babylon as manifest in the one whom they worship—the beast. John sees that the beast has a blasphemous nature (13:1) that manifests itself in three actions (13:6): (1) it blasphemes God—it does not acknowledge God to be God; (2) it blasphemes God's nature (lit., "name")—it does not allow God to be God in its life; (3) it blasphemes God's rule ("those who dwell in heaven," i.e., those who allow God to be God on God's terms)—it does not cast the crown. Just as the elders model the life and worship of New Jerusalem, the beast models the life and worship of fallen Babylon. Notice that the fallen Babylon's life is a negative relationship with God, the perverse reversal of the life of New Jerusalem.

This portion of John's vision provides us a good means of testing our citizenship. What are the deep inner dynamics of our relationship with God? Are our hearts continually falling before the throne, worshiping God, and radically yielding themselves to God? Or are there places in our lives where we do not acknowledge God, do not worship, and do not abandon ourselves to God? At those places in our lives we are still under the sway of fallen Babylon.

The last line of the elders' song proclaims a profound truth concerning our self-identity. The elders sing, "For you created everything; through your will they existed and were created" (4:11; my translation). The order "existed . . . were created" indicates that we existed in the heart of God before we became incarnate in our human existence. It is not that we were souls waiting to come to earth via the creation of birth, rather that we were beings already brought into being in the heart and mind of God. In the mystery of God's omniscience and foreknowledge we already existed before we were created (as John sees in 4:11)—the essence of our soul is the indwelling presence of God and existed in nascent form before our incarnation. One aspect here is an affirmation of God's omniscience—there are no surprises. Another aspect is what the Mothers and Fathers of the church have claimed, that we are beings who "emerge" from the being of God and have our true being in loving union with God who is present at the core of every person:

> *Love tends to union, to identification—expressed by Catherine [of Genoa] more boldly perhaps than by any other mystic. God is "my being, my self, my strength, my beatitude." She is speaking here of Love as identification to which one can attain ". . . not by sharing, but by true transformation into God."* (Saint 1986:313)

> *This Spirit of God, dwelling in us, given to us, to be as it were our own Spirit, enables us to know and experience, in a mysterious manner, the reality and presence of the divine mercy in ourselves. So the Holy Spirit is intimately united to our own inmost self, and His presence in us makes our "I" the "I" of God.* (Merton 1983:210)

We were not an unplanned pregnancy, an unwanted child, an accident. No. Long before a man and woman came together to conceive each one of us, God chose us before the foundation of the world. In the words of John's vision, all things existed in the heart of God before they were created—before each one of us was created, we were. Here is where we find our true identity and our true value. (For a fuller development of this, see Mulholland 2006:71-73.)

Before concluding this chapter, it should be noted that there is a remarkable similarity between John's vision of God on the throne here and his vision of New Jerusalem in chapter 21. Here in chapter 4 John sees God on the throne; New Jerusalem is the place of God's throne (21:1, 3). In chapter 4 God's appearance is like jasper; New Jerusalem, which has the nature of God ("[shining] with the glory of God"), appears like jasper (21:11). In chapter 4 God is surrounded by four living creatures; New Jerusalem is a "square"—i.e., four equal sides (21:16). In chapter 4 God is surrounded by 24 elders; New Jerusalem is surrounded by 24 elements (12 gates and 12 foundation stones; 21:12-14). These similarities suggest that John was describing the same reality in two different forms.

◆ 2. The redeemer Lamb (5:1-14)

Then I saw a scroll* in the right hand of the one who was sitting on the throne. There was writing on the inside and the outside of the scroll, and it was sealed with seven seals. 2And I saw a strong angel, who shouted with a loud voice: "Who is worthy to break the seals on this scroll and open it?" 3But no one in heaven or on earth or under the earth was able to open the scroll and read it.

4Then I began to weep bitterly because no one was found worthy to open the scroll and read it. 5But one of the twenty-four elders said to me, "Stop weeping! Look, the Lion of the tribe of Judah, the heir to David's throne,* has won the victory. He is worthy to open the scroll and its seven seals."

6Then I saw a Lamb that looked as if it had been slaughtered, but it was now standing between the throne and the four living beings and among the twenty-four elders. He had seven horns and seven eyes, which represent the sevenfold Spirit* of God that is sent out into every part of the earth. 7He stepped forward and

took the scroll from the right hand of the one sitting on the throne. [8]And when he took the scroll, the four living beings and the twenty-four elders fell down before the Lamb. Each one had a harp, and they held gold bowls filled with incense, which are the prayers of God's people. [9]And they sang a new song with these words:

"You are worthy to take the scroll
and break its seals and open it.
For you were slaughtered, and your blood has ransomed people for God
from every tribe and language and people and nation.
10 And you have caused them to become
a Kingdom of priests for our God.
And they will reign* on the earth."

[11]Then I looked again, and I heard the voices of thousands and millions of angels around the throne and of the living beings and the elders. [12]And they sang in a mighty chorus:

"Worthy is the Lamb who was slaughtered—
to receive power and riches
and wisdom and strength
and honor and glory and blessing."

[13]And then I heard every creature in heaven and on earth and under the earth and in the sea. They sang:

"Blessing and honor and glory and power
belong to the one sitting on the throne
and to the Lamb forever and ever."

[14]And the four living beings said, "Amen!" And the twenty-four elders fell down and worshiped the Lamb.

5:1 Or *book;* also in 5:2, 3, 4, 5, 7, 8, 9. **5:5** Greek *the root of David.* See Isa 11:10. **5:6** Greek *which are the seven spirits.* **5:10** Some manuscripts read *they are reigning.*

NOTES

5:1 ***right hand.*** This denotes the action of the person, the outward manifestation in behavior of the nature of the person. The scroll in God's right hand, therefore, has something to do with God's action, the implementation of God's purpose.

There was writing on the inside and the outside of the scroll. Whether the book was a scroll or a codex (suggested by Comfort 2005:27-30), the image here suggests that this book is completely full. There is no space for anything more to be added. It is, most likely, a representation of the fullness of God's purposes. (Ezekiel 2:9-10 also features a scroll written on both sides. The image from Ezekiel coincides with that in Rev 10:9-11, where, like Ezekiel, John is told to eat the scroll.)

seven seals. Since "seven" is the number of totality, or completeness, this image indicates total sealing, such that nothing can be taken from the scroll. John seems to have seen the immutable, complete purpose of God.

5:2 ***to break the seals on this scroll and open it.*** This is reversed in the Greek text, which reads "to open the scroll and to loose its seals." The NLT cuts through the puzzle, but doesn't solve it. If a sealed document is opened, the seals are necessarily broken. The vision seems to be placing the focus upon the disclosure of the scroll, the revealing of the purposes of God. It may also be pointing to the fact that the scroll and its "sealing" are not literal; the seals are an image suggesting that nothing can be taken from the scroll. The "opening" of each seal discloses another dimension of God's purposes, and the one "worthy" to open is the one who can disclose the fullness of God's purpose.

5:3 ***no one in heaven or on earth or under the earth.*** John saw that no one in the entire created order is able to disclose the purposes of God, neither heavenly beings ("no one in heaven"), living humans ("on earth"), or those who have died ("under the earth").

5:4 ***I began to weep.*** John wept because the disclosure of the consummation of God's purposes was seemingly unattainable.

5:5 ***the Lion of the tribe of Judah, the heir to David's throne.*** These are clear messianic images. The expression "lion of Judah" originated in Jacob's blessing of Judah: "Judah . . . is a young lion" (Gen 49:9). By the late intertestamental period it had clearly taken on messianic connotations: "as for the lion that you saw . . . this is the Messiah . . . who shall spring forth from the seed of David" (*4 Ezra* 12:31-32). (Though the final redaction of *4 Ezra* was early second-century AD, the "eagle vision" from which this citation is taken is generally dated in the late 60s AD, about the same time as John's vision.) Judah was the tribe of David (1 Chr 2:1-2, 5, 9-13), whose heir Isaiah prophesied would be the Messiah (Isa 9:6-7; 11:1-12).

has won the victory. He is worthy to open the scroll. The Greek structure indicates that the Lion of the tribe of Judah, the heir to David's throne, "has conquered to open" the scroll and its seven seals. The Greek syntax here is a finite verb followed by an infinitive (*enikēsen . . . anoixai* [TG3528/455, ZG3771/487]). Greek often uses this combination to denote the purpose of the finite verb. In this case, the purpose of the "conquering" was "to open." We will see throughout John's vision that the cross is the conquering that discloses the depths not only of God's purposes (see 1:18; 5:9b-10; 11:3-13; 19:11–20:3), but also of God's very being (see notes on 12:1-6).

5:6 ***I saw a Lamb that looked as if it had been slaughtered.*** Instead of a mighty, powerful, victorious Lion, John saw a Lamb—moreover, one that had been slain.

between the throne. The Greek text has "in the midst of the throne" (*en mesō* [TG1722/3319A, ZG1877/3545] *tou thronou*). This reading is confirmed by the instances where God and the Lamb are together on the throne (see note on 3:21). Wright (1996:625-626) traces the development of the image of the Son of Man as one who shares the throne with God from Ezekiel through the intertestamental period, which results in the image of the Son of Man as one who shares the throne with God. The Lamb is, therefore, in some measure, God.

among the twenty-four elders. But the Lamb is also "among the twenty-four elders." As such, he is fully identified with the redeemed just as he is present in the midst of the seven lampstands—the churches (1:13). Thus, in himself the Lamb conjoins God and redeemed humanity.

He had seven horns and seven eyes, which represent the sevenfold Spirit of God. Since horns are images of power, seven horns represent totality of power. The seven eyes depict the fullness of the Spirit of God (lit., "the seven spirits of God").

5:8 ***the four living beings and the twenty-four elders fell down before the Lamb.*** In 4:8-10 these two groups are portrayed as never ceasing to fall before God and sing his praises. We now see another dimension of that praise and adoration. This is yet another indication that the vision bonds Jesus and God together.

harp. This is the standard instrument mentioned for accompaniment in the Psalter, the songs of praise to God (e.g., Pss 33:2-3; 43:4; 71:22). The image appears again in 14:2 and 15:2.

gold bowls filled with incense, which are the prayers of God's people. This is an image deeply rooted in Jewish history. The morning and evening prayers in the synagogues were timed to coincide with the morning and evening incense offering at the Temple in Jerusalem. Even during the incense offering in the Temple, the people were outside praying (Luke 1:10). For the image of the "incense" linked to "the prayers of God's people," see notes on 8:3-5. One of the primary prayers of God's people in Jewish history was for deliverance from bondage and the restoration of the kingdom, bringing the fulfillment of God's covenant and promises. The following song suggests that these prayers have been answered because of what the Lamb has done.

5:9 ***new song.*** This is not something never sung before at all (in that case the Greek would have been *neos* [TG3501, ZG3742]), but a new version of something that previously existed (thus Gr. *kainos* [TG2537, ZG2785]). The previous song would have been the praise of God's deliverance and creation of his covenant people from bondage in Egypt with the purpose of making them a kingdom of priests (Exod 19:6). The "new song" is for the deliverance of people from bondage to fallen Babylon and making them a kingdom and priests (1:6; 5:10).

You are worthy to take the scroll. The Lamb is worthy to open the scroll, to disclose God's purposes, because he is himself the incarnation of God's purposes. He is the one in whom the fullness of God's power and presence has gone forth into the world.

you were slaughtered, and your blood has ransomed people for God. The opening of the scroll, the disclosure of God's purpose, could now happen because Jesus had been killed on the cross. In that act, his blood ransomed people for God. Just as the blood of the Passover Lamb "ransomed" Israel from bondage in Egypt to become God's people (Exod 12–14), so the blood of the Lamb ransomed people for God.

from every tribe and language and people and nation. This phrase, which threads its way through John's vision (7:9; 10:11 ["kings" instead of "tribes"]; 11:9; 13:7; 14:6; 17:15), represents those once held in the destructive and dehumanizing bondage of fallen Babylon. All citizens of God's kingdom, his New Jerusalem, began as citizens of fallen Babylon. The kingdom has now been expanded to include all people, thereby fulfilling the covenant promise to Abraham that through him all the families of the earth will be blessed (Gen 12:3).

5:10 ***to become a Kingdom of priests.*** This means becoming the restored and fulfilled covenant community of God's people (see commentary on 1:6). The image of a kingdom of priests was active in the intertestamental period, as seen in *Jubilees* 16:18.

they will reign. This is the reading of *a* $\mathfrak{M}^A$ it cop. Other mss (A $\mathfrak{M}^K$) read, "they are reigning," using a present rather than a future tense (so NLT mg). It is extremely difficult to understand why a later scribe would have changed a future tense to a present, but quite easy to understand why it would be changed from the present to the future, especially as Revelation became viewed in a more futuristic frame of reference. As we have noted up to this point, John's vision reveals that in Jesus as Messiah, God has restored the kingdom to Israel and fulfilled the promise of the old covenant. This, together with the likelihood of a change from a present to a future tense, strongly suggests that the present tense should be read here. At 20:4, the same phrase appears with the aorist tense (generally referring to completed action), while at 20:6 and 22:5 it is again in the future tense (see notes on these verses.)

on the earth. This image represents fallen Babylon, not the planet earth. John sees the kingdom of priests ruling upon the "earth" (Babylon) here. Similarly, in 15:2 John sees the same group (there described as "the people who had been victorious over the beast and his statue"), standing upon the sea, which is another symbol for the rebellious realm (see discussion of "earth" in note on 3:10, and the discussion of "sea" in note on 4:6). The symbols of earth and sea are used together in 10:2, 5, 8.

5:11 ***thousands and millions.*** Lit., "myriads of myriads and thousands of thousands," which computes to 100,000,000,000,000 (10,000 x 10,000 x 1,000 x 1,000), which is 100 trillion, an absolutely incomprehensible number for a first or twenty-first century reader.

angels around the throne . . . living beings . . . elders. This completes John's vision of heaven. Rather than a place, heaven is seen as a community whose center is God and the Lamb.

5:12 ***power and riches and wisdom and strength and honor and glory and blessing.*** This is the perfection or fullness of praise, as indicated by seven attributes.

5:13 ***every creature . . . on earth and . . . in the sea.*** Lit., "every creature . . . upon (*epi* [TG1909, ZG2093]) earth and . . . upon (*epi*) the sea." The use of *epi* is important because as pointed out in the note on 5:10, God's kingdom of priests are those whose posture is "upon" the earth (5:10) and "upon" the sea (15:2). The text later describes the citizens of fallen Babylon as "in" (*en* [TG1722, ZG1877]) the sea (20:13) and "in" the earth (13:12).

COMMENTARY

Human knowledge and wisdom cannot probe the depths of God's purposes—an important truth for us to remember. In our information age, it is easy for us to think that the human mind is capable of knowing all things. Given enough time, research, experimentation, coupled with the computer's ability to amass and synthesize data and the Internet's ability to bring multiple human minds into a larger community of knowledge, we think we can know all and do all.

John's weeping depicts the true human predicament. We are powerless to discern the fullness of the purpose of God. No matter how far-ranging our quest, we fail. We usually end by presuming that the purpose of God is defined by the narrow parameters of our own plans, purposes, and desires. Even when we have some general insight into God's purposes, their fulfillment usually surprises us.

The Jews believed, correctly, that "the Lion of the tribe of Judah," the Davidic Messiah, would come as a conquering warrior to defeat their enemies and reestablish Israel's kingdom as the premier kingdom of the world (Gen 49:8-10). But God's means of "conquering" was through the powerlessness of the cross, not the power of military might.

The cross is the deepest and fullest disclosure of the purpose of God for humanity. We have already seen John reveal that the cross was God's way of fulfilling two of the pieces of the Jewish expectations for the kingdom's restoration: Through the cross (1) God freed Israel from her sins—a basic prerequisite for the restoration, and (2) he made her a kingdom and priests—the purpose of the original covenant. There is more, however: Through the cross God has pulled the foundation from under the rebellious order (1:18), and now we see that all peoples can be included in the restored kingdom of God's people (5:9-10), a radical subversion of the Jewish expectation that limited the restoration only to Israel.

The image of a slain Lamb should have been clear to John's audience, given their familiarity with the Old Testament. The death of a lamb stood at the heart of Jewish identity, beginning with the Passover in Egypt (Exod 12:1-28), and the killing of a lamb was the essential sacrifice for a multitude of occasions in the Jewish sacrificial cultus. It was the death of the Passover lamb that began the creation of Israel as God's people, and the death of lambs that repeatedly cleansed Israel from its sins. The vision indicates that Jesus is the new Passover Lamb that begins the re-creation of God's people. This is clearly John's understanding: "[he] has freed us from our sins by shedding his blood for us. He has made us a Kingdom of priests"

(1:5b-6a), which was God's purpose for bringing the first people of Israel out of Egypt (Exod 19:6).

Because of his death on the cross, the Lamb of God is praised by all creation. The praise for God the Creator in 4:1-11 now merges with praise for God the Redeemer in 5:1-14; the Lamb shares the same ascriptions and therefore shares the same divine nature. Ascribing divinity to Jesus as Messiah is another subversion of Jewish expectations. There was nothing inherently divine about the Messiah in Jewish expectation. For example, Josephus informs us of many messianic movements in Judaism in the first century (*War* 2.258-263; *Antiquities* 20.97-99), and writings about the Bar Kochba revolt make it clear that Bar Kochba was viewed as the messiah, even proclaimed as such by the leading rabbi of the day, Akiba. In all instances, the supposed "messiah" was a human (Neusner 1973:99, 126-127, 137).

According to Jewish expectations, the Messiah was supposed to act on God's behalf to fulfill God's purposes. In John's vision, God acts on his own behalf in the person of Jesus. Paul had already come to this awareness when he wrote that "God was in Christ, reconciling the world to himself" (2 Cor 5:19). John's vision emphasizes this. First, Jesus is described in imagery that was normally ascribed to God (cf. 1:14, 17; 2:18; 3:1, 7). Second, John's vision presents the Spirit as one of the means of revealing the divine nature of Jesus as the Messiah. Anyone steeped in the Jewish understanding of God would know that the Spirit is one of the ways in which God is manifested in the world. John introduces his vision with a blessing from the sevenfold Spirit that is before God's throne (1:4), and in his vision of heaven he saw the sevenfold Spirit before the throne (4:5). Now, however, the Spirit is seen as an essential aspect of the Lamb (5:6) who, by clear implication, is the presence of God sent into the world.

The vision further confirms the identity of Jesus with God, first by giving to Jesus the same ascription of praise given to God (glory, honor, and power), along with additional ascriptions usually reserved for God—namely (1) wisdom (Job 12:13, 16; Ps 104:24; Prov 2:6-7; 3:19), (2) riches (Prov 3:16); (3) strength (Job 12:13, 16; Pss 18:1; 21:1, 13; 29:1; 59:9; 93:1), and (4) blessing (Pss 24:5; 129:8). Second, the vision affirms Jesus' divinity by joining God and the Lamb together in the final ascription of blessing, honor, glory, and power. By the time the reader gets to this point in John's vision, it has become clear that Jesus, the Messiah, is, in some profound sense, God—albeit God in a distressing appearance—a crucified God! This would have been a radical concept for those shaped by Jewish messianic expectations.

◆ C. The Seven Seals (6:1–8:5)

1. The four horsemen (6:1-8)

As I watched, the Lamb broke the first of the seven seals on the scroll.* Then I heard one of the four living beings say with a voice like thunder, "Come!"
2I looked up and saw a white horse standing there. Its rider carried a bow, and a crown was placed on his head. He rode out to win many battles and gain the victory.
3When the Lamb broke the second seal, I heard the second living being say, "Come!"
4Then another horse appeared, a red one. Its rider was given a mighty

sword and the authority to take peace
from the earth. And there was war and
slaughter everywhere.
5When the Lamb broke the third seal, I
heard the third living being say, "Come!"
I looked up and saw a black horse, and its
rider was holding a pair of scales in his
hand. 6And I heard a voice from among
the four living beings say, "A loaf of wheat
bread or three loaves of barley will cost a
day's pay.* And don't waste* the olive oil
and wine."
7When the Lamb broke the fourth seal,
I heard the fourth living being say, "Come!"
8I looked up and saw a horse whose color
was pale green. Its rider was named Death,
and his companion was the Grave.* These
two were given authority over one-fourth
of the earth, to kill with the sword and
famine and disease* and wild animals.

6:1 Or *book.* **6:6a** Greek *A choinix* [1 quart or 1 liter] *of wheat for a denarius, and 3 choinix of barley for a denarius.* A denarius was equivalent to a laborer's full day's wage. **6:6b** Or *harm.* **6:8a** Greek *was Hades.* **6:8b** Greek *death.*

NOTES

6:1 ***the four living beings say with a voice.*** It is significant that the four living beings are involved with the first four seals. As images of the creation (see note on 4:6), they suggest the vision is representing some aspects of the created order, such as its fallenness (seals 2-4) and its redemption (seal 1).

6:2 ***I looked up and saw a white horse standing there.*** The initial words in the description of the white horse and first rider are, in the Greek text, exactly the same as those regarding the Messiah at 19:11. In both places John uses "I looked" and "behold" (cf. KJV) to introduce the image of a white horse and one seated upon it. This suggests that the first rider is the Messiah (see commentary).

Its rider carried a bow. Is there significance in the fact that John reports no arrows? The term *toxon* [TG5115, ZG5534] (bow) is used in the LXX for the "bow" God set in the sky as a sign of his covenant with Noah and with "all living creatures" (Gen 9:12-13). The fact that the four living creatures around the throne (who represent in some manner all living creatures) are central participants in the opening of the first four seals, suggests that the "bow" may well represent the covenant God made with creation. Through the Messiah, God was working to redeem creation (cf. Beale 1999:390-393).

6:4 ***another horse appeared, a red one.*** "Red" (*purros* [TG4450, ZG4794]) is the same term used to describe the dragon at 12:3, the only other use of the term in the vision. This suggests that the second rider may represent Satan (12:9; see commentary).

6:5 ***a pair of scales.*** This is an economic, not a judicial image, as is made clear in the next verse.

6:6 ***A loaf of wheat bread or three loaves of barley will cost a day's pay.*** Lit., "A *choinix* [TG5518, ZG5955] (quart) of wheat for a denarius, and three *choinix* of barley for a denarius" (so NLT mg). The *dēnarion* [TG1220, ZG1324] represents a day's pay. A quart of wheat would sustain one person for a day; three quarts of barley would sustain a family for a day (Beale 1999:381). The imagery represents poverty conditions at the most elemental level of existence.

don't waste the olive oil and wine. The image could speak of the preciousness of all commodities during a time of crisis. Or the image may represent economic conditions in which the poor and marginalized are being ground down, but the wealthy are untouched, for they could afford the oil and wine. Later in the vision, John sees adverse economic dimensions in the human community as a result of Satan's rebellion (see commentary on 13:16-18). The third horseman is a variant image of the same reality.

6:8 ***Death . . . the Grave.*** The Grave is the NLT's rendering of *hadēs* [TG86, ZG87] (see NLT mg and note on 1:18). In John's vision, Death and Hades represent the foundational parameters of the rebellious realm. Death is the ultimate consequence of rebellion against God, and Hades is the realm of the dead. At 1:18, John sees that in the death and resurrection of Jesus, God has pulled the foundation from under the rebellious realm ("I hold the keys of death and the grave"). At 20:13-14, Death and Hades give up their citizens to judgment and are, with their citizens, thrown into the lake of fire.

one-fourth of the earth. While in the rest of the vision a "third" of numerous things are affected by the rebellion (8:7-12; 9:15-18; 12:4), only here is one-fourth of the earth affected (see commentary).

COMMENTARY

We have already seen John's dependence upon Zechariah for some of his imagery (see Introduction, "John's Narrative World"). There is a very tenuous connection between John's four horsemen and Zechariah, but John's vision moves in a much different direction. In Zechariah there are four chariots with red, black, white, and dappled gray horses, which represent the four winds of heaven (Zech 6:1-3). Earlier in his vision, Zechariah saw a man on a red horse with red, tawny, and white horses behind him, which have been sent by the Lord to patrol the earth (Zech 1:8). In both instances, however, the larger context is the restoration of Israel (Zech 1:12ff; 6:10ff), an expectation that John's vision reveals as accomplished.

In the four horsemen, John is seeing that two principal dynamics operate in the created order. The role of the four living creatures indicates that the riders are related to the created order. The first dynamic, represented by the Messiah as the initial rider, is God's redemptive victory over the rebellion. God is active throughout human history to conquer the rebellion. The second dynamic, represented by the last three riders, is the destructive and dehumanizing nature of the rebellion. Throughout human history Satan is active to destroy God's creation and to dehumanize humanity made in the image of God. John sees that for humanity the destruction is both physical and spiritual.

The first rider is Christ (see note on 6:2). Some have suggested it is an antichrist figure (see Beale 1999:375-377), but the attributes of the rider disprove this. First, in John's vision "white" is a color always associated with either heavenly beings or the redeemed (associated with Jesus or God: 1:14; 14:14; 20:11; associated with the redeemed: 2:17; 3:4-5, 18; 4:4; 6:11; 7:9, 13-14; 19:14). The color white never appears in association with any representative of the rebellious realm, fallen Babylon. Second, only heavenly beings or the redeemed have "crowns" (2:10; 3:11; 4:4, 10). The only seeming exception is 9:7, where the locusts have crowns, but John says "what looked like gold crowns on their heads." Third, the first rider goes forth "to win many battles and gain the victory." In the vision, "conquering" is almost exclusively related to the work of Christ and the redeemed (Christ: 5:5; 17:14; redeemed: 2:7, 11, 17, 26; 3:5, 12, 21; 12:11; 15:2). On only two occasions (11:7; 13:7) does the beast "conquer," but in the larger perspective of the vision this "conquering" is really his defeat by God (see notes on 11:7; 13:7). This imagery of the vision, therefore, coupled with the strong parallelism of the introduction of the first rider with the introduction of the Messiah in 19:11, makes it clear that the first rider is the Messiah.

Some are troubled by the incongruity of this image: If Jesus is the one opening the seal, how can he also be the rider? This is the mistake of taking the imagery of John's vision literally. There is no more difficulty here than the Lion of Judah being a slain Lamb (5:5-6). Vision imagery is fluid, multifaceted, polyvalent, and must always be understood within the larger flow of the vision. It would seem, then, that the first rider is the Messiah who comes to a fallen creation to bring God's victory over the rebellion.

The second rider on the red horse is probably Satan (see note on 6:4). The fact that this rider was "given a mighty sword" is an expression of God's sovereignty. Satan does not create his own sword or take a sword from someone; he is given a sword. Who would have given him this sword besides God? (In Jewish tradition, the passive voice was sometimes used to describe God's actions so as to avoid saying the name of God and, perhaps, thereby breaking the third commandment in Exod 20:7.) John also saw that this rider "was given . . . the authority to take peace from the earth," literally, "the peace" (6:4), a structure indicating a specific peace. In the context of Jewish history, this would be "God's shalom," God's order of wholeness and fullness of life and being, lost at the Fall. The consequence of the absence of God's shalom is "war and slaughter everywhere" in the created order. It would seem, then, that the second rider may represent Satan, who spreads his destructive and dehumanizing rebellion throughout creation.

The third and fourth riders bring further destruction to earth—specifically, to one-fourth of it. Other than normal uses of "fourth" in the Old Testament, one use may be significant for understanding John's use here. On numerous occasions the Old Testament indicates that God will bring judgment upon children for the iniquity of parents, to the third and the fourth generation of those who reject him (Exod 20:5, et al.). The string begins with the parents (first generation), moves to the children (second generation), and then to the grandchildren (third generation) and the great-grandchildren (the fourth generation). Why doesn't God ever continue to bring judgment upon further generations? Nowhere in the Old Testament does God bring judgment upon the fifth or a higher generation. In most cultures, and especially in Old Testament times, it would be rare for there to be four generations living together in a household, to say nothing of five or more. The living generational structure of human families is almost always truncated at the fourth generation, as great-grandchildren enter the picture and the great-grandparents pass from the scene. The vision seems to be indicating that death is the general consequence of the rebellion against God.

The vision adds another dimension when John sees that Death and Hades "kill with the sword and famine and disease and wild animals" (6:8). A more accurate translation of the Greek for the last two elements is "death and the beasts of the earth." When read this way, there is significance in the list. The "sword" was the instrument of the second rider (6:4), "famine" the instrument of the third rider (6:6), and "death" the nature of the fourth rider. In other words, even if one escapes warfare and famine, death will eventually come. But what about "the beasts of the earth?" The word John uses for "beast" here is the same term used for the beasts that appear throughout the rest of the vision (11:7; 13:1-4, 11-18;

14:9, 11; 15:2; 16:2, 10, 13; 17:3-17; 19:19-20; 20:4, 10). These beasts, as we will see, represent the incarnation of Satan's rebellion in human life. To worship the beast is to enter into the realm of spiritual death whose ultimate end is the "second death" (20:14). The vision seems to be indicating that there is something worse than physical death (sword, famine, death); there is a spiritual death (at the hands of the beasts of the earth) that is the ultimate destructiveness of the rebellious realm.

Human history is shaped by both the redemptive victory of God in the Messiah and the destructive and dehumanizing rebellion of Satan. We all ride through life either with the first rider or with the last three. If we "ride" with the Messiah, our lives increasingly become redemptive, healing, liberating, and a transforming means of giving God's grace in the world. We become those who have the word of God and the witness of Jesus (1:9). If we "ride" with the other riders, however, our lives increasingly contribute to the alienation, brokenness, and bondage that characterize so much of human existence in the world today. We become co-opted by values that dehumanize others and ourselves. We become participants in economic and political structures—and these marginalize some while exalting others.

In the end, we must confess that the vision in Revelation 6:1-8 demands a theodicy: If God is all powerful and all good, then why does evil exist? The vision doesn't provide an answer to this enigma. It simply indicates that the entire realm of rebellion is under God's sovereignty—inasmuch as the second rider "was given" (by God) a mighty sword and authority to remove peace from the earth, and Death and Hades "were given authority" (by God) over one-fourth of the earth.

◆ 2. Saints and sinners (6:9-17)

9 When the Lamb broke the fifth seal, I
saw under the altar the souls of all who
had been martyred for the word of God
and for being faithful in their testimony.
10 They shouted to the Lord and said,
"O Sovereign Lord, holy and true, how
long before you judge the people who belong to this world and avenge our blood
for what they have done to us?" 11 Then a
white robe was given to each of them.
And they were told to rest a little longer
until the full number of their brothers and
sisters*—their fellow servants of Jesus
who were to be martyred—had joined
them.

12 I watched as the Lamb broke the sixth
seal, and there was a great earthquake.
The sun became as dark as black cloth,
and the moon became as red as blood.
13 Then the stars of the sky fell to the
earth like green figs falling from a tree
shaken by a strong wind. 14 The sky was
rolled up like a scroll, and all of the
mountains and islands were moved from
their places.

15 Then everyone—the kings of the
earth, the rulers, the generals, the wealthy,
the powerful, and every slave and free
person—all hid themselves in the caves
and among the rocks of the mountains.
16 And they cried to the mountains and the
rocks, "Fall on us and hide us from the
face of the one who sits on the throne and
from the wrath of the Lamb. 17 For the
great day of their wrath has come, and
who is able to survive?"

6:11 Greek *their brothers.*

NOTES

6:9-10 ***altar.*** In Jewish history altars were focal points in the Temple. While John had not explicitly used Temple imagery up to this point, he had implicitly set a Temple context by indicating that the redeemed are "priests" (1:6; 5:10), and representing the redeemed as the 24 elders (corresponding to 24 courses of priests; cf. 1 Chr 24:1-19) around God on the throne. In Jewish history God's throne was often related to the mercy seat (NLT, "the place of atonement") on the Ark of the Covenant in the Most Holy Place, the innermost sanctuary within the Temple. (For the mercy seat, see Exod 25:17-22; 37:6-9. Note that the cherubim associated with the mercy seat have wings—a similar image to John's vision of four creatures with wings associated with the throne. For the throne of God associated with the Temple, see Ps 11:4; Isa 6:1; Jer 17:12; Ezek 43:7.)

There were two altars in the Jewish Temple. The first was the altar of sacrifice, located outside the Temple building, where the sacrificial fire burned continually and upon which the required burnt offerings and sacrifices were offered. Josephus, himself a priest, describes this altar as being 75 feet square and 22 ½ feet high (*War* 5.225). The second was the golden altar of incense, located just in front of the curtain that separated the Most Holy Place from the sanctuary within the Temple, upon which the morning and evening incense offerings were made (cf. Exod 30:1-10). We will see in the seventh seal (8:1-5) that John utilized both altars to convey his vision. Both altars represent the place of covenant relationship with God. The sacrificial altar was the place where impediments to perfect relationship with God were removed. The altar of incense was the place where the incense offering began and ended each day of covenant life with God. Whichever altar John implies here, and it could be both, it is a place where God's faithful people come to be in right relationship with God.

6:11 ***white robe.*** This represents the purity of the people of God (see note on 3:4).

their brothers and sisters—their fellow servants of Jesus who were to be martyred—had joined them. Lit., "their compatriots, their brothers and sisters, who were to be killed as they had been." The Greek text does not include "of Jesus," thereby opening the possibility that John was seeing all martyrs throughout the history of God's covenant history, both Jewish and Christian, comprising the souls under the altar. The answer to the martyrs' question of "when" is very similar to the answer found in *4 Ezra* 4:36: "Jeremiel the archangel answered and said to them, 'When the number of those like you is filled up.'"

6:12-14 Cosmic disturbances such as these are not to be taken literally but as images of radical reversal in the present state of things. Wright (1996:209) said that "language about sun, moon and stars being darkened or shaken has as its primary referent a set of cataclysmic events *within* the space-time universe, not an event that will bring that universe to its utter end." Buchanan (1993:179) also, rightly notes that "the notion that biblical authors expected the end of the cosmos and time was invented in nineteenth-century Europe." These images are frequently associated with the Day of the Lord in the OT. On some occasions the images relate to God's judgment of Israel, on others, God's restoration of Israel and judgment of her enemies. God's judgment of Israel: Jer 4:23-28 (earthquake, heavens black); Joel 2:1-11 (earthquake, sun, moon, stars). God's judgment of Israel's enemies: Isa 13 (sun, moon, stars, earthquake); Isa 34 (sky like a scroll); Ezek 32:1-7 (stars, sun, moon); Joel 3:15-16 (sun, moon, stars, earthquake). God's restoration of Israel: Isa 24 (earthquake, sun, moon); Joel 2:31 (sun, moon = Rev 6); Hab 3:6 (earthquake); Hag 2:6, 21 (earthquake).

earthquake. This image would have had an added force for John's readers, who lived in an active earthquake zone. The same is true of the images of "sun . . . moon . . . stars . . . mountains . . . and islands" in a maritime culture. The Mediterranean Sea was a significant element in the Roman culture. Both essential products as well as luxury goods were transported by ship. When traveling by sea, the sun, moon, stars, mountains, and islands are basic points of reference that enable accurate positioning and safe travel. If these points of reference are lost, total disorientation results—the whole structure of life comes apart. Whether relying upon the use of the images within the Jewish story, or the more immediate force of the images for his audience (or both), John's images reveal a vision of God's activity that is a radical disruption of the rebellious order.

6:15-16 The vision pertains to the rebellious order because it speaks to the entire citizenship "of the earth," which is the term for the rebellious realm of life (see note on 3:10). This entire citizenship (from kings to slaves) flees from God and tries to hide. John used an image from Isaiah related to God's judgment of the ungodly: "When the LORD rises to shake the earth, his enemies will crawl into holes in the ground. They will hide in caves in the rocks from the terror of the LORD and the glory of his majesty. . . . They will . . . crawl away into caverns and hide among the jagged rocks in the cliffs. They will try to escape the terror of the LORD and the glory of his majesty as he rises to shake the earth" (Isa 2:19-21).

6:17 ***the great day of their wrath has come, and who is able to survive?*** In the OT, the day of wrath was the time when God would judge the nations and restore the kingdom to Israel. One of the clearest expositors of this was Isaiah. Isaiah 10:20–12:6 foresees the restoration of Israel through the heir to David's throne. This is followed by the vision of the Day of the Lord against Babylon (Isa 13:1–14:23), "the terrible day of his fury and fierce anger" where no light will shine from stars or sun or moon, and the earth will be shaken (Isa 13:9-10, 13). John sees that through "the heir to David's throne" (5:5 = Isa 11:10), the Lamb, God's judgment has been enacted, and the rebellious order is shaken to its foundations.

COMMENTARY

For John's Jewish Christian audience, the fifth and sixth seals deal with an essential aspect of the Jewish expectations for the restoration of the kingdom to Israel. John's vision has already indicated that in Jesus, the Messiah—particularly in his death and resurrection—God has acted to fulfill his promise, consummate his covenant, and restore the kingdom to Israel. According to Jewish expectations, however, when this happened there would be two companion events: The righteous dead would be raised to participate in the restored kingdom, and the enemies of God's faithful would be overthrown. For John's audience, the affirmation of the restoration of the kingdom would raise the questions, "Why haven't the faithful dead been raised?" (cf. the fifth seal) and, "Why haven't the enemies of God's people been overthrown?" (cf. the sixth seal).

The resurrection of the righteous people is an integral part of the restoration of the kingdom to Israel. If, in the death and resurrection of the faithful martyr—the Messiah Jesus—God has indeed made his people a kingdom and priests (1:5-6), then why haven't the rest of the faithful martyrs been resurrected? The "rest" would be all those who, prior to Christ, were martyred for their faithful adherence to the covenant but who had not yet been resurrected to participate in the restored kingdom. The description of Jesus as the firstborn of the dead (1:5) implies that there are more to follow (i.e., the faithful martyrs). While the kingdom has, indeed, been restored, its final consummation is still in the future. The expectation of the resurrection of the faithful martyrs has now been shifted from the restoration of the kingdom to its final consummation. Thus, the martyrs underneath the altar are told they must wait a little longer (6:11).

John saw all who had been martyred for the word of God and for being faithful in their testimony. We have noted that many Jews believed that those who had been martyred for their faith would be vindicated when they would be raised from death to participate in the restoration of the kingdom to Israel. During the intertestamental period it was believed that their souls were held in a special place waiting for this moment. For instance, in *4 Ezra* 4:35, we read, "Did not the souls of the just in their storehouses ask about these things, saying, 'How long will we wait in this way? When will the harvest of our reward come?'" This is remarkably similar to John's vision: "O Sovereign Lord, holy and true, how long before you judge the people who belong to this world and avenge our blood for what they have done to us?" (6:10). While *4 Ezra* is generally dated in the early second century AD, it still reflects Jewish perceptions of the period. Dated about the same period as John's vision (late 60s AD), *2 Baruch* 30:1-3 says that the souls of the faithful are held in heavenly treasuries to be released at the end of the evil days when "the time of the advent of the Messiah is fulfilled." *First Enoch*, much earlier than either *4 Ezra* or *2 Baruch*, also envisions the righteous martyrs praying for justice (*1 Enoch* 47:1-4).

The question in Revelation 6 is whether the martyrs are Jewish or Christian martyrs. Since John and the vision intimate that the restoration has begun in the death and resurrection of the Messiah, these could represent both groups (as well as John's audience, made up of both Jewish and Gentile believers) asking when the resurrection of the righteous will come and God will overthrow the enemies of his people. This may be further confirmed in John's variation of the phrase, "those who kept the word of God and the testimony of Jesus" (6:9), which appears throughout the vision as a description of the citizens of New Jerusalem (see note on 1:2). By not limiting the martyrs to Christians, John intimates that the vision is representing all of God's faithful martyrs, both old and new covenant.

In John's vision, the martyrs are killed by "the people who belong to this world" (6:10). We have already noted that this phrase appears throughout John's vision as identifying the citizens of fallen Babylon (see note on 3:10). John was seeing that throughout human history God's faithful people experience martyrdom at the hands of the citizens of fallen Babylon. The two dynamics at work in history, as imaged by the four horsemen, are not merely two alternative modes of being, they are complete opposites. Those who bow before the one seated on the throne worship the one who lives forever and ever and cast their crowns before the throne (4:10), while those who worship the beast are those who blaspheme God, God's name, and God's dwelling (13:6). The enemies of God's people are engaged in warfare against them. That warfare brings tribulation on God's people (see 1:9).

While the vision clearly affirms that God has restored the kingdom through Jesus the Messiah, it also indicates that the final consummation of that restoration is still to come. The faithful martyrs, like the rest of the citizens of the kingdom, have already entered into the wholeness of life (the white garment) that characterizes the restored kingdom even though the final consummation is still ahead. At the same time, the citizens of fallen Babylon have already been radically affected by the restoration, even though it is not yet manifest.

The fifth and sixth seals also reveal the consequences of the four horsemen in human experience. The followers of the first horseman, the Messiah, are God's faithful people. They are the kingdom of priests, citizens of God's New Jerusalem. These are those who have the word of God and the testimony of Jesus, who are victorious over the destructive and dehumanizing values and perspectives of fallen Babylon. The followers of the other three horsemen, Satan and his cohorts, are those in rebellion against God. They are citizens of fallen Babylon, those "who belong to this world."

The fifth seal again reveals that God's faithful people experience tribulation, even martyrdom, at the hands of the fallen Babylon world (cf. 1:9 and the letters to Smyrna and Philadelphia). The sixth seal, however, reveals that fallen Babylon is shaken and disturbed by the presence of God and the Lamb in its midst. John has already seen that Jesus (the Lamb) is present in the midst of the churches, the communities of God's people (1:13, 20). They are the lampstand (1:20), which holds the lamp who is the Lamb (21:23), whose light is the very nature of God (21:23). That is, the church is the presence of God and the Lamb in the midst of the world. When the church is faithful, it becomes a disturbing and disruptive presence to the destructive and dehumanizing values and perspectives of its fallen Babylon world. This, in part, is why the early church was described as those who were turning the world upside down (Acts 17:6, KJV).

When the church is a faithful community of New Jerusalem citizens, its living witness to the values of God's kingdom becomes a sharp and threatening contrast to the prevailing values of the fallen Babylon world around it. The destructive and dehumanizing values of fallen Babylon cannot withstand the presence of New Jerusalem's values in its midst. If they are allowed to continue, they undermine and overthrow fallen Babylon. Therefore, fallen Babylon seeks to remove the witness of New Jerusalem from its midst.

◆ 3. Interlude: The composition of New Jerusalem (7:1-17)

Then I saw four angels standing at the four
corners of the earth, holding back the four
winds so they did not blow on the earth or
the sea, or even on any tree. 2And I saw
another angel coming up from the east,
carrying the seal of the living God. And he
shouted to those four angels, who had
been given power to harm land and sea,
3"Wait! Don't harm the land or the sea or
the trees until we have placed the seal of
God on the foreheads of his servants."
4And I heard how many were marked
with the seal of God—144,000 were sealed
from all the tribes of Israel:

5 from Judah 12,000
from Reuben 12,000
from Gad 12,000
6 from Asher. 12,000
from Naphtali 12,000
from Manasseh 12,000
7 from Simeon 12,000
from Levi 12,000
from Issachar 12,000
8 from Zebulun 12,000
from Joseph. 12,000
from Benjamin 12,000

9After this I saw a vast crowd, too great to
count, from every nation and tribe and

people and language, standing in front of the throne and before the Lamb. They were clothed in white robes and held palm branches in their hands. 10And they were shouting with a great roar,

"Salvation comes from our God who
sits on the throne
and from the Lamb!"

11And all the angels were standing around the throne and around the elders and the four living beings. And they fell before the throne with their faces to the ground and worshiped God. 12They sang,

"Amen! Blessing and glory and wisdom
and thanksgiving and honor
and power and strength belong to
our God
forever and ever! Amen."

13Then one of the twenty-four elders asked me, "Who are these who are clothed in white? Where did they come from?"

14And I said to him, "Sir, you are the one who knows."

Then he said to me, "These are the ones who died in* the great tribulation.* They have washed their robes in the blood of the Lamb and made them white.

15 "That is why they stand in front of
God's throne
and serve him day and night in
his Temple.
And he who sits on the throne
will give them shelter.
16 They will never again be hungry
or thirsty;
they will never be scorched by the
heat of the sun.
17 For the Lamb on the throne*
will be their Shepherd.
He will lead them to springs of
life-giving water.
And God will wipe every tear from
their eyes."

7:14a Greek *who came out of.* 7:14b Or *the great suffering.* 7:17 Greek *on the center of the throne.*

NOTES

7:1 *four corners of the earth.* This was a typical way of speaking of the bounds of the world (cf. 20:8; Isa 11:12; Ezek 7:2).

the four winds. These not only represent the bounds of the world (Ezek 37:9; Dan 7:2; 8:8; 11:4; Zech 2:6), but also God's judgment upon those opposed to him. For example, Jeremiah saw the four winds coming from the four corners of the sky upon Elam and scattering the people across the world (Jer 49:36). It is obvious that the latter image is the one John is employing here since, when they are released, they will harm the earth, sea, and trees.

so they did not blow on the earth or the sea, or even on any tree. The angels were holding back the wind from destructive action, as is confirmed in 7:3. We have noted that "earth" and "sea" are two of the vision's ways of representing the rebellious order (see note on 3:10 for discussion of "earth," and note on 4:6 for discussion of "sea"). The vision is revealing a delay in the consummation of God's judgment against fallen Babylon. But what is the role of the trees? As early as Deut 12:2, trees had become a place of idolatry, and Israel was warned not to plant any tree near the altar as a sacred pole (Deut 16:21). The prophets fulminated against the idolatry Israel had committed under every tree (Isa 57:5; Jer 2:20, 27; 3:6, 9, 13; 17:2; Ezek 6:13; 20:28). The image of the tree might well function, with earth and sea, to denote the idolatry of fallen Babylon against which God's judgment will come.

7:2-3 *angel coming up from the east.* Lit., "a messenger from the rising of the sun." For many Jews, this would have messianic connotations. Balaam's prophesy, "I see him, but not here and now. I perceive him, but far in the distant future. A star will rise from Jacob; a scepter will emerge from Israel" (Num 24:17), became part of the messianic expectations of the Jewish story (see "John's Narrative World" in the Introduction). Buchanan (1993:186-187) indicates that "the word *anatolē* [TG395, ZG424] means both 'east' and 'rising.' It was used to allude to Num 24:17, 'a scepter *shall arise* out of Israel.' Therefore the 'rising one' was a term given to the Messiah." Malachi moved in this trajectory of expectation when he wrote, "the Sun of Righteousness will rise with healing in his wings" (Mal 4:2).

the seal of the living God. The "seal" denotes ownership or control.

7:4 ***144,000.*** The entire vision does some interesting things with the number 144,000. Here it designates the full complement of God's faithful people within the 12 tribes of the old covenant. In 14:1-5, however, the 144,000 constitute those "redeemed from the earth" (i.e., fallen Babylon), those "purchased from among the people on the earth" (i.e., fallen Babylon); that is, God's people redeemed by the Lamb (in the new covenant) from every tribe, nation, language and people. Then, in the vision of New Jerusalem, the community of God's redeemed, John sees the community imaged as a cubic city 12,000 stadia on each side (21:16, NLT mg). The sum of the 12 edges of the cubic community totals 144,000.

7:5-8 ***12,000.*** The 12,000 of each tribe may be no more than evenly distributing the 144,000 across the 12 tribes of Israel since it is the latter number that plays a role in the vision. While it stretches credulity, it should be noted that the 12,000 stadia dimension of the 12 edges of the cubic community of God's people (21:16, NLT mg) might infer that New Jerusalem is the true Israel, composed of both Jews and Gentiles.

7:9 ***After this.*** See note on 1:19.

a vast crowd, too great to count, from every nation and tribe and people and language. As we have seen (see note on 5:9 for the discussion of John's use of this group), this phrase denotes the population of fallen Babylon. Here, however, John sees those of fallen Babylon who have been redeemed since they are "clothed in white." The reality of this is seen when John is informed that these are those who have "washed their robes in the blood of the Lamb and made them white" (7:14).

standing in front of the throne and before the Lamb . . . held palm branches in their hands. Palm branches were an essential part of Israel's worship of God. The directions for the celebration of the Festival of Shelters required rejoicing before the Lord with palm branches (Lev 23:33-43). The palm played a significant role in Ezekiel's vision of the restored Temple (Ezek 40–41). Celebrations of victory included the waving of palm branches (1 Macc 13:51). The first Hanukkah celebration included palm branches (2 Macc 10:7). (Hanukkah is the annual celebration of the rededication of the Jerusalem Temple after the Maccabees took control of Jerusalem in 164 BC.) Buchanan notes, "palm leaves were for Jews as green clover is for the Irish or the various tartans are for the Scots. They were their national symbols and were carried in processions and waved as flags" (1993:194). The imagery here conveys that Gentiles have now been included in God's restoration of Israel.

7:10 ***Salvation comes from our God who sits on the throne and from the Lamb!*** "Salvation" is the term describing God's deliverance of his people from their enemies and their restoration as his kingdom. The affirmation reiterates that it is through "the Lamb" that God has accomplished the restoration (salvation).

7:11-12 ***thanksgiving.*** With the exception of "thanksgiving," the heavenly ascription of praise brings together the qualities previously attributed to God (4:11—glory, honor, power), the Lamb (5:12—power, riches, wisdom, strength, honor, glory, blessing), and God and the Lamb (5:13—blessing, honor, glory, power). The placement of "thanksgiving" at the center of the ascriptions focuses not only on the attributes but also upon thankfulness that God has restored the kingdom to Israel.

7:13 ***Who are these who are clothed in white? Where did they come from?*** These questions focus attention upon the composition of the "vast crowd" before God's throne (7:9). For those shaped by Jewish expectations, the restored kingdom would, obviously, contain the restored 12 tribes of Israel. But what is this "vast crowd" doing before the throne with aspects that would normally be associated with Israel?

7:14 ***Sir, you are the one who knows.*** This response indicates that the 24 elders, who represent Christians as God's kingdom of priests, know the identity of the multitude.

the ones who died in the great tribulation. Lit., "the ones coming out of the tribulation" (cf. NLT mg). The Greek participle (*erchomenoi* [TG2064, ZG2262]) indicates a continual process—"continually coming out." The tribulation has been introduced by John as the experience faithful followers of Christ endure at the hands of a rebellious world (see notes on 1:9; 2:9-10). What, then, is the Great Tribulation? The continuing nature of this experience suggests John was seeing the redeemed of all Christian history who, in every age, experience tribulation at the hands of their particularized form of the rebellious order. Throughout history these faithful are "continually coming out" of a tribulation that persists until the end.

washed their robes in the blood of the Lamb and made them white. The "vast crowd" is also identified as those who have had their sins washed away. Cleansing of sin was one of the essential prerequisites for Israel before the restoration of the kingdom could occur, and John affirms that this has happened in the death of the Messiah Jesus (1:5). What is important here is that this group consists of those "from every nation and tribe and people and language" (7:9), that is, Gentiles. The vision makes it unmistakably clear that Gentiles have now been included in God's restoration of the kingdom (see note on 5:9).

7:15 ***they stand in front of God's throne and serve him day and night in his Temple.*** It is because of God's action in the Messiah, the Lamb, that Gentiles not only join Israel, whose place is to stand before God's throne, but also share the priestly role to serve God day and night in his Temple. Gentiles are clearly part of the kingdom of priests created by the Messiah (1:6; 5:10). In addition, God's promise that he would live among Israel and "shelter them" (see Exod 29:45; 1 Kgs 6:13) is now extended to Gentile believers.

7:16-17 The vision concludes its presentation of the Gentiles as participants in God's restored kingdom by including the Gentiles in a collage of promises that had been given to Israel. Woven together here are promises found in Isa 25:8; 49:10; Ezek 34:23.

COMMENTARY

In the interlude between the sixth and seventh seals, the vision fleshes out the answer given to the martyrs in the fifth seal (6:11). God's final judgment, the consummation of the victory already begun, will await until the full complement of God's people have been brought into his kingdom. The focus, however, is upon the nature and composition of God's people.

The vision in chapter 7 pertains to the separation of those who belong to God from those who do not. In Jewish history, the notion of a designating, distinguishing mark originated in the account of the Passover. There the mark was placed on the doors of God's people so they would be spared when judgment came upon Egypt (Exod 11–12). Ezekiel provides a variant of the image with the marking of the forehead of the righteous to spare them from God's judgment against the idolatrous in Israel (Ezek 9).

The seal is more than a mark; it has something to do with the very nature of those who are marked. As the vision progresses, John sees that the citizens of fallen Babylon are also marked on the forehead with a mark that has something to do with the "name," that is, the very nature of the beast (13:16-17). (We have previously noted at 2:13 and 3:12 that "name" has to do with the nature of the one named.

The NLT translation "reputation" at 3:1 captures some of the essence of "name.") John also saw that the citizens of God's New Jerusalem have the name of God and the Lamb on their foreheads (14:1; 22:3-4).

According to the Old Testament, the forehead represents one's inner posture of relationship with God. God's people were to be formed by the Torah—they were to bind it upon their foreheads (Exod 13:9, 16; 28:38; Deut 6:8; 11:18). When they turned away from God and became disobedient, they were said to have a brass forehead (Isa 48:4, ESV), a harlot's forehead (Jer 3:3, NASB), or a hard forehead (Ezek 3:7, ESV). When King Uzziah sinned against God and usurped the role of the priests, he was struck with a leprous forehead (2 Chr 26:16-21). The vision, therefore, seems to be responding to the query of the saints in the fifth seal. Judgment will be withheld until the full number of God's faithful has come to be.

The listing of the 12 tribes of Israel in Revelation 7 is unique. It does not follow the order of any of the lists of the tribes given in numerous places in the Old Testament. (Genesis 49; Num 1:20-43; 2:3-33 [=7:12-83; 10:14-28]; 13:4-15; 34:13-29; Deut 27:12-13; and Josh 13:8–19:48 give varying lists of the 12 tribes. While some of these lists agree among themselves as noted, none are the same as ch 7.) Most notable is the inexplicable absence of the tribe of Dan and its replacement by the tribe of Manasseh, the son of Joseph. While numerous theories have been developed to try to explain this, none to date has achieved a consensus. Since the vision subverts Jewish expectations at many points, here, too, it may be indicating that God's fulfillment of the restoration of Israel has taken on a different form than was expected. The fact that Judah is listed first may emphasize that Jesus is the Davidic Messiah, the "lion of the tribe of Judah." It is interesting to note that the tribe of Judah is listed first only in Numbers (Num 2:3 = 10:14; 34:19, et al.) and then related to leading the march into the Promised Land (the kingdom) and the allotment of the Promised Land (kingdom). In John's vision, the Lion of the tribe of Judah is the one who leads the people of God into the restored kingdom (note also that the faithful are those who follow the Lamb—14:4; 19:14).

God's people are those who have the seal of God upon their foreheads. This image has profound implications in that John's vision subsequently reveals that God's faithful have God's name and the Lamb's name on their foreheads (14:1; 22:4). Since a person's name is a manifestation of their nature, to have God's name upon one's forehead is to have one's nature conformed to the nature of God. The vision is revealing that being the people of God is not simply a matter of belonging to a particular group, being affiliated with a particular organization, or having one's name on a membership roll. Being the people of God is a matter of having one's very being restored to the image of God. In Paul's terms, it is being conformed to the image of Christ (see Rom 8:29; 1 Cor 15:49; 2 Cor 3:17-18; Eph 4:13, 15, 24; Phil 3:21; Col 3:10).

Who is eligible for such a transformation? The Jews of John's day tended to think that being the people of God was limited to those of Jewish blood or, at least, those nurtured in the Jewish heritage. Outsiders were presumed to be excluded from the possibility of belonging to the people of God. John's vision reveals that all humankind is eligible for membership in God's kingdom. The faithful in Israel are there, to be sure, but joined by all redeemed humanity.

Beginning in 7:9, we see the vast crowds "from every nation and tribe and people and language"—that is, the Gentiles—now standing before the throne of God and the Lamb. Gentile Christians are now included in God's kingdom. These Gentile believers are among the redeemed because they are clothed in white, hold palm branches in their hands (see note on 7:9), and have "washed their robes in the blood of the Lamb" (see note on 7:14). As part of the redeemed community of God, they share in the role of being priests to God and the Lamb.

John's vision gives only two criteria for being the people of God. First, we must be washed in the blood of the Lamb. This is the vision's way of describing what Paul calls being crucified with Christ (Gal 2:20), or what Jesus describes as losing oneself for his sake (Matt 10:39). This is the death to the false self created by the world's values and perspectives, the putting off of the whole self-referenced mode of being that governs every thought, word, and deed; it is the crucifying of the entire self-protective structure of relationships that manipulates others to our agenda. Again, in Paul's words, it is putting off the old nature with its deeds (Col 3:9). In other words, being "washed in the blood of the Lamb" is not simply a treatment for superficial stains and blemishes on the surface of our life that leaves us untouched at the deeper levels of our being. This is an opening of ourselves to God at the very deepest levels of our being, an abandonment of the old structures of our being, a radical release of who we are and have been to God.

Second, to be God's people we must become formed in the nature of Christ. We must allow God's name to be inscribed upon our foreheads. This means putting on the new nature, which is continually being renewed in the image of God (Col 3:10). This is a life of radical discipleship in which we allow God to mold us daily toward wholeness in the image of Christ. Such discipleship is a dynamic, ongoing process through which we "grow up in every way into him who is the head, into Christ" (Eph 4:15, NRSV) until "all of us come to the unity of the faith and of the knowledge of the Son of God, to maturity, to the measure of the full stature of Christ" (Eph 4:13, NRSV).

Such lives of radical discipleship are lives lived "before the throne." God and the Lamb become the formative center of our being, the primary reference for our life in the world. We "seek the things that are above, where Christ is" (Col 3:1, RSV). We live to serve God and the Lamb in all the circumstances of our lives, to be "priests of God" in all our relationships and all the situations of our living.

◆ 4. The power of prayer (8:1-5)

When the Lamb broke the seventh seal on the scroll,* there was silence throughout heaven for about half an hour.
2I saw the seven angels who stand before God, and they were given seven trumpets.

3Then another angel with a gold incense burner came and stood at the altar. And a great amount of incense was given to him to mix with the prayers of God's people as an offering on the gold altar before the throne.
4The smoke of the incense, mixed with the prayers of God's holy people, ascended up to God from the altar where the angel had poured them out.
5Then the angel filled the incense burner with fire from the altar and threw it down upon the earth; and thunder crashed, lightning flashed, and there was a terrible earthquake.

8:1 Or *book.*

NOTES

8:1-2 *silence throughout heaven for about half an hour.* What is this silence? I think it must be understood in its context, which is best understood as the incense offering in the Temple cultus on the Day of Atonement (see commentary). While there are, undoubtedly, multiple layers of nuance in the image, the liturgical setting of the scene would seem to point to the silent awe appropriate to approaching God, the silence in which God is known (Pss 46:10; 62:1, 5; Hab 2:20). In Zeph 1:7 and Zech 2:13, there is a call for all the people of the earth to be silent in the presence of God who is about to enact judgment and restore Israel.

seven angels . . . seven trumpets. This is an image of proclamation. What is subsequently proclaimed is God's judgment upon fallen Babylon (ch 9) and the consummation of the covenant with Israel (chs 10–11; see notes on 11:3-19). The image of trumpets, however, is also associated with the Day of Atonement in the Year of Jubilee (Lev 25:9)—the time when everything is restored. Caird (1966:108-110) notes several helpful antecedents for the use of trumpets in Israel's liturgies but fails to note the connection with the Day of Atonement. In the first century, the "Jubilee" had become an image for the restoration of the kingdom to Israel, the time when the Roman control of the Promised Land would be ended and the land restored to Israel (Buchanan 1978:4-5).

8:3-4 ***gold incense burner.*** The imagery is the incense offering in the Temple on the Day of Atonement (Lev 16:12-13), the one day in the Jewish tradition when the covenant community was restored in perfect covenant relationship with God—a preview of the restoration of the kingdom to Israel. The incense offering opened and closed the daily worship and sacrifices in the Temple in Jerusalem. On all other days of the year, a priest was chosen by lot from among those whose priestly order was on duty. (This is what Zechariah was doing according to Luke 1:5-23.)

stood at the altar. The Greek of 8:3 (*epi tou thusiastēriou* [TG2379, ZG2603]) uses *epi* [TG1909, ZG2093] with the genitive case and should be translated "stood upon the altar," not "at the altar." In contrast to this, "an offering on the gold altar," later in the verse, should be translated "at the altar" as it makes use of *epi* with the accusative case. Two different altars are involved here. The first is the sacrificial altar, a large structure outside the Temple, which had to be mounted by a ramp or stairs (cf. discussion at 6:9-10). The second is the golden altar of incense, a small altar located in the sanctuary of the Temple just before the veil that separated the sanctuary from the Most Holy Place.

8:5 ***the angel filled the incense burner with fire from the altar.*** The vision now adds a new element to the image of the incense offering. The angel filled the incense burner with the prayers of the saints, now incandescent through their mingling in the sacrificial fire from the altar (8:3), and threw them down into the earth.

threw it down upon the earth. Lit., "he threw it into the earth." There are a number of things that go "into the earth" in John's vision: the stars (6:13; 12:4; related to 9:1), hail, fire, blood (8:7; 13:13), locusts (9:3), Satan and his angels (12:9, 13), the angel's sickle of judgment (14:19), the bowls of wrath (16:1-2). In almost all cases, the image reflects the results of the actions of heaven in the midst of the rebellious realm. "The earth" is a term for the rebellious realm—fallen Babylon (see note on 3:10).

thunder crashed, lightning flashed, and there was a terrible earthquake. These are all signs of theophanies (see Exod 19:16; 20:18; 2 Sam 22:7-9; Pss 18:13-15; 77:18; Isa 29:6; and the discussion on 6:12-14).

COMMENTARY

John has already indicated that God began the restoration of the kingdom, and John will reveal in the interlude between the sixth and seventh trumpets (9:13; 11:15), and in the seventh trumpet itself, that God has, in Christ, consummated the old covenant and begun his reign. Revelation 8:1-5 introduces the next facet of the vision, as well as the breaking of the seventh seal.

In order to appreciate what is taking place in this vision, we need to understand what the priests did in the lighting of the incense altar. The priest would go up onto the sacrificial altar outside the Temple where the sacrificial fire burned continuously. He would carry a silver censer with which to gather coals from the sacrificial fire. He would then descend from the sacrificial altar and be given about half a pound of incense. The priest would then enter the sanctuary of the Temple and go up to the gold altar of incense that was situated before the veil that separated the sanctuary from the Most Holy Place where God's throne dwelt over the Ark of the Covenant. He would pour the coals from the censer upon the golden altar and then place the incense upon the coals. The smoke and aroma of the incense would then ascend to the presence of God in the Most Holy Place. On the Day of Atonement, this function would be performed by the high priest with a golden incense burner and as much incense as he could carry.

In the development of the synagogue liturgy, the morning and evening prayers were offered in the synagogue at the same time as the morning and evening incense offerings in the Temple in Jerusalem. Even during the Temple service the people were praying outside while the priest performed the incense offering (Luke 1:10). Thus, the incense offering came to be closely associated with "the prayers of God's holy people" (8:4).

John's vision gives us a profound understanding of the nature of prayer. For all too many Christians, prayer is either a "shopping list" of things we want God to take care of or a heavenly 911 call for rescue in the midst of difficulties. Prayer is viewed as something we "do," and rarely as something we "are." John's vision cuts through all our functional understandings of prayer and sets before us a profound vision of the true nature of prayer. John sees the nature and effects of the prayers of those who have been washed in the blood of the Lamb and have the seal of God upon their foreheads.

The first thing the vision reveals is that prayer is extremely costly. It is a participation in the sacrificial fire that cleanses and purifies by consuming all that is offered to God. True prayer cannot withhold anything of self from the consuming fire of God's holiness. This kind of prayer is a radical abandonment of oneself to God.

Second, the vision reveals that prayer is a radical relinquishment of oneself to God's purposes. The prayers of the saints are laid upon the altar in the presence of God. This kind of prayer is not a means of getting God to do what we desire, but a relinquishment of our lives to what God desires for us and our world. The prayer of the vision is much more a mode of being in relationship with God than a means of manipulating God to fulfill our, or even his, purposes.

Third, the vision reveals that abandoned, relinquished prayer becomes the means through which the presence of God is released in the fallen Babylon world in which we live. Like Israel, and even like the martyrs under the altar (6:9-10), we tend to think of prayer as getting God to fulfill his purposes in the world. The vision reveals that our lives are the means through which God acts to fulfill his purposes in our world.

For example, we tend to think of intercessory prayer as getting God to do something for another person. Rarely do we realize that genuine intercession is the offering of ourselves to God that we may become God's presence for the other person. This kind of prayer can be costly—in time, energy, and resources. When we truly abandon to God ourselves, our agendas, our desires, and our ways of resolving the matter; when we truly make ourselves available to God to be a means of his grace in the world; then the disruptive, disturbing, troubling, transforming presence of God will begin to become incarnate in and through our lives.

John's audience was expecting God to intervene in their fallen Babylon world to consummate the covenant and restore the kingdom to Israel. They thought they needed only to stand on the sidelines, be faithful to God, and petition God to intervene. John's vision reveals that God's faithful people are, themselves, the intervention of God in the fallen Babylon world. As God's kingdom of priests, God's New Jerusalem, live out their citizenship in God's realm, their presence and witness becomes a disruptive and disturbing presence that subverts the dehumanizing values and destructive dynamics of fallen Babylon.

◆ IV. The Problem and Its Solution (8:6–16:21)

A. The Seven Trumpets (8:6–11:18)

1. Flawed creation (8:6-12)

6Then the seven angels with the seven trumpets prepared to blow their mighty blasts.

7The first angel blew his trumpet, and hail and fire mixed with blood were thrown down on the earth. One-third of the earth was set on fire, one-third of the trees were burned, and all the green grass was burned.

8Then the second angel blew his trumpet, and a great mountain of fire was thrown into the sea. One-third of the water in the
sea became blood, 9one-third of all things living in the sea died, and one-third of all the ships on the sea were destroyed.

10Then the third angel blew his trumpet, and a great star fell from the sky, burning like a torch. It fell on one-third of the rivers and on the springs of water.
11The name of the star was Bitterness.* It made one-third of the water bitter, and many people died from drinking the bitter water.

12Then the fourth angel blew his trumpet, and one-third of the sun was struck, and one-third of the moon, and one-third of the stars, and they became dark. And one-third of the day was dark, and also one-third of the night.

8:11 Greek *Wormwood.*

NOTES

8:6 ***the seven angels with the seven trumpets.*** There are at least two textual echoes from the OT in the image of the trumpets. John has just seen an image that played upon the incense offering on the Day of Atonement (8:3-4). In the Jubilee year, on the Day of Atonement, trumpets were sounded to announce the Jubilee restoration of the land to its original status and the liberation of captives (Lev 25:9-17). Wright (1996:295) has suggested that "Jesus intended his cells of followers to live 'as if' the Jubilee were being enacted. They were, after all, to be the returned-from-exile people; and one of the emphases of the geographical 'return' of a few hundred years earlier had been Nehemiah's sharp dealing with the problem of debt and slavery within Israel, precisely as part of his attempt to create the true post-exilic people (Neh 5:1-13)."

The image of "seven trumpets" also recalls the original entry into the Promised Land (Josh 6), where the sequence of seven led to the destruction of Jericho and the beginning of the acquisition of the land for Israel. These echoes would not have been lost on an audience steeped in the OT. The vision of the seven trumpets suggests God's action to fulfill the covenant and restore the kingdom to Israel.

8:7 ***hail and fire mixed with blood.*** The images combine two of the plagues against Egypt (Exod 7:19-20; 9:23-24). In 2 Esdr 15:41-43, the image of fire and hail is used in God's judgment of Babylon.

earth . . . trees . . . grass. The action is against the earth and its life-support system, trees and grass. The earth, which has been affected by the rebellion of fallen Babylon, shares in its judgment. Earth is a fallen realm.

one-third. This image is without antecedent in the OT. It would seem to indicate that while fallen creation is already under God's judgment, its final, complete demise (and subsequent restoration) is yet to come.

8:8-9 ***great mountain of fire.*** This contains echoes of *1 Enoch* 18:13 and 21:3, where rebellious stars (heavenly beings) are like great burning mountains. Jeremiah envisions the fall of Babylon as a burned-out mountain ("I am against you, O destroying mountain, says the LORD, that destroys the whole earth; I will stretch out my hand against you, and roll you down from the crags, and make you a burned-out mountain," Jer 51:25, NRSV). The image indicates that creation must have been infected by the rebellion and is under God's judgment but not yet completely destroyed. Here the action is against the sea, which, as a consequence of the Fall, becomes dangerous and inimical to human living.

8:10-11 ***a great star fell from the sky.*** Isaiah seems to have originated the image in his description of the coming fall of Babylon: "How you are fallen from heaven, O shining star, son of the morning! You have been thrown down to the earth, you who destroyed the nations of the world" (Isa 14:12). This image was also used by Jesus: "I saw Satan fall from heaven like lightning" (Luke 10:18). *First Enoch* has the same image of one star (Satan) who falls to earth and then is joined by other stars (*1 Enoch* 86:1, 3).

Bitterness. This is an image associated with rebellion against God. The image originates with Jeremiah where God gives his rebellious people bitterness (lit., "wormwood") to eat and poison water to drink (Jer 9:15; 23:15). In John's vision, water, the essential for life, becomes less than wholesome for human refreshment. John is again seeing the effects of the rebellion upon creation and God's judgment as already present though not yet completed.

8:12 ***they became dark.*** Isaiah's vision of the restoration of Israel under a Davidic king (Isa 11–12) is followed by his vision of the judgment of Babylon (Isa 13:1–14:23) in which no light will shine from stars or sun or moon (Isa 13:10). The image is widespread in the OT of God's judgment associated with the restoration of Israel (see Ezek 32:7; Joel 2:10; 3:15; see also Matt 24:29; 2 Esdr 7:38-39). Here, however, not just the earth but the larger cosmos becomes less than it was created to be.

COMMENTARY

In the Old Testament, the fulfillment of the covenant and the restoration of Israel is coupled with God's judgment against the oppressors of Israel. John's vision, however, seems to expand this perspective to include the entire fallen creation (trumpets 1–4) as well as fallen humanity (trumpets 5–6) before God's fulfillment is seen (interlude; 10:1–11:14) and the victory song of fulfillment and restoration is sung (trumpet 7). Later in the vision, John sees a new creation that replaces the old (21:1). The vision seems to be indicating that the restoration of the kingdom to Israel is much more comprehensive than expected. Paul indicates this perspective when he tells the Romans, "the creation was subjected to futility, not of its own will but by the will of the one who subjected it, in hope that the creation itself will be set free from its bondage to decay and will obtain the freedom of the glory of the children of God" (Rom 8:20-21, NRSV). In other words, a restored creation will also be part of the restoration of the kingdom to Israel.

The Old Testament prophets used many images associated with the entire creation to describe God's judgment upon and overturning of the world order when God restores the kingdom to Israel. The Old Testament prophets, however, did not expect a literal cosmic catastrophe (see notes on 6:12-14). John's vision seems to move beyond the use of the images limited to the restoration of Israel and extends the restoration to the entire creation to recover its original perfection. At this point in the vision, John sees God's judgment already present within a fallen creation. Creation has fallen from its perfection and has become incomplete (the "thirds" that are missing, reduced, or otherwise affected). Creation no longer fully supports human wholeness and, to a certain degree, has become dangerous and destructive to that wholeness.

The vision reminds us that we live in a seriously flawed creation. Humanity attempts valiantly to bring the adverse powers of the created order under its control, but to no avail. El Niño and La Niña events continue to spread disruption and destruction, hurricanes and tornadoes continue to lay waste, earthquakes continue to uncreate human creations, floods continue to wash away human structures and livelihoods, and droughts continue to devastate and wild fires to ravage. We live in a creation that has been infected by the rebellion and manifests the inherent destructiveness that is the corollary of turning away from God. John's vision provides this glimpse of a fallen creation as a point of reference for the vision of a new creation (21:1), which is part of the ultimate consummation of God's restoration of the kingdom and the fulfillment of the covenant.

◆ 2. Fatally flawed creatures (8:13–9:21)

13Then I looked, and I heard a single ea-
gle crying loudly as it flew through the
air, "Terror, terror, terror to all who be-
long to this world because of what will
happen when the last three angels blow
their trumpets."

CHAPTER 9

Then the fifth angel blew his trumpet, and
I saw a star that had fallen to earth from
the sky, and he was given the key to the
shaft of the bottomless pit.* 2When he
opened it, smoke poured out as though

from a huge furnace, and the sunlight and air turned dark from the smoke.

3Then locusts came from the smoke and descended on the earth, and they were given power to sting like scorpions. 4They were told not to harm the grass or plants or trees, but only the people who did not have the seal of God on their foreheads. 5They were told not to kill them but to torture them for five months with pain like the pain of a scorpion sting. 6In those days people will seek death but will not find it. They will long to die, but death will flee from them!

7The locusts looked like horses prepared for battle. They had what looked like gold crowns on their heads, and their faces looked like human faces. 8They had hair like women's hair and teeth like the teeth of a lion. 9They wore armor made of iron, and their wings roared like an army of chariots rushing into battle. 10They had tails that stung like scorpions, and for five months they had the power to torment people. 11Their king is the angel from the bottomless pit; his name in Hebrew is *Abaddon,* and in Greek, *Apollyon*—the Destroyer.

12The first terror is past, but look, two more terrors are coming!

13Then the sixth angel blew his trumpet, and I heard a voice speaking from the four horns of the gold altar that stands in the presence of God. 14And the voice said to the sixth angel who held the trumpet, "Release the four angels who are bound at the great Euphrates River." 15Then the four angels who had been prepared for this hour and day and month and year were turned loose to kill one-third of all the people on earth. 16I heard the size of their army, which was 200 million mounted troops.

17And in my vision, I saw the horses and the riders sitting on them. The riders wore armor that was fiery red and dark blue and yellow. The horses had heads like lions, and fire and smoke and burning sulfur billowed from their mouths. 18One-third of all the people on earth were killed by these three plagues—by the fire and smoke and burning sulfur that came from the mouths of the horses. 19Their power was in their mouths and in their tails. For their tails had heads like snakes, with the power to injure people.

20But the people who did not die in these plagues still refused to repent of their evil deeds and turn to God. They continued to worship demons and idols made of gold, silver, bronze, stone, and wood—idols that can neither see nor hear nor walk! 21And they did not repent of their murders or their witchcraft or their sexual immorality or their thefts.

9:1 Or *the abyss,* or *the underworld;* also in 9:11.

NOTES

8:13 ***eagle.*** This is an image for God in the OT. At the inception of the covenant, God told Moses how he carried his people out of their Egyptian bondage "on eagles' wings" (Exod 19:4) in order that they might be a kingdom of priests (Exod 19:6). This, most likely, is the root of the image often used by the psalmists to describe God's faithful ones being sheltered under God's wings (Pss 17:8; 36:7; 57:1; 61:4; 63:7; 91:4).

through the air. Gr., *en mesouranēmati* [TG3321, ZG3547] (in midheaven). "Through the air" might be a logical translation if we weren't dealing with visionary imagery. The term "midheaven" appears again at 14:6, where an angel appears with an everlasting gospel to proclaim to the "people who belong to this world," the same group associated with the eagle! It appears again at 19:17, where an angel invites the birds of "midheaven" to feast on the vanquished enemies of God. In all instances, "midheaven" is the place of God's address or action related to the citizens of the rebellious order.

Terror, terror, terror. The vision here makes a distinction between the first four and last three trumpets. The last three trumpets are also three terrors. Greek *ouai* [TG3759, ZG4026] is an exclamation or interjection of grief, traditionally translated as "alas," or transliterated as "woe." The term appears also at 9:12; 11:14; 12:12; 18:10, 16, 19. "Woe" is used primarily in the OT to describe the deplorable state and coming judgment of those opposed to God (Num 21:29; 1 Sam 4:7-8; Isa 3:9-11; 6:5; 45:9-10; Jer 4:13; 13:27).

all who belong to this world. The last three trumpets relate only to this group of people. We have seen that this term is used to describe the citizens of the rebellious order (see note on 3:10). The last three trumpets reveal the grievous condition of those who are part of the rebellion against God. This infers that the first four trumpets portray a situation that relates to all humanity, both redeemed and unredeemed, contrary to Beale (1999:472ff), who sees the first four trumpets as God's deprivation of earthly security to the ungodly. He fails to note that in 8:13, John distinguishes the focus of the last three trumpets from the first four. Since the last three clearly affect the ungodly, the first four must affect a larger group—all humanity.

9:1 ***I saw a star that had fallen to earth.*** This is undoubtedly Satan (see note on 8:10 and commentary below).

he was given. This is another expression of the mystery of God's sovereignty over the rebellious order.

the key to the shaft of the bottomless pit. Satan was given the key to the "shaft," not the key of the bottomless pit itself. I think John was seeing that it was Satan's rebellion that opened the way into "death" (spiritual death), that Death and Hades (= the abyss or the bottomless pit) are the inherent consequence of rebellion against God. Satan's rebellion formed the path (access or "shaft") into death. All who turn away from God set their feet on this path. Sovereignty over the abyss, however, remains with God, for it is Jesus who has the keys of Death and Hades (1:18), another phrase that stands for "the bottomless pit" (*abussos* [TG12, ZG12]). For the "pit" as death (Sheol), see Job 17:14; Pss 16:10; 30:3; Prov 1:12; Isa 14:15; 38:17; Ezek 31:14; for the "pit" as abyss (deep), see Ps 69:15; for the "pit" as grave, see Ezek 32:23; for the "pit" as Hades, see Sir 21:10; 2 Esdr 7:36; *1 Enoch* 18:11-12.

9:2 ***smoke poured out as though from a huge furnace.*** This is an image of God's judgment, which appears first in the destruction of Sodom and Gomorrah (Gen 19:28). The image is used widely in the OT and is found in Joel in association with the sunlight becoming dark (Joel 2:30-31). It is Satan's rebellion that "opened" access to the place of death and judgment.

9:3 ***locusts.*** While locusts recall the plague upon Egypt (Exod 10:4-15), Joel used the image to describe God's judgment upon the ungodly (Joel 1:4), and Jeremiah used it of God's judgment of Babylon (Jer 51:14, 27).

scorpions. John's vision combines the destructiveness of locusts with the torment of scorpions, an image used in Sirach for the punishment of the ungodly (Sir 39:30).

9:4 ***not to harm the grass or plants or trees, but only the people who did not have the seal of God.*** We are dealing with imagery here, not literal swarms of locusts, for these "locusts" attack only "the people who did not have the seal of God on their foreheads." Whatever John was seeing relates to the situation of the citizens of fallen Babylon.

9:5 ***torture them for five months.*** John saw an image of limited torment for the people of fallen Babylon. There is no antecedent for the imagery of a five-month period. It may simply play off the locust image since locusts thrive only for the time that vegetation is available (about five months).

9:6 ***people will seek death but will not find it.*** They will long to die, but death will flee from them! This is a picture of deep distress and torment for which there is no relief. Job expressed this condition during his time of torment (Job 3:21).

9:7 ***locusts looked like horses prepared for battle.*** John saw another dimension of the locust-scorpions and their torment. His imagery is drawn primarily from Joel, who describes an invading army of locusts (Joel 2:4-5) whose "teeth are like lions' teeth" (Joel 1:6).

what looked like gold crowns on their heads. According to the Greek, these are something like gold crowns, but not actual crowns. This distinction undoubtedly relates to the vision's consistent image that only the redeemed or heavenly figures have "crowns" (*stephanos* [TG4735, ZG5109]; see note on 4:4; commentary on 6:2).

9:11 ***Their king is the angel from the bottomless pit.*** The magnificent locust-scorpion-horses, which appear to be completely self-sufficient, are actually under the control of this angel.

his name in Hebrew is* Abaddon, *and in Greek,* Apollyon—*the Destroyer. The vision then identifies this angel by the Hebrew and Greek terms for "destroyer"—"Abaddon" and "Apollyon." The Hebrew term appears in Job, Psalms, and Proverbs as a place of destruction or ruin often as a synonym for Sheol (translated in the Greek OT as "Hades"), the place of the dead (Job 26:6; 31:12; Prov 15:11; 27:20), or of death itself (Job 28:22; Ps 88:11). In these passages, the LXX employs the noun *apōleia* [TG684, ZG724] or the verb *apollumi* [TG622/A, ZG660], both having the same root as Apollyon. John appears to be employing two languages for his readers' benefit, since Hebrew would have been the primary language for some, while for most it was Greek. This identification of the "king" over the locust-scorpion-horses as the "Destroyer" indicates these are manifestations of the consequences of Satan's activity. In the Jewish pool of images, these three are representations of the consequences of Israel's apostasy and rebellion against God: (1) locusts: Deut 28:38 in the context of 28:15ff; 2 Chr 7:13; Joel 1:4; Amos 4:9; (2) scorpions: 2 Chr 10:11, 14—Rehoboam's threat to discipline those who were rebelling against him; (3) horses: Jer 6:23; 8:16; 50:42 (although here against the evil of Babylon); Ezek 23:23; Joel 2:4 (with strong parallels to Rev 9); Hab 1:8.

9:13 ***four horns of the gold altar that stands in the presence of God.*** This links to the imagery of the altar of incense in the sanctuary of the Temple (see commentary on 8:3-5). The entire image indicates that what follows is part of God's response to the rebellious mode of existence.

9:14 ***Euphrates River.*** This river was, for both Jews and Romans, an image of disaster (see commentary).

9:15 ***the four angels.*** These remind us of the angels in 7:1 who held back the four winds. The winds were designated to move destructively against the earth, sea, and trees, which, as we saw, represent the rebellious order.

hour and day and month and year. This suggests the inexorable reality of God's action against the rebellious order. John had already written about the events that had to happen (see note on 1:1), and this is a similar expression of the inescapable reality of God's response to the rebellion.

turned loose to kill one-third of all the people on earth. The image of "one-third" has already been related to the consequences of the rebellion (see commentary on 8:7-12).

9:16 ***200 million mounted troops.*** Another image of the inexorable reality of coming judgment is the size of the army. This is an unimaginable army in the first century, to say nothing of being an image of invincibility. Yes, the number is symbolic. The largest number of troops in the OT is 200,000 (1 Sam 15:4; 2 Chr 17:16-17). A thousand times that number would have been unimaginable in the first century.

9:17 ***the horses and the riders.*** These rider-horse beings, while often identified as a demonic cavalry or a demonic horde (Mounce 1977:201; Witherington 2003:154), represent, like the locust-scorpion-horse figures of the fifth trumpet, the destructive consequences of rebellion against God. The primary source for John's imagery seems to come from Jeremiah's vision of Babylon's destruction of Egypt (Jer 46), which includes a cavalry with breastplates (Jer 46:4), more numerous than locusts (Jer 46:23), and coming from the river Euphrates (Jer 46:2). An additional source might well be Jer 8:16-17, where the consequence of Israel's rebellion is imaged as a cavalry that devours the land (like locusts?) and is like serpents among the rebellious.

fiery red and dark blue and yellow . . . fire and smoke and burning sulfur billowed from their mouths. Fiery red is the color of fire, blue is the color of smoke, and yellow is the color of sulfur. The riders and horses are of a single piece. The image of fire, sulfur, and smoke appear first in the OT in the destruction of Sodom and Gomorrah where fire and sulfur rained upon the cities, and Abraham saw the smoke like the smoke of a furnace (Gen 19:24-28). The image is a regular one in the OT (for example, Ps 11:6 says, "He will rain down blazing coals and burning sulfur on the wicked"; and Ezek 38:22 says, "I will punish you [Gog] and your armies with disease and bloodshed; I will send torrential rain, hailstones, fire, and burning sulfur"). Especially interesting is Isaiah's prophecy of God's destruction of Assyria: "For his burning place has long been prepared; . . . the breath of the LORD, like a stream of sulfur, kindles it" (Isa 30:33, NRSV).

9:21 ***they did not repent.*** The vision suggests for the first time, but not the last (see discussion on the bowls of wrath in 16:1-21, especially 16:9 and 11), that God's action against the citizens of fallen Babylon has repentance as its aim, not punishment.

COMMENTARY

John's vision now reveals the terrible predicament in which people who have rebelled against God find themselves. The last three trumpets relate only to those people "who belong to this world" (8:13), those who do not have the seal of God on their foreheads (9:4). The vision also seems to connect the imagery of the fifth and sixth trumpets through the "horses" in them. In the fifth trumpet the horses have the teeth of a lion (9:8); in the sixth the horses have heads like lions. In the fifth, the power is in the tails of the horses (9:10). In the sixth, their power is also in their tails, although in the sixth the tails have heads like snakes in place of tails that sting like scorpions (9:19). It would seem that the vision is indicating two different aspects of the same reality.

The fifth trumpet reveals the activity of beings described as locust-scorpion-horses—with human faces. The human face adds the image of human control, a picture of humanity attempting to be in charge of its own existence. The locust-scorpion-horses also appear magnificent and invincible with their flowing manes "hair like women's hair," their "armor made of iron," and their "wings roared." While these magnificent, powerful creatures appear to be eminently desirable—who wouldn't want to be magnificent, invincible, and in control of their own existence?—their tails sting like scorpions. What appears to be desirable ends up being a terrible torment.

The king of the locust-scorpion-horses is the angel of the abyss, otherwise known as Satan. In the development of the Jewish story (see Introduction, "John's Narrative World"), Isaiah's description of the fall of Babylon (Isa 14:12-14) came to be understood as a description of Satan's fall from heaven. This is carried into the intertestamental literature: *2 Enoch* 29:4-5: "And one from out the order of angels, having turned away with the order that was under him, conceived an impossible thought, to place his throne higher than the clouds above the earth, that he might become equal in rank to my [God's] power. And I threw him out from the height" (see also *1 Enoch* 86:1-6).

The events related to the fifth trumpet give a stark picture of the nature and torment of sin. Sin almost always presents itself to us as something alluring, attractive, desirable, as something that will give power to our lives. It presents itself to us as something that enhances our control of our own existence. It offers us the opportunity to be in charge of our own behavior, to be "really human"—it has a human face and the semblance of a golden crown (see note on 9:7).

The first time we succumb to the temptation, we are in control. Often the experience is pleasant. We feel strong, powerful, in charge of our life. The sin, whatever it is, is merely something for us to have and use as we see fit. The same is true the second time we do it, as well as the third, the fourth . . . but somewhere down this road we cross an invisible line. Up to that point we really are still in control of the situation. Once we move across that invisible line, however, we are no longer in control. The sin has taken control of us. At first we don't notice the difference. Nothing seems to have changed. Gradually, however, we begin to realize that we are trapped. We begin to realize that the "sting" of sin is in its tail. We begin to experience the destructive torment of sin. The more we struggle against the sin, the stronger it becomes. We agonize over its destructive influence in our life and relationships. We desire to be free of its deadly power. We wish we could die to its insidious control over our life, but that death eludes us. We begin to realize there is a power working through the sin to destroy us. We are experiencing the "first woe."

The sixth trumpet unleashes events that take place when four angels are released from the great Euphrates River (9:13-14). The Euphrates had played a significant role in both the Jewish history and the perceptions of the Roman-Hellenistic world. Twice in their history, the Jews had been taken captive by dynasties from across the Euphrates. In 722 BC, the Assyrians took the 10 tribes of the northern kingdom, Israel, into captivity from which they never returned. In 587 BC, the Babylonians took the two tribes of the southern kingdom, Judah, into captivity. In both instances, this was understood to be God's judgment against the unholiness of the old covenant people (2 Kgs 17:5-24 recounts the conquest of the northern tribes of Israel; 2 Kgs 24:1–25:21 the conquest of the southern tribes of Judah). The Roman psyche had also been scarred by events associated with the Euphrates. In Rome's invincible conquest of its Mediterranean empire, its legions had never known defeat until they tried to extend their control into areas beyond the Euphrates. For the first time in their history, a Roman legion was defeated and their standards captured by the enemy in 53 BC, as Crassus attempted to invade Parthia (modern Iran). There grew up in Roman eschatology the belief that the end of the world would come when the hordes ("kings from the east," 16:12) beyond the Euphrates would sweep westward and overcome the Roman Empire (*Sibylline Oracles* 4.115-139). For those of Jewish and Roman traditions, therefore, this was an image of profound loss, destruction, and judgment.

In contrast to the fifth trumpet's torment of the rebellious, the sixth trumpet heralds the death of the rebellious, but only one-third of them. The suffering inflicted on one-third of the people comes in the form of a severe plague. But the people who did not die in the plagues still "refused to repent of their evil deeds" (9:20). Physical, emotional, psychological, and spiritual death can all be aspects of the destructiveness of sin. It is these kinds of things that the inhabitants of fallen Babylon saw all around them. Even though the citizens of the rebellious order saw their compatriots dying as a consequence of rebellion, they did not turn from their evil deeds (see *1 Enoch* 99:7 for a similar list of evil deeds). The sixth trumpet gives a stark picture of the deadliness of sin and its power to blind people to its deadliness. John saw that there is an inexorable progression from the torment of sin to the deadliness of sin. But the most tragic aspect of John's vision is the power of sin to blind those whom it enslaves. Even when they see others destroyed by their rebellious life, the people of fallen Babylon do not turn away from that life but persist in its destructive patterns.

Let me illustrate this reality with a personal experience. At one point in my life I had the opportunity to minister to a family who had a member dying from lung cancer. He had smoked all his life, even while undergoing cobalt treatments to kill the cancer. He literally screamed out the last days of his life in terrible, unbelievable agony, with the members of his family standing at his bedside. As soon as the interment service was over at the cemetery, every male in the family lit a cigarette! How true John's vision is: "the people who did not die in these plagues still refused to repent of their evil deeds."

Both the fifth and sixth trumpets give a vision of the anatomy of sin very similar to that of James. James says we are lured and enticed by our own desire. "These desires give birth to sinful actions. And when sin is allowed to grow, it gives birth to death" (Jas 1:14-15). The vision gives us a frightening picture of the hopeless condition of humanity in its rebellion against God. Rebellion places us in a situation from which we have no power or ability to extract ourselves. The next vision reveals God's response to this intolerable state.

◆ 3. Interlude: God's radical solution (10:1–11:14)

Then I saw another mighty angel coming
down from heaven, surrounded by a
cloud, with a rainbow over his head. His
face shone like the sun, and his feet were
like pillars of fire. [2]And in his hand was
a small scroll* that had been opened. He
stood with his right foot on the sea and
his left foot on the land. [3]And he gave a
great shout like the roar of a lion. And
when he shouted, the seven thunders answered.

[4]When the seven thunders spoke, I was
about to write. But I heard a voice from
heaven saying, "Keep secret* what the
seven thunders said, and do not write it
down."

[5]Then the angel I saw standing on the
sea and on the land raised his right hand
toward heaven. [6]He swore an oath in the
name of the one who lives forever and
ever, who created the heavens and everything in them, the earth and everything in
it, and the sea and everything in it. He
said, "There will be no more delay. [7]When
the seventh angel blows his trumpet,
God's mysterious plan will be fulfilled. It
will happen just as he announced it to his
servants the prophets."

[8]Then the voice from heaven spoke to me again: "Go and take the open scroll from the hand of the angel who is standing on the sea and on the land."

[9]So I went to the angel and told him to give me the small scroll. "Yes, take it and eat it," he said. "It will be sweet as honey in your mouth, but it will turn sour in your stomach!" [10]So I took the small scroll from the hand of the angel, and I ate it! It was sweet in my mouth, but when I swallowed it, it turned sour in my stomach.

[11]Then I was told, "You must prophesy again about many peoples, nations, languages, and kings."

CHAPTER 11

Then I was given a measuring stick, and I was told, "Go and measure the Temple of God and the altar, and count the number of worshipers. [2]But do not measure the outer courtyard, for it has been turned over to the nations. They will trample the holy city for 42 months. [3]And I will give power to my two witnesses, and they will be clothed in burlap and will prophesy during those 1,260 days."

[4]These two prophets are the two olive trees and the two lampstands that stand before the Lord of all the earth. [5]If anyone tries to harm them, fire flashes from their mouths and consumes their enemies. This is how anyone who tries to harm them must die. [6]They have power to shut the sky so that no rain will fall for as long as they prophesy. And they have the power to turn the rivers and oceans into blood, and to strike the earth with every kind of plague as often as they wish.

[7]When they complete their testimony, the beast that comes up out of the bottomless pit* will declare war against them, and he will conquer them and kill them. [8]And their bodies will lie in the main street of Jerusalem,* the city that is figuratively called "Sodom" and "Egypt," the city where their Lord was crucified. [9]And for three and a half days, all peoples, tribes, languages, and nations will stare at their bodies. No one will be allowed to bury them. [10]All the people who belong to this world will gloat over them and give presents to each other to celebrate the death of the two prophets who had tormented them.

[11]But after three and a half days, God breathed life into them, and they stood up! Terror struck all who were staring at them. [12]Then a loud voice from heaven called to the two prophets, "Come up here!" And they rose to heaven in a cloud as their enemies watched.

[13]At the same time there was a terrible earthquake that destroyed a tenth of the city. Seven thousand people died in that earthquake, and everyone else was terrified and gave glory to the God of heaven.

[14]The second terror is past, but look, the third terror is coming quickly.

10:2 Or *book;* also in 10:8, 9, 10. **10:4** Greek *Seal up.* **11:7** Or *the abyss,* or *the underworld.* **11:8** Greek *the great city.*

NOTES

10:1 ***another mighty angel coming down from heaven.*** This appears to be Jesus the Messiah coming as a messenger (*angelos* [TG32, ZG34]). Most of the attributes of this angel mentioned in this verse have already been associated with Jesus: "surrounded by a cloud" (cf. 1:7), "his face shone like the sun" (1:16), "his feet were like pillars of fire" (1:15). The "rainbow over his head" was an attribute of God (4:3), but already John had seen Jesus and God brought together on the throne where the rainbow is (3:21; 5:13; 6:16; 7:9-10, 17).

10:2 ***a small scroll that had been opened.*** This is in marked contrast to the sealed scroll in the hand of God (5:1). The image suggests something which had already been disclosed, perhaps the old covenant, since there are textual echoes here to the giving of the first covenant in that God appeared to the people in a cloud (Exod 16:10).

He stood with his right foot on the sea and his left foot on the land. This is repeated twice more (10:5, 8), emphasizing the significance of this image. The NLT's "land" represents the same Greek that is translated "earth" in 5:10—it is again a symbol for the rebellious realm of fallen Babylon. The "sea" is also a symbol of the rebellious realm (see discussion of "earth" in note on 3:10, and the discussion of "sea" in note on 4:6). Since "land" and "sea" represent the rebellious realm, this is a vision of Jesus' sovereignty over the entire realm of rebellion. Later in the vision John sees a beast coming from the sea and another from the earth (13:1, 11). *First Enoch* 60:7-8 gives witness to the imagery of two beasts in intertestamental Judaism, one related to the sea and one to the land. These two beasts represent an incarnation of Satan's rebellion in human history. John was seeing Jesus as the victor over the rebellion.

10:3 ***like the roar of a lion.*** This is the voice of Jesus, the Lion of Judah, the Lamb, whose death has conquered the rebellion (5:5). In the OT it is also an image of God's judgment against the ungodly (Joel 3:16; Amos 1:2, cf. *4 Ezra* 11:37; 12:31).

10:4 ***Keep secret what the seven thunders said.*** This command is typical in visionary experience. Paul heard things that could not be told (2 Cor 12:4), Daniel was told to seal up his vision (Dan 8:26; 12:4, 9), and here we see that John was prohibited from sharing a portion of his vision. The image of thunder is common in the Scriptures as an image for God's voice (Exod 19:9; Job 37:2, 4-5; Ps 29:3; John 12:28-29; and in 4:5 the thunder is used as an image for the one seated upon the throne). Since "seven" represents completeness and wholeness, John may be portraying the fullness of God's speaking in Jesus, the Lion of Judah, whose "roars" evoke the thunders. The prohibition against disclosing what the thunders said at least infers that there is more to God and the Lamb than John is allowed to reveal.

10:5-6 ***standing on the sea and on the land.*** Here for the second time Jesus is described in this victorious posture (see note on 10:2).

raised his right hand toward heaven . . . swore an oath. This echoes Deut 32:39-43, wherein God lifts up his hand to heaven, swears judgment upon his adversaries, and promises the restoration of his people. The image also appears in Dan 12:7. There, too, the focus is God's action against the enemies of Israel and the restoration of the kingdom.

who created . . . the earth and everything in it, and the sea and everything in it. This shows that God is also sovereign over the rebellious realm. This adds emphasis to the triple picture of Jesus as victor over sea and earth.

10:9 ***sweet as honey in your mouth . . . sour in your stomach.*** This image echoes Ezek 2:9–3:14. For Ezekiel, however, he was to prophesy to the rebellious house of Israel.

10:11 ***prophesy . . . about many peoples, nations, languages, and kings.*** John here uses a slight variation upon the usual "tribe, language, people, and nation" found in 5:9; 7:9; 11:9; 13:7; 14:6; 17:15, a phrase clearly identifying the composition of fallen Babylon, the people of the rebellious order.

11:1-2 ***Go and measure.*** The measuring called for here is not described, but may have its fulfillment in the measuring of New Jerusalem (21:15-17).

it has been turned over to the nations. John's image here is reminiscent of Jesus' prophecy regarding Jerusalem: "And Jerusalem will be trampled down by the Gentiles until the period of the Gentiles comes to an end" (Luke 21:24).

11:3 ***two witnesses.*** In Jewish tradition, at least two males were required as witnesses in order to bring judgment upon someone (Deut 19:15). In this case, the judgment is upon the entire rebellious order.

burlap. Or, "sackcloth." This is the garment of mourning (e.g., Gen 37:34). In the Jewish tradition it is especially associated with mourning for sin (e.g., Isa 37:1-2) and the judgment of God upon sin (e.g., Amos 8:7-14).

11:4 ***two olive trees and the two lampstands.*** The image is an echo of Zech 4 where two olive trees and a single lampstand figure prominently. The identity of the two olive trees is given only as "the two anointed ones" (Zech 4:14, KJV), and the larger context is the restoration of Israel (Zech 8–14).

11:5-6 The vision clarifies the identity of the two witnesses by describing their attributes. They are Moses and Elijah.

fire flashes from their mouths and consumes their enemies. For the identification with Moses, see Num 16:1-35; with Elijah, see 2 Kgs 1:10-12.

power to shut the sky so that no rain will fall for as long as they prophesy. This refers to what Elijah did (1 Kgs 17:1-7).

to turn the rivers and oceans into blood, and to strike the earth with every kind of plague. This refers to what Moses did (Exod 7:14–12:30). Moses and Elijah are archetypal representatives of the law and the prophets in the OT. John was seeing the old covenant as God's witness against the rebellious order.

11:7 ***When they complete their testimony.*** John employs *teleō* [TG5055, ZG5464] (complete) in his vision exclusively for reporting the completion or consummation of something (15:8, the seven plagues; 17:17, the words of God; 20:3, 5, 7, the 1,000 years). It is possible that the vision now reveals the completion of the old covenant (cf. Matt 5:17), which was consummated in the death, resurrection, and ascension of the Messiah.

the beast. The identity of this entity is clarified in ch 13, where it comes as the manifestation of the dragon's rebellion in ch 12, a rebellion that consists in devouring the Messiah, the child of the woman. (See the notes on the appropriate sections of chs 12 and 13, as well as the discussion in ch 17.) It will be seen that the beast represents the incarnation of Satan's rebellion throughout human history. For John and his hearers the beast was manifest as the Roman Empire and, particularly, in the emperor.

bottomless pit. This is a synonym for the abyss, Death and Hades, Satan's realm (see note on 9:1).

he will conquer them. Here is one of the two places where conquering is associated with the rebellious realm. The other is 13:7 (see note). All other uses of "conquer" are with the Lamb or the saints (see commentary on 6:2). The vision quickly reveals, however, that this "victory" is, in reality, a defeat for the beast and his realm.

11:8 ***Jerusalem.*** Lit., "the great city" (so NLT mg). Jerusalem was, of course, the historical and geographic place where the Messiah was crucified, but the vision is moving beyond mere historical and geographical realities. Later the vision identifies "the great city" as fallen Babylon (17:5; 18:2, 10, 16, 18, 19, 21), the rebellious order.

the city that is figuratively called "Sodom" and "Egypt." These were the archetypal places of rebellion against God and the oppression of God's people in Jewish history.

the city where their Lord was crucified. Historically this was Jerusalem, but the dynamics of a deeper reality were being enacted. The Crucifixion, at its deepest level, took place in the midst of the rebellious order, fallen Babylon.

11:9-10 ***the people who belong to this world.*** Lit., "those who dwell upon the earth." The vision now clearly reveals that the citizens of the rebellious order are designated by this phrase (see notes on 3:10 and 5:9).

celebrate the death of the two prophets. The rebellious order believes it has won the victory over God, and the people participate in the ultimate abuse and disrespect expressed in their refusal to bury the bodies of these two prophets (see, e.g., Jer 16:4-6 regarding the abomination of not being buried).

11:11 ***three and a half days.*** This expression is puzzling. There are no unambiguous antecedents for it in the Jewish story (i.e., Jewish tradition and worldview expressed in the OT and other literature; see the Introduction), nor is it clarified elsewhere in the vision. One possibility is that John is playing off of Daniel's "a time, times, and half a time" (Dan 7:25; 12:7), a unit of three and a half, especially since in Daniel it is associated with the tribulation and death that God's faithful people will experience at the hands of the wicked just before God acts to deliver them from their oppressors and restore the kingdom to Israel. While it is clear in Daniel that the time period represents years (plainly, the period of the Maccabean Revolt prior to the restoration of the Temple), we have already seen John modulate the imagery he employs from the Jewish pool of images, and we will see more of the same in what follows. The fact that John obviously uses the "a time, times, and half a time" from Daniel in Rev 12:14 (see note) should not detract from his alternate use here. For example, in 17:9 (see note), the seven heads of the beast upon which the woman sits are both seven mountains and seven kings. Thus, the imagery is polyvalent.

At the close of this period, God would end "the shattering of the power of the holy people" (Dan 12:7, NRSV). John here applies the imagery to the essence of the covenant, the law and prophets, indicating that in the death and resurrection of the Messiah, the shattering of the power of the holy people has come to an end and the kingdom has been restored to Israel. This would seem to be confirmed by the next image John uses.

God breathed life into them, and they stood up! The Greek text of the second clause reads *kai estēsan* [TG2476, ZG2705] *epi tous podas autōn* ("and they stood upon their feet"), which is exactly the same wording in Ezek 37:10, LXX. Therefore, it is unmistakable that John here draws upon the imagery of Ezek 37:10, which is also a vision of the restoration of the kingdom to Israel, including, in some form, resurrection (cf. Ezek 37:12-14). Thus, John sees in his vision symbols of the Messiah's death and resurrection that mark it as the fulfillment of both Daniel's (Dan 7:25; 12:7) and Ezekiel's visions (see commentary).

11:12 ***they rose to heaven in a cloud.*** This would seem to reflect the ascension of Jesus in Acts 1:9, further confirming the consummation of the old covenant in the death, resurrection, and ascension of the Messiah.

11:13 ***there was a terrible earthquake.*** This image is a representation of God's radical disruption of the structures and dynamics of the rebellious order (see notes on 6:12-14; 8:5), an image heightened by the fact that the audience lived in a very active earthquake zone.

destroyed a tenth of the city. The tenth represents the "tithe" in Jewish history, not merely as the portion that is given to God but as an acknowledgment that the entire amount from which the tithe is given has been received from God. Genesis 28:22 indicates this: "I will present to God a tenth of everything he gives me." It is seen again in Num 18:26: "When you [the priests] receive from the people of Israel the tithes I have assigned as your allotment, give a tenth of the tithes you receive—a tithe of the tithe—to the LORD as a sacred offering." Amos, too, provides a stark reminder of this reality, with God rebuking Israel for its greed and acquisitiveness even though it offers tithes every three days (Amos 4:4). In the context of Amos 2:6-7; 3:10, 15; 4:1, the desire for possessions and luxury resulted in the abuse of the poor and needy; also in the context of Amos 4:6-11, God had withheld their sustenance because of their abuse of his provision. Clearly here the role of the tithe extends far beyond the mere performance of a religious duty; it should be a manifestation of faithful stewardship of life before God.

In this context, therefore, when John uses the imagery of the tithe, the implication is that the *entire* rebellious city has been judged and is fallen. What John sees here seems to be the reality Jesus announced related to his death: "The time for judging this world has come, when Satan, the ruler of this world, will be cast out. And when I am lifted up from the earth, I will draw everyone to myself" (John 12:31-32). John was conveying the vision's revelation of how "Babylon" became "fallen Babylon." He was seeing God's judgment upon fallen Babylon and, at the same time, the mystery of fallen Babylon's continued sway in history. We will see John portray this mystery again in the image of the beast having a mortal wound that was healed (13:3).

Seven thousand people died in that earthquake. No translation can do justice to the puzzling Greek of this passage. A literal translation is "they were killed in the earthquake names of humans seven thousand." It is the use of "names" that makes this so strange. John could easily have written, "seven thousand people died," but he didn't. We have noted that "name" in the imagery of the OT represents the nature or essence of the one named (see notes on 2:13 and 3:12 concerning the meaning of "name"). Seven represents totality and is emphasized by the multiple of a thousand. What John seems to be seeing here is that in the cross the totality of fallen human nature, the essence of the rebellion, died. John saw here what Paul understood happened in the cross: "We are convinced that one [the Messiah] has died for all; therefore all have died. And he died for all, so that those who live [a smaller group within the "all" = John's "everyone else" who became fearers and gave glory to God] might live no longer for themselves [the essence of the fallen nature] but for him who died and was raised for them" (2 Cor 5:14-15, NRSV).

11:14 ***second terror.*** Lit., "second woe" (see note on 8:13). Both the destructiveness of sin (the sixth trumpet) and God's radical response to the rebellion (the interlude) are a great "woe" to the rebellious order. This woe, too, is the present reality of fallen Babylon—the reality of our world throughout all generations.

third terror is coming quickly. At the close of the vision of the seventh trumpet, John does not tell us that the third woe has come, as he does at the end of the fifth and sixth trumpets. It would appear that the final "woe" for fallen Babylon, its ultimate demise, is still ahead. John's term for "quickly" (*tachu* [TG5035, ZG5444]) is the adverbial form of the term used in a different structure in 1:1, which, as we saw, infers that things will happen in God's timing.

COMMENTARY

The interlude between the sixth and seventh trumpets reveals God's gracious intervention, as well as foretelling what will happen when the seventh trumpet sounds: "God's mysterious plan will be fulfilled. It will happen just as he announced it to his servants the prophets" (10:7). This mystery is the restoration of the kingdom to Israel. The fulfillment of this is seen when the seventh angel blows his trumpet and the heavens shout, "The world has now become the Kingdom of our Lord and of his [Messiah], and he will reign forever and ever" (11:15). There, too, the vision reveals God's judgment against his adversaries and the rewarding of God's faithful people and the prophets (11:18). John was about to see the fulfillment of the plan in God's action toward the rebellion and the restoration of the kingdom.

The mighty messenger, the Lord Jesus (see note on 10:1), declares "There will be no more delay" (10:6). This points to the Jewish expectation of the restoration of the kingdom, the consummation of the old covenant, and the fulfillment of the promises to the prophets that have been so long delayed. As we have already seen, John's vision reveals that in Jesus, God has begun the restoration. The rest of the interlude between the sixth and seventh trumpets confirms this. The "consummation of the old covenant" is the fulfillment of the purpose of the old covenant that Israel should be a kingdom of priests and a holy nation (Exod 19:6). It is this reality that John affirms in the introduction of his vision: "He has made us a Kingdom of priests for God" (1:6; cf. 5:10).

The voice comes from heaven and tells John to take the scroll from the messenger standing on the sea and the land, and then to eat the scroll (10:8-9). If this little scroll represents the old covenant, as suggested above (see note on 10:2), the images of sweet and sour make sense in light of the fifth and sixth trumpets. Those trumpets disclosed the terrible predicament in which humanity finds itself. Humanity is inescapably "imprisoned" by its sinful nature, which results in torment and death. The old covenant contained the promise of God's liberating response to this bondage; it was, indeed, sweet to the taste. But the promise had never yet been fulfilled, and this was sour in the stomach.

When we come to chapter 11, we see that John was told to measure the Temple. The imagery here relies upon Ezekiel 40–44, the vision of the restored Temple. In Ezekiel, however, the Temple, the altar, and the outer courtyard are measured, while in John's vision the outer courtyard "has been turned over to the nations" (11:2). John's vision again subverts messianic expectations. The vision intimates that the restoration of the Temple has begun, but that it is not yet fully consummated because it has been taken over by the nations.

John sees that the holy city of the restored Temple has been turned over to the nations who "will trample the holy city for 42 months" (11:2). The image of 42 months (cf. 13:5) is also represented as 1,260 days (11:3; 12:6), and three and a half years (12:14). This image originated with Elijah who prayed and the result was that there was no rain in Israel for 42 months (1 Kgs 17–18; cf. Luke 4:25). This was a time of intense tribulation for God's faithful people in Israel. The image was subsequently reinforced during the Babylonian siege and destruction of Jerusalem, which lasted approximately the same length of time. (The time from the refusal of tribute to Babylon by Zedekiah to the siege and destruction was roughly 591–587 BC.) The same time period occurred again during the Maccabean revolt. The time from the attack upon Jerusalem by Antiochus Epiphanes to its capture and cleansing by the Maccabees was approximately three and a half years (Dan 12:11 indicates the period as 1,290 days, one month longer than 42). This image became deeply ingrained in the Jewish psyche as representing a time of severe persecution for God's faithful people. This is reflected especially in Daniel 7:25 and 12:7, where the period describes the tribulations of faithful Jews at the hands of their enemies. John here is seeing that while the kingdom has been restored, this restoration is not complete. In the meantime, God's faithful kingdom of priests (1:5-6; 5:10) continue to experience persecution at the hands of fallen Babylon.

After hearing about the Temple, John is told about two witnesses, who are the prophets Moses and Elijah (see note on 11:5-6). These two prophets appeared with Jesus at the time of his transfiguration (Luke 9:28-36) and discussed "his exodus from this world, which was about to be fulfilled in Jerusalem." In his vision John sees the deeper dimensions of this discussion. Moses and Elijah, representatives of the law and the prophets, are joined with Jesus in his death, resurrection, and ascension. I say this because it seems to me that the two witnesses participating in Jesus' crucifixion (11:8, the only explicit mention of crucifixion in the vision) and subsequently being resurrected and then ascending to heaven forces the reader to associate this with Jesus' crucifixion, resurrection, and ascension.

This portion of John's vision would have been a radical message to those steeped in the Jewish story. John was seeing that in the crucifixion, resurrection, and ascension of Jesus the Messiah, the old covenant has been consummated. God has fulfilled the law and the prophets. Jesus, himself, had indicated as much. "I did not come to abolish the law of Moses or the writings of the prophets. No, I came to accomplish their purpose" (Matt 5:17). The consequence is the undoing of the entire rebellious order. God not only deals with sin and the sin nature, he deals with the entire realm of rebellion that engenders and nurtures the sin nature. God deals not with the consequences but the cause.

At the end of this section, we are told that "everyone else was terrified and gave glory to the God of heaven" (11:13). Thus, it appears that the response that enables persons to be redeemed from fallen Babylon and become citizens of New Jerusalem is to "fear God . . . give glory to him" (cf. 14:7). Here, then, John was seeing the two aspects of the cross for fallen humanity. Its fallenness is judged and pronounced dead. But for those who respond, it becomes their redemption from the destructive and dehumanizing bondage of fallen Babylon. John sees here what Paul understood happened at the cross: "Since we believe that Christ died for all, we also believe that we have all died to our old life. He died for everyone so that those who receive his new life will no longer live for themselves. Instead, they will live for Christ, who died and was raised for them" (2 Cor 5:14-15).

We must now step back for a moment and look at the "big picture" of John's vision, especially the centrality of the cross. Though John portrays the vision's focus on the cross somewhat obliquely, the cross stands at the heart of John's vision. In addition to the fact that John's vision portrays various aspects of the cross, this portrayal is set forth in seven dimensions throughout the vision. Some of these we have already seen, others are yet ahead of us. First, John saw that the cross undermines the rebellious order. In 1:18 Jesus says to John, "I died, but look—I am alive forever and ever! And I hold the keys of death and the grave." It was noted at 1:18 that Death and Hades represent the foundation of the realm of rebellion within which the dragon Satan "rules," the beast and false prophet operate, and fallen Babylon exists. John was seeing that in the death and resurrection of Jesus, control over the foundation of the rebellious order has been firmly placed in Jesus' hands. Second, John saw that the cross is the revelation of the fullness of God's purposes. At 5:5, we read, "the Lion of the tribe of Judah, the heir to David's throne, has won the victory. He is worthy to open the scroll and its seven seals." The sealed scroll at God's right hand represents the fullness of God's purposes (see note on 5:1). The vision notes that only the slain Lamb can disclose the fullness of God's purposes. The Lamb's conquering (via the cross) is what opens the scroll, what reveals the fullness of God's purposes (see note on 5:5). Third, John saw that the cross creates a new order of being. In 5:9-10 John describes the praise of the Lamb: "You are worthy to take the scroll and break its seals and open it. For you were slaughtered [the cross], and your blood has ransomed people for God from every tribe and language and people and nation. And you have caused them to become a Kingdom of priests for our God." Through the cross, the redeemed people of fallen Babylon are reconstituted as God's priestly kingdom. Fourth, as we have just seen, the cross consummates the old covenant. In John's only explicit mention of the Crucifixion, the two witnesses, Moses and Elijah, the law and the prophets, become integrated into the death, resurrection, and ascension of Jesus. This is John's way of portraying the vision's reality that in the cross the old covenant has been consummated.

Fifth, we are now coming to the point in John's vision where we see that the cross reveals the depths of God's being, that the cross reveals God's essential nature. As will be described in the next section, John sees God as a woman bringing forth her son into the mouth of the dragon (Satan). It will be noted that the vision reveals the cross, not as something God "did," but as a revelation of the very nature of God as cruciform love (cf. Gorman 2001; 2009).

Sixth, we will see that the cross defeats the beast. In 13:3 it will be seen "that one of the heads of the beast seemed wounded beyond recovery—but the fatal wound was healed!" This oxymoron is repeated twice more (13:12, 14), emphasizing the fact that the cross has inflicted a mortal wound on the beast even though the beast seems to continue as if nothing has happened. This mysterious reality is developed more fully in 19:20–20:3, the final vision of the cross.

Seventh, we will see that the cross breaks Satan's power over the people of fallen Babylon. It will be seen that the defeat of the beast and false prophet (19:20) is the result of the cross and is also the binding of Satan (20:2). Without the beast and false prophet, who represent the means of incarnating Satan's rebellion in human history, Satan's power over the people of fallen Babylon is broken.

For us this means that the entire structure of the world's false values, false perspectives, false behaviors, which have engendered and nurtured in us a false self shaped by those values, perspectives, and behaviors, has been judged and executed in the death of Jesus. This is why Paul reminds us that in the death of Jesus we all died (2 Cor 5:14). If that which held us in its destructive bondage has died, then we can be free from its debilitating hold upon our lives. But that freedom comes at a profound price. We must die to the false self if our true self, restored in the image of God, is to be nurtured to its maturity. This is what Jesus meant when he said, "If you cling to your [false] life, you will lose it; but if you give up your life for me, you will find it [your true life]" (Matt 10:39). Paul reiterates this reality when he tells the Galatians, "My old self has been crucified with Christ. It is no longer I [the false self] who live, but Christ lives in me" (Gal 2:19-20), and reminds the Colossians, "For you [the false self] died to this life, and your real life is hidden with Christ in

God" (Col 3:3). John sees this imaged in his vision in those who become fearers and give glory to God (11:13). The essence of the transforming transaction is the removal of self as our center of reference and allowing God to become the center of reference for our entire being and living.

The sixth trumpet is a stark picture of the inexorable destructiveness of sin. Paul reminds us that "the wages of sin is death" (Rom 6:23), and this is what John sees. We so often think we can "get away" with sin. After all, it is just a "little" sin. The action, however, is only the tip of the iceberg. The action is an outer manifestation of an inner posture of being that has turned its back upon God. At that turning, something deep within us begins its slow but inevitable journey down the broad and easy path toward spiritual death. Sin is a spiritual cancer that eats at the vitals of our very being. Like cancer in our physical bodies, its destructive growth often goes long undetected.

The real horror of sin, however, is its power to blind the one sinning to its destructive, cancerous growth. We observe others' lives being destroyed by some attitude, relationship, or behavior, but continue in the same path ourselves (cf. 9:20). Think, for instance, of the destructive power of AIDS. Much is known about the behaviors that lead to AIDS, yet how many have changed the behaviors that make them susceptible to contracting the virus? John sees that sin is spiritual AIDS. He also sees a greater problem—the entire human race is infected. Except for God's gracious intervention, we are in a hopeless condition.

◆ 4. The song of victory (11:15-18)

15 Then the seventh angel blew his trumpet, and there were loud voices shouting in heaven:

"The world has now become the
Kingdom of our Lord and of his
Christ,*
and he will reign forever and ever."

16 The twenty-four elders sitting on their thrones before God fell with their faces to the ground and worshiped him. 17 And they said,

"We give thanks to you, Lord God, the
Almighty,
the one who is and who always was,
for now you have assumed your great
power
and have begun to reign.
18 The nations were filled with wrath,
but now the time of your wrath has
come.
It is time to judge the dead
and reward your servants the
prophets,
as well as your holy people,
and all who fear your name,
from the least to the greatest.
It is time to destroy
all who have caused destruction on
the earth."

11:15 Or *his Messiah.*

NOTES

11:16 ***The twenty-four elders.*** These represent those redeemed by the Lamb, the kingdom of priests (see note on 4:4).

11:17 ***the one who is and who always was.*** The phrase "who is still to come," which was present up to this point (see 1:4, 8; 4:8 and notes), disappears here and is absent again in

16:5. What has happened that results in the omission? John has just seen (11:3-13) that in the cross of Jesus, God has come to deal with those who rebelled against him. I think John was seeing what happened in the cross, that it was there that "the kingdom of the world has become the kingdom of our Lord and of his Messiah" (11:15, NRSV). Thus, the cross becomes the long-awaited "is to come" that formed the center of the Jewish expectations for the restoration of the kingdom to Israel. From that point on, God would be "the one who is and who always was" as in 11:17 and 16:5, because in the cross, God has come to fulfill his covenant and his promises to the prophets.

you have assumed your great power and have begun to reign. In the death, resurrection, and ascension of the Messiah, God inaugurated the reign of his kingdom.

COMMENTARY

This section begins with the victorious proclamation that the world has now become the kingdom of our Lord and of his Christ. This affirmation is the fulfillment of Zechariah's prophecy of the restoration of the kingdom to Israel, "the LORD will be king over all the earth" (Zech 14:9). The image is prevalent in the prophetic vision of the restoration (Isa 2:2-3; 60:3-14; Dan 7:27; Mic 4:1-2). As in Handel's *Messiah*, the "Hallelujah Chorus" of Revelation is sung not at the end of the presentation but in the middle, at the point of God's victory that establishes his kingdom.

The vision reveals that God has acted decisively. The long-awaited and eagerly looked for coming of God has taken place in the life, death, and resurrection of the Messiah, Jesus. This means that God has overcome the enemies of his people, has given judgment in favor of the righteous martyrs who had given their lives for their faithfulness, and has fulfilled what he had promised through the prophets. However, as we have seen, the final consummation of this victory is yet to come.

B. What's Really Going On (11:19–15:4)

1. The real roots of the cross (11:19–12:6)

19Then, in heaven, the Temple of God was opened and the Ark of his covenant could be seen inside the Temple. Lightning flashed, thunder crashed and roared, and there was an earthquake and a terrible hailstorm.

CHAPTER 12

Then I witnessed in heaven an event of great significance. I saw a woman clothed with the sun, with the moon beneath her feet, and a crown of twelve stars on her
head. 2She was pregnant, and she cried out because of her labor pains and the agony of giving birth.
3Then I witnessed in heaven another significant event. I saw a large red dragon with seven heads and ten horns, with
seven crowns on his heads. 4His tail swept away one-third of the stars in the sky, and he threw them to the earth. He stood in front of the woman as she was about to give birth, ready to devour her baby as soon as it was born.
5She gave birth to a son who was to rule all nations with an iron rod. And her child was snatched away from the dragon and was caught up to God and to
his throne. 6And the woman fled into the wilderness, where God had prepared a place to care for her for 1,260 days.

NOTES

11:19 *in heaven, the Temple of God was opened.* This forms a bridge between the vision of the trumpets (8:6–11:18) and the next section (12:1–15:4), which then bridges to the seven bowls (15:5–16:21) with the same image: "the Temple in heaven . . . was thrown wide open" (15:5). The two references to the Temple form an *inclusio*:

A. 1:19—in heaven, the Temple of God was opened
B. 12:1—in heaven an event of great significance
B1. 15:1—in heaven another marvelous event of great significance
A1. 15:5—the Temple in heaven . . . was thrown wide open

Lightning flashed, thunder crashed and roared. Lit., "there were lightnings, and voices/sounds [so also in 4:5; 8:5; 16:18] and thunders." As already noted (see note on 4:5), these are images of the presence of God. Their appearance along with the Ark in this verse confirms that access to the Ark of the Covenant entails access to the very presence of God.

earthquake and a terrible hailstorm. For the rebellious order, the presence of God is seen in images depicting radical disruption and destruction. In the OT, hail often represented God's action against the ungodly (Exod 9:18-34; Pss 78:47-48; 105:32; Isa 28:2, 17).

12:1 *an event of great significance.* Lit., "a great sign." It is interesting, given all the magnificent and powerful imagery of John's vision, that it is only here and at 15:1 that John describes what he sees as an event of great significance. The NLT rendering skews our understanding somewhat because the Greek does not have "event" but "sign" (*sēmeion* [TG4592, ZG4956]), which indicates something that points beyond itself to a deeper reality that is only represented by the "sign." A "sign" may be an event, but not necessarily. In this case, the sign is not an event, but a person—"a woman."

clothed with the sun. This is most likely an image for God. In the Jewish pool of images, God is a pillar of fire (Exod 13:21); light (Job 24:13, 16; 38:19; Pss 4:6; 36:9; 44:3; 89:15; 104:2 [here especially, where God is "dressed in a robe of light"]; Isa 60:19-20; Dan 2:22; and the following NT passages that manifest this Jewish imagery: Acts 26:18; 1 Tim 6:16; 1 Pet 2:9; 1 John 1:5; Rev 21:23–22:5); a flame (Isa 10:17; 29:6); fire (Exod 3:2; 19:18; 24:17; Lev 9:24; 10:2; Num 11:1; Deut 4:12, 24, 36; 9:3; 2 Sam 22:9; Ps 50:3; Isa 66:15); and brightness (2 Sam 22:13; Ezek 1:4, 13; 10:4; Hab 3:4; Sir 23:19). John utilized a wealth of this imagery to describe his vision: Jesus' "eyes were like flames of fire [cf. 19:12]. His feet were like polished bronze refined in a furnace. . . . And his face was like the sun in all its brilliance" (1:14-16). John describes his vision of God: "From the throne came flashes of lightning [cf. 8:5; 11:19; 16:18] . . . And in front of the throne were seven torches with burning flames. This is the sevenfold Spirit of God" (4:5); the face of the mighty angel, Jesus, "shone like the sun, and his feet were like pillars of fire" (10:1); New Jerusalem "has no need of sun or moon, for the glory of God illuminates the city" (21:23; 22:5). *First Enoch* provides one of the clearest examples of how this imagery developed in the intertestamental period:

> And I beheld a vision, and lo! There was a second house, greater than the former, and the entire portal stood open before me, and it was built of flames of fire. . . . And its floor was of fire, and above it were lightnings [cf. Rev 4:5; 8:5; 11:19; 16:18] and the path of the stars, and its ceiling also was flaming fire. And I looked and saw therein a lofty throne: its appearance was as crystal, and the wheels thereof as the shining sun. . . . And from underneath the throne came streams of flaming fire so that I could not look thereon. And the Great Glory sat thereon, and His raiment shone more brightly than the sun and was whiter than any snow. . . . The flaming fire was round about Him, and a great fire stood before Him" (*1 Enoch* 14:15-22; cf. 71:2-6).

the moon beneath her feet. This image suggests God enthroned on the praises of Israel (Ps 22:3) since Israel's is a lunar-based cycle of worship (Num 29:6; 1 Chr 23:31; 2 Chr 2:4; 8:13; 31:3; Ezra 3:5; Neh 10:33; Ps 81:3; Isa 1:13-14; 66:23; Ezek 45:17; 46:3; Hos 2:11). It was apparently such a significant part of their worship of God that they were warned not to worship the moon itself as though it were God (Deut 4:19; 17:3; 2 Kgs 23:5). Another expression in Israel's worship is that they worship at God's "footstool" (Pss 99:5; 132:7) suggesting their position in worship is at God's feet. The Temple where Jewish worship took place was God's "footstool" (1 Chr 28:2; *4 Ezra* 6:4). Falling at someone's feet to worship is a well-established image for worship (19:10; 22:8; Matt 28:9; Acts 10:25). It seems clear that one image of worship is falling before God's feet; another is worshiping at God's footstool, the Temple. Again, these two images—a lunar-based cycle of worship and worship imaged as falling at God's feet—strongly suggest that John was imaging God as the woman.

a crown of twelve stars on her head. The number "twelve" suggests the 12 tribes of Israel, and in both Isaiah and Zechariah the restored Israel is seen either as a crown in God's hand (Isa 62:3) or like jewels in a crown (Zech 9:16). In Joseph's dream the progenitors of the 12 tribes are seen as stars (Gen 37:9). Beale (1999:625-626) provides extensive evidence for understanding the stars as Israel. If the stars are Israel, however, then the woman cannot be Israel, and if the crown is Israel as in Isaiah and Zechariah, the one wearing the crown cannot be Israel. It is not too much of a leap to see the crown in God's hand (Isa 62:3) as intended for his head (12:1). This image, also, strongly suggests that the woman is God. When the woman is understood in the light of Jewish imagery, therefore, rather than traditional allegorical interpretation, we can fairly well surmise that she symbolizes God.

12:3 *I witnessed in heaven another significant event.* Lit., "another sign appeared in heaven." This is another being who is a "sign" of a deeper reality.

red. While "red" is not an impossible translation for *purros* [TG4450, ZG4794], the basic meaning of the term is "fiery." The dragon is a bright, blazing being. The fact that the dragon is fiery suggests that his appearance is similar to God's, who has been imaged in John's vision as a fiery presence (see 1:16; 10:1). Jews saw Satan as originally standing next to God in brilliance, being, power, and authority.

dragon. This one is subsequently identified in 12:9 as "the ancient serpent" (cf. Gen 3:1), called the *diabolos* [TG1228A, ZG1333] (devil), a word often used in the LXX to translate the Hebrew word *satan* [TH7854/A, ZH8477] ("Satan"; cf. 1 Chr 21:1; Zech 3:1-2, LXX)—the author even supplies the Greek transliteration here—and "the one deceiving the whole world" (12:9). The basic sense of the terms *diabolos* and *satan* is "the accuser" (see note on 12:10). John is seeing here the source of the rebellion against God.

seven heads and ten horns. Both numbers signify totality or fullness. The head is the seat of being; horns are an image of power. John sees here that the dragon has fullness of being and power.

seven crowns. Lit., "seven diadems," an image of full authority. No rebellious figure in John's vision has a crown (*stephanos*). The dragon has diadems (*diadēmata* [TG1238, ZG1343]), as does the beast, the dragon's representative (13:1).

12:4 *His tail swept away one-third of the stars.* John seems to see that a third of the heavenly beings follow the dragon. The OT often depicts heavenly beings as stars, especially fallen beings. This has already been seen in 9:1 (see note). For other instances, see Job 38:7, where the parallelism has heavenly beings equal to morning stars; Dan 8:10, where again the "heavenly army" is parallel with "stars"; and Jude 1:13, where the apostate are described as "wandering stars."

he threw them to the earth. See note on 12:7-9.

12:5 ***gave birth to a son who was to rule all nations with an iron rod.*** This is an unmistakable pointer to the Messiah. The image originates in the messianic Ps 2, where the nations are said to plot against the Lord and his Messiah (Ps 2:2). The Lord then proclaims that his "son" (Ps 2:7) will break the nations "with an iron rod" (Ps 2:9). The image is also repeated in John's vision at 2:26-27 and 19:15. This confirms the echoes of Mic 5:2-5a in Rev 12:2 (see commentary).

her child was snatched away from the dragon and was caught up to God and to his throne. The NLT uses two verbs ("snatched away . . . caught up") for what is one verb in the Greek: *harpazō* [TG726, ZG773]. In the preponderance of uses in the NT, it means to be taken by force (Matt 11:12; 13:19; John 6:15; 10:12, 28, 29; Acts 8:39; 23:10; Jude 1:23; cf. the related words in Matt 7:15; 12:29; 23:25; Mark 3:27; Luke 8:29; 11:39; 18:11; Acts 6:12; 19:29; 27:15; 1 Cor 5:10-11; Phil 2:6; Heb 10:34). The exceptions are 2 Cor 12:2, 4; 1 Thess 4:17, where the word is used to denote "being carried away [to heaven]." I would suggest that the image is not just that of Christ being carried away to heaven but also ripped away from the dragon (= Satan). The NLT captures both ideas. In the context of 12:5, the image also represents God's victory over Satan who had the Messiah in his grasp (the Cross). I think this makes it unmistakably clear that the child was taken by force from the possession of the dragon. In this one term, John captures the Cross (the Messiah grasped by the dragon), the Resurrection (the Messiah taken away from the dragon), and the Ascension (the Messiah taken up to God).

12:6 ***the wilderness.*** As Beale notes, the wilderness "was not only where Israel was protected . . . but also an uninhabitable place of sin, evil, or judgment, where only fierce animals and evil spirits dwelled" (1999:645). Here we have the strange paradox of "wilderness" (or "desert") being both an image for God's presence with the covenant community, as well as the place of Satan's presence. The wilderness was where Israel was to go to meet with God (Exod 3:18; 5:1-3; 7:16). It was in the wilderness that God appeared to Israel (Exod 16:10). The wilderness was also where the goat bearing the sins of Israel was sent (Lev 16:10). It was in the wilderness that John the Baptist announced the advent of the restoration of the kingdom, calling Israel to cleansing from its sin in order to be ready (Matt 3:1). John's action reveals how the image of wilderness was further developed in the Jewish perspective as the place from which God would come to restore the kingdom to Israel (cf. Isa 40:3 [cited in Matt 3:3; Mark 1:3; Luke 3:4; John 1:23]). The wilderness became the staging area for messianic movements whose leaders announced the restoration of the kingdom (Acts 21:38; Josephus *War* 2.259-262, 433, 508; 6.351-352; 7.438; *Antiquities* 20.97-99, 168-172). Jesus warned his followers against such movements and their messianic pretenders (Matt 24:24-26). It was in the wilderness that Jesus encountered and defeated Satan's temptations (Matt 4:1). The ultimate outcome of the encounter of God with Satan in the wilderness is the transformation of the wilderness into a place of life (Isa 35:1, 6; 43:19). Thus, when John later sees the harlot, fallen Babylon, she is in the wilderness, seated upon the beast (17:3) to whom Satan gives his power, his throne, and his great authority (13:2). There all those allied with the beast make war on the Lamb, and the Lamb conquers them (17:14). In this broader context, therefore, God as the woman going into the wilderness is thoroughly consistent with John's Jewish imagery of the wilderness as a place of encounter with God.

God had prepared a place. Beale rightly notes that "elsewhere in the NT *topos* [TG5117, ZG5536] ('place') is a synonym for 'temple.' In the LXX it is a common synonym for 'sanctuary' [e.g., Lev 4:24; 7:2; 14:13; Deut 12:5, 11; 1 Kgs 8:29]" (1999:648). He adds, "In the Gr. OT, by itself or with adjectives (e.g., 'holy place'), [it] is often used of the temple" (1999:649). "Temple" in the Jewish pool of images is the dwelling place of God (2 Chr 7:1-3; Pss 11:4; 18:6; Isa 6:1; Ezek 43:4-5; Mic 1:2; Hab 2:20; Mal 3:1). The significance of John's use of *topos* in this perceptual milieu is that later John notes that there is no temple in the New Jerusalem because God and the Lamb are its temple (21:22), even though he has utilized temple imagery throughout to convey his vision. This suggests that the *topos* in 12:6 and 14 is the "place" of God.

1,260 days. This is a variant image of the "42 months" noted in 11:2, and a parallel to the 1,260 days given in 11:3 as the time of the activity of the two witnesses. As for "a time, times, and half a time" (12:14), it is widely understood (and often translated) as 3½ years, another expression of the 42 months (11:2; cf. 13:5) and 1,260 days (11:3; 12:6; 3½ years of 30-day months). The parallel between 12:6 and 12:14 confirms this. In all the other occurrences of this image, it represents the context of the tribulation of God's faithful people at the hands of the enemies of God (cf. 11:2 and 13:5-7). What John was seeing in the application of this image to the woman as God is that God was present in the midst of this context of tribulation of his faithful people.

COMMENTARY

Just as the open Temple in 11:19 is the bridge from the seven trumpets to the heavenly scene that begins in 12:1, at 15:5 the open Temple is the bridge to the vision of the seven bowls (15:6–16:21). The open Temple leads us into the second of the three heavenly visions. The first (4:1–5:14) was introduced with "a door standing open in heaven" (4:1) and was between the seven churches and the seven seals. The second (11:19–15:4) is introduced with "in heaven, the Temple . . . was opened" (11:19) and is between the seven trumpets and the seven bowls. The third (19:11–21:8) will be introduced with "I saw heaven opened" (19:11) and stands between the harlot, fallen Babylon (17:1–19:10), and the bride, New Jerusalem (21:9–22:9).

As this heavenly scene opened, John saw that the Temple of God was open and that "the Ark of his covenant could be seen inside the Temple" (11:19). In the Temple in Jerusalem, only the high priest could go behind the curtain into the Most Holy Place and then only once a year on the Day of Atonement. While other priests could enter the sanctuary outside the curtain that separated the Most Holy Place from the sanctuary, the "common" Israelite could only stand in the court outside the Temple. They could not even enter the sanctuary, to say nothing of the Most Holy Place. John's vision indicates that the Most Holy Place, the place where God's presence rested upon the Ark of the Covenant behind a curtain, has now been made accessible to all God's people. John sees here what the writer of Hebrews affirmed: "And so, dear brothers and sisters, we can boldly enter heaven's Most Holy Place because of the blood of Jesus. By his death, Jesus opened a new and life-giving way through the curtain into the Most Holy Place" (Heb 10:19-20). This reality is found in the Gospels in the account of the rending of the curtain (Matt 27:51; Mark 15:38; Luke 23:45).

In the beginning of chapter 12, we are presented with an image of a woman. Throughout the centuries, there have been three basic identifications of this woman: Israel, Mary, and the Church (or messianic community). Of these three, the last, though widely held in various forms (Beale, Mounce, Witherington, Harrington [the heavenly Israel]), seems to be the most prevalent. Yet it is the most difficult to sustain, since it is impossible to understand how the Church (messianic community) can birth its own Messiah around whom it is formed and from whom it derives its existence. The interpretation of the woman as Mary is, as might be expected, held by a number of Roman Catholic scholars, but here too, the difficulty arises with how Mary could be active in heaven even before Satan's rebellion. The identification of the woman as Israel is, actually, a subset of the identification as the messianic community, identified as "the people of God living both before and after Christ's coming" (Beale 1999:627). As with Mary, however, the question of how Israel could bring Messiah to birth before Satan's rebellion is insurmountable. Of course, Israel is the community of God's people through whom the Messiah was revealed, and Mary was the specific human agent of this revelation. What John was seeing, however, was the profoundly deeper reality that becomes manifest in the world through Israel and Mary.

The problem with most, if not all of these interpretations, is that they focus on the attributes of the woman and confuse the attributes with the woman herself. Yes, the crown of 12 stars does indeed represent Israel, but that is the crown, not the woman who wears the crown! Since, in the Jewish pool of images utilized by John, the attributes of the woman can be clearly identified as attributes of God, it makes sense to identify the woman as God—with God bringing forth God's own innermost being as the response to the dragon's rebellion even before the rebellion arose. John was seeing that Satan's rebellion had its ground in the desire to devour and thus to replace God. John was also seeing that God's "response" to the coming rebellion was not a response at all—the cross is not something God "did" as a response or reaction to the Fall, but a revelation of who God is in the essence of his being. In Christ we see God's cruciform love plumbing the depths of the human rebellion, God giving God's self to redeem humanity from the rebellion. God's likeness is not something God exploits (Phil 2:6) but is a self-emptying love (God bringing forth God's very being into the mouth of the dragon) for the sake of fallen humanity.[1] It is for this reason that John introduces his image of God as the woman and God's action toward the dragon as a "great sign" (see note on 12:1).

I realize that not one commentator has suggested that the woman is God, although Oecumenius comes close: "In order that the vision might show that the Lord, who was being carried in the womb, was the shelter of his own mother and the whole creation, it says that he was enclothing the woman" (Commentary on the Apocalypse 12:1-12, *Traditio Exegetica Graeca* 8.172). Primasius also hints at the idea that the woman could be God: "It is frequently said that a genus is divided into many species which are the same thing. For what was heaven itself [God?] is now a temple in heaven and now is the woman clothed with the sun and having the moon under her feet" (Commentary on the Apocalypse 12:1, *Corpus Christianorum. Series Latina* 92.179). Both go on to claim, in the typical allegorical exegesis of the early church, that the woman is the church.[2] Could the fact that no commentator has identified the woman as God be due to 2,000 years of male domination of the church, a domination heightened in our time in reaction to radical feminism, a domination only ever so slightly mitigated by the likes of Teresa of Avila, Julian of Norwich, and John of the Cross who suggested female images for God? Also, does apparent scholarly unanimity necessarily equate with reality? Until the Copernican revolution, the consensus was that the earth was the center of the universe. Entrenched paradigms yield only reluctantly and with difficulty to alternative possibilities. Yes, the identification of the woman as God is difficult in the light of prevailing sentiment, but the evidence of the imagery strongly suggests this.

I think the problem arises in that prevailing sentiment presumes an allegorical interpretation of the imagery, but nowhere is there evidence that John was engaged in the use of allegory to convey his vision. There are several places in the vision where an image is explained (1:20; 5:6, 8; 7:13-14; 11:4, 8; 12:9; 13:7; 16:14; 17:8-18; 19:8, 10; 21:23), but these give no warrant for interpreting John's imagery allegorically. Rather, John utilized his Jewish pool of images to portray a vision that both fulfills and transcends those images (see notes on the various images).

In the vision of chapter 12, John sees a great sign: a woman clothed with the sun, with the moon under her feet, and a crown of 12 stars on her head (12:1). The first question is, for what or whom is the woman a sign? In the Greco-Roman culture of John's day, people were identified by their attributes, especially divine figures. A male deity holding a trident with dolphins playing at his feet was Poseidon or Neptune (the Greek and Roman names of the same deity), the god of the sea. A female deity, with a hunting bow in her hand, a quiver of arrows over her shoulder, and hunting dogs at her side was Artemis (Diana), the goddess of the hunt. The attributes identify the person.

In chapter 12, John saw a woman who had labor pains and was in agony to give birth. In the Old Testament the image is often associated with the deliverance and restoration of God's people. The enemies of God's people have anguish like a woman in labor when God acts on behalf of his people (enemies in general: Ps 48:6; Babylon: Isa 13:8; 21:3; Jer 50:43; Moab: Jer 48:41; Edom: Jer 49:22; Damascus: Jer 49:24). God's people themselves suffer like a woman in labor prior to their deliverance and restoration (cf. Isa 66:7; Jer 30:6; Mic 4:8-10; Sir 48:19). Perhaps the most pertinent image is Micah 5:2-5a:

> But you, O Bethlehem Ephrathah,
>   are only a small village among all the people of Judah.
> Yet a ruler of Israel will come from you,
>   one whose origins are from the distant past.
> The people of Israel will be abandoned to their enemies
>   until the woman in labor gives birth.
> Then at last his fellow countrymen
>   will return from exile to their own land.
> And he will stand to lead his flock with the LORD's strength,
>   in the majesty of the name of the LORD his God.
> Then his people will live there undisturbed,
>   for he will be highly honored around the world.
>   And he will be the source of peace.

Here an unidentified woman in labor gives birth to a son (cf. 12:5) who brings about the return from the exile and the restoration of Israel. John's vision seems to place God in the role of the one who brings forth the "son" who restores Israel. It seems clear that John looked to the Micah passage as a source for his imagery of the woman in labor giving birth since this is a messianic prophecy of the one who will restore the kingdom to Israel. John, however, perceived the deeper reality that Micah only saw "through a glass darkly."

Another passage pertinent to this one can be found in the Dead Sea manuscript 1QH[a] 11:8-13 [=Sukenik 1QH[a] 3:7-13]. While it cannot be ascertained whether John would have had this document available to him, the passage can be read as utilizing the same powerful imagery of God as a woman:

> *For terrors and fearful pains have unfurled on its swell of waves that She who is with child might bring into the world (her) first-born. For the children have reached as far as the swelling waves of Death. And She who is big with the Man is in travail, in her pains. For she shall give birth to a male-child in the swelling waves of Death, and in the bonds of Sheol there shall spring from the crucible of the Pregnant one a Marvelous Counselor with his might; and he shall deliver every man from the swelling waves because of Her who is big with him . . . and at the time of the bearing of her first-born every terror unfurls over the crucible of Her who is with child.* (translated by Dupont-Sommer)[3]

A rephrasing of this in the light of John's vision could be as follows:

> *For terrors and fearful pains have unfurled on its [the dragon's] swell of waves [the sea an image for the demonic realm] that She [God] who is with child might bring into the world [her] first-born [the Messiah]. For the children [humankind] have reached as far as the swelling waves of Death [in bondage to the dragon]. And She [God] who is big with the Man [the Messiah] is in travail, in her pains [God's cruciform love for humanity]. For she [God] shall give birth to a male-child [the Messiah] in the swelling waves of Death [into the mouth of the dragon], and in the bonds of Sheol [into the mouth of the dragon] there shall spring from the crucible [cruciform love] of the Pregnant one a Marvelous Counselor [the Messiah] with his might [rule the nations with a rod of iron]; and he shall deliver every man from the swelling waves [Satan's rebellion] because of Her [God] who is big with him [the Messiah]. . . and at the time of the bearing of her first-born every terror unfurls over the crucible of Her who is with child.*

It seems clear from this that the image of God as a woman was not unknown in John's day, to say nothing of God as woman bringing forth the Messiah.

It is no wonder that John described what he saw as a great sign. It is here that John unveils the full depth of the revelation of Jesus the Messiah. We have noted already that the cross plays a focal role in John's vision of Jesus the Messiah. Through the cross God has cleansed his people from their sin (1:5), has restored his people as a kingdom and priests (1:6; 5:10), has utterly subverted the rebellious order (1:18), has revealed the fullness of God's purpose (5:5), has provided new being for his people (7:14), and has consummated the old covenant (11:3-13). John now sees the ultimate roots of the cross.

The vision reveals the true nature of the cross in an amazing image. John sees that the cross is far deeper than an event that took place outside Jerusalem about AD 30. The Crucifixion was the revelation in human history of the depths of God's very being. John sees that when Satan rebelled against God and, subsequently, seduced some of heaven's host and all humanity into his rebellion, that God did not have to come up with an effective response to this situation. Rather, God had already planned a revelation of the profound mystery of his very being. John sees God giving over God's very being to Satan in order to overcome Satan's rebellion (see note on 12:5).

Satan's rebellion was his desire to be God, to take God's place. In the pseudepigraphic *Life of Adam and Eve*, Satan is portrayed as refusing God's command, through Michael, to worship Adam as the image of God. When warned by Michael that he will be subject to God's wrath if he does not worship, Satan replies: "I will set my seat above the stars of heaven and will be like the highest" (*Life of Adam and Eve* 15:3). This is what John seems to see at this point in his vision—Satan's refusal to allow God to be God and his desire to usurp God's place. Isaiah's description of Babylon's fall also reveals the motives behind Satan's rebellion:

> *How you are fallen from heaven, O shining star, son of the morning! You have been thrown down to the earth, you who destroyed the nations of the world. For you said to yourself, "I will ascend to heaven and set my throne above God's stars. I will preside on the mountain of the gods far away in the north. I will climb to the highest heavens and be like the Most High."* (Isa 14:12-14)

The nature of Satan's rebellion is also seen in the temptation of Adam and Eve: "You will be like God" (Gen 3:5). John's vision reveals that rebellion, whether Satan's or ours, is always an effort to control God; to take God into our lives on our terms, not God's; to absorb God into our structures of life; and to assimilate God within our values and perspectives. Like Satan, we want to encompass God within our own being, to make God subordinate to our desires, our plans, our purposes.

The mystery of God's response is that God brings forth God's very being into the mouth of the rebellion. God overcomes evil by being overcome. God wins the victory by losing. God triumphs through death! The cross of Jesus is a revelation of the very heart of God's being before the foundation of the world. This is why, later in the vision, John sees that the Lamb "was killed before the world was made" (13:8; see note concerning the translation of this verse).

John saw that the response of God's being to the rebellion continues to be God's way of being in the rebellious order. We will see shortly that God is present in the midst of Satan's realm and Satan cannot drive God out (12:13-16). But God is present in the rebellious order, not as the almighty, invincible, victorious warrior, but as the vulnerable woman who brings forth her very being into the rebellion to overcome it. God acts in his love, and instead of simply ending Satan's existence with a command from heaven, God enters Satan's "realm" (the "wilderness," i.e., the earth). Satan's "realm," however, is under God's sovereignty and acts in God's behalf. There is, however, no place for Satan in God's realm (12:8)—but God has his place in Satan's realm. But then we also have the idea of care. In 12:6 and 12:14 we see that God enters fully into the circumstances of God's faithful people throughout the time of their tribulation at the hands of their fallen Babylon world. (We saw at 11:2-3 that the 42-month [1,260-day] period represents the tribulation and persecution of God's people at the hands of their enemies.)

The greatest puzzle of this section (12:1-6), according to the interpretation I have been presenting, is the statement that the woman fled into the wilderness "where God had prepared a place to care for her" (12:6). How can the woman represent God if God prepares a place for her? For God to "go" to God's place seems strange in the theological perspective of "omnipresence," as does the idea of God having already prepared this "place." But John's vision is not limited by our inadequate theological categories. The vision is revealing a great sign—that God is present in the midst of the wilderness, Satan's realm (see note on 12:6).

ENDNOTES

1. For an excellent development of this perspective, see Wright 1993:56-98. He writes (1993:84), "The real humiliation of the incarnation and the cross is that one who was himself God, and who never during the whole process stopped being God, could embrace such a vocation. The real theological emphasis of the hymn, therefore, is not simply a new view of Jesus. It is a new understanding of God. . . . Calvary reveals the truth about what it meant to be God. . . . Incarnation and even crucifixion are to be seen as *appropriate* vehicles for the dynamic self-revelation of God" (cf. also Gorman 2001 and Bauckham 1999). Additionally, if we take the syntax of Phil 2:5-8 seriously, the aorist participles modifying "he emptied himself" (Phil 2:7) and "he humbled himself" (Phil 2:8) indicate that before the emptying and humbling, Christ had already taken the form of a servant, already become in human likeness, already been found in a human nature, and already become obedient unto death.
2. For example, the inconsistencies of early allegorical exegesis can be seen in understanding the expression "the moon beneath her feet" to signify: (1) the church adorned with heavenly glory (Hippolytus); (2) that in the darkness of death the saints have light as of the moon (Victorinus of Petrovium); (3) the faith of those purified by baptism (Methodius); (4) the church of the heretics (Tyconius); (5) the law of Moses (Oecumenius); (6) the church trampling every mutable thing (Primasius); (7) hypocrites and evil Christians (Caesarius of Arles).
3. For variant translations, see Vermes (1962:157) and Martinez (1996:331).

◆ 2. The mother of all wars (12:7-17)

7 Then there was war in heaven. Michael and his angels fought against the dragon and his angels. 8 And the dragon lost the battle, and he and his angels were forced out of heaven. 9 This great dragon—the ancient serpent called the devil, or Satan, the one deceiving the whole world—was thrown down to the earth with all his angels.

10 Then I heard a loud voice shouting across the heavens,

"It has come at last—
salvation and power
and the Kingdom of our God,
and the authority of his Christ.*
For the accuser of our brothers
and sisters*
has been thrown down to earth—
the one who accuses them
before our God day and night.
11 And they have defeated him by the
blood of the Lamb
and by their testimony.

And they did not love their lives
so much
that they were afraid to die.
12 Therefore, rejoice, O heavens!
And you who live in the heavens,
rejoice!
But terror will come on the earth
and the sea,
for the devil has come down to
you in great anger,
knowing that he has little time."

13 When the dragon realized that he had
been thrown down to the earth, he pur-
sued the woman who had given birth to
the male child. 14 But she was given two
wings like those of a great eagle so she
could fly to the place prepared for her in
the wilderness. There she would be cared
for and protected from the dragon* for a
time, times, and half a time.

15 Then the dragon tried to drown the
woman with a flood of water that flowed
from his mouth. 16 But the earth helped
her by opening its mouth and swallowing
the river that gushed out from the mouth
of the dragon. 17 And the dragon was an-
gry at the woman and declared war
against the rest of her children—all who
keep God's commandments and maintain
their testimony for Jesus.

12:10a Or *his Messiah.* **12:10b** Greek *brothers.* **12:14** Greek *the serpent;* also in 12:15. See 12:9.

NOTES

12:7-9 ***war in heaven. Michael and his angels . . . dragon and his angels.*** In the *Life of Adam and Eve* 12:1–16:4, a pseudepigraphical writing dated from the first to third century AD, Michael brings Adam before the hosts of heaven and calls for them to worship the image of God. Satan and his angels refuse to worship. Satan responds to the threat of God's wrath by seeking to usurp God's place in heaven. As a consequence, in that story, like here, Satan was thrown down to earth with all his angels.

12:8 ***were forced out of heaven.*** This translation misses a vital feature of the vision. Lit., "no place was found for them in heaven" (cf. 20:11). We have already seen that God, imaged as the woman, has a "place" (12:6), which subsequently is seen to be in the midst of Satan's realm (12:14) and from which Satan is unable to expel God (12:15-16). The image is clear: Satan's rebellion, and all who follow in his train, have no "place" in God's realm; but God, and all who follow him, have an ineradicable "place" in Satan's realm (see note on 12:6).

12:10 ***It has come at last.*** This would be better translated as "it has happened just now." The word *arti* [TG737, ZG785] means "just now," "this moment," "at this very time."

the accuser. Satan's role as the accuser emerges first in the book of Job (Job 1:6ff), and is seen again in 1 Chr 21:1 and Zech 3:1. In this role, Satan held before God the sins of God's people that should disqualify them from God's realm.

has been thrown down. Lit., "has been cast out." The same essential term for "cast out" (*ekballō, ballō* [TG1544/906, ZG1675/965]) is used also in John 12:31, where Jesus says, "The time for judging this world has come, when Satan, the ruler of this world, will be cast out." The statement in the Gospel points to Christ's victory over Satan via crucifixion.

12:11 ***they have defeated him.*** A better translation would be "they conquered him," which carries forward the theme of "conquering" that is so essential in John's vision (see commentary on 6:2).

by the blood of the Lamb. Jesus washed the believers from their sins (1:5) and restored them as God's kingdom and priests (1:6).

by their testimony. The word *marturia* [TG3141, ZG3456] (testimony) carries here its basic meaning of martyrdom, as seen in the next phrase regarding the saints not being afraid to die.

12:12 ***terror will come on the earth and the sea.*** Lit., "woe to the earth and the sea." The statement is a present reality, not a future event. "Earth," as we have noted several times, is an image for the rebellious realm, as is "sea." John is here seeing the origin of that reality as well as its woeful condition.

he has little time. In light of the fact that two millennia of human history have transpired since this was spoken, this statement requires some explanation. "Time" here is *kairos* [TG2540, ZG2789], as in 1:3 where it was noted that the term was not being used chronologically (the Greek term would then be *chronos* [TG5550, ZG5989]) but metaphorically to describe the present reality of God's realm that has been inaugurated in the Messiah. The vision is now revealing to John that Satan's realm is severely proscribed.

12:14 ***she was given two wings like those of a great eagle.*** This is further confirmation that the woman is an image for God. In the exodus from Egypt, God tells Moses, "I carried you on eagles' wings and brought you to myself" (Exod 19:4). God is the one with eagle's wings. This is also depicted in Deut 32:10-12; Jer 48:40 (NASB); 49:22 (NASB).

for a time, times, and half a time. John used the term *kairos* (see note on 12:12) for "time, times, and half a time." This suggests that the vision is representing not a literal three-and-a-half-year period (because *kairos* by its very nature is an indeterminate term), but an undefined period during which the people of God and God himself experience tribulation at the hands of the rebellious order.

12:15-16 ***a flood of water.*** This is a regular image for the action of the realm of evil. The psalmist states, "floods of destruction swept over me" (Ps 18:4). The Hebrew literally says, "the torrents of Belial," one of the names for Satan in later Hebrew. The psalmist also speaks of God quieting "the raging oceans with their pounding waves" (Ps 65:7), praises God for being far mightier than the raging ocean (Ps 93:3-4), and affirms that God is enthroned above the floods (Ps 29:10). These are images of God's power and sovereignty over the forces of evil. Isaiah associates the ancient, evil dragon with the sea: "In that day [of Israel's restoration] the LORD will take his terrible, swift sword and punish Leviathan, the swiftly moving serpent, the coiling, writhing serpent. He will kill the dragon of the sea" (Isa 27:1). John saw Satan, the dragon, the serpent, bringing the full power of his realm (the sea) against God in an attempt to flush God out of his realm. But "the earth," another image for Satan's realm, works against him. Even Satan's realm is under God's sovereignty. (For further development of this perspective, see 2 Esdr [*4 Ezra*] 6:49-52.)

12:17 ***all who keep God's commandments and maintain their testimony for Jesus.*** This is a variant upon the usual description of God's faithful as those who have the word of God and the witness of Jesus (see note on 1:2; the phrase is found at 1:2, 9; 6:9; 20:4; with variants at 12:11 and 19:10, as well as here in 12:17). It may be that the vision is revealing the two components of God's people: The first is the old covenant community formed through the covenant at Sinai, those who keep God's commandments. The second is the new covenant community gathered to Christ from every tribe, language, people, and nation (see note on 5:9) and formed as a kingdom of priests (1:6; 5:10); they are those who maintain their testimony for Jesus.

COMMENTARY

John sees here the mother of all wars. It is a vision of Satan's rebellion against God. The vision gives us no idea of how Satan's rebellion relates chronologically to the creation. In Jewish tradition, as conveyed in Genesis, Satan is already fallen when present in the garden behind the serpent's disguise (Gen 3:1ff), which suggests that John was seeing an event prior to creation. This is confirmed by the vision of the cross seen in the previous section, a revelation of the essence of God's nature, which implies a reality that existed before creation. The vision of the cross is reiterated in the vision of the Lamb slain before the foundation of the world in the next section.

The war was between Michael with his angels and Satan with his angels (12:7). Michael had come to be understood as the archangel under whose care the people of God had been entrusted. The idea begins in Daniel (Dan 10:13, 21; 12:1) and was developed in the intertestamental period and beyond as seen in *1 Enoch* 20:5; *Testament of Levi* 5:6; and *Testament of Dan* 6:2. Even later rabbinic writings view Michael as the guardian of Israel (*b. Hagigah* 12b). Jude 1:9 cites *The Assumption of Moses* for the idea of Michael disputing with Satan for Moses. Michael is seen as the commander of angels in *3 Baruch* 11:4 and *1 Enoch* 24:6.

The role of "place" is very significant in this portion of the vision. John sees that there is no "place" for Satan and his rebels in God's realm (see note on 12:8), but there is a "place" for God in Satan's realm ("earth") from which Satan cannot drive him out (12:14-16). John sees that the victory of God, revealed in the cross of Christ ("the blood of the Lamb," 12:11), goes all the way back beyond Satan's rebellion in heaven. The cross is the response of God's very being to Satan's attempt to bring God's people under his control. The cross is not only a revelation of the heart of God, it is also a revelation of God's response to our rebellion, our attempt to have God in our life on our terms or to reject him altogether. The cross reveals that God gives himself to the depths of our rebellion and meets us there to offer us forgiveness and new life. John saw that the victory of God over Satan's rebellion, and ours, has its roots in the very nature of God's being. It was there that "salvation and power and the Kingdom of our God, and the authority of his Christ [Messiah]" (12:10) came into being. While this reality was manifest in human history in Jerusalem about AD 30, the reality itself belongs to the eternal nature of God, not a one-time event.

In this vision, John sees that God's people are protected from Satan for "a time, times, and half a time" (12:14). This expression first appears in Scripture when Daniel is told that one of the successors of Alexander the Great will "defy the Most High and oppress the holy people of the Most High. He will try to change their sacred festivals and laws, and they will be placed under his control for a time, times, and half a time" (Dan 7:25).[1] This was a vision of the time of Antiochus Epiphanes (175–162 BC), the king of the Seleucid dynasty, one of the four dynasties that arose out of Alexander's empire. It was Antiochus's effort to eradicate Judaism ("change their sacred festivals and laws") that led to the Maccabean Revolution (167–164 BC). During this three-and-a-half-year period ("time, times, and half a time") God's faithful people experienced extreme tribulation at the hands of their enemies. The same image is used again in Daniel 12:7. There, after the time of trouble,[2] God's people would be blessed. John is seeing that God is intimately present with his people in their tribulation at the hands of Satan and his rebellious realm—fallen Babylon.

The final words of this section indicate that God's people could well experience martyrdom for the sake of their testimony (see note on 12:11). Even today believers may be called to conquer Satan as the Messiah did—through death; in fact, more Christians have died as martyrs in the last 100 years than in the previous 1,900. We live in a world shaped by the rebellion of Satan. The values, structures, and dynamics of our world are, largely, those of fallen Babylon. They are dehumanizing and destructive of human wholeness in the image of God. Whenever we begin to live our lives by the values, structures and dynamics of God's kingdom (New Jerusalem), our lives become a challenge to the status quo of fallen Babylon. Fallen Babylon, and especially those whose power, position, and prestige are rooted in the values, structures, and dynamics of fallen Babylon, will seek to negate our witness, marginalize us, and silence us in whatever way is necessary to protect their status quo. When we commit ourselves to the lordship of the Messiah, we are called to live our lives as citizens of New Jerusalem in the midst of our fallen Babylon world.

A good contemporary example, mentioned earlier, is the faithful church in Romania. During the brutally oppressive communist regime, the church in Romania was besieged with tribulation at the hands of the authorities. Every sort of atrocity was inflicted upon the church and its leaders in an effort to drive it from the "realm." In the end, however, it was the Hungarian Reformed Church in Timişoara's parishoners' defense of their pastor, László Tőkés, that ignited the revolution and brought about the downfall of the regime (see further Deletant 1999).

The day after the fall of the communist regime, on the announcement board of the church was this proclamation: "The Lamb Won!" (Colson and Vaughn 2003:246-252). They knew they were living out the realities of John's vision in their fallen Babylon world. They were not afraid to die (12:11) for their life in New Jerusalem.

John saw that God's people ("the rest of her children"—12:17), whether the old or new covenant community, were living on the front lines of Satan's war against God. Paul made this abundantly clear to us: "We are not fighting against flesh-and-blood enemies, but against evil rulers and authorities of the unseen world, against mighty powers in this dark world, and against evil spirits in the heavenly places" (Eph 6:12). John will next see the nature of Satan's war against God's people.

ENDNOTES

1. The Greek Empire is the fourth beast in Daniel, which conquered the entire known world of that day (Dan 7:23). The "ten kings" (Dan 7:24) represent Alexander's successors.
2. "From the time the daily sacrifice is stopped and the sacrilegious object that causes desecration is set up to be worshiped, there will be 1,290 days" (Dan 12:11). This refers to Antiochus's desecration of the Temple in 167 BC by sacrificing a pig on the altar (1 Macc 1:41-61; cf. Josephus *Antiquities* 12.248-256 [12.5.4]) and setting up a statue of himself as Zeus in the Holy of Holies, which brought the sacrifices to an end since the Temple was defiled. At the end of the three and a half years, the Maccabees were able to cleanse the Temple, reconsecrate it, and reinstitute the sacrifices (1 Macc 4:36-59).

3. The nature of fallen Babylon (12:18–13:18)

18 Then the dragon took his stand* on the
shore beside the sea.

CHAPTER 13

Then I saw a beast rising up out of the
sea. It had seven heads and ten horns,
with ten crowns on its horns. And written
on each head were names that blas-
phemed God. 2 This beast looked like a
leopard, but it had the feet of a bear and
the mouth of a lion! And the dragon gave
the beast his own power and throne and
great authority.

3 I saw that one of the heads of the
beast seemed wounded beyond recovery—
but the fatal wound was healed! The
whole world marveled at this miracle and
gave allegiance to the beast. 4 They wor-
shiped the dragon for giving the beast
such power, and they also worshiped the
beast. "Who is as great as the beast?"
they exclaimed. "Who is able to fight
against him?"

5 Then the beast was allowed to speak
great blasphemies against God. And he was
given authority to do whatever he wanted
for forty-two months. 6 And he spoke ter-
rible words of blasphemy against God,
slandering his name and his dwelling—that
is, those who dwell in heaven.* 7 And the
beast was allowed to wage war against
God's holy people and to conquer them.
And he was given authority to rule over
every tribe and people and language and
nation. 8 And all the people who belong to
this world worshiped the beast. They are
the ones whose names were not written in
the Book of Life before the world was
made—the Book that belongs to the Lamb
who was slaughtered.*

9 Anyone with ears to hear
    should listen and understand.
10 Anyone who is destined for prison
    will be taken to prison.
Anyone destined to die by the sword
    will die by the sword.

This means that God's holy people must
endure persecution patiently and remain
faithful.

11 Then I saw another beast come up out
of the earth. He had two horns like those
of a lamb, but he spoke with the voice of
a dragon. 12 He exercised all the authority
of the first beast. And he required all the
earth and its people to worship the first
beast, whose fatal wound had been
healed. 13 He did astounding miracles,
even making fire flash down to earth from
the sky while everyone was watching.
14 And with all the miracles he was allowed
to perform on behalf of the first beast, he
deceived all the people who belong to this
world. He ordered the people to make a
great statue of the first beast, who was
fatally wounded and then came back to
life. 15 He was then permitted to give life
to this statue so that it could speak. Then
the statue of the beast commanded that
anyone refusing to worship it must die.

16 He required everyone—small and
great, rich and poor, free and slave—to be
given a mark on the right hand or on the
forehead. 17 And no one could buy or sell
anything without that mark, which was
either the name of the beast or the num-
ber representing his name. 18 Wisdom is
needed here. Let the one with under-
standing solve the meaning of the num-
ber of the beast, for it is the number of a
man.* His number is 666.*

12:18 Greek *Then he took his stand;* some manuscripts read *Then I took my stand.* Some translations put this entire sentence into 13:1. **13:6** Some manuscripts read *and his dwelling and all who dwell in heaven.* **13:8** Or *not written in the Book of Life that belongs to the Lamb who was slaughtered before the world was made.* **13:18a** Or *of humanity.* **13:18b** Some manuscripts read *616.*

NOTES

12:18 ***the dragon took his stand.*** Lit., "he took his stand"—the "he" referring to the dragon (12:17). This reading has the strong support of $\mathfrak{P}^{47}$ *a* A C it. A variant reading on this is

"I took my stand"—the "I" referring to John (13:1). This reading has the inferior support of 051 𝔐 cop. The verse is a literary pivot between the statement of the dragon's war against the children of the woman (12:17) and the nature of that warfare (13:1-18). Since John will now see one beast coming from the sea (13:1-8) and another beast coming from the earth (13:11-18), the "shore beside the sea" would be an ideal place for him to be located to observe both parts of the vision. But, at the same time, the two beasts are representatives of the dragon (13:2, 12), and the "shore beside the sea" would be the logical place for the dragon to be located to empower the beasts from the sea and earth. Thus, either reading works, though the reading with "he" (the dragon) has the stronger textual support.

13:1-2 ***a beast rising up out of the sea.*** It has been noted at several points that "sea" represents the realm of rebellion or, as Wright puts it, "the sea *represents* evil or chaos" (1992:289). See also notes on 4:6 and 21:1.

seven heads and ten horns. "Seven" and "ten" are symbols for totality, completeness, fullness (see note on 12:3).

ten crowns on its horns. Lit., "ten diadems on its horns" (cf. note on 12:3).

13:3 ***one of the heads of the beast seemed wounded beyond recovery—but the fatal wound was healed!*** Lit., "one of his heads as having been slain unto death, but his fatal wound was healed." The head doesn't "seem" to have a mortal wound. It *has* a mortal wound. John used "as" in this verse, as elsewhere (see "Literary Style" in the Introduction for the discussion of John's use of "like" and "as") to indicate that the image used doesn't really convey the fullness of what he experienced. The fact that this image is used three times for this beast (13:3, 12, 14) strongly emphasizes its condition, and the last two instances make it clear that there is a wound, not that it merely "seemed wounded."

The whole world marveled. Lit., "the whole earth marveled" (cf. ASV, RSV, ESV, NASB), a play on the theme of "earth" as the realm of rebellion.

13:5 ***forty-two months.*** The duration of the beast's activity is the same image John has used for the trampling of the holy city by the enemies of God's people ("nations"—11:2), the prophecy of the two witnesses (11:3), and God's presence in Satan's realm (12:6, 14). This is an image for the tribulation of God's faithful people at the hands of their enemies (see commentary on 11:2). John now sees what is behind such tribulation. It is Satan's war against God's children (12:17).

13:6 ***slandering his name.*** Since "name" has to do with the nature or essence of that which is named, to blaspheme God's name is to reject God's nature, to refuse to allow God to be God.

and his dwelling—that is, those who dwell in heaven. Lit., "his dwelling place—the ones dwelling in heaven." This reading has the manuscript support of *a** A 046^{c} 2053^{comm} 2344 Irenaeus. Another reading (adopted by the TR) is "his dwelling place and the ones dwelling in heaven," having the support of *a*^{2} 046* 051 P 2053^{txt} 𝔐^{A} it cop. The reading in 𝔓^{47} is "his dwelling place in heaven," and C reads "the ones dwelling in heaven." Comfort (2008:842) defends the NLT text by saying that this reading "has better documentary support (especially the combined testimony of A with *a**), is seemingly the most difficult reading, and is most likely the reading from which the others deviated. According to the syntax of this verse in Greek, the phrase 'those who dwell [lit., "tabernacle" as a verb] in heaven' is in direct apposition to 'his dwelling place [lit., "tabernacle" as a noun].' Thus, those who dwell in heaven are God's tabernacle in heaven; the people in heaven and the heavenly place are not two separate entities. This is made clear in versions like RSV, NRSV, NASB, NLT, HCSB, and NET. The image of God's people being the same as God's habitation is presented again in 21:1-3, where the New Jerusalem is depicted as the people of God becoming God's habitation."

13:7 *the beast was allowed to wage war against God's holy people.* This is an expression of God's sovereignty over the beast. To churches like those in Smyrna and Philadelphia, experiencing tribulation at the hands of their fallen Babylon world, the vision is an assurance that God is still in control.

and to conquer them. All the conquering in the vision is, with two exceptions, something that the Lamb does (3:21; 5:5; 6:2; 17:14) or the faithful people of God do (2:7, 11, 17, 26; 3:5, 12, 21; 12:11; 15:2; 21:7). The two exceptions are: (1) 11:7, John's vision of the cross as the consummation of the old covenant—a "conquering" by the beast that is really a terrible defeat; and (2) here, the beast's "conquering" of God's people.

13:8 *They are the ones whose names were not written in the Book of Life before the world was made—the Book that belongs to the Lamb who was slaughtered.* The alternative rendering (see NLT mg) is better: "They are the ones whose names were not written in the Book of Life that belongs to the Lamb who was slaughtered before the world was made." The progression of the Greek syntax is unmistakable: "the ones whose names were not written"—written where? "in the Book of Life"—what Book of Life? the Book of Life "of the Lamb"—what Lamb? the one "who was killed"—killed when? "before the world was made." The last phrase *apo katabolēs kosmou* [TG2602/2889, ZG2856/3180] (from the foundation of the world) immediately follows *esphagmenou* [TG4969, ZG5377] (having been slain). This translation is found in the KJV and NKJV. However, many other versions (RSV, NRSV, NJB, NET, NASB, ESV) agree with the rendering of the NLT. Why do these translations and commentators[1] interpret the last phrase of the verse so it modifies "written"? The primary rationale comes from considering 17:8, which literally reads, "And they will be amazed, those who dwell upon the earth, of whom has not been written the name upon the book of the life from (the) foundation of (the) world."

It would seem that many translators and commentators have taken 17:8 as the standard by which 13:8 is to be understood. The conventions of orality, however, would call for 13:8 to be the standard by which 17:8 is understood.[2] Originally, Revelation would have been read aloud to an audience (cf. 1:3—"the one who reads . . . and . . . all who listen"). One anomaly in the phrase "Book of Life" is the presence of the definite article (*tēs* [TG3588, ZG3836]) with "life" (*zōēs* [TG2222, ZG2437]), i.e., "the life" (3:5; 17:8; 20:15; 21:27; with a variant form in the Greek of 20:12—"the book that is the life"). I suggest the presence of the article raised expectations that John would identify what specific life was being noted. When the hearers heard the first instance of the phrase "the Book of Life" (3:5) it would raise a question in their minds, "the book of the life of what or whom?" From Jewish tradition and the OT, they would be aware of the fact that God had a book (Exod 32:32-33; Ps 139:16; Dan 12:1; Mal 3:16) and, of course, they would be well aware of "the book of the Law" (Deut 28:61; et al.) often further qualified with "of God," "of Moses, or "of the Lord." The phrase, "the book of the life," however, would be unusual, not being found in the LXX and only once in intertestamental literature (*1 Enoch* 108:3, but there "book of life," not "book of the life").

This appearance of the phrase (13:8; cf. NLT mg) resolves their question: It is "the Book of Life that belongs to the Lamb who was slaughtered before the world was made." This creates an entirely new framing of "the Book of Life" for the hearers, a framing which would then color all subsequent uses of the phrase. When, therefore, the listeners hear 17:8, they would naturally "fill in the gaps" from their remembrance of 13:8—i.e., it is the Book of the Life of the Lamb who was slain. This may possibly be confirmed by 21:27, where the qualifier "Lamb's" is added, presumably because of the distance between 13:8 and 21:27, and the absence of the qualifier in 17:8 and 20:12 and 15 requires its addition here to ensure the hearer goes back to 13:8 rather than to 17:8. The hearing of this new formulation in 13:8 would have been already framed by the vision of God, the woman, in 12:1ff where (as we have seen) John saw that the cross is a revelation of the very essence of God's nature even before Satan's rebellion, thus even before the world was created. This is the profound reality which, as Jesus indicated, was hidden from the foundation of the world (Matt 13:35), and which Peter affirms that Jesus, the Lamb, was destined before the foundation of the world to become our Redeemer (1 Pet 1:20).

13:14 ***a great statue.*** Lit., "an image." The word "great" is not found in the Greek text, and the word translated "statue" (*eikōn* [TG1504, ZG1635], "icon") was in wide use in the Roman world and "does not imply a . . . copy of something. It implies the illumination of its inner core and essence . . . in the image man somehow has the god himself present in his own being" (TDNT 2.389). This use can be seen in the NT where Paul speaks of believers being conformed to the image (*eikōn*) of Christ (Rom 8:29; 2 Cor 3:18), and of Christ as the image (*eikōn*) of God (2 Cor 4:4; Col 1:15).

who was fatally wounded and then came back to life. Lit., "who had the wound of the sword and lived." This rendering misses the significance of the image here, which does not speak of a fatal wound (13:3, 12; see note on 13:3), but of a wound of the sword. The vision here provides insight into the cause of the mortal wound—it is from "the sword." But what sword? From the rest of the vision the obvious candidate would seem to be the sword that comes from the mouth of the Messiah (1:16; 2:12; 19:15). The problem is that in 1:16; 2:12; and 19:15, the "sword" is *rhomphaia* [TG4501, ZG4855], not *machaira* [TG3162, ZG3479], the latter term being used for the sword of the second rider (6:4) and the instrument that gave the beast its mortal wound (13:14). It appears that the beast is mortally wounded by the sword of his own rebellion.

John seems to have introduced here, rather obliquely, a reality that the vision later clarifies. It will be seen in 17:16 that there is an internal warfare associated with fallen Babylon. The fallen Babylon/beast complex appears to carry within it the seeds of its own destruction. John sees the harlot, fallen Babylon, seated first on "many waters" (17:1), but also on the scarlet beast with seven heads and ten horns (17:3). The "many waters" are subsequently identified as "masses of people of every nation and language" (17:15), one of John's standard descriptors of the population of fallen Babylon (5:9; 7:9; 10:11; 11:9; 13:7; 14:6). Thus, the harlot (fallen Babylon), the citizens of fallen Babylon, and the beast are bound together in an unholy trinity. But John sees that the ten horns upon the beast destroy the harlot (17:16). The very essence of the rebellious order is self-destructiveness. It may be this reality John is alluding to when he sees that the beast's mortal wound was caused by the same kind of sword (*machaira*) introduced as an attribute of the second rider (6:4), who, it has been seen, is the dragon, Satan, who gives his power, authority, and throne to the beast (17:13).

Prior to 13:14, John has provided another hint at this same reality. In 13:10, those who are to be killed with the sword (*machaira*) will be killed by the sword (*machaira*). As explained in the commentary below, John was making a strong allusion to apostate Israel (Jer 15:2) and to Egypt, where those who refused God's word through Jeremiah had fled (Jer 43:11). The implication is that to rebel against God results in being killed (or mortally wounded) with the sword (*machaira*).

13:18 ***the number of the beast, for it is the number of a man.*** In the Roman world, as well as the Jewish, there was no system of numbers such as our Arabic numerals. Instead, the letters of the alphabet were used as numbers. This facilitated a process known as gematria—that is, using the values of the letters (i.e., alpha =1, beta = 2, gamma = 3, etc.) of a person's name to arrive at their "number." John is telling us that the number represents a man.

His number is 666. The number "666" has the support of 𝔓[47] *a* A P 𝔐 Irenaeus Hippolytus. A variant reading is "616," which has the support of 𝔓[115] C and other mss (according to Irenaeus). The textual history of this passage gives us another important clue to understanding the identity of the person. While strong textual evidence gives the number as "666," other manuscripts have "616." This opens an intriguing possibility.

In the Roman world of John's day the name of the emperor Nero would have appeared in two basic forms: Greek = Neron Caesar, and Latin = Nero Caesar. If the letters are transliterated into the Hebrew alphabet, the value for the first is 666, for the second 616! This may sound far-fetched, but John has already played with Greek and Hebrew at 9:11, and will do so again at 16:16. Since John conveyed his vision in Greek, the language of the eastern Mediterranean, the reading "666" (corresponding to the Greek spelling) appears in the earliest and strongest manuscripts. The reading "616" has only slightly less textual evidence, especially 𝔓[115], a third-century papyrus and the uncial manuscript C, a fifth-century manuscript that is a strong witness in Revelation. Since these are Greek manuscripts, however, it would seem that a scribe who knew Latin and, most likely, was preparing a copy of Revelation for a primarily Latin speaking audience "interpreted" the original "666" as "616" for his Latin readers. Another possibility is that the Greek manuscripts with "616" were developed from a Latin translation in which the shift from "666" to "616" had taken place. However it came into being, it seems most likely that the "616" reading was an adaptation of John's gematria for Latin speakers.

COMMENTARY

In this section John describes the nature of Satan's war against God's children—the human race. The war is fought on two fronts, represented by two "beasts." Each beast is an image for the way in which Satan's rebellion spreads through human societies.

The first beast that John saw (13:1) reflects Daniel's vision. Daniel saw four beasts rising up out of the sea: one like a lion, one like a bear, one like a leopard, and one with ten horns (Dan 7:2-7). John, however, saw a single beast that incorporates aspects of Daniel's four: It looked like a leopard, had bear's feet, a lion's mouth, and ten horns. This suggests that John was seeing the deeper reality that stood behind Daniel's four beasts.

Daniel's four beasts represent four human kingdoms (Dan 7:17), variously identified in the Jewish story, that were enemies of Israel. For Daniel they appeared to be the empires of Babylon, Persia, Alexander the Great, and the Seleucid successors to Alexander culminating in Antiochus Epiphanes, who sought to eradicate Judaism from his realm. John's modulation of Daniel's imagery suggests that he understood Daniel's vision to represent the dragon, Satan, who is incarnate in and energizes all the human empires of fallen Babylon. For John, the current incarnation of the dragon was the Roman Empire.

Since the dragon gives the beast "authority to rule over every tribe and people and language and nation" (13:7), it is obvious that the beast is a representative of the dragon. The dragon, however, had diadems on its heads, and the beast has the diadems (the Greek word is different from that translated "crowns" elsewhere—see note on 12:3) on its horns and a blasphemous name on its heads. This denotes a change between the dragon and its incarnation in the beast. Between John's vision of the dragon in 12:3 and the beast in 13:1, he has seen the war of the dragon against Michael. This has resulted in a radical change in the nature of the rebel. As was noted at 12:3, the diadems denote authority. The dragon's authority, prior to his rebellion, rested upon his "many heads," the seat of his being. After his rebellion, the dragon's authority rests upon his horns, the image of his power. This is the shift from integrity of being as the seat of authority to the exercise of might as the seat of authority. With this change comes a change of the nature of the dragon. He now has a name of blasphemy upon his heads. Biblically, "name" has to do with the very nature of that which is named (see note on 2:13). John saw that the dragon's nature, manifest in the beast, has become one of blasphemy toward God.

Revelation 13:3 tells us that the whole earth marveled at the beast who had a mortal wound but then was healed (see note on 13:3). "Earth" is one of the ways the vision represents the rebellious realm. This is now manifested clearly when John sees that "the whole earth" (NLT, "the whole world") marvels after the beast. The vision reveals that marveling after the beast is worshiping the dragon as well as worshiping the beast. In both cases, the cause of the worship is power (13:4). They worship the beast because of his invincibility—"Who is able to fight against him?" This is a classic expression of "might makes right."

"The beast was allowed to speak great blasphemies against God" (13:5). The beast's blasphemy of God is the antithesis of the elders' praise of God:

THE ELDERS (4:10)	THE BEAST (13:6)
Bow before God (Acknowledge God to be God)	Blasphemes God (Does not acknowledge God to be God
Worship God (Allow God to be God in their lives)	Blasphemes God's name (Does not allow God to be God)
Cast their crowns (Yield control of their lives to God)	Blasphemes God's dwelling (the place where God is in control)

If, as we saw, the actions of the elders represent the deep inner orientation toward God of the citizens of God's realm, New Jerusalem, then the blasphemies of the beast and those who worship him represent the deep inner orientation against God of the citizens of the dragon's realm, fallen Babylon.

In this section we also find the unmistakable identification of the two descriptions of the citizenship of the rebellious order, fallen Babylon. John sees that the beast was "given authority to rule over every tribe and people and language and nation" (13:7), thus defining this phrase for the entire vision. (The phrase, in some form, appears at 5:9; 7:9; 13:7; 14:6.) He also sees that "all the people who belong to this world worshiped the beast," also defining this phrase for the entire vision. (The phrase, in some form, appears at 3:10; 6:10; 8:13; 11:10; 13:8, 12, 14; 17:2, 8.) These are the people whose names are not found in the Book of Life. These are the people who have not been redeemed by the Lamb that was slaughtered before the foundation of the world (see note on 13:8).

After this, the proclamation is made: "Anyone with ears to hear should listen and understand" (13:9). This same phrase closed each of the letters to the seven churches; it serves to arouse the listeners to responsiveness. Following this, the text says, "Anyone who is destined for prison will be taken to prison. Anyone destined to die by the sword will die by the sword" (13:10). There are strong intertextual echoes of Jeremiah here. In Jeremiah 15:2, God uses a very similar saying against apostate Israel, and in Jeremiah 43:11 the warning is against Egypt, where a remnant of God's people have fled in rebellion against God's word to them through Jeremiah (Jer 42). It would seem that John was not predicting what will happen to the faithful, but indicating the inevitable demise of the beast and all those who participate in his war against God and God's people. While the beast may be "allowed" to conquer the saints, his victory only hastens his defeat. This is why John calls the faithful to "endure persecution patiently and remain faithful" (13:10), being assured that fallen Babylon's demise is inevitable.

Following this, John saw a vision of another beast (13:11). This, again, modulates Daniel's vision. In Daniel, the four beasts that come from the sea are subsequently interpreted as four kings who arise from the earth (Dan 7:17). John's vision of a single beast that comes up out of the earth suggests that John was seeing the deeper reality that stood behind Daniel's four kings. To understand this beast we must look at its attributes.

This beast "had two horns like those of a lamb" (13:11). The image is unmistakable in light of the Lamb throughout the vision. This beast masquerades as a savior of humanity, a "messiah" who will restore all things and establish God's rule over the earth. But as soon as the beast opens its mouth, it gives itself away; it speaks "with the voice of a dragon" (13:11). John was seeing what Paul describes: "Even Satan disguises himself as an angel of light" (2 Cor 11:14).

If the first beast is characterized by blasphemy, a deep inner rejection of God, the second beast is characterized by actions that incarnate that blasphemy in human life. The second beast puts into action the blasphemy of the first. He creates values, structures, and dynamics of life that have no place for God. In other words, the first beast represents a worldview or perceptual framework that rejects God. The second beast represents the lifestyle that incarnates that worldview. The first action of the second beast is to cause "all the earth and its people to worship the first beast" (13:12). "Its people" is literally, "those who dwell upon the earth," John's standard phrase for the citizens of fallen Babylon. The beginning of the loss of human wholeness is to worship something other than God as God. This worship takes many forms, including idolatry, hedonism, and materialism. For John and his hearers, the worldview and lifestyle of fallen Babylon were manifest in the Roman Empire and epitomized in its emperor.

The second beast did "astounding miracles" (13:13). In conjunction with calling people to worship the first beast, this image echoes Deuteronomy 13:1-3, where Moses warned Israel against false prophets who work miracles if, at the same time, they call for the worship of other gods. All sorts of charlatans abounded in John's day who, through various stratagems, did what appeared to be miraculous things, purporting to be the representative of one of the gods. Even "making fire flash down to earth from the sky" (13:13) would not have been out of the realm of possibility. Almost always, they induced their gullible audience to give them lavish gifts as an act of worship toward the god. (For an excellent contemporary account of this phenomenon, see Lucian's *Alexander the False Prophet*.) In 20:9, John will see all the forces of fallen Babylon surrounding God's people, the beloved city (New Jerusalem), and fire from heaven consuming the hordes of fallen Babylon. John may be previewing in 13:13 the ultimate demise of fallen Babylon in 20:9. The second beast leads the populace of fallen Babylon into a life of being contrary to God, a life which will finally be consumed by the fire of God.

The action of the second beast, who incarnates the blasphemous rebellion of the first beast, results in God's judgment upon the entire rebellious realm. Through such deception, the second beast leads humanity astray and induces them to construct an image of the first beast. This means that the second beast leads humanity into the development of values, structures, and dynamics of life that "image" the first beast's radical rejection of God (see note on 13:14). Such moral values, social and political structures, and economic dynamics come to life as the prevailing "voice" of the culture. This is what it means when it says the beast "was then permitted to give life to this statue so that it could speak" (13:15). Anyone refusing to worship the image must die. Fallen Babylon is remarkably intolerant of anyone who does not play by its rules. Anyone whose values, structures, and dynamics contradict those of the prevailing culture of fallen Babylon must be silenced.

One of the salient features of the Roman world of John's readers was the veneration, even worship, of the emperor. In a culture where emperors were often "divinized" after their death, the heir to the throne was generally perceived to be the son of a deity (*divi filius*). For example, in 42 BC Julius Caesar was formally recognized by the Roman Senate as a god—*Divus Iulius* (the divine Julius). Augustus, his adopted son and ultimate successor, subsequently became *divi filius Iulius* (son of the divine Julius). In some cases, the emperor proclaimed himself as a "god," like Gaius (Caligula, AD 37–41) who pronounced his deity and demanded worship. In the Roman province of Asia where John's readers lived, there was a long history of worshiping kings as divine beings, a tradition easily transferred to the emperor. In such a setting, refusal to worship, or at least venerate the emperor was viewed as seditious, and persecution of those behaving in this manner was usual.

John saw that the entire realm of fallen Babylon, the whole cultural spectrum—political ("small and great"), economic ("rich and poor"), and social ("free and slave")—are "marked" by the second beast. The placement of the mark is very significant, for the mark was placed "on the right hand or on the forehead" (13:16). In the Jewish pool of images, the forehead represents the seat of perception. The condition of one's forehead reveals the nature of one's relationship with God. God's faithful were to have their lives shaped by obedience to God's covenant. They were to have it on their foreheads (Exod 13:9, 16; Deut 6:8; 11:18). The high priest who represented God's people in his presence was to wear the signet with "HOLY TO THE LORD" on his forehead (Exod 28:36-38). Disobedience to God and turning away from God were also expressed on the forehead. When King Uzziah usurped the role of high priest, he was struck with leprosy on his forehead (2 Chr 26:19). Through Isaiah, God declared that apostate Israel's forehead is brass (Isa 48:4, KJV), and Jeremiah told them they had a harlot's forehead (Jer 3:3, NASB). God made Ezekiel's forehead harder than flint to withstand the hard forehead and stubborn heart of Israel (Ezek 3:7-9, KJV).

The other option for the placement of the mark is "on the right hand." Within the Jewish pool of images the right hand denotes the action or behavior of the one whose hand it is. God's right hand does great things (see Exod 15:6; Pss 20:6; 98:1). God's right hand is an expression of God's being in action. The right hand can be a cause of sin (Matt 5:30), obviously expressive of the action of a person rebelling against God. John has seen that another aspect of the beast is its "doing." It incarnates its blasphemy in action. To have the "mark of the beast" on one's right hand is to have one's behavior shaped by the actions of the second beast.

John saw that the mark of the beast is either the name of the beast (13:17) or the number representing his name (see note on 13:18). Because the second beast incarnates the first, the name in fact belongs to both beasts. Since "name" relates to the nature of what is named, the "mark" (which equals "the name") must relate to the nature of the beast. John had seen that one aspect of the beast's nature is blasphemy. The beast totally rejects God from its life and world. To have the mark of the beast on one's right hand or forehead is to have one's inner being shaped by the blasphemy of the first beast.

John saw that without the mark, people are not allowed to "buy or sell" (13:17). This may have had a very relevant meaning for John's audience. As long as Christians had remained within the context of the Jewish community, they participated in the privileged status of Judaism as a legal religion in the Roman world. When Christians were expelled from the Jewish community and became suspect in the eyes of the Roman culture, to buy from or sell to a Christian could place one in jeopardy of being suspect of being a Christian. Economic structures are one of the primary realities of any culture, and economic dynamics often reflect the underlying values of the culture. This is why, often, economic pressures are the primary means used to keep fractious elements in line or to marginalize them.

There are some important lessons that readers can take away from this chapter. First, we need to realize that the essential nature of the first beast is blasphemy, a deep inner posture of being which rejects God from any aspect of one's life and living. The beast's blasphemy is not so much an action as a way of being in relationship to God. Whenever persons live without proper reference to God in their life, whenever God plays no essential part in their values, perspectives, relationships, or actions, their inner being is shaped by the blasphemy of the beast. This is Satan's first strategy to bring humanity into the destructive and dehumanizing bondage of his rebellion. Whenever our being rejects God, as revealed in Scripture, from its frames of reference, it has the mark of the beast on its "forehead."

Second, we need to see that the second beast implements in actions and behavior the blasphemy of the first beast. It is a matter of worldview and lifestyle. The first beast represents a worldview devoid of God. The second beast represents a lifestyle that results from that worldview. Whenever our value system, our economic structures, or our social dynamics have no essential reference to God as God, then we have constructed in our world an "image" of the beast; we have incarnated in our individual or collective life the nature of a life without God. This is Satan's second strategy to bring humanity into the destructive and dehumanizing bondage of his rebellion. Whenever our behaviors reject God from their patterns of action, we have the mark of the beast on our "right hand."

Third, we need to realize the significance of the mark placed on the right hand or on the forehead. Sometimes our slide into Satan's rebellion begins not with a rationally constructed argument against the existence of God but with a single small act that undermines a God-referenced way of living. Often we are subtly and almost unconsciously drawn into the "world's" way of doing things, the "world's" values, the "world's" economic and political structures, the "world's" social and cultural dynamics. Modern technology makes these so pervasive that they become the "norm" of human life and action. "This is the way things are," many say. "You can't fight city hall." "You have to work within the system." Or, in John's terms, "Who is as great as the beast?" and "Who is able to fight against him?" (13:4).

The answer to these questions is found in the oxymoron of a mortal wound that is healed. If a wound is "mortal," by definition it cannot be healed. If a wound is healed, by definition it is not "mortal." What, then, is the "mortal" wound of the beast that is "healed?" John saw that the beast has already been defeated. God is the one who is greater than the beast and has not only fought against him but overcome him. John also saw that God's victory is not just one in an ongoing war. God's victory is total and complete—the beast is mortally wounded. That wound came because of the cross that has its roots in the nature of God's being from before the foundation of the world (see, e.g., the commentary on ch 11). Most redemption theologies have as their usually unspoken premise the idea that the cross is something God "thought up" after the Fall to deal with the problem of the Fall. This premise might be caricatured thus: God created a perfect creation. Adam and Eve "blew it" and creation itself became "fallen" (Rom 8:20ff). God then pondered the problem, finally coming up with the solution—"I will send my Son to die upon the cross. That will resolve the problem."

What John was seeing, however, is that the cross is not something God "did" but a revelation of the very heart of God's nature. Inherent in God's "decision" to create beings in his own image was that they could know their wholeness in a relationship of loving union with God. These beings were given the freedom to say "No" to that relationship because a love relationship always leaves the beloved free to say "No," otherwise it is not a love relationship but coercion. Inherent in God's decision was his commitment to enter into the depths of any rebellion in order to make possible the restoration of that relationship for those who would respond to his love as displayed in the crucifixion of Jesus. Thus, John sees God, imaged as the woman (12:1-5), bringing forth "her" very being into the mouth of the dragon.

Perhaps the image of a chess game would be helpful as regards the fatal wound of the dragon. The goal of a chess game is to "checkmate" your opponent. That is, to get your opponent's king in a position where the opponent cannot defend against the king being taken in the next move. Often in a chess game there comes a point where one player makes a move, usually a sacrificial one, which induces the opponent to make a response that sets the "mating net." This means that the game is already won at that point, even though there may be several moves left before the checkmate move. In other words, at that point the winner has already achieved victory, and the loser is mortally wounded. Should the loser continue to play the game, anyone looking on would think that the game was still undecided. The loser might still be capturing pieces from the winner, but each such "conquering" only moves the inevitable checkmate one step closer.

In the cross of Christ, God brought forth his very being into the face of the rebellion; God made the ultimately sacrificial move that "set the mating net." There Satan received the mortal wound. Satan, however, continues the "game" as though nothing had happened, as though he were "healed," but he is a defeated enemy.

For John and his readers, the second beast, like the first, was "incarnate" in Caesar Nero. While this was the primary focus for John, it does not preclude other figures throughout history who have used positions of power to persecute God's people. Again and again in human history, a particular historical incarnation of the beast has seemed invincible and nearly destroyed the people of God in its midst. But each of those incarnations has fallen and the people of God's New Jerusalem continue. This does not mean that life will be easy for God's people. In every age, faithful citizens of New Jerusalem experience tribulation at the hands of their particular fallen Babylon world.

Each fallen Babylon is notoriously intolerant of New Jerusalem. This is illustrated in a profoundly ironic manner in our early twenty-first century American culture today, where all "truths" are relative—all, that is, except for the "truth" that all "truths" are relative. This view results in a world where all values are also relative—all, that is, except for the value of toleration. In a pluralistic culture of relative truths and values, toleration is the only way to maintain any semblance of community. But notice what happens to this primary virtue of toleration whenever someone suggests that there are ultimate truths. Nothing is as malicious as the intolerance of a culture whose only virtue is toleration! This is why faithful citizens of God's New Jerusalem will always experience tribulation at the hands of their fallen Babylon world. But, as John will see shortly, all fallen Babylons carry within them the seeds of their own destruction because they have a "mortal wound."

ENDNOTES

1. Beale represents this group, although he seems to want it both ways. On the one hand, he writes, "these unbelieving multitudes were ordained not to have eternal life from before the creation of the whole [*sic*] world" (1999:700). On the other hand, he says, "the statement about the Lamb's death is immediately followed by the pre-creation temporal expression. And it is unlikely that the concluding temporal clause goes with 'written,' since twelve words separate them" (1999:702). He then "solves" this dilemma by presuming that 13:8 is dependent upon 17:8 and the distance between "written" and "from before the creation of the world" was created to insert "of the Lamb that was slain" as an identification of the Book of Life. As noted in the note on 13:8 and in endnote 2, this flies in the face of the logic of orality. Mounce, however, affirms the reading that indicates it was before the foundation of the world that the Lamb was slain: "It is better in this case to follow the order of the Greek syntax and read, "the Lamb that hath been slain from the foundation of the world" (1977:256). Witherington (2003:183) joins Mounce in this understanding.
2. The NT world was an oral culture. Kelber (1983:xv) argues effectively that "a disproportionately print-oriented hermeneutic" tends to govern contemporary biblical interpretation. Especially apropos for Revelation, Kelber notes, "The teacher lives a life that is paradigmatic in terms of his message. Because in oral hermeneutics

words have no existence apart from persons, participation in the message is inseparable from imitation of the speaker" (1983:151). John clearly expects his readers to make the reality of his vision the context of their life, thus identifying both them and himself with the same phrase, "having the word of God and the testimony of Jesus" (1:2; 6:9; 20:4), and beginning his communication with "blessed are those who hear and who keep what is written" (1:3, NRSV). How does one "keep" John's vision other than by entering into its reality? That Revelation is written orality can especially be seen in 1:3, where John clearly expects his recipients to hear the account of his vision. In such a setting, later abbreviated elements depend upon earlier introductions of the topic for their full understanding.

◆ 4. The nature of New Jerusalem (14:1-5)

Then I saw the Lamb standing on Mount Zion, and with him were 144,000 who had his name and his Father's name written on their foreheads. [2]And I heard a sound from heaven like the roar of mighty ocean waves or the rolling of loud thunder. It was like the sound of many harpists playing together.

[3]This great choir sang a wonderful new song in front of the throne of God and before the four living beings and the twenty-four elders. No one could learn this song except the 144,000 who had been redeemed from the earth. [4]They have kept themselves as pure as virgins,* following the Lamb wherever he goes. They have been purchased from among the people on the earth as a special offering* to God and to the Lamb. [5]They have told no lies; they are without blame.

14:4a Greek *They are virgins who have not defiled themselves with women.* **14:4b** Greek *as firstfruits.*

NOTES

14:1 *his name and his Father's name written on their foreheads.* This clarifies the "sealing" of the redeemed that John saw at 7:3 (cf. 9:4). The redeemed have God's nature ("name") and the Lamb's as the deep inner orientation of their lives (see commentary on 13:16-18).

14:3 *new song.* There are two words for "new" in Greek: *neos* and *kainos*. *Neos* [TG3501, ZG3742] designates something completely new, never before in existence. *Kainos* [TG2537, ZG2785] denotes something that has been made new from a former existence. The "new" song of the redeemed is a *kainos* song. It is, most likely, the song of the new covenant people of God composed as a result of the consummation of the old covenant (11:3-13), the fulfillment of the promise (11:18), and the restoration of the kingdom (1:6; 5:10). This interpretation may be confirmed when, later in the vision, John sees the redeemed "singing the song of Moses, the servant of God, and the song of the Lamb" (15:3). There the old covenant and new covenant leaders are brought together.

14:4 *They have kept themselves as pure as virgins.* As the NLT mg notes, the Greek says, "They are virgins who have not defiled [or, 'soiled'] themselves with women." At first blush it seems to be a radically chauvinistic statement, eliminating from redemption half of the church and demeaning half of the human race. There is no evidence of celibacy at this point in the history of the Christian movement, particularly in the Jewish tradition in which John's audience was steeped, either as Jews or as Gentiles who had been enculturated into the restored kingdom of God's people. Since there is no evidence of celibacy in first-century Christianity, and no evidence that women were viewed as causes of sin in the Christian community, what was John saying? Later in his vision, John sees the "great prostitute" (17:1). We will see that for John, the prostitute is the Roman Empire whose values and perspectives are in radical opposition to those of God's Kingdom. To be a virgin was to remain spiritually pure, rejecting false values and false deities.

a special offering to God and to the Lamb. Lit., "firstfruits to God and the Lamb" (so NLT mg). This highlights the priestly role of the kingdom of priests redeemed by the Lamb. In the Jewish story, the Levitical priesthood was the substitute for the consecration of the firstborn of Israel to God. Instead of each firstborn being consecrated to God, the Levitical priests took their place (Exod 13:2, 13; 22:29; Num 3:12-13).

14:5 ***They have told no lies.*** Lit., "in their mouth no falsehood was found." Falsehood is one of the attributes of fallen Babylon (21:8, 27; 22:15).

they are without blame. Blamelessness, found only here in the vision, is a vital attribute of the faithful. Those without blame will be delivered from their oppressors, that is, restored as God's kingdom (Wis 10:15), will endure forever (Ps 37:18), and are God's delight (Prov 11:20).

COMMENTARY

This visionary scene portrays "the Lamb standing on Mount Zion" accompanied by 144,000 faithful followers (14:1). The geography is significant because Mount Zion has always played a crucial role in Jewish history and expectations for the restoration of the kingdom. Mount Zion was God's dwelling place (Pss 48; 74:2; 78:68; Isa 8:18; *Jubilees* 1:28). It was also central in the restoration of the kingdom (Isa 4:5; 10:12; 18:7; 24:23; Joel 2:32; Obad 1:21; Mic 4:7; *Jubilees* 1:28). The writer of Hebrews used this image to confirm the fulfillment of the restoration (Heb 12:22). Outside of the canonical tradition, the image remains consistent: "Ezra" saw a great, numberless multitude (cf. 7:9) on Mount Zion praising the Lord with songs. They have "immortal clothing" and are being crowned by the Son of God (2 Esdr 2:42ff). Later, Ezra saw the Son of God standing on Mount Zion to judge the nations and restore Israel (2 Esdr 13:33-50). John saw "the Lamb standing on Mount Zion," a modulation of the Jewish image that again sets forth Jesus as the Messiah who, through the cross, has restored the kingdom.

Accompanying the Lamb were 144,000 followers. The figure "144,000" was previously used to designate the restored old covenant community, the 12 tribes of Israel (7:4-8). John saw, however, that this group had been redeemed (*agorazō* [TG59, ZG60]) from the earth (14:3) and purchased (*agorazō*) from among the people on the earth (14:4). Since "earth" represents the rebellious realm, and the only other place John used "purchased" (*agorazō*) in the sense of "redeem" is in 5:9 (cf. NLT, "ransomed"), where the Lamb purchased people for God with his blood "from every tribe and language and people and nation," it seems clear that John was modulating the imagery of the 144,000. It now represents the redeemed from all humanity, not just Israel, who constitute the members of God's restored kingdom.

John saw the redeemed kingdom of priests singing "a wonderful new song in front of the throne of God and before the four living beings and the twenty-four elders" (14:3) to the heavenly accompaniment "like the sound of many harpists playing together" (14:2). Only the 144,000 could learn this song (14:3) because they are the redeemed and they are virgins. The redeemed are said to be "virgins" (14:4; see note) because they are spiritually pure. We have already seen that John uses "adultery" to describe the activity of those who turn away from God and participate in the worship of other deities (2:14, 20). The primary image of such turning from God is fallen Babylon, which John will soon describe as a "prostitute" (17:1ff). In contrast, the primary image for God's faithful is New Jerusalem, which John will see as the bride of the Lamb (19:7-8; 21:9ff). It would seem that the vision is portraying the faithful as those who have not committed adultery with the harlot, fallen Babylon, but have kept themselves "virgins" for their bridegroom, the Lamb. The redeemed are also described as those who "[follow] the Lamb wherever he goes" (14:4), an image of radical discipleship to one who, among other things, went to the cross.

The brief description of the redeemed is set in stark contrast to the frightening pictures of the two beasts that shape the rebellious world of fallen Babylon. For readers steeped in Jewish history and literature of the time, the picture was abundantly clear. The Lamb is the Messiah whose rule from Mount Zion has already begun. What would have been new for these readers is the identification of the covenant community of God's people. Earlier in the vision (ch 7) John had seen the 144,000 representing the old covenant community of God's people—Israel. Now, however, the image represents a new Israel, a new covenant community, consisting of people from all humanity, not just Jews. Such a reality is part of the Old Testament, but a largely forgotten part. The covenant with Abraham indicated that through Abraham's descendants all the nations of the world would be blessed (Gen 12:1-3). This promise had largely been submerged by a variation that saw the restoration of Israel resulting in the nations becoming Israel's servants.

How easy it is for us to view God's actions on our behalf as giving us a position of superiority over our "enemies." We want God to "reverse the roles," to vindicate us and condemn "them." God's solution is more likely to break down the dividing wall of hostility and bring us together in a new unity (Eph 2:14-15). This may be why the redeemed in John's vision sing a "new" song (see note on 14:3). Their song is not simply a reprise of the Song of Moses, the old covenant, which expected the restoration for Israel alone (cf. Deut 32:43). Their song includes the nations in the restoration as indicated later in the vision in the song of the redeemed: "All nations will come and worship before you" (15:4). The fact that only the redeemed can sing this song indicates that John was seeing an experiential reality, not merely a propositional or cognitive structure. The new song, like the rest of the Christian life, is an incarnational reality. When the Christian life is reduced to a theological construct, a doctrinal structure, or a dogmatic position, it usually also becomes divorced from life. It becomes a set of propositions imposed upon life from without rather than the incarnation of a vital relationship with God in one's heart. For example, it would be possible for a person to study Beethoven's Fifth Symphony so thoroughly that they could reproduce the score from memory and could explain any point of the work in exquisite and exact musicological detail. But unless they joined an orchestra and performed the symphony, they would never really "know" Beethoven's Fifth. Thus it is with the "new song" of the redeemed. Their lives should sing forth in the world the incarnation of God's redemption.

Their lives should sing forth in the world because their character, their inner nature, is being transformed in the image of God. Having the Lamb's name and his Father's name on our foreheads, being spiritually undefiled, blameless, and without falsehood, are not forensic but formational realities. Such quality of being comes from "following the Lamb wherever he goes." This calls for an abandonment of our lives to God in all things. Our agenda, our plans, our purposes, our wants, our needs, our desires, and our goals all become expendable for God's purposes in and through our lives. Being spiritually undefiled comes from keeping God's purposes for us unstained by the overlay of our purposes. Being blameless comes not from obedient actions but from obedient hearts. Being without falsehood comes from the integrity of being who we are in God's love without pretense or facade. Only such persons are able to follow the Lamb to the margins of human existence, into the darkness of human lostness, into the brokenness of human despair, where the Lamb is present with the last, the least, the lowest, and the lost.

◆ 5. Opportunity and outcome (14:6-13)

6And I saw another angel flying through the sky, carrying the eternal Good News to proclaim to the people who belong to this world—to every nation, tribe, language, and people. 7"Fear God," he shouted. "Give glory to him. For the time has come when he will sit as judge. Worship him who made the heavens, the earth, the sea, and all the springs of water."

8Then another angel followed him through the sky, shouting, "Babylon is fallen—that great city is fallen—because she made all the nations of the world drink the wine of her passionate immorality."

9Then a third angel followed them, shouting, "Anyone who worships the beast and his statue or who accepts his mark on the forehead or on the hand
10must drink the wine of God's anger. It has been poured full strength into God's cup of wrath. And they will be tormented with fire and burning sulfur in the presence of the holy angels and the Lamb.
11The smoke of their torment will rise forever and ever, and they will have no relief day or night, for they have worshiped the beast and his statue and have accepted the mark of his name."

12This means that God's holy people must endure persecution patiently, obeying his commands and maintaining their faith in Jesus.

13And I heard a voice from heaven saying, "Write this down: Blessed are those who die in the Lord from now on. Yes, says the Spirit, they are blessed indeed, for they will rest from their hard work; for their good deeds follow them!"

NOTES

14:6 *flying through the sky.* Lit., "flying in midheaven." At 8:13 (see note), the eagle in midheaven proclaims "woe" to the citizens of the rebellious realm. Here, an angel in "midheaven" proclaims the Good News to the citizens of the rebellious realm. And at 19:17, the birds of "midheaven" are invited to feast on the slain citizens of the rebellious realm. "Midheaven" is one of the vision's ways to describe heavenly actions that have effects upon the rebellious order.

eternal Good News. John speaks of an "eternal" gospel because John's vision depicts followers of the Lamb as citizens of New Jerusalem in the midst of a fallen Babylon world. The angel with the "eternal gospel" calls to the citizens of fallen Babylon to become citizens of the eternal New Jerusalem.

14:7 ***Fear God. . . . Give glory to him. . . . Worship him.*** As noted at 11:13, fearing God and giving him glory is the action of those citizens of fallen Babylon who respond to God and become citizens of New Jerusalem. The vision characterizes the faithful as those who "fear God" (11:18; 19:5), as those who "fear" and "glorify" God (15:4), and, especially, as those who "worship" him (4:10; 7:15; 11:1; 22:3). The same triad of response to God is found at 15:4—"Who will not *fear* you, Lord, and *glorify* your name? For you alone are holy. All nations will come and *worship* before you" (italics mine).

14:8 ***Babylon is fallen—that great city is fallen.*** Lit., "Fallen, fallen is Babylon the great." The emphasis is upon the fallen nature of the citizens of the rebellious order. Destruction is the inevitable consequence of a fallen (or sinful) nature, but the destruction is still future (cf. 18:21).

passionate. Gr., *thumos* [TG2372, ZG2596], which also connotes "wrath" and "anger." It is likely that the "wrath" here is not Babylon's but God's (cf. 14:10).

immorality. Lit., "fornication," as throughout the vision (2:14 [see note], 20-21; 17:2, 4; 18:3, 9; 19:2). It represents the spiritual adultery of turning away from God to worship other gods. The chief characteristic of Babylon's fallenness is her orientation toward God, an orientation of rejection and rebellion as portrayed in the blasphemies of the beast (13:6).

14:9 ***Anyone who worships the beast.*** This leaves open the option of not worshiping the beast, of becoming citizens of New Jerusalem. For those who do not become citizens of New Jerusalem, however, there are dire consequences.

accepts his mark on the forehead or on the hand. As indicated in the commentary on 13:16-18, the forehead or right hand is the primary image, not the mark. The "forehead" represents the perceptual framework of the first beast (13:1-10), whose blasphemous nature totally rejects God from its worldview. The "right hand" represents the "performance" or lifestyle of the second beast (13:11-15), a mode of being devoid of God. Consequently, to "receive the mark of the beast" does not refer to having something tattooed upon your forehead or right hand, or having a computer chip implanted in your forehead or right hand. Rather, it means to be misshapen by the godless worldview and lifestyle of the fallen Babylon world. Anyone with a worldview that does not have any place for God as God has the "mark" upon their foreheads. Anyone with a lifestyle that doesn't manifest God as God has the "mark" upon their right hand.

14:12 ***God's holy people must endure persecution.*** Lit., "here is the endurance of the saints." In light of the dire consequences of belonging to fallen Babylon, the saints are exhorted to endure persecution at the hands of their fallen Babylon world rather than accommodate to it. This would speak strongly to those churches that were making such accommodations (Ephesus, Pergamum, Thyatira, Sardis, Laodicea).

obeying his commands and maintaining their faith in Jesus. Lit., "those who keep the commandments of God and the faith of Jesus." This is a variant of the usual description of the citizens of New Jerusalem as those who have the word of God and the testimony of Jesus (1:2 [see note], 9; 6:9; 12:17; 20:4). As noted at 1:2, to have the "testimony of Jesus" is to live a Christlike life in the world, i.e., to have the same "testimony" that Jesus manifested in his life. It would follow, then, that the alternative John uses here, where "faith" is substituted for "testimony," would indicate having the same "faith" Jesus had, i.e., living in the same relationship with God as Jesus had (see John 17:20ff). This understanding is further substantiated by John's use of an identical grammatical structure in 2:13 and 13:10.

14:13 ***says the Spirit.*** The Spirit speaking here is probably associated with the repeated litany in the letters to the churches, "listen to the Spirit and understand what he is saying to the churches" (2:7, 11, 17, 29; 3:6, 13, 22). This is especially appropriate since the letters deal with the "works" of the churches (2:2, 5, 19 [twice], 23, 26; 3:1, 2, 8, 15). Also, this is the second of the seven blessings in the vision (1:3; 14:13; 16:15; 19:9; 20:6; 22:7, 14) and would remind the readers that they are to listen to the message of the prophecy and "obey what it says" (1:3), again a connection to deeds.

good deeds. Deeds play a significant role in the vision. The churches are commended or confronted for their deeds (2:5, 6, 19, 22, 23, 26; 3:1, 2, 8, 15), fallen Babylon is condemned for its deeds (9:20; 16:11; 18:6), and all are rewarded according to their deeds (20:12-13; 22:12). Keeping Jesus' deeds (2:26; NLT, "who obey me") is to live a Christlike life in the world, to have the "testimony of Jesus." This is how faithful citizens of New Jerusalem "conquer" their fallen Babylon world. "Deeds" are the outer manifestation of the quality of one's being.

COMMENTARY

The first part of this passage presents an invitation for the citizens of fallen Babylon to become citizens of New Jerusalem. They are invited to hear the Good News, fear God, give him glory, and worship him (14:6-7). We must remember that all citizens of New Jerusalem begin as citizens of fallen Babylon. The vision makes this clear at several points: Through the cross the Lamb has ransomed people for God from every tribe and language and people and nation (5:9). John then saw this group standing before the throne of God and the Lamb and worshiping (7:9-12). John also saw that some of those from all peoples, tribes, languages, and nations, from those who dwell upon the earth, become ones who fear God and give him glory (11:9-13). The Good News is for fallen Babylon.

So much of the interpretation of John's vision emphasizes the antithesis of saints and sinners that we are liable to overlook the fact that the vision is full of images of God's redeeming love for the rebels. When John speaks of an "eternal Good News," he infers that God's love and grace for fallen humanity is everlasting. The Good News is not for the saints, it is for the citizens of fallen Babylon, emphasized here by John's use of both phrases for that citizenship—"the people who belong to this world" and those of "every nation, tribe, language, and people" (14:6).

The Good News is given as one last opportunity to the members of fallen Babylon before "the time has come when [God] will sit as judge" (14:7). Israel was eagerly awaiting this time because it was a time that signals the restoration of the kingdom and the demise of the Gentiles' control. There is still opportunity left for those in fallen Babylon to enter into that kingdom. Those who don't choose to remain in a world that rejects God. To participate in Babylon's rejection of God as God is to place oneself in a situation where the reality of God's holiness burns against all that is unholy in one's life. Holiness is ultimately destructive of unholiness and is perceived as "wrath" by the unholy.

Such people, it is said, "will be tormented with fire and burning sulfur in the presence of the holy angels and the Lamb" (14:10). This seems an uncharacteristically cruel picture of heaven, where the Lamb is seated on the throne surrounded by the holy angels (7:11, 17). The operative term here is "holy." As noted above, the holiness of God burns against all that is unholy, not in a vindictive, retributive, vengeful, punitive manner, but simply as the reality of holiness. John seems to have seen that those who are unholy spend eternity in the presence of the holiness of heaven. To spend eternity in the presence of holiness when one is, to the core of one's being, unholy, would be an endless torment. The same image of fallen Babylon in proximity to New Jerusalem is seen by John in chapters 21–22. There John sees that the gates of New Jerusalem are never closed (21:25), that outside is fallen Babylon (22:15), but nothing unclean is allowed to enter (21:27). It seems that fallen Babylon exists forever in the presence of the holiness of New Jerusalem. Jesus' parable of the rich man and Lazarus (Luke 16:19-31) is another image of heaven and hell being in close proximity to one another, but nothing of hell could enter heaven (cf. *1 Enoch* 48:9, which says "as straw in the fire so shall they [the wicked] burn before the face of the holy").

Rather than being discouraged by this scenario, the believers are told to be encouraged. They are also told that they will endure persecution at the hands of their fallen Babylon world (14:12) as they maintain their testimony for Jesus. At this juncture, a voice calls out from heaven saying, "Blessed are those who die in the Lord from now on" (14:13). This is the second of the seven blessings in Revelation (1:3; 14:13; 16:15; 19:9; 20:6; 22:7, 14.) The mention of "from now on" reflects the vision's subversion of Jewish expectations. They thought the faithful dead would be resurrected to participate in the restored kingdom. Once the kingdom was restored, there would be no more faithful martyrs since God's people would then reign over the earth, free from the oppression of their enemies. John saw that even though God had restored the kingdom through the Messiah, Jesus, God's faithful people continued to experience martyrdom at the hands of the enemies of God.

This section of Revelation (14:6-13) had much to teach the early church, as well as the church in our own times. Often it is as hard for the church today as it was for the early Jewish Christians to realize that the Good News is not a "private" possession. For Jewish Christians, the Good News of God's restoration of the kingdom in the Messiah and the fulfillment of the covenant and promises in the cross and resurrection of the Messiah were naturally seen as applying only to Israel. This is seen pointedly in the disciples' question to the resurrected Jesus, "Lord, has the time come for you to free Israel and restore our kingdom?" (Acts 1:6). One of the themes of Acts is God's work to get the Jewish believers to realize that the Gentiles were included in the restoration of the kingdom. Like the Jewish believers, we often look for God to act on behalf of our community of faith against its detractors, external or internal. God's focus, however, is on the redemption of our detractors. We are to proclaim the Good News in the midst of our world, and we are to incarnate the reality of the Good News.

Such incarnation is possible only when our own response to the Good News results in a change of our citizenship. When the "Good News" is merely a theological construct, a doctrinal structure, a cognitive perspective, or an ecclesiastical position, it fails to impact the world in transforming ways. The "Good News" must become the shaping reality of our very being if it is to be incarnated in our living. Without a change of citizenship, we are imprisoned in a fallen order. Often we try to put on a facade of Christianity but retain the values, structures, and perspectives of our fallen Babylon world. Such "Christianity" is never winsome to the world because it resorts to the world's methods to promulgate, establish, defend, and perpetuate itself. The "Good News" calls for a radical change of citizenship. A whole new set of values, structures, and perspectives come to shape and direct the lives of believers. They live in an atmosphere of awe toward God (i.e., they fear God). They desire that their lives manifest the very nature of God (i.e., give glory to him). They live lives that worship God in every thought, word, and deed.

Whenever the church forgets that the Good News is for the world, it forgets its primary purpose in the world. The church is not only the proclaimer of the Good News, it is also called to be the incarnator of the Good News. The Good News for citizens of fallen Babylon is that there is a way of life, a mode of being, a realm of existence in which healing for brokenness, forgiveness of sin, cleansing of unholiness, liberation from bondage, and transformation to wholeness can be found. But unless the world sees this reality incarnated in the life of the church, it will have no grounds for believing the proclamation.

When the church effectively incarnates the Good News of the wholeness of life in New Jerusalem, it casts into sharp relief the fallenness of fallen Babylon. How much better for the church and for believers to "condemn" the world not through harsh words of judgment, but through the witness of a radical alternative to the world's dehumanizing destructiveness.

This is why the church and believers must be so careful about accommodations to the dehumanizing values and destructive perspectives of their fallen Babylon world. If we "worship the beast," adopt its "image," live by its perspectives, we send an unclear signal to the world. The temptation to make accommodation with the world is powerful. Won't the world appreciate the church more if it "fit in" more readily with the world's values ("worship the beast")? Won't the world be more open to the church and its influence if the church operates more by the world's methods ("worship the image")? Won't the world be able to hear the gospel better if the church adopts the world's way of looking at things ("take the mark of the beast")? The answer is a resounding "No!" What happens is that the world simply comes to believe that its mode of existence is all there is because it is confirmed by the church. There is nothing to alert the world to the destructive direction in which it is going, to point out the dire consequences of its way of life.

Without such a radical change of citizenship, we are prisoners of "wrath." Fallen Babylon's existence is a life frustrated at every turn by its own brokenness. No matter how diligently we try to bring order to the chaos of our little portion of the world, no matter how hard we try to maintain control of our existence, no matter how much we try to promote ourselves and manipulate others, we always fail to achieve the peace, joy, and stability for which we hunger deep within. The problem is we are trying to play god in our life. There are only two options for human existence: Either God is God in our life, or we are god in our life. This is the root of our spiritual adultery, our turning away from God. This is the seat of all unholiness in our life.

Unholiness, however, always exists in the deeper context of the holiness of God. In that reality, the holiness of God becomes a terrible torment to our unholiness. Perhaps an illustration will help. If you are seated comfortably as you read this, your comfort and peace are the result of being in perfect harmony with the law of gravity. For the purposes of the illustration, let's presume that the room in which you are comfortably seated is on the top floor of a high-rise apartment complex. When you complete your reading, you decide to go out for a walk but, instead of taking the elevator to the ground floor, you decide to step out the window. When you step into space, what happens to the law of gravity? Does it suddenly undergo a transformation from a kind, beneficial, supportive reality to a mean, vindictive, punitive power? Of course not! It simply continues to be the law of gravity. By placing yourself in opposition to the law of gravity, you begin to experience the "wrath" of gravity. This, in some measure, illustrates the holiness of God. God's holiness is the context of our true wholeness, peace, joy, and stability. When we step away from holiness into unholiness, God doesn't change. God continues to be holy, and we begin to experience the destructive consequences of our unholiness. Unholiness is its own torment.

It is no surprise that as a culture becomes more and more shaped by the values and perspectives of fallen Babylon, human brokenness and its manifestation in violence increases more and more, both on the individual and the corporate level. Part of the violence is directed against any person or group who dares stand against the destructive and dehumanizing bondages of fallen Babylon. The pressure to conform is pervasive in fallen Babylon. Faithful followers of the Lamb must have increasing endurance, even in the face of pressures, to be faithful witnesses to the Good News in the midst of fallen Babylon. And God is with them in fallen Babylon, for God enters into the torment to offer redemption and restoration to holiness.

◆ 6. Harvest (14:14–15:4)

14Then I saw a white cloud, and seated on
the cloud was someone like the Son of
Man.* He had a gold crown on his head
and a sharp sickle in his hand.
15Then another angel came from the
Temple and shouted to the one sitting on
the cloud, "Swing the sickle, for the time
of harvest has come; the crop on earth is
ripe." 16So the one sitting on the cloud
swung his sickle over the earth, and the
whole earth was harvested.
17After that, another angel came from
the Temple in heaven, and he also had a
sharp sickle. 18Then another angel, who had
power to destroy with fire, came from the
altar. He shouted to the angel with the
sharp sickle, "Swing your sickle now to
gather the clusters of grapes from the vines
of the earth, for they are ripe for judgment."
19So the angel swung his sickle over
the earth and loaded the grapes into the
great winepress of God's wrath. 20The
grapes were trampled in the winepress outside
the city, and blood flowed from the
winepress in a stream about 180 miles*
long and as high as a horse's bridle.

CHAPTER 15

Then I saw in heaven another marvelous
event of great significance. Seven angels
were holding the seven last plagues,
which would bring God's wrath to completion.
2I saw before me what seemed to
be a glass sea mixed with fire. And on it
stood all the people who had been victorious
over the beast and his statue and the
number representing his name. They were
all holding harps that God had given
them. 3And they were singing the song of
Moses, the servant of God, and the song
of the Lamb:

"Great and marvelous are your works,
O Lord God, the Almighty.
Just and true are your ways,
O King of the nations.*
4Who will not fear you, Lord,
and glorify your name?
For you alone are holy.
All nations will come and worship
before you,
for your righteous deeds have been
revealed."

14:14 Or *like a son of man.* See Dan 7:13. "Son of Man" is a title Jesus used for himself. **14:20** Greek *1,600 stadia* [296 kilometers]. **15:3** Some manuscripts read *King of the ages.*

NOTES

14:14 ***seated on the cloud.*** This expression echoes multiple passages in the OT. At the formation of the old covenant community, God's presence is repeatedly depicted as a cloud. The "glory" (= presence) of God appeared in a cloud (Exod 16:10; 40:34ff; 1 Kgs 8:10; Ezek 10:4). In the Tabernacle, God appeared in a cloud over the atonement cover (Lev 16:2). God also appears on a cloud to judge the enemies of Israel (Isa 19:1) as well as Israel herself (Ezek 1:4ff). The psalmists repeatedly image God as present in a cloud (Pss 18:11; 68:4; 97:2; 104:3). In the account of Jesus' transfiguration, God speaks out of a cloud (Matt 17:5; Mark 9:7; Luke 9:35). Here, the imagery associating the Son of Man with a cloud indicates that Jesus is God.

someone like the Son of Man. This vision coincides with that in Dan 7:13 (see commentary for details).

gold crown on his head. It has already been noted that only the redeemed or heavenly beings have crowns in the vision (see note on 4:4; commentary on 6:2). "Gold" is an image for the very nature of New Jerusalem (21:18, 21).

14:15 ***the crop on earth is ripe.*** The image here is of the harvest of grain since the word for "ripe" (*xērainomai* [TG3583A, ZG3830]) means "dried." In Jesus' parable (Matt 13:24-30) the wheat represented the righteous, and this appears to be the case here. Also, in Jesus' teaching, it was the Son of Man who would gather the elect (Mark 13:26-27).

14:16 ***his sickle over the earth.*** Lit., "sickle upon (*epi* [TG1909, ZG2093]) the earth." The significance of the preposition "upon" becomes clear in contrast to the action of the angel in 14:19, who casts his sickle "into (*eis* [TG1519, ZG1650]) the earth" (cf. NLT, "over the earth"). The phrase "into the earth" plays an important role in the vision. The angel with the censer casts the fiery prayers of the saints "into the earth" (8:5, KJV), and fallen Babylon is shaken and disrupted by the presence of God. The angel of the abyss is cast "into the earth" (9:1), and becomes its Destroyer (9:11). The dragon, Satan, casts a third of the stars (rebellious angels) "into the earth" (12:4), and is himself cast "into the earth" (12:9, 13), which is the cause of the earth's woe (12:12). The beast from the earth causes heavenly fire to be cast "into the earth" (13:13). The first bowl of God's wrath is cast "into the earth" (16:1-2), and the citizens of fallen Babylon are tormented. We have seen that "earth" is an image for the rebellious realm, fallen Babylon. The redeemed are no longer part of fallen Babylon; they have become citizens of New Jerusalem. What the image seems to be portraying in the action of the Son of Man's sickle is that the citizens of New Jerusalem are not "in" the earth, but "upon" it.

14:18 ***power to destroy with fire.*** Lit., "authority over the fire." It has already been noted that "fire" is an image for the action of God's holiness against that which is unholy (see commentary on 14:9-11). John was seeing the action of the holy God (the angel comes from the Temple, from God's presence) against the unholy realm of fallen Babylon.

14:19 ***swung his sickle over the earth.*** Lit., "cast his sickle into the earth." See note on 14:16.

14:20 ***outside the city.*** "The city" would appear to be New Jerusalem. In his vision of New Jerusalem, John saw that fallen Babylon (represented by its wicked inhabitants) is "outside" the holy city (22:15). The same image appears in different form at 11:2, where God's faithful people and the temple and altar where they worship and serve God are surrounded by the nations (fallen Babylon) who trample the outside courts. In the OT, unclean things were to be taken outside the city (Lev 14:40-45), blasphemers were executed outside the city (1 Kgs 21:13), and the unclean were exiled outside the city (2 Kgs 7:3). At a deeper level, however, the city could be the earthly Jerusalem, outside of whose walls God's judgment was enacted in the cross of Jesus. In light of the Jewish image of what is "outside the city" (cf. Lev 16:27), it is interesting that the writer of Hebrews highlights that Jesus suffered outside the city (Heb 13:12).

blood flowed from the winepress in a stream about 180 miles long. This image is reflected in two noncanonical works. In 2 Esdr 15:24-37, concerning God's judgment against sinners, it is said "there shall be blood from the sword as high as a horse's belly." Similarly, in *1 Enoch,* where God executes judgment upon the rebellious by having sinners turn against one another and slay one another, it says "and the horse shall walk up to the breast in the blood of sinners" (*1 Enoch* 100:3). John's vision modulates this imagery by adding the length of the flow of blood.

If this is another image for the judgment of the cross, it heightens the image of the blood of the Lamb seen elsewhere in the vision. It is the blood of the Lamb that has cleansed people from their sin (1:5), ransomed citizens of fallen Babylon for God (5:9), washed the garments (beings) of the redeemed and made them white (7:14), and enabled them to conquer the dragon (12:11). It also gives new dimension to the image of the Lamb whose robe is dipped in blood (19:13), which, as shall be seen, is another image for the cross. John was drawing upon Isaiah 63:1-6 and Joel 3:13 at this point to portray his vision. In both, God's judgment is imaged as the treading of a winepress, and in Joel the grain harvest is conjoined with the grape harvest. In Joel, the vats overflow, and in Isaiah the blood of the peoples is poured out upon the earth (Isa 63:6). If with Joel, John's image is of a dual harvest (see Bauckham 1993b:94-98; *2 Baruch* 70:2 depicts a dual harvest) similar to that used by John the Baptist (Matt 3:12) and Jesus (Matt 13:30), then it would seem that there is one harvest with two consequences: the gathering of the redeemed (14:14-16), and the trampling of the rebellious. This would be another echo from Isaiah where both redemption and vengeance are conjoined in a single action: "For the day of vengeance was in my heart, and the year for my redeeming work had come" (Isa 63:4, NRSV). The fact that the winepress is "outside the city" echoes the crucifixion of Jesus outside the city (Heb 13:12). Since, for John, the cross is the source of salvation for the redeemed and, as just noted above, the blood of the Lamb the means of that redemption, does it not stand to reason that the cross is also the source of judgment for the rebellious, and the blood of the Lamb the condemnation of fallen Babylon? The blood of the Lamb gathers up the blood of the prophets (18:24), the saints (16:6), and the witnesses (martyrs) of Jesus (17:6) who have been slain by fallen Babylon. This is intimated by Jesus, "you will be held responsible for the murder of all godly people of all time—from the murder of righteous Abel to the murder of Zechariah son of Berekiah, whom you killed in the Temple between the sanctuary and the altar" (Matt 23:35). John picks up this image in 16:6: "Since they [the rebellious citizens of fallen Babylon] shed the blood of your holy people and your prophets, you have given them blood to drink." The blood that is cleansing for the redeemed is condemnation for the rebellious.

Thus, as I have suggested throughout this section, John may be seeing here not the final judgment (he sees that in 20:11-15) but another aspect of the cross (see notes and commentary on 11:7-14 for John's central vision of the cross). The redeemed (14:3) have already been "harvested" from the earth as "firstfruits for God" (14:4, cf. NLT mg), and the rebellious who are worshiping the beast and receiving its mark will drink the "wine of God's anger" (14:10), which John later images as "blood" (16:6). John was seeing the restoration of the kingdom in the cross of Jesus, a restoration with two consequences: the restored kingdom (New Jerusalem) for the righteous and a realm of death (fallen Babylon) for the unrighteous.

15:1 ***another marvelous event of great significance.*** John closes the unit begun in 11:19 by employing much of the same imagery and terms in the conclusion as in the introduction. He saw a sign (*sēmeion* [TG4592, ZG4956]) just as in 12:1. Then in 15:5, John sees the Temple in heaven thrown wide open, just as in 11:19. At the beginning of the seventh seal

(8:1-2), John sees the angels with seven trumpets (the next major unit) introduced before the details of the seventh seal are given. Here he sees the angels with seven bowls (the next major unit) introduced before the climax of this unit.

15:2 ***what seemed to be a glass sea.*** This is identical in Greek to the phrase in 4:6 (see note), suggesting this is the same "sea"—a symbol of the rebellious realm.

mixed with fire. Between 4:6 and this point, John has seen the judgment of God; now the holiness (fire) of God has entered into the rebellious realm (sea).

the people who had been victorious. The Greek has a present participle that should be translated, "the people who are conquering," thereby denoting a present and ongoing activity. This is the same use of "conquering" noted in the letters to the seven churches in which those who "are conquering" (present participle) are promised certain rewards (see 2:7, 11, 17, 26; 3:5, 12, 21).

statue. Gr., *eikōn* [TG1504, ZG1635], which means "image" (see note on 13:14).

harps that God had given them. This may give perspective to the earlier portion of the vision where, with the 144,000 accompanying the Lamb on Mount Zion, John hears a sound like "many harpists playing together" (14:2). The same term for "harp" is used of the instruments the 24 elders hold (5:8). Specifically, John writes of the cithara (*kithara* [TG2788, ZG3067]), which is "an elaborate lyre with eleven or twelve strings of equal length strung over a wooden sound box and fastened to tuning pegs on a crossbar, plucked with either the left or the right hand. It was used independently or with other instruments and also to accompany voices in singing" (IDB 2.526). The harp was used in general contexts of praise and worship, and in the LXX *kithara* translates the Hebrew terms *nebel* [TH5035A, ZH5575] and *kinnor* [TH2788, ZH3067]; cf. Pss 33:2 [32:2, LXX]; 57:8 [56:9, LXX]; 71:22 [70:22, LXX]; 81:2 [80:3, LXX]. Since John used this image in association with the redeemed who are imaged as priests (1:6; 5:10; 20:6), the main source for the image is the Levitical priesthood who used harps (among other instruments) to lead in the worship of God (1 Chr 15:16, 20; 16:5).

COMMENTARY

The image of Jesus as the Son of Man coming on the clouds seems to originate in Daniel (Dan 7:13) as a vision of the one who would restore Israel and rule the nations. This image was expanded upon in the intertestamental period and became part of Jewish expectation related to the consummation of the old covenant and the fulfillment of the promises to restore the kingdom to Israel. For example, 2 Esdras 13 develops the vision of the figure like a man (the Messiah) who rides the clouds to judge the nations and restore Israel. Jesus told the religious leaders who were judging him that they would one day see him, the Son of Man, coming on the clouds of glory (Matt 24:30; 26:64; Mark 13:26; 14:62; Luke 21:27). John's use of this image conveys his vision of the final consummation of God's victory.

The Son of Man was about to use his sickle to harvest crops on earth. This imagery coincides with that in Joel: "Swing the sickle, for the harvest is ripe. Come, tread the grapes, for the winepress is full" (Joel 3:13). For Joel, this is the "day of the LORD" (Joel 3:14), when the enemies of Israel will be judged and the kingdom restored to Israel. Hosea also used the harvest image for the time of God's judgment upon Israel for its rebellion (Hos 6:11) as the preliminary step to Israel's restoration (Hos 14:1-9). Second Esdras 4 also uses the image of harvest related both to the righteous and the evil, an image used by Jesus to describe the time of God's consummation (Matt 13:24-30). Jesus' depiction has wheat and weeds to represent the righteous and the wicked. John's vision also has a dual harvest, one of grain (14:15-16), representing the righteous, and one of grapes (14:17-20), representing the rebellious.

But how is it that an angel from the Temple orders the Son of Man to harvest the earth (14:15)? First, the Temple is the overarching image of this larger section of John's vision (11:19–15:4). It began with the Temple in heaven open (11:19), and it will close with the Temple in heaven thrown wide open (15:5). In the Old Testament, the Temple is God's dwelling place, from which God's action originates. Thus, the order comes from God the Father. Second, the vision may reflect the mystery Jesus set forth when asked when the consummation would be: "No one knows the day or hour when these things will happen, not even the angels in heaven or the Son himself. Only the Father knows" (Matt 24:36). John may have been seeing the enactment of this reality as God sent the angel from his presence (the Temple) to inform the Son of Man that "the time of harvest has come" (14:15).

John was not seeing two separate harvests. He was seeing two sides of a single harvest. Just as in Jesus' parable the wheat and weeds are harvested together, so John's vision portrays a single action of God that has two different results. The righteous are "harvested" into God's eternal realm; the wicked are "harvested" into eternal torment. The first harvest image (14:14-16) is a wheat harvest that both John the Baptist and Jesus imaged as the gathering of the righteous (Matt 3:12; 13:30, 38). The vision flows in the same imagery Jesus used in that angels are the agents who gather the wicked (14:17; Matt 13:41, 49-50).

The grapes sickled from the earth are those who will experience the winepress of God's wrath (14:19). This image of judgment was part of the Old Testament pool of images. Isaiah saw God, the redeemer and restorer of Israel, trampling the enemies of Israel in the winepress of his wrath (Isa 63:1-6). Jeremiah lamented that God had trampled Israel in the winepress of his wrath because of her sin (Lam 1:15). Joel saw God trampling in the winepress the enemies of Israel (Joel 3:13).

After this, John saw a vision of faithful citizens of New Jerusalem, God's kingdom of priests, who refused to accede to the values and perspectives of their fallen Babylon world. They are on the sea, depicting their trampling fallen Babylon under their feet. They are all holding harps, which is quite significant. Harps are frequently associated with the praise of God by the people of the Old Testament. The harp is clearly linked to the kingdom in the Jewish story:

By the rivers of Babylon—
there we sat down and there we wept
when we remembered Zion.
On the willows there
we hung up our harps.
For there our captors
asked us for songs,
and our tormentors asked for mirth, saying,
"Sing us one of the songs of Zion!"

How could we sing the LORD's song
in a foreign land? (Ps 137:1-4, NRSV)

In the psalm, the harps are the accompaniment for singing the Lord's song, songs of Zion, by the people of God. The psalm is also set within a context of restoration. The implication is that when they are restored to their land as God's kingdom, then they will once again take up their harps and sing the Lord's song. This is exactly what John sees in his vision. The redeemed are "singing the song of Moses, the servant of God, and the song of the Lamb" (15:3). Moses is the one through whom God established Israel as his covenant people, and the Lamb is the one through whom God restored Israel as his kingdom of priests, a kingdom that now includes the Gentiles. This inclusion of the Gentiles is the focus of the song as God is extolled as "King of the nations," and it is affirmed that all nations (or "Gentiles"—*ethnōn* [TG1484, ZG1620], as in the rest of the NT) will come and worship before him. As we have already noted at 11:13 and 14:7, to fear God and glorify him is the chief characteristic of citizens of New Jerusalem.

In the end, John's vision provides a profound picture of the saying, "You will always harvest what you plant" (Gal 6:7). In fact, Galatians 6:7-9 is Paul's succinct expression of what John sees in 14:14-20. Paul says, "Those who live only to satisfy their own sinful nature will harvest decay and death from that sinful nature [cf. Rev 14:17-20]. But those who live to please the Spirit will harvest everlasting life from the Spirit [cf. Rev 14:14-16]. So let's not get tired of doing what is good. At just the right time we will reap a harvest of blessing if we don't give up" [cf. Rev 14:12-13].

In John's vision of a harvest with two results, we see not a vindictive, punitive retribution by God against the citizens of fallen Babylon, nor a patronizing favoritism toward the citizens of New Jerusalem. In both instances, John's vision of the ripeness of the grain and the grapes suggests that the nature of the harvest is simply the natural consequence at the end of a process of maturation.

This puts our understanding of both salvation and judgment in a new frame of reference. Salvation is not merely a juridical transaction that removes a person from the list of those condemned and guarantees their being "harvested" into heaven when they die. Salvation is rather a process of maturation in one's relationship with God and others through which one is increasingly re-formed in the image of God and whose life progressively manifests Christlikeness in one's actions. Conversely, judgment is not merely a judicial fiat arbitrarily condemning one to punishment. Judgment is the consequence of a process of maturation in one's relationship with God and others through which one is increasingly self-centered, ever more fully usurping the role of God in his or her life, and whose self-centered actions progressively treat others as objects to be used or abused for the fulfillment of one's own purposes. In both salvation and judgment, the outcome is simply the final acknowledgment of the result of a long journey in a constant direction.

The image of Jesus ("someone like the Son of Man," 14:14) as the one who harvests the grain (those who are "saved") suggests that the consummation of the process of salvation is to be gathered in by Jesus, to be caught up into his nature and likeness. How often we think of salvation as "going to heaven when we die," as though "salvation" were simply an admission ticket to a better place. Salvation, however, is in essence a matter of relationship with God. This relationship begins in this life, grows and matures throughout our time in this world, and continues beyond death. Salvation is participation with God in God's realm of wholeness and life, even in the midst of life in this world.

This is precisely what John saw in his image of the faithful citizens of New Jerusalem ("all the people who had been victorious over the beast and his statue and the number representing his name," 15:2) standing upon the "glass sea mixed with fire" (15:2), which represents fallen Babylon—the realm of rebellion against God. As seen in the seven churches, it is difficult for the citizens of New Jerusalem not to succumb to the culture of fallen Babylon. Sardis (3:1-6) and Laodicea (3:14-22) had almost totally accommodated themselves to their fallen Babylon world. Pergamum (2:12-17) and Thyatira (2:18-29) were trying to live dual citizenships, faithful to both New Jerusalem and fallen Babylon. Ephesus, while not accommodating at all to fallen Babylon, had lost the love that would have enabled it to be a vital witness to New Jerusalem in its fallen Babylon world.

The church today is all too often characterized by its accommodations to the values, perspectives, worldview, and lifestyle of its fallen Babylon world than by its faithful and vital witness to a mode of being in which cleansing, healing, liberation, transformation, and true human wholeness are found. The church more often swims in the sea mingled with fire than dances upon it in exuberant life with God.

◆ C. The Seven Bowls (15:5–16:21)

1. Judgment on the citizens of fallen Babylon (15:5–16:9)

5Then I looked and saw that the Temple in heaven, God's Tabernacle, was thrown wide open. 6The seven angels who were holding the seven plagues came out of the Temple. They were clothed in spotless white linen* with gold sashes across their chests. 7Then one of the four living beings handed each of the seven angels a gold bowl filled with the wrath of God, who lives forever and ever. 8The Temple was filled with smoke from God's glory and power. No one could enter the Temple until the seven angels had completed pouring out the seven plagues.

CHAPTER **16**

Then I heard a mighty voice from the Temple say to the seven angels, "Go your ways and pour out on the earth the seven bowls containing God's wrath."

2So the first angel left the Temple and poured out his bowl on the earth, and horrible, malignant sores broke out on everyone who had the mark of the beast and who worshiped his statue.

3Then the second angel poured out his bowl on the sea, and it became like the blood of a corpse. And everything in the sea died.

4Then the third angel poured out his bowl on the rivers and springs, and they became blood. 5And I heard the angel who had authority over all water saying,

"You are just, O Holy One, who is and
who always was,
because you have sent these
judgments.
6Since they shed the blood
of your holy people and your
prophets,
you have given them blood
to drink.
It is their just reward."

7And I heard a voice from the altar,* saying,

"Yes, O Lord God, the Almighty,
your judgments are true and just."

8Then the fourth angel poured out his
bowl on the sun, causing it to scorch
everyone with its fire. 9Everyone was
burned by this blast of heat, and they cursed the name of God, who had control over all these plagues. They did not repent of their sins and turn to God and give him glory.

15:6 Other manuscripts read *white stone;* still others read *white [garments] made of linen.* 16:7 Greek *I heard the altar.*

NOTES

15:5 ***Then.*** See note on 1:19.

the Temple in heaven . . . thrown wide open. Like 11:19, this verse forms the "bridge" between this unit (11:19–15:4) and the next. The image of the Temple being open, together with the note of "significant events" in 12:1 and 15:1, forms the "bookends" that define this unit. The image of the "open Temple" is one of unhindered access to God, now made available through the cross. But, as will be seen next, this access is not without conditions.

God's Tabernacle. Lit., "the tent of witness," a phrase that appears elsewhere in the NT only in Acts 7:44. It is a common expression in the OT (appearing about 140 times) and is translated in the LXX by the same phrase John uses at 15:5 (*skēnēs tou marturiou* [TG4633/3142, ZG5008/3457]). It might echo Deut 31:26-29, where Moses places the Book of the Law beside the Ark of the Covenant to stand as a witness against the people when, in the future, they become rebellious toward God, provoking him to wrath. This would serve as the parallel to the bridge verse at 11:19, where the Ark of the Covenant is seen in the open Temple. It would also serve as the bridge into the vision of God's wrath (15:5–16:21).

15:6 ***The seven angels who were holding the seven plagues.*** These angels were introduced in 15:1.

spotless white linen. The white linen is similar to the garments of the bride (19:8), and suggests that these angels are in some way associated with the church. Linen was also the cloth for priestly garments (e.g., Exod 28:39, 42).

gold sashes. The priests wore sashes (Exod 28:39), although there is no mention in the Jewish tradition of the sashes being gold. Since the church is a kingdom of priests (1:6; 5:10), this may be yet another association of these angels with the church.

15:7 ***one of the four living beings.*** The living beings are an integral part of John's vision of God (4:6-9), introduce each of the four horsemen (6:1-8), appear regularly with the elders in the praise and worship of God (5:8, 14; 7:11; 14:3; 19:4), and now are associated with God's response to fallen Babylon. These are constant reminders that the created order, represented in the four living beings (see note on 4:6), is always an integral part of God's purpose.

who lives forever and ever. This ascription of God at this point highlights what was said about the wrath of God in the commentary on 14:8. Wrath is the experience unholiness has in the presence of the eternally holy God.

15:8 ***The Temple was filled with smoke from God's glory and power.*** This serves to further heighten the association of "wrath" with the holiness of God that burns against all that is unholy.

16:1-2 ***pour out on the earth the seven bowls containing God's wrath.*** Gr., *eis* [TG1519, ZG1650] *tēn gēn* (into the earth), as in 8:5 (see note); 9:1, 3; 12:4, 9; 13:13; 14:19. This suggests that God's wrath is related only to fallen Babylon. The confirmation comes when the first angel pours out his bowl into (*eis*) the earth and the consequences are for "everyone who had the mark of the beast and who worshiped his statue."

16:3 ***on the sea.*** Lit., "into (*eis* [TG1519, ZG1650]) the sea." Since "sea," like earth, is an image in the vision for the rebellious realm, John again saw that the holiness of God adversely affects the rebellious realm.

it became like the blood of a corpse. And everything in the sea died. In this case, the image is doubled: The sea doesn't just become like blood in a reprise of the plague in Exodus, it becomes "dead" blood. The holiness of God is death to all that is unholy.

16:4 ***on the rivers and springs.*** Lit., "into (*eis* [TG1519, ZG1650]) the rivers and springs." The image here is a reprise of the Egyptian plague (Exod 7:20ff) where the waters *became* blood.

16:5 ***the angel who had authority over all water.*** It is not clear if this is the angel who poured the bowl (Beale 1999:817) or another angel. In Jewish tradition, there were "spirits" or "spiritual beings" who were associated with the aspects of the created order (see *1 Enoch* 60:16-23; 61:10; 66:2—especially related to water; see Beale 1999:818 for a fuller list of Jewish sources that bear witness to this imagery). John echoes this imagery in the angels who hold back the four winds of the earth (7:1) and in the angel who has authority over fire (14:18). Since John indicates that it is one of the four living beings (4:6-7), who represent the created order (see note on 4:6), who gives the bowls to the angels, God's sovereignty over the created order is suggested. When Satan's realm rebels against God, creation itself is adversely affected and experiences the downside of its rebellion. Here is a simple illustration: When someone chooses to ignore the law of gravity and steps off of a 10-story building, inherent in that disobedience is a debilitating or even destructive consequence. John may be indicating something of this reality for fallen Babylon in the water becoming blood. Of course, this image also echoes Moses turning the waters of Egypt into blood (Exod 7:17ff), the consequence of Pharaoh's rebellion against God's people.

O Holy One. It is significant, in light of the proposed relationship between God's wrath and God's holiness, that God should be addressed here as the Holy One. Only here in the vision is God called the "Holy One" (*ho hosios* [TG3588/3741A, ZG3836/4008]; cf. 15:4 "you alone are holy" [*hosios*]). Jesus is named "the one who is holy and true" in 3:7, but the Greek is *ho hagios* [TG3588/40A, ZG3836/41], which is also the term used elsewhere in the vision for describing God (4:8; 6:10). In the OT, God is most frequently called "the Holy One of Israel" (2 Kgs 19:22; Pss 71:22; 78:41; 89:18; Isa 1:4; and 24 other uses; Jer 50:29; 51:5), particularly in the context of the unholiness of the Gentiles or of Israel itself.

who is and who always was. As in 11:17, the attribute "who is still to come," noted initially, has disappeared at the point where the vision reveals the consummation of the old covenant in the cross of the Messiah. Following these words, the Majority Text includes "is to come"; the transcribers who added this were influenced by 1:4, 8; 4:8, and did not realize why John had dropped the phrase in 11:17.

16:9 ***They did not repent.*** This highlights the redemptive nature of this action of the holiness of God in the midst of fallen Babylon. The opportunity to repent remains for those under judgment.

COMMENTARY

In the beginning of this section we see the seven angels, introduced in 15:1, who were holding the golden bowls of the seven plagues that will be poured out on those in fallen Babylon. These bowls, filled with God's wrath, come from the Temple aflame with God's holiness. In the middle of this section we hear an angel extolling

God as the "Holy One" (16:5), who executes true and just judgment (16:6). Thus, it is clear that the judgment of God is the result of holiness.

Throughout the Old Testament, God's holiness is depicted as a fire that consumes all that is unholy. When Nadab and Abihu, the sons of Aaron, offered unholy fire before the Lord, the fire of God's holiness consumed them (Lev 10:1-2). Isaiah spoke of how God (the "Light of Israel") will become a fire, and Israel's Holy One a flame that will devour the thorns and briers (the unholiness of Israel; Isa 10:17); and the sinners in Israel are afraid, and the godless tremble, for "who can live with this devouring fire? . . . Who can survive this all-consuming fire?" (Isa 33:14). In Zechariah the holiness of God is a wall of fire around Jerusalem (Zech 2:5), and for Malachi God's holiness is like a refiner's fire (Mal 3:2). This understanding is the basis for the many references that associate God's wrath with fire (Num 11:1; Pss 78:21; 79:5; Isa 30:27; Jer 4:4; 15:14; Ezek 21:31; Nah 1:6; Zeph 3:8).

John saw that "no one could enter the Temple until the seven angels had completed pouring out the seven plagues" (15:8). Nothing can come into the presence of the holy God until all its unholiness has been purged by the refining fire of God's holiness. To the unholy, this purging fire of holiness seems to be "wrath." This experience of the holiness of God was described by Isaiah. When he had his experience of God in the Temple in Jerusalem (Isa 6:1-8) and the Temple was filled with smoke, Isaiah was immediately aware of his terrible unholiness in the presence of the holiness of God. His unholiness was then purged by the fire from the altar.

Previously in John's revelation, he saw that the souls of the martyrs under the altar had called upon God to judge and avenge their blood upon the citizens of fallen Babylon who had killed them (6:9-10). John then saw that God's judgment in the bowls of wrath is not vengeance but justice. Unholiness brings its own consequences, not as a vindictive punishment but as the necessary result. The image of "blood for blood" carries the thrust of this inherent retribution. This is further highlighted—and the connection with the martyrs' plea in chapter 6 is confirmed—when John heard a voice from the altar saying, "your judgments are true and just" (16:7). All of this continues the revelation that the wrath of God is directed against fallen Babylon.

John saw that all the citizens of fallen Babylon are touched by the fire of God's wrath. There is no selectivity; all who are unholy experience the fire of God's holiness. Unfortunately, John says, "they did not repent . . . and give him glory" (16:9). Though this reaction is sad, it provides a vital clue to understanding the purpose of the bowls of wrath. The objective of the "wrath" of God is not punishment. It is not vindictive, retributive, or vengeful. The fire of God's holiness that burns against all that is unholy seeks the holiness of the unholy one.

It becomes clear that holiness is the issue when the citizens of fallen Babylon blaspheme the name of God. God's "name" is his nature, and his nature is holiness. The citizens of fallen Babylon blaspheme God (16:21), God's name (16:9), and the God of heaven (16:11). In this they incarnate the blasphemies of the beast who blasphemed God, God's name, and all who live in heaven (13:6).

People nowadays seem to have one of two basic perspectives about the "wrath" of God. They either think of it as a punitive, vindictive, retribution on the part of

God, or they dismiss it as a vestige of the cruel and darker perspectives of a less enlightened age. The first results in a God who is mean, authoritarian, even cruel; a God who is all too often incarnate in believers who are judgmental, critical, vindictive, punitive, retributive. The second results in a God who overlooks sin, who is not really concerned with the brokenness of people but who "blesses" human bondages as "normal" though "variant" lifestyles. Such a God is also incarnate in believers for whom the primary virtue is "tolerance" and whose values are but one set of relativities in a pluralistic world. It is readily obvious that such extremes have lost the creative tension of the paradox of reality.

When the writers of Scripture spoke of the "wrath" of God, they were searching for an image that expressed the fact that God's nature is unalterably and eternally holy. Some of the images that have been used to express this reality are the images of God's steadfastness and God's faithfulness. God's nature is the ultimate "fixed point" of all reality. Another set of images that is used is the pairing of righteous and true. This pair moves beyond the immutability of the first set and wrestles with the fact that God's nature establishes the ultimate values of human existence. Another set of images contains the ideas of holiness and purity. These terms convey the very essence of God's nature as the standard of human wholeness. Yet another set of images focuses upon God's mercy and grace. These images indicate that a God who is steadfast, faithful, righteous, true, holy, and pure still initiates a relationship with persons who are undependable, unfaithful, unrighteous, false, unholy, and impure. The crux of the matter comes in dealing with the impossible tension that exists between these opposites.

In human experience, such tensions are resolved in one of three ways. The first person accommodates to the second; the second accommodates to the first; or both accommodate to a compromise position. These options do not operate, however, in our relationship with God and God's relationship with us. This is because our relationship with God is not a relationship between equally fallible persons where neither has complete truth and wholeness. God is the ultimate reality within which we have our being. The nature of God is the context of our wholeness as well as our brokenness. God cannot and will not accommodate or compromise when it comes to sin and unholiness.

The resolution of the impossible tension finds its dynamic in the love of God. God's love enfolds us in our undependability, unfaithfulness, unrighteousness, falsehood, unholiness, and impurity. God's love, however, does not confirm our sinfulness. God's love confronts us with our brokenness, our incompleteness, our woundedness, and calls us to enter into transformation through his love. The confrontation of love can be disruptive to our status quo, disturbing to our structures of control, and painful and even tormenting at the points of our unlikeness to the image of God that is our ultimate wholeness. It is this aspect of the love of God that John describes as the "wrath" of God. It could be said that the "wrath" of God is the love of God that moves astringently, rigorously, unrelentingly against anything in our being that is inconsistent with God's will for our wholeness in his image. As long as we cling to our unlikeness to God, the love of God will be a constant torment.

Another aspect of what John sees in the bowls of "wrath" is the consequences of rejecting the love of God. Since the love of God is the context of our wholeness, our rejection results in a growing experience of brokenness. Spirit, mind, and even body are adversely affected by our abandonment of the love of God. These come, not as punishment from God, but as the inherent and immutable results of moving against the reality of our being. Whenever we break one of the physical laws of the cosmos, the adverse results are immediate and, often, tragic. Whenever we break the spiritual "laws" of our wholeness, the adverse effects, while not as immediate as with physical laws, begin to move our being toward destruction.

◆ 2. The results of the refusal of redemption (16:10-21)

[10]Then the fifth angel poured out his
bowl on the throne of the beast, and his
kingdom was plunged into darkness. His
subjects ground their teeth in anguish,
[11]and they cursed the God of heaven for
their pains and sores. But they did not
repent of their evil deeds and turn to
God.
[12]Then the sixth angel poured out his
bowl on the great Euphrates River, and it
dried up so that the kings from the east
could march their armies toward the
west without hindrance. [13]And I saw
three evil* spirits that looked like frogs
leap from the mouths of the dragon, the
beast, and the false prophet. [14]They are
demonic spirits who work miracles and
go out to all the rulers of the world to
gather them for battle against the Lord
on that great judgment day of God the
Almighty.

> [15]"Look, I will come as unexpectedly
> as a thief! Blessed are all who are
> watching for me, who keep their
> clothing ready so they will not have
> to walk around naked and ashamed."

[16]And the demonic spirits gathered all
the rulers and their armies to a place with
the Hebrew name *Armageddon.**
[17]Then the seventh angel poured out his
bowl into the air. And a mighty shout came
from the throne in the Temple, saying, "It
is finished!" [18]Then the thunder crashed
and rolled, and lightning flashed. And a
great earthquake struck—the worst since
people were placed on the earth. [19]The
great city of Babylon split into three sec-
tions, and the cities of many nations fell
into heaps of rubble. So God remembered
all of Babylon's sins, and he made her drink
the cup that was filled with the wine of his
fierce wrath. [20]And every island disap-
peared, and all the mountains were leveled.
[21]There was a terrible hailstorm, and hail-
stones weighing as much as seventy-five
pounds* fell from the sky onto the people
below. They cursed God because of the ter-
rible plague of the hailstorm.

16:13 Greek *unclean*. **16:16** Or *Harmagedon*. **16:21** Greek *1 talent* [34 kilograms].

NOTES

16:10 ***the fifth angel poured out his bowl on the throne of the beast.*** In case John's readers haven't realized that the bowls affect only fallen Babylon, it becomes perfectly clear with this bowl.

his kingdom was plunged into darkness. This is a reprise of the plague in Egypt (Exod 10:21-23). Darkness is an image for evil in the OT. Those who forsake righteousness walk in darkness (Prov 2:13), and the way of the wicked is deep darkness (Prov 4:19). John himself says that those who rejected Jesus "loved the darkness more than the light, for their actions were evil" (John 3:19). Perhaps the clearest textual echo is Ps 107:10-11, "Some sat in darkness and in gloom . . . for they had rebelled against the words of God, and spurned the counsel of the Most High" (NRSV). John was seeing this reality in the fifth bowl.

ground their teeth. Lit., "gnawed their tongues," which is a better rendering of the Greek and provides a more graphic expression of the torment of the citizens of fallen Babylon.

16:11 ***they cursed the God of heaven.*** This again emphasizes fallen Babylon's participation in the blasphemy of the beast against God.

pains and sores. This is the same as the "horrible, malignant sores" associated with the first bowl (16:2), suggesting that "pain" may be associated with the scorching of the sun in the fourth bowl (16:8-9). In any case, the citizens of fallen Babylon are in torment in the presence of the holiness ("wrath") of God.

16:12 ***Euphrates River.*** This river played a significant role in both the Jewish story and the awareness of people in the Roman-Hellenistic world (see the following note and the earlier discussion on 9:14).

dried up. When the Persians attacked Babylon, they captured the impregnable fortress of Babylon by diverting the Euphrates, which flowed under the wall of the city, and marching the troops down the dry riverbed into the heart of the city (Herodotus *Histories* 1.190-191). The image here recalls that event. "In the OT God is always the one who dries up the water, whether for redemption or judgment" (Beale 1999:827).

16:13-14 ***three evil spirits that looked like frogs leap from the mouths of the dragon, the beast, and the false prophet.*** The unholy trinity is the source of evil spirits that induce the rulers of the world, the human leadership of fallen Babylon, to the rebellion against God that leads inexorably to the judgment seen in the previous bowls as well as the final Judgment Day of God the Almighty.

16:15 ***I will come as unexpectedly as a thief!*** This interjection by Jesus and the blessing that follows seem to break into the natural flow from 16:14 to 16:16. The interjection reiterates Jesus' earlier warning (3:3) that he will come as unexpectedly as a thief. Jesus used the same image in the Gospels (see Matt 24:42-44; 25:13).

Blessed are all who are watching for me, who keep their clothing ready. This blessing is the third of seven in the vision (cf. 1:3; 14:13; 19:9; 20:6; 22:7, 14). In the Greek structure, the wording is "watching [i.e., staying awake] and keeping their clothing." These are parallel activities. In ch 3, it was mentioned that there were a few in Sardis who had not "soiled their clothes with evil" (3:4); they had kept their clothing pure from defilement by fallen Babylon. It is interesting that it was also the church in Sardis where the rest had fallen asleep and needed to awake (3:2-3), and the conquerors were promised white clothing (3:5). Keeping one's clothing is living a life undefiled by the contaminations of fallen Babylon.

to walk around naked and ashamed. This is an image of captivity in Jewish history. Prisoners of war were stripped and led away naked as a sign of their total defeat and humiliation (see 2 Chr 28:15; Isa 20:2-4; Ezek 16:39; 23:29). The implication is that unless the faithful keep themselves undefiled by fallen Babylon they will participate in her defeat.

16:16 ***the Hebrew name*** **Armageddon.** This term (along with "the mark of the beast") has generated more heat and less light than any other term in Revelation. John's attention to the fact that this is a Hebrew term is significant. It is the clue to its use, since it is a transliteration of the Hebrew, *har* [TH2022, ZH2215] *megiddo* (mountain of Megiddo). This reference is significant in Jewish history. The city of Megiddo was located on the edge of the plain of Megiddo, a place of decisive events in the history of the Jewish people. It was near

Megiddo that Deborah and the Israelites defeated Sihon's forces (Judg 4–5). Megiddo was where Ahaziah, the apostate king, died at the hands of Jehu (2 Kgs 9:27). It was at Megiddo that King Josiah attempted to stop Pharaoh Neco from attacking the Assyrians and was killed (2 Kgs 23:29). While there is no "Mount Megiddo," there is a significant mountain near Megiddo—Mount Carmel. It was there that Elijah overcame the prophets of Baal in a time when the faithful people of God were being pursued and killed by Jezebel (1 Kgs 18). John's play upon the Hebrew term, therefore, provides an image that denotes a place of decisive conflict between God and his enemies.

16:17 ***poured out his bowl into the air.*** This reminds us of the plague in Egypt that resulted when Moses threw soot into the air and boils came upon the Egyptians (Exod 9:8ff). The common perception of the day was that the "air" was peopled by spiritual beings and demonic forces. This is reflected in Paul's identification of Satan as "the commander of the power of the air . . . the spirit at work in the hearts of those who refuse to obey God" (Eph 2:2, NLT mg). John's vision is conveyed in the same perspective (9:2), when the "air" is affected by the smoke from the bottomless pit released by Satan's activity. Once again the realm of rebellion is the focus of God's holiness.

16:17 ***It is finished!*** In light of the entirety of Satan's realm being disrupted by the holiness of God (the "earth," the "sea," Satan's throne, and the "air"), this proclamation suggests that the rebellious realm has been totally impacted by God's holiness.

16:19 ***The great city of Babylon split into three sections.*** This image suggests a pertinent historical association for John and his readers. In AD 68, after the suicide of Nero, civil war broke out in Rome between three factions (cf. Tacitus *Histories* 1.2, 6; 2.8). The stability of the empire was threatened (the cities of the Gentiles fell). Since John saw the Roman Empire as the incarnation of fallen Babylon in his own day, it seems likely that John took advantage of the contemporary situation in Rome to illustrate that "God remembered all of Babylon's sins." The "remembrance" is the reaction of God's holiness to Babylon's unholiness.

16:21 ***They cursed God.*** Lit., "They blasphemed God." In conjunction with the blasphemies of 16:9 and 11, this concludes the repetition of the blasphemy of the beast seen at 13:6.

COMMENTARY

In this section we see the fifth, sixth, and seventh bowls. The last three bowls continue to depict the action of God's redemptive wrath toward fallen Babylon. The fifth bowl is poured on the throne of the beast (cf. 13:2), i.e., upon the political power structure of fallen Babylon. The resulting darkness alludes to the plague of darkness in Egypt (Exod 10:22). The sixth bowl is poured upon the Euphrates, whose drying up images the overthrow of the beast's kingdom (see notes on 16:12), as well as the deliverance of God's people (Exod 14:21f; Isa 44:27). The seventh bowl is poured into the air, another image for the demonic realm (Eph 2:2), and the consequent hail echoes another of the Exodus plagues (Exod 9:18-24).

The repetition of the three blasphemies of the beast (13:6) by the citizens of fallen Babylon (16:9, 11, 21) confirms the deep inner shaping of their being by the perspective of the beast. This perspective rejects God as having any relevant role in any aspect of individual or community life. The most dangerous aspect of this perspective, however, is how it creates an inability to respond to God's love and holiness in ways that enable cleansing, healing, liberation, and transformation toward wholeness. When citizens of fallen Babylon begin to experience the destructive and debilitating consequences of their life without God, they rarely see this as a touch of

God seeking to awaken them to their condition and call them out of their brokenness into God's wholeness. Instead, they blame others or society or government or big business or technology or leading nations for either causing their plight or failing to resolve their problems. Citizens of fallen Babylon rarely ever realize that the root of their condition lies deep within their own life and not in the circumstances and conditions of the world around them. They believe it is the surrounding world that needs to change to make things better, not they.

Such a perspective makes it extremely difficult to repent. It is much easier to curse the supposed cause of the problem than to acknowledge with Walt Kelly's "Pogo" that "we have met the enemy and he is us." Repentance emerges out of recognition of one's complicity in the root cause of the problem. Cursing emerges from a self-referenced structure of being that vigorously protects itself from any hint of complicity in the problem by locating its root cause outside one's self. Even when one's whole world is imploding under the weight of monstrous hailstones, the problem still lies "outside."

Even citizens of New Jerusalem can succumb, to some degree, to this tactic—something or someone "outside" is blamed, insulating the blamer from any complicity in the situation and thus "resolving" important issues. Perhaps this is seen most clearly in the multitude of failed predictions related to the end of the world that litter Christian history. Such predictions of final divine intervention to resolve all the problems of the world appear regularly through Christian history and, especially, as crucial times or significant transitions approach. It is difficult to comprehend why people persist in predicting the date of Jesus' second coming or the final judgment in light of almost 2,000 years of failures. It is even more difficult to comprehend in light of the consistent biblical injunctions against such predictions. Jesus made it unmistakably clear that the end will come suddenly and unexpectedly, even noting in a most puzzling statement that he himself does not know when it will occur. (On the sudden and unexpected nature of the final act of history, see Matt 24:37-44; 25:1-13; Mark 13:34-37. On Jesus' own unawareness of the time, see Matt 24:36.) Paul and Peter reiterated the same perspective (see 1 Thess 5:1-3; 2 Pet 3:10). In the book of Revelation, Jesus twice repeats the indication of his return at a totally unexpected time, for he will come like a thief in the night (3:3; 16:15; cf. 1 Thess 5:2). In all these instances, the issue for Christians is not prediction but preparedness. Citizens of God's New Jerusalem are called to live their lives in such true discipleship that whenever the end comes it does not find them unprepared but living fully in loving, responsive relationship with Christ in all the aspects of their lives.

What then of the "battle of Armageddon?" Surely the vision's identification of a specific place for the final battle indicates that it will be possible to know when the end is at hand. However, the vision does not identify a specific place (see note on 16:16). The very name "Armageddon" (meaning, "the mountain of Megiddo") is ambiguous, since there is no Mount Megiddo in Jewish history nor in the geography of Palestine. It is extremely difficult to avoid the implication that the vision here, too, is presenting us with an image of a deeper reality. As the notes indicate, "Armageddon" points both to Mount Carmel, which is near Megiddo, and the larger area near Megiddo where decisive events took place in Israel's history. For John's vision, and for us, "Armageddon" provides an image of a final victory of God over the forces of the rebellious realm. It is an image of confidence and assurance in God's final victory when everything else in present history suggests that fallen Babylon is on a path of unending conquest.

John's imagery in chapter 16 seems to imbue historical events with symbolic significance. We have noted that the image of Armageddon/Harmageddon, while not pointing to any geographical location for the battle with fallen Babylon, builds upon the historical role of Megiddo and Mount Carmel in Jewish history, both references to times of decisive encounter between God and the enemies of Israel (cf. Judg 5:13-20; 2 Kgs 9:27; 23:29; 2 Chr 35:22). Since both the Assyrian conquest of 722 BC and the Babylonian conquest of 600–587 BC originated from the region of the Euphrates, and especially with the drying up of the Euphrates being instrumental in the overthrow of historical Babylon by the Persians (539 BC), these historical realities shape an image John used to portray God's victory over fallen Babylon. With "the great city of Babylon split into three sections" (16:19), John appears to use a contemporary historical event, the civil war in Rome in AD 68, when three factions vied for control of the empire (see, e.g., Tacitus *Histories* 1.2), as symbolic of the demise of fallen Babylon.

◆ V. The Consequences (17:1–22:9)

A. Babylon's Present Fallenness and Future Demise (17:1–19:10)

1. Babylon's fragile facade (17:1-18)

One of the seven angels who had poured out the seven bowls came over and spoke to me. "Come with me," he said, "and I will show you the judgment that is going to come on the great prostitute, who rules over many waters. 2The kings of the world have committed adultery with her, and the people who belong to this world have been made drunk by the wine of her immorality."

3So the angel took me in the Spirit* into the wilderness. There I saw a woman sitting on a scarlet beast that had seven heads and ten horns, and blasphemies against God were written all over it. 4The woman wore purple and scarlet clothing and beautiful jewelry made of gold and precious gems and pearls. In her hand she held a gold goblet full of obscenities and the impurities of her immorality. 5A mysterious name was written on her forehead: "Babylon the Great, Mother of All Prostitutes and Obscenities in the World." 6I could see that she was drunk—drunk with the blood of God's holy people who were witnesses for Jesus. I stared at her in complete amazement.

7"Why are you so amazed?" the angel asked. "I will tell you the mystery of this woman and of the beast with seven heads and ten horns on which she sits. 8The beast you saw was once alive but isn't now. And yet he will soon come up out of the bottomless pit* and go to eternal destruction. And the people who belong to this world, whose names were not written in the Book of Life before the world was made, will be amazed at the reappearance of this beast who had died.

9"This calls for a mind with understanding: The seven heads of the beast represent the seven hills where the woman rules. They also represent seven kings. 10Five kings have already fallen, the sixth now reigns, and the seventh is yet to come, but his reign will be brief.

11"The scarlet beast that was, but is no longer, is the eighth king. He is like the other seven, and he, too, is headed for destruction. 12The ten horns of the beast are ten kings who have not yet risen to power. They will be appointed to their kingdoms for one brief moment to reign with the beast. [13]They will all agree to give him their power and authority. [14]Together they will go to war against the Lamb, but the Lamb will defeat them because he is Lord of all lords and King of all kings. And his called and chosen and faithful ones will be with him."

[15]Then the angel said to me, "The waters where the prostitute is ruling represent masses of people of every nation and language. [16]The scarlet beast and his ten horns all hate the prostitute. They will strip her naked, eat her flesh, and burn her remains with fire. [17]For God has put a plan into their minds, a plan that will carry out his purposes. They will agree to give their authority to the scarlet beast, and so the words of God will be fulfilled. [18]And this woman you saw in your vision represents the great city that rules over the kings of the world."

17:3 Or *in spirit.* **17:8** Or *the abyss,* or *the underworld.*

NOTES

17:1 ***the judgment that is going to come on the great prostitute.*** Lit., "the judgment of the great prostitute." The NLT rendering suggests that judgment is only a future event for the rebellious order when, as the vision has revealed, judgment has been present upon that order from before the foundation of the world. The judgment of Satan's rebellion took place at the point of the rebellion itself. In 12:7-11, John portrays the rebellion of Satan and his forces (12:7), their defeat (12:8), their expulsion from heaven (12:8-9), and the rejoicing of God's realm over God's judgment (12:10), which is also the victory of the redeemed over fallen Babylon (12:11). There will, indeed, be a final consummation of God's judgment upon fallen Babylon, but that will be the consummation of what is already a present and active reality in its midst. Also, this portion of the vision will reveal that judgment is operative in the very heart of fallen Babylon's nature (17:16-17).

many waters. This is explained in 17:15 as representing "masses of people of every nation and language."

17:2 ***committed adultery.*** Here, as elsewhere in the vision, adultery is an OT image for turning away from God and entering into life-distorting relationships with powers other than God. John sees that both the leaders (kings) and citizens (people who belong to this world—lit., "those who dwell upon the earth"; see note on 3:10) of fallen Babylon are shaped by such relationships.

17:3 ***in the Spirit.*** Four times John states he was "in the Spirit": 1:10 and 4:2 are connected through the "voice like a trumpet" (1:10; 4:1); 17:3 and 21:10 are connected through the angel who transports John. The Greek form is identical in each instance: *en pneumati* [TG1722/4151, ZG1877/4460]. This form, without the article, is quite commonly used for the Holy Spirit in the NT (Matt 3:11; 12:28; 22:43; Rom 8:9; 1 Cor 14:16; Eph 2:22; 3:5; 5:18; 6:18). All of these experiences "in the Spirit" were an integral part of John's visionary experience, a dynamic of visions attested also by Ezekiel (Ezek 3:14; 8:3; 11:1, 24; 37:1).

into the wilderness. The wilderness played a crucial role in Jewish history. It was in the wilderness that God formed Israel as his covenant people, yet the wilderness was also the place of rebellion against God (Num 27:14; Ps 78:40; Ezek 20:13). The goat bearing the sin of God's people was sent into the wilderness (Lev 16:9-22), yet it was in the wilderness that Israel was to prepare the way for the Lord's restoration of the kingdom (Isa 40:3; Hos 2:14; cf. Acts 21:38). This strange mixture of the wilderness both as a place of evil and the place of restoration is brought together in Jesus, who was led into the wilderness to be tested by Satan (Mark 1:12-13) and then began his proclamation of the restoration of the Kingdom of God (Mark 1:14-15).

17:4 ***purple and scarlet clothing.*** These were the colors worn only by the uppermost classes of Roman society, the emperor's family, the senators, and the equestrians.

jewelry made of gold and precious gems and pearls. This suggests those at the top of the economic life of the empire.

gold goblet. This echoes Jer 51:7, "Babylon has been a gold cup in the LORD's hands, a cup that made the whole earth drunk. The nations drank Babylon's wine, and it drove them all mad."

obscenities. Lit., "abominations." Israel was always warned of following the obscenities (NLT, "detestable practices") of the other nations and was judged for doing so (Lev 18:26-30; 1 Kgs 14:24; 2 Kgs 21:11; Ezra 9:1; Jer 7:10; Ezek 5:9).

immorality. Lit., "fornication." This is used in a spiritual sense, signifying the rejection of God, as evidenced in the blasphemies of the beast (13:6) and the parallel blasphemies of the citizens of fallen Babylon (16:9, 11, 21).

17:5 ***forehead.*** This represents the perceptual framework of the person, the deep, inner orientation of their life toward God (see commentary on 7:3 and 13:16 and note on 14:1), just as "name" is an image for the very nature of that which is named.

17:6 ***drunk with the blood of God's holy people who were witnesses for Jesus.*** Or, "drunk with the blood of the saints and the blood of the martyrs of Jesus." It is likely that John was seeing not only fallen Babylon's persecution of Christians in his own day, but also all the persecution of God's covenant people (the saints) throughout all of history.

complete amazement. The citizens of fallen Babylon were "amazed" at the beast (13:3; 17:8), and proclaimed, "Who is as great as the beast? . . . Who is able to fight against him?" (13:4). Apparently even John was moved to awe at the apparent invincibility of fallen Babylon over the faithful people of God.

17:8 ***whose names.*** Here, as in 13:8, the Greek has "name," singular, not "names," indicating that the issue is the nature of the citizens of fallen Babylon, not their individual identification.

were not written in the Book of Life before the world was made. Given the close parallelism of this passage with 13:8, it should be understood as a pointer back to 13:8, from which its meaning should be developed. That is, the phrase "the Lamb who was slaughtered" informs the abbreviated version of 17:8. Thus, this passage does not become a passage that teaches predestination, nor should 13:8 be interpreted on the basis of this passage (see note on 13:8).

will be amazed at the reappearance of this beast who had died. Lit., "they were amazed . . . because it was, is not, and will be."

17:9-11 ***seven heads . . . represent seven kings.*** John's clear delineation of the kings ("Five . . . have already fallen, the sixth now reigns, and the seventh is yet to come") is not so clear to scholars. There continues to be a lack of consensus on the identification of these kings. See commentary for discussion.

17:9 ***the seven hills.*** In the first-century world, the obvious reference is to Rome, which was built upon seven hills. Note that the prostitute, Babylon, is seated upon Rome. She is more than Rome, yet Rome is the bearer of her presence in the world in John's day.

17:12 ***The ten horns of the beast are ten kings who have not yet risen to power.*** The number "ten" represents totality, completeness, and fullness. There are Ten Commandments at the heart of the covenant, ten righteous persons would have saved Sodom (Gen 18:32), the Tabernacle had ten curtains (Exod 26:1), the full complement of Israel is ten thousand thousands (Num 10:36, ESV), and by the first century, ten Jewish men were the minimum required for a synagogue to be legitimate.

17:15 ***The waters . . . represent masses of people of every nation and language.*** The prepositional phrase in Greek is a variant upon the more usual, "people and tribes and nations and languages" (5:9; 7:9; 10:11; 11:9; 13:7; 14:6). These are the people of fallen Babylon.

COMMENTARY

The introduction to the vision of the prostitute (17:1-3), later identified as "Babylon the Great" (17:5) and fallen Babylon (18:2), is parallel to the introduction to the vision of the bride, New Jerusalem (21:9-10). Both are introduced by one of the angels who had the seven bowls. In both, the angel says to John, "Come . . . I will show you"—followed by "the great prostitute" (17:1) or "the bride, the wife of the Lamb" (21:9). In both, John is carried away in Spirit to see the vision.

The parallelism of the introductions is coupled with the later parallelism of the conclusions to these two parts of John's vision (19:9b-10; 22:6-9). In both sections, the angel tells John that the words are true; John falls down to worship at the feet of the angel; the angel subsequently prohibits John from doing this, telling him that he (the angel) is a fellow-servant and that John must worship God. By this close parallelism of introductions and conclusions, John is signaling his readers that there is an essential connection between the vision of the prostitute and the vision of the bride.

Within this literary structure, John's apparent disobedience (22:8) of the order not to worship the angel (19:10) demands attention. Throughout the account of the vision, John is seen as perfectly obedient. Why does he seem to break his record of perfect obedience only 13 verses from the end? The answer is, he doesn't—these are two accounts of the same event.[1] His first bowing at the feet of the angel is not disobedient since he had not yet been told, "Don't do that," and what appears to be a second bowing at the feet of the angel is, in reality, a reprise of the first. That is, 17:1–22:9 is the portrayal of a single, unitive vision at the close of which John fell at the feet of the angel to worship. In order to convey the experience, however, John broke it into three parts (17:1–19:10; 19:11–21:8; 21:9–22:9).[2]

In this vision, John saw "a woman sitting on a scarlet beast that had seven heads and ten horns" (17:3). The woman is called "Mother of All Prostitutes and Obscenities in the World" (17:5). John was seeing the profound reality that stands behind all historical incarnations of "Babylon the Great." At another level, however, John was seeing Rome as the incarnation of fallen Babylon in his time and suggesting that there would be "daughter" prostitutes that will follow her. Rome is just one in an ongoing historical sequence of "prostitutes."

The beast here is a paler version of the "fiery" dragon with seven heads and ten horns (12:3) who gives his power, authority, and throne to the beast from the sea with seven heads and ten horns (13:1). The prostitute rests upon the foundation of Satan's rebellion (the dragon) and its incarnation in human history (the beast). The vision emphasizes this by noting that the beast is full of blasphemous names—that is, the fullness of its very nature is rebellion against God.

Then the beast is described in a very mysterious way: This beast "was once alive . . . isn't now . . . yet he will soon come up out of the bottomless pit and go to eternal destruction" (17:8). This must be understood in the larger context of the vision. Later in the vision (20:1-10, see notes there), John sees Satan ("alive"; cf. 17:8) being seized, bound, and sealed in the bottomless pit ("isn't now"; cf. 17:8), and then coming up out of the bottomless pit and being thrown into the lake of fire ("eternal destruction"; cf. 17:8). This image seems to be something of a parallel to the image of the beast's "fatal wound [that] was healed" (13:3). Prior to the wound the beast was alive, it then received the mortal wound, but it was healed—it came up out of the bottomless pit (i.e., death).

It was this aspect of the beast that caused the citizens of fallen Babylon to be amazed and worship the beast (13:4), and in the present passage John sees that the same group (the people who belong to this world—lit., "those who dwell upon the earth"; see note on 3:10) are those who are amazed.

John is then told that the "seven heads of the beast represent the seven hills where the woman rules" (17:9). If we presume that "seven hills" equals "Rome," then John was seeing Rome as the incarnation of fallen Babylon in his day. It must then be presumed that the kings are Roman emperors. The first incontestably recognized emperor of Rome was Augustus (31 BC–AD 14). The next four were Tiberius (AD 14–37), Gaius (Caligula, AD 37–41), Claudius (AD 41–54), and Nero (AD 54–68). If we presume these are the five who "have already fallen," does this clarify the rest of the image? After Nero's suicide in AD 68, civil war erupted in Rome with three factions vying for control of the empire. Galba was put forward by the army in Spain and held control from the middle of AD 68 until he was assassinated by the Praetorian Guard in January AD 69. Was he the sixth king (17:10)? Otho was then placed on the throne by the Praetorian Guard but committed suicide in April AD 69. Was he "the seventh . . . [whose] reign will be brief" (17:10)? Before Vespasian inaugurated a new royal dynasty later in AD 69, Otho was replaced by Vitellius, the last emperor of the Julio-Claudio period, who was murdered in December of AD 69 and was perhaps the eighth king, who also incarnates the scarlet beast that was but is no longer, and who is of the seven and goes to destruction (17:11). If there is any truth in this application of the vision to Rome, then John was receiving his vision in AD 68–69, and was seeing in the historical events of that year the manifestation of the realities of fallen Babylon as incarnate in the Roman Empire.

Then John saw that the ten horns of the beast are ten kings (see note on 17:12). John seems to have seen the fullness or totality of kingdoms that will succeed Rome as incarnations of fallen Babylon. This is confirmed in the vision's note that "they will be appointed to their kingdoms for one brief moment" (17:12), and, especially, that they reign with the beast. Not only that, they "give him their power and authority" (17:13)—that is, their kingdoms are shaped by the values and dynamics of the beast's rebellion against God.

John saw the reality of their rebellion against God in that they "go to war against the Lamb" (17:14). This war, undoubtedly, takes the form of persecution of the citizens of New Jerusalem, the followers of the Lamb. When Saul, the zealous persecutor of the church, met the Messiah on the road to Damascus, Jesus said to him, "Saul! Saul! Why are you persecuting me?" (Acts 9:4).

In the face of the ongoing incarnations of fallen Babylon that seek to eradicate the church from their realms, John saw the one who can fight against the beast: "The

Lamb will defeat them" (17:14). The defeat of these powers is certain because the Lamb is already "Lord of all lords and King of all kings" (17:14). Each victory over an incarnation of fallen Babylon is an incarnation of the reality of who the Lamb is. John saw the citizens of New Jerusalem as "his called and chosen and faithful ones" (17:14). These terms, used throughout the Old Testament to describe Israel, God's covenant community, are used here for God's restored community, which now includes Gentiles.

Then John saw that the beast hates the woman, so much so that it "will strip her naked" and "eat her flesh" (17:16). The textual echo here is from Ezekiel 16:36-42, where it says that under God's judgment, Israel will be stripped naked for becoming a prostitute who gives her favors to the nations. The vision gives a new twist to the image, however. John saw that fallen Babylon is inherently destructive to itself. God's structure of reality is such that when people reject that reality, they put into effect the consequences of such rejection. Without God having to "act" in a retributive manner, the dynamics of reality God has established go into operation. This is what the vision is seeking to communicate when it says, "God has put a plan into their minds, a plan that will carry out his purposes. . . . So the words of God will be fulfilled" (17:17). Whenever individuals, communities, or nations "give their authority to the scarlet beast" (17:17), they are "destined" to experience the destruction that is inherent in such a way of life.

Finally, the mystery of the woman, the prostitute, is explained to John. She "represents the great city that rules over the kings of the world" (17:18). The explanation, however, doesn't really explain. Is this Rome, which in John's day incarnated fallen Babylon in human history? Or does the woman represent the deeper spiritual reality that lies behind every historical incarnation of fallen Babylon? Earlier in the vision, the great city was operative in Jerusalem where the Messiah was crucified (11:8). But the crucifixion was a Roman action. In 16:19, we have seen that the great city seemed to be Rome, convulsed by the civil war that followed Nero's death. In 18:10 and 21, however, the great city is identified as Babylon (previously described by John as "fallen Babylon"; cf. 14:8; 18:2), whose demise is mourned by kings (18:9-10), merchants (18:15-16), and seafarers (18:17-19). As we will see shortly, this also seems to be an illustration drawn from Rome's civil war. All this suggests that for John, the woman represents the malignant spiritual realm of rebellion against God, which in his day was incarnate in the Roman Empire.

Before concluding this section, it must be noted that it is significant that one of the angels with the bowls of wrath reveals to John both the prostitute, fallen Babylon, and the bride, New Jerusalem. If, as we have suggested, the bowls of wrath represent the holiness of God, then God's holiness is the foundation of judgment for fallen Babylon and the foundation of life for New Jerusalem. All human life exists in relationship with God. A life of unholiness exists in an inherently destructive relationship with God. Such a life has set itself against the very reality of its wholeness and, consequently, experiences the brokenness and destruction that results.

It is the reality of the inherent brokenness and destructiveness of fallen Babylon that John sees imaged in the prostitute. We can think of the prostitute as a spiritual order of being, a mode of existence in rejection of God. This order of being rests upon the rebellion of the dragon and its implementation in the blasphemy of the beast. John sees that this realm of rebellion becomes incarnate in the values, structures, and dynamics of life of human communities, institutions, and nations. There is a historical continuity of incarnations of fallen Babylon leading all the way down to structures we know today, including materialistic capitalism, equally materialistic socialism, hedonistic values, and aberrant lifestyles. The prostitute is the "mother of prostitutes." Each incarnation of fallen Babylon in human history ultimately falls, only to be replaced by the succeeding incarnation of fallen Babylon.

John also saw what seems to be the awesome power of fallen Babylon. The manifestation of its incarnation is seen in the social, political, and economic ordering of human life and community. It is seen in a diversity of social structures that marginalize some while elevating others to prominence. It is seen in a plethora of political structures that become the instruments of special interests to impose their control upon the community. It is seen in a variety of economic structures that enrich the wealthy and impoverish the poor and needy. But perhaps the most consistent aspect of fallen Babylon is its innate hostility toward New Jerusalem.

Every incarnation of fallen Babylon is "drunk with the blood of God's holy people" (17:6). Fallen Babylon is inherently intolerant of any values, perspectives, structures, or dynamics that threaten its "world." Those whose position, power, wealth, status, and control depend upon the dehumanizing and destructive order of fallen Babylon will be quick to sense a threat to their status quo and to come against that threat with all the resources at their command. If those who pose a threat cannot be subverted and integrated into the "system," they will be marginalized, isolated, and prevented from "infecting" the status quo with their disruptive values, perspectives, and lifestyle. If they resist marginalization or isolation, then they will be eliminated from the scene in some way. The means have varied throughout the history of fallen Babylon. Some have been simply executed. Others have been exiled or banished. Many have been imprisoned. Some have been "hospitalized" in psychiatric prisons. By whatever means available, fallen Babylon always acts against those whose lives turn its world upside down.

John also saw that fallen Babylon carries within itself the seeds of its own destruction. As awesome and powerful and invincible as fallen Babylon may appear, every incarnation is infected with the cancer of its own destructiveness. It turns upon itself and causes its own demise. This is an integral part of the inexorable victory of the Lamb. All previous incarnations of fallen Babylon in human history are gone, but New Jerusalem continues its incarnation through history. A good modern example is the Soviet Union. In 1985, I had the privilege of teaching John's vision to the pastors of the Methodist Church in the Soviet Republic of Estonia. When I used the Soviet Union as their "fallen Babylon," their heads nodded in agreement. Many in the group had loved ones disappear in the Gulag. Some had been imprisoned themselves. My translator had been interrogated by the KGB on multiple occasions. They knew the presence and power of their "fallen Babylon." When I began to tell them that the Soviet Union would fall, however, that it carried within it the seeds of its own destruction, they immediately began to shake their heads in disagreement. This would never happen! Never in their lifetime. Within six years their fallen Babylon was gone, and soon thereafter they were an entirely free and independent nation.

ENDNOTES

1. I am indebted to John Wesley (1976:730) for this insight.
2. It may well be that the entire visionary experience is a single unitive reality inasmuch as John's first and last response is to fall at the feet of the one he encounters (1:17; 22:8). A unitive reality can be illustrated with the "Battle of Gettysburg" Cyclorama at the Gettysburg National Military Park Museum. You stand in the middle of a circular room. On the walls and ceiling is a depiction of a location in the middle of the battle. You hear the cannon's roar, the whistle of cannon balls, the whine of mini-balls, the reports of rifles, the flashes of muzzles, the cries of the wounded and dying, the shouted orders of the leaders, etc. It is an "all at once" experience. To convey this experience to someone who has never been there, you would have to begin at one point in the diorama and proceed to describe what you see and hear for each portion of the scene. When you returned to where you began, you might well repeat something of your first description to let your reader know you have completed the account. This may be what John was doing in having his first and last response to the vision being his falling at the feet of the one whom he encountered.

◆ 2. Doom and gloom (18:1-24)

After all this I saw another angel come down from heaven with great authority, and the earth grew bright with his splendor. 2He gave a mighty shout:

"Babylon is fallen—that great city is fallen!
She has become a home for demons.
She is a hideout for every foul* spirit,
a hideout for every foul vulture
and every foul and dreadful animal.*
3For all the nations have fallen*
because of the wine of her passionate immorality.
The kings of the world
have committed adultery with her.
Because of her desires for extravagant luxury,
the merchants of the world have grown rich."

4Then I heard another voice calling from heaven,

"Come away from her, my people.
Do not take part in her sins,
or you will be punished with her.
5For her sins are piled as high as heaven,
and God remembers her evil deeds.
6Do to her as she has done to others.
Double her penalty* for all her evil deeds.
She brewed a cup of terror for others,
so brew twice as much* for her.
7She glorified herself and lived in luxury,
so match it now with torment and sorrow.
She boasted in her heart,
'I am queen on my throne.
I am no helpless widow,
and I have no reason to mourn.'
8Therefore, these plagues will overtake her in a single day—
death and mourning and famine.
She will be completely consumed by fire,
for the Lord God who judges her is mighty."

9And the kings of the world who committed adultery with her and enjoyed her great luxury will mourn for her as they see the smoke rising from her charred remains. 10They will stand at a distance, terrified by her great torment. They will cry out,

"How terrible, how terrible for you,
O Babylon, you great city!
In a single moment
God's judgment came on you."

11 The merchants of the world will weep and mourn for her, for there is no one left to buy their goods. 12 She bought great quantities of gold, silver, jewels, and pearls; fine linen, purple, silk, and scarlet cloth; things made of fragrant thyine wood, ivory goods, and objects made of expensive wood; and bronze, iron, and marble. 13 She also bought cinnamon, spice, incense, myrrh, frankincense, wine, olive oil, fine flour, wheat, cattle, sheep, horses, chariots, and bodies—that is, human slaves.

14 "The fancy things you loved so much
are gone," they cry.
"All your luxuries and splendor
are gone forever,
never to be yours again."

15 The merchants who became wealthy by selling her these things will stand at a distance, terrified by her great torment. They will weep and cry out,

16 "How terrible, how terrible for that
great city!
She was clothed in finest purple
and scarlet linens,
decked out with gold and precious
stones and pearls!
17 In a single moment
all the wealth of the city is gone!"

And all the captains of the merchant ships and their passengers and sailors and crews will stand at a distance. 18 They will cry out as they watch the smoke ascend, and they will say, "Where is there another city as great as this?" 19 And they will weep and throw dust on their heads to show their grief. And they will cry out,

"How terrible, how terrible for that
great city!
The shipowners became wealthy
by transporting her great wealth
on the seas.
In a single moment it is all gone."

20 Rejoice over her fate, O heaven
and people of God and apostles
and prophets!
For at last God has judged her
for your sakes.

21 Then a mighty angel picked up a boulder the size of a huge millstone. He threw it into the ocean and shouted,

"Just like this, the great city Babylon
will be thrown down with violence
and will never be found again.
22 The sound of harps, singers, flutes,
and trumpets
will never be heard in you again.
No craftsmen and no trades
will ever be found in you again.
The sound of the mill
will never be heard in you again.
23 The light of a lamp
will never shine in you again.
The happy voices of brides and
grooms
will never be heard in you again.
For your merchants were the greatest
in the world,
and you deceived the nations with
your sorceries.
24 In your* streets flowed the blood of
the prophets and of God's holy
people
and the blood of people slaughtered
all over the world."

18:2a Greek *unclean;* also in each of the two following phrases. **18:2b** Some manuscripts condense the last two lines to read *a hideout for every foul [unclean] and dreadful vulture.* **18:3** Some manuscripts read *have drunk.* **18:6a** Or *Give her an equal penalty.* **18:6b** Or *brew just as much.* **18:24** Greek *her.*

NOTES

18:1 ***the earth grew bright with his splendor.*** The term for "splendor" is *doxa* [TG1391, ZG1518], which is usually translated "glory"; it denotes the very nature of the being to whom it refers. This description echoes both Isa 60:1 and Ezek 43:2. In both, the earth is made bright with God's glory. The larger context of the passages is the restoration of the kingdom to Israel. As has been noted (see notes on 1:5 and 6:17), an essential part of the restoration of the kingdom was the judgment of the nations who had oppressed God's faithful people.

18:2 ***Babylon is fallen—that great city is fallen!*** This (in the Greek) is identical to the cry of the angel in 14:8: "Fallen, fallen is Babylon the Great." Since the ultimate future demise of Babylon isn't imaged until 18:21-24, the phrase reiterates the present nature of Babylon, its fallen condition, with defeat implicit in light of God's victory already accomplished in the cross (1:18; 3:21; 5:5; 11:15, 17; 12:10; 13:3, 12, 14).

hideout. The term *phulakē* [TG5438, ZG5871] indicates something akin to a prison. John used this term to indicate something of the nature of fallen Babylon. Everything unclean, foul, and hateful is "imprisoned" in fallen Babylon.

18:3 ***the wine of her passionate immorality.*** Lit., "the wine of the wrath of her fornication." To translate "wrath" as "passionate," though possible (ESV, RSV, NIV), misses the point of the text. As noted at 14:8, "fornication" is the spiritual condition of rejecting God. Such rejection places one in opposition to God's holiness, which becomes a consuming fire ("wrath") against all unholiness. Elsewhere in the vision, John makes it clear that "wrath" is related to God, the only clear exception being 12:12. It is fallen Babylon's spiritual fornication (i.e., turning away from God and having something other than God as a god) that evokes God's wrath (6:16-17; 11:18; 14:8-10, 19; 15:1, 7; 16:1, 19; 19:15).

The kings of the world. Lit., "kings of the earth." "Earth" is Revelation's term for "fallen Babylon" (see note on 3:10), used both here of the rulers and next of the merchants.

18:6-8 The vision employs imagery from Isaiah and Jeremiah to portray the demise of fallen Babylon:

Do to her as she has done to others. See Jer 50:15, 29.

Double her penalty for all her evil deeds. See Jer 17:18.

She glorified herself and lived in luxury, so match it now with torment and sorrow. See Isa 47:1.

I am queen on my throne. I am no helpless widow, and I have no reason to mourn. See Isa 47:7-8.

these plagues will overtake her in a single day—death and mourning and famine. See Isa 47:9.

She will be completely consumed by fire. See Jer 51:58.

for the Lord God who judges her is mighty. See Jer 50:34.

18:9-10 ***the kings of the world.*** Lit., "the kings of the earth" (see note on 18:3).

will mourn. Throughout this entire section, 18:9-19, there is a major translation problem with the verb tenses. The future tense used by the NLT in 18:10, 11, 15, 17, 18, 19 suggests that John saw an event that will take place in the future. The following instances are future tenses in the Greek: 18:9 ("will mourn") and 18:15 ("will stand"). The remainder are a mix of present, imperfect (continued action in the past), aorist (completed action), or perfect (past action with present consequences) tenses. The kings will weep and will mourn (18:9-10), but the merchants (18:11, 15) and the shipowners (18:19) are weeping (present). It seems that the future tense for the kings is required by the indefinite context set by the subjunctive mood ("whenever they should see the smoke of her burning"), since by its very nature the time reference of the subjunctive mood is the future. This suggests that John is indicating that whenever a historical incarnation of fallen Babylon comes to its demise, the political power brokers will respond in this manner.

The rulers (perfect, 18:10) and the shipowners (aorist, 18:17) stood far off, but the merchants will stand (18:15). This is the puzzle. Might it be that this future is extended from the subjunctive verb in 18:9? If so, then again John was indicating that whenever a historical incarnation of fallen Babylon comes to its demise, the economic power brokers, like the political, will respond in this manner.

This understanding would fit well with John's indication that the harlot is the "Mother of All Prostitutes" (17:5), as well as with the observation above that the political and economic leaders do not seem to be destroyed with her destruction. Were John seeing the final judgment of fallen Babylon, it is difficult to comprehend why those whose power and wealth depended upon her would not also be brought into judgment with her. The fruit for which fallen Babylon longed is gone (aorist) and will never be found (18:14). The use of the future here is grammatically necessary. If something is gone, "never to be found" extends indefinitely into the future. John's use of the aorist may be a reflection of fallen Babylon's true state—its entire mode of being has already been judged, and its future is bleak.

In any case, John once again may have been using the civil war in Rome as an illustration of the fragility of fallen Babylon (see the discussion on the city divided into three parts at 16:19, and the seven kings at 17:9-11, both of which could image the situation in Rome in AD 68–69).

18:10 ***How terrible, how terrible.*** Lit., "Woe, woe" (see note on 8:13). The double "woe" may have parallels to the woes associated with the last three trumpets (8:13). While the vision indicates three "woes" for fallen Babylon associated with the last three trumpets, it only states the fulfillment of the first two woes (9:12; 11:14) but not the third. It was suggested that the third "woe" would be fulfilled in the final consummation of God's victory. Since the kings, together with the merchants and shipowners, seem not to be destroyed with the demise of their fallen Babylon, it appears that the vision is not yet seeing the final consummation. Therefore, only two woes are expressed.

18:11 ***The merchants.*** It is significant that the largest block of material among the three groups (kings, merchants, and shipowners) is given to the merchants. They receive more "press" than the rulers and shipowners combined. (The merchants have 161 words in Greek, the rulers 51, and the shipowners 73.) This is due to the massive list of luxury items that form their existence.

18:13 ***horses, chariots, and bodies—that is, human slaves.*** Human slaves are at the bottom of the entire list. In fallen Babylon humans become just another commodity to be included in the same category as animals and things.

18:16 ***She was clothed in finest purple and scarlet linens, decked out with gold and precious stones and pearls!*** This image makes unmistakable the link to the prostitute seated upon the beast (17:4).

18:17 ***captains . . . sailors and crews.*** These men represent the commercial infrastructure of the Roman culture. The Mediterranean was the "superhighway" across which both the essentials and the luxuries of the empire were transported.

18:19 ***throw dust on their heads.*** This is an action of profound grief, mourning, and humility (cf. Josh 7:6; 1 Sam 4:12; Neh 9:1; Job 2:12; Lam 2:10; Ezek 27:30), apparently indicating the person is as good as dead so dire is their state.

18:20 ***Rejoice over her fate, O heaven and people of God and apostles and prophets!*** God's judgment of fallen Babylon is a common image associated with God's restoration of his people (Deut 32:43; Pss 48:11; 58:10; 96:11-13; Isa 44:23; 49:13; Jer 51:47-48).

at last God has judged her. The words "at last" are not present in the Greek text. Their insertion unnecessarily narrows the reference to the final consummation of God's victory. What follows in the vision (18:21ff) indicates that God's consummation is still in the future. The rejoicing here is over the fact that Babylon has already been judged even though it continues to be incarnate in human history.

18:21-24 ***the great city Babylon will be thrown down.*** John's vision now moves to the final consummation of God's victory over fallen Babylon. In this section, the NLT has faithfully represented the future orientation that the Greek stresses by a series of subjunctive moods that function to indicate an indefinite event in the future.

COMMENTARY

This section opens with the announcement: "Babylon is fallen—that great city is fallen!" (18:2). Babylon's condition is then amplified by a series of images. First, it has become the dwelling place of demons. John saw that as the result of Satan's war in heaven (12:7-8) there was no place for Satan and his angels in heaven. Fallen Babylon is their "place." Second, it is the prison of every unclean spirit, the prison of every unclean bird, and the prison of every unclean beast. Since there is no "place" for Satan and his demons, other than fallen Babylon, it is their "prison." In Jewish thinking, the opposite of "holy" is "profane," and "unclean" items are always profane and thus the antithesis of "holy." The triple repetition of "unclean" (NLT, "foul") indicates total and complete uncleanness, just as the triple repetition in "Holy, holy, holy" (4:8) indicates God's total and complete holiness. John was seeing that fallen Babylon is the unholy city, the antithesis of the holy city, New Jerusalem (explicitly noted as such at 11:2; 21:2, 10; 22:19).

It is because of this unholiness of Babylon that a heavenly voice shouts out, "Come away from her, my people. Do not take part in her sins, or you will be punished with her" (18:4). This is a recurring theme in the Old Testament. Lot was warned to get away from Sodom lest he and his family suffer its destruction (Gen 19:12-15). Moses warned the people to separate themselves from Dathan and Abiram lest they suffer their destruction (Num 16:26). Isaiah called God's people to come out of Babylon (Isa 48:20) and not to touch anything unclean (Isa 52:11). Perhaps the closest resemblance to John's vision is Jeremiah 51:6—"Flee from Babylon! Save yourselves! Don't get trapped in her punishment!" Jeremiah's next word, "It is the LORD's time for vengeance; he will repay her in full," is reprised by John's vision: "For her sins are piled as high as heaven, and God remembers her evil deeds" (18:5). Paul used the same exhortation to the Corinthians: "Come out from among unbelievers, and separate yourselves from them, says the LORD. Don't touch their filthy things" (2 Cor 6:17).

The text then presents a collage of quotations from Isaiah and Jeremiah depicting the demise of fallen Babylon (see note on 18:6-8). It is important to note that this collage of Isaiah and Jeremiah comes from contexts depicting the restoration of Israel. John's vision has portrayed the restoration of the kingdom (1:6; 5:10), the fulfillment of the old covenant (11:7-13), and the consummation of the prophets (10:7; 11:18) in the Messiah, Jesus. Yet faithful believers continue to experience tribulation at the hands of fallen Babylon. In Jewish thinking, the restoration of the kingdom included the judgment of Israel's enemies. John's vision separates these two elements, indicating that final judgment for fallen Babylon is yet to come. In what follows, however, John saw that there are judgments upon the historical incarnations of fallen Babylon prior to the final judgment (see note on 18:9-10). The vision depicts this in the actions of three groups associated with fallen Babylon: rulers (political interests) in 18:9-10, merchants (economic interests) in 18:11-17a, and shipowners (commercial interests) in 18:17b-19.

The rulers grieve the loss of their power base, Babylon, but they themselves are not destroyed by the fall of their particular incarnation of fallen Babylon—even though they are terrified by her great torment. It seems as if the rulers are simply waiting for the next incarnation of fallen Babylon to resume their leadership roles. The merchants of the earth weep and mourn the fall of Babylon but do not themselves experience fallen Babylon's destruction. They, too, seem to wait for the next incarnation of fallen Babylon so they can continue to grow wealthy from her. Likewise, the shipowners bemoan the loss of that which they served, but seemingly await the next incarnation of fallen Babylon to take up their roles. That they are looking for a replacement may be seen in their question, "Where is there another city as great as this?" (18:18). The same may be seen in various conflicts where leaders from a defeated regime reinvent themselves and reappear as part of the new order—the new incarnation of fallen Babylon.

Following these words we are shown an image of a great millstone thrown into the ocean. This is a modulation of Jeremiah's order to Seraiah to wrap his prophecy around a stone and throw it into the Euphrates and pronounce, "In this same way Babylon and her people will sink, never again to rise" (Jer 51:63-64). Seraiah was to enact a prophecy that had seen prior fulfillment in Jewish history. As the stone was thrown into the ocean, he shouted a litany of anathemas. The litany of destruction (18:22-23a) was also a common image in the Old Testament. Ezekiel (Ezek 26:13) and Isaiah (Isa 24:7-13) used a variation in their prophecies against God's enemies, and Jeremiah (Jer 7:34; 16:9; 25:10) used it against apostate Israel.

The vision then gives three reasons for Babylon's ultimate demise. First, her merchants were the greatest in the earth (18:23); John sees the primacy of economy in fallen Babylon, an economy that was oppressive and destructive of human wholeness (cf. 6:6; 13:17; 18:13). Second, she deceived the nations with her sorceries. Fallen Babylon is characterized by deceptive manipulation of its citizens. Third, the blood of the prophets and of God's people was spilled in her streets, and she slaughtered people all over the earth (18:24). God's faithful stand against the false values and deceptive dynamics of fallen Babylon, thus experiencing martyrdom at her hands.

John's vision of the deplorable situation of fallen Babylon is a stark contrast to her apparent power and wealth and status, at which he marveled earlier in the vision (17:6). Life in fallen Babylon is life in a prison. Fallen Babylon's rejection of God closes her in upon herself, her self-referenced structure of being, her self-generated identity, meaning, value, and purpose. Her life is driven by her need to maintain control of her own existence, advance her agenda, fulfill her purposes, and satisfy her desires. She becomes dominated by the demons of performance, possession, popularity, and power.

Whenever humans allow fallen Babylon to become the context of their life, they lose the freedom of being God's persons. As a beloved child of God, we find our identity in God's steadfast love. We find our value in God's sacrificial love. We find our meaning in God's loving purpose for our wholeness in his image. We find our purpose in God's will for us in the world. Without God as the center of our identity, value, meaning, and purpose, we are imprisoned in a structure of being that must develop its own center of identity, value, meaning, and purpose. We become controlled by the demons of performance who tell us that we are what we do. We become driven by the demons of possessiveness who tell us we are what we have. We become possessed by the demons of popularity who tell us that we are what others think of us. We become guided by the demons of power who tell us we are what we can control. Such a life is perpetually in conflict with others, with whom we must compete for performance, possessions, popularity, and power.

John sees that God calls us to separate ourselves from such a debilitating mode of being. Fallen Babylon's existence is doomed to destruction since it moves against the reality of God's holiness and against the reality of human wholeness. God's call is radically countercultural for every human society. As Kenneth Leech reminds us, "to take part in the Christian liturgy is to take on one's role in a new kingdom . . . It is the political act of all time and is therefore potentially seditious within the secular politics of a specific time and place. . . . The kingdom of God is not only a spiritual reality, but a universal revolution of the structures of the old world" (1985:294, 420). This is why the early church was accused of turning the world upside down (Acts 17:6, NKJV). To separate ourselves from fallen Babylon does not mean to remove ourselves from active involvement in the life of the world. It means to live our lives in the world as God's people, citizens of God's kingdom, New Jerusalem. When we are faithful, however, there is the real possibility that our blood will be added to that of the prophets and the rest of God's people in the streets of fallen Babylon.

John's vision reveals that one of the primary dynamics of fallen Babylon's imprisonment is the "power of luxury." It is noteworthy that the merchants play such a focal role in this portion of the vision. Perhaps one of the essential distinctions between fallen Babylon and New Jerusalem is in one's relationship to the created order. Fallen Babylon is characterized by possessiveness, New Jerusalem by stewardship. The vision is an astringent word to our culture, shaped as it is by acquisitiveness, conspicuous consumption, and the amassing of wealth and possessions. The "prosperity gospel" is but one sign of the terrible sickness of Western culture. We have become a culture that relies upon economic security and fulfillment as substitutes for trust and dependence upon God or, worse, as signs of God's favor. Perhaps the most significant result of Pentecost was not only the gift of the Holy Spirit, but the radical new perspective of the believers toward their "possessions." "All the believers . . . shared everything they had. They sold their property and possessions and shared the money with those in need" (Acts 2:44-45). Stewardship had replaced possession. This is one of the ways in which God calls us to separate ourselves from fallen Babylon.

The vision is saying loudly and clearly that spirituality is manifested in the economic dynamics of our lives. Nowhere is this more starkly evident than at the end of the list of luxury goods that characterize fallen Babylon. The "bottom line" is human souls (18:13). Our souls become commodities when possessiveness becomes the perspective of our lives. As we gradually "gain the whole world," we also lose our souls (Matt 16:26).

If John's vision gives an unmistakable illustration of Jesus' word about losing one's soul, it also provides an example of Jesus' parable about the shrewdness of the citizens of this world (Luke 16:8). When their current incarnation of fallen Babylon crumbles, the politicians, merchants, and commercial interests stand aside, avoid the debacle, and are ready to move ahead with the next incarnation when it comes. When communism crumbled in central Europe, the communist politicians in Bulgaria simply redesignated themselves as social democrats and moved forward in their positions of power and control. Their old fallen Babylon was gone, but they quickly adapted to the new fallen Babylon that emerged. When communism crumbled in the Soviet Union, the black marketeers quickly became the economic entrepreneurs and power brokers of the new economy. History is replete with such examples of what John sees in his vision.

The crumbling of historical incarnations of fallen Babylon is continual evidence of God's judgment. We often think of God's judgment as a single act that will be accomplished at some point in the future. John sees that God's judgment is a consequence of the very nature of God's being. That judgment is always operative at the very heart of every historical incarnation of fallen Babylon. Each manifestation of fallen Babylon in human history has crumbled because its rebellion against the holiness of God results in fatal brokenness in the very structures of its existence. This reality will continue until the final consummation of God's judgment when fallen Babylon itself, that realm of rebellion that had incarnated itself repeatedly throughout human history, is ultimately undone by God.

◆ 3. Praises for victory (19:1-10)

After this, I heard what sounded like a vast crowd in heaven shouting,

"Praise the LORD!*
Salvation and glory and power
belong to our God.
2 His judgments are true and just.
He has punished the great
prostitute
who corrupted the earth with her
immorality.
He has avenged the murder of his
servants."

3 And again their voices rang out:

"Praise the LORD!
The smoke from that city ascends
forever and ever!"

4 Then the twenty-four elders and the four living beings fell down and worshiped God, who was sitting on the throne. They cried out, "Amen! Praise the LORD!"

5 And from the throne came a voice that said,

"Praise our God,
all his servants,
all who fear him,
from the least to the greatest."

6 Then I heard again what sounded like the shout of a vast crowd or the roar of mighty ocean waves or the crash of loud thunder:

"Praise the LORD!
For the Lord our God,* the Almighty,
reigns.
7 Let us be glad and rejoice,
and let us give honor to him.

For the time has come for the wedding
feast of the Lamb,
and his bride has prepared herself.
8 She has been given the finest of pure
white linen to wear."
For the fine linen represents the
good deeds of God's holy people.

9 And the angel said to me, "Write this:
Blessed are those who are invited to the
wedding feast of the Lamb." And he added, "These are true words that come from God."
10 Then I fell down at his feet to worship him, but he said, "No, don't worship me. I am a servant of God, just like you and your brothers and sisters* who testify about their faith in Jesus. Worship only God. For the essence of prophecy is to give a clear witness for Jesus.*"

19:1 Greek *Hallelujah;* also in 19:3, 4, 6. *Hallelujah* is the transliteration of a Hebrew term that means "Praise the LORD." **19:6** Some manuscripts read *the Lord God.* **19:10a** Greek *brothers.* **19:10b** Or *is the message confirmed by Jesus.*

NOTES

19:1 *After this.* See note on 1:19.

Praise the LORD! As the NLT mg says, the Greek is *hallēlouïa* [TG239, ZG252], meaning "praise Yahweh."

glory and power. This ascription to God repeats the praise of the 24 elders (4:11), heaven's praise of the Lamb (5:12), and the redeemed's praise of God (7:12). The combination of "glory and power" is a fitting expression for God. God's power is not something God exercises or uses. God's nature (glory) is his power. It is the awesome power of God's absolute holiness. John has seen this in the Temple full of smoke from God's glory and power (15:8), and no one could enter the Temple until the fire of God's holiness (wrath) had done its work.

19:2 ***His judgments are true and just.*** This proclamation furthers the focus upon God's nature, not his action. For something to be just and true, it has to be in harmony with whatever is established as "just" and "true." The only standard of justice and truth in the OT is the very nature of God. God's nature is eternal and unchanging; thus, he is described as steadfast and faithful throughout the OT. It is against the unchanging reality of God's nature that fallen Babylon destroys itself. It is not that God *acts* and fallen Babylon is judged; God *is,* and fallen Babylon is judged. In other words, the unreality of fallen Babylon's perception, value system, and lifestyle is thrown into sharp relief in the presence of ultimate reality of God's nature as the center of true perception, the source of a true value system, and the context of a true lifestyle.

He has punished. Lit., "he has judged" (*ekrinen* [TG2919, ZG3212]), using a term from the same family as the term translated "judgments" (*kriseis* [TG2920, ZG3213]) earlier in the verse. Both are from the same verbal stem.

servants. These are those who have manifested God's image, God's nature, in their fallen Babylon world. They have God's name (nature) on their foreheads (14:1; 22:4). They have had "the witness of Jesus" in the midst of their fallen Babylon world. Fallen Babylon's rejection of God has resulted in their martyrdom, but their "justice" is vindicated in God's nature.

19:3 ***smoke . . . ascends forever and ever.*** This repeats the image from 14:11. There it was seen that the "burning" of fallen Babylon took place in the presence of the holy angels and the Lamb. The image here, in context with the previous verses, again emphasizes the holiness of God's nature, which is a consuming fire for all unholiness.

19:5 ***all who fear him.*** Throughout the vision, "fearing" God is an image for those who are faithful disciples (11:18; 14:7; 15:4).

19:6 ***the Almighty.*** This title is peculiar to Revelation in the NT (1:8; 4:8; 11:17; 15:3; 16:7, 14; 19:6, 15; 21:22) with the exception of 2 Cor 6:18, where Paul appears to be giving a free rendition of 2 Esdr 1:28. The term is much more widely used in the OT and intertestamental writings, however, and again lays emphasis upon the Jewish context of John's thinking.

19:8 ***linen.*** This was the garment of the priesthood (see Exod 39:27-29; Lev 6:10). Here is another image of the redeemed as priests (1:5; 5:10).

the good deeds of God's holy people. Lit., "the "righteousnesses of the holy ones." Here the images of garments and deeds come together. The lives of God's faithful people manifest righteousness because they are holy. The holiness of their being becomes incarnate in their living. Being generates doing.

19:9-10 The conclusion of John's vision of the prostitute, fallen Babylon, is parallel to the conclusion of the vision of the bride, New Jerusalem (22:6-9; see the analysis of 17:1).

19:9, 17 ***wedding feast . . . great banquet.*** The wedding feast (*deipnon* [TG1173, ZG1270]) of the Lamb is the ultimate consummation of New Jerusalem, of which the Eucharist throughout history is the proleptic manifestation. John uses *deipnon* again in 19:17 as the "great banquet [of] God," subsequently seen as the victory of God over the beast and false prophet (19:18-21). Since, as will be seen, John is here seeing another manifestation of God's victory through the cross, and since the Eucharist is the primary act of remembrance of this victory, in 19:17 John is seeing the "dark side" of the Eucharist for fallen Babylon.

19:10 ***who testify about their faith in Jesus.*** The NLT has somewhat clouded the understanding of the phrase "the witness of Jesus" by its translations, "testify about their faith in Jesus" and "witness for Jesus." In both places the Greek text has "the witness (*marturia* [TG3141, ZG3456]) of Jesus." To have "the witness of Jesus" is to live a Christlike life in the midst of the fallen Babylon world (see note on 1:2). This is far more than simply testifying about one's faith in Jesus or witnessing for Jesus.

COMMENTARY

Following his vision of the ultimate demise of fallen Babylon (18:21-24), John saw heaven's rejoicing at the consummation of God's victory. The sound "like a vast crowd in heaven" praising God is one of the themes that runs through the vision. At 5:13, John hears all of heaven and creation praising the Lamb. At 7:11, the angels in heaven sing God's praises. At 11:15, loud voices in heaven praise God and the Messiah for the restoration of the kingdom. At 14:2, John hears the heavenly multitude and the followers of the Lamb singing the new song before the throne. Here God is praised by heaven's multitudes for salvation, which includes the restoration of the kingdom and the overthrow of the enemies of God and God's people. John seems to have seen here the consummation of the restoration that was begun in the death and resurrection of the Lamb in conjunction with the culmination of the judgment of fallen Babylon.

The twenty-four elders and four living creatures affirm the praise of heaven's multitude by saying "amen," which means "verily, truly, yes" (19:4). This is followed by the invitation to all God's servants to "Praise God" (19:5) and the acclamation that the Lord "reigns" (19:6). The praise closes as it opened, with the assertion of God's salvation (19:1). "Salvation" is the restoration of the kingdom, over which God reigns.

Another essential part of the Jewish expectation of the restoration of the kingdom was the messianic banquet. This is amply illustrated by the sectarian community at Qumran, whose evening meal each day was a precursor of the great banquet of the kingdom where they would be joined by the Davidic (kingly) and the Aaronic (priestly) messiahs.[1] Jesus played upon the same expectations when he told his disciples that they would eat and drink at his table in the kingdom (Luke 22:30), and that many will come from east and west to eat with Abraham, Isaac, and Jacob in the kingdom (Matt 8:11). Isaiah envisioned a great banquet of God on a restored Mount Zion (Isa 25:6), to which everyone would be invited to come and eat and drink (Isa 55:1).

More specifically, John sees a wedding banquet (19:7), with God's people as the bride. The image of the marriage of God and his people is also threaded through the Old Testament. Isaiah says to Jerusalem, "Your new name will be . . . 'The Bride of God,' for the LORD delights in you and will claim you as his bride. . . . God will rejoice over you as a bridegroom rejoices over his bride" (Isa 62:4-5). God says to Israel through Jeremiah, "I remember how eager you were to please me as a young bride long ago, how you loved me and followed me even through the barren wilderness" (Jer 2:2). The entire prophecy of Hosea plays upon the image of God as the bridegroom and Israel as the bride, albeit an adulterous one. Jesus used this common image with his disciples, presenting himself as the bridegroom and them as the bride (Matt 9:15). He also described the end of the age as a marriage ceremony in the parable of the virgins (Matt 25:1ff). In John's Gospel, John the Baptist likens Jesus to a bridegroom and his disciples to the bride (John 3:29).

John's vision pulls together the two powerful images of the messianic banquet and Israel as the bride in the Jewish tradition to affirm that (1) Jesus, the Lamb, is the Messiah, the divine bridegroom, (2) the church is the bride, (3) the messianic banquet is a wedding feast, and (4) this is the consummation of God's victory through the Messiah.

An angel pronounced a blessing on "those who are invited to the wedding feast of the Lamb" (19:9). We find here the fourth "blessed" of the seven in the book (1:3; 14:13; 16:15; 19:9; 20:6; 22:7, 14). All of the blessings relate in some way to rewarding faithful discipleship. The first and sixth are for those who keep the words of the vision, that is, who incarnate its reality in their life in the world. The second and the fourth relate to the deeds of the faithful, which, as we have seen, are the outer manifestation of inner beings shaped in the image of God. The third, fourth, and seventh are associated with the clothing of the faithful, an image that pulls together the inner being and its manifestation in the world. The fifth is for those who experience the "first resurrection" and are, thereby, priests of God—an image that calls for holiness of both being and doing.

It is interesting to note how much praise-singing there is in John's vision (4:8-11; 5:9-14; 7:12; 11:15-18; 12:10-12; 14:2-3; 15:2-4; 18:20; 19:1-6). It is also interesting to observe that the Psalms are quoted or alluded to in the New Testament more than any other Old Testament book.[2] This is, undoubtedly, because the songs of Israel were deeply rooted in the lives of the human authors. The psalms formed their perceptions of God and their understanding of themselves as God's people in the world. The psalms wove themselves into the very fabric of their individual and corporate life.

Part of the genius of John and Charles Wesley was their use of Charles's hymns to ingrain the truths of Scripture and the faith into the minds, hearts, and lives of their followers. In Revelation, the songs of heaven and the faithful are the expressions of beings that resonate with the deep realities of God's realm. Paul seems to be aware of this dimension of discipleship when he exhorts the Colossians to "let the message about Christ, in all its richness, fill your lives," and then follows with two participial phrases that indicate how they are to do this. First, they are to "teach and counsel each other with all the wisdom he gives"; second, they are to "sing psalms and hymns and spiritual songs to God with thankful hearts" (Col 3:16).

A person who experiences deep overflowings of joy while singing a much-beloved hymn is experiencing the reality of their inner being resonating with the reality about which they sing. This seems to be what the singing in John's vision is all about. The singing of heaven and God's faithful is the expression of beings that resonate at their depths with the love and grace of God.

In the face of a world that marginalizes, demeans, belittles, persecutes, and even martyrs God's faithful, their beings resonate with a reality that has already overcome the world (John 1:5; 16:33). Paul and Silas had the full attention of their fellow prisoners when, after having been beaten and imprisoned, they were singing hymns at midnight (Acts 16:25). The Roman mobs could not comprehend the fact that many Christians went to their deaths singing.

The singing of John's vision is a powerful reminder that the faith is not an intellectual construct, a theological position, or an ecclesiastical standard; it is a life in vital relationship with God, a life of radical abandonment to God in love.

Such radical abandonment is how the bride prepares herself for her marriage to the Lamb. There is a revealing conundrum at this point in John's vision. He tells us first that the "bride has prepared herself." It sounds like "works righteousness," especially when we are told that her garments are "the good deeds of God's holy people" (19:7-8). But then John tells us that "she has been given the finest of pure white linen to wear." Now it seems that her preparation is God's doing. This puzzle is reminiscent of Jesus' teaching at the end of the Sermon on the Mount (Matt 7:21-23): Jesus first says, "Not everyone who says to me, 'Lord, Lord,' will enter the kingdom of heaven, but only the one who does the will of my Father in heaven" (NRSV). It would seem that works are the crucial factor in entering the kingdom. But then Jesus says, "On that day many will say to me, 'Lord, Lord, did we not prophesy in your name, and cast out demons in your name, and do many deeds of power in your name?'" Now, these people certainly had the "works," and Jesus didn't contradict their claim. They *were* prophesying in his name, they *were* casting out demons in his name, they *were* doing many deeds of power in his name. To all observers they would have appeared to be faithful disciples, even superdisciples, eminently successful in effective ministries. Jesus says to them, however, "I never knew you; go away from me, you evildoers." It becomes clear at this point that their works are not the outward manifestation of a vital relationship with Jesus. Such works are "evil deeds."

It is this reality that John seems to have seen in his vision of the bride. When John saw that she was given "the finest of pure white linen to wear," he was seeing that

God had opened the way for humanity to enter into a vital relationship with him in which they can be cleansed of their sins, healed of their brokenness, liberated from their bondages, and transformed into God's very own image. The bride becomes holy. At the same time, the bride must manifest the reality of this relationship in the way in which she lives her life in the world. Living out her relationship with God results in "righteousness," a life that manifests God's nature in the quality of its behaviors. It is the integration of being and doing. Being in vital relationship with God manifests itself in the way one lives with others. Jesus encapsulated it perfectly when he said that loving our neighbor is as important as loving God with all our heart, soul, mind, and strength (Mark 12:30-31; cf. 1 John 4:20). The bride is both holy and righteous. There can be no holiness that does not result in righteous deeds. There can be no righteous deeds except those that are the result of holiness. In John's vision, the image for such a life of holy righteousness is to "have the witness of Jesus."

The vision gives us a significant understanding of the nature of prophecy that links it to having this "witness of Jesus." Most people think of prophecy as predicting the future. The vision tells us here that "the essence of prophecy" is the "witness of Jesus" (19:10, my translation). A prophet is one who speaks for God in the world. The Old Testament prophets were the voice of the Lord for the people of their day in the midst of the situations of their lifetimes. While their proclamations often disclosed God's ultimate purposes for his people, those purposes were always related to the present faithfulness or apostasy of God's people in the prophet's day. The prophets were, in a sense, God's presence in the midst of the world. In John's vision, the ultimate presence of God in the world is the Messiah, Jesus. To have the "witness of Jesus," therefore, is to live lives of such radical abandonment to Jesus that Jesus is manifested to the world in which we live. In Paul's words, it is no longer we who live, but Christ who lives in us (Gal 2:20). Paul preceded this affirmation with the cost of such abandonment: "My old self has been crucified with Christ." The false self, shaped by the destructive and dehumanizing values and perspectives of our fallen Babylon world, must die in order that our true self, created in the image of God and restored in the image of Christ, might live.

ENDNOTES

1. For the Davidic Messiah at Qumran, see 4QFlor [4Q174] 1:10-13. For the priestly Messiah, see 1QS[a] 2:11-21. For a more complete discussion of the two messiahs at Qumran, see Vermes 1977.
2. See Appendix IV in NA[27].

◆ B. The Lamb's Present and Future Victory (19:11–21:8)

1. The Lamb's victory (19:11-21)

11 Then I saw heaven opened, and a white horse was standing there. Its rider was named Faithful and True, for he judges fairly and wages a righteous war. 12 His eyes were like flames of fire, and on his head were many crowns. A name was written on him that no one understood except himself. 13 He wore a robe dipped in blood, and his title was the Word of God. 14 The armies of heaven, dressed in the finest of pure

white linen, followed him on white horses. [15]From his mouth came a sharp sword to strike down the nations. He will rule them with an iron rod. He will release the fierce wrath of God, the Almighty, like juice flowing from a winepress. [16]On his robe at his thigh* was written this title: King of all kings and Lord of all lords.

[17]Then I saw an angel standing in the sun, shouting to the vultures flying high in the sky: "Come! Gather together for the great banquet God has prepared. [18]Come and eat the flesh of kings, generals, and strong warriors; of horses and their riders; and of all humanity, both free and slave, small and great."

[19]Then I saw the beast and the kings of the world and their armies gathered together to fight against the one sitting on the horse and his army. [20]And the beast was captured, and with him the false prophet who did mighty miracles on behalf of the beast—miracles that deceived all who had accepted the mark of the beast and who worshiped his statue. Both the beast and his false prophet were thrown alive into the fiery lake of burning sulfur. [21]Their entire army was killed by the sharp sword that came from the mouth of the one riding the white horse. And the vultures all gorged themselves on the dead bodies.

19:16 Or *On his robe and thigh.*

NOTES

19:11 ***a white horse was standing there.*** The introduction of the Messiah here is identical to that of the first horseman at 6:2 (see note). In that facet of the vision, John saw the Messiah going forth "conquering in order that he might conquer" (lit.). He now sees the full dimensions of that conquering.

named Faithful and True. Jesus affirmed for himself the same attribute in the letter to the Laodicean church (3:14).

he judges fairly and wages a righteous war. Lit., "in righteousness he is judging and making war." In the Greek, "judging" and "making war" are parallel terms aligned with "in righteousness." "Righteousness" appears only twice in the vision, although "righteous" is used several times: God is "righteous" (16:5; "just," NLT), as are his ways (15:3) and his judgments (16:7; 19:2). The clue to John's use of "righteousness," however, is found at 22:11, where the person who is "righteous" is exhorted literally to "do righteousness." Since the Messiah is righteous, he does righteousness—that is, his righteousness is what judges and wars against all that is unrighteous.

19:12 ***eyes were like flames of fire.*** This makes it clear that this is the Messiah who appeared to John at the beginning of the vision (1:14).

on his head were many crowns. Lit., "many diadems on his head." The diadems are representative of Jesus' victory over the dragon and beast, who also have diadems (12:3; 13:1), and they are consistent with the image of a victorious general who has the crowns of his vanquished foes.

A name was written on him that no one understood except himself. In Jewish tradition, the name has to do with the nature of the person or thing. John here sees that the nature of the Messiah transcends human comprehension.

19:13 ***He wore a robe dipped in blood.*** Whose blood? Since, in the vision, garments are related to the nature of the person who wears them (see note on 3:4), we must presume that it his own blood. Here is yet another aspect of the cross as a revelation of the very nature of God's being (see commentary on 11:19–12:6). Beale (1999:957) suggests that John was again utilizing imagery from Isa 63:1-3 (which he introduced in 14:20), and "the stained garments symbolize God's attribute of justice, which he will exercise in the coming judgment." Beale fails to realize that God's judgment has already been fulfilled in the cross. As noted in the commentary to 14:14-20, John portrays the cross as both gathering the redeemed into New Jerusalem and trampling the winepress of fallen Babylon.

the Word of God. The Messiah is, in the terms of John's Gospel, the Word become flesh, the very presence of God, expressing the nature of God (John 1:1, 14).

19:14 ***armies of heaven, dressed in the finest of pure white linen.*** The armies can be identified by their garments. John had just seen that the pure white linen garment of the bride of the Lamb is the righteous deeds of God's holy people (19:8). It may be that John saw the church, the citizens of New Jerusalem, the people of God's kingdom, as those who advance the victory of the Messiah.

19:16 ***On his robe at his thigh.*** The literal rendering is preferable: "on his robe and thigh" (cf. NLT mg). Since in John's vision a person's garments are the outer manifestation of their being, the appearance of this name/title both on his person and his robe emphasizes that Jesus really is "King of kings and Lord of lords." In the OT, the thigh plays a role in the taking of oaths (Gen 24:2, 9; 47:29). The precise significance is uncertain, but it seems to at least represent an act of fealty by the one who puts his hand "under the thigh" of the other—i.e., they are committing themselves to faithful obedience to the other. It would seem that it represents the establishment of a covenant that binds the participants to its fulfillment. Its use in the vision suggests that the Messiah's nature as "King of all kings and Lord of all lords" is an established reality that will be fulfilled.

King of all kings and Lord of all lords. This is an affirmation already noted at 17:14, where, once again, faithful disciples are included in the Lamb's victory over fallen Babylon, yet another pointer to the possibility that the army in white linen at 19:14 is the kingdom of priests created by the Lamb's death (5:10).

19:17 ***vultures.*** While "vultures" is a logical translation since the birds in this scene eat carrion, the Greek simply has "birds" (*orneois* [TG3732, ZG3997]) not "vultures" (*aetos* [TG105, ZG108]). One reasonable explanation for this is that John saw many types of scavenging birds, or had a passage from the LXX in mind (e.g., Ezek 39:4, 17; cf. Gen 40:19; Deut 32:24; 1 Sam 17:44; 2 Macc 15:33).

19:20 ***the beast.*** This one, first introduced at 16:13, is now identified as an image for the second beast of 13:11. This is seen in the fact that the false prophet is the one who did mighty miracles on behalf of the beast—miracles that deceived all who had accepted the mark of the beast and who worshiped his image (13:13-16).

COMMENTARY

The scene beginning in 19:11 is the final and fullest of the three "openings" in the vision: At 4:1, John saw a "door standing open in heaven"; at 11:19, "the Temple of God was opened"; now, all of heaven is opened. When the heavens were opened, John saw the triumphant Jesus on a white horse. This image may be a merging of two sources, Roman and Jewish. One of the features of the Roman world was the celebration of a "triumph" (see Versnel 1970). The Triumphator (the general or emperor who had won the war) would enter Rome in a triumphal procession riding in a chariot drawn by four white horses. He would be clothed in a red robe ("robe dipped in blood"; 19:13), and the crowns of the vanquished would be prominently displayed (see Payne 1962). The Triumphator would be followed by his army ("the armies of heaven . . . followed him on white horses"; 19:14). The triumph celebrated the Triumphator's victory over enemy nations ("strike down the nations"; 19:15) in a just war ("wages a righteous war"; 19:11). The Triumphator held in his hand a scepter symbolizing his rule over the vanquished nations ("rule them with an iron rod"; 19:15), and he was clothed in robes representing the god Jupiter ("on his robe . . . was written this title: King of all kings and Lord of all lords"; 19:16). While in the Roman context, no one would presume that the Triumphator was Jupiter in any way, John modulates the illustration to indicate that the title on Jesus' robe actually describes who he is. While there are also many Jewish images in John's portrayal as noted below, John used the imagery of a Roman triumph to reveal Jesus' triumph over the forces of fallen Babylon (Rome for John and his readers).

The vision then puts together several images of the Messiah seen before. We see again that from his mouth came a sharp sword (19:21), seen first in the inaugural vision (1:16) and reiterated in the letter to Pergamum (2:12). Its purpose, to strike down the nations, echoes the use of the sword at 2:16, where Jesus said he would war against the apostate with the sword of his mouth. Another image for the same reality is the iron rod, seen first at 2:27 in the allusion to Psalm 2:9, a messianic psalm. It is interesting to note that in 2:27, it is the faithful disciples who will rule the nations with the iron rod. This gives added weight to the possibility that the army that follows the Messiah is, indeed, the citizens of New Jerusalem—the church. The messianic image of the iron rod is seen again at 12:5, in the son of the woman (who most likely symbolizes God, see commentary). The final image is of the one who trod the winepress of the fierce wrath of God the Almighty (19:15). This image also appears earlier in the vision at 14:19-20. This triple imagery, sword from the mouth, iron rod, and winepress of wrath, all point to the unalterable reality of God's holiness, which is the undoing of the rebellious realm.

The sword of the mouth image appears in a negative context in Job 5:15, where God saves the needy from the sword of the mouth of those who oppress them. Those in positions of power speak forth an order of life that oppresses the poor. Their words form a world under their control, a world that is hostile to those not in power. A use of the image similar to John's is Isaiah 49:2, where God's servant who is to restore Israel is given a mouth like a sharp sword. As John's vision uses the image, it is coupled with the one who is also described as "the Word of God" (19:13). God thus speaks forth an order of being that is an expression of God's nature itself. God continues to speak forth this order of wholeness and life into the brokenness and death of the rebellious order. The wholeness and life of the Word of God is a sharp sword that penetrates to the heart of the rebellious order. It cuts through all the deception and lays bare the inner workings and hidden mechanisms of the fallen Babylon world.

Fallen Babylon tries to dull the edge of this sharp sword. It attempts to sheath the sword within its own structures of brokenness. It seeks to reinterpret the word of God so it becomes an affirmation of human brokenness and death. Fallen Babylon tries to subvert the word of God so that it will become a support for the dehumanizing perspectives and destructive structures of fallen Babylon. But God's unchanging reality is also an "iron rod," an image of unyielding, unbending strength and endurance. All that is contrary to God's order of wholeness and life will, ultimately, be shattered against the enduring reality of God.

Such shattering seems like "wrath" to the citizens of fallen Babylon. Here is something that threatens their entire order of being. Since fallen Babylon operates upon the premise that self usurps the place of God, each self-god seeks to bring others under its control. Instead of seeing others as children of the one God, others become objects in a world that is to be ordered according to one's own agenda. When others resist our control, when they thwart our agenda, when they upset our purposes, we become angry and lash out at them in wrath. It is this experience that we then apply to the experience of disruption that God's holiness brings into our unholiness. We presume that God is behaving as we do when our purposes are rejected. As fallen Babylon begins to experience the destructive consequences of its rebellion against God, it attributes its torment to a vengeful, punitive, retributive, wrathful deity.

It is as though the wholeness of God is a sharp scalpel in the hand of a skilled and loving surgeon. As the surgeon seeks to cut through our flesh to the cancerous growth that is destroying us, we could easily perceive the surgeon as a spiteful, sadistic, ogre who is seeking to inflict pain and suffering upon us when, in reality, the surgeon, the scalpel, and the suffering they cause are all directed toward our healing and wholeness.

Fallen Babylon fights against the scalpel, against the surgeon. It seeks to deflect the scalpel from its body and the surgeon from its world. John's vision makes a radical affirmation here. It suggests that the believing community, the bride of the Lamb, is the army that follows the Lamb and participates in his action in the midst of fallen Babylon. To continue our medical metaphor, the church becomes the presence of the surgeon in the operating theater and its proclamation the scalpel that cuts through to the diseased tissue in the body of the world. But its proclamation is more than verbal—the church is to incarnate wholeness and life in the midst of the brokenness and death of its fallen Babylon world. This is why John sees the "armies of heaven" clothed in "pure white linen," which he has just seen represents the "righteousness" of the people of God. The church doesn't "use" the scalpel of the word of God to slash away at the deadness of its world. It is itself the scalpel in the hand of God, and its presence in the midst of fallen Babylon is a terrible threat to the welfare and status quo of fallen Babylon. This is why, throughout the vision, John sees faithful disciples (citizens of New Jerusalem) experiencing tribulation at the hands of fallen Babylon. Holiness is a terror to unholiness.

We see here that there are two sides to holiness. For the citizens of New Jerusalem, holiness is wholeness and life. For the citizens of fallen Babylon, holiness is disruptive and, ultimately, deadly. John's vision portrays these two realities as two aspects of the Lord's Supper, God's banquet. For the redeemed, God's banquet is the marriage supper of the Lamb; it is life in all its fullness and abundance; it is life eternal. For the rebellious, however, God's banquet is a dinner of death. The vision of this banquet of death reflects Ezekiel's vision of God's defeat of Gog (Ezek 39:17-20), where God tells Ezekiel to invite the birds to the great banquet God has prepared where they will eat the flesh of mighty men (= kings) and all kinds of soldiers (= captains) and strong warriors and horses. John's vision, as usual, modulates the image from Ezekiel to encompass not just the army of God's enemies, but the entire citizenship of the opposing realm. In Greek, the word for "banquet" is the same as the term for the wedding "feast" (*deipnon* [TG1173, ZG1270]) of the Lamb in 19:9. It would seem that John is seeing the two sides of God's victory. For the faithful, it is the wedding banquet of the Lamb, for the rebellious, it is the banquet of their defeat. Thus, "the great banquet [of] God" both affirms the enduring reality of New Jerusalem and threatens the demise of fallen Babylon.

Following the vision of the great supper, John saw the demise of the beast and the false prophet, the two representatives of Satan's rebellion. The beast of 13:1-3 represents the inner posture of being that rejects God as God. The beast of 13:11, the false prophet, represents the lifestyle that results from the rejection of God. These two represent the being and doing, the worldview and lifestyle of fallen Babylon.

John saw that "the beast and his false prophet were thrown alive into the fiery lake" (19:20). This is the first mention of the lake of fire, which is also the ultimate destination of Satan (20:10), Death and Hades (20:14), and anyone whose name is not in the Lamb's Book of Life (20:15). This image is part of the diminution of the rebellious realm. It is imaged first as the "sea" (4:6; see note), then as the sea "mixed with fire" (15:2), now as a smaller "*lake* of fire," and finally as having disappeared (21:1).

It is significant that the beast and the false prophet were thrown "alive" into the lake of fire. When Satan, Death, and Hades, and all the citizens of fallen Babylon are thrown into the lake of fire (20:10, 14-15), the vision does not indicate that they are thrown in "alive." But the significance of "alive" here must await the next "scene" of the vision for its clarification (see comments on 20:1-4).

The removal of the beast and false prophet (19:20) also destroys the entire population of fallen Babylon because the "army" consisted not only of kings, captains, warriors, and cavalry, but also of "all humanity, both free and slave, small and great" (19:18). Their death is due to "the sharp sword that came from the mouth of the one riding the white horse" (19:21). The reality of God's holiness reveals the deadness of all that is unholy.

◆ 2. The firstfruits of victory (20:1-10)

Then I saw an angel coming down from heaven with the key to the bottomless pit* and a heavy chain in his hand. 2He seized the dragon—that old serpent, who is the devil, Satan—and bound him in chains for a thousand years. 3The angel threw him into the bottomless pit, which he then shut and locked so Satan could not deceive the nations anymore until the thousand years were finished. Afterward he must be released for a little while.

4Then I saw thrones, and the people sitting on them had been given the authority to judge. And I saw the souls of those who had been beheaded for their testimony about Jesus and for proclaiming the word of God. They had not worshiped the beast or his statue, nor accepted his mark on their foreheads or their hands. They all came to life again, and they reigned with Christ for a thousand years.

5This is the first resurrection. (The rest of the dead did not come back to life until the thousand years had ended.)
6Blessed and holy are those who share in the first resurrection. For them the second death holds no power, but they will be priests of God and of Christ and will reign with him a thousand years.
7When the thousand years come to an

end, Satan will be let out of his prison.
[8]He will go out to deceive the nations—
called Gog and Magog—in every corner of
the earth. He will gather them together
for battle—a mighty army, as numberless
as sand along the seashore. [9]And I saw
them as they went up on the broad plain
of the earth and surrounded God's people
and the beloved city. But fire from heaven
came down on the attacking armies and
consumed them.
[10]Then the devil, who had deceived
them, was thrown into the fiery lake of
burning sulfur, joining the beast and the
false prophet. There they will be tormented
day and night forever and ever.

20:1 Or *the abyss*, or *the underworld;* also in 20:3.

NOTES

20:1 ***angel . . . with the key to the bottomless pit.*** This can be none other than Jesus, the Messiah, who described himself to John as the one who has the keys of Death and Hades (1:18). See discussion at 9:1 for Death and Hades as the abyss or bottomless pit.

a heavy chain. This image was used in Jewish and Christian writings to describe how God bound the rebellious angels (*1 Enoch* 10:4-6; cf. 2 Pet 2:4; Jude 1:6).

20:2 ***the dragon—that old serpent, who is the devil, Satan.*** See notes on 12:3 and 12:18 and commentary on 13:7.

a thousand years. Here is one of the most hotly contested images in the entire vision, an image of what has come to be known as the Millennium. Many interpreters take the image to be literal, and they presume John was seeing a specific thousand-year period somewhere near the end of history. However, it is more likely that a thousand years signifies an extended period of time (see commentary).

20:3 ***so Satan could not deceive the nations.*** The Greek has the subjunctive mood, the mood of potentiality, which should be translated, "so Satan might not deceive the nations." It is not that he cannot, or will not, but that he might not. In other words, those who follow the Lamb (14:4), those who have the word of God and the witness of Jesus (1:2, et al.) will not be deceived since the "reality" of their life in Christ makes the falseness of Satan's realm clearly manifest. Others, however, have nothing by which to discern Satan's deception.

until the thousand years were finished. The Greek has the subjunctive mood, which should be translated, "until whenever the thousand years should be finished." This is the formulation used again at 20:5 and 7. If John had wanted to speak of a literal thousand years, he would have used the indicative mood. He uses the subjunctive mood, however, in support of his imagery of "a thousand years" as a huge period of time with an indefinite point of conclusion. The subjunctive mood is the mood of potentiality, which by its very nature points to an action in the indefinite, relative future.

20:4 ***thrones.*** John had previously seen the thrones of the 24 elders (4:4) who, we have noted, represent the redeemed citizens of God's kingdom, New Jerusalem.

had been given the authority to judge. There is an ambiguity in the Greek here. The text can be translated as in the NLT, but it can also be translated, "judgment was given in their favor," that is, God had adjudicated their case in their favor. In light of the plea of the martyrs in the fifth seal (6:10), the judgment on behalf of the prophets and saints (11:18), the revelation of God's judgments (15:4), the judgment of the prostitute (17:1-18), and the statement of God's judgment on behalf of the faithful (18:20; 19:2), it would seem that the second option is more likely here. Thus, the enthronement of God's faithful people is their vindication over those who had brought tribulation upon them.

the souls. This image links with 6:9-11; as such, it points to the fact that these people are souls who had not yet experienced a physical resurrection.

those who had been beheaded for their testimony about Jesus and for proclaiming the word of God. These are people who have been killed (whether by beheading or any other means) by their fallen Babylon world because their lives manifested the reality of God's holiness in ways that were intolerable for fallen Babylon. The martyrs are those who have been killed because their lives, shaped in God's image (i.e., by the word of God), manifested Christlikeness in their fallen Babylon world. It wasn't simply their testifying about Jesus that caused their death: It was their living like Jesus.

They had not worshiped the beast or his statue, nor accepted his mark on their foreheads or their hands. In the NLT this is a further description of the previously mentioned martyrs. Gr. *kai hoitines* [TG2532/3748, ZG2779/4015] allows for this interpretation because it can be translated "even those." But the Greek could also be rendered "and those"; as such, this could be a second group. If the Greek is speaking just of martyrs in all of 20:4, then only martyrs participate in the Millennium. If the Greek is speaking of martyrs and other Christians, then the verse is depicting all faithful Christians who are then blessed to experience the Millennium. The interpretation has ramifications for the judgment scene in 20:11-15. If only Christian martyrs participate in the millennial kingdom, then the "rest of the dead" to face judgment include both Christians and non-Christians. If all Christians participate in the Millennium, then the final judgment pertains only to those who were not Christians. Commentators are divided on this issue (for a good discussion, see Mounce 1977:360-370).

came to life again. Lit., "they came alive" (*ezēsan* [TG2198, ZG2409]). The vision clarifies the meaning of this image by adding, "This is the first resurrection" (20:5a). Several commentators think this means they were physically raised from the dead (for example, see Johnson 1981:579). The argument in their favor is that the same Greek word (*ezēsan*) is used in the next verse in the sense of physical resurrection: "The rest of the dead did not come back to life [*ezēsan*] until the thousand years had ended." However, I join a number of other commentators who think this means they were raised to new life from the deadness of their former life. I think John was using the same kind of imagery used by Paul to describe what happens when persons come to faith in Christ and are spiritually regenerated (see next note and the commentary below).

20:4-5 ***reigned with Christ for a thousand years. This is the first resurrection.*** John seems to be seeing in 20:4-5 what Paul describes in Eph 2:5-6: "Even though we were dead [cf. "the rest of the dead" in Rev 20:5b] . . . he gave us life [cf. "came to life again"; Rev 20:4] when he raised Christ from the dead [cf. "the first resurrection"; Rev 20:5]. . . . [He] seated us with him in the heavenly realms because we are united with Christ Jesus [cf. "thrones, and the people sitting on them"; Rev 20:4]." Both John and Paul used aorist verbs in a gnomic fashion, i.e., expressing a general truth or reality.

The rest of the dead. This presumes that another portion of the dead had already been identified—i.e., those previously referred to as those who "came to life again" (see previous note and commentary).

did not come back to life until the thousand years had ended. The "rest of the dead" come back to life at the end of the Millennium, but only to enter into the final judgment, which John sees in 20:11-15.

20:6 ***Blessed and holy.*** This is the fifth of the seven blessings (1:3; 14:13; 16:15; 19:9; 22:7, 14; see notes). This is the first time "holy" has been explicitly used to describe the faithful believers, although "saints" implies the holiness of the believers (cf. 5:8; 8:3; 11:8; 16:6; 19:8, KJV). God and the Lamb are "holy" (3:7; 4:8; 6:10; 15:4; 16:5), as are the angels (14:10) and New Jerusalem (11:2; 21:2, 10; 22:19). John's vision makes it clear that the way to holiness is through resurrection with Christ. This is also the way to escape the second death. John will see shortly (20:14-15) that the second death is the ultimate outcome of unholiness.

will reign with him a thousand years. The image of "reigning" appears also at 5:10, where the redeemed "reign on the earth." Why does John use a present tense at 5:10 (following A 𝔐[K]; see note on 5:10) and a gnomic aorist at 20:4, but the future tense at 20:6? At 20:6 the future simply reflects the essential nature of blessing: A blessing is a type of conditional statement in which, if the first part is fulfilled (in this case, if one shares in the first resurrection), then the consequence will follow (in this case, will be priests of God and will reign). In those places where someone or something is already blessed, the context makes it clear that a prior condition has been met from which the blessing flows. For instance, "Blessed are the poor in spirit, for theirs is the kingdom of heaven" (Matt 5:3, NIV)—participation in the kingdom is a consequence of a prior condition, poverty of spirit. This is confirmed in the statements about being priests of God. In both 1:6 and 5:10, the statement is a present reality, but at 20:6 the future tense is necessitated by the conditional nature of the statement.

20:7 *When the thousand years come to an end.* This is introduced in exactly the same form as at 20:3 and 20:5—by a subjunctive clause indicating an indeterminate time. John then sees the event that closes the Millennium.

Satan will be let out of his prison. Note that Satan does not escape. The use of the passive voice is a common Jewish way of indicating God's actions. The one who put Satan in prison also releases him; Satan is released so that he can be judged (20:8-9).

20:8 *Gog and Magog.* John used these images of the archetypal enemies of God from Ezek 39 to portray the entirety of fallen Babylon being gathered for the final act in the drama.

as numberless as sand along the seashore. This is used regularly in the OT to describe an immense number (see Jer 33:22 for its use for anything that cannot be enumerated; also Gen 22:17; 32:12; 41:49; Josh 11:4; Judg 7:12; 1 Sam 13:5).

20:9 *the broad plain of the earth.* Lit., "the breadth (*platos* [TG4114, ZG4424]) of the earth," indicating that the entire realm of fallen Babylon ("the earth") is involved in this action.

God's people and the beloved city. It is important to note the presence of God's people right in the midst of the action. The faithful of God have not been raptured out of the end time. In fact, they are at the very center of the action, surrounded by the innumerable forces of fallen Babylon. It even looks as if fallen Babylon is about to finally overcome New Jerusalem.

fire from heaven came down on the attacking armies and consumed them. This is the vision's image of what we have come to call "the Second Coming." John clearly sees that Christ's return is what brings the thousand-year period (the Millennium) to its close.

20:10 *thrown into the fiery lake.* John saw that the purpose of Satan's release from his prison is to be thrown into the lake of fire. Thus, the event that closes the Millennium is the final consummation of God's victory over Satan's rebellion, a victory revealed through the cross, which was the binding of Satan, the event that began the Millennium.

COMMENTARY

The primary exegetical focus on this passage in Revelation has been on the thousand-year reign, otherwise known as the Millennium. Historically, there have been three basic understandings of this portion of John's vision: premillennial, postmillennial, and amillennial. The premillennial view understands Revelation 20 as describing the imminent return of Jesus, usually at the close of a period of tribulation, to reign during a thousand-year period of peace on earth. The period will begin with the resurrection of the righteous, who are joined with believers who are still alive, and they will reign with Christ during the Millennium. The Millennium closes with the resurrection of the wicked for judgment. There are two variations on the premillennial perspective. Pretribulation premillennialists believe that Christ will return to gather the faithful prior to a period of tribulation on the earth and then return at the close of the tribulation to begin his millennial reign. Posttribulation premillennialists believe Christ will return at the close of the tribulation period to inaugurate his reign.

Postmillennialists believe in Christ's return at the close of a millennium of peace and prosperity under Christian dominance. Some postmillennialists believe in a literal thousand-year period, but most see John's thousand years as representative of a long, indefinite period of time. Most postmillenialists believe this period has already begun. During this time, the Kingdom of God will gradually displace the forces of evil until God's Kingdom comes "on earth, as it is in heaven" (Matt 6:10). There are two basic views of how this will take place. Revivalist postmillennialists believe the Kingdom will grow through the conversion of humanity one person at a time. Reconstructionist postmillennialists believe the Kingdom will come through changing the social, legal, and political institutions of society.

The amillennial perspective does not envision a thousand-year historical period, but understands this image in Revelation to be symbolic of the church age. At the end of this period Christ will return in final judgment and establish the new creation. The amillennial view was held by several of the early church leaders[1] and systematized by St. Augustine. It was the dominant understanding of Revelation 20 until the Reformation. It is this understanding of John's vision that seems most likely to me.

Statements in the Bible about a "thousand years" do not point to a literal one thousand calendar years; rather, they evoke the notion of longevity. The psalmist writes, "For you, a thousand years are as a passing day, as brief as a few night hours" (Ps 90:4). This image was varied slightly by Peter, "A day is like a thousand years to the Lord, and a thousand years is like a day" (2 Pet 3:8). It seems as if the psalmist and Peter were using antithetical imagery, contrasting the longest conceivable period of time with the shortest. If this is the case, then "a thousand years" would be better understood as "an eon" or "an era." This possibility seems to be confirmed by the writer of Ecclesiastes who states, "He might live a thousand years twice over" (Eccl 6:6). This translation is faithful to the Hebrew; it does not say "two thousand years," but "a thousand years twice." The Hebrew Old Testament has the number 2,000 frequently. There is no linguistic or grammatical problem with writing "two thousand." It would seem certain, therefore, that "a thousand years" is an image for the largest conceivable unit of time. If you want to emphasize it, as in Ecclesiastes, you do it twice.

If the thousand years is an image for an indeterminate period of time, its parameters are then established by the events that begin and end it. The thousand years commence with the binding of Satan by the Messiah. To determine this event, we must return to the beast and false prophet being thrown alive into the lake of fire

(19:20). John had seen (13:1-18) that the beast and false prophet incarnate Satan's rebellion against God and deceive humanity into the same rebellion. They are the means through which Satan holds the citizens of fallen Babylon in destructive and dehumanizing bondage. This might be illustrated thus:

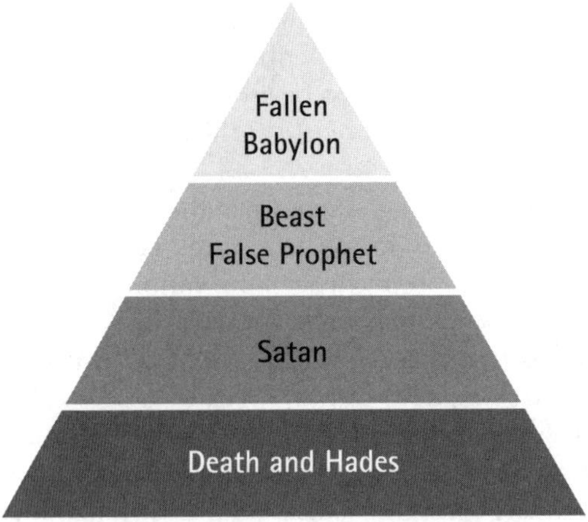

THE REBELLIOUS ORDER

If the beast and false prophet are removed from the structure, then Satan's power over the citizens of fallen Babylon is potentially broken. This is what John sees in 19:20. Through the cross of Jesus, the citizens of fallen Babylon were provided the possibility of liberation from the destructive and dehumanizing bondage of the beast and false prophet. They were "thrown alive into the fiery lake," so that Satan might not deceive the nations. If people become followers of the Lamb, Satan's power over them is broken. If, however, they choose to live in rebellion against God, then Satan still holds power over them because the beast and false prophet are still "alive."

John was seeing that the cross is the binding of Satan—a reality for believers and a potential reality for unbelievers. Jesus himself indicated this in John's Gospel: "The time for judging this world has come, when Satan, the ruler of this world, will be cast out. And when I am lifted up from the earth, I will draw everyone to myself" (John 12:31-32). John saw in his vision another dimension of the cross of the Messiah—it is the binding of Satan and the beginning of a new era of God's redemptive purpose for humanity.

The vision here gives new insight into the image of the beast's mortal wound that was healed (see 13:14, which literally reads, "who had the wound of the sword and lived"). For those who follow the Lamb, the cross is a mortal wound to the powers of rebellion—their destructive and dehumanizing bondage over those people is broken. To those who continue to worship the beast, however, the "mortal wound" is as if it never happened—they continue to be held in bondage.

If Satan is bound and shut up in the bottomless pit, as John claims, then why is there so much evil in the world? This is the mystery that the vision has been portraying in a variety of ways. Satan's realm is seen first as the "sea" under God's feet (4:6); obviously God is sovereign over that realm, yet it still exercises its destructive and dehumanizing power in human history. It is seen next as the three riders (6:3-8) who are allowed ("permission" is another expression of God's sovereignty over the realm of evil) to spread destruction, famine, and death through human history. Then John saw the fallenness of creation (8:6-12) and the torment and death caused by sin in human lives (8:13–9:21). He saw the beast and false prophet (13:1-18) who lead the citizens of fallen Babylon into a worldview and lifestyle of destructive rebellion against God. The rebellious realm is seen, finally, as the prostitute who leads the world into the dehumanizing bondage of her rebellion against God, a vision of a reality of such magnitude that even John was amazed (17:6). All of these images portray realities that have been incarnated consistently in human history since the cross of Christ. If the cross of Christ is, indeed, the binding of Satan, how is it that evil continues to reign as though nothing has happened?

This is what Paul calls "the mystery of lawlessness" (2 Thess 2:7, RSV). John's vision doesn't attempt to "solve" the mystery, except to consistently reaffirm that for those who follow the Lamb, for those "purchased from among the people on the earth [i.e., fallen Babylon]" (14:4), for those who refuse to worship the beast or its image and to receive its mark, Satan has no power to hold them in his destructive and dehumanizing bondage any longer. These overcome Satan by the blood of the Lamb. This does not mean that Christians will never experience tribulation at the hands of fallen Babylon. In fact, the vision makes it unmistakably clear that being a faithful follower of the Lamb all but ensures tribulation from fallen Babylon. The dragon is at war with God's children (12:17), and his agent, the beast, is allowed to make war upon them and to kill them (13:7). This becomes unavoidably clear when John sees that one group of those who are reigning with the Messiah are those who have been killed "for their testimony about Jesus and for proclaiming the word of God" (20:4).

Reigning with the Messiah is the reality of life for God's faithful people, the citizens of New Jerusalem. It is living, as Paul said, with our lives centered "on the realities of heaven, where Christ sits in the place of honor at God's right hand" (Col 3:1). But it is a "reigning" far different from the world's concept. Paul states it almost as strongly as John's vision:

> *Who will separate us from the love of Christ? Will hardship, or distress, or persecution, or famine, or nakedness, or peril, or sword? As it is written, "For your sake we are being killed all day long; we are accounted as sheep to be slaughtered." No, in all these things we are more than conquerors through him who loved us. For I am convinced that neither death, nor life, nor angels, nor rulers, nor things present, nor things to come, nor powers, nor height, nor depth, nor anything else in all creation, will be able to separate us from the love of God in Christ Jesus our Lord.* (Rom 8:35-39, NRSV)

It is this kind of "reigning" that enables faithful martyrs to go to death singing and forgiving their killers. It is this kind of "reigning" that enables God's faithful to love their enemies and pray for those who persecute them (Matt 5:44). It is this kind of "reigning" that enables the citizens of New Jerusalem to "offer the other cheek" (Matt 5:39), to go the second mile (Matt 5:41). It is this kind of "reigning" that enables a Mother Teresa to become a saint losing herself among the lowest and least of the dregs of Calcutta. It is a "reigning" in which one gains oneself by losing oneself, lives by dying, wins by losing, is strong through weakness, and is exalted through lowliness. It is a "reigning" that comes only by radical abandonment to the one who reigns forever and ever.

Such abandonment is the essence of the life of holiness, the kind of life that is fundamental to being "priests of God." Instead of spending our time and energies trying to determine when the end of the world might come and doing just enough to ensure that we will be on the "right" side when it happens, we should devote ourselves to the pursuit of that "holiness without which no one will see the Lord" (Heb 12:14, NRSV). John's vision asserts that being priests of God and reigning with the Messiah are two parts of a single reality. We "reign" when we are faithful "priests" of God in our fallen Babylon world. A "priest" stands between the holiness of God and the unholiness of the world. To be a "priest" is to bring the world into the presence of God to be made holy and to bring the presence of God into the world to offer it cleansing from its defilement, liberation from its bondages, healing of its brokenness, and transformation into wholeness. As John will see at the end of his vision, the leaves of the tree of life are for the healing of the nations (22:2).

This is undoubtedly why John saw that the people of God are in human history on earth right to the end. Misleading theories about the "Rapture" have horribly skewed the perceptions of many Christians. John's vision makes it unmistakably clear that God's faithful people are at the center of things right up to the end. Rapture theories, with their varied expectations that Christians will be taken out of the world before the end, have fueled escapist perspectives that are detrimental to a proper understanding of Christian life. Christians exist, not as some special group who will be spared the cataclysmic end of the world, but as those in whom God is present for the redemption of the world. Our role is to be priests, not prognosticators. As those who have been regenerated with Christ via his resurrection, we live in the era between the victory of God in the cross of Jesus and the consummation of that victory in his return at the close of human history. We are called to be faithful priests of God who "reign" with Christ in our portion of this period.

It is my view (as well as that of other commentators, cf. Kline 1976; Corsini 1983:379; Wall 1991:239) that the "first resurrection" signifies spiritual regeneration via union with Christ in his resurrection. However, since the time of the early church, there have been two different perspectives on the "first resurrection." One group of early writers viewed this as the resurrection of the righteous at the end of the age,[2] others as the resurrection out of spiritual death into life with Christ (which is my view).[3] It is interesting that most of the early writers understood the first resurrection as coming to the life of faith in Christ, but the preponderance of contemporary commentators hold that the first resurrection is of the righteous at the end of the present age.[4] This may be due to the strong influence of various dispensational interpretations of Revelation that have arisen in the last couple of centuries. One common feature of these interpretations is the idea that the Millennium (the thousand years of 20:2-7) lies in the future and that the first resurrection takes place before or at the beginning of the thousand years. But this idea seems to be contrary to other New Testament understandings of resurrection. Consider a few examples:

In response to Martha's affirmation of a physical resurrection at the last day (John 11:24), Jesus said, "I am the resurrection and the life. Those who believe in me, even though they die, will live, and everyone who lives and believes in me will never die" (John 11:25-26, NRSV). Note first, that Jesus equates resurrection with life.[5] Second, Jesus indicated that believing in him results in life, a life that not even death can obliterate. While Jesus made it clear that this is a life that transcends physical death, it is obvious he was speaking of a life that one who believes in him has in this world. Third, Jesus appears to equate this life with believing, "everyone who lives and believes in me." Fourth, Jesus indicates that one who has such life will never die. It might be argued that this point proves Jesus was speaking of a life beyond physical death, but the second point establishes the context for the fourth. Jesus was speaking of a life in him that one experiences in this world but that also extends beyond physical death. This is a common theme in John's Gospel (see John 3:15-16, 36; 5:24; 6:40, 47). John also records Jesus' saying, "Soon the world will no longer see me, but you will see me. Since I live, you also will live" (John 14:19). Here Jesus links the disciples' life with his resurrection. It would seem, therefore, that John understood resurrection life as a life of faith in Christ in this world.

Paul seems to have the same idea: "Therefore we have been buried with him by baptism into death, so that, just as Christ was raised from the dead by the glory of the Father, so we too might walk in newness of life. For if we have been united with him in a death like his, we will certainly be united with him in a resurrection like his" (Rom 6:4-5, NRSV). No one would argue that believers have died physically in their baptism. Rather, their existence apart from Christ, a spiritual deadness (Eph 2:1, 5) was dealt with, "buried." Paul then links the believer's "newness of life" with Christ's resurrection. This becomes even more explicit a few verses later: "We are sure of this because Christ was raised from the dead, and he will never die again. Death no longer has any power over him. When he died, he died once to break the power of sin. But now that he lives, he lives for the glory of God. So you also should consider yourselves to be dead to the power of sin and alive to God through Christ Jesus" (Rom 6:9-11). Resurrection is the focal theme of this passage, and death and life are the antitheses in which it is couched.

It seems abundantly clear that Paul links the resurrection of Jesus from death to life with the resurrection of the believer from deadness to life in Christ. The clearest statement of this is Ephesians 2:1-6:

> *Once you were dead because of your disobedience and your many sins. You used to live in sin, just like the rest of the world, obeying the devil—the commander of the powers in the unseen world. He is the spirit at work in the hearts of those who refuse to obey God. All of us used to live that way, following the passionate desires and inclinations of our sinful nature. By our very nature we were subject to God's anger, just like everyone else. But God is so rich in mercy, and he loved us so much, that even though we were dead because of our sins, he gave us life when he raised Christ from the dead. (It is only by God's grace that you have been saved!) For he raised us from the dead along with Christ and seated us with him in the heavenly realms because we are united with Christ Jesus.*

Here, Paul makes it unmistakably clear that believers have been resurrected with Christ out of their deadness into being alive with Christ. (See also Col 2:12; 3:1 for other instances of this understanding of resurrection.)

Interestingly, Paul provides us with another text that is strikingly similar to the final verses of this section of Revelation (namely, 20:8-10). In 2 Thessalonians 1:6-9 Paul wrote: "In his justice he will pay back those who persecute you [in John's imagery, Satan and his forces, Rev 20:8]. And God will provide rest for you who are being persecuted and also for us [in John's imagery, the camp of the saints, the holy city, Rev 20:9a] when the Lord Jesus appears from heaven. He will come with his mighty angels, in flaming fire [cf. Rev 20:9b, "fire from heaven came down"],[6] bringing judgment on those who don't know God and on those who refuse to obey the Good News of our Lord Jesus [cf. Rev 20:9c, "and consumed them"]. They will be punished with eternal destruction [cf. Rev 20:10, "thrown into the fiery lake . . . tormented . . . forever and ever"], forever separated from the Lord and from his glorious power." This is the holiness of God consummating the victory over the realm of unholiness, the victory that was won in the Lamb slain before the foundation of the world.

ENDNOTES

1. Justin Martyr, Origen, Clement of Alexandria.
2. See Victorinus of Petrovium *Commentary on the Apocalypse* 20.1-2.
3. Victorinus of Petrovium *Commentary on the Apocalypse* 20.1-2, (Johannes Haussleiter, *Corpus Scriptorum Ecclesiasticorum Latinorum* [Vienna, 1916], 49:3); Oecumenius *Commentary on the Apocalypse* 20.4-8, (M. De Groote, *Traditio Exegetica Graeca* [Louvain: Peeters, 1998], 8:253-255); Augustine *City of God* (Gerald G. Walsh, *Fathers of the Church: A New Translation* [Washington, DC: Catholic University of America Press, 1947], 24:279); Primasius *Commentary on the Apocalypse* (A. W. Adams, *Corpus Christianorum.* Series Latina [Turnhout, Belgium: Brepols, 1953] 92:277); Origen *Homilies on Jeremiah* 2.3.1-3 (John Clark Smith, *Fathers of the Church: A New Translation* [Washington, DC: Catholic University of America Press, 1947] 97:26-27); Caesarius of Arles, *Exposition on the Apocalypse* 20.5, Homily 18 (J.-P. Migne, *Patrologia cursus completus.* Series Latina [Paris: Migne, 1844–1864] 35:2448).
4. See Mounce 1977:354-359; Beale 1999:1003-1017; Witherington 2003:248-250.
5. This presumes that *kai* [TG2532, ZG2779] is paratactic—i.e., it joins two equal things. Thus, the phrase might well be translated "I am the resurrection—that is, the life."
6. The image of "fire from heaven" is used throughout the OT to depict the action of God's holiness against that which is unholy (Gen 19:24; Exod 9:23; Lev 10:1-3; Num 11:1; 16:35; 2 Kgs 1:10-12; Pss 97:3; 106:18; Ezek 38:22-23; 39:6-7).

◆ 3. The final fruits of victory (20:11–21:8)

[11]And I saw a great white throne and the one sitting on it. The earth and sky fled from his presence, but they found no place to hide. [12]I saw the dead, both great and small, standing before God's throne. And the books were opened, including the Book of Life. And the dead were judged according to what they had done, as recorded in the books. [13]The sea gave up its dead, and death and the grave* gave up their dead. And all were judged according to their deeds. [14]Then death and the grave

were thrown into the lake of fire. This lake
of fire is the second death. 15And anyone
whose name was not found recorded in
the Book of Life was thrown into the lake
of fire.

CHAPTER 21

Then I saw a new heaven and a new earth,
for the old heaven and the old earth had
disappeared. And the sea was also gone.
2And I saw the holy city, the new Jerusa-
lem, coming down from God out of heav-
en like a bride beautifully dressed for her
husband.
3I heard a loud shout from the throne,
saying, "Look, God's home is now among
his people! He will live with them, and
they will be his people. God himself will
be with them.* 4He will wipe every tear
from their eyes, and there will be no more
death or sorrow or crying or pain. All
these things are gone forever."
5And the one sitting on the throne said,
"Look, I am making everything new!" And
then he said to me, "Write this down, for
what I tell you is trustworthy and true."
6And he also said, "It is finished! I am the
Alpha and the Omega—the Beginning and
the End. To all who are thirsty I will give
freely from the springs of the water of
life. 7All who are victorious will inherit all
these blessings, and I will be their God,
and they will be my children.
8"But cowards, unbelievers, the corrupt,
murderers, the immoral, those who prac-
tice witchcraft, idol worshipers, and all
liars—their fate is in the fiery lake of
burning sulfur. This is the second death."

20:13 Greek *and Hades;* also in 20:14. **21:3** Some manuscripts read *God himself will be with them, their God.*

NOTES

20:11 ***great white throne.*** This seems to be an image of God's enduring holiness. White is associated with holiness throughout the vision. Some in Sardis had not "soiled their clothes" and so would walk with Jesus in "white" (3:4). The redeemed had washed their robes in the blood of the Lamb and made them "white" (7:14). The "white" garment consistently represents a life of holiness. God's throne is associated with God's holiness (cf. Pss 11:4; 47:8; Wis 9:10).

The earth and sky fled from his presence. The unholiness of the fallen creation cannot endure in the presence of God's holiness. Its fallen nature is made clear in 21:1, where John indicates that the first creation ("the old heaven and the old earth") had passed away and was replaced by the new creation ("a new heaven and a new earth").

they found no place to hide. Lit., "no place was found for them." This repeats the phrase used of Satan and his angels in 12:8, following their defeat in heaven. This seems to confirm that God's holiness and the fallen creation are the focal issues here. Judgment deals with the entirety of the fall: heavenly (Satan), earthly (all whose names are not in the Book of Life), and creation (earth and sky).

20:12 ***the books were opened, including the Book of Life.*** These are common images in Jewish writings. For "books," see Dan 7:10; 2 Esdr [*4 Ezra*] 6:20; *Pirke Aboth* 2:1; *1 Enoch* 81:4; 89:68-77; 98:7-8; 104:7; *2 Baruch* 24:1. For "the Book of Life," see Exod 32:32-33; Ps 69:28; Isa 4:3; Dan 12:1; Phil 4:3; *1 Enoch* 104:1; 108:3; *Jubilees* 36:10. For the books being opened on the Day of Judgment, see *1 Enoch* 47:3.

20:13 ***The sea gave up its dead, and death and the grave gave up their dead.*** This parallel structure by itself doesn't mean that "sea" equals "death and hades," but the fact that three verses later John indicates that there is no "sea" in the new creation indicates he was not speaking of the earth's oceans. He was, rather, using "sea" as an image for the rebellious realm as he had from the beginning (cf. note on 4:6). Since "Death and Hades" is another image for the rebellious realm, the parallelism of structure seems to also convey a parallelism of content.

20:14 ***This lake of fire is the second death.*** John is speaking here of spiritual death, existence alienated from God. He makes it quite clear in 14:10-11 that the citizens of fallen Babylon are existing in the presence of God ("the holy angels and the Lamb") in a condition characterized by fiery torment, the smoke of which rises "forever and ever." This is clearly not destruction (see commentary on 14:9-11).

21:1 ***I saw a new heaven and a new earth, for the old heaven and the old earth had disappeared.*** "Heaven" should be translated as "sky" (the Greek term for both "heaven" and "sky" is *ouranos* [TG3772, ZG4041]). This disappearance is what John noted at 20:11, there correctly translated as "earth and sky." John was seeing the new creation that replaces the old. That this is a new creation is confirmed in John's added note in this verse: "The sea was also gone." Since "the sea" has represented the rebellious realm, its absence from the new creation is to be expected (cf. notes on 4:6; 20:13).

21:6 ***I am the Alpha and the Omega—the Beginning and the End.*** This brings both the beginning and consummation of God's purposes together in the affirmation (see note on 3:14). This is strong assurance for John's readers, suffering tribulation at the hands of their fallen Babylon world, that God is in control of all things.

21:7 ***All who are victorious.*** These are the ones who appear throughout the vision as those in the process of "conquering." See 2:7, 11, 17, 26; 3:5, 12, 21; 15:2, where the Greek has a present participle, indicating the continual process of conquering, that is, living a New Jerusalem life against the grain and amid the pressure of the fallen Babylon world.

COMMENTARY

John now sees the final judgment at God's white throne. The throne plays a focal role in John's vision. It appears 32 times and is the center from which all the action of God emerges. John here sees God's holiness as the standard of judgment (see note on 20:11). The throne with one sitting on it is a reprise of the vision of God in 4:2. John saw "the dead . . . standing before God's throne" (20:12). Who are these? Since the redeemed have already been seen standing before the throne (7:9), it would seem that the group John saw here are the citizens of fallen Babylon, "the rest of the dead," who do not come back to life until whenever the thousand years should end (20:5). However, it is also possible that the dead are all those who were not Christian martyrs; hence, these dead would include both the righteous and unrighteous (see note on 20:4).

Then John saw that the books were opened, including the Book of Life. Many Jews believed that each person in the covenant community had a "book" in heaven in which were written all the deeds of their life (see note on 20:12). At the judgment, the books would be opened, and they would be "judged according to what they had done, as recorded in the books" (20:12). Their good and bad deeds would be totaled (cf. Pss 28:4; 62:12; Dan 7:10; Mal 3:16; Rom 2:6-8; *4 Ezra* 6:17-20; *1 Enoch* 81:1-4; 97:6; 104:7; *2 Enoch* 52:15). If the good outweighed the bad, you remained in the Book of Life and entered the kingdom; if not, you were erased from the Book of Life and were excluded from the kingdom along with the Gentiles. (See commentary on 3:5; notes on 13:8; 17:8 for the image of the "Book of Life.") Revelation 20:15, however, implies no such totaling as a basis for entering the kingdom.

"Anyone whose name was not found recorded in the Book of Life" (20:15) joined Satan, the beast, false prophet, and Death and Hades in the lake of fire (20:14; cf.

1 Enoch 90:26, which speaks of a place of fire as the destiny of the wicked). The entire realm of rebellion is thereby consigned to its eternal position in relationship to the holiness of God. This lake of fire is called the "second death." Apparently the "first death" is physical death, although neither John nor the vision clarify this. The image of fire is commonly associated with God's judgment in Jewish writings (Pss 11:6; 21:9; 68:2; 78:21-22; 97:3; 106:18; Isa 30:27, 33; 33:14; 66:15-16, 24; Dan 7:11; Sir 21:9; *2 Enoch* 10:1-6). Since fire is also an image for God's holiness, the vision suggests that the destiny of the unholy is to spend eternity in the presence of the holiness of God. John has already seen this reality at 14:10, where those who worship the beast and its image are "tormented with fire . . . in the presence of the holy angels and the Lamb." Another image of this reality is the holy city, New Jerusalem, pictured as right in the midst of fallen Babylon (22:15).

After John sees that all the negative elements are cast into the lake of fire, he sees a vision of the new heaven and new earth. This is a vision, using the imagery of Isaiah (Isa 65:17-19; 66:22), of the restoration of creation to its original wholeness, the final expectation associated with the restoration of the kingdom to Israel. Wright (1992:332) summarizes the first-century Jewish perspective well: "The Jews who believed in resurrection did so as one part of a larger belief in the renewal of the whole created order."

Again, playing off of Isaiah's imagery (Isa 4:4ff; 24:23; 27:13; 30:19; 33:20; 40:2; 52:9; 62:6-7; 65:18-19; 66:10ff), John saw the holy city, New Jerusalem, as the consummation of God's purposes, the fulfillment of God's promises. The vision conjoins the image of New Jerusalem with the earlier image of the faithful as the bride of the Lamb (19:7-8). John was seeing that New Jerusalem is not so much a "place" as it is the community of God's faithful people, the kingdom of priests.

Following this vision, Revelation provides a collage of prophetic images that fulfill God's old covenant purposes and promises:

TEXT FROM REVELATION 21:3-4	PURPOSE	PROMISE
"Look, God's home is now among his people! He will live with them."	Lev 26:11-12	Ezek 37:27; 43:7; Zech 8:8
"They will be his people."	Gen 17:7	Jer 31:33
"He will wipe every tear from their eyes."		Isa 25:8; 30:19; 61:3
"There will be no more death."		Isa 25:7
"These things are gone forever."		Isa 43:18-19 (cf. *2 Esdr* 7:113-114)

The vision indicates that the final restoration of the kingdom will be a new creation in which all the consequences of the rebellion will be absent.

Then John heard a voice from the throne that said, "I am making everything new!" (21:5). In light of John's vision of the final consummation of all things, we would expect here, "I *have* made all things new." But the present tense may relate to the subversion of Jewish expectations that John's vision reveals. We have seen that the vision reveals that in Jesus the Messiah, God has fulfilled his promises and restored the kingdom to Israel (but included Gentiles), and consummated the old covenant (but made his kingdom of priests from every tribe, nation, language, and people). But such claims flew in the face of the Jewish expectation that when the kingdom was restored, the enemies of God's people would be overthrown and Israel would rule over the Gentiles in a new creation. The vision has revealed that although the kingdom has been restored, its final consummation is reserved for the climax of history. Between the restoration and the consummation, the faithful people of God continue to experience tribulation at the hands of fallen Babylon. All of history, however, is moving toward the consummation of God's victory. Thus, God is continually making all things new, in spite of all appearances to the contrary in ongoing human history.

In 21:6b-8, the vision shifts from future fulfillment to present hope with a series of things that will be fulfilled in the future. That the vision has returned to the present from the view of future consummation is seen in the promise to all who are victorious (see note on 21:7). That the vision has returned to the midst of ongoing history becomes unmistakable when John sees that the "cowards, unbelievers, the corrupt, murderers, the immoral, those who practice witchcraft, idol worshipers, and all liars" (21:8) are still around. All these had been thrown into the lake of fire back at 20:15. Now that consequence of their rebellion once again lies in the future.

In this section of Revelation, we see that God's holiness is the ultimate reality, the enduring norm against which all creation is measured. God's throne is the seat of absolute holiness. Anything unholy is repelled by such holiness. But since God is the reality who encompasses all, where can unholiness go to avoid the presence of holiness? As the psalmist knew well, it is impossible to escape from the presence of God (Ps 139:7-12). God's holiness is a fire that burns against all that is unholy. For those who desire to be holy, the fire of God's holiness is a refining fire that burns out all that is unholy in them. For those who desire to be unholy, God's holiness is a consuming fire that continually burns against the very essence of who they have chosen to be.

Holiness, however, is primarily a matter of being, not doing. The holiness movement has often gone astray in placing its focus upon behavior. When holiness is defined only by behavior, the most destructive forms of legalism and works-righteousness can result. A person can be in perfect obedience to some holiness code, but their spirit can remain selfish, bitter, judgmental, and hard. If holy deeds are not the outer manifestation of holiness of being, they are empty and meaningless. In the terms of John's vision, our "book of deeds" may be exemplary; but if we are not in the Book of Life (i.e., we don't have holiness of being), then we have no part in God's realm.

The community of believers is the "holy" city (11:2; 21:2, 10; cf. 20:9), believers are "holy ones" (5:8; 8:3-4; 13:7, 10; 14:12; 16:6; 19:8; 20:9), those who participate in the first resurrection are holy (20:6), and the holy are to continue being holy in the midst of a fallen Babylon world (22:11). Furthermore, and perhaps most telling, is John's contrast between the "unclean" and those whose names are in the Lamb's Book of Life (21:27; see NLT mg). In Jewish tradition, "unclean" items are always profane and thus the antithesis of "holy" (cf. Lev 10:10; Isa 35:8; 52:1; Ezek 22:26; 44:23; cf. Paul's use of the terms in 1 Cor 7:14; 2 Cor 7:1; Eph 5:26). John seems to be indicating that holiness of life is commensurate with being in the Lamb's Book of Life.

To those who claimed exemplary deeds as their "ticket" into the Kingdom of God, Jesus said, "I never knew you. Get away from me, you who break God's laws" (Matt 7:23; see commentary on 19:1-10). Paul gives the same warning to the Christians of Colossae (Col 2:20-23). He begins by asking them, "If you died with Christ and thus were removed from the world's ways of ordering your life, why are you still living as though you were under the world's controls?" (my translation). One would then expect a catalogue of vices to illustrate how they were living. Paul does give a list, but it is a list of extreme holiness practices dealing with uncleanness (unholiness) by contact with unclean things (cf. Lev 5:2-3 [touch]; 11:8 [eat]; Deut 14:8 [taste and touch]). He singles out extremes established by human rules and traditions—"Do not taste, do not touch, do not handle." Paul warns that all these kinds of things only result in "perishing with use." What "perishes" if nothing is tasted, touched, or handled? Apparently the person following such practices! Paul admits that such practices have an "appearance of wisdom"; they make a person appear holy through "rigorous religiosity, a professed humility, even ascetic treatment of the body." His bottom line, however, is that such deeds are of no value to anyone, they only feed the "flesh life." For Paul, life in the flesh is a self-referenced life, life lived under one's own control (2 Cor 5:15). The worst form of the "flesh life" for Paul is when it becomes religious. Paul knew from his own efforts at trying to be holy as a Pharisee that this route is a dead end. Paul said about his own "book of deeds"—"as for righteousness [holiness], I obeyed the law without fault" (Phil 3:6). Paul's "book of deeds" was perfect, but he realized he would have ended up in the lake of fire (so to speak) had he not come to faith in Jesus as Messiah and been enrolled in the Book of Life (Phil 4:3).

Another significant image in this section is that of the New Jerusalem, the city of God and bride of Christ. The image of "city" has an interesting role in the Bible. There is a city early in the biblical narrative that stands as the antithesis of the New Jerusalem appearing at the end of the story. The result of Cain's departure from the Lord (Gen 4:16) was life in a land of "wandering" (Heb., *nud* [TH5110, ZH5653], cf. *nod* [TH5113, ZH5655], "Nod"), an existence without a center to give identity, meaning, value, and purpose. When Cain "left the LORD's presence," he began building a city (Gen 4:17). He attempted to create a structure that would give identity, meaning, value, and purpose to himself and his family. The characteristics of Cain's city are elucidated in the story of Babel (Gen 11:2-4). These people either came from the east (NRSV, NKJV, RSV, KJV), or migrated to the east (NET, NLT, NIV, NASB); that is, they either came from the place to which Cain went, or like Cain they went to the east (Gen 4:16). In either case, these city builders are associated with Cain, the first city builder. They wanted (1) to build a city for themselves (i.e., a self-referenced mode of existence); (2) to build a tower with its top in the heavens (thus bringing God under their control—they are the ones who determine the access to "heaven"); (3) to make a name for themselves (i.e., determine their own definition of what it is to be human). All of this was in order to avoid a decentered existence—"scattered all over the world" (Gen 11:4).

John's vision of New Jerusalem (21:2; 22:4) provides the antithesis to Cain's city, epitomized in Babel. New Jerusalem is (1) God's provision of a God-referenced mode of being for true human identity, meaning, value, and purpose; (2) the city coming down from heaven (i.e., this sphere of life is graced by God to humanity and not the results of their efforts); (3) the place where people find true human identity in the image of God.

John saw that New Jerusalem is both a present reality and a future consummation. At each place where the vision mentions New Jerusalem coming down (3:12; 21:2, 10), it uses the present participle, suggesting that it is the present reality within which believers live their lives in the world. This is especially the case at 3:12, where Jesus speaks to the church in Philadelphia about the New Jerusalem that is coming down. This is one of the focal themes of John's vision—Christians are to live as citizens of New Jerusalem in the midst of a world ordered by the destructive and dehumanizing perspectives and values of fallen Babylon. Another image for this reality is that of conquering. Our fallen Babylon world constantly pressures us to conform to its perspectives, to adopt its values, to order our lives by its lifestyles, and to be in relationships with others according to its principles. To move against this stream, to live counterculturally as a citizen of New Jerusalem, is to "conquer" (cf. note on 21:7).

◆ C. New Jerusalem's Present Hope and Future Glory (21:9–22:9)

1. The nature of New Jerusalem (21:9-21)

9Then one of the seven angels who held the seven bowls containing the seven last plagues came and said to me, "Come with me! I will show you the bride, the wife of the Lamb."

10So he took me in the Spirit* to a great, high mountain, and he showed me the holy city, Jerusalem, descending out of heaven from God. 11It shone with the glory of God and sparkled like a precious stone—like jasper as clear as crystal. 12The city wall was broad and high, with twelve gates guarded by twelve angels. And the names of the twelve tribes of Israel were written on the gates. 13There were three gates on each side—east, north, south, and west. 14The wall of the city had twelve foundation stones, and on them were written the names of the twelve apostles of the Lamb.

15The angel who talked to me held in his hand a gold measuring stick to measure the city, its gates, and its wall. 16When he measured it, he found it was a square, as wide as it was long. In fact, its length and width and height were each 1,400 miles.* 17Then he measured the walls and found them to be 216 feet thick* (according to the human standard used by the angel).

18The wall was made of jasper, and the city was pure gold, as clear as glass. 19The wall of the city was built on foundation stones inlaid with twelve precious stones:* the first was jasper, the second sapphire, the third agate, the fourth emerald, 20the fifth onyx, the sixth carnelian, the seventh chrysolite, the eighth beryl, the ninth topaz, the tenth chrysoprase, the eleventh jacinth, the twelfth amethyst.

21The twelve gates were made of pearls—each gate from a single pearl! And the main street was pure gold, as clear as glass.

21:10 Or *in spirit.* **21:16** Greek *12,000 stadia* [2,220 kilometers]. **21:17** Greek *144 cubits* [65 meters]. **21:19** The identification of some of these gemstones is uncertain.

NOTES

21:9 ***the bride, the wife of the Lamb.*** The vision has already presented "bride" as an image for the faithful followers of the Lamb (19:7), and for the holy city, New Jerusalem (21:2). "Wife" is added here to heighten the contrast with the "prostitute" in 17:1.

21:10 ***he took me in the Spirit.*** The experience of being transported in the Spirit was not unusual in the OT (cf. 1 Kgs 18:12; 2 Kgs 2:16; Ezek 3:14; 8:3; 11:1, 24; 40:2).

high mountain. The establishment of Jerusalem on a high mountain was one piece of the Jewish expectation for the restoration of the kingdom, seen especially in Isa 2:2, "In the last days, the mountain of the LORD's house will be the highest of all." John's vision plays upon Ezekiel's vision of the Temple-city (Ezek 40–46).

21:11 ***It shone with the glory of God.*** In the Greek text, the city "has the glory of God." Since the "glory" *doxa* [TG1391, ZG1518] is the very essence of God's nature (see note on 1:6), John was indicating that the nature of New Jerusalem is God's nature.

jasper. That the nature of the New Jerusalem is the same as God's nature is confirmed when John describes the city as having the appearance of jasper and, a few verses later, that its walls are jasper (21:18). In his vision of God in heaven (ch 4), John's first description of God is as jasper (4:3). New Jerusalem manifests the very nature and being of God.

21:12-13 ***The city wall was broad and high.*** The rebuilding of walls was an image of restoration (Ezra 9:9; Mic 7:11), since walls gave security against an enemy. *Second Enoch* 65:10 envisions the restored community ("paradise") having a "great indestructible wall." A broad and high wall emphasizes both the fullness of the restoration and the security of the restored community.

twelve gates . . . twelve tribes. John here reflects Ezekiel's vision of the restored Jerusalem (Ezek 48:31-34) where the gates have the names of the twelve tribes of Israel.

21:14 ***the twelve apostles of the Lamb.*** Since John is seeing the restored Israel, now consisting of both the tribes of Israel (7:4-8) and innumerable Gentiles (7:9), the apostles become the foundations of the New Jerusalem.

21:15 ***a gold measuring stick.*** John continues to play off Ezekiel's vision (Ezek 40–42) and Zech 2:1.

21:16 ***a square . . . 1,400 miles.*** Lit., "12,000 stadia." In Ezekiel's vision, the restored Jerusalem is a square of 25,000 cubits (slightly over 7 miles). John's seemingly extreme amplification of the size of the New Jerusalem may have significance in the context of his readers (cf. commentary below).

its length and width and height were each 1,400 miles. As a cubic dwelling place of God (21:22), John is envisioning the New Jerusalem as the "holy of holies" in the Temple, which was also a cubic dwelling place of God (1 Kgs 6:20).

21:17 ***216 feet thick.*** Lit., "144 cubits" (cf. NLT mg). The tremendous thickness of the wall is an image of total impenetrability. Since the walls are jasper, symbolizing the nature of God (see note on 21:11), this seems to be an image of God's holiness, which is an impenetrable barrier to all that is unholy. When John saw that the unholiness of fallen Babylon is outside the walls (22:15), and that nothing unholy can enter (21:27), it would seem that the vision reflects Zech 2:5, where God is a "wall of fire" around the restored Jerusalem. The dimension (144=12x12) is perhaps symbolically important, and Beale (1999:1076) comments that the 144-cubit thickness of the wall "echoes the 144,000 as the complete number of God's people" (cf. 7:4-8; 14:1).

21:18 ***The wall was made of jasper.*** The final confirmation of the idea that the wall is the holiness of God comes when John sees that walls are made of jasper, the vision's first representation of God at 4:3.

21:19-21 The jewels John lists are related to those found on the breastplate of the high priest (Exod 28:15-21; 39:8-14), although not all the same stones are listed. According to Beale (1999:1080), "the differently named stones in Revelation are semantic equivalents of the ones in Exodus." Their order, however, is completely disarranged. This is not necessarily unusual. Josephus lists the jewels in the breastplate in *War* 5.234 [5.5.7] and in *Antiquities* 3.168 [3.7.5] in yet two other orders. Various intriguing theories have been proposed to explain this, but what is most probable is that we have here another modulation of imagery to indicate that while God has consummated the old covenant in the Messiah, the nature of the fulfillment is radically different from what was expected. Beale is most likely correct when he suggests that the linking of the jewels with the apostles, whose names are on the twelve foundations (21:14), is John's way of indicating that the apostles are "the paramount witnesses and representatives of true end-time Israel" (1999:1080). Isaiah also saw the restored Jerusalem as constructed of jewels: "I will rebuild you with precious jewels and make your foundations from [sapphires]. I will make your towers of sparkling rubies, your gates of shining gems, and your walls of precious stones" (Isa 54:11-12).

21:21 ***The twelve gates were made of pearls.*** The rabbinic tradition held a belief that the gates of the heavenly Jerusalem would be made of pearls (see *b. Bava Batra* 75a; *b. Sanhedrin* 100a).

COMMENTARY

The introduction to the vision of the bride, New Jerusalem, is, as noted above, parallel to the introduction to the prostitute, fallen Babylon. John added, "containing the seven last plagues," to make unmistakable the connection of this introduction to that of the prostitute in 17:1-6.

John tells us that he saw the New Jerusalem "descending out of heaven from God" (21:10). Rather than a static state, an accomplished reality, John sees New Jerusalem in an ongoing process of coming into being (see commentary on 20:11–21:8 regarding the Greek grammar, which indicates that the city is continually coming down). Some Jews believed that the heavenly Jerusalem was being preserved with God in heaven and would make its appearance at the end of the age when God restored the kingdom to Israel (*2 Baruch* 4:2-7). The same image is at work in Hebrews 11–12, where Abraham was "looking forward to a city with eternal foundations, a city designed and built by God" (Heb 11:10). All the faithful of the old covenant "saw it all from a distance" (Heb 11:13), the "heavenly homeland" where God had "prepared a city for them" (Heb 11:16). The writer of Hebrews then affirmed that the followers of the Messiah have now "come to Mount Zion, to the city of the living God, the heavenly Jerusalem" (Heb 12:22). John was seeing that it was already coming into being.

Many people today, as in John's day, think of the heavenly city as something that exists only in a far distant future. For his Jewish audience, John's vision must have been as radical an idea as Jesus' proclamation that the Kingdom of God had come (Mark 1:15) and was already in the midst of his hearers (Luke 17:21). The vision is revealing that the promised future context of human wholeness is already a present and ongoing reality for those who follow the Lamb. This is why the vision is so insistent that we must resist the values and perspectives of our fallen Babylon world that want to shape our worldview and lifestyle. We are citizens of God's New Jerusalem, and our life should be an incarnation of this reality.

The city with 12 gates and 12 foundation stones forms a 24-element structure around God, just as the 24 elders were seen encircling God at 4:4 (see notes and commentary there). Here the 12 gates and 12 foundation stones respectively represent (1) the old covenant community, the 12 tribes of Israel (21:12), and (2) its consummation in the new covenant community represented by the 12 apostles of the Lamb (21:14).

Like Ezekiel, John saw three gates on each side. Ezekiel, however, uses various orders of the cardinal directions in his descriptions (e.g., Ezek 42:16-19 uses E-N-S-W; Ezek 48:16-17 uses N-S-E-W). Of primary interest is the order of the gates in Ezekiel 48:30-34, which begins on the north wall and moves clockwise (N-E-S-W). At Revelation 21:13 in Codex Alexandrinus, one of the strongest manuscripts of Revelation (see "Canonicity and Textual History" in the Introduction; cf. Beale 1999:72), the order begins on the east wall and moves counterclockwise (E-N-W-S), the reverse of Ezekiel's order in Ezekiel 48:30-34. (A later transcriber apparently changed the reading of 21:13 from the order in Alexandrinus to that of Ezek 42:16-19, resulting in the order found in English translations of the New Testament.) As we have seen so frequently throughout the vision, John once again modulates the images he uses to indicate that the old has now been fulfilled in the Messiah. As in Ezekiel's vision, the 12 tribes of Israel are the means of access into the presence of God.

Continuing Ezekiel's imagery (Ezek 40:3-5) as well as Zechariah's (Zech 2:1), John's angel "held in his hand a gold measuring stick to measure the city" (21:15). John's vision modulates the image, however, in that John saw a cubic city of tremendous dimensions—1,400 miles on each side and walls 216 feet thick (21:16-17). The length and breadth of the walls in Greek are given as 12,000 stadia. With 12 edges on a cube, this totals 144,000—the figure the vision uses elsewhere to represent God's covenant people. The number is seen first at 7:4, representing the old covenant people, then at 14:1, representing the new covenant people. Now it is seen again in the dimensions of New Jerusalem, which is constituted of both the old (12 tribes of Israel) and new covenant people (apostles of the Lamb).

John also noted that the city is pure gold (21:18). The image of a cubic, golden dwelling place of God points to the Most Holy Place in the Temple, which was a cubic space overlaid with gold (1 Kgs 6:20). Thus, the vision is portraying the redeemed community of God's people, New Jerusalem, as the Most Holy Place—the dwelling place of God. John saw what Paul described when he wrote that the redeemed community is built upon the foundation of the apostles (as is New Jerusalem—21:14) and is a holy temple, a dwelling place for God (Eph 2:19-22).

It is very likely that the dimensions of the city are significant in at least two ways. First, as noted above, each of the 12 edges of the cubic city is 12,000 stadia for a total of 144,000—the image representing the citizenship of God's covenant people. Second, this 1,400-mile cube makes a powerful statement when considered geographically. If you take a map of the Mediterranean and overlay upon it a square 1,400 miles on a side, with its center on the island of Patmos, the place of John's vision, you find that the western edge of the square is where Rome is found, the eastern edge is where Jerusalem is located, and the northern and southern edges roughly follow the northern and southern limits of the Roman Empire in the first century. While this in itself is interesting, what is most significant is that when John received his vision, almost every Christian alive in the world lived within the boundaries of that square! John was seeing that God's New Jerusalem is set down right in the midst of the fallen Babylon world of the Roman Empire.

If John were to receive his vision today, the dimensions of the cubic city would be 8,000 miles, encompassing the entire planet, since Christians are now found throughout the world. The vision calls us to a very different understanding of ourselves, our communities of faith, and our life in the world. It is not a call limited to John's vision, however. In the New Testament we are reminded that we are "resident aliens" in the world (Heb 11:13; 1 Pet 1:1, 17; 2:11), and Paul exhorts us, "If you have been raised with Christ, then seek the things that are above, where Christ is, seated at the right hand of God. Orient your entire being around things that are above, not things that are on earth" (Col 3:1-2, my translation). We live in a world in rebellion against God. All its perceptions, values, and behaviors are tainted by that rebellion even if they are not actual acts of rebellion in and of themselves. The letters to the seven churches reveal how easy it is for citizens of New Jerusalem to make accommodations to their fallen Babylon world.

Does this mean that Christians should isolate themselves from their fallen Babylon world? Not at all—fallen Babylon is the place of our ministry. We are to be fully engaged with our fallen Babylon world on behalf of the one whose death has broken the power of fallen Babylon and liberates persons from its destructive and dehumanizing bondages. Christians are revolutionaries in the best sense of the term. We do not revolt against fallen Babylon, living lives of negative reaction to it; we live lives that incarnate the reality of God's kingdom that turns the world upside down. When we do this, we incarnate the reality of New Jerusalem coming down from heaven in our world.

◆ 2. The people of New Jerusalem (21:22–22:9)

22 I saw no temple in the city, for the Lord
God Almighty and the Lamb are its tem-
ple. 23 And the city has no need of sun or
moon, for the glory of God illuminates
the city, and the Lamb is its light. 24 The
nations will walk in its light, and the
kings of the world will enter the city in
all their glory. 25 Its gates will never be
closed at the end of day because there is
no night there. 26 And all the nations will
bring their glory and honor into the city.
27 Nothing evil* will be allowed to enter,
nor anyone who practices shameful idol-
atry and dishonesty—but only those
whose names are written in the Lamb's
Book of Life.

CHAPTER 22

Then the angel showed me a river with the
water of life, clear as crystal, flowing from
the throne of God and of the Lamb. 2 It
flowed down the center of the main street.
On each side of the river grew a tree of life,
bearing twelve crops of fruit,* with a fresh
crop each month. The leaves were used for
medicine to heal the nations.

3 No longer will there be a curse upon
anything. For the throne of God and of
the Lamb will be there, and his servants
will worship him. 4 And they will see his
face, and his name will be written on their
foreheads. 5 And there will be no night
there—no need for lamps or sun—for the
Lord God will shine on them. And they will
reign forever and ever.

6 Then the angel said to me, "Everything
you have heard and seen is trustworthy
and true. The Lord God, who inspires his
prophets,* has sent his angel to tell his
servants what will happen soon.*"

7"Look, I am coming soon! Blessed are those who obey the words of prophecy written in this book.*"

8I, John, am the one who heard and saw all these things. And when I heard and saw them, I fell down to worship at the feet of the angel who showed them to me.
9But he said, "No, don't worship me. I am a servant of God, just like you and your brothers the prophets, as well as all who obey what is written in this book. Worship only God!"

21:27 Or *ceremonially unclean.* **22:2** Or *twelve kinds of fruit.* **22:6a** Or *The Lord, the God of the spirits of the prophets.* **22:6b** Or *suddenly,* or *quickly;* also in 22:7, 12, 20. **22:7** Or *scroll;* also in 22:9, 10, 18, 19.

NOTES

21:23 ***the Lamb is its light.*** The NLT translation has lost the power of the imagery here. It is God who "illuminates" (*ephōtisen* [TG5461, ZG5894]), but the Lamb is the "lamp" (*luchnos* [TG3088, ZG3394]). Earlier, John had seen that the church is the lampstand (1:20). The picture is complete: The lampstand (the church) holds the lamp (the Lamb), which displays the light (God).

21:27 ***evil.*** Lit., "common." John used a term here (*koinos* [TG2839, ZG3123]) that had great significance in Jewish thinking. "Common" was the opposite of "holy." It is often coupled with "unclean," a term that inherently implied unholiness.

shameful idolatry and dishonesty. Unholiness is characterized as doing, lit., "abomination and falsehood." The family of terms to which John's term "shameful idolatry" (*bdelugma* [TG946, ZG1007]) belongs was used predominately in the LXX to translate the Hebrew term *to'ebah* [TH8441, ZH9359] (e.g., in LXX Gen 43:32; Lev 18:22; Deut 7:25; 1 Kgs 14:24). The Greek term took on special meaning when it was used in the LXX to describe the desecration of the Temple by Antiochus Epiphanes in 167 BC (Dan 9:27; 11:31; 12:11; although Daniel uses the Heb. *shiqquts* [TH8251, ZH9199], this is also generally translated *bdelugma* in the LXX). Antiochus placed a bust of himself styled as Zeus in the Most Holy Place. "Falsehood" is used throughout the vision to depict the citizens of fallen Babylon (2:2; 3:9; 21:8; 22:15). The primary characteristic of those who follow the Lamb is that "they have told no lies; they are without blame" (14:5).

the Lamb's Book of Life. This repeats an image that has thread its way through the vision (see 3:5 and 20:12). The vision reminds the church that holiness comes through the Lamb, and not through self-efforts as some have believed.

22:2 ***tree of life.*** There is a most interesting passage in *Testament of Levi* 18, an early Jewish writing (cf. Beale 1999:235, 268). There the Lord will raise up a new priest (cf. 1:13), who shall execute righteous judgment (cf. 19:11) and shine forth as the sun on the earth (cf. 1:16; 10:1; 18:1). In his priesthood sin will come to an end (cf. 1:5), Satan will be bound by him (cf. 20:2), and his followers will tread upon evil (cf. 15:2) and eat from the tree of life. This emphasizes how John's vision draws from the Jewish pool of images and the Jewish expectations of the Messiah.

22:4 ***his name will be written on their foreheads.*** To have God's name on the forehead is to have God's nature as the foundation of one's life (see commentary on 7:3 and notes on 14:1).

22:5 ***the Lord God will shine on them.*** This is an image of fulfilled covenant relationship in the OT. Aaron and his successors in the priestly role were to bless Israel with the words, "the LORD make his face to shine upon you" (Num 6:25, RSV), and the psalmists repeatedly pray for God's face to shine upon his people, especially that they may be restored (Pss 4:6; 31:16; 67:1-2; 80:3, 7, 19). When God looks upon his people, they are then nurtured into God's own image.

they will reign. At 5:10 (see note), John indicates that the believers are reigning upon the earth. At 20:4, believers reign with the Messiah for a thousand years, i.e., during the period between the cross and the return of the Messiah (see note), a parallel statement to 5:10. Now, in 22:5, John sees that the "reign" of believers will continue on throughout eternity as that of the Lord and his Messiah (11:15—using the same phrase as 22:5, "forever and ever").

22:6-9 This portion is a bridge between the vision of the bride (New Jerusalem) and the beginning of the conclusion to the book. Just as John has previously interwoven the introduction of one unit with the conclusion of the previous unit,[1] here, too, he interweaves into the conclusion of the vision of the bride, New Jerusalem (22:6-9), an introduction to the conclusion of the vision (22:10-21). His introduction to the conclusion picks up a number of elements from the beginning of Revelation (1:1-3), thus bringing the vision full circle.

COMMENTARY

This section opens with John stating that he "saw no temple in the city, for the Lord God Almighty and the Lamb are its temple" (21:22). Needless to say, the Temple played a crucial role in Jewish history. It was the place of God's dwelling with his people and the place where covenant relationship with God was maintained through the sacrificial cultus. The Temple also played a central role in the expectations of the restoration of the kingdom to Israel. Ezekiel 40–46 originated the expectation for the eschatological Temple, filled with God's glory (Ezek 43:2-7), which would be at the heart of restored Israel. As Wright notes, "the Temple was for the Jews the centre of every aspect of national existence" (1992:225). Thus, to envision New Jerusalem without a temple would be a radical subversion of Jewish expectations. The vision has already provided the alternatives to the temple. New Jerusalem itself is the Most Holy Place where God's presence dwells (21:15-17), and the cross is the sacrifice that has fulfilled the old covenant (see commentary on 11:7-12) and cleansed God's people from their sin (1:5). This is why John saw that "the Lord God Almighty and the Lamb are its temple."

In 21:23-26, John's vision remarkably reflects Isaiah's prophetic visions for the New Jerusalem:

> "The city has no need of sun or moon, for the glory of God illuminates the city." (cf. Isa 60:19-20)
> "The nations . . . walk in its light." (cf. Isa 60:3)
> "The kings of the world [bring] their glory." (cf. Isa 60:5-7)
> "Its gates will never be closed." (cf. Isa 60:11)
> "There is no night there." (cf. Isa 60:20; see also Zech 14:7)
> "All the nations will bring their glory and honor into the city." (cf. Isa 66:12)

From these verses, it is obvious that Isaiah saw the Gentiles becoming part of God's people (Isa 2:2-4; 66:12). This is the fulfillment of the promise to Abraham, "All the families on earth will be blessed through you" (Gen 12:3). John was seeing the consummation of the promise to Abraham that was the foundation of the old covenant.

Having seen Gentiles welcomed into New Jerusalem, John's Jewish readers might well wonder if God had lowered the standards for membership in the people of

God. Thus, the last verse of this chapter makes it clear that there has been no change—nothing "ceremonially unclean" (21:27, NLT mg) will be allowed to enter New Jerusalem (cf. Acts 10:28; Rom 14:14).

The vision of Revelation 22:1-2 remarkably reflects Ezekiel's vision:

"river with the water of life" (cf. Ezek 47:1, 8-9)
"flowing from the throne" (cf. Ezek 47:1)
"on each side . . . a tree of life" (cf. Ezek 47:12)
"twelve crops of fruit, with a fresh crop each month" (cf. Ezek 47:12)
"leaves . . . to heal the nations" (cf. Ezek 47:12)

Since John had seen there is no temple in New Jerusalem but God and the Lamb are the temple (21:22), the river of life flows from their throne rather than the temple as in Ezekiel. The tree of life is a common fixture in the Jewish expectation of the restoration of the kingdom, and the vision modulates Ezekiel's "trees of all kinds" to this image. In 2 Esdras 8:52, the tree of life is coupled with the age to come and a city built, and in 2 Esdras 2:12, it is coupled with the kingdom prepared for the faithful. In *1 Enoch* 25:4-5, it is associated with the consummation of all things and will be given to the righteous and holy ones for food. In the *Apocalypse of Moses*, the throne of God is located where the tree of life is (*Apocalypse of Moses* 22:4; the same image is found in *2 Enoch* 8:3). And Adam is promised the tree of life when the resurrection comes (*Apocalypse of Moses* 28:4). The most striking modulation of Ezekiel's vision is that in John's vision the leaves of the tree of life are to heal the nations (i.e., the Gentile believers, cf. 5:9; 7:9; cf. Beale 1999:1107). In Ezekiel, it is presumed that the healing is for ethnic Israel, but in John's vision those who follow the Lamb constitute Israel. Once again the vision subverts the Jewish expectation by including the Gentiles in the restoration.

Revelation 22:3-5 provides an interesting summary of the New Jerusalem. Nothing of fallen Babylon (anything cursed) can endure (lit., "every accursed thing will not still be") where the throne of God and the Lamb is. What can be there are those who "worship him" (22:3), an image introduced first in the actions of the 24 elders who bow, worship, and cast their crowns (4:10). God's response to such worship is to reveal himself to his people: "They will see his face" (22:4).

The conclusion to the vision of the bride, New Jerusalem (22:6-9), is parallel to the conclusion of the prostitute, fallen Babylon (19:9-10; see discussion on 17:1). Woven into this conclusion is the beginning of the conclusion of the entire vision (22:10-21). John's vision returns to its starting point here with two repetitions of passages found at the beginning: (1) "God . . . has sent his angel to tell his servants what will happen soon" (22:6; cf. 1:1; where the Greek is very similar); and (2) "Blessed are those who obey the words of prophecy written in this book" (22:7; cf. 1:3, where the Greek is very similar). The repeated emphasis upon obeying the prophecy in 22:7 and 9, which will be emphasized again in 22:18-19, reminds us that the vision is not a cognitive, theological discussion of future events but a revelation of what it means to be faithful citizens of New Jerusalem in the midst of a fallen Babylon world. In addition to the two repetitions from chapter 1, the presence of Jesus once again enters into John's visionary experience (22:7) as it began the experience (1:10-20).

By way of application, it can be said that John's vision gives us a powerful picture of God's new realm of being, New Jerusalem, as the context in which Christians should live their daily lives. The absence of the temple is a forceful reminder that all of life is lived in the presence and worship of God. When there is a "temple" in the "city" of our lives, then there is a place where we can confine God. We can partition off our life into two parts, God's part, the "temple," and our part, the "city." Now, we may allow God some limited role in the life of our "city," we may even locate the "temple" at the very center of our "city," but we are the ones who have determined God's role in the structure of our life. We may be bowing and worshiping with the 24 elders (4:10), but we are not "casting the crown." We are not giving God unconditional control of our life. We are not allowing God to be God in our life on his terms.

Whenever we try to confine God to a portion of our life, we then must seek something other than God to illumine those portions of our life where we have closed God out. Something other than God becomes our "sun" and "moon" by which we seek to follow our own path through life. This, of course, permits us to control what comes to light in our life and what remains hidden. When God is allowed to be God, however, his light shines into every corner of our "city." The "slums" are exposed, the disreputable sections of our "city" are seen for what they are, and our questionable practices are disclosed.

God's order of wholeness and life is freely available to all. Its gates are never closed. All can enter and walk by God's light. All can bring what they are, their "glory," into the presence of God and be cleansed, liberated, healed, and transformed. But there is a catch! While you may come as you are through the gates of New Jerusalem into God's presence, you may not remain in your sin and bondage and brokenness. The fouled and polluted wellsprings of your old life must be abandoned, and you must begin to drink from the river of the water of life that flows from God and the Lamb. This river must be allowed to flow through the center of your "city," flushing the sewage out of the gutters, cleansing the grime from the streets, and becoming the source of refreshment and renewal. As you allow this grace of God to flow freely through the "city" of your life, you will begin to discover that long-buried "seeds" of life are beginning to sprout and bear fruit in you. As you move through each "season" of your life with God, the appropriate "fruit" will be there to strengthen and nurture you to wholeness, and the "leaves" of the tree will become a healing touch of God through you in the lives of others.

As you allow the river to flow ever more fully and freely through the "city" of your life, you will begin to realize that there is no longer anything cursed in your "city." You will have become one in whom God and the Lamb have taken up residence as promised (John 14:15-23; cf. Eph 3:16-19)—and they will not merely reside, but also rule. Everything in your life will be experienced while looking to God. His face will be your focus in all relationships, all circumstances, and all events of your life. God and the Lamb will be the light of your life, and you will begin to radiate that light to others. Your life will be increasingly conformed to the image of the Lamb as you live as a faithful citizen of God's New Jerusalem. This kind of life is the ultimate "interpretation" of John's vision.

ENDNOTE

1. In 8:2, the angels with the seven trumpets, the primary actors of 8:6–11:18, are introduced before John describes the action associated with the conclusion of the seven seals (8:3-5). In 15:1, John introduces the seven angels with the seven bowls, the primary actors of 15:6–16:21, before he concludes the section 11:19–15:4.

◆ VI. Conclusion (22:10-21)

10 Then he instructed me, "Do not seal up the prophetic words in this book, for the time is near. 11 Let the one who is doing harm continue to do harm; let the one who is vile continue to be vile; let the one who is righteous continue to live righteously; let the one who is holy continue to be holy."

12 "Look, I am coming soon, bringing my reward with me to repay all people according to their deeds. 13 I am the Alpha and the Omega, the First and the Last, the Beginning and the End."

14 Blessed are those who wash their robes. They will be permitted to enter through the gates of the city and eat the fruit from the tree of life. 15 Outside the city are the dogs—the sorcerers, the sexually immoral, the murderers, the idol worshipers, and all who love to live a lie.

16 "I, Jesus, have sent my angel to give you this message for the churches. I am both the source of David and the heir to his throne.* I am the bright morning star."

17 The Spirit and the bride say, "Come." Let anyone who hears this say, "Come." Let anyone who is thirsty come. Let anyone who desires drink freely from the water of life. 18 And I solemnly declare to everyone who hears the words of prophecy written in this book: If anyone adds anything to what is written here, God will add to that person the plagues described in this book. 19 And if anyone removes any of the words from this book of prophecy, God will remove that person's share in the tree of life and in the holy city that are described in this book.

20 He who is the faithful witness to all these things says, "Yes, I am coming soon!"

Amen! Come, Lord Jesus!

21 May the grace of the Lord Jesus be with God's holy people.*

22:16 Greek *I am the root and offspring of David.* **22:21** Other manuscripts read *be with all;* still others read *be with all of God's holy people.* Some manuscripts add *Amen.*

NOTES

22:10 ***Do not seal up the prophetic words.*** In Jewish apocalyptic literature, the writer was frequently ordered to seal up the document because it was for the time of the consummation of God's purposes. Daniel was told repeatedly to seal up his vision (Dan 8:26; 12:4, 9); Isaiah sealed up his prophecy (Isa 8:16); "Ezra" was told to put his writings in a secret place (*4 Ezra* 12:37). When John is told *not* to seal up the words "for the time is near," it is a signal to those of Jewish background in his audience that the time of restoration has come.

the time is near. This is in exactly the same form as in 1:3. It was suggested in the note on 1:3 that John was indicating that the kingdom had been restored in the Messiah, Jesus. Repeating the phrase, together with the order not to seal up the words, confirms this understanding.

22:12 ***Look, I am coming soon.*** This is identical to the phrase in 22:7 and is repeated once again at 22:20, without the word "look." In all three instances the context is one of obedient discipleship. In 22:7, there is the blessing for those who obey the prophecy; here,

Jesus brings his "reward . . . to repay all people according to their deeds"; and in 22:20, the saying closes another call to obedience in 22:18-19. The conclusion to the vision strongly reemphasizes the crucial significance of faithful discipleship (see note on 14:13).

22:13 ***I am the Alpha and the Omega, the First and the Last, the Beginning and the End.*** Once again, the vision merges the images for God and the Lamb. At 1:8 and 21:6, God describes himself as "the Alpha and the Omega," and at 21:6, as "the Beginning and the End" (see note on 3:14). To these the vision adds Jesus' assertion at 1:17, "I am the First and the Last," an image for God as both king and redeemer in Isa 44:6. As at the beginning of his vision, John saw a subversion of the Jewish understanding of Messiah. Jesus, the Messiah, is also God!

22:14 ***the tree of life.*** John draws the image of the tree of life from Gen 2:9. In the Genesis story, the expulsion of Adam and Eve from the garden was so that they might not "take fruit from the tree of life, and eat it . . . [and] live forever" (Gen 3:22). Obviously, the tree of life represents eternal life. In *1 Enoch* 25:5, the tree of life is "given to the righteous and holy. Its fruit shall be for food to the elect." The *Testament of Levi* says, "He shall give to the saints to eat from the tree of life" (*Testament of Levi* 18:11). In both *Enoch* and *Levi*, the perspective is of the consummation of God's purpose to restore all things to their original state. John indicates that this purpose has now been fulfilled in Christ. Those who have washed their robes (7:14) have access to the tree of life (22:14); they have entered into the life of New Jerusalem, which will endure forever. For John, the tree of life is the source of eternal life to which those who have participated in God's restoration in Christ have access.

22:15 ***dogs.*** This term was an epithet used by the Jews for Gentiles (cf. Jesus' use of the term in this fashion in Matt 7:6; 15:26). It denoted one who was totally unclean and outside the boundaries of God's covenant people.

the sorcerers, the sexually immoral, the murderers, the idol worshipers. Jesus listed four of the basic attributes of those in fallen Babylon previously noted in 21:8. In context, the term "sexually immoral" would be better translated "spiritual fornicators." The vision consistently uses the Greek term to describe, as in the OT, the actions of those who turn away from God to other things as gods (see note on 2:14). As in 21:8, the placement of "idol worshipers" and those "who love to live a lie"/ "liars" might possibly be meant to indicate that all the vices listed are manifestations of the "false self" that is the consequence of worshiping a false god.

who love to live a lie. This denotes people whose worldview and lifestyle are set against the truth of God.

22:16 ***I, Jesus, have sent my angel to give you this message for the churches.*** The identity confusion between Jesus (22:7, 12-15) and the angel (22:6, 8-11) is resolved with Jesus' statement here. As in the OT, there is a merging of an angel and God. See Gen 16:7-13, where Hagar meets an angel but knows she has really seen God; Gen 22:11-18, where Abraham is directed by an angel (Gen 22:11-15) and then is addressed by God (Gen 22:16-18); Gen 31:11-13, where Jacob is visited by an angel in a dream who says to him, "I am the God who appeared to you at Bethel"; Judg 6:11-24, where Gideon begins an encounter with an angel (Judg 6:11-13) who becomes the Lord (Judg 6:14-19) and then an angel again (Judg 6:20-22) and, finally, the Lord (Judg 6:23); and Judg 13:2-22, where an angel appears to Manoah and his wife but Manoah states, "We have seen God!"

this message for the churches. The reminder continues to ground the vision in the realities of being citizens of New Jerusalem in a fallen Babylon world.

I am both the source of David and the heir to his throne. Lit., "I am the root and offspring of David." Jesus closes his statement with messianic images from the OT. The first image echoes Isa 11:1: "A shoot shall come from the stump of Jesse, and a branch shall grow out of his roots" (NRSV).

the bright morning star. This second image echoes Num 24:17-19, where it is said that "a star will rise from Jacob. . . . A ruler will rise in Jacob" who will lead Israel in victory. The clear implication is that Jesus is the promised Davidic ruler who restores the kingdom to Israel.

22:18-19 ***If anyone adds . . . God will add to that person the plagues. . . . if anyone removes . . . God will remove that person's share in the tree of life.*** This strange warning has been terribly misunderstood and abused. Some have used it as a club to beat others into acceptance of their interpretation of the vision; others have used it as an excuse to avoid dealing with John's strange vision. The image used here is from Deut 4:2: "Do not add to or subtract from these commands I am giving you. Just obey the commands of the LORD your God that I am giving you." John's vision closes with the exhortation to incarnate the reality of the vision in one's life in the world. It forms a "bookend" with the first blessing (1:3) for those who listen to this prophecy and "obey what it says." The vision is not for futuristic speculation or prediction, but for New Jerusalem living in a fallen Babylon world. In light of Deut 4:2 and Rev 1:3, one might well understand that "removing from what is written" implies failure to obey. Some assert this statement has application to the Canon being closed, but the "book" John has in view is this book of prophecy (1:3, 11; i.e., the book of Revelation), so this doesn't seem likely.

22:20 ***I am coming soon!*** Jesus' promise elicits from the faithful the response, "Amen! Come, Lord Jesus!" New Jerusalem citizens live in the shadow of the return, the ultimate consummation of the victory already won in the Lamb slain before the foundation of the world.

22:21 ***May the grace of the Lord Jesus be with God's holy people.*** John closed his account of the vision with an epistolary conclusion. The same or similar closing is found in nearly all other NT epistles: Rom 16:20 (24); 1 Cor 16:23; 2 Cor 13:14; Gal 6:18; Eph 6:24; Phil 4:23; Col 4:18; 1 Thess 5:28; 2 Thess 3:18; 1 Tim 6:21; 2 Tim 4:22; Titus 3:15; Phlm 1:25; Heb 13:25; 2 Pet 3:18. Thus, the book of Revelation in its form is an encyclical epistle addressed to seven local churches.

COMMENTARY

Since instructions regarding the disposition of a book (22:10) were typical of conclusions to apocalyptic writings (cf. Dan 12:4; *4 Ezra* 14:46), it seems best to see 22:10 as the beginning of the conclusion to the vision. In case John's audience had not gotten the picture by this point, the injunction not to seal up the vision makes it unmistakably clear that the time for the restoration of the kingdom had come. Throughout Jewish history, prophecies were "sealed up" to be saved until the time when God would restore the kingdom to Israel (see note on 22:10).

The vision continues to follow Daniel's imagery here. Immediately following the order to keep his words secret, Daniel was told, "Many will be purified, cleansed, and refined by these trials. But the wicked will continue in their wickedness" (Dan 12:10). John's vision, in its larger context, gives the image a new twist. The restoration of the kingdom was also expected to include the judgment and removal of all wickedness from the world. If the restoration had indeed come, then why did wickedness continue in the world? John was seeing here what Jesus portrayed in his parable of the good seed and the weeds (Matt 13:24-43). Jesus indicated that the kingdom is already a present reality. The good seeds are the people of the kingdom, the weeds the people of the evil one. Both continue to exist together in history until the final consummation of the kingdom. The New Jerusalem is the present context of life for the followers of the Lamb, but they live as New Jerusalem citizens in a world shaped by the destructive and dehumanizing values of fallen Babylon.

For the citizens of New Jerusalem, the consummation is always imminent. We are to live as though each moment is the last. This does not mean abandoning the future, nor does it mean there is no need to plan ahead. It means living in such radical obedience to God each moment, that should the Lord return, we are not surprised or dismayed but experience the consummation of our own faithfulness in God's consummation. Our "deeds" don't earn us our place in the consummation; our "deeds" are the manifestation of a life lived in radical abandonment to God.

In this final section of Revelation, we read the final blessing of the book: "Blessed are those who wash their robes. They will be permitted to enter through the gates of the city and eat the fruit from the tree of life" (22:14). This seventh and final blessing (cf. 1:3; 14:13; 16:15; 19:9; 20:6; 22:7) forms a concluding summary of the vision's dynamics of New Jerusalem citizenship. People must "wash their robes," which, as John has seen, is accomplished through the blood of the Lamb (7:14). This brings two privileges: access to the fruit from the tree of life (22:2) and entrance through the gates of the city, which are never closed (21:25). Redemption through the cross of the Lamb results in new life in a new context.

The images of washing the robes, entering the city, and eating fruit from the tree of life are a paradigm of the spiritual life. The journey toward wholeness in the image of Christ at any point in our being begins with the "washing"—the release of our lives from the bondage of our uncleanness through the death of the Lamb. There can be no compromise, as was made plain in the letters to the churches (chs 2–3). When we are washed, we then need to enter into the "city." We need to allow New Jerusalem to become the context and structure of our life. This calls us to a radical change of our perspectives, our values, our structures of being and doing, and our dynamics of relating to others. We must abandon fallen Babylon's ways of being and doing and learn to live as citizens of New Jerusalem. This means we must find the essential nourishment for our life in the tree of life. Our fallen Babylon life feeds upon the poisons of a self-referenced existence. We feed upon possessions, upon power, upon prestige, upon performance, thinking that it is these that form our identity, give our lives meaning, shape our purpose, and establish our value. Once we are washed, we must feed upon God as the root of our identity, the source of our meaning, the shaper of our purpose, and the center of our value. Such nourishment drives the poisons from the body of our being and nurtures us to wholeness in the image of Christ.

The essence of fallen Babylon—our false self—enters into the sorcery of controlling our existence; the spiritual adultery of making ourselves "god" in our lives; the abuse of others that "murders" their identity, their wholeness, and their value; and the idolatry of making the false self the "norm" for all. The false self loves and lives a lie, because to do otherwise is to attack the very foundation of one's sense of being. This is why Jesus says we must "lose ourselves" for his sake (Matt 10:39, my translation). This is the "self" that must be denied in order to follow Jesus (Matt 16:24). If we try to save this false self, we will lose our true being as children of God; we will find ourselves "outside" the city of life.

The closing image (22:17) is the universal invitation to participate in New Jerusalem by drinking "the water of life." The Spirit of God invites those in fallen Babylon to "come." The Church (the bride) extends the invitation. And the redeemed ("anyone who hears"—the implication here is that those who "hear" are those who obey) each offer the invitation. The essential posture of New Jerusalem toward fallen Babylon is one of outreach and invitation. Anyone who wants to may come and "drink freely from the water of life." John saw the gracious inclusion of the Gentiles in God's restored kingdom.

Once we have washed our robes, entered New Jerusalem, and are feeding upon the fruit of the tree of life, evangelism becomes the essence of our living. Having known the destructive and dehumanizing bondages of fallen Babylon, we now yearn for those still held in its debilitating imprisonment to know the liberation and wholeness of God's people. Our very lives should become winsome witnesses to the wholeness of life to be found in God's New Jerusalem. New Jerusalem living is the incarnation of John's vision in the midst of the world.

In the face of the world's pressures and persecutions, it is a great temptation to diminish this vision, to accommodate it to the world, to add mitigating interpretations to the vision to make it easier to get along with the world, or to explain away its demands for radical discipleship. To do this, however, results in the loss of our true context of life and wholeness, and in a return to the destructive and dehumanizing bondages of fallen Babylon. It makes it impossible to live each day in the prayer of 22:20, "Come, Lord Jesus."

BIBLIOGRAPHY

Aune, David

1997 *Revelation 1–5.* Word Biblical Commentary 52A. Dallas: Word.

1998 *Revelation 6–16; Revelation 17–22.* Word Biblical Commentary 52B-52C. Dallas: Word.

Bauckham, R.

1993a *The Climax of Prophecy: Studies in the Book of Revelation.* Edinburgh: T&T Clark.

1993b *The Theology of the Book of Revelation.* Cambridge: Cambridge University Press.

1999 *God Crucified: Monotheism and Christology in the New Testament.* Grand Rapids: Eerdmans.

Beale, G. K.

1998 *John's Use of the Old Testament in Revelation.* Journal for the Study of the New Testament Supplement Series. Sheffield: Sheffield Academic.

1999 *The Book of Revelation.* New International Greek New Testament. Grand Rapids: Eerdmans.

Beasley-Murray, G. R.

1974 *The Book of Revelation.* New Century Bible Commentary. London: Marshall, Morgan & Scott.

Beckwith, Isbon

1979 *The Apocalypse of John.* Grand Rapids: Baker.

Buchanan, George Wesley

1978 *Revelation and Redemption.* Dillsboro, NC: Western North Carolina Press.

1993 *The Book of Revelation.* Lewiston, NY: Edwin Mellon.

Caird, G. B.

1966 *The Revelation of St. John the Divine.* New York: Harper & Row.

Colson, Charles, and Ellen Vaughn

2003 *Being the Body.* Nashville: W Publishing Group.

Comfort, Philip

2005 *Encountering the Manuscripts: An Introduction to New Testament Paleography and Textual Criticism.* Nashville: Broadman & Holman.

2008 *New Testament Text and Translation Commentary.* Carol Stream, IL: Tyndale House.

Corsini, Eugenio

1983 *The Apocalypse: The Perennial Revelation of Jesus Christ.* Translator, Francis J. Moloney. Wilmington, DE: Michael Glazier.

Deletant, Dennis

1999 *Romania under Communist Rule.* Rev. ed. Iaşi / Portland: Center for Romanian Studies / Civic Academy Foundation.

Dupont-Sommer, A.

1961 *The Essene Writings from Qumran.* Oxford: Blackwell.

Ekola, Timo

2001 *Messiah and the Throne.* Wissenshaftliche Untersuchungen zum Neuen Testament 2/142. Tübingen: Mohr Siebeck.

Ellul, Jacques

1977 *Apocalypse: The Book of Revelation.* New York: Seabury.

Gorman, Michael J.

2001 *Cruciformity: Paul's Narrative Spirituality of the Cross.* Grand Rapids: Eerdmans.

2009 *Inhabiting the Cruciform God: Kenosis, Justification, and Theosis in Paul's Narrative Soteriology.* Grand Rapids: Eerdmans.

Guthrie, Donald

1980 *The Relevance of John's Apocalypse.* Grand Rapids: Eerdmans.

Harrington, W. J.

1969 *Understanding the Apocalypse*. Washington, DC: Corpus Books.

Hemer, C. J.

1986 *The Letters to the Seven Churches of Asia in Their Local Setting*. Journal for the Study of the New Testament Supplement Series 11. Sheffield: Journal for the Study of the Old Testament Press.

Jastrow, Marcus

2006 *Dictionary of the Targumim, the Talmud Babli and Yerushalmi, and the Midrashic Literature*. Peabody, MA: Hendrickson.

Johnson, Alan

1981 Revelation. Pp. 397-603 in *The Expositor's Bible Commentary*, vol. 12. Grand Rapids: Zondervan.

Julian of Norwich

1978 *Showings*. Translators, Edmund Colledge and James Walsh. New York: Paulist.

Kelber, Werner H.

1983 *The Oral and the Written Gospel: The Hermeneutics of Speaking and Writing in the Synoptic Tradition, Paul, and Q*. Philadelphia: Fortress.

Kline, M. G.

1975 The First Resurrection. *Westminster Theological Journal* 37:366-375.

1976 The First Resurrection: A Reaffirmation. *Westminster Theological Journal* 37:110-119.

Ladd, George E.

1972 *A Commentary on the Revelation of St. John the Divine*. Grand Rapids: Eerdmans.

Leech, Kenneth

1985 *Experiencing God: Theology as Spirituality*. New York: Harper & Row.

Malina, Bruce

1993 *Revelation*. Sacra Pagina. Editor, J. Harrington. Collegeville: Liturgical Press.

Martinez, Florentino Garcia

1996 *The Dead Sea Scrolls Translated*. Grand Rapids: Eerdmans.

Merton, Thomas

1961 *The New Man*. New York: Noonday.

1983 The Inner Experience: Christian Contemplation (III). *Cistercian Studies Quarterly Review* 18.3:201-216.

Metzger, Bruce

1993 *Breaking the Code*. Nashville: Abingdon.

Mounce, R. H.

1977 *The Book of Revelation*. New International Commentary on the New Testament. Grand Rapids: Eerdmans.

Mulholland, M. Robert, Jr.,

1998 Life at the Center—Life at the Edge. *Weavings* 13(4):25-31.

2006 *The Deeper Journey*. Downers Grove, IL: InterVarsity.

Neusner, Jacob

1973 *From Politics to Piety*. Englewood Cliffs, NJ: Prentice-Hall.

Osborne, Grant

2002 *Revelation*. Baker Exegetical Commentary on the New Testament. Grand Rapids: Baker.

Payne, Robert

1962 *The Roman Triumph*. London: Abelard-Schuman.

Pliny

1938 *Natural History IV*. Loeb Classical Library. Translator, H. Rackham. Cambridge: Harvard University Press.

Powell, Mark Allan

1990 *What Is Narrative Criticism? Guides to Biblical Scholarship, New Testament Series*. Minneapolis: Fortress.

Rengstorf, Karl Heinrich

1964 ἑπτά. Pp. 627-635 in *Theological Dictionary of the New Testament*, vol. 2. Editor, G. Kittel, translator, G. W. Bromley. Grand Rapids: Eerdmans.

Safrai, S.

1976 *The Jewish People in the First Century*, vol. 2. Philadelphia: Fortress.

Saint, Max

1986 Catherine of Genoa. Pp. 313-314 in *The Study of Spirituality*. Editors, C. Jones, G. Wainwright, and E. Yarnold. Oxford: Oxford University Press.

Schürer, Emil

1979 *The History of the Jewish People in the Age of Jesus Christ (175 BC–AD 135)*, vol. 2. A new English version: Revisers and editors, Geza Vermes, Fergus Millar, and Matthew Black. Edinburgh: T&T Clark.

1986 *The History of the Jewish People in the Age of Jesus Christ (175 BC–AD 135)*, vol. 3. A new English version: Revisers and editors, Geza Vermes, Fergus Millar, and Matthew Black. Edinburgh: T&T Clark.

Smyth, Herbert Weir

1920 *A Greek Grammar for Colleges*. New York: American Book Company.

Tcherikover, Victor A.

1961 *Hellenistic Civilization and the Jews*. Philadelphia: Jewish Publication Society of America.

Tcherikover, Victor A., and Alexander Fuks

1960 *Corpus Papyrorum Judicarum*, vol. 2, papyrus no. 153. Cambridge: Harvard University Press.

Vermes, Geza

1962 *The Dead Sea Scrolls in English*. New York: Penguin.

1977 *The Dead Sea Scrolls: Qumran in Perspective*. Philadelphia: Fortress.

Versnel, H. S.

1970 *Triumphus: An Inquiry into the Origin, Development and Meaning of the Roman Triumph*. Leiden: Brill.

Wall, R. W.

1991 *Revelation*. New International Biblical Commentary. Peabody, MA: Hendrickson.

Wesley, John

1976 *Explanatory Notes on the New Testament*. Salem, OH: Schmul. (Orig. pub. 1754.)

Witherington, Ben, III

2003 *Revelation*. New Cambridge Bible Commentary. Cambridge: Cambridge University Press.

Wright, N. T.

1992 *The New Testament and the People of God*. Philadelphia: Fortress.

1993 *The Climax of the Covenant*. Minneapolis: Fortress.

1996 *Jesus and the Victory of God*. Philadelphia: Fortress.